THE RICH AND
THE SUPER-RICH

A Study in the Power of Money Today

THE RICH AND THE SUPER-RICH

A Study in the Power of Money Today

BY FERDINAND LUNDBERG

Lyle Stuart, Inc. • New York

EDITED BY EILEEN BRAND

PUBLISHED BY LYLE STUART, INC.

MANUFACTURED IN THE UNITED STATES OF AMERICA

Dedication:

To Bernie and Lillian,

Humanists of the Deed.

Molto Affetuoso

ACKNOWLEDGMENTS

I wish to acknowledge with gratitude the permissions granted by the following publishers to make somewhat extended quotations from the books here listed:

To The Free Press of Glencoe for permission to quote from Robert E. Lane, *Political Life*, 1965

To Harper and Row, New York, for permission to quote from Joseph S. Clark, *Congress: The Sapless Branch*, 1964, and W. Lloyd Warner and James C. Abegglen, *Big Business Leadership in America*, 1955

To Alfred A. Knopf, Inc., New York, for permission to quote from Alan Harrington, *Life in the Crystal Palace*, 1959

To Oxford University Press, New York, for permission to quote from C. Wright Mills, *The Power Elite*, 1956

To The Ronald Press Company, New York, for permission to quote from Louis Eisenstein, *The Ideologies of Taxation*, 1961, Copyright ©.

Beyond this I am obviously indebted and feel appropriately grateful to writers and publishers for all shorter quotations from other works, and to leading newspapers such as the *New York Times,* the late *New York Herald Tribune* and the *Wall Street Journal* for the many excerpts taken from their pages.

Obviously nobody could have developed so large a canvas as that of the present book without summoning many scholarly witnesses. To mention all such here would be superogatory, as they are all prominently mentioned in the running text as well as in the appended notes. Needless to say, my debt to such is great and without them much would have been obscure which is now precise. However, much more work remains to be done in many areas that are yet obscure.

Special thanks are due to the staff of the New York Public Library, Central Branch, which was unfailingly helpful over a long period in locating for me much not readily accessible or very well-known data.

F.L.

Contents

Let me tell you about the very rich. They are different from you and me. They possess and enjoy early, and it does something to them, makes them soft where we are hard, and cynical where we are trustful, in a way that, unless you were born rich, it is difficult to understand. They think, deep in their hearts, that they are better than we are because we had to discover the compensations and refuges of life for ourselves. Even when they enter deep into our world or sink below us, they still think that they are better than we are. They are different.

—F. SCOTT FITZGERALD

THE RICH AND
THE SUPER-RICH

A Study in the Power of Money Today

One ❧

THE ELECT AND
THE DAMNED

Most Americans—citizens of the wealthiest, most powerful and most ideal-swathed country in the world—by a very wide margin own nothing more than their household goods, a few glittering gadgets such as automobiles and television sets (usually purchased on the installment plan, many at second hand) and the clothes on their backs. A horde if not a majority of Americans live in shacks, cabins, hovels, shanties, hand-me-down Victorian eyesores, rickety tenements and flaky apartment buildings—as the newspapers from time to time chortle that new Russian apartment-house construction is falling apart. (Conditions abroad, in the standard American view, are everywhere far worse than anywhere in the United States. The French, for example, could learn much about cooking from the Automat and Howard Johnson.)

At the same time, a relative handful of Americans are extravagantly endowed, like princes in the Arabian Nights tales. Their agents deafen a baffled world with a never-ceasing chant about the occult merits of private-property ownership (good for everything that ails man and thoroughly familiar to the rest of the world, not invented in the United States), and the vaulting puissance of the American owners.

It would be difficult in the 1960's for a large majority of Americans to show fewer significant possessions if the country had long labored under a grasping dictatorship. How has this process been contrived of stripping threadbare most of the populace, which once at least owned small patches of virgin land? To this fascinating if off-color question we shall give some attention later.

Statements such as the foregoing on the rare occasions when they are ventured (although strictly true and by no means new)[1] are bound to be challenged by the alert propaganda watchdogs of the established order. These propagandists, when hard pressed, offer an incantation about a mythical high American standard of living which on inspection turns out to be no more than a standard of gross consumption. The statements must, therefore—particularly in this age of burgeoning one-sided affluence—be monumentally and precisely documented and redocumented. Not that this will deter the watchdogs, who have limitless resources of casuistry and dialectic to fall back upon as well as an endless supply of white paper from denuded forests.

Critical Scholarship Takes a Hand

But (fortunately for truth) critical scholarship, roused from its one-time somnolence by echoing charges and counter-charges over the years, has finally been led to make penetrating, detailed, exhaustive and definitive revelations of the underlying facts—although the findings of such scholarship are not featured in the controlled prints, are not publicly discussed and are not even alluded to in polite society. As far as the broad public is concerned in an age of unrestrained publicity, when even the martyrdom of a virile young president is made overnight into a profitable industry, the facts about the skeletons in the closet of the affluent society are shrouded in secrecy for all except those queer beings willing to delve for hours among dusty tomes in library crypts.

Nonetheless, irreproachable scholarly analyses of diamond-hard official data fully support my initial assertions, which to the average newspaper reader may seem incredibly iconoclastic, ludicrously wrongheaded or the maunderings of an idiot. Further along, some of the complex reasons for the odd situation will be touched upon, after the paramount position of the wealthy and the ways they are maintained have been fully depicted.

A Nation of Employees

Most adult Americans in the quasi-affluent society of today, successors to the resourceful (and wholly imaginative) Americano of Walt Whitman's lush fantasy, are nothing more than employees. For the most part they are precariously situated; nearly all of them are menials. In this particular respect Americans, though illusion-ridden, are like the Russians under Communism, except that the Russians inhabit a less technologized society and have a single employer. There are, of course, other differences (such as the fact that Americans are allowed a longer civil leash), but not of social position. And this nation of free and equal employees is the reality that underlies and surrounds the wealthy few on the great North American continent.

Those few newspapers that make a practice of printing foreign news occasionally survey Latin American countries. The writers are invariably grieved to find a small oligarchy of big landowners in control, with the remainder of the population consisting of sycophantic hangers-on and landless, poverty-stricken peasants. But I have never seen it remarked that the basic description, with the alteration of a few nouns, applies just as well to the United States, where the position of the landowners is occupied by the financiers, industrialists and big rentiers and that of the peasants by the low-paid employees (all subject to dismissal for one reason or other just like the peasants).

The Banana Republics

These same writers, focusing attention on Central America, refer caustically to the "banana republics"—those countries, economically dominated mainly by the United Fruit Company, where political leaders are bought and sold like popcorn and where ambitious *insurrectos* from time to time overthrow earlier *insurrectos* who run the government for their own profit. But the United States, sacred land of Washington, Jefferson, Franklin and Madison—"Of thee I sing"—itself often displays many similar aspects, mingled with a heady atmosphere at times reminiscent of rural carnivals, Oriental bazaars, raucous gambling houses and plush bordellos. If anyone thinks I exaggerate he should notice how the mingled images of Coney Island, Atlantic City, Miami Beach, Hollywood, Palm Springs, Broadway, Las Vegas and Madison Avenue often disconcertingly float into plain view at political conventions, state funerals, elections, court proceedings and congressional hearings, much to the glee of enchanted but I fear disrespectful and unconsciously alienated spectators.

Conditions in the United States, *mutatis mutandis*, are not nearly so different from conditions in other countries as North American natives are customarily led to suppose by imaginative editors. As in the "banana republics" we have assassinations and attempted assassinations of the chief of state at regular intervals—Lincoln, Garfield, McKinley and Kennedy shot dead; Truman and both Roosevelts the targets of would-be assassins; any number of local *jefes politicos* bullet-drilled. This is not to say that those differences that exist between the United States and the Central American republics may not be important. The point is that, while the differences in favor of the United States are endlessly stressed for public edification—such as the prevalence north of the Rio Grande of indoor flush toilets, an engineering marvel long antedating television sets—the grim similarities are seldom or never alluded to. To refer to them would be considered unpatriotic.

In the matter of domestic gunplay, for example, the United States far outdoes any of the "banana republics." Since 1900 more than 750,000 persons have died in the United States of nonmilitary gunshot wounds inside or outside the home, and the annual death rate from gunplay is now 17,000, or about 50 per day.[2] Other forms of violence are equally prevalent; and violence in general, to the dismay of the genteel, is the staple theme in American films and television, reflecting the external society. More than one and a half million have been killed by the automobile since its vaunted introduction into the United States.

Crime, to purloin a phrase, is rampant. From the Wickersham Report of 1931 down to a presidential commission in 1967, several national commissions have surveyed, recommended and wrung their hands as the tide of crime (much of which is not reported) has risen. In addition to frequently disclosed tie-ins of organized crime with local politicians, the associations of the organized underworld are openly traced up to the congressional level.[3]

In ancient days the messenger who brought bad news to the king was frequently executed. Those who produce unwanted messages such as these are now generally stigmatized as "muckrakers," themselves unclean, as though an epithet disposed of the phenomenon.

Even in such a presumably distinctive Latin American feature as the intrusiveness of the military, the United States now clearly overshadows anything in this line the Latin American republics are able to show. Compared with the political power and influence of the American military today, Hohenzollern Germany (at one time designated by horrified American publicists as the acme of cold militarism in modern times) was only a one-cylinder, comic-opera affair. The Pentagon of today—its agents busy in Congress and the Executive Branch, with the politicians obviously standing in awe of the bemedaled generals, with the defense-industry corporations loaded with retired officers—could flatten an entity like Hohenzollern or Hitler Germany with a few well-placed blows. The youth, too, are freely conscripted, as though they were German peasants.

Even the presidents are beginning to feel bewildered by it all. Dwight D. Eisenhower in his presidential "farewell address" called attention to "this conjunction of an immense military establishment and a large arms industry" and warned the country to be on "guard against the acquisition of unwarranted influence, whether sought or unsought, by the military-industrial complex." He said, "The potential for the disastrous rise of misplaced power exists and will persist," and the influence of the military "is felt in every city, every state house, every office of the federal government." With the military behind it if not over it, the federal government is assuming a dominating role in many directions, he said, "and is gravely to be regarded."

President John F. Kennedy felt that he had been duped by the Pentagon and the CIA into acquiescing in the long-planned invasion of Cuba, which foundered at the Bay of Pigs as Kennedy back-pedaled on ordering air support; this action gained him many infuriated rightist enemies. Many partisans of President Lyndon B. Johnson assert that he was misled by military advice into the costly Vietnam involvement that cast a deepening shadow over his administration. However, some leading generals from the beginning opposed the glorious adventure.

While American generals do not formally make political decisions, they (as have generals in many other countries since 1914) do evidently proffer advice that makes certain decisions and consequences a foregone conclusion.[4] They are far from inconsequential politically.

Except that the United States has such large numbers of industrial and office workers, rather than landless peasants, it has few features to which general descriptions of Latin American society do not apply. The United States is a great deal more like Brazil and Argentina, for example, than it is like France or England (two countries upon which most Americans are inclined to look with patronizing reservation).

Even in such a distinctive United States feature as the separation of church and state there is now a strong movement, led by politicians with their eyes on the least instructed voters, for a direct supportive involvement of the state in the affairs of the church, an involvement that would presumably gain these politicians the support of the church. In this feature, then, there is a movement to make the United States even more like Latin America and less like Europe, where church and state are tending to become more and more separate in most jurisdictions.

It might almost be said that there is a growing tendency to model the United States, apart from its industrial features, upon the "banana republics," thus making it the Banana Republic *par excellence*.

The Statistical Setting

The setting of our story is of necessity statistical. And statistics have the merit of being succinct. I am aware, however, that many readers cannot face statistics, a fact that leads seasoned editors to advise writers to dispense with them or to hide them in the back of the book. Apparently childhood encounters with arithmetic under inferior school conditions have developed in many people (even the cultivated) a distaste for numbers, and when they see them they merely skip. But it will repay readers to study and ponder carefully the following figures.

While good studies have been made for some decades, three recent high-level inquiries have developed the picture in sharper and more exact detail than ever before. They represent a long series of analyses of the extent and concentration of American wealth that was begun by G. K. Holmes in 1893. These analyses, showing greater and greater precision with the passing years, are listed in the chapter notes.[5]

The three recent studies were made, independently, by Professor Robert J. Lampman of the University of Wisconsin for the National Bureau of Economic Research; by the Survey Research Center of the University of Michigan as a continuing project in 1947, 1952, 1956, 1960 and 1963; and by the Harvard historian Gabriel Kolko as presented in his *Wealth and Power in America* (1962). I will touch upon these, as well as a resounding official clincher, in this order.

Running to 286 pages, containing 138 formidable tables and 37 charts (including 13 Lorenz curves) and employing the most sophisticated applicable mathematics, the Lampman study was published by Princeton University Press in 1962.[6]

What Professor Lampman did was to obtain basic data from federal estate tax returns for the years 1922, 1929, 1933, 1939, 1945, 1949, 1953 and in some cases for 1954 and 1956; but he concentrated attention on 1953. Such tax returns are required by law of all decedents with estates exceeding the level of exemption, which was $50,000 for 1922–26, $100,-000 for 1926–32, $50,000 for 1932–35, $40,000 for 1935–42 and $60,000 after 1942.

With the data in hand, Professor Lampman then employed the established estate-multiplier method. This requires that one multiply the number and property of decedents in each age-sex group by the inverse of the general mortality rate for each such group. One thereby arrives at an estimate of living persons and the amount of estate in each age-sex group and in each estate size.

Professor Lampman illustrates the method as follows: "Suppose that out of a population of 1,000 men aged 40 to 50, two men died in one year with estates of $100,000 or more. Suppose further that it is known that 5 per cent of all the 1,000 men aged 40 to 50 died in that year. Then it may be assumed that the two men who died with $100,000 were 5 per cent of all the living men in the group with $100,000. Hence, to estimate the number of living men with $100,000, we should multiply two by twenty (the inverse of 5 per cent) to get the answer of forty living men with $100,000 or more."[7]

The Lampman Findings

What Lampman found was as follows:

1. More than 30 per cent of the assets and equities of the personal sector of the economy (about 20 per cent of all wealth in the country being government-owned) in 1953 was held by 1.6 per cent of the adult population of 103 million.[8]

2. This group of 1.6 per cent owned 32 per cent of all privately owned wealth, consisting of 82.2 per cent of all stock, 100 per cent of state and local (tax-exempt) bonds, 38.2 per cent of federal bonds, 88.5 per cent of other bonds, 29.1 per cent of the cash, 36.2 per cent of mortgages and notes, 13.3 per cent of life insurance reserves, 5.9 per cent of pension and retirement funds, 18.2 per cent of miscellaneous property, 16.1 per cent of real estate and 22.1 per cent of all debts and mortgages.[9]

3. The following table shows the percentage of national wealth-holdings for the top ½ of 1 per cent and 1 per cent for the indicated years.[10]

	½ of 1 Per Cent of Adult Population (per cent)	1 Per Cent of Adult Population (per cent)
1922	29.8	31.6
1929	32.4	36.3
1933	25.2	28.3
1939	28.0	30.6
1945	20.9	23.3
1949	19.3	20.8
1953	22.7	24.2
1954	22.5	......
1956	25.0	26.0

4. The estimated gross estate size for the total adult population in 1953, obtained by extension of the same methods, was as shown in the table on the following page.[11]

In this table is found one verification of my initial paragraph. It shows that 50 per cent of the people, owning 8.3 per cent of the wealth, had an average estate of $1,800—enough to cover furniture, clothes, a television set and perhaps a run-down car. Most of these had less; many had nothing

Gross Estate Size (dollars)	Number of Persons Aged 20 and Over (millions)	Percentage	Average Estate Size (dollars)	Total Gross Estate (billion dollars)	Percentage
0 to 3,500	51.70	50.0	1,800	93.1	8.3
3,500-10,000	19.00	18.4	6,000	114.0	10.2
10,000-20,000	21.89	21.2	15,000	328.4	29.3
20,000-30,000	6.00	5.8	25,000	150.0	13.4
30,000-40,000	2.00	1.9	35,000	70.0	6.3
40,000-50,000	0.80	0.8	45,000	36.0	3.2
50,000-60,000	0.35	0.3	55,000	19.3	1.7
All under 60,000	101.74	98.4	7,900	810.8	72.4
60,000-70,000	0.18	0.1	61,000	10.5	0.9
60,000 and over	1.66	1.6	186,265	309.2	27.6
All estate sizes	103.40	100.0	10,800	1,120.0	100.0
Median estate size			3,500		

at all. Another group of 18.4 per cent, adding up to 68.4 per cent of the population, was worth $6,000 on the average, which would probably largely represent participation in life insurance or emergency money in the bank. Perhaps this percentage included some of the select company of "people's capitalists" who owned two or three shares of AT&T.

Another 21.89 per cent of adults, bringing into view 92.59 per cent of the population, had $15,000 average gross estates—just enough to cover a serious personal illness. This same 92-plus per cent of the population all together owned only 47.8 per cent of all assets.

Top Wealth-Holders

The number of persons in the top 1 per cent of wealth-holders through the decades was as follows:[12]

Years	Number of Persons (thousands)	Percentage Share of Gross Estates
1922	651	32
1929	744	38
1939	855	33
1945	929	26
1949	980	22
1953	1,030	25

But the top 11 per cent of persons in the magic 1 per cent (or 0.11 per cent) held about 45 per cent of the wealth of this particular group while the lower half (or 0.50 per cent) held only 23 per cent.[13]

Says Lampman: "The personally owned wealth of the total population in 1953 amounted to about $1 trillion. This means that the average gross estate for all 103 million adults was slightly less than $10,000. The median would, of course, be considerably lower. In contrast the top wealth-holder group had an average gross estate of $182,000. The majority of this top group was clustered in estate sizes below that average. Of the 1.6 million top wealth-holders, over half had less than $125,000 of gross estate and less than 2 per cent (27,000 persons) had more than $1 million."[14]

There were, then, in excess of 27,000 millionaires in the country in 1953—not only the greatest such aggregation at one time in the history of the world but a number greater than the aggregation throughout all of history before 1875 (as of 1966, millionaires numbered about 90,000). If consumer prices had remained stable from 1944 to 1953 there would have been fewer. "In 1944 there were 13,297 millionaires," says Lampman. "In 1953 there were 27,502 millionaires in 1953 prices, but only 17,611 in 1944 prices."[15]

What of the 1965-67 year-span? As the prices of stocks advanced tremendously in the preceding dozen years, one can only conclude that the proportion of wealth of the top wealth-holders also advanced impressively. For this small group, as we have seen, owns more than 80 per cent of stocks. The Dow-Jones average of 65 industrial stocks stood at 216.31 at the end of 1950; at 442.72 in 1955; at 618.04 in 1960; and at 812.18 in March, 1964. As of May, 1965, it was well above 900. The less volatile Securities and Exchange Commission index of 300 stocks shows the same quadrupling in value, standing at 41.4 in 1950; 81.8 in 1955; 113.9 in 1960; and 160.9 in March, 1964. How many employees have experienced a fourfold increase in salaries in the same period?

The rise in value of stocks, however, surely invalidates one of Lampman's speculations, to this effect: "Our finding that the share of wealth held by the top 2 per cent of families fell from about 33 to 29 per cent from 1922 to 1953, or about one-eighth, would seem compatible with . . . the general belief that there has been some lessening of economic inequality in the United States in recent decades."[16] The more recent rise in stock prices and in corporation earnings shatters even that slight concession.

Professor A. A. Berle, Jr., has rushed forward to hail the Lampman showing that the upper 1 per cent saw its participation reduced from 32 per cent of all wealth in 1922 to 25 per cent in 1953; but his celebration was premature and he did not fully report Lampman, who indicated that the participation had been reduced from 1922 to 1949 but thereafter was again increasing.[17]

The Lampman findings were extended to 1958 in an extremely sophisticated statistical critique presented in 1965 to the American Statistical Association by James D. Smith and Staunton K. Calvert of the Statistics Division of the Internal Revenue Service.[18]

After reviewing Lampman, revising him in a minor particular, Smith and Calvert conclude that "top wealth-holders owned 27.4 percent of gross and 28.3 percent of net prime wealth in 1953, but increased their share to 30.2 and 32.0 percent respectively by 1958. These data support Lampman's conclusion that the share of top wealth-holders has been increasing since 1949." Prime wealth, as they explain, is total wealth less the value of assets in trust funds and pension reserves.

This is where the question rests on the basis of the most recent data supplied by leading authorities in the field: Concentration of wealth in a few hands is intensifying.

Actually, in view of market valuations, the share of top wealth-holders at this writing is easily the greatest in history. It is my hypothesis that the share of the top ½ of 1 per cent now exceeds the 32.4 per cent of this group for 1929. Later studies should show that the proportions for all groups of top wealth-holders studied by Lampman have been significantly exceeded.

So much for Lampman although there is much else in his razor-sharp book that merits attention.[19]

The University of Michigan Study

Although showing some minor variations, the continuing University of Michigan survey dovetails with the Lampman study and fully supports it.

First, it was found that 3 per cent of spending units in 1953 had $60,000 or more total assets; this compares with 2.3 per cent of individuals in the Lampman study. A "spending unit" consisted of any one or more persons established as a household.

According to this University of Michigan "Survey of Consumer Finances," the upper 11 per cent of the nation's 54 million spending units held 56 per cent of the total assets and 60 per cent of the net worth of all private holdings in the country. "While this group held only 30 per cent of consumer capital," Lampman comments (p. 195), "they held 80 per cent of business and investment assets."[20]

According to the 1960 University of Michigan "Survey of Consumer

Finances," 86 per cent of all spending units in the country owned no stock whatever. Of incomes under $3,000, 95 per cent owned no stock; of incomes of $3,000–$5,000, 93 per cent owned no stock; and of incomes of $5,000–$7,500, 87 per cent owned no stock. The class of $7,500–$10,-000 incomes was 78 per cent without stock ownership, while even in the $10,000–$15,000 income class 61 per cent owned no stock. In 1963 a total of 83 per cent owned no stock. Stock ownership, it is clear, was being somewhat more widely diffused as long-term holders gradually unloaded at rising prices. Whereas in 1953 only 44 per cent of the income class above $15,000 owned no stock, in 1960 this same broad class included only 26 per cent without stock ownership.[21]

For some years the New York Stock Exchange and the Advertising Council, as part of a campaign to show that a "people's capitalism" exists with a widely diffused ownership in American industry, have been busily pyramiding figures. These computations show that in 1956 there were 8,630,000 American shareholders, and in 1962 there were 17,010,000.[22] The figure more recently being cited is 20 million.[23]

Even though the method of their compilation is challenged by statisticians, these computations could all be true and still not alter the implications of the Lampman analysis and University of Michigan surveys. For if 17 per cent of spending units owned stock in 1963, as the University of Michigan survey indicates, that would be well over 17 million persons. And anyone would qualify as a stockholder if he owned only one share worth 10 cents.

That most stockholders own trivial amounts of stock is shown by the University of Michigan figures for 1963. The 17 per cent of spending units holding stock broke down in this way: 3 percent held less than $500 worth; 2 per cent held $500 to $999 worth; 4 per cent held $1,000 to $4,999 worth; and 2 per cent held $5,000 to $9,999 worth. As far as stock ownership goes, these are all insignificant figures. Yet they make up 75 per cent of the households holding stock. Only 4 per cent of all spending units owned more than $10,000 of stock.[24] But most of this group, exceeding four million people, also owned little stock; for we are already aware that a group consisting of 1.6 per cent of the population owns more than 80 per cent of all stock, 100 per cent of state and local government bonds and 88.5 per cent of corporate bonds. Less than 20 per cent of all stock in 1963, then, was owned by some 15.4 million people.

Throughout this study, therefore, it is going to be taken as fully established that 1.6 per cent of the adult population own at least 32 per cent of all assets, and nearly all the investment assets, and that 11 per cent of households (following the University of Michigan study) own at least

56 per cent of the assets and 60 per cent of the net worth. It is even possible, as we have seen, that ½ of 1 per cent own more than one-third of all productive assets as of 1965–67. It is evident that this leaves very little to be apportioned among 90 per cent of the population. It will be recalled that Lampman showed 50 per cent owning virtually nothing, with an average estate size of only $1,800 as of 1953. This same study, according to my tabulation numbered 4, showed that 89.6 per cent of the adult population had available to it only 47.8 per cent of the assets, while 50 per cent had only 8.3 per cent. The University of Michigan figures and the Lampman figures, in short, coincide rather closely although developed by different methods.

Supporting Studies

Every other serious study supports these findings. The Senate Temporary National Economic Committee (TNEC) just before World War II inquired into the distribution of stock among 8.5 million shareholders in 1,710 major companies as of 1937–39 and found that 4 per cent of all common stockholders held 74.9 per cent of the stock, and 4.5 per cent of the preferred stockholders held 54.8 per cent.[25] Looking into the same situation as of 1951, the Brookings Institution of Washington, D. C., found that in 2,991 major corporations only 2.1 per cent of the holders owned 58 per cent of the common stock and 1.1 per cent of the holders owned 46 per cent of the preferred stock. Two-thirds of all common stockholders owned only 10 per cent of the shares.[26] Harvard's J. Keith Butters estimated that in 1949 the spending units (households) that owned $100,000 or more in marketable stock, comprising 1/5 of 1 per cent of all spending units and 2 per cent of stockholders, owned between 65 and 71 per cent of all marketable stock held by individuals.[27] None of these studies took into account the beneficial interest of individuals in stock held by institutions for the account of individuals, which swells the percentages proportionately.

The Lampman estate studies do not necessarily reveal the sizes of fortunes. This is because many of the fortunes are systematically distributed during the lifetime of the owner, mainly for the benefit of heirs. At the time of death the fortune is reduced.

Again, in extrapolating from the estates to the rest of the population, at least two distortions are discernible. First, only adults are considered by Lampman, whereas a considerable number of children are millionaires owing to having had trust funds settled upon them. Second, the economic position of age groups is not strictly comparable between the affluent and the poor because of an average earlier death rate for the latter.

But, on the whole, the Lampman study came closer than anyone had yet come to showing the asset position of all adult age-sex groups.

Definitive Data from the Federal Reserve

Strongly persuasive though all these studies are, it is possible to be definitive about the distribution of wealth in the United States, on the basis of findings put forth recently under the highest official auspices.

In a complex and comprehensive study prepared for the Board of Governors of the Federal Reserve System on the basis of Census Bureau data under the title *Survey of Financial Characteristics of Consumers,* the cold figures are officially presented on asset holdings as of December 31, 1962, removing the entire subject from the realm of pettifogging debate.

On that date the number of households in the country worth $500,000 or more was carefully computed at about 200,000.[28] The number of millionaires at the year-end was more than 80,000, compared with Lampman's 27,000 as of 1953. Only 39 per cent of these 200,000 had no inherited assets.[29] These 200,000 at the time held 22 per cent of all wealth, while 57 per cent of the wealth was held by 3.9 million individual consumer units worth $50,000 or more.

The panorama of wealth-holding throughout the populace was as follows (in millions of units):[30]

	Millions	Percentage of Households
All consumer units (households)	57.9	100.0
Size of wealth:		
Negative	1.0	1.8
Zero	4.7	8.0
$1–$999	9.0	16.0
$1,000–$4,999	10.8	18.0
$5,000–$9,999	9.1	16.0
$10,000–$24,999	13.3	23.0
$25,000–$49,999	6.2	11.0
$50,000–$99,999	2.5	5.0
$100,000–$199,999	.7	1.25
$200,000–$499,999	.5	Less than 1.0
$500,000 and up	.2	Less than 0.4

In stating that 200,000 households held 22 per cent of the wealth there is some danger of suggesting that the power of these 200,000 is less than it actually is. The nature of the wealth held is of determining importance here. In general, the lower wealth-holders mostly own inert assets such as automobiles, small amounts of cash and some residential equity, while the upper wealth-holders mostly own corporate equities in an aggregate amount sufficient to show that they are in full control of the productive side of the economic system.

Households in the number of 200,000 worth $500,000 and more held 32 per cent of all investment assets and 75 per cent of miscellaneous assets, largely trust funds, while 500,000 worth $200,000 to $499,999 held 22 per cent of investment assets. The 700,000 households worth $100,000 to $199,999 held 11 per cent of investment assets.[31]

Center of Economic Political Control

We see, then, that 1.4 million households owned 65 per cent of investment assets, which are what give economic control. Automobile and home ownership and bank deposits do not give such control. The economic power of the upper 200,000 is greater than indicated by their ownership of 22 per cent of all assets; it amounts to 32 per cent of investment assets.

Experts concede that a 5 per cent ownership stake in a large corporation is sufficient in most cases to give corporate control. It is my contention that *general* corporate control lies in this group of 200,000 very probably and almost certainly lies in the combined group of 700,000 wealthiest households, slightly more than 1 per cent, owning assets worth $200,000 and more.

There is a danger here, as the erudite will recognize, of perpetrating the logical fallacy of division—that is, arguing that what is true of a whole is true of its individual parts. That argument here would be that because 200,000 households own 32 per cent of investment assets they each hold a stake of exactly 32 per cent in the corporate system. I do *not* make such a ridiculous argument. First, this upper group concentrates its holdings for the most part in leading corporations, bypassing the million or so paper-tiger corporations of little or no value. Again, as just noted, far less than 32 per cent of ownership in any individual corporation is required to control it. *Control*, as we shall see, is the relevant factor where power is concerned. Usually comparatively little ownership is necessary to confer complete corporate control which, in turn, extends to participation in political control.

A man whose entire worth lies in 5 per cent of the capital stock of a corporation capitalized at $2 billion is worth only $100 million. But as this 5 per cent—and many own more than 5 per cent—usually gives him control of the corporation, his actual operative *power* is of the order of $2 billion. Politically his is a large voice, not only because of campaign contributions he may make but by reason of all the legislative law firms, congressional and state-legislative, under retainer by his corporation; for every national corporation has law firms in every state. There is additionally to be reckoned with all the advertising his corporation has to dispense among the mass media as a tax-free cost item, the lobbyists his corporation puts into the field and the cultural-charitable foundations both he and the corporation maintain.

Such a man, worth only $100 million net, is clearly a shadowy power in the land, his ownership stake vastly multiplied by what he controls—other people's property as well as his own. And there are more than a few such.

On the other hand, many intelligent citizens today complain in the face of the alleged complexity of affairs of feelings of powerlessness. Their feelings are justified. For they are in fact politically powerless.

The actual power of such concentrated ownership, therefore, is much greater than its proportion in the total of investment assets. The corporate power of the top 200,000, and certainly of the top 700,000, is actually 100 per cent. The *power* of this top layer corporatively would be no greater if it owned 100 per cent of investment assets. Actually, it might be less: It would then receive no support from many tremulous small holders but would probably find them in political opposition.

As to distribution of investment assets among smaller property holders, 1 per cent are owned by the $5,000 to $9,999 group, 7 per cent by the $10,000 to $24,999 group, 11 per cent by the $25,000 to $49,999 group and 15 per cent by the $50,000 to $99,999 group, or 34 per cent in all. In this group of comparatively modest means one finds some of the most voluble supporters of the established corporate way. Within their own terms they are all winners, certainly hold some financial edge. Most of them, as their expressions at stockholder meetings show, greatly admire the larger stockholders. In their eyes, a divinity doth hedge the large stockholders.

Net Worth in the Populace

Approached in terms of net worth (assets less debt) the situation of the lower populace is more unfavorable, as shown in the following table.[32]

Net Worth	Percentage of Consumer Units
Negative (deficit)	11
Zero	5
$1–$999	12
$1,000–$4,999	17
$5,000–$9,999	15
$10,000–$24,999	23
$25,000–$49,999	10
$50,000–$99,999	4
$100,000–$199,999	1
$200,000–$499,999	1
$500,000–$999,999	Less than ½ of 1 per cent
$1,000,000 and more	Less than ½ of 1 per cent

As this table shows, 28 per cent of the households had a net worth of less than $1,000; the 11 per cent with a deficit, on balance in debt in varying amounts, greatly exceeded the percentage of those worth $50,000 and more. The less than 1/10th of 1 per cent who were millionaires (from time to time pointed to with pride by *Time, Fortune* and the *Wall Street Journal*) were offset by 11 per cent of households worth less than zero. Add the zero-group and one obtains 16 per cent of all households. Forty-five per cent of all households had a net worth of less than $5,000. Is this affluence?

The View from the Bottom

A sensitive statistical analysis meriting the closest attention by all students of the distribution of wealth is that of Harvard's Dr. Gabriel Kolko, *Wealth and Power in America*. Not only does he develop essentially the same perspective as Lampman and the University of Michigan—"Since World War II, one-tenth of the nation has owned an average of two-thirds of liquid assets" (p. 49)—but he attacks the problem from below. He has no difficulty in showing, on the basis of official figures that, as of affluent 1957, 44 per cent of the spending units (households) lived below the maintenance level set by U.S. Bureau of Labor Statistics budgets, and that 27.5 per cent lived below the emergency level.[33] These figures represent a slight improvement over 1947, when the figures were 51.2 per cent and 27.5 per cent.

Dr. Kolko approaches the problem via income from all sources, employment as well as assets. As he shows, using Bureau of Census and University of Michigan figures, the distribution of income in the United States is fantastically lopsided. Whereas the lowest tenth of the population in all years from 1947 through 1955 received only 1 per cent of national personal income after federal taxes, the upper tenth in the same years received from 27 to 31 per cent. The second from the lowest income-tenth received 3 per cent of income from 1947 through 1955 except for the years 1953 and 1954, when it received 4 per cent. The third from the bottom income-tenth received 5 per cent throughout these years.

For 1947–55, in other words, the three lowest income-tenths, or 30 per cent of recipients, received 9 per cent of national income after taxes compared with a varying 56–58 per cent for the three upper income-tenths.[34] These figures spell poverty in all starkness—particularly in view of the greater concentration of children on the lower and poorly guided levels. Oddly, the prospect does not improve very much as one ascends until one gets to the very top. For the fourth income-tenth from the bottom received only 6 per cent of income, and the fifth income-tenth received only 8 per cent. It is not until the sixth tenth from the bottom that one finds 10 per cent of the receivers obtaining 10 percent of the income, balanced distribution. The next highest got 11 per cent, the next received 13 per cent and the next to the top got 16 per cent.

But if the top income-tenth, which received 27 per cent of income in 1955, were to be broken down into 1 per cent groups, we would find, as established by Lampman, that the top 1 per cent got the lion's share. For the higher one ascends, the fewer the number of persons involved, the greater the percentages of participation in economic advantages. Again let me remind readers, these incomes are from employment as well as from assets. It is the asset-derived income that is the most desirable, involving little or no strain on one's time or energy. With that kind of income one is not chained to a job, often ungratifying in itself. With asset-income one can choose one's line of endeavor or choose to be completely idle while others work.

Inadequate Counter-Measures

Not only is poverty in the United States very deep and widespread, Dr. Kolko clearly shows, but the various New Deal measures devised to mitigate it—Social Security, unemployment insurance, disability relief, minimum wage laws and the like—are quite inadequate in their coverage. There is no such thing, as newspapers repeatedly insist, as an embryonic Welfare State in the United States. This is evident in the fact that the average monthly old-age insurance payment in 1963 was $77.03, or $924.36 per year.

As to savings by each income-tenth, the lowest income-tenth has long lived on a deficit. From 1929 to 1950 this deficit varied from 2 to 35 per cent, standing at 16 per cent in 1950. Not only does this group not own anything but it is deeply in debt. The lower 50 per cent of income receivers in 1950 had a net savings deficit of nearly 18.5 per cent; the sixth income-tenth from the bottom had only 4 per cent of net national savings, with the figures rising thereafter by income-tenths from 10 to 11 to 20 and to 72 per cent for the top tenth. During the depression years of 1935–36, the net savings of the top income-tenth amounted to 105 per cent, of the next income-tenth 13 per cent, of the next income-tenth 6 per cent and of the fourth income-tenth 2 per cent—adding up to 126 per cent. But 60 per cent of the lower income receivers incurred debt of 25 per cent as an offset.[35] In this numbers game much of what one saves another owes.

To all this some hardy souls respond by saying, "Well, that's the way the ball bounces, that's the way the cookie crumbles." In other words, all this is the consequence of the inevitable interplay of chance factors in which some persons are the lucky winners or the more intelligent players.

Planned Consequences

But actually the results at both the top and the bottom are contrived. They are the outcome of pertinacious planning. For example, it is known on the basis of other careful studies that the lower income levels are disproportionately populated by Negroes and poor southern whites. They don't account for all of the lowly by any means; but they do account for very many. And the economic plight of both the Negroes and the southern whites is the consequence of a longstanding political power play. Southern Democratic Party gravy-train politicians after the Civil War, seeing a popular local issue in "restoring slavery in all but the name,"[36] asked for and received northern Republican acquiescence that would insure personally lucrative Democratic one-party dictatorial rule in the South. In return they agreed to deliver unbroken congressional support to the Republicans in blocking the rising national clamor, mainly from organized labor, for needed social legislation. For nearly a hundred years the scheme has worked perfectly, and the politically confused southern white in holding the Negro down, culturally and economically, has kept himself down to the same level. The scheme has had wider effects, as it has enabled the wealthy backbone of the Republican Party to keep a good portion of the rest of the country deprived, particularly of needed educational and social measures. The social role of the Republican Party ever since the death of Lincoln has been delay and obstruction, even though off and on there have emerged responsible, forward-looking Republicans.

This isn't to say that the foregoing paragraph accounts for the existence of deep and widespread poverty in the midst of fabulous wealth, but it accounts for some of it.

The Mild War on Poverty

President Lyndon B. Johnson in 1964 startled average newspaper readers by suddenly announcing, out of a seemingly cloudless sky, his "war on poverty." This was widely interpreted, cynically, as a pure vote-getting ruse, of no intrinsic merit. For was it not a fact, as newspapers vowed, that there was no genuine poverty in the prosperous, high-living United States? But since then, as a result of official speeches and the passage of an initial anti-poverty measure exceeding $1 billion, the country has been gradually introduced to the strange, even subversive, notion that poverty is prevalent in the United States.

The argument has now shifted, as it is always bound to in the nimble hands of the dialecticians, to what precisely constitutes poverty. Sargent Shriver, director of the Office of Economic Opportunity and former President John F. Kennedy's brother-in-law, suggested that a family of four with a yearly annual income under $3,000 and an individual with an income under $1,500 be classified as poor, which would put more than 30 per cent of all families in the poverty-stricken category according to University of Michigan figures. For the University of Michigan *Survey of Consumer Finances* showed for 1962 that, while the figures of the lowest tenth of all spending units (households) were not then available, the figure for the next lowest tenth was $1,510 for each household; and for the third from the lowest tenth it was $2,510. For the fourth tenth from the bottom it was only $3,350.[37] Mr. Shriver subsequently raised his figures to $3,130 and $1,540.

The United States Chamber of Commerce predictably challenged Mr. Shriver's first gauge of poverty as too high. "The Chamber of Commerce based its criticism of the old gauge," said the *New York Times*, "on the fact that a small family living in a warm climate and growing most of its own food could live comfortably on $3,000 a year."[38] As the patient could rest easily on this amount of income, why introduce him to luxuries—such as medicine?

Mr. Shriver, himself a wealthy man, more recently indicated that 35 million American families are "poverty-stricken," untouched by existing programs for assisting the poor.[39] If one assigns only 3 persons to a poor family, many of which have many more, one obtains 105 million persons out of a population of 180-plus million.

Rather obtusely the Chamber of Commerce people did not recognize that the Administration, in dealing with a serious situation (for whatever motives, humanitarian or self-serving) had produced a deceptive new official yardstick for measuring poverty: income. Down through history poverty has always referred to lack of property. The man who had no property was defined as poor; the more property a man owned the less poor he was. Most people in the United States own little more property than do Russian peasants, and by that standard they are poor.

By the Shriver standard, if a family had income from uncertain employment of twice $3,130 a year it would not be poor. While many Americans by the Shriver standard are poor, most are not—even though they own nothing worth speaking of. But the Shriver standard makes it appear that most people are well off, which is hardly true.

Poverty Defined

For my part, I would say that anyone who does not own a fairly substantial amount of income-producing property or does not receive an earned income sufficiently large to make substantial regular savings or does not hold a well-paid securely tenured job is poor. He may be healthy, handsome and a delight to his friends—but he is poor. By this standard at least 70 per cent of Americans are certainly poor, although not all of these by any means are destitute or poverty-stricken. But, as was shown in the 1930's, Americans can become destitute overnight if deprived of their jobs, a strong support to mindless conformity. As a matter of fact, many persons in rather well-paid jobs, even executives, from time to time find themselves jobless owing to job discontinuance by reason of mergers, technical innovation or plant removal. Unable to get new jobs, they suddenly discover, to their amazement, that they are really poor, and they also discover by harsh experience to what specific conditions the word "poverty" refers. And even many of those who never lose their jobs often discover in medical and similar emergencies that they are as helpless as wandering beggars. They are, in fact, poor. In such eventualities the man of property is evidently in a different position. He is definitely not poor. And this is all I say.

Conditions in England and India

The United States, in the short period since the public lands were distributed to the people, often through the intermediation of profit-skimming railroads, has rather quickly been brought close to the position of older countries such as England. In 1911–13 the small fraction of 0.63 per cent of persons over age 25 in England owned 57 per cent of all capital, compared with 1.84 per cent of such persons owning 51.92 per cent of capital in 1946–47. In 1911–13 1.53 per cent owned 66.9 per cent of capital compared with 4.56 per cent owning 63.27 per cent of capital in 1946–47.[40] Observers see a slight tendency to equalization in these figures.

But in superstition-ridden India about 1 per cent of the population gets half of all income.[41]

Apart from the differences in the proportions, a difference between the United States on the one hand and England and India on the other is that in the latter there is a much longer history behind each condition. In the United States it is recent.

Some Preliminary Conclusions

It should be evident in studying the Lampman and Federal Reserve figures on estates that the United States now has a well-established hereditary propertied class such as exists in Europe, which Americans have long looked upon disdainfully as the stronghold of class privilege. Great wealth in the United States, in other words, is no longer ordinarily gained by the input of some effort, legal or illegal, useful or mischievous, but comes from being named an heir. Almost every single wealth-holder of the upper half of 1 per cent arrived by this route.

Lampman's figures clearly indicate this. He noted that 40 per cent of the top wealth-holders are women. Now, while some women have garnered big money by their own efforts—Mary Pickford, Greta Garbo, Helena Rubinstein and a sprinkling of others in the world of entertainment and fashion—few women have been even modest fortune builders. Women simply do not occupy the money-making positions in finance, industry and politics. But they have been heirs.

It is true that estate splitting between husband and wife is increasingly resorted to in order to take advantage of tax provisos. But this works both ways. Women can split estates with men just as men can with women. And on the upper level of wealth it is usually wealthy people who marry each other. Otherwise it is front-page news. Even if it is contended that not so many as 40 per cent of the men are in the picture because of estate splitting, the men are, as heirs, prominent among the wealthy for another reason. Many men, having inherited a smaller estate, have expanded their wealth through shrewd operations. J. Paul Getty, whom certain English newspapers insistently refer to as "the richest man in the world," inherited $7 million from his father many years ago, thus placing him well in the millionaire class. He has through operations in the oil business gone well beyond this level. Nevertheless he is not "self made." There are more than a few Gettys among the top wealth-holders.

It can therefore be concluded that *at least* 40 per cent of the men, or 24 per cent of all the top wealth-holders, are heirs, bringing to more than 60 per cent the hereditary proportion. I believe, on other grounds, that the proportion of male heirs in the group is much larger. Women, owing to their inexperience with financial affairs, are generally poor estate managers, Hetty Green notwithstanding. They are more easily victimized by specious schemes, fail to take advantage of obvious opportunities, and so tend to drop out of the group and to be under-represented. Men are usually financially more capable and their greater staying power entitles them statistically to a larger representation among the heirs than women. More conclusively, it is directly observable among the super-rich that the possessors—men or women—are simply heirs. They got there by listening to a will being read, not by schemes that fill some observers with unaccountable transports of delight, that others consider unspeakably ignoble. There are few newcomers, as we shall see in the next chapter.

Although a man who amassed his own money would figure only once among the propertied, some who are heirs are heirs many times over, having inherited from many testators. This has taken place on the upper, intermediate and lower levels of wealth. And this occasional process leads to further concentration.

The federal estate-tax statistics since 1916 show that an avalanche of wealth has been transferred over fifty years by testamentary bequest. Individuals inherited in nearly every case. Whatever the presence of rags-to-riches moneymakers in the past the acquisitors now are largely gone. The inheritors are in possession.

Extended Family Groups

Lampman's figures relate to individuals. They do not show that most of the people in the upper ½ of 1 per cent that now probably own at least 33 per cent (by value) of all assets are members of extended family groups. There are more than 1,600 Du Ponts, not all individually in the upper circle. There are sizable clusters of Rockefellers, Vanderbilts, Whitneys, Mellons, Woolworths, Fishers, Phippses, Hartfords and others. Through distaff marriages part of the big fortunes are concealed behind offbeat names, such as Cecil (Vanderbilt). The well-groomed heirs or their representatives often sit together amicably on the same boards of directors. Most belong to the same metropolitan clubs.

But the rather well-populated group that Lampman calls top wealth-holders also certainly contains many blanks as far as big wealth is concerned. It will be recalled he stressed that more than half of his top group had no more than $125,000 of assets—a paltry sum, even though in thousands of neighborhoods around the country a man with such wealth would be looked upon as a Croesus.

Owing to intermarriage among the wealthy, property holdings tend to concentrate in fewer and fewer hands. For the propertied, not without sound reason, often suspect the marital motivations of the nonpropertied.[42]

These processes cannot help but concentrate wealth and make the scope of new estate builders less ample. There is less and less room at the top for new moneymakers. Although there are new successful enterprises, they are all comparatively small. Some are absorbed by the bigger enterprises on advantageous terms. None shows the slightest sign of becoming another Ford Motor Company. All the big bets seem to be down. *Rien n'a va plus.*

Apologists on the Defensive

But this panorama of contemporary private wealth and power throws some doubt on the doctrines of earlier apologists for the big fortunes. It was once widely preached from pulpits as well as editorial pages that great wealth was either the reward for social service (such as graciously building a vast industry to cater to an undeserving public) or it represented the inevitable, natural and wholly acceptable outcome of an evolutionary struggle in which the fittest survived and the unfit landed in the gutter. On the basis of this doctrine the present top wealth-holders are the offspring of public benefactors and the fittest of a past generation. Fortunately, they are not themselves facing the same tests of fitness.

It was also once often said that, if all money were equally divided among all the people, in less than a generation it would be back in the same hands. While this may have been true when the original fortune-builders were alive, it is hardly true any longer, when the heirs would have to contend with gentry like Mr. James J. Hoffa and Mr. Frank Costello. In a struggle waged outside the Marquis of Queensberry rules (which is where the fortune-builders operated) most of the present wealth-holders, many of them personally attractive, would hardly be voted most likely to succeed. Could they make much headway against Jake Guzik and Tony Accaro? Al Capone and Machine-Gun Jack McGurn?

Down through the years all the estates have been subject to taxation—federal and sometimes state—but to much less than is commonly supposed, as we shall see. There is no process of estate destruction taking place in the United States through taxation, as is commonly suggested by propagandists of the Establishment. And few estates, unless there are no heirs, pass to institutions. But many estates pass indirectly as well as directly to heirs through various arrangements such as delayed-action trust funds, endowments and foundations. The indirectly conveyed portions are operated by the heirs for their own beneficial interest.

The Fortress of Interlaced Wealth

What has developed, then, under the operation of inheritance laws handed down from days when property ownership was far more modest to a day when vast properties have been created mainly by technology, is a huge, solid fortress of interlaced wealth against which even clever new wealth-seekers, try as they will, cannot make a tiny dent. About the only way one can get in (and that way isn't always rewarding) is by marriage. If a potential new Henry Ford produces an invention and sets out with friends to market it he generally finds (as did Professor Edwin H. Armstrong, inventor of wide-swing radio frequency modulation, the regenerative circuit for vacuum tubes, ultra short-wave super-regeneration and the superheterodyne circuit) that it is boldly infringed by established companies. After he spends the better part of a lifetime in court straining to protect his rights he may win (usually he does not); but if he wins he collects only a percentage royalty. What the infringers can show they have earned through their promotional efforts they may keep, with the blessings of the courts, who are sticklers for equity: All effort must be rewarded. And then the overwrought inventor, as Professor Armstrong did in 1954, can commit suicide.

Henry Ford came up when there were only small competing companies in the field. When established companies are in the field, inventors must sell out, or suffer a fate similar to Professor Armstrong's.

The Role of the People

The inheritance laws have played a major role in the development of great fortunes. But they haven't been the only factor. A small group, unless possessed of direct dictatorial power, could not unaided have served itself so generously, even if masters of stealth. Writing about the wealthy in *America's Sixty Families*, page 5, I remarked: "The situation, for which the people themselves are in a great measure to blame. . . ." The public itself has facilitated and continues to facilitate the building of vast hereditary private power within the American elective system of government. This public is in many ways a self-made victim, as sociologists now regard many victims of crimes.

The contrast I have posed between concentrated wealth and widely distributed poverty may seem to suggest that I am arguing for the equalization of wealth. But though there is obviously considerable room for some equalization I shall not argue for it because there are millions of people who could not hold on to $10 for five minutes or $10,000 for five months.

If wealth were equalized, what would we have? As Lampman showed, if all asset-wealth as of 1953 were equally apportioned, there would be about $10,000 for each adult. Let us suppose that a share in this amount were held for each adult in a national trust supervised by the United States treasury. The income from each share at 5 per cent would be $500 per annum. If one adds this to the present amount of each person's earned income it would not amount to much, however welcome it would be for some in the lowest brackets.

If inequality of income is not the main question, what is?

Policy-Making Power of Wealth

First, the present concentration of wealth confers self-arrogated and defaulted political policy-making power at home and abroad in a grossly disproportionate degree on a small and not especially qualified mainly hereditary group; secondly, this group allocates vast economic resources in narrow, self-serving directions, both at home and abroad, rather than in socially and humanly needed public directions.

When, through its agents, it cannot enlist the government in support of its various plans at home and abroad it can, and does, frustrate the government in various proceedings that have full public endorsement. It involves the nation in cycles of ferocious wars that are to the interest of asset preservation and asset expansion but are contrary to the interest of the nation and the world. It can and does establish connections all over the world that covertly involve American power in all sorts of ways unknown until some last-minute denouement even to Congress and the president.

It doesn't do any of this maliciously, to be sure, any more than an elephant feels malice when it rubs against a sapling and breaks it in two. An elephant must behave like an elephant, beyond any moral stricture. And power of any kind must exert itself. Historically it has invariably exerted itself in its own self-visualized interests.

So, concentrated asset-wealth not only brings in large personal incomes, but confers on the owners and their deputies a disproportionately large voice in economic, political and cultural affairs. Thus the owners may make or frustrate public policy, at home and abroad.

Low Incomes of Vital Personnel

Managers of concentrated asset-wealth determine, among other things, how much is to be paid for various services—who is to be paid a great deal and who is to be paid very little. Some people, for the convenience purely of asset-wealth, are rewarded munificently for services of comparatively slight social importance—for example, certain leading company executives. Other persons are paid poorly for what are universally insisted to be superlatively valuable services—for example, scientists, engineers, artists and teachers. The pay of scientists in the United States in the 1960's, according to the National Science Foundation, is in the range $6,000-$15,-000 per annum,[43] far less than that of an astute salesman of encyclopedias or vacuum cleaners. Referring to "starvation wages," Paul Woodring, educational consultant to the Fund for the Advancement of Education of the Ford Foundation, said: "There are dozens of liberal arts colleges which pay average salaries as low as $3,000 per year and minimum salaries much lower still."[44] If it is said that such compensation has more recently been increased (which isn't generally true), one may still ask: Is it anywhere near the astronomical level of executive salaries?

Of salaries of scientists and teachers, a company director would say: "What have we to do with those? They aren't in our jurisdiction. The executive salaries, I admit, are."

My response to this is: When the leading cadres of wealth want to be the government, as we shall see, they are the government. When they don't want to be, when there is some delicate problem to be solved, they say, "Go to Washington about that. It's out of our jurisdiction." But even in Washington they have many friends who believe that teachers and scientists should not be spoiled by being paid ample wages.

Marxism and the Workers

Marxists hold that it is the workers—factory workers—who are being deprived to insure profits for the rich. And this may be so to some extent in some times and places, and at one time it was so universally in the United States. But the workers would not likely be paid more and would probably be paid less than they are now in thoroughly unionized industries under such so-called Marxist regimes as we have yet seen.

In some instances, owing to organization and the balance of external forces, some categories of unionized workers in the United States today are probably disproportionately rewarded, are paid more than many trained scientists. Their leaders have simply seized opportunities to exert leverage in the power structure, threatening to disrupt production.

Lest I leave a misleading impression of American workers, it must be said that the position of the unorganized and unskilled is very bleak, in the depths of poverty. So-called white collar workers are also poorly paid. Since World War II the custom has spread among low-paid skilled people, particularly teachers, of working at two jobs, a practice known as "moonlighting." Police and firemen, too, participate in the practice, and so do even skilled factory operatives who wish to keep above the poverty level. At a time when many sociologists discourse fervidly about a coming thirty-hour week and assert increasing leisure to be a basic human problem, many moonlighters work sixty and seventy hours a week, hardly a step forward from the nineteenth century twelve-hour day. The moonlighters drive taxis, tend bar, act as property guards, work in stores, etc.

But if the workers in general are indeed deprived for the sake of profits they wouldn't be benefited much directly by an egalitarian distribution of assets, nor would anyone else. For it isn't the factor of ownership of assets in itself that is crucial. It is the factor of general *control* that *concentrated* ownership confers that needs to be understood. Owing to the strength given them by their *concentrated* and *combined* assets, the big owners and their paid managers have a major if not always decisive voice in running the economic system, in backing the political parties and their candidates and in influencing if not determining national policies from the highest to the lowest. The ownership titles, reinforced many times over from the vantage point of banks and insurance companies, are what constitute the ticket of admission. The amount of ownership at the top of the pyramid necessary to insure such control for any group may be only 5 per cent. Scattered smaller owners, if there are any, cannot gather enough stock to overcome the leading blocks and would not know what to do if they could.

The Radiation of Control

This control at one or a few points radiates through all of industry, with a few central groups participating in a cooperative manner. The industrial control (to be shown later) gives command over vast resources, some of which are used to influence political parties and candidates, newspapers and other publications. A tacit, uncriticized scheme of values is put into action and is absorbed by many people far from the scene. The point to be raised is this: Is this scheme of values always conducive to the security and well-being of the Republic? Whether it is or not, it is often decisive at crucial historical turning points. And it isn't subject to review in any public forum.

I don't assert that every single individual—man, woman and child—in the circle of great wealth has an active role in this process of control. Many are far from the centers of power, leading *la dolce vita*, and hardly know what goes on. Some are utterly incapable, confined in sanatoria, the wards of family trustees. Still others, present in full command of able faculties, disapprove of the general trend but are unable to prevail against what is basically a group momentum.

Many people own some stock. Each share is entitled to a vote. An owner may refuse to vote, in which case decisions are made despite him. Usually he sends in his proxy to be voted for the management, which is the way the Russians vote: for a single ticket. However, he may decide that he wants to vote against the management, in which case he must at great cost and effort round up many other stockholders. This task in any company is about as great as putting an opposition slate in the field in a Russian "election." Occasionally it succeeds, although not when initiated by small stockholders. One must have some large blocks of stock to begin with if one hopes to check or unseat any established management—blocks of 5, 10 or 15 per cent of all outstanding stock. If one has that, one appeals for other large blocks to join, or buys additional large blocks in the market (for vast sums, which one must be presumed to have). *For it is ownership blocks that determine who the managers shall be.*

If one miraculously wins the election, one has the task of installing new managers, men more to one's liking. But the one who can do this is himself one of the top dogs. He is not a small stockholder.

Such control is exercised not in one company or in a few companies (contrary to what is often supposed) but through a long series of inter-locking companies. It is what constitutes power in the American system. It may not be power as great at a single moment as that possessed by some elected officials, such as the president, but it is a more *continuous* power. An elected public official, even a president, must from time to time undergo the hazards of a formal election at regular intervals. And even a president is limited to a maximum term of eight years, whereas the head of a big corporation or bank can remain in office for forty or fifty years and can see many presidents of the United States come and go.

Deficit in Public Services

The converse of the great concentration of personal wealth is the great deficit in needed public social services. On the corporation front, the country is obviously extremely lusty. But in education and medicine, to cite merely two areas, everything suddenly becomes extremely meager, scroung-ing and hand-to-mouth. This disparity is curious in a wealthy country and forcefully reminds one of Benjamin Disraeli's allusion to two na-tions, the rich and the poor. But the deficits in these areas, the dialecticians will be quick to point out, are gradually being met now by government out of taxes. As we shall see later, however, the contribution of the top wealth-holders to taxes is disproportionately low. The wealthy, like every-one else, dislike to pay taxes and, unlike most other people, they know how to minimize them through the exercise of political influence. This is one of the nice differences between being wealthy and being poor.

The Constitution of the United States bars the bestowal of titles of nobility. But in many ways it would clear up much that is now obscure if titles were allowed. Not only would they show, automatically, to whom deference was due as a right but they would publicly distinguish those who held continuing hereditary power from people who are merely temporarily voted in or appointed for limited terms. The chroniclers of High Society—that is, the circles of wealth—recognize this need and, in order to show hereditary status and family position, they allude to males in the line of descent by number, as in the case of royal dynasties. Thus in the English branch of the Astor family there is a John Jacob Astor VII.[45] But there are also George F. Baker III, August Belmont IV, William Bird III, Joseph H. Choate III, Irénée and Pierre du Pont III, Marshall Field V, Potter Palmer I, John D. Rockefeller IV, Cornelius Vanderbilt V and so on.[46]

It is names such as these that would properly be found in an American Almanach de Gotha.

Two ❧

ROOM AT THE TOP: THE NEW RICH

Were it not for the miscellaneous batch of hard-bitten, shirt-sleeved Texas oil-lease speculators and wildcatters that since World War I has risen on a tide of special tax privileges like science-fiction dinosaurs, it could well be said that the day of accumulating gargantuan new personal fortunes in the United States is just about ended, leaving the tubbed, scrubbed and public-relations-anointed inheritors of the nineteenth-century money scramble holding most of the chips. As it is, fortune-building continues—albeit at a greatly subdued pace outside the lushly flowing oil industry. For just about everything else of marketable value is tightly vaulted down, much of it resting comfortably in trust. But even in the oil industry, magnitudes are exaggerated, Texas-style, by writers who desire to bedazzle readers with a modern if oil-soaked Arabian Nights tale.

New personal wealth is dealt with in this chapter—that is, great individual wealth that has shown itself since World War I and, more particularly, since World War II. For the most part it is wealth not known to Gustavus Myers, historian of the first waves of American fortunes and, partly because of the give-away oil depletion allowance, it postdates *America's Sixty Families* (1937). Classification of these new fortunes with respect to wealth and super-wealth and their comparison with the old fortunes are deferred until Chapter IV.

Actually, before larger sums are bandied about in these pages, let it be noted that a person worth only $10 million (insignificant though $10 million is compared with many modern fortunes) is very, very wealthy indeed. If a prudent, hardworking, God-fearing, home-loving 100 per cent American saved $100,000 a year after taxes and expenses it would take him a full century to accumulate such a sum. A self-incorporated film star who earned $1 million a year and paid a 10 per cent agent's fee, 10 per cent in business expenses, a rounded 50 per cent corporation tax on the net and then withdrew $100,000 for his own use (on which he also paid about 50 per cent tax) would need to be a box-office rage for thirty-four unbroken years before he could save $10 million. Yet some men do acquire such sums—and much more. But never by offering mere talent, whatever it is, in a free market. Even the most talented bank robbers or kidnappers have never approached such an accumulation before being laid low by the eager gendarmerie.

The incandescent Marilyn Monroe, as big as they come in filmdom and a veritable box office Golconda, died broke—an old story with the mothlike entertainers and professional athletes. She bequeathed $1 million to friends but, despite posthumous earnings of $800,000 accruing to her estate, nothing was left after taxes and creditors' claims. Clearly she was in need of a tax lawyer. There was even nothing left to establish a trust fund to generate a paltry $5,000 a year for her invalid mother. Yet Miss Monroe, obviously a true-blue American, reportedly drew $200 million to the box office from 1950 to 1963.[1] More recent reports indicate that something was salvaged for her mother.

Hard to get, $10 million shows its power in another way. If invested in tax-exempt securities it can generate about $250,000 a year. Now if the owner exercises initial frugality and invests this *income* similarly each year, it will produce $6,250 the first year and (disregarding compound interest all along) $12,500 the second year, $18,750 the third year, $25,000 the fourth year and so on. In the tenth year the income of the accumulated *income* of the original $10 million will be $62,500 on a new capital sum of $2.5 million, which automatically doubles itself every ten years. The owner might even do a bit better by investing in taxable securities and paying taxes, particularly on the second accumulation, but I have focused on tax-exempt securities in order to keep to the simplest terms. Yet the ordinary man on his 4 or 5 per cent in the savings bank must pay full taxes. This sort of accumulating on the income of the *income,* thus generating new capital sums, has long been the investment style of old Boston and Philadelphia families. Careful to a fault, they own only *small* yachts, drive only *old* (but well-maintained) cars and are accustomed to wear old but *expensive* clothes of the first class so that they look quaintly dowdy. And they intermarry with *old* families, unfailingly. They are people who would rather study the fine engraving on a stock certificate than the brush strokes of an old master. They are, in short, respectably, unobtrusively rich.

How the sizes of new fortunes were obtained will appear in the text. The most conservative available figures are used throughout and are critically evaluated. For precise figures it would be necessary to get certified copies of net worth, which (not being voluntarily proffered) could be obtained only in the unlikely event of a congressional *subpoena* with the acquiescence of the Supreme Court. The sacred right to privacy is used to screen the dimensions of great wealth, although privacy becomes expendable when young men are summoned into the armed forces for "police" duty at coolie pay and are unceremoniously ordered to strip naked for minute scrutiny and examination. And if subpoenaed the figures might not be even momentarily accurate because, owing to the undeveloped state of a part of many large holdings, the owners themselves honestly don't know how much, at going market prices, they are worth. Seeking such accuracy in the figures amounts to committing the fallacy of misplaced precision.[2]

The Fortune Study

Fortune, stepping into the data vacuum decreed by a delicately sensitive Congress, has given us the latest *précis* on the largest individual contemporary fortunes.[3] Beginning our exposition with it and selecting only the relative newcomers, we find that with few exceptions the newer fortunes rose on the basis of oil and its generous depletion allowances, and upper executive position in General Motors Corporation.

Fortune assumed, reasonably enough, that an income of $1 million or more per year (some incomes range much higher—up to perhaps $25 to $50 million) might suggest asset-holdings of at least $50 million. But some large incomes are nonrepetitive, derive from unloading assets (which might have been procured very cheaply) at a large profit; they are not the same as continuing incomes from investments. The incomes swollen by relieving oneself of assets at higher prices (capital gains) are reflected in boom times in the sharp rise in million-dollar *incomes*—from 49 in 1940 to 398 in 1961. But no steady million-dollar incomes at all blossom from the sale of services or talent; not even the most extravagantly rewarded executives or film stars pick up that much in straight across-the-board pay.

The point of departure for *Fortune* was a Treasury official's estimate that in 1957 there were between 150 and 500 $50-million-plus assetholders; there were actually 223 incomes of $1 million-plus, according to the Treasury's subsequently published *Statistics of Income: 1957* (p. 20). *Fortune* to its own satisfaction identified 155 of them by name. Of this group it published the names of half, the ones thought to possess assets of $75 million upward, and gave estimates of their net worth in broad ranges. *Fortune* also named a few other steady big-income beneficiaries at random in its text, outside its list, giving no reason for this deviation. The list, confined to then living people, did not name all the big post-1918 fortunes, although here and there some persons who had recently died were mentioned. Some such fortunes omitted from the *Fortune* list will be mentioned further along.

Before scanning the *Fortune* list and then noting qualifications of it, the reader will be better prepared if he ponders over the tables in Appendix A that provide a broad statistical background since 1940 on the larger incomes and lay the ground for some incisive observations. In the upper brackets at least, these income recipients abstractly impaled like skeletal insects in the tables are unquestionably included among Lampman's 1.6 per cent of adults that compose American wealth-holders. No doubt the *Fortune* list in its entirety, with some additions to be supplied, represents a part of the moneyed elite of the Lampman higher strata. But in the group of Appendix A incomes below $100,000 or so, many are only those of potential wealth-holders—for the simple reason that they are from salaries.

Property and Politics

Nonetheless the varying totals shown in Appendix A of incomes in excess of $25,000—numbering 49,806 in 1940 and 626,997 in 1961—certainly represent the cream of the take in the American system. This is not a large group and, in relation to a population of nearly 200 million, of which more than half are adults, it is not any different in relative size from the small group of tight-fisted landowners found in Latin American countries or from the Communist Party of Soviet Russia.

In order to participate in politics in the Soviet Union one must be a member of the Communist Party. This is a formal condition. Similarly, in order to participate meaningfully in politics in the United States one must be a property owner. This is not a formal requirement; formally anyone may participate. But, informally, participation beyond voting for alternate pre-selected candidates is so difficult for the nonpropertied as to be, in effect, impossible. The nonpropertied person in the United States who wishes to attain and hold a position of leverage in politics must quickly become a property owner. And this is one reason why unendowed budding American politicians, not being property owners, must find or create opportunities (legal or illegal) for themselves to acquire property. Without it they are naked to the first wind of partisan adversity and gratuitous public spitefulness.

Politically the nonpropertied carry little efficient influence in the United States—that is, they have at best only marginal individual leverage—which is not the same as saying that all property owners participate in politics. But, when all the chips are down, these latter rule or significantly modify the situation in committee rooms and cloakrooms, directly or through amply rewarded intermediaries. In the United States the ownership of property, often evidenced by possession of a credit card, gives the same personal amplitude that possession of a party card confers in Soviet Russia.

Although different, the political systems of Soviet Russia and the United States are not basically so different as widely supposed. The United States can be looked upon as having, in effect, a single party: the Property Party. This party can be looked upon as having two subdivisions: the Republican Party, hostile to accommodating adjustments (hence dubbed "Conservative"), and the Democratic Party, of recent decades favoring such adjustments (hence dubbed "Liberal"). The big reason third parties have come to naught—a puzzle to some political scientists—is simply that no substantial group of property owners has seen fit to underwrite one. There is no Anti-Property Party.

In general, American politics are not nearly so brusque, arbitrary and doctrinaire as Russian politics. But those carried away by the lullaby of American democracy should consult the harsh experience of the Negro and other repressed groups in the American system. There matters begin to take on a distinctly Russian complexion.

As to the sources of the big incomes (those above $500,000 and over $1 million), Appendix A shows that the aggregate received in this category includes comparatively little in salaries or partnership profits. Receipts in the form of dividends and capital gains, interest and other forms of property return, were comparatively colossal. The 398 persons in the $1 million-plus income class in 1961, for example, took only $18,607,000 in salaries, an average of $46,753, and $10,503,000 in partnership profits but took $259,574,000 in dividends, $434,272,000 in capital gains, $8,754,000 in interest, $3,163,000 from trust funds (not including capital gains from such) and $2,371,000 from rents and royalties. The group as a whole also absorbed $7,915,000 of business loss, more than offset by the interest it received. This, in brief, is not a group of workers even of the upper executive class, and the same holds true of the $500,000–$1,000,000 group of income recipients.

Fortune differentiated between inherited and personally assembled wealth. We will leave the inheritors for Chapter IV; examined below is the *Fortune* list of the new big wealth-holders, thirty-five in number.

Left off the *Fortune* list but referred to in its text were Dr. Martin Miller, New Orleans surgeon, with a reported annual income of $7–

BIG NEW WEALTH-HOLDERS

Name	Stated Net Worth (millions)	Financial Activity	Age in 1957	Schooling	Children
1. J. Paul Getty (Los Angeles)	$700–$1,000	Integrated oil companies	65	Oxford (A.B.)	5 (1 dead)
2. H. L. Hunt (Dallas)	$400–$ 700	Oil operator	67	Fifth grade	4
3. Arthur Vining Davis (deceased 1962)	"	Alcoa executive	90	Amherst (A.B.)	none listed
4. Joseph P. Kennedy (Boston)	$200– 400	Market operator	69	Harvard (A.B.)	9 (3 dead)
5. Daniel K. Ludwig (New York)	"	Ship operator	60	Public school	unmarried
6. Sid Richardson* (Fort Worth)	"	Oil operator	60+	Some college	unmarried
7. Alfred P. Sloan, Jr. (New York)	"	General Motors executive	82	M.I.T.	none listed
8. James Abercrombie* (Houston)	$100–$ 200	Oil operator			
9. Stephen Bechtel (San Francisco)	"	Public construction	57	Some college	2
10. William Blakley* (Dallas)	"	Railway Express and airlines		Some college	
11. Jacob Blaustein (Baltimore)	"	Integrated oil companies	65	Some college	none listed

BIG NEW WEALTH-HOLDERS (Continued)

Name	Stated Net Worth (millions)	Financial Activity	Age in 1957	Schooling	Children
12. Clarence Dillon (New York)	"	Investment banker	75	Harvard (A.B.)	
13. William Keck* (Los Angeles)	"	Oil operator			1
14. Charles F. Kettering (deceased 1959)	"	General Motors executive	81	Ohio State	
15. William L. McKnight (St. Paul)	"	Minnesota Mining and Manufacturing Co.	70	Public school	none listed
16. John Mecom (Houston)		Oil operator	45	Some college	3
17. C. W. Murchison (Dallas)	"	Oil operator	62	Some college	3 (1 dead)
18. John L. Pratt* (Fredericksburg)	"	General Motors executive			
19. R. E. Smith* (Houston)	"	Oil operator			
20. Michael Benedum (deceased 1961)	$ 75– 100	Oil operator	88	Public school	1 (dead)
21. Donaldson Brown (Baltimore)		General Motors and Du Pont executive	72	Virginia Polytechnic Institute	6
22. George R. Brown (Houston)	"	Public construction	59	Some college	3

BIG NEW WEALTH-HOLDERS (Continued)

Name	Stated Net Worth (millions)	Financial Activity	Age in 1957	Schooling	Children
23. Herman Brown (deceased 1962)	"	Public construction	65	Some college	none listed
24. James A. Chapman* (Tulsa)	"	Oil operator			
25. Leo Corrigan (Dallas)	"	Real estate and hotel operation	63	Public school	2
26. Erle P. Halliburton* (Duncan, Oklahoma)	"	Oil well equipment			2
27. Henry J. Kaiser (Oakland)	"	Public construction	75	Public school	
28. John W. Kieckhefer (Milwaukee)	"	Paper, containers	not given	not given	not given
29. John E. Mabee* (Tulsa)	"	Oil operations			
30. John D. MacArthur (Chicago)	"	Insurance promotion	60	Public school	2
31. H. H. Meadows (Dallas)	"	Oil operator	58	Law school	1
32. Charles S. Mott (Flint)	"	General Motors executive	82	Stevens Institute of Technology	3
33. James Sottile, Jr. (Miami)	"	Banking	44	Public school	5

BIG NEW WEALTH-HOLDERS (Continued)

Name	Stated Net Worth (millions)	Financial Activity	Age in 1957	Schooling	Children
34. George W. Strake* (Texas)	"	Oil operations			
35. Louis Wolfson (New York)	"	Financial operator	45	Some college	4

* Not listed in *Who's Who* 1956–57, 1964–65.

$8 million from oil royalties; E. V. Richards, New Orleans real estate oper-
ator estimated by *Fortune* to be worth $50–$100 million; and Matilda
Geddings Gray of New Orleans, who inherited an oil fortune of unstated present value from her father. *Fortune* also mentioned a sprinkling
of new names in the $50–million bracket, but these persons need not
detain us here.

Revision of the List

Under critical analysis, this list requires some pruning and rearranging,
both with respect to the number of inclusions among the new big rich
and to estimated size of holdings.

Only the probates of estates of those who have died since 1957 can give
us a clue to the value of the fortune, although even they cannot be
decisive. But Michael Benedum, "King of the Wild-Catters," died in 1961
at the age of ninety-two and the probate of his will in Pittsburgh showed
a net estate of $68,199,539, putting him only some 10 per cent below
Fortune's $75–$100 million range in which he appears.[4] I count
this estimate a direct "hit," as holdings of this size can easily vary in value
by 10 to 25 per cent from year to year, up or down.

Benedum left half his estate to the inevitable tax-evading foundation
and after a number of specific bequests to relatives he left the residue to a
nephew, Paul G. Benedum, who now ranks as a wealthy man of the lower
ranks and directs the Benedum oil properties through his own holdings
and those of the Benedum foundation. In passing, it may be noted that
Benedum, as *Fortune* relates, had the amiable and rare habit of cutting
younger and even menial employees in on some of his lucrative ventures;
thus, a chauffeur who looked for no more than a steady $50 per week was
so favored and predeceased his benefactor worth some $17 million.

Arthur Vining Davis, former head of the Mellons' Aluminum Corporation of America, died in 1962. The press report of his will played back the
Fortune estimate of $400 million on his wealth,[5] but the probate showed
that *Fortune* had missed wildly on this one; it was too high by about 370
per cent.[6] The actual size of the Davis estate was $86,629,282.83, not
including $5 million of Cuban property. As there is no record of early
Davis gifts large enough to have ever put him in the $400– to $700-
million class of wealth-holder, on this one *Fortune* must be debited with
a very bad miss.

There is no public evidence to justify such a high estimate by *Fortune*.
As of December 11, 1939, according to a Securities and Exchange Commission study (TNEC study, Monograph No. 29, to be cited later), Mr.

Davis owned 11.4 per cent of Aluminum Company of America common and a brother owned .96 per cent. Mr. Davis also owned 5.41 per cent of the cumulative preferred. At the 54¾ close for 1962 a block of 12 per cent of Aluminum common then outstanding was worth $140,397,615; 5.5 per cent of the preferred was worth $3,128,547 at the year's high. At the record high of 133½ in 1956, 12 per cent of Aluminum was worth $329,262,364.

This block of stock never could have put Davis into the $400– to $700– million class even in a momentary market flurry. As it was, he had obviously sold much of it at lower levels or transferred it to others off the record. He could not have sold at or anywhere near its high point because then the proceeds exceeding $300 million would have been in his estate; he was too old at the time to divest himself of any by gift under the provisions of the tax code.

The Davis will, after assigning $1 million and his home to his secretary, divided the estate into 100 shares. Of these, 50 were put into a public trust with the First National Bank of Miami, a nephew among the co-trustees; 25 were put into a public trust with the Mellon National Bank and Trust Company of Pittsburgh, the nephew and a son-in-law among the trustees. Ten shares went to the heirs of a deceased brother, 10 shares to a stepdaughter and 5 shares were set aside for inheritance taxes. Thus, 75 per cent of the estate escaped taxes. The tax-free income of the trusts was broadly designated for the usual charities and scientific, educational and religious work. But the trustees, like those of many similar establishments, will continue to exercise the corporate voting power of the Davis holdings, which is what counts. Davis thus passed his financial power, diminished only by an overall tax of 5 per cent, on to his relatives.

In 1952 Davis had established another foundation, the Arthur Vining Davis Foundation, which, according to the *Foundation Directory*, 1964, at the end of 1961 had assets of only $1,379,672. So no earlier Davis wealth of substantial proportions appears to have escaped notice.

A report is not yet available on the estate of Herman Brown of the construction firm of Brown and Root, Inc., of Dallas, who died in 1962.

Charles F. Kettering, research director of General Motors, died in 1958 and left an estate "conservatively" estimated at a little more than $200 million but no inventory was cited.[7] The bulk went to the Charles F. Kettering Foundation and a trust. At the end of 1962 the Foundation had assets of $72,020,128, according to the *Foundation Directory*; and as Kettering in his lifetime placed large sums for medical research, there seems no reason to question seriously the *Fortune* rating of the $200– million range. (One of the surer ways of spotting truly big wealth is that it shows itself in huge public transfers of assets during the lifetime of the owner.)

Alfred P. Sloan, Jr., also appears to be justifiably rated. By the end of 1962 Sloan had conveyed to the Alfred P. Sloan Foundation assets then worth $222,715,014 at the market. Charles Stewart Mott, also of General Motors, had at the end of 1960 put assets worth $76,754,317 into a foundation bearing his name. The John L. Pratt Foundation of Fredericksburg, Virginia, however, at the end of 1962 had assets of only $88,753. But this structure can be looked upon as a prepared financial tomb to receive a large portion of the Pratt fortune, which can be tentatively accepted as close to or in the range laid out by *Fortune*.

It is evident that the *Fortune* estimates as checked against available probates show extremely wide variations, approximately correct at times but at other times far off the mark. It would, in fact, be remarkable if *Fortune* had found an unofficial way to being even approximately correct in all cases.

Ambiguity of the New Wealth

Additionally, one must notice that much of this "new money" is concentrated in real estate, promotional effort and uncertain oil prospecting. The owner of real estate or of oil-producing land holds something not readily translated into dollars. The independent oil prospector is subject to price fluctuations, curtailment of politically arranged tax privileges and, in many parts of the world, confiscation. In any event, his wealth consists largely of *estimated* below-ground reserves, which may be erroneous. The real estate operator, in order to cash in, must find for his properties buyers, who are relatively scarce; and often the big realty operator is sitting on a slippery cushion of bank loans and mortgages. His own equity is seldom as imposing as the facades of his properties.

Few men on the list are in manufacturing or banking, where there is not only solid evidence of what an enterprise is worth but where the heavy money is found. And even big oil operators fall on evil days. Glenn McCarthy, who in 1949 threw open the Shamrock Hotel of Houston to a less-than-astounded world and who is more recently financially in an ambiguous position, is a case in point. Hence I would place a question mark after the name of nearly every independent oil prospector on this list with respect to the rated extent of his wealth. I do this for two reasons: Most of them own purely private companies and few publish balance sheets and income statements. Those that do, such as Murchison's Delhi-Taylor Oil Corporation, have years of deficit operations alternating with profitable years. What nonfinancial observers do is to look at a heap of assets, usually no more than leases and land concessions, and put some figure on the heap. They do not take into consideration offsetting liabilities—cost of leases, drilling equipment, political contributions and the like. This is not to deny that the oil men mentioned are wealthy in varying degrees.

Nor is this a point made in passing. The issue underlying my remarks is this: Are large fortunes, solidly comparable in size to the inherited fortunes, still being made in profusion by free-as-air rugged entrepreneurs in the American economy? *Fortune*, the *Wall Street Journal* and most newspapers that follow the "party line" laid down by these over-arching publications say "Yes." I say, most respectfully, "No." In the upshot, the reader can make his own choice.

We have already seen that Arthur Vining Davis drops like the proverbial plummet from *Fortune's* $400-million class to the $86-million class in probate autopsy and I venture to say that most of the independent oil operators will, when they throw in their final hands, show similar downward variations from ebullient outside estimates. But I incline to keep Jacob Blaustein pretty much in the position *Fortune* assigned him because he is a full-scale operator, is high in national political councils and is a known big stockholder of the muscular Standard Oil Company of Indiana—a solid, old-line Rockefeller enterprise.

The J. Paul Getty Story

J. Paul Getty may be worth less than *Fortune* rates him, but Getty does not belong to the list of new wealth. Getty himself provides this information as well as his own comments on the *Fortune* estimate. As wealthy people seldom contribute to the discussion of their affairs, Getty's action was most unusual.

Getty, incidentally, was scarcely known except to business associates until the *Fortune* article appeared, crowning him the world's richest man. "Illustrative of the extent to which I had been able to maintain my anonymity through the years," Getty writes in his memoirs, "was a chance encounter with a former classmate I had not seen since my undergraduate days at the University of California at Berkeley. Meeting accidentally on a Los Angeles street in 1950, we recognized each other and stopped to reminisce for a few moments. 'By the way, Paul,' my former schoolmate asked me at one point in our conversation, 'who are you working for these days?' "[8]

Right after the article appeared, Getty relates, he became a sitting duck for a parade of interviewers, cranks, money-seekers and spongers.

As to the source of his wealth, Getty writes, his father died in 1930, worth $15,478,137. As early as 1916 the elder Getty was a millionaire oil prospector. He left the bulk of his estate to his wife but by 1916 he had entered into a 70–30 partnership with his son, allotting the latter, gratis, 300 of 1,000 newly issued shares of the Getty Oil Company. By the terms of his father's will Getty got only $500,000; "but I had no real need for more money; I had several millions of my own."[9] He owned, in fact, more than 30 per cent of Getty Oil.

Getty, in brief, is an inheritor. The son of a wealthy oil operator, he completed his formal education at Oxford University before World War I and was brought in on the ground floor as a junior partner of a going business where he did well.

In 1930 Getty was elected vice president and general manager of George F. Getty, Inc., but the controlling interest remained with his mother and former associates of the elder Getty. Young Getty, in order to protect the company's position, urged the acquisition of additional shares of companies in which the Gettys already had interests, but his elderly associates held back and young Getty went ahead on his own account. He first bought 160,000 shares of Pacific Western Oil Company at $7 a share: $1,120,000. He next started buying Tidewater Associated Oil Company in the open market at $2.50 a share, depression-low prices, and acquired 285,004 shares for $923,285.30 or an average price of $3.59.[10]

Getty, schooled by his father to reach only for aces, was out to get control of Tidewater. He found himself blocked by the powerful Standard Oil Company of New Jersey but, with some unexpected luck, delicately outfenced this giant and finally got control of Tidewater and the Mission Corporation, which the New Jersey company had formed to hold its own Tidewater stock. He also picked up at bargain prices the Hotel Pierre in New York, and the Skelly Oil Company, which owned the Spartan Aircraft Company. In the meantime, his mother had assigned her Getty shares to a trust for her grandchildren, with J. Paul Getty as sole trustee.

In 1963 Getty, after accepting Getty oil stock for his various independent holdings, held 12,570,939 shares of the Getty Oil Company, which now owns all or nearly all of Tidewater, Mission, Mexican Seaboard, Skelly and a good many others.[11] These shares in the same year, by the company's audited computation, had a net *tangible* underlying value of $31.21. This single holding alone, then, was solidly worth $392,339,006.19 and is only part of the family holding. By late 1967 the market value of J.

Paul Getty's Getty Oil holdings had advanced to around $1 billion $200 million.

As Getty personally has always liked to stand free and clear of banks, one may suppose none of it is up for collateral against hidden loans. Add here and there any stray properties Getty may own, consider that he has made provisions for his sons and grandchildren going beyond those of his mother's trust fund, and one sees looming before one an authentic very large fortune, new in its latter-day magnitude at least, although not in its origin. Aside from the Sloan, Kettering, Pratt and Mott General Motors fortunes, all post-1918 jobs, it is one of the few so-called new big ones we can accept without demur (other than denying it is new) from the *Fortune* list. Had Getty not had money and insight provided by his father he could not have picked up these companies.

Getty, commenting on his elevation to hyperbolic billionaire status, said "there is no such thing as a billionaire among active businessmen, not in the sense that most people would understand the term. An individual may own or control business enterprises worth a billion dollars or even more, but little of his rated wealth is available to him in cash. A millionaire or billionaire does not have his millions on deposit in his personal checking account. The money is invested in his businesses.

"It is impossible for him to know what his investments are really worth at any given time. The values of a businessman's holdings fluctuate greatly. The price of stocks may rise or fall, corporations may show major increases or decreases in their net worth, innumerable variables may multiply the value of an investment or wipe it out completely."[12]

Getty's entire life has been subdued in pitch. He went to school quietly —first to the University of Southern California, later to the University of California and then to Oxford. He traveled the world quietly, went into business with his father quietly and later bought large amounts of stock very cheaply—and quietly. He was married quietly seven times and as quietly divorced, with no hint of scandal. In his memoirs he quietly takes the blame for his marital failures and speaks with quiet commendation of his various wives. He appears to have quietly evaded politics and politicians at all times. In more recent years he has lived quietly in the baronial halls of Sutton Place, his English manor house, and will one day no doubt die quietly and quietly leave his swollen fortune to foundations and to his four sons and many grandchildren. Getty, beyond doubt, has been the all-time ghostly atypical presence in the procession of American wealth. When he speaks—and he has been interviewed on TV—he speaks, yes, very quietly.

H. L. Hunt and the Politics of Oil

Haroldson L. Hunt, No. 2 on *Fortune's* list, has been variously estimated as worth $250 million to $3 billion.[13] Forced to choose, I'd incline toward the lower figure; *Fortune* pegged him at $400–$700 million, leaving a good deal of leeway. But Hunt's fortune, like that of all the oil prospectors, rests literally in the sands and in money-inflamed politics, domestic and foreign. He no doubt holds a good hand, but one may doubt that it harbors a royal flush.

Hunt, a small-town cracker-barrel philosopher (in this aspect very much resembling the late Andrew Carnegie and Henry Ford) and overburdened with wildcatted possessions beyond his own wildest, wildcatting dreams, first came to national political notice during the 1950's (much as Henry Ford did in the early 1920's) as a rabble-rousing propagandist for hard-nosed right-wing political points of view. For Hunt takes seriously what he has heard around the town cracker-barrel. The violence of the diatribes in his subsidized radio programs—carried to 331 cracker-barrel stations—led many observers to see them as having at least helped nurture the mood for the assassination of President Kennedy. The programs, seeming overtures to *schrecklichkeit*, are prepared and taped by a stable of about twenty-five henchmen Hunt maintains in Washington, D.C. In general, views blandishing to the Ku Klux mentality are broadcast.[14]

On the very morning of President Kennedy's assassination—in Texas—the Hunt radio program in Dallas and other areas predicted pessimistically that a day was soon coming when American citizens would not be allowed to own firearms with which they could oppose their rulers, an important function of red-blooded free citizens in the cracker-barrel point of view. Of a communist society (thought by cracker-barrel pundits to be imminent in the United States) the Hunt commentator said forebodingly: "No firearms are permitted the people because they would then have the weapons with which to rise up against their oppressors."

Hunt staged his alarmist programs through a series of incestuous foundations—Facts Forum, Inc., the Life Line Foundation and Bright Star Foundation, none of which is listed in the very complete *Foundation Directory*, 1964, issued by the Russell Sage Foundation. Until early 1965 (after the assassination of President Kennedy, that is), despite many strongly sponsored protests, Hunt seemed to have mysterious and powerful friends in or behind the Internal Revenue Service, which granted these propaganda foundations complete tax exemption. The Life Line Foundation originally got tax exemption as a religious organization! To his fingertips the pecuniary man as well as cracker-barrel philosopher, Hunt further improved his position by soliciting business donations for his foundations and giving his own food and patent-medicine companies reduced advertising rates on his radio programs. For H. L. Hunt believes in killing whole flocks of birds with a single stone.

One of Hunt's many immortal quoted sayings is: "Everything I do, I do for a profit."

There is also the H. L. Hunt Foundation, founded in 1954, a financially anemic affair with assets at the end of 1961 of only $799,553, according to the *Foundation Directory*, and which in that year made charitable grants of a stupendous $17,500. No doubt it is this little creation that is destined to receive and immortalize any portion of Hunt holdings in flight from inheritance taxes.

Although Hunt—silver-haired, soft-spoken, frugal, a food faddist—is very rich, few people are able to say they have ever seen the color of his money. He has never been known to contribute in the presence of witnesses more than $250 to $500 to any single political candidate; and in 1956 he gave the Republican Party, over the counter, a mere $38,000. In 1952 the Republicans tried to entice $300,000 from him, but Hunt came up with only $5,000—this, at least, is according to the public role of penny-pincher that he plays.

But owing to the vastness of his landholdings, sprawling over the Southwest and the Middle East, and his seemingly uncanny ability to obtain high-level political chaperonage at crucial moments, realistic observers surmise that Hunt is passing out large sums under the table. "He must have a front man he spreads his money through," hostile Senator Ralph Yarborough of Texas has said. "A man with that kind of bank roll is bound to have."

It is rumored in Texas, according to the *New York Times* (August 17, 1964), that Hunt put up $150,000 to get General Douglas MacArthur the Republican presidential nomination in 1952 and that he put up $100,000 for the Kennedy-Johnson ticket in 1960 owning to his longstanding friendship with Lyndon B. Johnson. Booth Mooney, the Hunt public relations man in Washington, wrote the authorized *The Lyndon Johnson Story* in 1956, updated in 1964; and Lyndon Johnson is an old friend of the oil depletion allowance as well as of Hunt. Although Senator Barry Goldwater in 1964 stood forthrightly for straight Hunt political wisdom, Hunt testily denied that he was supporting Goldwater against the old Huntsman, L. B. J.

One must agree with Senator Yarborough that Hunt and other Texas oil men are passing money (or some equivalent) to political figures. If they didn't, they wouldn't have the depletion allowance, ostensibly passed as a defense measure to stimulate the search for oil but also serving the useful function of providing a politician's entering siphon into the oil Golconda. There might instead be a special high tax on oil!

Here we touch the edge of a problem: Why, if the independent oil men are so favored by nature and politicians, do they show this political rancor? True, not all the oil men are so perturbed as Hunt and some others, who apparently feel that their easy-come wealth could as easily be whisked away; many of the more realistic, less anxiety-prone Texas oil crowd speak of themselves as just plain lucky and see no need for making the world safe for future wildcatters.

But H. L. Hunt is an expression in exaggerated form of the irritation and resulting apparent meanness of many oil independents, even though most oil men appear to regard him as more than a little kooky. What produces this irritation? There is, first, the annual tax bill. Some of the successful oil men write annual checks for the Internal Revenue Service in amounts that would stagger the ordinary man. And most of the oil men are ordinary men who early in their lives worked long hours for small wages. The men who write these checks still think in terms of the original $20-a-week roustabout. And while it is frequently said that one wouldn't mind writing big tax checks if one had the big incomes, to have worked in one's early life on the supposition that what one acquired one could keep and then to learn after hitting it big that one must share to some extent with the government—or politicians—is more than some persons can swallow gracefully. Some of the oil men, Hunt included, feel very much the way a man earning $60 a week would feel if he was told the withholding tax was to be $50. They just aren't psychically attuned to their new positions. On top of the tax bite, very much softened by the depletion allowance and drilling write-off, the oil men find they must share what is no doubt a good part of the depletion benefits with hungry politicians in the form of "campaign contributions." And for these political contributions they feel the politicians ought to deliver more. The politicians, to extenuate their less than totalitarian success, no doubt report that there are various obstacles in the form of Liberalism, Communism, Socialism, Eastern Capitalists, Labor Unions, Welfarism and a world full of Wrong-Thinking People all the way from college professors and journalists to Supreme Court justices. The enormity of it all, the injustice of all these misguided people stirring a witch's brew with which to annoy Horatio Alger's own darling boys out on the oil frontier, finally becomes more than human flesh—or at least H. L. Hunt's flesh—can stand.

Hunt has seen it all at first-hand, indeed. He has regularly attended the national conventions of both parties, keeping his ears close to the ground, his eyes sharp and his nose clean for any whiff of Godless un-Americanism. And there is, as God only knows, much of it around, in the very Constitution itself!

There is, too, the milieu of Texas as a force shaping Texas consciousness. For Texas has very much the economic and political status of a colony, as also have many far less bustling western states. In the words of Senator Wilbert (Pappy) Lee O'Daniel, Texas is "New York's most valuable foreign possession."

The widely traveled John Gunther in 1947 found that "Texas reminded me a good deal of Argentina . . . cattle culture, absentee ownership, vast land holdings by semifeudal barons, a great preoccupation with weather, an under-developed middle class, interminable flatness and open spaces, and fierce political partisanship and nationalism. And . . . reaction closely paralleling that of Argentina."[15]

Most of the state is in fact absentee-owned by big eastern capital. The largest enterprise in the state is the Humble Oil and Refining Company, subsidiary of the global Standard Oil Company of New Jersey, the annual gross revenue of which exceeds the *combined* revenues of thirty state governments—$11.471 billion versus $11.375 billion in 1965. The operations of the huge eastern enterprises—Du Pont, U.S. Steel, General Motors, Dow Chemical and various others—are splattered right and left. And many of the prominent men in the state, Hunt included, originate elsewhere, are in effect colonial concessionaires. Many Texas oil men are not native Texans at all.

With a thin layer of native wealthy and imported representatives of big corporations at the top, bellowing the glories of Texas in history and contemporary culture, most Texans find themselves somewhat dazedly in the low-income classes, dirt poor—in fact, *colons*. Gunther was told in Texas that twenty corporations ran the state, but he thought this exaggerated. I don't think so. At least, the rank and file *colons*, many close to peons, do not run it—and they know it.

Texas boastfulness, free-swinging behavior and loud talk about independence of spirit are all a compensatory reflex to the feeling, deep in many Texans, that they are dusty puppets manipulated from outside. Some informed Texans amuse themselves sardonically by giving visitors the home addresses in New York, Boston, Philadelphia, even Amsterdam, of the owners of prominent items of Texas property.

One word fits the general Texas political consciousness from high to low: resentment. And some of Hunt's outpourings have awkwardly expressed simply this.

As to colonialism, it shows itself everywhere in this way: One can see a great deal going out—cattle, cotton, oil, minerals, chemicals—but little or nothing coming in. The dividends go out, too. Texas, like Pittsburgh seventy-five years ago, is being bled grey, if not white.

The niggardliness of Hunt's *known* political handouts is thought to derive from the position that, although Hunt may like a man's political stance, he does not like to back losers. His political contributions, like those of the old-line magnates, are not made to support or propagate principles so much as to purchase instant influence in government. In this respect he seems, if reports are true, cut from the same bolt as the late Henry J. Havemeyer, the sugar magnate, who testified before the United States Industrial Commission that he habitually contributed to both political parties (as do the oil men) and explained: "We get a good deal of protection for our contributions."

Hunt, lamentable to relate, has had some hard times with cruel politicians. When he bid $17 an acre on offshore oil tracts that the government ordinarily leased at $406 an acre he was unsympathetically rebuffed by Secretary of the Interior Frederick Seaton. Hunt thereupon procured Senator Everett M. Dirksen and Representative Charles A. Halleck, statesmen of the purest Republican strain, to convoy him to a protest interview with Seaton. This eyeball to eyeball confrontation came to naught. But after the tidelands were transferred under Eisenhower to state jurisdiction—for which the well-heeled oil lobby had worked every bit as hard as wildcatters on a hot tin roof—Hunt found Texas Governor Allan Shivers, a board member of Hunt's Facts Forum, far more accommodating. In this matter Shivers's land commissioner, Bascom Giles (before he was bundled off to the state penitentiary for getting caught cheating the state in another quarter), approved all of Hunt's bids for more than 100,000 acres of tidelands leases, even though Hunt bid an average of $6 an acre while the average over-all bid was $78. As I remarked, Hunt is frugal and this frugality—aided by his knowledge of governors—has helped make him wealthy in a nation where people are so foolish as to pay whatever it says on the price tag.

The last president of whom Hunt fully approves was Calvin Coolidge; even Herbert Hoover he finds too soft. Both Eisenhower and Kennedy he regards as disasters of virtually Rooseveltian proportions. Although backing haughty Douglas MacArthur for the presidency, Hunt literally doted on Senator Joseph McCarthy, with whom he zestfully played cards and exchanged fraternal favors. For governor of Texas he backed morose General Edwin Walker, whose right-wing propagandizing forced him out of the Army, to the regret of a considerable congressional bloc.

The political ideology of William Buckley, Jr., himself a scion of a small-bore Texas oil fortune, makes a strong appeal to Hunt although he believes the volubly rhetorical Buckley uses too many big words. Hunt, unlike Buckley, sees nothing to be gained by repackaging a muted kluxishness in fancy language as a tortured endeavor in high moral aspiration. Hunt deeply admires Candyman Robert Welch, founder of the John Birch Society, George (Stand-in-the-Doorway) Wallace of Alabama and others who stand forthrightly for the trammeling of common equity. According to the *New York Times,* Hunt's ideal Democratic ticket of 1964 would have been Harry F. Byrd of Virginia for president and Frank J. Lausche of Ohio for vice president with a Republican ticket consisting of Bourke B. Hickenlooper of Iowa and Roman L. Hruska of Nebraska.

Showing the earnestness of his beliefs, Hunt spends a good deal of priceless wildcatting time bombarding newspaper editors with cracker-barrel messages. For he believes that if the American people would only remove the scales from their eyes they would see that the nation is being subverted right and left. Among the subverters, as he sees it, are the governesses, nurses, tutors and teachers of the children of the established rich who grow up to become extreme leftists like W. Averell Harriman, Nelson Rockefeller, John Lindsay, G. Mennen Williams and John F. Kennedy —all alien to the cracker-barrel. One can see what they did even to language-frenzied William Buckley, Jr. It is very insidious. But although he almost from the first unpatriotic rejection of his cheap bid for valuable tidelands disliked Eisenhower, Hunt has not yet turned on his close friend Lyndon B. Johnson, of whom he said early in 1964:

"Johnson is the kind of President who can lead Congress around by its nose. I wouldn't mind seeing him in there for three terms."

Hunt was born in Vandalia, Illinois, in 1890. He could read at age three and early displayed a phenomenal memory, which he has retained throughout the years. Like Henry Ford basically an intelligent but very partially informed man, he quit school in the fifth grade and became a drifter at thirteen. After wandering through the West as a barber, cowhand, lumberjack and gambler (Hunt still likes to gamble and claims to trounce the racetrack bookies) he settled in Arkansas, where he became a moderately prosperous cotton farmer. Ruined by the collapse of cotton prices in 1921, he turned for lack of anything better to oil, and was literally swept off his feet toward riches. According to the Hunt legend, he struck oil on the first try with a drilling rig he bought with a $50 loan. Another version is that he won the money, or the rig itself, in a card game.

A wildcatter with little or no money must strike oil right away because, as Hunt himself testifies, only one in thirty attempts to get oil succeeds and the average cost of each attempt now is about $250,000. Hunt attributes his continued success to following the law of averages: If one keeps trying, one will eventually strike oil. He claims he has drilled as many as 100 dry holes in succession, which at $250,000 average per hole is $25 million.

After much successful drilling in Arkansas, Hunt shifted to East Texas, not then considered likely territory. But there aging C. M. (Dad) Joiner brought in the world's largest producing field. Hunt bought Joiner's discovery well, took a lease on 4,000 nearby acres and wound up with most of the Joiner land in a deal that many chroniclers profess to find mysterious. Hunt says he paid $1 million for the lands, money he had made in Arkansas. But Joiner, like most wildcatters, died broke, while the bubbling East Texas field swirled Hunt upward to oildom's Pantheon. He now, like most of the Texas oil men, operates all over the world, hobnobs with the Arab sheiks and plays oil politics wherein the white chips cost anything from $1 million to $10 million.

Suspected of being the financial angel of various far-out right-wing agitational groups, Hunt is regarded by some observers as dangerous. And in a sufficiently intense atmosphere he might be. But all of the various right-wing groups to which some politically unsophisticated wealthy people contribute as yet show no signs of being more than money-cadging rackets set up to squeeze a profit out of the fears of rich neurotics. No doubt they stir passions but their leaders couldn't stage a cracker-barrel putsch, much less set fire to the Capitol wastebasket. If Hunt is giving any of them money, it can only be his version of a share-the-wealth movement.

Hunt has been overheard introducing himself to strangers by chirping: "Hello, I am H. L. Hunt, the world's richest man. . . ."

Clint Murchison and Sid Richardson

Joseph P. Kennedy is sufficiently recognizable as the sire of the late president to need no further identification. His career has been exhaustively investigated by Richard J. Whalen in *The Founding Father*, which is almost clinical in its penetration. *Fortune* seems to me to rate him on the high side.

Many of the people on the *Fortune* list deliberately avoid public notice, attempting to blend, chameleonlike, into the background. One who confesses to this sort of shyness is Daniel K. Ludwig. The General Motors fortune-hunters and Henry J. Kaiser are rather fulsomely known to the public through newspaper reports and need not detain us.

Two oil men of a cut somewhat different from H. L. Hunt perhaps should be noticed. They are Clint Murchison and Sid Richardson, who often make a team with the Murchison sons. In some ways more ambitious than Hunt, they have also been more realistic. Although rightists politically, they have never showed a desire to play the role of a Fritz Thyssen in the American system.[16]

Murchison is the plain man as a multimillionaire, shirtsleeves, unassuming manner and all. His grandfather and father owned the First National Bank of Athens, Texas, which Clint now owns, and Clint had a short stay at Trinity University, Texas, before entering the bank. Upon his demobilization from the Army in 1919 he encountered his boyhood friend Sid Richardson, who had also tried college and who was now dealing in oil leases. Because he liked trading for the sake of trading he joined Richardson. After a period of buying, selling and exchanging leases throughout the Southwest, barely keeping ahead of the game, Murchison pulled Richardson out of a poker game in Wichita Falls one night to investigate the rumor of a wildcat well near the Oklahoma border. They sneaked past guards close enough to smell oil, and the next morning they spent $50,000 buying regional leases. The following day they unloaded the leases for more than $200,000 and were off and running in a business way.

During the depression Murchison built up the Southern Union Gas Company and the American Liberty Oil Company, both later sold. Then he formed the Delhi-Taylor Oil Corporation, always rising higher on a flood of new oil.

Murchison is distinguished from most of the other Texas oil men by the breadth of his diversified non-oil interests and by his participation in a number of national financial coups with the alert Allen Kirby and the late Robert R. Young of the Alleghany Corporation.

As to his diversified interests, he is virtually the sole owner of the Atlantic Life Insurance Company of Richmond, Martha Washington Candy Company of Chicago and Dallas, Waco and Austin taxi, bus and transit lines among various smaller interests. He is or was the dominant owner of the American Mail Line, Ltd., of Seattle; Delhi-Taylor Oil Company; Holt, Rinehart and Winston, New York publishers; Diebold, Inc., office equipment; and a chain of small Texas banks as well as miscellaneous other goodies. He has a substantial interest in the Transcontinental Bus System; American Window Glass of Pittsburgh; and Southeastern Michigan Gas Company. Of course, even as this is being written, his holdings and those of his sons may shift in the unending succession of deals for which he is noted. His general strategy appears to be to pick up cheaply properties that do not appear to be living up to their potential and to make them into good earners by installing skilled managers. He gets wind of these properties, as do most wealthy men, through professional investment locators.

He was approached by the late Robert R. Young, a fellow Texan and the financial mentor of Woolworth's Allen Kirby in the Alleghany Corporation, and was asked to join the Young-Kirby forces in the 1950's in seeking control of the Morgan-Vanderbilt New York Central Railroad, the Piéta of railroad cognoscenti. Alleghany already controlled the Chesapeake and Ohio Railroad, a lush earner. Murchison joined Young and brought Richardson with him. Between them Murchison and Richardson put $20 million on the line.

Clint, after talking with Young over long-distance, told Sid about the transaction on the telephone. "When the calls were over," says Cleveland Amory, who researched the Texans in their native habitat, "Richardson thought the deal was for only $10,000,000. Informed it was twice that, he called his partner back. 'Say, Clint,' he said, 'what is the name of that railroad?'"

The capture of the prize New York Central by this group made financial history, as they say.

Murchison and his sons also followed Alleghany Corporation and took a position in the stock of Investors Diversified Services, which controls a tangle of investment trusts with aggregate assets of more than $1 billion.

Richardson, Amory informs us, is a bachelor and lives around in various hotels and clubs. Amory assigns him a wealth exceeding a billion dollars, a figure few others agree with. But he owns an island in the Gulf of Mexico where he hunts and fishes. He declines to write letters and has no secretary; his office is in his hat. He owns a fleet of Cadillacs in Dallas and one each in every city he regularly visits.

In 1947 Richardson established the Sid W. Richardson Foundation of Fort Worth, Texas, which for the end of 1962 reported to the *Foundation Directory* net worth of $69,554,801. Benevolent grants for the year totaled $14,500, which hardly spread much sunshine among the heathen. In the meantime the income on this big accumulation most of the time since the fund was started would have been subject to maximum tax rates up to 91 per cent, more recently 77 per cent. The foundation, however, in a neat stroke, preserved all this income intact and saw to it that none of it went to paying for the costs of sacred national defense.

Murchison, widowed and remarried, owns a 75,000-acre ranch in Mexico's Sierra Madre Range. Here he has entertained the Duke and Duchess of Windsor and other ultra-magnificoes. In fact, he owns several homes; one has a room with eight beds "so a group of us boys can talk oil all night."[17]

The Wolfson Story, in Brief

The only other person of special interest on the *Fortune* list is Louis Wolfson, assiduous wheeler-dealer of Miami Beach who has engaged in much shuffling about with New York Shipbuilding Corporation and the construction-dredging firm of Merritt-Chapman & Scott among others. Wolfson is one of the standard Roman-candle phenomena of American society, one of hundreds that come and go across the financial horizon like fireflies, and *Fortune* itself demoted him from the list of heavyweights in 1961.[18] Having no reason to gainsay *Fortune* here, I accept its last judgment on Wolfson.

Wolfson and an associate were convicted on September 29, 1967, in federal court on nineteen counts of criminal conspiracy and illegal stock sales. Gaudily overdramatizing, newspapers pointed out that Wolfson faced a possible ninety-five years in jail. When it came to sentencing the judge meted out sentences of one year on each of the nineteen counts, with the sentences to run concurrently. If over-ruled on appeal, Wolfson will then serve one year with the customary time off for good behavior.

Nominees of the Satevepost

Thus far I have confined myself to the *Fortune* list of alleged new builders of alleged big fortunes; but others, too, have their candidates.

Accepting and endorsing *Fortune's* nominations of John D. MacArthur, John Mecom, Daniel K. Ludwig, Leo Corrigan, William Keck, R. E. Smith and James Abercrombie as financial big-shots and dispensing a bit of scuttlebutt about them, the *Saturday Evening Post* in 1965 put forward six additional candidates: Dr. Edwin Land, inventor of the Polaroid camera, whom the *Post* credits with $185 million, a doubtful figure despite the soaring market prices of Polaroid stock; Henry Crown, head of the General Dynamics Corporation (government contracts) and dabbler around in building supplies, real estate and railroads, whom the *Post* says is worth $250 million; Howard Ahmanson, California insurance and savings-and-loan wizard, worth $300 million according to the *Post*; and W. Clement Stone, insurance promoter, worth $160 million on the *Post's* nimble abacus. The *Post* did not turn up any new information on ultra-shy Ludwig (who it averred had made a round billion dollars since World War II); none on Charles Allen, Jr., of the investment banking firm of Allen and Company, other than that he is a "financier." And no more on John Erik Jonsson than that he is the major stockholder in market-zooming Texas Instruments Company and the possessor of a "huge fortune."[19]

All these figures, even those bearing on Land, are little more than curbstone estimates. Land's could be about right, for he owned 51 per cent of the Polaroid Corporation stock at the inception of its productive phase. But one does not know yet to what extent he may have revised his holdings. As Land is a technical man, an inventor who sticks closely to his work and has ready access to all the capital he thinks he needs (he was bankrolled to the tune of $375,000 by the old-line heavy money of W. Averell Harriman, James P. Warburg and Lewis Strauss, all vastly enriched by their Polaroid stock) he retains a large interest. Precisely how much we shall see later.

Of all the persons named thus far in this chapter, Land is the only one who has created a ground-up new free enterprise. All the others jumped aboard existing merry-go-rounds or hung onto government coattails, although Kettering and Donaldson Brown did significantly creative jobs at General Motors.

Land did far more than invent the Polaroid camera, which develops its own pictures. He has more than 100 inventions to his name in the field of optics and was inventing while still a student at Harvard, which he quit. He is not a bit interested in money and resents being categorized primarily as a rich man. He lives in moderate middle-class style in Cambridge, Massachusetts, and has a small farm in New Hampshire. Like Pasteur, Edison and other creators, he lives mainly in order to work.

His impact on the world has been far more than adding to its marketable gadgetry, for he played the chief role in developing cameras (such as those used in the famous U-2 espionage plane) that would take detailed pictures at more than 70,000 feet of altitude. It was his cameras that exploded the idea of a "missile gap" and detected the Soviet missiles in Cuba. He is currently interested in ways of humanizing machine society, eliminating the "problem of mass boredom and mental stagnation" in American life, particularly among industrial workers. Whether he cracks this nut or not, his mind is soaring in an empyrean far above that of Hunt, the wildcatters and the wheeler-dealers.

Most of the men mentioned on both the *Fortune* and the *Post* lists are obviously of wheeler-dealer stripe, the kind that can well be, financially speaking, here today and gone tomorrow. In a steadily continuing inflation they will all no doubt come through with burgees flying; in the event of a substantial recession, some could find themselves in disturbed relations with their banks if not on the streets selling apples.

The *New York Times*, September 13, 1963, offered a few additional names of supposedly new rich: Thomas J., Jr., Arthur K. and Mrs. Thomas J. Watson, their mother, collectively then worth $108 million in International Business Machines stock; Sherman M. Fairchild, son of a founder of IBM and dominant owner of Fairchild Camera and Instrument and Fairchild Stratos; Archibald G. Bush, with a $103 million holding in Minnesota Mining and Manufacturing; Cyrus Eaton, Cleveland banker; and a variety of others.

But very few of the names mentioned by the *Times* additional to those named by *Fortune* and the *Post* are of men who made their own fortunes. Like the Watsons and Fairchild, they are mostly inheritors: Howard Heinz II, the pickle king; Joseph Frederick Cullman III of Philip Morris, Inc.; J. Peter Grace of W. R. Grace & Co.; Lewis S. Rosenstiel of Schenley Industries; Norman W. Harris of the Harris Trust and Savings Bank (Chicago); and others.

More Entries for the Pantheon of Wealth

These are by no means the only names of possible new big-money nabobs that could be mentioned. And while there can be no guarantee that some sleeping prince has not been missed—a super-solvent wraith like J. Paul Getty—the law of diminishing returns sets in after these listings. We are not, of course, stooping to mention the ignoble wretches, the proletariat of Dun & Bradstreet, evaluated at less than $75 million by wealth-watchers, even though some of them are interesting characters and are given compensatorily reverent treatment by *Fortune* from time to time.[20] We'll run into a few occasionally further along, resolutely plowing their golden ruts.

But, to consider one of a number of rejected nominations and the reasons for banishing him from the financial Pantheon (lest the reader suppose I am being arbitrary in those I flunk out), let us consider the late William F. Buckley, Sr., publicly saluted as having been worth $110 million on his death in 1958.[21] Money of this specific gravity should have put him high in the *Fortune* hierarchy; but *Fortune* did not so much as mention him, with what to me seems ample justification.

Buckley, an authentic on-the-spot imperialist concession-hunter, before his death stirred desultory attention by founding a private school in Sharon, Connecticut, dedicated to safeguarding small children "against contamination by the theories of so-called 'liberalism.'"[22] His son, William F. Buckley, Jr., carries his father's torch of anti-New Dealism in the oil-slick *National Review* and in books embarrassingly revelatory of elementary intellectual inadequacies such as *God and Man at Yale*, *McCarthy and His Enemies* and *Up from Liberalism*. A McCarthy-lover, the son has also collaborated on a rousing defense of the House Un-American Activities Committee. Education, to the son as to the father, is guided indoctrination with ancient unwisdom.

Apart from the elder Buckley's authoritarian views on education (he decreed that his children be trilingual and study the piano whether musically inclined or not) he was reportedly an ardent admirer of Theodore Roosevelt, particularly of Roosevelt's penchant for sending threatening battle cruisers to objectionable (small) countries.[23]

When he gave up the ghost, Buckley *père* was not widely known. It is hardly an exaggeration to say that his death recalled him from oblivion to obscurity. He was not immortalized in *Who's Who, Current Biography 1940–1960* or *Poor's Register of Corporations, Officers and Directors.* The *New York Times* carried no *précis* of the probate of his will, which it usually does on large estates. It seems fair to say that attention has focused on him retrospectively only because of the verbal political posturings of his son and namesake.

While there is no reason to doubt that the elder Buckley may have left his ten children and twenty-eight grandchildren (as of 1957) more money than might be good either for them or for the country, there is no external evidence justifying his placement in the $110-million, the $50-million or even the $25-million class. Compared with grizzled Clint Murchison or old Sid Richardson, he simply does not rate. I omit any detailed analysis of the Buckley enterprises, all small.[24]

Buckley's Pantepec Oil, of which John W. Buckley is now the family director, in 1962 had total assets of only $3,435,011 and working capital of $35,544. It had three million shares outstanding, all valued on the market as low as $600,000. But in 1956 it sold its Venezuelan concessions to the Phillips Petroleum Company for $4.9 million, a respectable sum to which I genuflect. Priced a while back in the $2.00 range, the stock of Pantepec slid down to 20 cents a share in 1963.[25]

Coastal Caribbean Oils, Inc., another Buckley company, in 1962 had total assets of $3,632,216 and a deficit in working capital of $138,286. Like Pantepec it was pretty much a hollow shell consisting of (1) stock issue and (2) arbitarily valued exploring concessions. It boasted 3 employees and claimed 16,453 stockholders, no doubt all praying madly for the blessed increment in the form of gushers.[26] Canada Southern Oils, Ltd., a holding company, in 1964 had stated assets of $9,653,393, a working capital deficit of $469,704, 10 employees and 15,000 stockholders.[27]

James L. Buckley is an officer and director of some Pantepec subsidiaries but he is also vice president and a director of United Canso Oil and

Gas, Ltd. William F. Buckley, Jr., in person, is a director of Canso National Gas Company, a subsidiary. *Moody's* assigns United Canso assets in 1963 of $10,599,807, net working capital of $1,474,118, net loss for the year of $304,562 and an accumulated deficit of $7,382,815, 45 employees and 10,400 stockholders.

To what extent other stockholders divide the clouded prospects with the Buckleys the record does not show. But even if one concedes all these stated assets (less liabilities, such as accumulated deficits) to the Buckley family and doubles the total for good measure one doesn't get within rocket-range of $110 million. Nor have the Buckleys established the usual wealthy-man's foundation nor made telltale large transfers to universities or hospitals.

This is not to deny that Buckley senior in his lifetime probably collected more legal tender than 95 per cent of Americans have ever eyed wistfully through the bank teller's wicket. But he was just not rich of the order of $110 million unless he held assets well concealed from public view. This is always possible but there are considerations for holding it improbable.

That the elder Buckley was never a really large operator is strongly suggested by the history of his son's *National Review*, which the father admired as something of a time bomb under the pallid outlines of an American Welfare State projected by the New Deal. I reason that a super-wealthy father, admiring this curious publication so much, would have underwritten it completely, using any deficits to charge a tax loss against real income. This wasn't done.

The *National Review* was founded in 1955. Capital of $290,000 was importuned from 125 angels, not from Buckley alone, although this was a trifling sum to a man reputedly worth $110 million even if he did have a wife and ten children. By mid-1958 the *Review* had accumulated a deficit of $1,230,000. How this was paid off or written off is not yet clear. But, in order to offset continuing deficits, in 1957 the parent company, National Weekly, Inc., bought a radio station in Omaha for $822,500 and in 1962 an Omaha FM station. These have reduced the deficits, it is said, although they continue—happily for liberalism, progressivism and plain reason.[28]

But a big fortune would hardly find it necessary to run around juggling obscure radio stations with which to offset relatively small publication losses, which could be used to reduce taxes on any very large income. A wealthy man might enjoy owning a minor money loser like *National Review*, with up to 77 per cent of the loss a tax saving. My conclusion, then, is that there are no vast Buckley assets.

Buckley, Jr., has postured before the country in various guises, mainly as a neo-conservative with ill-concealed negative intentions toward the disconcessioned. But he has also made a public display of the fact that he is a particularly devout Catholic. His supposedly profound Catholicism, however, did not prevent him from teeing off on Pope John XXIII when that lamented pontiff, respected even by many unreconstructed Protestants and atheists, issued the humane encyclical *Mater et Magistra,* which urged aid for the underdeveloped peoples of the world via welfare programs. The encyclical, the Buckley concession-heir pronounced, was "a venture in triviality" and was not sufficiently alert to "the continuing demonic successes of the Communists." If these latter and their dupes have successes in odd corners of the world, life will manifestly be difficult for Pantepec.

America, the Jesuit weekly, responded that to imply that "Catholic Conservative circles" accepted the Church as Mother but not as Teacher was "slanderous" and that "It takes an appalling amount of self-assurance for a Catholic writer to brush off an encyclical. *The National Review* owes its Catholic readers and journalistic allies an apology."

Never at a loss for an unexpected word, Buckley stigmatized these comments as "impudent."

All of which reminds one of the remark of John F. Kennedy when he found that he was opposed by wealthy Catholics: "When the chips are down, money counts more than religion."[29]

Owing to the many bizarre positions taken by the *National Review* in projecting its oddly tailored version of "conservatism," observers have wondered at odd moments about the Buckley motivations. Not only has he been opposed to the New Deal at home, with accents here and there of McCarthyism and Birchism, but in the foreign field he has stood forth valiantly as the defender of Moshe Tshombe of Katanga Province in his struggle with the United Nations (which Buckley despises) and as the defender of the white *coup d'etat* in Rhodesia. Buckley himself in 1961 organized the American Committee for Aid to Katanga Freedom Fighters, which had the ring in its name of an old-fashioned Communist front group.

Critics rightly disparage as "vulgar Marxism" attempts to account for anyone's total personality in terms of direct economic motivation. But if anyone will read the *National Review* with the Buckley oil concessions in mind, the political mentality of William F. Buckley, Jr., will be at least partially explained. *Whatever and whoever threatens the well-being and future of those concessions—Communism, liberalism, Socialism, New Dealism, the Supreme Court, Congress, the United Nations, the president, nay, even the pope—is going to feel the touch of the rhetorician's venom.* Young Buckley—he is now past forty, is referred to as an aging *enfant terrible*—in his political stances is almost an automaton of Marxist motivation who would have been clinically fascinating to Karl Marx himself. And this, in all simplicity, is neo-conservatism in a nutshell.

The otherwise inexplicable Buckley infatuation for Moshe Tshombe is readily understood the moment one recalls that Tshombe was the native proconsul in Katanga Province for the Union Minière du Haut Katanga, S.A., of Belgium, envied concession-holder to the rich mineral lands of the Congo. A blow at Tshombe was a blow at concession-holders everywhere, and Buckley brought the *National Review* phrase-crazy spears to bear on the United Nations as he did on the pope.

A Note on Neo-Conservatism

All the neo-conservatives from H. L. Hunt and Barry Goldwater on down resemble Buckley in that, whatever their rated wealth (which is usually small), they are insecure. Some feel subjectively more insecure than others; all are objectively insecure in a changing world. They are caught between big corporations on the one hand and big government, Communist or liberal, on the other. But, envying the big corporations and wishing to be included among them, they direct most of their fire against the cost-raising social aspirations of the people—from whom established capital does not feel it has so much to fear. (If necessary, entrenched capital can stand social reform as in Sweden, passing the costs on in price and taxes. It has, in any event, more room for maneuver and holds all the strong positions.)

But the Goldwaters and Buckleys, with their obscure department stores and oil concessions, are in a different boat. They have begun to suspect that they may never make it to the top, there to preen before the photographers. Sad, sad. . . . Hence, they cry, government should not be used to meet the needs of the people, despite the constitutional edict that it provide for the common welfare; government should merely preside over a free economic struggle in which the weak submit to the strong stomachs. As for the Big Wealthy in the Establishment, in the Power Structure, the Power Elite, they should not, say the neo-conservatives, allow themselves to be deluded by infiltrating nurses, governesses, tutors, teachers, wandering professors, swamis, university presidents and others bearing the *spirochita pallida* of political accommodation. For accommodation has its own special word in the vocabulary of neo-conservatism. It is: Communism.

The neo-conservatives or radical rightists, like the radical leftists, are discontented. There is, however, a different economic basis to the discontent of each. The leftists own no property, therefore see no reason to embrace a property system; the rightists still have some but feel their property claims slipping, feel they are being precipitated into the odious mass of the unpropertied. They foresee being thrown out of the Property Party; for many of them, in fact, are heavily indebted to the banks. The illusion of the radical rightists is that they can yet save their property claims, not by restoring free competition and subduing the rivalrous Rockefellers, Du Ponts, Fords and Mellons (whom they admire and fear as well as envy) but by inducing these latter to join in an all-out assault on the *sans-culottes* and *descamisados*.

However, established wealth, seeing no good for itself in upsetting a smoothly running operation which it feels fully capable of controlling, is not interested in this vexing prospect. Hence the outcries of the neo-conservatives against "the Eastern Establishment" and the "socialism" of Nelson Aldrich Rockefeller. In Buckley's *National Review* these self-dubbed conservatives sound like inverted Marxists in yachting clothes.

Obiter Scripta

Those interested in more on William F. Buckley, Jr., and his success in selling his Pantepec-conservatism to a goodly number of unwary college students as well as seven million buyers of cracker-barrel newspapers that carry his weekly column should consult Forster and Epstein, *Danger on the Right.*

These writers say, however, "There is a unanimity as to Buckley's attractiveness, erudition, charm, intelligence and wit." On this, permit me to register a demurrer. As to erudition and intelligence, nobody would claim it for him who had counted up his frequent logical fallacies, semantic confusions, apparent inability to distinguish between fact and value and his historical gaffes, such as tracing the political disequilibrium of the world to Wilsonian "idealism." Buckley is, in fact, a free-flowing wordsmith, a rhetorician, with a property fetish.

Other names that have been put forward here and there as new wealth-holders of the first magnitude, like that of the senior Buckley, similarly disintegrate under analysis.

Some Half-Forgotten Big Shots

Some new rich who died before *Fortune* staged its round-up ought, in the interests of a fully rounded picture, to be noticed. There were a few, mainly Texas wildcatters and General Motors executives.

It will be recalled that the American political economy went into a severe decline in the 1930's and was brought out of its long coma only by World War II. What happened was reflected by the million-plus incomes. These numbered only twenty-one in 1921, but under the expert ministrations of the Harding-Coolidge Administrations, installed by big wealth as the public list of campaign contributions shows, millionaires-plus numbered 207 in 1925. They rose to 290 in 1927.

In Spanish bullfights there comes a moment when the bull, maddened, bleeding and covered by darts, feeling his last moment has come, stops rushing about and grimly turns to face the man with scarlet *muleta* and sword. It is known to Spaniards as "The Moment of Truth."

It seemed for a while in 1928 that this was the Moment of Truth for the American economy, when stocks in the bull market were pushed up to unprecedented heights, discounting not only the future but the hereafter. In that year there were 511 million-dollar incomes.

But this was a tough bull. Thousands of people, as they said, "believed in" the United States—by which they meant they thought there was no limit to American expansion and, most importantly, free-and-easy money-making.

Gushing blood-money from every orifice, the bull market again in 1929 faced its tormenter, the big American money-maker. There was again the swift, profit-taking thrust that produced 513 million-dollar incomes for the year, a record.

But the sacred bull, though dying now, was not cleanly slain. In 1930, million-dollar incomes, as the blood drained from the bull, sank to 150; in 1931 to 77; and in 1932 to 20 (all figures from *United States Statistics of Income*). The market had come full circle since 1921; millions of dollars had been made and put away in the final push (for not everybody lost money in 1929) and millions were trudging the streets out of work in an extremely flexible labor market—that is to say, employers could name their terms in a way delightful to all neo-conservatives. Put another way, alien to economists, millions of Americans were crying into their pillows at night—that is, those who did not merely set their jaws and lose all feeling or give up the ghost.

What the Moment of Truth disclosed about the American economy was this: It can't take any and every kind of abuse, can't be left to the infinitely greedy wheeler-dealers and over-reachers of the market place.

The 1930's were not good times for fortune-building. Million-dollar-a-year incomes gradually rose to sixty-one in 1936 and then sank to a dull fifty-two in 1940. But the vultures were still getting scraps from the old bull and would try their hands again with sword and cape after the war.

Against this background of economic carnage, few new fortunes could have been assembled, although we have seen how J. Paul Getty vastly reinforced his family holdings by picking up tidbits from the dying bull.

Largish new fortunes of recent contemporaries who died prior to 1957, similar to the living snared in the *Fortune* survey, stemmed mainly from General Motors and from oil wildcatting and lease-trading. There were, of course, exceptions.

But *Fortune,* too, appears to have missed completely a few of the big on-the-surface post-1918 money-piles of interest to connoisseurs.

Neither the public record nor *Fortune,* for example, showed how Henry R. Luce himself, late founder and head of the *Time-Life-Fortune-Sports Illustrated* complex of high-powered mass media, deployed his assets; but even though his enterprises were initially bank-financed, his reported net worth exceeded $100 million upon his death in 1967. Again, Mr. and Mrs. DeWitt Wallace, founders and sole owners of the multilingual, globe-circulating *Reader's Digest,* deserve more than a pious thought in this connection; for they have already conveyed some small fortunes to various schools and colleges. The Wallaces have more giving-away money than many well-heeled persons have spending money.

Just how far, if at all, the following stalwart entrepreneurs fell below the $75-million mark at their peaks would be a quest to put a crew of accountants on their mettle:

Donald W. Douglas, chairman of the Douglas Aircraft Company, born in Brooklyn in 1892, M.I.T. graduate, an Episcopalian and a Republican.[30]

Walter E. (Walt) Disney, motion picture producer, born in Chicago in 1901, died in 1966; although he never attended college he was graced by honorary degrees from Yale and Harvard.[31]

William S. Paley, born in Chicago in 1901, son of a successful cigar manufacturer and an apprentice in that business. A graduate of the University of Pennsylvania, he joined the now opulent Columbia Broadcasting System at its modest inception and became president, chairman and chief stockholder as well as a power in the land. He is president and director of the William S. Paley Foundation (assets as yet nominal), trustee and director of numerous important educational boards, an officer of the Legion of Honor, holder of the Legion of Merit, Croix de Guerre with Palm, Order Crown of Italy, etc., etc.[32]

Juan Terry Trippe, born in New Jersey in 1899. A Yale graduate, he became president, then chairman of the emerging Pan American World

Airways; a director and member of the finance committee of the Metropolitan Life Insurance Company; trustee of the Yale Corporation, the Carnegie Institution, the Phelps-Stokes Fund, etc., etc.[33]

All these men, like nearly all on the *Fortune, Saturday Evening Post* and *New York Times* lists and like most of the nineteenth-century acquisitors, were escalated financially by organizing readily available new technology which they did not create. This observation does not hold true of such rare birds as Dr. Edwin H. Land nor the late George Westinghouse and George Eastman (Kodak), themselves skilled technologists and inventors. Nor would it apply to merchandisers like the late Frank Woolworth, who simply took advantage of urbanization (based on technology). Steady population growth on a resource-rich continent was, of course, a necessary pre-condition to the organization of emerging technology. Few of these people could have made their marks in such a noisome way if they had been confined to the limits—and laws—of Switzerland or Holland—or even England or Germany.

The Saga of A. P. Giannini

It is the general time-tested assumption that the chief of an enterprise is taking care of himself in rococo style. But this assumption would have been wrong if applied to Amadeo P. Giannini (1870–1949), the Italian Catholic fruit and vegetable peddler who built the colossal Bank of America of San Francisco, still the biggest in the world; the Transamerica Corporation, chain-bank super-holding company; and beat the Morgan interests in their attempt to wangle into control.

Giannini, although he had plenty of opportunities at the hands of grateful directors who pressed upon him the customary slushy stock bonuses (which he refused), believed that $500,000 was a sufficient personal fortune for any man. And his estate at his death was under $600,000. He was succeeded at the helm of his enterprises by his son Lawrence.[34] From the outside looking in one would have thought that Giannini, because he was in a position to do so, would have helped himself greedily to all sorts of fiscal bon bons. But Giannini, in his lordly disdain for personal gain and his personal pride in the vast enterprise he had built, was one of the few American moneymen with a truly aristocratic view of his role.

Deceased Magnates

There were, too, a number of recently deceased men that *Fortune* did not mention, although their accumulations by no means passed out of existence with their deaths. They should be reckoned.

William L. Moody, Jr.

First, there was little noticed William L. Moody, Jr. (1865–1954), with a rated net worth of $400 million at his death.[35] According to the *Foundation Directory, 1964*, The Moody Foundation of Galveston, which he established, retained tax-sheltered assets of about $188 million at the end of 1962. Among the trustees were two sons, William L. III and Robert L., chairman of the board. Moody III was grimly cut off with $1 in his father's will but through litigation was able to get a settlement of $3,640,-898; most of the residual estate went to the tax-saving foundation.[36]

Moody was in banking, cotton-processing, real estate, insurance, printing and newspapers. With his father he founded W. L. Moody and Company, bankers of Galveston, later merged with the National Bank of Texas. He founded in 1920 the American Printing Company, which he owned; bought the Galveston *News* and *Tribune*; founded and owned the American National Insurance Company, one of the biggest such enterprises in the Southwest; and founded and owned the National Hotel Company. He built various skyscrapers here and there, and at his death owned thirty sizeable hotels—any one of which spelled Easy Street for the owner. What he did not put into his foundation he left to two daughters and one son. As this big fortune had its roots back in the nineteenth century it should probably not be considered new, although awareness of it is new. Like many others, Moody mushroomed with the region around him. He was in the mainstream of American property acquisition.

Hugh Roy Cullen: A Texas Regular

Hugh Roy Cullen (1881–1957), Texas wildcatter, left more than $200 million, according to common report. He established the Cullen Foundation to which he assigned $160 million, say standard sources;[37] but the *Foundation Directory, 1964*, accords the foundation a net worth of only $2,434,610 at the end of 1961. Possibly the estate was still being processed. Cullen also allotted more than $30 million to the University of Houston, specializing in vocational training, there to establish a memorial for his only son, and at least $20 million more to hospitals and the like.

Cullen, a man of little schooling, son of a cattleman, went to work at age twelve and eventually emerged as a cotton broker. He went into oil in

1917 and at various times was closely associated with Rockefeller and Mellon companies. His personal instrument was the Quintana Petroleum Corporation, and with it he found many big new fields. But he followed the lead of someone else in applying scientific methods to the discovery of oil.

Like H. L. Hunt he believed the American public needed instruction in political basics, and in 1951 he bought the Liberty Network of radio stations with outlets in thirty-eight states, to facilitate the flow of cracker-barrel interpretations of the Constitution.

Cullen was one of the earliest of the ultra-conservatives. He was against the New Deal from the beginning. Like Herbert Spencer, he was opposed to all government regulation, was opposed to the Marshall Plan, to the United Nations, to unionization and to the lowering of tariffs. In this latter respect an inner contradiction shows in his theory of self-effacing government, for tariffs are a government regulatory device in favor of domestic producers. Cullen's true position, like that of almost all the anti-regulation business people, is that he opposed government regulation that in any way might conceivably sandpaper business profits but he joyfully favored any sort of government regulation, interference, intrusion, intervention, support or action if it was price-raising or promised to be directly profitable to business. This is the actual principle governing the pecuniary man, who is at bottom an unconscious anarchist, hostile to all government not his personal instrument.

Back in the 1930's Cullen organized what was known as the Texas Regulars, still the hard core of the ultra-conservative movement. In 1948 he supported the Dixiecrats, but in 1952 he led the revolt in the Texas Republican delegation against Taft in order to get on the ground floor with Eisenhower. He gave money lavishly in politics to any counter-clockwise movement.

Cullen, like H. L. Hunt, took his acquisition of wealth as a sign from on high that he possessed unique virtue, that he was of the elect, a prophet to lead the boobs to the Promised Land. His sudden riches not only gave him an excess of confidence but a feeling of omniscience and clairvoyance in all human affairs. Although he had never studied these matters, was indeed like Hunt anti-intellectual, he thought he knew all about foreign affairs, world politics, history and, above all else, the needs of the domestic political economy. These were quite simple: What was needed was a general application of the Horatio Alger philosophy within a simple Spencerian setting, each individual striving upward toward the kindly light of money with no intervention from government either to block or assist (except established businessmen).

In seeing the businessman as omniscient, Cullen was simply echoing an early American point of view. It was often said by the bullying Major Henry Lee Higginson, founder of the Boston banking firm of Lee Higginson and Company, that "Any well-trained businessman is wiser than the Congress and the Executive."[38] And, if one gives full value to the operative word "well-trained," the major may have had an arguable point of view even though some fastidious minds might consider it faint praise to concede anyone more wisdom than Congress. But businessmen rarely limit omniscience to the well-trained and tend to feel that anyone who has made some money has given ample proof of his general wisdom.

Although a simple but forceful mentality such as Cullen's may evoke uneasy smiles among the more knowledgeable, it must not be forgotten that such men, by reason of their ability to put up money, have much to say in politics. Arrogating to themselves the role of supreme legislators, they use formal legislators, chosen in the catch-as-catch-can political process, as their cat's paws, mainly to block socially necessary measures. Cullen and his cracker-barrel colleagues placed their distinctive stamp on the internal colonialist politics of Texas, and they had more than a little to do with returning the Republican Party to power in 1952–60. They are always working at it, with money and main, and will never be satisfied until they install the straight Coolidge-McKinley ticket. They keep the lambent glow of the horse-and-buggy age bright in the thermonuclear-missile-automation-computer age.

James A. Chapman

Still another oil baron whose fortune reached awesome dimensions was James A. Chapman of Tulsa, Oklahoma. Chapman died in 1966, aged eighty-five, leaving about $100 million, most of it to the University of Tulsa, the balance to other educational and medical institutions.

Self-floated with $700 in 1907 on a tide of oil, Chapman was rated by insiders as Oklahoma's most successful oil operator. During his lifetime Chapman, said his attorneys, had secretly "given away" more than $75 million. His will made no provision for his wife and conveyed only $1,000 to his forty-seven-year-old son because, as it noted, "adequate provisions" had already been made for them (*New York Times*, October 15, 1966; 1:1).

De Golyer: A Man for Most Seasons

But not all of the oil men are cracker-barrel fugitives from textbooks,

it is gratifying to report. Some are impressive figures and would unquestionably have risen to prominence in any socio-political system.
One such was Everette Lee De Golyer (1886–1956), of remote French
descent, who compares with most oil hunters as does a Stradivarius with a
banjo.

De Golyer, a geologist and a geophysicist, was many times a millionaire,
and is indeed credited with bringing applied geophysics to the United
States. He is known in scientific circles, where he was very much at home,
as "The Father of American Geophysics." To De Golyer more than to any
other one man goes the credit for the discovery of so much underground
oil since 1910. Without De Golyer—or some counterpart—the world oil
supply would unquestionably be much lower than it is today. For the
oil industry from the beginning was very wasteful, haphazard and slap-
dash, full of apprentice barbers performing as surgeons.

De Golyer's father was a mineral prospector and De Golyer, born in a
Kansas sod hut, initially took an interest along these lines. He joined the
Wyoming Geological Survey in 1906 and later worked with it in Colorado
and Montana. But soon tiring of rule-of-thumb methods, he enrolled in
the University of Oklahoma where he was graduated in 1911 at the age of
twenty-five. In the summers he worked as a field geologist and in 1909
joined the Mexican Eagle Oil Company, then owned by British interests
and later sold to Royal Dutch Shell.

On his first trip out in the area near Tampico, later known as "The
Golden Lane," relocating the search in accordance with his knowledge of
structural trends, he brought in Potrero del Llano No. 4 well, one of
the most spectacular gushers of all time. This well produced 110,000
barrels daily and cumulatively produced more than 100 million barrels.
De Golyer was promoted to chief geologist and then chief of the land
department.

Some sources say he was a millionaire before finishing college; others relate that Mexican Eagle put him on a salary of $500 a month—fairly good
money in 1909—while he went to school. He continued with the company
in a consultative capacity until 1919, although he left it officially in 1914
to open his own offices as a consulting engineer to the petroleum industry.

Called to England in 1918 to participate in the sale of Mexican Eagle
to Royal Dutch Shell, he was then backed by Lord Cowdray of Mexican
Eagle to form the Amerada Petroleum Corporation, of which he was made
vice president and general manager, then president and finally chairman. He retired from highly successful Amerada in 1932. He continued,
however, with the Geophysical Research Corporation, which discovered
oil fields by scientific methods for the big oil companies. He also formed

Core Laboratories, Inc., and the Atlatl Royalty Corporation to carry on oil discovery and ownership.

De Golyer's method was to apply the knowledge of a trained, scientific mind nourished widely in the theoretical literature about the causal processes of earth formations. He picked up some of his most valuable insights by applying early European theory to his work. The presence of underground salt domes is now known to predict the presence of oil. How are salt domes formed? Then prevalent theory held them to be of volcanic origin, the result of the expansion of growing salt crystals or deposits from rising columns of brine from deep sources. De Golyer came to accept the European theory that they are formed by plastic flow, the salt having flowed owing to the weight of overhanging rocks. Once the salt dome has been found, the oil prospector must determine the formation of the underlying rocks in order to get through. All this careful inquiry was quite out of harmony with the practical, common-sense, feet-on-the-ground, down-to-earth, no-nonsense, rule-of-thumb guesswork in the field by the boys who had just recently left the cracker barrel.

De Golyer implemented his insights by introducing the use of the seismograph, gravimeter, torsion balance, electro-magnetic surveys and explosives to send shock waves through the varieties of underground formations, thereby determining their texture. Using these appliances he found field after rich field in Texas, Oklahoma and the Gulf region. Cullen and others, sweating for money, copied his methods, which are now standard all over the world in oil prospecting.

Basically a scientist, a student and a scholar, De Golyer was widely read, not only in his technical specialty but in the literature of the Southwest. He published a long, impressive list of original scientific papers and wrote about the history and personalities of the Southwest. From a money-making point of view he wasted tens of millions of dollars of time reading and writing. He collected priceless rare books—on the Southwest, on geology and geophysics and on scientific method and the history of science—and left them, a treasure, to the University of Oklahoma, the University of Texas and other institutions. He established the De Golyer Foundation to add to these valuable collections of books.

In the late 1940's, hearing that the *Saturday Review of Literature* was in financial straits, he came forward to give it a lift and was made chairman of the board. De Golyer served on literally scores of national and local cultural and scientific bodies and boards, lectured to serious audiences at M.I.T. and Princeton and served in 1940 as Distinguished Professor of Geology at the University of Texas. He held well-deserved honorary degrees from many American and foreign universities and was frequently decorated.

Although a moderate Republican, he served willingly under Franklin D. Roosevelt as oil adviser to the New Deal, later in the war, and as chief of the technical mission at the Teheran Conference. The number of his trusteeships, directorships and organization memberships was far too extensive to list here.

He is memorialized by the National Academy of Science (of which he was a Fellow) in Volume XXXIII of its *Biographical Memoirs* together with Thomas Hunt Morgan, the biologist; Robert A. Millikan, the physicist; Lewis M. Terman, the psychologist; and Josiah Royce, the philosopher. He was clearly much more than an oil prospector, businessman or capitalist. The *Memoirs* give a bibliography of his writings from 1912 onward, encompassing fifteen pages of titles.

After an illness of six years De Golyer shot himself at the age of seventy.[39]

What De Golyer was worth is less interesting than what he could have been worth had he devoted himself solely to accumulating wealth. There is no doubt he could have been worth billions had he been interested in nailing down for himself every likely claim. As it was, his retained wealth was estimated at $10 million to $100 million at his death, a wide range.[40]

Looking on his fellow oilmen with considerable reserve, De Golyer "frequently remarked that the talent for making money can imply a lack of talent for leading a useful life."[41] De Golyer certainly did not suffer from this deficiency.

But like some of the other oil men, De Golyer did believe in luck. "I hate to tell you," he once said, "how many times I've made money by going against my own judgment."[42] On this same theme realistic R. E. Smith, one of the *Fortune* listees, said, "My West Texas oil field was solely luck. It has 38 million barrels in reserve and cost me $5 an acre. It was the same with Hugh Roy Cullen. The first money he made was on some land he didn't want; the oil company kept the 'A' acreage. They gave him some 'D' property—the lowest grade—as consolation and he hit. The company never did hit anything on their 'A' property. The lesson you learn as you get older is that it's luck." Again: "The fortune of Matilda Geddings Gray," explained a Louisianian, "came mostly from her father. He made it on a herd of cattle; found an oil well under every cow."[43]

Without some element of luck, no matter how hardworking, ingenious, greedy or unscrupulous the protagonist, nobody ever made much money. The general luck of the nineteenth century entrepreneurs was to have a great deal of new technology thrust under their noses—steam engines, steel-making processes imported from abroad, internal combustion engines, new electrical apparatus and the like. Few of the entrepreneurs participated in the creation of any of this but they did know how to convert it under lucky circumstances into titles of extravagant ownership—in their own names.

Raskob of Du Pont

John J. Raskob (1879–1950), one of the upper executives of the General Motors Corporation, prepared with a knowledge of stenography, got his start by becoming secretary to wealthy Pierre S. du Pont. Raskob's big coup some years later was to suggest General Motors as a likely investment for surplus Du Pont money, and he thereafter alternated rising lucrative employment with General Motors and E. I. du Pont de Nemours and Company. The leading figure in trying to make Al Smith president in 1928 and the Democratic Party a replica of the Republican, he was made Private Chamberlain to the Pope. He founded the tax-shy Raskob Foundation for Catholic Activities in 1945; it had assets of $29,281,060 in 1960 and four Raskob sons among its officers. On his death he left his wife and each of ten surviving children trust funds of unspecified amounts.[44] One presumes they were generously proportioned. As Raskob was a pecuniary man to his fingertips with no other apparent interest in his life, his fortune before he started redeploying it may well have exceeded $75 or $100 million.

William S. Knudsen

William S. Knudsen (1879–1948), former president of the General Motors Corporation and Director General of the Office of Production Management during the war, had one of the "ten biggest incomes in the country"[45] but the expanse of his holdings at the end is fogged. Standard reference media, including the New York Times, give no accounting of his estate, which was presumably disposed of before his death; he established no foundation, left three daughters and one son, all presumably financially soigné.

A Note on Probate

There is nothing conclusive about the probate of an estate. In his lifetime a wealthy man might make tax-free dispositions to foundations or other endowments (which usually show on the record) or he might make regular low-tax distributions to members of his family. At a gift-tax cost of $325,700 as of 1965, an unmarried person could transfer $1 million to an individual. If he did this every year for twenty-five years to five persons, thus transferring $125 million cumulatively, he would have to pay $40,-712,500 additional in taxes, a tidy sum. If he waited to bequeath $165 million at death to individuals, the tax bite would be $125,438,200, or about $85 million more than by the installment-transfer procedure.

But by halving his individual gifts each year and putting the other half of the money into a tax-free foundation (which his heirs could play with as it suited their tastes) he would pull his total transfer taxes down to a low, low $6,119,375 or a little less than 4 per cent on $165 million. His saving over the first procedure, for the benefit of his heirs and their foundation, would be $34-plus million; over the second procedure, a little under $119 million.

Delightful though this prospect is, if the man is married he can make the original transfer of $125 million solely to individuals at only double the cost of 4 per cent, paying a little more than $12 million, under special provisions for estate division written into the law in 1948. His saving here over the first direct transfer is $28-plus million, which he can slam into a foundation for so much extra gravy. Whoever said we didn't have a thoughtful Congress to write such thoughtful laws? In the meantime, newspapers and "spokesmen"—that is, paid propagandists—go about talking loosely about high taxes on the big estates. When one gets down to the fine print, those high taxes just aren't there.

A man might, indeed, die stony broke and still have ruled over a large fortune if he had concentrated a goodly sum in a foundation. As head of the foundation he would naturally set himself a substantial salary. He would not, legally, own anything; he'd just control the assets of the foundation by charter and the disposition of its income. Until he drew his last breath, even though he was only on straight salary, he'd have corporate, political and other power through his foundation as well as the satisfaction of knowing that he hadn't helped the rustics in Congress with their eternal problem of budget balancing. So the mere fact that a man dies without leaving traces of large assets really proves nothing.

Jesse H. Jones

Jesse H. Jones (1874–1956) was for many years a power in the land and a top-level, hardbitten wheeler-dealer. A banker and politician based in Houston where he owned the *Chronicle*, banks, buildings and other properties as well as properties in Dallas and Fort Worth, Jones became chairman of the Reconstruction Finance Corporation and Secretary of Commerce under Roosevelt II. As chairman of the RFC he is said to have made the decisions to lend more money than any other man in history, getting himself involved, too, with some of the borrowers. His father was a Tennessee tobacco planter, and young Jones came to Dallas at age twenty to find a place under an uncle in the lumber business. His estate at death was only $8,765,302,[46] but he had earlier made large distributions to children and a foundation, The Houston Endowment (1937), which in 1962 had assets of $43,939,169 and had just made grants of $7,249,765.

Amon G. Carter: Texas Ueber Alles

Amon G. Carter (1879–1955), son of a blacksmith, went to work at age twelve selling newspapers á la Horatio Alger, graduated into selling photographs and then, in 1904, into the not-so-great game of advertising. In 1906 he became advertising manager for the Fort Worth *Star* and by 1923 was president and publisher of the merged *Star-Telegram*. He also weaseled into radio and television but made his biggest money in oil wildcatting. Under his ownership was drilled the discovery well of the big pool in the Wasson lease in Gaines and Yoakum counties, Texas. He sold out there for $16.5 million and put the money into the Amon G. Carter Foundation, which at the end of 1962 had total assets of $32,519,-275 (*Foundation Directory, 1964*). An aviation enthusiast, he was a founder of American Airlines and a major political influence in bringing various military aviation installations, bomber plants and missile enterprises to Texas. He is credited with using his influence to make Texas second only to California as an aviation center. He was a noisy Fort Worth and Texas booster and was said hyperbolically to own all of Fort Worth. He left two daughters, a son, the *Star-Telegram,* various pregnant properties and the foundation. No probate of his will was published in standard reference media available to this inquirer but if one assumes only half his wealth was left in the foundation he was worth more than $65 million at some time in his later life, probably a bit more.[47]

William H. Danforth: Apostle of Purina

William H. Danforth (1870–1955) of all American millionaires probably most deserves the much-abused characterization of philanthropist. For Danforth genuinely liked people in general and was obviously stimulated by them.

Born in the backlands of Missouri, Danforth went to St. Louis at four-teen to go to school and remained to be graduated from Washington University. With $4,000 borrowed from his father he went into a horse-feed partnership with two men in 1894: the Robinson-Danforth Commission Company. A natural salesman, Danforth traveled through the Middle West selling Purina Horse Feed in a folksy way ("Purina Feed will make your horse laugh," one of thousands of bucolic Danforth slogans) and buying ingredients from farmers. The day after one of the partners sold out to Danforth in 1896, the business already booming, a tornado blew down their sizeable plant. With an unsecured bank loan of $25,000 he rebuilt, and the business extended into all varieties of farm feeds under the Purina label. It also went into the production of whole-wheat cereals for human consumption (the new health fad) under the familiar checker-board label. This latter was adopted from a farmer's shirt design and for some reason had such an hypnotic effect on customers that it was widely infringed but successfully defended in the courts.

Danforth was quite spontaneously an enthusiastic extroverted Christian, a YMCA man (he served in France as a YMCA secretary in World War I), a believer in the social gospel and a true, corn-ball do-gooder. He seemed to feel that good will, good humor, enthusiasm and energy were all that were needed to put the world to rights. A Congregationalist Sunday School teacher and superintendent, he believed in helping young people help themselves. He gave thousands to finance camping trips and outings in the woods and on the shores for the young. He was a pioneer in helping finance mostly somewhat bucolic college educations, for which in 1927 he established the Danforth Foundation (assets in 1962: $125,-694,089, mainly in Ralston Purina stock). Danforth believed in college as much as he believed in the Bible.

Danforth ran his business pretty much like a folksy husking bee with plenty of homespun high jinks. He required his employees to exercise to-gether and sing together, and was the originator of widely copied em-ployee welfare programs such as contests, office messages and personal items, employee theatricals, awards, parties, picnics, square dances and general one-big-happy-family stuff. He produced mottoes tirelessly and wrote inspirational books and pamphlets in the school of Dr. Frank Crane, Elbert Hubbard and Orison Swett Marden.

Everybody around Danforth was caught up in a blizzard of activity, all happy Christian soldiers marching onward and upward and holding forth the holy grail of Purina. Somehow, money filtered artlessly through the whole like molasses in a bran mash. Danforth unquestionably be-lieved in everything he did. There was probably not an insincere bone in his body. And the good Lord just made that cash register ring, ring, ring.

Danforth was extremely wealthy by 1929, when Jehovah suddenly signaled that he was unaccountably displeased. All of Danforth's holdings were wiped out in the stock market crash with the exception of his ownership of Ralston Purina. The sign probably meant that the good Lord wanted him to stay out of the wicked stock market and stick to healthy, whole-wheat food.

After the crash, business for Purina slacked off so badly that Danforth, depressed, had to lay off old employees. As grain prices continued to tumble Danforth found that he was constantly having to sell for less than he paid for the raw materials and labor. He was, in short, going broke in a big way. Satan was in command.

But the Lord had not forsaken His earnest worker. In 1932 Danforth relinquished control of the business to his son Donald, recently out of sleek Princeton University and in his father's estimation not much of a businessman. But the boy's mother spoke up staunchly on his behalf, Donald took hold and, giving the business the old college try, he made good in such a way as to amaze the elder. In the general inflation, sales were whirled up from $19 million in 1932 under Donald's shrewd Ivy League ministrations to $400 million in 1956, when Ralston Purina chugged into eighty-seventh place on *Fortune's* list of the mightiest corporations. In the distance such giants as AT&T, General Motors and Standard Oil of New Jersey could dimly hear the corn-belt juggernaut slowly creeping up on them.

Danforth himself was a "natural" in a world of counterfeits. Personally likeable and uncomplicated in his views, he was simple-minded and naïve and perhaps just lucky never to fall into the sights of the financial sharpshooters all around him. He took no visible interest in politics. His early heroes were Hill, Harriman, Rockefeller, Astor, McCormick, Carnegie and their like, whom he saw as builders of the nation, Daniel Boones of the dollar. He longed to emulate them. He always sought out the business great in an effort to learn their "secrets." He looked up John Wanamaker, whom he admired both as a businessman and as a Christian layman. (In Danforth's view "businessman" was just about synonymous with "Christian." Jesus was after all, as it has been said, a salesman. Danforth would gladly have given him a job selling Purina.) Once Danforth followed Henry M. Flagler, the Standard Oil tycoon and Florida promoter, around a golf course in Florida, pencil and notebook in hand, and asked the great man many questions, to which he was graciously given answers. Danforth also sought out Henry Ford for prayerful discussions about philanthropy.

As far as the record shows, Danforth (unlike many of his prominent business contemporaries) never engaged in any shady practices, was never involved in any swindles, was never the defendant on criminal charges and was never accused of exploiting his workers. Nor was he, it seems, ever seriously criticized, knocked, called to account or rebuffed in good times or bad. For a portrait of the American capitalist as an extremely good, wholesome, honestly Christian earnest outgoing do-gooder one must turn to William H. Danforth.

The name of Ralston got into the Ralston Purina label in a curious way. Early in this century there was a Dr. Ralston who established health-food clubs around the country. Danforth, in order to get into the human food market with his whole-wheat cereals made a money-for-name tie-in with the good doctor and Ralston Purina was off on the heels of Quaker Oats and Kellogg's Corn Flakes. Health foods, big money and religion all gathered at the shore of the mighty Mississippi river.[48]

New–Old Fortunes

Although all these noninherited fortunes have been treated as new, they are new only in a relative sense. Almost all the big individual nonin-herited fortunes mentioned in this inquiry date back before World War II and, indeed, the bulk of them date before 1929. Most of the Texas oil fortunes were founded between 1910 and 1925. The General Motors fortunes were all in foetal existence in the 1920's. Although the names of the owners are less familiar than Rockefeller, Morgan and Vanderbilt, every single one was already rich on the eve of Pearl Harbor and nearly all were rich in 1929.

Many clearly date from before World War I—Danforth, Moody, Jones, Getty.

Unless processes are going on inaccessible to inquiry it can be said that big new individual property accumulations are now taking place, if at all, at a decidedly diminished pace. And this is understandable in view of the entrenched position established by hereditary wealth. No man, how-ever puissant, can come along and simply say "move over" to the Standard Oil Company of New Jersey, E. I. du Pont de Nemours and Company or dozens of similar enterprises. Nor can such a puissant man by any method yet disclosed take them over as his own.

Whirling Dervishes of the Mass Media

Although the barrel has been scraped in the search for new or nonhereditary wealth on the American scene, and just about every likely candidate appears to have been noticed, there can be no guarantee that some big "sleeper" has not been overlooked. We have ignored, for reasons of space, stuff ranging from $25 to $75 million.

Most of the names of new fortune-builders put before the public are those of men who are little more than speculative entrepreneurs backed by banks or some syndicate. As long as these whirling dervishes stand upright they receive rapt attention. But most of them vanish in a cloud of debt and tears to become skeletons in the Death Valley of newspaper files.

Newspapers are interested in such worthies for at least two reasons:

1. They want new names and faces to present to the public, and many people as well as editors seem to find it thrilling to read of some immigrant who arrived in this country with five dollars and went to work as a rag picker, quietly saved his pennies, gradually bought real estate and finally emerged as the greatest real-estate tycoon of all time. Or so they say until the banks start calling loans.

2. They cite these putative geniuses of pecuniary derring-do in order to prove that anyone who is willing to work hard, live right and tend to business can make at least a million and probably more in the United States—the American dream. A curious feature of this thesis is that the money-cult editors and writers who expound it are themselves not notably pecunious, are apparently unable to apply their own profound insight.

In the 1920's, in the aftermath of World War I, names to conjure with in the press were William C. Durant, founder of General Motors and possessor of a fresh fortune several times in his life; Jesse L. Livermore; Arthur W. Cutten; Frank E. Bliss, "The Silver Fox of Wall Street"; Benjamin Block; Michael J. Meehan; Joseph E. Higgins; Louis W. Zimmerman; George Breen; and Harry Content.[49] All went down the financial drain without a gurgle.

Arthur W. Cutten, as big as they used to be verbally blown up, died in 1936 while under indictment for income-tax evasion. His estate of $350,-000, once reputed to be worth $100 million (press reports of the holdings of market operators are usually vastly exaggerated, thus attracting more suckers), had tax liens against it of $644,000 and was confiscated.[50] Rumors that he had funds in Canada, where he was born, were checked without affirmative result.

Cutten, for years a drab bookkeeper in a Chicago brokerage house, in the early 1920's became a speculator-manipulator in the grain pits. He finally had perhaps a few million drably to his credit and drably came to New York in 1925 at the age of fifty-four in search of drab new puddles to conquer. He engaged in buying and bulling stocks, assisted by hordes of even drabber men and women who bought anything they heard Book-keeper Cutten was buying. Distributing to the suckers as the top he had set was approached, Cutten pocketed the profits. This process was endlessly repeated and would no doubt still be going on if the "Moment of Truth" had not come in October, 1929. Cutten was, with poetic justice, one of the many picadors and bandilleros whom the dying bull managed to gore fatally before expiring. His career may be summarized as a transit from bookkeeper to gambler to nothing. There is no hard evidence that I can find that Cutten was ever worth $100 million, $50 million or even $10 million net; he was carried by the banks.

There were, too, in those salad days, high-flying dervishes like Samuel Insull, Charles E. Mitchell, Ivar Kreuger, Albert Wiggin, Howard Hopson, Edward Doherty—all men with complex Rube Goldberg schemes afoot and in the end all speculative flat tires, personally as undistinguished as any pushcart peddler. But in their day the newspapers ecstasized over them as proof positive that under the great American system of godly democracy any right-thinking, right-living man who had faith in the United States should, could and would acquire a fortune.

The biggest flops of all, as one would expect, were those men widely regarded as the soundest. The superlatively sound men of the time were Oris P. and Mantis J. Van Sweringen of Cleveland, presented in the press as masters of railroading (although they were actually two obscure provincial real estate brokers). With the backing of the J. P. Morgan bloc the Van Sweringens busily floated vast railroad holding companies, busily issued watery securities, busily merged, unmerged and submerged rail-roads and busily carried on general financial wildcatting in search of profit. Their bubble burst in the depression, removing two geniuses of bank-press creation from the scene.

Just how big the Van Sweringens were considered in the 1920's may be seen in the fact that they were listed in 1930 by James W. Gerard, former ambassador to Germany, as one of the sixty-four shoguns who "ruled the United States." President Herbert C. Hoover was, correctly, not on this list, which was headed by John D. Rockefeller I, Andrew W. Mellon, J. P. Morgan II, George F. Baker, John D. Ryan (copper), Henry Ford I, seven Du Ponts of high dynastic numbering, the five Fisher brothers of Detroit ("Body by Fisher"), A. P. Giannini, Daniel Guggen-heim, a few corporation executives and some dubious elements no doubt included by the diplomatic Gerard to be complimentary: William Green, Matthew Woll, Roy W. Howard, William Randolph Hearst and, of all people, Adolph Zukor and Harry F. Warner, the film moguls.

But although one might quarrel with the catholicity of Gerard's choices, he did adhere to the theory, bitterly denied by all party-liners of the American myth, that some sort of dimly visible shogunate lies behind major trends in American policy. The country was not being run from Washington by duly elected representatives of the people, Gerard sensed, but by a group of remote-control drivers, masters of the cash register. Its ringing was, to them, the Liberty Bell, signaling their own freedom from want.

One could go on for many pages reviewing the lists of the financial also-rans, a fevered crowd—all duly celebrated in their day. In order to bring things down to date, we may notice in parting the name of William J. Zeckendorf, the big builder, operator and general juggler of office buildings and hotel properties, since World War II given much press attention as an authentic coast-to-coast tycoon. The Zeckendorf story, a reader's thriller for many years, may be now told very briefly: His enterprise went decisively bankrupt in 1965 as the banks called the loans, a process irreverently known as "pulling the plug."[51]

Fallacious Logic in Media Celebrations

The notion that new fortunes are being made right and left in the United States, selectively documented from time to time by *Fortune* and the *Wall Street Journal*, may now be looked at briefly. In general, these publications perpetrate several fallacies in logic in supporting this thesis, notably those of untypical instances and of neglected aspect.

Fortune (January, 1952) presented a survey titled "The New Rich," cueing it in with the substatement that "A lot of enterprisers you probably never heard of are proving you can still strike it rich in America."

"Since 1945," said *Fortune*, "a brand-new crop of rich men has risen in the U.S. Mostly shirt-sleeved enterprisers who started from scratch, they are hardly more than well off compared to the 'Pittsburgh millionaires' of the nineteenth century or the 'Detroit millionaires' of the Twenties. What makes them spectacular is their profusion. Every state in the Union has them by the hundreds, and their collective wealth, glittering from coast to coast, has given the whole country a pleasant golden hue."

(I find it difficult to believe that any responsible writer of such a line is not being exaggeratedly ironic.)

"They are the core of that fast-growing group whose 15,000-odd members report incomes between $100,000 and $300,000 a year; their affluence is neither freakish nor unstable. Right behind them, ready to step into their shoes, are roughly 50,000 individuals who in 1948 reported incomes of $50,000 to $100,000 a year, and 175,000 who reported $25,000 to

$50,000." *Fortune* takes no account of the carefully established fact that most of these incomes are old-line asset-incomes, not the incomes of new men.

"Nationally their presence is recorded in the 400,000 Cadillacs sold since 1945, the 37,000 pleasure craft registered since 1946, the doubling of Chris-Craft's 1951 big-boat sales (forty-two feet and up), and the introduction, under the pressure of demand, of a sixty-two-footer, priced at $125,000. A score of the splashier restaurants have become fabulously successful as a result of their patronage; their private planes, as many as two hundred at a time, fly in for the bigger Texas football games; and their dexterity with an expense account since pleasures and business are hard to sort out in wholly owned enterprises, gives them a spending power far above others making the same amounts in straight salary."

Fortune soberly names some of the new paragons as follows:

William Mullis (frozen shrimp, Georgia); Jeno Paulucci (frozen chop suey, Minnesota); Sam Joachim (burlap bags, Texas); Ross Sams (church furniture, Texas); Abe Katz (plastic toys, New York); Ralph Stolkin (punchboards, oil, cattle, movies, TV, Chicago, valued by *Fortune* at $35 to $50 million with no source evidence cited); Vern Schield (power shovels, Iowa); Dr. Earl Carpenter and John C. Snyder (baby beds, Wisconsin); Winston Smillie (floor cleaners, Missouri); Malcolm Lee McLeod (timber, South Carolina); Milton Brucker (plastics, California); Harry E. Umphrey (French fried potatoes, Maine); Hugh B. Williams (earth-boring machines, Texas); "Smiling Jim" Moran, "The Courtesy Man" (auto dealer, Illinois); Sam Eig (real estate, Maryland); Kenneth Aldred Spencer (chemicals, Kansas); Herman Delmos (Breezy) Wynn (sporting goods, Georgia); Fred Hervey (supermarkets; restaurants; hog farms; mayor of El Paso, Texas).

All these are instances, says *Fortune*, of "individual success." What they all are, in fact, are fairly run-of-the-mill marginal businessmen, hailed by *Fortune* as the new rich. No balance sheets are revealed, no listing of bank loans. How many will emerge with a substantial net worth is not shown, nor how many will go the way of Zeckendorf and thousands of others.

In many cases, especially where annual sales are cited, one can make certain hard deductions. The baby-bed makers, said *Fortune*, had run their sales up to a million dollars a year. Now, some of the most successful U.S. enterprises regularly have around 14 per cent profits on sales, an envied figure even if sometimes exceeded. If we gratuitously give this superb percentage to the baby-bed makers they were making $140,000 a year. Split two ways this is $70,000, which after taxes leaves less. Allowing each entrepreneur to live very frugally, let us say he saves $50,000 a year. In ten years he will then be worth $500,000, in twenty years $1 million. The point is that few small businesses keep up this way. They run into competition and other vicissitudes, mostly from larger enterprises.

But Kenneth Aldred Spencer is doing well, says *Fortune*. "Besides a $50,000 salary, in 1950 he received $377,000 in dividends on his 236,000 shares of common stock and realized $118,000 through sale of the purchase rights of a new issue." "Smiling Jim" Moran has set up a $1,450,000 trust fund for the children." Not too bad but, really, chicken feed.

But these simple annals of the merely well-to-do, whom we always have with us, hardly prove that new fortunes are in the offing. Successful business entrepreneurs though all these men may be, one can scarcely regard them as "the new rich." They are small fish in a pond full of large fish. And the odds against any of them becoming big fish—authentic barracudas—are enormous.

As instances of the ability to make new fortunes on the American scene, we must pronounce a Scotch verdict: not proven.

Where the reportorial fallacy enters in is the citation only of these minor winners, no losers. But of the many who answer the siren call to riches few are chosen, as the record of bankruptcies shows. Business failures in the United States, according to annual reports by Dun & Bradstreet, national credit raters, have in most years since 1950 exceeded 10,000 and in some years 15,000. Between 1950 and 1953 they ranged between 7,611 and 9,162 and have not to date fallen below 10,000. In 1963 they totaled 14,374 with total liabilities of $1.3 billion, the value of a largish supercorporation. For every businessman in a given year who makes enough of a splash to come to the attention of *Fortune's* editors, about 10,000 split a gut trying and cough blood in the bankruptcy court. If it weren't committed to dispensing sunshine, *Fortune* could write a melancholy article every year on business failures and issue a thick supplementary directory merely giving names and addresses.

Nor do these figures show the panorama in its full sweep. The special monograph on small business of the Temporary National Economic Committee, a joint Senate and Securities and Exchange Commission operation, in 1939 revealed that "in the first thirty-nine years of this century, 19 million enterprises opened their doors and 16 million closed them." This was a four-decade failure rate of 85 per cent.

Henry Thoreau, writing in *Walden* in the mid-nineteenth century, concluded that the failure rate of businesses in his day was 97 per cent.

The Failure System

In business, under the American system, each year the failures exceed the new successes by a very, very, very wide margin. In business, under the American system, hundreds of thousands more have failed, generation after generation, than the few who have succeeded. If we are to judge by the preponderance of individual successes over failures or vice versa, then the American system, businesswise, is a record of steady, almost unrelieved failure. It has failure literally built into it. It is indeed a near-miracle, front page news, when anyone really makes it. This judicious observation sounds paradoxical only because it contradicts conventional propaganda.

As it is observed by Professor Paul A. Samuelson of M.I.T. in his standard textbook, *Economics* (McGraw-Hill, N.Y., 7th edition, 1967, p. 76), the average life expectancy of an American business is six (6) years!

While it is true that no particular blame attaches to anyone for the high rate of small business mortality, blame can be leveled for the misleading propaganda about the business system. By the one-sided stressing by propaganda organs of the few successes, many are led to lose their hard-earned savings in establishing new businesses. Sound advice to 85 to 95 per cent of Americans contemplating opening their own businesses would, in the light of the facts, simply be: "Don't."

The belief of a wide public that it can succeed in business supplies a lucrative crop of suckers for established equipment suppliers, usually big corporations. Banks, too, participate in this merry game by making loans against resalable equipment. The same fixtures are sold and resold to a long string of losers incited into action by florid accounts of success in the *Wall Street Journal, Fortune* and other media.

Today, the new man going into business, like the individual consumer, does not realize that all the possibilities in almost every situation have been determined down to decimal places by batteries of computers and the results have been evaluated by staffs of exceedingly acute experts. In pitting himself against these computers and highly paid experts, the ordinary man is very much like an amateur chess player who elects to pit his skill against a consulting collection of chess masters. His doom is virtually sealed with his very first move.

Fortune's valedictory for its inspiring group of minor successes was that "The new rich symbolize the abundant health of the U.S. economy, for they have been pushed up by a general prosperity below. A fair guess is that money in the hands of millions at the base will keep them at the summit and in the decade ahead swell their number by the thousands."

More Fuel from the Wall Street Journal

The editors of the *Wall Street Journal* in 1962 put somewhat similar findings about thirteen men and one woman into the form of a book.[52]

The foreword by Warren H. Phillips, managing editor, makes it clear that the presentation is designed to prove something: that it is as easy as it ever was to make a fortune in the American economy, that it is desirable to do so and that fortunes are being made right and left. Like the *Fortune* group of 1952 the *Journal's* group of 1962 embraced only modest fortunes, men who might be called the "poor man's millionaires." They did not pretend to be like the all-time heavyweights of the *Fortune* 1957 list.

As Mr. Phillips observed, "It is often said that today it is infinitely more difficult to amass great wealth than during earlier periods in the nation's history; that the nation's economy has matured, and the rags-to-riches legend belongs to its period of youthful growth; that business opportunity today is highly limited, not only by high taxes, but by stiffer competition from large corporations and by pronounced restrictions based on education, race, religion, sex and age.

"The evidence sharply contradicts this impression."[53]

The only "evidence" Mr. Phillips cites is the number of postwar million-dollar incomes that we have already examined, incomes from established assets.

"All such statistics suggest that the opportunities for making fortunes in this country are as wide today as in any earlier period of history."[54]

The statistics on large incomes provide no evidence whatever for concluding that new fortunes are being made or that there are opportunities for making fortunes. Without the identities of such large income receivers one cannot tell whether the income is from an old or a new fortune, from asset-wealth or from earnings in the form of salaries or commissions. In view of the fact that, despite pertinacious work by *Fortune*, the *Saturday Evening Post*, the *New York Times* and myself, so few authentic recent fortunes have been turned up, it is a practical certainty that nearly all the million-dollar incomes as well as $50,000 and $100,000 incomes come from *old* fortunes.

An individual fortune may bring in $500,000 one year and, as business conditions boom and dividends rise, increase its income to more than $1 million. It is then a *new* million-dollar income but not indicative of a new fortune. It may, too, have had a million-dollar income many times in earlier years. But it is always the same good old fortune, whatever the income. Nothing new has been added.

In the United States, Mr. Phillips also wants us to believe, "Material success is more within the realm of the possible than in most European societies, with their cartelized business systems and more rigid social class structures."[55] And with this statement it is easier to agree, but on other grounds; for "most European societies" takes in a group that either has no business system at all or one so rudimentary—as in Spain, Portugal, Greece —as to afford few trading opportunities. If one adds Russia, Poland, Hungary, Czechoslovakia, Bulgaria and Yugoslavia—all under statist regimes—and looks at small places like Finland, Austria, Switzerland, Lichtenstein and Denmark, there isn't much of a playground left for "material success." The United States could outdistance this combination with one new millionaire a decade.

As for the rags-to-riches legend being still valid, none of the names presented by the *Journal* editors supports it. Nearly all were merely non-asset-holders before they started their modest climbs.

Although only one of the cases cited comes within hailing distance of heavy money—$34 million, if this is his authentic net worth—it may be interesting to peep at some of these small operators briefly as a contrast with our coming glimpses at truly impressive super-wealth.

Thomas F. Bolack, says the *Journal,* was an oil-field laborer before he rose to become lieutenant governor of New Mexico and a gentleman farmer. He did it by buying oil leases at 25 cents an acre in the San Juan Basin, which he sold for $5,000 an acre. He was worth $3 million in 1951, says the *Journal,* and possibly more later.[56]

Then there is Winston J. Schuler, Michigan restaurateur, who was worth only $50,000 in 1946 but is now worth more than $3 million.[57] Schuler got a lift toward immortality when his father gave him and a brother a run-down restaurant. The upcoming entrepreneur sagely added a bowling alley and generally refurbished the place. It was a hit and began to boom. Schuler opened other restaurants and soon had a chain. A prudent man, he formed a separate corporation for each restaurant, say the *Journal* editors, thus avoiding any large cumulative taxable income. He also decreed that the corporations not pay out any dividends and although each one necessarily paid corporation taxes (each getting the initial deduction) he would not be taxed on any dividend income. Earnings were ploughed back into expansion, so that Winston J. Schuler is presumably getting richer and richer minute by minute.

Peter Kanavos of Dedham, Massachusetts, presents a simple story to the *Journal* editors. His father was a Greek barber and Pete started with a lowly saloon on borrowed money in 1947. He went into real estate on the side and in a decade had made $5 million, so they say.[58]

A stalwart woman, Mrs. Catherine T. Clark, baked her way to new-found wealth. Finding a chink in the capitalist armor in the form of soggy corporate bread, she decided in Oconomowoc, Wisconsin, to bake a palatable whole-wheat loaf. She began in 1946 and by the time the *Wall Street Journal* got around to her she was head of Brownberry Ovens, Inc., selling non-soggy bread to an insatiable market, had moved to San Francisco and was now, the *Journal* editors guarantee, wearing $50 hats and Paris clothes. The account is vague about her net worth but it seemed to be biggish.[59]

Again, there is James J. Ling of Ling-Temco Electronics, Inc., now Ling-Temco-Vought, of Dallas, Texas, who quit school at fourteen, the son of an oilfield laborer. He learned electronics in the Navy, began business in 1947 and was worth around $14 million when the *Journal* editors got to him. He has since gone much higher, may become a terrific tycoon.

Robert Peterson, his father an immigrant mechanic, found himself in 1948 low man on the totem pole as a California press agent. But he started *Hot Rod Magazine,* which was such a success among teen-agers that it swept him up to a reported net worth of $3 million in short order.[60]

Ralph E. Schneider, in the 1940's a lawyer from the Harvard Law School, '32, with at most a meager $15,000 a year income, started the Diner's Club credit-card system and was worth at least $7 million by 1960.[61] The *Journal* editors also suspect that he has a string of other juicy investments.

Kell H. Qvale, born in Norway in 1919, his father a Norwegian sea captain, in 1947 found himself a California Jeep salesman and rapidly getting nowhere in typical American style. But he became an M-G dealer, had vast success with a restless public and now owns British Motor Car Distributors, Ltd. His net worth: $3 million at least.[62]

James A. Ryder, a day laborer in 1935 and later a truck driver, now owns the Ryder System, Inc., of Miami, truck, car and equipment leasers and highway freight haulers. His stated net worth: $7 million.[63]

And now comes Sydney S. Baron, whose father owned but lost a shoe factory in the 1929 smash-up. Baron is a public relations man who in 1949 was worth only $25,000. He has since handled various accounts, but the most talked-about have been Tammany Hall and the Dominican dictator, Rafael Trujillo, whose points of rare excellence were put before the American people by Baron. By 1959 Baron had a net worth of at least $1 million, say the *Journal* editors, and wore $160 suits. And say what one will about Trujillo, and echo if one will the French saying that money has no odor, it isn't everyone who can wear $160 suits. But in the United States a successful moneyman wears them like a halo.[64]

The most impressive of the *Journal's* meager bag appears to have been Samuel Rautbord, a lawyer who before World War II drew up some papers for a partner of the American Photocopy Equipment Company of Evanston, Illinois. Interested, Rautbord bought a share and in time became president, chairman and principal stockholder, with the company now listed on the New York Stock Exchange. Worth only $20 million the year before the *Journal's* editors spotted him, his holdings at press time were worth $34 million.[65]

This is by no means all of the Rautbord saga. The former lawyer also had paternally conveyed to his two sons $35 million in securities in two trust funds and had induced friends to invest and become rich. One, Edward Flann, invested $20,000 in 1944 and was at press time worth $3 million. A sister did likewise, with similar consequences. As the *Journal* editors say, he has "the Midas touch."

Rautbord found the taxes of the partnership running so high in 1953— 91 per cent—that he reorganized as a corporation, which brought taxes down to the 52 per cent corporation bracket. Then he astutely formed the Clay-Bob Realty Company and exchanged much of his Apeco stock for *its* stock. The advantage here apparently was that Clay-Bob paid a lower tax than his personal tax would have been. The proceeds received by Clay-Bob, as the *Journal* tells the story, are not paid out to Rautbord, who has plenty of other lucre, but are invested. That ends all nonsense about taxes and helps Rautbord keep his head above water.

The way this worked out is as follows: Apeco as a partnership had roughly only $9 left after taxes out of every $100 of income. As a corporation it had $48 left (disregarding the tax-free initial $20,000 of corporate income). So large were Rautbord's holdings of Apeco that he would have had to pay a good deal more than half of this $48 in taxes. Instead, as the *Journal* editors indicate, Clay-Bob received it and paid at most $24.96 tax, retaining $23.04 for investment purposes. If Rautbord's income had been up in the $1 million range, as the value of his holdings suggests it was, he would be back in the 91 per cent tax range and instead of Clay-Bob's $23.04 to invest he would have had only $2.07. Since then, the top income-tax rate has been reduced to 77 per cent and the corporation rate to 48 per cent. But even so a personal holding company, which pays at most only 48 per cent (and in most cases less) is a distinct advantage over paying a 77 per cent personal income tax, which is one good reason there are so many personal holding companies.

Naturally all this affluence has wrought some changes in Rautbord's life. He owns a Rolls-Royce, a big yacht and seventy pairs of cuff links.[66]

Hans Fischer, born in Vienna, heads H. Fischer and Associates of Cleveland. A consulting engineer, he came to the United States in 1939, as yet, alas, a non-American. Around 1950 he had only $4,000 and with only that much was practically an un-American but—such had been his success when the *Journal* editors looked him over—he, now fully American, was worth $1.2 million, owned a Cadillac, a Jaguar and a forty-five-foot Chris-Craft, and lived in a big house in Shaker Heights, Ohio, near other true-blue Americans.

But J. W. Walters did somewhat better, possibly because he was American-born and therefore by nature anointed. A Navy veteran driving a truck in 1946, he was looking for a really cheap house, all he could afford. He saw an ad for a "shell" structure at $1,195 and went with borrowed money to buy from a man named Davenport. Instead, he went into partnership with this man. Davenport, evidently a person of little faith or having other worlds to conquer, sold out to Walters in 1948 for $48,000; Walters was then thirty-eight years old.

The lowly enterprise went on to become National Homes Corporation, producer of prefabricated homes, which the *Journal* men say has made more than $1 million for each of seven persons and left Mr. Walters with a net worth in 1960 of $8,700,000.[67] Walters, who quit school after the twelfth grade, has acquired a 1,700-acre Florida hunting ranch as well as other dazzling properties. National Homes now makes prefabricated apartment buildings, shopping centers and schools as well as individual houses. It will build whole prefabricated towns, and has done so, at the drop of a nail.

But these people, though we salute them as true-blue American enterprisers, are all really small potatoes, hardly worth a feeble cheer from the House Un-American Activities Committee. The new crop, either the one of *Fortune*, 1952, or the *Wall Street Journal*, 1962, simply does not rate on the scale of wealth even though its members may be having the time of their lives in their cruisers, Jaguars, $50 hats and $160 suits.

The Sweetest-Smelling Real Estate Empire

The *New York Times* in 1965 introduced two formidable contenders into the arena of big new wealth, as if to replace the void left by the departure of bulky William Zeckendorf.

These new tycoons, said the *Times*, are Sol Goldman, forty-seven, and Alex Di Lorenzo, Jr., forty-eight, who have built a real estate empire on a pyramid of mortgage loans.

When the *Times* studied them in April, 1965, they quietly owned more than twenty office buildings, including the seventy-seven-story Chrysler Building; extensive harbor terminals; a growing flotilla of hotels; various "sprawling" industrial buildings; shopping centers; and large apartment houses. More than 20,000 persons were employed in keeping these properties operative.

Cruising under the firm name of Wellington Associates (presumably it would be unlucky to be Napoleon Associates), they have followed the technique of "mortgaging out"—that is, borrowing enough money with first and second mortgages to cover the full purchase price of a property, literally "nothing down." If, through improvements or other devices, the buyer can increase the rent rolls, he can go to a bank in a year or two and borrow enough money on a new mortgage at lower rates to wipe out the high-interest mortgages, sometimes leaving a surplus above the original purchase price. This surplus is then invested in other properties and the process goes on like a rolling barrage. A neat feature is that the surplus is tax-free because it is technically borrowed money, on which one pays no tax, naturally.

Wellington Associates bought the Chrysler Building in 1942 for $42 million, mostly carried on first and second mortgages charged against them. Some four years later they borrowed $47 million at 5½ per cent from a Wall Street syndicate, which spread the paper around the country, and paid off on the old paper. In the meantime by amortization out of rents they had reduced their original obligation by $3 million, so they had $8 million of technically borrowed nonrepayable tax-free money to play with, the best kind there is.

Now the Chrysler Building alone is producing for them $1.5 million a year, tax-free, for their investment in other properties.

Proceeding in this way, if nothing goes wrong (such as an interruption in rents or balkiness of the banks), Goldman and Di Lorenzo should in time own all of the United States, cost free. They have already bought more than 250 pieces of property in Manhattan and own more than 450 properties "conservatively estimated," says the *Times,* to be worth more than $500 million. The equity of the two partners in this chunk is set at about $150 million, a worthy figure. But it could shrink—or expand.

The *Times* got wind of Wellington Associates because its swift rise had set alarm bells ringing in nearly every investigative agency in the country, including the FBI. The latter was instantly fascinated because of the persistent rumor that underworld money is finding its way into American business, that "bad guys" born in Sicily and other unhallowed places are infiltrating "good guys" with names reminiscent of Astor, Vanderbilt and Rockefeller. No basis whatever for these rumors was found in the Goldman-Di Lorenzo set-up, which emerged smelling as sweet as any real estate empire ever smelled. It appeared, indeed, to be the sweetest-smelling real estate empire that the investigators had ever encountered.[68]

The Rising Tide of Wealth

But wealth is apparently rising around us like a tidal wave even as inquiry proceeds. Herman P. Miller, assistant to the Director of the Census Bureau, reports that "The rich among us are flourishing as never before. And not only millionaires, but multi-millionaires." The figure of 27,000 persons owning $1 million or more of property in 1953, according to the Lampman study, must now be raised to close to 90,000 in 1965, says Miller.

It is this *increase* in the wealth of wealth-holders that is taken to prove that newcomers are making big money in droves.

"The 90,000 millionaires are a diverse lot," says Miller. "They include men and women, young and old, creators and contrivers, new rich and established rich.

"Since their number is rapidly growing, it suggests that the new millions are largely earned [sic!] and not simply passed down through inheritance—that is, they come from the creation of goods and services we can all enjoy. A large proportion of today's new millionaires derive their wealth from scientific inventions, home construction, new products and other things that enrich our lives in many ways."[69]

There is nothing in the set of figures presented to justify this disarmingly pleasant conclusion. The simple fact is this: In the general rise in prices holdings previously valued below $1 million are now valued at $1 million or more. No doubt some new earning properties have been created out of inventions and the like but most of these million-dollar-plus properties are owned by the same people who in most cases inherited them. It is not the case, as far as these bare statistics show, that "the new millions are largely earned"; that remark is thrown in from nowhere, with no evidential basis cited. A man worth $200,000 in 1940 may now be worth $2 million and may in five or fifteen years be worth $800,000 or $5 million, depending upon the swing in the economy and the nature of his property.

But it is not the case that there are 90,000 newly moneyed millionaires, 9,000 or even 900. It is clearly incumbent upon anyone who contends this to show it. Some few persons have in the past twenty years come up from nothing to $1 million or more; but they represent only a minor fraction of this phalanx of 90,000, who are simply the old-line upper property holders.

A New String from Time

But reports such as these are quickly followed by others, all with the same message but a different cast of characters. Thus *Time*, December 3, 1965, under the title "Millionaires" presented a new list of men who had allegedly made a million or more before they were forty. Editors should notice that there is still to be presented a list of women, like Lucille Ball, who have made a million or more before forty and even of children who had become worth more than $10 million before they are five years old.

Said *Time*:

"As a land passionately devoted to free enterprise, the U.S. has always been the best place for a man to make his million. The fabled 19th century millionaires . . . all began poor. Despite their often controversial actions, they, like most American millionaires, basically enriched themselves by enriching a growing nation [a statement that might be seriously questioned.—F.L.].

"The U.S. still offers countless opportunities for the man who wants to accumulate a personal net worth of $1,000,000 or more—and thousands [sic!] seize them every year. The number of U.S. millionaires, reports the Federal Reserve Board, has swelled from 40,000 in 1958 to nearly 100,000 at present. How do they do it? In a variety of individual ways, but their common denominator is that they find an economic need and fill it."

My readers are aware, to the contrary, that nearly all of these 90,000-plus do it by inheriting, with the increasing number of millionaires traceable to the rise in prices.

But *Time* goes on to present its own meager bottom-of-the-barrel list of new wealthy:

	Net Worth*
Arthur J. Decio, 35, Elkhart, Ind., Skyline Homes	$5 million
Charles Bluhdorn, 39, N.Y.C., Gulf & Western Industries	$15 million
Harold Smith Prince, 37, N.Y.C., Broadway producer	$1 million
Arthur Carlsberg, 32, Los Angeles, real estate	$5 million
Merlyn Francis Mickelson, 38, Minneapolis, computer parts	$47 million
John Diebold, 39, N.Y.C., management consultant	$1 million plus
Eugene Ferkauf, 44, N.Y., Korvette, Inc., cut-price stores	$55 million

* *Time* cites no public record for its figures.

Jerry Wolman, 38, Philadelphia, football impresario	"Millions"
Art Modell, 41, Cleveland, football impresario	"Millions"
Michael Mungo, 37, South Carolina, ex-cottonpicker, real estate	$2 million
John F. Donahue, 41, securities salesman	$1.5 million
Alvin Weeks, 41, Atlanta, frozen pastries	Not stated
Joseph McVicker, 35, Cincinnati, toys	"Millionaire"
Walter Davis, 42, Texas, trucking	$7 million
Ernest Stern, 45, Pittsburgh, theater magnate	Not stated
Robert K. Lifton, 37, N.Y.C., real estate	$4.75 million
Fletcher Jones, 34, Los Angeles, computer programmer	$20 million
Del Coleman, 40, Chicago, jukeboxes	Not stated
James Thomas, 37, Los Angeles, real estate	"Millionaire"
Michael Rafton, ?, Oakland, portable classrooms	"Huge profit"
Charles Stein, 37, Chicago, orange juice	"Millionaire"
Al Lapin, 38, Los Angeles, coffee vending, pancakes	"Rich"
Jerry Lapin, 36, Los Angeles, coffee vending, pancakes	"Rich"
Fred Bailey, 39, Los Angeles, ordnance parts	$2 million
Charles Gelman, 33, Michigan, chemist, filter manufacturer	$1.3 million

Accepting all these valuations as authentic, what do they prove? Not, surely, that big wealth is new wealth or *vice versa*. Nobody denies that a few score or even a few hundred men in business ventures make a temporary million or more. The point is that most of these sums mentioned are chicken feed and the larger figures might require some further examination. Again, how many of these will survive economic downdrafts? How many will follow William Zeckendorf into sterile impecuniosity?

A list of hundreds of names could be drawn up under the title "Men Once Worth a Million or More Who Went Broke." As Thomas Mellon remarked, it is harder to hold onto money than to make it.

The Big Winners in Review

What remains to be said about this heterogeneous collection of names? Some have arrived, some are in the process of arriving (or departing), some are only pseudo-*arrivistes*.

To return to the *Fortune* list of thirty-four, taking it at face value and disregarding any of the qualifications offered, most of the men on it are neither builders, inventors, constructors of new-type industries nor job creators. The predominant oil crowd play an enlarged version of the childhood game of finders-keepers under a big tax shelter. They provide little employment, at most pour low-tax high-price oil into a pre-existent world pipeline.

Kaiser and the Browns of Brown and Root, Inc., are construction men, buoyed up a long part of the way by politically wangled government loans and contracts. Kaiser has shouldered his way heavily into private enterprises of various kinds—aluminum, plastics, cement, steel. Perhaps he has bulldozed a pattern for the future in which government will finance new private enterprises via low-cost loans, contracts, tax schemes and other aids, thereby providing jobs lower down for the multitudes that the old-line monopolists allowed to spawn without reckoning on the ability of the economic system to sustain them.

Stewart Alsop found that all on his *Post* list but Land had made good in a big way mainly by taking advantage of special government shelters over oil, insurance and real estate. All the oil men—Mecom, Keck, Smith and Abercrombie—get the depletion allowance and are able to take large deductions for "intangible drilling expenses." "Thus," as Alsop remarks, "an oilman with a good tax lawyer can pay little or no income tax on a real income of millions of dollars." In real estate, depreciation plays the role of depletion in oil and there is always "mortgaging out." In insurance, the key word is "reserves"; for in order to build reserves generous tax allowances are made which apply as well to the equity of the owners of insurance companies such as Stone, MacArthur and Ahmanson. The latter, doubling in the building and loan business, is propped up also by government insurance up to $15,000 per individual depositor.

Kettering, as I have noted, was an inventor; Mott and Sloan, engineers; Kennedy, Wolfson and Getty are market operators who, like most of Alsop's list, never made any weighty contribution to the gross national product. Getty became king-size by buying underpriced shares in the Depression. Halliburton, Ludwig and MacKnight are company organizers and rationalizers, able to find chinks in an established market. MacArthur simply offered through mass advertising as little insurance as anyone wished to buy, from $1 per month up. Like the Woolworth plan this one was admirably suited to an economy in which few people have money beyond immediate pressing needs.

All the noninheritors on the *Fortune* list were born in the United States. Of the twenty-three for whom the information is of record, thirteen were born in small towns or semi-rural areas.

A few started as poor boys, notably H. L. Hunt, who was dirt-poor. But most had comfortable beginnings. Getty's father was rich, Richardson's and Murchison's were well-to-do, Sloan's father was a successful small-businessman and Kennedy's father a prosperous-enough saloonkeeper-politician. In general, those who never entered college appear to have had the more modest beginnings; but except for Hunt the rags-to-riches theme applies to none. At least one married well from a financial point of view, although he was also endowed with technical ability.

A notable pattern emerges in the large number of school dropouts on the list, from early grades to college. Stewart Alsop noticed the same thing in his *Saturday Evening Post* list of thirteen, of which five are on the *Fortune* list.

Most of the *Fortune* men identify themselves educationally as having attended "public schools," which may mean anything from first grade to completing high school. And most of those I have added—Amon G. Carter, Jesse Jones, John J. Raskob, Hugh Roy Cullen, William L. Moody and even A. P. Giannini—had scant schooling. With few exceptions, the fortune-builders of more recent date, like their nineteenth-century fore-runners, had little interest in school even when it was available to them. Not especially well-educated or well-read either, they are obviously truants from high culture. Many who weren't high school dropouts were grade-school dropouts.

Educators, trying in desperation to rally popular support for education and mulling over statistics, like to point out to rugged philistines that on the average educated people earn more than the meagerly educated. And this is true when it comes to offering marketable skills and personalities at modest salaries in an existing Establishment that requires ever-increasing skilled personnel for its complex operations. But it has never been true where really big money is concerned. An education can be a severe handicap when it comes to making money.

The reason for this is that in the process of being educated there is always the danger that the individual will acquire scruples, a fact dimly sensed by some of the neo-conservatives who rail against the school system as "Communistic." These scruples, unless they are casuistically beveled around the edges with great care, are a distinct handicap to the full-fledged money-maker, who must in every situation be plastically opportu-nistic. But a person who has had it deeply impressed upon him that he must make *exact* reports of *careful* laboratory experiments, must conduct *exact* computations in mathematics and logic, must produce *exact* transla-tions and echoes of foreign languages, must write *faithful* reports of *cor-rect* readings and must be at least imaginatively aware of the world in its diversity, and who has learned these lessons well, must invariably dis-cover that some element of scrupulosity—even if he hasn't been subject to moral indoctrination—has been impressed on his psyche. If he enters upon money-making in a world bazaar where approximate truths, vague deceptions, sneak maneuvers, half promises and even bald falsehoods are the widely admired and heavily rewarded order of the day he must make

casuistic adjustments of his standards. The very process of laboriously making the adjustment, even if he succeeds, puts him at a disadvantage *vis-à-
vis* the unschooled, who need waste no energy on such adjustments, who
pick up anything lying around loose as easily as they breathe. Some educated people can't make even a partial adjustment to the market bazaar,
and their disgraceful bank accounts show it. They are, as even their wives
sometimes kindly inform them, failures, though they are doing something
conceded to be useful such as instructing children or enforcing the law.
They can inscribe after their names a big "F" and go stand in a corner
under a dunce cap as the propaganda dervishes scream about "success."

But, so as not to alarm appropriations-conscious educators, mere schooling (which is not the same as an education) may prove no great handicap in the race for money, which is one reason some heavily schooled
persons turn out to be pecuniary successes. For many persons dutifully
put in the required number of years in a national school system noted
for its permissiveness without ever acquiring dangerous scruples. One
could cite hundreds of names. Among other things, they learn to cheat
handily in examinations—excellent training for the market. They learn to
bluff overworked teachers with verbal balderdash. And they do well subsequently as loose-talking salesmen, jobbers, advertising men, promoters,
agents, brokers, morticians, lobbyists, fixers, officeholders and smooth
workers in the film and television industries. They all learn to be practical
—that is, judiciously unscrupulous. After all, as any of them can testify
truthfully, the world isn't perfect and they piously feel no obligation to
alter its skewness. They may even become tycoons, and it is only other
tycoons who stand in their way.

An education, it is widely and correctly thought, should prepare the
individual for life. But the preparation is not for life as the philistines
preconceive it. Educators have prolixly explained what an education is so
many thousands of times without denting the popular notion that it is
vocational preparation that it would be piling prolixity on prolixity to
attempt it again. Put most briefly perhaps, an education is designed solely
to humanize the individual, and if it has done that it is a "take." The
idea of an education is to raise the individual above the level of mere
animality, or at least to qualify his animality significantly. If such an individual makes out better-than-average financially it may be due to recognition of his worth. But thousands of thoroughly educated people have
never been appraised by their contemporaries as worth a living wage.
T. S. Eliot, Harvard-schooled and widely hailed as the most significant
poet writing in English in the past half century, earned his living as a
bank teller and, much later, as a publisher's reader. Financially speaking,

Eliot as poet, teller or editor wasn't worth so much as a cuss word. Yet it seems probable that his writings will be appreciatively read long after every single existing American corporation and bank, and the memory thereof, has passed out of existence. Curious. . . .

An education, truth to say, has nothing whatever to do with making or not making money, except perhaps as a hindrance. The educators, in extolling the money-rewarding features of education, are indulging in a benevolent deceit, trying to hornswoggle a public with a peasant view of life to support the schools and perhaps lift themselves by their bootstraps above simple animality. Vocational trainees sometimes get sidetracked into true educational paths.

There is no evidence that any of the men on our list who had a higher education, except the General Motors engineering group, ever made use in their careers of what, if anything, they learned at college. There is little in the careers or expressions of either Getty or Kennedy to reflect the influence of Oxford or Harvard. Each could as well have finished off in a business college just as Raskob did. Harvard never endorsed either stock market pools or the general conduct involved in such pools. These were strictly extracurricular.

The General Motors men were all technicians and applied their knowledge of technology strictly to making money, not to engineering the best possible cars. Donaldson Brown, who married a Du Pont girl, is credited by Alfred P. Sloan, Jr., in his memoirs with developing a penetrating method of ascertaining rate of return on investment by company subdivisions, a method taken over as well by Du Pont.[70]

Most of the men on the *Fortune* list, as on Stewart Alsop's list, were unsuitable employees, a facet that Alsop takes note of. Few of these men could fit into a pre-arranged job, except for the General Motors executives. As far as employment was concerned, they were maladjusts, nonorganization men. In whatever brief employment some of them had early in their careers, they were like restless panthers, looking only for a chance to break out and track into the jungle. Again except for the General Motors crowd, who were team workers, nearly all the others mentioned were "loners." And most of them remained "loners," detached, nongregarious. Exceptions would be found among some of the Texas oil men, although Hunt is very much of a "loner."

Alsop found other peculiarities among those he interviewed, which apply, with some exceptions, to the *Fortune* listees. None played golf, supposedly the businessman's game. All were physically restless, standing up, moving about, scratching themselves, drumming their fingers, chain-smoking cigarettes, twiddling and twitching—all of which may merely have been restiveness at having to submit to an interview. Alsop takes it as a general character trait.

Some who have been in the armed forces made out poorly under military discipline, couldn't take it. John D. MacArthur, Alsop reports, was discharged from the Navy in World War I, "unsuited to naval discipline." Despite the many big wars the United States has fought in the lifetime of all these men, none stands forth as a major or minor military figure. Where a *Who's Who* record is available it shows few in military service even when by age classification one would have expected to find a man in uniform. But some perhaps common deviant characteristic appears to have led the military to pass them by. Money-making and military service do not appear to mix.

As to religion, few on the *Fortune* list make a point of mentioning it. Two were Jews and one was a conspicuous Catholic, Mr. Kennedy. While a few of the others who do not give such information may be Catholics, the probability is that all thirty-one are at least nominally Protestants or religiously disinterested. Catholics do not appear among money-makers proportional to their numbers in society probably for the same reason that they do not loom large in any department of upper-hierarchical American life except local politics and trade-union leadership: They have been self-segregated from the mainstreams of American life by a clergy apparently afraid that contact with non-Catholics will cause their submissiveness to the Church to diminish. With the history of Europe before us we cannot conclude that Catholics as such are not interested in money and power.

Many of these men, dead or alive, are saluted as philanthropists by newspapers (that carry the advertising of their enterprises) because they have, before or at death, established foundations formally classified as charities under the law. Of these Kennedy, Sloan, Kettering, Kaiser, Benedum, Richardson stand out thus far, although virtually all of them will in the normal course of operations establish foundations. Such action has now become standard procedure in reducing estate taxes and keeping controlling shares either in a family or a friendly group, at the same time previsioning considerable posthumous social influence through the financial patronage the foundation is able to bestow.

Who among the noninheritors has made the deepest national impress? This question is easy to answer and one must say Mr. Kennedy, at second remove, mainly through his children. Although John F. Kennedy was not trained by his father to become what he became, not merely president of the United States but a president fantastically visualizing the United States as something more than a pettifoggers' paradise, the father did not impede him and in many ways must be conceded to have indirectly helped him, as the sire's biographer, Richard J. Whalen, skillfully brings to light. Through JFK, and possibly through his other sons, Mr. Kennedy (and his wife) enters History (that is, he comes under analytical individual consideration of the historians) instead of merely being part of history like his financial contemporaries and the rest of us. Between History and history there is a vast difference: The former invokes the canons of aesthetics and morality; the latter is nonevaluative, shapeless. Mr. Kennedy also made a signal contribution as the aggressive first chairman of the Securities and Exchange Commission.

If we continue beyond the *Fortune* list we find no significant alteration in these patterns although we do, here and there, run into odd variations in the form of Land, De Golyer and Danforth. These are untypical cases, sports.

As to the general human type of American wealth-builder, new and old, it can be said that he is usually an extrovert, given to little reflectiveness until perhaps he approaches senility. He is more often unschooled than schooled, and unread, and has for the most part a naive view of the world and his role in it. A man of action, he is compulsive and repetitive in his single-minded acquisitiveness. He simply does not know what else to do. As De Golyer remarks, he substitutes money-making for living and often believes that he is engaged in a great crusade. He rarely, as far as the record shows, has qualms or doubts about himself. He is almost invariably devoid of a sense of humor. Color him grey.

"Beyond certain minima, economic gain is inevitably associated with prestige and status, self-validation called 'success,' opportunities for assertion against others, autonomy from disliked persons, tasks, or situations, and so forth. What gives economics its power to command such energy as is invested in the pursuit of gain is often its instrumental value as a means to some other objective. Money buys more than commodities; it buys psychic gratifications of all sorts—although never so completely as the money-seeker thinks it will."[71]

The winner is consequently usually restive. For he evidently feels that with all his wealth he ought to strike a blow for something tremendous. But what? And how? Christianity? Science? World peace? Progress? Education? Free enterprise? Democracy? Health? In many cases he ends up feeling frustrated and morosely retires to some *House and Garden* paradise to meditate on the freakishness of the world and its people. In no case yet of record has he developed a sense of mission that the world can identify itself with. By his position alone he is alienated. For all he has, in fact (apart from deviants like De Golyer, Land and Danforth), is money.

Three 🌿

CRIME AND WEALTH

In the quest for new wealth there are shadier avenues yet to scan. For the organized underworld has been designated by a number of recent observers as the luxuriant seeding ground for new fortunes of menacing portent.

This theory grew out of hearings before the Special Senate Committee to Investigate Crime in Interstate Commerce, May 10, 1950, to May 1, 1951, under the chairmanship of Senator Estes Kefauver of Tennessee. In 1952 Kefauver was the Democratic candidate for vice president of the United States.

The germ of the theory appears in Kefauver's book based on the hearings, *Crime in America* (1951). With minor variants the story has since developed: Underworld characters with local political protection are acquiring legally established businesses as "fronts" and are snatching working control in various large corporations—especially in hotels and hotel chains, motels and motel chains, in divers pleasure resorts and perhaps also in banks. Such characters, it is held, have made a bundle in the underworld—through gambling operations, houses of prostitution, bootlegging, assassination, smuggling, the narcotics traffic—and they are now pyramiding their illicit gains in the labyrinthine corporate world.

Various dangers loom: They will loot companies from the inside, they will rig markets and defraud the public, they will be better able to procure politicians, they will prey on "legitimate" businessmen. They will turn a happy, honest corporate world into a devil's den, with consequent demoralization of an orderly society. They will, in short, act like fairly typical businessmen.

As the senator himself put it, "I cannot overemphasize the danger that can lie in the muscling into legitimate fields by hoodlums . . . there was too much evidence before us of *unreformed* hoodlums gaining control of a legitimate business; then utilizing all his old mob tricks—strong-arm methods, bombs, even murder—to secure advantages over legitimate competitors. All too often such competition either ruins legitimate businessmen or drives them into emulating or merging with the gangsters.

"The hoodlums also are clever at concealing ownership of their investments in legitimate fields—sometimes, as Longie Zwillman said, through 'trustees' and sometimes by bamboozling respectable businessmen into 'fronting' for them. Virgil Peterson of the Chicago Crime Commission testified that 'hundreds' of hoodlum-owned businesses are successfully camouflaged. He told us of having been consulted by a friend of his who had been offered a $25,000-a-year job to head a 'new corporation.' Peterson investigated and found that 'the fellow who had contacted him was part and parcel of the Capone Syndicate.' "[1]

Senator Kefauver said he feared legitimate business would be used as a "front," a cover for tax-evading illegal operations; that unreliable men would arise in industries vital to health and safety. "I, for one," he said, "do not like to think of food products necessary to the health of my children, or of medicine that can mean life or death to a good many people, coming from plants controlled by gangsters whose code of ethics is the dollar sign, and who do not care if that dollar sign is stained somewhat with blood."[2]

But the senator nowhere gave definitions of "legitimate" and "respectable" businessmen.

Kefauver showed that mobsters were established on the fringes of seventy different industries, including drug manufacturing, baking, candymaking, food distribution and hotels.[3]

While he did not enlarge Kefauver's theory, Robert F. Kennedy, chief counsel of the Select Committee (McClellan Committee) of the United States Senate on Improper Activities in the Labor or Management Field, subsequently attorney general of the United States, and still later senator from New York, did reinforce it in his book based on the McClellan investigation, *The Enemy Within* (1960). For the investigation found, as Kennedy reports, direct tie-ups between extremely vicious underworld characters, spurious labor unions and various leading corporations.[4]

The object of these tie-ups was to prevent effective unionization of employees, a criminal violation of the National Labor Relations Act. Many other crimes, such as murder, were allegedly committed out of sheer exuberance of spirits.

After diplomatically saluting "the majority of American businessmen" as "above crookedness and collusion in labor-management negotiations,"

Kennedy wrote that "we found that with the present-day emphasis on money and material goods many businessmen were willing to make corrupt 'deals' with dishonest union officials in order to gain competitive advantage or to make a few extra dollars. . . . We came across more than fifty companies and corporations that had acted improperly—and in many cases illegal—in dealings with labor unions . . . in the companies and corporations to which I am referring the improprieties and illegalities were occasioned solely by a desire for monetary gain. Furthermore we found that we could expect very little assistance from management groups. Disturbing as it may sound, more often the business people with whom we came in contact—and this includes some representatives of our largest corporations—were uncooperative."[5]

"By and large," wrote Kennedy, "little accurate information came to us from the business community. We received 150,000 complaints during the Committee's life. Seventy-five per cent of them came from representatives of organized labor, mostly rank and filers. Some came from people outside the labor-management field. Only a handful came from people in the business world. Certainly no investigation was touched off by any voluntary help we received from management. And this was not because management had no information to give. I believe 90 per cent of the corrupt deals between business and labor could be eliminated if business officials would simply talk to proper authorities."[6] Why business people, as the instigators of the corrupt actions, would do this he didn't say.

"Often," Kennedy related, "we found that corrupt deals involving management were handled through attorneys who played the role of 'middleman,' or, as we came to think of them, 'legal fixers' or 'legal prostitutes.' More often it was the labor relations consultant who played the 'middleman.'"[7]

Kennedy reeled off a list of names of offending companies that reads like a miniature Social Register of big business. "Although I thought I had become case-hardened," Kennedy remarked, "I discovered I still was not shock-proof when I studied the results of our investigation of the A. & P. . . ."[8]

The thesis that the underworld is a direct bridge into new propertied wealth for latecoming frontiersmen is laid down flatly by Professor Daniel Bell, chairman of the department of sociology of Columbia University.[9]

"The jungle quality of the American business community, particularly at the turn of the century, was reflected in the mode of 'business' practiced by the coarse gangster elements, most of them from new immigrant families, who were 'getting ahead' just as Horatio Alger had urged.[10]

"For crime, in the language of the sociologists, has a 'functional' role in society, and the urban rackets—the illicit activity organized for continuing profit, rather than individual illegal acts—is one of the queer ladders of social mobility in American life. Indeed, it is not too much to say that the whole question of organized crime in America cannot be understood unless one appreciates (1) the distinctive role of organized gambling as a function of a mass-consumption economy; (2) the specific role of various immigrant groups as they, one after another, became involved in marginal business and crime; and (3) the relation of crime to the changing character of the urban political machines."[11]

Crime, in other words, was the road taken by many immigrants, imbued with the Horatio Alger ideal of 100 per cent Americanism to become property holders and escape the repressive wage yoke imposed upon them by foresightedly frugal Anglo-Saxon corporations.

As business became more organized so did racketeering and gambling, until in the 1920's and 1930's it had become "industrial racketeering" through the medium of labor disputes, a fertile field.[12]

Leading entrepreneurs here were Arnold Rothstein (shot after a high-stakes card game), Louis Lepke Buchalter (executed in Sing Sing), Gurrah Shapiro, Dutch Schultz (assassinated), Jack "Legs" Diamond (assassinated) and Lucky Luciano (deported). Buchalter and Shapiro, as Professor Bell notes, in New York in the 1930's dominated sections of the clothing industries, house painting, fur dressing, flour trucking, etc. "In a highly chaotic and cutthroat industry such as clothing, the racketeer, paradoxically, played a stabilizing role by regulating competition and fixing prices. When the NRA came in and assumed this function, the businessman found that what had once been a quasi-economic service was now pure extortion, and he began to demand police action."[13]

Seeking other worlds to conquer, says Professor Bell, the criminal racketeer shifted his emphasis from production to consumption, mainly gambling, without wholly yielding his interest in the productive side—as his deep involvement in labor racketeering in the 1950's and 1960's attests.

The Kefauver investigation revealed the tentacles of the gambling and vice syndicates; the McClellan investigation disclosed the seamy labor racketeers in full bloom. The latter performed the economic function of keeping labor costs down for the owners (a function performed by the political police in Soviet Russia). The gambling entrepreneurs performed the political-economic function of helping finance surreptitiously the major local political organizations—"machines" to critics—in Boston, Providence, New York, Philadelphia, Pittsburgh, Buffalo, Cleveland, Detroit, Chicago, St. Louis, Kansas City and other large urban areas.

Properly rejecting the Kefauver Committee's idea that a Mafia rules the underworld, Professor Bell points out that the committee failed to understand "(1) the rise of the American Italian community, as part of the inevitable process of ethnic succession, to positions of importance in politics, a process that has been occurring independently but also simultaneously in most cities with large Italian constituencies—New York, Chicago, Kansas City, Los Angeles; (2) the fact that there are individual Italians who play prominent, often leading roles today in gambling and the mobs; and (3) the fact that Italian gamblers and mobsters often possessed 'status' within the Italian community itself and a 'pull' in city politics."[14]

The road of crime, in other words, was taken by some latecoming immigrants trying to become property owners: Italians, East European Jews in the garment trades and Irish.[15] The urban political machines levied on all of these a heavy tariff.[16]

In the process many of these men became "legitimate" property holders —"legitimate" here meaning that a court will uphold one's property claim. "Many of the top 'crime' figures" (I don't know why Professor Bell puts 'crime' in quotation marks, since they were court-certified criminals— F.L.) now derived their income from "legitimate investments (real estate in the case of Costello, motor haulage and auto dealer franchises [Ford] in the case of Adonis) or from such quasi-legitimate but socially respectable sources as gambling casinos."[17]

One arrives, in short, at the big shots of the underworld, their names paraded anew in the Kefauver and McClellan investigations, and including such "labor leaders" as Jimmy Hoffa, Dave Beck and their henchmen—topsy-turvy Robin Hoods who gleefully robbed the poor for the benefit of the rich. These are men who, it is widely asserted, have traveled the latest highroad to wealth and secretly own large shares in the largest corporations. They have indeed the requisite qualities of ruthlessness and unscrupulousness but lack finesse.

Without harrowing the reader with details of the lengths to which I have gone to verify this notion of the criminal underworld as the source of great new wealth, let me categorically say this: There is nothing to it. While it is no doubt true that people like Costello have accumulated a nest egg of dimensions that might be envied by the common man I doubt that it is very great in the terms under discussion. If Costello or any other underworld character as of 1965 had a net worth of more than $5 million it would be surprising. No available evidence shows great underworld wealth unless Wall Street is located in the underworld.

Senator Kefauver cites incomes of various gambling groups taken from income-tax returns, which the underworld dislikes falsifying since Capone and others were caught at it and jailed for long terms, but though some of these figures are impressive, even if understated, it is only in a small way. They seem in the category of the marginal speculative businessmen scanned toward the end of the previous chapter, at best.

The reason for this low pecuniary estate is simple. The underworld in its public operations—gambling, prostitution, other variants of vice (as distinct from secret operations such as dope peddling)—is subject to "the split." It must share its receipts (Kefauver estimated the gambling turn-over alone at $20 billion a year) with local politicos, and the police from the beat patrolman up to the precinct captain.

This necessity diminishes the net return to the operators who, themselves a group, must also split. I should imagine the net return on total "sales" to be a good deal less than 1 per cent. On $20 billion (a figure pulled from the air) 1 per cent is $200 million, and even $200 million is far more than is likely to reach underworld coffers. For in addition to pay-offs to winners, the gamblers must make heavy payouts for judicial fixes and lawyers. They must constantly yield tribute to hijackers. And when the residue is split among hundreds of operators there isn't much left for each. The "take" in prostitution is less and subject to a bigger overhead.

Someone who was known to be "on the take" for many years was Mayor Frank Hague of Jersey City, long a power in national councils of the Democratic Party (he might just as well have been a Republican). For Hague the revenue from gambling was steady. As a formal Catholic he frowned on prostitution. At his death he left an estate valued at $5 million.[18] If Hague, starting as a poor youth and never leaving the receiving end, could do no better than that, what must the so-called syndicate heads have made? Even if we allow that Hague spent $5 million additional in high living, his receipts would not have been more than $10 million for a very large, enduring and central gambling-political operation. While a goodly sum, this is not really "big" money. And Hague was not himself a gangster.

According to the newspapers, some criminal—usually Italian, Irish or Jewish—establishes an organization. Then he shops about for "political protection" and manages to seduce some respectable churchgoing American official with a charming wife and children and a dog, cat and canary. A really decent chap, you know, until sweet-talked and bribed by an agent of the Mafia.

What actually almost always happens is that an established group in business and/or politics, having decided what the prospects are, looks about for a strong-arm man. If he can't be found locally he is imported, as Costello was imported into New Orleans to run slot machines, as Johnny

Torrio and Capone, Brooklyn men, were imported into Chicago to dominate vice in general and as Harry Bennett was brought to Detroit by
Henry Ford.

Something to notice about nearly all the underworld figures in their
public appearances is that they are unsure of themselves. In fact, if they
didn't have sponsorship they wouldn't have the assurance to set up
extensive public operations. The newspapers require one to believe, for
example, that the Anastasia brothers jumped ship and then proceeded
autonomously to establish themselves on American soil as general strong-
arm men and assassins. If one will only notice one's own uncertainty in a
strange city (much less a strange country with a strange language) one
will see how unlikely it is that lower-class people who don't know the
language would take to large-scale lawbreaking in a strange land. But—if
someone in authority convinced them it was all right to break the law,
that they would be protected and paid, and if he was able to prove this on
numerous touch-and-go occasions—one would produce the pattern of sul-
len, defiant, wordless behavior of lower-class thugs at the bar with which
the public is familiar.

The core of the Chicago prohibition mobsters, now world famous, was
originally recruited by Chicago newspaper publishers who were engaged
in literal gun battles for newsstand position—the "Circulation War."
All of the gunplay of the 1920's had a long dress rehearsal before World
War I in the newspaper war. The participants learned through the Chicago newspaper attorneys how "the fix" worked and, later under political
protection, they functioned the same way in the prohibition gangland
wars.[19]

Newspapers also purvey the fiction that once an operation has begun
another independent comes along and tries to "muscle in," and then gang
warfare breaks out. This is seldom true, although some independents
(perhaps misled by reading the newspapers) have lent color to the theory,
to their own undoing.

*Most cases of urban gang warfare in the United States, apart from
juvenile gangs, are expressions of factions in the local political party
structure.* Local branches of the two major parties or factions thereof
extend protection to different strong-arm men, in gambling, prostitution, bootlegging, "protecting" small businessmen, and similar enterprises. Out in the field the cohorts of one gang infringe on the supposed
territory of another, each catering to the *hoi polloi.* Formally outside the
law, there is no way out for them except to fight or retreat. In some cases,
no doubt, there have been retreats. In the known cases, violence has
been the arbitrator.

The strong-arm men occasionally trip over the law (though there has not been a single conviction other than for the murder of a newspaperman for hundreds of gang murders in Chicago since World War I), but rarely are their political protectors laid by the heels. One exception was James J. Hines, Tammany district leader and the political connection for the Dutch Schultz gang, who was convicted and sent to jail in the late 1930's by Thomas E. Dewey, later governor of New York and twice the Republican candidate for president. Somewhat later James J. Moran, fire commissioner under Mayor William O'Dwyer, was imprisoned for simple extortion as a result of disclosures before the Kefauver Committee. O'Dwyer himself stood clear.

But political protectors usually stand apart from gang affrays and may or may not come to terms among themselves. If they don't, as in Chicago in the 1920's, the various gangs—Gennas, Capones, Morans, O'Bannions, O'Donnells et al.—fight a war of extermination. Capone swept the field, in part through greater cunning, in part because he introduced the machinegun into his operations, a technological advance with devastating results. (Capone was a machine-gunner in World War I.)

Kefauver named a number of the Republican and Democratic Illinois legislative connections of Capone's successors.[20] The list could be greatly extended.

Sometimes outsiders do "muscle in." One such was Vincent "Mad Dog" Coll in the 1930's, who preyed on various "banks" and "drops" of the rackets in New York City and is reported to have kidnapped for ransom some leading mobsters. Coll was abruptly shot to death in a telephone booth.

On rare occasions, a member of the underworld approaches officials with a view to buying political protection. A danger in doing this, shown in a case Kefauver cites, is that the official may be untouchable and may successfully turn and prosecute his tempter. For attempted bribery is, odd as it may seem, illegal.

But in these operations, the strong-arm men—agents of political parties or business groups—are the low men on the totem pole rather than the swashbuckling chiefs depicted by the newspapers. For it is they who are investigated, put on trial, pilloried in newspapers, sometimes jailed or executed, and murdered. It hardly seems a desirable way to make a living. Their ulcer rate must be high. Even Frank Costello, referred to as "The Prime Minister of the Underworld" and in the 1940's a modest Warwick in elevating chosen men to local office, has been shot, narrowly escaping with his life. Most of the men summoned before Kefauver showed either physical scars or the ravages of tension and dissipation. None, despite possession of massive houses, swimming pools and cars, is really a winner. In their public appearances, they look congenitally unhappy. One pities their wives and children. A hard life, all in all, in the great American quest for property.

Crime: The Highroad to Wealth

Either sound instinct or a certain knowledge led Kefauver, Kennedy, and Bell to link notorious underworld figures with the business world. For crime is an historically established highroad to American fortune-building, as was first detailed by Gustavus Myers in *The History of the Great American Fortunes* and later by Matthew Josephson in *The Robber Barons*. If earlier men came into the upper propertied class by means of violent crime, it would seem that later criminal practitioners might be heading toward the same dubious salvation. So assiduously and unscrupulously did the earlier fortune-builders work that one might suppose they believed that in attaining wealth they were attaining eternal life.

Honoré de Balzac (1799–1850) held that behind every fortune there is a crime, a judgment with which I would disagree if he intended to suggest that in every case the fortune is conceived in crime. Another Frenchman, Pierre Joseph Proudhon (1809–1865), in soaring hyperbole simply stated: "Property is theft." With these notions—flares on a distant horizon—we need not concern ourselves here. But today, in view of what we are now about to consider, it could be said with some justness in paraphrase of Proudhon: "Business is crime." And if this were so, businessmen would be, in all simplicity, criminals.

Both the Kefauver and Kennedy investigations were rooted to a considerable extent in newspaper preconceptions. And the standard newspaper pattern of crime in the United States is based on and has itself shaped the FBI's annual *Federal Uniform Crime Reports,* with variations here and there to suit individual editorial prejudices. These reports consist solely of crimes known to the police.

In this pattern thousands of individuals each year commit crimes ranging from petty larceny to murder. Some of these offenses, particularly theft, are committed for gain; many, particularly murder, are committed under emotional stress. Most convictions for theft, rape and assault involve members of the lower socio-economic classes. The culprits number few property holders except an occasional embattled husband and wife, lover and mistress, or small-business arsonist.

Deviating a bit now from the annual *Federal Uniform Crime Reports*, the newspapers also recognize organized underworld crime and crime committed by politicians. The latter in the main, according to the press, receive bribes and graft, and are seldom caught; it is usually a red-letter day for the newspapers when one is convicted, providing much ground for editorial moralizing: the sanctity of the home, American institutions, the Founding Fathers. . . .

But the most threatening sort of crime to news editors is organized crime, carried on by Mafias, Cosa Nostras, Syndicates, gangs, mobs, and other nefarious enterprises. Sometimes these appear as coast-to-coast operations, under a shadowy board of sinister directors, wrong guys all. At other times they are purely regional but interlocking with other regional enterprises. The syndicates rule over gambling, prostitution, white slaving, drug peddling, smuggling, counterfeiting, fencing stolen goods, shady hotels, night clubs, bootlegging, labor racketeering and all manner of systematic evil, public and private. They are protected by politicians, a disturbing special species, who participate in the ill-gotten gains and snicker all the way to the bank.

Although these phenomena are indeed all present in profusion, as a full pattern of American crime the picture is false and has been shown to be so by the scientific experts in the field—the criminologists. Nonetheless, every newspaper continues to present it, which is much like ignoring Pasteur's germ theory of disease in reporting on medicine.

Nearly all of these newspaper-featured crimes are crimes reported, if reported at all, to the police, although bribery of public officials and of the police themselves is rarely so reported. But criminologists, interested in all crime, cannot confine themselves to police-reported crimes. They are interested as sociologists (criminology is a subdivision of sociology, the study of group behavior) in (1) crimes that may not be reported at all and (2) crimes reported to administrative agencies other than the police, such as juvenile boards. Many crimes are never reported. Rape is often not reported—some say 80 per cent of the time—because the victim, subject to twisted puritanical values, feels disgraced, stigmatized. Again, special agencies have been established for taking cognizance of many crimes, as of juvenile delinquents and businessmen, and newspaper reporting of the work of these agencies is extremely tentative.

Upper-Class Crime

The sorts of crimes ignored by newspapers in their bulk and persistence are what the late Professor Edwin H. Sutherland (1883–1950) of Indiana University called "white collar crime." Sutherland was known as "the dean of American criminologists." He was a former president of the American Sociological Association and chairman of his department. Out of his work, as out of Pasteur's, albeit on a smaller scale, there has grown an internationally reputed school of specialized researchers.

Sutherland like other criminologists was interested in the causes of crime, for which there are many divergent and irreconcilable theories.[21] He analyzed these theories, showed them defective. As a sociologist Sutherland was impressed as long ago as 1925 with the fact that more than 98 per cent of the prison population came from the lowest socio-economic classes; less than 2 per cent came from the upper classes.[22] To explain this disparity criminologists had developed two special theories: that crime is caused by poverty, that crime is caused by mental illness.

But Sutherland could accept neither as overarching in its explanation. He noticed, first, that well-to-do people showing no signs of mental disease commit what everybody agrees are serious crimes (murder, for example) and he then noticed that most of the poor were painfully law-abiding. And if poverty was not a cause of crime it did not account for the patent fact that most people in prison were very poor.

Reaching for a more enveloping standard, Sutherland concluded after prolonged study that crime—apart from impulsive crime—is no more than learned behavior that deviates from some prescribed norm. It may be learned in various ways or by face-to-face association with dominant persons who prescribe and approve the deviant behavior, giving rise to Sutherland's differential-association theory. The criminal, in acting, simply substitutes a different norm in accord with the teachings of those on whom he is dependent, usually the younger *vis-à-vis* the older on all social levels. Sutherland did not pursue the question of why some personalities made apt learners and others did not.

But, if this is so, it does not account for the preponderance of poor people in prisons unless one is to conclude that they alone have been instructed in deviant values. Why this preponderance? And why do some well-to-do law-breakers land in prison and not others?

Sutherland after much inquiry noticed that the laws are written and administered with different emphases. In general, crimes in which property or the propertied might be injured, even though the nonpropertied might be injured by them as well, were implemented with much more severe sanctions than other crimes.

Most offenses open to members of the upper socio-economic class other than those traditionally proscribed, as he found, were dealt with by special administrative tribunals. The offenses were mostly variants of fraud or conspiracy. Where they were committed against the broad public they called for relatively light penalties, seldom prison terms. Verdicts against the offender were often carefully phrased so as to be non-stigmatic. But the crimes accessible to the lower classes, involving violence or direct theft or some of each, called for penalties that were physically severe and were intensely stigmatic in their language, some so stigmatic that the victims themselves could not use it—e.g., rape and blackmail.

Even when a member of the upper socio-economic class was found guilty of a stigmatic crime and was about to be sentenced, there was a marked difference in language of the judge. Often in the case of a culprit of the lower classes the judge administered a savage tongue-lashing, while the defendant hung his head and his family sobbed, terrorized. But when upper-class culprits had been convicted in criminal court of using the mails to defraud the general public, the judge (as quoted by Sutherland) typically said: "You are men of affairs, of experience, of refinement and culture, of excellent reputation and standing in the business and social world." They were in fact, as the judicial process had just disclosed, *criminals*. This difference in attitudes of judges is often pronounced. Severely reprehending toward members of the lower classes, the judges become wistful, melancholy or sadly philosophical when sentencing men of the upper class. (After all, this isn't strange as they both come from the same class, may have gone to the same school and may belong to the same clubs.) And a sad duty does indeed confront the judge in contrast with those joyful occasions when he can say to some despicable specimen just convicted of armed robbery: "I sentence you to twenty years at hard labor."

When Sutherland inquired closely he found, contrary to the established supposition, that many members of the upper classes did commit offenses for which the government held them accountable. But in most cases special arrangements had been made to handle them with kid gloves and in many cases to administer by way of punishment a slap on the wrist.[23]

Nor was the reason for differential formulation and application of the law hard to find. The class whose members were being proceeded against was the class that had the dominant influence in the government and supported the political parties at the top. It was, indeed, their government and their political parties engaged in running their very own plantation.

As to the vast volume of crimes of all kinds in modern society, upper-class and lower-class, Sutherland is very clear about general background. "After the disappearance of the nobility," he says, "business men constituted the elite, and wealth became respected above all other attainments; necessarily, poverty became a disgrace. Wealth was therefore identified with worth, and worth was made known to the public by conspicuous consumption. The desire for symbols of luxury, ease, and success, developed by competitive consumption and by competitive salesmanship, spread to all classes and the simple life was no longer satisfying. . . . High crime rates are to be expected in a social system in which great emphasis is placed upon the success goal—attainment of individual wealth—and relatively slight emphasis is placed upon the proper means and devices for achieving this goal. In this type of social organization the generally approved 'rules of the game' may be known to those who evade them, but the emotional supports which accompany conformity to the rules are offset by the stress on the success goal."[24]

What Sutherland referred to as white collar crime did not concern some kind of newly discovered crime nor was it an extension of the concept of crime. He employed the white collar notion as Alfred P. Sloan had employed it in *The Autobiography of a White Collar Worker*. It referred simply to crimes open to commitment only by the upper, respected, approved and socially preferred class. Not reported to the police, these were of little interest to simple-minded police-oriented newspapers; they were reported to special administrative agencies.

Sutherland first presented his thesis in a speech in 1939 to the American Sociological Association. He later published a series of monographs and in 1949 a book, *White Collar Crime*.[25] This book is already a classic of sociology, ranking in the opinion of some professionals with works like Emile Durkheim's *Suicide* and perhaps even Max Weber's *Protestant Ethic and the Spirit of Capitalism*. It is required reading for anyone who wants to understand American society as well as crime and modern criminology.

"The thesis of this book, stated positively," says Sutherland, "is that persons of the upper socio-economic class engage in much criminal behavior; that this criminal behavior differs from the criminal behavior of the lower socio-economic class principally in the administrative procedures which are used in dealing with the offenders; and that variations in administrative procedures are not significant from the point of view of causation of crime. Today tuberculosis is treated by streptomycin; but the causes of tuberculosis were no different when it was treated by poultices and bloodletting."[26]

Sutherland accepts the combination of two abstract criteria used by legal scholars to define crime: a legal description of an act as socially injurious and a legal provision of a penalty for the act.[27]

White collar crime, as Sutherland makes clear, is far more costly than crimes customarily regarded as constituting the "crime problem."[28] The crimes committed mostly by the propertied and wealthy in the course of managing their property include embezzlement; most big fraud; restraint of trade; misrepresentation in advertising and in the sale of securities; infringements of patents, trademarks and copyrights; industrial espionage; illegal labor practices; violations of war regulations; violation of trust; secret rebates and kickbacks; commercial and political bribery; wash sales; misleading balance sheets; false claims; dilution of products; prohibited forms of monopoly; income-tax falsification; adulteration of food and drugs; padding of expense accounts; use of substandard materials; rigging markets; price-fixing; mislabeling; false weights and measurements; internal corporate manipulation, etc., etc. Except for tax fraud the ordinary man is never in a position to commit these crimes.

A distinction between most white collar crime and most ordinary crime is that the white collar criminal does not usually make use of violence; he depends chiefly on stealth, deceit or conspiracy. In the case of illegal labor practices, however, he does often through agents employ violence leading to death of workers. And there may be violent, even fatal, reactions to some of its nonviolent forms, such as the consequence of adulteration or improper preparation of foods and drugs.

The "white collar criminals, however, are by far the most dangerous to society of any type of criminals from the point of view of effects on private property and social institutions."[29] For their predations gradually tend to undermine public morale and spread social disorganization.[30] Large-scale stock swindles, bank manipulations and food and drug adulteration administer particularly convulsive shocks to broad segments of the populace. The volume of total violations, much of it officially unchallenged, leads to a spreading mood of public cynicism and more and more rank-and-file lawbreaking. It is finally echoed in the statement: "There's one law for the rich and another law for the poor." Government itself stands impugned. The stage is set for anarchy, sometimes emerging in riots.

An equally grave consequence, which Sutherland does not notice but upon which I shall later touch, is that the attempt to gloss over, conceal, minimize and apologize for white collar crime in general and in specific cases trammels the channels of public communication, undermines the terms of public debate and clouds the critical faculties even of many scholars.

The laws relating to white collar crime, as Sutherland remarks, tend to "conceal the criminality of the behavior" and thus do not reinforce the public *mores* as do other laws.[31]

Sutherland surveyed the laws and took note of those instances in which white collar crime is explicitly stated to be crime and those where it is only implicitly indicated. White collar crimes are committed by individuals and by corporations, mostly the latter as the transmission mechanisms of widespread illegal planning. They are committed against a small number of persons in a particular occupation or against the general public; it is rarely a case of individual versus individual. Individuals only commit such white collar crimes as embezzlement and fraud, and when they do they come under statutes clearly labeled criminal.

But there are many newer statutes, developed incident to the emergence of machine technology and the modern corporation.

There are, first, the antitrust laws—the Sherman Act, the amendment thereto establishing the Federal Trade Commission, the Clayton Act and other amendments. The Sherman Act is explicitly stated to be criminal law, and various of its amendments explicitly define violations as crimes. The amendments are largely under the jurisdiction of the Federal Trade Commission, which may issue cease-and-desist orders or enter into stipulations for the termination of some behavior. If a stipulation is violated there may be issued a cease-and-desist order, and if this is violated there may be issued a court injunction, the violation of which is punishable as contempt of court, provided for in the original Act. If the interim procedures (similar to probation in the ordinary courts) are not effective, fines and imprisonment may be imposed for contempt. An unlawful act, as Sutherland remarks, is not legally defined as criminal by the fact that it is punished but by the fact that it is *punishable*. It follows from these and other considerations that "all the decisions made under the amendments to the antitrust law are decisions that the corporations committed crimes."[32]

Laws against false advertising, designed to protect competitors and consumers, and the National Labor Relations Law, designed to protect employees against coercion and the public from interference with commerce, are adaptations of the common law to modern conditions. Laws against false advertising relate to common-law fraud. There are, too, laws against infringement of patents, which relate to the common-law prohibitions of restrictions on freedom in the form of assault, false imprisonment and extortion. Prior to the enactment of these and other laws the basic common law already expressed itself against restraint of trade, monopoly and unfair competition.

False labeling, a variant of false advertising, is defined as crime in the

Pure Food and Drug Act. False advertising in the Federal Trade Commission Act is defined as unfair competition, and comes under the same criminal procedure as its other violations. It is fraud.

As to the National Labor Relations Act, "all of the decisions under this law, which is enforceable by penal sanctions, are decisions that crimes were committed."[33]

Most white collar criminal statutes are relatively nonstigmatic—that is, they don't arouse an automatic reaction of reprehension in the broad public. That someone has been convicted of using the mails to defraud, or has restrained trade, does not sound as heinous as if he had been convicted of robbing post boxes even though in the first cases very large sums may have been illegally taken from millions of people and in the latter case perhaps only a Social Security check from a single individual.

The crimes of the lower socio-economic classes, however—most of them embalmed in the *Federal Uniform Crime Reports*—do carry with them deep social stigmas. They are, in part owing to newspaper emphasis, socially disgraceful. They exclude one from respectable society and curtail one's civil privileges.

In the case of most crimes in the white collar area, too, the penalties are notably lighter than for crimes reportable to the police. Few of these crimes, even when they individually involve sums greatly exceeding all the burglaries and bank holdups in a year, call for prison sentences. Most call for nominal fines, and some require that the defendant merely not repeat the crime. In a few the action is broken off with the defendant signing a consent decree agreeing to terminate a lucrative course of illegal action.

There would be difficulty in imposing jail sentences or executions in many of these cases, because the defendants are usually corporations. While the courts have decreed in their wisdom that corporations are "persons" and are entitled to all the protections of persons, it is a fact that one can't jail or execute a corporation. And officers of a corporation, being quite different persons, cannot, it seems, justly be held responsible by a careful Congress for the acts of the corporation. Even where the acts of the corporation have netted millions in illicit gain, the fines prescribed by a benevolent Congress are trivial compared with the gains. It is true that the legislation establishing the Sherman Act and the Federal Trade Commission did provide for prosecution of officers of offending corporations; but such prosecutions have rarely been launched by business-minded public officials. And prosecutions under the Sherman Act are wholly at the discretion of the Attorney General. They are not mandatory, hence are subject to political juggling.

Corporate Crime

Sutherland centered his study on the behavior of corporations, the instruments of much steadily continuing crime.[34]

He took the seventy largest nonfinancial corporations as given on two lists, that of Berle and Means in *The Modern Corporation and Private Property* (1933) and that of the Senate Temporary National Economic Committee (1938). He then excluded from these lists public utility corporations (he examined fifteen power and light companies separately) and the corporations in one other industry. Left with sixty-eight corporations, he added two that appeared on the list of 1938 and not on the list of 1929. It was a list representative of the cream of corporate society, the elite.[35]

The average life of these corporations was forty-five years. Their criminal histories were traced through official records, which Sutherland names.

He found a total of 980 decisions against these corporations, with a maximum of 50 for one and an average per corporation of 14.0. No fewer than 60 (or almost all) had decisions against them for restraining trade, 53 for infringements, 44 for unfair labor practices, 43 for a variety of offenses, 28 for misrepresentation in advertising and 26 for rebates. In all there were 307 adverse decisions on restraining trade, 97 on misrepresentation, 222 on infringement, 158 on unfair labor practices, 66 on rebates and 130 on other cases.

One hundred and fifty-eight of these decisions were entered in criminal court, 296 were in civil court, 129 were in equity court, 361 were by commission order, 25 were by commission confiscation and 11 were by commission settlement.

Even if the analysis had been limited to explicit criminal jurisdiction, 60 per cent of the corporations (or 42), with an average of four convictions each, had experienced that particularly stigmatic jurisdiction. As Sutherland points out, in many states persons with four convictions are defined as habitual criminals or "repeaters." Applying this concept to corporations, on the average at least 60 per cent of the leading corporations are habitual criminals.

Few cases initiated after 1944 are included in the Sutherland study, and the author warns that his work does not include all violations that have taken place because not all administrations were vigorous in enforcing the law and not all cases were systematically recorded. In general, there was lax enforcement under Republican Administrations—only 40 per cent of the cases from 1900 to 1944 date from prior to 1934—and more alert enforcement under Democratic Administrations. The most serious attempts at enforcement occurred under the New Deal, although the bulk of the laws had been on the books for many decades. One gets some insight here into reasons for the pre-Johnsonian enthusiasm of the corporate world for the foot-dragging Republican Party as well as some understanding of the *quid pro quo* for heavy national campaign contributions.

Of these seventy corporations, Sutherland found, thirty were either illegitimate in origin or began illegal activities immediately thereafter. Eight others, he found, were "probably" illegal in origin or in beginning policies. The finding of original illegitimacy was made with respect to twenty-one corporations in formal court decisions, by "other historical evidence" in the other cases.

Sutherland does not attempt any estimate of the total loot (all depressing to the common living standard) produced by these and unadjudicated violations. But, as many violations continued for long periods of time, it must run into large sums that make the work of Mafias, Cosa Nostras, and spurious labor unions look like extremely petty operations. One cannot, of course, attribute the entire income of these corporations to criminal behavior although a part of net income was the consequence of criminal activity. In the case only of the twenty-nine that were born in crime—to which Balzac's phrase would certainly apply—could one attribute all the subsequent earnings to criminal behavior. But the total criminal haul, throwing a garish light on the maxim "Crime doesn't pay," ran into billions upon billions of dollars for these seventy corporations alone. Crime, carefully planned and executed, is demonstrably the royal highroad to pecuniary success in the United States.

Corporate crime is, indeed, crime in the grand manner. But it isn't part of the pattern of crime as presented by the newspapers. Why the newspapers aren't fully alert to this sort of wrongdoing apart from ineptitude, why they don't include it in the standard pattern of crime, is not difficult to decide. Nearly all the advertising revenues of the newspapers and mass magazines, as well as of radio and television stations and networks, come from these same corporations and their smaller counterparts. Although reporting individual large cases as they arise (not always prominently or fully) the newspapers have never despite recent sociological revelations ventured statistical summaries of the situation as they regularly do with lower-class, police-reported crimes—a marked case of class bias. Even the large individual cases are only reported fully in a few leading metropolitan papers. They tend to be ignored by the many hundreds of others.

Not only are acts of commission unreported or diminished in significance, but those who commit these acts with the corporations as pliant tools are in their general *modus operandi* held up to public view as the cream and bulwark of society, the very pillars of the nation. Such a strange state of mind is inculcated in the public that a correct statement of the facts inevitably seems bizarre, overdrawn, tendentious and even perversely subversive.

The leading stockholders in these corporations—80 per cent of all stock being held by 1.6 per cent of all adults—consist of the wealthiest property owners in the country. The leading company executives are the most highly paid group in the country, drawing remuneration astronomically exceeding that of skilled professional people.[36]

Corporations as Ideal Delinquents

Sutherland compares the behavior of corporations and their officers with that of the professional thief, "the ideal delinquent," of which he made a special almost classical study.[37] Both are "repeaters," persistent operators; illegal behavior of both is more extensive than complaints and prosecutions show; neither loses status with associates but may instead be admired; each customarily orally expresses contempt for law, government and governmental personnel; and the crimes of both are not only deliberate but organized. They are, however, different in their self-conceptions. The professional thief recognizes himself as a criminal and is so regarded by the public; the corporate man thinks of himself as respectable and is generally so regarded by the public.

But white collar criminals often, as Sutherland points out, admit to being "law violators," a distinction without a substantial difference. Another difference is that the crime of the professional thief is plainly visible whereas the crime of the corporation is camouflaged, hard to detect. Corporate men, unlike professional thieves, rationalize their acts by semantic substitutions. Fraudulent representation is excused as merely puffing one's wares, and so on. Extravagant or insistent claims are called "the hard sell," conspiracy in restraint of trade is "a gentleman's agreement," price fixing is "stabilizing the market," monopolistic practices are suggested as laudatory evidence of "a hard competitor." Yet both the professional thief and the corporation use aliases, the latter by forming subterfuge subsidiaries, dummy companies, inventing new brand names for the same product to escape new regulations or developing "fighting" brands. In public defense both employ "mouthpieces." The professional thief usually has only a lawyer, but the corporation and the corporate man have lawyers, advertising agents and public relations counselors. These latter influence lawmaking and law enforcement as they relate to the corporation as well as defend the company in court and before the public. The object is the same in both cases: to get the client off scot free.

But although different from the professional thief in that it is directed by a group and thus invokes for itself the maximum of rationality, the corporation is similar, says Sutherland, in that it selects crimes risking the least danger of detection and identification and against which victims are least likely to struggle. It selects crimes that are difficult to prove and it engages in the wholesale "fixing" of cases. The corporations when they encounter officials they cannot "fix" have gone as high as the president of the United States to remove them. In general, says Sutherland, the "fixing" of white collar criminals is much more extensive than that of professional thieves. It is also much more costly, and he cites the case of the bribe of $750,000 by four insurance companies that sent Boss Pendergast of Missouri to jail, later to be pardoned by President Truman (who originally belonged to the Pendergast organization). It was almost ten years before the insurance companies were convicted. Then they were only fined; no insurance executives went to jail.

There was, too, the case of Federal Judge Martin Manton who was convicted of accepting a bribe of $250,000 from agents of the defendant when he presided over a case charging exorbitant salaries were improperly paid to officers of the American Tobacco Company. While the attorney for the company was disbarred from the federal courts, the assistant to the company president (who made the arrangements) was soon thereafter promoted to vice president: a good boy.

In the case of white collar crimes of corporations, if any individual is punished (usually none is) it is only one or a very few. The authorities do not dig pertinaciously with a view to ferreting out every last person who had anything to do with the case. But, as Sutherland points out, it is different with crimes of the lower classes. In kidnapping, for example, the FBI, in addition to seizing the kidnappers, flushes to the surface anyone who (1) rented them quarters to conceal the kidnapped person or to hide out in; (2) acted as unwitting agents for them in conveying messages or collecting ransom; (3) transported them; (4) in any way innocently gave them aid and assistance; or (5) was a witness to any of these separate acts. The government men do such a splendid job that almost everyone except the obstetricians who brought the various parties into the world are brought before the bar, where the aroused judge "breaks the book over their heads" in the course of sentencing. Sovereignty, it turns out after all, is not to be trifled with.

It may be argued that kidnapping, which resorts to violence, is a more serious crime than bribing a judge. With this I would disagree. Gravely serious though kidnapping is, its commission strikes directly at only a few, and in most cases involves comparatively small sums—even though they seem large to the ordinary man. But bribing a judge—and in the Manton case far more than any known kidnap ransom was at stake —strikes at a very broad public and, indeed, at the foundations of social institutions in general. It is subversive in the deepest and truest sense.

Emulatory Crime in the Ranks

What is of particular interest is the vast amount of emulatory crime white collar crime inspires among underlings, insiders and outsiders, much of this never reported to the police. Companies, as many reports since World War II show in *Fortune*, the *Wall Street Journal* and other business papers, are increasingly subject to constant depredations. Specialty, department and chain stores are subject to a continuous pressure of theft, which led one security officer to state his opinion publicly that 25 per cent of the public is absolutely honest and wouldn't steal under any circumstance, 25 per cent is systematically seeking opportunities to steal and 50 per cent is ready to steal at any time it feels certain of escaping detection.

There is a constant assault on the corporate fortress from the inside as well, by employees who steal from stockrooms and loading platforms and who have in some cases organized truly gigantic withdrawals of goods. Embezzlement is rife. Only a few years ago some of the police in Chicago and Denver were found to be practicing old-fashioned burglary on a large scale as a supplement to low salaries.

If money is evidence of personal worth, then many persons are out to prove they are as worthy as anyone in Wall Street.

In eight and one-half concentrated pages Sutherland gives a synopsis of crime in the United States.[38] Fraud is extensive in the professions— legal, medical, clerical—although he rates physicians and surgeons rather favorably on the whole. Bribery of officials, particularly by businesses selling goods to municipalities, counties and states, is common. But within private business itself corruption is internally quite common. He reports: "Buyers for department stores, hotels, factories, railways, and almost all other concerns which make purchases on a large scale accept and sometimes demand gifts of money payments." Again, "The police constantly break the laws. The laws of arrest are rigidly limited, but the police exercise their authority with little reference to these limitations and in violation of law. Hopkins refers to illegal arrests as kidnappings, and in this sense, the number of kidnappings by the police is thousands of times as great as the number of kidnappings by burglars and robbers. The courts, similarly, are not immune from criminal contagion, and this is true especially of the lower courts."

The United States, the plain unvarnished facts show, is a very criminal society, led in its criminality by its upper socio-economic classes.[39]

Contemporary Big Business Crime

Has the ominous outlook altered since Sutherland terminated analysis as of 1944?

It has not changed in the slightest. In the two decades since 1945 the acts cited by Sutherland continued—in many cases with redoubled force; for the penalties imposed by law are obviously not of sufficient weight to deter. One can make large sums of money in business by breaking the law up to the point where one is ordered to stop or is indicted.

In the Federal Trade Commission alone, from January 1, 1945, through fiscal 1965 as given in annual reports, there were 3,991 cease-and-desist orders for violations by enterprises large and small.[40] The largest corporations were conspicuously represented, along with ambitious small fry. The specific violations were: false or misleading advertising, using a misleading trade or corporate name, using false or misleading endorsements, removing or concealing law-required markings, disparaging competitors' products, misrepresentation and deception, false invoicing, misbranding and mislabeling, deceptive pricing, failing to make material disclosures, offering deceptive inducements, obtaining information by subterfuge, using misleading product name or title, shipping for demand-payment goods not ordered, etc., etc.

In the Food and Drug Administration, which administers the amended Food, Drug and Cosmetic Act of 1938, there were 5,208 criminal prosecutions from 1945 through 1961, an average of 306 per year.[41] Many of these were for distributing poisonous or contaminated products. Fines and jail sentences were usually meted out.

In its 26th annual report, the United States Securities and Exchange Commission, empowered to supervise the issuance, sale and resale of securities, reports that "From 1934, when the Commission was established, until June 30, 1960, 2,777 defendants have been indicted in the United States District Courts in 645 cases developed by the Commission, and 1,385 convictions obtained in 585 cases. The record of convictions obtained and upheld is over 85 per cent for the 26-year life of the Commission."[42]

"During the past fiscal year," says the 1960 report, "53 cases were referred to the Department of Justice for prosecution. This is the highest number of referrals in the past 18 years and the second highest in the Commission's history and is in line with the continuing increase in the number of referrals during the past several years. As a result of these and prior referrals, 43 indictments were returned against 289 defendants during the fiscal year."[43]

The Securities and Exchange Commission, of course, deals with thousands more cases each year in which it issues orders to discontinue illegal practices.

The National Labor Relations Board, which processed only a few more than 1,000 cases in 1936 and now processes more than 25,000 a year, enforces fair labor practices as defined in the twice-amended National Labor Relations Act of 1935. Most of its rulings on appeal to the courts have been sustained. Of 2,719 cases subjected to judicial review up to June 30, 1964, the orders of the NLRB were fully affirmed in 57 per cent of the cases and affirmed with modifications in 20 per cent. In only 18 per cent of the cases was the Board completely overruled. In appeals to the Supreme Court, the Board was affirmed in 63 per cent of the cases and affirmed with modifications in 8 per cent. The Supreme Court overruled the Board completely in 17 per cent of the cases.[44]

This Board, a quasi-judicial tribunal similar to the Federal Trade Commission, the Securities and Exchange Commission and the Food and Drug Administration, issues injunctions and supervises violators and, according to the National Labor Relations Act, "Any person who shall willfully resist, prevent, impede, or interfere with any member of the Board or any of its agents or agencies in the performance of duties pursuant to this act shall be punished by a fine of not more than $5,000 or by imprisonment for not more than one year or both." Complaints under this criminal statute are brought by individuals and unions against employers and by employers against unions.[45]

Business or white collar crimes are usually thought of as nonviolent, thus placing the culprits in public opinion at least a peg above such unorthodox businessmen as Frank Nitti, Tony Accardo and Frank Costello. But this differentiation is clearly false, as is shown in many cases of record before the National Labor Relations Board. A recent pattern, as brought to light by the McClellan Committee is for Company X to hire "labor relations adviser" A who in turn enrolls certified thugs T_1, T_2 and T_3 to beat up, bribe, drive away or destroy labor organizer L.

Up to 1945, according to Sutherland, labor relations decisions had been made against 43 of the 70 large corporations, or 60 per cent, with

149 decisions in all. All 43 were "repeaters": 39 used interference, restraint and coercion; 33 discriminated against union members; 34 organized company unions; 13 used labor spies; and 5 used violence. Such violence was largely confined to the steel and automobile industries.

The late Henry Ford was quoted as saying in 1937: "We'll never recognize the United Automobile Workers Union or any other union." The Ford Motor Company had long maintained a service department under Harry Bennett, a former pugilist, staffed with 600 men equipped with guns and blackjacks. With reference to this service department Frank Murphy, then governor of Michigan, said: "Henry Ford employs some of the worst gangsters in our city."

According to undisputed testimony before the NLRB, in 1937 the United Automobile Workers Union started to organize employees at Ford's River Rouge plant. It was announced that organizers would distribute literature outside the plant at a specified time, and reporters and photographers were present in force. Said a guard to a reporter: "We are going to throw them to hell out of here." Upon arrival the organizers went up an overhead ramp to one of the entrances, where they were told they were trespassing. Witnesses said they turned and started away. As they left they were assaulted by service department guards—beaten, knocked down and kicked. Witnesses testified that it was a "terrific beating" and "unbelievably brutal." Among those severely beaten were Walter Reuther and Richard Frankensteen, officials of the United Automobile Workers Union.

The guards followed out into the street. One man's skull was fractured, another's back broken. Cameras of photographers were seized by guards and the films destroyed. Two reporters were chased by automobile at eighty miles an hour through Detroit streets until they reached the sanctuary of a police station. Later when women organizers attempted to distribute literature outside the plant they were attacked by guards, knocked down and beaten. City policemen who were present during these events stood by and did not interfere—testimony to the local power of Henry Ford.[46]

From fiscal years 1959 through 1965, inclusive, the Antitrust Division of the Department of Justice won 147 formally designated criminal cases against companies and lost 24. It won 206 civil cases and lost 9.[47]

Other disciplinary bodies to which one should turn for a more complete picture of such business violations as are judicially decided are the Federal Communications Commission, the Civil Aeronautics Authority, Federal Aviation Agency, Federal Power Commission and the Interstate Commerce Commission.

There is no federal agency that compiles, correlates and makes public the statistics on corporate crimes as the FBI does with diverse police-reported crimes in the *Federal Uniform Crime Reports*. If there were, there would be shown a much larger volume of corporate crime than reported here. It is well recognized by experts that the enforcement of laws against corporate crimes is at best of a sporadic token character carried on by understaffed and underfinanced agencies.

The *Federal Uniform Crime Reports* serve a purpose beyond merely informing the public of the incidence of crime, which they do only very lopsidedly and exaggeratedly for these particular crimes. The *Reports* have the intent, as evidenced in many public expressions by J. Edgar Hoover, the redoubtable G-man, of encouraging greater public support for more repressive police measures and stiffer penalties (against errant members of the lower socio-economic classes, who generally commit these direct-action crimes). Some future reader may assess the sagacity of this writer when he says that after this disparity in reporting lower-class and upper-class crimes has been sharply pointed out there will be no change: No federal agency will make a comprehensive annual statistical report on corporate crimes as such, although Washington is literally crawling with expert statisticians who could whip the figures together in a trice. Nor will the penalties for corporate crimes likely be increased to the point where they realistically deter. The offenders will continue to be treated as though they were somewhat crotchety but beloved maiden aunts who have been inexplicably naughty.

The Great Electrical Industry Conspiracy

While the bulk of the cases cited have involved the uncamouflaged criminal jurisdiction, with the judges properly accoutered with everything except the black cap, there have been many recent thumping reminders that carefully planned crime is an inseparable companion of big business. Three cases involved whole basic industries: the electrical, aluminum and steel industries. None of the protagonists was sponsored by the Mafia. They clearly prove that "the bad old days," thought to be conquered by the New Deal, are still with us.

The Great Electrical Industry Case came to a climax in 1961. It involved forty-five individual blue-ribbon defendants and twenty-nine corporations, including ultra-ultra General Electric Company and Westinghouse Electric Corporation, which together lovingly shared more than 75 per cent of the market. As *Fortune* remarked, it was the "biggest criminal case in the history of the Sherman Act."

United States District Judge J. Cullen Ganey heard the case in Philadelphia. The prosecution was by the attorney general of the United States, in full panoply. It was crime, crime, crime all the way, front and back, up and down, back and forth. This needs to be emphasized because Fred F. Loock, president of Allen-Bradley Company, one of the defendants, said: "It is the only way a business can be run. It is free enterprise."

The charge was specifically the dark one of conspiracy—in this case to fix prices, rig bids and divide markets in a series of secret cartels on electrical equipment valued at $1.75 billion annually. The leading defendants pleaded guilty to the most serious counts, no contest to the rest. The conspiracies extended over many years, going back prior to World War II and in the opinion of some observers to 1896. Surprisingly, this conspiracy was carried on with all the guilt-conscious cloak-and-dagger techniques known to spies: secret codes, mysterious meetings in hotel rooms, queer notes, guarded telephone calls, concealed records, fictitious names, burned memoranda and the like. No patron of TV or the films, watching the actors, could have failed to recognize that an authentic, vintage conspiracy was afoot. Only sinister music was lacking.

Although operating departmental executives stood in the dock and the top managements of GE and Westinghouse virtuously disclaimed knowledge of the whole affair, Judge Ganey felicitously remarked before sentencing: "One would be most naive indeed to believe that these violations of the law, so long persisted in, affecting so large a segment of the industry and finally involving so many millions upon millions of dollars, were facts unknown to those responsible for the corporation and its conduct. . . . I am not naive enough to believe General Electric didn't know about it and it didn't meet their hearty approbation." But although the government had gathered monumental evidence it had not been able to connect the very top executives directly to the conspiracy in ways required by law.

Judge Ganey imposed total fines of $1,924,500. General Electric was fined $437,500 and Westinghouse $372,500. Damages of $7,470,000 were also assessed. Upon twenty-four individuals in the case jail sentences were imposed—and suspended owing to their advanced ages. William S. Ginn, vice president of General Electric, was given thirty days in jail and fined $12,500. Six other company officers drew fines of $1,000 to $4,000 and thirty days in jail. And it was the unusualness of sentencing these high-salaried company men to thirty days in jail, the usual police-court sentence for disorderly conduct, that attracted special attention. Corporation executives are rarely sent to jail even for brief sojourns. Indeed, they are far more immune to jail terms than high Russian Communist Party officials.

The Great Electrical Industry Conspiracy emerged in a curious way. The Tennessee Valley Authority one day in the 1950's received identical sealed bids from various suppliers of heavy electrical equipment. The fact came to the attention of Senator Estes Kefauver, who threatened to start his own investigation if the Eisenhower Administration did not act. The Department of Justice was alerted and began looking into the case, but at first found it difficult to pick up the threads of wrong-doing. It decided to subpoena various records of the companies and finally obtained an account of conspiracy from the official of a small company. His story implicated General Electric.

Queries to General Electric provoked an internal inquiry by top management, which was truthfully informed by some of the operating vice presidents of what went on. Top management professed to be shocked, put pressures on the men and eventually forced all to resign or fired them. This strong line by GE sent angry insiders and their lawyers scurrying to the government with their stories, and the net of evidence wove itself more tightly. In the other companies men were not removed.

General Electric had for many years had a policy formally calling for strict compliance with the antitrust laws. This policy was implemented by written orders conspicuously sent from time to time to operating executives. Nevertheless, General Electric was an old offender, in the 1940's alone being snared in thirteen antitrust cases.

The convicted executives maintained that they had simply inherited procedures carried on by predecessors and were acting under direct orders from higher ups. One of the men knew that he held his job "under risk" for two years unless he increased profits. There was evidence of men who had held some of the same positions earlier, who had refused to enter into collusive arrangements with competitors and who had lost their jobs. Top officials denied everything. Judge Ganey clearly did not believe them.

Policy for General Electric was set by Chairman Ralph Cordiner, who, president since 1950, became chairman in 1958; his predecessor, Charles E. Wilson, had left to become chief of national defense mobilization. While Cordiner has been criticized for rudely dumping his men for doing what everybody did in this and in other industries (illegal price-fixing is standard business practice) his theoretical position was much sounder than that of others. Cordiner was an avowed devotee of competition, and public policy avowedly requires competition. There is, however, little competition in the American economy. But if this fact were to be formally admitted or authoritatively asserted the way would be paved for sweeping changes costly to big proprietors.

General Electric in sacrificing its men as it did acted in the style of governments who, having found some diplomat or espionage agent embarrassing, simply disavow him. (Most of these men, happily, were later hired by other companies, some at advanced levels.)

Origins of Anti-Monopoly Doctrine

The anti-monopoly doctrine was originally developed by individual business people in Europe who struggled against Crown monopolies in late medieval times. The earliest reported case in England was *Darcy v. Allen* in 1602 (11 Coke 84). In 1623 Parliament passed the Statute of Monopolies, abolishing nearly all existing monopolies as unlawful (St. 21 James 1, c. III). Englishmen from early times were always opposed to voluntary self-restraints of tradesmen by contract, and English courts refused to uphold such agreements (William Howard Taft, J., Addyston Pipe case, 85 Fed. 271). The "business revolutions" of 1688 in England and 1789 in France were in part directed against such monopolies. Trade was to be free and open; and the public, in return for granting the trading privilege, would benefit from the resultant low prices wrought by competition. This, too, was the American idea.

In time, particularly in the United States, small businesses grew into large quasi-sovereign businesses and the large businesses found they had become (usually through illegal behavior) large monopolies such as the Aluminum Company, the Standard Oil Trust and many others. Broken up by government action or evolving in separate units, the various industries find in time that two to five or six companies did 75 to 90 per cent of the business and many small companies—tokens of competition—the remain- This pattern is what economists call oligopoly or rule by a few. Prices usually set by one company, the "price leader," and others follow the When the few tacitly agree so to "follow the leader," as they do, there is in effect a general subtly maintained monopoly.

But if monopolies are indeed tolerated in the American system, if enterprises are not competing so that buyers get the lowest possible prices, what is the constitutional warrant? How does the situation constitute equal protection under the law? There is, in fact, no constitutional warrant. Monopoly is fundamentally illegal, with or without the Sherman Act, which refers to it as a "high misdemeanor." Why should a select few have the *public* market as a private plaything?

But, having broken up the electrical and various other clearly proved monopolies, can we not say that the government is keeping the market open to free competition? While many would so argue, concentration and monopoly grow steadily. In view of the steady denunciations, official and unofficial, and of specific laws against monopoly, how can this be?

Issues and Solutions

The mystery, if such it ever was, is neatly dispelled by Judge Thurman Arnold in his *The Folklore of Capitalism*. Arnold was from 1938 to 1943 in charge of the antitrust division of the Department of Justice, and knew whereof he spoke. The operative function of the Sherman Act, Arnold holds, is to make possible from time to time ceremonial observances of the American belief in competition. These ceremonial observances take the form of criminal prosecutions, so that a concerned fraction of the public may believe the competitive situation is being defended. Meanwhile concentration and monopoly advance in rapid strides from decade to decade as in Europe. Those convicted do not alter their behavior.

And now we come to the basic issue, which the General Electric upper moguls perhaps had in mind in talking and acting as virtuously as they did for the record. If these industries are indeed monopolies that continually strengthen their position and do not give the public the advantages of competition, then they should be subject to regulation at least as strict as that accorded the public utilities in their "natural" monopolies. But it is just this sort of cartel regulation that the corporations fear. They would particularly abhor effective regulation even with stabilized prices. For at what level would the prices be set? At the other extreme from regulation there would be outright government ownership, wi[th] profits beyond the recovery of costs going, *a la Russe,* into the gene[ral] government operating fund.

No accepted politician in the United States takes either of these positi[on] All profess themselves in favor of the present situation, which im[plies] only that they fundamentally line up with the big proprietors who fi[nd the] present situation precisely to their taste: monopoly with ceremonia[l] tones of pseudo-competition.

A third course might be to break some of the big companies into their constituent parts. General Electric under Cordiner, for example, was found to be organized into twenty-seven autonomous divisions consisting of 110 small companies. Each of these latter was run as if it were a single enterprise, with the boss of each making up his own budget. But there was constant pressure from the top executive suite on the boss of each unit for greater profitability.

This particular course of action, too, would be distasteful to the big companies, most of which are cannibalistic agglomerations, although their physical productivity would not be adversely affected by it. Indeed, it might be enhanced. One consequence of such action would be to produce more top executive jobs, which should be of interest to ambitious middle-class people.

The behavior of corporate man shows that he entertains certain unconscious beliefs, which he never expresses: that it is "his" market, filled with vassals in the form of "his" customers and "his" employees, and that government officials are "his" officials. While in legal theory the corporation exists to serve society, in the unconscious and correct belief of corporate man, society and government operationally now exist to serve the corporation—the be-all and end-all of everything.

In the electrical industry both the men and the companies came in for somewhat rougher treatment than is usually the case. As heavy equipment was involved, the companies were deluged by lawsuits from public utility companies, municipalities and government agencies. In 1965 a judgment was turned in against GE, Westinghouse and some others for $16,863,203 on behalf of a group of midwestern power and light companies. In all, 1,912 civil antitrust suits were filed against the companies, costing GE a reported $225 million, Westingthouse about $110 million and Allis-Chalmers $45 million. Most were settled out of court for undisclosed sums but, all in all, the moneys involved were considerable even if they came short of erasing illegal profits.

The Prevalence of Price-Fixing

Has price-fixing been terminated by the electrical industry case? The rea⌐ can supply the answer for himself by checking competing products in h⌐ various stores. Somehow they are all priced about the same—soap, sugar, milk, salt, cereals, automobiles, appliances, cigarettes, etc. By regions the same grades of gasoline have the same prices under various brand names, except for an occasional "price war." But a "price war," which is ordinary competition for business, is rare, as everyone knows. Established business considers price wars pathological and will do anything to avoid them. For while business believes in free enterprise—freedom to do whatever it desires—it abhors free competition, whatever it may say to the contrary. The government for its part, while condemning price-fixing, itself supports agricultural prices.

T. K. Quinn, a former vice president of General Electric, has recorded his belief that a third of the American economy—automobiles, steel, ciga-

rettes, cement, oil products, chemicals, roofing material and machinery—
is price-stabilized through agreements of the leading companies. But corporation men, precisely like members of the underworld, have their own
peculiar definitions for every situation. Thus, Roger Blough, president of
United States Steel, has said "a price that matches another price is a
competitive price," with which doctrine few nonbusiness people would
agree. If every baseball game ended in a tie most fans would begin to
suspect that the outcome was "fixed."

Westinghouse stockholders, when called upon to pass on the conduct of
their management, voted overwhelmingly to endorse it. General Electric
stockholders simply shouted down any attempt to question the management and approved it by 98 per cent.

Yet this elaborate charade about monopoly, in which many people (including the judge in the case) seriously believe, is played at a price:
The big companies, backbone of the American economic system, are
formally stigmatized as criminals.

In this respect General Electric (along with many other companies) is
what Professor Sutherland calls a "repeater." Attorney General Robert
Kennedy in what was perhaps a grandstand flourish after the trial suggested that an injunction be brought against General Electric, which had
twenty-nine adjudicated convictions on its record, to keep it from repeating its conduct under the threat of more severe penalties; this was much
as though a lawbreaking ex-convict should be enjoined from breaking the
law. To implement this directive the Justice Department in December,
1961, sought a court order to make General Electric subject to unlimited
fines if it ever again violated any requirement of the antitrust laws. In
support of its action the Justice Department cited 39 antitrust actions
against GE, 36 filed since 1941, including here the 29 convictions as well
as seven consent decrees and three "adverse findings" by the Federal Trade
Commission. Such a record, the Justice Department said, revealed "General Electric's proclivity for persistent and frequent involvement in antitrust violations" in all branches of production. The record of Westinghouse
was hardly less immodest.[48]

"Has the industry learned any lessons?" asked *Fortune*. " 'One thing
I've learned out of all this,' said one executive, 'is to talk to only one other
person, not to go to meetings where there are lots of other people.' Many of
the defendants . . . looked on themselves as the fall guys of U.S. business.
They protested that they should no more be held up to blame than many
another business man, for conspiracy is just as much 'a way of life' in
other fields as it was in electrical equipment. 'Why pick on us?' was the
attitude. 'Look at some of those other fellows.' "

In so saying these men showed they did not understand the ceremonial uses of sacrifice. The high Indian civilizations of South and Central America had the custom each year of sacrificing to the gods, by burning or other violence, the most beautiful maidens of the city. By destroying what was manifestly so desirable, the men of the nation showed piety. By stigmatizing with criminal convictions these high-salaried executives, paragons of the mass media, the United States similarly testified to its pious belief in competition even as competition approaches the vanishing point.

As an immediate aftermath to the case, President Robert Paxton of General Electric at the age of fifty-nine, with six years still to go before his compulsory retirement, resigned "because of ill health."[49]

Of a pending series of seven criminal indictments of the steel industry, in the summer of 1965 the companies were first found guilty in two highly significant decisions.

In the first case eight companies were found guilty in federal court of conspiracy to fix prices on carbon sheet steel, which makes up an annual market of $3.6 billion—far larger than the electrical industry haul—and enters into a wide range of consumer products from automobile bodies and kitchen cabinets to refrigerators, washing machines and office furniture. The companies were fined $50,000 each, the maximum under the applicable section of the law; and sentencing of two principal officers was deferred.

The guilty companies composed most of the steel industry—the United States Steel Corporation, the Bethlehem Steel Company, the National Steel Corporation, The Great Lakes Steel Corporation, the Jones and Laughlin Steel Corporation, the Armco Steel Corporation, the Republic Steel Corporation and the Wheeling Steel Corporation. Named as co-conspirators in the indictment but not as defendants were the Youngstown Sheet and Tube Company, the Granite City Steel Company and the Pittsburgh Steel Company. The companies had felt emboldened to commit the sinister offenses complained of between 1955 and 1961, when a Republican Administration had briefly returned to power.

A curious comment at the time the indictments were handed up was made by Edmund F. Martin, vice chairman of Bethlehem Steel: "Even assuming that the matters charged were true, the Department of Justice is seeking not to correct any illegal or improper present-day situation, but only to harass the industry for practices which, even under the allegations of the indictment, have been abandoned." This is much as though a man charged with a three-year-old burglary were to claim that authorities were not dealing with current crime but were harassing him, since he had been "going straight" ever since.[50]

A few days later another federal judge fined four leading makers of steel forgings and a steel trade association a total of $150,000 after finding them criminally guilty of price fixing and bid rigging in the sale of open die steel forgings to the Army and Navy as well as to private companies from 1948 to 1961, an interval that embraced the Korean War. Bethlehem Steel, second in the industry, was fined $40,000; United States Steel, $35,000; the Midvale-Heppenstall Company of Philadelphia, $35,000; the Erie Forge and Steel Corporation, $25,000; and the Open Die Forging Institute, Inc., $15,000. The defendants did an estimated $100-million business a year in this line.

While ship shafts for the Navy and cannon for the Army were involved in the forgings, an interesting sidelight was that the defendants were found to have illegally set identical prices for rotors and generator shafts sold to General Electric, Westinghouse and Allis-Chalmers, the top defendants in The Great Electrical Industry Conspiracy. The difference in the size of fines in the steel and electrical cases stemmed from the number of indictments on each charge. The Sherman Act as amended permits a maximum fine of $50,000 on each charge. In the electrical case there were twenty charges in all, although every company did not fall under each charge.

Asked by the *Times* whether they intended to start civil suits for treble damages against the steel companies, General Electric said nothing had been decided and Allis-Chalmers said it had no comment; but Westinghouse valiantly reported: "So far as we know, we have received full value for our purchase of steel which we believe to have been made at competitive prices."

In this case five executives of the companies were fined an aggregate of $44,000 on October 25, 1962, on the same criminal indictment, which they did not contest.[51]

The fines in these cases, in relation to the amount of illegal business done, were obviously of the order of a $5 slap on the wrist for grand larceny.

The number of big recent cases—in oil, asphalt, milk, steel, electrical goods and the like—is too great to detail here. No fewer than ninety-two antitrust suits, a record, were begun in 1960 under the Republicans, although enforcement actually eased off sharply under President Kennedy and came to a virtual halt under President Johnson.[52] The Johnson Administration has practically given Big Business the green light on mergers and regulation in general, in return for which the presidential Business

Advisory Council, composed of about 100 chairmen and presidents of the biggest corporations, appears to have given its full endorsement of Mr. Johnson's personally engineered disastrous Vietnam war.[53]

In these upper reaches of power everything is strictly on a *quid pro quo* basis.

The New Higher Politics

Let us look at all this lawbreaking from another point of view. Perhaps the statutes are somehow misbegotten, as many corporation heads freely assert, even though they are simple expressions of the common law upon which the entire Anglo-American legal system rests. But possibly this legal system, too, is misbegotten and should be scrapped or radically overhauled.

In his devotional biography of John D. Rockefeller I, Professor Allan Nevins, the Columbia historian, suggests that the common view of Rockefeller as the epitome of ruthless Pecuniary Man, freely breaking the law in quest of profits in any and every accessible field, is entirely mistaken. Professor Nevins in his summation (which may be taken as applying just as well to any industrial tycoon) indirectly suggests that Rockefeller is representative in his way of Political Man—that is, a person planning and providing for the entire community even if in ways not readily understood by lesser mortals. This is evident, for example, when Professor Nevins says: "Behind this organizing genius, which had analogies with Richelieu's or Bismarck's, lay a combination of traits not less interesting because of their simplicity, conspicuity, and harmony." And Rockefeller's singlemindedness, says Professor Nevins, "reminds us of Cecil Rhodes."[54] In brief, Rockefeller reminds Nevins of commanding political leaders.

Had Professor Nevins chosen for comparison political personalities from nearer home, readers might more readily have detected the untenability of offering Rockefeller as an example of Political Man, acting according to some conception of the general welfare of society rather than milking society for personal gain through the most effective monopoly of all time. Rockefeller in his heyday in fact stood adverse to the common interest and this was formally found to be so by United States courts.

Professor Nevins has generalized beyond Rockefeller: "The architects of our material progress [if such they ever were—F.L.]—the men like Whitney, McCormick, Westinghouse, Rockefeller, Carnegie, Hill and Ford—will yet stand forth in their true stature as builders [if indeed they ever were—F.L.] of a strength which civilization found indispensable."

In this connection Professor Nevins went on to contend grotesquely that these and other men like them "saved the world" in World War I and later helped the world meet "a succession of world crises." He thereupon called for a revision of history, at which historians so far look with deep reserve, to give these unjustly evaluated men their proper due as builders and saviors of civilization.[55]

As to the role in 1914–18 of the industrial tycoons, American and foreign, far from saving the world, they were the chief operative factors in producing World War I, as a wealth of research conclusively shows. Again, it was the American business leaders who pushed the United States into that war from far out in left field on fantastic grounds of insuring freedom of the seas, terminating militarism and saving the world for democracy.[56] Nearly every major difficulty of the contemporary world can be traced directly to the governments of the major powers, the United States included, in 1914–18, and the leading property holders who stood solidly behind them. They produced, among other things, totalitarian communism as an outgrowth of the situation.

But even though Professor Nevins and others who argue like him are not plausible, there does exist this view that Corporate Man is a disguised Political Man. And if this were so, then the lawbreaking in question might not only be condoned but might even be praised. For if these men are merely trying to get rid of a series of progress-stifling, retrograde laws by wholesale violation and evasion in order to establish industrial feudalism, they may be looked upon as forward-planning political saboteurs, even revolutionaries, who should be compared with and differentiated from Lenin, Trotsky, Gandhi and Mao Tse-tung. It is true that no such general intention has been openly avowed; but perhaps the intent is secret. Perhaps there exists a clandestine political conspiracy to undermine the present form of government and produce the Good Society according to the conception of the U.S. Chamber of Commerce—that is, industrial feudalism. As for Richelieu, Bismarck and Rhodes, none of them was at odds with the system in which he found himself. None was ever found guilty of serious crimes in his nation's courts.

But although the corporation leaders do not seem to be consciously political beyond seeking at all times to install opportunistic puppets and cat's-paws in office, it is a fact, as Professor Sutherland notes, that:

During the last century this economic and political system has changed. The changes have resulted principally from the efforts of businessmen. If the word "subversive" refers to efforts to make fundamental changes in a social system, the business leaders are the most subversive influence in the United States. These business leaders have acted as individuals or in small groups, seeking preferential advantages for themselves. The primary loyalty of the businessman has been to profits, and he has willingly sacrificed the general and abstract principles of free competition and free enterprise in circumstances which promised a pecuniary advantage. Moreover, he has been in a position of power and has been able to secure these preferential advantages. . . .

The restriction of free enterprise has also come principally from businessmen who have constantly sought to increase government regulation in their own interest, as in the case of tariffs, subsidies and prohibition of price-cutting on trademarked items.

In fact, the interests of businessmen have changed, to a considerable extent, from efficiency in production to efficiency in public manipulation, including manipulation of the government for the attainment of preferential advantages. . . . But the most significant result of the violations of the antitrust laws by large business concerns is that they have made our system of free competition and free enterprise unworkable. We no longer have competition as a regulator of economic processes; we have not substituted efficient government regulation. We cannot go back to competition. We must go forward to some new system—perhaps communism, perhaps co-operativism, perhaps much more complete governmental regulation than we now have. I don't know what lies ahead of us and am not particularly concerned, but I do know that what was a fairly efficient system has been destroyed by the illegal behavior of Big Business.[57]

One can, then, take these various behaviors of the corporations, owned 80 per cent by 1.6 per cent of the populace, in one of two ways. If the corporate men and their principals are struggling to undermine the political system of 1789, the one established by the Founding Fathers, in order to achieve a new one nearer their heart's desire, they may be looked upon as political engineers and (at least from the point of view of the big property interests) as admirable men such as Professor Nevins finds Rockefeller to have been. But, on the other hand, if the system of 1789 is the good one, and to be defended (as in my own prejudice I suppose it generally to be), then the corporate men stand before history as convicted habitual criminals, true subversives and enemies of established society.

In any event, returning to our initial inquiry, in looking for criminals in the business system one need not look for denizens from the underworld who have wormed their way in. There is, furthermore, no concrete evidence that underworld figures have done so, although anyone may buy stock in the open market. The big criminals consist of the ordinary corporations and their officers—agents and instrumentalities of the rich—and this is a fact repeatedly certified by the federal courts and the quasi-judicial tribunals of the United States of America.

We must confess, then, to failure in the attempt to find members or agents of any Mafia, Cosa Nostra or underworld syndicate of any kind high in the business world, although the established entrepreneurs, securely installed, give a lusty account of themselves in the matter of lawbreaking. Comparatively they make Mafias and Crime Syndicates look like pushcart operations.

Four ❧

THE INHERITORS: I

Large sums and wealthy individuals have been scrutinized for two chapters, but the concentrated core of private American wealth is yet to be examined. This chapter reports the findings of such an examination.

Private wealth acquired by new entrepreneurs, new in the sense of first showing themselves since World War II or even World War I, does not amount to much relatively, as we have observed. The conclusion is evident: Although there are indeed new fortunes large and small, either post-1918 or post-1945, they are neither numerous, of unusual amplitude nor especially potent in politico-economic affairs. With the exception of the Kennedy fortune, none of the later fortunes has played a prominent role in public affairs, and the political activities of the Kennedys have not been a consequence of their financial interests. The Kennedys were political long before they had money, though money has proved to be a fortuitous aid to their political inclinations. Except for Joseph P., the Kennedys—grandfathers and grandsons—have all been political rather than pecuniary men.

Nearly all the current large incomes, those exceeding $1 million, $500,000 or even $100,000 or $50,000 a year, are derived in fact from *old* property accumulations, by inheritors—that is, by people who never did whatever one is required to do, approved or disapproved, creative or non-creative, in order to assemble a fortune. And, it would appear, no amount of dedicated entrepreneurial effort by newcomers can place them in the financial class of the inheritors.

Some 2,000 to 3,000 incomes, more or less, in the range of $50,000 to $500,000 (a very few higher) accrue to salaried corporation executives, the stewards and overseers of vast industrial domains for the very rich.

These men came into these revenues rather late in life, in their late forties and fifties mostly, and face early retirement from the scene. Few are heavily propertied. Independent small businessmen—a small enterprise being generally accepted now by connoisseurs as one with assets below $50 million—account for perhaps the same number of such incomes.

A considerably smaller number accrue to a scattering of popular entertainers and athletes, whose earning power usually diminishes steeply with the fading of their youth. Very few large incomes, contrary to popular supposition, accrue to inventors. None whatever, as the record clearly shows, accrue to scientists, scholars and trained professionals of various kinds; only a handful to highly specialized medical doctors working mainly for the propertied class, and to an occasional executive engineer. Top-rank military officers are paid meagerly, although some manage to find their way to the tag-end of the corporate gravy train for their few years remaining after official retirement. In brief, few members of the most highly trained professional classes even late in life receive incomes approaching the level of $50,000—or even $30,000. They are, income-wise, strictly menials, necessary technicians on the economic plantation. In the world's most opulent economy they, together with the less skilled bulk of the populace, must count their pennies in an economy of widespread personal scarcity.

Increases in the number of large incomes paralleling cyclical increases in prices and quickened economic activity therefore do not indicate, as naive financial observers conclude, that new fortunes are being made right and left. They signify only that established accumulations are profiting by the cyclical trend. Whether the income is high or low the property always remains, ready to show its truly magnificent earning power in upward cyclical phases, showing its brute staying power in downward slides.

In the combined *Fortune, Saturday Evening Post* and *New York Times* roundups of the new and established big-wealthy it turned out that about half of the seventy-five-plus given close scrutiny are new-wealthy and the other half old-wealthy. The situation, on the face of it, seems to be about half-and-half, evenly balanced as between the old and the new. This implication tacitly conveyed by the manner in which *Fortune* in particular presented its list in 1957 will be flatly challenged here, where it will be shown that even granting the new-wealthy all that *Fortune* claimed for them, they represent little more than a shadow on the surface of a deep, silent and generally unsuspected pool. This pool consists simply of the estates, including trust funds, shown to view by Professor Lampman, cited in Chapter I.

These estates, the owners comprising 1.6 per cent of the adult population as of 1953 (the percentage is the same or smaller now owing to the disproportionate increase in the nonpropertied through the higher postwar birth rate) that held $60,000 or more of revenue-producing assets, constitute the nearly absolute bulk of the holdings of the propertied class. But more than half of this class own no more than $125,000 each of assets, as Lampman points out, bringing down to 0.8 per cent those in the group holding more than $125,000 of assets. And most of this 0.8 per cent can be considered only moderately wealthy, what is usually meant by the sayings "well fixed" or "comfortably off."

The *Fortune* rainbow of individual inheritors holding $75 million or more of assets will now be presented but there will, first, be some further demurrer leveled against its categorization of new-wealthy and old-wealthy. It will be recalled that, according to the Lampman findings, there were 27,000 owners of at least $1 million as of 1953, so the *Fortune* list represents only a very small sample off the top. There were about 90,000 such as of 1967 owing largely to the rise in market values.

As a beginning, the name of J. Paul Getty will be placed now on the list of inheritors, where it properly belongs; he was placed on the list in Chapter II only to appease, temporarily, those who suppose on the basis of public reports that he made the grade strictly on his own. One other name will be included among the inheritors that *Fortune* classified as new-wealthy; reasons for the reclassification will be given and the reader may judge for himself as between *Fortune* and this writer.

The name added to the list, termed one of the new-wealthy by *Fortune*, is that of Godfrey L. Cabot of Boston, who died in 1962 at 101. He was a member of the famous Cabot family of Boston (who proverbially speak only to God) that was founded by Jean Cabot or Chabot who came to America in 1700 from the Anglo-French island of Jersey. Cabot soon became one of the large landowners of the new colonies, and the family ever since has been distinguished by propertied business and professional men, diplomats and political figures. It and the allied Lowell and various other Boston families have been "in the money" all along, some from earlier than Paul Revere's ride.

Godfrey Cabot, after his graduation from Harvard in 1882 and some study abroad, went to western Pennsylvania where he engaged in the new oil and gas business and soon, responding to his chemist's training, became interested in carbon black, a byproduct of natural gas that to others was plain soot. He invested money, of which he had more than a

INHERITED WEALTH-HOLDERS, 1957

	Stated Net Worth (millions)	Financial Activity	Age in 1957	Schooling	Living Children
1. J. Paul Getty London	$700–$1,000	Executive Getty Oil Co.	65	Oxford (B.A.)	5
2. Mrs. Mellon Bruce (Ailsa Mellon) New York	$400–$700	Rentier			2
3. Paul Mellon Upperville, Virginia	$400–$700	Director Mellon National Bank, etc.	50	Yale (A.B.) Cambridge (A.B.)	2
4. Richard K. Mellon Pittsburgh	$400–$700	Executive Alcoa, Gulf Oil, etc.	58	Attended Princeton	4
5. Mrs. Alan M. Scaife* (Sarah Mellon) (Died, 1965)	$400–$700	Rentier	54		2
6. John D. Rockefeller, Jr. (Died, 1960)	$400–$700	Standard Oil Group Stockholder	83	Brown (A.B.)	6
7. Irénée du Pont (Died, 1963)	$200–$400	Executive E. I. du Pont, General Motors	81	M.I.T. (B.S., M.S.)	8
8. William du Pont Wilmington	$200–$400	President Delaware Trust Co.	61		5

INHERITED WEALTH-HOLDERS, 1957 (Continued)

	Stated Net Worth (millions)	Financial Activity	Age in 1957	Schooling	Living Children
9. Mrs. Frederick Guest* (Amy Phipps) Palm Beach	$200–$400	Rentier			
10. Howard Hughes Houston	$200–$400	Executive Hughes Tool Co.	52	Attended Caltech	None
11. Vincent Astor New York (Died, 1960)	$100–$200	Real estate owner	66	Attended Harvard	None
12. Lammot du Pont Copeland Wilmington	$100–$200	Executive E. I. du Pont General Motors	52	Harvard (B.S.)	3
13. Mrs. Alfred I. du Pont	$100–$200	Company Director	N.A.	Attended Longwood College	None listed
14. Mrs. Edsel Ford* Detroit	$100–$200	Rentier			4
15. Doris Duke* New York	$100–$200	Rentier			
16. Amory Houghton Ex-Ambassador to France	$100–$200	Corning Glass	58	Harvard (A.B.)	5
17. Arthur A. Houghton, Jr. New York	$100–$200	Corning Glass		Attended Harvard	4
18. Roy Arthur Hunt	$100–$200	Executive Alcoa	76	Yale (A.B.)	4

INHERITED WEALTH-HOLDERS, 1957 (Continued)

	Stated Net Worth (millions)	Financial Activity	Age in 1957	Schooling	Living Children
19. Mrs. Jean Mauze* (Abby Rockefeller)	$100–$200	Rentier			
20. Mrs. Chauncey McCormick* (Marion Deering) Chicago	$100–$200	Rentier			
21. Mrs. Charles Payson (Joan Whitney)	$100–$200	Rentier	54	Attended Barnard	4
22. John Hay Whitney Ex-Ambassador to Britain New York	$100–$200	Publisher Investor	53	Attended Oxford Yale	2
23. David Rockefeller	$100–$200	Executive Chase Bank Standard Oil	42	Harvard (B.S.) Chicago (Ph.D.)	6
24. John D. Rockefeller III New York	$100–$200	Chairman Rockefeller Bros. Fund	51	Princeton (B.S.)	4
25. Laurance Rockefeller New York	$100–$200	Executive Rockefeller interests	47	Princeton (A.B.)	4
26. Winthrop Rockefeller Governor, Arkansas	$100–$200	Rockefeller interests Land development	45	Attended Yale	1
27. Nelson A. Rockefeller Governor, New York	$100–$200	Government	49	Dartmouth (A.B.)	6
28. John Nicholas Brown Newport	$75–$100	Real estate operator	57	Harvard (A.B.)	

INHERITED WEALTH-HOLDERS, 1957 (Continued)

	Stated Net Worth (millions)	Financial Activity	Age in 1957	Schooling	Living Children
29. Godfrey L. Cabot (Died, 1962)	$75–$100	Chairman Godfrey L. Cabot, Inc. Chemicals	96	Harvard (A.B.)	5
30. Mrs. Horace Dodge, Sr.* Palm Beach	$75–$100	Rentier			3
31. John T. Dorrance, Jr. Philadelphia	$75–$100	Beneficiary Campbell Soup Trust	38	Princeton (A.B.)	2
32. Benson Ford Detroit	$75–$100	Ford Motors Vice President	38	Attended Princeton	2
33. Henry Ford II Detroit	$75–$100	Ford Motors Chairman	40	Attended Yale	2
34. William C. Ford Detroit	$75–$100	Ford Motors Vice President	27	Yale (B.S.)	2
35. W. Averell Harriman New York	$75–$100	Government service, investments	66	Yale (A.B.)	2
36. Robert Kleberg, Jr. King Ranch, Texas	$75–$100	Cattle, oil	61	Attended University of Wisconsin	1
37. John M. Olin Alton, Illinois	$75–$100	Executive Olin Mathieson Chemicals	65	Cornell (B.S.)	3
38. Spencer T. Olin Alton, Illinois	$75–$100	Executive Olin Mathieson Chemicals	57	Cornell (M.E.)	4

INHERITED WEALTH-HOLDERS, 1957 (Continued)

	Stated Net Worth (millions)	Financial Activity	Age in 1957	Schooling	Living Children
39. J. Howard Pew Philadelphia	$75–$100	Executive Sun Oil Co.	75	Attended M.I.T.	None listed
40. Joseph N. Pew, Jr.	$75–$100	Executive Sun Oil Co.	71	Cornell (M.E.)	4
41. Mrs. M. Merriweather Post Washington, D.C.	$75–$100	Director General Foods	70	Finishing School	3
42. Robert Woodruff Atlanta	$75–$100	Executive Coca-Cola, etc.	68	Attended Emory	

* Not listed in *Who's Who*, 1956–57, 1964–65.

little, in carbon black plants (he soon owned ten), and in natural gas pipelines. He could well be called "Cabot the Carbon Black King." Carbon black has many uses in the chemical industry, in which Cabot and a brother were long leading figures. Cabot, in short, was a moneyed investor-entrepreneur, as good as they come, and ran his original stake up to a level recently worthy of notice from *Fortune*. He clearly classifies as an inheritor, albeit personally more creative than most. All the extant Cabots are inheritors.[1]

An Incomplete List

There is no way to guarantee that this list of forty-two exhausts all individuals with inherited holdings, improved or unimproved, of $75 million or more. The list is probably incomplete even with the terms laid down by *Fortune*. Thus, not included on it was William Rand Kenan, who died July 28, 1965, aged ninety-three, leaving an estate for probate tentatively estimated at $100 million. He was a founder of the Union Carbide Company.[2] That the Kenans were no financial midgets is attested by the fact that William Rand Kenan, Jr., is at present chairman of the board of the Niagara County National Bank and Trust Company; president of the Peninsular and Occidental Steamship Company, the Florida East Coast Railway Company, the Florida East Coast Hotel Company, the Florida East Coast Car Ferry Company, the Model Land Company, Perrine Grant Land Company, West Palm Beach Water Company, Caroline Apartment Company and Western Block Company; and a director of various other companies including the Florida Power and Light Company. So many presidencies suggest large personal holdings.

Just how many similar big fish may have escaped our dragnet one cannot be sure. The big-wealthy Rosenwalds of Sears, Roebuck were omitted. We have already seen how J. Paul Getty moved along in shadowy anonymity most of his life. The Mellon family, already astronomically rich, was nationally unknown until Andrew Mellon, his name never before printed by the *New York Times*, was made secretary of the treasury by President Warren G. Harding. (This was much like making Casanova headmaster of a school for young ladies, as the sequel showed. For Mellon dished out with a lavish hand huge unexpected tax rebates to the surprised rich and, as a distiller himself, did not prevent distillers' stocks from inundating the Volstead Act, which was under his official jurisdiction.)

Although the list, then, is not exhaustive, it may be taken as tentatively indicative of those who in 1957 individually possessed inherited wealth in excess of $75 million. But the prime value of the list is that it points the way to far larger concentrations of wealth that *Fortune* chose to ignore.

Family Holdings: The Key

It is noticeable that most of these individuals belong to a financially prominent family, their fortunes a slice from a single source. As the holdings are now vested in individual names they each, from one defensible point of view, hold a single fortune. Generically, however, their family-derived holdings together constitute a single fortune. And without the family holdings they would amount to little financially.

On a generic basis, indeed, many clusters of individually inherited fortunes, no single one as large as $75 million, do in fact exceed some of the strictly individual large ones such as that of Howard Hughes. For five related and cooperating persons holding a mere $50 million each from a single source—and there are many in this pattern—would represent a generic fortune of $250 million.

What I term super-wealth is prominently, although not completely, represented on this list. Super-wealth simply consists of a very large generic fortune that may or may not be split into several parts. It has other characteristics: First, it generally controls and revolves around one or more important banks. It absolutely controls or has a controlling ownership stake in from one to three or more of the largest industrial corporations. It has established and controls through the family one to three or four or more super-foundations designed to achieve a variety of stated worthy purposes as well as confer vast industrial control through stock ownership and extend patronage-influence over wide areas. It has established or principally supports one or several major universities or leading polytechnic institutes. It is a constant heavy political contributor, invariably to the Republican Party, the political projection of super-wealth. It has extremely heavy property holdings abroad so that national, foreign and military policy is of particular interest to it. And it has vast indirect popular cultural influence because of the huge amount of advertising its corporations place in the mass media.

Critics mistakenly blame a shadowy entity called "Madison Avenue" for the culturally stultifying quality as well as intrusiveness of most advertising. But here it should be noticed that Madison Avenue can produce only what is approved by its clients, the big corporations. If these latter ordered Elizabethan verse, Greek drama and great pictorial art, Madison Avenue would supply them with alacrity.

Beyond this, the dependence upon corporate advertising of the mass media—newspapers, magazines, radio and television—makes them editorially subservient, without in any way being prompted, to points of view known or thought to be favored by the big property owners. Sometimes, of course, as the record abundantly shows, they have been prompted and even coerced to alter attitudes. But the willing subservience shows itself most generally, apart from specific acts of omission or commission, in an easy blandness on the part of the mass media toward serious social problems. These are all treated, when treated at all, as part of a diverting kaleidoscopic spectacle, the modern Roman circus of tele-communication. As Professor J. Kenneth Galbraith aptly remarked, in the United States it is a case of the bland leading the bland. No doubt it would be bad for trade if there was serious stress on the problematic side of affairs. It would disturb "confidence."

On this *Fortune* list, valuable in its way, we find among the super-wealthy, among others less prominent, the Du Ponts, Mellons, Rockefellers and Fords as well as the Pews. The primary but not exclusive sources of their wealth have been E. I. du Pont de Nemours and Company, the Aluminum Corporation of America, the Standard Oil group of companies and the Ford Motor Company. Each of these companies has many times been formally adjudicated in violation of the laws, the first three repeatedly named in crucial successful prosecutions charging vast monopolies. Aluminum, Standard Oil and Du Pont achieved their positions precisely through monopoly, as formally determined by the courts.

The Du Pont Dynasty

The combined wealth of four Du Ponts, as given by *Fortune*, was minimally $600 million and at a maximum stood at $1.2 billion. But here, it becomes clearly evident, it is possible to understate greatly the size of a generic fortune by singling out for notice only a few of its most prominent representatives.

For there are many additional wealthy, *soigné* Du Ponts. Perhaps they do not individually hold as much as $75 million, but many of them out of a total group (exceeding 1,600 persons descended from Pierre-Samuel du Pont [1739–1817]) hold somewhat lesser fortunes that stem directly or indirectly from the central Du Pont financial complex. Not included on the *Fortune* list were Alexis Felix du Pont, Jr., born 1905; Alfred Rhett du Pont, born 1907; Alfred Victor du Pont, born 1900; Edmond du Pont, born 1906; Henry B. du Pont, born 1898; Henry Francis du Pont, born 1880; Pierre S. du Pont III, born 1911; and a variety of active highly pecunious Du Ponts bearing the Du Pont name or alien names brought into the golden dynastic circle through exogamous marriages of Du Pont women. Endogamous marriages among the Du Ponts, however, have been frequent.

The financially elite among the Du Ponts number about 250 "and most of the family's riches are in their hands."[3] There are, then, 250 Big Du Ponts and many Little Du Ponts.

The generic Du Pont fortune appears to be the largest, now, of the four here under scrutiny. Not only is the Du Pont company the oldest of them, but as a prolific clan the Du Ponts have included many individual entrepreneurs, none perhaps individually as outstanding as Rockefeller or Ford but collectively more persistent. Again, as an ordnance enterprise in an era of big wars Du Pont grew astronomically, attaining its biggest growth in World War I, and thus provided the sinews for branching out into at least four of the biggest modern industries: chemicals, automobiles, oil and rubber. It is the American Krupp.

But, the question should be raised, is any violence being done the facts in examining a generic fortune rather than its individual slivers? The picture would indeed be distorted if the individual heirs had gone their separate ways and an analyst nevertheless insisted upon treating them collectively. But the Du Ponts, as well as others, have not gone their separate ways with their inheritances; they have, despite intra-family feuds, acted as a collectivity. In Note 2, Chapter II, I mentioned a C. Wright Mills reference to an earlier work of mine in which he says chidingly that I once generalized "cousinhood *only*" into political and economic power. In the Du Ponts, however, we have a literal, closely cohering financial and political cousinhood, as in the case of the Mellons. In the case of the Fords and Rockefellers we have, staying within these terms, brotherhoods.

The Du Pont cousinhood coheres, tightly, through a network of family holding companies and trust funds which, under a unified concentrated family management, gives a single, unified thrust to the family enterprises. There is danger of distortion in treating any single one of this cousinhood, financially, as an individual. It is misleading because it shows only a few facets on top of the huge iceberg, neglects the concealed major portion below the surface.

The precise size of the generic Du Pont fortune would be difficult to determine. But the Christiana Securities Company alone, largest of the family holding companies, at the end of 1964 held investments valued by itself at $3.271 billion in E. I. du Pont de Nemours, the Wilmington Trust Company, the Wilmington *News-Journal* and the Hercules Powder Company.[4] This, be it noted, was after E. I. du Pont had divested itself of sixty-three million shares of General Motors common, in which others than the Du Ponts, of course, had some equity.

The Christiana portion of this GM distribution was 18,247,283 shares,[5] worth $1.788 billion at a closing price of $98 a share for 1964. At that time the whole original E. I. du Pont GM block had a market value of $6.174 billion.

E. I. du Pont paid an average price of $2.09 a share for this stock, according to Senator Harrison A. Williams, Jr., of New Jersey, or $131,670,-000 in all.[6]

With 10,026 formally registered separate common stockholders at the end of 1964, Christiana has stockholders other than Du Ponts and their in-laws; these other stockholders are mainly company officers and employees. But the extent of Du Pont family participation in Christiana before World War II, according to a government investigation of dominant owners of the 200 largest nonfinancial corporations, was 74 per cent.[7]

Assuming that the financial core of the Du Pont family still held 44 per cent of E. I. du Pont de Nemours stock (as per the TNEC study), the recent record stands approximately as follows:

	Market Value Dec. 31, 1961	Market Value Dec. 31, 1964
44 per cent family interest in 45,994,520 E. I. du Pont shares at 247½ for end 1961, 241¾ for end 1964	$5,001,257,472	$4,892,433,792
44 per cent family interest in 63 million General Motors shares divested by E. I. du Pont at 1964 closing price of 98. (Individual Du Ponts holding GM not included)		$2,716,560,000
Christiana Securities direct holding in GM (added since TNEC study) at 57⅞ for end 1961, 98 a share for end 1964	30,962,102	52,430,000
Totals for above	$5,032,219,574	$7,661,423,792

Less: Sales of 1,050,000 shares GM by Christiana Securities for taxes and cost of distribution at average price of about 62		62,193,750
Corrected totals	$5,032,219,574	$7,599,230,042
Less: Further planned sale of 457,312 GM shares by Christiana at beginning of 1965 at estimated minimal price of 100		45,731,200
Revised totals	$5,032,219,574	$7,553,498,842
Add: 10.5 per cent Du Pont interest in U.S. Rubber Co., as shown by TNEC study held by individuals and the Du Pont-owned Rubber Securities Company	$ 34,316,836	$ 38,232,179
Add: Holdings of Christiana Securities other than E. I. du Pont and General Motors		$ 37,749,136
Add: Various assorted individual investments by Du Ponts and ownership in extensive landed estates	?	?
Total		$7,629,480,000 plus

The figure of $7.629 billion for 1964, as indicated above, is an approximation, but one close to the figures available. In view of the many individual Du Pont investments not included—for various of the Du Ponts have long branched into other fields—it is beyond doubt an understatement.

On what grounds can one assume that the family investment in E. I. du Pont de Nemours remained at 44 per cent? First, the investment of this company in General Motors itself was not diminished. Second, since the TNEC study, a new investment was made in General Motors by Christiana; whether this represented an increase in over-all General Motors holdings or a transfer from some other part of the Du Pont exchequer is not shown, but presumably it represented an enlarged investment. If anything, the family investment, through individuals, was increased since 1937, the date of the TNEC data. For the Du Ponts in the intervening years were in receipt of vast cash dividends. In the meantime, many of them had reduced their once-opulent and ultra-expensive scale of living. Unless they had, off the record, somehow disposed of large sums it would seem inevitable that their investment position was enlarged. Their foundations did not, in the meantime, show any large new accretion of funds.

It is true that the family participation in General Motors cannot be computed accurately at the figure given for the end of 1964 even after allowing for the sales of GM by Christiana because the Du Pont trust funds were also required to sell whatever GM they received in the distribution. But the equivalent value in money, depending upon what point in the rising market GM was sold, would remain in Du Pont hands.

Taking into consideration various factors such as these, and others, the entire family holding should be at least $7.629 billion, rather than the vague recent estimate of $3 billion by a family historian.[8]

I conclude, therefore, that the financially cohesive Du Pont family is capable of throwing something around a $7.5-billion "punch" at any time in the American political-economy on the present price level. Its members should not, despite their partial setback in General Motors, be looked upon as a miscellaneous collection of financial tabby cats. The individual Du Ponts, it should be noticed, retain their GM holdings, constituting the largest identifiable block in General Motors stock.

The Du Ponts have additionally established a string of at least eighteen foundations,[9] the most recent assets of which are reported by the *Foundation Directory, 1964*, at an aggregate of $148,046,401. These foundations are Bredin, Carpenter, Chichester du Pont, Copeland Andelot, Crestlea, Good Samaritan, Irénée du Pont, Jr., Eleutherian Mills-Hagley, Kraemer, Lalor, Lesesne, Longwood, Nemours, Rencourt, Sharp, Theano, Welfare and Winterthur.

The largest of these, Longwood and Winterthur, with combined assets of $122,559,001, are largely devoted to maintaining in all their splendor former Du Pont estates as public museums and botanical gardens.[10] The estates, thus dedicated to public uses, were not required to pay *ad valorem* inheritance taxes.

But the invested voting power of these assets, funneled through banks and trustees, provides some additional Du Pont strength in politico-economic decision-making.

Even if one were able to pinpoint the value of the family holdings at $7.629 billion this would not be especially significant. The big fortunes rise and fall in value with the economy so that in one decade their values are up and in another down. But the significant fact is that throughout economic changes the big fortunes, and the companies underlying them, outperform expansions of the economy. Put another way, more and more of the economy is constantly being preempted by fewer and fewer generic interests even though through inheritance the generic property income is distributed among a greater number of individuals. There are, in brief, more Du Ponts, Rockefellers, Mellons and their like today than there were in 1900. But they each share in much enlarged central stakes.

The divestiture of General Motors stock took place after the United States Supreme Court ordered it upon finding E. I. du Pont de Nemours and Company guilty of violating Section 7 of the Clayton Act, which forbids any stock acquisition whose effect "may be substantially to lessen competition or tend to create a monopoly." This case of closing the barn door after it had been wide open for more than thirty years began in 1949 under President Harry Truman. The Supreme Court, overruling a lower court, found that Du Pont's ownership of 23 per cent of GM, which it controlled, placed it in a favored market position in the sale of automobile finishes and fabrics, to the detriment of competitors. GM, in fact, was a captive customer. As the *New York Times* incidentally reported, "Few if any large companies have been the subject of so many anti-trust suits as du Pont."[11] Since 1939 nineteen have been counted.

But Du Pont holdings, as indicated, are by no means all channeled through Christiana Securities. During the GM proceedings it was reported to the court, for example, that William du Pont, Jr., personally owned 1,269,788 shares of E. I. du Pont de Nemours. And, unless the family investment pattern has changed greatly since the TNEC study, other Du Ponts are heavy individual holders in E. I. du Pont de Nemours and other companies.

The TNEC study showed the following individual Du Ponts directly holding stock in E. I. du Pont de Nemours: Pierre S.; Eugene; Archibald; M. L.; H. F.; Eugene E.; Ernest; trustees for Philip F.; trustees for Elizabeth B.; trustees on behalf of William du Pont, Jr., and Mrs. Marion du Pont Scott; and Charles Copeland. This group held 5.75 per cent.[12]

One member of the family and the Broseco Corporation, another family holding company, held stock directly in General Motors, substantial even by Du Pont standards.[13] A family trust held much more.

But twenty-two other Du Ponts, none named above, held stock in the Delaware Realty and Investment Company (since absorbed by Christiana Securities), which in turn held 2.75 per cent of E. I. du Pont de Nemours stock.

Thirty-nine other Du Ponts, none named above or included in the Delaware Realty group, held stock in Almours Securities, Inc. (since dissolved), which held 5.24 per cent of E. I. du Pont de Nemours stock as well as an interest in the Mid-Continent Petroleum Corporation.[14]

The TNEC study uncovered eight Du Pont family securities holding companies[15] and seven separate trust funds.[16] This variety of financial instruments was in part at least the residue of earlier feuds and financial squabbles in the family with charges of individual overreaching and tricky dealing aired in public. In recent decades most of these quarrels appear to have been composed in favor of consolidating family interests.

The government in its General Motors case held that the Du Ponts were a "cohesive group of at least 75 persons." But it named 184 members of the Du Pont family in its complaint.

Spokesman for the Du Ponts, after the GM decision was given, said that GM stockholders closely affiliated with the Du Pont management would sell an additional three million shares of General Motors.[17]

The TNEC study showed that individual Du Ponts, their family holding companies and/or their trust funds held stock in many other companies. The largest of these additional stockholdings was in the giant United States Rubber Company, which the Du Ponts in effect controlled. Here the Rubber Securities Company, a Du Pont family company, and seven individual Du Ponts owned 10.5 per cent and constituted the largest cohesive stockholding group. The continued presence of the Du Pont interest in the United States Rubber Company as of 1965 is signaled by the presence on the board of directors of J. S. Dean, president and director of the Nemours Corporation and a director and member of the executive committee of the Wilmington Trust Company, and of George P. Edwards, chairman of the Wilmington Trust Company. Other companies in which various of the Du Ponts, their family companies and/or trust funds held smaller ownership positions were the American Sugar Refining Company, the Mid-Continent Petroleum Corporation, Phillips Petroleum Company and the United Fruit Company. At various times they have been interested in still other companies.[18]

Du Ponts are also found in other pecuniary pastures. Thus Edmond and A. Rhett du Pont, sons of Francis I. du Pont, a member of the reorganized main corporation in 1903, have independently developed (using family-derived money) Francis I. du Pont and Company into the second largest brokerage house in the United States, with branches at home and abroad. Du Pont in-laws are the chief partners of the highly rated brokerage house of Laird, Bissell and Meeds. Still other Du Ponts, outside the main financial line, have established themselves in a variety of varyingly lucrative enterprises large and small.[19]

E. I. du Pont de Nemours and Company, since its beginning in 1803 with an initial capital of some $36,000, is now one of the world's industrial giants. Because, despite some recent adverse publicity, its history is not nearly as well known as that of the Standard Oil Company or the Ford Motor Company, highlights of its rise may provide insight here into some ways large fortunes are made.

After early difficulties the company became successful because its French-trained owners made a better gunpowder. Helped along by the War of 1812, the company was made prosperous by the Civil War.

In 1872, with the market glutted by postwar surplus powder, the Du Ponts organized other leading powdermakers and themselves into the Gunpowder Trade Association, which dictated prices and ruled the market for hunting and blasting powder with an iron hand. Hostile competitors were undersold until they capitulated or went out of business, when prices would again be raised. This enterprise, later known as "The Powder Trust," continued without challenge into the first decade of the twentieth century.[20]

Under one-man rule for many years and with wars scarce, by 1902 the company seemed to be losing ground and its weary chief owners thought of selling it to outsiders. But one, Alfred I., the "Savior of the Du Ponts," objected and, bringing to the fore younger cousins T. Coleman of the Kentucky branch of the family, and Pierre S., made a purchase offer that was accepted. The price was $15,360,000, more than $3,000,000 above what it had been hoped to get from outsiders. The new owners soon found, moreover, that the property was worth more than $24 million. Best of all, the new owners put up no cash but gave $12 million of 4 per cent notes plus $3,360,000 in stock of a new company just founded, a company purely on paper. This company, without assets, took over the old company. Only incorporation expenses of $2,100 were paid out by the three up-and-coming cousins.

As part of a feud that in time developed, Alfred I. was later forced out of the management by T. Coleman and Pierre S. Meanwhile, Pierre had brought in his brothers Lammot and Irénée and, after the withdrawal of Coleman, these three ran the show. In a deal from which Alfred I. was excluded, Pierre, Lammot and Irénée purchased the shares of T. Coleman in 1915 with money borrowed from J. P. Morgan and Company. Furiously Alfred I. charged that Pierre had used the standing of the company to borrow for the purchase and freeze him out. He brought suit against Pierre but lost. He was never reconciled.

Although the power play by Pierre and his brothers was not illegal it seemed—and with this Alfred I. would agree—very much like self-centered overreaching, not against the outside *hoi polloi*, always fair game, but against an original sponsor and benefactor—an all-too-familiar story on the power levels of world history.

The company in the meantime had blossomed unbelievably under T. Coleman's merger policy and it stood on the threshold of its present eminence. The diverse members of "The Powder Trust" had now, one by one, been bought up or otherwise absorbed by Du Pont.

"With breathtaking speed, companies were merged into the parent Du Pont corporation. By 1906, sixty-four corporations had been dissolved. A year later, Du Pont was producing from sixty-four to seventy-four per cent of the total national output of each of five types of explosives, and one hundred per cent of the privately produced smokeless military powder. Only the Standard Oil trust was as well organized."[21]

In 1907 complaints finally led the government to file languid suit against the company for violation of the Sherman Act, and after five years it was absent-mindedly convicted. Since 1903, when its investment was valued at a maximum of $36 million, it had earned nearly $45 million.[22]

But because the companies absorbed by Du Pont had been dissolved, the court was in a mild quandary about how to separate the blend. It asked the government and the company, as partners in the minuet, to work out a plan of reorganization. Alfred I. went to see President William Howard Taft.

"At the White House, Alfred insisted that it would be to the advantage of the government and of the nation as a whole for du Pont to retain its one hundred percent monopoly of smokeless military powder: du Ponts were aware that war might break out soon in Europe. When it was pointed out that du Pont had been found guilty of violating the law, Alfred turned to Taft's Attorney General, George W. Wickersham, who was present, and reminded him that he had been du Pont's lawyer at the time the violations had taken place. If du Pont had broken the law, it was because the company had received bad legal counsel."[23]

At special court hearings a long procession of generals and admirals appeared to testify for the Du Ponts, contending that it was absolutely vital to national security that Du Pont retain its monopoly of smokeless military powder.

"Unbelievably," says the not unsympathetic but frank and independent family historian, "the court accepted these arguments. To split up the military powder business among several competing companies would do damage to the close co-operation between du Pont and the government and thus jeopardize the security of the nation without any corresponding benefit to the public. Or so the court held in its final ruling in June, 1912. Thus du Pont was permitted to keep its one hundred percent monopoly of military powder."[24]

The less strategic powder divisions were placed in two new companies: the Atlas Powder Company and the Hercules Powder Company, the stocks and bonds of which were turned over to E. I. du Pont stockholders. The effect of the court order was merely to replace control of the new companies by the Du Pont company with control by the collective Du Pont family.[25]

But in 1942 E. I. du Pont de Nemours and five other companies, including Atlas and Hercules, were indicted in an antitrust suit and pleaded *nolo contendere,* automatically bringing a judgment of guilty. "Since the case was a criminal cause, no injunction was in order. Thus the only deterrent effect was the penalty."[26]

Substantially, however, "It is quite clear that the government lost the case," said Harvard economist Edward W. Proctor. "No permanent or even temporary restraint was placed on any of the practices of which the government complained. In fact, the companies calmly continued doing business the same way they had been doing it before the government brought suit. The case solved nothing—it really did not punish the law offenders nor did it alleviate the restraints on competition."[27]

As William H. A. Carr, the already-cited family historian, remarks, "This may not be as bad as it sounds. Proctor and other economists believe the wartime prosecution was politically motivated. Supporting this suspicion is the fact that the Department of Justice first tried to obtain an indictment in Norfolk, Virginia, but the grand jury there refused to return a true bill. Then the government took its evidence to Philadelphia, where another grand jury went along with Washington's demand for action."[28]

Actually, every proper prosecution or official act of any government official is politically motivated as an act in the management of the State (*polis*). The pejorative connotation that has become attached to the word "political" in popular American usage has developed owing to the frequent charge, usually made by anti-regulation business spokesmen, that questioned political acts are improper acts for personal advantage, which they may or may not be.

But whatever the motivation of the prosecutors, the companies did not deny the charges and the court made its decision on the basis of them. If the companies were indeed blameless, then the court itself became the partner in an improper action. And we are always faced with this alternative whenever it is argued that companies brought before the bar are being persecuted: If the companies are innocent, even when they plead guilty or no contest, then there is a grave fault in the American constitutional system. But the schools and leading privately owned agencies of public information all say the American constitutional system is excellent, the best in the world. The intelligent citizen, therefore, must feel not a little confused when he hears charges made of improper political motivation. If that is the kind of system we have, some will reasonably conclude, it ought to be changed in the interests of simple justice.

World War I saw the swift rise of E. I du Pont to industrial stardom. "Forty percent of the shells fired by the Allies were hurled from the cannon by du Pont explosives. At the same time, the company met fully one-half of America's domestic requirements for dynamite and black blasting powder."[29] Eighty-five per cent of production was explosives. In brief, without Du Pont the Allies could hardly have fought what has been appropriately called the most unnecessary big war in history.

At the same time the company's capital flooded upward from $83 million to $308 million on the basis of a wartime gross business of $1 billion. Net profits for four war years reached $237 million, of which $141 million were paid out in dividends. "Those dividends could be reckoned at four hundred and fifty-eight percent of the stock's par value."[30]

With $49 million of wartime profits not paid out in dividends, E. I. du Pont de Nemours bought its initial interest in General Motors Corporation, then the product of the merger of twenty-one independent automobile companies.[31] Du Pont soon took control.

German interests having been driven from the postwar domestic chemical field, where they had been entrenched, E. I. du Pont de Nemours branched into the general chemical field, in which it previously had only a small foothold. It did this not through some inherent scientific capability, as is sometimes suggested, but by buying up with wartime profits one independent chemical company after the other: Viscoloid Company, National Ammonia, Grasselli Chemicals, Krebs Pigment and Chemical, Capes-Viscose, Roessler and Hasslacher Chemical, Commercial Pigments, Newport Chemical, Remington Arms Company and others. Individual Du Ponts, now well supplied with funds, bought into North American Aviation, Bendix Aviation and United States Steel.[32] Provided with enough money, anyone could have done this.

Offered during World War II a cost-plus-fixed-fee contract to build atomic bomb plants for the Atomic Energy Commission, E. I. du Pont de Nemours, which alone had gathered to its capacious bosom the engineering facilities and personnel for such a gigantic task, set the fee at $1.

What led the company to make this resoundingly modest charge is said in the official history of the Atomic Energy Commission to have been the following considerations:

"The tremendous military potential of the atomic weapon posed a possible threat to the company's future public relations. The du Pont leadership had not forgotten the 'merchants of death' label slapped on the company during the Nye Committee investigations in the 1930's. Certainly it was clear that the company had not sought the assignment; but to keep the record straight, du Pont refused to accept any profit. The fixed fee was limited to one dollar. Any profits accruing from allowances for administrative overhead would be returned to the government. Walter S. Carpenter, Jr., the du Pont president, disavowed not only profits but also any intention of staying in the atomic bomb business after the war. In his opinion, the production of such weapons should be controlled exclusively by the government. The contract provided that any patent rights arising from the project would lie solely with the United States."[33]

And so we come to the present when the labyrinthine Du Pont enterprise, no longer specializing exclusively in the merchandisable means of death, is devoted to making thousands of peacetime products, what it calls "better things for better living through chemistry."

The Mellons

Four leading Mellons on the *Fortune* list are given a minimal combined worth of $1.6 billion and a maximum of $2.8 billion. As market values up to this writing have risen sharply, these figures now embody considerable understatement.

The Mellons are another close family group, with holdings concentrated as shown in the TNEC study in a broad group of leading companies: Aluminum Corporation of America, Gulf Oil Company, the Allis-Chalmers Manufacturing Company, the Bethlehem Steel Corporation, the General American Transportation Corporation, Jones and Laughlin Steel Corporation, Koppers United Company, Lone Star Gas Corporation, Niagara Hudson Power Corporation, Pittsburgh Coal Company, Pittsburgh Plate Glass Company, The Virginian Railway Company, Westinghouse Electric and Manufacturing Company and various others. Of this group the Mellons controlled Aluminum Corporation, Koppers United and Gulf Oil. Five Mellons held these interests directly and through two family holding companies, three closely held insurance and securities companies, six trust funds, one estate and one foundation.[34]

In Aluminum Corporation common stock the Mellons held 33.85 per cent; in the contingent voting preferred stock the family and its foundation held 24.98 per cent. In Gulf Oil Company the Mellon family and its personal companies owned 70.24 per cent of the common stock, an unusually large single family stake in so large an enterprise. The Mellons held 52.42 per cent of the common stock of Koppers United and 1.52 per cent of the contingent voting preferred.[35]

Applying the TNEC percentages of ownership at closing 1964 market prices the value of the Mellon holdings in the three leading companies alone would be:

7,127,725 shares of Aluminum Company common (33 per cent of outstanding 21,413,177 shares) at 61½	$ 438,970,087
164,477 shares Aluminum Company preferred (25 per cent of outstanding 659,909 shares) at median price of 85½ (1964 price range 83–88)	$ 9,128,468
72,579,487 shares Gulf Oil Corporation (70 per cent of outstanding 103,684,981 shares) at 58⅝	$4,254,972,426
1,166,567 common shares Koppers (52½ per cent of 2,222,032 outstanding shares) at 55⅜	$ 64,599,968
Other companies	?
Total	$4,767,669,949

This computation is made without considering the Mellon holding in the Mellon National Bank of Pittsburgh, not included in the TNEC study, and in various other banks and in many companies with Mellon participation as reported in the TNEC study. But although the preceding table shows the *pattern* of the family holdings in general, there have been shifts in Mellon holdings since the TNEC study, notably through the establishment of a series of foundations in the 1940's.

These foundations, whose holdings should not be necessarily considered as additions to those already indicated, are as follows:

	Date Founded	1962 Assets
The A. W. Mellon Educational and Charitable Trust (included in TNEC study)	1930	$ 24,197,042
Avalon Foundation, N.Y. (Mrs. Ailsa Mellon Bruce)	1940	$ 99,182,784

Sarah Mellon Scaife Foundation	1941	$ 20,098,157
Old Dominion Foundation, N.Y. (Paul Mellon)	1941	$ 65,082,139
Bollingen Foundation, N.Y. (Paul Mellon)	1945	$ 6,013,881
The (Richard K.) Mellon Foundation	1947	$ 82,028,250
The (Matthew T.) Mellon Foundation	1946	$ 160,775 (as of 1960)
Foundation Total		$296,763,028

Although the income and any capital distribution from these foundations must be used for legally prescribed public purposes, the capital investments, as long as they remain undistributed, represent Mellon voting power in industry. But the foundations established since 1940 do not, as comparison with the first tabulation shows, diminish by much the personal Mellon holdings of today when computed according to the TNEC pattern. The family, all lovers of the old-time capitalism will be cheered to note, does not appear to be dissipating its fortune in riotous charity.

Andrew Mellon (1885–1937) was himself an inheritor, the son of Thomas Mellon, a rich Pittsburgh private banker and the pre-Civil War Horatio Alger source of the family fortune. From his father's bank Andrew and his brother, Richard B., began branching out and initially acquired a commercial bank and an insurance company. It was a small beginning, with far greater deeds of financial derring-do to come.

The first really big Mellon opportunity came, however, when two metallurgists told Andrew in 1889 of a successful new process for smelting aluminum discovered by Charles M. Hall. In return for $250,000 credit with T. Mellon & Sons, the Pittsburgh Reduction Company, owner of the process, gave Mellon control of the company. It was common at the time for banks to demand a "piece of the action" in any promising enterprise that applied for loans, which is how Mellon and other bankers turned up with toothsome participations in so many burgeoning enterprises.[36] For these participations in many if not most cases, they paid nothing whatever but sat in their money-nets like intent spiders and let the flies walk in one by one.

The Mellon participation in Gulf Oil came about similarly. Anthony F. Luchich, a Yugoslav prospector, brought in the great Spindletop gusher in Texas in 1901, which quickly led to more oil than all the Pennsylvania fields had since 1859. Money was now needed to handle the flow and build pipelines, and Pittsburgh interests were appealed to. Among these were William Larimer Mellon, nephew of Andrew and himself an heir of Thomas Mellon. In the upshot there was formed the J. M. Guffey Petroleum Company, capitalized at $15 million. Andrew W. Mellon bought the prospector's interest for $400,000 and altogether put $4.5 million into the new company, of which Colonel J. M. Guffey, who had an interest in the Spindletop lease, was given the presidency, $1 million and a promise of $500,000 from future dividends. Andrew W. Mellon and his brother, Richard B., took 40 per cent of the stock and sold 60 per cent to six Pittsburgh capitalists.[37] Guffey Petroleum soon was renamed Gulf Oil. Guffey himself was dropped.

Mellon utilized the same technique again and again with other entrepreneurs who came to him for the means necessary to launch or tide over their enterprises.

The Aluminum Company was eventually judicially designated a monopoly but not until it had enjoyed a long charmed life. It repulsed a number of private suits under the Sherman Act early in the century and on a few occasions outmaneuvered the Federal Trade Commission, which could not prove its bone-deep belief that the company was engaging in unfair competition. In 1912, however, the Aluminum Company consented to a practically meaningless decree in an action brought by an unenthusiastic Department of Justice charging unfair trade practices.

Again in 1937 the Department of Justice brought suit, holding that the company held a 90 per cent monopoly. In 1945 the United States Court of Appeals, Second Circuit, concluded that the company indeed held prewar monopoly control of ingot production. But the court did not force the company to dispose of any plants pending disposition of government aluminum-making facilities built in wartime 1942–45.

During the war, with aluminum in short supply, Reynolds Metals Company with government encouragement began primary production, the first competitor in the field since 1893. After the war the government, bypassing Aluminum Company, offered its plants to 224 different companies—some of them large—and strangely found no buyers. Surplus Property Administrator W. Stuart Symington then accused Aluminum Company of blocking the surplus plant sale by its patent control. After denying this, Alcoa relinquished to the government its many patents, gobbled up during the years, thus throwing them open to free licensing.

Reynolds Metals now bought or leased various of the government plants created around these patents. Kaiser Aluminum, formed for the purpose, took over other government-built plants. Since then the Anaconda Copper Company and Revere Copper and Brass, Inc., have entered the lucrative field, with still others likely to come. The long Mellon monopoly in aluminum was finally broken, but not before the Mellons made millions from it. And the country is now for the first time well supplied with aluminum.

Who are the Mellons today? There are Paul Mellon, son of Andrew Mellon, director of the Mellon National Bank and various Mellon funds; his children, Timothy and Catherine Conover (Mrs. John W. Warner); Richard King Mellon, Jr., son of Richard Beatty Mellon, nephew of Andrew, director and officer of various leading Mellon enterprises; his children, Richard, Cassandra, Constance and Seward; Ailsa Mellon (Mrs. Mellon Bruce), daughter of Andrew and mother of Audrey Mellon Bruce; Sarah Mellon (Mrs. Alan M. Scaife, died 1965), daughter of Richard Beatty Mellon and mother of Richard Mellon Scaife, who is a director of the Mellon National Bank and of various Mellon funds and trusts; William Larimer Mellon, M.D., and others. By no means as numerous as the Du Ponts, the Mellons nevertheless constitute more than the glittering quartet named by *Fortune*.

The Rockefeller Monolith

Fortune, without mentioning Rockefeller guidance over huge foundation endowments, credited seven Rockefellers with a minimum combined holding in 1957 of $1 billion and a maximum of $1.9 billion. Although the Rockefeller name is now synonymous with extreme wealth it is probable (owing to its earlier head-on conflicts with the law and consequent attempts to propitiate an aroused public opinion by contributions to publicly approved activities) that the combined Rockefeller fortune today is below that of the Du Ponts, who apparently have not as yet felt it necessary to indulge in baroque endowment operations to appease public opinion. The concentrated Rockefeller financial punch, however, both because of controlled foundations and many personal trust funds, is demonstrably more than double the maximum weight indicated by *Fortune*; beyond this the Rockefellers have acquired considerable moral influence. To some small extent the larger figure I produce is attributable to the rise in market value between 1957 and 1964; but *Fortune* left a great deal out of its calculations.

The death of John D. Rockefeller, Jr., in 1960 provides us with a concrete case for checking on *Fortune's* estimate of inherited wealth. The probate of the Rockefeller will showed that *Fortune* was again astray (in this case very far astray) in estimating JDR, Jr., as personally worth $400–$700 million in 1957; the probate showed his holdings added up to no more than approximately $150 million.[38] For he had over the years, as it was announced, established trust funds for six children and twenty-two grandchildren.[39] From these trust funds the children receive only income, with the principal sums presumably accruing to the grandchildren. There is thus assured a steady future supply of well-propertied Rockefellers.

If it was not evident before this, it should be clearly evident now that *Fortune* had no confidential information and no special expertise in computing the value of the large fortunes, individual or collective. Sometimes its procedure produced acceptably accurate results; at other times it was far off the target. Its listing, however, provides a convenient springboard for getting more deeply into the basic data.

The JDR, Jr., estate paid virtually no inheritance taxes because it was left half to the widow and half to the Rockefeller Brothers Fund, a foundation. Under the inheritance-tax law as revised in 1948, over a presidential veto, half of any estate going to a spouse is nontaxable under what is pleasantly called the marital deduction. Who could be so disagreeable, except one hostile to marriage and possibly home, children and dogs as well, as to object to such a deduction? But the effect of this deduction was to more than halve inheritance taxes for married property holders, a vast majority. The greatest money benefit, obviously, accrued to the very largest property holders, and it was undoubtedly they who deviously pressed for the measure through their many staunch friends in Congress.

As the half of the Rockefeller estate left to the fraternal foundation was also nontaxable, the whole was nontaxable.

However, when, as and if the widow disposed of her trust fund, which she was empowered to do, it became estate-taxable (in lower brackets, to be sure, than if it were still part of the original whole estate). If left to charity it would be nontaxable. But if the widow made no disposition of the capital, it was all to accrue to JDR, Jr.'s, children, when it would be taxable as in the case of any noncharitable disposition.

For many years Rockefeller, Jr., son of the original self-made tycoon, had been prudently reducing his taxable estate by (1) establishing trust funds for members of his family and (2) allocating money to foundations controlled by the family. Thus, early in the 1930's he had begun transferring large holdings into trust funds for the children, according to the federal record.[40] As of December 18, 1934, when stock prices were abnormally low, two trusts for Abby Rockefeller were launched giving 2.13 per cent ownership of Standard Oil Company of California; one for John D. III giving .99 per cent ownership; and one for Nelson A. Rockefeller giving .92 per cent ownership—4.04 per cent in all. Similar trusts were set up at the same time for the same children in Standard Oil Company of New Jersey.[41] Later, as the will disclosed, trusts had been established for all six children and the twenty-two grandchildren. The family was now resting quietly in trust.

As a general pattern, the TNEC study disclosed that 30 per cent of the Rockefeller holdings were in foundations, 30 per cent in family trust funds and 40 per cent in the hands of individuals, a judiciously balanced diversification.[42] Trust fund holdings are now apparently higher, individual holdings lower.

There are reputed to be a large number of Rockefeller trust funds. According to the *Washington Daily News*, June 8, 1967, page 69, there may be as many as seventy-five family trust accounts "set up by John D, 'Junior,' for his six children and by those children for their 22 offspring. The later generation—known as the 'cousins'—have begun setting up trust accounts for their 44 children."

In pointing out the low taxability of the JDR, Jr., estate I do not intend to imply that some sort of impropriety was practiced. Rockefeller, Jr., acted according to the prescribed laws and like any prudentially motivated parent in making the best possible material provision for his children. My reason for stressing the tax-free status of his estate is only to counter the notion, widely spread by newspapers and right-wing demagogues, that the tax laws in general are breaking down, dispersing or seriously trimming property holdings of all kinds. The dominant effect of the tax laws actually (and not surprisingly in a society dominated by property holders with abundant money and patronage to dispense) is to preserve and solidify private property in general, especially big private property. The latter type, naturally, derives the most substantial benefits from the equal protection of the law which, as Anatole France remarked, majestically allows rich as well as poor to sleep under bridges.

There was the same sort of low-taxable estate left when Rockefeller, Sr., died in 1937. The probate disclosed that he had left a pitiful $25 million, of which state and federal taxes took about half; nearly all of the remainder was left to a granddaughter, Mrs. Margaret Strong de Cuevas, and her children and to the Rockefeller Institute for Medical Research.[43] The bulk of the fortune he had amassed through the original Standard Oil Trust had already been transferred to his son and to foundations. Whatever may have been transferred before 1914 was tax free; whatever may have been transferred between 1924 and 1930 bore the low tax rates of the Mellon era in government finance; whatever was transferred in the 1930's was at depression-low values.

In brief, the amount of inheritance taxes collected from John D. Rockefeller Sr. and Jr. has been virtually nil. And despite the continual references in the public prints to how taxes are breaking up big fortunes, the Rockefeller fortune, like the Du Pont, Mellon and many others assembled in the nineteenth century, is still intact, fully fleshed and going strong.

As *Fortune* was very much in error on the JDR, Jr., holding, there is no reason to suppose it was any more accurate in placing each of the six children in the broad $100–$200 million bracket. The surer procedure, it seems to me, is to ascertain as I have done before what the TNEC, under power of subpoena, found to be the pattern and percentage of total family holdings by individuals, trust funds, family holding companies and foundations, and to assume at least tentatively that this pattern and percentage still persist. When anyone argues (as some are bound to) that holdings in a company may have been altered, it should be pointed that such alteration would not seriously call this method into question. Whatever was sold in one place would be invested somewhere else—probably to better effect, as these large holdings are all under skillful professional supervision and tend to take maximum advantage of circumstances and to minimize disadvantages. New investments outperform old, as in the case of W. Averell Harriman's investment in Polaroid. As for the modest sums paid out in gift taxes it is standard trust doctrine that these can be recovered gradually out of the income of the trust. On top of all this, the big fortunes have an unending stream of dividends, the spending of which would wear anyone out and has indeed worn out some flamboyant spenders. Much of these dividends (after taxes) are reinvested, thus tending to increase the fortune.

The Rockefellers, like the Du Ponts and Mellons, could be relatively poorer today than they were at the end of 1937 (the date of the TNEC data for this phase of the inquiry) only if they had (1) sold substantial interests and hoarded the proceeds in uninvested cash or placed them in fixed-interest securities; (2) if they had burned or flung away the cash proceeds of investment sales; (3) if they had sold good investments and made bad investments; or (4) if they had given huge properties into the absolute ownership of others. As there is no evidence available that they did any of these things, we may dismiss the idea that their total vested interest is smaller, either absolutely or relatively, than it was at the end of 1937. It must, in fact, be larger owing to the steady receipt of big revenues and the normal use of skilled professional advisers. The TNEC percentages, carried up to the present, must be, if anything, understatements in the case of the Rockefellers as in the cases of the Du Ponts and Mellons.

It should be stressed that the TNEC study did not embrace all the holdings of these groups. It did not include holdings in strictly financial enterprises, such as banks and insurance companies, any real estate or any stockholdings that aggregated less than the twenty largest in any single company. As to the Rockefellers, there was not included their dominant interest in the Chase National Bank, one of the international "Big Three" among commercial banks, colossal Rockefeller Center in New York City and a variety of extensive real estate and landholdings. Indeed, a substantial fortune for each of these big families was deliberately left out of consideration in the TNEC study. If a man were to own whatever the Rockefellers, Du Ponts or Mellons held that was not even counted in the TNEC study, he would be considered one of the nation's nabobs.

The following table applies the percentage of ownership of the Rockefeller interests, including foundations, as they appeared among the twenty largest stockholders as ascertained by the TNEC, and shows the value of these same percentages and at closing 1964 prices.[44]

	Largest Stockholdings (percentage)	1937 Prices	1964 Prices
Atlantic Refining Co. (S.O.)	1.16		$ 6,821,025
Bethlehem Steel Corp.	.41		$ 10,379,268
Consolidated Edison (N. Y.)	.28		$ 10,170,255
Consolidated Oil Corp. (S.O.)	5.71	$ 7,000,000	$ 49,058,436
Continental Oil Co. (S.O.)	.84		$ 14,055,174
Illinois Central R. R. (now Illinois Central Industries)	.32		$ 536,364
Int'l Harvester Co.	2.31		$ 24,604,360
Middle West Corporation (now constituent companies)	2.11		$ 8,272,495
Missouri-Kansas-Texas R. R.	1.14		$ 115,679
Norfolk and Western Ry.	.32		$ 782,073
Ohio Oil Co. (now Marathon Oil Co. [S.O.])	19.52	$ 16,000,000	$ 190,165,807
Pere Marquette Ry. (exchanged for Chesapeake & Ohio R. R. stock)	1.45		$ 23,927
Phelps Dodge Corp.	.74		$ 5,381,811
Radio Corporation	.22		$ 4,362,775
Santa Fe Railway	.38		$ 1,576,563
Socony Vacuum Oil Co. (now Socony Mobil Oil Co. [S.O.])	16.34	$ 76,000,000	$ 771,303,099
Standard Oil Co. of Calif.	12.32	$ 47,250,000	$ 664,330,693

Standard Oil Co. (Indiana)	11.36	$ 58,000,000	$ 334,335,677
Standard Oil Co. (New Jersey)	13.51*	$163,000,000	$2,628,070,253
U.S. Steel Corp.	.12		$ 3,361,473
Western Pacific R. R.	4.79		$ 3,916,487
		Total	$4,741,515,014

Considering only the largest holdings, it will be seen how magnificently these properties have risen from depression-level valuations—from seven to nearly seventeen times in less than thirty years (the latter in the case of the giant Standard Oil Company of New Jersey). How many persons in the same period have seen their salaries or propertied status improve by as much? If a school teacher, starting out at a salary of $3,000 a year in 1937, had experienced the same ratio of gain in remuneration he would now be paid in the range of $21,000–$51,000. Actually, the school teacher now receives in the range of $6,000–$10,000, if that, and is facing early retirement at half pay. There never comes a time when property, large or small, is put on half pay because of age.

In the case of the Rockefellers, as of the Mellons, it has been publicly announced that they have sold some of these holdings: JDR, Jr., in Socony Mobil Oil and the Mellons in Gulf Oil. What the proceeds were used for—new investments or trust funds for others—is not indicated. At any rate, the foregoing table should not be taken as a recent breakdown of major Rockefeller investments, which in some cases may be larger or smaller, in others may include different properties. But, I argue, whatever the present holdings are, their relative value is almost certainly not smaller than the total for the tabulation and is, for a variety of sound reasons, very probably larger.

What the TNEC study singled out as the personal largest industrial holdings of the Rockefeller family, individuals and trust funds, is shown in the following table computed at closing 1964 prices:

	Largest Personal Stockholdings (percentage)	1964 Closing Market Value
Atlantic Refining Co.	1.16	$ 6,812,085
Bethlehem Steel Corp.	.41	$ 10,379,268
Consolidated Oil Corp.	5.71	$ 49,058,436

* The Rockefellers actually had voting power over 20.20 per cent of the vast New Jersey Company, in assets the largest industrial enterprise of the world, enough to assure control, by reason of New Jersey stock owned by the minority-controlled Standard Oil Company (Indiana).

Ohio Oil Co.	9.83	$ 190,165,807
Socony Vacuum Oil Co.	16.34	$ 771,303,099
Standard Oil Co. of Calif.	11.86	$ 639,326,406
Standard Oil Co. (Indiana)	7.83	$ 236,721,770
Standard Oil Co. (New Jersey)	8.69*	$1,691,696,720
	Total	$3,595,463,591

If we subtract from this $100 million for the widow (assuming her holdings had appreciated to this level since 1960) there is left for each of the six third-generation Rockefeller children *personally* $570,077,232 (including whatever is laid up in trust for the grandchildren, which has lightened the financial burden of the parents). In view of the many ancillary Rockefeller holdings that are not here considered, this figure is far nearer what one should have for each more recently rather than the *Fortune* figure of $100–$200 million. Market values rose between 1957 and 1964, it is true, but broadly allowing for the rise and excluding grandchildren's trusts, it would seem that each of six Rockefellers must be worth *at least* in the range of $425–$475 million, including trust funds, and possibly more than $570 million. The apportionment ratio of trusts as between children and grandchildren is not publicly known but, as the grandchildren take from the parents, it is probable that direct trust provision for the grandchildren was made, if at all, on a much smaller scale than for their parents. To venture further into the labyrinth of family trusts without possessing the accountants' figures could only be unwarrantably speculative.

As the foundations make public reports of their holdings, there would be a way of partially checking the correctness of these computations if the same foundations were now in existence as figured in the TNEC study. Unfortunately, the structure and number of Rockefeller foundations have greatly changed since 1937 and only the sketchiest sort of check is possible. Just as the Rockefellers have probably shuffled their personal investments, so have they publicly shuffled their foundations consonant with the introduction of a third generation into the management of affairs.

The foundation holdings, reckoning by the TNEC percentages, should have stood at $1,146,051,423 at the end of 1964. At the end of 1962 (the only figures yet available) the actual foundation holdings, when market values were somewhat lower than at the end of 1964, were $823,-

---

* By reason of the Standard Oil (Indiana) interest in the New Jersey company, the personal Rockefeller voting power in the latter company was 15.38 per cent, enough to give practical control or "dominance," in the language of the TNEC study.

485,972, according to the *Foundation Directory, 1964.* My computations, it is clear, produce a figure that is $322,565,451 higher than seems to be the case.

Before we consider this not inconsiderable discrepancy and what may account for it, the recent foundation holdings should be examined. The *Foundation Directory* shows them and their stated assets to have been as follows:

	Date Founded	Assets at End of 1962
General Education Board	1902	$ 342,834
Rockefeller Foundation	1913	$632,282,137
Sealantic Fund (Community fund for Seal Harbor, Me., and Pocantico Hills, N.Y., where Rockefellers reside)	1938	$ 11,639,033
Jackson Preserve, Inc.	1940	$ 21,939,398 (1961)
Rockefeller Brothers Fund	1940	$152,386,637
American Int'l Ass'n for Economic and Social Development (part Rockefeller)	1946	$ 752,585 (1961)
Council on Economic and Cultural Development	1953	$ 3,360,950
Chase National Bank Foundation (part Rockefeller)	1958	$ 782,398
Total		$823,485,972

At the time of the TNEC study there were only the Rockefeller Foundation, the General Education Board and the Spelman Fund of New York in the field. The latter has gone out of business and six others have been added since 1938.

Applying the TNEC pattern, which found that 30 per cent of Rockefeller holdings were in foundations and 30 per cent in personal trusts, with 40 per cent individually held, and using the 1962 foundation holdings as the base of computation, one would have the following as the figure of dominated and owned holdings in 1962:

Foundations—30 per cent	$ 823,485,972
Individual trust funds—30 per cent	$ 823,485,972
Individual holdings—40 per cent	$1,077,981,296
Total	$2,724,953,240

Using recent foundation holdings as the base to which the TNEC percentage is applied appears to me to result in a downward distortion, first because the individual holdings were concentrated in the upward-spiraling oil industry while much of the foundation investment is in fixed-interest securities, and secondly because the foundation pattern has been altered. My conclusion is that proportional to individual holdings and trust funds the foundation holdings are now either less than 30 per cent of the whole or that their assets by 1964 had moved up in value closer to the projected figure of $1,146,051,423 obtained by my computation.

As the foundation reports are issued at a more leisurely pace than company reports and are not available for 1964 at this writing, direct comparison cannot be made. But critical readers can make the comparison at any time, when the reports become available, provided they always apply market values rather than book values of holdings.

If one wishes to examine still another possibility, one can put together the figure of $3,595,463,591 for the 1964 value of the personal holdings obtained by my computation with the 1962 figure of $823,485,972 for foundation holdings. This gives a total of $4,418,949,563 for the combined holdings. I still believe, however, that my original figure of $4,741,-515,014 is an understatement of the combined family holding, because the TNEC did not survey all the family properties (only the largest) and notwithstanding the fact that Rockefeller, Jr., had to pay gift taxes in the establishment of his chain of trust funds for children and grandchildren.

When one throws the Chase Bank, Rockefeller Center and various real estate properties into the pot and considers that Laurance Rockefeller has blossomed in his own right as a venture capitalist in luxury hotels and advanced-technology enterprises, the combined Rockefeller financial "punch" should be above $5 billion. Although apparently outpaced by the Du Ponts in the super-wealth sweepstakes, the Rockefellers seem to me to be running at least neck and neck with the Mellons.

The TNEC study, it must again be stressed, did not pretend to produce the totals of wealth held, for it confined itself only to the twenty largest stockholdings in the 200 largest nonfinancial companies and ignored ownership of banks, insurance companies, bonds, real estate and smaller stockholdings. Relying on the TNEC method alone there might have been missed even larger concentration of wealth, for example if the twenty-first largest stockholder in all 200 companies had been the same person or family; but on other evidential grounds it is known that such a logical possibility did not hold in fact.

The Fords of Dearborn

Mrs. Edsel Ford and her three sons—Henry II, Benson and William—were assigned a combined minimal wealth of $325 million and a maximum of $500 million by *Fortune* in 1957. Her daughter Josephine (Mrs. Walter Buhl Ford II) was not noticed by *Fortune*.

It is always fairly easy to compute the collective personal wealth of the Fords because they own 10 per cent of the outstanding stock (but 40 per cent of the voting power) of the Ford Motor Company (always assuming there have been no secret sales or purchases and that there are no side interests). On the face of it (although not really) 10 per cent of the entire stock issue of the company appears to be the sole personal financial strength of the family.

What slightly impedes any computation of Ford wealth is the rather complicated capital structure of the company as created under the wills of Henry and his son Edsel.

At the end of 1964 this capital structure, after split-ups in each class, stood as follows:

	Shares
Common stock (owned by investors)	52,338,152
Class A stock (owned by the Ford Foundation)	46,283,756
Class B stock (owned by the Ford family)	12,267,794
Total	110,889,702

The Class A stock is nonvoting until it is either sold by the foundation or given by it to some approved nonprofit organization, when it acquires one vote per share; but never at any time can all the common stock cast more than 60 per cent of the vote at a stockholders' meeting. For, as noted, 40 per cent of voting power is concentrated by charter in all the Class B stock, giving the Ford family very nearly absolute control of the company at all times. All classes of stock participate equally, share for share, in dividends. Control is what counts.

At the closing 1964 quotation of 54½ per share this capitalization had a gross market value of $6,043,488,759. This left the Fords 10-plus per cent apparently valued at $604,348,876. But, considering the factor of control, the Ford family stock has as much voting power as two-thirds of the common, which was valued in the market at $1,901,619,450. Anyone who owns two-thirds of the common stock would have as much voting power as the Fords but would get more dividends—on 34,892,100 shares as against 12,267,794 shares—and to that extent would have more value in hand. But the Class B stock, owing to the heavy weight of voting privileges embodied in it, is worth more, share for share, than the market value of the common stock (although nobody would seek to get that value unless he sought control of the company). If, however, a buyer of control were to show himself, the Ford-held stock at closing 1964 prices would have, in relation to the common, the value of close to $2 billion I have assigned it by this computation. While the Ford stock gets dividends of only about a third of the equivalent amount of voting-power common, this isn't too much of a hardship as the Fords are in an income-tax bracket that hits such soaring dividends hard. Besides, the men all drew high salaries as officers of the company. They have plenty of pocket money.

So, at a price of around 54 for the present outstanding stock of the company, I would rate the value of the family holding at a minimal $2 billion, although any syndicate interested in buying the company would probably have to pay more for it (assuming current or higher levels of profitability).

Compared, then, with the Du Ponts, Mellons and Rockefellers, the Fords are in comparatively modest circumstances although individually the members of the three latter families are on the average richer owing to the participation of a greater number of Du Ponts in the heady Du Pont mixture.

Since 1964, however, there has been a slight alteration in the foundation holdings, which does not affect my computation nor the conclusions drawn from it. In June, 1965, the foundation marketed more shares. Originally it received precisely 88 per cent of all stock in the form of Class A nonvoting shares. Adjusting for stock splits after the 1965 sale it had disposed of very nearly half or 46.9 million present shares. The 45.7 million shares it retained composed 35.8 per cent of the entire capital stock of Ford Motor.

In terms of its own book values of the various securities it held, Ford Motor plus others, the foundation at the end of 1964 was worth $2.4 billion.

The great care taken by the two elder Fords to see that control remained in the family is shown by the voting provisions for the stocks. If the outstanding Class B stock falls below 5.4 million shares (which it can do only if it is called in by the family) the total voting power of the common rises to 70 per cent; and if the B stock outstanding falls below 3 million shares it votes equally with the common.

Until the family, then, quixotically decides to call in the B stock (thus cutting its own throat as far as control is concerned) it holds 40 per cent of voting power in the company, tantamount to absolute control. Should some syndicate attempt to buy control in the market the Fords need purchase only 16⅔ per cent of outstanding common to give it 50 per cent voting power, whereas a syndicate would have to purchase 83⅓ per cent of all common to reach the same dead-heat point. In such an unequal race the Fords would necessarily win.

But even if a syndicate turned up with *all* the common, giving it absolute control, the Fords have an ace in reserve. And this ace shows one of the many ways foundation control can be synchronized with industrial control. The Fords control the foundation. And the A stock held by the foundation acquires voting power as it is sold or given to a nonprofit institution. Faced with an opponent who owned all the common, giving him a 60 per cent vote and control, the Fords need merely activate the voting power of the foundation stock by selling it or giving it to friendly hands, thus diluting the voting power of the outstanding common. By converting all its remaining Class A stock into voting stock the foundation could dilute the voting power of the presently outstanding common to 30 per cent of the present capital structure. With the 30 per cent of the voting power in the newly converted common plus the 40 per cent of voting power in the Class B stock the Fords would actually have, as they now potentially have, 70 per cent of the voting power. The foundation, indeed, could sell somewhat more than half of its remaining Ford stock and leave the Fords able to muster 55 per cent of the voting power in any critical showdown.

The ins and outs of this situation may have puzzled some readers. The point to be made is only to show the great care taken to guard control, revealing what the wealthy intend. In acting as they do they are only being reasonable; for the humanly normal thing to do is to guard one's possessions. But we have many propagandists around, led by such errant professors as A. A. Berle, Jr., who apparently are not afraid of being judged certifiably silly by contending that control as well as ownership of the large companies is being widely spread around, that the big fortunes are being broken up to right and left. The Berle thesis, refuted on every hand by the facts, is that as ownership is dispersed (which it is not in fact), free-lance company managements install themselves in the drivers' seats as something of a new corporate breed. These new managers—the "managerial revolution"—proceed in this fairy tale to elbow aside the Du Ponts, Mellons, Rockefellers, Fords, Pews, Gettys and various others —and thus introduce a new set of actors on the stage of history, a set of actors that conquer by sheer bureaucratic techniques.

Such being the case, reason many readers, we can all just sit back and watch the fun as bright young men rise to conjure the corporations away from the big owners. Like all fantasies, this one has quite a coterie of be-mused devotees.

The surviving Fords would have been a great deal richer today than they are if Henry Ford, founder and original master mind of the automotive behemoth, who died in 1947 at eighty-three years of age, had been personally less grasping and if the deaths of central figures in the family had not occurred before the very rich could get a tractable Congress around to trimming the New Deal inheritance taxes. This trimming process was no doubt hastened by the example of the tax-speared disaster that engulfed the massive Ford fortune.

Ford's only son, Edsel, a far more likeable, intelligent and informed man than his flinty father but kept unhappily subordinate all his life, died prematurely at age forty-nine in 1943. The oldest grandson, Henry Ford II, at the age of twenty-five, inexperienced in business and up to 1940 a sociology major at Yale, was hastily spirited out of the wartime Navy where he was an ensign and installed as a director and executive vice president of the vast company, a miraculous corporate success story. His brothers Benson and William, twenty-five and eighteen years old at the time, trailed him into the company later, where they also showed their mettle by quickly rising to the top. Their mother, whom I have perhaps ill-advisedly listed as a rentier, played a strong and constructive role (from a family and property point of view) on the board of directors with Henry II. She backed him particularly, if she did not indeed take the lead, in getting rid of much accumulated deadwood in the cracker-barrel executive suite of Henry I.

Holding tightly (and tax-expensively) to 58½ per cent of the company's voting stock, Henry Ford at his death was publicly assigned a net worth of $500–$700 million.[45] The value at the time of the Ford Motor Company, since reorganized and vastly improved internally by the grandsons, was in the vicinity of $1 billion. Ford's death came none too soon for the family fortunes, as the company under his old-style heavy-handed administration had for more than fifteen years been losing ground to free-swinging General Motors and stepped-up Chrysler and had long since tumbled from the top of the motor heap. Definitely on the skids, the company was thought in the automobile industry to be headed for the junk-yard that had already engulfed scores of automobile companies.

But the deaths of Edsel and Henry, with the company slipping mainly because the views of Edsel were continually overruled by the feudal owner and his sycophantic cronies in the management, also came at an inopportune time with respect to the tax laws. For the marital deduction

and the option of estate splitting had not yet been enacted. Both Edsel's
and his father's holdings were faced by a flat 91 per cent inheritance tax,
designed under the New Deal expressly to break down big fortunes top-
heavy with political power. Had the later law been in effect, the two
Fords could have assigned half their holdings to their wives, tax free,
and the wives could have worked their funds with the help of lawyers
into much lower tax brackets. This splitting, it should be noticed, also
often puts the testator into a lower tax bracket as well, although it could
not have had that effect with the two Fords unless they had made free use
of trust funds for the grandchildren. Henry Ford was apparently too
tightfisted to do that, which would have cost him only bargain-counter
gift taxes.

A partial way out of this tax disaster was engineered in The Ford
Foundation for Human Advancement established by Edsel in 1936.
(Henry Ford himself was hostile to public benefactions and spoke out
freely against them.)[46] But even with the help of the Ford Foundation, the
personal Ford fortune, which under standard tax management would
have been much larger today, was literally decimated nine times over.

Edsel left the greater part of his holdings to the Ford Foundation, thus
escaping the big tax, and his father eventually had to do the same or see
his money go largely to Washington and its hated New Dealers.

In this flukey way the Ford Foundation received nearly 90 per cent of
the stock in the Ford Motor Company, all of it nonvoting as long as the
foundation held it but participating equally in dividends.[47] As far as
Henry Ford himself was concerned, the foundation was an unwilling
benefaction, the lesser of two ghastly evils.

"On the Foundation's books, this [Ford money] was given the value,
for tax purposes, of $416,000,000, but its real value, as measured by the
earnings of Ford Motors, was at least $2,500,000,000. This is considerably
more than half as much money as all the other foundations in the country
have among them."[48]

Still salvaging what they could in a bad situation, the Fords stipulated
that the stock made over to the foundation should be nonvoting, leaving
the 10 per cent in the hands of the family with an initial 100 per cent
voting power.

Asked whether he would rather have all the Ford Motor dividends or
company control, the average man would probably choose the dividends.
He would be mistaken, for those in control determine whether there shall
be any dividends at all. One in control could decide to invest earnings
elsewhere until the designated dividend-receiver came to some sort of
terms, not disadvantageous to a controller. *Control* is always the prime

objective of the true leaders in all large organizations—political, financial, economic, philanthropic, educational or otherwise. For control determines everything that is subject to the will.

And, finally, the family, now controlling the company, was also placed by the elder Fords' testaments in control of the foundation. Although it could not receive foundation income or any part of it, the family could manage the foundation (as it has since done) to the advantage of the Ford Motor Company, the goose that lays the golden eggs.

The Ford Foundation, which when Henry Ford was alive was devoted purely to community projects in and around Detroit that were beneficial to the Ford Motor Company, began its national operations only in 1950, when it started spewing forth huge grants for educational and other purposes in unprecedented fashion. Ordinarily hard-to-get money began to float around the country in huge gobs. In 1954 the foundation bestowed $68 million, four times the annual Rockefeller contribution to the charitable kitty and ten times that of the third largest foundation, The Carnegie Corporation. This figure, a mere taste of what was yet to come, was as much as all American foundations combined spent in any single year up to 1948 and was about a quarter of the spending of all foundations in 1954.[48] If the Ford Foundation is a good thing, as many maintain, then it must be attributed to New Deal tax laws.

In connection with trust funds earlier, the reader may recall there was a somewhat cryptic reference to "standard doctrine." The two Fords relied on standard doctrine in creating the Ford Foundation. Just what is standard doctrine? Most broadly and informally, and applicable in all social and political contexts, standard doctrine was perhaps most pungently expressed by the late W. C. Fields when he voiced the deathless maxim: "Never give a sucker an even break." But, more specifically, it relates in our social system to known legal ways of maximizing advantages and minimizing disadvantages for property, especially under existing tax laws. Moreover, it shows one in detail how to accomplish these ends. With reference to the tax laws in all their ramifications the doctrine is now well codified, notably in a series of multiple-volume loose-leaf publications titled the *Standard Federal Tax Reporter* published by the Commerce Clearing House in New York. Supplementing the income-tax series there are the sub-series titled *Federal Excise Tax Reporter* and *Federal Estate and Gift Tax Reporter*.

With respect to a structure like the Ford Foundation, standard doctrine holds:

"Charitable giving through the channels of charitable, tax-exempt foundations has achieved a position of importance in estate planning. Apart from the humanitarian aspects involved, the family foundation can be an effective means of reducing income and estate taxes and of continuing control of a closely held corporation in the family of the donor."[50] These are precisely the ends that were achieved by the testamentary dispositions of the Ford estates.

Foundations, in other words, are a way of reducing taxes, and this is part of standard doctrine. Newspapers and other propaganda media, however, have long referred to them in their whimsical way as benefactions (which in certain cases they may also be) and their creators as philanthropists rather than as tax-sensitive acquisitors (which they may or may not be), and invariably refer to the transferred money as donations and gifts (which they are not necessarily). The donations, so-called, are the consequence of big tax write-downs offered by the government precisely for such a possibly benign placement of funds.

But a large section of the public has been instilled with the unwarranted belief that something is being given away for nothing. And, anomalously, as I have had occasion before to point out[51] these huge so-called gifts sprang from the hoards of men who in their active lifetimes left no stone unturned to amass for themselves great wealth. The most acquisitive, it would seem in this fantastic newspaper scenario, turn out to be the most benevolently inclined.

More broadly, standard doctrine holds that one should always pay the lowest possible wages and taxes, charge the highest possible prices and rents, and never give anything away unless the gift confers some hidden possibly overcompensatory personal benefit. The big propertied usually do their level best to adhere to it.

This may sound cynical to some, but only because they have witlessly allowed themselves to be deluded by unrealistic propaganda lullabies. It is not only standard but sound doctrine in any social system that pits its citizens competitively against each other and makes property ownership a cornerstone of well being. Would any property owner be considered sensible if he elected to pay maximum wages and taxes, charge minimal prices and then, if he had anything left, gave it away to Tom, Dick and Harry? Even to steer a middle course between the two extremes would not be considered very astute.

Although Henry Ford died worth $500–$700 million at 1947 values, he met his final tax problem well even though until then he had steered a less than canny course. His federal tax was only $21,108,160.91 on a taxable estate of $70 million which consisted of $31,451,909.36 plus some Ford stock.[52]

Edsel paid about $12 million, or 6 per cent, on an estate then estimated to be worth $200 million.[53] But in 1935 he had established trusts for his four children. In addition to Ford stock, he owned most of the stock of the Manufacturers National Bank of Detroit, which he left to his widow. As it was disclosed, Henry Ford owned 55 per cent of the stock of Ford Motor, Edsel 41½ per cent and Mrs. Henry Ford 3½ per cent.[54] Together Henry and Edsel paid inheritance taxes of a little more than $30 million. The elder Ford would have done better, as the elder Rockefeller did, by giving his son, wife and grandchildren stock over a period of years.

But if Edsel and Henry had not had recourse to the foundation—at the last moment almost—the estate would have been forced to pay a 91 per cent tax. This would have left a mere 9 per cent of outstanding ordinary stock in Ford family hands, hardly enough to control the corporation. Instead, they were left with 10 per cent of the stock (clothed by charter with 40 per cent voting power) and 100 per cent control over the asset-logged foundation, which as it engages in good works cannot help but generate friendly feelings for the Ford Motor Company in many worthy bosoms.[55]

A further advantage in the plan adopted (for which some unsung lawyer deserves a *summa cum laude*) is that its provision for selling foundation stock created a horde of stockholding allies for the Ford family, which was dangerously isolated when it was the sole owner. Now when anyone wishes to make a face at the Ford Motor Company, the Ford Foundation or, indeed, at any of the Fords, he must reckon not only with all the grateful beneficiaries of foundation grants but with thousands of dividend-hungry small stockholders. Big owners have many small partners.

The Realm of Super-Wealth

The Du Ponts, Mellons, Rockefellers and Fords, in any event, are the four cardinal points of the compass in the realm of super-wealth. The Fords must be included by reason of the sheer magnitude of their controlled holdings even though they do not yet have as varied an organizational task force as their peers.

On the basis of sheer magnitude, again, J. Paul Getty should probably be thought of in the same class, although we do not yet know what will be the *post mortem* status of his holdings.

The other major clear-cut claimants to super-wealth status—and theirs would be minor super-wealth—are the Pews of the Sun Oil Company.

Neither the Houghtons of Corning Glass nor the Olins of Olin Mathieson Chemical appear to quite make it. But the Hartfords and

Rosenwalds should be considered. The Houghtons, incidentally, were missed by the TNEC dragnet.

Fortune mentioned only two Pews, but the TNEC study showed them to be a numerous clan: J. Howard Pew, Mary Ethel Pew, J. N. Pew, Jr., Mabel Pew Myrin, Walter C. Pew, Albert H. Pew, Mrs. Mary C. Pew, Arthur E. Pew, Jr., John G. Pew, Helen T. Pew, Alberta C. Pew and others. The Pews collectively—individually and through estates and trust funds—owned 70.6 per cent of Sun Oil Company common stock as of February 15, 1938.[56]

Assuming that this same percentage of ownership was maintained, they would be collectively worth $708,458,121 at closing prices for Sun Oil in 1964.

But the Pews since TNEC days have also set up foundations. As of March 2, 1965, the Pew Memorial Trust (through The Glenmede Trust Company) owned 21.7 per cent of Sun Oil stock and held as fiduciary for other Pew trusts and estates 20.9 per cent.[57] The *Foundation Directory, 1964,* states the 1960 assets of the Memorial Trust alone, leaving out its fiduciary holdings, at $135,309,481.

Before we pass to lesser but interesting wealth-holders (the extremely wealthy as distinguished from the super-wealthy), we may scan those we have examined in this chapter for common characteristics apart from their holdings of wealth.

Characteristics of the Super-Wealthy

All were born American citizens; their families have been in the United States for generations. All are inheritors in greater or less degree and, except for the Du Ponts who sprang from a revolutionary savant, all are far better educated than their family founders. Such being the case, they have a broader awareness of the world and its vagaries. None of these groups has its younger members placed in less than the third generation of wealth; the Du Ponts stand at least seven generations in the stream of gold. Such being the case they all together contradict the American folk-belief that a family passes from shirtsleeves to shirtsleeves in three generations. None of these gilt-edged people, obviously, are having any of that.

Offhand it would be said that they are all white, Anglo-Saxon Protestants; but such a statement would be somewhat misleading. The Du Ponts are of French Huguenot origin, and there is a Jewish crossing (Belin) in one of their lines of descent. Nor can it be said categorically that they are all Protestants. For Henry Ford II became a convert to Catholicism on the occasion of his first marraige and, through the foundation, funnels large sums to Catholic schools and colleges. As a consequence of his divorce and remarriage outside the Church, he is now automatically excommunicated but remains a Catholic. His children are Catholic.

Despite the fuss made by outsiders about being white, Anglo-Saxon and Protestant (or Catholic-Jewish) it is doubtful that any of these people attach much importance to the point. Most of them, from all indications, are pretty worldly wise and wear their ethnicity and religiosity debonairly. Money, they know, is what counts in the established scheme.

Sinews of Republicanism

A far more significant common characteristic of all these super-wealthy families is that they have long been the main supporters nationally of the Republican Party, the party of plutocratic oligarchy. They have been its big sinews. Except for some minor Democratic deviants among the Du Ponts (and the Du Ponts can show many kinds of deviants from the basic family pattern) all leading members are Republican and their forebears were Republican.

With the exception of the Fords each has at various times played strong forward roles in the Republican Party—the Rockefellers particularly under the McKinley Administration; the Mellons under the Harding-Coolidge-Hoover Administrations; the Du Ponts with the Liberty League in fighting a strong rearguard action during the 1930's against the resurgent Democratic Party; and the Pews ever since in being the wealthiest supporters (among many) of unreconstructed right-wing Republicanism down to the present. If not kings themselves, they are king-makers.

The Rockefellers have in recent years come again to pay a forward role through the person of Nelson A. Rockefeller. Thrice elected governor of New York, until his divorce and remarriage to a divorced woman he was considered a chief Republican presidential prospect. Every professional politician in the country agrees that if the personable and outgoing Nelson had pressed for the Republican presidential nomination in 1960 he would have obtained it and beaten John F. Kennedy. While his divorce might not under other circumstances have kept him from the presidency its inflation to a major issue by ultra-rightist Republicans tended to have that effect in the 1960's.

But the Rockefellers still play a very strong role in Republican politics and Winthrop has become the Republican governor of Arkansas. Ultra-rightist Republicans, however, give them credit for too much by blaming them chiefly for the electoral disaster that overtook their implausible darling, Barry Goldwater, in 1964.

As important wheels in the political process these families have always had quick and direct access to the White House, no matter what the party of the president. Not only in times of war (when gossamer party lines tend to blur) but in times of peace, representatives of these families have always been able to obtain an audience even with a Democratic president, and sometimes have been summoned for counsel, comfort and advice by dazed Republican presidents. But the name of Rockefeller was once under such a public cloud that on a visit to the White House the younger Rockefeller was spirited in by a back entrance to talk to President William Howard Taft.[58]

Yet these and other magnates of extreme wealth had been far from strangers to the Democratic Party. Both the political parties have been supported—the Republican mainly by weightily propertied elements. The parties are opposite sides of the same coin. Instead of saying that the United States has a two-party system, it would be more nearly correct to say it has a dual-party system.

After the Civil War, with the plantation owners self-destroyed, the Democratic Party always attracted large propertied elements whenever it made strong bids to win national elections. The Cleveland Administrations were as close to Wall Street, manned by Wall Streeters, as any Republican Administration. William Jennings Bryan, although anathema to the Wall Street Establishment, was supported by western mining interests, for whom "free silver" was so much extra gravy. The Wilson Administration was as completely under the thumb of Wall Street as the subsequent Harding, Coolidge and Hoover Administrations.[59] John W. Davis, the Democratic candidate for president in 1924 was a Wall Street corporation lawyer.

In 1928 Al Smith had his chief backing, financial and emotional, from fellow-Catholic John J. Raskob, prime minister of the Du Ponts. If Smith had won he would have been far less a Catholic than a Du Pont president, although the religious question was what was pushed to the fore by a politically obtuse electorate. Hoover, the Republican, was a J. P. Morgan puppet; Smith, his democratic opponent, was in the pocket of the Du Ponts, for whom J. P. Morgan and Company was the banker. By 1936 Smith was a roaring Liberty Leaguer. The victory of either man put J. P. Morgan and the Du Ponts into the presidential driver's seat. W. Averell Harriman was one of the leading wealthy Republicans who crossed the line to the Democrats in 1928 and has been a Democrat, and a high government official, in all subsequent Democratic Administrations.

Under Franklin Delano Roosevelt, owing chiefly to troubled circumstances, for the first time it appeared that some of the magnates might be unwelcome at the White House. The wealthiest, especially the Du Ponts, opposed him bitterly, which meant that he was opposed by the banks and heavy industry. Those numerous wealthy persons who became staunch Rooseveltians were mainly of the second or third tier of wealth and nearly all in merchandising and light industry, immediately dependent upon the stagnating mass-consumption market. They were down-the-line New Dealers but not, as misconceived Republican propaganda had it, Socialists, Populists or even Welfare-Staters.

But owing to the disastrous Republican-fostered and Wall Street nurtured economic depression, which interrupted seventy-two years of unbroken rule by the magnates through either Republican or Democratic puppets, the Democratic Party became the inheritor of vast social problems informally created largely by Republican neglect. The big special problems in the United States always develop through neglect, in part because so many active and intelligent elements are permanently siphoned off into the chicaneries of the money-making process. If profitability cannot be shown for an activity, such as raising the cultural level and tending to the lame, the halt, the blind and the stricken, such activity is left to quixotic and somewhat suspect elements—quixotic at least by prevailing standards.

Not that the Democratic Party moved very far to the Left in coping with domestic disaster, as hostile propaganda has it; for the magnates had ready to their call almost the entire southern congressional delegation, which had been their ready tool ever since Reconstruction days in a deal that left the Negroes to the mercies of their former masters in return for giving southern support to the Republican magnates in Congress. The southern wing of the Democratic Party, rooted in grass-roots ineptitude, was as much a political tool of big wealth as was the Republican Party.

Under the impact of the depression the Democratic Party became the national spokesman for the suddenly risen industrial city with all its problems. Its mass base was urban. The mass base of the Republican Party had always been in the small towns and rural areas, close to the fly-blown cracker barrel, although its telltale inaction in the 1920's lost it the over-exploited western farmers. But behind these disparate mass bases—city dwellers for the Democrats and country dwellers for the Republicans, with southern Democrat politicos spiritually in harmony with the Republicans, and western Republicans veering into the Democratic fold—there was at all times, in both parties, big wealth pulling the strings and arranging the scenes in its own succulent interests, a grotesque spectacle.

It simply so happened that the biggest wealth, shaped by policies since the Civil War, was Republican, and included the Rockefellers, Du Ponts,

Mellons and Fords. The Democrats had with them, however, plenty of heavy money, committed to different handling of the domestic mess created by the Republicans.

Although Roosevelt and his New Deal became the hated devil of big wealth, which brought 85 per cent of the newspapers to bear against him through its control of corporate advertising, with the advent of war and the adoption of a bipartisan foreign policy it was Roosevelt who made the first overtures toward bringing the less fanatical Republicans into the government. He brought into his Cabinet, for example, Colonel Frank Knox, Republican vice presidential candidate of 1940; Henry L. Stimson, Hoover's secretary of state; E. R. Stettinius, Jr., of J. P. Morgan and Company; and James V. Forrestal of the investment banking house of Dillon Read and Company. He gave Nelson A. Rockefeller his first leg up in political office by making him Coordinator of Latin-American Affairs. With these and similar appointments Roosevelt made his third administration seem a Bar Harbor, Newport and Park Avenue affair. As FDR himself said, "the New Deal is out the window."

After two Republican Administrations from 1952 to 1960, gained by using a clearly apolitical war hero as a stalking horse, the country again went Democratic under John F. Kennedy, himself a wealthy heir although basically a political man from a political family. Kennedy, even with no war providing an excuse for a coalition, awarded his chief Cabinet posts to Republicans from the camp of big wealth. Douglas Dillon, Republican and very wealthy heir of the founder of Dillon Read and Company, Forrestal's old firm, was made Secretary of the Treasury. Robert S. McNamara, Republican president of the Ford Motor Company, was made Secretary of Defense. McGeorge Bundy, Republican, was made liaison man to the CIA. Dean Rusk, a Democrat, but president of the Rockefeller Foundation from 1952 to 1960, was made Secretary of State.

The basic government posts, in other words, went to men deep in the camp of big wealth. But those posts that required dealings with the *hoi polloi* in social contexts went to party men versed in the rhetoric of inspirational ambiguity.

Dillon resigned under Johnson and was replaced by Henry H. Fowler, a career Democrat; but most of the rest of the Kennedy team continued, with the distant goal a mirage: the Great Society. The laudable stated ends of this Great Society are the end of want and of inequalities of opportunity.

As Princeton University political sociologist Richard F. Hamilton remarks,

In an affluent society, a liberal, welfare-oriented party can go a long way toward satisfying the wishes of its followers. Rather than preside over a drawn-out struggle between the people and the interests, as if it were an either/or game, the new style is to give both what they want and pay for it out of the returns from a stable and rapidly growing economy. In essence this is the Galbraithian solution—not to struggle over the "take" but to increase its size. Thus, the typical new figure on the political scene is the liberal demagogue—one who can cater to the masses because he is willing to pay them off and can do so without depriving the interests of what they want. He can be for civil rights, for improved housing, for urban renewal, for a poverty program, and at the same time can vote against a reduction of the depletion allowance. The Great Society synthesis overcomes that age-old problem of liberal politics: how to reward the clientele. Before affluence, the result was a long, hard and usually indecisive fight with the interests or it was capitulation. The new liberal, however, does not have to fight or switch.[60]

The attraction of the Great Society for the wealthy, however, is the new opportunities it creates for making money on huge government contracts. In the area of defense there is a huge tax-supported military establishment making constant highly profitable demands—up to 40 and 50 per cent profit—on industry for complex new weapons. In urban renewal there is the vast profitable enterprise, replete with windfalls, of rehabilitating the commercial heart of the big cities. In slum clearance and school buildings there are vast slushy construction projects of low quality in the offing. And in the antipoverty program itself there is vast roadbuilding, as in Appalachia (which needs few roads), as well as opportunities for the local political machines.

As Dr. Hamilton remarks, "Large numbers of entrepreneurial types have recently discovered that 'there's money in poverty.'"

We have, then, as he notes, now developed "liberals of convenience" as contrasted with "liberals of conviction," and staunch Republicanism is no longer to be taken for granted among the big wealthy, whatever their past history. For big wealth cannot afford to back political losers.

Everything about the Great Society as blueprinted spells lucrative contracts for someone. Hence the party of the Great Society now has special attractions for the wealthy that the Republican Party, fallen into the hands of dervishes of the cracker barrel, no longer has. The defections of the professional elite and leading mass media from the Republican cause in 1964, when a "true" Republican ran, clearly show the way the wind is blowing.

In point of fact, the Johnsonian Democratic Party is the new political rallying ground of big wealth, which is forced by circumstance suddenly to see some validity in the Democratic approach ("Me-Tooism"). The social programs of marginal rehabilitation and repair will go forward, but at a snug profit, provided the military can spare the money. And big wealth will continue to get its depletion allowances, tax cuts and big deduction write-offs.

Lest we be carried away by the prospect of an early marriage of old-line Republicans with the Democratic Party we are reminded of difficulties by no less a personage than David Rockefeller, president of the mammoth Chase National Bank (1964 assets: $13 billion). Explaining in a television interview that he had "great admiration for the president [Johnson]," Mr. Rockefeller said he was nevertheless "disturbed by the Government's move in the aluminum price increase" that was rescinded after the government moved to sell stockpiled aluminum. In words that his grandfather would have unhesitatingly endorsed the Chase bank chief said "the aluminum industry was the best judge of whether prices should go up" and added that he was "in disagreement with the attitude of Government that prices should be controlled."

The problem of inflation should be dealt with through "natural economic forces within the capitalist system," the *Times* said he observed, without specifying just what these natural forces were and to what extent they included greed, which is certainly a sturdy, old reliable natural force. An assumption in his position, as in that of the early classical economists, is that if something is natural it is acceptable, which tenet would make tuberculosis or cancer acceptable. A further assumption was that if someone intervenes in any process, as in regulating industry or practicing surgery, there is something "unnatural" and to be condemned about it. Actually, whatever any human being does—spit on the sidewalk, paint monstrosities on the walls, set fire to buildings, fornicate with lower animals, or regulate the actions of other people—is entirely natural. For if it weren't natural they couldn't do it. Mr. Rockefeller, like many others, reserves natural as a description of that of which he approves.

Said the *Times* report: "Mr. Rockefeller said the manner in which President Johnson handled the aluminum increase, even though he remained largely behind the scenes, was not appreciated by business [read: persons of wealth] anymore than President Kennedy's halting of a proposed steel increase."[61]

But the reason Democratic presidents must be sympathetic toward the big wealthy at all times, short of allowing them to upset the new synthesis, is simple: All these people, even if Republican, carry great weight in American affairs because of their intimate hereditary involvement through professional subordinates in complex enterprises penetrating into every corner of society. They may no longer be self-made—they may have been sired by trust, testament or codicil out of holding company, foundation and monopoly—but they are independent power wielders. They aren't average citizens. And this is a political *fact*, not likely to be overlooked by any serious politician.

Any criticism of Presidents Kennedy and Johnson for the nature of their top appointments should face up to this question: Where should they look for Cabinet officers? Kennedy and Johnson looked for them where Eisenhower looked for them, and where Roosevelt looked: in the large financial and industrial organizations. These organizations belong to the wealthy. They are part of their plantation, which in its broadest sweep is the market place itself.

Experts of greater if not complete independence of judgment are to be had, to be sure, from the leading universities, and Franklin D. Roosevelt and John F. Kennedy both drew heavily upon them for certain tasks. But scholars have neither the habit of command nor is their authority apt to be recognized by men practiced in the arts of expedient manipulation—Plato's men of the appetites. Any president has to look to the big enterprises, selecting competent men who are least compromised by egocentric self-service.

To be sure, it is not the quintet of Du Ponts, Rockefellers, Mellons, Fords and Pews that alone has supported the Republican Party in its struggles to protect and nourish big wealth and is now playing around the edges at least of the Democratic Party. They have had many collaborators among groups of lesser wealth, most of them strong Republicans in the past as now, even though some of them seem inclined to take fright as latter-day woozy fanatics come to the fore in the Republican Party.

When, as and if they become Democratic the Democratic Party will have to become more tractable along the lines David Rockefeller suggests; it will have to become more Republican. This not too difficult process may take place gradually and stealthily. But the power of money is such that it can easily come about.

Five ❧

THE INHERITORS: II

Approximately 200,000 households of the upper layer of American wealth-holding assets of $500,000 or more own 22 per cent of the private wealth of the country and 32 per cent of the investment assets, while another 500,-000 households (worth $200–$500,000) own another 13 per cent of wealth and 22 per cent of investment assets—54 per cent in all of investment assets for 700,000 households out of 57.9 million households. Add another 700,000 households—those worth from $100,000 to $200,000—and one has accounted for 43 per cent of all private wealth and 65 per cent of all investment assets.*

It is these huge percentages of ownership that give these relatively small groups their enormous leverage in the American political economy and justify our referring to the ownership as "leverage wealth."

It should, therefore, be evident that the super-wealthy and big-wealthy are settled within a somewhat larger contingent of contemporaries who differ financially only in that their holdings are less extensive in the pyramidal hierarchy of property. Relating to this property there is an all-pervading cult, forming a large part of what some refer to as the American ideology. The part of this ideology that relates to property is, basically, Standard Doctrine, heavily sugar-coated.

For preliminary guidelines to the big holdings, we can do no better than to turn to the compendious TNEC report, based as it was on official questionnaires filled out by the companies.[1] The data in them are as "hard" as government surveillance can make them.

Summarizing this valuable governmental study in a report to Senator

* Board of Governors of the Federal Reserve System, *Survey of Financial Characteristics of Consumers*, Washington, D.C., August, 1966; pp. 136, 151.

Joseph C. O'Mahoney, chairman of the TNEC, Sumner T. Pike, chairman of the Securities and Exchange Commission, under date of September 24, 1940, wrote:

Thirteen family groups—including these three (Du Ponts, Mellons and Rockefellers)—with holdings worth $2,700,000,000, own over 8 per cent of the stock of the 200 [largest nonfinancial] corporations.

Only one-half of the large shareholdings of individuals in the 200 corporations are in the direct form of outright ownership, the other half being represented by trust funds, estates, and family holding companies. The study clearly shows the importance of these instrumentalities for perpetuating the unit of control over a block of stock held by an individual or the members of a family.

Each large interest group has shown a strong tendency to keep its holdings concentrated in the enterprise in which the family fortune originated. . . . The branching out of the Mellon family into a dominating position in half a dozen important corporations in as many industries is rather unusual and not duplicated among the other interest groups controlling any of the 200 corporations. Many large family interest groups, however, have greatly expanded their industrial sphere of influence by indirect means, viz., the acquisition of control over additional enterprises by the corporations which they control, such acquisitions being financed mainly out of undistributed profits.

In the case of about 40 percent of these 200 largest corporations, one family, or a small number of families, exercise either absolute control, by virtue of ownership of a majority of voting securities, or working control through ownership of a substantial minority of the voting stock. About 60 of the corporations, or an additional 30 per cent, are controlled by one or more other corporations. Thus, a small group of dominant security holders is not in evidence in only 30 percent of the 200 large corporations. [Emphasis added.]

[Note: Although the TNEC confined itself to nonfinancial corporations, approximately the same pattern of ownership is shown by informal inquiry into purely financial enterprises such as banks and insurance companies. The same people own these that own the industrial corporations: Rockefeller, Du Pont, Ford, Mellon and others.]

The financial stake of officers and directors in their own corporations is relatively small. [Note: This is because they, like workers lower down, are merely employees, subject to dismissal. The largest holdings of officers, said the report, are in the hands of those who represent dominant or controlling family groups.]

The 20 largest shareholdings in each of the 200 corporations account, on the average, for *nearly one-third of the total value of all outstanding stock. In the average corporation the majority of the voting power is concentrated in the hands of not much over 1 percent of the stockholders.* [Emphasis added.]

As the study showed, the value of the twenty largest record holdings in 208 common stock issues as a percentage of total value was:

	Per Cent
Manufacturing companies	26.7
Railroads	24.9
Electric, gas and water utilities	45.3
Others	17.3

The relatively small percentage in the fourth category is accounted for by the fact that it included AT&T with its widely dispersed comparatively small shareholders.

But for the twenty largest stockholders to own such large percentages, *on the average*, of the leading companies testifies to the extremes of concentrated ownership in the American economy.

Most of the millions of individual stockholdings in the hands of a variety of run-of-the-mill people made up only 6 per cent of the ownership and voting power. The general anonymous stockholders, although up to twenty million by count in 1965, all together own very little and have as much to say as the Russians have over their rulers in the Kremlin.

"The great bulk of the 8 to 9 million domestic stockholders own only small amounts of stock and the dividends they receive represent but a minor proportion of their total income. About half of all stock-holders have an annual dividend income of less than $100 and holdings worth less than $2,000. The group which depends economically to a large extent on the dividends from corporate stocks or the market value of these stocks is very small and probably numbers not much more than 500,000 people.

"The ownership of the stock of all American corporations is highly concentrated. For example, 10,000 persons (0.008 percent of the population) own one-fourth, and 75,000 persons (0.06 percent of the population) own fully one-half, of all corporate stock held by individuals in this country."[2]

Foreign investors, it was pointed out, own more than 6 per cent of the common and nearly 4 per cent of the preferred stock of these companies, and "Foreign ownership exceeds 10 per cent of total stock outstanding in about one-tenth of the 200 corporations." [Note: These foreign holdings are held by comparable individual large European interests.]

These patterns persist down to the present, as shown conclusively by the Lampman, University of Michigan, Federal Reserve and many other studies, and also in what I shall refer to as The Dartmouth Study: *Corporate Concentration and Public Policy*, by Professors Martin L. Lindahl and William A. Carter of Dartmouth College.

Noting that the patterns persist does not mean that the position of the owners has remained stationary. Although the percentage of ownership in the economy may conceivably be no greater than the concentration of control, owing to the steadily increasing concentration of assets, it is unquestionably greater now than it ever was before. The only dropouts from the upper strata of ownership have been produced by the ending of a family line. None of the big fortunes pinpointed in the TNEC study has gone bankrupt. Under the impetus of economic and technical change, of course, some of the minor big fortunes have lost ground relative to the leaders; but as other elements have thrust their way forward, the essentials of the panorama have scarcely changed.

While it might be of some interest to pinpoint changes for the better or the worse within some fortunes, it is not within the scope of this exposition to make such an attractive digression. We may, therefore, be spared the details of who is worth $100 million more or less. The Ford Motor Company is reported to have taken a $250 million loss on its unsuccessful Edsel model, but the Ford family remains in the leading quartet of wealth. These big fortunes can afford to take big losses, and they do have their ups and downs. What they lose one day in one place they make up another day in another place. What permits them to do this is: heavy reserves, affording maneuverability.

The TNEC study broke itself down into types of control, either by family or corporation, as follows:

a. By majority ownership
b. By predominant majority
c. By substantial minority
d. By small minority

But in most cases control of one corporation by another saw the controlling corporation itself under single or multiple-family control.

The Thirteen Largest TNEC Family Interest Groups

As measured by market or calculated value at the end of 1937, the thirteen wealthiest family interest groups, led by the Du Ponts, Mellons, Rockefellers and Fords, also included the following:[3]

Family	Main Corporations
McCormick (Chicago)	International Harvester
Hartford (New York)	Great Atlantic & Pacific Tea
Harkness (New York)	Standard Oil (New Jersey)
	Standard Oil (Indiana)
	Standard Oil of California and
	Socony Vacuum Oil

Duke (North Carolina)	Duke Power, Aluminum Co. of America
	Liggett and Myers Tobacco
Pew (Philadelphia)	Sun Oil
Pitcairn (Pittsburgh)	Pittsburgh Plate Glass
Clark	Singer (sewing machines)
Reynolds (North Carolina)	R. J. Reynolds Tobacco
Kress (New York)	S. H. Kress (variety stores)

To be sure, as the study warned, "Many members of these groups undoubtedly had stock investments in one or more of the 200 corporations which did not appear among the 20 largest record shareholdings. . . . Many also had investments in other corporations, particularly in large financial corporations which are not covered by the study, and investments in other forms such as corporate bonds, tax-exempt securities, real estate, and bank deposits. It is quite possible that for some groups these outside investments had a larger aggregate value than their identified holdings in the 200 largest corporations."[4]

A point never made by the TNEC study is that this same pattern of concentrated ownership and control extends below the 200 largest companies to the 500 largest, the 1,000 largest, the 10,000 largest, etc. What is remarkable about the TNEC showing is not that there were shown ownership and control by such tiny groups but that there were such concentrated ownership and control over such mammoth corporate entities, which standard propaganda insists are widely owned by the rank-and-file citizenry as stockholders. As enterprises get smaller and smaller there is even less public participation in their ownership than in the biggest companies until one soon runs into the 100 per cent family-owned or individually owned closed corporation. It is no exaggeration to say that all money-making enterprises of whatever size, including the widely owned AT&T, are owned by a very small class of proprietors. Whatever property is scattered among nearly 90 per cent of the populace is mostly non-revenue-producing: much-used cars, TV and radio sets, furniture—in brief, chattels.

The Standard Oil branch of the Harkness family, now with few surviving members and its once vast funds largely distributed, mainly to leading educational institutions, was found to be among the twenty largest stockholders in no fewer than 24 of the 200 largest companies, apparently a record.[5] While this particular ownership is no longer concentrated, the fact that it recently existed shows what is possible within the system.

Family Control by Majority Ownership[6]

	Single Family	Main Corporation	Percentage of Ownership
1.	Dorrance	Campbell Soup	100
2.	Duke	Duke Power	82
3.	Ford	Ford Motor	100
4.	Hartford	Great Atlantic & Pacific	100
5.	James	Western Pacific RR	61.18
6.	Kress	S. H. Kress	79
7.	Mellon	Gulf Oil	69.5
8.	Mellon	Koppers	52
9.	Mellon	Pittsburgh Coal	50.9
10.	Pew	Sun Oil	69
	Multiple Family		
1.	Anderson-Clayton	Anderson, Clayton (Houston)	94-plus
2.	Clarke-Bourne-Singer	Singer	50-plus
3.	Phillips-Olmsted-Childs	Long Island Lighting	47-plus
4.	Bell-Darby-Cooper-Biddle-Duke *et al.*	American Cyanamid	88.77

A peculiarity about this last holding was that while most of the Class A voting stock was owned by eight senior officers—almost 29 per cent by W. B. Bell, president—most of the equity was represented by the Class B nonvoting stock. The twenty-two leading stockholders, with three tied for twentieth place, held 88.77 per cent of the voting stock.[7]

The holdings of the Hartford family in the Great Atlantic & Pacific Tea Company, which does more than 6 per cent of all retail grocery business in the United States, are not precisely ascertainable now on the basis of the TNEC report. The Hartfords owned at least 61 per cent of the old preferred stock, exchanged for three shares of common in the recapitalization of 1958, and all of the voting common, exchanged for one share of new common. In the old arrangement there were 935,812 shares of nonvoting common, also exchanged share-for-share for new common, but because the TNEC did not inquire into the Hartford ownership, if any, of this stock, its possible present ownership position (assuming no sales or purchases) cannot be completely deduced.

But, assuming the Hartfords owned none of the nonvoting stock and retained all their other stock in the exchange, they would now own very close to 70 per cent control of the company. At the end of 1964 all its outstanding common had a market value of $936,850,025, leaving the Hartford share at about $650 million. At the end of 1959, 33.98 of this outstanding stock was held by the John A. Hartford Foundation. I conclude, then, that the Hartford family through nominees still retains majority controlling ownership of this huge company by a wide margin.

Predominant Minority Control[8]

A predominant minority was defined in the TNEC study as consisting of the ownership of 30 to 50 per cent of the stock.[9]

Single Family (approximate number of income recipients)	Corporation	Percentage of Ownership
1. Du Pont (about 250)	E. I. du Pont de Nemours (controlling General Motors by 23 per cent)	44
2. Mellon (about 10)	Aluminum Co. of America	34.4
Mellon	Pittsburgh (Consolidation) Coal	50.9
3. Cudahy (about 32)	Cudahy	48.7[10]
4. Deere (4)	Deere	34.12[11]
5. Pitcairn (4 or more)	Pittsburgh Plate Glass	35.34[12]
6. Straus (14)	R. H. Macy	38.67[13]
7. Kresge (6)	S. S. Kresge	44.24[14]

Multiple Family[15]

1. Field-Simpson-Shedd	Marshall Field
2. Rosenstiel-Jacobi-Wiehe-Schwarzhaupt-Gergross	Schenley Distillers
3. Weyerhaeuser-Clapp-Bell-McKnight	Weyerhaeuser

The largest number of family interest groups was found to use the device of control by means of a substantial minority ownership of stock, which permits controlling positions to be taken in some cases in a wide spectrum of big companies. These were as follows:

Control by Substantial Minority[16]

Single Family	Corporation	
1. E. I. du Pont de Nemours & Co. (family controlled)	General Motors	
2. Crane	Crane	
3. Colgate	Colgate-Palmolive-Peet	
4. Firestone	Firestone Tire & Rubber	
5. Gimbel	Gimbel Brothers	
6. McCormick	International Harvester	
7. Hanna	National Steel	
8. Palmer	New Jersey Zinc	
9. Rockefeller	Ohio Oil (now	10
	Marathon Oil)	to
	Socony Vacuum Oil Co.	30
	(now Socony Mobil Oil)	per cent
	Standard Oil of California	in
	Standard Oil (Indiana)	each
	Standard Oil (New Jersey)	case
10. Levis	Owens-Illinois	
11. Mellon	Pullman	
12. Rosenwald	Sears, Roebuck	
13. Avery	U.S. Gypsum	
14. Du Pont	U.S. Rubber	
15. Williams	North American Co. (since dissolved into constituent public utility operating companies)	
Multiple Family		
1. Walters-Jenkins-Newcomer	Atlantic Coast Line RR	
2. Stone-Webster	Engineers Public Service Co. (since dissolved into constituent operating units)	
3. Davies-Woodward-Igleheart	General Foods	
4. Block-Ryerson-Jones	Inland Steel	
5. Rand-Watkins-Johnson-Peters	International Shoe	
6. Widener-Elkins-Dula-Ryan	Liggett & Myers Tobacco	10 to
7. Hillman-Shouvlin-Chalfant	National Supply (oil well supplies)	30 per cent
8. Miller-Volkman-Schilling	Pacific Lighting	in

9.	James-Dodge-Hanna	Phelps Dodge (copper)	each case
10.	Procter-Gamble-Cunningham	Procter and Gamble (soap)	
11.	Lynch-Merrill	Safeway Stores (groceries)	
12.	Kirby-Woolworth-Donahue-McCann	F. W. Woolworth	
13.	Hochschild-Loeb-Sussman	Climax Molybdenum	
	Hochschild-Loeb-Sussman	American Metal	

Small Minority Control[17]

	Family	Corporation	
1.	Moore	American Can	
2.	Zellerbach	Crown Zellerbach	
3.	Crawford	Lone Star Gas	Less
4.	Moore	National Biscuit	than
5.	Cornish	National Lead	10
6.	Du Pont-Phillips	Phillips Petroleum	per cent
7.	Swift	Swift	
8.	Warner	Warner Bros. Pictures	

We have named fifty-seven single families and combined, cooperating multiple-family groups that exercise control of the largest corporations by majority, predominant minority, substantial minority and small minority ownership. There were thirty-seven single-family-control entities, although some of these, such as the Mellons, Du Ponts and Rockefellers, each controlled several big companies. There were sixty-four single families in the multiple-family groups named, although in some cases the names are not given in this text. Perhaps as many as 400 families composed the various multiple-control groups in the 200 largest corporations.

Some of these companies, as noted, have changed their *modus operandi*, notably the public utility companies. Some have changed their names, like the Ohio Oil Company. Others have gone out of existence by the merger route. It is neither necessary nor expedient to trace here each company through various subsequent permutations and combinations, for equities are what concern us.

Have the percentage positions of these families remained the same in all these companies? Probably not. In some cases they have undoubtedly increased their holdings, in others they are known to have decreased.

Some may even have closed out their holdings. But, as pointed out earlier, if anyone has sold out in one place he has reinvested elsewhere, and possibly to better advantage. He is, therefore, still rich.

Knowing the value of the property from the inside, all these groups know when the stock is overpriced and when to sell. As the income-tax returns since the war show, the higher income groups have been steadily taking capital gains, which are taxed at a maximum of 25 per cent, a bargain in relation to the upper income taxes. Wealthy holders usually show a strong tendency to sell some holdings in rising markets and to buy again in declines, thus increasing their percentile position (Standard Doctrine). So their percentages of ownership change from time to time. Sales would not necessarily show on the books of a company. For a man can always sell the stock short.

With the exception only of two as far as I have been able to ascertain, all these families are still extant and still highly solvent. The exceptions are the Harknesses and Arthur Curtiss James (1867–1941), who died leaving no heirs. James left his money to a foundation with the fairly unusual stipulation that the principal was to be distributed in twenty-five years, which was done.[18] Like James himself, the foundation is now defunct.

There remains the case of one big company holding control of another big company. (Control of scores to hundreds of smaller companies by many of the big companies is the common pattern now in the American economy.) Nearly all of the 200 largest nonfinancial companies of the TNEC study, like most of the 500 industrials regularly featured by *Fortune,* are in fact holding companies, not operating companies at all. Just about all the big companies that are familiar household words in the United States are holding companies, contrary to the general public belief. AT&T, for example, is a holding company.

Corporate Control by Majority Ownership[19]

Holding Company	Operating Company	Per Cent
Armour (Illinois)	Armour (Delaware)	100
Cities Service	Empire Gas and Fuel	100
Royal Dutch Petroleum	Shell Union Oil	64
AT&T	Pacific Telephone & Telegraph	78.17
AT&T	New England Telephone & Telegraph	65.31
Chesapeake & Ohio Ry	New York, Chicago & St. Louis RR	57

Reading Company	Central Rail Road of N.J.	55
Atlantic Coast Line RR (under multiple Walters-Jenkins-Newcomer control)	Louisville & Nashville RR	51
Many public utility holding companies	Many public utility operating companies now cut loose	100

In many cases, particularly in railroads and public utilities, two corporations shared control.

A predominant minority as well as substantial and small minority control was exercised by many corporations, particularly in the railroad and electric utility fields. In this latter field, long subject to gross manipulative abuses, the companies holding widely scattered properties were finally dissolved by congressional decree and the equities in operating companies were distributed to individual stockholders.

Until very recently the most salient instance of a predominant minority control of one mammoth corporation by another was that of E. I. du Pont de Nemours and Company of the General Motors Corporation (discussed in Chapter IV).

While there were some cases where the big owners were underrepresented in the management by reason of "youth, old age, sex, preoccupation with other financial or nonfinancial interests or other considerations" heavy representation or even overrepresentation was "much more common."[20] Thus, although members of the Swift family owned only 5 per cent of the voting stock, the remainder of the stock being distributed mainly in slices of 100 to 500 shares each, the Swift family held six of the nine directorships. In the Crown Zellerbach Corporation the Zellerbach family, owning 8½ per cent of the stock, provided the president, a vice president and three directors out of a board of thirteen. It is not necessary, then, for a family to own a majority or near-majority of stock to control a company and the disposition of its total weight. A small family block of stock and many small general stockholders are enough to secure control of the board of directors and officers.

Nor did the revelations to the TNEC in all cases show the true center of control, owing to a complicated network of company ownerships. An example is the Tidewater Associated Oil Company which as of December 15, 1939, the date of the TNEC questionnaire, was already well in the pocket of J. Paul Getty, although unknown to the world. The TNEC report shows that 3.07 per cent of the common was owned by George F. Getty, Inc., which in turn was 43 per cent owned by J. Paul Getty in person and 57 per cent as trustee for his children. But Pacific Western Oil Corporation owned 3.93 per cent, and was in turn owned 67.9 per cent by George F. Getty, Inc., and 2.62 by the Mission Corporation. Again, the Mission Corporation owned 16.52 per cent, and was in turn owned 46.53 by Getty's Pacific Western Oil Corporation and, observe, 7.39 per cent by the Tidewater Associated Oil Company!

Directly and indirectly J. Paul Getty at the time, undetected by the TNEC analysts, already owned 23.52 per cent of the mammoth Tidewater enterprise. Actually, his percentage of control was somewhat higher than this because the South Penn Oil Company, of which Tidewater owned 17.27 per cent, reciprocally owned 2.77 of Tidewater. Mission Corporation was originally established to hold the interest of Standard Oil (New Jersey) in Tidewater but Getty, as he reports in his memoirs, talked John D. Rockefeller, Jr., into selling him his Mission stock and then in a quiet campaign prevailed on other stockholders to follow the Rockefeller lead. At the time of the TNEC study Standard Oil (Indiana) owned 1.05 per cent of Tidewater through the 98-per cent-owned Pan American Southern Corporation.[21]

The TNEC made a supplemental study of 10 interesting large companies that were not included on the list of the 200 largest. Some of them were as follows:[22]

Family	Corporation	Percentage Owned
Dorrance family (by trust indenture)	Campbell Soup	100
Woodruff-Nunnally-Stetson-Candler-Illges	Coca-Cola International (controlling Coca-Cola Co.)	nearly 50
Twenty individuals	Crucible Steel	45.55
Mainly members of the Bell family among twenty stockholders	General Mills	20.14
Havemeyer family, H. O. Havemeyer estate, and the Ossorio, Thatcher and Boettcher families	Great Western Sugar	43.34
Heinz family	H. J. Heinz	82.10
Twenty individual stockholders, mainly investment companies	International Utilities	26.71
Ajax Pipe Line	Standard Oil (Ohio)	24.77

Rockefeller Foundation	Standard Oil (Ohio)	17.63
Harkness-Flagler-Prentiss (Rockefeller)-four other individuals and 11 trust companies and brokerage houses for others	Standard Oil (Ohio)	10.92
St. Regis Paper	United Corporation (utility holding company)	8.332
American Superpower	United Corporation	6.640
J. P. Morgan & Co., Brown Brothers Harriman & Co., and 16 brokerage houses and investment firms	United Corporation	9.846

The tenth company on this supplemental list was the Electric Bond and Share Company, then a utility holding company and now an investment trust. Its twenty-one largest stockholders were banks, brokerage houses and investment companies, and the names of the beneficial owners of the stock were not elicited.

Leading family names not yet mentioned that were strewn through the twenty largest stockholders in the 200 largest nonfinancial companies —in many cases appearing in more than one company—were as follows:

Adler, Astor, Cabot, Clapp, Doris Duke Cromwell, Cunningham, Doherty, Drexel, Fleischmann, Forstmann, Goelet, Goldman, Guggenheim, Hanna, Hearst, Hillman, Hutton, Jones, Laughlin (Jones and Laughlin Steel), Lynch, McClintic, Miller, Milbank, Palmer, Payson, Penney, Pillsbury, Rosenwald, Schott, Skaggs, Vanderbilt, Watkins, Whitney, Widener and Winthrop.

Names of wealthy families that did not appear because their stockholdings were not among the twenty largest and were probably widely distributed in smaller blocks, rentier-style, through many companies or were in real estate or bonds, were the following:

Baker, Bedford, Berwind, Curtis-Bok, Fisher, Frick, Gould, Green, Hill, Kahn, Lehman, Metcalf, Patterson, Pratt, Phipps, Taft, Timken, Warburg and others.

These omissions, not at all to be deplored, came about because the TNEC study was not directed to ascertaining the names of all wealthy families—what it gleaned here was a byproduct—but merely of determining who controlled the 200 largest nonfinancial companies. Anyone who was concentrated mainly in real estate, banking, insurance or in widely diversified, nonconcentrated investments the study necessarily missed. All the new Texas oil men were missing. Joseph P. Kennedy's name did not appear.

Even if one had before one an up-to-date list of all the largest income-taxpayers, names of some extremely wealthy people could readily elude us, such as anyone who, like Mrs. Horace B. Dodge, had converted all her holdings into tax-exempt state and municipal securities. One could, theoretically, own a billion dollars worth of these, drawing a tax-free income of $25–$30 million a year, and never show up on the income-tax list at all.

What the TNEC analysis made incontrovertibly clear was that the family, not the individual, is now the significant wealth-holding and wealth-controlling entity in the United States, a thesis I had antecedently asserted, for the first time as far as I know.[23] While the proposition may seem firmly established to some it is, curiously, often denied or blandly ignored even though the SEC continues to supplement the TNEC findings in detail. One man may amass the fortune, as in the case of John D. Rockefeller, but if the fortune is to remain intact it must have heirs. Where the fortune-builder is a bachelor or fails to establish a family, the fortune simply disappears in a foundation or institutional grants. Heirs, then, are as important to a fortune as to a title of nobility. Most American fortunes, easily by a majority of 70 per cent, are in the hands today of heirs.

And, in saying that the family holds the fortune, one cannot suppose this to suggest that its members fend individually for themselves to all points of the compass. They must hold together, for their predecessors have in almost all cases entangled them in a network of trusts and family holding companies that assure unified action at all times.

No less than half of all these controlling corporate holdings were in "trust funds, estates, and family holding companies."[24] Even if an heir wished to go away on his own, all he could take with him would be income; the holding itself would remain in a center, massed with other individual holdings and directed by some individual or small family committee. This circumstance puts all the holdings into a tight fist, generating power that is played out in the political and cultural arena. Anyhow, who would want to walk away from the goose that lays the golden eggs?

Family Holding Companies

There are thousands of personal and family holding companies, large and small, in the United States. In most cases their names have never been seen or uttered by 99.9 per cent of the citizenry because these entities are private, are under no obligation to make any report to anyone except the tax authorities. No public compilation of them exists.

Their names usually only come to public attention through court proceedings or as the byproduct to certain government investigations, such as the TNEC inquiry. That particular inquiry did provide information about the existence of some extremely large family holding companies.

A family holding company may have a score or more participants of beneficial interest in it—infants, teen-agers, the superannuated, the mentally retarded, absent big game hunters, scholars and normal persons in the prime of life. But the slices of beneficial interest, apart from the income pay-out, are all managed as one entity by a single person or a family committee, which in turn is either adept in the management of large properties or has the benefit of expensive professional advice. An heir may seem deficient in business acumen to all who know him, but he may be the constant beneficiary of the best legal and investment advice available, perhaps even against his own wishes. He might prefer to take his stake and invest it in various attractive schemes, or spend it, but he is firmly deterred from this course by the family holding company. And it functions, up and down the line, according to Standard Doctrine.

We have already noticed, in connection with the Du Ponts, that the TNEC found a large role being played by the Christiana Securities Company and Almour Securities, Inc., both family holding companies. But other huge family companies were also uncovered in the report.

There was, first, the Bessemer Investment Company, instrument of the Phipps (Carnegie Steel) family that included, among many persons named Phipps, such names acquired by distaff marriages as Douglas, Janey, Sevastopoulo, Martin, and Winston and Raymond Guest. In all, twenty or more Phippses were beneficiaries. All appeared to have the financial status of rentiers and were well known social registerites and polo players. Bessemer Investment Company was found to be a principal stockholder in New England Power Association, International Hydro-Electric System and International Paper Company, whatever else it held of lesser dimensions.

Oldwood, Inc., was 66.58 per cent owned by the Bessemer Investment Company and a group including the Chace, Gammack, Majes, Cox Brady and Phipps families. It was a leading stockholder, too, in the New England Power Association.

More than twenty Du Ponts had a participation large enough to list for Christiana Securities Company, which had among its stockholders other Du Pont family holding companies such as Delaware Realty and Investment Company, Archmere, Inc., and Du Pont trust funds.

The Cliffs Corporation, the personal instrument of the Mather family, owned all the common stock of the Cleveland Cliffs Iron Company, which was among the principal stockholders of the Wheeling Steel Corporation and the Republic Steel Corporation.

The Coalesced Company was owned 50-50 by Paul Mellon and Ailsa Mellon Bruce, and in turn was among the top stockholders in Koppers United Co., The Virginian Railway Co., Pittsburgh Coal Company and General American Transportation Company.

The Mellon Securities Company, owned by Richard K. Mellon, Sarah Mellon Scaife and various Mellon trusts, was a leading stockholder in Aluminum Company of America and the Gulf Oil Corporation.

The Curtiss Southwestern Company belonged to Arthur Curtiss James and Harriet P. James and in turn was a principal owner of the Phelps Dodge Corporation, the Western Pacific Railroad Corporation and the Missouri-Kansas-Texas Railroad Company.

The Empire Power Corporation was the instrument of the Laurimore Corporation (owned by Ellis and Kathryn Phillips), the Delaware Olmsted Company (owned by the Olmsted family), the Eastern Seaboard Securities Corporation (a joint Olmsted-Phillips venture) and individual Olmsteds and Phillipses. Empire Power was a principal stockholder of the Long Island Lighting Company.

The Falls Company was a holding company for the very numerous Rosengarten family and was a principal stockholder of the United Gas Improvement Company, the Duquesne Light Company and the Philadelphia Electric Company.

The M. A. Hanna Company, monument to Mark Hanna of McKinley era fame, belonged to the Hanna family and its numerous inter-related genetic lines. It was a principal stockholder in Phelps Dodge, Lehigh Coal and Navigation and the National Steel Corporation.

The Illges Securities Company belonged to the numerous Illges-Chenoweth-Woodruff and other families and was a principal stockholder in the Coca-Cola Company.

The Illinois Glass Company was the holding company of the numerous Levis family and was a principal stockholder in Owens-Illinois Glass Company and National Distillers Products Corporation.

Light and Power Securities Corporation belonged to the Starling W. Childs family and was a principal stockholder in four large public utility companies.

The Miami Corporation, a holding company for the Deering estate, was a chief stockholder in International Harvester Company and the Chesapeake and Ohio Railway Company.

The New Castle Corporation, owned by Mr. and Mrs. Alfred P. Sloan, held the Sloan stock in the General Motors Corporation and the Phillips Petroleum Company, both among the big holdings.

The North Negros Sugar Company belonged to the Ossorio family and was a principal stockholder of the Great Western Sugar Company and the American Sugar Refining Company.

The Phillips family, quite numerous, owned the T. W. Phillips Gas and Oil Company, which in turn was the dominant stockholder of the Federal Water Service Corporation.

The Pitcairn Company, a leading stockholder in the Pittsburgh Plate Glass Company, the Consolidated Oil Corporation and the Columbia Gas and Electric Corporation, was owned by the Pitcairn family of Pittsburgh.

The Provident Securities Company was owned by William W. Crocker, Helen Crocker Russell, Charles Crocker and Ethel Mary de Limur and in turn was a leading stockholder of the Tidewater Associated Oil Company, General Mills, Inc., Pacific Telephone and Telegraph Company, Pacific Gas and Electric Company and the Southern California Edison Company.

The Rieck Investment Company belonged to the Rieck-Woodworth families and was a principal stockholder in the National Dairy Products Corporation and the Firestone Tire and Rubber Company.

The Taykair Corporation, which held a large number of serially numbered trusts, belonged to the Benjamin family and was a big stockholder in The Virginian Railway Company, Gimbel Brothers, Inc., and the Brooklyn Union Gas Company.

Serial and paralleling family holding companies are not uncommon. For example, the Colgate family, of the Colgate-Palmolive-Peet Company, reported a tangle of holding companies that with a few other relatively small interests made up 31.85 per cent of the twenty largest Colgate-Palmolive stockholdings. There was the Beechwood Securities Company; the Oakbrook Company; the Bertco Company; the Holly Security Company, which was 100 per cent owned by the Filston Security Company, itself a holding company for family members; and the Orange Security Company, owned 100 per cent by the Beechwood Securities Company; and then there were individual holdings by individual Colgates and distaff descendants.

One could go on at great length exhuming the names of hundreds of additional family holding companies but nothing would be added except repetitive detail to the essentials of this report.

It is not usually the case, then, that a big fortune is subject to the ownership and direction of some single individual, some dominating Croesus.

It is usually directed by a small family committee with access to expert professional advice, each member of this committee owning only a small percentage of the big pie. But the decisions respecting the big pie are the same as far as the world outside is concerned as if one man owning hundreds of millions made his will effective.

Under American law the entailment of estates is prohibited, but the prohibition has in effect been nullified through what may be termed serial entailment. For property owners of the third generation make provisions for placing property once again in untouchable trusts extending to three more generations, and so on *ad infinitum*. Boston is a particular center of such long-range serialized trusts.[25]

As in England under legal entailment, in the United States huge properties are thus secured for generations unborn. The future beneficiaries can never have made any compensatory social contribution and may never make any after they are born. They are simply privileged by prescription as under the longstanding American-despised European system.

Trust Funds

Whereas private family holding companies are a favorite way of keeping big holdings intact and under central direction (even though the beneficial interest in income may be spread among scores or hundreds of cousins, aunts and in-laws), there are also individual trust funds, usually under the direction of a bank. The concentration of many trust funds in large banks, of course, concentrates just this much industrial voting power under the boards of directors of the banks. It makes them powers in the land.

Some of these trusts are relatively small. But, altogether, they add up to an enormously big financial punch. And, as the banks largely maneuver according to the same point of view, they in effect act in concert in voting these securities in various corporations. Indeed the size of the holdings they represent often enables them to name members of corporate boards of directors, which is one of the reasons so many bank officials are found strewn among the corporate boards. The large amount of stock that places them in position is not their own. But it gives them a great deal of veiled authority.

In some cases, various apparently unconnected members of the boards of directors of the corporations are like so many horses running out of the same stables, carrying the same ownership colors. The family that is the biggest stockholder in Corporation X, holding 20 per cent, is also the biggest stockholder in the bank with many trust fund holdings in relatively small amounts of stock of Corporation X, also perhaps adding up to 20 per cent. Another bank, also holding a great deal of trust stock, perhaps 12 per cent in hundreds of trust funds, may not be controlled by any of the first parties but is merely a friendly back-scratching ally. Together the two groups absolutely control the corporation, name its officers, determine its policies, apply its influence.

To what extent are funds now under trusteeship?

"At the end of 1964, trust departments of commercial banks had investment responsibility for assets of approximately $150 billion, of which about $50 billion represented employee benefit accounts. In addition, bank trust departments provided investment management for agency accounts with assets of at least $35 billion."[26] In these last the banks acted as agents for other trustees. We see, then, that nonemployee or individual trust funds amount to at least $135 billion, although the true figure is actually larger than this, for there are nonbank trustees who do not make use of banks even as agents.

Of the trust holdings of national banks, "More than 59 percent of these assets were invested in common stocks; about 52 percent of the employee benefit accounts, and approximately 62 percent of the other accounts."[27]

Most of these trust funds were concentrated in a few large banks. "Twenty-one banks with investment responsibility for trust assets of more than $500 million held approximately 56 percent of the total, and the 100 largest trust departments held more than 80 percent of the trust assets of national banks. Asset concentration was greatest among employee benefit accounts for which the 21 largest national bank trust departments held almost 80 percent of the assets where national banks acted as trustee. Large trust departments, for the most part, are concentrated in the largest commercial banks, although there are many exceptions where moderate-sized banks have very large trust operations and vice versa."[28]

"National banks with trust assets in excess of $5 million reported having approximately 580,000 trust accounts, including 68,500 corporate accounts, and 340,000 accounts where they exercised investment responsibility."[29] These figures indicate, excluding the corporate employee accounts, that there are at least 920,000 individual or private trust accounts in national banks alone. Some persons, of course, are the beneficiaries of many trust funds. Not all trust funds are large, may indeed be as small as $5,000 or $10,000, but the larger banks will not accept these. The larger New York banks do not like to be named as trustee for anything under $100,000 even for inclusion in their collective trust funds, in which there is a mingling of many smallish trust funds with proportionate participations, as in an investment trust.

The average size of trust accounts where the bank exercised invest-ment responsibility, excluding employee benefit accounts, was $173,000; but in the larger banks the average size was $300,000. Smaller banks car-ried trust accounts at an average size of $53,000.[30]

But "Investment management accounts tend to be larger than the aver-age for other trust accounts, since many banks set a relatively high min-imum size or minimum fee on such accounts."[31] Thus the average size of such accounts was $582,000, and in the bigger banks it was $735,000.

In addition to national banks there are the state-chartered banks to be considered.

"We estimate that state-chartered banks have investment responsibility for trust assets, apart from those of employee benefit accounts, of approxi-mately $51 billion, bringing the total of such assets for all banks to approximately $105.5 billion."[32] Employee-benefit accounts in such state-chartered banks were estimated at $29.5 billion, with the New York State Banking Department alone accounting for $23.6 billion as a definite non-estimated figure. For all state-chartered banks, investment management accounts were estimated at $20 billion.[33]

Total trust accounts for which banks have investment responsibility, then, amounted to $155.8 billion at the end of 1964, of which $105.5 bil-lion represented nonemployee benefit or individual accounts.[34] There was another $35 billion for which the banks acted as investment advisory agencies and an unknown amount in the hands of individuals or corpo-rations that did not make use of banks as advisory agencies.

There are two significant aspects of these trust-fund figures.

First, they represent an entirely new set of statistics, the gathering of which was begun by the comptroller of the currency only in 1963.

Of greater significance, however, is that the figures show the deep foun-dations of vested inherited wealth in the United States. Trust funds are popularly thought of as solely for the benefit of widows and minor or-phans, and such are no doubt included among the beneficiaries. But, by and large, most of the beneficiaries are able-bodied adults, unwidowed, unorphaned and, as often as not, pleasantly idle. In many cases the first generation in receipt of trust-fund benefits never collects the princi-pal at all, which is left to the next generation. When principal is paid out, it is often in dribbling installments throughout the recipients' lifetimes. In the case of the original Marshall Field, trusts were established that did not allow the grandchildren to collect the last part of principal until they were fifty years of age.

Such provisos keep the fortune from being dissipated through the exer-cise of immature judgment. The first generation cannot disturb the principal and the next generation does not get all of it or, sometimes, any of it until its members are quite advanced in age. At that point many of them lock the principal, Boston-style, back in new trusts for the benefit of the next two generations. Again, too, inheritance taxes are bypassed except at those points where principal is paid over.

From a property-ownership point of view all this undoubtedly has great merit. But what it signifies for the unpropertied is that they will never lay hands on any of this property no matter how they perform, short of overturning the legal system and the military forces behind it. The beneficiaries cannot even be swindled out of their benefices. Obviously, economic opportunities, legal and illegal, are considerably narrowed for the multitude when so much property is closely sequestered for the benefit of unborn generations.

The trust funds, like the family holding companies, point up the fact that the United States, like the Europe it proposed to surpass in equality of opportunity, has developed a permanent hereditary propertied class. Indeed, owing to the far greater proportion of public ownership now in western Europe, the United States actually has more of a hereditary property system than does Europe.

And if this seems paradoxical, one may notice this even greater paradox: There are kings now in Europe who are far more democratic in their attitudes than the average American citizen.

What stocks are trust funds concentrated in? This is not difficult to ascertain. Although individual trust funds may, by stipulation, be concentrated in one or a few stocks, when there is no such stipulation the principle of diversification is resorted to by competent trust officers. This amounts to invoking the principle of the investment trusts that limits their holding of any issue to no more than 2 per cent of the entire capital. The big New York banks issue to interested parties the portfolio list of their collective trust funds—that is, those where many smaller trusts are mingled together, with each trust participating proportionately to its size. A small trust is defined in different ways by different banks and may be as much as $500,000. "Small" here means too small to be managed profitably by itself.

As these lists of collective trust funds show, the stock investment is mainly in the list of the 200 largest companies and the 500 largest industrial companies and the 50 largest merchandising, public utilities and railroads, respectively, on the annual *Fortune* lists. Trust funds are not invested in the biggest companies *per se* but in the relatively well-performing stable companies that are relatively cheapest at each time of purchase. Public utility and insurance company stocks have for some time especially attracted trust accounts.

While questionable practices were uncovered in some trust accounts in the 1930's, such as stuffing them with dubious issues for which the bank was in an underwriting syndicate (now no longer possible with the separation of underwriting from banking under the law), in an advanced jurisdiction like New York the trust companies are under strict state supervision. The trust company has come to the fore as an institution because of the many cases in the past where individual trustees have exercised bad judgment or turned out to have sticky fingers with respect to the trusteed property. The very life of a trust company depends upon its proper operation within average limits.

Before leaving this topic of trust funds one may ask: What is their major utility? The trust funds are designed to keep principal intact and impervious to error of inexperienced heirs, and to hold inheritance taxes to a minimum.

Family Holding Companies Revisited

The personal and family holding companies also perform this function, and more. A personal holding company is defined in the Revenue Code as a company owned 50 per cent or more by no more than five stockholders with income derived primarily from certain types of investments. The two Mellon entities already named are examples. The family holding companies are the equivalent of close investment trusts and operate under tax laws appropriate to such entities.

Says Standard Doctrine: "A personal holding company is a close corporation, organized to hold corporate stocks and bonds and other investment assets, including personal service contracts, and employed to retain income for distribution at such time as is most advantageous to the individual stockholders from a tax point of view."[35]

As of 1958, the latest date available, there were 6,285 personal holding companies. Another type of closely held corporation, similar in many cases in its functions, is the legally defined Small Business Corporation. There were, as of 1962, more than 120,000 of these. They are taxed through their stockholders, of which there may not be more than ten.

The personal holding companies are purely investment companies. The total assets for all of them were $5,236,429,000, but $4,304,158,000 of the assets were concentrated in only 652 with assets of $1 million or more; 25 had assets exceeding $50 million, 12 exceeding $25 million and 48 exceeding $10 million. Total income of these entities was $361,916,000, of which $216,822,000 came from dividends. Whatever their size, these were instrumentalities of larger property holders.[36]

A remaining advantage in both corporate forms is that they concentrate corporate voting power for the special benefit of all the beneficiaries. Let us, for the sake of simplicity, suppose that there is a family group of 200 individuals, each owning precisely $1 million stock in the mythical Super-Cosmos Corporation whose outstanding stock is valued at $1 billion. Each one of these persons would on the basis of his personal equity have little to say about the company, it is clear, but would be part of the rabble of minor stockholders. Combined, however, possibly in a group of personal holding companies, they own 20 per cent of the stock and thus name members of the board and are always well advised in advance of inner-company developments. Their representatives, too, can trade such inner-company information with similar groups in other companies for investment orientation. They are, also, politically powerful as a group.

Again, under existing tax laws it is the general strategy of the very rich to keep dividend pay-outs low in relation to earnings. The family investment company can hold back some of its income as corporate reserve, thus reducing the tax liability of its members. This corporate reserve, in turn, is reinvested.

In the sphere of operating corporations as a whole, producing goods or services for the public, the average dividend pay-out is ordinarily about 50 per cent of earnings. Some of the earnings are retained to replace worn-out equipment, to expand and to keep dividends stabilized in less profitable years. But corporations differ in their pay-out rates, even among good earners, ranging from zero to 80 per cent. Small stockholders tend to favor those with high pay-out rates. But many big stockholders have come to prefer those with small pay-out rates, for then personal income taxes are lower.

Control of companies, however exercised, enables one to have something to say on this important subject of pay-out rates.

But in recent years many of the large corporations have retained earnings greatly in excess of replacement and future dividend needs. Such earnings have been used in the acquisition of companies in unrelated fields, as part of a policy of investment diversification, and in buying control of foreign companies, which might be classed as economic imperialism. The advantage to the big stockholders is that the money is not paid out in taxable income but is continually ploughed back to increase the underlying value of equities. However, if any big stockholder wants more income he can take it in the form of low-taxed capital gains by selling some of his stock. The large yearly aggregates of capital-gain income reported to the Internal Revenue Bureau since 1950 reveal what is happening.

A fairly recent concept that has emerged in the corporate world is that of the "growth company." A growth company, manifestly, is a company that grows. The name is attached rather indiscriminately by brokers to new companies in technologically novel fields: electronics, space-age, atomic power, etc. Not all of these are growth companies for, as experience shows, not all of them grow. But any company that ploughs back a large proportion of its earnings steadily is obviously a growth company. With taxes in mind such companies are advantageous.

The very wealthy, in brief, are less interested in increasing their taxable incomes than in increasing their nontaxable ownership stake. This, when necessary, can always be cashed.

Observations En Passant

There remain some observations to be made about the American hereditary owners, contradicting common beliefs.

It is generally supposed that the heirs of the big fortune-builders are comparatively incompetent playboys or at best poor copies of the original Old Man. While wastrels have been seen among some of the very wealthy, most of them women or some man intent upon impressing some woman (Astor, Vanderbilt, Hearst and others), in all the big surviving fortunes the heirs seem to show greater and greater finesse in applying Standard Doctrine under more and more complex conditions. The original fortune-builder might not understand everything they were doing but he would have to admit they are getting results as good as or better than he ever got. One reason for this is that the heirs now have available to them much more highly developed professional experts, deeply versed in the intricacies of each situation: economists, statisticians, analysts, engineers, psychologists, lawyers and the like.

Two original Du Ponts did very well in launching E. I. du Pont de Nemours and Company and deserve a reverent salute from all deeply committed money fans. But they seem to have been outdone by every succeeding generation of Du Ponts, each of which appears to have missed no opportunity to enlarge that part of the fortune it inherited.

The same with the Fords. After his first great success Henry Ford, set in his ways, dogmatic, began to lose his touch. He refused to defer to his son Edsel, who close observers believe would have put the company on a sounder footing than it found itself in the 1940's. But Henry Ford II, a grandson in his twenties, later aided by two younger brothers, brought the Ford Motor Company up to new heights of wealth, public esteem and prestige. In a little more than ten years the grandsons more than sextupled the value of the company, outperforming the economy as a whole, and have no doubt engaged in unknown side *coups* of more than modest proportions.

Judge Thomas Mellon's sons outdid his financial feats, and his grandchildren do not appear, under more difficult circumstances, to have lost the golden touch. The Mellons are still going strong, surrounded by family holding companies, trust funds and banks.

As to the Rockefellers, it might appear that none of them will ever be able to outdistance the wily old monopolist who put the family on the financial and political maps. But many authorities would argue that John D. Rockefeller, Jr., performed a far more difficult feat in holding the fortune together under strong political attack. Judge Mellon's opinion that it is harder to hold on to money than to make it has been explicitly made part of Standard Doctrine.[37]

If this is so then Rockefeller, Jr., who inherited a difficult situation, must be considered to have surpassed his father. The grandchildren are doing even better, for in addition to advancing the family fortunes they have performed the difficult feat of making themselves the idols of a considerable public.

As to it being more difficult to retain money than to make it, probably few would readily agree with this proposition. But slight reflection will show that it is true. Most adults have jobs and are paid. But how long does the weekly pay check last? Could one resolve not to spend it? Most people could not make such a resolution unless they wished to starve. Actually, most persons are unable to save as much as an average 5 per cent of their earnings. This state of affairs illustrates the point.

The average man in the street might contend that if his pay were only higher he would retain some of it; and in some few cases, let us agree, he would. But from time to time there are big sweepstakes and lottery winners, suddenly possessed of goodly sums. How old Judge Mellon would smile if he could hear them excitedly telling newspaper reporters what they are going to do with their windfalls: a new house, a new wheelchair for grandma, crutches for Tiny Tim, a new car, a trip to Florida and then some government bonds of declining purchasing power! A year or so later, as it turns out, they are all where they were financially to begin with, looking back wistfully to the time they were suddenly rich. What happened to the money? they ask. Where did it go?

What defeats most people in holding onto money, reinforcing the judgment of Judge Mellon, is that they are basically childish spenders. And therein lies part of the opportunity of acquisitive moneymakers. One task of the marketplace is to separate people from their money, often giving them something meretricious in return.

Present Status of 200 TNEC Corporations

What has happened to the two hundred corporations of the TNEC in the twenty-five years that have elapsed? Have any fallen by the wayside, carrying their owners to disaster? Have any slipped from the top of the heap?

"Analysis of the 1937 group of 200 non-financial corporations," according to The Dartmouth Study[38] "reveals on the surface a number of things. In terms of *current* dollar values there has been great growth for the group as a whole. In terms of *constant* dollars (values adjusted for depreciation of money), the total growth is probably not much greater than the rate of growth of our economy. This point cannot be pressed further, however, in the absence of detailed information about the accounting adjustments which the various firms have made as the value of the dollar has declined and as new assets have been added."

The TNEC list is set forth parallel with the 1964 list of biggest non-financial corporations in Appendix B.

There have been changes of detail in the list (although not significant) with respect to who owns and controls the wealth. With the exception of a few newcomers, the same groups own the companies as owned them in 1937.

Certain companies have moved off the master list of the leading 200, not because they have lost out entirely but because they have been squeezed off by mergers or by the emergence of new industries such as aviation and natural gas pipelines.

Except for the Mellon (Pittsburgh) Consolidation Coal Company, all coal companies have been pushed off the list, replaced by gas pipelines. Railroads have moved down on the list and some have moved off; but a merger kept Erie-Lackawanna on the list. Pullman, Inc., a Mellon enterprise, has declined, partly because of an adverse antitrust decision. It is evident that the loss of a monopoly position in the face of new means of transport is what has taken the bloom off the railroads. In meat packing, the "big four" have been supplanted by the "big two"—Swift and Armour.

The electric utilities on the two lists are not strictly comparable. On the later list are many new regional companies that are the outcome of the dissolution of the old holding companies. But in essentials the same electric power properties are on both lists, though often under different names.

Film companies have been pushed off the list, owing to the competitive advent of television and adverse antitrust decisions. Their owners were never seriously classified among the big-wealthy.

In all, close to fifty companies appear to have been pushed off the list. In addition to three coal companies, two packers and fifteen old-line utility holding companies, they are: Texas Gulf Sulphur, American Sugar Refining, American Woolen (Textron), Hearst Consolidated, International Shoe, New Jersey Zinc, U.S. Smelting, National Supply, United Shoe Machinery, Gimbel's, Marshall Field, R. H. Macy, Hudson and Manhattan Rail Road, six interstate railroads and two film companies. No really big interests experienced a decline.

Some newcomers are the product of split-offs. Western Electric came out of AT&T and now ranks twenty-fifth in size. The only other newcomer in the first twenty-five is Tennessee Gas Transmission, representing new capital mobilization. The only newcomer in the second twenty-five is El Paso Natural Gas, owing to similar circumstances.

The second fifty have among them as new faces only Sperry Rand and Olin Mathieson, outcomes of mergers.

The most recent list, in brief, represents the same old crowd with a few additions produced mainly by mergers and subtractions by squeezing.

At the very top there is no change except that the companies have grown much larger. AT&T, largest company in the world, leader of both lists and the stock of which is widely held, had total 1964 assets of $30.306 billion compared with $3.859 billion in 1937. Standard Oil (New Jersey), largest purely industrial company in the world in point of assets, had assets of $12.49 billion compared with $2.06 billion in 1937, and was in second place both times.

The smallest company on the TNEC list was Texas Gulf Sulphur, with assets of $62.9 million. The smallest company on the later *Fortune* list was Scott Paper, closely shadowed by Allied Stores, with assets of $413.8 million.

The TNEC list was compiled during a depression, the *Fortune* list after a war and twenty years of boom, heightened concentration and inflation.

As to the owners and controllers, there has been no significant change except that they are more firmly established in the ascendancy than before. Four Rockefeller companies appear among the first twenty-five compared with 3 in 1937, and there are 6 of them on the TNEC list and 7 on the *Fortune* list. The two big Du Pont companies have moved up among the first twenty-five, improving relatively. One of the chief Mellon properties, Gulf Oil, has moved into the first twenty-five, in eighth place, where it was not to be found in 1937. The Ford Motor Company has moved up from twenty-third to fourth place.

One of the most spectacular improvements in the approximately thirty or so years separating the two lists was Sears, Roebuck and Company, which moved from sixty-ninth place, with assets of $284 million, to ninth place, with assets of $4.271 billion, making it the world's leading retail merchandiser. The position of the dominant Rosenwald family has been correspondingly improved, making it easily worth more than $500 million and on the threshold of super-wealth. An even more spectacular growth company was International Business Machines, leader of the computer-automation field, which moved from one hundred eighty-fifth to twelfth place in size of assets.

Most of the newcomers to the list, however, are the result of mergers, spin-offs or the rise of new industries such as aviation and gas pipelines on the basis of new capital. But, although there are newcomers, few of the newcomers are new properties. Mergers either brought companies onto the list, moved companies up on the list or kept them on the list: General Telephone, American Metal Climax, International Telephone and Telegraph, Olin Mathieson, Burlington Industries, Erie-Lackawanna, Georgia-Pacific, General Dynamics, United Merchants and others.

While the lists in both cases represent only a small sample of American companies, these companies represent almost 70 per cent of U.S. output. Basic economic activity outside these lists represents the lesser portion of the pie.

Aluminum Company of America moved from seventy-ninth to thirty-eighth place even though its monopoly position was broken by the sale of wartime government aluminum plants to competitors. The Kaiser interests —one of these competitors, and nurtured by government patronage—have put no less than three new companies on the master list: Kaiser Aluminum, Kaiser Industries and Kaiser Steel.

The Pew family's Sun Oil Company moved up from one hundred thirty-eighth place to seventy-fifth. Although J. Paul Getty's Tidewater Oil is only sixty-ninth on the list, up from ninety-second place, it should be remembered that Getty owns most of it and has many other oil interests whose lesser dimensions fail to qualify them for this list.

Viewed again purely from the perspective of this most recent list of the biggest American proprietors, the financial grand dukes of the United States appear still to be, individually and collectively, the Rockefellers, Du Ponts, Fords, Mellons, Rosenwalds, Pews, Gettys, Phippses, Mathers, Hartfords, McCormicks and individuals like Allen Kirby, who in addition to his New York Central and Woolworth holdings is a leading stockholder of the big Manufacturers Hanover Trust Co. of New York.

The old question pops up: Have positions in these companies been maintained at the same level throughout the years? In some cases, as in that of the Du Ponts, we know they have. There have been some shifts in Rockefeller holdings, and the Ford holdings are about what they were when Henry Ford I died. At the time of the TNEC study the Rosenwalds held 12.5 per cent of Sears, Roebuck. In view of the steady strong growth of this company one would not suppose they would have sold out. If anything, guided by Standard Doctrine, they would have increased their holdings.

As groups like railroads and coal companies declined in the economy, no doubt leading holders tended to sell them out. But they may also have reestablished positions at lower prices, and in recent years the railroads have shown great improvement, both in earnings and in market action of securities.

No big interests such as Hartfords, Zellerbachs, Weyerhaeusers, Dukes, Pitcairns. Mathews, Swifts and others are reported to have cleared out. Among smaller interests there have undoubtedly been inter-company shifts of holdings, as into oils, aviation, natural gas and gas pipelines.

Old money, though, has found its way into successful new enterprises, as in the Harriman-Warburg-Strauss ground-floor investment in Polaroid.

We have seen that concentrated ownership is a more prominent feature of small companies. This circumstance and the fact that there is such concentrated ownership of very large companies show that concentration of ownership and control in few hands is a built-in feature of the American economy. While twenty million or more stockholders have an equity (usually trifling) in these and hundreds of other companies, it is a fact, as the TNEC study showed, that from two to three up to twenty of the largest stockholders own very large to total percentages of the companies. Total ownership by small inter-related groups was shown for Great Atlantic & Pacific Tea Company, Ford Motor Company and Campbell Soup Company. The small stockholders are therefore no more than insects crawling on the backs of rhinoceri.

Six

WHERE ARE THEY NOW?

As the TNEC data are more than twenty-five years old the question naturally arises: Are these large holdings of wealth still extant? Have they not been destroyed by ruthlessly vicious taxation? Aren't the large heirs—under pressure not only of a monstrous tax burden but of militant trade unions, draconic government regulation, intense competition with each other, hostile legislators, public welfare schemes at home and Communist inroads at home and abroad—really in reduced and increasingly precarious circumstances?

The sociologist C. Wright Mills, as noticed in Chapter 2, note 2, found difficulty in ascertaining who was wealthy. He spent a good deal of time making inquiries of people supposed to know and who, though sympathetic to his quest, found the question of identities equally mysterious. He was reduced to culling names as they had been more or less randomly mentioned in various books and by authors dealing with unsystematic data and constructing his own architectonic symmetries from them.

While it cannot be claimed on the basis of any available collection of data that one has unearthed every wealthy person and clan, the means are at hand for making far better contemporary determinations than did Mills, who was apparently not aware of the monumental TNEC data. But even the TNEC findings are continually being supplemented in monthly reports of significant securities transactions, required by law, to the United States Securities and Exchange Commission (SEC). Moreover, any new issuance of securities by an existing company, or in the launching of a new company, requires that information be supplied to the SEC about major individual participations in ownership. This information is open to public scrutiny.

The reports to the SEC are tabulated alphabetically and published each month in the *Official Summary of Security Transactions and Holdings,* published by the United States Securities and Exchange Commission. All persons can consult back numbers in any central metropolitan public library or can subscribe to the publication at $1.50 per year.

Under the Securities and Exchange Act, 1934, all corporate officers, directors, closed-end investment companies and individual nonofficer owners or beneficiaries of 10 per cent or more of any securities issue of any company offering securities for sale in the American market must report each month all purchases, sales or other transfers of securities in any company in which they have a direct or indirect interest.

This requirement in some ways provides far more data than did the TNEC study. For it relates to *all* security-selling companies, not merely the 200 largest. And while, unlike the TNEC study, it does not single out the largest stockholders as such, the requirement that stockholders owning 10 per cent or more of any issue report changes in investment position often discloses the biggest elements. If someone owned only 2 per cent of an issue but was among the twenty largest stockholders, the SEC reports, unlike the TNEC study, would not disclose him unless he was also an officer or a director.

To some extent the 10-per cent requirement partially screens big wealth, which is held mainly in family phalanxes. For if three buyers or sellers each held 9.9 per cent of the stock of a big company, amounting to 29.7 per cent control, the SEC reports would not show them unless they were officers or directors. The same would be true if ten members of a family each owned 5.5 per cent of the stock, amounting to 55 per cent or absolute control. They could be represented on the board of directors by nominess, their own lawyers or bankers, who might hold only a few directors' qualifying shares.

Not only do the SEC reports show purchases and sales but also acquisitions or dispositions by bequest or inheritance, compensation, corporate distribution, exchange or conversion, stock dividends, stock splits, redemptions and gifts. While personal gifts of stock are strewn throughout the year (apparently in observance of birthdays), Christmas appears to be a favorite time of the propertied for giving stock. The Christmas gifts are expecially reflected in the January and February reports for each year.

What the SEC reports do *not* tell us about wealth-holdings would perhaps be a better guide than the statement of what they do contain.

The SEC reports do not inform us at all about (1) federal, state and municipal bondholdings (although they do inform us about corporate bondholdings and about all senior and junior issues); (2) noncorporate real estate, land or mortgage holdings; (3) personal interests in enterprises abroad that do not offer securities in the American market; (4) holdings of noncorporate promissory notes, options, cash, foreign exchange, insurance policies and collections of jewels or *objets d'art*; or (5) miscellaneous personal property, such as Swiss bank accounts, racing stables, foreign islands, yachts, airplanes and cars.

It is not our intention to determine the exact extent of participation of any fortune in a particular property, although the TNEC study did make such a determination possible with respect to the largest corporations. Nor is it our intention to determine the exact investment position of any fortune at any given moment. Such a determination could only be made by a new government study or by a Permanent National Economic Committee; even the TNEC study did not inquire into stockholdings below the top twenty, although a person could be incalculably wealthy if he was the twenty-first largest stockholder in many companies. Nor is it our intention to trace shifts in holdings among various companies, although in certain cases such shifts are clearly shown by SEC data.

Despite the logical possibility of concealment of a fortune in, say, tax-exempt bonds or jewels, it should be noticed that no big fortune was ever *made* in such investment media. The modern corporation, plus engineering technique, more recently aided by huge government contracts, is the big and virtually exclusive instrument of modern fortune-building, and a fortune once made cannot disappear from view merely by going into tax-exempts or real estate. One can usually trace it, as in the case of Delphine Dodge, at least up to the point of its conversion into more static media.

Even with the help of the voluminous SEC reports, it is possible to lose exact trace of some large fortunes although, having no evidence of their destruction, one knows they must still exist in some form. Individuals or groups owning 15 per cent of enterprises scrutinized by the TNEC may have halved their participation and spread the proceeds of sale among various companies. If they do not function as officers or directors or hold at least 10 per cent of some company, their further transactions are not reported by the SEC.

Lamentable though this may appear, it does not impede us by much for most of the large interests stay put. They are more likely to increase their holdings as J. Paul Getty and the Du Ponts have steadily done to the date of this writing, than to reduce them. If they merely retain their holdings, new investments are apt to be made with income from the old investments, thus obtaining desirable diversification as a shield against changes of various kinds: technological, political, cultural, economic and social.

Aims of SEC Reports

The object of the SEC reports was to terminate the rigging of securities markets, prevalent before the passage of their enabling law. Before the law was passed, company officers, directors and leading stockholders (while issuing optimistic or pessimistic reports) would secretly sell or buy the company's stock on the basis of knowledge at variance with the reports. A large public of gullible small stockbuyers was in this way repeatedly stung and tended gradually to lose faith in the riproaring Republic for which an earlier gullible horde had bled and died.

Under the securities law, insiders cannot long keep to themselves favorable or unfavorable turns in a company's outlook. Again, what they say can be evaluated in relation to what they actually do in their own securities.

Buying and selling by insiders do not invariably indicate something about a company. Insiders, too, have been wrong in their estimates of a company's position in the context of public policies and conditions. Sometimes insiders sell some of their holdings because they need money for taxes, because they see a better opportunity elsewhere or because they have a fixed policy of taking low-tax capital gains in companies with low dividend payouts. Usually it means only that they are taking profits or avoiding losses.

Some small market operators mechanically follow the buying and selling of insiders, but not with universally fortunate results. Everything else being equal, as it seldom is, it is not a bad policy to pay heed to company officers and directors when they buy or sell heavily. For this reason the SEC monthly reports are closely studied by market *aficionados*. But company officers, playing only for swings in the market, often sell as quickly as they buy and the knowledge is only available a month later—sometimes too late for outsiders.

One thing the SEC reports show clearly is that in many companies the officers and directors repeatedly buy and sell as a block. Presented to the country as masterful managers of giant enterprises that are the envy of the world, as builders of the nation indeed, they nevertheless in many cases seem interested in playing this private poker game which has no economic justification. It does nothing for gross national product. In so doing they show they are basically Pecuniary Men willing to turn their attention to anything that will swell their bankrolls. If they could go out on the corner and make money by trading baseball cards or stamps the way children do, or lagging pennies, one would find them out on the corner. Their icon is the stock ticker.

Different companies have different policies about timely flutters in the securities market by officers and directors. In some cases such transactions are rare. In many companies it is apparently thought to be one of the perquisites of officers to trade up and down in a percentage of their holdings, thus incurring low capital-gains taxes while getting more income so their wives and children won't fall behind on country-club dues.

With such factors in mind the monthly SEC reports on holdings have been selectively checked with a view to updating the TNEC data, thus reassuring anxious critics that our material is all fresh and new. But, in general, in-and-out trading by mere company officers and directors has been ignored here except when it has seemed to be of significant proportions or by significant officers.

Attention has been concentrated pretty much on the original TNEC list and the 1964 *Fortune* list of the largest nonfinancial companies, although there is also presented an extensive listing of control groups in other well-known companies.

As to the method used in examining the SEC reports, which embrace thousands of companies and tens of thousands of individuals: The reports have been closely scrutinized in their entirety from 1960, inclusive, through 1965. As every transaction registered requires that the net remaining holding be given, one is assured of what the latest position is, confirming or not the TNEC finding at a distance of about twenty-five years. In this way, too, latecoming names of big holders (if they buy or sell) are brought into view.

Where significant large holdings have not turned up in this 1960 decade, a special tracing backward by individual companies was made prior to 1960 to ascertain the latest date when a net position was given for some family member (thus showing the continued presence of the family).

In certain companies the holdings were traced back to 1945 or to the point that yielded the latest total holding. Such a complete tracing was made of all the major Rockefeller, Mellon, Ford, Du Pont and Rosenwald properties; it was not necessary in the case of others because their presence is fully revealed by the data of the 1960's in almost all cases.

What may seem to be a defect in this method, and perhaps it is a genuine defect, is that by stopping the retroactive survey with 1960 we won't pick up any new investments made by either new or old wealth-holders prior to 1960. But the objective here is not to show the entire investment position of either new or old wealth-holders or to trace all these elements from one company to another in such cases in which they have transferred investment allegiance. All I am trying to do is to show who is rich *now* and who is a big newcomer to riches by presenting some large samples.

Nor am I trying to develop in detail the names and holdings of every one of 90,000 or more millionaires. Limited space makes it necessary to confine attention to the cream of the crop.

In the case of some of the new companies, I have examined the original prospectus filed with the SEC, as required by law, to ascertain any significant changes in holdings and identities. Particular attention was given to the new public utility operating companies organized out of the old holding companies, because as matters stood in the earlier chapter we tended to lose sight of the owners in the shuffle. The question is: Are they still there? If not, who has taken their place?

We are initially armed with the fact that these companies aren't owned by just anybody out of 190 million-odd in the population. Even the most tenuous kind of ownership puts the owner into about 10 per cent of the populace. And any holding of any kind worth minimally $60,000 net as of 1953 places him within 1.6 per cent of the population. The holdings with which we are most concerned are limited to a circle consisting of 0.11 of 1 per cent of the population.

Thus narrowed, our attention is focused directly on the biggest American proprietors—the magnates, the big shots.

The SEC requires that reports of a person's entire interest be made if there is any change in any holding in which he has a beneficial interest. This means that his personal holdings, those in which he has an indirect beneficial interest as from a trust or family holding company, those held by a spouse, those for which he acts as trustee or custodian, must all be reported if more than 100 shares are bought or sold in any part of the holding, direct or indirect. A good picture is therefore given of particular beneficial interests.

While such reporting is for individuals—except when made by a closed-end or family investment company—the holdings of big financial groups are revealed through different transactions on behalf of various members of a family.

It is true that this method will not reveal the holdings of an entire family group in a particular company unless every member of the group engages in transactions, as they sometimes do. But we already know the names of the big family groups so that if we see one member altering his investment position it may be deduced that the others are still solvent but are merely not interested in buying or selling.

We cannot tell in every case who is better off or worse off. A family group may have closed out a very large holding and diversified its ownership in smaller slices in many companies. The new diversified position may have improved its position or not. In dollar values, owing to the general inflation of prices, probably all positions have been improved. At the very top, among Mellons, Du Ponts, Rockefellers, Rosenwalds, Fords and Pews, we know that relative positions have been improved because their companies have outperformed the economy, sometimes by very wide margins. Comparisons can be made here by relating gross sales to gross national product, gross income to national income and net income to net national income.

The reports are set down by the SEC in the following general form:

John Doe	Transaction $\pm$ X shares	Net Holding X shares
Trust	X_1 do.	X_1 do.
Savings fund	X_2 do.	X_2 do.
Employer's fund	X_3 do.	X_3 do.
Wife or family	X_4 do.	X_4 do.
As trustee	X_5 do.	X_5 do.
As custodian	X_6 do.	X_6 do.
Investment company	X_7 do.	X_7 do.
Partnership	X_8 do.	X_8 do.

The plus-or-minus, indicating a purchase or sale, is credited in the SEC report to whatever individual or instrumentality did the buying or selling.

It would require too much space here to report individual by individual in this way. A somewhat different form of presentation has been adopted to convey the same information.

Our findings will be set forth as much as possible in semi-tabular form. Although share totals will be given, they will not be translated into market values. This task may be left as an exercise for the interested reader, who will be given the 1965 prices for the biggest companies.

As a foretaste of what we are after let us ask, for example, how do matters stand in the late 1960's with J. Paul Getty? Is he still rich? The SEC *Official Summary*, September, 1965, informs us that he personally owned 4,610,217 shares of the Getty Oil Company and was an indirect participant in trusts with 7,948,272 shares—a total of 12,558,489 shares or about 80 per cent. At a price of 34⅞ for Getty Oil on November 22, 1965, this holding had a market value of nearly $438 million; in late 1967, $1.2 billion.

This figure by no means represents everything owned by Getty, who is interested directly and indirectly in many other companies, but it does satisfy us that he is still very rich, probably worth more than a billion. And that is all we are concerned with. For many years, he and his companies have been steadily adding to their holdings. The SEC report for July, 1965, showed Getty Oil owned 4,077,240 shares of Mission Development, a different company. The report for December, 1963, showed that Getty Oil, after buying 21,169 shares, owned 2,748,883 shares or 63 per cent of Tidewater Oil Company, in which J. Paul Getty through a trust fund owned now only 4,225 shares. He owned none directly, having exchanged his earlier Tidewater stock for Getty Oil stock. The report for June, 1964, showed that Mission Corporation in turn, after buying 8,500 shares, owned 3,431,280 shares of Skelly Oil Company. These are all majority ownerships.

We could go on in this way analyzing the multifarious holdings and interholdings of J. Paul Getty but we would never get to the bottom of it in any event. For Getty, like many others, is a big foreign operator and unquestionably does not have all his holdings registered on the American record.

Getty is clearly officially certified as still in possession of vast wealth. But we must continue, as there may be gnawing doubts about others, such as Rockefellers and Pews, Pitcairns, Du Ponts, McCormicks and Rosenwalds, Clarks and Dukes.[1]

In requiring reports of a beneficial interest in trust funds and of holdings as a trustee, the law reveals a large portion of the social security system of the rich. It is an excellent system, and provides much security for its beneficiaries. But in considering it, one wonders about the oft-heard thesis of many conservative and ultra-conservative spokesmen and newspapers that the federal Social Security System, the Family Welfare System and the trade-union system all carry great danger of destroying the characters of the participants. They might, among other things, become mercenary or lazy.

The rich themselves very evidently do not believe that being the beneficiaries of huge trust funds has undermined their characters, or that establishing trust funds for their children will distort the children's characters. No case has come to light where the children of the wealthy have been left penniless for their own benefit. All known cases of disinheritance are punitive, because the children have displeased the parents. Why, if drawing benefits without labor from a big trust fund does not destroy character, will drawing benefits in old age from Social Security or a pension system do so? Why would a true Welfare State be injurious to the general pub-

lic when a private welfare system of trust funds is not apparently injurious
to its limited number of beneficiary heirs?

The Du Ponts Today

As it is never wrong to begin with the Du Ponts in any discussion of
American wealth, let us begin with this fabulous clan, leveling our fundamental question: Where are they now, financially speaking? The evidence strongly suggests that they are still massively concentrated in
Christiana Securities Company, E. I. du Pont de Nemours and Company,
General Motors, Remington Arms and other enterprises of the kind they
were partial to in the 1930's. They stand approximately where they were
shown to be in the TNEC study. They have neither gone elsewhere,
suffered diminution, become bored with property ownership nor disap-
peared. Taxes have not exterminated them or even visibly shaken them.

Some revelatory SEC reports by members of the Du Pont family in the
1960's are, incompletely, as follows (dates refer to monthly issues of the
Official Summary of Security Transactions and Holdings):

Christiana Securities Company   Price range 1965: $232–$315

	Shares	Date Reported
Irénée du Pont, Jr.	150,460	March, 1965
Trust	22,322	
A. Felix du Pont, Jr.	20,510	
Trust	92,132	
L. du Pont Copeland	252,657	August, 1964
Trust	100	
Crawford H. Greenewalt	52,848	
Trust	4,410	
S. Hallock du Pont	140,000	March, 1964
William Winder Laird	88,546	August, 1963
R. R. M. Carpenter, Jr.	11,520	February, 1963
Trusts	130,995	
Pierre S. du Pont	29,472	October, 1961
Lammot du Pont Copeland, through Delaware Realty and Investment, merged with Christiana	52,299*	

These holdings vary from year to year. Some of the Du Ponts are, from

* Shares of Delaware Realty and Investment

time to time, fairly active traders in a marginal percentage of their hold-ings. And while they do not reflect the entire holding of the Du Pont family in Christiana Securities, for which the TNEC study showed the family owning 73.958 per cent of common and 58.541 of preferred prior to its absorption of Delaware Realty (of which the family owned 83.985 per cent), what these deals since 1960 do positively show is that the Du Pont family is today still ensconced where it was found to be by the TNEC inquiry.[2]

As for E. I. du Pont de Nemours and Company, the world's largest chemical company, the SEC reports show the following incomplete recent holdings:

E. I. du Pont de Nemours   Price range 1965: $225¼–$261

	Shares	Date Reported
Christiana Securities	13,416,120	February, 1965
Crawford H. Greenewalt	11,710	
Co-trustee	4,000	
L. du Pont Copeland	69,297	November, 1963
Andelot, Inc.	40,668	
Trust	86,072	
Irénée du Pont, Jr.,	7,562	August, 1963
Trusts	20,000	
Pierre S. du Pont	2,926	March, 1963
William du Pont, Jr.,	8,000	February, 1963
Trusts	1,261,888	
Irénée du Pont, Jr., Trust	143,864	September, 1962
Henry B. du Pont	12,407	September, 1961
Emile F. du Pont	8,766	March, 1961

These are by no means the only transaction dates for Du Ponts in stock of Christiana Securities and E. I. du Pont de Nemours in the early 1960's. They merely represent some of the latest positions.

A more thorough disclosure of the identities of some leading Du Pont stockholders was made in the *Monthly Summary* for June 11, 1949, on the occasion of a stock split in E. I. du Pont de Nemours. Then the hold-ings of Du Ponts who were officers and directors and holders of more than 10 per cent were as follows:

	Common Shares
Donaldson Brown, married to Greta du Pont Barksdale Broseco Corp. (Brown Securities Corporation)	20,000

J. Thompson Brown	49,096
W. S. Carpenter, Jr.	47,256
Christiana Securities	12,199,200
Lammot Copeland	110,680
Trust	92,572
Delaware Realty & Investment	1,217,920
Emile F. du Pont	2,248
Wife	180
Eugene du Pont	203,212
Henry B. du Pont	10,844
Henry F. du Pont	173,000
Irénée du Pont	12,000
Lammot du Pont	63,836
P. S. du Pont III	6,940
Pierre S. du Pont	32,896
C. H. Greenewalt	4,236

$4.50 series preferred
shares

Lammot Copeland through	
Delaware Realty	16,256
Emile F. du Pont	15
Eugene du Pont	6,405
Henry B. du Pont through	
Delaware Realty	16,256
Henry F. du Pont	14,184
P. S. du Pont III	11
Pierre S. du Pont	34
Trust	1,611

The way titles stood at the end of 1965 was as follows: Members of the Du Pont family own more than 75 per cent of Christiana Securities, which in turn owns at least 29 per cent of the stock of E. I. du Pont de Nemours. Individual Du Ponts separately own additional E. I. du Pont stock or are beneficiaries of trust funds, so that the entire family holding exceeds 44 per cent in gigantic E. I. du Pont de Nemours.

E. I. du Pont de Nemours itself, until recently, owned 23 per cent of the stock of General Motors Corporation, saleswise the world's largest industrial company. After it and other Du Pont holding companies and trust funds were ordered by a federal court to distribute this stock to individual equity owners, each owner of each share of E. I. du Pont de Nemours received 1.36 shares of General Motors. Upon receiving their share of the GM distribution, Christiana Securities and other Du Pont family funds (selling some to pay capital gains taxes) passed the GM shares they received on to individual Du Ponts.

The question now is: How much General Motors stock remains in the hands of individual Du Ponts? Assuming that they sold none since the court order took effect in 1962, on the face of it they still hold *at least* 17.25 per cent of General Motors outstanding stock. This minimal figure is arrived at by assuming the payment of a 25 per cent capital gains tax on the entire holding in GM, an overgenerous assumption because the holding was not all interpreted as capital gains.

However, the Du Pont company management announced that, going beyond the court order, members of the family closely associated with the Du Pont company management would voluntarily dispose of their General Motors stock, but such sale would hardly bring holdings below 17.25 per cent because no tax at all was required on the GM shares distributed to *individuals* by E. I. du Pont de Nemours.

The SEC reports do not show holdings for Du Ponts in other companies where they are not officers, do not own more than 10 per cent individually or have not engaged in stock transactions. But that they are interested personally in other companies is shown by the September, 1965, *Official Summary* where Henry B. du Pont is reported holding 6,000 shares in Remington Arms after selling 500 shares. E. I. du Pont de Nemours owns 60 per cent of Remington common and 99.6 per cent of the preferred. Transactions were not traced for this study in companies like U.S. Rubber and Phillips Petroleum, where Du Pont interests are represented on the boards of directors.

But in Remington Arms another big old-line family holding was shown in the December, 1961, report for M. Hartley Dodge, son of the founder, who was reported as retaining 510,787 shares after selling 9,072 shares to other members of his family. Mr. Dodge, son-in-law of William Rockefeller, held 50,000 additional Remington Arms shares through a holding company and 28,407 shares in a trust fund. (The SEC reports provide similar information on the other old-line wealthy families: Phipps, Clark, Danforth, Knudsen, Baker, Anderson-Clayton, Dollar, Fisher, Heinz, Swift, Prince, Pew, Harriman, Block, Ryerson, Pitcairn, Hanna, Levis, Warburg, Kresge, Timken, Armour, Grace, Bedford, Firestone, Rosenwald, Colgate, Peet, Milbank, Crocker, Jennings, Olmsted, Cudahy, Havemeyer, Cabot, Lehman, Woolworth, Gimbel, Jones-Laughlin, Candler, Rosengarten, Hochschild, Wrigley, Rosenstiel, Reynolds, and others.)

With very few exceptions, and a few additions, the roll that was called in the formidable TNEC study is echoed and reechoed today in the SEC monthly reports.

What has been proved in these foregoing pages? Not very much, one would be forced to agree: Merely that the Du Ponts are still alive and thriving, and are richer and more powerful today than they were in 1940. And one can predict that they will continue to grow richer and more powerful as long as the continually amended New Deal, Square Deal, New Frontier and Great Society politico-economic synthesis prevails.

The Ford Family

There isn't much doubt about the financial endurance of the Ford family, because the holdings of Henry and Edsel Ford were transferred only after 1947 to the present heirs. Those who believe they may be suffering extinction under the impact of metaphorically brutal taxes or other forces may gain reassurance from recent records.

The Fords did not turn up in the SEC reports until September 1956, when it was shown that Benson Ford held 1,025,915 shares of Ford Motor Class B stock and Henry Ford II held 1,055,346 of the Class B. The Class B stock, all of which went to the Fords, holds 40 per cent of the voting power. The way this Class B holding came to the SEC record was explained as follows: "Reported that by the terms of a trust created by a relative, Benson Ford and Henry Ford II had in common with two others an option expiring 6/26/56 to acquire 15000 shares of Class B stock. Benson Ford, on 6/20/56, by gift, delivered an assignment of his portion (3750 shares) of the option. On 6/26/56 Henry Ford II, for a consideration, delivered an assignment of his portion (3750 shares) of the option."

In the February, 1957, *Official Summary* it was reported that Henry Ford II disposed of 9,000 shares of Class B and in September, 1957, it was shown that he disposed of 100,000 shares and acquired 100,000 shares of the common. The March, 1959, report showed him disposing of 19,415 Class B shares in a private sale and that he had established a holding company that owned 3,284 shares; he retained 815,901 Class B shares at this point. By September, 1959, he had reduced his common holdings to 90,500 shares.

As of September, 1964, Henry Ford II no longer held any common in his own name but did hold 43,846 shares through a trust.

In March, 1964, it was reported that he now owned 1,319,576 Class B shares, held 75,000 B shares in trust, 12,000 B shares through holding companies and was trustee for 316,398 B shares. He now held 99,846 common shares in a trust.

In January, 1962, it was reported that Benson Ford had reduced his direct holdings of the Class B to 894,147 shares but indirectly held 5,987 in holding companies and 105,456 in trust.

These are the latest positions through 1965 shown for the two men. No positions are shown for William or Charlotte Ford, which presumably were originally identical.

As reported earlier in this account, the Ford family effectively controls the Ford Motor Company and would continue to control it even if a considerable amount of additional common stock were given voting power through sale by the Ford Foundation.

The Mellon Family

The SEC report of March, 1965, showed Richard King Mellon clearing out his last 100 shares of Aluminum Company of America $3.75 cumulative preferred stock, leaving his holdings in this issue at zero. In July, 1963, however, he was shown as holding 861,200 common shares of Alcoa ($61½–$79⅝) after disposing of 291,552 shares. Alcoa is the world's largest aluminum producer. And in June, 1963, he retained 2,809,-922 shares of Gulf Oil ($87–$94¼) after disposing of 1,943,580. But in July, 1961, he held 4,666,929 shares of Gulf after selling 400,000 shares.

On the basis of the above facts one might reasonably conclude that the Mellons were still flourishing, without taking into account their other manifestations in the form of directorships and the like.

But a more positive showing can be made. In December, 1945, according to SEC reports, some years before six-for-one stock splits, Richard King Mellon owned 1,070,637 shares of Gulf Oil, and his sister, Sarah Mellon Scaife (who died late in 1965) owned 1,041,144 shares. Donaldson Brown of General Motors and Du Pont intermarriage owned 100 shares of Gulf Oil in July, 1947, and held 93,400 through the Broseco Corporation. Alan M. Scaife owned 9,300 shares of Gulf Oil, according to the January 10, 1949, SEC report, and by January, 1950, had raised his holding to 10,300 shares. He owned 30,600 shares in June, 1951.

Down through the years various other transactions in Gulf Oil and Alcoa are shown for this branch of the Mellon family but there is no present point in tracing them; the Mellons are, obviously, still in the ascendant.

The SEC reports show no transactions since 1945 in Gulf Oil or Alcoa for Paul or Ailsa Mellon or transactions for either of these two Mellons in the securities of any companies since 1960. Paul Mellon has been less active than his older cousin in corporate affairs, has more particularly applied himself to foundation and cultural affairs.

The TNEC study found that this clan had a finger in some hundred companies. Even if one had records of recent transactions in them all it would be awkward to set them forth. Exposition is defeated by the very extent of holdings. Recent SEC reports show, for example, that the Consolidation Coal Company, formerly the Pittsburgh Coal Company, of which Richard, Paul, Sarah and Ailsa Mellon owned more than 50 per cent (according to the TNEC study), now holds a 7 per cent interest in the Chrysler Corporation. To trace all such ramifications would be a virtually endless task.

Nor can we undertake to scrutinize all overlappings of large interests. The M. A. Hanna Company is a very large stockholder in Consolidation Coal, the SEC reports, and has heavy investments in many other large companies. H. Barksdale Brown, of the Du Pont clan, owns 3,317 shares of Gulf Oil (SEC, May, 1965); and the Broseco Corporation, instrument of the Brown family, held 666,684 shares on that date. We have already seen that Donaldson Brown, former high General Motors executive, and the Broseco Corporation are heavy stockholders in E. I. du Pont de Nemours. Donaldson Brown and the Broseco Corporation are also substantial stockholders in General Motors (SEC, October, 1950). Down through the years there has been much talk, much of it uninformed, about interlocking directorships. It is more significant that there is a great deal of interlocking ownership among the big interests.

The Pew Family

The TNEC study found the Pew family of Philadelphia in firm ownership-control of the huge Sun Oil Company ($56⅝-$67¾). Recent SEC reports confirm that the family is still in charge with a large dominant interest, 41.5 per cent. John G. Pew recently held 44,139 shares (September, 1965). Arthur E. Pew, Jr., held 37,170 shares and a John G. Pew trust 217 shares (December, 1964). Walter C. Pew held 434,214 shares (November, 1964). J. Howard Pew held 794,416 shares (April, 1964). A trust for A. E. Pew, Jr., held 32,207 shares (November, 1963). J. N. Pew, Jr., held 647,335 shares (November, 1960). And so on. Whatever the precise Pew ownership position is at any given time, one is obliged to conclude that the Pews are still in full charge of the Sun Oil Company.

The Pitcairn Family

This Pennsylvania family, shown by the TNEC study to dominate the giant Pittsburgh Plate Glass Company ($67¼–$85), in the SEC report for August, 1965, was shown to still hold 3,121,296 shares (about 30 per cent) through the Pitcairn Company, the family holding company. Nathan Pitcairn, according to SEC reports (August, 1963) owned 2,912 shares of the Pittston Company ($23⅛–$32⅜), big coal, oil and transportation holding company; and the Pitcairn Company held 42,-000 shares of Pittston. Whatever else they own the available record showeth not.

The Rockefeller Family

The SEC reports fail to show any dealings in any of the Standard Oil Company stocks by the six leading Rockefellers since 1940. This lacuna is perhaps to be expected, as none of them is a director in the Standard Oil cluster and apparently none individually owns as much as 10 per cent of any Standard Oil stock. As far as the SEC reports show, the Rockefeller position in the Standard Oil group has remained basically unchanged since the time of the TNEC study, although there could have been sales or purchases without their being reflected in the SEC reports. There were indeed sales of Socony in the early 1950's by the late John D. Rockefeller, Jr.

The SEC report for July 10, 1947, showed the Rockefeller Foundation holding 345,902 shares of Standard Oil of Ohio after selling 6,782 shares. Various SEC reports show recent holdings for old-line Standard Oil families such as the Jennings and Bedfords.

But a few dealings in stocks of non-Standard Oil companies of which they are directors are shown in the reports for David and Laurance Rockefeller, suggesting that they still command ample resources. Whether they have sold out any Standard Oil holdings in order to participate in other companies the record does not show, but there is no reason to suppose they have. Apart from their foundation trusteeships the Rockefeller brothers, with the exception of New York Governor Nelson A. Rockefeller, are currently all directors of Rockefeller Center, Inc., and Rockefeller Brothers, Inc.

David Rockefeller is chairman of the Chase Manhattan Bank, second largest in the country, and is known to hold stock in companies in which he holds directorships. The SEC, November, 1962, showed that he held

8,950 shares of B. F. Goodrich stock through trusts. As of 1965 he was a director of Goodrich, Rockefeller Brothers, Inc., Equitable Life Assurance Society; and chairman of Morningside Heights, Inc., a real estate development.

Laurance S. Rockefeller is often described as a "venture capitalist" and, in addition to his foundation trusteeships, was in 1965 chairman of Rockefeller Brothers, Inc., Caneel Bay Plantation, Inc., Rockefeller Center, Inc.; director of Filatures et Tissages Africains; chairman of Estate Good Hope and of the Dorado Beach Hotel Corporation. The SEC reports, September, 1961, show that he held 183,274 shares, more than 15 per cent, of the Marquardt Corporation ($8¾–$19½) after selling 1,300 shares. In Itek Corporation he sold 425 shares as reported by SEC in July, 1965, retaining 152,080 shares ($41). His investment orientation is said to be toward growth enterprises.

Winthrop Rockefeller, a self-described investment manager, has established himself in Arkansas as an extensive operator in land and large-scale agricultural projects. He is a director of the Union National Bank of Little Rock. The most martial of the Rockefellers, he entered the army as a private in 1941 and emerged as a lieutenant colonel; he was with the 77th infantry in the invasion of Guam, Leyte and Okinawa and was decorated with the Bronze Star with oak leaf cluster and the Purple Heart.

If one were to base one's conclusions about the financial status of the Rockefellers from the SEC reports alone, there would be little to tell. A stranger to the scene, with only the SEC reports to go on, would never conclude the Rockefellers amounted to much financially. But we do know from court records that the extensive Standard Oil holdings of John D. I passed to his children, chiefly to John D. II, whose will in turn indicated that he had established trust funds for his six children and many grandchildren. We are thrown back in this case to the TNEC study for basic data.

The family could have divested itself of Standard Oil holdings but, if it had, the fact would have become known through SEC reports or other channels. The Rockefellers do not actively associate themselves with the management of the Standard Oil enterprises, apparently allowing them to be run according to standard big-business practices; but the general opinion of investment specialists is that directly and indirectly they hold a decisive veto power over any policy or action of these companies. No conceivable financial syndicate in the world would undertake to challenge the unobtrusive Rockefeller dominance of Standard Oil Company (New Jersey), the largest oil company and the largest industrial enterprise by assets of any kind in the world.

My conclusion is that the relative financial position of the Rockefeller family is now the same as or better than it was at the time of the TNEC study. It may be surpassed a bit by the far more numerous Du Ponts; but no single Du Pont appears to be as wealthy as any one of the six oldest Rockefellers. The financial strength of the Du Ponts is spread unevenly among some 250 persons. So, while the collective net worth of the Du Ponts may or may not be somewhat greater than that of the Rockefellers, only the Mellons can compare with the latter individually.

The general strength of the Rockefellers and Mellons, net worth to one side, also appears notably great because it is more widely diversified in high priority enterprises—especially banking. The Du Ponts seem more deeply entrenched in frontier technology, although neither the Standard Oil companies nor Gulf Oil should be overlooked as huge science-oriented enterprises. They are more than producers and distributors of petroleum.

But the very vagueness of our recent *specific* data on the Rockefellers, their failure to trade in and out of their stocks, should in itself be taken as a sign that they preside over enterprises too vast to permit distraction into minor operations.

The Rosenwald Family

About 25 per cent of the stock of Sears, Roebuck and Company, largest merchandising enterprise in the world, is owned by the employees' pension fund. The TNEC report showed the Rosenwald family holding 12.5 per cent of the stock, worth now about $500 million. While the Rosenwalds do not engage in many stock transactions in this company, there have been a few, enough to signal that they are still present. Whether their percentage holding is now greater or less than it was there is no way of determining through the SEC reports. In view of the vast expansion of the company since the war, one would surmise that they had simultaneously added, net, to their holdings. The most recent Rosenwald holding was shown in the SEC report for October, 1964, when Edgar B. (Rosenwald) Stern, Jr., was shown as owning 25,017 shares directly, 1,762 shares as community property and 312,844 shares through a trust fund. He is a director of the company and an occasional trader in the stock. The July 11, 1949, SEC report showed that Julius Rosenwald II held 7,248 shares after selling 750 shares. As neither of these are the major living Rosenwalds, who are Lessing and William, we may safely conclude that the family still maintains a large financial presence in the company, with the management of which they have always been actively associated.

Miscellaneous Large Holdings

Similar large holdings by family and investment groups in major companies can be set forth. In order to economize on space there will now be summarily reported, on the basis of the SEC reports, some concentrated large stockholdings in the largest companies of 1964, mostly of old-line families. The dates are of the SEC monthly reports. Prices are the 1965 range.

Some such holdings are, incompletely, as follows:

		Shares	Date
Armour	($35¼–$53⅛)		
Frederick Henry Prince Trust of 1932		356,000	Sept., 1965
Modestus R. Bauer		136,400	March, 1965
William Wood Prince		63,625	Jan., 1965
Reynolds Metals	($33⅝–$48)		
David P. Reynolds		175,090	Jan., 1965
Trusts		180,264	
Minor daughters		4,720	
Davreyn Corp.			
R. S. Reynolds, Jr.		64,075	
Trusts		252,256	
As custodian		323	
Rireyn Corp.		42,472	
William G. Reynolds		108,486	
Trusts		84,878	
Wilreyn Corp.		240,577	
Singer	($56–$83¼)		
Stephen C. Clark, Jr.		113,432	Sept., 1965
Trusts		193,872	
F. Ambrose Clark		259,264	Jan., 1964
Trusts		650,110	
American Sugar	($19⅜–$31⅝)		
Frederick E. Ossorio		51,325	Sept., 1965
Ossorio family		35,759	
As custodian		21,896	
Inland Steel	($41⅞–$48)		
L. B. Block		61,500	Aug., 1965
Trusts		123,900	

	Shares	Date
Joseph L. Block	51,563	May, 1965
Trusts	123,900	
Phillip D. Block, Jr.	143,694	Feb., 1960
Trusts	19,500	
Alleghany ($8¾–$13¾)		
Allan P. Kirby (Woolworth)	3,451,913	Dec., 1963
Holding company A	632,900	
Holding company B	9,400	
Scott Paper ($33–$40⅛)		
Thomas B. McCabe	865,752	Nov., 1963
Minnesota Mining & Mfg. ($54–$71⅝)		
Ralph H. Dwan	1,000	Aug., 1965
Trust	876,000	
Trust	371,800	
John D. Ordway	4,500	Aug., 1964
Foundation	1,500	
Ordway Trust	4,682,504	
William L. McKnight	2,711,801	May, 1963
Archibald G. Bush	1,797,895	May, 1961
General Guarantee Insurance	25,000	
Owens-Illinois ($49⅝–$67¼)		
Robert H. Levis II	12,980	July, 1965
R. G. Levis Estate	4,200	
Trust	60,000	
J. Preston Levis	25,450	Aug., 1964
Trust	2,000	
William E Levis	53,592	July, 1960
Partnership	8,000	
Polaroid ($44¼–$130)		
Edwin H. Land	1,313,520	July, 1965
James P. Warburg		
Holding company	36,885	
Bydale Company	169,776	
Fontenoy Corporation	1,216	
(Both of these holdings are reduced from originals)		
International Business Machines ($404–$549)		
Arthur K. Watson	56,111	May, 1965
Trusts	34,315	

		Shares	Date
Thomas J. Watson, Jr.		37,072	
Trusts		34,315	
Sherman M. Fairchild		164,795	
Magellan Company		3,750	
Dow Chemical	($65⅛–$83¾)		
Herbert H. Dow		272,832	March, 1965
Corning Glass Works	($49⅛–$58¾)		
Amory Houghton		51,350	Feb., 1963
Trusts		918,651	
Amory Houghton, Jr.		400	Oct., 1961
Trusts		22,500	
As Trustee		1,130	
Arthur A. Houghton, Jr.		265,465	
Trusts		990,401	
International Paper	($28¼–$36⅛)		
Ogden Phipps		1,513	March, 1965
Trust		14,599	
Holding company		909,226	
W. R. Grace	($47¼–$61⅜)		
J. Peter Grace		240,678	March, 1965
Trusts		50,715	
Michael Phipps		8,641	Dec., 1963
Holding company No. 1		370,897	
Holding company No. 2		9,146	
John H. Phipps		10,028	July, 1962
Trust		752	
Holding companies		372,590	
Weyerhaeuser	($41½–$49⅜)		
C. D. Weyerhaeuser		117,069	Feb., 1965
Trust		165,963	
Corporation		1,422	
John H. Hauberg		15,658	Dec., 1964
As guardian		7,050	
Trusts		170,732	
Corporations		13,500	
Nonprofit corporation		2,125	
Herbert M. Kieckhefer		298,278	
John M. Musser		76,356	April, 1964
Trusts		162,800	
As trustee		110,257	

	Shares	Date
F. K. Weyerhaeuser	142,646	Jan., 1964
Trusts for children	64,000	
Green Valley Co.	35,360	
Winn-Dixie Stores ($35⅛–$43⅞)		
Four members of Davis family	2,714,897	Feb., 1965
Anderson, Clayton ($26⅛–$33½)		
S. M. McAshan, Jr.	55,326	Jan., 1965
S. C. McAshan Trust	129,838	
William L. Clayton	111,652	Oct., 1964
Leland Anderson	31,103	Dec., 1962
Hunt Foods & Industries ($24¾–$33⅞)		
Donald E. Simon	236,921	Jan., 1965
Trusts for children	3,422	
Frederick R. Weisman	11,025	Nov., 1964
Lerand	80,293	
Robert Ellis Simon	260,649	Aug., 1964
Georgia-Pacific ($51⅝–$65⅝)		
Julian N. Cheatham	61,086	Dec., 1964
J. N. Cheatham Corp.	21,173	
Owen R. Cheatham	217,189	
R. B. Pamplin	22,329	
R. B. Pamplin Corp.	22,943	
Trusts	31,300	
Robert E. Floweree, Jr.	37,644	March, 1965
H. J. Heinz ($38⅝–$49⅜)		
H. J. Heinz II	405,839	Sept., 1963
C. Z. Heinz Trust	577,728	
Distillers Corporation–Seagrams ($30⅜–$39⅛)		
S. Bronfman Trusts	3,382,026	Aug., 1963
Rohm & Haas ($151½–$181½)		
F. Otto Haas	13,936	Jan., 1965
Trustee	23,707	
John C. Haas	20,446	
As trustee	23,708	
Trusts	638,702	
Charitable trusts	644,767	
(Also see Feb., 1963, for larger holdings)		

		Shares	Date
William Wrigley, Jr.	($92¼–$104¾)		
Philip K. Wrigley		364,256	Dec., 1964
Trusts		60,845	
Corporation		15,000	
Firestone Tire & Rubber	($40⅞–$50¼)		
Roger S. Firestone		267,452	Nov., 1964
H. S. Firestone, Jr.		27,346	April, 1947
Raymond C. Firestone	SPLIT 6 FOR 1	35,914	
Roger S. Firestone		28,390	
Upjohn	($52¼–$77)		
Dorothy U. Dalton		465,299	June, 1964
Rudolph A. Light		247,587	
Trusts		72,331	
Preston S. Parish		16,083	April, 1964
Trusts		242,152	
E. Gifford Upjohn		44,617	
Trusts		50,649	
Donald S. Gilmore		188,750	Jan., 1964
Trusts		211,065	
Consolidation Coal	($46⅜–$66⅜)		
M. A. Hanna Co.		2,010,000	April, 1964
National Steel	($51–$65¾)		
M. A. Hanna Co.		3,402,780	April, 1964
Columbia Broadcasting	($33⅝–$47⅞)		
William S. Paley		1,391,968	March, 1964
Holding company		297,430	
As trustee		9,178	
Olin Mathieson Chemical	($41–$58¼)		
Spencer T. Olin		28,984	Feb., 1964
In voting trust		380,930	
Ralston Purina	($34⅞–$41½)		
Donald Danforth, Jr.		40,304	Jan., 1964
As custodian		61,346	
Crown-Zellerbach	($47–$60¼)		
J. D. Zellerbach		104,462	July, 1963
Texas Eastern Transmission	($44½–$53¾)		
George R. Brown (Brown & Root)		0	June, 1963

		Shares	Date
Partnership		747,066	
Foundation		16,850	
Trusts		16,528	
Brown Engineering		19,232	
John F. Lynch		249,566	Jan., 1963
Fairchild Camera	($27¼–$165¼)		
Sherman M. Fairchild		457,396	Feb., 1963
Partnership		35,000	
Holding Company		22,000	
Smith Kline & French Laboratories	($70¼–$86¾)		
Miles Valentine		856	Dec., 1962
Trust A		42,570	
Trust B		2,116,000	
Allied Chemical	($46⅛–$58¼)		
William A. Burden		94,485	Sept., 1962
Trust		80,661	
Company		136,135	
Merck	($48½–$75)		
Adolph G. Rosengarten, Jr.		33,710	Sept., 1961
Estate A	SPLIT 3 FOR 1	60,600	
Estate B		43,000	
Schenley Industries	($22¼–$39⅞)		
Lewis S. Rosenstiel		636,958	Sept., 1961
Wholly owned company		66,183	
Trust A		1,500	
Trust B		217,859	
American Metal Climax	($40¾–$54¼)		
Harold Hochschild		510,558	Aug., 1961

Concentrated Control in All Companies

Having shown the persistence into the present of these very large interests, it will now be demonstrated that virtually *all* companies—large, medium and small—are ultimately controlled and/or mainly owned by a few large interests manifested mainly as families.

One could show this by direct citation of the SEC reports, which would necessitate literally thousands of references. But these SEC reports are utilized by investment analysis services in reporting to their pecuniary-minded readers. These services summarize the SEC reports of large holdings. We may therefore refer to a highly reliable secondary source which picks up and summarizes these facts, a source available in major public and university libraries. It is *The Value Line Investment Survey*, published by Arnold Bernhard and Company of New York. This *Survey*, devoted to analyzing investment properties, keeps a large number of well-known listed companies under a thirteen-week cyclical survey each year. The facts about to be listed were taken from the summaries of this *Survey*, which were compiled from the SEC monthly *Official Summary*.

The contention to which we are addressing ourselves, once again, is this: American companies are widely owned by at least twenty million stockholders, a number that is increasing. While this is true, because anyone owning a single share of stock worth $5 is a stockholder, we have already seen that most people do not own any stock at all. The thesis that stock ownership is widespread and the further thesis that most stock owners hold a great deal of stock is false. Only a very few people own stock in significant quantities. Just how few is shown by the cited University of Michigan studies.

In certain companies, it is true, stock ownership is widespread compared with most companies, and much of the stock is held in small quantities. But the fact that a person holds a small quantity of stock in a company like AT&T—100 to 500 shares—does not prove he is a small stockholder. He may and often does hold stock in many companies.

Although a company like AT&T does indeed have many small stockholders—persons owning 50 to 100 shares and perhaps little or no other stock—the carefully nurtured propaganda even about AT&T is grossly misleading. This propaganda asserts that no *individual* owns as much as 1 per cent of the stock of AT&T.

Now, if any person owned only ½ of 1 per cent of the stock in AT&T he would be enormously wealthy, worth about $160 million, but AT&T has large stockholders whose exact percentage of holdings today would be disclosed only by a government investigation addressing itself to this question. The United Kingdom government, for example, was until recently a very large stockholder in AT&T as well as in other American and European companies. European governments are large stockholders in many American and European companies. Additionally, private investment holding companies and family trust funds are large holders. The stockholding interest even in AT&T, then, is not so completely generalized as one might conclude upon being informed that no *individual* owns as much as 1 per cent of its stock.

But if only ten individuals held ½ of 1 per cent each, that would be 5 per cent of the stock, worth about $1.6 billion, and a long step toward working control.

In presenting the following list of dominant interests in a wide variety of companies it should be noticed that the big stockholders are usually characterized as a family or group of officers and directors. This is done to save space; anyone can look up officers and directors in standard reference manuals if he is interested in identities. Scores of companies reported in *The Value Line Investment Survey* are not listed. In general, those are not listed in which no large interest is *reported*.

But just because large interests do not trade in a stock and because directors own only a few shares there is no reason to believe that large interests are not in the immediate background. In the General Electric Company, world's largest manufacturer of electrical appliances, directors own only 1 per cent of the stock and the SEC reports do not show any single stockholder or family group holding more than 10 per cent of the stock. Nevertheless, stockholdings in General Electric are quite concentrated.

The TNEC study, for example, as of November 24, 1939, showed that 86.2 per cent of the stockholders, owning 19.4 per cent of the stock, held fewer than 100 shares each. But 13.8 per cent of the stockholders, owning 80.6 per cent of the stock, held in blocks of more than 100 shares each.[3]

Actually, out of 209,732 stockholders at the time, 522, or .2 per cent of all stockholders, held 33 per cent of outstanding General Electric stock, while 1.5 per cent of all stockholders held 53 per cent of the stock.[4] At that time in E. I. du Pont de Nemours, known by current SEC data to be still closely held by the du Pont family, .4 per cent of stockholders held 65.7 per cent of all stock.[5] There is not much difference, then, between a company closely owned and one supposed to be widely owned.

At that same prewar period the TNEC study showed that in AT&T .02 per cent of stockholders held 7.8 per cent of the stock, .1 per cent of the stockholders held 15.3 per cent of stock and .4 per cent of the stockholders held 21.2 per cent of the stock (these figures being cumulative).[6]

In a large company only 5 per cent of the stock, particularly if it is voted by the management, is generally considered to be a long step toward working control, and 15 per cent is said to be well-grounded working control. Only a powerful syndicate contending for the support of medium and small stockholders can hope to challenge the control of a 15-per-cent block in a big company. Naturally, the closer the controlling block approaches 51 per cent of the stock the nearer it is to absolute control.

But working control is ordinarily sufficient for running the company and determining its policies.

AT&T in 1965 had 2,674,000 stockholders. If we assume there is now the same distribution of large stockholders as before World War II, then 534 stockholders now vote 7.8 per cent of the stock, 2,674 vote 15.3 per cent and 10,679 vote 21.2 per cent of the stock. Thus is refuted the contention that in this most widely owned of American companies there is no power-center of concentrated ownership. And if these percentages do not now actually prevail, some closely similar set of percentages surely holds and it may well be that relatively fewer stockholders own larger percentages of the stock now than in 1939.

The management of AT&T, far from representing a generalized wide interest in its stock, in fact acts at the behest of a small group of large stockholders and trust fund managers. The directors themselves hold less than .1 per cent of the stock.

By consulting this same TNEC source anyone can ascertain that in every large American company, no matter how many individual stockholders it may have, extremely large blocks are held by a handful of people. Indeed, the same statistical presentation of TNEC showed some large companies to be 100 per cent owned by a single shareholding: Great Atlantic and Pacific Tea Company, Ford Motor Company and Hearst Consolidated Publications. In the 1930's it was quite common for big public utility operating companies to be 100 per cent owned by a holding company and for entire issues of preferred stock to be owned by a single stockholder.

The TNEC study showed, in fact, that almost always only a fraction of 1 per cent of the stockholders (usually only a small fraction) in all the large companies own huge controlling blocks of stock.[7] Numerous small stockholders collectively usually own only a minor percentage of outstanding stock.

Let me here cite the TNEC percentages for a few companies commonly regarded as widely held. American Can, .2 per cent of stockholders owned 29.9 per cent, .8 per cent owned 45.2 per cent; Coca-Cola, .7 per cent owned 66.1 per cent; Corn Products, .4 per cent owned 37.3 per cent; Consolidated Edison, .2 per cent owned 30.8 per cent; Eastman Kodak, .1 per cent owned 16 per cent; General Motors, .6 per cent owned 65.5 per cent; Sears, Roebuck, .2 per cent owned 44.9 per cent; Texas Corporation, .3 per cent owned 31.8 per cent, etc. The pattern rarely varies. And when it does it gives no support to those who argue that stock is widely held. Thus, in Anderson, Clayton & Co., then and now the largest cotton merchandisers in the world, 10 per cent of stockholders held 73.6

per cent of common stock; and 26.7 per cent held 95.8 per cent. But the 10 per cent consisted of three shareholdings and the 26.7 per cent of eight shareholdings; for this was a company with very few stockholders.

The fact that all companies are not cited in what follows, therefore, does not indicate that there are companies without very small groups of large stockholders. All it indicates is that there has been no recent citation of such evidence for some companies in the SEC reports.

This can flatly be said as a fact: *There is no American producing company that is controlled through a representative directorship by or primarily on behalf of a set of stockholders each of which owns or has a beneficial interest in only an infinitesimal proportion of outstanding shares.* "People's capitalism" has this in common with "people's democracy": The rank and file doesn't have much to say, which is what common sense alone would lead one to suppose.

The method of disproving this sweeping statement (what logicians call a universal statement) is extremely easy. All anyone has to do is to point to the exceptional company and the statement is falsified. The company usually pointed to as the exceptional case, AT&T, is clearly not such a case; nor is General Electric. There is no company on the TNEC list, analyzed with a view to disclosing such data, that meets the requirement.

Bearing all this in mind, let us now look at the broad evidence of large interests that has been revealed in recent SEC reports. The dates heading each section of companies are the dates of the separate weekly issues of *The Value Line Investment Survey.*

The additional companies with recently revealed large controlling owning individuals or groups of stockholders are as follows (instances repeating our findings from the SEC reports have been retained):

October 1, 1965

Allied Supermarkets	Officers control about 50 percent of shares
Broadway-Hale Stores	Hale Bros. Associates owns 20 per cent of stock
City Stores	Bankers Securities Corp. owns about 75 per cent; G. A. Amsterdam, Chairman, and associates own majority control of Bankers Securities
Emporium Capwell	Broadway-Hale Stores, Inc., owns 23.9 per cent

Gimbel Brothers	Directors and associates interested in about 15 per cent of shares
W. T. Grant	W. T. Grant owns 14 per cent common stock; Grant Foundation, 12 per cent
S. Klein Dept. Stores	McCrory Corp. owns 18.6 per cent of outstanding stock
E. J. Korvette	E. Ferkauf and family own 28 per cent of stock
Sears, Roebuck	Employee pension fund owns 24 per cent (Rosenwald family owns at least 12.5 per cent by TNEC study and scattered SEC reports)
Bond Stores	Directors interested in 14.1 per cent
Diana Stores	Directors vote 26.2 per cent of outstanding stock
Lane Bryant	Directors vote 28 per cent
S. S. Kresge	Directors vote about 3 per cent of stock; Kresge Foundation, 21.6 per cent
McCrory	Rapid-American Corporation owns 50.5 per cent of common
Neisner Brothers	51 per cent of stock controlled by Neisner family
J. J. Newberry	Newberry family controls about 40 per cent common
Peoples Drug Stores	Trusts of the Gibbs family control about 13 per cent of stock
Colonial Stores	National Food Products Corp. holds 33 per cent common; directors own about 17 per cent Colonial common, 21 per cent National Food
Food Fair Stores	Friedland family controls about 35 per cent common

Food Giant Markets	Management controls about 35 per cent common and 51 per cent preferred stock
Food Mart	Management controls about 10 per cent of shares
Grand Union	L. A. Green, director, and relatives own 9.0 per cent common and 10.9 per cent convertible debentures
Great Atlantic & Pacific Tea	Hartford Foundation and members of family own 72 per cent of stock
National Tea	Company controlled by W. Garfield Weston
Penn Fruit	Directors own about 35-40 per cent common
Von's Grocery	Von Der Ahe family owns 43.6 per cent of stock; Hayden family owns 19.5 per cent
Winn-Dixie Stores	Davis family of Florida owns 28 per cent common
Beaunit Corp.	El Paso Natural Gas owns 32 per cent
National Sugar Refining	H. Havemeyer, Jr., and H. W. Havemeyer and their associates own 28 per cent
North American Sugar	Kaiser family owns 25 per cent
American Crystal Sugar	North American Sugar holds 9 per cent
Sucrest Corp.	Taussig family controls about 42 per cent

October 8, 1965

Columbia Broadcasting	W. S. Paley and directors control about 15 per cent
Desilu	Lucille Ball, actress, owns 50 per cent common and Class B combined

Disney Productions	Directors own or control about 41 per cent
MCA, Inc.	Directors own 45 per cent common
Hilton Hotels	Conrad Hilton and directors own 27 per cent of stock
Howard Johnson	About 38 per cent is owned by Johnson family
Sheraton Corporation	Henderson and Moore families own 22 per cent

October 15, 1965

Only banks and insurance companies, involving secondary holdings of assets, are listed in the issue of this date, and usually the dominant interests are not shown because there are few changes in key holdings from year to year.

The known dominant interest of the Mellons in the Mellon National Bank or of the Rockefellers in the Chase National Bank is therefore not alluded to. On the basis of either the SEC or TNEC reports there is no direct evidence of such interests, which are known on other grounds such as presence among directors. If a Mellon, Rockefeller, Du Pont or similar personage is on the board of directors of a bank one has no reason to suppose that he is contributing his widely informed insight to a profit-making institution in which he has no beneficial stake.

In general, among banks and insurance companies there is an even smaller distribution of small holdings than in some of the well-known industrial companies because they are more apt to attract a rarer sophisticated type of investor with a better understanding of these relatively complicated media. Values in the shares of financial companies are leveraged by more subtle factors than are those of most industrial companies and often the true values are concealed. In general, in the mid-1960's, the values of most banks and insurance company stocks were understated in market price while the values of most industrial companies were grossly overstated. These discrepancies correct themselves in time. But a sophisticated investor, buying a stock at 50 which he knows to be worth 100 (and such situations can be pointed to), does not mind if the price does not immediately advance or even if it declines still further. He knows that eventually it must work out at its true value. Meanwhile, he can presumably afford to wait.

But in this issue of *The Value Line Investment Survey* it is pointed out that the Transamerica Corporation, an investment company, holds an 11 per cent interest in Crocker-Citizens National Bank of California. Transamerica was established by the Giannini interests, which built a Bank of America of California into the biggest commercial bank in the world.

October 22, 1965

Aerojet-General	General Tire owns 84 per cent of voting stock
Beech Aircraft	Mrs. O. A. Beech controls 17 per cent; directors 4 per cent
Douglas Aircraft	J. S. McDonnell controls 5 per cent
McDonnell Aircraft	J. S. McDonnell, Jr., owns 14 per cent common; other officers 5 per cent
Fairchild Hiller	Sherman M. Fairchild and other directors own/control 7 per cent
General Dynamics	Henry Crown controls almost all of $96.7 million preferred stock
Grumman Aircraft Engineering	Directors control 8.5 per cent
Marquardt Corporation	Laurance Rockefeller owns 16 per cent
Piper Aircraft	W. T. Piper controls about 18 per cent
Chrysler	Consolidation Coal (Hanna-Mellon) owns 7 per cent, directors 1 per cent
American Metal Products	Directors own about 6.5 per cent
Champion Spark Plug	Management owns about 66 per cent
Dana	C. A. Dana owns 9.5 per cent common; Dana Foundation 16.4 per cent
Eltra	American Mfg. owns 33.4 per cent of stock
Fram	S. B. Wilson and family control 11 per cent

Gulf & Western Industries	Directors control about 20 per cent common
A. O. Smith	Smith family owns about 53 per cent of stock
Timken Roller Bearing	Directors have 22 per cent
General Battery and Ceramic	Officers/directors control about 26 per cent common
Globe-Union	Sears, Roebuck owns 12 per cent
Gould-National	Directors own about 24 per cent
Divco-Wayne	Directors own 28 per cent
Deere	Directors own 14.5 per cent
Armstrong Rubber	Sears, Roebuck owns 9 per cent; directors about 11 per cent
Firestone Tire & Rubber	Firestone family owns about 21 per cent of stock
General Tire & Rubber	Directors control 17 per cent

October 29, 1965

Braniff Airways	Greatamerica Corp. owns 58 per cent
KLM Royal Dutch Airlines	Dutch government owns 51 per cent
National Airlines	Directors own about 13 per cent
Northeast Airlines	Storer Broadcasting owns 87 per cent
Trans World Airlines	77 per cent of stock held in trust for Hughes Tool Co., owned by Howard Hughes
New York Central RR	Allan P. Kirby controls; he owns 4.5 per cent directly and controls 15 per cent through Alleghany Corp.
Pittsburgh & Lake Erie RR	81 per cent owned by New York Central
Soo Line RR	Canadian Pacific owns 56 per cent
Pittsburgh Forgings	Directors own/control 12 per cent

American Commercial Lines	16 per cent closely held
American Export Isbrandtsen	Isbrandtsen Co. owns 26.3 per cent common
Lykes Bros. Steamship	Directors own 15 per cent; another 50 per cent closely held by Lykes family interests
McLean Industries	Directors own 60 per cent
Moore and McCormack	Directors interested in 34 per cent
Cooper-Jarrett	About 35 per cent of stock closely held
McLean Trucking	About 20 per cent of stock closely held
Merchants Fast Motor Lines	G. and C. L. Whitehead own 47.2 per cent
Roadway Express	Galen J. Roush family owns about 52 per cent
Ryder System	Directors control about 53 per cent
Spector Freight	Directors own about 47 per cent

November 5, 1965

Amerada Petroleum	United Kingdom government owns about 10.8 per cent
British American Oil	65 per cent owned by Gulf Oil (Mellon)
Creole Petroleum	95.4 per cent owned by Standard Oil (New Jersey) (Rockefeller)
Hess Oil & Chemical	Leon and Moses Hess interests control 66 per cent
Imperial Oil	70.2 per cent owned by Standard Oil (New Jersey) (Rockefeller)
Kerr-McGee	McGee interests control more than 11 per cent of stock
Murphy Oil	Management controls 56 per cent

Pacific Petroleums	Phillips Petroleum (Du Pont presence) owns 45 per cent
Richfield Oil	Sinclair and Cities Service did own 61 per cent (Atlantic Refining [Rockefeller] now owns)
Shell Oil	69.4 per cent owned by Royal Dutch/ Shell group
Signal Oil & Gas	Officer-directors own majority of Class B voting common
Superior Oil	More than 50 per cent owned by Keck family
Coastal States Gas Producing	Directors own about 19 per cent
Texas Gas Transmission	Hillman family owns 11 per cent common
Transcontinental Gas Pipe Line	Stone and Webster, Inc., owns 11 per cent common; directors 2.6 per cent
Ayrshire Collieries	B. F. Goodrich and associates own 43 per cent common
Consolidation Coal	M. A. Hanna controls with 15 per cent of common stock; dominant Mellon presence
Eastern Gas & Fuel Associates	26 per cent closely held
Peabody Coal	Directors own 16.3 per cent of voting stock
Pittston	Directors control about 11 per cent common; Pitcairn family presence
United Electric Coal	General Dynamics owns 53 per cent

November 12, 1965

Diamond Alkali	Directors own 6.2 per cent common; Mellon National Bank as fiduciary 12.7 per cent

International Salt	The Fuller family holds about 10 per cent
Koppers	Directors control 10 per cent, but long-time Mellon interest
Minerals & Chemicals Philipp	50 per cent stock closely held
Minnesota Mining & Mfg.	Directors own 19 per cent
National Starch & Chemical	Mr. and Mrs. F. K. Greenwall own more than 20 per cent
Occidental Petroleum	Directors, including Armand Hammer and Frederic Gimbel, own 14 per cent
Olin Mathieson Chemical	Olin family and directors own 15 per cent
Pittsburgh Coke and Chemical	Directors own or control about 57 per cent
Reichhold Chemicals	H. H. Reichhold owns 14 per cent of common
Remington Arms	E. I. du Pont de Nemours owns 60 per cent common, 99.6 per cent preferred
Rohm & Haas	70 per cent of stock closely held (mainly by Rohm and Haas families)
Stauffer Chemical	16 per cent of stock controlled by directors
Sun Chemical	N. E. Alexander, president, owns about 20 per cent common
U.S. Borax & Chemical	73 per cent owned by Borax, Ltd.
Wallace & Tiernan	Wallace, Tiernan and Strasenburgh families own 54.5 per cent
Witco Chemical	Directors control 56 per cent
American Hospital Supply	Directors own 13.6 per cent
Baxter Laboratories	Management controls 25 per cent common

Carter-Wallace	CPI Development Corp., controlled by Hoyt family, owns 51.9 per cent
Johnson & Johnson	42.4 per cent controlled by Johnson family
Kendall	Directors own 20 per cent common
Eli Lilly	Lilly Endowment, Lilly family and associates own 100 per cent of Class A voting stock; only 25 per cent of Class B nonvoting stock publicly held
McKesson & Robbins	Foremost Dairies owns 25 per cent
Mead Johnson	Directors hold 49.6 per cent of voting stock
Miles Laboratories	Management controls about 12.4 per cent of outstanding stock
Plough, Inc.	A. Plough, president, owns 13 per cent
Rexall Drug	Directors own 12.3 per cent
W. H. Rorer	Rorer family owns 36 per cent
G. D. Searle	Searle family controls 46 per cent
Smith, Kline & French Laboratories	Directors control 32 per cent
Syntex Corp.	Allen & Co., investment bankers, own 20 per cent; directors about 7 per cent
Upjohn	Upjohn family owns 47 per cent
Warner-Lambert Pharmaceutical	Directors own 12.2 per cent common
Anheuser-Busch	Busch family and directors own about 24 per cent
Drewrys	Directors interested in about 10.1 per cent
Falstaff Brewing	Directors control about 13.3 per cent
Pabst Brewing	"Management stockholdings are understood to be large"

Joseph Schlitz Brewing	Owned 93 per cent by Uihlein family
Brown Shoe	Directors control about 8.5 per cent
Edison Bros. Stores	Edison family owns 15 per cent
Genesco	Officers and directors own 21 per cent common
Green Shoe	Officers and families own about 26.5 per cent
International Shoe	Directors own 9.5 per cent
U.S. Shoe	Directors own about 15 per cent
Wolverine Shoe and Tanning	Krause family controls 45 per cent

November 19, 1965

Duke Power	Doris Duke, Doris Duke Trust and Duke Endowment control 73 per cent common stock

(Note: In most of the electric power and light companies directors usually own 1 per cent or less of the stock and the large stockholders in recent years do not trade; the large holdings, therefore, are not reflected in recent SEC reports but must be sought in the original SEC prospectuses.)

November 26, 1965

American Cement	Directors own about 25 per cent of stock
(Philip) Carey Mfg.	Directors and families own about 10 per cent
Congoleum-Nairn	Power Corporation owns 26.3 per cent; directors 7.5 per cent
Corning Glass Works	Houghton family owns 33 per cent
Crane	Directors own 18 per cent
De Soto Chemical	Sears, Roebuck owns 52 per cent common

Kaiser Cement & Gypsum	Kaiser family and directors own 24 per cent common
Kaiser Industries	Kaiser family owns about 50 per cent common
Marquette Cement	Directors own 18.7 per cent common
Masonite	Directors own 14.5 per cent
National Homes	Officers and directors own 32.7 per cent
Owens-Corning	Owens-Illinois Glass (Levis) and Corning Glass (Houghton) each own 31.1 per cent common
Pittsburgh Plate Glass	Pitcairn family owns 30 per cent stock through The Pitcairn Co.
Screw and Bolt	Directors control 26.4 per cent
Wallace-Murray	About one-third of common and two-thirds of convertible preferred owned by Charles H. Dyson and F. H. Kissner
Walworth	General Waterworks owns 49.9 per cent
Welbilt	Hirsch interests own 70 per cent common
Hudson Pulp and Paper	Abraham Mazer Family Fund, Inc., controls 60.25 per cent common with management interests
Riegel Paper	Directors control about 10 per cent
American Distilling	Directors own about 20 per cent
James B. Beam Distilling	Directors control about 55 per cent
Brown-Forman Distillers	Directors own about 25 per cent of Class A, 20 per cent Class B
Distillers	Bronfman family holds more than 38.8 per cent

Heublein	Directors own 16 per cent of stock; additional 25 per cent held in trust for insiders and families
National Distillers	12 per cent common owned by Panhandle Eastern Pipe Line
Publicker Industries	S. S. Neuman owns 25 per cent common, controls additional 30 per cent
Schenley Industries	Directors and associates own 30 per cent common

December 3, 1965

Admiral	Siragusa family owns about 40 per cent
Amp	Directors own or represent about 33 per cent
Avnet	Avnet family owns 25.8 per cent
Bunker-Ramo	Martin Marietta owns about 62 per cent
Bundy	Officers and directors own 35 per cent
Collins Radio	Collins family owns 24.4 per cent
Consolidated Electronics Industries	U. S. Philips Trust owns directly and indirectly about 33 per cent common
CTS	Directors own about 43 per cent
Emerson Electric	Directors own 8 per cent
Emerson Radio	Directors own more than 33 per cent
Fairchild Camera	S. M. Fairchild of IBM owns 20 per cent
Cornell-Dubilier Electric	98 per cent owned by Federal Pacific Electric
Pioneer Electric	100 per cent owned by Federal Pacific Electric
Foxboro	About 49 per cent is closely held

General Instrument	Directors own about 20 per cent
General Precision Equipment	Directors own about 10 per cent
Hoffman Electronics	H. Leslie Hoffman and his family own about 22 per cent
Indiana General	Directors control about 7.9 per cent
International Resistance	Directors control about 10 per cent
Magnavox	Officers and directors own about 9 per cent
Maytag	Directors own about 15 per cent
McGraw-Edison	Officers and directors own 9.4 per cent
Motorola	Galvin family controls 24 per cent; other insiders own additional 12 per cent
Robertshaw Controls	Reynolds Metals, largely owned by Reynolds family, owns 30 per cent
Ronson	Directors control more than 15 per cent
Sangamo Electric	Bunn and Lamphier families control 25 per cent
Schick Electric	Eversharp and Technicolor own 25 per cent
Schlumberger	Schlumberger family controls about 50 per cent
Sunbeam	Directors own about 13 per cent
Tung-Sol Electric	Directors own or control about 22 per cent of common
Varian Associates	Directors and officers own about 17 per cent of stock
Whirlpool	RCA owns .5 per cent; Sears, Roebuck 7.5 per cent; directors 6 per cent
Zenith Radio	Directors own 7 per cent
Carolina Telephone & Telegraph	Bell System owns about 18 per cent

Comsat	50 per cent owned by the common carriers; balance by general stockholders
New England Telephone	AT&T owns about 69 per cent
Pacific Telephone	AT&T owns about 90 per cent
Southern New England Telephone	AT&T owns 18.4 per cent
Central Telephone	Western Power and Gas owns 57 per cent common
Addressograph-Multigraph	Directors own about 15 per cent of stock
American Photocopy	Rautbord family owns about 27 per cent
Control Data	Directors own about 6 per cent

December 10, 1965

Cyclops	Directors own about 6 per cent
Detroit Steel	Directors control 13.7 per cent
Eastern Stainless Steel	Officers and directors own about 8 per cent
Firth Sterling	Directors own 11.7 per cent common
Harsco	Directors have about 10 per cent of stock
Interlake Steel	Pickands Mather & Co. own 9.2 per cent common; directors 3.4 per cent
Kaiser Steel	Kaiser Industries, owned by Kaiser family, owns 79 per cent
Lukens Steel	Huston family owns 38 per cent
National Steel	M. A. Hanna Co. owns 22 per cent, insiders 3.5 per cent
Phoenix Steel	Insiders own about 25 per cent common

Pittsburgh Steel	Directors control about 21 per cent common
U.S. Pipe & Foundry	Directors own about 2 per cent, Freeport Sulphur 5.7 per cent
Wheeling Steel	Hunt Foods & Industries own 11.1 per cent; Cleveland Cliffs Iron 4.8 per cent; directors 1 per cent
Woodward Iron	Woodward family holds about 15.4 per cent; directors about 8 per cent common
American Metal Climax	Selection Trust owns 12.2 per cent common; directors 4.2 per cent; Phelps Dodge 4 per cent
American Zinc, Lead & Smelting	Consolidated Goldfields of South Africa owns 61 per cent
Bunker Hill	Hecla Mining owns 9.75 per cent common
Campbell Red Lake	Dome Mines, Ltd., owns 57 per cent
Cleveland-Cliffs Iron	Directors own about 5 per cent; Detroit Steel 22 per cent
Consolidated Mining	Canadian Pacific owns 51.5 per cent
Copper Range	American Metal Climax owns 17.5 per cent; Blacton & Co. 12.5 per cent
Great Northern Iron	In trust for lifetime of 18 persons
Harvey Aluminum	Harvey family owns all Class B stock
Hudson Bay Mining	Anglo-American Corporation owns 18 per cent common
Inspiration Consolidated Copper	Anaconda Co. owns about 28 per cent of stock
Kaiser Aluminum	Kaiser interests own 45.2 per cent common
Magma Copper	Newmont Mining owns 80.6 per cent common

McIntyre-Porcupine Mines	Shares closely held
Newmont Mining	Directors own more than 15 per cent common
Reynolds Metals	Directors, mainly members of Reynolds family, control about 19 per cent
United Nuclear	Olin Mathieson and Malinckrodt Chemical Works own nearly 30 per cent
Vanadium	Directors control about 11 per cent
Calumet & Hecla	Directors control about 9 per cent common
Continental Copper	Directors control 7 per cent common
Fansteel Metallurgical	Directors control 9 per cent of stock
General Cable	American Smelting owns 36 per cent
Howmet	Pechiney (France) owns 49 per cent common; directors control 8 per cent
International Silver	Directors control 9 per cent common
Revere Copper & Brass	American Smelting owns 34 per cent of stock

December 17, 1965

American Chain & Cable	W. T. Morris Foundation owns 17.8 per cent of stock; directors 3.1 per cent
Baker Oil Tools	Directors hold about 16 per cent common
Clark Equipment	Directors and families own about 12 per cent of stock
Continental Motors	Ryan Aeronautical owns about 47 per cent
Foster Wheeler	Directors own 5.7 per cent; Financial General Corp. owns 13.5 per cent
Gardner-Denver	Directors represent 7.1 per cent

Halliburton Co.	Directors own about 8 per cent
Ingersoll-Rand	Directors own 6 per cent common
Leesona	Directors own about 17 per cent
Link-Belt	Directors own about 6 per cent
McNeil	Directors own 11 per cent
Mesta Machine	Directors own about 6 per cent common
Outboard Marine	Ralph S. Evinrude owns/controls 14 per cent of stock
Rockwell Manufacturing	Rockwell family controls 19 per cent
Symington Wayne	Directors own 10 per cent
Textron	Directors own 6.5 per cent common
S. S. White	Directors own about 6 per cent common
Brown & Sharpe Manufacturing	Henry B. Sharpe, president, and family own 34 per cent of stock
Carborundum	Mellon family and related interests own about 21 per cent common
Cincinnati Milling Machine	Directors and families own 21.7 per cent common
Giddings & Lewis	Directors and families own 21 per cent of stock; Motch & Merryweather Machinery 10 per cent
Kearney & Trecker	Trecker family owns about 50 per cent
Norton	Officers and directors own 11 per cent common
UTD	Directors interested in 25.3 per cent of stock
Dr. Pepper	Directors hold about 11 per cent

Royal Crown Cola	Directors hold 14.6 per cent; Pickett and Hatcher Educational Fund 2.9 per cent
General Baking	Goldfield Corp. owns 51 per cent common
United Biscuit	Directors own 18 per cent of stock
Ward Foods	Directors interested in 32 per cent of stock
John Morrell	Directors hold 18 per cent
Campbell Soup	Dorrance estate owns in trust about 64.3 per cent
Chock Full O'Nuts	William Black, chairman and founder, controls about 15 per cent common
Consolidated Foods	Nathan Cummings owns 9.4 per cent of stock; Union Sugar 8.2 per cent
Gerber Products	Gerber family and directors own about 30 per cent common
H. J. Heinz	Heinz family owns more than 37 per cent common
Hershey Chocolate	Milton Hershey School owns 66 per cent of stock
Hunt Foods & Industries	Directors own about 7.9 per cent common
Libby, McNeill & Libby	Foreign interests own 40 per cent common
A. E. Staley	Staley family owns 60 per cent common
Stokely-Van Camp	A. J. Stokely, president, and directors own or control 31 per cent common
William Wrigley, Jr.	Wrigley interests and directors control about 35 per cent common
Eversharp	Directors own about 15 per cent of stock

Max Factor	Directors own 99.9 per cent common and 33.5 per cent Class A shares
Helene Curtis Industries	Directors own 53 per cent of stock
Revlon	Directors own 99.9 per cent Class B and 11 per cent common
Pet Milk	Leading stockholders own about 65 per cent common
Anderson, Clayton	Directors control 48 per cent of stock
Kellogg	W. K. Kellogg Foundation controls 51 per cent common
Pillsbury	Directors control about 6 per cent of stock
Bulova Watch	Directors control 19 per cent
Hewlett-Packard	Directors own about 70 per cent
Polaroid	Directors control about 25 per cent
Tektronix	Directors and officers own 57 per cent
Alleghany	Allan P. Kirby owns about 40 per cent common in this company with big holdings in New York Central RR, Missouri Pacific RR, Transamerica and Investors Diversified Services
General American Investors	Directors own about 11 per cent common
Investors Diversified Services	Alleghany owns 43 per cent voting stock

The burden of proof has clearly been shifted in this chapter to those who contend that stock ownership and corporate control are widely dispersed among many small stockholders. All available evidence, direct and statistical, stands as an insurmountable barrier against the contention.

Any low percentages of participation in the foregoing list should not be taken as implying that they exhaust the concentrated interest. All they indicate is that this is the concentrated interest as shown under the rules of the SEC. In every single case, even where only a 5 per cent interest is shown, deeper inquiry would show, almost invariably, that far fewer than 1 per cent of stockholders owned the bulk of the stock or enough to give working control.

Even *Fortune*, after many years of surrender to the Berle-Means fantasy that ownership is divorced from control in most of the big companies, has now (June 15, 1967) come over to recognizing that the big owners have more than a little to say. What Berle-Means did, initiating the fantasy, was to confuse control with operating direction. Company managers, whether themselves owners or nonowners, are always in charge of operations, by tacit or explicit leave of the big owners. The issue of control is seldom raised. But when it is, as most recently with a big company in the case of the New York Central Railroad, the nonowning management walks the plank. In this case the big owners turned out to be the Young-Kirby-Murchison group.

"After more than two generations during which ownership has been increasingly divorced from control," says *Fortune* rather misleadingly, "it is assumed that all large U.S. corporations are owned by everybody and nobody, and are run and ruled by bland organization men. The individual entrepreneur or family that holds onto the controlling interest and actively manages the affairs of a big company is regarded as a rare exception, as something of an anachronism. But a close look at the 500 largest industrial corporations does not substantiate such sweeping generalizations.

"In approximately 150 companies on the current *Fortune* 500 list, controlling ownership rests in the hands of an individual or of the members of a single family. Significantly, these owners are not just the remnants of the nineteenth-century dynasties that once ruled American business. Many of them are relatively fresh faces. In any event, the evidence that 30 per cent of the 500 largest industrials are clearly controlled by identifiable individuals, or by family groups, is something to ponder. It suggests that the demise of the traditional American proprietor has been slightly exaggerated and that the much-advertised triumph of the organization is far from total."

While it is true that the big owners are not "*just*" remnants, they nevertheless, among other things, are indeed remnants. And while true that many are "relatively fresh faces," nearly all show strong ancestral resemblances or bear established ancestral names already mentioned many times in this book. They are heirs.

Fortune's list of 150 concerned only an individual owner or a single family that holds the controlling interest and is active in the management. In the case of the 350 other largest industrials, which were not touched upon, control also rested with a small number of owners (as distinct from nonowning managers and many small stockholders): either multi-family ownership groups consisting of as many as five to seven families or individual members of a functionally related financial group. In no case, except when a company is under court-sanctioned trustees, can it be shown that ownership is divorced from control, although in many cases it is divorced from active management.

While taking cognizance of the *Fortune* article, and largely endorsing it as far as it goes, I, for my part, learned nothing from it that I have not known for thirty years. Its significance was not that it told something new but that it represented some open backtracking from the Berle-Means contention that ownership has been, or is being, divorced from company control and that full control rather than delegated management is being exercised by professionally trained nonowning managements.

What is most interesting—to me, at any rate—is why steps are now being taken to abandon, at least partly, the Berle-Means fantasy, which has been widely disseminated and has many quite distinguished followers. There was nothing inherently marvelous about the theory; what led to its being given wide currency was that it served to gull an always gullible public with the idea that property was losing its power and that something akin to socialism (but better) was evolving before our eyes. The United States was going to retain private property but at the same time it was going to have collective nonprofit-oriented, professional management in the corporations; if the owners, particularly the big owners, did not like this they would be powerless. As far as that went, big ownership itself was going out of existence.

In brief, this was a useful myth in manipulating restive public sentiment, particularly in the Depression and spectacular World War II. The idea that big stockholders were either impotent or vanishing was widely relished.

As I surmise, the myth is being abandoned precisely because of this depiction of the stockholders, particularly the big ones, as impotent. As a psychiatrist might say, the stockholders are shown in the Berle-Means script as castrates, displaced by bright young men up from Swampwater College with nothing but technique to offer: know-how and can-do. Objectively serviceable though the myth has been for the big proprietors, it has been subjectively and personally humiliating. Instead of being seen by his wife, children and friends as an authentic bigwig, the boss (which he is), the top owner-manager has had himself publicly presented as something of a corporate tabby cat. As the *Fortune* sample list of 150 shows, he is anything but this. He is, in fact, far more autonomous and far-ranging than any Soviet industrial commissar, who is always under the tight leash of the Communist Party. The commissar accepts policy; the big owners make or shape policy. They are not the puppets of nonowning corporate managers.

What must have happened in a general way, it seems to me, is that somebody grumbled about this constant depiction of stockholders as the pawns of puissant corporate officials who came from nowhere, and the grumbling was finally heard by the big ears up at *Fortune*. And now we see the beginning of the dismantling of what had become a sturdy myth, although quite a few academicians are still bemused by it and see something akin to socialism (only better) developing by gradual administrative fiat promulgated by expert nonowning managers to whom profits are secondary, public welfare primary.

Seven 🌿

THE AMERICAN
PLANTATION: A PROFILE

It has been abundantly shown that the members of a small coterie, comparable in relative size to the owning class of the Banana Republics and other unbenign polities, own and control all important economic enterprises in the United States. And now that we have a latter-day insight into the ownership and control of the individual parts, it remains to be shown into what whole these parts fit.

The thesis of this chapter is that the economic system as a whole is principally owned, and mainly though not wholly controlled but certainly decisively influenced, by or on behalf of hardly many more than 500,000 biological individuals (as distinguished from fictitious persons such as corporations). In turn, the political system is very concentratedly influenced. The instrument of this highly personal influence-control is the large corporation, an Archimedean lever. Ownership in some degree may be claimed by perhaps 10 per cent of the population, most of it in tiny bits, but outside this slice it is largely confined to chattels. Few Americans own more productive property, directly or indirectly, than do benighted Russians, Chinese or Latin American *descamisados*. This fact is no doubt difficult for those conditioned by domestic mass-media propaganda to accept; yet intractable fact it unquestionably is.

Firms in Operation

The number of American firms in operation as of 1963, the most recent date for which the information is available, was 4,797,000, an increase of 22,000 over 1962.[1] This figure did not include agricultural enterprises or firms of professionals such as physicians and lawyers. Nearly half, or 2,032,000 firms, were in retail trade, most of them small local retail stores, often in hock to local banks.

Sole proprietorships at the end of 1961 totaled 9,242,000 and partnerships 939,000.[2]

Gross national product, or the totality of goods and services transferred to consumers by all agencies, public and private, amounted to $554.9 billion in 1962.[3] It approximated $600 billion in 1965 and may have exceeded $700 billion before this book is published. The national rate of economic growth rose to 5.5 per cent in 1965.

Sales of the 500 largest industrial corporations amounted to $229.08 billion in 1962, or nearly 42 per cent of gross national product. About 65 per cent of these sales, or $149.4 billion, were made by the 100 largest industrial corporations, $36.2 billion by the next 100, $20.5 billion by the third 100 and $13.2 by the fourth 100.[4]

The Treasury Department for tax purposes has a category of "active corporations," numbering 1,190,286 in 1961. This category with sweeping catholicity includes corporations in finance, insurance, real estate, services, nonallocable businesses and agriculture, forestry and fisheries. Excluding all such and retaining only the mining, construction, manufacturing, transportation, communication, electric, gas and wholesale as well as retail trade industries in order to obtain a category comparable with that of the big industrial enterprises we have been considering, we have 675,074 active industrial enterprises.[5]

The total assets of all these 675,074 active industrial and trading enterprises were $561.778 billion in 1961[6] compared with total assets in the same year of $186.769 billion for the 500 largest industrial companies, $125.734 billion for the 100 largest.[7] In 1962 the assets of the 500 had risen by more than $10 billion. More than 30 per cent of the industrial assets of the country, then, was confined to 500 of the largest companies.

Actually, in 1961 companies with assets of $50 million and more among all active corporations, industrial and nonindustrial, well above the range of "small business," held the bulk of assets and most of the net income.

The number of such companies was 2,632 or .2 per cent out of the 1,190,286. The $50-million-asset-plus companies held $812.396 billion out of total corporate assets of $1,289.516 billion, or nearly 65 per cent. Their net income was $30.027 billion out of $45.894 billion, or 66 per cent of all corporate net income.

Confining ourselves once again to active industrial and trading companies, we find that 1,073 constituting the $50-million-plus class had assets of $346.922 billion out of total industrial and trading assets of $561.-

778 billion, or more than 60 per cent, and net income of $24.151 billion or 70 per cent, out of total net income of $35.916 billion.[8] Again, one central corporation often owns many other large ones. The big corporations are not always detached entities.

Summarizing, 2,632 active corporations or slightly more than .2 per cent of all active corporations (almost always dominantly owned and controlled by less than .1 per cent of their stockholders) held nearly 65 per cent of all corporate assets for 1961 and got 66 per cent of net corporate income. These 2,632 corporations were those with individual assets of $50 million or more. In the industrial-trading category alone less than .2 per cent (1,073 out of 684,075) of corporations, with assets of $50 million or more, held more than 60 per cent of assets and derived 70 per cent of net income.

The vast number of enterprises below the $50-million asset class (and almost 60 per cent of them had assets of less than $100,000) perform only a shrinking marginal amount of the business of the country. We can therefore with the utmost caution say that most of the productive activity of the United States is in the hands of a tiny number of very large corporations largely owned and completely dominated by a small coterie, almost a junta.

This fact is shown, too, in the figure of $302.536 billion for total sales of the 1,073 largest industrial and trading corporations for 1961, which was nearly 60 per cent of gross national product.[9]

What have been cited are official government figures and as such may be suspect to some persons who profess deep distrust of all government activity. Let us, then, turn to strictly business sources.

"The 7,126 U.S. companies with more than 100 or more employees (2.5% of the nation's 286,817 manufacturing corporations) account for 90% of total manufacturing assets and 83% of sales," says a widely circulated business directory in referring to 1961.[10] "The nation's top 13 employers, firms with 100,000 or more workers, have assets of $37.9 billion (15.3% of total U.S. manufacturing assets) and sales of $47.1 billion (13.6% of total sales)."

No matter which source one turns to, the same prospect unfolds: intense concentration. Slightly more than 7,000 managements, often interlocked, account for 83 per cent of all sales!

Whoever owns and/or controls the large corporations, then, obviously owns and/or controls the lion's share of the productive system. We have already shown how untenable is the idea that such ownership is widely diffused among millions of small shareholders. The small shareholder in the United States stands in the same relative position to the large shareholder as the rank-and-file Communist in Russia stands to the party leadership. Useful, he nevertheless need not be seriously consulted. He carries no more weight than the rank-and-file employee. Corporatively speaking, he is a nonentity, an unperson.

The Cannibalistic Merger Movement

The smaller enterprises, moreover, are being steadily squeezed out of business or absorbed by the giants, most of which became giants by the cannibalistic process.

There have been three periods in this century marked by waves of American mergers—1900–10, the 1920's and the years since World War II. From 1920 through 1929 there were 6,818 mergers; from 1930 through 1939 there were 2,264; from 1940 through 1949 there were 2,411; from 1950 through 1959 there were 4,089; and from 1960 through 1963 there were 1,978. In most cases larger companies absorbed smaller ones; in some cases many small companies were suddenly combined into large ones.[11]

The word "merger" in actual practice almost invariably indicates that large companies are involved; it is rare for really small enterprises to figure in mergers. Thus in the decade 1951–61, of 3,736 mergers involving the 500 largest industrial and 50 largest merchandising firms—almost all the mergers there were—the largest 100 industrial companies absorbed 884 firms, the next largest 100 absorbed 1,059, the third largest 100 took in 577, the fourth largest 100 absorbed 453 and the fifth largest 100 absorbed 431 firms. Among the merchandising companies the largest 50 took in 332 other companies.[12]

In the years 1948–60, 33.4 per cent of assets acquired by merger went to companies with assets of $50 million or more and 34.3 per cent of acquired assets went to companies with assets of $10–$50 million. Assets acquired by companies with less than $1 million of assets amounted to only 1.6 per cent. The same trend continued into the 1960's up through 1962, the latest date available.[13] Since then, the merger movement has taken a new spurt.

The small enterprise, at least rhetorically beloved by many small-town congressmen, has also been steadily driven out of business by failure, a traditional hazard of genuine businessmen as distinct from corporate manipulators. In the period 1921 through 1935 there was a yearly average of more than 20,000 failures (excluding railroad bankruptcy proceedings), with aggregate liabilities averaging more than $500 million and average individual liabilities between $21,000 and $27,000. From 1936 through 1940 the yearly average was 12,064 and in the 1940's it was a little more than 5,000. But in the 1950's the figure started burgeoning again, from 8,058 in 1951 to 14,053 by 1959. In the 1960's it is exceeding 15,000 annually.

Most of these failures are of very small firms. Only in 1961 did aggregate annual liabilities cross $1 billion, where it remained thereafter through 1963, our latest date. In no year has the average individual liability exceeded $100,000.[14]

The figures tell little of blasted hopes in the uneven race toward business success.

It is almost a cardinal rule that only small businesses go out of existence through bankruptcy. The word is encountered only academically on the higher corporate circuit.

One of the effects of the propaganda about business success (propaganda based on a meager number of instances) is to encourage each year thousands of illusion-ridden citizens to jump into the business whirlpool. Unskilled in logical analysis, they optimistically accept the lopsided findings of *Time, Fortune* and the *Wall Street Journal* as representative fact. All they accomplish in most cases, sooner or later, is to enrich with their small bankrolls the coffers of suppliers of business equipment, which is later knocked down to the highest bidder at bankruptcy auction sales. There is a thriving business in the United States dealing, year in and year out, with bankruptcy itself.

By every known sign, entering into business for oneself in the United States is now, and always has been, a highly risky affair. Many are called; few are chosen. And most who remain in business do so on the thinnest of survival margins, constantly financed by short-term bank loans, the constant prey to recessions, regional strikes or even vagaries of the weather. A simple run of unseasonable weather regularly drives out of business hordes of hopeful operators of small resorts, hotels, stores and service enterprises. Many are hopelessly in debt. But in addition to misfortunes of local circumstance there stand in the background the asset-heavy large enterprises, which survive all vicissitudes, like granite cliffs against the sea. Not many German enterprises survived the military disasters that engulfed the Reich this century; but the Krupp family's steel enterprises, for one, did survive and, indeed, are flourishing now as never before. Krupp in Germany could no more be vanquished by overwhelming national calamity than could Du Pont in the United States. What would survive any event, perhaps even atomic warfare, would be titles, patents, formulas, certain key personnel and organization charts. One would, as the saying goes, have to get the country "moving" again. And who can do this better than Krupps, Du Ponts, Rockefellers, Fords, Pews, Gettys, Rosenwalds and their kind? For, among other things, they have gathered unto themselves administration of the technical "know-how." This is what they have, over and beyond money: general far-ranging administrative authority.

Business versus the Corporation

As applied to the larger enterprises the term "business" has become a euphemism, no longer expressing the intended content of the word. The man who owns and operates a small independent shoe store is a businessman. So, it is implied, are Henry Ford II, J. Paul Getty, Crawford H. Greenewalt and Roger Blough. Yet these latter basically have no more in common with the small tradesman, either in outlook or mode of operation, than has a juke-box entrepreneur with a musician.

Among the defining characteristics of any business enterprise is that it can fail, can go out of business through bankruptcy. It is risky, in short. But the major corporations can no more fail than can the public treasury. Their risks are all marginal. Their massed financial reserves and other assets are absolute guarantees against total risk and failure. Beyond this, they are so thoroughly woven into the very warp and woof of society that they are the peculiar anxious and constant concern of sovereign power itself.

This last has been shown in this century in particular in the case of railroads, many of which through gross financial mismanagement—"milking"—have gone through bankruptcy proceedings in which unpreferred creditors were squeezed out with heavy losses. But reorganization proceedings under the supervision of the federal courts have restored them to formal financial health, often under the same management, bankers and holders of senior obligations. For the railroads serve a vital function in modern society.

The large industrial corporations have never yet had to be individually bailed out of financial difficulties by the government, for they have not experienced overwhelming individual financial difficulties. Their financial position has been made too secure by monopolistic and semi-monopolistic practices, at times formally adjudicated illegal.

What kind of business is it, then, that is impervious to failure, one of the most basic possible experiences of business in history? If it is indeed a business, then it is something distinctly new in business history.

Close students of corporations feel driven to employ various devices to differentiate the big corporation from the ordinary corporation, which may indeed fail. There was first widely used the rather imprecise term Big Business. But, as we have noticed, the big corporation is different from the smaller corporation in crucial ways other than mere size. It is not only big but it cannot fail, cannot (as the saying goes) go out of business. Some specialists then introduced the term super-corporation,[15] which is better, as it indicates at least some sort of superiority or supremacy. But what is the superiority? The fact of being failureproof? Size?

The big corporation, as a matter of fact, is not a business enterprise at all, at least not in the sense that business enterprise has been understood through history and as it is commonly understood even today. The linguistic habits of people have simply not kept abreast of institutional change.

The big corporation, it is true, *does* business, engages in trade. But so do the government trading enterprises established by Soviet Russia, which seek profits but which are nevertheless not thought of as businesses or business enterprises. By definitional ukase they are excluded from the business category.

A writer on economic affairs, reflecting on AT&T, shows awareness of the inapplicability of the term "business" to the functioning of the large companies when he says: "AT&T today is less a company than a quasi-political state."[16]

But not only is AT&T a quasi-political state; many other large corporations are in the same category and, indeed, like AT&T have foreign governments among their large stockholders. The stock is held as a national treasury asset. But it is not the participation of governments as investors that makes these entities quasi-political states; they are that even without any government stockholding. They are, too, more than an integral part of the economy. They are an integral part of the functioning political system, their acts and plans focusing the attention of legislators and political administrators, just as the acts of legislators and political administrators are of paramount concern to them. Their interests and those of government officials at many points overlap and interlock.

The big stockholders and managers of these quasi-political states, again, are stockholders and managers in some sense different from people ordinarily so recognized. They not only have more power than the common run of stockholders and managers but they must continually pass judgment and act on a wider spectrum of eventualities, a spectrum as wide indeed as that of any top government leader. What the president of the United States is thinking about is, more often than not, precisely what the big corporate people are thinking about, often in the same terms: war or peace, balance of international payments, treaties, unemployment and wages, gross national product, interest rates, consumer finance, national debt, taxes, etc., etc.

Because referring to these men as corporate leaders or big stockholders or magnates is imprecise, and confusing as well to many (for what, really, is a big stockholder, a man owning a million shares worth $1 each or a million shares worth $500 each?), I have coined a new term for them. They are, according to this term, *finpols*—financial politicians. Their political mentalities and acts are shaped by their propertied and institutional positions.

Although not recognized by the general public as politicians, whom cartoonists still regressively depict as men in broad-brimmed black hats wearing string ties and black frock coats, much of the daily activity of the biggest property holders—the *finpols*—is identical with the work of government leaders. They are, first, diplomats—so much so that they can be quickly shuttled into the highest formal diplomatic posts. They are, too, manipulators of public sentiment through advertising, public relations subordinates and corporately controlled mass media in general. They make or cause to be made speeches on fundamental public questions, seeking to persuade. They select subordinates, conduct negotiations with governments, hire and fire high-level corporate personnel, manipulate political parties and, above all, make decisions of national and international import. Most crucially, they have, like the very top governmental leaders, vast financial resources at their fingertips, resources for which they are far less strictly accountable than most government leaders working within constitutional frameworks. They can, and at times do, buy legislators and judges. Most—repeat: most—legislators are on their payrolls.

As far as that goes, many of them or their aids can and do without so much as shifting gears go right into top government posts, where they feel perfectly at home. When Robert McNamara went from the presidency of the Ford Motor Company to become secretary of defense, he simply stepped from one to another large organization. The horizon of Nelson A. Rockefeller hardly broadened when he stepped into the governorship of New York. Even though he had not previously been in any very high administrative post, the transition from the universal concerns of the Rockefeller family to those of New York State was hardly a move into a wider domain.

These quasi-political states or super-enterprises, then, are a reality. The men with the biggest stakes in them and at their helms are little different from government leaders in function, outlook or means at their disposal. In most cases they far overshadow the domains of all except the highest political leaders. Revenues for AT&T in 1964 exceeded revenues of the thirty smallest American states, nearly equaled the three richest. No governor of any American state presides over an enterprise nearly so vast, complicated or minutely far-reaching. No senator has in his jurisdiction any comparable domain. As Desmond Smith points out, the *net income* of AT&T's Bell System, *after taxes*, is approximately equal to the *national income* of Sweden. Bring a few of the other large companies into a cluster and one sees how many other long-established nations they together exceed. France becomes a minor operation, comparatively. The big corporations account for most of the American gross national product itself, and most of the national income as well. One can almost justifiably say: They *are* the United States. Take them out of the picture and what would be left?

AT&T is certainly a gigantic affair, an octopus or super-octopus if you will. But it has many near counterparts at home and abroad: General Motors, Standard Oil (New Jersey), Ford Motor, U.S. Steel, Socony Mobil Oil, Du Pont, Bank of America, Chase Manhattan Bank, First National City Bank, Manufacturers Hanover Bank, the big life insurance companies (Metropolitan, Prudential, Equitable, New York and John Hancock), Sears, Roebuck, Great Atlantic & Pacific Tea, Royal Dutch Shell, Unilever and still others.

These are not businesses at all as the term has been historically understood. They are clearly more like governments, or government departments, and would be more aptly termed *finpolities*. Their influence on formal government, direct and indirect, conscious and unconscious, is enormous. Their influence, indeed, is so often peremptory that it might better be described as in the nature of quasi-decretal. For such entities, through agents, often tell governments, in secret conference (the United States government included) what they must do and what they cannot do. That, I submit, is power. And, if governments fail to comply, at the very least they will lose the considerable cooperative power of the *finpolities*.

"The 'top' or 'pure' executive largely symbolizes organizational authority. He is a politician," says David T. Bazelon in a general analysis (*The Paper Economy*, Random House, N.Y., 1963, p. 37).

Crown, Baronage and Church

Historians in surveying the late Middle Ages of Europe often organize their narrative around three focal centers: the Crown, the Baronage or Nobility and the Church. These were the three often rivalrous, sometimes embattled, power centers of the times. The Crown came to be held by a family line that had emerged from the Baronage and gradually extended its sovereignty over it. In its struggle it ran into a powerful rival in the Church, represented by the pope, who claimed universal dominion in the name of God. In time the Crown, linked to rising nationalism, was victorious over the barons and, finally, also over the Church. Strongly centralized national governments emerged, these contending brutishly down through the centuries with each other for imperial power. The most recent climactic acts of this recurrent European drama were colossal World Wars I and II.

Utilizing this same sort of schema it is possible to discern analogous power centers in the United States today. There is the central government roughly (and blindly) occupying the position of the late medieval Crown. There is the restless baronage in the form of the *finpols* and upper corporate magnates (*corp-pols*), seeking to bend the Crown to the purposes of their corporate baronies and dukedoms. Crown, Church and Baronage in medieval times, although contending for power against each other, were not always at swords' points; sometimes they cooperated, sometimes they fell apart and fought or intrigued one against the other. At times the Crown itself was overturned, to be succeeded by some dominant baron.

Among many additional differences in the situation, though, is the fact that the modern financial baronies have emerged under the protection of the Crown; the medieval Crown, *per contra*, emerged from among the competing Baronage, subdued it. The medieval Crown rose as a challenge to the Baronage; the modern financial Baronage has risen as a power challenge to duly established pseudo-democratic government.

In their overlapping aspects, government and *finpolities* are almost identical, a fact most apparent in time of war and in matters of defense. The so-called defense industries are such an indispensable part of government today as to have given rise to the concept of the Warfare State. Company boardrooms are departments of the Department of Defense or, looked at another way, the Department of Defense is a special branch of the big-company boardrooms.

In dealings with the upper strata of government the *finpols* appear as equals, very much as prime ministers of a foreign state. When the chairman of AT&T, General Motors, Standard Oil or U.S. Steel sits down with the president of the United States to discuss some issue of mutual concern we witness a genuine political "summit conference." It is far more than a conference between a big leader and an informed citizen. It is more like a conference between a medieval king and a powerful baron, a potential kingmaker or kingbreaker.

On the whole, most of the time, the relations between the president of the United States and the leading *finpols* have been cordial. Actually most of the presidents of the United States appear to have admired and stood in awe of the *finpols*—men who have mastered or have been put in mastery of the mysterious life-giving market.

There have been periods, usually short, when relations between the two, like relations between the medieval Crown and the Barons, have become strained. But much of this strain, arising from groping attempts of government to regulate the far-ranging *finpols*, has been a sham, improvised to deceive a gullible populace. The aim has been to leave the president of the United States looking good in the eyes of the populace, preserving his image as a strong and puissant leader, but to give the *finpols* their way concretely although perhaps in some new package. Thus, although we live under increasing government regulation, much of the regulation is purely token. And if the *finpols* do defy the government and break the law in some billion-dollar foray—they will, if caught, be forthrightly fined up to perhaps $50,000 or $100,000!

National policy with respect to the *finpolities* has been paralyzed by ambivalence relating to two ideas. There has been, first, the strong national belief in competition. Without competition the national history itself would be seen as without meaning, simply a record of random activity. On the other hand, there has been admiration for advancing technology, linked purely by association with the corporations, and with bigness. Americans generally admire competition, advanced technology and pure bigness. The fact that one must choose between competition and corporate bigness has been evaded. It is logically impossible to have *finpolity* and competition, yet few are willing to make a choice between the two.

"Bigness itself is no crime" is a statement often made in classrooms and in writing by apologetic academicians with their eyes on the big corporations. And they are tautologically correct; bigness cannot be a crime because it is a pure abstraction. But to be a big *corporation*, as we have seen, is almost always and invariably, as the fact happens to be, to be an adjudicated *criminal* corporation. The proper reply to the professor who utters the empty truism is this: "But bigness in a corporation always, as a factual matter, involves crime."

Presidents McKinley, Theodore Roosevelt, Taft, Wilson, Harding, Coolidge, Hoover and Eisenhower were deep in the confidence of the *finpols* and, despite harsh words at times purely for public consumption, got along very well with them. Theodore Roosevelt demagogically referred to them as "malefactors of great wealth." But the *finpols*, always, despite harsh public language, managed to get their way, sooner or later. Corporate concentration, for example, continues apace despite the hullabaloo of antitrust.

Where the desires of the *finpols* and the government became clearly divergent was in the 1930's, with the country beset by the deep crisis of unemployment initiated by the *finpolities*. The formula under which the *finpols* had prospered finally came apart, and government felt the need to improvise. There ensued a period of tension and genuine hostility between *finpols* and government, which was finally poulticed over by the advent of World War II, in which the *finpols* and *finpolities* were very much needed. The fusion of the *finpolities* with the national government, with many *finpols* taken boldly into the national government under the rubric of patriotic effort, was again complete, and was solemnly recemented during the Eisenhower Administration. President Eisenhower freqeuntly expressed his admiration for the *finpols* and gave them a prominent role in his administrations.

In the 1960's the *finpols* remain restored to grace in national affairs. Most of them at the moment seem to agree that the government should be allowed to engage in somewhat wider social maneuvers than *finpolity* would ordinarily approve. Presidents John F. Kennedy and Lyndon B. Johnson, seeking to rebuild Franklin D. Roosevelt's synthesis of electoral support, have been allowed to engage in much social-program maneuver. And the *finpols* have been conceded many of their demands—removal of price controls, lower taxes, etc. President Johnson, like President Eisenhower, has professed great admiration and respect for the *finpols* who are, after all, under the equal application of the laws entitled to as much consideration as, say, the ordinary workman. The *finpols*, then, are an integral part of "The Great Society," in which there is obviously a great deal of lucre to be made filling profitable government contracts for cement, steel, aluminum, copper, textbooks, rockets, space machines, tanks, recoilless rifles, schools, hospitals, sanitoria and bird baths.

In place of the Church today, there are the Intellectuals. In so saying I realize that my remarks lose credibility for many American readers, for intellectuals are not highly esteemed in the American mass-media or, presumably, among most of the populace. As I don't want to take the space to lay down a detailed argument supporting my case for the Intellectuals as a domestic Third Force let me, aiming right between the eyes of the dubious, simply remark that Karl Marx and V. I. Lenin were intellectuals. So, for that matter, were Winston Churchill, Albert Einstein, Thomas Jefferson, Benjamin Franklin and John F. Kennedy. Not all intellectuals, to be sure, have attained comparable eminence. But they are nevertheless present in their various ways.

It is the intellectuals, as a group, who preside and wrangle over the undulating frontiers of ideology, philosophy, scholarship and science, in all of which they may be said to have, by popular default, a vested interest. Most broadly (and abstractly) they preside in some disorder over values. And although their concrete power today is not comparable with the power of the medieval churchmen (themselves the intellectuals of their day, supported by the propertied and psychological power of the Church), it is nevertheless implicit. It is the general task of the intellectuals to make sense out of the established order, if that is possible; but the more the established order fails to make sense in the minds of the intellectuals the nearer it is to ultimate rejection or modification. If a basic political operating rule is that all men are entitled to the equal protection of the law and Negroes and others are flagrantly denied such protection, it is the intellectuals who are most sensitive to the contradiction between rule and action and who therefore deny that the system is what it virtuously claims to be. By the test of its own rules, by the way, ours is not an operationally virtuous system.

The fact of the importance of the intellectuals as a class has nothing at all to do with the strength or virtue of the intellectuals as individuals but has everything to do with the ultimacy of systematically applied thought. Hitler threw the intellectuals out of his system, preferring to rely upon what he called his intuition. As a consequence he lost, among many other things, priority in the matter of the atom bomb. The currently split and diminished Reich stands as a monument to his folly. The Russian politicians, supposing Leninism to be ultimate political revelation rather than a restricted set of tactics, keep the intellectuals under close restriction; the expression of free thought is not permitted in contemporary Russia. Nevertheless, the Russian intellectuals do maintain some under-the-surface ferment in the Soviet Union. They are a force, however feeble, but of vast potential.

One of the latter-day difficulties of the *finpols* and the *finpolities* on the American scene is that since 1929 they have lost the sympathy of a considerable segment of intellectuals. Far fewer today than in the 1920's believe that what's good for General Motors is good for the United States. Much about the specific enterprise of General Motors, indeed, increasingly fails to make human sense in the minds of intellectuals, despite the herculean labors of public relations men. And in view of the emergence of a vast hereditary establishment of property, it is blindingly clear that huge money rewards are not merited compensation for some overpowering social contribution as in the creation of an industry. If Carnegie, Rockefeller, the original Du Ponts, Westinghouse, Ford, Hartford and other nineteenth-century men made such a contribution, a debatable point in itself, it is certainly plain that their heirs have not. Today, the biggest money rewards in the American system come from simply sitting and listening to the reading of a will, which can scarcely be construed as a social contribution. Intellectually, it looks medieval.

It is a mistake, though, to suppose that it was the post-1929 denouement alone that caused the defection of many intellectuals from the old and easy ways of thinking. It was the literary intellectuals more particularly, committed to humanistic values, who reacted most strongly to the national experience after 1929. But public policy with respect to the new weaponry, from the atomic bomb onward, raised increasing doubts about the direction of events among scientific intellectuals, many of whom now look upon the joint policies of the government and the *finpolities* with an increasingly dubious eye.

Yet it is the relations between the *finpols* and the *pubpols* or public politicians that occupy the foreground, with the intellectuals kept in enfeebled attendance under steady public disparagement as "long hairs" and "impractical theorists" rather than in forthright restriction as in Russia. *Finpols* and *pubpols* are generally bedfellows, the latter probably the more ardent in the relationship, but increasingly there are signs of strain as the *pubpols* recognize, with some bewilderment, that in many ways their interests are incompatible. Can it be, they seem to ask themselves in dismay, that what is good for General Motors is not always good for the administration in Washington? What Big Business wants, in short, no longer always seems to harmonize with what the White House believes is required. The naive king, friend to all men, begins to feel that the barons are perhaps plotting against him.

The divergence of interests, not wholly closed since it widened under Franklin D. Roosevelt in the 1930's, seems likely to grow wider in the course of world change. The *pubpols*, like the medieval kings, may be obliged to struggle against the baronage, a prospect few of them can relish in view of their not too secret admiration for them. But as interests diverge and strains grow greater, the central government (like the medieval Crown, simply by reason of its wider responsibilities and inherent powers) seems bound to triumph, although by that time the central government may have been transformed into a more viable version of the Corporate State than was ever seen in Italy and Germany prior to 1945. There is indeed a discernible swing toward such a Corporate State, of which the *finpolities* would be integral and guaranteed formal parts (with big ownership stakes assured under some saving, perhaps socialistic, formula), and most of the smart money would no doubt bet on its emergence. Yet, in the time remaining before its advent, will the intellectuals look upon its coming with favor?

Informally, we are already well into the era of the Corporate State, of which the Warfare State is only a subdivision. Practically, it already exists as long as the *pubpols* find their interests running parallel with those of the *finpols*. A difficulty for the latter, though, is that the *pubpols* are sometimes obliged by the far-scattered facts confronting them to interpret the general situation differently, as President Kennedy did in the case of steel prices and as President Johnson did in the case of aluminum, copper and steel prices.

Although AT&T is a *finpolity*, a vast dukedom little short of a full polity, the domain over which it presides is parochial in comparison with the relatively universal domain of the United States government. AT&T is, comparatively, narrowly specialized in its interests.

And it is the narrow specialization of profit-interests of all the *finpolities* that, at times, makes their acts and policies inharmonious with those of the government of the United States, whose necessary task is to harmonize, at least roughly, a wide variety of foreign and domestic problems and interests. The government, often to its distaste, must deal with a far more complicated situation than any *finpolity* deals with.

Such being the case there is always the potentiality of a clash—perhaps a serious clash—between the central polity and all or some of the *finpolities*. There can be no doubt which way the hand would go *if* all the chips were ever down. A question that arises at this point, unanswerable yet, is this: Will the intellectuals be able to come forward with some solution or set of solutions more attractive than the looming and gradually emerging Corporate State or ultimate *finpolity*?

Although the medieval Crown won out in its struggle with the barons and the intellectuals of the day, when it attained its final victory it was by no means the same Crown. It had been modified and battered in the struggle. For the intellectuals in the course of time caused it to be changed almost beyond recognition, most dramatically in the French Revolution. While much remains the same today, as the effort to re-establish something like the Holy Roman Empire in the guise of a United Europe, the content, the outlook and the methods of the European governments are all different, largely owing to the efforts of the now secularized intellectuals. The slogan "Liberty, Equality and Fraternity," which exploded the emotions of men, did not come from king, nobleman, soldier, peasant or businessman. It, like modern science as a whole, came from the intellectuals.

No suggestion is intended here that some sort of established script or historical cycle is being followed or even that the same sort of structure confronts us that confronted medieval Europe. It is only that the interactive, usually muted, tug-of-war among government, the big corporations and the intellectuals stirs memories and seems to be at least a dim replica of an earlier internal struggle.

My own view is that although the big corporations and their dominant owners and managers, the *finpolities* and the *finpols*, are still unquestionably powerful they are in a long-term slipping position as far as ultimate general dominance is concerned. Too many counter-forces are emerging on the world scene.

That this is so has been shown both by Presidents Kennedy and Johnson, neither of whom was personally hostile to the corporate crowd. President Johnson has appeared to admire it as intensely as President Eisenhower and maintains close relations with it.

Yet situations arose which showed that, when the chips were down, a president who knows his own mind and interests can and must quickly bring the *finpolities* to heel. It has been demonstrated, in brief, that a political leader with a firm knowledge of the mechanics of government and the balance of forces in society can successfully assert the priority of the general interest over the special interests. Franklin D. Roosevelt did it most spectacularly, able as he was to act in the name of an unquestioned emergency. But neither Presidents John F. Kennedy nor Lyndon B. Johnson needed the excuse of an overriding emergency when they vetoed, only temporarily to be sure, the price increases of some of the most powerful industries. President Johnson, by releasing stockpiled government aluminum and by threatening to reallocate government orders for steel, showed that indirect government counter-action is always possible if the *finpolities* threaten to run away with any situation. This fact was probably always known to dominant Republicans, for which reason they have shown such marked partiality for a long line of mediocre and subservient presidents from Grant to Hoover and Eisenhower. Not a single Republican president since Lincoln, nor most of the Democratic, causes the pulse of a reader of American history to quicken even slightly. When honest, they were dull and inactive. When energetic, like Theodore Roosevelt, they were fakers; and when stupid they were calamities. No historian of any standing among his peers would deny it.

In a certain sense every big corporation is a hostage to presidential and even congressional ire, which alone explains the Republican partiality for figurehead presidents and congressmen of the worm's-eye view like Dirksen, Halleck, Hickenlooper, Curtis, Mundt and Hruska. Any corporation can be investigated and, in fact, the entire community of wealth can be inquired into via officially mobilized scholarship as was shown in the Temporary National Economic Committee's investigation. And all investigations disclose some state of affairs hitherto unsuspected and deplored by the more intelligent segment of the populace, leading to cries for change.

Trend toward Multi-Finpolity

The *finpolities*, in any event, are much more than merely large corporations. Indeed, even in their purely functional aspects they are not simply what the public thinks them to be.

AT&T, the man in the street supposes, is devoted to telephony, General Motors to making automobiles, Sears, Roebuck to merchandising, Great Atlantic & Pacific Tea to distributing groceries—all true. But these companies, and others, do much more, and the trend of each corporation now is to become a general enterprise engaging in any and every sort of activity that is profitable, related or not to its original line.

Let us examine a few of these multifaceted corporations, or *multi-finpolities*, from among the largest corporations, taking as our model one from real life.

What happens, let us first ask, if a big corporation loses its customers, its *raison d'être*, as the old-time wagonmaking companies lost their customers with the advent of the automobile? Does it then go out of business? As many cases attest, the answer is No. As a huge financial reservoir it merely enters into one or many other businesses, provided they seem potentially profitable. They do this, too, if their original business enters upon a prolonged downtrend. The big corporations, in short, are Protean.

As good an example among many is International Telephone and Telegraph Corporation, the world's tenth biggest industrial employer with 195,000 workers in 55 countries, and the thirty-fifth largest American company assetwise. Its name suggests it to be devoted to international telegraphy and telephony but such is not at all the case. For as the *Wall Street Journal* justly remarked, it "sometimes seems no more than a scavenger-like monster, madly grabbing up everything in sight, always ready to strike again."[17]

It is difficult to tell precisely what business IT&T is really in aside from the business of making money. In this respect it is like a bank, and all the big corporations are, banklike, large pools of capital; what they produce, aside from profits, is secondary. And if what they produce does not bring in profits they simply switch to producing something else. Nearly all are holding companies, not operating companies as commonly supposed.

IT&T was founded in 1920, originally to run the telephone and telegraph companies of Cuba and Puerto Rico. It expanded into other countries: Spain, Belgium, Rumania, Australia, Latin America, the Philippines, etc. It also built up a manufacturing arm second in its field only to Western Electric.

But international political upheavals and wars deprived it of much of its operating territory. IT&T was quite literally forced out of business in many places.

After World War II it took a new lease on life and became a general holding company for all manner of enterprises. As its president told the *Wall Street Journal*, its criteria for buying a company are only two: "The company should be growing faster than ITT. And it should have plenty of room to grow as the industry it is in grows."

"The executive steps into his Avis rent-a-car," begins the *Wall Street Journal* account, "drives to his broker's to check on his Hamilton Mutual fund shares, mails the quarterly premium for his American Universal Life Insurance policy, checks on financing some capital equipment through Kellogg Credit Corp., fires off a cable to Britain and then motors to Camp Kilmer, N.J., for a session with the purchasing agent at the Federal Job Corps there. It's just a routine morning dealing with a variety of matters, but so far the man's business has been entirely with divisions or operations of the inappropriately named International Telephone & Telegraph Corp."

IT&T now owns and operates the Aetna Finance Company; the American Universal Life Insurance Company; part of the Great International Life Insurance Company; Hamilton Management Corporation and Hamilton Funds, Inc.; Avis, Inc.; Kellogg Credit Company; the Mackey Telegraph and Cable System; Coolerator Company; Kellogg Switchboard and Supply; Kuthe Laboratories, Inc.; Federal Caribe, Inc.; Airmatic Systems Corp.; Hayes Furnace Manufacturing and Supply; Royal Electric Corp.; the telephone system of the Virgin Islands; L. C. Miller Co.; Jennings Radio Manufacturing; American Cable and Radio; Alpina Buromaschinen-Werke and Edward Winkler Apparatebau of Germany; a large group of Finnish, French, Swiss and English companies; National Computer Products; General Controls Co.; etc. It owns scores of companies throughout Latin America and Europe in almost everything related in any way to using or producing electrical equipment, as well as many companies without the slightest relation to electrical equipment. It is a credit-insurance-investment-electrical equipment-general world communications-transportation-chemical-computer-engineering-general service company. You name it, IT&T does it, almost, so long as it is highly profitable.

An extreme case, it will be said, but far less extreme than one might suppose. IT&T is more like a standard model of the emerging Protean *finpolity*. AT&T itself is not radically different.

General Motors makes automobiles at home and abroad. But it also makes giant Diesel locomotives, industrial apparatus, a full line of household electrical appliances (refrigerators, stoves, washing and drying machines, dishwashers, etc.), airplane motors, earthmoving equipment and a variety of other items, and it can retool and make anything whatever in the electro-mechanical line. As easily as not, it could make airplanes, intercontinental missiles, submarines or space ships. Whatever it does not make it does not make because it doesn't want to. Thus far its automobile line is its main source of profit. Ford Motor is similarly in the household appliance field and heavily committed to electronics, including TV sets. Both own an assortment of underlying material-supplying companies. Both are really multi-faceted states, and with their credit companies and dealership-franchise arms are not very different from IT&T.

The diversified mixture of products of each was achieved by combining many different existing companies, as IT&T has done in a broader spectrum. In the case of some companies the product mixture has come about gradually. In the case of others the decision to diversify has come suddenly, as though recognizing an opportunity that others stumbled upon earlier. Companies suddenly and radically shift their operating emphases, always in quest of maximum return on capital.

Thus, W. R. Grace and Company, eighty-fifth in corporate size, originally operated ships to Latin America (the Grace Line) but more recently has diversified its activities so that it is now a big chemical and fertilizer producer, banker, Latin-American manufacturer, exporter-importer and oil company. This former ship operator and banker now derives 65 per cent of its sales and 66 per cent of its pretax earnings from its chemical division. As in the case of IT&T, we may ask of W. R. Grace: What, really, is its business?

Sears, Roebuck and Great Atlantic & Pacific Tea would be defined, correctly, as merchandising enterprises. But each owns a great many supplemental manufacturing and financial enterprises which have been developed or acquired. Each does much more than mobilize, stock and deliver a wide variety of merchandise. A&P, like many of its counterparts, would ordinarily be described as a vast retail grocery chain. Yet it now also carries a big line of cosmetics, pharmaceuticals, household hardware and certain items of clothing (aprons, gloves, etc.). It and Sears, Roebuck and their smaller counterparts are obviously on the way to becoming general national manufacturing and merchandising enterprises oriented toward the ultimate consumer. Sears, Roebuck is usually thought of as a mail-order house; yet it operates chains of department stores as well, and engages in the general insurance business. In many phases it is a manufacturer. Both are giant transport companies.

What is Du Pont? A big chemical combine, it will be said. But it is also a big manufacturer of synthetic textiles, paints and explosives. It can build, and has built, nuclear energy plants. It could just as easily build cities. The big oil companies are chemical companies as well as huge operators of seaborne shipping, tank-car fleets and continental pipelines, and some of the big chemical companies are becoming to some extent oil companies. What is Tennessee Gas Transmission? A transmitter of natural gas, of course; but it is also a huge chemical, petroleum and fertilizer enterprise as well as other things.

The trend among all the big companies is increasingly toward non-specialization and to the merging of seemingly incompatible enterprises, as when Columbia Broadcasting acquires the New York Yankees baseball club and IT&T acquires American Broadcasting. Radio Corporation and other electronic firms acquire big book publishers with a view to gaining literary and educational properties. Many big newspaper enterprises also publish books, magazines and operate TV and radio stations, pulp and paper mills, deepwater ships, etc.

AT&T itself, publicly looked upon as "the telephone company," operating about 85 per cent of the nation's telephones, long owned 99.8 per cent of Western Electric, manufacturer of telephones, switchboards and a wide array of electrical apparatus. AT&T is also heavily committed to research and holds patents relating to the whole electronic field, including computers. It is deep in the satellite enterprise.

What all the expansion reflects is: investment of earnings not paid out. As we have noted, payouts incur additional taxes for stockholders; retained invested earnings are not taxed, are like money in the bank and get accelerated depreciation allowances. As there are not sufficient opportunities at home, the companies are now acquiring foreign enterprises at a great rate—in France, Germany, Belgium, Switzerland, Japan, everywhere—and since World War II have invested abroad about $40 billion. Ownership is preferred over income.

The cases cited are not at all untypical. One could go on for a long time detailing odd combinations of corporate activity. Thus, Hunt Foods & Industries, Inc., originally the Ohio Match Company, in addition to making and marketing a broad line of food products operates companies in lumber, glass, aluminum, real estate, chemicals, glass and metal containers, gin, paints, varnishes, wallpaper, floor coverings and so on. It has a line of big corporate investments that is every bit as odd as the IT&T labyrinth. It is, first, the largest stockholder in Wheeling Steel, with 8.8 per cent. It owns 22.7 per cent of Canada Dry and 35.8 per cent of the McCall Corporation, publisher of *McCall's Magazine, Redbook, Bluebook* and the *Saturday Review*. It has a 4.5 per cent interest in ABC-

Paramount, giving it a foothold in film-making, radio and television broadcasting.

Let us take a more sober-seeming company, the Mississippi River Fuel Corporation, originally formed to transport natural gas by pipeline from Louisiana to St. Louis. There was first formed the Mississippi River Corporation to exchange stock with it, and this company now owns 94.2 per cent of the Mississippi Transmission Corporation, 100 per cent of several cement companies and 58 per cent of the Class A stock of the big Missouri Pacific Railroad. As the change in its name suggests, it is apparently going to concern itself with everything in the Mississippi Valley, perhaps the Valley as a whole.

The Illinois Central Railroad may become its rival, might even merge with it. For the railroad has caused to be formed Illinois Central Industries, Inc., with which it exchanged 95 per cent of its stock; and Illinois Central Industries has already acquired a big electrical equipment maker. As its name suggests, it is ready to operate anything along its right of way from Chicago to Florida and the Gulf of Mexico.

Operating companies become holding companies and some of the holding companies become general investment companies such as Adams Express Company, until 1918 a leading express and money-order house that sold out its business to American Express and transformed itself into a closed-end investment trust. The chief difference between a standard investment trust and a heterogeneous holding company is that the latter holds a dominant to 100 per cent interest in companies in which it plays a directorial role; the investment trust has only a fractional position in each company and is not involved in the management. The investment trust is a pure *rentier*.

The time, then, is near at hand when a company's name will give no clue at all to its line of business apart from the business of making money.

Studying the reasons for the crazy-quilt expansion, the Federal Trade Commission in 1955 noted them as follows:

Building new capacity adds to existing capacity and intensifies competition; but by buying, a manufacturer acquires additional capacity without adding to total capacity and may also reduce some external competition. "These competitive considerations are especially important if he is diversifying into products new to him, but in the production of which others are well established."

Selling companies are motivated to sell because they lack the financial resources for expansion. Here lies the opportunity of the resource-rich company.

"The same factor is to be noted in instances in which a company having surplus cash not immediately needed in its operations invests it in the securities of other companies, either in the same or an unrelated industry. Such investments may subsequently prove to be the initial step in acquisitions carried out either as further investment and diversification of the acquirer's business, or as a means of salvaging the investments already made.

"Tax savings possible under various provisions of the Internal Revenue Act granting more favorable rates on capital gains as compared with the rates applicable to operating profits of corporations and personal incomes of individuals, the provisions covering tax-free exchanges of stock, and the provisions governing the carrying forward of past operating losses as credits against future earnings are also important factors."[18]

Said the Federal Trade Commission stiffly: ". . . the economic forces and motives discernible are not *per se* different from those upon which all business judgments are based respecting the ownership and exchange of property in a free economy. The operation of these forces on a large scale, however, carries with it such adverse economic effects on third parties, and on the economy as a whole, as to bring their unrestrained operation into conflict with public policy and law."[19]

What is happening may perhaps be better depicted by showing it as a small fictitious model, as follows: One man, owning all of the highly profitable Super-Cosmos Corporation, is causing it to hold back most of its earnings, thus enabling him to bypass personal income taxes. With these withheld tax-free earnings he is gradually buying up *all* other companies, large and small, causing them also to hold back earnings in order to buy other companies which in turn generate profits to buy others, etc., etc. If this Super-Cosmos Corporation paid its earnings to him in dividends he would be heavily taxed and not richer but poorer. As it is, he grows richer and richer, owns more and more property, expands and expands, so that finally he owns every shoe-shine stand and peanut stand. He finally owns every single enterprise there is.

It is not true, of course, that one man is doing this. But several clusters of men, capitalists, are doing something like it and are producing the strange multifarious sort of companies we have noted, which are becoming *typical* companies among the biggest ones. And concentration is being intensified.

What of the antitrust laws? Why don't they prevent the erection of these huge, expanding multifarious trusts or *finpolities*?

The average citizen is not aware that the antitrust laws are highly selective in their application at those relatively rare times when the *pubpols* decide to make them operative. Their application is permissive, not mandatory. The avowed purpose of the antitrust laws is to protect competition. Thus, if a company in one line of business tries to take over a company in the same line of business they may be called into play; also, if a company through ownership in a functionally unrelated company —such as Du Pont in General Motors—seems likely to divert subsidiary business from others to itself, they may also be put into play.

As it is said, the antitrust laws forbid only horizonal mergers or horizontal restraint of trade. Under those laws General Motors could not acquire Ford Motor or *vice versa*.

But other kinds of mergers are not forbidden.

There are possible, for example, vertical mergers. Here a manufacturing company may acquire suppliers, all the way back to the mine or field, or may acquire distributors to the retail market. This does not appear to be illegal unless competition is *directly* affected with someone in the same line of endeavor. Actually, the company that engages in vertical mergers, far from ending competition, is externally intensifying it, forcing others to do likewise or to fall behind in the blind race for dominion.

There are, too, circular mergers, in which a company acquires a good many companies, neither in exactly the same line of business, but the whole tending to come back into a closed circle so that all these companies only or largely do business with and for each other, excluding others from the magic circle. Such a combination might well come under fire of the antitrust laws, particularly if the White House occupant decided to parade his muscle.

There are, finally, these latter-day heterogeneous mergers and acquisitions we have discussed and in which the large companies now so largely figure. The antitrust laws do not apply against them because the various acquisitions are not in directly competing lines. A ship company that acquires chemical companies, an automobile company that acquires a household-appliance-maker or a telegraph company that acquires insurance companies does not appear to have acquired any of its competitors.

But in a very real sense basic competition is diminished. For large pools of liquid capital, retained profits, acquiring most of the economy for themselves, *are gradually ending competitive endeavors in making money and in running enterprises.* As far as economic creativity is concerned, competition has been stifled at its very roots. Most of the population is in the process reduced to the passive status of the Russian and Chinese populations but by different means.

The antitrust laws, as Justice Oliver Wendell Holmes noted, are a joke. They have signally failed to preserve competition, their avowed intent. While the economists go about vainly seeking perfect monopoly, a single company in a single industry making a single item, and debate among themselves the semantic differences of oligopoly, monopoly and price leadership, we see around us a rising and all-embracing *financial monopoly*, quasi-monopoly or semi-oligopoly. It isn't that there is monopoly in one industry—such as steel, oil or motors—but that industry in general totality is monopolized in ownership, control and direction by a very few people, the rich and super-rich. The *moneybund* is a concrete literal reality rather than a hyperbolic figure of speech.

The next step may be the merging, as it becomes profitably tax-saving, of the huge heterogeneous trusts. There is nothing in the antitrust laws as now written, seemingly, that would prevent the merger of U.S. Steel with Great Atlantic & Pacific Tea and the fusion of this combination with IT&T and W. R. Grace. Another possible combination among many is General Motors, Sears, Roebuck, Standard Oil of New Jersey and Heinz pickles. Why not? They don't offer competing products or services. They are simply competitive in making money, which is the mainspring of all the activity. Take away the money-making incentive in the form of extremely peculiar tax laws and such mergers would not occur.

What is happening is not only of economic and political concern but is of profound cultural concern. Under the system of many competing enterprises, each independent of the other, independent and candid voices were encouraged. The old-time merchant, for example, was often a man of forthright, informed opinions, which he forcibly expressed. The object of going into business for oneself in the American ethos was to become "independent," so that one needed nobody's permission to speak out or anyone's aid or charity.

The institutional foundations of independent expression, however, are being as eroded under spreading corporate giantism as under Communist or Fascist totalitarianism. Neither *finpols*, their managers or employees dare speak out on anything for fear of compromising the corporate image before a heterogeneous public. What does the corporate crowd really think about birth control, religion in the schools, civil rights, conscription and the like? Nobody knows because they play it cool, say nothing. The mass media under their control are similarly noncommunicative, carrying water on both shoulders, reflecting the world as an entertaining circus of clowns, idiots, heroes, villains and random events. The growing corporate philistinism spreads slowly over the seats of learning.

To what extent can an employee of any one of the multiple parts of the corporate octopi commit himself on public questions? As a middle-range executive of the Super-Cosmos Corporation, to what extent can he express himself on, say, traditional versus progressive education? If he manages to make himself effectively heard on either side he is sure to make a large emotion-ridden crowd angry. Indeed, the more effectively he speaks on any aspect of a topic the angrier they get. They send letters to the management of the company, threatening to raise a boycott against its many branches, subsidiaries, affiliates and coordinates. But rarely do matters go this far; if they do, the offending middle-range executive is told to "lay off, forget about different approaches to education, stick to business."

As nearly everybody works for one or the other of these *finpolities*, nearly everybody is reduced to mouthing mild banalities if called upon to speak at all. Everybody toes the approved corporate line, designed to avoid making anybody angry about anything. "Don't be a trouble maker," is the operational motto. Meanwhile, the world itself poses more and more difficulties.

As for politics, leave that to the *pubpols* and their minions. As General Motors goes, so goes the nation: I'd die for Standard Oil: I have but one Ford to give to my country: Fifty-four-forty or AT&T: Nylon *ueber alles*.

Independent merchants and lawyers, once noted for their forthright views on public affairs, spoke out as the occasion seemed to require. Now that they are gone down the corporate drain, theirs and other voices are frozen in corporate silence. In their place the *finpols*, if they feel anything of public concern requires attention, summon their public relations men, legislative representatives and lawyers and map out a quiet under-cover campaign—but only as the interests of the *finpolity* itself dictate. Do the political parties themselves need an overhauling? That is something best left to the *pubpols*. "Mind your own business" becomes the prevailing rule. "Live and let live."

The outcome is much the same as though a totalitarian regime had imposed its will. The organization man in the grey flannel suit becomes endemic, not only on the corporate circuit but in politics and the groves of academe. The independent, autonomous mind is more and more seen as an eccentric, a knocker, a trouble-maker, an agitator. "Don't rock the boat," he is admonished. "You are simply playing into the hands of our enemies abroad. Be patriotic and rally behind the four-square guesswork of Mr. Big."

The uniformity is perfectly reflected in the glacial technical slicknesses of the watered-down mass media. The pay-off comes in one catastrophe or the other—Bay of Pigs, Vietnam, Watts. Catastrophe itself becomes endemic, built-in—as in the ghettos.

The source of it all surely is found in the need to preserve the well-being of the really huge investments of the *finpolities*. Any real or apparent deviation from a bland public-relations norm, in word or deed, can hurt profitability, and this is the new unforgivable sin. For as profits go down, unemployment rises, parents despair, children grow hungry. Then riots begin, suicides proliferate. It is easy to see that the general well-being depends wholly upon the well-being and good temper of the *finpolities*. The national maxim becomes, "Shut up."

Engineering Enterprises

A difficulty in writing about corporations is that the idea of a corporation brings different things to people's minds.

What people usually think of when they think of corporations is the engineering structure owned by the corporations. People sometimes visit corporations, as they say, by which they mean they visit their plants or offices.

Nevertheless, nobody, not even a corporation lawyer, has ever seen a corporation, which as a juridical concept is beyond sensory experience and almost as impalpable as a metaphysical abstraction. Yet one can sue or be sued by a corporation, injure or be injured by one. The corporation is actualized, concretized, only in a set of papers, the provisions of which the courts stand ready if necessary to implement. Whatever is tangible about the corporation is in these papers—its charter of incorporation, its by-laws and the titles to its properties. Even when a corporation owns a single plant and office combined, one cannot go and look at it; one can look only at its properties, which it can sell or otherwise dispose of and still remain intact in full corporativeness.

Public relations departments, in presuming to show the corporation to public view, in almost all cases show only some of its property, mostly consisting of engineering enterprises. All the leading 200 corporations listed in Appendix B are the legal representatives of such engineering enterprises. The corporation itself is a business—or *finpolity*; the business is an adjunct of an engineering process, which could be carried on by other legal means.

While there may be little difficulty in seeing U.S. Steel, General Motors, AT&T and their industrial counterparts as operators of engineering enterprises (a brief visit to their plants will convert doubters), there may be some difficulty in seeing certain other companies as conducting such operations. The electric, gas transmission and railroad companies, of course, all clearly stand out as operators of engineering enterprises. But there might be some opposition to the assertion that Sears, Roebuck, Great Atlantic & Pacific Tea and R. H. Macy and Company are also operators of engineering enterprises. It is nevertheless herewith asserted that they are.

Even if we eliminate all manufacturing—that is, machinefacturing— from their jurisdiction, they remain engineering enterprises, their engineering function being to gather, transport, store, display, deliver and offer to view a great variety of merchandise. Their engineering task is logistical. Of course, if anybody wishes to deny that R. H. Macy & Company is engaged in engineering we need not worry; one either sees the point or not. But it cannot be rationally denied that all the so-called industrial and public utility companies are engaged in pure engineering as well as in trade for profit.

Engineering is one form of applied science, and we find the industries, taken altogether, using the full range of mathematics, physics, chemistry, biology and even, more or less to suit the taste, the social proto-sciences. With more or less growing consciousness they apply pure science to their problems of production. The discovery of a new scientific principle, such as is involved in the transistor, is instantly incorporated into radios. New self-directed machines (automation) are installed on production lines as soon as they are created.

Now, if anyone wishes to contend that all these corporate engineering plants are marvels of modern human ingenuity, he will not hear any demurrer from this observer. He may find, instead, that he has a rival in eloquent advocacy, for I would be the first to agree that all these big corporations in their engineering aspects are among the wonders of the modern world.

But we are not considering them in this aspect—we are taking this showy aspect wholly for granted. We are considering them only in their corporate aspect, their juridical and quasi-political as well as financial-economic aspects. One not only concedes but proclaims and insists upon the fact that E. I. du Pont de Nemours and all the others have marvelous plants and general offices, based upon the latest scientific principles.

Few of the *finpols*, however, are *au courant* with their enterprises in their scientific and engineering aspects. Like the man in the street, they couldn't tell one much about molecules, atoms and sub-atomic particles nor about the principles of mechanics. Their knowledge has to do largely with principles of accounting and finance, law, cost analysis, taxes, prices, political negotiation, marketing, general organization—and profitability. They are largely creatures of the executive suite and boardrooms and the higher political caucuses rather than of the plant. They know far more about tax structure than about atomic structure.

And it is just these societal aspects, *their* particular area of interest, that is *our* area of interest. We take for granted the work of the scientists in the laboratory and the technicians and engineers in the plants. They have those, too, in Soviet Russia and Communist China where, however, they do not have *finpols*.

Portent of good or evil, depending upon one's point of view, it is nevertheless a differentiating descriptive fact.

What most basically confronts us is not only different legal systems but different types of legal systems. The *finpols* and *finpolities* have come into historic view, chiefly with the aid of modern technology which they neither invented nor developed, in our sort of political system. They constitute *our* problem, if problem they are, and this problem is in the truest sense political rather than economic or technical.

We are, then, interested in the *finpols* and *finpolities* from a political point of view. We do not identify the corporations in their essence either with their plants, which are among the most praiseworthy structures in the land, or with their products. While nylon to the average citizen may connote Du Pont, to us it connotes only chemistry. What Du Pont connotes to us—and Ford, Rockefeller, Mellon and the rest—is *finpolity*.

Eight 🌿

UNDERSTRUCTURE OF
THE FINPOLITAN ELITE

As the various *finpols* and *finpolities* are rivalrous at least in respect to making and retaining money, how and in what way do they act in concert, if they act in concert at all? Do they, in fact, act in concert in imposing *faits accompli* and policies on the nation?

To conclude that they more or less loosely act together as a *moneybund* is to proclaim oneself at once an adherent to what is pejoratively called the conspiracy theory, widely frowned upon by latter-day organizational academics in grey flannel suits (many of them briskly on the way up to the State, Defense or Treasury Departments or to the foundation refreshment troughs). In a broad sense, as it has been observed by unabashed exponents of the conspiracy theory, all history is a conspiracy. In this sense the word no more than broadly and perhaps privately and even unconsciously indicates coordinated action toward some mutually agreed upon end or ends at variance with public expectations; manifestly it does not have its specialized meaning in law.

In any event, overeager members of the financial elite have been caught and convicted in American courts of many literal subconspiracies, so that even in the narrow juristic sense many of them stand forth individually as certified, simon-pure conspirators. Consequently, even if there is not a single all-embracing conspiracy in juristic terms, it is a fact that there are and have been hundreds of adjudicated single conspiracies. The conspiracy theory, then, has a little more to it than honors-bound academics concede.

Three Theories

There are in fact three major sociological theories, academically certified in all solemnity, to account for the phenomenon of socio-economic decision-making, the recondite problem being to determine: Who, if anybody in particular, really makes the basic decisions that govern society? Who calls the shots?

To a considerable extent this is a pseudo-problem, for virtually every person knows that *he* isn't calling the shots nor are any of his neighbors, co-workers or acquaintances. Everybody knows it is some distant and obscure "they." But this fact (evident to any intelligent person) is not at all evident to many academics, who have made quite a scholastic mystery out of the whole business. Doubt is raised by some that any individual whatever makes any decisions; the theory is advanced that the entire process is occultly collective.

There is, first, the theory of an elite, which is employed by some masterful investigators.

Next, there is the theory of an inert, apathetic, partially alienated mass society, consisting largely of P. T. Barnum's myriad suckers and H. L. Mencken's swarming booboisie—the denizens of the grandstands and taverns. According to this theory, as most people are supine, unresponsive, childishly credulous and seeking no more than a job, diversion and comfortable mediocrity for themselves, the few who are seriously active emerge spontaneously at the decision-making level, more or less by default. As Tom, Dick and Harry won't bestir themselves and George the doer does, George finds himself willy-nilly among the decision-makers, a natural leader. But he got there more by chance than design, chosen if at all merely by fitting into the pattern of things and events. No conspirator he, no boob and no elitist.

There is, finally, the pluralist theory, according to which many diverse groups, individuals and forces confront each other in various ways, and under various cultural auspices arrive after debate by consensus or compromise at decisions, a notion that fits in neatly with democratic prescriptions. The process is presented as one of mutual accommodation.

There is something to be said for each of these theories, as each explains some of the data. Obviously a single synthesizing theory would be preferable. Lacking such, one can, and many sociologists do, attempt to blend them or to use them all. But as this is eclectic, theoretical purists are offended. The world, however—even the small world of society—is more complex than any all-embracing theory about it.

My own tacit use of these theories with respect to our subject is hierarchical and eclectic in the order stated. The facts strongly suggest to me, in other words, that the elitist theory best explains the facts. Whatever it fails to explain is then explained by the concept of the mass society. Finally, in many matters, less paramount in almost every single case, the pluralistic theory does come into play as it finds supporting data. But it is far less often significantly applicable than its sponsors suppose.

Actually, the elitist theory presupposes or implies the theory of the mass society. One could hardly have an elite without a mass. If everyone was alert and on his toes, how could an elite ever show itself? The mass itself, paradoxically, would be an elite, and perfect high-level democracy would prevail. The mass-society theory, then, does not stand separately. If one has an elite, one must have a mass and, if society is to survive, *vice versa*. The uninspired mass team, in brief, must have a quarterback and, preferably, a coach or set of coaches. If the elite is truly aristocratic, selecting only the best, so much the better.

These theories and some of their prominent adherents are briefly dealt with by a young sociologist in an interesting book;[1] there is, of course, a rather large literature about them. He himself found it necessary to apply them eclectically, although he believes in the greater inclusiveness of the pluralist view. As his attention was centered upon community decision-making in a small California town, the pluralist view is most serviceable; for its most fruitful application is on lower levels that are of little interest to the financial elite. But it would plainly be useless if applied to a company or white-supremacy town.

He objects to the elitist theory because it allegedly imputes motivations to covert leadership groups. If they are covert by definition they cannot, he believes, be investigated by rational methods. Next, he holds, the elitist theory smooths over and obscures the many internal struggles over decisions within an elite. With such struggles in mind, it would seem that one must apply the pluralist theory to the operations of the elite itself, a logically well-taken point certainly germane to the paramountcy of theory. Thirdly, the theory of the elite must rely on the impact of events outside the elite system to explain changes within the system itself; for the elite, which does indeed change, does not change spontaneously. Most importantly, "elitist studies of community power typically do not present data to support their contentions that *all* major decision-making rests in the hands of single leadership groups."

While I recoil from the operative "all," which I have emphasized, it is clearly incumbent upon anyone utilizing the elitist approach to show major decisions emanating from the elite group—decisions at variance with some established consensus. If such decisions are made, and are made to stick, then I think it may fairly be deduced that other decisions are similarly made. It isn't the general consuming public, we may say in a preliminary way, that decides to raise the prices. Nor is it, in view of the system of corporately administered prices, an automatic free market. It is clearly some distant and popularly distasteful "they" who decide this.

The elitist theory, most broadly stated, holds that the United States, for example, is a society of many dominant elites. The elite levels of science, scholarship, the arts, entertainment and sports (but not politics or finance) are open to anyone of ability. These are, therefore "open" elites, and consonant with the democratic bias. But there is, it is asserted or implied by a variety of writers, a politico-economic elite of elites, which is a "closed" elite. It is closed because something other than personal ability is required to belong to it. The main although not exclusive qualification for membership, it is here contended, is money. This elite has been referred to as the *moneybund*—the complex of *finpolities*. Its leading members, I suggest, are *finpols*. This moneybund is different from C. Wright Mills's "power elite," which is a somewhat fanciful and highly personal embroidery upon the old-established basic idea of a moneyed elite. Take the money crowd away and Mills's "power elite" crumbles into verbal dust.

Now, while the moneyed elite no doubt is pluralistically structured internally, toward the outside world it presents itself as a rather solid, small, coherent entity. Its decisions once having been taken or not taken (a decision in itself)—and we can obtain at least glimpses of some of its decision-making processes—it presents to the world pretty much of a united front even if it is not always unified internally in its views. Its members, at any rate, have various ways of knowing the difference between insiders and outsiders.*

As for motivations, it is, first, surely possible to deduce certain over-riding motivations in the moneyed elite by the way its members conduct

---

* The idea of an elite does not necessarily imply that it is homogeneous. Thus, Albert Mathiez, the French historian on the subject of the French nobility, says: "The nobility consisted, in fact, of distinct and rival castes, the most powerful of which were not those who could point to the longest pedigrees. Side by side with the old hereditary or military nobility, there had sprung up in the course of the last two centuries a nobility 'of the long robe' (*noblesse de robe*); that is to say, an official nobility which monopolized administrative and judicial offices. This new caste, which was as proud as the old nobility, and perhaps richer, was headed by the members of the parlements, or courts of appeal." This new nobility, as Mathiez goes on to show, was in many ways more powerful than the old nobility. Albert Mathiez, *The French Revolution*, Alfred A. Knopf, Inc., N.Y., 1926; Universal Library, N.Y., 1964, pp. 6–7. One could similarly divide the American elite into the old and new money and the leading corporate officials and corporation lawyers.

their worldly affairs. One doesn't need to tap their telephones or induce their psychoanalysts to break confidences to see that they are nearly all motivated (1) to retain their money and power; (2) to add to money and power if possible; (3) to make use of all the resources of modern science, technology and politics in the retention and expansion of their power; (4) to keep their share of the tax burden as low as possible; (5) to support whatever politico-economic policies support or improve their position and to struggle against those which seem likely to diminish it; and (6) to have themselves presented to the world as especially worthy people.

What they want more specifically is shown by their legislative lobbyists, trade association spokesmen and newspapers. *Fortune*, the *Wall Street Journal* and similar publications consciously and unconsciously tell us much about what they want. Beyond this, public inquiries, the taking of testimonies, the massing of evidence in the courts and occasional books by insiders have done much to reveal motivations. There have been memoirs such as those of the late Clarence W. Barron, critical and friendly biographies and even letters (although collections of letters, as in the case of the elder J. P. Morgan, have often been ordered burned by testamentary prescription). This in itself seems a bit conspiratorial.

The major ends of the moneyed elite are clearer, it must be confessed, than the devious means often used to attain those ends.

In view of this elite (judging purely by their outward behavior) what's good for them is good for the United States. They see their personal pecuniary interests as identical with the complex interests of the nation. This elite is known to favor, among other things, a minimum of government regulation of their corporate instrumentalities; they openly talk to this end and work to achieve it. Society, they feel, should be subject to minimal direction. Would anyone wish to assert there is any doubt about this?

As far as motivations go, it is not a difficulty that inheres peculiarly in the theory of an elite; in this day of Freudian psychology the motivations of every individual are a mystery even to himself. What are the motivations of participants in a pluralist decision-making process? If it is said, "How can we know what the elite is up to and why?" one may reply with another question: "How can we know what pluralists are up to and why?" Not being able to look inside people's heads, one makes deductions from external behavior. If a man hoards money in a hole in the floor we conclude that he is a miser. Can we be wrong? Can it be that he is in fact a spendthrift? As to why he does it, we turn to the psychoanalyst and hear talk about feelings of insecurity, inadequacy, rejection, alienation. Hoarding, it seems, makes him feel less anxious. Yet, he remains a miser *vis-à-vis* others, an objective phenomenon. He is not *merely* a psychiatric case.

The theoretical objections to the theory of the elite, at any rate, are not nearly so compelling as they may seem when viewed only dialectically on the purely theoretical level, before testing against the facts.

But there are stronger reasons, compelling to any rational mind, for rejecting the idea of the greater serviceability of the pluralist theory in explaining decision-making on the national level. For if the pluralist theory indeed held, if major decisions in the United States were in fact the product of countervailing and balanced groups, with each group element of society making itself fully heard, the outcome in terms of money, position and prestige would be a great deal more equitable than it is. Sociologists can indeed show many decisions arrived at by pluralist means. But we are talking now about the humanly fundamental decisions—the decisions about who gets what, where, how and why. Those decisions, I assert, are elitely determined, sometimes against considerable opposition.

If the decision about the distribution of the basic economic means is arrived at pluralistically, why is the payoff so uneven? If one goes along with the pluralist view we must conclude that people have acquiesced in their relatively low reward by the economic system. Yet millions of people protest all the time that they are being underpaid. They sound as though they had not consented to the decision-making about the distribution of money.

Most people in the United States, including very many outstandingly intelligent and highly trained, are much like the participants in a dice game in which the opponent throws a long series of 7's and 11's, losing seldom; but when the dice change hands it develops that they follow the laws of randomness and show no runs of 7's and 11's. In a real dice game, most such losers would quickly conclude that the dice were loaded and they were being rooked.

Now, if the social dice weren't subject to manipulation from behind the scenes, would so many people be so far below par in the matter of money and property? Such subparity elements, it is often said by way of explanation, are the no-goods, without ambition or energy. But, we may ask, is this also true of Nobel laureates, university professors in general, the trained professional classes, whose pay in comparison with that of corporation executives and big dividend recipients is absurdly meager? Are we to suppose that highly skilled professionals have acquiesced in their relatively niggardly compensation? Hearing them complain, reading their complaints in professional journals, one would not suppose so. They sound very much as though they are complaining futilely against loaded dice.

Again, to look at the bottom of the labor force, are we to suppose that the poverty-stricken itinerant agricultural worker or the ghetto denizen has acquiesced through some pluralistic decision-making process in his low estate?

In looking at the history of organized labor, the long record of anti-labor violence and counter-violence, one gets the strong impression that basic decisions were imposed upon unwilling and eventually maddened victims. Those who worked in Andrew Carnegie's steel mills at $10 for a seventy-two-hour (and longer) week of punishing effort under intense heat had never willingly agreed to perform in this manner. Nobody had ever asked them or their representatives. They were driven by stark necessity to accept a one-sided bargain.

It is true that all the persons to whom I refer have their compensation determined by a market. The elite, however, do not have their revenues impersonally determined by a market, to the dictates of which they submit. They make market rules pretty much to suit their inclinations.

It does, then, look as though members of the labor force, high and low, have come up against a decree that says: So far and no further. They have not acquiesced in this decree; they have not been consulted about it. They are often opposed to it, but are as powerless to push it aside as Russian workers are powerless to push aside a state decree.

It looks very much as though this decree has been handed down from some esoteric group, for there is no general rule against having an expansive income in a booming economy.

In any play against the socio-economic elite of *finpols* with a view to participating in its inner decisions, few—indeed, none—of the members of the various open elites find they can make it. They don't have the hereditary tickets; and even if they had the tickets they might not possess other qualifications.

What, precisely, is the understructure of the top elite of *finpolity*?

Intermarriage of the Elite

Largely headquartered in the East, this elite, first of all, is heavily intermarried. This fact has been shown in great detail and need not detain us.[2] Most of the world of *finpolity* and its environs is interlaced by complicated cousinages, as in the case of the longer established European nobility. Intermarriage among the big propertied elite—the bourgeoisie, the *finpols*—continues, as the "society" pages of newspapers show nearly every week.

As a fairly recent and uncomplicated example of upper-crust family structure let us take the Fords. Edsel, the only child of grass-roots Henry, had four children. Henry Ford II, one of Edsel's three sons, married Anne McDonnell, a Catholic socialite by whom he had three children. His daughter Charlotte, twenty-four, in 1965 married the off-the-beach Greek shipping magnate Stavros Spiros Niarchos, fifty-six, reputed to be worth a minimal $260 million.[8] Her coming accouchement was duly announced early in February, 1966; not long thereafter a prospective divorce. Her debut in 1959, according to the *Times,* took a year to plan, was attended by 1,200 guests and cost about $250,000, of which $60,000 went for flowers alone. Recalled the *Times* nostalgically (December 17, 1965): "Two million magnolia leaves were flown from Mississippi and were used to cover the walls of the corridors leading to the reception room in the Country Club of Detroit, which had been redecorated to look like an eighteenth-century French chateau." Sister Anne Ford, twenty-two, was married with less fanfare a few days later to Giancario Uzielli, an international stockbroker of New York. Henry Ford II in his second marital venture, after a divorce that led to his excommunication from the Catholic Church, married the divorced, also excommunicant, Mrs. Maria Christina Vettore Austin, of Italy and England, who is more particularly one of the European Rothschilds of pecuniary repute. William Ford, another of Edsel's sons, married Martha Firestone of the rubber fortune, by whom he has three children.

Here, among the comparatively late-arriving Fords, one finds a rococo interlacing of diverse elements the common social denominator of which is property; and this is typical of the upper ownership strata.

As to inward and outward twining cousinages among the moneyed elite, the Du Ponts provide perhaps the most spectacular example, interlinking with a number of other established and unlikely cousinages such as the Peabodys and Roosevelts. It is not usually easy in the hereditary strata of wealth to find someone unjoined to one or more other wealthy families by cousinly ties, and many of them link with what in Europe is known as nobility. Cousinage threads through many apparently disparate propertied families.

To avoid detention here by details readily available elsewhere, let it simply be said that much about the affairs of the *finpolities* is a family matter. These families, it is true, are often subject to strains within themselves and *vis-à-vis* other families (pluralism); but they together present pretty much of a unified front to the world (eliteness).

Pretensions to Aristocracy

The American wealthy, as Cleveland Amory shows in considerable diverting detail, have confused money, ostentatious partying, politico-economic position and far-ranging power with aristocracy, of which they very commonly think themselves representative.[4] By the hundreds they have dug up for themselves, or caused to be devised, European coats of arms, more than 500 of which have been suitably proved and registered with the New England Historic and Genealogical Society, "easily the country's outstanding authority on coats of arms."[5]

The stress on coats of arms, both among bearers and disappointed non-bearers, suggests that the wealthy themselves, unlike some unaccountably obtuse outside investigators, regard themselves as part of family enterprises, not as isolated persons who have won in an individualistic rat race. These families, to be sure, are placed within a certain setting of historically developed institutions of which American children sing innocently in school.

As the redoubtable H. L. Mencken remarked in 1926, "the plutocracy, in a democratic state, tends to take the place of the missing aristocracy, and even to be mistaken for it. It is, of course, something quite different. It lacks all the essential characters of a true aristocracy: a clean tradition, culture, public spirit, honesty, honour, courage—above all, courage. It stands under no bond of obligation to the state; it has no public duty; it is transient and lacks a goal. Its most puissant dignitaries of to-day came out of the mob only yesterday—and from the mob they bring its peculiar ignobilities. As practically encountered, the plutocracy stands quite as far from the *honnête homme* as it stands from the Holy Saints. Its main character is its incurable timourousness; it is forever grasping at the straws held out by demagogues. . . . Its dreams are of banshees, hobgoblins, bugaboos. The honest, untroubled snores of a Percy or a Hohenstaufen are quite beyond it.

"The plutocracy, as I say, is comprehensible to the mob because its aspirations are essentially those of inferior men . . . money. . . . What it lacks is aristocratic disinterestedness, born of aristocratic security. There is no body of opinion behind it that is, in the strictest sense, a free opinion. Its chief exponents, by some divine irony, are pedagogues of one sort or another. . . . Whatever the label on the parties, or the war cries issuing from the demagogues who lead them, the practical choice is between the plutocracy on the one side and a rabble of preposterous impossibilists on the other . . . what democracy needs most of all is a party that will separate the good that is in it theoretically from the evils that beset it practically, and then try to erect that good into workable system" (*Notes on Democracy*, Alfred A. Knopf, N.Y., pp. 203–6).

Schools of the Elite

The children of the *finpols* and their higher servitors are early separated from the common run of children by being sent to special private schools, which exist as part of a different world. This point was inquired into by C. Wright Mills.[6] Not all the children in these schools are from the elite, because such a prescription would defeat educational ends. The private schools are "democratic," in that they take students, many on scholarships, from a wide social spectrum. Some now take able Negroes, although their quest is not exclusively for intellectual ability. But firmly sandwiched into the unquestionably mixed and in part subsidized mass are the children of the moneyed elite.

The formal education offered by the best of these private schools is no better, as far as any evidence shows, than that offered by the best public schools. But they do a better job for laggards, who are numerous in all strata, because their classes are smaller, the schools are isolated from distracting influences and the faculty supervision over studies is stricter. A highly motivated student in a good public school (which is not too frequently encountered) can get as much out of his school experience as he could at one of the better private schools; but the less scholastically motivated will probably get greater benefit from the good private school, which is more of a hothouse.

The products of the older private schools, at least, tend to form much closer ties to each other than are formed at the public school or college level. They are cemented, as it were, by the bonds of exile. Indeed, if asked about his educational background, the private school product is far less apt to say that he went to Harvard, Yale or Princeton, even though he did so, than to say he went to Exeter, Andover, Choate, Groton, Hotchkiss or whatever the case may be.

Few children of the rich attend public schools, although there are rare exceptions. As inquiry will convince anyone, most of them attended one of the old-line private "prestige" schools. People who like to make the point, as though it was significant, that Jack Kennedy attended Harvard and Adlai Stevenson Princeton, simply aren't aware of the nuances. Both were Choate school boys and would still be Choate boys if they had gone on to Swampwater College, Okefenoke University or Oxford. Anybody might go to Harvard, Yale or Princeton. But anybody cannot go to Choate.[7]

As Mills points out, the private-school boys do tend to stick together and to be found disproportionately later in or near the upper echelons of insurance companies, banks, investment trusts and general corporations. For the big owners of these enterprises are themselves products of the same schools.[8] The schools serve as unintended centers to bring bright members of lower social classes in as corporate personnel.

Until the recent past, the products of the private schools tended to monopolize Harvard, Yale, Princeton and other Ivy League universities. This trend has been diminished as private universities have intensified the intellectual rigor of their undergraduate colleges with a view to producing more teachers and scientists and fewer executives and salesmen.

The big rich, then, are more and more closely intermarried and generally send their children to a relatively small number of private schools. Some send them abroad to Switzerland or England.

Upon graduation from college, the children of the rich find themselves entering a world wherein many of their relatives are big owners of property and perhaps ensconced in important corporate or near-corporate positions. They move largely in a world which in England, whence the pattern came, would be familiarly described as the world of upper-class families, hunt clubs and the Old School Tie. The chances are high that they are going to marry someone whose family, like their own, is at least in the Social Register. They are on the estate and trust-fund circuit.

If they do not marry someone of the world of established property, if they marry instead a Rumanian chauffeur or the daughter of a Lithuanian iron puddler, they become the subject of excited newspaper accounts. For whenever wealth marries nonwealth it is a case, to the newspaper editors, of man bites dog. Although such marriages are not uncommon, the plain implication of all the fuss is that the marriage should not have taken place, any more than the King of England in the eyes of British Tories should have married Mrs. Simpson. Readers await news of the almost inevitable divorce.

The Exclusive Clubs

Neither family, coats of arms, nor attendance at private schools guarantees elite soundness. Elite families, lamentably, sometimes produce odd characters. The best private schools unfortunately turn out people who sometimes become song-writers, actors, photographers or even Kennedys, Stevensons or Roosevelts.

The higher elite must therefore mark itself off more precisely than either family, coat of arms, school or the possession of money can do. It does mark itself off through the system of private clubs, which in the East are so exclusive that neither the pope nor most presidents of the United States could qualify for membership.

The private clubs are the most "in" thing about the *finpol* and *corppol* elite. These clubs constitute the societal control centers of the elite.

There is at least one central club of the wealthy in every large city—the Chicago Club, the Cleveland Club, the Houston Petroleum Club, the Duquesne Club of Pittsburgh, etc. These are all imitations or outgrowths of earlier Boston, New York, Philadelphia and Baltimore clubs, which were imitations of English clubs. But the New York clubs are now the most important because the big money is centered in New York and the leading New York clubs include the wealthiest of the out-of-towners and many foreigners.

Which of the New York clubs is most exclusive, or most important, is a matter of opinion. The Knickerbocker Club requires that its members be either born New Yorkers, of New York descent, or at least occasional New York residents. But The Links, formed in 1921 ostensibly to promote the game of golf, seems to represent heavier money on the whole. Distinctions among the leading clubs are obscure to outsiders. "At the Metropolitan or the Union League or the University," Cleveland Amory quotes a clubman, "you might do a $10,000 deal, but you'd use the Knickerbocker or the Union or the Racquet for $100,000 and then, for $1,000,000 you move on to the Brook or the Links."[9] Some big wheels, to be safe, belong to them all.

My own rating of the New York clubs in order of *finpolitan* weight is as follows:

1. The Links. 2. The Knickerbocker Club. 3. The Metropolitan Club. 4. Racquet and Tennis Club. 5. The Brook. 6. The Union. 7. The Union League.

These are, except perhaps the last two, the exclusive, highly restricted inner-circle clubs. The University Club, in addition to claiming a larger membership, also includes professionals, administrators and below-the-top executives—that is, not only chairmen, presidents and executive vice presidents of corporations. Although it includes unquestionably elite elements like Allan P. Kirby, Cleveland E. Dodge, the Goelets and others, it is more like a transmission connection between the elite clubs and the world of general management. The Union and the Union League also have much of this transmission character in the club hierarchy.

An even broader transmission link or meeting ground between the higher club strata and the world of public affairs is The Century Association, the membership of which is heavily composed of approved artists, musicians, columnists, writers, lawyers, editors and book-reading executives (a rare and special breed!). A very few of the members of the top elite clubs mingle with the comparatively bohemian and always literate element of The Century. A careful review of the 1965 list of members—showing names like Dean Rusk, Isaac Stern, Eric Sevareid, Walter Lippmann, Yehudi Menuhin, James Reston and Arnold Toynbee along with three Rockefellers and other indomitable men of the supra-corporate spaces—suggests that few would be inclined to question the essential rightness and goodness of the *finpolitan* world. Many of its members are its eloquent spokesmen and apologists; some express mild and at times melancholy dubiety. None flatly challenges the essential beneficence of the *finpolitan* course.

But the brains and wit of the big New York clubs are unquestionably concentrated most conspicuously in The Century, a few of whose members at least seem capable of arriving at independent judgments. The membership list has never wandered far enough to the left to take in people like Norman Thomas, Scott Nearing, C. Wright Mills, Thorstein Veblen or even John R. Commons, all keen discussants. It did, however, include Franklin D. Roosevelt and Herbert Hoover, which about fixes its political poles. Investigators and questioners of the social frontiers are conspicuously lacking among its scholars.

An examination of its membership list up to 1965 fails to disclose the names of able organizational Negroes like Thurgood Marshall, Whitney Young, Martin Luther King, Roy Wilkins or Robert C. Weaver. Walter White never belonged.

The precise scope of The Century, founded in 1847, can perhaps best be shown by citing the names of some others who never belonged. These were H. L. Mencken (but Andrew Mellon did), Mark Twain (but Cornelius Vanderbilt did), Lincoln Steffens, Joseph Pulitzer, Charles Beard, Edmund Wilson, Sinclair Lewis, G. Stanley Hall, Eugene O'Neill, Herbert Bayard Swope, Theodore Dreiser, Henry David Thoreau, Herman Melville (but J. Pierpont Morgan I and II did), Morris Rafael Cohen, Cleveland Amory, Bennett Cerf, William James of Harvard and so on. But John Dewey, Oliver Lafarge, Oswald Garrison Villard and Charles Peirce did belong.

In any event, The Century does not appear, either today or yesterday, to be intellectually, morally and artistically representative. Its precise rationale for membership selection does not readily show itself. The heterogeneous membership shows little common denominator, and some mighty big intellectual guns, past and present, are conspicuously missing. Deeply critical temperaments or anyone who "comes on strong" are notably absent.

But a function the University and Century Clubs also perform is that of reciprocal transmission: The *finpol* members in them also hear much about the outside world, the below-stairs world as it were, from the more bohemian elements who may move easily from the club precincts to a Greenwich Village coffee house or Yorkville saloon and then back. The bohemian element's greater down-ranging mobility may at times be the envy of some of the *finpols*.

Each of the leading clubs appears to have spawned a cluster of offspring or imitators, founded sometimes by dissidents. They specialize in various things, some such as The Brook (touchingly named after Tennyson's poem) in continuous twenty-four-hour service.

Lesser clubs, in the opinion of Amory and other alert club-watchers, appear to be the nonexclusive Manhattan, Lotos, the Coffee House (of which Nelson A. Rockefeller is a member), the Harvard, the Yale and the Princeton. Better known to the public perhaps because of their association with the entertainment world are the Lambs, the Friars and the Players but these, in all candor, are the bottom of the barrel in relation to the clubdom with which we are concerned and should really not be mentioned except by way of indicating what an upper-class club, properly speaking, is *not*.

The only one of the New York clubs John D. ("Big John") Rockefeller got into was the Union League. His son, "John the Good," had no interest in belonging and was advised against it by his investment mentor, Frederick T. Gates. However, he did join the University and The Century. The grandsons belong to the cream—variously The Links, Knickerbocker, the Metropolitan of Washington and others. None lists the Union League.

The original Rockefeller was not only in bad odor with radicals, populists and liberals but, it may come as strange to some readers, he was looked upon askance in the old-established elite. Says Cleveland Amory, "Only a generation ago, for example, Mrs. David Lion Gardiner, dowager empress of New York's proud Gardiner Family, was informed that her young grandson, Robert David Lion Gardiner, was about to go out and play with the Rockefeller children. Mrs. Gardiner forbade it. 'No Gardiner will ever play,' she said, 'with the grandchild of a gangster.'" And De Golyer, dean of oilmen, told Amory he could never decide "whether John D. Rockefeller was the greatest oil man who ever lived, or a goddam lying pirate who made a monkey out of the whole capitalistic system."[10]

Nelson Rockefeller is looked upon today as the savior of the Knicker-bocker Club, which in 1954 was nearly submerged into the Union Club out of which it had sprung. A few leading members agreed to accept ten cents on the dollar for its bonded indebtedness and Rockefeller bought the premises and permitted the club to occupy them rent-free for ten years and then rent-free for ten more years if he was still alive.[11] It seems fair to conclude that the Rockefellers have an interest, perhaps only senti-mental, in keeping this distinctive club extant.

It should not be thought that the top clubs are purely sociable haunts where the rich idle away the time, although such is the impression con-veyed by Amory, Wecter and the long line of cartoonists and satirists who have shown elderly members snoozing over newspapers in the windows and who have derisively quoted club nincompoops. The clubs, one may be sure, enjoy being mildly derided as centers of futility and senile naivete. As they say in spydom, this gives their serious members a good "cover" for serious purposes.

Nor should it be thought that the big tycoons are in constant attendance. The membership of even the biggest clubs is obviously layered or hierarchi-cal, and consists of inner coteries according to specific serious and frivolous interests. There are, of course, always some amiable hangers-on and some retired from active life, and these provide something of a background Greek chorus or mob scene for the members with weightier concerns on their minds.

The clubs, in point of fact, have underlying deeply serious systemic functions behind their facades, as follows:

1. Their membership hierarchies from the leading to the minor clubs show in general who is A.O.K. by degrees in what is now variously re-ferred to as the national power structure, the Establishment (in imitation of English jargon), the power elite (after Mills) and so on. Newer designations for the phenomena will no doubt turn up and, as the reader will recall, I seem to find the situation best summarized in the term *finpolity*. If one wants to know who really matters behind the scenes of national affairs, in the order that they matter, one can hardly do better than to line up the memberships of the New York clubs in the order given. Now add each of the central non-New York clubs: Boston, Philadelphia, Chicago, Pittsburgh, Washington, Cleveland, etc., in about that order. Strike out duplications as they appear.

Here one gets, with few exceptions, the entire power structure. Every-body on the list will be A.O.K., rarely voicing anything except what John Kenneth Galbraith calls "conventional wisdom"—that is, trite and shallow commonplaces.

2. The clubs are the scene, at least in the preliminary stages, of some of the biggest deals in the capitalist world. It is not denied that such deals are also broached on golf courses, yachts and perhaps even in exclusive executive washrooms and Turkish baths; it is only asserted that a very heavy documentation could be supplied showing that some of the biggest deals, consortiums, syndicates, raids and campaigns were first proposed in one of the clubs.

3. The clubs are to the general corporate world of *finpolity* what the boardrooms are to individual corporations and what Congress is to the American populace. They are the places where attitudes are shaped toward proposed national policies. Once a consensus has been reached, the clubs serve to hand down a general "party line" of *finpolity* to members, who carry it to the world in their various functional capacities. For with the big proprietors sit the big executives, many big (usually Republican) political figures and leading owners of the biggest enterprises in mass media.

In saying that a party line is handed down, I do not suggest that members must accept the verdict of an always free and informal running discussion. Some members do object to and refuse to implement conclusions in whole or in part. Nobody is formally bound by any preponderant opinion, but everybody appears to be influenced by tendencies.

How, for example, should a particular president of the United States be presented in the mass media? Should the verdict be favorable, on the fence or unfavorable? Club talk will determine something of this. And if the drift is toward accepting him as favorable or unfavorable, some member or members may interpose a cogent objection that reverses or halts some emerging conclusion. One will get the verdict, whatever it is, in one's favorite newspaper or periodical.

Of one thing all club participants may always be sure: Views are invariably expressed in the light of some propertied interest. The discussions are never cluttered with extraneous and (by definition) ridiculous considerations that might occur to single-taxers, pacifists, social reformers, social workers, socialists, communists, populists, trade unionists, antivivisectionists, idealists, civil libertarians, utopians, New Dealers, unconventional ideologists, uplifters or even detached on-the-target scholars. The ideological center of all the discussion is, odd though it may seem, freedom, pointed simply to freedom of these elements to preserve and expand their propertied interests.

These clubs are the most intense partisans of freedom—*their* freedom— in the world today. While considerable imagination and ingenuity often enter into club discussions, to judge by leaked reports from occasional defectors, one element is invariably lacking: sympathy or concern for the rabble in the outer world.

In an earlier work I pointed out that often a uniform attitude comes suddenly to be expressed in the press from coast to coast on some topic, as though a hidden *politburo* had come to a decision. Never a dissent, never a deviation appears, as though one were reading the Russian press. The source—or sources—of such uniformity, as in the 85 per cent press opposition to Roosevelt, is the deliberations of the tycoons and tycoonlets in their clubs.

Unlike Congress, whose members must go home now and then to get re-elected, the clubs are always in session, unimpeded by parliamentary procedures, and the members need not fear being deposed from their positions. Congressmen and presidents come and go. The club members continue until death or disability does part them from the club discussions.

Discussions through the entire hierarchy of clubs, New York and provincial, are an important part of the informal process of government in the United States—far more important, say, than the political conventions, which often merely ratify what has been antecedently decided in the clubs. For these are the places where citizens of *weight*, of property, lawfully assemble and freely air their views and criticize the views of their peers. These are the democratic debating grounds of the *first* citizens, the people with the means and instrumentalities for making their views effective in the world. There are thousands of lesser clubs and associations throughout the United States; but a difference between them and the metropolitan clubs is that the formal resolutions of the lesser clubs, as contrasted with the purely informal resolutions of the metropolitan clubs, are usually ineffective. Nothing much, if anything, happens nationally after the passage of the solemn formal resolutions.

To control or influence public policy one is better placed if one has a strong voice in the clubs than if one has a strong voice in the Senate of the United States, yet the clubs draw little attention from the sociologists or political scientists, a serious oversight.

The leading clubs, such as The Links and the Knickerbocker Club, in their yearly alphabetical directories list members living and dead. These are like roll calls of American *finpolity* and *corp-polity*, past and present. Among the dead are many extensive family groups still with living members. Included among these, of course, is the coat-of-arms and inner private-school crowd.

The Links directory for 1964 includes such significant names as Winthrop Aldrich, former chairman of the Chase National Bank; Lester Armour of Chicago; Stephen D. Bechtel, Jr. and Sr., of San Francisco;

Charles H. Bell of Minneapolis; August Belmont; George R. Brown of Houston; Nicholas F. and James C. Brady; Paul C. Cabot of Boston; Lammot du Pont Copeland of Wilmington; C. Douglas Dillon; William H. Doheny; John T. Dorrance, Jr.; William Hincks Duke; Pierre S. du Pont III; Benson Ford; Henry Ford II; G. Peabody Gardner of Boston; Robert Goelet; Joseph P. Grace, Jr.; Crawford H. Greenewalt of Wilmington; E. Roland Harriman; John A. Hill; W. E. Hutton; Amory Houghton, Jr. and Sr.; B. Brewster Jennings; Robert E. McCormick; William G. McKnight, Jr.; Paul and Richard K. Mellon of Upperville and Pittsburgh, respectively; Jeremiah Milbank; Henry S. Morgan; John M. and Spencer T. Olin of East Alton; Howard Phipps, Jr. and Sr.; John S. Pillsbury of Minneapolis; Frank C. and William B. Rand; David, James S., Laurance S., Avery, Jr., William and Winthrop Rockefeller; Charles P. Stetson; Oliver de Gray Vanderbilt III; John Hay Whitney, publisher of the now defunct New York *Herald Tribune*; Robert E. Wilson of Chicago, and others.

The foregoing list culls the names of a few of the big proprietors. But The Links includes among its members also top-level corporation executives, bank presidents, special-entree journalists, upper-echelon Pentagon and diplomatic figures, corporation lawyers and Republican political figures of the inner sanctum—people like Joseph W. Alsop of Washington; Owen R. Cheatham of Georgia-Pacific Plywood; General Lucius D. Clay; S. Sloan Colt of Bankers Trust; Ralph J. Cordiner, former chairman of General Electric (during its conspiracy conviction); Arthur H. Dean of the key law firm of Sullivan and Cromwell and numerous top-level diplomatic conferences; Thomas E. Dewey; Nelson Doubleday of the book publishing world; Lewis W. Douglas of Arizona; Frederic W. and Frederick H. Ecker of Metropolitan Life Insurance Company; Dwight D. Eisenhower; the late Walter S. Gifford, former head of AT&T; Gabriel Hauge, president of Manufacturers Hanover Trust; Herbert C. Hoover; George M. Humphrey of Cleveland and the U.S. Treasury; Grayson Kirk, president of Columbia University; the late Henry R. Luce of *Time-Life-Fortune*; Air Force General Lauris Norstad; and, to arbitrarily end a list replete with many other gilt-edged rag-paper names, Jean Monnet of Paris, architect of the European Common Market.

Financially and corporately speaking, there is little or no deadwood in the Links roster. If its membership does not exactly run the country it has much to say about its course. Here are what the Russian and Chinese press morosely refer to as "American ruling circles."

A similar and sometimes overlapping cross-section of the upper elite is displayed by the 1965 list of the Knickerbocker Club. Here we obtain many other history-evoking names, past and current, such as Prince Amyn M. Aga Khan; Giovanni Agnelli, Italian industrialist; Winthrop W. Aldrich; John D. Archbold; Count Alessandro de Asarta Guiccioli; John Astor; Count Bertil Bernadotte of Sweden; Oliver C. Biddle; Francis H., Henry B., Jr., and Powell Cabot; Lord Camoys; Rear Admiral Grayson B. Carter; Anthony Drexel Cassatt; Rear Admiral Hubert Winthrop Chanler; Charles W. Chatfield; Joseph H. Choate; Grenville Clark, Jr.; Henry Clews; Count Charles-Louis de Cosse Brissac; William D. Crane; Seymour L. Cromwell; Lieutenant Colonel Charles C. Crossfield III (USMC); Major Robert Dickey III (USMC); C. Douglas Dillon; Colonel Joy Dow; John R. Drexel III; Henry Francis du Pont; Dwight D. Eisenhower; Thomas K. Finletter; Hamilton Fish, Jr.; Peter O. Forrestal; Caspar C. de Gersdorff; Francis, John and Robert Goelet; George and Michael Gould; Charles B. and William Grosvenor; Ogden H., Jr., and William C. Hammond; Henry Upham Harris; Abram S. Hewitt; James T., Nathaniel P., and Patrick Hill; Arthur A. Houghton, Jr.; R. E. K. Hutton; Vice Admiral Stuart H. Ingersoll; Ernest and O'Donnell Iselin; Commander John Dandridge Henley Kane; Hamilton Fish Kean; Moorhead C. Kennedy, Jr. and Sr.; Count Jean de Lagarde; Brigadier Charles L. Lindemann, DSO; Count Marc de Logeres; Townsend M. McAlpin; Charles E. Mather III; Paul Mellon; Edmund C. Monell; Ivan Obolensky; Count Ogier d'Ivry; Cecil C. Olmstead; Thomas I. Parkinson, Jr.; George B. Post; Sir Alec Randall; David, Laurance S. and Nelson A. Rockefeller; Kermit Roosevelt; Elihu Root, Jr.; Prince Sadduddin Aga Khan; Ellery Sedgwick, Jr.; Jean de Sieyes; Mortimer M. Singer; Alfred P. Sloan, Jr.; Chauncey D. Stillman; Count Anthony Szapary; Marchese Filippo Theodoli; Brigadier General Clarence P. Townsley; Count Mario di Valmarana; Harold S. and William H. Vanderbilt; F. Skiddy von Stade; Count Leonardo Vitetti; George D. Widener; William Wood Prince; Lieutenant Commander Cameron Mc. R. Winslow; Admiral Jerauld Wright; and Sophocles N. Zoullas.

This partial list, through which shine sections of Debrett and the Almanach de Gotha, also reads in part like a diplomatic and military roll call of the upper echelons. The list of deceased members is even more impressive; it reads like the index of names to a complete financial and industrial history of the United States.

Through the memberships of The Links and the Knickerbocker Club one could obviously obtain instant entree to any financial-political circle in the world. These are the very penthouses of *finpolity*.

Where does the harried staff of a new president of the United States look for candidates for Cabinet and other high-level posts? The membership lists of the leading clubs serve at least as *aides-memoires*. Not all the members, admittedly, are of sufficient personal calibre; but it is a fact that many names, previously little known to the public, have appeared on these club rosters long before they emerged in Washington and on the world scene. Interspersed with the playboys and club hangers-on are names that recognizably belong only on the upper circuits of *finpolitan* affairs, the fellows who in the shadow of the heavy weaponry finally get down to talking very cold turkey with De Gaulle, Gromyko, Nasser, the oil sheiks, Chou En Lai, Erhard, and Ho Chi Minh about who takes over what lush terrain and who gets the dirty end of the international stick (which one fears is pretty much the general myth-befuddled populace all over).

The leading clubs, though, are decidedly Republican in statistical orientation. This fact does not, of course, prevent Democratic Administrations from making use of valuable members such as Douglas Dillon. Nearly everybody in high appointive office, indeed, can be traced to one of the clubs, either the high or the lesser ones.

As Amory observes, the leading freedom of the top clubs is the freedom to be anti-democratic and (self-deludedly) pro-aristocratic; in an earlier day they would have been Federalist, although now one hears in them lamentation about lost states' rights that would have astonished the Founding Fathers.[12] Truman was merely disliked by most of the New York clubmen, Amory notes, but Franklin D. Roosevelt was apoplectically feared and consequently hated. Opinion about FDR even at the relatively cosmopolitan Harvard Club was sharply divided and feelings were intense. FDR, who did more to save their rickety world than any other man, was the *bête noir* of the clubmen.

Many of the upper club members look back nostalgically to the good old days under Harding, Coolidge and Hoover and do not show much enthusiasm over Eisenhower, much less over Kennedy. But as of well into 1967, the clubs were reported to feel rather enthusiastic about Lyndon B. Johnson, a big depletion-allowance man, who could, if he continues to deal his cards right, become a club member himself. After all, Eisenhower, born in Abilene, made The Links. Tap day could well come for the statesman of the Pedernales River valley who is committed to the proposition that a bomb is mightier than any valid syllogism or statement of fact.

Decision-Making by the Elite

We have been setting the stage for an answer to the question that opened this chapter: How and in what way do the *finpolitan* elite act in concert, if they do act in concert?

Any elite, in order to be an elite, must possess considerable autonomy within its special jurisdiction. This is true of all elites: of lawyers, artists, scientists, entertainers, philosophers or whatever. If the conditions are correctly stated here, they must also hold for a politico-economic elite. One would hardly have an elite if it had to be bound by ordinary rules or by some hard-and-fast tradition—if it had no area of privileged action.

The freedom to improvise as it sees its own interests must belong to any elite. If it doesn't have this freedom then it is just part of the mass. Physicists and mathematicians, for example, don't submit their differences to popular polls.

The closed American politico-economic elite, like any elite, does make its own rules, and it enforces its rulings in those areas where it believes its vital interests are involved; other areas it ignores. The task, now, is to show such elite rulings, and to show that they stick even against the opposition of Congresses, Supreme Courts, presidents and popular opinion. To claim that there is a privileged class and then not to be able to show it exercising privileges would be absurd.

Returning to the higher clubs, then, it should first be noticed that they do not allow any outright or avowed Jews to become members. Jews are not specifically barred in the by-laws but the procedure for admitting new members is such that none gets in, a fact noted by close students of the clubs.[13]

The term "outright Jews" is used advisedly because in certain cases Jews on the family tree, as in the case of the Belin line of Du Ponts or the Belmonts, do not apparently provide sufficient ground to bar from membership in the leading metropolitan clubs like The Links and Knickerbocker where names such as Rosenwald, Warburg, Lehman, Baruch, Schiff, Kuhn, Loeb, Gimbel, Guggenheim and the like simply do not appear even though their holders are of big-money stature and even though the grounds for claims to gentility of some, such as Baruch and Warburg, antedate those of the most ancient transplanted Bostonians. Gentility has nothing to do with it. But what all this shows is only that the Hitlerian racist definition of what constitutes a Jew is not applied. What Professor Baltzell calls "gentlemanly anti-Semitism" is not, in fact, racist or religious. It relates to property and position.

But even in the case of approved persons with Jews in the family tree, the barriers often go down slowly, as in the case of Douglas Dillon, member of The Links and the Knickerbocker Club, whose "paternal grandfather was Sam Lapowski, son of a Polish Jew and a French Catholic, who emigrated to Texas after the Civil War, adopted his mother's maiden name of Dillon, prospered as a clothing merchant in San Antonio and Abilene, and finally moved to Milwaukee, where he entered the machinery-manufacturing business."[14]

But while a very few topranking people with Jews on the family tree are found in the top New York clubs, there are no avowed or full-fledged Jews, whatever their qualifications, none at all such as the otherwise technically eligible Meyer Kastenbaum or corporate bigwig Sidney Weinberg of Goldman Sachs and Company, with multiple upper-level corporate directorships and yachting companion of the mighty.[15] It is Weinberg who is credited with the scheme for preserving the Ford fortune in the Ford Foundation, thereby eluding a mountain of taxes. How much more cooperative can anyone ever be?

The first of the well-known middle-level clubs in which unambiguously Jewish names are encountered is The Century, with two Warburgs as well as others. The Manhattan Club, founded in 1865, has many Jewish as well as a few local Italian and Irish names. Its roster shows that it is obviously a non-elite Democratic opposite number to the Republican Union League Club; it included Franklin D. Roosevelt, Herbert and Irving Lehman, Alvin and Irwin Untermyer, Joseph M. Proskauer and Alfred E. Smith. But the Manhattan, like the Century, is not considered by club experts to be an upper-strata club. Clubwise, in terms of inner corporate power, it is merely so-so. This isn't where the massed armored divisions of *finpolity* are controlled.

Hope is expressed by some optimists that the pattern of club exclusion may be changing: "In Boston, Chicago, Minneapolis, Newark, New York, Philadelphia, Pittsburgh, Portland, Syracuse and other cities, prestige clubs have admitted Jews—in some cases ending nearly a century of exclusion," say two observers. "The change has begun to affect all three of the major groupings of prestige clubs in the country; the University Club, Union Club and Union League Club. In addition, new, equally distinguished clubs without discriminatory policies have been launched in Atlanta, Dallas and Denver. . . .

"In 1960, only two of the 28 University Clubs in the country had any Jews on their rolls. Two years later, the University Club of New York City . . . began to accept Jewish members. This breakthrough paved the way for similar developments elsewhere. . . . As of 1965, seven University Clubs had accepted Jews to membership, one was about to do so, and five were engaged in exploratory discussion. . . . Thus, thirteen University Clubs had dispensed or were about to dispense with the discriminatory process, in contrast to two only five years earlier.

"The Union Club in Boston has enrolled its first Jewish members, and the Union League Club in Philadelphia is taking a similar step. The latter development is truly historic; for one of the founders of the Union League Club more than a century ago was the banker Joseph Seligman, who is remembered today as the first prominent victim of social discrimination against Jews. In 1877, Seligman and his family were refused accommodations at the fashionable resort of Saratoga Springs, New York; in the years that followed, the anti-Semitic virus spread rapidly, and soon Seligman's own club instituted an exclusionary policy."[16]

While the foregoing is true of what the authors call prestige clubs it is not yet true of the five top *finpolitan* elite clubs nor, for that matter, of the central elite club in each of the leading cities. The Union, University and Union League constitute pretty much a national club chain, offering inter-regional club privileges mainly to intermediate people. There may, in time, be a breakthrough, so that at least some token Jews are accepted as members of the very top clubs; but even that is doubtful, for reasons we shall see.

Something to be noticed is that the anti-Semitic bias, never prior to the 1870's a feature of American life, entered with the new industrialists, themselves from the Fundamentalist grassroots, poor boys like Rockefeller, Carnegie, Frick and others who "struck it rich."

Professor Baltzell ascribes the barring of Jews to "Protestant values" but here I think he commits the *post hoc* fallacy. True, the members of the clubs are almost exclusively if nominally Protestant; but they would just about all find the writings of Martin Luther, John Calvin and Sören Kierkegaard so much gibberish, the utterances of far-out clowns. The club members of late industrial derivation, the top dogs, came from the grassroots Horatio Algers who introduced the anti-Semitic rules. In addition to being nominally Protestant they were culturally and educationally of no higher level than the nineteenth-century immigrants from Europe whom they despised. Not only were they of poverty-stricken origins but they were all educationally distinctly *en retard*. It was the attenuated and confused cultural values of this element, straight from the cracker barrel, that were applied. To trace it to Protestantism, especially in view of the long European Catholic anti-Semitic tradition, seems to me off target.

Earlier American attitudes toward Jews, though tinged here and there with the European virus of anti-Semitism, were on the whole respectful, perhaps unduly so, for Jews were widely regarded as children of the Holy Book. Some Americans claimed to belong to "lost" Jewish tribes. American Protestant colleges made a point in the eighteenth and early nineteenth centuries of offering Hebrew as well as Latin and ancient Greek as the classical languages, in part because of the mistaken belief that the original New Testament had been written in Hebrew and that Jesus spoke this language. An early American classicist had to know Hebrew as well as Greek and Latin. Jews were friends and collaborators of a number of the Protestant Founding Fathers, were received into leadership circles North and South and were associated in vital early federal affairs. The idea of treating Jews as pariahs would have been deemed aberrant.

The exclusionary treatment of Jews in American life stemmed from a decision by the new financial elite, which elbowed to one side persons of the earlier aristocratic temper. Money became king, not Protestantism. The stock ticker became the dominant symbol, not the flag or the cross.

The exclusion of Jews from the inner metropolitan clubs is also imitatively enforced in elite and nonelite country clubs and in the old-line college fraternities. Actually, the Jewish exclusion serves to confer the special cachet of distinction on such clubs, most of the members of which are tedious Babbitts. A club or fraternity that does not exclude Jews is by this token advertising itself as an undistinguished affair, which it really is on the ground that its members are almost invariably persons of no intellectual or moral distinction. That the country-club and fraternity crowd consists in large part of simple animals, not always fully housebroken, one can ascertain by reading the novels of F. Scott Fitzgerald, John O'Hara and others who specialize in doings on the country-club circuit.

Catholics, although few and far between because most important Catholic money is concentrated in the hands of the Church hierarchy and because Catholics until very recently have been something of a self-segregated caste in American society, are not barred from the metropolitan clubs and one sees Nicholas F. Brady, Consolidated Edison tycoon, for example, as a member of The Links. There are others, such as Henry Ford II, but not many. John F. Kennedy became a member of The Brook.

It is doubtful if any Negro has ever been so much as proposed for membership. It would be erroneous to say Negroes are barred. They are simply not noticed. Negroes fall under the latter-day integrationist rule: They are not discriminated against as Negroes but it so happens they are found to be unqualified because of a tragic history over which the latter-day keepers of the keys have no retroactive control. The point is only: They couldn't get accepted even if they could fly to the moon and back in a kite.

Beyond this, as far as the clubs are concerned, Negroes not only lack titles to property (as quite a few Jews do not) but no one of them seems to be within 250 years of ever having them in any significant proportions. Who would a Negro be likely to inherit from?

As large property holdings are now mainly inherited and hard even for an occasional white nonproprietor to come by, it would seem that Negroes are forever circumstantially barred from becoming considerable American property owners. This is not to deny that some Negro, some day, may in some flukey situation run a small stake up into a big corporate nest egg and then turn out to be one of the larger swindling wheeler-dealers.

One can see two roads opening up to a very few Negroes, even though not to an entire stratum of wealthy Negroes.

One of these roads might be the entertainment or sports world, where a successful Negro might use his earned stake to become an impresario, then perhaps an owner of chain hotels, eventually the Empire State Building and perhaps a 5 per cent cut of one of the big banks.

Another road would be through politics and the participation in its many slushy inside contracts of the kind that have lifted many shadowy political figures from hamburgers to affluence. Early in 1966 a New York State investigation of large-scale housing developments in Harlem with public money indicated that a Negro political leader who had put up $2,000 stood to make $250,000, not a bad or unusual prelude to larger operations. For great family oaks from such little acorns have grown all over the American scene since the Civil War.

But that this sort of thing is going to happen to many Negroes and that they or their increasingly light-skinned progeny are going to be taken readily into the caste-iron clubs seems improbable.

We find, then, that at least 15 per cent of the population (Jews, Puerto Ricans and Negroes) is effectively barred from the clubs on intrinsic grounds. The remainder of the population is barred on extrinsic grounds: It has neither large properties nor high functional positions.

All this, it might be argued, is perfectly reasonable. These are private clubs, and clubs may choose their own clubmates. But these are not only social clubs; they are the staging areas of national policy and of the big deals that make Harlem real-estate deals look like pennyante poker.

Some of the clubs, indeed, in court actions over tax privileges have denied pointblank that they are social clubs, have claimed that they are in fact business clubs. This is true of the ninety-year-old Merchants Club of New York, located in the old textile district and allowing no Jews to belong, and it is true of the ultra-ultra Duquesne Club of Pittsburgh.[17]

As it can be shown that many of the progenitors of club members came into their money via party politics, such as through early public utility and railroad franchises, and as their members shuttle in and out of high government posts with almost metronomic regularity, and are big political campaign contributors, it must be evident, *prima facie*, that they are also political clubs. They are concerned with finance and with politics. They are, in brief, *finpolitan*, perhaps 45 per cent devoted to business, 45 per cent to politics and 10 per cent to blessed sociability.

While the inner pattern of arrangements differs from club to club, we may take a look at the redoubtable Duquesne Club to find out what they are all really about.

"It is when you go upstairs in the Duquesne that you begin to enter the substratosphere of executive power," says Osborn Elliott. "On the second floor there are no fewer than five dining rooms, including the main one; and in each of these, day after day, the same people sit at the same tables. As you enter the main dining room, the Gulf Oil table is across the way; Gulf's chairman David Proctor sits facing the door, surrounded by his senior vice presidents. In the corner over to the right is the Koppers table, populated by most of the top men in that company, and next to it is the U.S. Steel table, where sales vice presidents break bread together. In another smaller room nearby, Pittsburgh Coke & Chemical's president, chairman and vice presidents gather daily; in still another, Pittsburgh Plate Glass has a central spot, while Alcoa's executive committee chairman, Roy Hunt, holds forth in the corner—next to Jack Heinz's table.

"If the Duquesne's second floor feeds the captains of industry, many of the field marshals are to be found on the fourth and fifth floors, where thirty-five suites are rented out by the year (at $12,000 and up) to such companies as U.S. Steel, Gulf Oil, Jones & Laughlin, Blaw-Knox, and Alcoa, to name just a few. These attractively decorated apartments usually have a bedroom, living room and dining room; they are used by the companies' topmost brass for meetings and lunch almost every day, and for dinners perhaps two or three times a week, particularly when a visiting fireman, or rather fire chief, comes to town. . . .

"In these company suites new products and mergers are planned, bargaining strategy for labor negotiations is hammered out, multi-million-dollar financing arrangements are made. Here, and in the public dining rooms below, the professionals of production get together and exchange ideas, day by day. There is a daily exposure of people to people who are all of the same mold or forced into the same mold. This tends, no doubt, to channel their interests and energies toward the mono-purpose goal of production; and it may well be, as has been said, that Pittsburgh would not be the production marvel it is without the exchange of information, techniques and ideas that take place every noontime at the Duquesne."[18]

This continuous-performance center is obviously a caucus room and continuous seminar of *finpolity*. Jews, of course, and anyone without big money or high position, are barred. Baltzell relates that "Even today there is in Pittsburgh an executive at the very top level of leadership in one of the nation's major corporations who has never been taken into the Duquesne because of his Jewish origins (even though he has never been associated in any way with the city's Jewish community). But as this executive's high functional position would ordinarily demand Duquesne Club membership, other arrangements have been made. In other words, although it may seem absurd, he is *allowed* and *encouraged* to entertain important business associates in his company's private suite on the upper floor of the Duquesne. And he does this in spite of being barred from membership in the club! It may seem hard to believe that such a dehumanizing situation would be tolerated either by this talented executive of Jewish antecedents or by his gentile office colleagues who are also leaders at the Duquesne."[19]

Baltzell also tells of a high Jewish executive in Chicago who was denied the presidency of a corporation founded by Jews because he would be barred from membership on "religious" grounds from the leading club. He resigned and, a man of proper temper, refused to reconsider when the board of directors changed its mind.[20]

"Many such dreams of corporate and financial empire-building have been consummated within the halls of America's more exclusive clubs," notes Professor Baltzell after relating how Cecil Rhodes had used his club to buy out Jewish Barney Barnato in the De Beers diamond syndicate. "The greatest financial imperialist of them all, J. Pierpont Morgan, belonged to no less than nineteen clubs in this country and along Pall Mall. One of his dreams was realized on the night of December 12, 1900, in the course of a private dinner at the University Club in New York. Carnegie's man, Charles M. Schwab, was the guest of honor and the steel trust was planned that night."[21]

Not only are the big deals arranged in the comfortable privacy of the interlocking clubs, where nosey journalists, repelled by the claim of privacy, are not about watching the comings and goings of the sociable principals but, as already indicated, general policy governing the interlocking corporate world, as distinct from the specific policy of each company, is there determined. Even big tycoons must eat; and they eat together in their clubs. As it happens, during the meals, arrangements are made for organizing the world after their hearts' desires.

The Corporate Rule: Gentiles Only

The club rule against Jews, not at all strangely, turns out also to be the corporate rule. Some writers deplore, directly or by implication, the nonadmittance of Jews (and Negroes) to the clubs; but even if they were admitted matters would be little different. What significant alteration of the world for the better would follow if Sidney Weinberg, Meyer Kastenbaum or Thurgood Marshall were made members of The Links or the Knickerbocker Club? Could they, even if they wanted to, change the *finpolitan* outlook? For the clubs make sure, in advance, that anyone taken in agrees broadly with their *weltaunschauung*.

If Jews were suddenly admitted to the clubs and upper corporate positions would it be a gain for liberalism? In view of Baltzell it would (and he is probably right in this) result in a strengthening of the ruling class, in making it more competent, less mindlessly castelike. It would make the ruling class more effective, would make it, as far as sheer merit is concerned, more aristocratic. But merely the selection of the best people in a certain limited scale of values is no guarantee of *general* aristocracy. The best gangster, although he may be an aristocrat among gangsters, can hardly be taken as an aristocrat.

Baltzell defines aristocracy as follows: "By an aristocracy I mean (1) a *community of upper-class families* whose members are born to positions of high prestige and assured dignity because their ancestors have been leaders (elite members) for one generation or more; (2) that these families are carriers of a set of traditional values which command *authority* because they represent the aspirations of both the elite and the rest of the population; and (3) that this class continue to justify its authority (a) by contributing its share of contemporary leaders and (b) by continuing to assimilate, in each generation, the families of new members of the elite. As with the elite concept, I do not conceive of the aristocracy as the 'best' or the 'fittest' in the sense of the term 'natural aristocracy' as used by Jefferson. The aristocratic process means that *the upper class is open*."[22]

He is not, however, making a plea for aristocratic rule but, as he stresses, "it is the central thesis of this book that no nation can long endure without both the liberal democratic and the authoritative aristocratic processes."[23] He sees the true aristocrat as a public leader.

But aristocrats, in Jefferson's sense of the naturally best, are not produced invariably or even generally from a community of hereditary upper-class families, as Baltzell's tracing of the class origins of Abraham Lincoln shows.

"If an upper class degenerates into a caste, moreover," as Baltzell so well puts it, "the traditional authority of an establishment is in grave danger of disintegrating, while society becomes a field for careerists seeking success and affluence." And this is the present American position.

A *true* aristocracy developed in the clubs (or elsewhere) might indeed change the world for the better. But merely lowering the barriers to Jews and Negroes would not accomplish this, as the clubs also bar on other caste grounds. It is the general values of the clubs more than their exclusionary policy that are most open to question.

The very caste structure of the American propertied elite—as Baltzell agrees—shows it not to be an aristocracy, shows that it is afraid of competition from natural excellence. Plato, an aristocrat, would not have barred a man from his Academy because he was a Jew but he did bar him if he did not know geometry. Nor would he have barred from discourse a man just because he disagreed with him; he even reported for history the crucial difficulties for his beloved theory of ideas raised by Parmenides.

The nonadmittance of Jews (and Negroes) to the upper ruling clubs is cited here not to reiterate the truism that the *finpols* are illiberal and narrow-minded or to imply that Jews and Negroes should in the name of democracy or aristocracy be admitted to their circle. My observations, unlike those of Baltzell and others, are made only descriptively, to establish a tracer, as is done when physicians inject radioactive isotopes in order to make some determination about an organism. The nonadmittance of Jews to the central clubs enables us to make a vital determination: that decisions made in the clubs hold with rigor out in the corporate world and in society. If Jews and Negroes should now suddenly be admitted, the determination here made would still stand, for all time. It would signal only that the *finpols* had changed their minds: The acceptance of Jews and Negroes in the clubs and corporations would still show they had determining power. Whatever they do in this matter, pro or con, *it is still their decision before history*.

Jews, we may remind ourselves, are and have been members of the United States Supreme Court, the Cabinet and both houses of Congress. They have been high in the armed forces, often charged with the most vital matters of national defense, as in the case of Admiral Hyman Rickover. They have been governors of leading states such as New York and Connecticut, have been deep in the construction of delicate national policy in war and in peace. They are neither formally excluded by American public institutions nor informally excluded by the popular political process. The instrumentality of their entrance into political life has been, largely, the post-Civil War Democratic Party, and in this sense the latter-day urban Democratic Party has been more democratic (as well as more republican) than the Republican Party. Jews like Jacob Javits, Louis Lefkowitz and even Barry Goldwater in the Republican Party are distinct odd numbers.

But Jews, although very much to the fore in public life, and quite distinguished (Brandeis, Cardozo, Frankfurter, Lehman, Rickover, Baruch, Arthur J. Goldberg, Morgenthau, Ribicoff and others), disproportionately distinguished in the fields of learning and the arts and disproportionately few in prisons, are rarely acceptable as middle-range executives of the leading corporations and seldom appear as chief executive officers.

Now, it may be purely coincidental that we have before us these two parallel facts: exclusion of Jews from the leading clubs and from the corporate ranks. But this seems extremely doubtful. For the clubs have as their members virtually every leading stockholder, higher executive and key corporation lawyer. The policy *vis-à-vis* Jews which they collectively enforce in the clubs in the name of personal selection of associates is the same policy they separately enforce in the quasi-public corporations.

Considering the wide acceptance of Jews in public life and in the elites of science, scholarship, professions, the arts, entertainment and organized sports and their simultaneous nonadmittance to the entirely private metropolitan clubs and quasi-public corporations, we are forced to conclude that elitist decisions have been made, pro in some quarters, contra in others.

It might be argued in the light of the evidence thus far that Jews are not admitted to the clubs because they are not admitted to the corporations, that the corporations control the club people rather than the club people the corporations. But as this is a uniform policy and the corporations have no unified meeting ground of their own, it seems evidentially preferable to conclude that the unified ruling must come from the locus of unified membership, the clubs.

In any event, we know on the basis of very careful direct research that the club is primary to the corporation. For if one is not admitted to one of the clubs first—in New York the leading clubs that have been mentioned or in one of the provincial cities to the central club, such as the Duquesne in Pittsburgh—one will never move into the upper corporate executive echelons. Admission to one of the prime clubs of, say, a vice president or general manager, is the general signal that one is regarded as a Coming Man, that one is either at or very near the top. Shades of deference the man was never before accorded now become his due. Not being admitted usually signals that a man has reached the end of his climb.

This general fact is precisely established by E. Digby Baltzell.[24] The evidence, says Professor Baltzell, shows that the club is the tail that wags the corporate dog.

Others, such as Osborn Elliott, traversing the same ground, cite evidence pointing to the same conclusion.[25]

As a purely mechanical matter it would be difficult for a ruling by the corporations to be transmitted to the clubs; but it is easy for a consensus ruling to go from the clubs to the corporations. The leading stockholders and corporate officers all meet and mingle in the clubs; they do not meet and mingle in the corporations where they are limited to one or a few companies each. Unified policy comes, then, from the clubs, not from the corporations. The clubs are the centers of *finpolitan* eliteness.

For the purposes of this presentation it makes no difference where the discrimination begins—the clubs or the corporations. But by reason of the fact that it prevails in the leading clubs as well as the leading corporations, in the private sanctuaries of the controlling large stockholders, it seems clearly evident that the discrimination is the consequence of a *decision* in a closely knit group at the top. As we have seen, the corporations are controlled by very small groups, with ownership stakes ranging from 10 to 100 per cent. If these owner-controllers wished policy to be otherwise they could easily order it, in the corporations as well as the clubs. They do not want a different policy, however—at least not yet—so the present policy prevails.

As this is a policy neither required by law nor sanctioned by formal public policy, it clearly emanates from control quarters outside the framework of formal government or public discussion. It is policy based upon an autonomous elite decision. That decision was probably never taken after a full-dress discussion but originally emanated from, and has since been repeatedly endorsed in, innumerable informal club conversations.

Now, what are the grounds for saying that Jews are excluded from corporate managerial employment?

"In the United States," says a key University of Michigan study, "Jews are no longer disadvantaged with respect to education or income. Their training and educational background are conspicuously underutilized, however, in the executive ranks of most major corporations. The evidence need not be recapitulated here; every serious effort to collect data on this subject has yielded the same general conclusions. In recent years, for example, Jews have comprised 12 to 15 per cent of the graduating classes of the Harvard Graduate School of Business Administration, an institution to which the executive recruiters of many large companies regularly turn. Among the executives of such companies appearing at Harvard's seminars and training programs for businessmen, fewer than 0.5 per cent were estimated to be Jewish."[26]

Exclusion is contrived, says this study, by the ostensible utilization of easily manipulated "nonability" factors in evaluating prospective personnel —social connections, religious background, attendance at the right schools, membership in the right clubs and fraternities, appearance, residence in good neighborhoods and circumspectly self-assured deportment. Baltzell, however, cites instances where highly competent applicants for corporate entry who had all the "nonability" factors on their side in abundance, and seemed to be on the way in, were turned down as soon as it became clear they were Jewish. One sees this, in fact, very frequently.

"Approximately 8 per cent of the college-trained population of the United States is Jewish," says Vance Packard; "against this, consider the fact that Jews constitute less than one half of 1 per cent of the total executive personnel in leading American industrial companies."[27] This figure should also be considered in relation to the fact that 3 per cent of the population is Jewish. Jews, very clearly, are glaringly underrepresented in corporate management in relation to their frequency in the population and among college graduates.

Out of 2,000 management people at U.S. Steel a researcher for the American Jewish Committee could find only nine or ten who were Jews, less than 0.5 per cent.[28]

The facts are established as well in a number of careful special studies, national and local. Even in cities with large Jewish populations, like New York and Philadelphia, where frequency in the population might be expected to be reflected at least locally in management ranks, the percentage of Jewish participation is negligible.[29]

Exceptions have been few. Gerard Swope, one-time president of General Electric, was never accepted by the leading clubs, nor was David Sarnoff of the Radio Corporation of America, which was developed with Jewish money. Sears, Roebuck, although built by Jews, goes along with the practice of preferring non-Jewish executives.

Of perhaps more significance to most people is the fact that this exclusion extends to lower levels of employment in companies and industries. Many companies and industries discriminate boldly in lower-level employment of Jews as well as Negroes; some discriminate only against Negroes.

It was reported in 1965 to Secretary of Labor W. Willard Wirtz that major corporations, recipients of huge government defense contracts financed out of public tax money, were discriminating against Jews and Catholics as well on managerial and lower levels. Secretary Wirtz promised to seek laws to stop the practice.[30] When discrimination against Catholics can be shown, it becomes political dynamite owing to the frequency of Catholics in the national electorate. Jews, in addition to being fewer, are more concentrated in certain regions, and anti-Jewish discrimination is more easily and slyly applied. It is, moreover, approved by the mindless generally, Catholic or Protestant.

Because corporations have grown so that they extend over such a great portion of daily life, discrimination in corporations on managerial and lower levels serves to cut people off from positions where they can function. Among the many things corporations are tending more and more to monopolize are human functions. Most members of the labor force now work for a large organization—the $50-million-asset-plus corporations, government or the public-private educational system; it is increasingly difficult to find people who do not work for one of these. When corporations, thrusting into larger and larger areas of local and personal life, practice discrimination it simply cuts the victims off from a chance to function. Jews particularly, and Negroes, sometimes Catholics, are denied such functional opportunities, although some Jews have unwittingly benefited by being forced into independent though marginal enterprises of their own.

The most keenly felt loss, perhaps—and loss to the country—stems from the fact that many positions are classified as managerial when they are really technical and semiprofessional.

But the reason the barriers will not be as easily removed as some seem to suppose is this: The modern corporation is organized very much along military lines, although its military lineaments are carefully cloaked in all sorts of public-relations formulas. There is a chain of command, from the directors and top officers down to the department foremen. In this chain of command one obeys orders. The orders are not usually passed on brusquely, as in an army, and failure to obey the orders does not bring one before a court-martial. The process is much subtler. The successful organization man can hear orders that are never uttered. In order to move up in the managerial ranks one must be "smart" enough to "catch on" without being told everything.

As William Whyte makes clear in *The Organization Man*, the members of the managerial chain of command are carefully selected with the minutest attention to detail. One can be shunted into numberless corporate Siberias, never to emerge, for all sorts of sins of omission and commission. If one's wife does not qualify for the country-club set this can impede promotion. Queer people in the family like pacifists or single-taxers can create doubts. Wearing the wrong clothes—too gay, too funereal, inharmonious—can earn disapproval and lack of promotion.

One is usually fired only for some overt infraction or glaring blunder. But not being promoted is often tantamount to being fired.

What is wanted, as Whyte makes clear, is the pleasantly agreeable conformist—an intellectual and moral castrate. Like the German soldier, it is not for him to reason why, but only to follow orders or to anticipate unvoiced orders. The aim of it all is maximum profitability amid public acceptance for the corporation.

The basic rule of the corporation is that which Theodore Roosevelt said was the ultimate criterion of his social class: "Does it pay?"[31]

This chain of command in the corporations with their huge assets is obviously very important. It is no place for deviants, real or supposed. And the big owners of property are extremely nervous, very defensive, as some of their memoirs show.[32] One could deduce the same conclusion by considering their elaborate electronically guarded safe-deposit vaults, high electrified fences and stone walls around estates and complicated systems of guards, watchmen and locks in their dwellings. And it is true, as demonstrated by the existence of bank robbers and safe crackers and the utterances of radicals of the Left, that many persons have designs on their enormous wealth and position.

They are, therefore, unduly sensitive, perhaps hypersensitive, about their propertied domains. They don't want any wrong elements in their precious chain of command, and any element they don't fully understand is apt to seem unsuitable.

While Jews—and Catholics and Negroes—like other groupings of people, distribute according to the normal curve of probability, showing certain percentages of every type and most of them concentrated in the middle area, Jews like Negroes have a higher visibility. In the case of Jews the higher visibility, where it is present, comes from cultural differences.

Again, a number of prominent Jews appear to have taken seriously, too seriously, the formal documents of the American legal system, the Declaration of Independence, the Constitution and perhaps Lincoln's Gettysburg Address. Such were, obviously, Joseph Pulitzer and Louis D. Brandeis, who did not see the emerging corporation as an unalloyed boon. These were public men rather than *finpols*. How many other Jews, the *finpols* no doubt ask themselves, are like these?

Within the corporations, as the recent electrical-industry scandal shows, many things go on that are bound to be viewed askance by the public. When the milk is watered it is necessary to have a line of loyal managers, to have nobody present who is apt to blow the whistle and call in the police. To insure this one needs carefully screened people. People who are excluded are, then, not basically excluded on racial or religious grounds—for the corporate men have no more interest in ideology than has a giraffe—but on grounds of reliability, real or supposed. Anyone about whom there is doubt that his *primary* loyalty will be to the corporation must be left out—and this goes for Jew, Catholic, deeply committed Protestant or any overt moralist, unorthodox ideologist or detached scholar.

In objecting to the exclusion of Jews it is overlooked that corporations exclude on other grounds as well. They wouldn't knowingly hire a David

Thoreau for example. They aren't partial to liberals, and Jews are associated historically with liberalism. The exclusion of Jews, then, even by some corporate people who marry Jews, traces back today to the general fear of any disturbing influence along the chain of command. It is not that the corporations want passive people. They want aggressive, ambitious people, but aggressiveness and ambition must be channelized toward one goal: making money. Any other interest is disturbing.

While it is no doubt galling for any people, especially people within a supposedly democratic society, to be stigmatized in advance of performance, this whole prospect is not as bleak as it at first seems. Corporations (on behalf of their owners) get their way in society by both the proper and improper use of money. In one of the approved ways, they constantly entice personnel away from government, the educational system and other socially supportive areas. A man may be doing an excellent job as a personnel director for a school or hospital at, say, $8,000-$9,000 a year when he is spotted by an alert corporation scout, who offers him, say, $18,000 a year plus other prospects. As the saying goes, the man cannot afford to turn down this opportunity to better his condition, and few would ask him to; his family stages a celebration over father's "promotion." He joins the corporation, where his work may not be nearly as socially effective as it was; it may, indeed, be socially destructive, depending upon what policies he is required to implement. He may have chosen people before on the basis purely of talent; now he must take into account "nonability factors."

The corporations in this way constantly drain to themselves directing personnel of talent, whose talent they often misuse in the service of profitability and a sense of corporate security.

But an uncalculated social advantage to the barring of Jews by the corporations, although not relished by Jews themselves, is that they are left undisturbed in society as free-lance teachers, lawyers, physicians, editors, publishers, writers, surgeons, accountants and what-not. As the corporations don't want them, they come to form something of a reflex professional caste. Their services, thus, are available to noncorporation elements.

Lest some readers think I strain at a minor point, let it be noticed that many lawyers, physicians, surgeons, even publishers, refuse to handle certain types of cases or accounts for purely caste reasons. They feel the eye of Big Brother in the clubs, in the newspapers, is upon them. Many lawyers won't take certain cases because the elite of the community frown on the plaintiff or defendant (who presumably is not entitled to due process). Some doctors won't heed the wishes of those who call them if handling the case by purely medical canons violates the rule of some perhaps religious caste to which they belong (won't abort at the request of a patient but will remove a wart or lift a face, won't give godless injections, etc.). Certain publishers won't publish books that reflect upon the nobly born and well connected or upon caste-approved ideas although they will publish books that show such in a deceptively favorable light. It is an advantage, then, for the majority of noncaste people to have available to them the services of competent people uncontrolled and left at liberty by the corporations. One is more apt to get untrammeled skill.

We see in prospect, similarly, the lifting of Negroes from a caste of unskilled workers to one of prizefighters, athletes, entertainers and purely Negro politicians—the American Dream converted into a comedy of errors.

The unsought creative effects of barring Jews from corporations are perhaps most evident in publishing, although they may be found elsewhere as well. For the American cultural scene is incalculably richer for the presence of Jewish publishers, originally barred as higher functionaries for the older Anglo-Saxon publishing houses. Jewish publishers have been willing to publish all sorts of books that caste-minded Anglo-Saxon publishers were afraid to publish. Thus Simon and Schuster published Bertrand Russell, an Anglo-Saxon; and Alfred Knopf published the books of the very Saxon H. L. Mencken. Random House, Inc., and Viking Press have been right up in line also publishing various non-Establishment Anglo-Saxon writers. There was, too, Joseph Pulitzer.

Now, if the Jews who founded these and other publishing houses had been initially taken into the older houses they would have been absorbed into the Anglo-Saxon nest, their best ideas blunted in the name of organizational *gemutlichkeit*. This is not to say there are no independent publishers other than Jews; but Jews were clearly the pace-setters who kept the publishing tracks wide open, as anyone can see by looking up the early experiences of American writers like Theodore Dreiser.

The most threatening feature about Jewish and Negro exclusion by elite establishments, though, is that it reinforces the ever-present biases of the mindless, who are always with us. "Gentlemanly anti-Semitism" in Germany, as Baltzell points out, paved the way for the later demonism of Nazism. "Gentlemanly anti-Semitism," in other words, is a charge of unfused dynamite lying about, waiting for the circumstance and the paranoid personality to supply the fuse.

Baltzell, citing memoirs and biographies, tells of a number of instances in which rejection of Jews in the financial world by the clubs induced much anguish of spirit. But just how sympathetic one ought to feel about someone—Jew, Gentile or Negro—being denied acceptance in the inner *finpolitan* world I wouldn't know, because I feel that being barred by The Links is about on a par, from a purely human point of view, with being barred by The Elks. The clubs, in other words, are not centers of excellence.

Baltzell relates that Bernard Baruch, an admirer of clubman J. P. Morgan, felt hurt at being excluded from the inner club circles of *finpolity*. Doesn't it seem as though his admiration was misplaced? Moneyed Jews, instead of feeling personally affronted at what would pass for insulting behavior in the world of ordinary men, surely ought to be able to see that *finpolity* precedes ordinary civility. What matter the opinions of curbstone moralists and liberals when billions are felt to be at stake?

What this pattern of discrimination imposed by the elite clubs on the corporate world, the country clubs and the college fraternities shows (leaving aside the alleged good or bad effects or the reasons for it all) is that (1) an elite decision has been effectively imposed on the country without leave of the government or any pluralist plebiscite and (2) that it is possible to impose effectively such elite decisions.

If it is possible to impose such decisions—in corporations, college fraternities and suburban residential areas—it is equally possible to impose them with respect to any *individual* or to any *types*—ethnic, political, intellectual. The prejudices of the upper clubs, in other words, have the force of effective law throughout the land.

It is not unusual in history for the prejudices of a ruling class to prevail over a society as law, but it is the general supposition that the United States is sharply divorced from such a state of affairs. The supposition, however, is mistaken. Operatively the United States is not so new a model in the world as commonly thought.

The question now is: Are other such elite decisions made and imposed?

Other Finpolitan *Elite Decisions*

A casuist might counter what has been shown with this response: It is true that an effective decision has been made by the financial elite against Jews, Negroes and sometimes Catholics but this does not prove that similar decisions of sweeping effect are imposed. All that has been shown is that it is possible to impose such decisions and that one has indeed been imposed.

It is necessary, then, to show that the same sort of decision-making takes place in various momentous areas whenever the *finpolitans* feel their vital interests are concerned. It is not denied that other people make decisions, that there is a formal governmental structure for decision-making, as when President Truman decided in person to drop atomic bombs on Japan or President Johnson decided after consultation only with the Joint Chiefs of Staff to involve the United States in futile large-scale warfare in Vietnam.

What is asserted is that often, in contravention or supplementation of formal government, effective, informal and momentous decisions are made by the financial elite without consulting anyone else. These decisions pragmatically have the force of law. They enable certain things to happen, prevent other things from happening. Furthermore, these decisions relate to fundamental dollars-and-cents areas in the life of the American people.

Our next area for consideration will be that of regulation of the corporations, long a vexing subject.

Many laws have been placed on the books for the ostensible purpose of regulating corporations, and they do regulate the corporations in those respects in which the corporations resign themselves to being regulated. Among these laws are the Sherman Anti-Trust Act as amended, the Clayton Act and various others that can be read about in a wide literature devoted to describing, analyzing and criticizing the anti-trust laws.

The proclaimed purpose of these laws is to preserve competition. Supplementing the work of the courts in applying these laws is the Federal Trade Commission and other quasi-judicial regulatory bodies.

Yet, despite token prosecutions under these laws and repeated investigations and disclosures by Congress and the regulatory agencies, competition dwindles steadily in American economic life. Fewer and fewer companies, as we have seen, control wider and wider areas of economic activity, more and more jobs. Except on the margins, small, independent owner-operated businesses are being slowly squeezed out of existence, nearly everybody is being forced to work for the corporations—or not to work at all.

As Professor Sutherland of Indiana University has pointed out, the token regulation of corporations follows the same lines as the probation system for juvenile delinquents, who are irresponsibles of tender years. The corporation like the delinquent is found to be doing something forbidden by law and is hailed before the court or commission. Light punishment and a suspended sentence are prescribed for both, and from each is exacted a promise not to repeat the forbidden act. In fact, each is enjoined against a repetition and is told that if it does repeat it will be called back and—now—seriously treated; the delinquent will be sent to jail, the corporation could be fined for contempt of court. This last proviso is a criminal sanction, held in reserve.

But the corporation, unlike the juvenile, may offend against some other law, and may indeed be a constant offender over the legal spectrum, as many have been. If the juvenile delinquent did this he would be locked up for a long stretch.

Despite the continuous outcry about antitrust law enforcement it was demonstrated to the country recently in The Great Electrical Industry Case that the big enterprises are no more impressed by the government than are gangsters by a "fixed" police force. It will also be recalled that those officers who were convicted and fined and either made to serve thirty days in jail, or given suspended sentences, felt greatly put upon *because they had done nothing that was not being done throughout every industry.*

Not all monopolistic trusts break the law so precisely as the electrical industry brazenly did, carefully touching all the illegal bases, and those that do are careful to avoid having the proof as available as it was in the electrical industry case. The same situation prevails, there is strong reason to believe, in many industries but the judicial proof is not at hand or is not sought.

The laws usually, except in the case of vague charges like obscenity and blasphemy, state precisely what series of acts constitute the offense and under what conditions. Evidence must show that these acts and conditions were plainly present. In the case of something so complicated as a conspiracy to restrain trade, it is often difficult to muster the requisite evidence.

Not many open-and-shut convictions, therefore, have taken place under the antitrust laws. And they have not been much of a deterrent, as the electrical-industry case showed.

But, as we have seen, monopoly proceeds to establish itself also in many ways not stylistically forbidden by law, as in the case of heterogeneous or conglomerate mergers. Here we see companies in one central industry gobbling up companies in all sorts of directly unrelated industries, finally producing a giant *finpolity* of massive proportions with much concentrated economic and political power. There is up to this writing no law whatever against such combinations, which have the effect of giving a small group of owners and controllers monopolistic control over huge sectors of the economic system itself.

The antitrust laws did not apply at all to the public utility holding companies which had acquired operating companies all over the country and were "milking" them for excessive service charges, which were passed on to the public in the form of higher rates. The participants favor mergers because they broaden opportunities for screened internal, intra-divisional lucrative transactions, all ultimately affecting the prices paid by the public. Prices in the wake of the merger movement, as anyone can see, do not go down; they go up, and up, and up.

Instead of proving monopoly now, so much of it having been shown in hundreds of court cases, Federal Trade Commission hearings, congressional investigations and a voluminous scholarly literature devoted to the subject, the burden of proof has shifted to the other side. What must now be done as far as a public defense of the big corporations is concerned is to show a single clear instance of free competition on the upper corporate circuit. One doubts that this can be shown.

Now, it will be noticed that virtually *all* the leading stockholders, *all* the leading executives and *all* the leading lawyers of (1) big corporations that have been convicted in open court of monopoly or restraint of trade or related practices, (2) big corporations that have consented under threat of judicial proceedings to desist from certain practices, (3) big corporations that have been shown in congressional and Federal Trade Commission investigations to be monopolistic or quasi-monopolistic and (4) big corporations that have been found guilty in open court of breaking other laws and ordered either to desist or fined—*all* these leading stockholders, executives and lawyers are members of the restricted clubs of the *finpolitan* elite.

If it could be shown as positively that they were all members of the Communist Party everybody would agree that the corporate practices were unquestionably part of a subversive Communist plot, directed from Moscow. The cry of "subversive conspiracy" would be raised from coast to coast.

There is, of course, no "plot." There are certain shared attitudes and ways of doing business in a small continually consulting group, and these are reflected in the public behavior of the corporations. In a group committed to pecuniary aggrandizement as a major aim in life there will, naturally, be calculated breaking of rules made by plebeian outsiders who are, by definition, cranks, screwballs and crackpots.

The dominant feeling in the clubs, one may surmise from publications owned and religiously patronized by club members, is basic opposition to any and all effective antitrust laws. For regulation of the corporations by government agencies amounts to "interference" in private business affairs, one of the worst sins government can commit in the *finpolitan* view. Less bad, to be sure, is purely token regulation, which is mere insistence upon a principle, but even it is bad enough. "Hands off the corporations" is the covert club slogan *vis-à-vis* the government. No club member would seriously disagree with it.

Still Other Finpolitan Decisions

In the clubs, too, are matured various campaigns to influence public opinion with a view to making it possible for basically accommodating government to modify policies. As such campaigns number into the hundreds, there will be mentioned here only the postwar campaign to remove price controls, which were very irksome to the corporations. The case was loudly made throughout the press that the economy would do much better with the controls removed. They were removed and the economy moved on, as predicted by experts, into endlessly troublesome inflation. Leading club people, such as Henry Ford II, spoke out in this campaign. But as profits outpaced the inflation, and eventually outpaced lower taxes, the decision to remove price controls was correct from the *finpolitan* point of view. The populace as a whole, however, grew poorer and proceeded to run over its neck into personal debt.

Here we may ask: Did the populace want higher prices? Does it ever?

Another type of case is this: It is shown by the government that some huge consolidation is clearly illegal and the Department of Justice calls for its termination under the threat of submitting the issue to the courts, whose ruling is a foregone conclusion. The offending party thereupon sets its agents to work on Congress with a view to getting the law changed so as to permit the particular consolidation, and succeeds in its efforts. This, of course, takes power, especially as many congressmen initially opposed to passing the enabling legislation must be won over. But, apparently so strong is the case for the consolidation, or the radiant power of money, that even the most antitrust congressmen finally agree.

Such a case was in 1965 and 1966 provided by the giant Manufacturers Trust Company of New York (Kirby), which had merged with the competing Hanover Bank and Trust Company and had absorbed the many directly competing Hanover branches into its system. The more the Department of Justice studied this merger, undertaken without anyone's by-your-leave, the more it was convinced that it violated the applicable law all around. The Department served notice it was going to the courts.

Efforts thereupon began with Congress, which in 1966 passed the enabling legislation that permitted this and some other challenged bank mergers to stand.

Here is a clear case of a corporate decision that was made in violation of the law, with the law later changed in order to permit the initial elite-level decision to stand.

Again, many persons, some in Congress, made pointed note of how rapidly Congress (after the Supreme Court ordered Du Pont to divest itself of improperly held General Motors shares) acted to exempt the recipients of the General Motors distribution from a capital gains tax. The oldest and largest holders, owners of the greatest capital gains, were the Du Ponts themselves. Many observers thought it would have been more seemly if Congress had at least dragged its feet (as it ordinarily does) before passing this special bill. But congressional leaders, it seemed, were anxious in this matter to give especially rapid service, thus showing profound deference. Had Congress not acted as it did the Internal Revenue Service would have reached out for all the taxes it could get in the situation, as it usually does whether gains have been made legally or illegally.

So here is a case of another after-the-fact law being passed to facilitate top elitists in holding on to gains made out of what the Supreme Court considered a legally dubious situation.

Controlling Police Actions in Personal Affairs

Private elite decision-making extends to more personal matters involving the violation of the law, literally to murder. For the elite decision-making process can interfere with and prevent investigations and prosecutions for murder.

Cleveland Amory notes that in the case of at least seven notorious "Society" murders since 1920 the investigations were quashed "for the sake of the families."[33] The greatest amount of publicity had attended all these cases, and yet investigations fizzled out. The killings were all "unsolved."

The pattern in every case was of wealthy, black-sheep philanderers or cut-ups—rebels—who were variously shot, stabbed or bludgeoned, sometimes in the proximity of other people, often in peculiar, veiled circumstances.

While the plea of dropping investigations "for the sake of the family" has a sentimental appeal, in all the cases the waywardness of the victims was known to family and social set and in some instances had been bruited about in the tabloids. News about the black sheep would hardly be novel or unduly shocking to family or friends.

But a broader reason for quashing the investigations is found, perhaps, in the idea that ventilating all the circumstances would tend to indict a broad class of moneyed people in the eyes of the populace, which retains certain illusions about the gentry. The painstaking presentation of evidence in court, then blazoned in the circulation-hungry tabloids, and the sketching in of sordid background high jinks, would tend to document many doubts about the aristocratic pretensions of the moneyed "social leaders."

There is no suggestion here that initial steps to quash investigations were taken in any of the metropolitan clubs—although they could have been—or that the police were the initiators of negative action. The police, as professionals, are normally inclined to proceed with investigations. Nor, in any of the cases, is it necessary to suppose that any of the families in any of the cases initiated the negative action.

The mechanics of these affairs are, in general, as follows: After the crime, with the police beginning to set up their lines of investigation, prominent individuals in the same social set, with at least the consent of the family (which could rightfully insist upon full investigation) get in touch with the leading politician or politicians upon whom the police are dependent for their jobs. The right politician, responsive to the halo of money, tells the chief of police: "Drop this investigation, for the sake of the grief-stricken family. The guy got what he deserved anyhow and the family knows it."

Here the police instincts are satisfied on two counts: first, on sentimental grounds (and most police are basically conventionally sentimental) and, second, on retributional grounds. Lost in the shuffle is the fact that someone, no doubt of high social position, has committed murder and is about to get away with it, law or no law.

Now, in the case of most murders, the victim has a family; and in many cases the family is as sick of the victim as any Society Family of its black sheep. But this does not deter police from delving into every aspect of his career that might point to his murderer. Even if it is thought the victim got precisely what he deserved, the police probe in every direction, and family now be damned. For the family involved is not an Important Family.

Whatever one thinks of all this, one must agree that the police in such quashed cases act in response to an elite decision.

Congressional Endorsement of Elite Decisions

Elite decisions are most often, perhaps, implemented by legislative bodies, Congress or the state legislatures. It would take hundreds of pages to show all of these in detail. Here I shall take space only to mention two conclusive examples, leaving Congress for scrutiny until later.

In the early 1960's there were before Congress two proposals, one to terminate tax-free expense account privileges of corporation executives and another to enforce by law greater truth in advertising. After some minor trimming with respect to the first, much to the disgust of the *New*

York Times editorial board, which favored an end to the tax privileges, the tax-free fringe benefits were allowed to stand virtually unchanged. In the second instance, with newspapers and magazines taking a hand behind the inspiriting slogan of "freedom of the press," the call for more stringent policing of misleading advertising claims was defeated. Similarly, the cigarette industry succeeded in having watered down the anti-cancer warning proposed for cigarette packages.

Even though the outcome was determined in Congress it can hardly be doubted the decisions were made on high, for special interests, and were simply validated in congressional horse trading.

Who in the country, apart from the corporations, corporation executives and pleasure resorts, want these executives to have untaxed expense-account privileges, which amount to a hidden, untaxed raise in pay? The ordinary citizen cannot deduct the cost of carfare to or lunch on his job even though these are clearly expenses in his way of doing business.

Again, who in the country aside from advertisers and their publications and other outlets will stand up in favor of free and easy deception in advertising?

Both of these are clearly elite decisions carried out against what would be the true wishes of nearly all people if the issue were ever effectively submitted to them.

Let us recall another among many salient cases wherein Congress obliged. In 1948, as mentioned earlier, Congress changed the inheritance tax law so that half of a married person's estate would be untaxed—the marital deduction. As most people are married, they no doubt favor anything that favors the marital state, and "marital deduction" has a fine, solid, home-building ring. Who would be so abandoned as to oppose a marital deduction?

Again, as we live under the principle of equality before the law, it is well to notice that this law applies to everyone—provided only that he have a taxable estate, which means that it does not in fact apply to about 95 per cent of people.

In the present law the first $60,000 in any estate is tax free. Thus, if a married man dies and leaves a net estate of $100,000, only $40,000 of it was taxable before the revision of the law and only $20,000 after the revision. In each case only a small tax was paid.

But after the law was revised a married man who left an estate of $100 million was subject, first, to the deduction of $60,000 of taxable estate and then of $50 million! As of 1966, the estate would have paid a tax under the pre-1948 law of $75,342,000. But under the revised law such an estate would pay only $36,149,000! This represents a saving of $40 million, worth going to some trouble to obtain.

Cui bono (Who benefits?) was a Roman principle used for determining the instigator of an action. Could anyone claim that the decision to revise this tax law, of appreciable benefit to very, very few people, was the consequence of some pluralist process? The country was not even aware that the law was being revised in this sleight-of-hand fashion, thus tending to preserve the very large estates and giving a minor tax benefit to small taxable estates.

The decision to revise this law was obviously taken among some wealthy discussants, possibly in one of the clubs, and the assignment to procure its revision was obviously given to some legislative representative of the elite.

Not only do the *finpolitan* elite make decisions such as the foregoing, mostly in their clubs, but they make all other decisions deemed relevant to their vital interests—on taxes, wages, prices, price controls, interest rates, ethnic and religious employment policies, investment expansion or contraction, the evaluation of public personalities in the mass media, etc., etc. Hence the propriety of referring to them as a ruling class.

But they don't, it will be said, make the decisions on war or peace. This is usually true, although they did make the decision to involve the country in World War I, a decision fraught with many troublesome consequences for themselves and the world. But at other times they are usually not heard on the question of war or peace, which they leave to constitutional officers, because they are ready to play their cards either way. Whether there is war or peace, they adjust their profit enterprises to the situation and make out very well in either case. No doubt, like most people, particularly in the age of catastrophic weapons, they prefer peace. But if constitutionally formal decision makers decide for war they interpose no visible objection. They are, however, always interested in "defense" contracts.

None of these decisions is made conspiratorially. All are arrived at after purely informal discussion, although now and then leading figures may retire to some private club room when delicate subject matter is to be broached. But the general atmosphere in the clubs is quite free and easy, open and aboveboard, with no hint of conspiracy afoot. These matters are just part of the ordinary course of *finpolitan* affairs, like shop talk in any professional or vocational club. New ways of contriving mergers, avoiding taxes or circumventing labor unions amount to so much club chit-chat, but one should always note that club chit-chat on various matters becomes translated into external effective action in society. If club members happen to feel that Jews are not suitable as corporation executives it just so happens, without any fuss or noise, that Jews do not become corporation executives. Smooth, smooth. . . .

Everything about club decisions is in this way informal, offhand, in a low key—unhurried, unhysterical, gentlemanly. The high pressure atmosphere of the corporation sales meetings is noticeably lacking.*

As it seems to me, it has been shown that the *finpolitan* elite unilaterally makes momentous decisions that in one way or the other, in contexts large or small, are imposed on the country whenever the elite feels its vital interests are affected. Where it does not see its vital interests involved, either collectively or singly, it simply stands aside and lets others decide in issues such as, say, whether or not a new school should be built or whether a park should be located here or there. The *finpolitans* have little interest in such details and allow anyone who presses to make the decision.

There may be some, however, who will say that I haven't proved my case. Although many other supporting instances could be mentioned in this chapter, it should be evident that for those determined not to accept the clearly warranted conclusion there would be no admission that the case was proved if instance were piled on instance in detailed profusion for hundreds of pages.

One either intelligently sees the force of the proof offered or goes on muttering idiotically forever, no matter how much evidence is adduced, "Not proven, not proven."

Toward a Domestic Kremlinology

Since World War II and the upthrust of Russia there have emerged "Russian Institutes" in various of the universities, devoted to studying all things Russian. Some of the scholars focus directly on the ruling group in the Kremlin, attempting at a distance, amid considerable difficulty, to deduce

---

* Here, if not elsewhere, the judicious reader may pause and ask himself: "How can a writer, and an outsider at that, be so sure projects are handled so easily on the upper strata?" The answer is: one turns to entirely credible, literal reports. Thus, George Santayana, long a professor of philosophy at Harvard and for many years an intimate friend of Charles A. Strong, son-in-law of John D. Rockefeller, reports an incident in the first decade of this century at Rockefeller's Lakewood, New Jersey, between-seasons residence: "One day when I had mentioned Spain, he (Rockefeller) asked me, after a little pause, what was the population of Spain. I said I believed it was then nineteen millions. There was another pause, this time rather longer, and then he said, half to himself: 'I must tell them at the office that they don't sell enough oil in Spain. They must look the matter up.'" George Santayana, *Persons and Places: The Middle Span*, Vol. II, Charles Scribner's Sons, N.Y., 1945, p. 134.

Santayana makes this penetrating observation about Rockefeller: "He was beyond comparing himself with his competitors; he compared himself with himself." *Ibid.*

what is going on at the top. They pore over Russian newspapers, study the order of precedence of names of officials, examine budgets, make note of who appears and who does not appear at diplomatic receptions, analyze Russian jokes, and subject every conceivable aspect of Kremlin affairs to minute scrutiny.

Many problems challenge attention: Who is the No. 1 man, who is No. 2 and what is the likely line of succession? What are the rivalrous groups within the top leadership and what policies does each stand for? What is the current dominant policy? What are the temperaments of the top men—irascible, bland, suspicious, etc.?

With this in mind, it may be said that a purely domestic variety of Kremlinology or American *finpology* could well be developed as a subsection to university departments of political science.

What is the main current orientation of the *finpols*? What are their alternate policies in the event of a variety of possible occurrences?

Who, if anyone, is the chief arbiter of the *finpols*? If they have no chief arbiter do they have a committee, a sort of sub-executive committee of the ruling class; or may any accredited person take a hand?

This sub-executive committee, if it exists, has how many members—five, eleven, twenty-six? Where, if it exists, does it meet—at The Links, The Knickerbocker Club or in one of the suites at the Waldorf Astoria Hotel? What does it call itself, if it answers to a name?

Who is the top man or is there collective leadership? What are the respective orders of priority among Richard King Mellon, Crawford Greenewalt and, say, David Rockefeller? Do these ever consult? Does Nelson Rockefeller join them with an admonitory word? Is anyone else ever consulted? Where do they go? What do they say? Do their jokes, if any, have hidden meanings of national or world significance?

Or, if they do exchange views, is such exchanging done through underlings? What, in other words, is the procedure, always assuming there is some sort of at least informal procedure?

The answers to these questions I do not know. That would be something for *finpologists* to determine. Not to know the answers is not to know what is taking place in an important sector of American government.

But we do already possess certain deductions in *finpology* analogous to those in Kremlinology in our knowledge of how to determine who is moving to the top in the corporations. As E. Digby Baltzell and Osborn Elliott tell us, one can spot the Coming Men in the corporations by their admission to the metropolitan clubs. This is as good as seeing a name unaccountably moved up nearer the top in a list of officials published in *Pravda* and *Izvestia*. Some corporate vice president, not a member of the clubs, suddenly is made a member. We know enough now to know he is next in line for executive vice president or president.

Again, we know where to look for who really counts. We look to the metropolitan clubs. There we find future Cabinet officers and diplomatic negotiators. If I have arranged the clubs in their right order of priority we know in what layer of eminence personalities are to be found. Some other *finpologist* might want to dispute the point. Some, I know, would have their reasons for rating The Brook and the Racquet and Tennis ahead of the Metropolitan Club. They should make their reasons known and we might, as the Kremlinologists do, thrash it all out in a weekend seminar at Aspen financed by the Ford Foundation.

It is more difficult today than it was thirty-five years ago, it seems to me, to determine precisely where the center of gravity in all this lies. Perhaps there is now no center of gravity and perhaps the issue of dominance in *finpolity* is being left in abeyance or quietly fought out behind the scenes. Is there, as in the Kremlin, a behind-the-scenes struggle for power?

Thirty-five years ago, prior to the disruption caused by the Depression and the New Deal, any knowledgeable Wall Streeter could have named the inner executive committee in the exact order of precedence: J. P. Morgan (or 23 Wall Street), John D. Rockefeller I (or 26 Broadway) and Andrew W. Mellon of Pittsburgh. Anything these three agreed on happened as they said it would, including sometimes as in 1916–1917 the decision to enter the war.

One thing they agreed upon basically: not to meddle in each other's respective domains. None wished to tangle at close quarters with either of the others.

But 23 Wall Street, without downrating the others, made its words felt over the most varied domain. That was where newsmen went for tips on what was likely to happen—in Washington, in London, in Paris, at the Federal Reserve. If no tips were available there, the pickings were apt to become slim; although sometimes Winthrop Aldrich at the Rockefellers' Chase Bank, only figuratively at 26 Broadway, might be able to give some special insight.

But when Aldrich spoke, newsmen understood that although the words were his the dramatic line was surely approved by "Big John," doddering along the golf course at Ormond Beach and manically handing out shiny dimes to everyone who came near. J. P. Morgan II rarely spoke. In his place spoke Thomas W. Lamont, the *eminence grise* of the firm whose mind perceived so many aspects to any simple question that he could, if he had wished (which he rarely did), have discoursed with visitors for hours about them. Mellon, except when he was Secretary of the Treasury, rarely bothered to cue any outsider into his thinking.

But Morgan's, 23 Wall Street, was the center of the action, a fact often alleged but rarely *shown*. For example: A. P. Giannini, the self-erected San Francisco banking tycoon, in 1928 bought control of the 116-year-old Bank of America, of New York, from Ralph Jonas and associates, paying $510 a share for 35,000 of 65,000 outstanding shares. He then absorbed the Bowery East River National Bank and the Commercial Exchange National Bank and formed the Bancamerica Corporation as a securities-underwriting affiliate.

But before he bought the Bank of America Giannini needed the consent of J. P. Morgan and Company.

"I don't want it unless I have the consent of 'The Corner,'" Giannini told his agent.

"I can get that consent," the agent said.

A meeting was arranged between Giannini and Morgan.

"I'll see Seward Prosser and the Federal Reserve officials at once," the New York tycoon told him. "You will certainly be welcomed into the banking picture here."[84]

Said Seward Prosser, chairman of the New York Clearing House and president of the Bankers Trust Company, to Giannini:

"We don't favor ownership of banks by holding corporations. However, we'll be glad to welcome you to the Street if you will agree to do away with all but twenty per cent of your holdings of this consolidated bank."[85]

Giannini agreed reluctantly. While he was distributing this stock, says his biographer, he was informed that an official of the commercial bank-controlled Federal Reserve Bank of New York, speaking for the chairman, had said the Reserve Bank would not transmit to the Federal Reserve Board in Washington the application for trust powers unless Bancitaly Corporation of San Francisco agreed to divest itself of every share it owned of Bank of America in New York.

Giannini immediately went to Washington, where he was told by Roy Young, governor of the Reserve Board, that the Board had no legal right to take over the trust department. Whereupon Giannini refused to distribute the remainder of the stock and went into the market to buy back what he had sold.

"If you don't conform to our wishes here," said Francis D. Bartow, a Morgan partner, to Giannini back in New York, "we must ask you to take your various accounts out of J. P. Morgan and Company. Right or wrong, you do as you're told down here."

"The hell I will," retorted Giannini. "If you boys want a fight I'll see that you get it."[36]

The next day, reports Julian Dana, a meeting was arranged with Jackson Reynolds, head of the First National Bank, a Morgan satellite. "Reynolds, always an admirer of Giannini, had a word of caution for his ear. 'You have made such a tremendous success that I'm not trying to give you advice on what you should do, A. P.,' said Reynolds frankly. 'You know your own business better than I do. You may have been badly treated—have all the law on your side. But if I were you I'd take my orders and say nothing. If you don't—well, they'll knock you down and walk all over you.'

" 'They can't do that to a red-blooded California boy,' said A. P. coolly. 'If they try it they'll have the biggest damn scrap on their hands they ever tackled.' "[37]

Several years later Giannini, by rallying his stockholders, fought back a complicated attempt by Morgan associates to take over his giant Transamerica Corporation from the inside. The story is told in detail by Giannini's biographer.[38]

Morgan dominance, so thorough that no outsider could enter Wall Street without Morgan consent (gained at a price) was broken by a host of New Deal banking laws that shifted control over many key financial matters to Washington—to the Federal Reserve Board, which had previously been informally circumvented by the Federal Reserve Bank of New York, to the Securities and Exchange Commission and other agencies. Morgan power thereafter declined; in its day it was great.

This is the way it was, at any rate, up to the date that A. P. Giannini successfully challenged it and until the Depression and New Deal laws undermined it. The Morgan word in Wall Street and far beyond, without the consent of Congress or any president, was law. Morgan's ran Wall Street, not in the sense that it initiated whatever went on down there but in the sense that it could veto anything it didn't like. Mellon and Rockefeller stayed out of its way; only A. P. Giannini was foolish and lucky enough to put the Morgan power to the final test, when Morgan's was under other pressures.

Says Elliott V. Bell, a one-time member of the staff of the *New York Times* (writing in 1938) and more recently chairman of the executive committee of McGraw-Hill Publishing Company and a director of the Chase Manhattan Bank, the New York Life Insurance Company, the New York Telephone Company, the Tri-Continental Corporation and other stratospheric entities:

"The position of the House of Morgan is unique and in those days [prior to the New Deal] its right to leadership was undisputed. The basis of the Morgan power is not easy to explain. It is not a large bank, as Wall Street banks go. A dozen other institutions have much larger resources. True, the firm exercises a strong influence over a number of these larger banks—the so-called Morgan banks—but it has never been established to what extent that influence is based on financial control. The sheer money power of the Corner is, of course, great; but my own belief is that this is a minor factor in the firm's leadership. What really counts is not so much its money as its reputation and brains. . . .

"But to get back to the Corner. It is not a mere bank; it is an institution. It has become a symbol of Wall Street itself, viewed variously as a predatory creature, exercising a 'spider-web' control over most of the banking and business resources of the country, or, at the other extreme, as a semiphilanthropic organization whose benign ministrations cause great banks and corporations to flourish, giving employment to millions of workers and causing the stocks of 'widows and orphans' to rise in value and give off dividends.

"There was a time, still within the memory of many in Wall Street, when financial titans booted the stock market about to satisfy their own feuds or ambitions; a time when the elder J. P. Morgan could call a handful of bankers into his awe-inspiring presence and bark out orders that would stop a panic. There was a time, much more recent, when government turned first to Wall Street's leaders for advice and means in meeting economic problems; when it almost seemed as though Wall Street regulated Washington.

"In the early years of the depression it was not unusual for one of the big bankers to tell me that he had just been talking to President Hoover on the telephone about this or that proposal to accelerate prosperity's coming around the corner. The comments on these consultations were often by no means flattering to the Chief Executive."[39]

Although the Rockefellers and Morgan partners never tangled and sedulously kept to their own back yards as far as they were each concerned, Mr. Bell relates succinctly the Rockefeller thrust that really undid Morgan's. John D. Rockefeller, actually, had never liked the bullying elder Morgan.[40]

This thrust was administered in 1933 by Winthrop W. Aldrich, then head of the Chase Bank, when he publicly proposed precisely those banking reforms that struck at the heart of the Morgan financial empire and which were later enacted into law: notably the elimination of joint investment and deposit banking.

"In openly challenging the Morgan system," says Mr. Bell, "Mr. Aldrich displayed at its most daring his flair for anticipating events. Probably few people realized at that time, despite the attendant collapse of the banking system, how greatly the power and prestige of the Morgan firm had been impaired and how much it was to be clipped in the events that were to come. Mr. Aldrich by his action made certain that the searchlight of the Senate investigation (already bearing upon his own bank) should be turned with full force upon the Morgans."

What has been shown here, now, is what once *was* and is no more. But the crucial question is: What, if anything, has replaced the old order behind the scenes, if it has been replaced?

To believe that all the strings have been moved to Washington would be too naive, although elected officials now do unquestionably have more to say about the country than they had prior to the New Deal. But they don't appear to have enough say-so to open all opportunities in the economic and social system to Jews—or Negroes, Puerto Ricans, Mexican-Americans or intellectual independents—or to stop the continuing concentration of more and more assets into fewer and fewer hands. One assumes, as they don't oppose it, that they tacitly consent to all of these as well as other practices such as informal publication censorship.

The *finpols* we do know, after actions by Presidents Kennedy and Johnson, can no longer dictate prices; they must at least get acquiescence from Washington, which appears to have moved into a closer partnership with *finpolity* whether the *finpols* like it or not. They can no longer dictate interest rates either.

As long as affairs proceed more or less smoothly, this unsolemnized partnership will no doubt continue: Money talks. But when, as and if matters get out of hand and crises strike, it will again be a case of each for himself. While the Crown and the Baronage appear to be honeymooning just now in the Welfare-Warfare State it is probable that in some great crisis analogous to the Great Depression they will find they are pulling in different directions, have different basic interests.

Should that happen, should the *finpols* find they are once again confronted by *pubpols* with overwhelming problems on their hands, what will happen? Assuming that the crisis is not too great it seems that the *pubpols,* always able to wrap themselves in the flag and point to the apostolic succession since George Washington, will have the edge. The *finpols* are at their best in behind-the-scenes maneuvering. When public questions must be openly dealt with the *pubpols* are able to make use of the vast (if temporary in the life of every *pubpol*) reserve powers conferred upon them by the Constitution.

What will happen, though, if the *pubpols* in charge are abject servitors of the *finpols*, their sincere admirers? What happens to *pubpols* who follow too slavishly the *finpol* script was shown by Herbert Hoover. They expire in futility and the national situation deteriorates. Sooner or later (and for the sake of the public one hopes it is always sooner) the *pubpols* must be guided by the remorseless logic of the situation as it confronts them and must address it forthrightly in terms of the values their culture has provided them.

The newspapers, largely owned, controlled or patronized with advertising by the *finpols* do, with the emphasis on Washington affairs, practice *pubpology* assiduously. Not much in the goings, comings and doings, even private thinking, of the *pubpols* escapes minute scrutiny and repeated review. It would be too much to expect these same *finpolitan* newspapers to turn the spotlight of critical attention on their esteemed friends, the *finpols*. But what the newspapers don't do, perhaps some nonconformist political scientists might do.

Very possibly what we have today at the top is not a tight little committee that hands out the "party line" of *finpolity*. The leading clubs appear to function more as a Committee of the Whole, with no personality presently thrusting itself forward. They function, not as an open Vatican Council nor as an organization under a pope, but more as the secretive Roman Curia; though always very, very informally. Their determinations, however, are far-reaching and penetrating, having the operative force on true believers of a papal decree.

Nine ❧

THE GREAT TAX SWINDLE

If the propertied elite can enforce basic socio-political decisions—such as denying employment in the labyrinthine corporate bureaucracy to large numbers of qualified people on irrational ethnic grounds when the basic laws do not support such discrimination—the experience of history would suggest that they would go farther and also deal themselves enormous tax advantages. For down through history the dominant classes, groups, factions, clans, interests or political elites have always been scrupulously prudent in avoiding taxes at the expense of the lower orders. The aristocracy of France before the French Revolution, for example, gave itself virtually total tax exemption. The burden of supporting a profligate royal court with its thousands of noble pensioners was therefore laid upon commoners, thus supplying not a little fuel for the onrushing tidal wave of blood.[1]

It would be foolish to contend that there is a propertied elite in the United States and then not be able to show that this elite accords itself fantastic tax privileges down to and including total exemption. And, true enough, the large-propertied elements in the United States see to it that they are very lightly taxed—many with $5 million or more of steady income often paying no tax at all for many years while a man with a miserable $2,000 income, perhaps after years of no income, denies his family medical or dental care in order to pay tax!

Taxes "are a changing product of earnest efforts to have others pay them. In a society where the few control the many, the efforts are rather simple. Levies are imposed in response to the preferences of the governing groups. Since their well-being is equated with the welfare of the community, they are inclined to burden themselves as lightly as possible. Those who have little to say are expected to pay. Rationalizations for this state of affairs are rarely necessary. It is assumed that the lower orders will be properly patriotic."[2] And, as anyone may ascertain any day, aggressively expressed patriotism increases markedly in intensity, readily crossing the borderline into spontaneous violence, the further one looks down the socio-economic and cultural scales into the lower middle class and downward.

There is a fundamental view, widely shared and often overtly expressed in schools and in the mass media, that the American socio-political system is, if not completely fair, as fair to everybody as the ingenuity of man can devise. This belief is monumentally false, as analysis of the tax structure alone discloses.[3]

What Is to Be Proved

Prosecutors at the opening of a case in the law courts customarily state to judge and jury what they intend to prove. In adopting this procedure here, let it be said that it will be proved beyond the shadow of a doubt:

1. That the American propertied elite with the connivance of a malleable, deferential Congress deals itself very substantial continuing tax advantages at the expense of the vast majority of the population.

2. That the national tax burden is largely shouldered, absolutely and relatively, by the politically illiterate nonmanagerial labor force rather than by big property owners or by upper-echelon corporate executives (who are often tax free).

3. That the resultant tax structure is such that it intensifies the abject and growing poverty of some 25 to 35 per cent of the populace (about whom latter-day *pubpols* theatrically wring their hands), and grossly cheats more than 95 per cent in all.

Quite an order, the judicious reader will no doubt say to himself. But let such a reader armor himself in skepticism and let us consider the proof.

Some Preliminary Remarks

While the American propertied element is not ordinarily completely tax exempt it is subject in general to extremely low taxes. In many salient areas it is *absolutely* tax exempt, like prerevolutionary French aristocrats. This happy condition derives, as Eisenstein often points out, from special obscurely worded congressional dispensations. The situation, far from being mixed or a matter of shading, is absolutely black and white. The United States is widely supposed to have a graduated tax system, based on ability to pay, but there is very little actual graduation in the system and what graduation there is turns out to be against the impecunious.*

It is not being urged that the results to be shown were obtained through some centralized secret plot of bloated capitalists and paunchy cigar-smoking politicians. For it would indeed take a confidently jocund group of autocrats to deliberately plan the existing tax structure—what conservative tax-expert Representative Wilbur Mills, Democrat of Arkansas, in a bit of judicious understatement has called a "House of Horrors." The late Senator Walter George of Georgia (never regarded as a friend of the common man) called the present scale of exemptions "a very cruel method by which the tax upon the people in the low-income brackets has been constantly increased."[4] Senator Barry Goldwater of Arizona, no liberal, radical, or starry-eyed reformer, said "the whole tax structure is filled with loopholes"; Senator Douglas of Illinois, a liberal and a professional economist, asserted that the loopholes have become "truck holes."[5] Referring to the fantastic depletion allowance, conservative Senator Frank Lausche of Ohio, no extremist or reformer of any kind, said: "It is a fraud, it is a swindle, and it ought to be stopped."[6]

One is, therefore, in fairly sedate baby-kissing company if one says (perhaps overcautiously) that the tax structure is a pullulating excrescence negating common sense, a parody of the gruesomely ludicrous, a surrealist zigzag pagoda of pestilent greed, a perverse thing that makes the prerevolutionary French system seem entirely rational. One takes it that Congressman Mills had something like this in mind with his "House of Horrors."

Representative Mills in further explication of his "House of Horrors" characterization said the tax laws are "a mess and a gyp," with some taxpayers treated as coddled "pets" and others as "patsies."

---

* I prefer the somewhat pretentious-sounding "impecunious" to the simpler "poor man" because it is semantically cleaner, less streaked with the crocodile tears of latter-day politicians and professional social workers. A poor man, after all, is only a man without money and is often very little different in cultural attainment or outlook from many beneficiaries of multiple trust funds. He does not wear a halo; worse, he is never likely to. The recreations of a bayou Negro are little different from those of many denizens of Fifth and Park Avenues; each hunts, fishes, copulates, eats, sleeps, swims and boats and neither is much of a reader, thinker or art patron. The main social difference between them is money and its lack. The defensive idea of some sociologists that there is a "poverty culture," insuring the continued poverty through generations of its participants even though they were given trust funds, must be rejected as untenable. What is called the "poverty culture" is merely the reactive creation of impecunious people rejected for one reason or the other, often arbitrary, from the labor force as unsuitable. But if they were given an ample regular income without the performance of any labor, like members of the trust-fund cult, they would quickly emerge from this "culture," perhaps to comport themselves like "Beverly Hillbillies" or Socialites.

But the tax laws would have been no surprise or cause for consternation to someone like Karl Marx with his doctrine that government is inherently the executive committee of a ruling class. Indeed, they document that dictum—if not to the hilt—then a good distance up the blade.

One can apply to the present American system the exact words of French Finance Minister Calonne in 1787 on the soon-to-be-destroyed French system: "One cannot take a step in this vast kingdom without coming upon different laws, contradictory customs, privileges, exemptions, immunities from taxation, and every variety of rights and claims; and this general lack of harmony complicates administration, disturbs its course, impedes its machinery, and increases expense and disorganization on all sides."[7]

To refer to this system, then, as another but bigger Banana Republic is not merely a bit of misplaced literary hyperbole.

The American tax system is the consequence of diligent labors by diversified parties of major property interest working down through the years to gain their ends. Two congressional committees of seemingly over-easy virtue have been their target. A public demoralized by a variety of thoughtfully provided distractions, and liberally supplied with Barnum's suckers and Mencken's boobs, would not know what takes place even if it were fully attentive because it could not understand the purposely opaque syntax of the tax code, the inner arithmetic or the mandarinic rhetoric of the tax ideologists.

Has the result been spontaneously achieved in hit-or-miss fashion or is it intentional? As there are always those observers who want to interpret all human actions blandly, and who decry any suggestions of conniving or underhandedness, let it be said that on every hand in the tax laws there is clearly revealed (1) intent to deceive and (2) self-awareness of intent to deceive. First, those laws are demagogically sugar-coated in various ways—with entirely illusory and deceptive rates up to 70 or 91 per cent, with a variety of homespun seeming concessions to ordinary people and with numerous items of sentimental bait such as apparent (but only apparent) concern for the handicapped. Next, many seeming concessions to weakness, such as age, are actually supports for financial strength. The opacity of the language, often putting skilled lawyers at odds, alone testifies to intentional deceptiveness. Also, the couching of special bills of benefit to only one person or corporation in general terms, without naming the unique beneficiary, testifies to the same intent. A comparison of the verbiage of the tax laws with the language of the Constitution shows entirely different mentalities at work—devious in the first instance, straightforward and to the point in the second.

The deviousness does not, as some profess to believe, reflect modern complexity of conditions. It is the deviousness that induces much of the complexity. The writers of the tax laws evidently consider the broad populace —and, what is worse, the rational critic—as yokels at a country fair, to be trimmed accordingly.

In referring to the broad public it may seem that I have suddenly enlarged the scope of this inquest from a very small to a very large group. But we are confronted here with something of a puzzle: How could nearly 99 per cent of a large population be put into such a wringer by some 1 per cent or less, as though the 99 per cent were the victims of a particularly brutal military conquest? How could such an apparently free population be reduced to the financial status of peasant slaves?

A variety of factors has conspired to this end, but the populace has been handled by a smooth governing technique. In a process that has unfolded partly by sincere stealth, partly by sincere subterfuge, partly by convenient self-deception and partly by barefaced sincere chicanery, the people have been led to accept the tax laws by being offered many apparent advantages over each other in pseudo-exemptions and pseudo-deductions. But the bitter mixture to which the electorate has step by step acquiesced, under the plea partly of necessity and partly of undue advantage, it has finally been forced to swallow with the compliments of Congress—a lesson in adroit political manipulation as well as practical morality.

The tax laws, as drawn, appear to be a loaded gun pointed at the rich and affluent. But this is a tricky gun; as the ordinary man pulls the trigger in high glee he shoots himself! For the true muzzle of the weapon, as in a fantastic spy film, points backward.

As Congress now may appear to be cast as the villain of this opus (which is really without a villain), it should be conceded that there are many excellent public servitors in that body, functioning far beyond any reasonable call of duty. But Congress collectively is very different from congressmen and senators individually. Congress tends to function according to the least common denominator, the worst element in it. Congress, indeed, torn between different factions as it settles toward the least common denominator, becomes very much like a crazy king who doesn't know his own mind. The will of this king is reflected in the laws.

Tax-Free Fortune Building

Until the passage of the income-tax amendment to the Constitution in 1913, and the subsequent estate tax, the big industrial proprietors were virtually tax free, subject after the Civil War mainly to minor local real

estate taxes. The biggest fortunes—among them Du Pont, Mellon, Rockefeller—were all largely amassed in the tax-exempt era. Corporation lawyers,
such as Rockefeller's Joseph H. Choate, fought with every legal and political means at their disposal against the imposition of even a token income
tax, which they correctly sensed might be the opening wedge to heavier
taxes.

What it became, finally, was a siphon gradually inserted into the pocket-
books of the general public. Imposed to popular huzzas as a class tax, the
income tax was gradually turned into a mass tax in a jiu-jitsu turnaround.
Thus it provided the *pubpols* with the present stupendous sums for reckless overspending in the areas of defense (Over-Kill) and the letting of
lucrative construction contracts in the sacred names of education, medicine, housing and public welfare. Consequently, as far as disposable moneys at their fingertips are concerned, the *pubpols* are now on a basis of
approximate parity with the *finpols*. Whereas in 1939 only 4 million people
paid income taxes, and in 1915 only 2 million did, today more than 46
million do so—truly a case of turning the tax tables on the lowly!

Nearly all of the revenue, moreover—86 per cent of it—comes from the
lower brackets, from the initial rate that all must pay, which is the lion's
share of the $41 billion taken from individual incomes in 1960. The so-
called "progressive" rates leading into the high brackets contribute only
14 per cent.[8] The politicians will never willingly give up this Golconda.

Differently put, the less than 1 per cent of the individuals who own upward of 70 per cent of productive property throw only 14 per cent into the
tax caldron as their distinctive, differentiated contribution, while their
own publications metronomically salute them as pillars of society. It is truly
a piece of sleight-of-hand that would have been the envy of the French
Bourbons. In the United States, as it has been said, if you steal you will be
hailed as a great man, provided you steal everything in sight.

To get this one-sided tax burden off the backs of the common people
will, one suspects, require a political upheaval of first-class dimensions.
Nothing less would do it. For the *pubpols*, with the constant self-sustaining
threat of defensive warfare on the one hand (neither Vietnam, Lebanon,
Guatemala, Cuba nor the Dominican Republic attacked the United States)
and the convenient excuse of profitable open-ended welfare on the other
(the Great Society), can now work an oscillating double-pronged assault
on the patriotic low-income man. It should always be remembered that
the higher incomes pay for little of all this. They merely increase.

In general, the higher the income in the $10,000 and upward class of
income receivers, comprising no more than 10 per cent of all taxpayers, the
more lucrative tax privileges and absolute exemptions are progressively en-

joyed. As one moves into the top 1 per cent of income receivers (the $25,000-plus class) the exemptions become still greater until in the top 2/10ths of 1 per cent (the $50,000-plus class) the exemptions and disparities become boldly and, in a presumably enlightened age, ludicrously profligate. The greater the income, the greater the legal tax exemption—up to 100 per cent. Conversely, the smaller the income the greater the proportion of taxes it pays, mainly through tax-loaded prices of goods and services among very small incomes.

Taxation is a complex subject and will be dealt with here in as compressed and clear a fashion as possible.[9]

Four Types of Tax System

The United States, broadly, has four separate tax systems: federal, state, county and municipal. Including the counties and municipalities, there are thousands of separate tax jurisdictions. While all of them together gather in much money for local uses and abuses, separately they are of small importance and are mentioned here only as a means of dismissing them. The federal per capita tax collection in 1962, for example, was close to $450, whereas all state and local taxes were about $230, so that about two-thirds of all taxes collected are federal.[10]

The biggest nonfederal tax is on local real estate and personal property, to which everybody contributes something either as occupant-owner or as residential-business tenant. Depending on the region, the realty tax varies; although wherever it is low, local services are attenuated. A tax growing in use in states and municipalities and almost as productive of revenue is the sales tax, which levies up to 5 per cent on most retail purchases and, obviously, hits the poorest man hardest. This tax will, no doubt, be increasingly relied upon to squeeze money from the patriots.

Some states and municipalities also, aping the federal government, have income, excise and special-purpose or use taxes. Excise and most special-purpose taxes—gasoline, liquor, cigarette, business, documentary, etc.—are like the sales tax in that they hit the rank-and-file buyer directly.

But, as we have seen, the biggest tax-gathering jurisdiction, singly and collectively taken, is the federal, which imposes income, estate, excise and customs taxes. The latter two are percentage taxes on retail purchases and, except when placed on luxury goods, hit the common man hardest.

This exposition will largely confine itself to the federal income and estate taxes, for with respect to most other taxes the unmoneyed man pays exactly the same as the rich man although *the proportion of income paid by the impecunious man is always astronomically higher.*

The Sales Tax Steal

In order to make this clear initially, we may note that a man who pays sales taxes of $60 a year out of a $3,000 income has paid 2 per cent of his income on this tax. He would incur such an outlay at 5 per cent, enough to buy a good deal of medicine or dental care, on purchases amounting to $1,200. As the same amount of purchases by a man with $100,000 income incurs a tax of only six-hundredths of 1 per cent, the lower income-receiver pays at a rate more than 3,300 per cent higher in relation to income!

In order to incur a recurrent sales tax that would be 2 per cent of his income (at a 5 per cent rate) the $100,000-a-year man would have to buy $40,000 of sales-taxable goods—hard to do unless he buys a Rolls-Royce or a seagoing vessel every year.

But the disparity is often greater even than this, difficult though it may be to believe. The lower income is almost always in already taxed dollars. For on a $3,000 income an individual has already paid $620 in income taxes at the pre-1964 rate, $500 at the post-1964 rate. The $500,000 income, however, is often tax-exempt or, owing to the diversity of its sources, is taxed at a small fraction of the cited 88.9 per cent pre-1964 or 60 per cent post-1964 rates.

As in all these tax matters there are always further ramifications, let us in this instance pursue one, allowing readers to work out the ramifications of others. Whatever is paid in sales taxes in one year is deductible on the federal return the next year and has an in-pocket value to the taxpayer at whatever percentage tax bracket he is in. The individual with $3,000 taxable income is in the 16.6 per cent bracket as of 1966, which means that the following year his sales tax of $60 will be good for $10.00 against his federal taxes. But the $100,000 man who paid $2,000 sales tax on $40,000 (improbable) sales-taxable purchases is in the 55.5 per cent bracket and will on his return receive a federal tax credit worth $1,110. The leveraging influence of the higher brackets greatly reduces the impact of sales taxes on his purse. If he, like the low-income man, bought goods sales-taxed at only $60, he would get a tax credit of $33.30, or more than three times that of the low-income man.

But a married man with four children and a gross income of $5,000, and who paid no federal tax, would get no compensatory reduction in any federal tax at all. Those low-income people, in other words, who have no federal tax to pay, are hit flush on the jaw by the sales tax. A married couple with one child and $2,000 of gross income ($40 per week), not uncommon in the American economy, might pay 5 per cent of sales taxes on $1,000 of goods, clothing and medicine. This would be $50, or more than a week's pay. If one traces indirect taxes they pay through prices and rent, one sees that they pay many weeks' income in taxes.

The sales tax clearly is a heavy levy directly on the least pecunious citizens.

Tax-Exempt Corporations

Corporations as well as individuals *apparently* pay income taxes.

In 1965, for example, the official statistics tell us that every dollar received by the government came from the following sources: individual income taxes, 40 cents; corporation income taxes, 21 cents; employment taxes, 14 cents; excise taxes, 12 cents; miscellaneous taxes, 11 cents; and borrowing, 2 cents.[11] Corporations on the face of it appeared to contribute 21 per cent of federal revenues, and individual income-tax payers 40 per cent. Of these collections, 44 cents went for "national defense."

But corporations do not really pay any taxes at all (or very, very rarely) —surely a novel and (to most people) no doubt a thoroughly wrong-headed, erroneous and even stupid assertion. For are there not daily allusions to corporation taxes and don't official statistics list corporation taxes? Corporations, however, are no more taxed than were the aristocratic pre-revolutionary French estates.

The evidence is plain, in open view; there is nothing recondite about the situation. *All* taxes supposedly paid by corporations are passed on in price of goods or services to the ultimate buyer, the well-known man in the street. This is not only true of federal and state taxes (where levied) but it is also true of local real estate and property taxes paid in the name of corporations. The corporations, in nearly all cases, merely act as collection agents for the government.

The scant exceptions to this rule are those corporations (none of the large ones and very few of any) that are losing money or that make a considerably below-average rate of return on invested capital. The money-losers pay no income tax at all, and may be forced to absorb local property taxes. Those making a below-average return may be required to pay some taxes, the payment of which does indeed contribute to the low return.

A glance at the income account of any large corporation shows that before share earnings are computed, every outlay has been deducted from total sales. The General Motors income account for 1964, for example, shows that the foreign and domestic income taxes are computed on the basis of income after deduction of all costs, salaries, wages, charges, depreciation, obsolescence, interest on debt and managerial expense accounts and bonuses. Now, after the deduction of federal income taxes, there remained the net income available for preferred and common dividends and for reinvestment. This was the net return or *profit*, more than 20 per cent on invested capital.

The money for every cent of it, close to $17 billion, came from sales of products. All this money, obviously, had to be absorbed in prices apportioned among millions of sales units, mainly cars. The car buyers obviously paid the income tax as well as a federal excise tax. In many cases, they paid local sales taxes as well.

But, the ever-present casuist will object, if the company did not have to pay income taxes at 48, 50 or 52 per cent, it would have had this much more available for dividends. The argument is that prices would remain the same, tax or no tax. Instead of refuting such a contention by citing long and involved economic analyses one may simply consider the figures on rate of return on invested capital either for one corporation or for all corporations over a period of decades.

This rate of return does vary in response to a complex multiplicity of factors but, *pari passu* and *mutatis mutandi*, it remains fairly fixed within certain maximal-minimal secular limits. It averages out. Rates vary from industry to industry and company to company and the average, median or mode for all companies does no more than tell the general story, which is that the average rate of return on invested capital is not significantly affected by taxes. The taxes are largely absorbed in price as an item of cost, and prices rise as corporate taxes are imposed. That prices don't instantly fall when taxes are reduced derives from the fact that corporations are slow in passing on tax benefits. But removal of the taxes would in time bring prices down; rates of return would remain about the same.

No heretical or offbeat argument is offered here. For it is commonly recognized by knowledgeable persons that corporations pay no taxes. The *Wall Street Journal*, for example, trenchantly observes that the corporation income tax is "treated by corporations as merely another cost which they can pass on to their customers."[12] Tax or no tax, the customers pay for everything, including a fairly stabilized average rate of return on invested capital.

In further support of the point, the late Representative Daniel Reed, sponsor of the Eisenhower dividend credit, held that "inordinately high" consumer prices prevailed partly because "all products are increased in price in the exact proportion of taxation"; and the former Republican Speaker of the House, Representative Joseph Martin of Massachusetts, reminded listeners that "any graduate economist can tell us that corporations compute profits after taxes, and not before, and their price scales are adjusted accordingly."[13]

There are some economists who contend that not all corporations are able to pack taxes into prices but instead force workers to absorb some of them in unduly low wages. Here the workers partly subsidize the customers. But the corporation, if it can help it, does not allow any tax to come out of its resources or its return on capital. The so-called "corporation tax," then, is a misnomer and a deception on a gullible public, which itself pays all corporation taxes. The corporation tax is a disguised sales tax.

Indeed, at least two-thirds of American corporations even add payroll taxes to their prices.[14] These consist largely of their legally designated proportion of Social Security taxes, which they are theoretically supposed to pay out of their own pockets. These taxes, in greater part, are paid half by the employee individually and directly, and the balance by consumers, who are themselves mainly employees. It would hardly be erroneous, then, to say that employees pay nearly *all* of Social Security. The only way to make employers pay for them is to deduct from dividend checks or retained profits. Even if this were done, the companies would simply, by inner bookkeeping shifts, transfer money now earmarked for payroll taxes (and passed on in price) to money available for dividends. A greater sum would be made available for dividends and retained profits so that after any deductions for employees' Social Security the same amount would go to dividend recipients. Rate of return would remain the same.

There is really no way of forcing a successful profit-making corporation to pay taxes other than by levying on its capital, thereby reducing it at least as fast as retained earnings build it up. But this action is ruled out under our legal system as confiscatory. It is absolutely taboo. So it is clear that the existent legal system forever protects the going corporation from taxation, like a nobleman's estate. But this system could be altered by a simple constitutional amendment: "Capital may be taxed directly."

While undermining the growth power of corporations, for good or ill, and giving politicians another weapon, such a law would profoundly alter our economic system by making it possible to shift the tax burden at least in part to corporations. This would no doubt induce many tax ideologists to protest that thrift and virtue were being taxed; for "thrift" is the ideological code word for inherited corporate wealth, "virtue" the code word for wealthy man. Would that one could be as thrifty as third-generation inheritors! While the power of the *finpols* would no doubt be curtailed by such taxation, that of the *pubpols* would be relatively enhanced. Whether this would be all to the good is questionable. One might be willing to take one's chances with a Franklin Roosevelt, Adlai Stevenson or John F. Kennedy but be doubtful about taking them with a Lyndon B. Johnson, Barry Goldwater or Richard Nixon. For statesmen are few, "practical" politicians are many, in the world of *pubpolity*.

The dim feeling that this kind of out-of-pocket tax is now paid by corporations is part of what makes the average man feel fairly complacent about the tax situation. But that federal taxes are no impediment to corporations we can see by observing their rates of return. General Motors in 1964, for example, enjoyed a rate of return of 22.8 per cent on invested capital. Although some rates of big companies exceeded that of General Motors, ranging up to 38.2 per cent, industry medians ranged from 8.6 per cent in textiles to 16.3 per cent in pharmaceuticals, the highest. Smith Kline and French Laboratories had a rate of return of 31 per cent.[15]

Various annual series on rates of return by industries are available and should be consulted with a view to ascertaining that income-tax rates do not significantly affect rate of return.[16]

What is not realized by most people is that nearly all investment down through the years consists of corporate reinvestments in varying proportions of their post-tax profits. According to one estimate, from 1919 to 1947, of gross capital formation in the amount of $770 billion in the United States only 2 per cent was contributed by individual savings invested in common stocks.[17]

But aren't corporate people always decrying corporate taxes? If the corporations don't pay taxes, why should they object? Their objections are made on grounds other than that they pay the taxes, although they claim this is the issue. Taxes packed into the price of goods and services obviously reduce the purchasing power of individual buyers and place much purchasing power into the hands of government officials who (1) have in mind the purchase of other kinds of goods and (2) can if they wish have purchases handled by sophisticated hard-to-please purchasing agents. The government cannot be gulled unless it wants to be gulled or unless it has faithless employees. Again, the government may buy mountains of cement and heavy equipment but it cannot be induced to buy chewing gum, fashions and millions of automobiles.

Corporations obviously prefer the less sophisticated, happy-go-lucky types of purchasers to the *pubpols* who, beyond any orders they place, may also require extraneous payments for their patronage such as campaign contributions and retainers. In one way or another, the *pubpols* exact kickbacks for their massive tax-supported business.

In any event, corporations rarely pay any taxes but merely act as collection agents for the government. This fact is shown most formally and precisely in the case of the utility companies, which are always trumpeting to the world how much they pay in taxes. Because these companies hold a franchised monopoly, they are subject to rate regulation, usually within states but in some cases nationally; but by reason of many court rulings against confiscation of capital they are legally entitled to a certain minimum generous return on invested capital—at least 7 per cent. Taxes therefore may not be allowed to intrude upon rate of return but, as they are imposed, must be followed by increased consumer rates. Thus the users (the customers) pay all federal income and other taxes of the utility companies.

The point here is that the situation is the same with the non-utility companies, except that they don't have their prices set by a regulatory commission. The market, subject to monopolistic manipulation, supplies whatever limitation there is.

Landlords and Business Partnerships

It is the same with the revenues of landlords and of business partnerships. Unless they happen to be running at a loss or doing less well than average, all their taxes—local, state and federal—like other costs, are packed into the price of goods or services they sell. The buyer pays the taxes.

Where a landlord owns an apartment building his tenants obviously must pay his taxes as well as all other costs in order to leave him with a profit. Yet it is the landlord who constantly laments about the taxes, which he collects for the government, and the tenants who live lightheartedly unawares. If anyone is to lament about taxes paid, it is obviously they; but they are inattentive to the actual process.

Multiple Taxation

The Eisenhower Administration became very indignant about multiple taxation, holding it to be, if not unconstitutional, at least unfair. It felt stockholders were most unfairly treated in this respect, and puckishly devised a system of dividend credits (4 per cent of dividends discount on the tax itself) that gave very little to many small stockholders but a great deal to a few big ones. A small dividend-received credit remains in the tax laws, but the theory on which it is based—unfair double taxation—is false from beginning to end. For stockholders as such have not, directly or indirectly, paid any tax prior to receiving their dividends. Again, multiple taxation has long prevailed on every hand.

The way these dividend credits worked in 1964 was as follows: Any person receiving dividends could deduct up to $100 of dividends received

($200 for a married couple). Up to $200 of dividends, in short, were tax free for a married couple, and so remained in 1965 and 1966. Beyond this, 2 per cent of all dividends received from domestic taxpaying corporations were deducted *directly from the tax total*. If a man had $1 million of dividend income, he could deduct a flat $20,000 from his final tax. But a married couple receiving $500 of dividends beyond the tax-free base could deduct only $10.

The dividend credit, in other language, was of significant value only to very wealthy people. Before the Eisenhower law was revised, it had twice the value of 1964.

Expressing his indignation, in the 1952 presidential campaign Eisenhower complained that there were more than a hundred different taxes on every single egg sold, and he was probably correct.[18]

But this serves only to point up the fact that it is the rank-and-file consumer who pays most taxes. When, for example, one buys a loaf of bread one pays fractional multiple taxes—the farmer's original land tax; the farmer's income tax (if any); the railroads' real-estate, franchise and income taxes; storage warehouse taxes for the ingredients (income and realty); the bakery's income and realty taxes; the retailers' income and realty taxes; and, possibly, a climactic local sales tax. If all these and many more taxes did not come out of the price of the bread, there would be no gain for anyone along the line of production. So it is the buyer of the bread as of other articles and services who pays the taxes.

How to Get Rich by Not Paying Taxes

By way of introducing an always sharp exposition Philip M. Stern points out that in 1959 five persons with incomes of more than $5 million each, when the public supposed such incomes paid 90 per cent tax, paid no federal tax at all. One with an income of $20 million paid no tax. Another with an annual income of nearly $2 million had paid no tax at all since 1949. In 1961, seventeen persons with incomes of $1 million or more and thirty-five others with incomes of $500,000 or more paid no taxes whatever. In 1960 a New York real estate corporation with $5 million of income paid no taxes but showed, instead, a bookkeeping loss of $1,750,000. And various persons with huge investments in tax-free bonds regularly pay no tax whatever on their aggregate incomes. Not only is this sort of thing continuing, year after year, but the number of tax-free big incomes is multiplying like the proverbial rabbits.

The United States, very evidently, has gone a long way toward aping prerevolutionary France, where court-favorites were given complete tax exemption. Corporations, like noble French estates, are not taxed.

Techniques of Government

In order to bring about these results, politicians have drawn lessons from history and developed techniques for treating their demoralized constituents more as adversaries, to be manipulated, than as a consenting public. And they use the very strivings, selfishness and divisiveness among people to bend them to their own dubious purposes.

When Jack Dempsey was the world's heavyweight boxing champion he went on an exhibition tour of the hinterland. As a feature, a goodly sum was offered to any man who could stay in the ring for three rounds with him. In a certain region of the Tennessee hills the champion was challenged by the local strong man, who had beaten men for miles around in boxing and wrestling and who could bend iron bars with his bare hands. A large local crowd turned out at the arena to see the outside smart-aleck get a dose of real country medicine.

"Look out for this fellow, Jack. He's awfully strong and could hurt you," said one of his handlers to the champion as they watched the strong man jump into the ring.

"Watch him walk into my right," said the champion coolly, according to newspaper men who reported the event.

Need one continue?

As they squared off, the champion flatfooted, the strong man suddenly rushed. The champion's left glove flicked stingingly into his face and was instantly followed by a powerful right cross to the jaw. The strong man, without ever having landed a blow, sank unconscious to the floor. The audience sat bewildered. They had just seen a champion against a novice.

Dempsey figures in this story as the politician, the controlling element, and the strong man symbolizes the people. The governmental method used by Dempsey was that of *letting them come to you and then belting them.*

This method alone does not work with large groups. With them it is necessary to play either on their inherent divisiveness or to divide them arbitrarily in order to rule. This Napoleonic method is well exemplified in the tax laws, which divide and subdivide the populace into many bits and shreds. It is Napoleonic because the general strategy of the little Corsican was to strike successively each section of divided forces with his full, massed force.

Government uses these methods, it should be noticed, when the public is reluctant or unwilling. Apart from taxation, it is used to good effect in conscription. Let us briefly examine it there in order better to understand the tax outcome, which otherwise, in the absence of a hostile conquering force, is inexplicable.

Most men are instinctively reluctant to serve in the armed forces, where one may be killed or maimed. We know this because, if they were not, all they would have to do is to join at any of the many recruiting stations scattered around. Most of them must be *ordered* to serve.

If, as in World War II, the government wants some thirteen million men it is obviously difficult to order them forward all at once, risking the political ire of such a multitude. Again, government at no time possesses the manpower to force thirteen million to obey. The FBI, resourceful though it is, could hardly cope with this situation.

The government here brings into play two tactics—Dempsey's lethal punch and the doctrine of divide-and-rule.

First the government divides the manpower into classes—by ages and by marital and parental status. It then summons first those who are politically and psychologically weakest, the single youths aged eighteen to twenty-one who don't even have the vote. Excepting the few true-blue patriots and excitement-hunters who rush to the recruiting offices, all others, thankfully feeling they have been excused from danger, cheer in approval and tell the bewildered youngsters they are only doing their patriotic duty; older men and women hurry off, like often-criticized Germans, to better-paying jobs in munitions plants. Next to be summoned are single men aged twenty-one to twenty-five, while married men approvingly urge the victims on. For the government gets much assistance from that part of the populace it is not at the moment corralling. Any of those who have shown strong signs of not wishing to go are shouted down by their fellow men, shamed. Some who have watched and cheered the process meanwhile have rushed off to get married to the first unattached female they could find; for the government, it seems, has a soft spot in its heart for married men—whom it is not calling.

But now, with a considerable force in training under arms, the government has enough men to deal handily with any late-showing dawdlers. Moreover, the men under arms feel scant sympathy for those who have not been called. The conscript army would, in fact, relish an order to go and get them at bayonet point. As in a wrestling match, the weight has been shifted. Where at first the forward-thrust of weight was with those not called, who chivvied the tender youths into service, this weight has now shifted to the youths under arms who now regard others as slackers and are ready to kill on command. The slackers are summoned—first the battle-shy married men and then those stalwarts with children up to a dozen and beyond.

On the battle line, finally, one finds single men eighteen to forty-five and married men with a dozen or more children—men wearing glasses, with fallen arches, flat feet, no teeth and leaky hearts. As the rule was finally explicated by the soldiers themselves in World War II, "If you can walk, you're in." They are now all, as the soldiers themselves pronounced, "dogfaces," nobodies. (They were that, too, in civilian life but didn't know it.)

Most of the populace initially acquiesced in this process because it seemed that somebody else was going to be soaked. On this basis they gave their full-hearted consent to the process that finally snared them.

A similar technique is used with respect to the imposition of unfair taxes. For it always appears in reading the tax laws that somebody else is going to be soaked, or at least soaked more than the reader. Does it not clearly appear that some are going to be soaked up to perhaps 91 per cent? On $1 million of income, that is $910,000, leaving the bloody no-good bastard only $90,000 or about twenty times too much. Three cheers for Congress!

The tax laws divide people into many more groups than the conscription laws. There are, first, the single, the married, the married with children and the heads of households; next come minor students, adults and persons over sixty-five. Those over sixty-five retired and unretired, with and without income, blind or still with vision. But this is only the beginning. People are divided also according to sources of income. The basic division is between earned and unearned income, the latter of many varieties. But there is also taxable and non-taxable income, foreign and domestic income, etc.

While to the general public the basic division appears to be between single and child-blessed married persons, the true basic division is between earned and unearned income. It is invariably true that *earned* income is taxed most heavily, unearned or property-derived income most lightly down to nothing at all.

But the average taxpayer is quickly made to feel that he is getting away with something at someone else's expense, that he is, as Mr. Stern says, a "tax deviate." The way the laws are drawn most of us are forced into being tax deviates. The only persons who cannot qualify are single persons with earned incomes, some seven million individuals. They are the low men on the tax totem pole.

The government encourages everyone to feel he is getting away with something by advising all to be sure to take all the deductions—exemptions they are entitled to on the labyrinthian tax form. And they are many. After correctly filling out this form the average taxpayer has the delicious feeling that he has once again outwitted a grasping bureaucracy. But he has only succumbed to Jack Dempsey's strong right hand. He has, literally, walked into the punch.

It is much like participating in a crooked card game in which, one is assured, everyone is cheating. So why not take what comes one's way? But where an ordinary player is allowed to "get away" with $200, favored players somehow get away with $200,000, $2 million or even $20 million. The small players pay for this in the end.

Thus, as Mr. Stern ably shows, the variations from the posted schedules in what is paid increase very steeply as one rises in the tax brackets. Whereas the income below $5,000, calling for 20.7 per cent of tax, actually pays on the average 9 per cent ("What a steal!" we may imagine the simple man saying to himself), the income of $1 million and more calling for a viciously punitive 90.1 per cent on the schedule (if it is taxable at all) actually pays on the average only 32.3 per cent, and the incomes over $5 million pay only 24.6 per cent. The demogogic arrangement of the rates conceals this.

Whereas the average under-$5,000 income receiver, who probably had to work hard for his paltry dollars, saved $274 by his allowable deviation from the posted rate, the *average* multi-millionaire taxpayer saved $5,990,-181 below the apparent rate. While the small man was allowed to cut small corners by an apparent 50 per cent, perhaps to his intense satisfaction with a benign Congress, the recipient of $1 million cut big corners by 66 per cent, and the $5-million man by 75 per cent!

Put in other terms, how much trouble would a person go to in order to chisel $274 and how much to chop out $5,990,181?

The Con-Game Pattern

What the many tax-deviation opportunities provided by Congress for the small payer are is what is known in the underworld as "the come on" or bait. It is especially used in the "con game," the essence of which consists of an approach to a formally respectable person with an offer of great gain to be made by engaging in an operation that is safe but frankly shady. In the end the person being "conned" is tricked through his own illicit greed.

The tax laws, with their many deductions and exemptions, are thus (cynically?) set up in the precise pattern of the "con game." One is invited to step in and chisel on the government by availing oneself of the many small opportunities strewn about for chiselers. One takes up the invitation—or challenge—like Dempsey's strong man. One walks very confidently right into the punch.

Somewhat of an improvement over the "con game," however, most of the victims do not even suspect that it is they who are being unmercifully fleeced in the big delayed thrust.

Four Cases in Point

Mr. Stern dramatically shows what happens to four men who each received $7,000 annual income. A steel worker paid $1,282 in federal taxes after all deductions (not considering all the indirect taxes he has already paid in the market through prices). A man who got all his income from dividends paid only $992.30. Another who sold shares at a profit of $7,000 paid only $526. A fourth who got his income from state and municipal government bonds paid no tax at all. The latter, incidentally, might have had the same tax-exempt status if he had invested in oil or mineral royalties. It hardly pays, as anyone can see, to work for wages. The tax laws thus grossly discriminate, at all times and in all directions, against salaried and wage workers. Grossly, grossly, grossly. . . .

The higher professionals are similarly brutally discriminated against—perhaps most brutally.

Let us take a busy, highly skilled, unmarried brain surgeon, his fees his sole source of income. If his income was, $100,000 after all expenses, then his tax prior to 1964 was $67,320; after 1964 was $55,490. Another man, who sold (possibly inherited) shares at a profit of $100,000 since acquisition, paid only $22,590. A third, who got his income from state and municipal government bonds or possibly from oil or mineral royalties, paid no tax at all. Indeed, in some cases of remote participation in profitable mineral or cattle operations one may make a profit and have the government owing one money in tax credits!

All higher professionals with ample earned incomes are subject to the full force of the graduated tax laws, with the exception of persons in the entertainment field who may incorporate themselves, sell themselves as a "package" and come under the low-tax capital gains provisions.

Again, two men may each take $300,000, one by laboriously writing a best-selling novel, the other by inventing a trivial machine—perhaps, as Mr. Stern says, a new kind of pretzel-bender. The novelist must pay three times the tax of the machine maker.

The Question of Tax Exemption

Should there, first, be any absolute tax exemptions, as of the French nobility? In a national poll the majority answer to this question would probably be "No." But what of religion? Ah, yes, most people would probably murmur, that surely ought to be exempt because it is "a good thing." If one so agrees, the *principle* of total exemption is accepted, and can be applied elsewhere, as indeed it is. Actually, religion in any event could not be taxed by any government. What the so-called religious exemption boils down to in operation is the grant of tax-free status to *beneficiaries of ecclesiastical investments*. This is obviously something different from religion. While most of the more than 200 sects own very little property and rank-and-file clergy even in wealthy churches certainly are paid little, the *managers* of the heavily propertied ecclesiastical establishments gain from this provision, which splits them from the rest of the populace as accessories before the fact. The high-living upper ecclesiastics of the tax-favored churches are usually thick-and-thin pro-government men, upholding the *pubpols* in whatever they do. Naturally, they tell their communicants they ought to be glad to pay one-sided taxes and walk into cannon fire.

The leading property-holding church is the Catholic Church, although most Catholics are quite poor. An unusual feature of the Vietnam war, as widely noted, was the strong opposition to it of many American clergy. But, said the *New York Times*, "The main exception to the general trend, of course, is the American hierarchy of the Roman Catholic Church, which has largely been silent or, in the case of several leaders such as Cardinal Spellman of New York, supported the war effort. The position of the American Catholic hierarchy, however, contrasts sharply with the peace efforts of Pope Paul."[19]

Cardinal Spellman, indeed, on television declared "My country right or wrong" in a strengthened version of Stephen Decatur's "In her intercourse with foreign nations may my country always be in the right, but my country right or wrong." Spellman was, evidently, a *churchpol*.

The Catholic Church similarly, in return for its retention of properties and privileges, was a strong supporter of the Hitler regime, even as tens of thousands of French, English and American Catholics fought to the death against German and Italian Catholics to depose him.[20] It has supported the dictator Franco in Spain, supported Mussolini in Italy. It supports, indeed, any government that gives its large investments tax exemption.

The *pubpols* of all nations, in short, get something in return—thick-and-thin support—for the clerical tax exemption when it becomes substantial. And what the higher clergy doesn't pay, others must.

But although churches under American tax laws may and do operate businesses tax free, in competition with tax-collecting businesses, a university that does this is not tax exempt. Very evidently if a business does not have taxes levied on it, it is in a competitively favorable position pricewise. As the Catholic Church uniquely among churches does not issue financial statements, one does not really know how many investments and businesses it owns. In other cases the ownership is known. The tax base is constantly being narrowed by exemption of church property which, untaxed, is increasing.

The *principle* of total exemption now being established as the pipe organs thunder their approval, it can be extended to whatever else is designated as especially worthy. After religion, what is most worthy? Obviously, it is education. Anything that is educational now becomes tax exempt, and as "education" is a word very elastic in referential meaning it is found, in practice, to cover political propaganda. Organizations and radio stations that emit rightist political propaganda, such as those of oilmen H. L. Hunt and Hugh Roy Cullen, now become tax exempt. And so it goes.

What else is worthy of substantial exemption? As a sagacious Congress has decreed, the powerful oil industry, like religion and education, deserves from 27½ per cent to 100 per cent tax exemption.

Meanwhile, for every exemption and deduction granted, in the low as well as high brackets, for every narrowing of the tax base, the tax squeeze must become more stringent elsewhere; for the government must get whatever money it says it needs. If the government granted complete tax exemption to everybody except one person it is evident that this one person would have to supply the government with all the revenues it required!

The Baited Trap

In order to set the public up for the big tax swindle, the proceeds of which accrue only to the wealthy elements, the government must dangle before it various obvious injustices in which it participates as a beneficiary. The public is, thus, "conned" into a baited trap.

The first, as noted, is the religious exemption (which turns out to be of generalized service as well to propagandists, investors in local government bonds and oil men). But it sounds good to the rank-and-file, who see it as some kind of blow against vicious atheists and freethinkers (all, oddly, created by an all-powerful God).

But, among those paying taxes, the next division takes place between single and married people. In con men's language this is known as "sweetening" the "set up," and is only the beginning of the process. As married people constitute more than 60 per cent of the adult populace, Congress obviously has a majority on its side in discriminating against the single. One should notice again the use of the principle of divide and rule.

Taxwise, the apparent remedy of the single is to get married, but as a practical matter everybody is married who feels able to be married. Those disabled from marriage for one reason or another are simply taxed more heavily.

Thus, under the 1965 tax law, as under previous laws, the taxable income of the single person incurs an initial tax at a much lower sum.

The tax of a single person using the tax tables begins at $900 of actual income, that of a married couple at $1,600. On the first $500 of taxable income (1966), after all deductions, the single person pays 14 per cent; the married couple pays 14 per cent on the first $1,000. Whereas the married couple pays $140 on the first $1,000 of taxable income (after all deductions) the single person pays $145. The disparity gains force as one ascends the tax ladder. On a taxable income of $8,000 the single person incurs a tax of $1,630, the married person only $1,380. On $20,000 the single person pays $6,070, the married person $4,380.

While what the average married person saves on the lower brackets compared with the single person is not enough to maintain a spouse, as one ascends the brackets one finds the tax saving alone can maintain one very well. Congress does not favor marriage through taxes by very much, as will appear, but it does favor marriages by rich people. Congressional tax favors, wherever they fall, do not actually fall according to the stated category but invariably fall according to the category of greater wealth.

This becomes apparent in the $50,000-bracket, where the single man pays $22,590 on taxable income (after all deductions) but the married man pays only $17,060, an advantage of $5,530, enough to support his wife. But at $100,000 of taxable income the wealthy man gets more than ample support for his wife, for he pays $45,180 while the single man pays $55,490. Even a girl with a healthy appetite can be maintained very well on the differential of $10,310.

Before proceeding, the reader should be warned not to pay too much attention to the fact that $50,000 incomes pay $22,590 and $17,060 of taxes respectively for single and married persons. These seem like rather substantial rates. But this is on *taxable* income. We have yet to come to wholly nontaxable incomes.

Mr. Stern argues that taxes ought to be the same for married and single persons. But married people and parents apparently feel there is something onerous about their condition, for which they require a tax concession. Congress lets on that it agrees, gives them a minor concession and then belts them down to the floor by fantastically widening the concession for wealthy people!

Married people get a deduction not enjoyed by the single if they have children. Each child is good for a deduction of $600, which to many seems fair, as children are expensive. But the expense of maintaining children is not proportionately as great in the upper brackets, where the deduction broadens in value with the formal tax rate—the usual story.

Valuable Wives

In the upper income stratosphere, wives (or husbands for wealthy women) are extremely valuable, as Stern shows in detail.

Here is the cash asset value of a spouse at different taxable income levels under pre-1964 law (it is only slightly less now):

Taxable Income	Asset Value of Spouse
$ 10,000.00	$ 11,818.25
25,000.00	131,931.75
75,000.00	1,000,000.00
100,000.00	1,891,875.00
445,777.78	5,996,994.00

But at $1 million of income, the capital value of a spouse, oddly, begins to decline, as follows:

Taxable Income	Asset Value of Spouse
$1,000,000.00	$2,766,153.75
$1,399,555.55 and higher	Zero
Under $ 2,889.00	Zero

The point about capitalizing a wife in these ways is that one can compute at going rates of return what a wife is worth to one in yearly retained income. The wife capitalized at a value of $1 million at 4 per cent is worth $40,000 a year in income to her husband; the $6,996,994-wife is good for $279,877.66. But in the tax bracket below $5,000 a wife is worth in tax benefits only 73 cents per week, no bargain.[21]

Tax Support for Rich Children

A married man with a taxable income of $8,000 under the tax law as of 1965 paid $1,380 (against $1,630 for a single man). If the married man had four children his tax liability was reduced to $924. Under the law four children have gained a married man $456 or $114 per child over the child-less married man. But the married man in the $50,000 bracket, who without children paid $17,060 tax, with four children and the same income pays $15,860 tax, a gain for him of $1,200 or $300 per child. His children are worth in tax benefit about three times what the children of the $8,000 man were worth.

Whose Congress writes this sort of a law? Is it a Congress that represents the $8,000-a-year man or the $50,000-a-year man? As I can't ask this question after showing each such disparity, let it be said here that as one crosses the income-mark of about $15,000 the tax laws boldly and brazenly always progressively favor the richer and always absolutely favor unearned income over earned income.

While the tax laws subsidize only very slightly the wives and children of the poorer man at the expense of single people, they do *absolutely* subsidize those of the wealthier. Here is a flat statement of incredible fact: The upkeep of wives and children of the wealthy is subsidized generously by the existing tax laws. It would, in other words, cost a wealthy single man nothing additional if he suddenly married an impecunious widow with four children. He would retain as much in-pocket spending money as he had before marriage and might also gain a fine ready-made family. If a single man earning $8,000 a year and itemizing deductions did this he would gain only $820 compared with a gain of $7,030 for the $50,000-a-year man. Most families live on far less than a $50,000-a-year bachelor would get in annual tax reduction by marrying a hungry widow with four children.

But the lower taxpayers, while computing their paltry marital and children's deductions, perhaps feeling pity for the single persons, get the feeling of "getting away" with something, or at least of getting some concession from the government because they are married and have children. Actually, however, they are only being "conned" by a wily Congress.

In any case, whatever encouragement the tax deduction gives to the birth rate is distinctly against the general interest at a time of obvious over-population and a seemingly intractable unemployment rate of 4 per cent. By all present signs at least 4 per cent of children born, and perhaps more, will not be able to get jobs.

There are many other ways of dividing the formidable army of tax-payers, throwing first this one and then that one a sop, always under a sentimental camouflage. A single person, incidentally, who is contributing less than half to the support of a disabled or aged relative gets no tax rebate. Unless a person is more than half dependent, which would exclude almost everybody, he cannot be deducted.

Other Ways of Income Splitting

The treatment of married people is known as income splitting, producing two incomes that are taxed at lower rates.

One can, once the principle is established, carry out this process of in-come splitting further, producing three, four or more smaller incomes, less taxed, instead of one that is large and subject to much tax. These ways are all practiced by the wealthy.

While the tax laws basically divide the populace between the single and the married and between the childless and parents, its greatest discrimina-tion is with respect to earned income as against unearned or property-derived income.

This salient feature is carried forward in the extension of income splitting.

One way of income splitting is to allot partnerships in businesses to children, thus giving them a taxable income. If the partnership can be split many ways, among children, grandparents and other dependents, into smaller incomes, substantially smaller taxes will be encountered all around. Retained income for the family group will be much larger.

Another way, as we have seen, is to establish trust funds, and the use of trust funds has grown enormously. While trust funds have many aims, one of the objectives they serve is to split assets and incomes among many people, often among many trust funds for the same person.

But the income of such a recipient is not limited to the trust funds. He may also draw salary, have low-tax capital gains and tax-free income from government bonds or oil-mineral royalties. He may, indeed, draw every kind of income there is, taxable and nontaxable.

Does anyone actually do this? They do much better! As President Roose-velt observed in a message to Congress in 1937 "one thrifty taxpayer formed 64 trusts for the benefit of four members of his immediate family and thereby claimed to have saved them over $485,000 in one year in taxes." But that is ancient history. More recently the Stranahan family, the leading owner of Champion Spark Plug Company, created more than thirty trusts and thus saved $701,227.48 in three years, according to Mr. Stern.

But a certain Dr. Boyce, misled by the logic of the tax laws, in one day established ninety identical trusts to hold a mere $17,000 of stocks and bonds. The $100 dividend exemption left them each tax exempt. Appealed to the tax court, the plan was found "preposterous." "Straining reason and credulity," the learned court said, "it ought to be struck down forthwith." And, as Mr. Stern remarks, "It was."

Another device for income splitting, thus obtaining lower taxes, is to establish many corporations in place of one. In one of many instances a finance business split into 137 corporations to avoid $433,000 of taxes annually, and a retail chain divided itself into 142 corporations to avoid $619,000 annually.[22] The surest way of keeping money today is to steer a proper course through the crazy-quilt tax laws.

Additional Tax Dodges

A man who is sixty-five or over, in the best of health, gets an additional deduction of $600 whether his income is $1,000, $10,000, $100,000 or $1 million, although most people over sixty-five have little income at all beyond meager Social Security. But if he is in chronic poor health, unable to work except spasmodically, and under sixty-five, even if he is sixty-four—no extra deduction. A blind person gets an extra exemption of $600, suggesting to the reader of tax instructions that he lives under a Congress with a heart. But if a person retains his sight and is stone deaf, without hands, has had a stroke or is paralyzed from the waist down he does not get this compassionate exemption.

Whenever such a disparity is pointed out to Congress it usually gladly, in the name of consistency and equity, spreads the inequity to include others. We may, therefore, soon see Congress giving an exemption to all disabled or physically handicapped people, thereby further narrowing the tax base.

The point here is not whether a person is handicapped but whether he has income. What value is an extra exemption to a blind, disabled or aged person who has no income? The only person such an exemption could benefit would be one with an income. And all such special exemptions are taken by persons with incomes—often very substantial incomes. They are props to financial strength, not supports of weakness.

Just how much good the exemptions for over age sixty-five do may be seen by considering the income statistics for 1962, the latest year available.

Of 7.4 million male income recipients over sixty-five years old, 18.6 per cent got less than $1,000 gross; 34 per cent, from $1,000 to $2,000; 18.4 per cent, from $2,000 to $3,000; and 9.9, from $3,000 to $4,000—80.9 per cent under $4,000 gross. Of 7,491,000 female recipients 56.2 per cent got less than $1,000; 30 per cent, from $1,000 to $2,000; and 6.7 per cent, from $2,000 to $3,000—92.9 per cent under $3,000 gross.[23] Much of this income was from tax-free Social Security, which averaged $74.33 per month in October, 1965.

In other words, exemptions for persons over sixty-five can be of significant advantage only to affluent persons, property owners, retired corporation executives on large pensions with big stock bonuses and upper professionals who have managed to save and invest. Like marital income splitting and deductions for children, it is of significant advantage only if one has a large, preferably unearned income.

For a man in the 70-per-cent tax bracket each such exemption is worth in cash 70 per cent. For a person with zero income it is worth zero. In order to benefit slightly from the extra exemptions for being over sixty-five and blind, a single person using the standard deduction must have in excess of $2,000 taxable income. If he receives $4,001, he will pay tax on $1,800 (standard deduction plus three exemptions) or $294. But, having saved $80 by being blind, he will then be in a minority income group of less than 20 per cent of over-aged males! He will, despite the smallness of his income, be in a small, highly privileged income group. If it is a woman with an income of $3,001, she will pay $146—but she will then, despite the smallness of her income, be in a restricted group of less than 8 per cent of over-aged females!

The tax deductions for the aged, blind and retired are of significant benefit only if one belongs to a small group of persons with taxable incomes higher than 81.8 per cent of the males and 92.9 per cent of the females actually do have. The ones most benefited are the affluent aged, blind and retired.

These income statistics for the aged throw a curious light on the propaganda about the United States as a land of opportunity, the richest country in the world and the home of the individual-success system. Under this system, most people, economically, appear to be failures at the end of the road. And were it not for Social Security, the figures in each of the income brackets cited would, on the average, be about $900 less.

Some hidden hand, force or influence appears to cause most people, after a lifetime of effort, to show up very patently as losers. Could prices, taxes and overpersuasive advertising, as well as individual shortcomings, have anything to do with the result? With only 19.1 per cent of over-age males having a gross income above $4,000 and 7.1 per cent of retired females above $3,000, economic success does not appear to have crowned the efforts of most survivors in the most opulent land ever known to history.

In drawing the tax laws Congress is no more being sentimental than when it temporarily exempts the father of twelve from battle duty. Although individual congressmen no doubt have their personal points of view on all of this, collectively Congress in drawing the tax laws is absolutely indifferent to whether one is poor, married, has children or has personal disabilities. But it is not indifferent if one has property or a well-paid position. Then it is most enthusiastically on one's side.

Congress, as we have noted, likes students. It likes them so much that if one is able to gain a scholarship or fellowship he need pay no tax at all on it, an educational exemption, up to $300 a month for thirty-six months and even if the scholarship adds considerably to family income. Scholarships are awarded by many endowed colleges and special bodies, but many corporations now earmark scholarship funds given, for example, to the National Merit Scholarship Fund. Some funds are not earmarked, but the earmarked funds are for the children of employees (usually executives) of the company. The granting of the scholarship has the hidden effect of giving the father an untaxed pay raise and the corporation a pre-tax deduction, paid by consumers and small taxpayers. The father will not now have to pay his own taxed money for tuition. And in known cases students of *lower* standing in test examinations and lower academic standing have drawn earmarked scholarships while students of *higher* standing have drawn none, even as the public supposes the scholarships are awarded on the basis of strictly on-the-record merit.

For nonability factors are taken into consideration in this quarter, too, as in the hiring of people of negative ethnicity.[24]

Divide and Prevail

My object in going into this small stuff is to make this point: Congress is not really sentimental at all but is just busy dividing the taxpayers into separately manageable little bands of over-reachers, each of whom feels particularly and unwarrantably virtuous about some feature of his status—that he is married, has children, has a student in school, contributes to a church, has one out of many possible disabilities, is over sixty-five or was never arrested while robbing the Bank of England on a bicycle ridden on a high wire with a monkey on his back.

A congressman might deny this, might hold that the body is really sentimental, and point out that payments under Social Security and the Railroad Retirement Act are tax exempt entirely. But every recipient of Social Security and retirement provisions is not automatically entitled to special sympathy. A number of them are survivors from among many who have succumbed before them and as such, someone might argue, ought to pay a special tax—or at least be taxed equally with others. A long-employed utility-company executive, no risk competitor, who retires at age sixty-five with a pension of $40,000, a rather standard figure for his industry, plus owning accumulated stock, money in the bank and a large home, may draw the maximum Social Security payment, tax free, plus the special exemption for over age sixty-five. Upper-bracket officials of long service in their personally owned corporations as well as lower-bracket wage-earners are equally under Social Security, and get the same tax exemption whether they need it or not.

When the average man retires, his income drops sharply. But when an executive or owner who has worked over the years for his own company retires, his income from stocks, bonds, pensions, annuities, etc., does not decline. Yet he gets untaxed Social Security payments as well as the poorer man, showing again the equality of the law in all its majesty.

Untaxed Income

While the average man, chuckling to himself, is stooping over picking up the sops a cynical Congress has laid out for him, his pocket is being emptied from behind. As he has elected to trade punches with the champion, let us see how he fares.

Ninety per cent of people, more or less, own no stock and receive no dividends. But people who own stock receive the first $100 of dividends tax free; a husband and wife each owning stock get $200 tax free. However, so-called dividends from mutual savings banks and building and loan associations, usually received by low-income people, do not qualify for this strange deduction.

Furthermore, dividends paid in stock or in "rights" to subscribe to stock pay no tax at all even though the company has taken money from earnings with which to increase invested capital. This feature of the laws explains the popularity of the stock dividend: It is tax free.

The stockholder is in a more favored tax position than even this shows because most companies do not pay out all their earnings in dividends. The dividend payout rate varies among companies from zero to 80 or 90 per cent but averages at about 44 per cent.

What this betokens is that accrued earnings, not paid out, are credited to the capital account and amount to so much untaxed money at work for the stockholder.

Let us imagine that someone owns 100 shares in a company that earns an average of $10 a share but pays out an average of $5 a share in dividends. The stockholder receives $500, deducts $100, and puts $400 into his gross taxable income. But the $500 not paid out is at work for him in the company, growing each year. It is tax-free unearned capital. But if a wage worker receives a $500 bonus at year-end and the employer deposits it in a bank for his account, the $500 must be reported as taxable income and will be taxed. Not to pay a tax on it would be a violation of law, and punishable.

Some companies, although they are big earners, pay no dividends at all. Known as "growth companies," they grow by leaps and bounds. If a man invests $10,000 in such a growth company and it grows at 10 per cent a year (rather modest for a growth company) the investment will be worth $16,105 at the end of five years and $20,000 in a little more than seven years. On all this accrual he has paid no taxes, yet is becoming wealthier and wealthier.

If he decides to take his profit at $20,000 he will pay a maximum of 25 per cent (he might pay less) on $10,000, or $2,500. But he need not do this at all, need never sell and never pay a tax.

When he eventually dies, his heirs will not be liable at all for a capital gain tax even if the original investment of $10,000 has grown to $50 million. Nor need they even pay estate taxes if he has prudently placed it in trust funds for their benefit. While his heirs may receive from him stock worth $50 million, his estate tax may be zero, so that all along there has been incurred no income tax, no capital gains tax and no estate tax.

But if he split the original investment of $10,000 among four trust funds, at his death four beneficiaries would have estates worth $12.5 million each, on which there had never been paid income taxes, capital gains taxes, gift taxes or estate taxes. All would be completely legal.

This road to wealth is not only theoretically possible but is actually traveled in various degrees by many of the rich, as their final accountings show. They die stripped of assets.

The amount of untaxed undistributed profits of corporations each year is very large. In 1950 it was $16 billion. It was $16.5 billion in 1955, lowered to $10.8 billion in 1958, rose to $15.9 billion in 1959. Since then it has ranged between $13.2 billion to $16.8 billion in 1963.[25] Since 1946 it has always been each year more than $10 billion. Like money in the bank, the beneficiaries pay no tax on any of it. It is this feature that enables major stockholders to become constantly richer, tax free.

Retained corporate profits, mostly reinvested, have *exceeded* dividends since 1962 and in 1965 totaled $25.6 billion against $18.9 billion of dividends. They also exceeded dividends in every year from 1946 through 1959, with the exception of 1958, often by a very wide margin; in 1947 and 1948 they were more than double the dividend payout.[26]

From 1945 through 1965 total corporate dividends paid out amounted to $226.9 billion compared with $296.2 billion of profits retained, as shown by the immediately preceding source. The actual payout rate has been a shade more than 44 per cent. Retained profits and increased earnings on them have been among the more solid reasons for the increase in market value of stocks.

Not to pay dividends is an accepted maxim of tax economists. In the words of one tax advice service, "paying dividends is clearly a tax waste."[27]

The retention and reinvestment of corporate profits is the royal road to tax avoidance and financial expansion, at home and abroad. Abroad it is the basis of what is known as American economic imperialism. It requires, of course, the maintenance of a vast "defensive" military establishment largely paid for by the less affluent lower taxpayers. The aggrandizing foreign investments, like the domestic investments, are largely made by corporations with tax-free money!

Under the Eisenhower Administration, as we have observed, the dividend tax credit passed in 1954 enabled big stockholders to make a killing while small stockholders gained very little, the usual pattern of the tax laws. With fewer than 1 per cent of all families holding more than 70 per cent of all stock by value, it is clear that very few could be advantaged by this law. As Mr. Stern shows, a man who had a tax bill of $2,020 and had received dividends of $500 would reduce his tax by $20 under the Eisenhower law. But for 306 top taxpayers, with an average dividend income of nearly a million dollars, we have noted the dividend credit meant an average $40,000 in cold cash for each. Quite a difference![28]

Tax-Exempt Medicine—for the Rich

As the wealthy person has more money available, he can always purchase more tax-deductible medical services than the average man. A married taxpayer is limited to a maximum $20,000 medical deduction, a great deal even for a rich man, and to the excess over 1 per cent of taxable income for drugs and medicines.

But if the taxpayer has an employer who pays his medical and hospital expenses, these exempt from taxes, which is very handy for the company executives who often enjoy this "fringe benefit." For the ordinary taxpayer any wages paid as "sick pay" are exempt up to $100 a week after a waiting period, but not many figure in such arrangements. Those persons retained by companies that make this a practice obviously enjoy a differential tax advantage over most taxpayers.

Corporation executives often enjoy free medical services, for themselves and their families, from fulltime company medical departments. This amounts to so much tax-free medicine, which is charged to consumers in price and to general taxpayers. High public officials, it must be noted, also often come in for such free medical services at various of the up-to-date governmental military hospitals. Former high officials also participate through the courtesy of incumbents, whom they publicly back when controversy rises.

If he has no organization he can charge for the medical services, the rich man does have up to $20,000 of medical attention each year as a tax-free deduction from spendable income, thus reducing his taxable income. In the 70-per-cent bracket this is worth $14,000, cash.

Most persons in the country never enjoy the services of a doctor until they are *in extremis* or a doctor must be called in to pronounce them dead. This is because they cannot afford a doctor and instead rely on the nearby pharmacist, in all poorer neighborhoods referred to as "Doc." Their prescriptions are whatever proprietary drugs he recommends. The pleasant-sounding medical deduction, then, is of no service to the many persons without money to spare for doctors and medicine.

Lucrative Charities

One may deduct up to 30 per cent of gross adjusted income for contributions to charities, and if contributions exceed 30 per cent in any one year they may be spread over five years. As most taxpayers manifestly cannot make contributions on such a scale, the provision is obviously of service only to the wealthy.

While the contributions may be made to existing bodies, most of the wealthy prudently decide to make them to their own charitable foundations, which are run as helpful adjuncts to their other affairs.

Oddly enough, one's financial power in society increases as one "gives" money to a personally owned foundation, proving that it is more profitable to "give" than to receive. If a certain man has a million-dollar *taxable* income (he has made all deductions), he is liable for $660,980 in taxes under the 1965 law, or nearly 70 per cent flat. But he can still make a charitable contribution for a deduction of $300,000. If he does, his tax will be only $450,980, a tax saving of $210,000. But as he has "given" $300,000 it looks as though he is deprived of $90,000 more than if he had paid straight tax.

But what he has "given" he has given to his own foundation, and he can invest this money in stocks of his own companies and thereby maintain profitable control. Again, the earning power of this $300,000 (at least $15,000 a year) is now tax free itself, greatly increasing its effectiveness. It will recoup his $90,000 out-of-pocket cost in at most six years and thereafter show a tax-free profit. He has more income to dispose of now in "philanthropic" patronage than if he had retained his taxed earnings and invested or spent them, for the proceeds of such retained money would be taxed.

What does his foundation contribute to? It contributes, as actual cases show, to laboratories seeking cures for various diseases. Surely this is entirely worthy, and so it is. But what do the corporations make that he controls? They may make medicines that are sold at a profit for the cure of various diseases, and any discoveries made by the laboratories to which his taxfree foundations "give" money will be utilized by his medicine-making corporations in making further profits. But few such discoveries will be available to impecunious people. It usually takes money to buy medicines.

"Charity" under our tax laws can be highly profitable. It can be monetarily more profitable, indeed, than noncharity.

Big Killings via Interest

Interest received, except from tax-exempt bonds, is taxable. Every man who gets interest from a bank account, a mortgage or on a federal or corporate bond is liable for taxes on it.

Interest paid out, on the other hand, is 100 per cent deductible. The man who buys an automobile or household appliance on the installment plan may deduct the interest paid before computing his income tax, just like the man who deducts for the payment of $100,000 of interest a year on a margined stock-market account. For the latter, the interest is deductible as an expense of doing business, and in the 70-per-cent bracket is worth to him $70,000. His true interest outlay is only 30 per cent of the face amount.

All such big interest payments are of major advantage to the big operators in stocks, real estate and oil lands who borrow a great deal in order to contrive their killings, which are sometimes sure things—as in the case of the metropolitan realty operators who "mortgage out."

Where interest paid as a deduction most obviously divides the population, placing another large number in the role of sucker and an apparent large number among the advantaged, is in the matter of home ownership. While tenants, in the form of rent, pay all costs, including mortgage interest and taxes of the owner, the home owner may deduct on his federal tax return interest he pays on his mortgage and his local real estate taxes. On a $30,000 house in which he has a $10,000 equity the home owner may pay 5 per cent perhaps on a $20,000 mortgage, or $1,000; his taxes may be $500; and he may reasonably figure 3 or 4 per cent for depreciation, repairs and maintenance, or $900–$1,200. His rent, then, exclusive of heating, is minimally $2,400. But if he is married and has a $10,000 taxable income he may first deduct the interest payment of $1,000 and then the real estate tax of $500. At the 22 per cent rate for that bracket the deduction is worth $330, bringing his actual rent down to $2,070 or $172.50 per month. A tenant would have to pay considerably more per month plus some entrepreneurial profit to the owner; he would probably have to pay from $225 to $275 per month, possibly more.

While this seems to give home owners a bit of an edge over tenants (I have omitted items like cost of insurance), Congress is not especially fond of home owners either. It has much bigger game in mind. With home owners sitting contentedly chewing their little tidbit, knowing they are slightly better off taxwise than tenants, the interest deduction meanwhile has opened some large gaps in the tax laws through which profit-hungry elements churn like armored divisions through Stone Age club-wielders.

First, for the wealthy man with many houses and country estates, both the realty tax and interest deductions amount to windfalls. If a million dollars of such residential property is mortgaged up to half at 5 per cent, there is a total interest charge of $25,000. But in the 70-per-cent bracket only $7,500 of this represents an out-of-pocket payment. Whatever the realty tax bill is, only 30 per cent of it represents an out-of-pocket payment. The same situation applies with respect to personally owned cooperative luxury apartments; the general taxpayers defray up to 70 per cent of the interest and realty tax outlay.

The interest and realty tax deductions, then, are extraordinarily valuable—to holders of extensive properties.

But this is only the beginning of the story.

Metropolitan real estate operators, as we have observed, use interest as a lever with which to "mortgage out" and then obtain tax-free income.

Here, in other words, is the real milk of the interest deduction coconut. Whereas the average home owner is getting away with peanuts at the expense of tenants, both tenants and home owners in the end must make up out of other taxes they pay, mainly in the form of prices, what the big operators have been able to avoid paying on their profits.

Congress, although not loving home owners, is surely infatuated with big real estate and stock-margin operators. And why not? It is these chaps who have the money to kick in for campaign funds, always a matter of concern to the officeholder.

One may agree that the ordinary citizen is entitled to complain. He knows he is in some sort of squeeze. But, politically illiterate, he clearly does not realize its nature nor does he see that he won't get out of it by obtaining some petty advantage over the single, the childless, the tenants and other fellow rank-and-file citizens. He cannot understand that it is the very *type* of person he likes as a legislator that is his undoing. For he prefers "con men" to seriously honest men.

Tax-Exempt Bonds

One of the biggest tax-exemption loopholes consists of state and municipal government and school bonds. Here, whether one draws $1,000 or $50 million of income, one pays absolutely no tax ever.

Very few people invest in such bonds and nearly all who do are very rich. Tax-exempt bonds are, clearly, a rich man's investment vehicle and are provided for this very purpose.

In the last available Treasury report issued about such bonds, the top 1/10 of 1 per cent of the population owned 45 per cent of all outstanding, the top 3/10 of 1 per cent owned 66 per cent and the top 1½ per cent owned 87 per cent.[29] In short, no down-to-earth people own such bonds.

How many such bonds are outstanding? As of 1963 there were $85.9 billion outstanding compared with only $17.1 billion in 1945.[30] One can see they are very popular with their buyers. At an average interest rate of 3 per cent, this amounts to $2.577 billion of untaxed annual revenue falling into the hands of wealthy individuals and a few banks and insurance companies.

The ordinary man would not find such investments attractive, as he can get from 4 to 5 per cent on savings. The advantage enters through the leverage exerted by the tax-free feature as one ascends the formal income brackets.

As Mr. Stern has worked it out, for a person with a taxable income of $4,000 a 3 per cent tax-free bond is equal to a stock yielding 3.75 per cent; for a person in the $20,000–$24,000 bracket to 4.8 per cent; for a person in the $32,000–$36,000 bracket to 6 per cent; but to a person in the $88,000–$100,000 bracket it is equal to 10.7 per cent on a stock.

On $140,000–$160,000 income it is equal to 15.8 per cent on a stock, on $300,000–$400,000 income to 30 per cent on a stock and on everything above $400,000 it is equal to a blessed, flat, cold 33 per cent on a stock! Such a percentage return in a tax jungle is obviously worth reaching for.

As these bonds are secured by a lien on all the real estate taxes in their respective jurisdictions, they are absolutely without risk as to capital or payment of interest. In order to make as much taxable money, a high-income person would obviously have to invest in very risky enterprises that paid dividends of at least 33 per cent on invested capital. Not many established companies do this.

While some persons, like Delphine Dodge, put all their holdings into such securities, the average wealthy man puts only part of his fortune in them, thus reducing his total tax bill. A possible diversified portfolio and the taxes paid on it might be as follows:

Investment	Income	Tax
$100 million tax-free bonds	$3 million (cash)	None
$100 million oil royalties	$15 million (cash)	None
$100 million growth stocks earning 15 per cent but reinvesting all; no dividend payout	$15 million (accrued)	None
Total Investment $300 million	Total cash income $18 million	Total tax None
	Total accrued income $15 million	
	Total real income $33 million	Total tax None

But such a man's chauffeur, if single and receiving $6,000 a year, would have paid a tax of $1,130 a year at 1965 rates.

Not only is it possible, but it actually happens, that the house servants—chauffeurs, cooks, maids, gardeners—of some ultra-wealthy people pay income taxes and the employers pay none at all, year after year. For this, as one must understand, is a democracy where the lowly pay taxes but many of the rich do not.

In passing, very few Americans can afford to hire servants, and there are in fact few servants in the United States, which some naive souls take as proof of how "democratic" the country is. According to the 1960 census, there were only 159,679 private household workers "living in" in the entire country; they had a median wage of $1,178, were of a median age of 51.6 years and only 26.4 per cent of them were nonwhite. As some large estates harbor huge staffs of servants it is evident that this number distributes among a very small percentage of rich families. Private household workers "living out" numbered at that time 1,600,125, had a median wage of $658, were of a median age of 44.2 years and were 57.3 per cent nonwhite. This latter group obviously makes up the part-time help of some of the urban middle class.

Even suburban families with two or three children in the $25,000 income-bracket find they cannot pay for a servant after taxes, educational and medical costs, car operation and ordinary running expenses. And even part-time servants in the United States are now a luxury confined to an extremely small group of people.

The Expense-Account Steal

A corporation that rewards its top executives opulently, so that after personal deductions each has $500,000 of taxable income a year, is cognizant that each must pay, if married, an income tax of $320,980 or 60-plus per cent. According to one line of doctrine this "reduces incentive" to work like crazy for the dear old company; another doctrine feels it has little dampening effect on executive performance.[31]

As the ascendant view, Congress concurring, is that incentives to make the United States *ueber alles* are reduced by high taxes on executive salaries, ways have had to be devised for putting additional but refreshingly taxfree money into the hands of discouraged upper corporate executives, among whom some of the big hereditary stockholders are included. The two major additional ways are (1) expense accounts and (2) cut-rate stock options. *Many* corporation executives derive most of their take-home pay from these two sources, insouciantly allowing the government to clip their direct-cash salaries up to 70 per cent.

In conducting a business, as anyone can see, an executive naturally incurs nonpersonal expenses for travel, hotel rooms, meals and tips away from home. If a good customer is casually present at mealtime the custom has also been long established of inviting him for a meal and perhaps a convivial drink or two.

But controversy over expense accounts does not relate to these facts of ordinary business life, which may be termed "proper expenses." The controversy centers on "improper expenses," which are a much-criticized way of directing tax-free revenue into the hands of a corporation executive or representative, either giving him money he would not otherwise have had or relieving him of paying for luxurious recreation and diversion out of his own pocket and thereby reinforcing his personal finances while he has fun, fun, fun.

The controversy over expense accounts has succeeded in removing some of the more ludicrously blatant abuses, but in essentials the expense account remains a perfectly legal tax-evading racket. In the 1930's, for example, wealthy people formed special corporations to operate their yachts, racing stables and country estates; the operating cost was deducted as a business expense, thus reducing taxable income. One woman caused her personal holding company, which ran her country estate, to hire her husband at a generous salary to manage the place. His ample salary was a deductible expense before taxes![32]

In such cases standard corporate methods were applied to personal finances. And why not? If a corporation can do it, why not a profit-seeking individual? A spouse, from an accounting point of view, is clearly a deductible expense.

But, despite a narrowing of some expense-account latitude, the field is still rather wide open to free and fancy improvisation.

Almost institutional now are the business convention and regional sales meeting for industry and company go-getters. Here the tab for the milling throng is picked up by the company or companies as a deductible expense. Everything is "on the house"—meals, cigars, wine and liquor, music, entertainment and fancy-free girls. The amount of business transacted at such affairs would be hard to detect with an electron microscope. Anthropologists have compared them with primitive saturnalian festivals, a lusty change of pace from the austere rigors of higher business life.

At one such hilariously confused affair the comely profit-oriented wife of a conventioneer, having heard to her innocent astonishment from some of the call girls in the powder room about the high fees they were getting, got herself on the payroll as a part-time nymph without informing her husband. She was duly installed in a hotel room and a blind date was arranged for a certain hour. As she melodiously called "Come in" to the knock on the door at the appointed time, in walked her own husband.

Those sheltered readers who may consider this story farfetched and untrue are not aware of what has long been known to close observers of High Society: Some socialite women function as professional prostitutes—a fact finally recognized by the *New York Times* (August 14, 1967; 24:1) in its allusion during a survey of contemporary prostitution "to the socially prominent woman who grants her favors for up to $500 in a suite in one of New York's best hotels."

From a pecuniary point of view there are distinct advantages to plying this trade at this social level. At $500 per seance, and with only one such choice seance per week, such a practitioner would gross $26,000 per year *tax free*. For the politicians have yet devised no way of levying a tax on this traffic or bringing it into the range of reportable income. The quest for tax-exempt income naturally turns the thoughts of some pecuniary-minded women in this direction.

Proper business expenses would be those defrayed by a salesman in traveling about to call on customers, or an executive on a plant-inspection tour. But such outlays on expense accounts are minor.

The larger expenses are incurred in providing elaborate entertainment for actual or potential customers, unnecessary entertainment for colleagues and business peers when the sole business topic is ordinary shop talk, and in providing executives with a wide range of recreational expenses. It is a succession of Roman holidays financed by the public.

As to lavishly entertaining customers, if it is done by individuals for their own account, the cost is tax deductible up to 70 per cent, which makes the government (i.e., the general public) pay for it up to 70 per cent. If the bill is paid by a corporation, all of it is deductible as a cost of doing business, paid for in prices.

Under the entertainment feature, corporations make lavish gifts to customers, particularly at Christmas time. A very minor gift is a case of whiskey, and corporation liquor purchases have been estimated at more than $1 billion annually.[33] Corporate gifts in general, involving Cadillacs and jewels, are estimated to exceed $2 billion.[34] The public bears such costs in price directly. Here is a big patronage sewer.

The Internal Revenue Bureau has fought many of the weirdest claims for deductions but has often lost in the tax courts to corporate-minded judges. The owner of a large dairy and his wife were allowed to deduct the $16,443 cost of a six-month African safari as an "ordinary and necessary" business expense because the showing of movies of their trip resulted in presumably beneficial advertising for the dairy. A well-known actress was allowed to deduct the cost of expensive gifts to her agent, dialogue director and dress designer. As she was in the upper brackets, the cost of the gifts was borne almost entirely by the government; she would, had she not made the gifts, have had to pay out most of this money to the government—that is, the general public. As it was, she garnered for herself some personal good will with it.[35]

President John F. Kennedy proposed some mild curtailments in expense-account deductions but was largely over-ruled by Congress. Under his scheme the government would have picked up an estimated additional $250 million in taxes and would no longer have allowed deductions at public expense for theater and sports tickets, night clubs and the maintenance of yachts, hunting lodges and Caribbean hideaways.

Congress allowed such expenditures to remain tax deductible but stipulated that the maintenance of facilities like yachts, hunting lodges and tropical resorts would be disallowed unless they were used more than half the time for business purposes, not a difficult provision to comply with. Making it a bit more annoying, Congress now required itemizing of expenses; previously itemizing was not necessary. But itemized lists are not difficult to supply.

Furthermore, country club dues could continue to be deducted only if more than half of club use was for business purposes (not difficult to show as business associates and customers are about all the average business member knows). The heavy dues and expenses of membership in the big metropolitan clubs, when in showdowns claimed as business clubs, are all deductible.

Under the new law, for business entertaining to be deductible, there must be some "possibility of conducting business affairs" and there may not be present "substantial distractions." This appears to rule out theater parties, sports events and nightclubs though it does allow entertaining in luxury restaurants and at-home dinner parties. But there may be participation even in the presence of distracting events "directly preceding or following a substantial and bona fide business discussion," which opens the door wide again to sports events, bullfights, theaters, nightclubs and the like. As in the shell game, now you see it, now you don't.

"Some skeptics," says Stern, "foresee this major exception resulting in the strategic scheduling of 'substantial and bona fide business discussions' at such select times as the eve of the Rose Bowl game, or the Kentucky Derby —or even the heavyweight title fight."

As one threads one's way back and forth through the yes-and-no fine print it becomes evident that anything goes for which the shadow of a claim can be made, including all-expense trips to Caribbean resorts, gifts of Cadillacs and *objets d'art* to key customers and the placing at the disposal of executives of fully serviced, chauffeured cars for business *and* personal use.

Said one businessman, a member of a coterie of business acquaintances whose companies picked up their lunch bills serially: "I haven't paid for my lunch in thirty-one years." Credit cards are largely paid for by corporations; hence their wide use.

The basic intent of the improperly used expense account is to pay most of the recreational-entertainment bill of executives and some of the recreational bill of customers, and to siphon directly tax-free money into the pockets of upper sales personnel who are given expense accounts, no questions asked, of up to $700 to $900 per week.[36] They pay no tax on such largesse.

There is really no point in picking one's way through what is paid via the expense account and what is not paid: Basically, the whole recreational bill is put on the shoulders of the public, thereby relieving the beneficiaries of this considerable out-of-pocket expense.

Expense money may serve in lieu of salary and has the advantage of being nontaxable. In one case an unmarried president of a small eastern corporation was paid a salary of $25,000 on which he paid $8,300 taxes. He wanted no more because his company paid his apartment rent, club dues and expenses (meals and drinks), entertainment expenses and an occasional trip abroad "to study business methods overseas and improve his firm's competitive position." He thus had the equivalent of a $98,000 salary on which income taxes would have been $62,600, nearly eight times what he actually paid![37]

Where a man has a stipulated expense account it is, of course, understood that he does not have to spend it all. Some of it is "keeping money," tax free. After all, who knows the difference?

One of the subjects faced by Congress in slightly revising the expense-account provisions was the business-mixed-with-pleasure trips of corporate husbands and wives. These latter are an indispensable feature of many business affairs and are fully tax deductible. When the ordinary citizen takes his wife out for a trip or entertainment he foots the bill fully; but for a man on the expense-account circuit she is fully deductible, a pleasant feature of corporate matrimony.

Whereas before Kennedy on a business-mixed-with-pleasure trip the whole cost was deductible, even if a brief conference in Europe or the Caribbean were followed by a prolonged vacation, under the new law when a trip lasts more than a week and where the pleasure component is greater than 25 per cent, only a partial deduction of transportation costs will be allowed unless it can be shown that the pleasure component was the prelude or the aftermath to portentous discussions. Then, apparently, the sky is the limit.

While the percentage stipulated seems very precise it cannot, in fact, be applied.

What if a business executive and his wife (he can't do without her presence) journey to Rome where there is a business conference of half a day about a possible oil deal of $250 million? Now the man and his wife tour the Mediterranean for three to six weeks. Does one now measure the pleasure component by time, by intensity or by magnitude of outlay? If it is the latter, then it is a flea-bite in relation to the magnitude of the possible deal; if it is by time, then close to 99 per cent of the component has been pleasure. If the whole trip cost $12,000, how can this be reasonably questioned as an adjunct to a possible $250-million deal? The fact is, of course, that big deals can be, and have been, arranged with the expenditure of just 10 cents for a phone call. A large deal does not necessarily require expense outlays commensurate to its size, does not need to be arranged in a palace in the presence of dancing girls, whirling dervishes and musical clowns at a Lucullan feast. These are thrown in because they are diverting —and are at public expense.

Clarence B. Randall, former chairman of the Inland Steel Company, is a sharp critic of the expense-account racket, which he rightly sees as adding nothing of value to the economy and as conveying a damaging image abroad of the American businessman's way of life.[38] But he is a minority of one in the business community, as far as the record shows.

The New York pleasure-belt, extending roughly from 34th to 59th Streets and First to Eighth Avenues, is largely supported by expense-account deductions—that is, by the general public. This was made evident when leading restaurateurs and theatrical producers, supported by their congressmen, protested to Congress that they would go out of business if the Kennedy proposals became law. A host of expensive shops would also presumably go under.

Although all these establishments are regarded as play areas of the rich, not many rich people would patronize them if they had to pay for them with their own money. For a wealthy man, often in mortal fear of being considered a sucker, is more apt to overrate than to underrate the value of a dollar. If he spends, he prefers that it is other people's money.

This whole area, where the mere serving of a meal may be a ceremony rivaling the High Mass of the Catholic Church, is underwritten by the general public in the price paid for goods and in lost tax money made up by the lower brackets.

New York City is the Mecca of the nation's big retail establishments, which send buyers there by the hundreds. These buyers, man and wife, are ordinarily royally entertained, providing many a tale for telling at the home-town country club. If, however, no entertaining whatever were done, tax deductible or not, would the nation's total of business suffer? Would the buyers refuse to buy and the customers at home go unappeased?

While it is true that all this may make business more pleasant and exciting, it would make everything more pleasant and exciting if such tax-supported antics were available to everyone. If two scholars have lunch and incidentally discuss the number of commas in Chaucer's writings, should not the lunch be tax deductible? If a physician or lawyer takes acquaintances to dinner, should the cost not be tax deductible on the ground that they might some day become patients or clients? What if two philosophers meet to discuss the cosmos? This is obviously a large matter, larger than a merger of all companies into one. Should they not be tax exempt for life? Does not the government really owe them billions in view of the magnitude of their task? Why should not the ordinary office worker's lunch be tax deductible? Is not the lunch an "ordinary and necessary" expense ancillary to carrying on business?

Should not, by the same line of reasoning, everybody's outlays for anything—food, housing, clothing, chewing gum, tobacco, entertainment—be tax deductible? Is not clothing an "ordinary and necessary" expense for attending to one's job? Could one show up for work clad only in a pair of slippers?

If business expenses, proper and improper, are all deductible, why should not all personal expenses be similarly deductible under the principle of equality under the law?

The Stock-Option Racket

A far more lucrative way of deriving income and evading taxes is by means of executive stock options, which have become increasingly used since World War II.

The essence of the stock-option scheme is that it allows its designated beneficiaries, few in number, to purchase stock at steeply reduced rates. Some price is arbitrarily set at which a favored group of executives, often including large hereditary owners, may buy stock after a certain date. The benefiting executives are supposed to scheme harder in order to enhance the underlying value of the company, thus giving themselves profits. Naturally, if the economy were sinking, no matter how hard they schemed the value of the company would not increase; it increases only as the company participates in an expanding economy, which has nothing to do with the efforts of the executives (with some exceptions).

The way it works is as follows:

Certain high-salaried executives are told that they may within three years buy a block of stock in the company, if they wish, at $50 a share. It is now selling at $45. After three years, let us say, the stock has risen to $125. As they each decide to buy the allotted number of shares, usually running into many thousands, they pay $50 for a stock worth in the market $125, or $75 per share instant profit. If they now sell this stock they pay a maximum 25 per cent tax on the gain or they may retain the stock and pay no tax at all.

But what if the stock fails to advance or declines? This is too bad and in that case the options, with nothing lost, are not exercised and expire. But in many cases of record, when this has happened, the board of directors simply voted that the option price be reduced, from perhaps $45 to $20. This made it possible to buy the stock at a discount of $25, and the purchase of sufficient additional shares might be allowed to permit as great a profit as if the stock had advanced to $125 under the original option.

The option plan clearly allows its preferred beneficiaries to buy stock at a discount and hold on to it, paying no tax, or to sell it and pay a relatively low tax on the increment. An executive need not, indeed, put any of his own money into the deal at all because most issues listed on the Stock Exchange are good for a bank loan at 50 per cent of their market value at any time. If the option price is at least 50 per cent of the market price, a bank will put up all of it, gladly, and the executive need then, after holding the shares a few months, simply sell them to lift off the low-tax capital gain. Smooth, smooth, smooth. . . .

But stock options always dilute the equity of stockholders, large and small. In the case of large stockholders, these sometimes participate in the option plans themselves, thus experiencing no dilution of equity; but in some cases large stockholders concur without participating, apparently feeling it is worth it to them to get this tax-favored extra compensation into the hands of aggressive higher executives.

If a group of executives elect to keep their stock, as did the leading executives of General Motors over the years, they may in time become independently wealthy. Alfred E. Sloan and others of the well-known executives in Du Pont-controlled General Motors from the 1920's to the 1950's were big stock-option men.

There is no risk involved in exercising these options. It is all as difficult as shooting fish in a barrel. And much of the gain involved stems from the reduced or nonexistent tax. If these acquisitions of value were taxed at the same rate as the corporate salary, it would be virtually impossible for big corporation executives to become tycoons on their own account, as a few have become. It is the tax-exempt feature, paid for all the way by the public, that enables them to emerge as financial kingpins, without performance of any commensurate service.

Specific cases under these general observations fully support everything that has been said.

International Business Machines (IBM) in 1956 granted to Thomas J. Watson, Jr., the president, a ten-year option to buy 11,464 shares at $91.80. Five years later Mr. Watson exercised the right to buy 3,887 shares, when the market price was $576. Had he sold at this price his instant profit would have been $1,882,085.40, taxable at 25 per cent. If he was in the 75-per-cent bracket, his tax saving over direct income amounted to $950,000.

The president of a manufacturing company was enabled to buy 30,000 shares at $19 while the stock sold at $52, an instant no-risk profit of $990,-000. The president of an electric company bought 25,000 shares at $30, while the stock sold at $75, an instant no-risk profit of $1,125,000. The president of a drug company bought 27,318 shares at $7.72 while the stock sold at $50, an instant no-risk profit of $1,100,000.

What is made from stock options often exceeds regular salary by a wide margin. Charles H. Percy, head of Bell & Howell and more recently Republican senator from Illinois, in the 1950's got $1,400,000 in option benefits, twice his salary; L. S. Rosensteil of Schenley Industries made $1,267,000, 2¼ times regular salary; and W. R. Stevens of Arkansas-Louisiana Gas Company got option benefits ten times regular salary. It would take a separate book to list all such option benefits.

As salaries are taxed at standard graduated rates, it is only natural for corporate officials to prefer compensation in some untaxed or low-taxed form.

But the potential gain of outstanding options, as yet unexercised, is tremendous. For U.S. Steel executives it was recently $136 million, for Ford Motor executives $109 million and for Alcoa officials $164 million.[39]

There are various arguments on behalf of the option system, all of which fall apart under analysis.[40]

One is that the options attract and hold high-powered executives. But one firm gave more than half its optional stock to nine executives averaging more than sixty years of age and thirty-five years of service.

Watson of IBM at the time of his option purchase already held more than $40 million of the stock, which he had largely inherited. Would he have left the company without the option allotment? Was the option necessary to make him feel a proprietary interest?

Actually, the option scheme was only a method of passing to him a large bundle of additional no-tax or low-tax money.

Another argument is that the options enable companies to compete for executive talent. But as more and more companies come to have option plans no competitive advantage actually accrues.

A third argument is that executives with a big option stock interest will make the company boom. But, as Stern shows, even as a company's position is deteriorating, its stock often rises sharply in price under buying in speculation on a recovery, enabling officials to cash in on options. In a comparison between the performance of companies with and without option plans, more companies without option plans did well than companies with option plans.[41]

Still another argument is that the option plan enables officials to become stockholders and thus have a strong personal interest in the company. But many officials sell out their option stock as quickly as they can and in fact hold no continuing ownership in the company. They are simply profit-hungry.

It is further contended that the options make company officials work harder to make a good showing. But there have been cases, as with Alcoa, where the stock has moved down in price and the option price has thereupon been moved down. The option plan has often worked profitably for insiders whether the stock goes down or the company deteriorates.

Again, it has been charged that company officials, in order to kite the price of the stock in the market and thus make possible an option "killing," have reduced necessary company outlays in order to show misleadingly high and entirely temporary profits.

Objections to the option schemes, particularly to their tax shelter, far outweigh any alleged public advantages, as one can see by reading Mr. Stern's analysis. The option schemes are simply a method of passing tax-free or low-tax money into favored hands and are often voted into effect by their own direct beneficiaries. But they always dilute the equity, reduce it, of nonparticipating stockholders. When an option plan is introduced into a company the book value of all nonparticipating stock is shaved or clipped, much as gold and silver coins used to be clipped by money dealers before governments introduced the milled edge.

In some cases minority groups of stockholders have successfully gone to court to have option plans of big companies either set aside or modified. This has been done in American Tobacco, Bethlehem Steel and General Motors, among others. A General Motors option plan in one instance was set aside by court order on grounds of fraud.[42] But most small stockholders cannot afford to go to court and many big stockholders go along with the option plan on the ground that if officials were not able to chisel in this way they would find some other arcane and possibly more subversive way of nibbling into the property.

As, in theory, a purely money-oriented person, a top big-corporation official is by definition pretty much of a tiger. The stockholder wants him to be a fierce hunting tiger *vis-à-vis* the world in general but a tame tiger toward his masters. Yet a tiger, as many cases in corporate history show, has a strong tendency to direct himself toward the fattest and nearest carcass, the company itself. The option scheme partly deflects this purely theoretical tiger by giving him at least a piece now and then of this rich carcass which he is supposed to guard and enhance.

Well paid, the top company official is supposed to be a faithful servant, dedicating himself to his master. But history knows of many cases of well-paid servants who for their own profit undercut their master's interest. Companies in the corporate jungle have been looted by psalm-singing, God-fearing paid officials.

Options, among other things, are held to be cheaper for corporations, although not for stockholders, than straight bonuses. On this point one must disagree with Mr. Stern, who believes that the corporation pays some tax. Whatever a corporation pays out in cash bonus is so much paid out of net return or added on to price; it is not merely an additional cost of operation reducing a true taxable income. On a stock option the corporation has no out-of-pocket expense at all. But while not costly to the corporation, the stock option is costly over the long term to the nonparticipating stockholders.

Something to notice about the stock option is that it is one of the valuable perquisites of company control. Earlier it was noted that control of a company may be exercised with from 5 to 100 per cent ownership. Whatever the percentage of ownership, control is control. The bigger the ownership stake, of course, the more is the *retention* of control assured. But a 5 per cent control is as effective as 100 per cent.

Among the advantages of controlling a company are these: (1) Dividend payout rates may be determined, and for large stockholders the smaller the payout rate and the larger the tax-free reinvestment rate the richer they become by evading taxes on dividends. (2) Cut-rate stock-option plans may be adopted, with the controllers participating and, indeed, increasing their degree of control by diluting the equity of non-participants. (3) In making outside investments with company money properties personally acquired for a song can be unloaded on the big company at a high price, thereby making a concentrated personal profit but spreading the inflated price among many other persons. (4) Personally beneficial expense-account features can be arranged such as renting a tax-deductible permanent luxury suite in some tropical hotel which, when not used for allowable business purposes, may be used for extracurricular pleasures. (5) Relatives to whose support one might be expected to contribute may be placed on the payroll, often at a substantial figure, thus allowing others and the public to pay for their support. And this is only the beginning.

Control, of and by itself, is valuable because it is a means of directing tax-favored revenues toward oneself.

Depletion and Depreciation Allowances

We have not yet touched upon some of the more spectacular congressionally sanctioned large-scale special tax dispensations.

One of these is the oil depletion allowance. And at the outset it must be made clear that this depletion allowance applies to far more than oil. While it began with oil it now includes all the products of the earth *except*, as Congress finally stipulated, "soil, sod, dirt, turf, water, mosses, minerals from sea water, the air or similar inexhaustible sources." But it does include farm crops, trees, grass, coal, sand and gravel, oyster shells and clam shells, clay and, in fact, every mineral and naturally occurring chemical or fiber on land.

The percentage depletion, according to the Supreme Court, is an "arbitrary" allowance that "bears little relationship to the capital investment" and is available "though no money was actually invested."[48]

But as more than 80 per cent of depletion benefits accrue to the oil and natural gas industries, the discussion can be confined to them.

Dating back to 1919 but with many tax-evading embellishments added since then, the depletion scheme works as follows:

1. The original investment by a company or individual in drilling a well—and under modern discovery methods three out of five wells drilled are producers—is wholly written off as an expense, thereby reducing an individual's or corporation's tax on other operations toward zero. Investment in oil drilling, in other words, offsets other taxable income. If an ordinary man had this privilege, then every dollar he deposited in a savings account would be tax deductible. The law permits, in short, a lucrative long-term investment to be treated as a current business expense.

2. As this was an investment in the well there is to be considered another outlay, or development cost, for *the oil that is in the well*. This cost is purely imaginary, as the only outlay was in drilling the well, but it is nevertheless fully deductible.

3. There remains a continuing, recurrent deduction, year after year, for making no additional investment at all!

The way these steps are achieved is through a deduction of 27½ per cent (the figure was arrived at in 1926 as a compromise between a proposed arbitrary 25 per cent and an equally arbitrary 30 per cent) of the gross income from the well but not exceeding 50 per cent of its net income. If after all expenses, real and imaginary, a well owned by a corporation has a net income of $1 million, the depletion allowance can halve its ordinary liability to a corporation tax and it may maintain prices as though a full tax was paid. Through controlled production of some wells as against others, the tax rate can be reduced still further so that leading oil companies can and have paid as little as 4.1 per cent tax on their net earnings.[44] Some pay no tax at all although earnings are large. Oil prices are "administered" by the companies; they are noncompetitive.

As Eisenstein sets forth this triple deduction, "For every $5 million deducted by the oil and gas industry in 1946 as percentage depletion, another $4 million was deducted as development costs. For every $3 million deducted as percentage depletion in 1947, another $2 million was deducted as development costs."[45] The process continues, year after year, through the life of the well. Income often finally exceeds investment by many thousands of times.

A widowed charwoman with a child, taking the standard deduction which leaves her with $1,500 of taxable income pays taxes at a much higher rate, 14 to 16 per cent, than do many big oil companies and oil multimillionaires in the great land of the free and the home of the brave.

This depletion deduction "continues as long as production continues, though they may have recovered their investment many times over. The larger the profit, the larger the deduction."[46]

"For an individual in the top bracket, the expenses may be written off at 91 per cent while the income is taxable at 45.5 per cent. For a corporation the expenses may be written off at 52 per cent while the income is taxable at 26 per cent."[47] A company may work this percentage a good deal lower and even to nothing.

We have noted that the Supreme Court has called the depletion allowance "arbitrary"—that is, as having no basis whatever in reason. Eisenstein examines in detail all the excuses given for permitting the depletion and in detail shows them all to be without a shadow of merit. Instead of reproducing any of his analysis here, I refer the interested reader to his book. The depletion allowance is a plain gouge of the public for the benefit of a few ultra-greedy overreachers and is plainly the result of a continuing political conspiracy centered in the United States Congress.

What it costs the general public will be left until later.

Even more sweeping results are obtained by means of legally provided accelerated depreciation, long useful in real estate and under the Kennedy tax laws applicable up to 7 per cent annually for all new corporate investments. In brief, whatever a corporation invests in new plant out of its undistributed profits it may take, up to 7 per cent of the investment, and treat it as a deductible item. On an investment of $100 million this would amount to $7 million annually.

Because Stern traces, step by step, the process by which accelerated depreciation operates in the real estate field to eliminate taxes entirely the reader is referred to his book.[48]

But the results in real estate alone, as related by Stern, are as follows:

In 1960, the following events occurred:

—Eight New York real estate corporations amassed a total of $18,766,200 in cash available for distribution to their shareholders. They paid not one penny of income tax.

—When this $18,766,200 was distributed, few of their shareholders paid even a penny of income tax on it.

—Despite this cash accumulation of nearly $19 million, these eight companies were able to report to Internal Revenue *losses*, for tax purposes, totaling $3,186,269.

—One of these companies alone, the Kratter Realty Corporation, had available cash of $5,160,372, distributed virtually all of this to its shareholders—and yet paid no tax. In fact, it reported a *loss*, for tax purposes, of $1,762,240. Few, if any of their shareholders paid any income tax on the more than $5 million distributed to them by the Kratter Corporation.[49]

All of this was perfectly legal, with the blessing of Congress.

According to a survey by the Treasury Department, eleven new real estate corporations had net cash available for distribution in the amount of $26,672,804, of which only $936,425 or 3.5 per cent was taxable.[50]

The Great Game of Capital Gains

Capital gains are taxed, as we have noted, at a maximum of 25 per cent, although this rate is lowered corresponding to any lower actual tax bracket; but up to and including people in the highest tax brackets the rate is only 25 per cent. Thus, capital gains are a tax-favored way of obtaining additional income by the small number of people in the upper tax brackets.

Something to observe is that 69 per cent of capital gains go to 8.7 per cent of taxpayers in the income group of $10,000 and up; 35 per cent go to the 0.2 per cent of taxpayers in the income group of $50,000 and up.[51] The cut-rate capital gains tax, like many of these other taxes, is therefore obviously tailored to suit upper income groups only.

The total of capital gains reported to Internal Revenue for 1961, for example, was $8.16 billion. Of this amount $465 million of gains were in the $1 million and upward income group; $1.044 billion in the $200,000 to

$1 million income group; $1.63 billion in the $50,000–$200,000 income group; $1.6 billion in the $20,000–$50,000 income group; and $1.3 billion in the $10,000–$20,000 income group. Only $2 billion was in the less than $10,000 income group.[52] It is, plainly, people in the upper income classes who most use this way of garnering extra money.

What is involved in ordinary capital gains is capital assets—mainly stocks and real estate.

The theory behind the low-tax capital gain is that risk money for developing the economy is put to work. If the capital gains tax were applied for a limited period, say, to new enterprises, giving new employment, the theory might be defensible. But, as it is, it applies to any kind of capital asset, to seasoned securities or to very old real estate. Most capital gain ventures start nothing new.

There is some risk in buying any security, even AT&T. The risk here is that it may go down somewhat in price for a certain period; but there is absolutely no risk that the enterprise will go out of business. The theory on which the capital gains tax discount is based is that there is *total* risk; yet most capital gains are taken in connection with basically riskless properties. There would be some risk attached to buying the Empire State Building for $1; one might lose the dollar in the event a revolutionary government confiscated the property. But the amount of risk attached to paying a full going market price for the building is in practice only marginal. One might conceivably lose 10 per cent of one's money if one sold at an inopportune time. But one would not risk being wiped out.

In real estate, capital gains serve as the icing on a cake already rich with fictitious depreciation deductions. Depreciation is supposed to extend over the life of a property. Yet excessively depreciated properties continue to sell at much higher than original prices. When so much capital value is left after excessive depreciation has been taken, there must be something wrong with the depreciation schedule. What is wrong with it is that it is granted as an arbitrary and socially unwarranted tax gift to big operators. It is pure gravy.

Depreciation for tax purposes in real estate is taken at a much more rapid rate than is allowed even by mortgage-lending institutions.

First, a certain arbitrary life is set for a building, say, twenty-five years. But a bank will usually issue a mortgage for a much longer term. On such a new building in the first year a double depreciation—8 per cent—may be taken, but on an old building with a new owner a depreciation rate of one and a half may be taken in the first year. The depreciation taken in the first year and subsequently generally greatly exceeds the net income, leav-

ing this taxless. The depreciation offsets income. For a person in high tax
brackets it is, naturally, advantageous to have such tax-free income.

In a case cited of a new $5 million building the tax savings to an 81-
per-cent bracket man amounted to nearly $1 million in five years.

The book value of this building, by reason of accelerated depreciation
deductions of nearly $1.7 million, was now $3.3 million. The owner was
offered $5 million for the building, the original cost. He decided to accept
this offer. The tax deductions he had already taken had saved him 81
cents on the dollar and the tax rate he would get on his "book profit"
would cost him only 25 cents on the dollar. The seller's net tax gain was
$942,422.78.[53]

The new owner of the building could resume the depreciation cycle
again on the basis of the $5 million cost and the old owner could go and
start the process again with some other building. Real estate operators
repeat this process endlessly. Many buildings in their lifetime have been
depreciated many times their value. Best of all, the land remains.

Depreciation charges, deducted from before-tax profits, are an increasingly important way of concealing true earnings, as the *Wall Street Journal* notes (August 29, 1967; 18:3-4). "These funds don't show up as
profits in corporate earnings reports, but are regarded by many investors
as being nearly as good as profits . . . such funds can be put into new
facilities that eventually may bring bigger sales, earnings and dividends
for stockholders.

"At no time during the 1948–57 period did depreciation funds amount
to more than 80 cents for each dollar of after-tax earnings, Government
records show," the *Journal* said. "In some of the earlier years, in fact,
depreciation cash came to less than 40 cents per dollar of earnings. But
in 1958—the year that the price-earnings ratio climbed so sharply—depreciation for the first time in the post-World War II era approximately
equaled the after-tax earnings total. Through the Sixties, depreciation
funds remained relatively high, so that for every dollar of corporate earnings there was nearly another dollar of cash for expansion programs or
other such programs."

Depreciation, in brief, amounts to a second line of profit, not acknowledged as such and now approximately equaling the acknowledged profit.

While this tax-deductible depreciation feature is not present with the
purchase of stocks, the leverage of a loan at interest, as in the case of the
real estate mortgage, is often present. For at least half the purchase price
of the stock may be financed with a broker's loan at the standard rate of
annual interest. The percentage of profit in relation to the input of investment becomes very great.

If 1,000 shares of stock are purchased at $50 a share, with a bank supplying half the money, the investor's share is $25,000. The interest he pays on the $25,000 of bank money is itself deductible. If the stock in six months doubles in value and is sold, the price realized is $100,000. As the bank loan is paid off and the initial investment is recovered there remains a profit of $50,000 or 200 per cent. On this there will be paid a capital gains tax of $12,500, leaving the profit after taxes at 150 per cent (or 300 per cent at a yearly rate).

It isn't usual that a stock doubles in value in six months, but many have done so. A post-tax profit of 150 per cent in as much as five years will amount to 30 per cent tax-free per year, which is not in itself a poor return. Compared with 5 per cent from a bank or a high-grade bond, which is taxable, it is an excellent return, making chumps out of most ordinarily thrifty citizens.

Whether the owner is using only his own money or is borrowing some, he is obtaining a tremendous tax advantage over the ordinary citizen.

Individual Tax Bills

A completely different sort of tax privilege, far less widely known and not even suspected by most persons, is gained by having one's Congress pass a special bill giving one special tax exemptions. Many such special bills are enacted, all reading as though they applied in general.

Actually, when they are incorporated after secret committee sessions into the tax laws the experts in the Treasury Department have no inkling of what they may mean. In order to ascertain their meaning they must wait until a certain return comes in, citing the relevant section of the law as authority for some unusual step being taken. Then it is seen, in a flash, that the return fits the law as neatly as a missing piece fits into a jigsaw puzzle.

One such case among many described by both Eisenstein and Stern concerned Louis B. Mayer, the movie mogul. The experts in the Treasury Department were mystified upon first reading Section 1240 of the Internal Revenue Code of 1954, written in the customary opaque tax language. They had not the remotest idea of what it meant. What it said was:

Amounts received from the assignment or release by an employee, after more than 20 years' employment, of all his rights to receive, after termination of his employment and for a period of not less than 5 years (or for a period ending with his death), a percentage of future profits or receipts of his employer shall be considered an amount received from the sale or exchange of a capital asset held for more than 6 months if (1) such rights were included in the terms of the employment of such employee for not less than 12 years, (2) such rights were included in the terms of the employment of such employee before the date of enactment of this title, and (3) the total of the amounts received for such assignment or release is received in one taxable year and after the termination of such employment.

Stern supplies a translation into English of this paragraph in its generality. But what it meant specifically was the following: Louis B. Mayer, and only Louis B. Mayer, may receive all future profits in the company to which he will be entitled after retirement in one lump sum and this lump sum will be taxed at 25 per cent as a capital gain even if it is not in any sense a capital gain.

Had Mr. Mayer received these profits after retirement as they were generated he would have had to pay maximum taxes on them each year. The special bill for his benefit—Section 1240—gave him $2 million of pin money.[54]

How did it come to be enacted? His attorney was Ellsworth C. Alvord, who appeared before the Senate Finance Committee not as Mr. Mayer's lawyer but as a spokesman for the United States Chamber of Commerce. And the section was so drawn as to be of no use to anyone else, although since then other measures have been passed that enable certain large lump-sum settlements of pension or income rights to be treated as capital gains.

A ludicrous sidelight of this and other tax sections is that the states sometimes copy the federal tax laws, as California copied the tax law of 1954. But much of what they copy has no possible applicability to any tax situation that may arise because some sections are specially tailored to a single situation. Sub-section 2 of Section 1240, which reads "such rights were included in the terms of the employment of such employee before the date of enactment of this title" made it applicable only to Mr. Mayer, who alone had such particular terms before the passage of the bill. Unless one can show one had a contract containing such provisions *before the passage of the bill* one cannot cite the section on one's tax return.

It should never be thought that the leaders of Congress do not know what they are doing.

Many such special sections exist in the tax laws, of benefit only to a single individual or estate (one-shotters) or of continual benefit to certain industries; and Stern discusses a number of them. To obtain such special tax sections for oneself one must, obviously, have a "friend at court," somebody who has the king's ear.

Many companies get such special tax laws, of benefit only to them; and otherwise illegal gains from mergers of various corporations or banks are covered either by one-shot or multiple-shot laws. Sometimes one company is able to squeeze itself into provisions especially tailored for another, but not often.[55]

Low Estate Taxes

Not much will be said here about estate taxes other than to point out that entirely illusory rates are posted here as elsewhere. Many very rich men's estates pay little or no tax. The public supposition that the big estates are being dismantled by estate taxes, often repeated in newspapers, is entirely false.

According to the rate schedule in the law, estates exceeding $60,000 are now taxed from 3 per cent for the first $50,000 to 77 per cent for amounts over $10 million. Offhand, one might suppose that a man who left $100 million net would pay a tax of $67,566,150. But no taxes like this are ever paid and, as we noted earlier, John D. Rockefeller Sr. and Jr. and Henry Ford I paid low estate taxes.

Some persons, below the top levels of wealth, do indeed pay full estate taxes. But this is because they have either through personal peculiarity or unusual moral standards refused to seek and follow the advice of an experienced tax lawyer. Usually it is a personal peculiarity that leads them in this direction, according to what lawyers say. They are unable to understand the steps outlined for them to take or fear they are in danger of losing something.

An anecdote of record about the late Somerset Maugham, the well-known and affluent writer, will illustrate the point. It was explained to Maugham that if he took certain steps to divest himself of nominal control over his assets for the benefit of his children, with whom he was not on good terms as such are generally understood, his estate under English law would almost entirely escape taxes.

"I won't do it," Maugham said as the situation was explained, "because I am too aware of what happened to King Lear."

It is mainly, among the law-cognizant, persons with a strong feeling of alienation who do not avail themselves of the many profitable loopholes in the estate-tax law. Henry Ford, it appears, was one such, and only the last-minute recourse to the Ford Foundation saved control of the company for his family. Ford was obviously either a tenaciously grasping person, indifferent to his family, or simply could not understand the ins and outs of the law, which one assumes were thoroughly explained to him by able lawyers. We know he did not want the government to get his money.

Ford, of course, did not have the advantage of the marital deduction, which was passed the year after his death. Had it been in existence a half of about a billion dollars would have been, right off, tax free. As matters now stand, one half of the taxable value of all estates where there is a surviving spouse is tax exempt.

A $100 million net estate, instead of paying $67,566,150 under the posted rates, therefore seemingly pays only $32,566,150. This is quite a bit but it isn't anything like the posted 70 per cent; it is 32.5 per cent.

Even this 32.5 per cent is illusory under the various leveraging amendments to the estate-tax law and, to make a long story short, we may simply show in this table what the real against the posted rates are:[56]

Gross Estate	Scheduled Rates (Per Cent)	Actual Average Tax (1958) (Per Cent)	Percentage of Discount (approximate)
$500,000–$1 million	29–33	15.3	50
$1–$2 million	33–38	18.2	50
$2–$3 million	38–42	19.3	50+
$3–$5 million	42–49	21.2	50+
$5–$10 million	49–61	23.2	50–60
$10–$20 million	61–69	24.4	60+
$20 million and higher	69–77	15.7	80+

One may obtain the actual rate for any year by averaging the actual payments in each bracket as reported by the Treasury Department. From year to year the actual rates vary slightly.

So, when one reads in a newspaper about high estate taxes one is reading something untrue. The maximum actual estate tax by percentage is about the same as the income tax on an individual $10,000–$20,000 income.

Similar low actual rates prevail on large incomes as shown by the Chase Manhattan Bank in 1960 in its bimonthly news letter, as follows:

Adjusted Gross Income	Scheduled Rates (Per Cent)	Actual Rates (Per Cent)	Percentage of Discount
Under $3,000	20	19	5
$ 10,000–$ 14,999	25	20	20
$ 20,000–$ 24,999	36	23	35+
$ 50,000–$ 99,999	55	38	33+
$200,000–$499,999	80	42	48
$1,000,000 and up	87	38	57.5

But a man with a family will not ordinarily pay anything even like the actual rates on a $100 million estate. For, being sensible and knowing that he must some day die, he has long before death begun transferring assets to his wife and children. Let us suppose he has two children.

He can transfer $100,000 a year to each of them at a gift-tax cost of $15,525 each or 15.5 per cent, with the sums held in trust. In thirty years $9 million will have been transferred. He can make his own law firm trustees.

He can transfer an equal amount, at once or gradually, to his family-controlled foundation, entirely tax free up to 30 per cent of annual income.

He can increase his transfers at slightly higher gift-tax rates. Whatever he transfers brings the actual estate tax lower.

But he can do even better than this. He can transfer to members of his family, at extremely low gift-tax rates, properties of grossly understated value whose true value he alone knows. Such, let us say, would be mineral-bearing but unexploited lands, since privately surveyed and "proven." If such land had been acquired at $100,000 it could be transferred for purely nominal taxes, and this big asset would be in the hands of his heirs long before his death. Times of downswings in the market, as during the Depression, are a good time to make corporate gifts. Overdepreciated real estate or foreign property, with a low book value but a high actual value, is another good thing to transfer by gift. The heirs can sell it at full value without paying any capital gains tax.

At no stage need he lose practical control over any of his properties, leaving aside his moral authority over his family. Many of those who do not avail themselves of these provisions apparently feel they have no moral authority over their heirs or believe their heirs will take these properties and leave them in the lurch, as Mr. Maugham publicly feared. While such a possibility may exist in some families, even it can be guarded against by a knowledgeable tax lawyer.

The value of wives here is again outstanding, as in the case of the marital deduction in the upper brackets.

It might be asked what value it is to a man that half his estate escapes any taxes if his wife gets that money. But the first advantage is that she halves the tax. He must be interested in this feature because he could avoid all taxes by simply leaving all the money to the public in some form. As he usually doesn't do this, one must conclude that he is interested in preserving the fortune for some reason.

What he leaves to his wife can be left in a life trust, he naming the ultimate beneficiary but giving her the right to change this. By doing this he has clearly reduced the taxable amount by one half. His children ultimately take from the mother's estate, so at least two-thirds of the fortune is preserved. But much better than this can be done by means of lifetime distributions in the form of trusts and by taking advantage of other provisions in the fine print of the law.

And through the use of trusts, assets can be kept intact for at least three generations. The dead man can assert his will for at least 100 years. If the final recipients, having full control over the property, now replace it in trust according to family doctrine, the holdings can be preserved in trust for another three generations. If it is a series of multiple trusts that have been established, the tax rates can be very, very low.

While the Constitution forbids the entailment of property as in England it is nevertheless practically possible to practice serial entailment, as Cleveland Amory reports many of the old Boston families have done. Serial entailment is achieved if the third-generation recipient, loyal to family teaching, replaces the property in trusts.

Estates, in fact, are not broken up by the tax laws; they grow larger through the generations, assuring the presence of an hereditary propertied class. This fact has many implications, one of which is that latecomers in the game of grabbing property face a shrunken hunting ground.

The whole point is this: Plenty of escape hatches exist in the estate-tax law for those who wish to avail themselves of them. Some, like Henry Ford, do not, and prefer to clutch nearly every last dime they own until the undertaker forces open their hands. For the heirs of such, the tax outlook is rather bleak, although by no means so hopeless as often reported. There is always the foundation escape hatch, and the foundation, all else failing, can give remunerative employment to members of the family, who become *philanthropols* or, somewhat paradoxically, philanthropist-politicians.

In summary, it should be noticed that the rich, who contrary to Ernest Hemingway are different in other respects than that they simply have more money, live in a specially favored tax preserve which could not have taken form without considerable elitist prompting. Congress alone would not have had the Kafka-esque imagination to devise this labyrinth of fiscal illusion. The public itself did not demand these tax laws.

All deductions and exemptions available to rank-and-file taxpayers in trifling amounts, as we have seen, have far greater weight when applied to the receivers of big incomes from property and its manipulation. Deductions for wives, children, general dependents, education, medicine and social investment have an in-pocket value up to the maximum of the tax rates for the rich. Beyond this are all the special tax dispensations provided especially for big property holders: accelerated depreciation, depletion allowances, expense accounts, low-tax capital gains, specially tailored exemptions, mortgage and interest leverages, tax-exempt bonds, multiple trust funds, light estate taxes, family partnerships, low-tax lump sum settlements of a large variety of fictitious capital gains, etc.

It is very evident that, as government expense has gone up attendant upon fighting corporately profitable wars, the rich have decided to play very little part in defraying it.

Results such as those depicted could have been attained only as the consequence of much elitist work, thought and conniving. Can anyone believe the results are accidental? Or that they are remotely equitable?

Taxpayer Terrorization

While the tax rates gouge the general populace, the Internal Revenue service in recent years, by all accounts, has been conducting a highhanded reign of terror against small delinquent taxpayers, often confused by the crazy-quilt tax forms. "Tax disputes more than any other have given many harassed citizens a glimpse of the other face of Uncle Sam when he scowls," writes Washington political columnist Jack Anderson. The face of Uncle Sam that many citizens now see closely resembles the skinflint depicted by hostile foreign cartoonists.

While making advantageous settlements with delinquent large taxpayers, says Anderson, "the government was relentlessly pursuing a host of small tax debtors, poor but loyal Americans, many of whom were in debt for reasons beyond their control. Uncle Sam garnisheed their wages, seized their property, confiscated their bank accounts, and deprived them of their jobs, stripping them of almost everything they possessed except the mere clothes on their backs. . . . More than one hard-pressed taxpayer has found himself in trouble because of a trivial or unintentional error in an old return, the failure of an employer to withhold the correct tax, or a personal tragedy that cleaned him out of the money he set aside for Uncle Sam. The files at Internal Revenue are stuffed with complaints from taxpayers who say they have been hounded, bullied, and browbeaten by collectors whose methods would put a loan shark to shame. Many a widow's last mite has been snatched from her. Men have been stripped of their livelihood and, along with it, their only means of paying the government."

A committee of twenty-two tax lawyers and accountants appointed by Chairman Wilbur Mills of the House Ways and Means Committee found many acts of "overzealousness" by tax agents that infringed "the vital rights and dignities of individuals."[57]

If a taxpayer subjected to arbitrary Internal Revenue rulings is affluent enough to be able to hire a lawyer he on the average, in appeals, has 85 per cent of the tax assessments sharply reduced or eliminated.

"Only a small percentage of individuals whose deductions are disallowed, whether right or wrong, *do* use existing systems to challenge IRS auditors," writes William Surface. "Why not? 'The small taxpayer's first and usually last impulse is to quit,' says Senator Warren Magnuson of Washington. 'Just throw in the towel, pay the deficiency, no matter how unjust he believes it is, rather than face the tiers of faceless bureaucracy. The small taxpayer is faced with staggering disadvantages in his dealings with the Federal Government in comparison with large, corporate taxpayers.'"

The bigger taxpayers proceed otherwise. About 10 per cent of those assessed additional taxes request an "informal conference" with the auditor's supervisor, and about half of those who do this win some concession. In 1965 a total of 26,301 corporations and individuals who were assessed additional taxes, or 1 per cent, appealed their cases to the Appellate Division, an autonomous body. No less than 85 per cent of the cases so appealed each year have their cases settled for about $200 million a year less than what IRS originally assessed. Beyond this there is the Tax Court, where an average of 8,500 appeals from IRS rulings are heard each year. "Four out of five cases that reach Tax Court are settled without trial for only 31 per cent of the amount that Internal Revenue had initially demanded."[58]

On this showing, IRS is clearly overzealous in many cases, and most people readily knuckle under in fear of being suddenly confronted, apparently, by an unbenign Uncle Sam. Anderson, Surface and various congressmen blame it on petty bureaucrats in IRS, with which judgment I emphatically disagree. IRS people are civil service employees, all of them small people. They only follow instructions from higher up. They act only in response to orders passed down along a chain of command from the White House and the Secretary of the Treasury. When they get very tough and arbitrary it is because they feel their jobs are in jeopardy if they do not make a good showing.

It is true that underlings in all large organizations, governmental and corporate, often tend to be overzealous in carrying out very mild orders, thus giving the organization eventually a bad name. Mild orders from on high tend to gain strength as they are passed down, and at their point of final execution are often brutal.

At times, with the approval of higher-ups, the Internal Revenue Service acts illegally. The Commissioner of Internal Revenue has admitted that for seven years, from July, 1958, to July, 1965, agents had made "improper" or "questionable" use of electronic eavesdropping devices on 287 occasions. The information was elicited by the Senate Judiciary Committee. One senator charged that electronic devices were used "during routine investigations of ordinary taxpayers"; the charge was denied. Planting of such devices by means of trespass, the Supreme Court ruled in 1961, is unconstitutional (illegal), violates the prohibition against unreasonable search and seizure, invalidating evidence so obtained.[59]

Whereas the Bourbons, drunk with power, proceeded forcibly against the peasants *en masse* to collect unfair taxes, in modern states, including the United States, the full force of sovereignty is brought to bear against single individuals. Intimidated in advance by any sort of authority, the ordinary citizen here is in no position, even under constitutional government, to invoke his rights. He does what many intimidated innocent people do in the courts: He pleads guilty to a lesser charge.

General Remarks

What has been put down so far represents only part of the story of shoving the tax burden onto the patriotic labor force by the *finpols* and *corp-pols* with the consent of the *pubpols*, who in turn thoughtfully misapply (Over-Kill) at least 30 per cent of the tax money they do take in. This percentage of profitable misappropriation, largely on the excuse of "defense," more recently of "welfare," is put very conservatively; a thorough direct examination of what is obtained by the expenditures would probably show a larger percentage.

A careful comparison of the fiscal situations in the United States and eighteenth-century France, which was under candid autocratic rule, shows that the American populace is being short-changed far more efficiently than was the French populace under Bourbon rule. Indeed, the American process is more effective because most of the people are not even aware they are being trimmed under the twin banners of anti-Communism and anti-poverty; most rank and file citizens would be the first to deny it vehemently while bursting into strains of Yankee Doodle. The French were fully aware of the process because many of their taxes were collected by force, often after pitched battles between the peasants and the troops. The American process of making the labor force shoulder most of the tax burden takes place in much subtler ways, behind the formidable barriers of deceptive language, high-flown ideology, simple arithmetic and the full panoply of sovereignty arrayed against isolated individuals.

In this atmosphere the withholding tax, levying on earned income before received, was nothing short of a *pubpolic* political inspiration.

The General Results

What is not paid by the higher-ups must be paid by the rank-and-file. The government, despite all the tax loopholes, is never deprived of whatever revenue it says it needs, even for waging fierce undeclared wars of its own bureaucratic making. What revenue the government decides not to take from the influential *finpols* it must take from the poor and needy over which the *pubpols* weep and wail like the Walrus and the Carpenter did over the happy trusting oysters they had eaten.

Stern has reported various shrinkages in the tax base and the attendant cost to the Treasury (which cost must be made up by the patriotic rank and file).[60]

Here these various shrinkages and costs are presented somewhat differently: first, those shrinkages and costs of advantage solely to the wealthy; secondly, those shrinkages and costs participated in and preponderantly of advantage to the wealthy; and, thirdly, those shrinkages and costs generally of advantage only to rank-and-filers.

Lump-Sum Tax Evasions of the Wealthy Only

	Shrinkage of Tax Base (billion dollars)	Cost to Treasury (billion dollars)
Depletion deductions	$ 3.7	$ 1.5
Intangible oil and gas drilling deductions	———	.5
Excessive expense account deductions	———	.3
Real estate depreciation	———	.2
Dividend credits	———	.5
Capital gains deductions	6.0	2.4
Estate tax evasions	12.5	2.9
Interest on tax-free bonds	2.0	1.0
Undistributed corporate profit*	25.6 (1965)	12.8 (est.)
Totals	$49.8	$22.1

* Stern does not include this significant item.

The wealthier class of taxpayers, in brief, fails to pay $22.1 billion of taxes which it might properly pay. Nor is this all, because it participates in tax loopholes available to others.

Lump-Sum Tax Evasions in Which the Wealthy Participate with the Less Wealthy Middle Classes

	Shrinkage of Tax Base (billion dollars)	Cost to Treasury (billion dollars)
Extra exemptions for the aged and blind (most of these deductions percentagewise and in totality must go to those few with substantial income—the higher the income the greater the deduction)	$ 3.2	$ .9
Nontaxable income from social security, unemployment and veterans' benefits, etc. (except for unemployment benefits, the wealthy participate to some extent)	11.9	3.6
Rent equivalent (deducted mortgage interest, etc.) on owned homes (greatest advantage to wealthy as residents and as real estate operators)	6.5	2.0
Itemized deductions (most profitably used by wealthy)	43.0	11.9
Income-splitting for married people (of most percentage and dollar value for wealthy persons)	——	5.0
Totals	$64.6	$23.4

Lump-Sum Tax Dodges in Which the Wealthy Probably Have Little Participation

	Shrinkage of Tax Base (billion dollars)	Cost to Treasury (billion dollars)
Fringe benefits (some participation by well-paid executives)	$ 9.0	$3.0
Interest on life insurance savings	1.5	.4
Sick pay and dividend exclusions (some participation by wealthy)	.9	.3

Standard deduction	12.0	2.6
Unreported dividends and interest (mostly small people)	3.7	.9
Totals	$27.1	$7.2

According to this approximate computation, which would vary in detail from year to year, there is a total tax diversion from the Treasury of $52.7 billion a year. This diversion must be compensated for, with national budgets now rising above $100 billion, and it is compensated for at the expense of the smaller taxpayers, who pay more than $20 billion of corporate and other taxes in price and also pay most of income and excise taxes. The rates on the lower incomes are far higher than they would be if an equitable system of taxation existed.

While the less pecunious classes are able to evade most of $7.2 billion (for which they nevertheless pay elsewhere), the more affluent classes (with the wealthy participating by individual proportions most extensively) evades paying $23.4 billion (for which most of their members pay elsewhere). The wealthiest class as a whole evades directly a total of $22.1 billion, which it unloads on the impecunious and less pecunious classes.

What the extent of its participation is in the evasion of $23.4 by the middle group can only be surmised. If we estimate the participation at only $5 billion then we find the wealthiest have evaded $27.1 billion of taxes in addition to whatever they have merely generally pushed over on the lower orders.

If anyone believes there is suggested here too high a figure of what is really owed in taxes by the wealthy, it should be recalled that the upper 10 per cent of the population owns *all* of the nation's productive private property while 1 per cent of the population owns more than 70 per cent of it. Such being the case one would not reasonably expect that a single employed person who is paid $1,000 in a year—about $20 a week—would be obliged to pay a tax of $12. Nor would one expect that a married man with a salary of $4,000 would be obliged to pay a tax of $350, a month's pay. But so they had to do in 1966 if they took the standard deductions.

To shift the scene a bit, it may be recalled that national elections now require the spending by the political parties of more than $100 million. This is without considering the many costly local elections in off years or parallel with the national elections. The rising figures, often cited, are considered stupendous. These campaign funds are supplied by the wealthy and the propertied who, it should be clear, get a manyfold return on what they pay for. As the political parties (in default of effective popular participation) are to all practical purposes theirs, they obtain preferential treatment from government. So it has been all down through history. The United States is not an exceptional case. It is a typical historical case, contrary to what the Fourth of July orators would have one believe, except that the people have been subdued through their own ineptitude.

People in the Tax Net

In 1940 there were filed 14,598,000 individual income tax returns. In 1961 61,068,000 were filed. The greatest increase took place in 1944 under the wartime tax laws; in 1945 the total stood at 49,751,000.[61]

Having brought this great additional throng into the tax net under the income tax, originally an upper-class tax, does anyone believe the *pubpols* will ever remove the net?

By far most of these taxes are withheld from salaries and wages, earned income. In 1962 there was withheld $47.583 billion compared with $15.317 billion not withheld; in 1963 it was $51.839 billion against $15.205 billion.[62] The income tax has been transformed largely into a permanent *wage tax*, a Gargantuan political joke on the workers.

One often hears of tax-cheats, individuals and organizations, that are proceeded against unceremoniously by the government. As this chapter should make blindingly clear, however, the greatest tax cheat (perhaps in all history) is the United States government itself, which by means of the federal tax code stupendously cheats the vast majority of its trusting citizens on behalf of its political pets. Not only does the government do this but its prime beneficiaries daily boast to a bemused world that in the United States everyone enjoys full equality under the law. The government, of course (to give it its due), is staffed by the weird people put into office by an idiotic electorate, which is fittingly hoist by its own petard. The boobs are overwhelmed by boobs of their own choice!

The Chances of Reform

What are the chances of reforming the tax laws?

Here it must suffice to say that most experts see little prospect of reform. At most there will be further deceptive rearranging and ideological tinkering. And even if taxes were fairly apportioned, past gains would remain in the hands of the advantaged.

A colossal historical inequity like the American tax structure, a mechanism subtly fastened on a people with a view to extracting from them the produce of their labors not necessary for subsistence, is never removed by means of elections or the passage of laws. At least, it never has been thus far in history. The beneficiaries, having gone to a great deal of trouble and expense to devise and maintain this structure, are not going to stand idly by and see it dismantled. They will use every considerable power at their command to defeat all substantial reforms.

In history fantastic, capricious and arbitrary structures such as this have vanished only in some sort of climactic explosion—revolution, conquest or collapse. A far less onerous tax structure in the early American colonies was terminated not by reform but by revolution and war.

These remarks, needless to say, are purely descriptive, intended to bring out the very serious purpose underlying these laws. This earnest purpose, which is to run a vast society in a certain way for certain hereditary beneficiaries and their retainers and emulators, cannot be lightly pushed to one side, particularly when it is well wrapped in the accepted ideology of freedom. Anyone who proposed such action at this time, indeed, would be very foolish, as the populace is hardly aware—and shows no signs of wishing to be aware—that it is fastened in a straitjacket only slightly less tight than in many other ideologically unhallowed societies that could be mentioned.

Anyone who doubts that this is so may set about the task of tax reform. If he succeeds, these concluding observations will have been set at naught. And whether he fails or succeeds he will get a sound political education.[63]

(Note: The reader should not suppose that this chapter is a full treatment of the tax situation. It touches only the highlights and allots no space at all to many publicly costly ludicrous oddities such as the decision allowing Kathleen Winsor to pay 25 per cent capital gains taxes for the sale of her book *Forever Amber* because under a tax-court ruling she was not a professional writer and had written the book "primarily because she enjoyed the research and writing which went into its composition. . . ." The interested reader should refer to sources cited and pick up enlarged bibliographies from them. He will soon see that everything in this chapter is written in a spirit of understatement.

As to the cause of it all, the socialist will murmur "capitalism." Yet the American tax structure has no intrinsic relationship to capitalism and can, indeed, be shown as functionally inimical to it. Other capitalist countries such as England, Western Germany or Japan do not have similar tax structures. The source of the tax structure is clearly the popular electoral system and an inept electorate, which places in office smooth-talking men of a disposition to trade tax and other favors in return for personal emoluments. This the legislators do, in stages and by bits and pieces, resulting in an increasingly peculiar tax structure that may be subtly undermining the capitalist system itself.

Capitalists clearly would be paragons of unusual virtue if they did not, for inner competitive reasons, take full advantage of the fact that a politically inept public had placed into strategic offices men who are deviously accommodating on a *quid pro quo* basis. If capitalists—and a gullible public—were faced by a preponderance of true public men in office they would hardly seek to have written into the laws these various tax monstrosities. But the kind of electorate one finds in the existing political system is unable to insure the presence in office of a preponderance of true public men. Instead the electorate gives us people of the stripe of Senator Thomas Dodd, Congressman Adam Clayton Powell, Bobby Baker, the late Senator Robert Kerr, Judson Morhouse, Senator Everett Dirksen *et al.* The basic causes obviously lie out in the broad electorate.)

The over-riding problem in the United States is not economic. It is political.

Ten 🌿

PHILANTHROPIC VISTAS: THE TAX-EXEMPT FOUNDATIONS

Wealthy men and women today are almost all freely labeled by the public prints as philanthropists. In such mindless parroting the word has acquired the operationally extended meaning of "wealthy person"; and "wealthy person" means, reciprocally, "philanthropist." As hardly anybody in society is more welcome than a philanthropist, it follows that nobody is more welcome in all his beneficence than a wealthy man. By American propagandic decree the wealthy man thus has strangely been transmogrified into the quintessential cream of humanity. Simple people, the majority, accept him without reservation in this guise.

It is, furthermore, extremely rare to find the public prints, particularly the corporate press, labeling anyone other than a wealthy person as a philanthropist. Journalists now appear to make a subtle distinction between philanthropists as merely rich persons and humanitarians as functional benefactors without money: Jane Addams, Lillian Wald, Jacob Riis, Clara Barton, Florence Nightingale.

Oddly at variance with the common perspective of the wealthy person as an overreacher of others in competition for worldly goods and power, the prevalent one is quite in harmony with the Alice-in-Wonderland treatment of contemporary affairs in public prints. As it is practiced on the American scene it is a variant of Orwellian "New-Speak," in which war means peace, peace means war, and liberation means enslavement. For the United States as much as Soviet Russia has its own "New-Speak" in which "defense against Communism" means "invasion of Vietnam" (or the Dominican Republic). Defense means attack. Patriotism means doing physical injury to someone. Inflation means prosperity. Bigness means greatness. And wealth means philanthropy. According to the public prints all is not as one might simple-mindedly suppose in the realm of wealth; contrary to reasonable supposition and statistical fact the wealthy are not endeavoring to increase their wealth but are feverishly endeavoring to give it away for good works.

The basic misinformation sedulously conveyed is this: Whatever the people's government is not taking away from the wealthy in huge tax bites is being given away to the lame, the halt, the blind, the needy, and the worthy with a lavish hand. Therefore, it seems, one should forget about the wealthy; they are not a serious factor of power in the social situation.

Instead of the wealthy, who are measurable and palpable, we are assured by approved savants that what is really involved in the social situation is something elusively unmeasurable and impalpable, discernible only to rarely subtle minds, masters of arcane and delicate methodology. These minds, more and more of late eschewing the troublesome concrete in favor of the pleasantly abstract, limn for us The Power Structure, The Establishment, The Power Brokers, and The Power Elite who face, not the poor, the exploited or the unpropertied, but The Disadvantaged, The Culturally Deprived, The Under-Privileged, The Unfortunate and The Lower Socio-Economic Strata. (All these Disadvantaged may escape their plight by climbing the golden staircase of Upward Mobility.) Taboo entirely in the cleansed new social metaphysics are such coarse and unmannerly terms, worthy only of unwashed boors and churls, as Class and Caste, with their connotations of past and present turbulence. Very much favored is Strata, a cool and cleanly word. People are people, it seems—all pretty much the same according to democratic dogma but found in different Strata, some merely flying by choice or temperament at lower altitudes than others. And in the emerging new social metaphysics or rhetorical whitewash there are few Unemployed. In their place we have the Disemployed, even the Involuntary Leisured. There are, too, Senior Citizens in place of Old People. Persons unable to detect the difference are obviously deficient in understanding—cannot tell the difference between a war and a massive overseas police action.

"Class" is a particularly troublesome word; for one can, unless one is very careful, slip and slide on into "class warfare." But in the elegant variance of the aseptic new terminology one can hardly make the mistake of saying "power-structure warfare," "power-elite warfare" or "lower socio-economic strata warfare." The fashionable new terminology protects against such deplorable gaucheries. Yet the basic phenomena remain in all their harshness.

Puzzles of Philanthropy

As we are not engaged here in an embroidery upon journalistic fantasies we are confronted by a number of puzzles. To what extent are the wealthy giving their money away for good works if they are giving it away at all? This is somewhat similar to the question faced in the last chapter: To what extent are the wealthy being taxed out of existence? And, if they are not giving wealth away, what is it that they are really doing with their numerous foundations?

As many persons are involved in all this so-called philanthropy one must not, heeding the caveats of methodological vigilantes of the Establishment, impute motivations without warrant, although the very term philanthropy (to which the Establishment methodologists oddly do not object) does already unwarrantably impute motivations. What the individual motivations are of those thousands who now transfer money to foundations one cannot say one really knows.[1] But one can trace certain indubitable nonphilanthropic effects of such activities.

The first of these is the public relations effect. The founder may have been publicly disliked, like John D. Rockefeller I, or not very well liked, like Andrew Carnegie. But the forming of foundations had the effect of altering opinion in an unsophisticated population, turning the supposed bad guy into a supposed good guy.

Just how far down in public esteem a wealthy man may sink can be seen from the following acerb vignette of John D. Rockefeller I by Ida Tarbell, writing in the widely circulated *McClure's Magazine* in 1905:

No candid study of his career can lead to other conclusion than that he is a victim of perhaps the ugliest . . . of all passions, that for money, money as an end. . . .

It is not a pleasant picture . . . this money-maniac secretly, patiently, eternally plotting how he may add to his wealth. Nor is the man himself pleasanter to look upon . . . portraits show . . . craftiness, cruelty, something indefinably repulsive. . . .

Hypocrite, intriguer, freak of nature, it is not for us to say. The great public does not deal in nice psychological distinctions. . . . It says this man has for forty years lent all the power of his great ability to perpetuating and elaborating a system of illegal and unjust discrimination by common carriers. He has done this in the face of moral sentiment, in the face of loudly expressed public opinion, in the face of the law, in the face of the havoc his operations caused. . . .

He has fought to prevent every attempt to regulate the wrong the system wrought, and . . . turned his craft and skill to finding secret and devious ways of securing the privileges he desired. . . .

He has turned commerce from a peaceful pursuit to war, and honeycombed it with cruel and corrupt practise; turned competition from honorable emulation to cut-throat struggle. And the man who deliberately and presently does these things calls his great organization a benefaction, and points to his church-going and charities as proof of his righteousness. To the man of straight-forward nature the two will not tally. This, he says, is supreme wrong-doing cloaked by religion. There is but one name for it—hypocrisy.

To have blotted out of popular consciousness largely by foundational activity this once prevalent estimate has been a notable achievement in public relations engineering.

Another effect is the tax-saving benefit. Nearly all of the American foundations have come into view since the enactment of the income tax and estate tax laws: The foundations are completely exempt not only with respect to income taxes but also capital gains taxes. One does not know in each case that the founder sought to escape taxes, but common reason would indicate it. Many standard tax-advisory services explicitly point to these factors as attractive features of foundations.[2]

A third effect is the corporate-control effect. Corporate control, which would otherwise be undermined by the tax laws, is preserved to perpetuity by many foundations, permitting the hereditary transmission, tax free, of vast corporate power.

A fourth effect is that the foundations extend the power of their founders very prominently into the cultural areas of education (and propaganda), science, the arts and social relations. While much that is done in these areas under foundation auspices meets judicious critical approval, it is a fact that these dispensations inevitably take the form of patronage, bestowed on approved projects, withheld from disapproved projects. Recipients of the money must be ideologically acceptable to the donors.

There is a positive record showing that by these means purely corporate elements are able to influence research and many university policies, particularly in selection of personnel. While the foundations are staunch supporters of the physical sciences, the findings of which have many profit-making applications in the corporate sphere, among the social disciplines their influence is to foster a prevailing scholastic formalism. By reason of the institutional controls that have been established, the social disciplines are largely empty or self-servingly propagandistic, as careful analyses have disclosed.[3]

Whether or not these various effects were sought by the foundation creators, they are present, and the realistic observer must suppose they were what the realistic founders had in mind. (We must be particularly impressed by the frank analyses of their tax advisers.) Via the foundations they get more mileage out of their dollars—and retain more dollars.

The Foundation Panorama

There are now so many tax-exempt foundations in the country that the number cannot be precisely ascertained.

The *Foundation Directory*, 1964, published by the Russell Sage Foundation, lists 15,000 foundations but says the number is increasing heavily year by year.[4] In this figure it challenges the total of 45,124 given by Representative Wright Patman, chairman of the Select Committee on Small Business of the House of Representatives. Patman's figure, the *Directory* holds, included civic, educational, welfare and religious organizations as well as pure foundations.[5] But the Patman investigation of the foundations in the early 1960's is the most complete available and will be cited throughout this chapter. It was focused, moreover, on the 534 largest foundations (within the Russell Sage meaning of the term) with total book-value assets exceeding $10 billion at the end of 1960.

As of early 1967, a total of 6,803 foundations in the United States had total assets of $20.3 billion by market values (as distinct from book values), an increase of almost $6 billion in three years, according to the foundation-supported Foundation Library Center of New York, as reported in the *New York Times*, April 4, 1967 (32:3-4). These were record high figures, a measure of lush prosperity in Foundationland.

Total foundation assets in the period 1960–63, according to the *Foundation Directory*, were $14,510,765,000; so it is evident that Patman's inquiry covered most of the field.[6] Of these, $8.161 billion were concentrated in New York; Pennsylvania came next with $853 million; then Michigan with $752.9 million; and Texas with $744 million. New York is far in the lead here as in all other aspects of finance.

Prior to 1910 there were only eighteen American foundations, with just one exceeding $10 million. (Until 1913 there were no income taxes, until 1916 no estate taxes.) In the next decade 76 were launched, in the 1920's 173, in the 1930's 288, in the 1940's 1,638 and in the 1950's 2,839. Of 5,050 leading foundations, 32 per cent were launched in the 1940's and 56 per cent in the 1950's.[7] In their magnitude and pervasiveness, then, the foundations are something recent, a new thing. They are plainly a reflex to the tax laws which give them exemption.

The *Foundation Directory* sets forth thirteen foundations with $100 million or more in assets.[8] But this listing, although impressive, is misleading because some interests have established many foundations, and small foundations in their various ways are themselves significant. Patman more revealingly shows them by groups.

The thirteen leaders according to the *Foundation Directory* are:

	Source	Assets (millions)
Ford Foundation	Ford Motor	$3,320
Rockefeller Foundation	Standard Oil	632
Duke Endowment	Duke Power	478
John A. Hartford Foundation	Great Atlantic & Pacific Tea	360
W. K. Kellogg Foundation	Kellogg cereals	310
Carnegie Corporation	Carnegie Steel	268
Alfred P. Sloan Foundation	General Motors	223
Moody Foundation	W. L. Moody, Texas oil, realty, newspapers and banks	188
Rockefeller Brothers Fund	Standard Oil	152
Lilly Endowment, Inc.	Eli Lilly pharmaceuticals	151
Pew Memorial Trust	Sun Oil Company	135
Danforth Foundation	Purina cereals	126
Commonwealth Fund	Harkness family; Standard Oil	125

The inadequacy of the above listing on the side of understatement is readily shown. Patman detailed eleven out of fourteen Rockefeller-controlled foundations with aggregate assets of $1,016,440,732. These represented about one-seventh of all foundation assets. Among six in all there were four Mellon-controlled foundations, none with assets of $100 million but with aggregate assets of $160,651,388. Nine Mellon foundations, according to the *Foundation Directory*, held $372 million of assets. There were eight Ford-controlled foundations. Seven of these were infinitesimal in size compared with the monster Ford Foundation, which holds nearly a quarter of all foundation assets. Five Carnegie foundations had aggregate assets of $413,465,429. Out of nine Du Pont foundations six were stated to have aggregate assets of $18.9 million, but the Alfred I. du Pont estate, set up in the form of a trust destined for The Nemours Foundation, had aggregate assets of $292 million at the end of 1962 compared with its originating valuation of slightly less than $40 million in 1935.[9]

Patman in his text seriously understated the value of the Du Pont foundations as compared with the showing in his detailed table of foundation assets, which shows the Longwood Foundation, Wilmington, Delaware, alone with total assets of $122,712,483, and the Winterthur Corporation, a foundation, with assets of $32,271,151. Putting these together with the Nemours Foundation and other Du Pont foundations mentioned in earlier chapters, one finds Du Pont foundations totaling nearly $500 million.[10]

Protean Uses of Foundations

While the largest foundations and flotillas of foundations have been mentioned, size is not alone important. Smaller foundations act as conduits and control points, useful in all sorts of secret business affairs and especially in tax evasions. Nearly every large corporation and many of the large banks now have their own foundations. And small foundations often suddenly flower into huge growths.

Among other things, as Patman found, foundations can become tax-free receptacles for capital gains. An individual or corporation may have an investment it wishes to liquidate but which stands to incur a huge capital gain on large long-term appreciation. Payment of a capital gains tax may be avoided by turning the investment over to a foundation (no gift tax) and then having the foundation sell the investment (no capital gains tax). The foundation may now lend the entire liquid sum back to the donor at a nominal interest rate (no law requires that the foundations seek maximum earnings), or it may with the untaxed money obtain a controlling block of stock in some company the original donor wishes to control. With this control he can raise or lower the company's dividend rate, obtain power over its possibly large cash funds and management and perhaps even obtain for himself some further low-interest loans.

With low-interest loans received, a donor can make lucrative investments. He could, for example, with a loan on which he paid 1 per cent, itself tax deductible, go out and buy tax-free local government bonds paying him a tax-exempt 3 per cent.

Let us suppose that an original investment of $10 million was now valued at $100 million. If it were sold it would incur a capital gains tax of approximately $22.5 million. But if it were all given to a foundation the foundation could sell it and pay no gains tax. Now if the foundation lends the whole sum back to the donor at 1 per cent he pays it $1 million a year. And if he makes $3 million on a tax-free investment in government bonds he keeps $2 million annually, tax free. But if he had sold the original amount he would have had only $77.5 million after-tax capital which, invested at 5 per cent, would have brought him $3,875,000. After payment of about $2,712,500 (or 70 per cent) income tax, he would have remaining $1,162,500 annually or almost a half less than by the first procedure. It was clearly financially advantageous to filter the money through the "charitable" foundation.

If he so desires he can in fifty years build the original sum in his personal name back, all tax free. After fifty years he or his family can possess, in fee simple, $100 million in free *new* assets and also control the disposition of the original $100 million in the foundation, which may satisfy legal requirements by using its small income to assist crippled newsboys or homeless dogs.

But this is only a minimal sort of deal that can be arranged either once or preferably in a confusing series through the handy medium of a foundation. Patman showed that foundations can do anything that is financially possible, without any sort of public supervision or regulation. In the sphere of finance, name it and they can do it, tax free.

It is mainly because of the Protean utility of the foundation, particularly in the evasion of taxes, that nearly everyone in the community of wealth has come now to share the original insight of only a few such as the pioneering Carnegie and Rockefeller. Actually, the Rockefeller foundations appear to be the most efficiently run of the foundations, although their major function is definitely not the simple allocation of money to various worthy causes.

Whether they were so intended or not, the Rockefeller foundations are instrumental in keeping in being and under family control the Standard Oil empire that the Supreme Court ordered dissolved in 1911.

At the close of 1960, 7 Rockefeller-controlled foundations owned 7,891,567 shares of common stock of Standard Oil of New Jersey with a market value of $324,946,110. The same 7 foundations owned 602,126 shares of the common stock of Socony Mobil Oil Co. with a market value of $23,610,770. Two Rockefeller foundations owned 306,013 shares of Continental Oil capital stock with a market value of $17,060,224 (the Rockefeller Foundation itself held 300,000 of these shares with a market value of $16,725,000); 4 Rockefeller foundations owned 468,135 shares of Ohio Oil common stock with a market value of $17,998,495; 5 Rockefeller foundations owned 1,256,305 shares of the common stock of Standard Oil Co. of Indiana with a market value of $59,736,991; and the Rockefeller Foundation, itself, owned 100,000 shares of the capital stock of Union Tank Car Co. with a market value of $3,100,000.

If Standard Oil Co. (New Jersey) were to attain substantial ownership in its competitors, it would certainly tend to eliminate competition and again tend toward monopoly, and engage the Department of Justice in inquiry.

The use of a subterfuge—in the form of Rockefeller-controlled foundations —in effect produces the same result as if Standard Oil Co. (New Jersey) owned substantial stock interest in Continental Oil, Ohio Oil, Standard Oil Co. (Indiana), et al.[11]

The Rockefellers also have stock holdings in these companies through personal trust funds, as shown by TNEC, Monograph #29, and perhaps directly.

One is impeded from ascertaining precisely what the Rockefeller interest now is in each of the Standard Oil companies through the spreading around of stock ownership in foundations, personal trusts and personal accounts. Under the law establishing the Securities and Exchange Commission, as we have noted, any holding of a publicly offered stock by any individual or enterprise in excess of 10 per cent of the issue must be reported. But, as I pointed out earlier, a man could secretly hold most of the stock in a company by having 9 per cent in his name and 9 per cent in each of various trusts. If he never changed his holdings the fact would never be reported. He could hold more by adding foundations to the scheme, although the foundation holdings would be on the public record. Just what the percentage of Rockefeller ownership/control now is in any of the Standard Oil companies cannot be ascertained from the record because apparently no individual or trust owns as much as 10 per cent of any issue.

"It is a well-known fact that the Rockefeller family controls Standard Oil Co. (New Jersey), and the Rockefeller-controlled foundations own a substantial part of the corporation," Patman remarks in the same place.

Only once has Rockefeller dominance ever been challenged. That was in 1929 when strong-willed Colonel Robert W. Stewart, chairman of the Standard Oil Company of Indiana, appealed to general stockholders over the heads of the Rockefellers for control of the company. In the showdown vote all the Rockefeller foundations, funds, trusts, personal holdings and holdings of old Standard Oil families were massively counted against Stewart. He was ignominiously snowed under.

Rockefeller family control of the giant Standard Oil flotilla is unchallenged and unchallengeable. Foundation-held stock helps insure it to perpetuity. No possible combination of financial interests under existing law could dislodge that control.

I am not suggesting that this control should be altered. I am simply stating a fact of financial-political life. One may be entirely satisfied to see the Rockefellers rather than some other group in control. But control is what is at stake. One deduces this because this is the way it is. This, one must suppose, is the way it was planned by the wily master architect of Standard Oil.

True, one could suppose that the major intent was philanthropic. It is not logically impossible that the outcome of control was unplanned. But John D. Rockefeller I, whatever else he was, was a planner. I conclude, possibly erroneously and uncharitably, the situation is the consequence of a plan that visualized the retention of control as a goal.

The Rockefeller foundations, as Patman found, are by no means unique as mechanisms for corporate control.

Two Du Pont foundations owned 6,931 shares of Christiana Securities Company worth $83.8 million, and 358,105 shares of E. I. du Pont de Nemours worth $20.4 million.

Six Mellon foundations held 120,294 shares of Aluminum Company worth $8.2 million, 3,729,933 shares of Gulf Oil Corporation worth $124.5 million and 48,750 shares of First Boston Corporation worth $3.2 million.

The Herbert H. and Grace A. Dow Foundation owned 645,238 shares of Dow Chemical Company worth $48.1 million. The Howard Heinz Endowment owned 314,104 shares of H. J. Heinz Company worth $42.5 million. The Timken Foundation owned 427,760 shares of Timken Roller Bearing Company worth $20.5 million. The Charles A. Dana Foundation held 500,000 shares of Dana Corporation worth $16 million. The Gulf Oil Foundation held all the stock of Pontiac Refining Corporation, worth $32 million.

Foundations as Untaxed Holding Companies

Foundations often serve as tax-free holding companies that maintain working control by means of 10 to 100 per cent ownership of many large corporations, the Patman inquiry made certain. But 73 foundations out of 534, including some large ones, did not report such ownership positions to the Treasury as required by law.[12]

Some of the leading corporations in addition to the Standard Oil group entirely or supplementarily controlled by foundations are as follows:[13]

(Asterisks mark those not reporting ownership as required by law.)

Controlled Corporation	Untaxed Foundation	Percentage of Ownership
Kaiser Industries	Henry J. Kaiser Family Foundation	15.4
Callaway Mills	*Callaway Community Foundation	100.
Coca-Cola	Emily and Ernest Woodruff Foundation	15.21
George D. Roper	Sears, Roebuck Foundation	11.77

Controlled Corporation	Untaxed Foundation	Percentage of Ownership	
Midwest Oil	*Standard Oil Foundation, Inc.	18.34	
Eli Lilly	Lilly Endowment, Inc.	46.24	common
		10.40	class B
Kellogg	W. K. Kellogg Foundation	58.	preferred
	W. K. Kellogg Foundation Trust	51.	common
S. S. Kresge	Kresge Foundation	34.	
United States Sugar	Chas. Stewart Mott Foundation (General Motors)	48.2	
B. Altman (N.Y.)	Altman Foundation	84.59	
Connecticut Railway and Lighting	Charles Ulrick and Josephine Bay Foundation	99.25	preferred
		51.07	common
Duke Power	*Duke Endowment	57.24	common
		82.02	preferred
Ford Motor	Ford Foundation	100.	class A
W. T. Grant	Grant Foundation	10.7	
Great Atlantic & Pacific Tea	*John A. Hartford Foundation	33.98	common
S. H. Kress	Samuel H. Kress Foundation	41.9	
American Chain & Cable	William T. Morris Foundation	17.8	
Federal Cartridge	*Olin Foundation	100.	preferred
Reinsurance Corp. of N.Y.	Richardson Foundation	14.	
Faberge	*Samuel Rubin Foundation	100.	common
		100.	1st preferred
		70.	2nd preferred
Electrolux	Wenner-Gren Foundation for Anthropological Research	24.2	
Enna Jettick	Fred L. Emerson Foundation	100.	
Pittsburgh Steel	Donner Foundation	10.	A preferred
Sun Oil	Pew Memorial Trust	21.29	
National Bank of Commerce, Houston	Houston Endowment	23.4	
Allen Bradley	*Allen-Bradley Foundation	64.62	preferred
Miller Brewing	De Rance, Inc., Milwaukee	29.	
National Lead Co. of South America	*National Lead Foundation	100.	preferred

James S. Kemper	*James S. Kemper Foundation	34.2	preferred
Wieboldt Stores	*Wieboldt Foundation	90.6	preferred
Sahara Coal	*Woods Charitable Fund	20.7	preferred
Tecumseh Products	Herrick Foundation	23.	
Hormel	*Hormel Foundation	11.69	
Ralston Purina	*Danforth Foundation	23.4	
American National Insurance	*Moody Foundation	34.55	
Beaunit	*Rogosin Foundation	24.5	
Jonathan Logan	*David Schwartz Foundation	15.	
Cudahy	*Patrick & Anna Cudahy Fund	86.66	B common
Springmaid of the West	Springs Foundation	100.	

Some additional significant enterprises under foundation control were the following:[14]

Edgewater Beach Hotel Chicago	*The Boston Foundation	100.	
First National Bank, Ligonier, Pa.	*Avalon Foundation (Mellon)	21.5	
North American Accident Insurance	*Field Foundation	30.	
Field Enterprises	*Field Foundation	100.	preferred
Reinsurance Corporation of N.Y.	*The Richardson Foundation	14.	
Cannon Mills	*Cannon Foundation	11.69	
First Boston	*Sarah Mellon Scaife Foundation	43.33	

In all, no fewer than 111 foundations were found to own more than 10 per cent of one class of stock, usually the voting stock, in one or more of 263 different important corporations as of December 31, 1960.[15] This was a considerable number of corporations in which to exercise tax-free control even though not all of them were of the commanding size of Great Atlantic & Pacific Tea, Kresge, Ford Motor or Sun Oil. The Ford Foundation does not directly control Ford Motor, but its holding of nonvoting stock enables the Ford family, which also controls the foundation, to control the company absolutely with its own block of stock of weighted voting power.

But at the end of 1960 all 534 foundations in the study held investments in the stock of more than 2,000 corporations, assuring considerable dispersion of voting influence.[16]

The point about foundation control, full or partial, is that it is tax free all the way, giving the foundational enterprise a big competitive edge over nonfoundational businesses, a facet Representative Patman was especially interested in. He cited reports from various businessmen on how they were being undercut in the market by foundation-owned enterprises.

The 534 foundations "had aggregate untaxed receipts of almost $7 billion during the period of 1951 through 1960. During the one year 1960, their total receipts were $1.34 billion as against $554 million in 1951. I find it difficult to reconcile the withdrawal of $1 billion annually from the reach of the Treasury with the federal government's pressing need for revenue.

"During the period of 1951 through 1960, the contributions, gifts, grants, scholarships, etc., paid out by the 534 foundations totalled $3,448,-867,894 (see Schedule 3A for details)—roughly 50 per cent of their aggregate receipts of $6,981,180,819. They claimed expenses, including administrative and operating costs, of $721,199,586—almost 10 per cent of the total receipts."[17]

The foundations in the aggregate, it is readily seen, are as prudent as the corporations in what they pay out. They pay out only about half of income, plus 10 per cent for administration, while the corporations pay out only 44 per cent. The remainder, in both cases, is used for reinvestment and growth. The capital position of the foundations over the years is thus enlarged on the basis of their tax savings. What they don't pay in taxes, it must always be remembered, must be paid in other ways—mainly by the rank-and-file, flag-waving patriots.

To show the magnitude of income for only 534 foundations, Patman points out that 7,213,000 families in 1960 had incomes of less than $2,000 each before taxes, aggregating $8.04 billion. Foundation income the same year was 13 per cent of this total.

But the foundation income of $1.034 billion for 1960 was more than 20 per cent greater than the $864,435,000 net operating earnings after taxes of the fifty largest banks in the United States![18]

At the end of 1960, indeed, the net worth of the 534 foundations studied was 23 per cent greater than the capital, surplus and undivided profits of the nation's fifty largest commercial banks.[19]

As to accumulation of income, the Patman findings, apart from showing payouts in *pro forma* beneficences of only 50 per cent of earnings on the average, placed into view some startling findings. Retained earnings of only some of the largest foundations, which are supposed to be doing the most public good, were as follows through 1960:[20]

	Retained Earnings through 1960
Ford Foundation	$432,916,492
Carnegie Corporation	65,854,287
William Volker Fund, California	17,204,824
Carnegie Institution of Washington	30,334,316
Callaway Community Foundation, Georgia	7,173,911
William H. Miner Foundation, Chicago	13,963,496
The Cranbrook Foundation, Michigan	8,187,872
W. K. Kellogg Foundation	7,524,832
T. B. Walker Foundation, Minneapolis	8,436,379
Danforth Foundation	15,799,676
Charles Hayden Foundation	16,064,615
John and Mary R. Markle Foundation	9,589,958
Milbank Memorial Fund	9,412,828
William T. Morris Foundation	8,831,544
Olin Foundation	15,239,780
Research Corporation	10,070,661
Rockefeller Foundation	51,019,677
Alfred P. Sloan Foundation	33,152,735
Fred L. Emerson Foundation	9,394,815
Thomas J. Emery Memorial	6,847,411
Samuel Roberts Noble Foundation	8,154,763
Sarah Mellon Scaife Foundation	6,198,566
Houston Endowment	27,110,937

While such saving is excellent investment procedure, it does not represent giving away either income or principal. Yet the law (only since 1950) in allowing tax exemption to such enterprises stipulates that there shall be no unreasonable accumulations of income. Prior to 1950 foundation income could be retained without even nominal restriction.

Untaxed, Unfair Competition

Representative Patman's main concern was that the foundations steadily shrink the tax base, thereby increasing the tax burden for others. At the same time they gain a competitive advantage by escaping corporation taxes of 48 to 52 per cent which other business entities must load onto costs. This tax saving they use to build their capital position higher. They in fact literally, almost to the penny, capitalize their tax savings and grow. The wealthy churches do this, too.

The general panorama revealed by Patman was that through the foundation device this privileged part of the American capitalist structure had been able to move itself back into the earlier position of unregulated, uncontrolled, untaxed capitalism. Through the foundations, unless they are restrained by law or public criticism, the old unregulated capitalism may well be restored behind the screen of fitful and halfhearted *pubpolic* corporate regulation in the foreground.

The Internal Revenue Service of the Treasury Department, Patman showed, paid only the most cursory attention to the foundations, apparently taking them at their face value as beneficences. It rarely conducted field audits, kept very haphazard statistics, did not require proper reports, accepted any and all schemes of accounting, did not hold the foundations to existing regulations, did not hold them to the requirement in law forbidding "unreasonable" accumulations of income, gave tax exemptions for straight-out big-profit big-business deals, allowed the tax base to be eroded and, in general, after a few feeble token gestures, allowed anything called a foundation to do whatever it wanted to do.[21]

As a first step in correcting this situation Representative Patman called, futilely thus far, for a moratorium on the granting of further tax exemptions.

He showed, further, no less than twenty-eight accounting defects in the law-required reporting procedures of foundations.

Among other questioned practices he showed that big New York banks turned over to their own foundations appreciated assets, which the foundations then sold, thus evading a capital gains tax.[22]

In the matter of holding controlling blocks of stock he showed them to be agents of more intensive corporate concentration.[23]

He showed foundations operating wholly owned enterprises in competition with taxpaying enterprises, with the foundation-owned enterprise paying no taxes because it was ostensibly operated for charity.[24]

Funds were given by certain foundations to certain universities which used them in *applied*, profit-making research for enterprises with which the foundations were connected rather than in *basic* research available to everybody. Such activities were carried on in competition with taxpaying firms of engineering consultants which should, it was suggested, more properly have been hired. But as the whole ride was tax free on gifts to university and institute research departments, there was more mileage to be had from the money. Had the services been purchased, the purchaser would have had packed into the price he paid (as the ordinary consumer has) profits and the business income taxes.[25]

Certain large enterprises are established, indeed, to carry on applied research, without any shadow of charitable intent, and yet are given sweeping tax exemption.[26]

Foundations, as the Patman inquiry showed, carry on, tax free, the following kinds of operations:

1. They buy up properties from large companies and lease them back, thus providing the companies with ready cash so that they need not enter the competitive capital market.

2. They lend money at cut rates to very large corporations, thus enabling the latter to bypass banks and the capital market.

3. Some of their donors are given convenient cut-rate loans.

4. The foundation stockholdings are used in struggles for corporate control. "In 1960 [the Patman report said], during the battle for control of the Endicott Johnson Corp. the Albert A. List Foundation, of Byram, Conn., received 54,000 shares of Endicott Johnson from the J. M. Kaplan Fund, of New York City. These shares were used by Mr. Albert A. List in his unsuccessful attempt to acquire control of the corporation. According to press reports, during the struggle over the Alleghany Corp. between Allan P. Kirby and the Murchison brothers, the Fred M. Kirby Foundation purchased Alleghany shares, which had not previously paid a dividend."

5. They return capital to donors when, as and if the latter need it.

6. They render research, market study and other services to related businesses on a preferential basis; staffs of large foundations serve as a minor governmental advisory staff for the donors. Parenthetically one should observe that foundation staffs regularly interchange high- and middle-level personnel with formal government. The Barons at times serve the Crown, and officers of the Crown at times serve the Baronage. For a good many years secretaries of state have mainly been foundation officers, corporation lawyers or both. Among the former has been Dean Rusk. Among combinations of the two have been John Foster Dulles, E. R. Stettinius, Jr., Henry L. Stimson, Frank B. Kellogg and Charles Evans Hughes. Corporation lawyers in the post have been Elihu Root, Philander C. Knox and Robert Lansing, to go no further. Secretaries of the treasury have long been drawn for the most part from banks or investment funds. John W. Gardner, recent Secretary of Health, Education and Welfare, was drawn from the presidency of the Carnegie Corporation. Government reciprocally supplies, from time to time, high foundation personnel; McGeorge Bundy skipped from the position of presidential adviser on for-

eign affairs to the presidency of the Ford Foundation. Rusk originally went from the State Department to the presidency of the Rockefeller Foundation. The reciprocal interchange of personnel is heavier on the middle levels between government on the one hand and foundations, investment houses and corporate law firms. Only here and there on both middle and top levels does one find professional politicians, disparagingly referred to in the newspapers as "political" appointees. This means, between the lines, that the man is more or less incompetent for the job but useful in snaring votes. Foundations, law firms and investment houses form in relation to government part of what is known in football as The Platoon System; they have entire specially trained teams ready to be sent into the highest strata of government as conditions require. As all of these are Organization Men of the finest tooling, they fit as though pre-engineered into whatever slot they are assigned. And the reason for this is that the world of *finpolity* is itself a world of government.

7. They pay excessively for certain assets.

8. They sell certain assets to certain parties for unaccountably low prices.

9. They accept contributions (kickbacks?) from persons or organizations that supply goods and services to companies interlocked with the foundation.[27]

10. They also often grossly understate their assets, either in whole or in part. This includes the biggest among them such as the Ford Foundation, Samuel H. Kress Foundation, John A. Hartford Foundation, the Carnegie Corporation of New York and the Howard Hughes Medical Institute. Extraordinarily valuable properties are often carried on the books at $1.[28] Patman concluded all foundations understate asset values.

It cannot be said surely that any of this is done with intent to deceive; one simply does not *know* what the intent is and must infer from results.

Additionally, the foundations are big operators in the stock market, acquiring huge tax-free capital gains.[29] They do, in fact, whatever banks and investment trusts do except issue securities. They are like closely held private family banks and trusts, with virtually no limitation on their operations.

Despite substantial payouts over the years from time of inception to the present, the retained assets of the leading foundations, thanks to their tax exemption and average half payout rate, have piled up astronomically.

Much of the research and other contributions of the foundations pertain to areas of special high pecuniary interest to the donors.

Some of the foundations, such as the Howard Hughes Medical Institute, are used in concert with large corporations such as the Hughes Tool Company and the Hughes Aircraft Company in achieving very large tax savings on assets shuffled back and forth. The Hughes Medical Institute started out by buying $75 million of commercial business assets and assuming liabilities of $56 million, at the same time becoming additionally and directly liable for $18 million on its own note. Said Representative Patman: "This sounds more like high finance to me than charity."[30]

So increasingly scandalous did the Patman findings become in the course of the investigation that the staid *New York Times* took to distinguishing in its reports between "reputable" and "disreputable" foundations, without listing either or laying down criteria for the distinction.

By "reputable" it presumably referred to the largest foundations. And the Ford Foundation is presumably as reputable as any.

But Patman in his very first report teed off on the Ford Foundation as well as other big ones and showed it to be as free-wheeling as any.

First, the Ford Foundation is engaged in large-scale money-lending activity in competition with taxpaying banks. It lends money to a large variety of leading corporations, the interest to them tax-deductible, such as Chris-Craft, the New Haven Railroad, the Chesapeake & Ohio Railway, Continental Air Lines, Standard Oil of California, Shell Caribbean Petroleum Company, El Paso Natural Gas Company and many others. Stockholders in taxpaying lending enterprises such as banks are certainly undercut by such tax-free activity.

Moreover, whenever it wishes it can lower its interest rate to preferential levels. "Why, for example," Representative Patman asked, "was the Duke Power Co. of Charlotte, N. C., charged only 2.65 percent interest on a $3 million, 20-year loan, while other borrowers paid 6½ percent? Duke Power, incidentally, is owned 57 percent by the Duke Endowment, another tax-exempt foundation."[31] Here is one foundation washing the hands of another.

Even more fundamental questions were raised about Ford operations by Patman.

I have already referred to the $33 million the foundation loaned overseas during the 1961 balance-of-payments crisis. This, in effect, amounted to a Government subsidy being used, without Government control, in operations in conflict with government policy. Treasury Secretary Dillon on May 17, 1962, warned that the mounting flood of European bond issues sold in the U.S. capital market is undermining our Government's efforts to defend the dollar. Precisely such an outflow of dollars—to industrial nations like France, Belgium, and Canada—was involved in the Ford Foundation's loans, as shown on Schedule 4, pp. 83–84.

The Ford Foundation loans to foreign corporations and governments create a somewhat bewildering paradox. Our Government brought home soldiers' families so as to save dollars overseas. Yet the Ford Foundation exported $33 million in the year 1961. Also, in 1960 the Ford Motor Co. arranged to export $358 million to purchase minority stockholdings in British Ford which they already controlled.

The result was that a substantial part of the dollars we saved by separating our soldiers from their families was sent back overseas by the Ford Foundation and the Ford Motor Co. And the irony is that the Ford Foundation operates on a subsidy from the taxpayers—in the form of tax exemption.

Moreover, we do not know the purpose of the Ford Foundation loans to the foreign corporations and governments. For example, if the loans are used by foreign businesses—which are not bound by our antitrust statutes—to help them gain entry to our market, those foreign firms have a great competitive advantage. Trade practices in the United States and the Common Market are quite different. In Europe, an industry cartel can cut up the U.S. Market, assigning to certain members exclusive territorial rights in certain sections of the country. Our firms cannot do this without facing a violation of our antitrust laws. Hence, the Ford Foundation's loans could conceivably be helping our competitors who are not bound by the Sherman Act, the Robinson-Patman Act, etc.[32]

But Mr. Patman appeared to be overzealous when he took the Ford Foundation and others to task for contributions to nonprofit educational television stations, which appear to be entirely defensive activities. Only if Mr. Patman's unstated premise is valid, that all activities must be profit-making, can his argument here hold.[33] If this is so, then contributions to nonprofit hospitals and schools are questionable.

The Patman inquiry, one must conclude, fits well the thesis of sporadic friction between the Crown and the Baronage, between *pubpols* and *finpols*. Patman's, it is evident, is not the prevalent view of the foundations among *pubpols*. But the *pubpols* in their various calls for regulation, supervision, revision or reform of one or another aspect of the realm of *finpolity*—sometimes corporations, sometimes foundations—do appear to be playing some part of the role of the medieval Crown *vis-à-vis* the restless Baronage. This will no doubt continue until the day arrives, if it ever does, when they effect a transition either into the corporate state or into the collective corporation: One corporation under God, indivisible, with liberty and justice for all directors and major stockholders. . . .

Seven Wildcat Foundations

Thus far Patman dealt with the foundations in their generality. In the second and third parts of his report, which ran to 872 large pages, he concentrated on seven foundations with a view to showing just how freely foundations could operate under existing laws and regulations.

In the second part he dealt with the David, Josephine and Winfield Baird Foundation ($10.2 million), the Winfield Baird Foundation ($17.4 million) and the Lansing Foundation ($779,546), all established by David G. Baird of Baird and Company, member of the New York Stock Exchange; the Jessie Smith Noyes Foundation, established by Charles F. Noyes, a New York real estate broker; the Lawrence A. Wien Foundation and the Harry B. Helmsley Foundation.

The third part was devoted entirely to The Nemours Foundation and the originating Alfred I. du Pont Estate of Jacksonville, Florida.

As commentaries around the country showed, Mr. Patman at this stage had made a deep if fleeting impression.

The report revealed that the Baird foundations engaged in just about everything conceivable in the way of loose practice. They had trustees and directors who were employees of Baird and Company or relatives and friends of Mr. Baird, "mere figureheads." All were "subservient" to him. "The abuse of public privileges" by the Baird foundations recalled findings in 1948 about three trusts established by Textron, Inc., under Royal Little, which were held by the Senate Commerce Committee to exist "for purposes of tax avoidance and providing risk capital to Textron, thereby giving Textron an unfair advantage over the orthodox manufacturer." One of the Baird foundations was involved, as it happened, with Textron.

Patman detailed a number of exact similarities between the Textron operation and the Baird foundations. From very small beginnings in the 1930's and 1940's both groups grew to large size.

The Textron foundations consisted of the M.I.T. Trust, the Rhode Island Charities Trust and the Rayon Trust.

Said the Patman report:[34]

The M.I.T. Trust, created in 1937 with assets of $500, had earned almost $1 million net by October 1948. Its beneficiary, the Massachusetts Institute of Technology, had not received any contributions.

The Rhode Island Charities Trust, created in 1937 with assets of $500, earned $4.5 million by September 1948. The Providence Rhode Island Community Chest, the sole beneficiary, had received only $85,000 contributions. The bank handling the investments and the trustees, however, had received over $140,000 during the same period.

The Rayon Foundation, created in 1944 with assets of $100, earned $750,000 by October 1948. The Rhode Island School for Design, the sole beneficiary, received only $75,000 in contributions.

All of this was tax exempt.

Benefits accruing to Mr. Baird and associates were set forth as follows:

1. Substantial commissions for Baird and Company were generated by large and continuous securities transactions of the Baird foundations.

2. The foundations received contributions from others which should have been treated, and taxed, as income to Mr. Baird for services he rendered to the "donors," or at least as income of the foundations rather than as tax-free increments to their capital funds.

3. Loans were made to business associates of Mr. Baird "for purposes of swinging deals."

4. The foundation funds were freely used to "prop up" a series of Baird-dominated companies, companies controlled by the Baird foundations and companies in which Mr. Baird was a director or stockholder.[35]

All of this had gone on for at least twelve years without any intervention from the Treasury Department. There is little "interference" by government with business conducted by foundations, as Patman showed conclusively.

The records of the Baird foundation "prove beyond doubt that these organizations have operated as multi-million-dollar, tax-free securities dealers—dispensing millions of dollars of credit to prominent businessmen-customers."[36]

". . . no less than 70 persons and companies used the Baird Foundations as securities dealers and/or uncontrolled lenders for securities purchases."[37]

Inter-dealings of the Baird foundations with similar foundations were frequent.

The significance of such sources of unregulated credit is that fiscal authorities have no way of preventing the credit, under existing law, from entering into wild speculative sprees that terminate in crises like the stock-market collapse of 1962. While nominally facets of capitalism, such operations in fact undermine formal capitalism at its very wellspring. These operators, despite protestations, have no more piety toward capitalism than a Lenin or Trotsky. They appear as no more than pecuniary anarchists.

The Patman report, in many pages and exhibits, details many of these deals.

"The records of the Baird Foundations have been kept in a state of total disarray, indicating a shocking disregard of the most elementary accounting principles. The Foundations' books have never been audited by independent accountants, and numerous discrepancies are evident in the accounts. . . ."[38]

These foundations accumulated income at a great rate, failing to live up to charitable pretensions and, over a period of ten years, carried on "log-rolling" of assets among each other and with foundations established by business associates. According to the tax returns of the Baird foundations, they paid out $28,476,567 in contributions, gifts, grants, scholarships and the like for the decade through 1960. But about half of this sum represented solely "wash" transfers to each other and to nine other foundations owned by business associates![39] Not a vestige of public charity was involved in such transfers.

According to the Patman findings, the foundations made unsecured loans to friends, failed to report stock ownerships as required by law, engaged in purchases and lease-back transactions that should have been taxable, made loans at "usurious" rates, collected fees in the form of "contributions," accepted gifts from business associates of Mr. Baird, engaged in unlicensed private banking, etc.

On the basis of an avalanche of these and other alleged abuses it is difficult to characterize the operations of the Baird foundations. They appear to have been carried on without imaginative limitation as though no government or laws existed, as though they were infinitely privileged.

While the Baird foundations, like many others, are not individually of great size in the foundation world, the Patman analysis of their operations showed what *any* foundation can do if it likes under the existing law and regulations. The sky is literally the limit on foundation operations.

Broadly similar states of affairs were shown to exist with respect to the Jessie Smith Noyes Foundation, the Lawrence A. Wien Foundation and the Harry B. Helmsley Foundation.[40] The last two, with participations in the Empire State Building, were in many deals with the Baird foundations.

With respect to The Nemours Foundation, the Patman inquiry traced the building up of a huge foundation fund over the years on the basis of property left by Alfred I. du Pont, who died in 1935.

"Laid bare here for the first time," said the report somewhat melodramatically, "is the detailed anatomy of one of America's great fortunes—a fortune that will one day slip away forever from the payment of any income taxes."[41]

This Du Pont estate, only one among many, and The Nemours Foundation were not included in the prior reports.

[The Du Pont estate] has been used to build up an extraordinary economic empire controlling wide banking, industrial, railroad and real estate interests. These interests center in the State of Florida, but they also spread into many other states.

The fortune represented by the Du Pont Estate was worth no less than

$292,720,413 at the end of 1962, according to reports received from The Nemours Foundation. By way of comparison, the Estate was valued at $39,374,-845.38 on April 29, 1935, based on an appraiser's valuations.

According to the Du Pont Estate's Federal income tax returns, it had total income of $74,392,126.47 in the 12 years 1951 through 1962, including dividend income of $72,885,402.93. In the year 1962 alone, the Estate received total income of $8,196,244.50, including dividend income of $8,038,636.14.

Most of the Du Pont Estate's income down through the years has been paid out as annuities of certain beneficiaries. These annuities are taxable income to the taxpaying beneficiaries, subject to Federal and State income tax. After the death of the annuitants, their portion of the Estate's disbursements will go to the tax exempt Nemours Foundation. Thus all income from the Du Pont Estate's vast fortune will in time escape Federal and State income taxes entirely.[42]

Nor will the fortune pay any estate tax.

Taxable distributions to beneficiaries in twelve years exceeded $67 million, with $7,597,675.25 distributed in 1962 alone. Of this last, $6,633,-482.22 went to Jessie Ball du Pont, widow of Alfred I., $877, 293.03 (non-taxable) to The Nemours Foundation and the balance, all taxable, to eighteen members of the Du Pont clan.[43]

At the time of the inquiry Mrs. Alfred I. du Pont was eighty years old, living in comfortable hothouse retirement on the social security funds provided by her husband after a life constructively spent in the harvesting of vast hereditary revenues.

Upon the death of the beneficiaries the estate will pass, tax free, to The Nemours Foundation. "Once again," according to the Patman report, "the 'cream' of one of our Nation's great fortunes will go completely tax free. Once again, the 'skim milk' incomes of the hardworking majority of the American people will be forced to bear a still heavier share of the total tax burden."[44]

The major assets of the estate were found to be as follows:

1.   Direct ownership of 44 per cent to 87.5 per cent of thirty banks in the "Florida National" group of banks, indirect ownership in the thirty-first and control in all cases. These banks held 11 per cent of all bank deposits in Florida. The trust department of the Jacksonville bank alone had assets of well over a billion dollars, thus exercising far-reaching corporate influence.

2.   Direct ownership of 75.01 per cent of the common stock of the St. Joe Paper Company of Jacksonville worth $35,515,148. This company in turn owned a million acres of woodlands, the Apalachicola Northern Railroad, the St. Joseph Telephone and Telegraph Company and 52 per cent

of the common stock of the $90-million Florida East Coast Railway as well as other securities of this enterprise.

3. Direct ownership of 764,280 shares of E. I. du Pont de Nemours and Company worth $198 million on February 25, 1964.

4. Direct ownership of 444,618 shares of General Motors common with a value on the same date of more than $35 million.

5. Direct ownership of numerous parcels of real estate including the estate of "Nemours" in New Castle County, Delaware. A standard guide-book to Delaware in the *American Guide Series,* 1955, Hastings House, N.Y., publishers, describes it as follows: [45]

"On the 300-acre property there are the chateau of Nemours itself, a carillon tower, and the several hospital buildings of Nemours Foundation. . . . The residence of Nemours, built in 1908, is of formal French chateau style throughout, the exterior finished in Indiana limestone. . . . The colonnade, grand basin, fountains and statuary, pool and water courses, urns and lawns, all suggest the Garden of Versailles. . . . The front terrace is flanked by two white marble sphinxes formerly at the Chateau de Sceaux (in France). . . . Behind the sunken gardens, on an eminence, stands a classic 'temple of love.' "

The three trustees are self-perpetuating. When one dies the surviving trustees select a new one. The corporate trustee may be changed at any time by the individual trustees.

What, now, is all this wealth destined to accomplish by way of beneficence?

Quoting the will, the Patman report relates that it is first to maintain the out-of-the-way mansion at Nemours "mainly for the purpose of providing a library and exhibiting to the public interesting and valuable literature, works of art and any articles of historic and artistic interest for the advancement of education" and to maintain the mansion, grounds and gardens of Nemours "for the pleasure and benefit of the public." Next, on the grounds at a "proper distance from the Mansion House" a charitable institution is to be maintained "for the care and treatment of crippled children, but not of incurables, or the care of old men or old women, and particularly old couples," with first consideration to residents of Delaware. Finally, any surplus income "may from time to time" be given to "other worthy charitable institutions" for the care of crippled children, old men, old women, old couples, with Delawarians preferred.

The other two big Du Pont foundations, Longwood and Winterthur, are similarly established primarily in order to enable the public to visit foundation-maintained former Du Pont mansions and grounds, there to contemplate the splendor in which past Du Ponts lived in the heyday of the munitions trust. The Du Ponts themselves, as *Fortune* has observed, prefer to look upon themselves as "Armorers to the Republic," suppliers of the weapons, one concludes, with which the sturdy, God-fearing American yeomanry goes abroad and faces the myriad black-hearted rascals of the world to establish freedom, super-markets, hamburger stands, filling stations and, presumably, 100 per cent American slums.

Wells of Patronage

Two main areas of interest to observers and critics of the foundations are evident. In addition to their corporate holdings and investment operations, neglected by most inquirers, the second area of interest is the disposition of the funds they disburse in grants: their patronage. Not all funds disbursed by all foundations, as we have seen, go into what would be called beneficence by any standard. Some are simply paid over to other foundations for the profit of donors.

Let us attend now to what is claimed to be constructive outlay—at least by the formally reputable foundations. Here we find a somewhat larger literature, featured most recently by a briskly readable study of the Ford Foundation by Dwight Macdonald.[46]

Although he presented a most perceptive guide to the fund-dispensing activities and public-relations tribulations of the Ford Foundation, Mr. Macdonald showed little or no interest in it as a financial control-center. But for information about how it conducts itself in the matter of payouts, his book is indispensable (although now in need of supplementation on later history).

On one of his generalizations about foundations, the weight of available evidence is strongly against the conclusion he sets forth. Commenting somewhat cavalierly on the late Dr. Eduard C. Lindeman's *Wealth and Culture*, Harcourt Brace and Company, N.Y., 1936, Macdonald characterizes it as "a muck-raking survey, from a conventional-liberal point of view, that is now outdated as to many of its specific complaints (as, that philanthropists are arrogant and secretive) but which is still to the point in more general criticisms (as, that business types are over-represented on foundations boards and intellectuals represented hardly at all)."[47]

On this disputed point Lindeman was clearly right and Macdonald wrong, as Patman's findings subsequently showed in monumental detail. As to arrogance, perhaps it was as Macdonald said about the philanthropoids, a term for the fund-dispensing executives coined by one of them as distinct from my term of *philanthropols* for the financiers who establish and supervise the investment portfolios. *Philanthropols* are merely an ultra-sophisticated version of *finpols*. But Macdonald studied only one foundation in detail and he was obviously, as alert public relations would dictate, accorded the red-carpet treatment suitable under such circumstances to a sharp and frank critic with a commission from a widely read magazine. Any display of arrogance under the circumstances would have been self-defeating.

Concerning arrogance and secrecy on the part of foundations in general, Patman reports that he had difficulty getting information on almost every hand. Records provided by many foundations, when they were provided at all, were illegible, incomplete, lacking in required identifications of securities, personalities and other details, did not distinguish between income and principal, meandered from one accounting system to another and were generally obscure and misleading.[48] In many instances, repeated letters and subpoenas had to be issued to get required information.[49] The net effect of much foundation activity purporting to comply with requests for clarifying information was concealment.

Obtaining the information from the foundations has been a struggle [said the Patman report]. In many cases, it has taken four or five letters and a reminder of the committee's subpena power to obtain the information needed for this study. Many foundations have taken from 30 to 60 days to reply to a letter. We have been compelled to issue subpenas to 17 of them who failed to furnish information requested. These 17 foundations had been given ample opportunity to furnish the information voluntarily—in many instances, several months. In the case of the five members of the Ford family of Detroit, the Pew Memorial Trust of Philadelphia, and the Allen-Bradley Foundation of Milwaukee, the committee first asked for the information in October 1961. When followup letters did not produce the documents and data, we issued subpenas in February and March of 1962.

The attitudes of far too many of the foundations under study suggest an unmatched arrogance and contempt for the Congress and the people whom we represent. They appear to have adopted the attitude that tax exemption is their birthright—rather than a privilege granted to them by the people, through the Congress, for a public purpose.

The reluctance to cooperate takes many forms. Some only furnished information under subpena, demonstrating something less than a charitable attitude toward public knowledge and democratic processes. Others have sent us incomplete, or partially or wholly illegible, documents. Frequently, principal officers seemed to be in Europe when our letters arrived, leaving no one in the office with access to the records.[50]

Perhaps what looks like it to the observer is not really arrogance but a genuine misunderstanding by adverse parties of the nature of political reality. Mr. Patman, like many others, appears to believe that the United States government is a supreme entity. But many persons of wealth, on the basis of their entire life experience, have developed the notion that it is they who are supreme; they believe this because of the many instances in their own experience when they have seen their will become either law or public policy. The Ford fortune and others like it will outlast Patman and *pubpols*—reason enough to foster some feeling of greater durability in the possessors. Patmans come and go; Rockefellers, Fords, Du Ponts, Mellons and others roll on seemingly forever under the laws of inheritance and congressionally dispensed tax loopholes. Which is permanent and which transitory, which is substance and which shadow?

When challenged by a man like Patman the objects no doubt feel no more than the amused contempt of a French grand duke of the time of Louis XIV when accosted by a peasant or a minor official: "Is the man mad?" The challenge is something to be brushed aside, treated lightly, courteously ignored.

But although the Baronage is powerful, individually and collectively, it cannot win every encounter with the officers of the Crown. And on rare full-dress showdowns, which the Barons usually try to avoid, the Crown will always win. This will be true whether the Barons secretly control or influence the mercurial Crown or not.

The Fords, as relative latecomers to the realms of higher *finpolity,* apparently still need to learn the lesson long ago absorbed by the Rockefellers, Du Ponts, Mellons and a few others: No flexing of muscles in public, thus provoking invidious attention. Henry Ford II is much given to doing just this, issuing peremptory statements on public policy (usually opposing reforms) as though he were an elected official or an obscure citizen in a saloon. Although thus far he has aroused only desultory interest, he may some day find himself in hot water by touching some hidden public nerve.

Not only did many foundations, including some of those belonging to the Fords, *seem* arrogant by *seeming* to attempt evasion of the Patman inquiries but some, after field audits by the Treasury had disclosed irregularities, returned at once to the irregular practices.[51] In doing this they certainly showed overweening arrogance and contempt of government. And, in general, I believe they are justified in feeling contempt for the *pubpols,* a sorry crew.

The unwilling objects of Patman's scrutiny in the upshot had this edge on him: The newspapers, even the *New York Times,* did not give him the opulent coverage his findings seemed to merit sociologically. A news editor could with good conscience play down and bury these reports as overly complicated for a culturally benighted readership. Again, the Patman reports were confusing to many simple-minded readers because, owing to the public-relations image developed by the foundations over the years as whited sepulchres, the Patman reports no doubt seemed to many worthy souls like aspersions upon motherhood. For many readers the Patman conclusions about such entities as the Ford and Rockefeller foundations no doubt, somehow, connoted headlines like: *Motherhood Scored. Congressman Recommends Its Abolition.* Indeed, Patman later was written about (as in the Luce publications) as a kooky, highly intelligent and informed, well-intentioned maverick in a china shop, perhaps not to be taken too seriously.

One need not rely on Patman and Lindeman alone, with Macdonald dissenting, for a glimpse of secrecy in foundation operations. The *Foundation Directory* reports difficulty in gathering data over the years from foundations, many of which in past years have failed to disclose their existence even to Russell Sage, their friend and associate. Thus the latest directory notes that the 1939 directory was able to list only 243 noteworthy foundations, whereas the 1960 directory, using data made available by the Treasury since 1950, shows that 600 noteworthy foundations had been in existence through 1939. As the *Foundation Directory* bleakly observes, "the records before 1950 are grossly inadequate."[52]

Foundations, although ostensibly not involved in politics or money-making, are curiously anxious about their public image. We know this because some big ones have used their tax-exempt revenues (in which the government—that is, the general populace—paid 91 per cent of the bill) to hire public relations counselors. From 1952 through 1961 the Ford Foundation had the public relations firms of Newmyer Associates, Inc., and Carl Byoir and Associates, Inc., on the payroll for $172,583.80 in all. From 1955 through 1960 the Howard Hughes Medical Institute paid Carl Byoir and Associates $46,417.55; and the Hughes Aircraft Company, reciprocally associated with the Medical Institute, paid Byoir from 1956 through 1962 a fee of $166,666.66 and expense money of $545,773.69.[53] As foundations professedly have nothing to sell, this is strange.

Let us say a foundation is doing 100 per cent good but the public misunderstands, believes it is really doing harm. If an investigation would show it is really doing only good by catering to the lame, the halt, the blind and the diseased, what difference does it make what the ill-informed public thinks?

Influencing public opinion with tax-free money in favor of a foundation can only have the purpose of warding off investigation. It can only have the effect of suggesting: Don't investigate that perfectly good institution. But if it is as good as it claims to be, what objection can there be to investigation?

The objection can stem only from a desire to conceal the functioning of a link in the *finpolitan* chain of politico-economic control. Or so I conclude. Nobody in possession of his senses can possibly object to anything the foundations do if it is truly philanthropic and charitable. Nobody can object to the disinterested scattering around of blessed money.

As to the large number of corporation-controlled foundations that have sprung up in recent years, the *Foundation Directory* says the following about their purposes:

"A wave of foundations of a new type has crested in the past decade. The 'company-sponsored' foundations are tax exempt, nonprofit legal entities . . . with trustee boards consisting wholly or principally of corporation officers and directors . . . their programs are likely to be confined to communities in which they have offices, and to center upon philanthropic agencies that benefit the corporation, its employees, its stockholders or its business relationships."[54] They are, otherwise put, like other foundations.

Constituting 28 per cent of 5,050 leading foundations, the straight-out corporate foundations had total assets of $1.177 billion in 1962. Their annual receipts were $201,444,000 and their grants $142,694,000. The flow-through of heavy annual receipts made them, in the characterization of the *Directory*, "conduits."[55]

Foundations in their Protean potentiality have also been found to provide good "cover" for the activities of the Central Intelligence Agency, whose sensitive fingers are in many pies, long ears at many doors. Useful to the *finpols* in their operations, they have been found useful, too, to the *pubpols* in international espionage and possibly, too, in domestic surveillance of non-communist heretics and offbeat thinkers. Secret dossiers abound in the land of the free.

According to an intensive review of CIA activities by the *New York Times* in 1966, "The CIA is said to be behind the efforts of several foundations that sponsor the travel of social scientists in the Communist world. . . . Congressional investigation of the tax-exempt foundations in 1964 showed that the J. M. Kaplan Fund, Inc., among others, had disbursed at least $400,000 for the CIA in a single year to a research institute. This institute, in turn, financed research centers in Latin America that drew other support from the Agency for International Development (the United States foreign aid agency), the Ford Foundation and such universities as Harvard and Brandeis.

"Among the Kaplan Fund's other previous contributors there had been eight funds or foundations unknown to experts on tax-exempt charitable organizations. Five of them were not even listed on the Internal Revenue Service's list of foundations entitled to tax exemption."[56]

Publishers of the *Foundation Directory* informed the *Times* they had no knowledge of the eight associated foundations: the Gotham Foundation, the Michigan Fund of Detroit, the Andrew Hamilton Fund of Philadelphia, the Borden Trust, the Price Fund, the Edsel Fund, the Beacon Fund and the Kentfield Fund."[57] These were presumably pure cloak-and-dagger outfits. Later there were more disclosures of cloak-and-dagger CIA operations by "reputable" and fraudulent foundations with respect to student and labor-union activities abroad.

Foundation Channels

To what channels do foundations allocate grants?

According to the *Foundation Directory,* grants of $10,000 each or more were given in 1961 and 1962 to the following broad fields:[58]

Fields	1961			1962		
	Grants	Amount (millions)	Per Cent	Grants	Amount (millions)	Per Cent
Education	614	$107	31	563	$145	46
International Activities	448	62	17	418	52	17
Sciences	210	37	11	320	45	14
Health	313	68	19	238	32	10
Welfare	417	43	12	268	20	6
Humanities	120	25	7	123	16	5
Religion	98	9	3	53	5	2
	2,220	$351	100	1,983	$315	100

Total annual grants by 6,007 foundations in 1961–62 came to $779,475,-000, so that the above total represents only about half the "flow of funds."[59] It is evident, therefore, that not all disbursements are statistically accounted for in the murky world of foundation activity. More recently total annual disbursements have exceeded $1 billion.

As to breakdowns, most of these grants are to existing institutions, few to individuals. In "religion," for example, 84 per cent of the grants went for theological seminaries, church and temple support, buildings and equipment and religious welfare agencies. Buddha, Jesus or Mohammed might be hard put to find the specific religious element in the recipients of the grants.[60] In the humanities 37 per cent went to museums.[61] Grants for education and science went, as was to be expected, largely to institutions.

It has been theorized by philanthropoids that the private foundations have a special role to play in financing constructive activities to ease the travail of a society in the course of change and to provide necessary special improvements. But as Dwight Macdonald notes, they only serve at best to lubricate existing machinery.[62] He here concurs with many earlier observers.

What happens when a foundation attempts to stray from the straight and narrow path of middle-road conformity was shown when the Ford Foundation in the early 1950's emerged on the national scene under the presidency of Paul Hoffman, former president of the Studebaker Corporation and original Marshall Plan administrator. Hoffman, coaxed into the job by Henry Ford II, selected a nonstodgy team of assistants, including the sharp-witted, outspoken Robert M. Hutchins; and the foundation was charted on a course not only more extensive but somewhat more imaginative than those of the established foundations.

Almost from the beginning there was trouble, to the dismay of Henry Ford II, who merely wanted to flood the roads with millions of cars, thus contributing to the world traffic jam, and to put the foundation money to the seemingly most constructive moderate use.

The opening gun in the trouble was fired in 1951 by the anti-Ford *Chicago Tribune* with a pseudo-news story under the headline: LEFTIST SLANT BEGINS TO SHOW IN FORD TRUST. This bias, the *Tribune* argued, showed in the presence of Hoffman, who as head of the governmental Marshall Plan had "given away ten billion dollars to foreign countries"; of Dr. Reinhold Niebuhr, distinguished professor of Applied Christianity at Union Theological Seminary, who had "pinko tieups"; of Supreme Court Justice Owen J. Roberts, "a world government advocate"; and of Frank Altschul, "a Roosevelt Republican and retired international banker." In the *Tribune* lexicon anything international borders on high treason; and "international banker" has the same connotation, for those who read below the belt, as the Nazi use of the term.

Although this newspaper is hard for some people to understand, the *Tribune* model of patriotic uprightness is really very simple. It is Mark Hanna, who not only was William McKinley's political mentor but was related by marriage to the *Tribune's* McCormick family. Anything in American history that deviates in the slightest from the brass-tacks, nononsense, cash-on-the-barrelhead Mark Hanna model is suspect to this paper's publishers, accounting for the fact that long before Hanna appeared it waged its own McCarthyite campaign of vilification against Abraham Lincoln. It has never hesitated to replay this campaign against any morally aspiring person or movement. The bare implication, whether from the left, right or center, that there is anything about American life that can stand elevation or modification is enough to send the *Tribune* and its sister *New York Daily News* into tantrums of ecstatic editorial rage.

It was at once apparent that the *Tribune* by its enterprise had touched a rich vein. For instantly a coven of Hearst columnists, abetted by radio commentator Fulton Lewis, Jr., and others, moved into the arena, which they filled with their lurid phrasomania for several years. Lewis opined that because "Many books and various studies have been financed by tax-free grants from these foundations. . . . In effect, the American people are paying more taxes to finance so-called scholars who work diligently to beat out our brains and change our traditional way of life into something more Socialistic." George Sokolsky mused: "Henry Ford . . . made nearly all his money in this country, but Paul Hoffman, who is spending that money, seems to prefer to pour it into remote bottomless pits and to expend it for meaningless purposes, such as an investigation as to why the world is full of refugees, when, as a matter of fact, it always has been. . . . Why cannot some of the money the Ford Foundation is piddling away on trivia be used constructively for the saving of opera?"

Westbrook Pegler fulminated fantastically, calling Hoffman "a hoax without rival in the history of mankind." He took a hard bloodshot look at the eight other trustees of the period. Four, including two Fords and the dean of the Harvard Business School, seemed "sound enough," he said, but "the best that can be said of the political wisdom of the others is that they are flighty." These others included a former chairman of Standard Oil of New Jersey and a former president of General Electric.

The Ford funds, Pegler held, "are in reckless hands. . . . That is the way queer international things get going." Later, under the headline FORD FOUNDATION IS FRONT FOR DANGEROUS COMMUNISTS, he misinformed that Associate Director Milton Katz, professor at the Harvard Law School, was "a Frankfurter man of the same group that insinuated dangerous Communists into our government" and noted a "connection" between the Foundation and President Eisenhower, Henry (China Boy) Luce and "the Marshall Plan squanderbund." "I find it beyond my ability at the moment to establish the master plan of these strange associations and activities," Pegler madly wrote. "I will continue, however, to offer you verified facts and my best efforts at interpretations."

Later, traitors all around, he enlarged: "There is a very important and sinister political mystery concealed in the mixed activities of the Ford

Foundation under Paul Hoffman and Robert Hutchins, the *Time-Life* propaganda empire of Henry Luce, and the political works of William Benton, the Social-Democratic Senator from Connecticut."

No facts were offered to sustain these gaseous charges, which eventually led to a dazed Henry Ford II being shrilly accused by a distraught woman at a social gathering of being a Communist.[63] This was much like charging Andrei Gromyko with being a secret director of Standard Oil.

Nevertheless, the uproar—sustained by advertising-hungry publishers—has provided the background noise for three congressional investigations of the foundations since World War II. The first two, as Macdonald observes, were inspired by intra-party political animus. There was, too, obvious non-party economic animus in the Patman inquiry of the 1960's. But the fact that the investigations sprang out of political animosity provides no reason to ignore whatever they produced in the way of fact and insight.

As Macdonald sees the first two investigations, correctly I believe, both were merely episodes in Republican factional politics.[64] It was disappointed Taft Republicans, disgruntled at the Eisenhower capture of the Republican nomination, who were active behind the scenes in both early investigations in their own variation and fugue on the Joe McCarthy smear tactics.

The first investigation was directed by a House committee under the chairmanship of the late Eugene Cox, Georgia Democrat who was responsive to the general McCarthyite view of extreme Taftists. However, "the strategy misfired, because the Democratic leaders, who were still in control of the House, boxed in the impeccably Americanistic chairman with less dedicated colleagues."[65]

Because the committee members went about the investigation in a matter-of-fact way, the final report cleared the foundations of being infiltrated by Communists, of recommending socialism, of weakening, undermining or discrediting the entirely laudable system of American free enterprise. It cleared them too of the suspicions that moneys they spent abroad were devoted to purposes less than praiseworthy. The hearings even led rock-ribbed Chairman Cox to say he had undergone "some change of heart."

One member of the committee, however, remained discontented. This was the late Representative Brazilla Carroll Reece, of Tennessee, former chairman of the Republican National Committee, who at once demanded a new investigation. Reece has been one of Taft's campaign managers "and so was especially disappointed by the Cox Committee's failure to 'get' the Fords' and the Rockefellers' foundations."[66] The Fords and Rockefellers, along with other leading elements of wealth, had in 1952 supported the bewildered Eisenhower, the only sure winner owing to his public standing as a war hero, the mighty conqueror no less (by grace of public relations techniques) of the baleful and infinitely resourceful German General Staff.

Reece got his investigation in 1953 and 1954, conducting it along murky McCarthyite lines. The premise, as stated by Reece, was that "there is evidence to show there is a diabolical conspiracy back of all this. Its aim is the furtherance of Socialism in the United States." The Ford Foundation, he held, was the main offender in undermining a free market, working in concert with such subversive organizations as the Advertising Council, Republic Steel, General Motors and Standard Oil of California.

The hearings and the final report, all expertly reported by Macdonald, were a confetti of nonsense. And they were assailed as such by the corporate newspapers, ten to one.[67]

Prior to the Reece investigation, a Gallup poll showed 63 per cent of sturdy grass-roots Americans had never heard of the Ford Foundation, 13 per cent were indifferent to it, 23 per cent favored it and 1 per cent were hostile. After the frenzied hearings another Gallup poll showed 60 per cent had never heard of it (the power of the press!), 11 per cent had no opinion, 27 per cent were favorable and 2 per cent were hostile. Of Republicans queried, 46 per cent had heard of the foundation; only 35 per cent of the less literate Democrats had ever heard of it!

When Patman began his inquiry in 1961–62 he was seemingly entering a thoroughly ploughed field. The attention of his committee, however, was turned in a different direction. The Cox investigation, which ran to great length and heard from officials of most leading foundations, was largely limited to the question of ideological purity and the nature of fund grants. The Patman inquiry concentrated on the investment maneuvers and policies of the foundations, turning up some of the strange monsters of the financial deep we have scrutinized.

Patman's inquiry was also obviously fueled by animus. As Macdonald points out, all public investigations of the foundations have been unfriendly, critical in various degrees, from different points of view. The Walsh investigation of 1915 was directed from a Populist or native-leftist, quasi-socialist point of view, and socialists, communists and leftist liberals have always been more or less critical of the foundations as instruments of an ascendant, vulpine capitalism. But the more recent investigations, Patman's included, have been oriented from a rightist, small-business point of view, a fact that brings into focus a revelatory perspective on contemporary American politics.

That Congressman Patman did not develop the whole foundation story is vouched for by *The Nation* of December 4, 1967. Patman, although very close politically to their sponsors, did not delve into a variety of Texas foundations, the owners of which feel rivalrous toward the "Eastern Establishment" and their foundations.

According to *The Nation*, the Brown Foundation, Inc., of Houston, established by the late Herman Brown and brother George R. Brown of the big government contractors, Brown and Root, channeled money into at least one Central Intelligence Agency conduit foundation and into at least one organization partly supported by the CIA. Brown and Root, incidentally, is politically close to President Johnson.

In 1963 the Brown Foundation gave $150,000 to the Vernon Fund and in 1964 it gave $100,000, these being the latest available figures. It gave $50,000 in 1963 to the American Friends of the Middle East and $150,-000 in 1964. By no kind of elastic interpretation can these donations be regarded as in the cause of sweet charity.

There are now at least seven CIA-conduit foundations known to be operating in oil-lush Texas; the others are the San Jacinto Foundation, the Marshall Foundation, the Anderson Foundation, the Hoblitzelle Foundation, the Jones-O'Donnell Foundation and the Hobby Foundation. The latter was set up by Oveta Culp Hobby, former Secretary of Health, Education and Welfare under Eisenhower, and by her son William Hobby, Jr., executive editor of the *Houston Post*. Both Hobbys are close to President Johnson.

"In the eight months that have elapsed since the CIA was discovered to have polluted the world of the foundations," said *The Nation*, "neither the IRS nor Patman has shown any interest in discovering just how deeply the spies have penetrated the supposedly charitable organizations. Patman's investigations into charity, like charity itself, should begin at home. He might even tell us what good works have been supported lately by the Lyndon Johnson Foundation, established a few years ago by the President."

Political Perspectives

It is customary in the public prints, as part of the lofty centrist stance, to portray rightists and leftists as crackpots of various degrees. For how could anything possibly be wrong with the ineffably beautiful *status quo*? McCarthy and Reece were, it is true, both crackpots in that they had a fantastic, paranoid vision of reality. Leftists succumb to the same malady when they see capitalism as the quintessence and autonomously unique source of personal and institutionalized evil. Was Stalin a capitalist?

Crackpottism is most clearly revealed in methods pursued, which in the case of both sides at the extremes boil down to inciting to riot and civil disorder. Whatever within ideological limits will bring about this eventual result is pressed into service. For neither political extreme has the least chance of success without a breakdown of order—spontaneous or induced. Political extremism in all cases—in Russia and China, in Germany and Italy—gained the ascendancy during genuine, war-induced breakdowns. In Spain in 1936 the breakdown was induced by a contrived military uprising.

But this freehanded, irascible labeling of leftists and rightists as crackpots obscures the incontestable fact that both groups are respectively irked by something. In some way a shoe is pinching their adherents. While crackpottism often stems from or is reinforced by purely subjective disorders, objective factors must be present to make it plausible to large numbers of people. Crazy though Hitler undoubtedly was, something was patently askew in Germany and Europe when he rose to power. There may, too, behind a bland exterior (a fact often overlooked), be crackpottism at the center—a moderate, reassuring, tranquilizing crackpottism that bids man accept everything as he finds it, as though heaven-sent. A strong argument could be developed that there is at least as much crackpottism at the center as on either the right or the left—the crackpottism of paralyzed navel-gazing inertia.

Patman, like his investigational predecessors left and right, was obviously deeply disturbed by something, and he plainly stated it. He was irked, on behalf of his major constituents, by the incontestable fact that Big Business with its various instrumentalities, including the foundations, was crowding small business to the wall. In standing up for historically doomed "small business," Patman was not speaking generally for what the ordinary person would consider especially small. For Patman's political underpinnings are found among Texas entrepreneurs of corporations with assets ranging up to $50 million. These latter-day economic individualists feel pressed by the bigger enterprises, in part because of the ducal tax exemptions and other political boons enjoyed by the giants. Furthermore, although the total assets of some of the so-called small corporations may seem large to the onlooker, the equity of the nominal owner is often darkly overshadowed by heavy issues of senior securities and bank loans. The nominal owner often clings to a slender stake in his enterprise.

Patman, in other words, approached the situation as a business analyst. He was a realistic even though unconscious participant in a late phase of what Karl Marx called "the class struggle," what our own James Madison termed "faction." He didn't make charges to hear himself talk, nor did he strive to stir an uproar for political revenge or to engender turbulence. He was after facts upon which to recommend concrete limiting legislation.

Patman was entirely successful, as we have seen, in his attempt to show one aspect of how big interests squeeze smaller interests. His effort fit snugly into the Marxist concept of class struggle which, contrary to vulgar supposition, does not alone pose big capitalists against workers or the poor. In the class struggle under capitalism, Marx pointed out, the capitalists themselves contrive each other's destruction. Some become bigger as others are crushed. In the impersonal process (and Marx went astray on this prediction) everybody is proletarianized except the big capitalists. Marx's error of anticipation stemmed from the fact that he failed to see the emergence with proliferating technology of a white-collar horde of corporate technicians and administrators, many of whom were to identify themselves psychologically, purely through physical association, with the upper owning classes. Nor did he see the emergence of new interstitial enterprises, late reverberations as it were of an earlier upthrusting industrialism.

Even though accelerated by two gigantic wars, developments under capitalism proceeded at a slower pace than Marx predicted. But, in a Marxian view, the phenomenon of small capitalists being squeezed by big capitalists in their adroit manipulation of the state apparatus (which is Patman's basic thesis) is an important readily verifiable facet of class struggle.

Is it morally justifiable to feel politically irked? This is obviously a foolish question. If one is irked one is irked, a psycho-physical fact. How one now behaves, rationally or otherwise, is determined by one's intellectual analysis and program for eliminating or avoiding felt difficulties. Marx in his recommended political program, visualizing the forcible overthrow of capitalism by factory workers, was far more of a visionary than in his theoretical analysis, which was an attempt to find broad intellectual sanction for remedial political action of a fundamental nature. And even in his political program calling for revolution, Marx was far less of a visionary than many subsequent self-styled Marxists, notably Lenin.

For the Marxist revolution, Marx very practically held, could take place only in a very advanced capitalist country, such as England, the United States or Germany. And when it took place, just about all of the people—now all proletarians—would favor it. The actual revolution would be a small affair, easily throwing the few surviving big owners out. All very simple. Remaining would be a smoothly running technical system with the profit motive removed, everybody happy.

What confuses many who are superficially informed is that what is represented as Marxist revolution has taken place only in backward agricultural countries such as Russia and China, in the wake of debilitating wars. Although these were indeed revolutions, and might well have recommended themselves as such to Marx, who was by temperament as well as conviction a bone-deep revolutionary, they were far from *Marxist* revolutions.

No Marxist revolution, violent or peaceful, has ever taken place anywhere. But certain processes within capitalism, some of which Marx first discerned, some of which he foresaw and some of which he neither discerned nor foresaw (such as the effectiveness of piecemeal reform in modifying many conditions), continued to hold sway, transforming capitalism into its many different national guises. On the basis of his premature observations Marx considered all reform a misleading hoax.

But in the concept of class struggle, even though all history is surely not (as he asserted) the history of class struggle, Marx achieved an intellectually fruitful insight. And what are seen as leftist and rightist deviations from centrism (which upholds the *status quo*) are clearly instances, however ineffective, of class struggle or at least class protest.

Whereas the earlier leftist movements in the United States from Populism through Socialism and on into Communism of the 1930's were ventures in class struggle or protest carried out at least nominally on behalf of lower elements of society, the more recent rightist movements are ventures in the same sort of struggle waged by and supposedly for persons who futilely (in the long run) resist being squeezed out of existence or into less lucrative positions. As Marx pointed out, when men feel cornered they often elect to fight.

While earlier Populists and other leftists waged their struggles, which produced a certain amount of mild increasingly diluted reform (though it did not arrest a large and spreading impoverishment among the unskilled), persons situated in society at the levels where contemporary rightists now find themselves did not feel stirred. This was no doubt because they still identified themselves with the Rockefellers, Carnegies, Du Ponts, Fords, Mellons *et al.* Soon, too, they would be ascending those blessed golden peaks! Soon, too, their address would be 1 Wall Street, their summer address Newport or Bar Harbor.

Under the impact of recent pressures, however, it has begun to dawn on many of them that their address is far more likely to be the bankruptcy court. Many have already been displaced from the middle class, sons of former corporation executives who cannot "make it," inheritors of deflated estates and others of the nouveau dispossessed.

Looking about, they have concluded that one of the causes of their difficulties is the variety of social legislation called into being in three decades under the pressure of concrete phenomena such as unemployment. This legislation has had the effect, among other things, of depriving small operators of much cheap, profitable labor. This, they conclude, is tantamount to socialism and the sponsors are in effect socialists or communists.

And the big corporations, instead of continuing to fight this rise of "socialism," have finally compromised with it. Wealthy persons such as Henry Ford II and the Rockefellers now accept the mild, often diluted New Deal reforms. The only very wealthy hereditary group that still appears to support openly rightist causes is the Pew family of Philadelphia. Many medium corporations, however, join the Pews.

The big corporations, with their greater productivity and reserves, have indeed more or less acquiesced in the process after the failure of their political struggle in the 1930's against it, when the big Du Ponts led heavy industry, the banks and the newspapers against the New Deal. The big corporations are easily able to meet the major demands of organized labor, thus avoiding trouble and a poor public image, by passing increased costs on to consumers in administered prices. Most of the state right-to-work laws, forbidding the union shop, are noticeably located in the less industrialized regions. Attempts to supersede these low-wage laws by a federal law that would facilitate unionization are desperately fought by small high-cost producers as the encroachment of soul-destroying socialism.

It isn't the big companies, by and large, or the foundations, that lead this latter-day fight against the unions. For the big entities have found it profitable to fall into step with the welfare-warfare state. It is the small, often rightist businessman who favors the anti-union laws. Many of the regulations that small-business elements find distasteful were in fact devised over the years and made into public policy by representatives of the wealthiest and most Republican interests.[68] They wanted to squelch the small, market-upsetting wildcat operators. Only big, stabilizing centrally controlled units were wanted.

Not only are the small operators annoyed that the big corporations pay better wages and no longer fight the unions but they are annoyed at the ease with which the big operators, with the many fringe benefits they offer, are able to hire the cream of available personnel. Left to the small employer are the misfits, the restless, the inefficient.

As the rightists generally put their case, the small businessman is being squeezed between Big Unions and Big Government (the latter imposing more and more New Dealish "socialist" rules and thereby strangling freedom to deal properly with employees and customers). All this regulation smacks of what rightists understand as regimented socialist society. In most of its versions the analysis is unrealistic because canons of middle-class respectability lead most rightists to overlook the fact that Big Corporations are implicated in the squeeze. But to say this would make them sound like old-time long-haired socialists, thus defacing their self-image of respectability.

Political realists like Patman, however, do not overlook this factor in the equation. Nor were the ill-behaved Republican rightists at the famous convention of 1964, when they hissed and booed Nelson A. Rockefeller, unaware that he represented a genuine, blandly powerful adverse interest. Rockefeller, as a "liberal" Republican—that is, one willing to accept the New Deal approach—had become anathema to Republican rightists, many of whom more recently denounced him as a socialist.

The small businessman, if he were to read the signs in a Marxist way, would see that he is being slowly expropriated. He should, according to Marxist prescription, join the Marxist ideologues in seeking the day of mass deliverance. As he is biased by his middle-class point of view, envisioning himself as a potential original Rockefeller, Du Pont, Mellon or Ford—like them finding salvation in an unregulated market and society—he will have nothing to do with the doctrinaire Marxists. He therefore, wishfully, analyzes the situation not as one of big enterprise versus small enterprise but as "New Deal socialism" versus free enterprise. He lives within an economic as well as political myth, fails to see that free enterprise itself has long since been superseded by corporate monopoly, leaving him uncomfortably in one of the remaining dead ends. He does not see that in the impersonal, at times slow, process of economic development he is marked for eventual destruction. He is expendable.

There is, alas, no place for him at 1 Wall Street—unless, perchance, he can inflame the masses with the demonic idea that Eisenhower, Henry Ford II and Nelson Rockefeller are secret card-carrying Communists. If he could get enough people to believe this, and to exert themselves appropriately, then perhaps the strait jacket of New Deal regulations and labor union contracts could be broken. With plenty of cheap labor again available, perhaps he could make a big low-tax profit, build up cash reserves and finally rent a palatial suite of offices at 1 Wall Street. Then all the people who laughed at him when he said he was going to be rich would change their tune. Then they would all see that he was, all along, really a superior fellow, sure to be a success, as good as Rockefeller or Carnegie and maybe even better. Then his wife or mistress would be particularly impressed as he circled his yacht and private island in his own jet plane after he took off for large conferences in Washington or Hong Kong.

But this crude fantasy, although firm in its lineaments, tends to vanish under the weight of heavy unequal taxes, rising labor costs, tightening New Dealish regulations, monopoly, high prices of materials and corporate automation. The outlook becomes darker as he looks across the way and sees one of the hundreds of plants of the Super-Cosmos Corporation churning out trainloads of goods in a profitable torrent. The Super-Cosmos parking lot is filled with the cars of union workers, who denounce him as a fink, a rascal, a Goldwater crackpot and his employees as incompetent, low-paid scabs. If not incipient socialism all this is surely something just as wicked.

Because the rightists have no program upon which to base a convincing mass appeal they are reduced to bringing forward whatever emotional irrelevancy they believe will gain them mass support. Thus they represent themselves as bone-crushing super-patriots, anti-internationalists, anti-foreigners, anti-Communists, anti-Socialists, anti-Semites, anti-atheists, anti-Negroes. They are anti-fluoridation of water, anti-vaccination and, indeed, against whatever is offensive to low-level mass pockets of folklore, superstition and misinformation.

It is in consequence of this kind of electorally necessary appeal that one finds in the rightist entourage such a variegated assortment of screwballs. But all movements when they promise the excitement of combat—left, right or center—have a similar appeal for the demented and half-demented. In time of war the center, for example, draws unfastidiously to its bosom every latent or overt votary of violence—sadists, xenophobes, paranoids, the suicidal. I put all this down because I don't want to be put into the position, generally taken by the left and the center, that there is something inherently deranged about the rightist position. Rightists, like other politicians, take people as they find them and try to bend them to their purposes. And all political positions—left, right and center—leave much out of account in their neat formulas.

If they were fully logical in their prescriptions for the Good Society, the rightists would call forthwith for the dissolution into their constituent parts of United States Steel, General Motors, Standard Oil of New Jersey, AT&T and the other big holding companies. They do not make such a demand because in fact they deeply venerate these enterprises, would themselves like to possess them, only wish that their own Calabash Oil and Swampwater Steel were similarly flourishing. As it is, when Standard Oil of New Jersey breathes a little more deeply than usual, Calabash Oil is suffocated.

Barring some extremely unusual set of developments, the center, the Establishment, seems likely to continue in its triumphant balancing act despite the noisome antics of the rightists. Little more than clamor seems likely to come from the political right, less even in the way of enforced minor adjustments than came from the reformist demands of the more numerous working masses. The center, the Establishment, with its corporations, foundations, trust funds and family holding companies, clearly rules the roost, whether under Truman, Eisenhower, Kennedy or Johnson. And there is a deep reason for this, which is that by the Law of Inertia the center is bound up in golden links with the Good, the Beautiful and the True. Truth, or at least the routine profession of truth, is solidly on the side of the *status quo*. All else is error. . . .

Critics and the Foundations

In their patterns of granting funds the foundations display their power in ways that appear most fascinating to casual observers. While most citizens appear to accept dutifully the verdict of the corporate press that foundations exist in an unalloyed good cause, there are many critics of foundation patronage—insiders and outsiders, friendly, unfriendly and temperately judicious. These worthies bring into view a little noticed but wryly instructive aspect of the foundation phenomenon.

The individual critic in Foundationland, whoever he is, is much like a tourist in the Soviet Union. Upon his return home he tells what he liked, what he disliked. Here was a modern laboratory, there an advanced clinic, in another place a special school for backward children and there was, of course, the resplendent Moscow subway system—all of this the tourist liked very much. On the other hand, what he saw of collective farms, country roads, new apartment houses, most stores and the Kremlin itself—these he disapproved. Still other things he had mixed feelings about, like the schools: too traditional and authoritarian but, on the other hand, very high standards and well equipped, teachers excellent.

And the judicious critic in Foundationland is like the tourist in the Soviet Union also in that whether or not he approves what he sees *this is the way it is and this is the way it is going to be*. In both cases his judgments, no matter how finely spun, count for naught. He is a cipher in a society of ciphers.

Naturally the managers of the foundations, like the managers of the Soviet Union, prefer that the observer like everything he sees. If not, it is nice that he finds something to endorse. But whether he likes everything or nothing, it is—general public-relations blarney apart—fundamentally of no concern to the managers *because this just happens to be part of their plantation*. And merely because one finds something on the tour that one likes does not imply, any more in Foundationland than in the Soviet Union, that the tourist and the higher-ups are enrolled in a common cause.

Visitors to big houses of the rich that have been thrown open to the public as museums show the same irrelevantly and futilely judicious attitude. They like the drawing rooms and the library—"Really magnificent, you know." But, unfortunately, "They certainly showed poor taste in the décor of the bedrooms. And the solid gold bath tubs are ridiculous." But whether the masters showed a lapse of taste in this or that matter or not, this is the way it was and no word of the visitors will change a bit of it.

Foundation Organization

Let us, in order to understand foundations better, leave off attempts to evaluate their distributive worth on a scale of zero to 100. Let us instead concede that they are perfect in their expenditures, thus bypassing an argument apparently as fruitless as the one about the Soviet Union. And let us now look to their organization.

At the top we find a board of trustees, all concededly doing only good. Among the Ford Foundation trustees we find Benson Ford and Henry Ford II and thirteen others of whom at least nine are surely from the world of *finpolity* and *pubpolity*. All of these are very able men; about this we need not dispute. But, except for the two Fords, all were selected . . . by the Fords. The Fords, though, were neither selected, elected, co-opted or chosen by public examination. Nobody at all asked them to assume these arduous philanthropic duties, for which it might seem they chose themselves.

But neither they (nor the Rockefellers, Du Ponts, Mellons and others) did even this, although this is what the Soviet managers did. For the Soviet managers, out of the kindness of their hearts, themselves chose to lead a disbelieving world to the Promised Land of Communism, where the lion shall lie down with the lamb, the unicorn shall shed his horn, the meek shall inherit the earth and the State shall wither away.

The Fords, like their peers, were chosen before birth for their roles, which are (oddly in a democratic, republican or merely parliamentary context) purely hereditary. They are hereditary oligarchic philanthropists!

It is, then, by hereditary right that all these concededly beneficent expenditures are made. If it is not all done in the pure spirit of sacrifice it is, we are repeatedly assured by the corporate press, very close to it. It amounts, simply, to *noblesse oblige*.

As there are far too many foundations, even large ones, to scrutinize here in any detail, our attention will be largely confined to a few, including the Ford Foundation.

Orientation of Patronage Grants

Those foundations that regularly make substantial payouts—and as we have noticed they altogether paid out only 50 per cent of income through the 1950s—are in philanthropoid jargon said to be "discipline-oriented" or "problem-oriented" or a little of both. They are also "friend-oriented," "company-oriented," "profit-oriented" and "market-oriented."

The discipline-oriented, like the Rockefeller group, mainly allocate money to institutions harnessed by intellectual disciplines—physical and social sciences, medicine and (much less so) the humanities. Except for the last, in the opinion of a leading philanthropoid (a very mentor of philanthropoids) these have been overstressed.[69] But heavily financed science (and perhaps this is pure coincidence) has thousands of profitable industrial applications of which the corporations have freely availed themselves. And medical advances are immediately available to the rich, much later if at all to the non-rich. There is little if any monetary profit in the humanities, however (perhaps only another coincidence).

The stress on science in American society has at least been reinforced if not originally invoked by the foundations, an obvious exhibition of power, and a scientist cited by Abraham Flexner believes it has been overstressed. The foundations, thus seen, are centers of self-serving hereditary power.

The Ford Foundation is problem-oriented. It is out to solve or at least make more manageable public problems of various kinds.

After the death of Henry Ford, the foundation, originally organized in 1936, began its larger operations on the basis of a Study Report.[70]

The report laid out five Program Areas, as follows:

I.   The Establishment of Peace. (Involving international programs; "peace" here, as Macdonald remarks, "means trying to make other nations more friendly to us and less to the Communists.")

II.   The Strengthening of Democracy (domestic civil liberties and politics).

III.   The Strengthening of the Economy.

IV.   Education in a Democratic Society. (As Macdonald remarks, the democratic society "is apparently ours.")

V.   Individual Behavior and Human Relations. (Macdonald believes this section could more accurately have been titled "Mass Behavior and Social Relations." The Ford Foundation, however, does not formally concede there are "masses" in "our democratic society.")

It was in the attempted implementation of this report that Paul Hoffman ran into the trouble with the rightists that led to his resignation two years later.

More recently the Ford Foundation has broken its problem areas down as follows: Education in the United States, Economic Development and Administration in the United States, Public Affairs, Humanities and the Arts, International Training and Research, Science and Engineering, International Affairs, Population and Overseas Development. These subdivisions in the voluminous annual reports are further subdivided into an astonishing array of grants for projects and individual scholarships and fellowships. The sun never sets on the works of the Ford Foundation.

So massive was the task of transferring its vast revenues found to be that the foundation early established and separately financed a number of independent sub-foundations, all under the guidance of philanthropoids: The Fund for the Advancement of Education, the Fund for Adult Education, The Fund for the Republic, Resources for the Future, various television entertainment-educational programs and its own special programs.[71]

While the entire original program of the foundation came indiscriminately under attack from rightists, The Fund for the Republic, presided over by the far from diplomatic Robert M. Hutchins, provoked their especial ire because it was established for the entirely laudable purpose of bringing about "the elimination of restrictions on freedom of thought, inquiry and expression in the United States, and the development of policies and procedure best adapted to protect these rights in the face of persistent international tension."

It aimed, quite simply, to defend civil liberties. As Hutchins took his commitment seriously, the rightists were doubly incensed; for, concerned only with their petty material affairs, they are opposed to civil liberties—for others—at all times.

As Chief Justice Earl Warren remarked in the middle 1950's, it is doubtful that Congress would pass the Bill of Rights if it were introduced today. By the same token, it is doubtful that more than a small minority of Americans favor it. For Americans, of all western peoples, are most committed in the grass-roots mass to the general denial of civil liberties to dissenters, outsiders and deviators. No doubt owing to the general insecurity of their social position, most Americans are rigidly and narrowly conformist, quick to smell out heresies (thus proving their loyalty) and to call for summary punishment of deviators in such a spontaneous way as to make them the envy of any Gestapo, GPU, MKVD or KGB functionary. Under appropriate circumstances, one is melancholically led to believe, rightists in the United States would have more of a field day than they ever had in Germany or Italy. Whereas in other countries the secret police are invariably unpopular, in the United States the FBI and the CIA have generally had the standing of folk heroes—mute testimony to the superior effectiveness of American propaganda methods and to the trend of popular feelings.

The foreign program under Hoffman, set to achieve an era of greater world friendliness for the United States, was attacked as communistic. It was, plainly, "internationalist," itself evil. (Whatever isn't American, *inter alia*, is wicked.) And the educational programs, supporting progressive and adult education, were obviously communistic in that they deviated from traditional paths, trod by no others than our sainted pluperfect forebears.

The broad rightist attack, which according to Macdonald frightened Henry Ford II, although surveys showed that wild calls for boycotts had not hurt Ford Motor sales, was finally subdued in an ingenious way. Hoffman and his aides were ushered out and the attack was simply smothered in money. Unselectively, heavy grants in the hundreds of millions were ladled out year after year to *all* accredited colleges and universities, *all* hospitals and, later, *all* museums, all symphony orchestras; all of everything in the *status quo*. In the grants to colleges and universities, Catholic institutions were included (to their gratified consternation) in the greatest deluge of money they ever experienced. Nobody was spared.

This silenced the rightists, possibly because all the dry emotional tinder out in the grass roots had been thoroughly saturated in floods of money. It was difficult to maintain the idea before the public that the Ford Foundation was evil when it was spewing forth lifegiving money to all points of the compass like lava from a volcano. As no standards were observed it was all obviously democratic.

If the continual widespread distribution of money in large amounts is a good thing, then the Ford Foundation must be one of the best things that ever happened. *Cui bono?* The *status quo* is clearly made more bearable as its various cracks and fissures are plastered over, while thousands cheer. And the Ford Motor Company, the goose that laid this golden egg, is surely not hurt. The public-relations value of the Ford Foundation to the automobile company was not lost upon the more than 8,000 Ford dealers in the United States, who earlier in the 1950's were among those protesting that too much foundation money was being spent abroad on benighted aliens.[72] But, apparently unknown to them, Ford Motor is a big operation abroad as well.

Public Relations and Influence over Attitudes

Apart from their roles in corporate control, the big foundations, at home and abroad, have a public-relations "splash value." What they give to approved medical, scientific and educational institutions tends to bathe in reflected radiance corporate enterprises that some critics quixotically consider ominous. It appears, on closer analysis, that this is a mistaken and possibly deranged judgment, and that all effort is really being expended for the benefit of humanity, naturally without forgetting the stockholders. If not socialism, the panorama seems to have overtones about it at least of quasi-socialism or, we may say paradoxically, capitalist socialism or social capitalism.

The foundations, it is clear, represent to some degree a line of public-relations defense of the large corporations. General Motors, too, is not without its surrounding foundations—the Alfred P. Sloan Foundation, the Mott Foundation and a number of others. The big foundation, indeed, is the hallmark of corporate super-wealth.

As to giving money away, it is evident that these endowments could have been transferred in one original move to extremely capable hands. In education they could have been turned over to the Association of American Universities and similar bodies, in science to the American Association for the Advancement of Science, in medicine to the American Medical Association, and so on. But this would be the end of it all. The donor and his heirs would have no more participation in it.

By making serial gifts each year out of income from a perpetual principal fund the donor can keep prospective worthy recipients sitting around forever like a circle of hungry dogs, awaiting the next handout. In such an arrangement prospective institutional recipients are not likely to voice unwelcome socio-economic or politico-economic ideas. They are more likely to be careful to give utterance only to impeccably sound ideas, the kind one might hear in the top clubs. The general foundations, then, with their serial gifts, function pretty much as a carrot, rewarding those who are cooperative and constructive, passing over the unworthy, the carping, the critical, the nonadmiring, the unsound.

Institutional administrators consequently find that it pays to stay clear of public controversies and to voice at best only tried-and-true platitudes: to show themselves at all times as sound men. While this reticence to some extent dims their true brilliance, in the long run it seems most rewarding. Robert Maynard Hutchins is one of the few on this circuit who for a long time seemed able to have his cake and eat it too, to function as a big institutional wheel and still enjoy the luxury of delivering himself of tart remarks at the expense of the many sorry spectacles around him. But after he rose to great foundation heights the forces of conformity at last caught up with him, in a latter-day version of a preordained cut-rate Greek tragedy. For the Fund for the Republic was cut loose from the Ford Foundation and left to face the hostile hordes with a dwindling mere $15 million.

The critic is often challenged to say how he would do it better, as though a judge who found an apple to be sour was under obligation to grow a sweeter one. But in the case of the foundations such a challenge would be easy to meet. In the case of the Ford Foundation a much more consequential commitment of its money would have been to devote it to making an adequate secondary-school education available to all promising students. Secondary education is the weakest link in the American educational chain. What the Ford Foundation could have done, and can still do, is to see that all promising students get into a good school, all expenses paid. As such schools are only rarely found in home neighborhoods it would be necessary that the students be boarded, sometimes clothed and supplied with travel expenses. Some could be placed in existing private schools, although they, too, are crowded. For others, regional private schools with highly motivated, well-paid faculties would have to be supplied.

The task could be left to other agencies, public and private, to see the Ford-grant graduates through college. As it is, a very large percentage of those entering colleges are poorly prepared to profit by college-level work. In my proposed Ford-grant system defects of preparation would be removed.

While the immediate impact of such expenditure would not be apparent, the long-term consequences would be enormous and beneficial.

Politically there is very little that could be said against this plan from any point of view.

Effects of Grants, Good and Bad

That the various foundation emphases in their grants are not without vast social effects we can see from the judgments of informed critics wandering more or less like unheeded ghosts through Foundationland.

As an example of what he considers mischief, Macdonald cites an early cause taken up by the Carnegie Foundation for the Advancement of Teaching. Andrew Carnegie had it brought to his attention how poorly teachers were paid, and he decided to do something about it—thus privately assuming a legislative function (which all the foundations do). So in 1905 he established his foundation to improve teaching, with the objective of giving every down-at-heels college professor in the country a free pension. When it became evident toward 1920 that all of Carnegie's money could not fill this bill, existing contracts were frozen. There was then established the Teachers Annuity and Insurance Association, supported by contributions from teachers and colleges as well as by Carnegie money. Carnegie's heart, however, had been in the right place.

It had been initially necessary, though, to have a criterion of who was a worthy teacher and what was a college. Many places that call themselves colleges, then and now, are not. The then president of the Carnegie Corporation, Henry Pritchett, composed an "Accepted List" of colleges eligible for Carnegie pensions. An admirer of the German university system, Pritchett laid it down that qualifying colleges must have Ph.D.s as department heads. Many already had such cherished department heads and the Ph.D. up to that time had merely been a degree sought by people committed to research scholarship.

"This put pressure on colleges to qualify, which put pressure on professors to get Ph.D.s, which brought about the present Procrustean situation where no amount of scholarly brilliance or teaching flair will make up for lack of a doctorate. There are those who see in the Ph.D. obsession a major cause of the sterility and mediocrity of our academic life today, and the moral of *that* is: Doing Good Is a Complicated Business."[73]

Without intending to do so but by incautiously exerting their great power, the Carnegie interests, it is contended, actually devalued the Ph.D. degree to its present estate when it is most conspicuously borne by routine jobholders and bureaucratic academic administrators. As hordes of prospective jobholders, looking forward to tenured academic employment and distant pensions, besieged the graduate schools (of which many new ones set up shop to supply the demand) the graduate curriculum was purposely made mechanically more arduous in order to deter all except the most hardy plodders (getting the prized degrees began to take up to ten and twelve years in the less formalized subjects such as history, literature and philosophy). Brilliant minds, superior either as teachers or as scholarly producers, increasingly declined to subject themselves to what was often a creatively sterile grind.

While the Ph.D. requirement lent itself readily to the organizing American corporate approach, in England, not similarly scourged by the Ph.D. mania, one still saw hundreds of brilliant teachers and scores of internationally recognized scholars without the degree. Visiting the United States these English scholars, flaunting only a meager M.A., often lecture to halls filled by goggle-eyed American Ph.D.s. Bertrand Russell was one such.

The point in all this is not that there is anything wrong with the basic idea of the Ph.D. The point is only that it is no longer indicative of a true scholarly interest, which can indeed be shown only by the nature of work done. Many Ph.D.s, too, have come to be awarded in ridiculous fields. Hutchins found one granted for work in automobile driver training!

So this heavy-handed Germanizing of American scholarship traces back to an original *ex parte* foundation decision.

Not all foundation efforts, by any means, have had such a disputatious outcome.

Carnegie money, for example, financed Abraham Flexner's great investigation of American medical schools. The report, which appeared in 1910, found nearly all of them far below par and some to be rackets, leading to extensive reforms that drove out the worst and converted the remainder from among the worst in the world to the best.

Again, Carnegie money financed Gunnar Myrdal and associates in the monumental study of the American Negro before World War II, titled *An American Dilemma*. It was on the basis largely of the findings in this report that the Supreme Court rendered its epochal school desegregation decision of 1954.

Rockefeller money largely financed Dr. Alfred Kinsey and associates in the study of sexual behavior which, despite methodological and other controversies that ensued, appeared to represent a long step toward greater light in a puritanically degraded area.

As Macdonald notes, "The Rockefeller agencies made medical history with such exploits as their worldwide campaigns to control malaria and yellow fever, and their detection—and subsequent elimination—of hookworm as a drain on the vitality of rural Southerners."[74] It is evident that there is much one can find to set up on the credit side of the foundations.

And, yet, the critics still find many serpents coiled in the garden. William H. Whyte, in *Fortune* (November, 1955), held it a bad thing that foundation grants went more and more to institutions or to research teams, less and less to individual workers. As Macdonald reminds us, the greatest work has been done by individuals, and in the "soft" disciplines.[75]

Not only must the foundations, with an eye to the cultural vigilantes, stick to safe, tried and true areas, but they cannot support pioneers, who automatically have the animal mobs ranged against them. Had they existed in an earlier day the foundations could not have sponsored Copernicus, Galileo, Vesalius, Darwin, Pasteur, Marx, Freud or many others. These were all, by public acclaim, reprehensible men; some still are.

As recently as the 1920's they could not, owing to low-grade public opinion, support Mrs. Margaret Sanger in her timely but frustrated campaign to disseminate information about birth control. Margaret Sanger, like Socrates, fought as an individual and went to jail as an individual. The birth control movement was stalled, has been revived only recently under dire eleventh-hour necessity.

The original program of the Ford Foundation grew out of criticism by Edwin R. Embree, former president of the Julius Rosenwald Foundation, advanced in an article in *Harper's Magazine* in 1949 entitled "Timid Billions." Embree held that, because foundations—mainly those of Carnegie and Rockefeller—had pioneered in medicine and health nearly fifty years before, these now highly developed fields had become placid foundation preserves, with about half of all grants going to them, another third to routine universities and colleges, and the rest to routine welfare agencies. He thought it time that new ground was broken, with the results seen in the successful know-nothing attacks on the Ford Foundation.

Embree criticized the foundations for "scatteration." And in its more recent policy this is precisely what the Ford Foundation has come to.

The Guggenheim Foundation more conspicuously than others has awarded grants to the humanities and to individuals. Hundreds of writers and artists have received sustaining funds from this source.

As part of the favorable tax-financed public-relations image the foundations develop for corporations and founders that grew rich in questionable ways, they present the aspect of being highly civilized by proxy association with cultural heroes. Avoiding in their lifetimes creative persons like Margaret Sanger or Socrates who are invariably suspected by the ignorant multitudes of being up to no good, the foundations fondly embrace all *established* cultural heroes and those potential heroes working in popularly approved cultural channels. Not heroic themselves, they nevertheless exist in a soft, derived heroic light, invoking in the thoughtless gaping multitudes some feeling of being in the shadow of a cathedral. They are, on the contrary, basically demagogic; for the main thrust of their effort is not in any sense the deliverance of man but the protection of their sponsors' plantation. While this is surely narrowly intelligent of them, it is not, as I see it, something to induce public celebration.

And the fact that it is all done, really, with public money certainly puts anyone in the position of being gulled who applauds them more than mildly for good works. It should never be forgotten that if the Ford Foundation had never been founded every cent of the money would have been taken in inheritance taxes by the United States government, thus lightening the tax load for everybody. If the Fords, now, should achieve something humanly tremendous through their foundation they would not achieve it with *their* money but with *our* money. While not impugning the achievement, whatever it was, or the judgment that led to it, recognition of the nature of the transaction would certainly place it in a somewhat different light.

What the subsidy is in the case of any foundation of any considerable size one can readily ascertain by looking up what the estate tax rate was when it received its funds. This rate, ranging more recently up to 90 per cent, represents the portion of principal saved from taxes. Where income on the principal exceeds $100,000, the amount of taxes avoided, at present rates, is at least 70 per cent and has been as high as 91 per cent.

So, whatever good is accomplished by the foundations is largely accomplished with other people's money, a familiar *finpolitan* practice. And if one wishes to salute the original source of this beneficence it should be Congress, making free use of *our* money.

Money funneled into education has to some extent no doubt been of general benefit. However, much of this educational effort has been devoted to producing corporate personnel, with the primary mission of making profits. The Du Ponts have poured heavy sums into M.I.T.; and Carnegie established the Carnegie Institute of Technology in Pittsburgh, a prime source of local plant and departmental managers and company officers. Even more general applications of educational funds can be shown destined primarily for the support of the corporate world.

It is a common experience in the United States for people to read in newspapers and magazines of great new medical advances and discoveries, but they little realize that most of these advances will never be available to them, will be available only to those who can afford them in a few centrally located medical centers. As I gave extended attention thirty years ago to these problems in which there has been little change since, the contemporary reader may be left to the references.[76]

Scientific findings have been applied most assiduously in the amassing of corporate profits.

While it is generally gratifying to see so much human ingenuity displayed and developed, it is worth noticing that the fruits of all the effort are for the most part restricted in their distribution. The wide prevalence of slums would suggest to a visitor from another planet that there was little education, science or medicine available to anyone at all in the United States.

If it is nevertheless insisted that all this foundation effort represents philanthropic activity, then it is governmentally coerced philanthropic activity, under the threat of taking the principal in taxes if the income is not devoted to narrowly applied good works. The government, in brief, forces the rich to tend their own plantation.

Intellectual Sleight-of-Hand

I therefore cannot help seeing the entire American philanthropic movement, hailed as something unique in the world, as intellectual sleight-of-hand as far as its claimed disinterested benevolence and general distribution of benefits are concerned. There may have been some gain in allowing private dispositions of the money to be made, where it has been made in good faith, because one cannot suppose it would have been expended more judiciously if left to run-of-the-mill *pubpols*. The prospect might have been far less entrancing if it had been left to the manipulation of the more self-oriented of these.

The Ford Motor Company does not claim to be philanthropic. But the Ford Foundation, which grew out of it and is the public halo of the company, is claimed to be philanthropic even though it is managed by the same people. When Henry Ford II presides over the Ford Motor Company he is nonphilanthropic, a business barracuda; but when he steps into his role as a trustee of the Ford Foundation he, like a Jekyll-Hyde, suddenly becomes a philanthropist. With the Ford Motor Company he endeavors to garner all the money possible; with the foundation he endeavors to give money—*our* money—away.

Is he—on balance—richer or poorer? As a result of establishing their many foundations and "giving away" hundreds of millions of dollars, are the Rockefellers and other foundation impresarios richer or poorer, more or less esteemed, more or less solidly ensconced, stronger or weaker?

The answer in every case of a surviving foundation family group is that the foundation has benefited its sponsors more than it benefited the world. Whatever benefit it has wrought for the world it has wrought, too, for the family group. For the world is their village, through which their personal interests ramify in a bewildering network. Why should they not wish to benefit the world as they, too, must live in it? And any benefit wrought, however minor, brings to them vast credit, enhances their status as exalted citizens of the world. They all rate at the highest level in mass-media esteem.

The main point I extract from this is that these are very subtly powerful people, far more powerful even than they are portrayed by a deferential press. Nor are they, despite the deft airbrush of the public relations man, especially benign, as is plainly evident in the heavy commitment to systematic extreme violence of the political system in which they have, by enormous margins, the largest stake.

Never registering opposition to any of the many wars, foreign police actions and military missions against the heathen in which the seemingly detached government engages, usually instead registering enthusiastic approval and giving full support, they must be considered integral to this way of conducting affairs. At the time of this writing this political system is using some of its vast firepower, much of its manpower, with which to establish new foreign bases, as in Vietnam. Although Vietnam is popularly accepted as an heroic dirt-level president's maximum effort, the operation has been formally and enthusiastically endorsed by Governor Nelson A. Rockefeller. It is, obviously, a venture carrying the highest *finpolitan* sanction.[77]

While the Vietnam venture will indeed make all of us more secure against the devil of Communism (or will it?), it is surely going to make some persons far more secure than others. To be entirely fair, we must concede that even the denizens of the slums, thanks to a foresighted president, will be made more secure in their slumminess. This boon happily works both ways: The rich *and* the poor are benefited by being fully protected in their respective statuses.

Proposed Foundation Reforms

Representative Wright Patman advanced concrete proposals for reforming the foundations, tightening the regulatory leash so they would not be quite so free to maneuver self-servingly as now. His recommendations were as follows:

1. Limit their life to twenty-five years, as in the voluntary cases of the Julius Rosenwald Fund and the foundation established by the late Arthur Curtiss James.

2. Prohibit them from engaging in tax-exempt business in unfair competition with taxpaying businesses.

3. Prohibit them from engaging in tax-free lending and borrowing.

4. Require them to engage in arm's length relationships—that is, prohibit them from extending intramural benefits, say, to the employees of a controlled company, a form of subtle unfair competition with others.

5. Prohibit them from soliciting or accepting contributions from suppliers to and patrons of their companies.

6. Prohibit foundations from owning more than 3 per cent of any corporation, thus shrinking them as factors in corporate control.

7. Make them conform to certain rules in the case of proxy fights in corporations where they hold stock ownership.

8. Prohibit them from trading in and out of securities in quest of capital gains.

9. Allow no tax exemption on contributions to a foundation until the money has been actually put to approved charitable use.

10. Deny tax exemption to any foundation if it has clearly been established for tax avoidance or to obtain financial benefits for the founder.

11. Compute donations of property to a foundation at cost or market value, whichever is lower, rather than on the present basis of market value which permits the evasion of taxes on appreciated assets.

12. In contributions made by corporations, let such contributions be credited to the stockholders, thus keeping untaxed contributions to present limits prescribed by law.

13. Treat all capital gains by foundations as expendable income and do not allow them to be converted into new capital.

14. Add money unreasonably accumulated by corporations controlled by a foundation under present laws to the foundation's own accumulation as if the two were one. "The use of subsidiary corporations should not be permitted to cloak actual accumulations, as is the case in the Howard Hughes Medical Institute of Miami Beach."

15. Corporations controlled by foundations should be subject to taxes on unreasonably accumulated earnings, as prescribed by law for foundations.

16. From the base for the marital deduction there should be excluded amounts left to foundations that are henceforth untaxed. And while money given to foundations is not subject to gift and estate taxes, the rate brackets to be applied to moneys that are taxable should be the same as if the prescribed foundation portions were part of the taxable gifts or estate.

17. Regulation of the foundations by the Treasury Department should be tightened in many specifically indicated ways and the Treasury Department should be obliged by law to function actively in this area.

"These and other reforms," Mr. Patman gravely concluded, "are vitally necessary."[78] For what little it may be worth, I concur.

The Patman investigation has already influenced the passage of new laws regulating foundations in New York State, where most of them are chartered. The effect of these New York laws will probably be to drive many to states of easier virtue, as in the case of corporations that finally found lax regulatory states in Delaware and New Jersey. In general, regulation in any of the states, of any kind of activity, is about on a par with the regulation of a frontier saloon, which is why entrepreneurs of all kinds prefer state to federal regulation.

Said the *New York Times* about the new situation in New York:

A sampling of reports filed as the result of a new law this year has shown that many purportedly charitable foundations are tax dodges, according to Attorney General Louis J. Lefkowitz. He said that the foundations were also sources of funds for the personal use of their directors.

The charitable organizations . . . operated without supervision or regulation before last January. . . .

A random sampling of 400 registrants, and examination of the 500 financial reports, has turned up numerous examples that show sufficient evidence of improper manipulation of the funds to justify the calling of an investigation, according to the Attorney General.

Often the manipulators who used the funds for their personal gain had already profited by large tax deductions based on their gifts to the foundations, he added.

. . . some charities have already received millions of dollars this year that they would not otherwise have obtained as a result of his staff's work.

Tax-free ostensible charitable funds had been used (Mr. Lefkowitz discovered tardily) for business purposes, to buy expensive paintings and sculpture for the donors' own homes, to pay salaries to relatives and for a variety of other personal accommodations—facts which anyone could have ascertained in 1937 by reading *America's Sixty Families*. Most of the New York foundations funded at more than $1 million—and this the authorities now thought suspicious—were set up to make distributions for charitable purposes "to be selected by the directors."

Under the new law the attorney general of the state may at his discretion bring action to remove directors who fail to comply with the law and may compel accountings and order reimbursement for loss of funds resulting from improper activities of directors or trustees.[79]

All this, however, will not lock the barn door even tardily because there are forty-nine other states.

Concluding, whatever foundations do, for good or ill, for self or humanity, they do for the most part with publicly conferred money.

Eleven 🌿

MINISTERS OF FINPOLITY: THE UPPER EXECUTIVES

Top executives of top American corporations are, after the Kremlin rulers, the most anxiously studied and written about small group of persons in the contemporary world of affairs. Each group is more sedulously and continuously scrutinized, in sober truth, than the much larger and far more crucial collection of scientists.

More numerous than Russian politicos, American upper corporation executives are nevertheless very few. If we take the elite *Fortune* list we have before us only 500 industrial companies, 50 commercial banks, 50 public utility companies, 50 transportation companies (rail, air, highway and water), 50 life insurance companies and 50 merchandising enterprises—750 in all. This is the cream, with assets ranging from as low as $7.444 million (Needham Packing) to $30.906 billion (AT&T).

Each of these enterprises glories in a chairman, a president, usually at least one executive vice president, sometimes a comptroller and always a treasurer and a secretary, the three latter rarely involved in policy formation. The array of vice presidents varies by size of enterprise but, no matter how large it is, these men are usually mere divisional or departmental managers, direct instruments of top management but not in top management themselves.

So truly imperial is the domain of the largest *finpolities* such as AT&T, General Motors and Standard Oil that the executive vice-presidential function is often divided among several men, who meet as an executive committee. General Motors in 1964 had three executive vice presidents; Standard Oil of New Jersey, five; but Ford, only one.

In the ordinary case the top officers are a trio: chairman, president and executive vice president. The president's duties correspond to those of the captain of a ship, are virtually as routinely formalized; and those of the vice president correspond to the ship's executive officer.

If we allot to big management an average of five men we have 3,750 upper executives. Because some of the larger companies have more than five in top management, it may be that as many as 5,000 should be reckoned. As there are smallish fairly important companies not included in *Fortune's* compendium, the number of top management people may be as great as 10,000, the number set forth in *Business Executives of America,* published by the Institute for Research in Biography in 1950. But this total included men in Canadian as well as United States companies.

Important corporation executives certainly do not exceed 10,000. More probably there are fewer than 5,000, a restricted group. Naturally, if one looks down the entire nondemocratic para-military chain of command to junior executives and foremen, the number of executives is much greater. None of these shapes policy and few ever will. They are cogs of the order of middle-range Soviet commissars and lower bureaucrats. The system is indeed very much like the Soviet's, which was modeled after it.

Corporations generally are run by the executive vice president (or vice presidents), the president usually supervising and intervening directly only when he feels it advisable. In newer, reorganized or problematic companies the president, it is true, may be a dynamo of activity. The chairman is available for consultation on nice points of policy; only rarely if ever, one gathers, does he tell the president, unbidden, what he ought to be doing.

Within the bounds of determined policy and the nature of the business the president is a complete autocrat. Such being the case he usually acts with great restraint, like a jet pilot who knows that the slightest touch on the rudder may cause a wide deflection of course.

The chairman comes into fullest bloom at meetings of the directors, over whom he presides. These are held quarterly or semi-annually; and are mostly routine affairs. Top officers are directors, and one may ascertain who is and who is not in top management by noticing whether he is or is not a director as well as an officer, a point in elementary corporatology.

The chairman, president and executive vice presidents are invariably directors; the vice presidents sometimes are. In Ford and Standard Oil of New Jersey some vice presidents are; in General Motors at present only executive vice presidents are.

Apart from company officers, directors usually consist of officers of other friendly companies or friendly banks, of lawyers, sometimes foundation officers and college presidents, former officers and large stockholders (sometimes themselves former officers). Directors who actively question or suggest are usually owners or representatives of large blocks of stock or senior obligations. In most cases the outside members are passive, merely listening and taking note of what is reported by the executives. They evaluate what they hear in terms of their own business experience.

Except where forbidden by law, as in the case of banks, directors are usually cogs in widespread interlocks, a phenomenon abhorrent down through the years to many congressmen. Congressmen who dislike this practice of interlocking directors—that is, a few directors from a cluster of key companies spread around among a large number of satellite companies—would like it forbidden on the ground that it signals central moneybund or "Wall Street" control. They would prefer that a man be a director of only one company at a time, thereby bringing in many "unsound" outsiders.

My own objection to forbidding interlocking directors is that it would be ineffective in breaking the true interlock, which exists by prior dispensation in a small ownership coterie through blood relationships, intermarriages, private school associations and club memberships. We must not forget that the entire corporate situation directly concerns no more than 2/10ths of 1 per cent of the adult population (fewer than 200,000 people); with some 8/10ths of 1 per cent less involved; and never more than 10 per cent even infinitesimally involved except as rank-and-file employees and consumers. Abolishing corporate interlocks would not alter any basic situation, would at most provide only one more futile pseudo-reform. If it led anyone to believe some basic change had taken place, it would be grossly deceptive.

Those who oppose interlocking directorates, if they were seriously consistent in their recommendation, should call for the outlawing of intermarriage, hereditary trust funds, common schooling and common metropolitan club membership among large property holders and corporate families. One could isolate each one, incommunicado, in a private telephone booth.

Except where they represent large blocks of stock or are officers of the company, directors are seldom vital to the conduct of affairs—serve mostly as window dressing. There is a school of corporate thought that contends directors should direct; but this is a minority view. Directors generally do not direct unless they are also big stockholders or officers; as outsiders they usually don't know enough about the specific situation. Even the notion that some bring to bear an indispensable broad-gauged public point of view, valuable in preserving the corporate image as a benign entity, won't hold water because efficient public relations departments tend to this simple detail. A few directors, in fact, are invited on boards solely because they are witty or eccentrically knowledgeable fellows, thus tending to perk up otherwise dull meetings of essentially stodgy men.

In crises directors may be collectively called up to tap their general business experience. Some internal dispute over fundamental policy may be submitted to them, in which case they function as a board of judges. If they cannot resolve the dispute it will be resolved at the next meeting of stockholders, where the big shareholders will assert themselves. But such an occurrence is rare because among the directors it is known who speaks for large stockholdings. It is known where the ultimate power lies.

Despite all the devotion to voting in corporations, the process is hardly democratic because the vote, in any showdown, is by shares of stock, not by individuals. All the thousands of rag-tag stockholders in the Ford Motor Company could not outvote the Ford family. The situation is absolutely or effectively the same in every company, which means that a very large and paramountly vital part of internal American affairs is under essentially autocratic rule, as in Russia. At variance with democratic ideology this statement surely is but nevertheless, alas, it is true, true, true.

As long as matters progress smoothly, as they ordinarily do, the point of view of the managing officers prevails at board meetings. Organizational trouble appears only if a very large stockholder, or someone speaking for large blocks of stock, seriously opposes the management.

While newspapers report from time to time on internal struggles for company control, such reports rarely involve the biggest companies. Control is seldom an issue in the big smoothly running enterprise. Whenever it is, the issue is quickly resolved, either by internal vote or by court decision.

The Executive Mystique

Corporation officers are of interest in this inquiry mainly because they are the front-line deputies of the rich and the super-rich when they are not themselves of the rich. They are the watchdogs and overseers (usually hired) of great wealth. As such, their earned take-home pay is rivaled only by that of persons in the sports and entertainment worlds who become tremendous box office attractions—home-run hitters, knock-out punchers or seducers-seductresses of the screen. Because only a handful of these fire-flies maintain their box office charisma for any considerable time, as a group they are not in the income class of the executives, who even in retirement continue to be handsomely rewarded. Entertainers and athletes in general are paid little.

Just what is it that makes an upper corporation executive worth his pay, ranging on the record from $200,000 to $800,000 a year in the merely cash portions? A standard answer, part of what I shall hereafter refer to as *the executive mystique,* is that "the value of an upper-echelon executive lies in the decisions he makes and influences."[1]

It is made evident that the decisions for which he is rewarded so handsomely are money-making decisions. While he may at times make wrong decisions, most of his decisions (at least the big ones) must be the right ones, the winning ones. Or so it is argued.

One cannot deny that the top executives are decision makers. But this observation is not very profound because, paradoxically, not to make any decision is a decision. We are all, as it happens, decision makers. But we are not—most of us—money-making decision makers.

The kind of decision making the big executive engages in, according to theory, is as follows:

He makes one big decision (or a series of decisions) that vastly improves the relative position of his company, reflected in earnings; that slightly improves or holds steady the relative position of his company among rivals; that in any general economic decline leads his company to lose ground less rapidly than others; or that enables his company, at the bottom of a slump, to spring up again, phoenixlike, and astonish the world—or at least the editors of *Fortune* and the *Wall Street Journal.*

More exactly, he is not supposed to make those decisions by himself, out of the whole cloth, but to fit together the advice and insights of many others, like a master craftsman, and extract the winning decision.

In theory the decisions he makes must be winning decisions. Because if one is paying for decision making, as the big stockholders are supposed to be doing, one surely does not want to pay for losing decisions. And yet, highly paid executives often make momentous losing decisions, sometimes all together, sometimes in industry groups and sometimes in single companies.

In the early 1930's, the leading corporate executives all made a collectively losing decision. They decided to maintain their economic positions amid sudden price declines through cost-cutting, mainly by wholesale discharges of unprotected workers, the rank-and-file patriots. The theory was that as demand for goods was restimulated at lower price levels, business would pick up at more normalized levels than in the 1920's, workers could be rehired at lower wages as in the slump of 1920–22. Then the process of money-making could resume on a "sounder" basis.

There was no pick-up, however, because during the serial process of wholesale layoffs workers exhausted their meager savings and credit.

When prices reached low levels they continued to fall to still lower levels, except where they were "administered." Much less business was done because many people had no money. The economy began stagnating, the Communists gloated because Marx had predicted capitalism would lose the ability to govern in one of these slumps. The Great Depression was on, produced by master minds who instead of living up to their reputation as entrepreneurs had become, turtle-like, solely interested in preserving working capital.

Ironically, surrounding conditions from a business point of view were perfect. There was no government interference with business. There had been twelve years of uninterrupted lax Republican rule under figurehead presidents. Taxes under Treasury Secretary Andrew Mellon had been brought to very low levels. Tariff walls against odious foreign goods were at record high levels. Big Business ruled the roost more fully than it did later under Lyndon B. Johnson.

If it were a fact that executives are paid as decision makers they would all have been fired. For they had all, acting according to crowd psychology as they usually do, made a general losing decision, reflected in steady corporate deficits. There never was a major winning decision in this situation in the sense of one company moving ahead of others. No corporate master mind showed himself, for the simple reason that there were no corporate master minds. The emperors were all stark naked. In national self-defense the government moved, slowly, to intervene with its own programs, amid witless cries from the corporate press of "creeping socialism."

One often sees the same sort of collective losing decision making in an entire industry, as in the railroad industry since World War I. Suddenly faced with new competition—from pipelines, trucks, buses and airplanes— the railroad industry down through the decades, instead of adjusting services to meet new conditions, instead of participating by one avenue or the other in new forms of transport, decided to curtail services. The industry decided, forsooth, to go out of business on the installment plan.

Where one company clearly falls behind all others in the same industry through having failed to adapt to new currents or to take advantage of some innovation, it is obvious that the chief executive (or his subalterns) has not been alert and he is, unless he is a big stockholder, usually dropped. This was the case with respect to Charles Luckman, president of Lever Brothers after World War II and widely touted as a "wonder boy." The rest of the industry stole a march on him in the introduction of detergents in place of soap powders, and Lever Brothers underwent setbacks in the market until it tardily took up detergents. Luckman was fired. But when Ford Motor Company lost a reported $250 million on its hapless Edsel model in the 1950's, Henry Ford II did not walk the plank. He, along with other stockholders, simply took it in the pocketbook. He could not be fired because he was a chief owner. This simple fact revealed the source of true power in an executive.

Aging Sewell Avery, a big stockholder, stubbornly held to his position at the head of Montgomery Ward and Company after World War II and decided to retrench in expectation of a resumption of the depression. Ward's arch-rival, Sears, Roebuck and Company, decided to expand in expectation of an inflationary boom, and soon passed on to astronomic heights of latter-day success. Here we have a case of a losing and a winning decision, both made by experienced managements, one rather inflexible. To argue that Avery was a poor executive because he made a less advantageous decision is like arguing that Napoleon was a bad general because he lost the battle of Waterloo.

In all the loose talk about executive decision making it is overlooked that corporate decisions are usually made collectively, more recently on the basis of a vast mass of information assembled and digested by computers. After careful sifting by low-paid technicians—statisticians, economists, mathematicians, psychologists and even at times anthropologists—a set of alternatives is laid before the executive board. If the correct data have been fed to the computers these mechanisms may themselves have the answer: Expand, branch out, retrench, stand pat, fight, submit, deny. Again, the decisions are rarely of life-and-death caliber. They are usually fairly routine and marginal.

John F. Kennedy, it is reported, faced divided counsels among his advisers on the religious issue in 1960. Some said he should avoid it, some said he should stress it, others felt he should touch on it, but lightly. The problem was put to a computer into which a mass of data was fed on the characteristics of the American population. The computer replied: Stress the issue. And this was done. While one cannot say that this is why Kennedy won, it obviously did not cause him to lose. So it was presumably the right decision—made by a computer. The masterly decision in this case was evidently to turn to the computer.

Corporation officials often face issues that arise from a set of losing decisions of long- or short-term nature. And they know they are losers. What they often do then is to make no decision, ride with the tide in the hope that something of a saving nature will turn up. They are not, then, paid primarily to make dramatic "right" decisions, although they participate in corporate serendipity and will be penalized for obviously bizarre judgments, now increasingly eliminated by expert analysts and computer technology. But corporations, their nets spread wide, are not run by ear, as the decision-making theory suggests. If they sometimes gamble, it is only in small ways. Almost never do they stake their lives on a single line of policy. They do indeed have alternative policies, sometimes all in effect in different areas at the same time. They play both ends against the middle and the middle against both ends.

There is much else, which need not detain us, to show there is little in this contention that high compensation is given for profitable decision-making. The decision-making theory is part of the executive mystique. This mystique, dubbed "Management," has been developed partly for psychological reasons: To give executives in a long chain of command down to the newest junior executive and foreman a sense of worth in essentially boring jobs. It also provides an impressive rationale for the payment of grotesque salaries. For as decision makers, most company chairmen and presidents could not fight their way out of a paper bag, as is repeatedly shown when they are dragged into full public view and subjected to searching questioning under *subpoena*. Then they almost invariably wilt, show themselves as very ordinary men.

This is not to say that corporation executives are without ability. They are able people, the ablest that can be found for the task. Their ability resides in a varying combination of qualities. The big factor that enters into their selection and compensation is that they are custodian-trustees and overseers of vastly valuable properties. As they are agents of often absentee large owners, and are sometimes caught in tight situations where one decision is as bad as another or is a Hobson's choice, their pay is in part an inducement to guarantee loyalty at the beginning of a chain of command. Below the top, loyalty can be enforced by sanctions. But the initiator in the chain of command has a wider sphere of action.

Owing to their strategic position at the head of complex properties the top executives are in excellent positions for self-enrichment. They hold the combination to the office safe, know many inner company secrets. They are exactly in the positions of Rockefeller and Carnegie with their early enterprises, except that they are not the chief owners. (They usually own very little of the company.) But, as corporate history shows, they are in a prime position to help themselves to goodies at the expense of the company and its stockholders. Many have done so, a few from time to time are still caught in the act.

Though partly a crowning reward for long service in a variety of lower positions throughout the company, their compensation is mainly a shield against the temptation of helping themselves at the company's expense. Such temptations are guarded against in many technical ways, as by outside audits and analyses, but the basic way is to make it always evident that a sure and comparatively high earned income awaits the man who avoids the dark risks of high adventure at the company's expense.

That astronomic executive compensation has nothing whatever to do with decision making or competitive wizardry is proved by the fact that executive compensation in the noncompetitive electric utility industry is as high as, often higher than, in straining, striving industrial companies. Copious figures on the compensation drawn by executives in these utility sinecures, which could easily be filled by bright collegians, are presented for twenty pages by Senator Lee Metcalf of Montana in his *Overcharge* (David McKay Company, N.Y., 1967), a study of fancy financial capers by the entire contemporary electric utility industry.

There is even more to the need for high compensation. As the company wants the top executive's undivided attention, it wants him to feel free of all the nagging worries that beset other men. As far as these problems can be met by money—big life insurance, schooling for the children, residence in soothing surroundings, a contented wife—they are met in the compensation awarded. Problems that cannot be solved by money, such as problematic wives, will cause a likely prospect to be passed over because the company cannot afford to have its affairs in the hands of a brooding man. Much has been made of the fact that an alcoholic or socially withdrawn wife will cause a man to lose the nod of advancement. But anything at all bizarre or worrisome about the wife will have the same result. It is not minded if she is a big spender, but if she overspends or in any way *shows she is out of control*, she will certainly jeopardize his chance. Indeed, any member of the family far out of control and thus the object of worry to the man will count heavily against his selection for a top position.

Hence the high salaries, elaborate fringe benefits and deference in the corporate press to ostensibly brilliant decision makers.

The hired top corporation man, then, as distinguished from the hereditary owner-executive, is much like the cormorant or fishing bird, still used in China. A strap is fastened around the bird's neck, permitting him to breathe but not allowing him to swallow his catch. He dutifully brings the fish back to the boat. Now and again (paydays) the strap is loosened and he is allowed to swallow a fish. The bird is a percentage participant in the process, which was established by and for others.[2]

It is part of the corporation mystique that the corporation executive is inherently a powerful person—that he freely and autonomously extemporizes. But if such ability were either extensive or crucial it would be easy to shift top officials out of industries where the average net return on capital was high, such as automobiles, cosmetics or pharmaceuticals, into industries where it was low, such as coal, railroads or steamships. The wizard decision makers would then be able to make decisions that would move the lagging enterprise far above the traditional rate of return for the industry.

This is not done. Executives are not attracted from booming industries to lagging ones, from whaling and pearling to sponge fishing. When an industry hits the skids all the enterprises in it go down, some perhaps faster and further than others. No amount of experienced executive decision making in a single company is able to arrest the process.

There is in fact no consistent relationship between high executive pay and company success. Even in a company on a downhill course, paying no dividends, executives may be paid better than in more profitable companies. Thus for years Bethlehem Steel, although paying no dividends and running at deficits, paid Eugene P. Grace as president up to $800,000 a year, a record as of 1956 in cash emoluments. Somebody, including himself, apparently wanted Mr. Grace in charge of the properties.

That the British take a somewhat jaundiced view of inordinately high executive salaries was shown recently by the case of Wilfred Harvey, sixty-seven-year-old, $750,000-a-year chairman of the British Printing Corporation. Four fellow directors forced his resignation on the ground that his salary scale was "grotesque and ridiculous." He also had a special expense account. The annual earnings of the company were those of General Motors for a single day. So exercised did the British become that acidulous editorials were written and questions were asked in Parliament.[3]

The chief executives of the big companies, in addition to directing internal affairs, also represent the company *vis-à-vis* the world, government, labor unions and the general public. Their role is, basically, that of politicians and diplomats. As shrewd politicians some, irrespective of the prosperity of the company, are able to make a better deal for themselves than others among the various factors of major owners, small stockholders, government officials, labor leaders, banks and customers. Some are where they are because they are married to a daughter of the chief stockholder or the daughter of the banker that holds the company's notes. They may, indeed, just be a friend of the bank, which is interested only in its notes, not in record earnings.

Henry Ford II, aged twenty-five, was not spirited out of the Navy in 1943 to become vice president of Ford Motor (executive vice president the next year) because he was considered a wizard decision maker. He had failed to graduate with his class of 1940 at Yale, couldn't make the grade. Nor, years before, was his father Edsel at age twenty-six made a vice president because of any then evident great decision-making ability. Henry Ford, when he appointed Edsel, told newspapermen it showed what a remarkable country the United States was that so young a man could achieve such a high post so early. On this score Bourbon France was a far more remarkable country, for Louis XIV became king at age five.

The Power Elite according to Mills

That the top corporation executive is a person of commanding power in his own right is part of the executive mystique and is uncritically incorporated into his theory of the power elite by C. Wright Mills, the American sociologist. As originally argued by the Italian sociologist, Vilfredo Pareto, in every branch of human activity people can be given an index number on a scale. To those with the largest accumulated indices of achievements or specific qualities, in whatever category, he gave the name of *elite*. There is, obviously, an elite for every function and quality: barbers, violinists, scientists, bankers, seductive women, politicians.

People, too, possess powers, from zero to 100, in asserting themselves over large areas of affairs. Those able to assert their wills, thus affecting many others, perhaps even against *their* wills, are said to have power. And, paraphrasing Pareto, Mills said that those with the most such power are to be regarded as a Power Elite.

Where Mills becomes original, or quasi-original, is in his description of what purports to be the more recent American power elite. He constantly uses the words "new" and "today," so that the situation as it stands is evidently something freshly perceived by Mills.

Although the corporate rich or big owners belong to the elite of Mills, he says their role has been reduced in phases—first by big politicians as in the New Deal and more recently by generals, admirals and corporate officials of the Warfare State.[4] The big rich are being phased out or down and are being replaced by executive types, either military or civilian. If Mills is correct, the message of these pages is somewhat *passé*.

The inner core of the power elite consists, first, of those who interchange commanding roles at the top of one dominant institutional order with those in another: the admiral who is also a banker and a lawyer and who heads up an important federal commission; the corporation executive whose company was one of the two or three leading war materiel producers who is now Secretary of Defense; the wartime general who dons civilian clothes to sit on the political directorate and then becomes a member of the board of directors of a leading economic corporation. . . .

The inner core of the power elite also includes men of the higher legal and financial type from the great law factories and investment firms, who are almost professional go-betweens of economic, political and military affairs, and who thus act to unify the power elite. The corporation lawyer and the investment banker perform the functions of the "go-between" effectively and powerfully. . . .

The outermost fringes of the power elite—which change more than its core —consist of "those who count" even though they may not be "in" on given decisions of consequence nor in their career move between the hierarchies. Each member of the power elite need not be a man who personally decides every decision that is to be ascribed to the power elite. Each member, in the decisions he does make, takes the others seriously into account. They not only make decisions in the several major areas of war and peace; they are the men who, in decisions in which they take no direct part, are taken into decisive account by those who are directly in charge.

On the fringes and below them, somewhat to the side of the lower echelons, the power elite fades off into the middle levels of power, into the rank and file of Congress, the pressure groups that are not vested in the power elite itself, as well as a multiplicity of regional and state and local interests. If all the men on the middle levels are not among those who count, they sometimes must be taken into account, handled, cajoled, broken or raised to higher circles.[5]

There has in fact been accomplished a Managerial Revolution, Mills implies. Power in the United States has insensibly shifted from the owners to the managers, from property to technical function (Berle-Means, James Burnham, J. K. Galbraith). Here he echoes a long line of modern writers increasingly emboldened in what they assert.[6]

According to Mills, within the new managerial grouping, power is in the flux of coalition among managers. It follows that if the Fords, Mellons, Rockefellers, Du Ponts and others still count, they count for much less than they once did. If money once talked, now it only whispers in the halls of power, hushed by the presence of the organization man.

The major new segment in the managerial group, according to Mills, consists of "the warlords," the military. Owing to the emergence of a big cold-war military establishment and the infusion of corporations with hundreds of retired officers (who were really available because 13½ million men were mobilized for World War II), the military establishment has become an independent political segment, Mills contends. War and peace are dictated, not in Wall Street as socialists and populists used to claim, not in Congress and the White House as formal constitutionalists believe, not in the populace as naive democrats believe, but in the Pentagon. The Joint Chiefs of Staff, professionals, have the determining voice in this matter and Rockefellers, Mellons, Du Ponts et al. must just tag along.

Although the situation as projected by Mills creates a complicated and dramatic picture, one must object to it on compelling grounds. Mills has raised what are clearly subordinate advisers and technicians into his elite of power. Many of the persons he mentions as power wielders are known, in Wall Street and Washington, as "office boys," "fat boys," court jesters and errand boys. Even by categories they do not rate. Lawyers and bankers, as such, do not rate. The point is: *Whose* lawyer or banker are they?

Mills's classification was purely subjective, externally applied. Most of the members of his elite are subject to the decisive will of others. They do not have a wide range of power in their own right, as do Communist leaders, but derive it. They are but *the representatives of power,* held in reserve by others. Yet Mills claims that "the higher agents" of the economic, political and military domains "now often have a noticeable degree of autonomy" and "that only in the often intricate ways of coalition do they make up and carry through the most important decisions."[7] He asserts in effect that if the Pentagon says "No" to Wall Street and the White House there ensues at least an internal power crisis.

As to this, it can be shown that on "important decisions," such as the discontinuance of manned bombers as well as on other matters, the Joint Chiefs have been flatly, pointedly and publicly overruled amid cries of anguish from friends of the bomber program in Congress. The present weakness of manned airpower has been dramatically shown in Vietnam, where American plane losses against a minor foe have been staggering.

A salient fact about any elite is that it is not only a classifiable entity but it really has what it is supposed to have. The elite heavyweight punchers can really outpunch other men. All the orchestral conductors in the world, in meeting duly assembled, could not vote Leonard Bernstein out of the category of elite conductors. This is because Bernstein has all the characteristics stipulated for an elite conductor. One might meaningfully say, "I don't like Bernstein's conducting"; but one could not meaningfully say, "Bernstein is not an elite conductor."

And this is particularly so of anyone in a *power* elite. If someone can say of anyone in a supposed power elite, "You no longer have power," and this statement is true, did the object of the remark really have power?

But most of the members in Mills's power elite are readily removable, or may be ignored, by other members. Most of the members of Mills's power elite are indeed no more than advisers and technicians. They were hired and can be fired, hold their positions only during satisfactory conduct. This is not to say that while in office they are not powerful. But their power is *derived power, not their own, not autonomous.*

All of Mills's military officers, first, are subject to retirement under pre-existing rules. Moreover they can all be retired early. None of them can say, "I don't believe I shall retire just yet." Furthermore, none of them made the rules.

Again, each can be ordered to change his command, his driving will thwarted. In a salient case President Truman relieved General Douglas MacArthur of the Far Eastern command. MacArthur did not want to be relieved. But when all the chips were down, he was *powerless*. The same goes for the Joint Chiefs. In speaking of the autonomous power of the American military, Mills sounds as though he were speaking of the German and French officer corps of an earlier day, when a faction of landed (propertied) army families actually had deputies sitting in the legislature. The General Staff was a legislative force, could unseat ministers. The United States has no such independent politically ensconced officer corps and it is misleading to imply it. In the United States, generals (even loud talkers like Curtis E. Le May and George Patton) can be moved around like pieces on a chessboard.

Corporation officials, similarly, are retired on schedule and are always dismissible at the behest of the large blocks of stock. While they may be powerful, it is not their own power on behalf of which they speak. It is derived power.

In all of Mills's collection of power-elite people, only the big owners (the *finpols*) and the upper *pubpols* cannot be dismissed. Here and there, too, some underling is established through the dialectic of intrigue, usually in a limited way. Members of the Supreme Court are ensconced for life, collectively have ultimate power in the area of interpreting the laws; they can void statutes, can precipitate an inner nationwide power crisis (as with the school desegregation and state legislative redistricting decisions). The president has full executive power, but only for a limited term; all appointed national officials are subject to his whim. Congressmen each wield fractional power for formally limited terms. Only a very few of these in the Senate have some national stature based on inner rank or on constituencies they have attracted outside their home states. Those in office for many terms from noncompetitive electoral districts come, on the basis of deals and understandings with each other, to constitute a powerful inner directorate. In combination this directorate can easily frustrate newcomers. They are the "old boys" in the school, know where all the jam pots are hidden. They are the "power elite" in each house. Collectively, they "run" Congress. State governors, legislators and judges are clearly second-rank figures: they may be secure, but in very limited areas.

The upper hierarchy of the Catholic Church, too, owing to its psychic hold on many voting church members, should be considered pretty much as high-ranking *pubpols*, between the first and second ranks. It consists of *churchpols*.

This is the end of the power elite as far as *pubpolity* alone is concerned.

Two people of a type not here included who fit into Mills's conception of the power elite are Secretary of State Dean Rusk and former Secretary of Defense Robert McNamara, respectively derived from the Rockefeller and Ford stables. These men meet all the Millsian criteria and I wouldn't suggest that they should be regarded as ciphers. It is, however, noteworthy that each significantly changed his tune if not his entire public personality in the transition from service under President John F. Kennedy to service under President Lyndon B. Johnson. Each, indeed, changed from ostensibly reasonable and moderate men to fire-eating hawks, from cosmopolitan men to provincial men. In each case, it is obvious, their public script was supplied by the president, who held the power of dismissal over both. Each, no doubt powerful as a go-between, was powerful only as an underling.

J. William Fulbright, Richard B. Russell, John C. Stennis and others of the Senate Directorate in the interim experienced no such change of attitude. They remained implacably themselves.

There has in fact been no such phased change since 1930 as Mills and others refer to, although there have been changes—mostly in the way of more intense concentration of wealth with some greater preemption of roles by *pubpols*. *Pubpols* and *finpols* have both enhanced their powers, not with respect to each other but with respect to the public. One of the hundreds of external evidences of this is the shift of the major tax burden to the lower labor force. But these changes have not been basic changes that have altered the structuring of power in the United States.

What is the case is that American society has grown very large and complex and requires a more complex hierarchy of managers and officials with delegated powers. But to ascribe autonomous, initiating power to this hierarchy, as though it or any member of it below the very top could initiate or veto policy, is to befog the picture. The decisive power is at the very top, as was shown by the futile outcry of almost the entire intellectual and academic community against President Johnson's ruinous Vietnam policy. This policy was given the endorsement of leading *pubpols* and of big owners and corporation officials. And this was, for those with a stomach for it, a demonstration of *power*.

Let us look at a few recent big decisions of history and ask ourselves what role the Millsian power elite played in them.

In 1940 the facts of atomic theory were put to President Roosevelt. It seemed possible to develop an atomic bomb, Hitler might do it. Beyond scientists (not in Mills's power elite) telling the president of the technical possibilities, what elite led to the decision to go ahead with the Manhattan

Project? None, as far as the record shows. If it had proved a costly failure who, besides the president, could have been blamed?

When it came to dropping the bomb on Japan, who was consulted on the pros and cons? Only President Truman figured in the decision to do it. The dropping of the bomb, like its manufacture, came as a surprise even to the corporate press. Similarly, who joined in the decision to oust General MacArthur? Only President Truman. As the saying goes, he wasn't asking anybody, he was telling them. This is, clearly, demonstrated power.

During the Cuban missile crisis many advisory voices counseled President Kennedy: Invade Cuba, bomb it, blockade it, go to the United Nations, consult foreign governments, ignore the whole business, stick to economic blockades. Most suggestions, it is clear, were ignored. One course of action was selected—by President Kennedy.

The Bay of Pigs operation, however, appears to have been a true Millsian power-elite decision (Pentagon and CIA) which the president doubtfully accepted, with a crucial modification (withdrawal of air support) that in effect scuttled the whole thing.

When it came to committing American military power openly in Vietnam in 1965 the whole idea, as far as the record shows, arose in the mind of President Johnson, who appeared to believe he could pull off an easy coup, a grandstand play that would show him a political wizard. As far as the record shows, no combined group such as Mills talks about recommended any such action, and the president in the campaign of 1964 had explicitly opposed militant action as recommended by Barry Goldwater. Key Democrats of the inner Senate Establishment, such as Richard B. Russell of Georgia and John C. Stennis of Mississippi (elite of the elite as far as inner political power is concerned), were opposed to the procedure. Yet the president, and the president alone, gave the fateful signal that put the United States on the course toward blundering and costly slaughter and the loss of valuable friends all around the world. The operation, indeed, put the United States on all fours with Soviet Russia in its brutal suppression of the Hungarian uprising of 1956, stripped from the United States all pretensions to humane superiority over what is described on every hand as a sinister totalitarian power.

In all of Mills's collection of alleged power-elite people only the big owners (what I have called the *finpols*) and the upper *pubpols* cannot be questioned, and they never were in question. While the big owners can be proceeded against with much hue and cry, investigated, chivvied, demagogically denounced or even fined, they cannot be knocked out short of revolutionary change; for their position is woven into the very warp and woof of the legal system. The upper *pubpols* can at most be gradually undermined in a series of electoral defeats. Even in defeat the *pubpols* often still have much power, like mortally wounded pythons.

This being ineluctably so, the situation is precisely where it was before Mills introduced his dazzling array of underlings. Necessary instruments of it, they are not members of the power elite although in the ruling class; they are its fringes, at most its dispensable advisers. Whatever power they have is by appointment unless they become big owners, which they may do by marriage, or win big elections. Nelson A. Rockefeller, Robert F. Kennedy, Edward Kennedy, W. Averell Harriman and a few others hold elite rank on both counts.

Members of the topmost elite are not answerable to anyone for what they do in the ordinary course of affairs. This condition eliminates the *pubpols,* who are ultimately answerable to the electorate and to peers. The *pubpols,* for example, must spend a good part of their time conspicuously entering and leaving churches; the *finpols* can take the churches or leave them alone, as they usually do. Nelson A. Rockefeller no doubt diminished his standing as a *pubpol* by his divorce and remarriage; he did not diminish himself a bit as a *finpol.* Nor did Henry Ford II diminish himself as a *finpol* by divorce and remarriage. He even weathered automatic excommunication from the Catholic Church, which a *pubpol* could not have done.

A *finpol* may be an alcoholic, a drug addict or a homosexual; a *pubpol* would hardly have those choices. A sybaritic *finpol* can swing elections; his checks are as good as those written by a puritan. A known sybaritic *pubpol* could not make it. The *finpol,* in short, has a surer and more generalized power base: money.

Finpols spend much of their time abroad, often maintain foreign residences—*palazzos,* ranches, plantations, haciendas, *latifundias* and even resort hotels. *Pubpols* must remain close to the home soil, with an occasional junket abroad on "fact-finding" trips. They can't even be seen at Las Vegas.

Finpols, with no dilution of their essential power, can also lead *la dolce vita* fully orchestrated, with a full entourage of Corybantic girls. Tendencies in this direction have been moderated of late amid tightening world tensions, as a slight concession to public sensibilities. But jollification continues here and there—in Rome, Marrakech, Monaco, Rio and St. Moritz —behind closed doors.

Best of all, the *finpol* cannot be toppled by elections. If one party loses out he has many *pubpol* friends in the other party. As long as the factories are running he is right in the swim. Reforms come and go; trimming in the back committee rooms goes on forever.

As a *finpol* one obviously has a surer footing.

The difference with Mills on the structure of the power elite and other details mentioned earlier does not mean that his book is without merit: Mills wrote as a moralist and a political analyst rather than as a sociologist. As a sociologist he was unable to make contact with readily available data, he did not have the underlying facts. Yet Mills, despite much shuffling with ranks and cadres of underlings, always and despite everything comes around to the paramountcy of money in the situation. He is especially mordant in his final chapter, "The Higher Immorality," where he writes:

Whenever the standards of the moneyed life prevail, the man with money, no matter how he got it, will eventually be respected. A million dollars, it is said, covers a multitude of sins. It is not only that men want money; it is that their very standards are pecuniary. In a society in which the money-maker has had no serious rival for repute and honor, the word "practical" comes to mean useful for private gain, and "common sense," the sense to get ahead financially. The pursuit of the moneyed life is the commanding value, in relation to which the influence of other values has declined, so men easily become morally ruthless in the pursuit of easy money and fast estate-building.

A great deal of American corruption—although not all of it—is simply a part of the old effort to get rich and then become richer. But today the context in which the old drive must operate has changed. When both economic and political institutions were small and scattered—as in the simpler models of classical economics and Jeffersonian democracy—no man had it in his power to bestow or to receive great favors. But when political institutions and economic opportunities are at once concentrated and linked, then public office can be used for private gain.[8]

The Big Money

Just as one cannot be sure how much a man is worth by ascertaining how much stock he owns directly, so one can tell little about the true compensation of a top corporation executive by ascertaining what his salary is. It is pointless to mention specific formal salaries. There was a time when a corporation executive kept all of his generous salary. But with the introduction of the graduated income tax, cash income was eroded.

The tax laws seriously undermined the objective of purchasing the loyalty of worry-free essentially pecuniary men, and ways had to be found to make up the difference. Cash bonuses would not do because these required that the corporation expend (as the laws stood up to 1964) $100,-000 for every additional $10,000 that found its way into the executive's pocket.

The two thoroughly sound ways that were found to avoid this contre-temps turned out to be cut-rate stock options, a concealed untaxed gift, and lavish expense accounts. These latter have more recently been deli-cately trimmed, but the stock-option plan is flourishing as never before.[9]

The effect of the stock-option plan on executive take-home pay, assuming a doubling in value of the stock spread annually over a decade, was as follows in one company under the law as it stood in 1961:[10]

Total Cash Compensation	Estimated after-Tax Income on Cash	Capital Gain after Taxes on Options per Year	After-Tax Income Plus Capital Gain as Percentage of Cash Compensation
$240,000	$72,000	$144,000	90
150,000	59,000	79,000	92
95,000	46,000	43,000	93
65,000	37,000	26,000	97
45,000	29,000	14,000	96
30,000	21,000	5,400	85

The effective yearly executive tax in this company ranged, then, from 3 to 15 per cent, or less than the rate applicable to the lowest taxed ordi-nary income receiver in the country. The pecuniary advantages, direct and *sub rosa*, of being an upper executive are obvious.

We need not detain ourselves by reviewing untaxed expense account money, applied to some extent to entertainment and diversion and other-wise simply pocketed, or to other perquisites in the way of retirement funds and investment tips handed around among insiders on the top cor-porate level.

Depending on the extent of the stock-option plan and the nature of the company, this new wrinkle turned out to be the new royal road to riches in some companies. In pioneering General Motors, as we have noticed, it converted a long string of successive top executives into multi-millionaires: Raskob, Sloan, Knudsen, Mott, *et al.*

Stock options dilute the equities of stockholders—that is, outstanding stock is insensibly reduced in book value as blocks of stock are parceled out at cut rates. Until limitations were imposed outright, stock bonuses were popular, and in these the dilution was more plainly evident. The question now is: Do the stockholders, particularly the large stockholders, know what is taking place?

Leading stockholders always know precisely what is taking place, want to whet the acquisitive appetite of eager-beaver officers. In General Motors the Du Ponts, with a 23 per cent stake, obviously knew what was going on, acquiesced in it and possibly planned it that way. In at least one case some General Motors stockholders objected and terminated a then existing plan in court. In other companies stockholders are not at first aware of what is taking place and, when some do become aware, they may go to court to have the plans struck down, as in the 1930's in American Tobacco and Bethlehem Steel among others. In those cases a largely nonowning management had set up the plans as a way of subtly obtaining enlarged ownership of the company at bargain-counter prices.

Where some of the large hereditary owners, as in IBM among others, are executives and therefore participants in a stock-option plan, they experience less dilution of equity. The equity of the stock they already hold, true enough, is diluted but the dilution is partly or wholly compensated for by the participation in the juicy options.

Executives as Nonpecuniary Men

It is evident from the various schemes of corporate executive compensation that the acquisition of property and more property appears to be the overriding goal. One so concludes upon considering the large formal salaries, stock bonuses, stock-option plans, generous expense accounts and lucrative retirement plans, without considering various fringe benefits: long vacations, medical services, college scholarships and the like. This is all, very plainly, Easy Street in the latter-day corporate era.

And yet it has been seriously suggested that corporation executives are not really interested in money and money-making. We shall come to more items in this black-is-white mythology later, but right here seems a good place to attend to the notion that executives are not interested in making money.

The line, echoed in many management utterances, is stated succinctly by Osborn Elliott: ". . . the top men of U.S. industry possess the kind of drive and energy that separate the winners from the also-rans. Yet strangely enough, in a society based on the profit motive, these staunchest defenders of private profits are not themselves primarily motivated by money. Many of them, it is true, quite naturally entertain a healthy regard for the six-digit pay check. For when a man steps into a top job, his pay is likely to accelerate almost to escape velocity."

There follows a review of some of the opulent salaries, up to Eugene Grace's $800,000 in 1956.

"Yet," Elliott resumes, "the promise of money is not what keeps most top executives coming to the office every day. For one thing, high taxes make a raise almost meaningless. . . ."

We have, though, already seen how that little impediment is bypassed. "This is certainly the way Crawford Greenewalt [of Du Pont] feels about his own pay as president of du Pont," Elliott continues. "It is a well-known fact that on Greenewalt's wedding day in 1926, his father-in-law Irénée du Pont gave him 1,000 shares of Christiana Corp., the holding company that owns gobs of du Pont stock. By 1959, Greenewalt owned 4,096 shares of du Pont common (at $250 a share) and 687 shares of Christiana common (at $17,000), for total holdings worth $13 million. Thus Greenewalt does not exactly depend on his $300,000-odd yearly salary and bonus from du Pont to keep body and soul together. . . ."

But Greenewalt's pay check, Elliott admits, nevertheless has at least emotional meaning to him. He would not like to work for nothing. For, Greenewalt is quoted, "Money is a symbol in the same way that a Nobel Prize is a symbol to the scientists. You can't eat a Nobel Prize. Of course, you can eat the $50,000 that goes with it, but that's not why people want to win one."[11]

So, this strange spectacle of elaborately large pay taken in various tax-skipping forms, does have a rational if recondite explanation. It is, we are assured, purely symbolic, analogous to a Nobel Prize in science. A slight difference is that the Nobel Prize usually comes only once, cannot be solicited and is for a modest $50,000. It carries with it no stock options, gifts or retirement pay that amounts to more in one year than the average worker makes in twenty to forty years.

And the recipients of the pay, we are assured, are akin to scientists, but better paid.

Lest it be thought that I dismiss the strange contention out of hand let us prayerfully consider it together. There may be some subtle point here, as in higher mathematics, which lesser mortals have difficulty in grasping. All this money is a symbolic prize apparently for rare and profound management insight exercised to keep the infinitely complex industrial system going.

Looked at coldly, the contention in the light of all surrounding circumstances is an insult to intelligence. Comparison of year-in-year-out executive pay to the Nobel Prize compounds the insult. If the money were a mere symbol it could be hung on the wall, like a diploma. As it is, it is treasured, carefully invested, locked into the strongest vaults. If a stranger gains access to it without permission, he is liable to be shot out of hand. It is, then, more than a symbol. It is the substance, the ultimate goal.

It is entirely possible, of course, for a man to say honestly that his salary of $300,000 or so means little to him (especially when 70 or 91 per cent of it is taxable) in the light of the fact that he has other large income steadily accruing to him in dividends, undistributed profits, retirement funds, prepaid life insurance and perhaps capital gains from cut-rate stock options. Anyone might feel this way about $300,000 in such circumstances. But that this disproves an interest in money is hardly tenable. Rather could it be interpreted more reasonably as showing an interest in money that has been so well satisfied that $300,000 additional before taxes is a trifle!

Still, Osborn Elliott may be exactly correct in the letter of what he says, although he is certainly errant in rendering the essence. For he said, the close reader will note, that these men are not *primarily* motivated by the prospect of large gain. What primarily motivates any man might be difficult to say. Most men appear to be *primarily* motivated by a desire to continue breathing from moment to moment. But somewhere along the way the big money-makers, after primary motivations have been served, appear to be grasped by a very strong, compulsive, overriding motivation to gather in large sums of money by a variety of devious avenues.

Careful studies of executive inter-company mobility, based on large numbers of companies, are inconclusive in showing a clear pull of money alone in the attraction of executives. This is in part because the effect of stock options, which became pervasive only after 1950, has not been fully studied and because the effect of hidden perquisites like wide-open expense accounts cannot be measured. But even though pre-1950 data do not clearly show the pull of bigger money[12] it is agreed by observers in the field that either money or greater responsibilities and higher positions invariably associated with money are factors.[13]

Business Week in 1953 found that 422 job-changing executives gave the following reasons for moving: bigger job, more responsibility, 29.9 per cent; greater opportunity for future growth, 21.6 per cent; increased income, 17.8 per cent; disagreement with management policies, 16.1 per cent; discharged, 14.7 per cent; need for change of activity, 10.9 per cent; all other reasons combined, 50.9 per cent.

As Roberts points out, on the executive circuit the first two reasons are usually associated with more money, so that in this group 69.3 per cent of the reasons given concerned money-making. The total of reasons exceeds 100 per cent because some of the men stated more than one reason.[14]

"Many similar surveys have been made and, while they differ in the weight given to individual factors, they point to a complex web of motivations in which money *by itself* [my emphasis—F. L.] appears to be relatively unimportant, but in which money contributes to an unknown degree to the attractiveness of non-financial factors."[15]

All that this indicates, after tracing through the fine print, is that a salable executive will not ordinarily stay in a well-paid job if he is seriously humiliated, mistreated or frustrated and will not seek a better-paying job if it doesn't offer him at least as much security of treatment and status. But none of it suggests that executives are not attracted by better money offers. A man paid $100,000 net by Du Pont might not respond to an offer of $200,000 from Podunk Arms but, unless he saw better things in sight for him at Du Pont, he would almost certainly examine carefully an offer of $200,000 net from Allied Chemical or Union Carbide. He would, as everyone recognizes, owe it to his wife, his children, his mother, his pastor, his Alma Mater and the family dog to do at least this much.

If executives were not drawn by better money offers, despite all labored statistical analyses, such offers would not be made (and often accepted) as they commonly are. The fact that all the offers are not accepted shows the weight of the old maxim: Money isn't everything.

Yet the asserted disinterest of the high executive in money, attested to by Greenewalt of Du Pont, has achieved high academic certification, as have many other strange notions relating to wealth in the United States. Professor Daniel Bell, Columbia University sociologist, thus assures us that the new corporate men "were a special breed, often engineers, whose self-conscious task was to build a new economic form, and whose rewards were not *primarily* [there it is again—F. L.] money—few accumulated the large fortunes made by a Carnegie, a Rockefeller, a Harriman, or a Ford —but status achievements and, ultimately, some independent power of their own. Thus T. N. Vail, who created American Telephone and Telegraph, Elbert Gary, who became the public relations face of U.S. Steel ('He never saw a blast furnace until he died,' said Ben Stolberg once, bitterly), Alfred P. Sloan, who fashioned the decentralized structure of General Motors, Gerard Swope, who held together General Electric, Walter Teagle, who rationalized Standard Oil" are representatives of a new social upward mobility.[16] And this last may be true.

The big corporation man here stands forth as a status achiever, not *primarily* interested in money. (It has never been established, one should notice, that Carnegie, Rockefeller, Harriman, Ford or any of the progenitor moguls were *primarily* interested in money. For my part, I should say they were not.)

All these men—Vail, Gary, Sloan, Swope and Teagle—were agents. Behind Vail, Gary and Swope stood J. P. Morgan and Company. Behind Sloan was the Du Pont family and behind Teagle were the Rockefellers.

The only one of these to amass a very considerable fortune, thanks to stock options and a preternaturally skyrocketing large industry, was Sloan.

Professor Bell's thesis here is that family capitalism, once dominant, is breaking up, making way for the New Men of power, the new managers, who are very much akin to the members of Mills's power elite, although Bell has many well-taken critical reservations about Mills. Like Mills, he believes in the managerial revolution, in new coalitions of men not *primarily* interested in money (except as collectors) but interested in status, achievement and play with power. The power of the "ruling class" has been dissolved. Everything is in flux.[17]

That the concrete evidence shows this has not happened—at least not yet—the reader is now well aware.

What I suggest is that the big executives, the new men, are interested in money, perhaps not primarily but prominently. I deny that ultimate power either in a company or nationally lies with the executives, unless they are also big owners.

I don't by any means suggest that the big executives are straw men, water boys. They would be of slight use to the powers-that-be if they were. Considering what little is expected of them by their superiors they are perfectly capable. They just do not call the shots, either singly or in coalition. Their role is advisory. If, creatively, they develop large plans, these plans are subject to approval—in politics by the president and the congressional Establishment (with the concurrence of the Supreme Court) and in industry-finance by the big and few stockholders (not by the twenty million shareholders of the Stock Exchange's "People's Capitalism").

To show that what I assert is not so, all anybody has to do is to cite a single case wherein a single executive or coalition of executives, lawyers, military men or others carried out any project whatever in government against the will of the president and Congress, and in industry-finance against the will of the big owners either directly present or always ready to step in. Berle in *The Modern Corporation and Private Property* shows a string of big companies under management control by one legal device or other, but a few years later the managers, who were often big owners elsewhere in the economy, were knocked out by legislation and most of the companies were also knocked out of existence, especially in public utilities.

All this is so even though, as I am aware, there are cases of big owners who haven't the foggiest notion about anything until they consult the president of their company and their lawyer. They are completely dependent for guidance upon these far more knowledgeable men, who exercise power by proxy. In the circles of power, too, everybody knows for whom they speak. But I see no validity in looking upon such representatives of absentee power as "new men" of power. To me they look like old-fashioned agents, overseers, by no means to be disparaged. At the same time, they should not be enthroned—at least, not until after a coronation.

Social Origins of Executives

The origins and backgrounds of big business leaders have been studied under the most refined academic auspices and their careers statistically traced with fine-caliper methodology.[18] We may profitably take note of some of the findings.

Of the large sample studied for a period of twenty-five years, 52 per cent had fathers in business and 22 per cent had fathers in professions or white-collar work. Only 9 per cent had sires who were farmers, and 15 per cent laborers.

The fathers of 8 per cent were owners of large businesses, of 15 per cent were major executives, of 18 per cent were owners of small businesses, of 8 per cent were minor executives and of 3 per cent were foremen.[19]

This finding was widely at variance with the distribution of occupations in the population as of 1920, when 47 per cent of all adult males were classified as laborers. If big business leaders had been 47 per cent the sons of laborers, the mobility rate for laborers would be 100. As it was it was only 16, while that of sons of farmers was only 40. The upward mobility rate for the sons of owners of small business was 360, of sons of professional men 350 and of sons of foremen was 133.

Most significantly, the upward mobility rate of men whose fathers were business executives or owners of large business was 775, nearly eight times the statistical projection. The sons obviously either had friends at court or got proper coaching.

As the University of Chicago sociologist W. Lloyd Warner sees it, the "royal road" to high executive success was higher education. Whereas in 1928 only somewhat more than 30 per cent of big business leaders had a college education, by 1952 the quota was nearly 60 per cent. In 1928 only 15 per cent had some college study but by 1952 20 per cent had at least been to college.[20]

Of 505 business leaders as of 1952 as many as 216 went to only 14 different colleges, and these same 14 colleges were mentioned 87 times as the ones attended secondarily, either for graduate work or in transfer. Yale, Harvard, Princeton and Cornell were named most often, with Harvard as the dominant choice for graduate work.[21] Very nearly a third went to Harvard and Yale as undergraduates or graduates.

In no fewer than 62 cases the men went to a second "select" group of 10 colleges, of which Northwestern, Pennsylvania State, Stanford, Wisconsin and Western Reserve were tied for first place.[22]

"Education has become the royal road to positions of power and prestige in American business and industry," says Warner. "That this royal road is open to all men is given ample testimony by the large number of educated men from the bottom social layers who appear in our sample."[23]

That this royal road, so optimistically saluted, may not in fact be such is suggested by the continuing merger movement and the steady progress of computer analysis. Decision making, whatever its role in the past, is inevitably being narrowed in scope by the increasing refinement and elaboration of computers; live decision makers, whatever their role in the past, are becoming increasingly dispensable. Furthermore, the merger movement is continually reducing the number of top executive posts. Every merger, while it does not necessarily reduce the total of vice presidents and executive vice presidents, does reduce the number of chairmen and presidents. If all companies were combined into a single company there would be places for only one chairman and one president, and at most twenty-five members of the board.

That education is not the true gateway to the "royal road" is shown by the concentration of elite schools, long the special wards of the propertied. These schools, eclipsing others, produced most executives because they were most patronized by the upper classes. In view of the fact that sons of members of the business elite, owners or big executives, were disproportionately represented and showed the highest index of upward corporate mobility, it would appear that belonging to the business in-group and the socially related professional group was a more significant factor than level or place of schooling in obtaining big-business position. Sons of owners, executives and professionals as a matter of course are more likely to go on to college, particularly to elite colleges, and after that into the higher executive posts. True, as Warner shows, men of lower social origins can and do make the grade, but in far lesser proportion than the incidence of low social origin in the population. Otherwise put, those who are already in at the beginning are more likely to be in at the final reckoning.

The typical business leader of the 1950's was 54 years old, had been with his firm 24 years, achieved his high position 24 years after entering business and had held his job for almost 7 years. Most men began business between age 21 and 22, freely shifted jobs and companies until about 29 years old when they joined their permanent firms. Typically, the man was 45 or 46 years old when he clearly emerged as a top dog.[24]

But the longer his period of schooling the quicker he made it to the top. Graduate students made the very top in 19.9 years, college graduates in 22.9 years, college dropouts in 24.5 years, high school graduates in 27.9 years, high school dropouts in 30.6 years and grade school products in 31 years.[25]

So, the more schooling the successful entrants have (or the more affluent early circumstances) the quicker they make it to the top. At any rate, neither education nor in-group standing retard one in his ascent.

In beginning occupations, 43 per cent started as clerks and salesmen, 24 per cent as professionals, only 14 per cent as skilled or unskilled laborers. "Few at any point in their careers were entrepreneurs in the sense of owning or establishing their own businesses. Also, while there have been a number of cases of men moving from top-level military positions into key positions of late, these form only a minor proportion of the total business elite."[26] So much for Mills's switchovers from the military to the corporate circuits.

The Horatio Alger hero, as Warner notes, is not very much in evidence.

"Careers are built largely on formal education, acquisition of management skills in the white-collar hierarchy, and movement through the far-flung systems of technicians and lower-level management personnel into top management. Traces of the legendary patterns remain, and spectacular examples of the type exist; they tend to be unique."[27]

Upward mobility toward the elite corporate level, Warner found, was especially marked in the area of marriage because most business leaders in all categories married above or below their levels of origin. Those of laborer origin married most frequently at their level of origin, 42 per cent; big-business people married next most frequently at their level of origin, 35 per cent. Professionals and white-collar people, exogamous at 77 and 81 per cent respectively, married most frequently outside their levels of origin, but nearly 20 per cent in both these cases married into the big-business class, took to wife a tycoon's daughter.

When a man marries above or below level of origin—and most of all categories did—there is upward social mobility toward corporate elite status involved in marriage for the man *or* the woman. As the leaders all have elite status, it matters not how they got it, although women born below the elite obviously got there only through marriage. A woman is either in the elite to begin with, marries into it or marries a man who drags her along into it.[28]

People who make it to the top or are born into the top are mobile in non-social ways. They are, first, geographically mobile, easily moving around the country from place to place. They are functionally mobile, readily adapting to a considerable range of jobs in which Warner detects much special educational stimulus; they are adaptable men. Those in the birth elite, however, tend to be less conspicuously geographical gadabouts.

External signs of steadiness and "stability" were most noticeable in the birth elite. The others, at least early in their careers, were more akin to rolling stones, willing to switch jobs and locations.

The number of men in the same firm as their fathers, compared with sons of the elite who achieve high position in other business organizations, is relatively small. There can be no doubt that each group of men was advantaged by being born to high estate. Only a few were directly aided by extra privileges and financial assistance; but the immediate factor of being born to families accorded high rank by the community provides such fortunate men with social and economic advantages, such as being in the higher levels of prestige where the powerful are, going to the "right" preparatory schools, having the right social relations and clubs and fraternities in college, and going with and courting young women of their own social set, knowing what to do and not to do (while the parvenu by trial and error is struggling to learn that there are such ways). They get a head start in life that can be overcome only by hard work, grim determination, and watchfulness of personnel offices, or the eager quest of great corporations for young men of promise. The birth elite are advantaged because their families learn "superior" values, goals, and standards by living in the subculture of an upper class. Their earliest adaptations from infancy on—nursing, weaning, cleanliness, likes and dislikes, admiration or dislike of intimate figures about them, later childhood goals and ambitions—are set within the learning maze of a "superior" family.[29]

It may be hypothesized that there are far more heart attacks among the nonelite upward strivers than in the birth elite: the Horatio Alger boys who never made it, dropped dead on the ten-yard line. I have found no studies of fatal illness in the candidates for success on the corporate ladder that compare the rate of such illness for groups of different social origin. One may surmise, however, that the man who makes it from laborer to retirement as chairman of the board has an exceptionally strong constitution. The road ahead somehow seems less rough with Scarsdale, Yale and Skull and Bones as take-off points.

Life around the Executive Suite

Life in the corporations, and in and around the executive suite, has been as closely studied as other phases of the executive terrain and has often been portrayed in best-selling novels and popular films. William Whyte's *The Organization Man* is one of the better known of the more mordant studies of the corporate bureaucracy and its foibles, and there are others.

But for an impressionistic study of the headquarters office of the large *finpolity* there is nothing to excel Alan Harrington's *Life in the Crystal Palace*, written by one of its Harvardian denizens. Grimly forbidding to the Socialist, Communist and more generalized radical, the organizational generating point of human exploitation and debasement, the corporation on the inside is indeed nothing so much as a crystal palace, a place of shining light, elevated attitude and sweet benignity. "I think that our company resembles nothing so much as a private socialist system," says Harrington.[30]

The whole of his book is a banteringly persuasive, penetrating embroidery on this theme.

What Marx suggested socialism might be like after it took over an irrational capitalism from a handful of selfish owners one finds here—at the headquarters of the giant corporation. Here the byword is: From each according to his capacity without any great pressure, to each according to his needs in an ascending hierarchy of greater and greater privileges, boons and opportunities. Harsh voices are never heard in the Crystal Palace, nobody is ever bawled out, nobody is ever fired no matter how much he deserves it, everything is cushioned—benefits all around for everybody from day of employment until death.

"A mighty fortress is our Palace; I will not want for anything. I may live my days without humiliation. I will not be fired. It nourishes my self-respect. I am led along the paths of righteousness for my own good. I am protected from tyrants. It guards me against tension and fragmentation of myself. It anoints me with benefits. Though we pass through hard times, I will be preserved. These strong walls will surely embrace all the days of my life, if I remain a corporation man forever."[31]

And all this applies down to the lowliest clerk and office boy of the Crystal Palace, each of whom has in hand his plan of sure benefits until retirement and beyond. Everything is bland, bland, bland . . . and genteel, subdued.

But "As for the young man who has not gone to college, he is virtually untouchable so far as a middle-level job with a corporation is concerned. If Henry Ford were reincarnated he could never land a job at the Crystal Palace. In fact, on the technical side, an applicant will have quite a bit of selling to do if he can't produce a graduate school degree."[32]

"I suspect," says Harrington, "that most jobs in a corporation and elsewhere can be mastered in a few months, or at any rate in a year or two. What cannot be learned that quickly is the corporation minuet—the respectful dance with the right partners. The watchful corporation man gradually finds out who is important and who is not; what is acceptable and what is not; what type of project will advance his fortunes and what is not worth bothering about. The secrets of gauging and responding to the power of others—superimposed on a normal intelligence—will move him slowly upward."[33]

In the upshot Harrington found paradise boring. The hardest task was standing quietly on the escalator as it quietly swept one upwards toward the quiet stratosphere of quiet corporate power.

There was one cardinal sin at the Crystal Palace, Harrington found, and it could get one into serious difficulty. This was to be without the capacity for belief in the absurd, at least for believing in believing. Not to be a true believer of some acceptable sort stamped one as dangerous. As Harrington saw it, the hierarchy of acceptable beliefs from highest to lowest was as follows:

1. Belief in the product. "The highest and most satisfying form of commercial belief is the conviction that the product I am working for is essential, or at least helpful, to mankind. If I can't have that, I should be able to assume, at any rate, that our product is the best of its kind on the market. Lacking that, let me have faith that it is not positively the worst of its kind. Take even that away, and please assure me that it is not poisonous. Without such assurance, I will have to justify my job in another way." The product, in short, is making the world a better place, at least not worse.

2. Belief in making money. "Money . . . measures the length and strength of my manhood. It is the skin of the dangerous leopard, the bacon from the wily pig that I bring home because I am strong and know my way around the forest. . . . The possession of money makes men more masculine and women more feminine. Cash enlarges the soul. Money creates beauty where there was none before. It is positively erotic and can buy gaiety. When I have money I am a much nicer person, tolerant, kind and understanding, and I forgive the sins of others. . . ." Moneymakers are great people, the greatest.

3. Belief in getting ahead. Attainment of status is the end in view here. You are what people think of you.

4. Belief in being a "pro," in doing a job professionally well whether one likes the job or not.

5. Belief in sheer process. "I believe in production."

6. Belief in the company, whatever one's lack of belief in any of the foregoing. Not at the very least to believe in the company disqualifies one entirely.

For if I am lost in the split-level values of modern business, the High Corporation will serve as my High Church. Like the church, my Crystal Palace removes the burden of belief from me. It removes my need for decision. I have found my rock. I only believe in the company.

Like the church, our company is good and wise. In the context of business enterprise, it is the inheritor and vessel of a mighty tradition. Our company has achieved high ethics and kindness, and cares for me, and will see me through to sixty-five, and send me checks after that. Church and Palace alike are sanctuaries in the jungle of unbridled competition. At the head of the church is God. On the top floor of the Crystal Palace . . . it doesn't matter, since I will never arrive there.[34]

The Big Money

The plush fortunes, few excepted, belong almost entirely to original owners of properties, mainly in the form of corporations, or their descendants. Leading executives, no matter how much they are paid, rarely put together overarching estates.

The way one becomes ultra-rich on the corporate circuit is to gain an early ownership participation in a rapidly developing company (preferably unnoticed) in a new field, precisely as in the nineteenth century. The trick is to see the new field opening up or to open it up. Most nonowner executives, as we have seen, make it to the top at about forty-five years of age, with only some twenty years to go before mandatory retirement. Even if they were able to put aside as much as $1 million a year out of cash salary, stock options and participation in undistributed profits this would guarantee only $20 million prior to retirement, not a pauper's portion by any means but still not up in the imperial range of the General Motors executives between 1920 and 1960 nor in the range of the $90-million estate left by Arthur Vining Davis of Alcoa.

In order to get into the really top money an executive must have taken his top position very early, which means that except in the case of an hereditary owner it must certainly have been a small or smallish little-known company when he took his position. Thereafter his fortunes became those of the burgeoning company; as a member of the inner family he becomes rich enough to arouse widespread envy.

Not many big new companies have emerged since 1920. Running down the *Fortune* list of the first hundred industrials we find International Business Machines, North American Aviation, Boeing, Radio Corporation, General Telephone, General Dynamics, Sperry Rand, United Aircraft, Allied Chemical, Minnesota Mining and Manufacturing, Mc-

Donnell Aircraft, Olin Mathieson, Textron, Celanese, Litton Industries, Douglas Aircraft, Reynolds Metals, Grumman Aircraft and United Merchants and Manufacturers. Even some of these embrace, through mergers, properties extant before 1920; most of them, however, are representative of new technology, mainly aviation, electronics and chemicals, and have been well served by war. Some started out rather big. It is in companies such as these that early executives who remain for many years turn up with estates that are large but seldom within hailing distance of the big established fortunes multiply distributed among many family members. In this collection no fortunes have been produced to compare with the stupendous accumulations of Henry Ford and the General Motors crowd.

A rather fruitless running debate takes place desultorily between those who assert that the American economy is so developed that nobody can any longer scrape together a big fortune and those who claim there are as many opportunities for fortune-builders as ever. That there are lush opportunities cannot be denied. But that, in view of the great increase in population and the solidly established titles of hereditary wealth, the opportunities are nearly so many as once was the case is extremely doubtful. Concentration alone limits opportunities for financial devilment by newcomers.

While new technology does lift new men to positions of wealth, it should not be forgotten that old wealth-holders are usually careful to see that they are participants in the new technology. Thus, while the development of Polariod made newcomer Dr. Edwin H. Land a very wealthy man —one of the few really wealthy inventors—he was in partnership with Harriman and Warburg money.

Corporation executives are the most highly consistently paid people in the American economy. If salary is a symbol of worth, as commonly supposed, they are the most worthwhile people in American society. In general, pay for administering large properties or organizations exceeds all other types of *recurrent* pay. The pay of top executives even in nonprofit organizations, such as foundations and national trade unions, also tends to be high, in the range at least of $50,000 to $100,000.

The most systematically, subtly and thoroughly trained people in the country, it will be generally agreed, are the scientists. Yet the median annual salary of 223,854 registered scientists in 1964 was only $11,000 a year, about the expense account of a middle-level salesman.[35]

The highest median for highly experienced scientists was for those in the age range 50–54, where the figure was $13,400. Scientists employed in industry and business had a median salary of $12,000. In the management or administration of research and development scientists had a median of $15,500. The median for the upper tenth of income receivers among scientists was $18,000; for the lower tenth, $7,100.[36]

The median for scientists in education, trainers of new scientists, was $9,600; in the federal government, $11,000; in other government, $9,000; in the military, $7,800; in nonprofit organizations, $12,000; and among the self-employed, $15,000. Scientists with a medical degree had a median of $15,500 compared with $12,000 for the holders of the Ph.D.[37]

The highest pay as of 1965 reported for any pure scientist in the United States was $45,000 annually paid to Dr. C. N. Yang, Nobel physicist of the University of the State of New York. The highest salary reported for a non-scientist working scholar was $30,000 assigned to Dr. Arthur Schlesinger, Jr., historian formerly of Harvard and more recently with the City University of New York.[38]

When Dr. Albert Einstein, one of the most fundamentally creative brains of modern times, just before World War II accepted an invitation to join the Institute for Advanced Study at Princeton, New Jersey, he was asked by Dr. Abraham Flexner, the director, to name his price. Einstein, writing that he was "flame and fire" for the position, suggested $3,000 a year. Flexner quietly set the pay at $16,000.[39]

The salary of Dr. Yang would be considered barely adequate by any middle-range corporate executive. It would be a small "gift" for any legislator. It would hardly buy the gowns for one year for any one of scores of nubile heiresses who would probably have difficulty threading a needle. Einstein's salary, even by pre-World War II standards, was that of a very lower-rung man.

If we take Dr. Yang's salary of $45,000 as an index of maximum sophisticated earning ability, it is clear as crystal that 75 per cent or more of the salaries of top corporation officials is paid for nonability factors—mainly loyalty. The salaries of scientists, academic and nonacademic, range far higher than those of college professors in general or even most college presidents, as shown in annual reports on salaries by the American Association of University Professors. Many professors as of 1967, even at what are taken as "good" schools, were paid down in the range of $7,000 and less. Most of the schools' teaching staff is paid far lower.

Professionals in general are paid on a similar low level. The most highly paid professionals are dentists, physicians, surgeons, lawyers and judges, and their median earnings in 1959 were somewhat about $10,000 annually, according to *Statistical Abstract,1964*, page 229. The medians for other professionals were far lower—$4,020 for clergymen, $4,653 for musicians and music teachers, $7,207 for college presidents, professors and instructors, $5,827 for secondary school teachers, etc. Engineers, so vital to an industrial system, had a median of $8,361.

The reader should be reminded that the median indicates that half are paid *below these levels.*

Leaving aside the factor of scientific creativity, the man in science must have precise, detailed knowledge of thousands of minute and of all-enveloping aspects of his field, within which he must be able to reason subtly, usually mathematically, and he must maintain over long periods of time steadiness of purpose even though results are meager. He is rarely buoyed up by the great "breakthroughs" alluded to so facilely by journalists. Nor can these when they occur be patented and capitalized.

Neither in input of thought, effort, preparation or concentration is the work of any corporation executive remotely comparable. Indeed, on the basis of "inside" or friendly accounts the intellectual attainments of corporation executives appear to be slight. *Fortune* finds they do not do much reading, are weak in intellectual powers.[40] Others wonder how many of them have functional reading ability at all because so many seem poorly informed, constantly need assistance from public relations men (usually ex-journalists).

There is a great concentration of brains in a corporation. But it shows itself, not in the top executives as a rule, but in the lower-paid lawyers, engineers, scientists, market analysts and public relations men. These specialists usually work up the script for the trusted top men. When some of the executives decide to "go it alone" in public expressions of their conventional wisdom, one gets derisive reverberations, as in the case of Charles E. Wilson's what's-good-for-General Motors homily to Congress. Speaking out on his own, the top corporation man often sounds like a goof, a super-Babbitt, and the lower professionals in his company writhe uncomfortably. Indeed, in some companies the professional staff is under standing instructions to keep the top man so "boxed in" and isolated that he cannot put his foot in his mouth in public, cannot deliver himself of dazzling shafts of cracker-barrel wisdom.

It is sometimes argued that it is the vast concentrated responsibilities of the top corporate men that make them worth their pay; responsibilities of scientists and teachers, although not denied, are held to be more diffuse, less immediately decisive. Top military officers, however, certainly have organizational responsibilities that transcend those of any corporate officials. Their moment-to-moment decisions involve far more men, equipment, money and organizational niceties as well as the very safety of the nation. This is especially so in time of war.

Yet the Chief of Staff as of 1966 drew a maximum base pay of $2,140 a month or $25,680 per year. The men serving as Chairman of the Joint Chiefs of Staff, Chief of Staff of the Army, Chief of Naval Operations, Chief of Staff of the Air Force or Commandant of the Marine Corps receive basic pay for the grade of $2,019.30 per month regardless of cumulative years of service. A Chief of Staff or Chief of Naval Operations also draws $4,000 per year in personal money allowance. A four-star general or an admiral gets $2,000 a year in money allowance and a maximum annual salary of $17,796. Corporately speaking, all this is taxable chicken feed.

When we ascend to the ineffable level of the Commander in Chief himself, the president of the United States, we find the salary is $100,000 a year and fully taxable. There is also a taxable expense allowance of $50,000 for officially connected duties and a nontaxable annual travel allowance of $40,000. Living quarters are also provided and an alert president can latch on to many free rides and free lunches. There now goes with the job a lifetime pension of $25,000 a year, $10,000 annually for presidential widows and up to $50,000 a year (plus free mailing privileges) for the office help of ex-presidents. The maximum time a man may enjoy this comparatively modest salary and expense account is ten years.

Owing to the tax bite the in-pocket effectiveness of both the salary and the nontravel expense account is reduced by more than 50 per cent. For a president like Lyndon B. Johnson, who was thriftily able to build up from hard-pan poverty an estate of some $13 million or more on his salary as a congressman, there was no particular problem involved. And for a big inheritor like President John F. Kennedy there was no problem.

This office carries with it vast responsibilities. Yet there is probably no president or chairman of any one of 750 or more of the largest corporations who is not paid far more. So much for responsibilities and the emoluments therefor.

The corporate executive, as I said, is no wizard. He is paid as he is because he is in a position to do much harm to big property holders. There is a further nuance that should perhaps be noticed. A big stockholder, everything else apart, wants his chief executives to feel identified as closely as possible with him. Hence he sees to it that their take-home pay is as close to $1 million a year as possible. He knows their expense account is phoney because he probably set it up himself and knows there is no such legitimate expense involved. It is all readily explainable as serving to keep up appearances.

The executives at various times must entertain foreign notables, public officials or other wealthy men. It would hardly do for them to entertain in meager surroundings. The residences of the top executives should say at a glance: The Super-Cosmos Corporation is an extremely rich and powerful entity, to be treated respectfully. Again, big executives must make political campaign-fund contributions.

No implication is here intended that executives, considering all circumstances, should really be paid less. They are paid by people who seldom overpay, who pay only what they feel they must pay in every situation. All I intend to say is that, despite all the ballyhoo about esoteric executive skill to cover up what the pay is really for, the executives are not paragons, are not superior people—superior to scientists, high military officers and *pubpols* —to the degree that their compensation might suggest. They are basically politicians, with all the popular connotations of the term. They are paid as they are to guarantee proper performance by people who are anxious about that performance.

The comparatively astronomic pay of corporate executives as stand-in overseers of large properties and manipulators of large numbers of employees, consumers and common citizens is shown in still another perspective when compared with the compensation, before taxes, of the entire American labor force. Here the pay of at least some scientists begins to look pretty good, although at least half the scientists are paid on the level of the lower labor force.

The following chart-profile of family income in the United States from 1947 to 1964 in 1964 dollars is taken from *Current Population Reports: Consumer Income* of the United States Department of Commerce, issued September 24, 1965.

About 20 per cent of *families* as of 1964 had incomes above $10,000 a year. While only 10 per cent of individual incomes exceeded $10,000, with only 1 per cent exceeding $25,000, substantial family participation in plus-$10,000 income stems from the fact that some persons hold two jobs, some families have two or more wage earners and many families in this bracket own property. Nevertheless, 80 per cent of the families shown on this chart had incomes below $10,000, mostly from wages, no matter how many earners they had. From somewhat more than a quarter in the income-group under $3,000 in 1947 the families in this range by 1964 were slightly less than 20 per cent in dollars of 1964 value.

The United States is usually alluded to in the corporate press as a country of large incomes, high wages. And so it is in comparison with nonindustrial countries where incomes are very low. But in relation to the incomes of corporate executives and the owners of large inherited properties, and to American tax-padded price levels, Americans draw coolie pay. A few weeks out of a job and most of them are stony broke, on the relief rolls.

The careful reader should not suppose that the reference to "coolie pay" is hyperbolic.

Per capita "real" income from all sources in the United States in the first quarter of 1966—that is, income after personal taxes and in terms of the dollar stabilized at 1958 prices—was at an annual rate of $2,260, up from $1,900 in the first quarter of 1960 and from $1,831 in 1958. In terms of the 1966 dollar the rate was $2,490, showing an inflation of $230 or about 10 per cent over the "real" rate.[41]

These figures, of course, are averages, applicable to every man, woman and child. In order to have the latest figure applicable to members of his family, a married man with three children in 1966 would have required an income of $12,450, after taxes, in current dollars, which would yield a "real" income of $11,300 in 1958 dollars. If such was his income, though, he would have been well up among the upper 10 per cent of income receivers.

Owing to the very great incomes received by 1 per cent and less of the population, mostly from investments, the actual participation of some 90 per cent of the population in "real" income takes place at levels ranging far below the stated average of $2,260 per person.

Single persons who received from $2,490 and upward in 1966 after taxes were, of course, at or above the average. But a married man with a nonworking wife would have had to receive twice this much to be at the average and would need $2,490 of income in current dollars, always after personal taxes, for each of his children in order for them all to be at the average. Few persons participate at the "average" level!

This bedrock figure computed by the government, moreover, does not allow for the substantial taxes incorporated in prices.

In order to show the splendor of American workers' incomes it is often shown how much longer one must work in Russia for a loaf of bread, a pair of shoes, a bottle of milk, etc. What is shown is true specifically, but misleading. For some costs in Russia, such as of available housing, are less. Again, many services are provided at no direct cost. In Russia and throughout Europe, no college tuition is charged and a variety of services, costly in the United States, are provided at low cost.

The median figure on real income would necessarily be much lower than this average, for the lower half necessarily includes many with zero income —the publicly institutionalized sick and delinquent. There are also the low-paid seasonal agricultural workers, the unemployed and the only occasionally employed.

Total income in the United States is, of course, great—the greatest in the world. But popular participation in this vast income ranges from zero to very

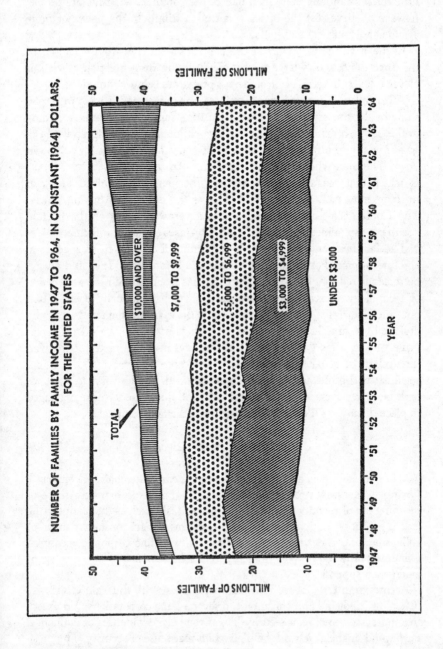

NUMBER OF FAMILIES BY FAMILY INCOME IN 1947 TO 1964, IN CONSTANT (1964) DOLLARS, FOR THE UNITED STATES

$10,000 AND OVER

$7,000 TO $9,999

$5,000 TO $6,999

$3,000 TO $4,999

UNDER $3,000

TOTAL

MILLIONS OF FAMILIES

YEAR

little for substantially more than half of the populace. Most literate people, however, believe just the opposite is true, a tribute to the power of propaganda and statistical manipulation.

In the 1930's large sectors of the population suffered from deflation. In the 1950's and 1960's large sectors are suffering from inflation as well as elevated taxes. In terms of income most people are being "whipsawed."

What inflation over the long term has done to income is shown in a 1966 study by the conservative National Industrial Conference Board. According to this study, a man with a wife and two children today must receive $13,-324 annually to buy the same amount of goods he could get for $5,000 in 1939. The man who received $10,000 in 1939 must now receive $27,288 to match that year's buying power and the man who received $100,000 in 1939 must now get $307,734 to have the equivalent buying power. The Conference Board concluded that a very large part of the fivefold rise in per-capita income has been eroded by taxes and price inflation.[42]

The family-income chart, too, is misleading if it is taken as a guide to absolute income. For these figures are stated *before taxes*. It should always be remembered that as labor productivity has risen through the application of technology, as real wages have risen, there has gradually been shifted onto the labor force, especially since 1940, the high income taxes originally designed for large income receivers, as well as new sales taxes. In Chapter Nine we saw some (a small part) of the ways in which taxes for the warfare-welfare state have been largely shifted onto the working population, scientists and professionals of all kinds included. We also saw to what extent large receivers of income, salaried and investment, have managed to place themselves like Bourbon favorites in the tax-exempt class.

Bolstering Executive Egos

Yet, despite high pay, all is not well along the corporate chain of command. Owing to tensions, stress and, no doubt, the failure to extract a sense of meaning out of repetitious, essentially routine tasks such as the manufacture and distribution of soap, many executive egos are in constant danger of collapsing, and they need to be reinforced by heroic corporate measures. Obtaining little ego support from any solid achievement, they need constant emergency support.

According to Dr. Robert Turfboer, psychiatrist with the Yale University School of Medicine and consultant to several large corporations, "an executive must have emotional security like anyone else. Evidences of eminence, far beyond financial reward, help give him that sense of security. The president of a company can be as fearful of failure as the office boy or assistant sales manager is of being fired."

Sagging executive egos are bolstered in two ways apart from money, says Dr. Turfboer: by special privileges and by special status symbols (although there are grave dangers in the utilization of the wrong status symbols).

Special privileges are of the following order: a $10,000 sauna in the executive suite of a new mid-Manhattan building for the sole benefit of the president and a few other top-echelon wizards; an $8,000 billiard room in the executive suite of another large corporation; in the Chase Manhattan Bank building $510,000 worth of fine art for private executive offices and executive reception rooms and, in general, office massage tables, office barber chairs, executive dining rooms, telephonic company automobiles (so that the great man need never be out of touch for an instant with GHQ), private executive planes, ultra-modern office furniture and plenty of service flunkies. There is, too, the expense account.

"Just as a king needs a crown for people to know he is a king, so an executive often needs the first-class symbols for his position as well as his self-esteem," says Dr. Turfboer.

How status symbols and special privileges are to be apportioned within the executive group is a problem; it is solved in accordance with an executive's putative importance. His importance is judged according to a criterion laid down by Dr. Elliott Jaques, British psychiatrist, who says, "The level of employment work can be measured in terms of the time span of discretion authorized and expected without review of that discretion by a superior." Otherwise put, the more a man can be trusted to be on his own the more important he is. Thus, the corporation president need not report to his board for six months—very important. All who have to report to somebody once a month, once a week, once or more a day are obviously progressively less important. People under constant surveillance are of no hierarchic importance at all.

"Status symbols, therefore," says Dr. Turfboer, "should be assigned or permitted according to a man's 'time span of discretion.'" The more discretion, the more *costly* the symbol. A company limousine costing $50 an hour should not, it is evident, be assigned to an office boy—or even to a junior vice president. Such a gadget can only be for Mr. Big himself.

Dr. Turfboer then goes into some subtle points of higher corporatology: how to distinguish at a glance among the guardians of big property. In the hierarchy of the average establishment, the third or lowest grade of vice president may be distinguished by Venetian office blinds and absence of carpeting. The second echelon generally merits wall-to-wall carpeting (at

$14 a yard) and draperies or curtains to the sill. For top executives, there are floor-to-ceiling draperies and carpeting at $17 a yard. As Vance Packard has pointed out, a mahogany desk outranks walnut, walnut outranks oak or metal. The man entitled to carpeting is likely to display a water carafe, which long ago displaced the brass spittoon as a symbol of flag rank. At one broadcasting company, only secretaries of executives above a certain specific level of advancement are entitled to electric typewriters.

What really determines the cost and number of status symbols is "the number of people an executive affects and the intensity with which he affects them," the doctor assures us.

But there are dangers in flaunting status symbols around indiscriminately, the doctor warns. "I refer to flashy office furniture and gold faucets, teak countertops, and Picassos in executive washrooms. The nonintellectual who displays books with fancy leather bindings, or the executive who hangs collectible art but does not appreciate what he has, may be marked as a fraud. A too-gadgety bar (except behind a sliding panel) should not be accepted as a proper status symbol. . . .

"The wrong kind of authoritative emblems can have negative consequences. In subordinates, they may inspire envy or ridicule. While an executive may make himself often inaccessible to subordinates as a symbol of his importance rationalized by his need for privacy, needless exclusiveness can arouse antagonism within his organization."

Symbols are assigned or self-selected, and in both cases there are grave dangers. A minor executive, for example, may acquire a desk set exactly like the one used by the chairman of the board, which "may be permissible, but it may also turn out to be poor strategy." Will the chairman, one wonders, feel burned up?

As to assignment of symbols, Dr. Turfboer cites the sad case of a marketing executive given a much larger and more palatial office; yet the man had the effrontery to say he felt uncomfortable in his new de luxe surroundings. "Evidently," says Dr. Turfboer, "his self-esteem had not had a chance to rise to the level of the symbol bestowed on him."

Offhand, a strictly part-time curbstone psychologist would assume that the man had very little self-esteem to begin with if it depended on anything so contrived as an office and its furbishings.[43]

All is not well, as it is readily seen, along the corporate chain of executive command. Many of the men have doubts—about their worth, their importance, the value of their presence, their identities in the scheme of things, perhaps even about their potency. They need to be bolstered in a world of basic achievers, such as scientists.

Another study, however, finds top executives to be "Basically sound, above-average in effective intelligence. These men deal best with practical or tangible data in relation to problem-solving situations. They are as a group only fair conceptual thinkers. They do not do too well in dealing with theoretical, abstract or conceptual thoughts or ideas."

As students they had above-average grades and were in the upper 25 per cent of their class at college, although not all were college graduates.

Most of them had engaged in some form of commercial venture before age fifteen and they are "Generally not socially aggressive. None were 'big men on campus' although some held fraternity offices. However, they were as a group somewhat lacking in the degree to which they participated in traditional student activities."

Most of them married late, had children, and their wives played little noticeable role in their business affairs.

One fact applied to all: None came from poverty-stricken backgrounds. In other words, none was a poor boy who "made good."

These findings were made by Dr. Louis F. Hackemann, president of Hackemann & Associates, an international management consulting company with headquarters in San Francisco.[44]

Professor Mabel Newcomer, near the conclusion of a study based upon a very large number of cases—882—of top executive officers, says:

"Athough he [the typical executive of 1950] has specialized training, he has never practiced independently, nor has he at any time run a business of his own as his father did. He is a business administrator—a bureaucrat —with little job experience outside his own corporation. His investments in 'his' company are nominal, in terms of potential control—less than 0.1 per cent of the total stock outstanding. He is a Republican in politics; he attends the Episcopalian church, if he attends church at all; and he served the federal government in an advisory capacity during the war. He was, in 1950, sixty-one years of age, and he will probably be seventy when he retires."[45]

Of note here, direct verification in a study of the top executives themselves of what has been indicated before, is that the corporate executive is not ordinarily much of an owner. He is a hired man, the tool of big owners, never the servant of myriad small stockholders as in the fable of "People's Capitalism."

Professor Newcomer makes the important point that corporations rarely comb the field looking for what would objectively be considered the best or most capable man for the top job. Why, in other words, do they "promote from within so frequently? And why do they promote so late? The reasons appear to be first, that the talent within the company is better known, and to that extent safer [*nota bene*—F. L.], than outside talent. Also, there is always a feeling that one's own company is different and that intimate knowledge of its problems is important from the start. The president or chairman is likely to select his successor in advance and to groom him personally for the job. And loyalty to the company is stressed. Moreover, there is a sense of obligation to the officers with whom the chief has worked, and a conviction—which is doubtless justified—that morale will be higher and the chance of retaining able executives greater, if they are aware that the top offices will be filled from within."[46]

Corp-politan *Vistas*

To attempt anything like a complete survey of the executive and his sphere would be impossible short of encyclopedic format. Under the rubric *Management* the central reference room of the New York Public Library indexes nearly 4,000 volumes; under *Executives*, nearly 400. There is, too, some score of periodicals devoted to the topic.

So it is clear that the subject of management is a large one in a postulated democratic society where the individual is pretty much supposed to manage himself. Americans, in fact, are under constant political and economic management manipulation.

While many of the works on management are serious analytical and descriptive studies, the executive mystique, tending to show the superlative worth of the executive and his technique as such, occupies much attention. Management of property itself, it turns out, is an arcane science, worthy of graduate study in the universities.

For those who want a compressed view of the field there might be recommended the *Reading Course in Executive Technique*, published in eight volumes with many authors by Funk and Wagnalls Company, New York, 1948. The volumes are given a lengthy introduction, "Modern Executive Techniques," by the editor, Carl Heyel, who is president of Executive Techniques, Inc.

The books in this course are titled: *Systematic Solution of Management Problems* (how to think, operations control, management controls, manual of organization, use of statistics, charting the course); *Human Relations* (employee morale, employee suggestion systems, supervising women, hints on psychology, human relations in industry); *Personnel and Industrial Relations; Creative Training Programs; Manufacturing Control; Distribution; Financial Control and General Office Management;* and *Public Relations*. Thus armed, the aspiring executive can take over with confidence.

Management, it turns out, consists of a melange of many things, a smattering from many disciplines that turns into an *ad hoc* empiricism resembling a pseudo-science.

Much of the literature in management can be reduced to cautionary injunctions, applicable generally or in various specific situations to "Always do this," "Never do that," "Usually do this," "Usually do that," "Be very careful in doing this," etc. Concrete situations are cited from experience, sometimes careful observational studies such as those of Elton Mayo on how most easily to get maximum output from a work force. Taking all the injunctions together one is given what some writers term a "philosophy of management." Troublemakers, so much sand in the gears, are especially unwanted and the place to spot them is at the personnel office, where the latest in psychological testing is put to use. Potential non-believers, doubters, scoffers, misfits and persons with "negative attitudes" generally must be weeded out lest they contaminate a basically sound work force and impede the smooth flow of profits.

Critics from time to time commiserate with the bureaucratic aspirant in the Leninist countries who must, before he arrives at the top, read the metaphysical works of Marx, Engels, Lenin, Stalin and many lesser dialecticians. The American executive, however, to judge by the tomes he must read, is much worse off. For most of these writings are at best stodgy, usually turgid. And beckoning the American is no future society of shining mirages but, at most, an office with wall-to-wall carpeting, a gold key to the executive washroom and membership in a country club.

Not only are there special periodicals devoted to the executive and his sphere, but magazines of more general appeal do not overlook him. *Fortune* rarely lets a month slip by without at least one article on executives, of which a few since 1950 have been: "The Case of Charles Luckman," "The Nine Hundred," "Boards of Directors," "Do Stock Options Pay?" "How Hard Do Executives Work?" "Can Executives Be Taught to Think?" "How Executives Get Jobs," "Is There an Executive Face?" "The Executive Bonus," "Are Executives Paid Enough?" "How Executives Invest Their Money," "How Top Executives Live," "The Executive Crack-Up," "How Much Is an Executive Worth?" "Young Executive in Manhattan," "Executive Qualities," "Life in Bloomfield Hills," "The Pirates of Management," "Those American Managers Don't Impress Europe," "Executive Compensation: The New Wave," "How to Pay Executives," etc.

In "Those American Managers Don't Impress Europe" (*Fortune*, December, 1964) we were given a story of disillusion. American companies entering the European market, either by merger or establishing new plants, necessarily sent along American executives. Keyed by all the hoop-la from the American corporate press about high-powered, lynx-eyed American executives, Europeans proceeded to pay very close attention. Now, they apparently thought, they were going to see the very soul of American puissance in action. Alas, it was once again the story of mighty Casey at the bat. For the American wizards were found to be very so-so, nothing remarkable. After watching them Europeans felt reassured.

It might be argued that the Americans did not send their first team to play in a strictly bush league, and this was probably true. To see the varsity all-stars in action the backward Europeans will have to come to the United States. Once they glimpse the Picassos in the executive washroom they will know they are in the very uterus of the big time, at the altar of the executive mystique. Now they will see how big, really big, decisions are made . . .

Twelve ❧

THE REPUBLIC OF
MONEY: THE PUBPOLS

As everything thus far inquired into has obviously flowered under the benign providence of government it is evident that government and politics have more than a little to do with the gaudy blooms of extreme wealth and poverty in the feverish American realm. It has not, to begin with, prevented whatever is the case. What it has ministered to, and how and why, will now be our theme.

How the government of the United States functions in all its ramifying complexity is the theme of ponderous treatises running into the proportions of Sears, Roebuck catalogues—composed by academicians somewhat left-handedly known as political scientists. Whatever they say is almost invariably correct in a formal sense as anatomical description, apart from any decorative filigree provided by such heady words as "democracy" and "freedom."

What we are really interested in, however, is process, function—political physiology, as it were. Although many political scientists profess to deal with this aspect as well, they all tend to lose sight of the actual ball in play or to avert their eyes in horror at the clinches. They are as physicists would be who had never been in a laboratory, as members of a vice squad who had never been in a brothel or taken money under the table from a madame. They themselves were never in the celebrated smoke-filled backrooms, never on hand when the price was set, the bodies buried, the papers burned, the ballots destroyed, the payoff made, the *double entendre* arranged, the people bilked.

Like nearly everyone else in this sphere, the political scientist is dependent on reports, rumors, memoirs, documents, statistics, interpretations, deductions and more or less shrewd surmise. And, like everyone else, he is limited by his position as a strict outsider. Journalists are far more privy to what goes on than he, and indeed he depends on journalists for much of his information. It is one field where certain participants know more about it in its nook-and-cranny aspects than those self-dedicated to its systematic study.

The difference between government as reported by political scientists and government as it actually takes place is much like the difference between learned descriptions of *amour* and *amour* itself. The difference is far greater than that between description in general and phenomena in general, between symbol and act. The political scientist is in much the same outside position as a biologist or psychologist studying *amour*. What each says may be entirely correct, moderately enlightening or even exhilarating; but what the dedicated acolyte misses are the nuances these experts haven't been able to encompass even by delicate imaginative projection. Their often assumed delicacy is elephantine. Again, they often misinterpret simple rutting for *amour*, intrigue for politics.

Even more than the theoreticians of *amour*, who sometimes have the advantage of being tentative practitioners themselves, the political scientist is at a disadvantage: For he has never actually been in the situation, does not occupy a privileged position denied, say, to the editors of the *New York Times*. The terrain, clearly, belongs in the particular jurisdiction of someone else, as *amour* lies in the jurisdiction of the poet or madman. A poet, even a madman, now and then has something revealing or poignant to say about *amour*; it would be astonishing if a political scientist ever said anything about government that approached a Machiavelli or a Hobbes who, be it noticed, were nonscientific "insiders."

The indubitable experts I call upon to bear witness in this chapter (leaving to one side the delicate question of my own expertise) will all be far, far closer to what goes on than any political scientist has ever been, valuable though the compilations, commentaries, commonplaces and occasional insights of these gentry may be as *aides-memoires* and reference classifications.

As most people have some more or less accurate conception of the gross mechanics of the United States government, seen mostly in rose lights and soft-focus, I omit the citation of basic supposed facts on which we might be improbably supposed to agree in advance. Let us simply descend on the phenomenon oozing in its habitat.

In much of what follows for quite a way I lean heavily on first-hand analysis by the erudite and resolutely democratic Senator Joseph S. Clark of Pennsylvania, until his election in 1956 the Democratic burgomeister of dingy Philadelphia, *magna cum laude,* Harvard, '23—in brief, a man of parts. Having Clark on hand is pretty much like having a literate psycho-analyst stationed right on the vice squad itself, an entrancing and unex-pected combination. Here and there I shall set the focus a little more sharply than does the truly able but somewhat romantic senator. He, although sufficiently forthright, is a gentleman and becomes queasy at spelling out certain details which I, here as a pathologist, will have no more hesitancy in scrutinizing in the light of the evidence available than has a coroner in examining a mildewed cadaver.

As Senator Clark has made microscopically clear, no doubt to the con-sternation of the more polite observers, each house of Congress is under the tight control of a dour inner clique, the general intended aim of which is to cater to favored ultra-acquisitive interests and to frustrate the general lightheartedly nonacquisitive interests. As far as these cliques are con-cerned, the general populace can go and slide on its collective buttocks if it has any complaints to make—and stick its finger in its ear for good measure.

To these twin cliques, composed to a man of self-certified back-country patriots, we owe the gamey tax laws, among others. Senator Clark stylishly refers to the cliques as "The Senate Establishment" and "The House Estab-lishment." They run Congress, when necessary with a heavy hand, at times in opposition to any president, sometimes as under Lyndon B. John-son in close harmony with him. When they are in full-blown opposition, the government simply deadlocks, freezes, as far as rational adjustment to events is concerned.

The special merit of Senator Clark's analysis is that he shows at first hand the precise inner mechanics of Establishment control, so that even a child can understand it.

The senator endorses the conclusion of James Macgregor Burns that there are always two governing parties in power, a Congressional party and a Presidential party. The Presidential party is national, necessarily concerned with broad interests, and is at least halfheartedly oriented to-ward carrying out the cloudy party platform submitted every four years to the bemused voters. The Congressional party is devoted to particularistic self-seekers (as shown by near-the-spot sources other than Senator Clark); these include most of the members themselves as on-the-sly entrepreneurs. It is bipartisan—a coalition of standpat Republicans and Democrats. It is generally opposed, usually by indirection, to the party platform, most of which it covertly sabotages. The function of the party platform is only to stir enthusiasm in Presidential voters. After serving this purpose it is sub-ject to discard.

The Establishment, moreover, is as permanently and fixedly in power as the Communist leadership in Russia. Nothing about it alters over the decades except the fall of a few of its aging personnel by the wayside. Only extreme force and violence could remove it. It is anchored, in sober fact, in extra-legal violence, intimidation and terrorism as religiously practiced especially throughout the South but visible at times elsewhere.

The findings of Senator Clark were expressed at considerable personal risk. For no professional can ever give such pointedly documented critical testimony to the outside heathen without thereafter having every hand of the Establishment secretly raised against him. All that can now save Senator Clark from political oblivion is the popular constituency—by itself a weak reed, as every practicing politician knows.

Barriers against the Majority

Barriers to the expression of majority will at the governmental level are, among others, the following:

Many persons do not vote—some for the intelligent reasons that they suspect the electoral process is rigged or they do not know enough about the issues or candidates; most from indifference, apathy, intimidation, terror stemming from localized violence, simple mental or physical ill health or because they are barred from voting by peculiar residential requirements devised by local politicos with little enthusiasm for voting.

Only a bit more than 60 per cent now vote in presidential elections (presidents have never been true majority officers). On statewide bases, the voters always number fewer than 50 per cent in purely congressional elections and range downward to less than 10 percent in other elections.

In 1962 only 46.7 per cent of civilians of voting age cast ballots for House congressmen, a record high in a nonpresidential year.[1] In many states (all Establishment Country) the percentage of voters was far lower: 13.7 per cent in steamy Mississippi; below 20 per cent in Arkansas, Georgia, Louisiana and Virginia; between 20 and 30 per cent in Alabama, Florida, South Carolina, Tennessee and Texas; and between 30 and 40 per cent in Kentucky, Maryland and North Carolina. The largest statewide vote for House congressmen that year was in Idaho with 66.5 per cent. Only eleven states attained 60 per cent or better.[2]

In 1964 even the presidential vote was below 40 per cent in Alabama, District of Columbia, Georgia, Mississippi (33.3 per cent), and South Carolina. Usually it attains lower levels in these and some other states.[3]

It is often said that the Democratic primaries are the true elections in the South, the election itself just a formality. But even so they do not involve a significantly large segment of the population. Again, it is often said that the poor showing in the South is traceable to the exclusion of Negroes; yet most of the abstentions are of low-grade whites. In 1960, Mississippi, with the largest proportion of Negro population, had less than 40 per cent Negroes in its population of voting age.[4] So it is not only the exclusion of Afro-Americans that accounts for the poor voting record of the South. It is mainly whites (or pinks and rednecks) who abstain from voting, in part because they are culturally as retarded as the sepia shades and in part because they are dissuaded by the local *padrones*.

The vast disparity of participation between presidential and congressional elections—in 1960 the presidential vote drew 64 per cent—reveals the degree of purposeful abstention and lack of ardor in many people for an electoral process widely suspected of being greased and rigged and at least ineffective as a means of producing tangibly gratifying results. Too many people have seen too much remain the same after too many high-flown elections to be carried away by the prospect of another.

Many of those who vote do not vote their interests intelligently, perhaps do not even know what they are. Again, many of those elected obviously do not themselves know what the score is, as they show by asinine pronouncements. One must be very much of a mystic to believe that, at variance with rational criteria, there is something intrinsically valuable about a popular vote. It is at best a rough way of selecting somebody, even a Lyndon B. Johnson.

Having voted for one of the two handpicked puppets of backroom schemers (except where there are open primaries), usually with some childish ethnic or religious bias most prominently in mind, the functioning portion of the electorate favors a man (as often as not deemed unfit by the community for other walks of life) who is then thrown into close working contact with others of like mind arrived in the halls of government by the same dubious road. There are some 750,000 elective offices in the land and, considering the fact that there is at least one aspirant arrayed against every incumbent, it is evident that the mere filling of offices amounts to quite an industry in an economic sense—gives employment to many people.

Despite all hosannahs to the collective sagacity of the people (what politician or newspaper editor would publicly question it?) the arrangements under which popular elections have been held since their inception have been as crooked as a fixed wheel in a low gambling house. Long asserted by the tough-minded, denied by the tender-minded, the plain fact was only recently underscored in terse decisions by the United States Supreme Court. Various transparent devices, the Court found, were traditionally used in many states to keep Negroes and other *a priori* undesirables from voting, thus trammeling gloriously free even if obtuse popular expression at the very source. A wider and subtler abuse was found in the legislative districts, federal and state, which had been traditionally gerrymandered by one-party and two-party establishment-controlled state legislatures so that in some cases enormous numbers of distraught voters, mostly urban and suburban dwellers, had only one dubious representative; while in other cases very few voters, mostly functionally illiterate rural hinds, also had a dubious representative. A handful of rustics thus were the means for stifling the representatives of thousands of trapped city patsies. The consequence was that even if a majority of a legislative body was allowed to prevail (not always the case, as we shall see) the majority did not reflect the majority of the voting population either in its wisdom, folly or confusion.

Although the Court has now issued its ukase against these practices, the men borne to prominence by them will remain on the scene and in office until they wilt; and there is no guarantee that something equally objectionable, or more so, will not be devised by the always cunning *pubpols*.

Americans, it is often said unthinkingly, believe in majority rule. Yet, oddly, they never have had it; they have always had oligarchic rule, usually of a rather low order. The farther one moves away from a gerrymandered, intimidated, meagerly educated, emotionally immature and partly disqualified electorate the fewer become the participants in any decision until in the legislatures it is always and invariably far less than a majority, either representatively or among those present. For all those brain-laundered with the doctrine of majority rule this is, admittedly, a strange, even unpatriotic notion. Yet it is an exact statement of the case.

"The primary and overriding duty and responsibility of each member of the House of Representatives is to get re-elected," it has been well said by Adam Clayton Powell, long a proficient preacher of the Gospel and a successful and highly affluent congressman since 1945.[5]

The Establishment legislator in Congress—and some not so classifiable— has three further informal, off-the-record duties: (1) to work loyally with the legislative Establishment as an organization man; (2) to insure his own position whenever possible as a member in good standing of the affluent sector of society by acquiring any available cash, securities, real estate, franchises, market tips or whatever else may be of value; and (3) to share his affluence with indispensable offstage key figures of his home district organization grouped around the state or district party chairman. Nobody, it is plainly evident, plays the game alone.

Not to do this is to leave himself at the mercy of the shifting whims and moods of a potentially unstable constituency, wide open to the claims of eager rivals for his office. Despite careful planning by the legislator, he is at times the victim of political upsets and internal feuds. Yet if he is of the Establishment he is never wholly extinguished even if he has not had time to become affluent, because he has made many Establishment friends who remember him as a "regular." They see to it that his post-legislative life is enriched by various appointments suitable to a "lame duck"—commissionerships, judgeships, receiverships, lobby clients and the like. He belongs to a *bund*.

The Congressional Establishment, as Senator Clark proves, has a life of its own, policies of its own, aims of its own. These either have no connection with the needs or desires of the nation as a whole or harmonize with them only occasionally, fitfully, incidentally and, as it were, accidentally. It is a parasitical oligarchy. It produces results of its own predetermined stamp. It explains much about the chills, fevers and shudders of American society—its volume of crime, riots and lynchings.

The Bottom of the Bird Cage

"The trouble with Congress today," writes Senator Clark, "is that it exercises negative and unjust powers to which the governed, the people of the United States, have never consented. . . . The heart of the trouble is that the power is exercised by minority, not majority rule."[6]

As in Soviet Russia and Red China, power is in the hands of solidly installed intriguing manipulators, with the difference that in the United States the intrigue takes place behind a facade of reasoned if blurry constitutionality. In Russia and China the bayonets show through the periodic purges. The difference is enough to make the reasonable man prefer the American system with all its blemishes, about as one would unjoyfully prefer dysentery to cholera.

"Our forms of government are heavily weighted against any kind of action, and especially any that might alter significantly the status quo. It takes too many units of government to consent before anything can be done."[7] This, of course, is a truism. The constitutional bulwarks against tyranny, placed there by the Founders' hands, are used to produce a creeping, low-key tyranny.

It is the third branch of government, the legislative, where things have gone awry. Whether we look at city councils, the state legislatures or the Congress of the United States, we react to what we see with scarcely concealed contempt. This is the area where democratic government is breaking down. This is where the vested-interest lobbies tend to run riot, where conflict of interest is concealed from the public, where demagoguery, sophisticated or primitive, knows few bounds, where political lag keeps needed action often a generation behind the times, where the nineteenth century sometimes reigns supreme in committees, where the evil influence of arrogant and corrupt political machines, at the local and state level, ignores most successfully the general welfare, where the lust for patronage and favors for the faithful do the greatest damage to the public interest.

. . . the legislatures of America, local, state and national, are presently the greatest menace in our country to the successful operation of the democratic process.[8]

Lest the sheltered reader, tucked away in his bower, think that Senator Clark here delivers himself of an extravagant opinion or resorts to hyperbole, it is a settled conclusion among seasoned observers that, Congress apart as a separate case, the lower legislatures—state, county and municipal—are Augean stables of misfeasance, malfeasance and nonfeasance from year to year and decade to decade and that they are preponderantly staffed by riffraff or what police define as "undesirables," people who if they were not in influential positions would be unceremoniously told to "keep moving." Exceptions among them are minor. Many of them, including congressmen, refuse to go before the television cameras because it is then so plainly obvious to everybody they are what they are. Their whole demeanor arouses instant distrust in the intelligent. They are, all too painfully, typecast for the racetrack, the sideshow carnival, the back alley, the peepshow, the low tavern, the bordello, the dive. Evasiveness, dissimulation, insincerity shine through their false bonhomie like beacon lights.

The *New York Times,* customarily referred to as staid, has vouched editorially that the Massachusetts legislature is the most corrupt in the country. If this is so, the Commonwealth lawmakers have nosed out many others, including neighboring Rhode Island, merely by millimeters. The *Times* based its opinion on a solid report of the Massachusetts Crime Commission, submitted by impeccable leading citizens of the Bay State to Governor John Volpe in response to frenetic public clamor. "Corruption permeates the state, the report said, from town governments to the state house and involves politicans, business men, lawyers and ordinary citizens."[9]

This official report, a state document, cited wide-scale bribery by corporations and lawyers and the fact that legislators are on the payrolls of companies doing business with the state. Corruption was encouraged, the report said, because of "the lack of backbone" in the legislature.

As to this particular legislature, the *Boston Globe* analyzed it during the week of April 11, 1966, revealing elements of a pestilent tale. Most of the legislature, the *Globe* indicated, is composed of Babbittian local real estate dealers, insurance brokers, fixing lawyers, loan sharks, used-car entrepreneurs, miscellaneous fast-buck operators and obscure local hangers-on and roustabouts—many of them types who if they could not become attached to a public payroll, there to divert commerce their way, would be local misfits and perhaps panhandlers, vagrants, con men, family dependents, procurers or on local relief or unemployment rolls. The net impression given by the *Globe* (a rather reserved family paper) was of a political *lumpenproletariat*, a scabrous crew.

As to other legislatures, Senator Estes Kefauver found representatives of the vulpine Chicago Mafia ensconced in the Illinois legislature, which has been rocked by one scandal of the standard variety after the other off and on for seventy-five or more years. What he didn't bring out was that the Mafians were clearly superior types to many non-Mafians.

Public attention, indeed, usually centers on only a few lower legislatures —Massachusetts, New York, New Jersey, California and Illinois—and the impression is thereby fostered in the unduly trusting that the ones they don't hear about are on the level. But such an impression is false. The ones just mentioned come into more frequent view because their jurisdictions are extremely competitive and the pickings are richer. Fierce fights over the spoils generate telltale commotion. Most of the states are quieter under strict one-party quasi-Soviet Establishment dominance, with local newspapers cut in on the gravy. Public criticism and information are held to a minimum, grousers are thrown a bone and not many in the low-level populace know or really care. Even so, scandalous goings-on explode into view from time to time in Florida, Texas, Louisiana, Oklahoma, Missouri and elsewhere—no states excepted. Any enterprising newspaper at any time could send an aggressive reporter into any one of them and come up with enough ordure to make the Founding Fathers collectively vomit up their very souls in their graves.[10]

The territorial base of the Establishment lies in the low-down one-party states. Ten have been found by careful political scientists to be generally one-party. They are Alabama, Arkansas, Florida, Georgia, Louisiana, Mississippi, South Carolina, Texas, Vermont and Virginia. Twelve were found to be practically one-party: Iowa, Kansas, Kentucky, Maine, New Hampshire, North Carolina, North Dakota, Oklahoma, Oregon, Pennsylvania, South Dakota and Tennessee.[11] Ignoring for the moment still others that alternate over long periods as one-party jobs, like Florida recently, it is noticeable that the above array is nominally Republican as well as Democratic. Among the clearly Republican one-party strongholds are Vermont, Iowa, Kansas, Maine, New Hampshire, North Dakota, Oregon and South Dakota. At least twenty-two states, then, or nearly half, are one-party set-ups, with some dozen others coming very close to qualifying. Public political scandals, it will be noted, are much less frequently heard of in the one-party states. Here it is as in one-party countries.

The single point to emphasize here is that Senator Clark is entirely correct, even reserved, in his sweeping reference to the legislatures. He does not exaggerate. As the lawyers would say, he is a sound witness. He does not, however, delve into the processes that brought such uncomely personnel into the legislative bodies. How did the honest electorate come to elect such *canaille?* That is, manifestly, another story, and is left to the next chapter.

As Senator Clark sees it, there is no continuing discipline in Congress whereby a majority of the members of a party are able, by simple vote, to discipline recalcitrant members interested only in blocking national measures and in feathering their own nests. The recent Powell and Dodd cases were token ceremonies. Although the parties have various committees, the policy committees give out no policies, the steering committees do not steer but block; and, in general, every man is for himself. And yet, important decisions are made.

The Congressional Establishment

The Congressional Establishment "consists of those Democratic chairmen and ranking Republican members of the important legislative committees who, through seniority and pressures exerted on junior colleagues, control the institutional machinery of Congress. . . . The official leadership group of the Congress—Speaker of the House, Senate Majority Leader, *et al.*— are usually captives of the Establishment, although they can sometimes be found looking out over the walls of their prison, plotting escape."[12]

"It is important to note that the views of the Congressional Establishment are not shared by a majority of their colleagues, who, left to their own devices, would be prepared to bring the Congress into line to cope with the necessities of our times."[13] This, as we shall see, may be gravely questionable.

The Senate Establishment is "almost the antithesis of democracy. It is not selected by any democratic process. It appears to be quite unresponsive to the caucuses of the two parties. . . . It is what might be called a self-perpetuating oligarchy with mild, but only mild, overtones of plutocracy.

"There are plenty of rich men in the Senate, but only a few of them are high in the ranks of the Establishment; and none of them would admit [sic!] to a belief that the accumulation of great wealth is a principal object of life. This is another distinction between the American and the

Congressional Establishments. The former [consisting of the prime bene-ficiaries of the *status quo*] has, despite its slightly liberal orientation, def-inite overtones of plutocracy, although its tolerance is much more for inherited than for recently acquired wealth."[14]

Senator Clark now comes to the ties that bind the Congressional Estab-lishment. They are: a common militant belief in white supremacy, a stronger devotion to property-ownership rights than to rights of the per-son, strong support of the military establishment at all times, marked bel-ligerence in foreign affairs and an absolute determination to block internal congressional reform.

"A substantial number of the members of Congress in both parties are the product of political forces which give them a rural, pro-business, anti-labor, isolationist, conservative perspective with an attitude toward civil rights which ranges from passive unconcern to outright hostility."[15]

It is plain that the legislative strength of the Big-Business Establishment is, ironically, mainly in the agrarian districts. What are the "political forces" to which Senator Clark here refers in a somewhat opaque manner? They may be summed up in a word: money. The rural legislator—not directly tied to the business system, which is invariably weak in his home district (few stockholders, consumers, corporation employees or factories are found there)—has something to sell: his vote. And he sells it in a cir-cumlocutional way, wrapped in some rococo principle such as states' rights, sacred privacy, economy, government anti-centralism, economic in-dividualism or plain pure Americanism. This is the kernel of support by rustic solons for softly regulated big-city industrialism.

Politics, popularly thought to consist mainly of elections, really begins only after elections, when those elected come together to divide the spoils. The meetings of any legislative body, as of a floating crap game, must be under rules, which like laws themselves must emanate from the legislative body itself. The Constitution does not stipulate how Congress must govern itself. This is a "political question," wide open.

One of the Senate rules is that there may be unlimited debate; no senator may be silenced, unless, under Rule XXII, two-thirds of the senators pres-ent vote to terminate debate. With all senators present, this rule requires 66 votes to end debate. If only 35 refuse to limit debate, those who have the floor may go on talking endlessly, in relays. Such filibustering blocks all business until an agreement is reached to withdraw some proposal disliked by a sometimes very small minority.

As Senator Clark notes, the United States Senate is the only open legisla-tive body in the world under such an extravagantly absurd rule, which calls to mind the veto power held by any member in the House of Nobles of the old Polish Kingdom. There the rule, more severe than ours, so effectively paralyzed the country as to leave it an easy prey to neighboring Prussia, Russia and Austria.

From 1789 to 1806 the Senate rules included the motion for the previous question, as provided for in Jefferson's *Manual*. On two occasions it was used to close debate. Since 1811 the motion has been used frequently in the House to end debate and is provided for in House Rule XVII. Virtually all the state legislatures allow the procedure, which, as Jefferson pointed out, was used in the British Parliament as early as 1604. It is not, as Senator Clark reminds us, alien to hallowed Anglo-Saxon parliamentary procedure. It is, in truth, almost sacred and not to allow it full rein is ground for the deepest suspicion.

May a majority of the Senate at the beginning of a new Congress vote to terminate debate in order to pass on a change in the standing rules? This question was put point-blank as recently as 1963 by the vice president as the presiding Senate officer. In response there were only 44 ayes and 53 nays, with no roll call. The Establishment had triumphed, by a clear majority. (The question has since been put at the opening of every term with a similar outcome.)

Early in 1964 on a cloture petition that would have ended further debate on the question of a change of the rule—and which, under the rule, required a favorable vote of two-thirds of those present—the Clarkian majority lost by 54 for and 42 opposed. Senator Clark draws comfort from the fact that, including 4 absentees, the Senate at the time stood 56-44 in favor of cloture, only 10 short of the necessary two-thirds. But the earlier vote, with 53 nays, showed the full fire-power of the Establishment on the bedrock issue. On such showdowns the Establishment has thus far been able to muster far more than a third—pointedly, more than a half.

The Establishment itself is not a majority but it can, owing to the many strings in its octopal fingers, pull many unhappy non-Establishment senators into line when all the chips go down. On basic questions affecting its own power it is, in sober fact, a majority.

The sole contemporary full-face defeat of the Establishment was on the Test Ban Treaty, which came to a vote September 24, 1963, after a long debate. Two-thirds of those present and voting were required for ratification under the Constitution. The vote was 80 to 19 in favor.

Those who voted "No" at the time constituted the stone-faced core of the Senate Establishment in Senator Clark's view: Russell and Talmadge of Georgia, Stennis and Eastland of Mississippi, Long of Louisiana, Byrd and Robertson of Virginia, Byrd of West Virginia, McClellan of Arkansas, Thurmond of South Carolina, Curtis of Nebraska, Goldwater of Arizona,

Simpson of Wyoming, Jordan of Idaho, Margaret Chase Smith of Maine, Bennett of Utah and Tower of Texas. Most of these were from rule-by-terror states, nearly all from one-party states. Mundt of South Dakota, who usually votes down the line with the Establishment, defected.

But for changes in Rule XXII and cloture all of these, with Mundt, voted "No," including the following Establishment people who had defected momentarily on the Test Ban Treaty: Ellender of Louisiana, Hayden of Arizona, Holland of Florida, Johnston of South Carolina, Hill and Sparkman of Alabama, Cannon of Nevada, Cotton of New Hampshire, Williams of Delaware and Dirksen of Illinois. Half of these were also from rule-by-terror states; most were from one-party states.

It is the men mentioned in these two paragraphs, according to Senator Clark, who constitute the nucleus of the present Senate Establishment, which has its counterpart in the House. How one stands on Rule XXII determines whether one is for or against the Establishment.

A few of those mentioned are not present as of 1968. Such absence makes no difference to the Establishment because fresh replacements are always available approximately from the same states. When death approached Byrd of Virginia, the ailing senator retired and had his fifty-year-old son appointed in his place—an hereditary senator! Hardly any of the states represented by Establishment senators are industrialized—only Illinois and Delaware. The rest are predominantly rural and agricultural or extractive; most are nonurbanized and are of exceptionally low general educational levels—defective schools, few libraries and bookstores, mediocre newspapers, poor radio-television programs, etc. Money for these is shot away nationally in wars. The core of the group is the southern Democratic bloc, which has been said to be the South's revenge on the rest of the country for the loss of the Civil War. But it has many members from parts of the country that are as economically and culturally retarded—in general, the Bible Belt, which tends to look indulgently on terror and intimidation.

The Establishment people are not men of parts; they are devoid of generally esteemed talents. None, possibly excepting McClellan and Sparkman, is a persuasive speaker. Many such as Eastland show themselves conspicuously deficient in reasoning powers, confidently propounding howlers in elementary logic that would shame most college freshmen. Nearly all appear to be quite innocent of acquaintance with semantics. Although most are members of the bar, none is rated high as a practicing lawyer. Few seem to be well read. None, as far as the record shows, is a writer; Goldwater's books of shabby notions were ghost-written. Few if any are soundly schooled. Their knowledge of the world—and of the language itself—appears to be meager. Their talents lean almost entirely to simple intrigue.

Everett Dirksen is their prototype of a prophet. They are a drab crew.

If these people did not band together as they do behind Rule XXII, if they relied on their own capabilities in open debate on the merits of issues, they would stand forth in all hollowness among more talented men. And this is one reason for the Establishment: It is a refuge for the untalented, a closed trade union of the meagerly endowed.

What do Establishment members want? Are they merely interested in preserving the ties that bind them together and give them factitious substance: Rule XXII, white supremacy, the celebration of property and military derring-do and a truculent stance in foreign affairs? So to suppose would be to credit them with very limited, purely symbolical objectives. Actually, as Senator Clark stresses, many members of the Establishment go along with other measures, some with quite liberal measures, as long as Rule XXII and white supremacy remain inviolate. They are political traders, keen for cheap jack opportunities.

When blockages arise under Rule XXII, the Establishment is in a position to trade. In return for concessions it becomes its turn to make demands, to enforce its gloomy will on the country.

Customary analyses of Congress distinguish Republicans from Democrats, Southerners from Northerners and Westerners and conservatives from liberals. The latter distinction suggests, misleadingly, that there are reasoned attitudes present rather than rationalization for narrowly pecuniary self-interest. Political scientists are united in believing that national party affiliations are meaningless, that congressmen nearly all stem from purely local state and district factions.[16] Nor is the regional distinction fundamentally any more important than that of party.

There are, in truth, more fundamental distinctions to be observed. There is, first, the Establishment and anti-Establishment distinction that Senator Clark brings to view, with most of the Establishment people organization men from Soviet-style one-party districts or states. As unchaperoned strangers in them quickly discover, most of these states have extremely inquisitive *polizei*. Few such states are industrialized, few are very rich, and the rich ones, like Texas, are largely absentee-owned, obvious colonies of Wall Street and State Street. In all, organized politics offers one of the few sure roads to personal affluence, functional latitude and renown. In the industrial states there are many such roads.

Much about American politics would be clearer if one thought of a metropolitan and a colonial or provincial United States. Metropolitan United States consists of southern New England, New York, New Jersey, Pennsylvania, Ohio, Indiana, Michigan, Illinois, Wisconsin, California, perhaps the state of Washington and the very eastern portions of Missouri,

Iowa and Minnesota. Just about everything else is nonmetropolitan, culturally below par and holds nearly all one-party politics. It is more like eastern Europe than like eastern United States.

Economically, this division is generally made as between agrarian and industrial states. Yet the congressional politics of the representatives of the agrarian states are not distinctively agrarian. Elected by a politically illiterate, often very small electorate unaware of the true drift of affairs and with few vital demands of its own to make, congressmen from these states are far freer than those of the metropolitan states to place their votes where the most money is, on the side of big property. For doing this they are allowed to join the propertied class by backstairs methods and are impressively referred to as conservatives.

Leadership in the nonmetropolitan states is noticeably below par (one of their basic deficiencies) owing to the steady drainage of homegrown talent into the metropolitan sector. It is not that the nonmetropolitan region fails to produce talented leadership material. It does produce it but discourages it and loses it steadily to the metropolitan sector, culturally more attractive. New York, Chicago, Boston, San Francisco and other metropolitan centers fairly crawl with talented people from Georgia, Mississippi, Kansas and other retrograde provinces. On trips back home they are careful to keep a tight rein on their tongues lest they face the prospect of being expertly tarred and feathered and ridden out of town on a rail by the local authorities, acting through local thugs.

Many organization politicans inside and outside Metropolia are known to feel, self-righteously, that their party ties provide a *democratic* device for the distribution of some of the industrial wealth—to themselves. They are sadly mistaken. No distribution of wealth to public-spirited connivers is taking place by this route. What is available, in various ways, is only a small percentage of the untaxed industrial *revenues* in the form of "campaign" contributions, gifts, fees and retainers. These are tips to menials.

It is not being suggested here that members of the Establishment and their veiled supporters are in all cases *primarily* trying to gain affluence for its own sake. Rather is it a fact that they must have affluence in order to function on their chosen level. The organization men split their "take" with other organization men in the home party organization. Many, it can be plainly shown, are eager estate builders—Johnsons, Dodds, Dirksens, Kerrs *et al.* Some, probably most, are a combination of the two. The prospect of money is definitely in the picture except in a very few cases.

Money is needed to get into electoral politics. Money is needed to remain there. And money is needed to carry one over the bleak days if one is voted out.

In saying this, one is not saying something that would have astounded the Founding Fathers. Under the Constitution as it originally stood, there were property qualifications for voting even for members of the House of Representatives and the state legislatures. Only as the various states gave the franchise to the nonpropertied in the early nineteenth century was this qualification removed, thus opening the way to office for poor men. This was a dangerous development because the poor newcomers to politics, seldom themselves partisans of the poor, needed money going far beyond the paltry pay of office, originally designed purely as honoraria for men of property and still on this level in many jurisdictions. The unpropertied man in politics was in time, according to an unwritten convention, expected to use ingenuity in providing for himself. Imaginative and defensible schemes were devised by some, but the sheer logical possibilities of making adequate monetary provision outside of meager salary without going beyond the law or the proprieties are few and largely boil down to writing, lecturing, making after-dinner speeches or practicing ordinary law—all of which take some talent. Promotions in which the name of the officeholder was used to confer prestige were legitimate—when the promotions themselves were legitimate. But for most of the new off-the-soil officeholders, always with noteworthy exceptions, it all boiled down to acquiring money in some questionable way. They were necessarily purchasable men. In the practice of law the purchase price took the form of heavy retainers from big interests.

In order to attain congressional or any political office one must, as many experts have attested: (1) be independently wealthy either as an inheritor or a builder of better booby traps; (2) have the backing of a wealthy individual, group or organization; or (3) have the backing of a local party organization which in turn has access to suspect supporting funds. Sometimes a "bad" organization supports a man of impeccable probity as a way of disarming critics. The supporting funds, it is true, could come from thousands of "little people" chipping in quarters or dollars; but the "little people" are either not sufficiently interested, do not understand or cannot afford to contribute—or a combination of the three. They have money for booze, soft drinks, tobacco, cosmetics, gadgets, high installment interest rates and the whole range of stuff at Woolworth's but not a cent as expense money for their tribunes. They may well suspect, too, that the candidates have already been spoken for by higher bidders.

What I say here is by no means original with me, arising from some internal distemper. It is the consensus of sophisticated observers. "Many people are asking the question," says Drew Pearson in his nationally syndicated column, " 'Do Congressmen steal?' Our answer is that they do not unlawfully take money from the government but they do take money lawfully for representing 'anti-government' interests. In this sense they do steal the right of the voters to have a man in Congress who represents them, instead of representing his law firm and its big business clients."[17] There are, however, many ways of legally putting money into a congressman's hands apart from attorneys' "fees" and "campaign" contributions. Attention will be given this lush aspect of standard garden-variety "democratic" politics further along.

The Establishment Method

How does the Republican-Democratic Establishment extend its will over the rest of the Congress? It does this, first, by its power to block anything, which forces others to trade with it. But its general control derives from its minute control over committee appointments. As the work of Congress is quietly done by committees, not through rational debate on the floor, such control is fundamental.

Any newcomer to Congress, whatever he has rashly promised his constituents, has as much to say over surrounding affairs as if he stepped into the rush-hour crowd at Grand Central Terminal or into the midst of a Bombay riot. If he managed to get the floor to make the most rousing speech ever delivered, there would be nobody present to hear it except the bored clerks and some flabbergasted tourists in the galleries. As soon as he rose to deliver himself of his deathless remarks, all the members would walk out as they customarily walk out on each other.

What he must do, Senator Clark informs us, is to keep quiet and watch what goes on. And the way to "get along," he further tells us, is to "go along"—with the older hands. If he continually "goes along" with those who are solidly ensconced, he will soon find that he is a member of some friendly bloc. It might seem that the smart thing to do would be to join the Establishment at once but this cannot always be managed because Establishment ideas are under some dispute in the more crowded and variegated parts of the country. The next smartest thing to do is to be against the Establishment on the record but to support it on showdowns, as many do in voting that a majority of a new Senate may not vote to close off debate in order to pass on a change in the rules. He can, also, be a "maverick" like the forty-four senators of 1963, although not many of these are very far-ranging.

If the new member continually "goes along," particularly with the Establishment, he finds that he is able to get various things done of interest to himself and to his standing in the eyes of his constituents. He may even

be allowed to get his name on bills—the "Sascha Schmaltz Bill to Extermi-
nate Poverty in Our Time" or something similarly astonishing. Also, his
bank account, if he so desires, will steadily improve. His banker and
broker will know he is now running with a well-heeled crowd.

Committee appointments, especially the powerful chairmanships over
(not *of*) the most powerful committees, are commonly supposed to go to
the members with the most seniority. Senator Clark shows conclusively,
citing chapter and verse, that the Establishment freely deviates from the
seniority rule whenever it wishes to push some member for reasons obscure
to the observer.

Committee appointments are made by two party groups—the Democratic Steering Committee and the Republican Committee on Committees.
The Establishment holds a majority of both, and, through its ability to
entice new members, holds its power as an hereditary fief.

The Democratic Steering Committee varies in composition from time to
time. By custom its members serve until they die, resign or are defeated at
the polls, the last not likely in the one-party states and districts from which
they emanate. As of 1959 it had fifteen members, seven southerners plus
Lyndon B. Johnson, majority leader, and Carl Hayden, president *pro tem-
pore* of the Senate, thus giving the Establishment a majority of nine. Johnson all along has been a 200-proof, sour-mash Establishment man.

Because the composition of Congress changed with the election of 1960,
bringing in more Democrats, Senator Clark wanted the Steering Committee
changed. He did get himself and three others put on, but the Establishment still controlled with nine votes. In 1963 at a Democratic Conference,
composed of all the Democrats in the Senate, he proposed that the Steering
Committee be increased to nineteen members.

Such an increase would have brought about geographical and ideological
balance, in Clark's view, and Majority Leader Mike Mansfield promised to support him. "To my chagrin and surprise, Mansfield opposed my
motion and [Hubert] Humphrey failed to support it. They told me later
Bobby Baker had told them the votes were not there to approve the increase. Perhaps this was right. . . . Had the Majority Leader and Whip
supported Senator Anderson and me, I believe we would have won."[18]
The point, though, is that they did not. On the secret ballot the Establishment vote was highest.

Within the Democratic Conference itself on a secret ballot the forces of
reform represented by Clark were outnumbered nearly 2 to 1. The Republicans, the nonurban element of them Establishment people from the
cradle up, have no need of such stacking in their Committee on Committees, which Senator Clark finds to be regionally and ideologically rep-

resentative. With the Democratic Party in the majority, the Republicans get few committee appointments anyhow. Yet their members plus the southern Democrats constitute the Establishment power.

As the Republican Party has been deflated to a minority since 1932, it is clearly the congressional wing of the Democratic Party that is now the chief block to legislative forthrightness. Yet the Democratic Party is the one that is popularly regarded as liberal, even radical. When the Republicans have a president he usually sees pretty much eye to eye with the Establishment; but since the accession of Democratic Lyndon B. Johnson as president, the Establishment is now in closest harmony with the White House. On the basis of Senator Clark's analysis, it would appear that the Establishment controls all the positions except the Supreme Court.

Through its power of appointment the Establishment in both houses "stacks" the committees of Congress with its supporters. "In the Eighty-sixth Congress [House] members from seven [backward] states controlled 97 of the 153 committee votes."[19] As Senator Clark shows, the Establishment dominates all vital committees and keeps off non-Establishment men with seniority.

In the crucial committees of both houses there is a frequent installation of the same pro-Establishment men, although in the Senate no person may be a chairman of more than one committee. A small percentage of pro-Establishment men hold majority votes, with few exceptions.

The effect throughout, from the party committees to the standing legislative committees, with only minor exceptions, is as though a permanent bureaucracy were installed, Senator Clark notes. In Russia the same sort of phenomenon, differently arrived at, is known as the Politburo. What Senator Clark calls the Establishment is indeed very much like the Politburo in its permanence and indestructibility, although not perhaps in its specific objectives. The methods of holding and wielding power are similar. But one does business in rubles, the other in dollars.

Owing to the large number of intra-party and legislative committees the Establishment people sit on, they are heavily worked. Russell, leader in recent years of the Establishment as the most senior member, always managed the opening-session struggle against changing Rule XXII, masterminded meetings of the Democratic Steering Committee, was active in the Policy Committee, chairman of the Armed Services Committee, was a member of the Appropriations Committee and chairman of its subcommittee on defense, member of the Aeronautical and Space Sciences Committee, the Joint Committee on Atomic Energy and a member of the commission to investigate the Kennedy assassination and of the Boards of Visitors to the

Military, Naval and Air Force Academies. And similarly with other Establishment people.[20]

Senator Clark makes much of the distinction between liberals and conservatives in the Senate, but just how little it signifies was shown in 1966 on the vote to allow the Foreign Relations Committee and Appropriations Committee to share supervision of the Central Intelligence Agency with Senator Russell's Armed Services Committee. Russell was opposed to the change; Senator Fulbright, chairman of Foreign Relations, favored it.

Russell won on the show-down, 61 to 28. While no Establishment people sided with Fulbright, plenty of liberals sided with Russell, namely: Anderson of New Mexico, Douglas of Illinois, Magnuson of Washington, Neuberger of Oregon, Pastore of Rhode Island, Ribicoff of Connecticut (all Democrats) and Kuchel of California. (It is this sort of thing that earns liberals the label of "fuzzy-mindedness.") Clark and Scott of Pennsylvania were not present—not that it would have made the slightest difference.[21]

The CIA is ideologically a straight Establishment agency, designed as an identical opposite number to the Soviet para-military intelligence network. Whatever its model, the Soviet apparatus, does the CIA can and does do as well—or better.

The committees of the Senate are rated in order of prime importance about as follows: Finance (taxes), Armed Services (military supplies), Foreign Relations (world markets), Appropriations (domestic allocation of money), Rules and Administration, Banking and Currency (monetary policy and credit), and Judiciary and Government Operations. Committees such as Agriculture and Forestry, Commerce, District of Columbia, Interior and Insular Affairs, Labor and Public Welfare, Post Office, and Civil Service and Public Service are far less important (possibly excepting Agriculture) because they exert less leverage.

It is the power to block plus leverage in vital situations, often involving stupendous amounts of money, that makes certain committees paramount. Chairmen of committees are powerful because they are permanently installed as the senior member, are alone empowered except in the case of a very few committees to call committee meetings, and alone set agendas, call up bills for consideration, regulate hearings and terminate committee debates. Within the jurisdiction of each committee the chairman is almost a dictator. He can kill any bill in his jurisdiction by simply pigeon-holing it. Although it is possible to call meetings at the demand of a majority of committee members, practically this is rarely done because most committee members are more handpicked than the chairman, with whom they have many convenient understandings. They may even have been picked by the chairman himself. Until a bill is reported out by a committee it cannot come before the Senate unless two-thirds of the senators want it out. A bill could be ordered out on a majority vote, of course, but only if the Establishment approved.

In the House the chief committees are Rules, Ways and Means (taxes), Armed Services, Interstate and Foreign Commerce, Banking and Currency, Appropriations and Judiciary. Before going to the floor, unless a hard-to-get majority votes to bring it out, a bill must first be reported out by the Rules Committee. Most proposed bills, many of them having wide public approval, are never reported out. Filed with the Rules Committee, they might just as well have been dumped in a wastebasket. A majority of the House may order a bill discharged from committee, but ordinarily such a majority is hard to get.

Even though the House does not allow unlimited debate it has a more complex set of rules than the Senate. These rules are used to strangle or whittle down proposals unwanted by the House Establishment.

"Committee and subcommittee chairmen have more naked power in the House than in the Senate," Senator Clark notes. "There is no tax legislation if Wilbur Mills of Arkansas, chairman of the Ways and Means Committee, doesn't want any, nor a wilderness bill against Aspinall's wishes."[22]

The various committee chairmen are kingpins in the House and form the nucleus of its Establishment. "While power seems more fragmented in the House than in the Senate," Senator Clark remarks, "it is probably because the former body is so much larger. Thus it is easier for chairmen to become more powerful. For the same reason there is less cohesion. There appears to be less sense of a 'band of brothers.' While the South is to some extent in the saddle, it seems less obviously so."[23] Still, the men from the nonmetropolitan sector rule.

Yet the Establishment coalition "operates on many an occasion even more effectively in the House than in the Senate" and has killed or whittled down a long line of useful bills—federal aid to education in 1960, area development in 1963, the Mass Transit Bill and Youth Opportunities Act, health care for the aged in earlier versions, improvement of foreign aid. "It cannot stop civil rights legislation because of the urban and suburban Republicans. But it can usually stop if it really wants to what the Establishment likes to call 'spending programs.' "[24]

It did not, however, stop or whittle down Administration requests in 1965 and 1966 for additional appropriations for the undeclared presidential war in Vietnam. Although costing some $20 billion or more annually, the Vietnam operation is not construed as a "spending program." It is, more properly put, a patriotic program. Opposed to expenditures for domestic improvement programs, the Establishment in both houses is religiously devoted to all military spending, sometimes votes more than is asked for by the president.

Committee control and the two-thirds rule are only part of the Establishment method. The American constitutional system at best, as all scholars know, yields a cumbersome government that operates much like a Rube Goldberg threshing machine. With everybody giving his best the machine will work according to the intention of the designers, not efficiently but surely. But when the delays inherent in the checks-and-balance system are added to, as by Rule XXII and other contrivances not found in any parliamentary manual, the machine simply stops.

Rule XXII and the dominance of committee chairmen in the House by no means constitute the only devices of delay.

As Senator Clark notes, certain procedures have been adopted that use up more than half the time of Congress with a view to keeping new business from coming up even if it could be dislodged from the dilatory committees. There is, first, a requirement that the *Journal* of each Senate session must be read the following day unless unanimous consent to skip it is obtained. Says Clark: "It is utilized only for purposes of delay. . . ."[25] Next, the morning period reserved for minor business, using up a valuable legislative hour or more, "makes for delay."[26] Senators speak at exhaustive length; Clark believes speeches should be limited to two hours. Often the subjects talked about haven't the remotest connection with anything taking place; they may be a description of the scenery of the solon's native state, memories of boyhood, a disquisition on the culinary arts, the national flower or the care of dogs—all with a view to using up time.

Again, "A motion to take up a bill on the calendar made by the Majority Leaders should be determined by vote without debate. At present such a motion is subject to unlimited debate, thus giving the opponents of the bill two chances to filibuster instead of only one. . . ."[27]

Establishment senators, with a keen instinct for wasting time, introduce all manner of irrelevancy in their speeches, violating the rule of Jefferson's *Manual* that "No one is allowed to speak impertinently or *beside the question,* superfluously or tediously." Says Clark: "No other legislative body in the world, so far as I have been able to discover, operates without a rule of germaneness."[28]

Clark's staff in a survey of the *Congressional Record* for 1961 found that nongermane speeches, excluding written insertions made only for the record, took up one-third of that gangrenously swollen publication.

While the Senate is in session, committees may not sit. Thus committee work can be delayed. When quorum calls go out, senators check in on the

Senate floor, then fade out, leaving nobody to vote on measures. Thus arises the amusing distinction between a "live" quorum and a *pro forma* or on-the-record quorum.

The Appropriations Committee, however, sits continuously. It obtains unanimous consent at the beginning of each session to sit at any time whether or not the Senate is in session. It would be just too bad if appropriation bills were not ready for railroading on time.

Still another way of slowing down the legislative process is by requiring separate House and Senate hearings on the same bills, thus making witnesses appear twice at different times. As Clark points out, such time-consuming duplication could be eliminated by joint hearings.

Again, when there are joint House and Senate conferences with a view to harmonizing different bills, Establishment leadership sees to it in both houses, very often, that the representatives of the stronger bill are men who voted against it and are unsympathetic to it. These men tend to favor the weaker bill and to compromise accordingly.

It is sometimes an election ploy by a rival for his seat to charge a House congressman especially with a long series of absences from roll calls and votes, implying that he has not been attending to business. But if he is not a member of the Establishment and does not have many committee appointments, there is really no need for him to be present most of the time. He knows the votes on most matters coming up are cut and dried in advance. There is no issue on which his presence can make a difference. The sensible thing to do is to be absent until such time as he can function meaningfully.

It would look better on the record, it is true, if he hung around and answered the roll calls. But such roll-call response can be misleading with respect to the significant activity of a congressman. Some merely sit and read and entertain visitors in their offices between roll calls and votes.

I have given here only a taste of Senator Clark's revealing work. The student of American government, steadily fed on formalistic pap, can do no better than turn to it, read it, memorize it, put it into blank verse and set it to stately music.

Why doesn't somebody, it may be asked, point out in detail to the senators themselves precisely what is taking place? As men of goodwill, the naive will suppose, they will quickly respond and mend their ways. Senator Clark, however, has already performed this bootless task, without avail.[29]

Clark's books offer many concentrated grotesque details—tabulations on the stacked committees, on the ages of the principals, etc. Congress in truth is ruled by a collection of old men, like a primitive tribe. The average age of chairmen of leading Senate committees in 1963 was 67.5 years, with one chairman aged 86 and the youngest 51.[30] In the same year the average age of chairmen of the important House committees was 68.7 years, with the oldest 84 and the youngest 54.[31] A reason advanced by agile Establishment spokesmen against the invariable application of the seniority rule is that it would, unless relaxed from time to time, leave senile dodderers in charge. Yet such are in fact left in charge despite variations in application of the rule to others.

In general, these committee chairmen are unimaginative, insensitive, uncultivated, set in their ways and nurture a vision of social reality long since vanished—always with the inevitable exceptions such as J. William Fulbright of the Foreign Relations Committee, Clinton P. Anderson of the Aeronautical and Space Sciences Committee and perhaps a few others.

The preponderance of the lawless South on key committees is clearly evident. There were twenty-three Democratic senators in 1963 from Dixie —eleven Confederate states plus Arkansas and Oklahoma (23 per cent of the Senate). Yet they held 50 per cent of the seats on the Appropriations Committee, 42 per cent on Armed Services, 55 per cent on Finance, 42 per cent on Foreign Relations, 47 per cent on the Democratic Steering Committee and 33 per cent on the Democratic Policy Committee—this last their true proportion among sixty-seven Democrats.[32] Among Democrats on the committees their disproportion is far greater than given above.

Something not realized by Senator Clark and his on-the-record anti-Establishment cohorts (generally styled liberals and reformers in both parties) is that they themselves lend plausibility to the Establishment game, which is to seem part of a representative body. Without Clark and his stalwarts, playing according to the democratic book, Congress would be visible to all as a heavy-handed affair, like a Russian Constituent Assembly, redolent of the hangman. As it is, the anti-Establishment opposition makes it look at times like a representative legislative body, full of enticing nuances and shadings. The opposition gives the Establishment a brisk diaclectical workout from time to time, keeps it on its toes. Whenever it wishes to, the Establishment can submit its power to a test vote, play for real and knock the opposition through the floor with solid "democratic" votes.

Agreeing with Senator Clark's analysis, up to a point, I must dissent from the final chapter of his *magnum opus*. There, no doubt remorseful for the way he has thrown a scare into the stray American reader by showing how he is ruled by nothing very different from a grim Politburo, he gives way to optimism and looks forward to changes. Simply the many required conditions for changes that he mentions show that it is an all but impossible dream.

Actually, if only thirty-five senators were as demonically opposed to Rule XXII as the Establishment is in favor of it they could destroy it in a matter of weeks, perhaps days. All that a determined opposition need do is to start filibustering on the first item of Establishment business brought to the floor. When there finally came a call for a termination of debate, by the Establishment this time, on the showdown vote there would not be the necessary two-thirds. The hardy thirty-five (or more) would stand adamant. So the filibuster would go on, if necessary for weeks, and Senate business would grind to a halt. Appropriation bills would not get passed and the government would need to resort to financing through the banks in a large way.

As the price of ending the filibuster all the opposition would do is to demand the end of Rule XXII. If the rule stayed, the filibuster would continue.

It is highly doubtful if thirty-five senators, or even fifteen, are this resolutely determined to end Rule XXII. They have, it is true, no mandate for such action from their constituencies. The latter for the most part do not even know of Rule XXII. The non-Establishmentarians are not so determined to abolish it as the Establishment is to keep it, nor are they sufficiently numerous. It follows that the Establishment rules completely, with no sign of an early break in its grip. Such a break—when, as and if it comes—is not likely to develop on the basis of a Clarkian appeal for fair dealing. It can come only as a consequence of some profound upheaval in American society.

The discarding of Rule XXII would not in itself break the power of the Establishment, although the alignment of forces within it would no doubt shift. One sees this by looking at the House, which is run by full-time self-centered *intrigants* without resort to unlimited debate as a threatening weapon. Rule XXII, while convenient, is not really needed.

The remedy for all this, some will say, is in the electoral process before the people. How inadequate a refuge this is one can see by noting that most of the members of Congress occupy "safe" seats, are always virtually sure of election. In the House, supposed paladin of the people, hardly more than a hundred seats are ever in doubt, as Senator Clark admits. More than three-quarters of the occupants know they will invariably be re-elected. An even larger proportion of the Senate holds completely safe seats. Under the impact of a social cataclysm as awesome as the Depression, seats change hands slowly, and after the cataclysm the new incumbent is usually in for the rest of his life.

Such exceptions as there are can be cited from only a few highly competitive, transitional and variegated regions, mainly California and New

York, New Jersey and Connecticut, etc. Inertia in the stuporous electorate is a large factor in holding seats. Not only do the voters usually dislike change but they see no reason for it, can discern no more merit in new contenders than in incumbents. All promise heaven. Unless one can raise the strong suspicion that an officeholder is a Communist, a homosexual, a freethinker, a dabbler in science, a sexual athlete, a practitioner of divorce, a reader of prohibited books or something equally esoteric, he will be hard to dislodge if he has conducted himself according to the established routines of the electoral game.

Senator Clark, like others who feel as he does, lays great stress on public opinion, the need to mobilize it in order to put the government on a course conducive (as he sees it) to the long-term interests of the people and the very safety of the Republic. Such stress on the need for an informed public opinion is an indirect confession of the inadequacy of representative government. If everyone must be fully informed on every question and press insistently for government action, it means we simply now have a more cumbersome form of the New England town meeting when the populace as a whole was the legislative body. If public opinion must be so rampant, and at variance with its own standards, what is the need of representatives? Why not submit all proposals to direct popular vote?

The Establishment in Action

Devoted conscientiously to blocking adjustments in the ramshackle *status quo*, the Establishment can be cooperative and quick-moving when it wishes. It is most cooperative and retiring, Senator Clark points out, in time of war. Then it endorses anything asked for remotely likely to help in crushing the enemy. War, in fact, seems most effective in unlocking its springs of action, in quickening its pulse, in arousing its ardor. It is as bellicose as any Prussian *Junkerverein*. It equates patriotism with war.

Bills affecting its special pets among the *finpols* also get rush-order treatment. Thus, the emergency bill to exempt Du Pont stockholders from the capital gains tax in the distribution under Supreme Court mandate of General Motors stock held by E. I. du Pont de Nemours was galloped through *prestissimo*, as Senator Clark notes. It was as though the Establishmentarians knew that now they were being watched by the gentry and were anxious to show what really fine work they could do—all of which was no doubt very reassuring to Wilmington, Delaware.

How the Establishment works to ensnare the country in something the electorate finds distasteful is more interesting and more revealing of Establishment ways and is best shown in the matter of taxes.

Congressmen in general are not well informed on taxes—or on much else, for that matter. They are, to put it bluntly, conveniently ignorant and depend on the word of floor leaders, whips and committee chairmen.

> Needless to say [as the infinitely expert Eisenstein remarks] members of Congress are not as well versed in taxation as they should be. Of course, they are also inadequately informed on other matters which are entrusted to their care. It is no secret that votes are commonly cast without a firm grasp of the issues involved. In taxation, however, knowledge comes with unusual pain and suffering. The statutes are enveloped in a peculiar verbal fog of their own. The Internal Revenue Code, indeed, is a remarkable essay in sustained obscurity. It has all the earmarks of a conspiracy in restraint of understanding. The conspiracy never ends because amendments never cease. Year after year many minds combine anew against the grave danger of being understood. . . . Surely, the nimblest member of Congress can hardly hope to perceive in a day what the alleged experts are unable to understand over the years. Most members are soon lost and bewildered when they move beyond the rates and personal exemptions. As Representative Patman gently understated the ignorance of Congress, "the tax laws are passed with the Members not knowing exactly what they mean."[33]

Rank and file Republicans and Democrats, right and left, complained at its submission that they did not understand the tax law of 1954,[34] which still provides the main base.

> A vote on a tax bill, then [says the legist Eisenstein] is an act of faith. With few exceptions the members of Congress helplessly approve whatever the tax committees may choose to offer. They "must take the word" of the committees. While the committees usually provide reports for each bill, the reports hardly qualify as guides for the perplexed. As a rule, they merely fortify the sense of organized confusion. If the members look for enlightenment during debate, they rarely learn much more. Complex tax bills are poorly discussed and hastily enacted. At times there is no discussion at all. . . .
>
> The House, in fact, proceeds on the theory that individual members should generally abstain from thinking for themselves. This principle of parliamentary behavior is known as the "gag rule." The members are discreetly denied the right to offer any amendments or to vote on separate sections of a bill. They can only accept or reject the bill as a whole. Since their function is so limited, they have little incentive to be enlightened. In any event, too many questions cannot be asked because debate is carefully curtailed . . . too often the explanations on the floor sound as if the halt were leading the blind.[35]

Within the tax committees and among their technical staff writers—the people who compose *taxese* or tax prose—there is a clearer view of affairs.

Among them, Republicans and Democrats alike, there is full understanding of the workings of special dispensations or "loopholes."[36]

"The story is always the same," Hubert Humphrey admitted when he was a senator. "Higher rates are imposed and at the same time loopholes are carefully framed which permit the wealthy to get out from under the higher taxes."[37]

Says a leading tax expert: ". . . the average congressman does not believe in the present high rates of income tax, especially those applicable in the upper brackets. When he sees these rates applied in individual cases he thinks the rates are too high and therefore unfair. . . . True believers in these rates would long ago have torn down the tax shelters and resisted all pressures for special relief. Instead, the reverse is true."[38]

Astronomic rates, headlined hysterically by newspapers, impress the general public. The rich, it is presumed, are being made to bleed and disgorge by a stern socialistic or at least fanatically liberal government. Rightists fulminate. With the left hand, however, a trucksize loophole is chopped that cancels the high rate, in some cases allows no tax at all to be paid.

For one oil and gas virtuoso, for example, on a total income of $14.3 million in five years, all subject *prima facie* to a 91 per cent tax, the total taxes were only $80,000 or 3/5 of 1 per cent. Still another artist in oil did even better. He tenderly groomed properties that brought in nearly $5 million one year—on which there was no tax due. "In escaping tax on his oil income, he also escaped tax on most of his other income. His total taxes for the period were less than $100,000, but his income from sources other than oil averaged about $1 million a year."[39] At the same time the lowest rates for ordinary taxpayers, the fevered patriots in the streets—rates they could not escape—ranged from 19 to 23 per cent. Theirs not to reason why. . . . Some ultra-large oil companies find the tax at times so infinitesimal that they do not even list it as a separate item in reports to stockholders.[40]

The politically illiterate common man pays what others do not. The government always gets all the money it says it needs. It never permits a "raid" on the Treasury.

The committee process by which the rambling Internal Revenue Code is amended is childishly simple, yet difficult and fatiguing to follow, much like a long-drawn tournament between chessmasters. Like a chess game, too, it is tedious to describe in its inwardness for noninitiates owing to the ramifying effects of simple little moves.

It is in committee hearings that one sees men of C. Wright Mills's executive "power elite"—all figures of distinctly secondary rank, many of them subject to the pleasure of the president as temporary appointees in the

Executive Branch. If committee chairmen or members feel like it, they rake them with sarcasm, challenge them point blank, give them the lie direct.

Before these committees a good deal of careful deference is shown by visiting executives and lawyers. It doesn't all run one way because there is a good deal of reciprocal respect and there is the knowledge among committee members that the witnesses are, after all, connected as underlings with big distributors of pecuniary patronage. Such knowledge is not always controlling because, as the front men in well-entrenched one-party state political factions, the committee members already have plenty "going for them" both politically and financially. If he felt sufficiently irked, one of these committee chairmen could tell the Du Ponts, Rockefellers and Mellons combined precisely where to head in and never feel even slightly threatened by the possibility of any successful electoral reprisal. It has been done, simply as a bravura finger-exercise.

Critics charge that the major tax forces represent narrow and selfish private interests as against public and presumably broad and generous interests. But as Eisenstein points out, it is not possible to isolate public and private interests as separate determinate essences.

In the eyes of these critics, "The taxing process emerges as an unceasing struggle between good and evil. The 'general taxpayer,' the 'general public,' the 'people' are on one side; 'organized groups,' 'special groups,' 'pressure groups,' on the other." But "The 'public' or the 'people' necessarily consist of individuals, and individuals fall into various groups. Not even the adherents of ability insist that all taxpayers should be similarly treated. If they are not to be treated alike, they must be treated as distinctive groups."[41]

Some groups, each of the tax proponents feels, are more vital to the public interest than others, and are entitled to special consideration. This, basically, is the point. Some people count, most do not.

How it plays out is well shown by Eisenstein:

The same generalities are perennially repeated because they are vacant expressions. Everyone may freely put into them whatever he wishes to take out. That is why they are beyond dispute. For the same reason they are also very useful. Dispensations may be broadly condemned and then selectively approved without fear of engaging in any contradictions. Senator Wiley of Wisconsin, for instance, declares that taxes "should be as fair and equitable as possible." They should be "based primarily on ability to pay," and they should not discriminate "as between different groups." But at the same time the senator also maintains that taxes should, "as a matter of principle," provide a "reasonable incentive to earn, to grow, to expand." Therefore, he warmly recommends such special dispensations as a credit for dividends and a reduced rate for income from foreign investments. Apparently dispensations which remove barriers and deterrents do not discriminate "between different groups." The public interest similarly enables Congressman Mills to distinguish between one dispensation and another. Our income tax, he charges, is "riddled with preferential benefits." The statutes are "full of special provisions through which a shrewd or lucky tax-payer can often escape paying anywhere near his full share." But having said all this, Congressman Mills indicates that it would not be "desirable to eliminate all the special provisions that we now permit." Those who fail to pay their "full share" may also serve the public interest.[42]

Whatever is said at these tax hearings, and whatever one may think about what is said, the result (whether explicitly intended or not) is clear: Most of the tax burden is shouldered over, directly and indirectly, on the non-propertied, free-spending labor force, which constitutes the main body of patriots upon which the future of the Republic depends.

After protracted hearings the tax committees go into "executive session," excluding the profane. Staff writers get their instructions. Whatever is not of sentimental appeal is put into the customary opaque language, but what is of sentimental appeal such as high rates on the big incomes and baited deductions for blindness, medicine, children and superannuation is left crystal clear.

When ready the bill is reported out on the floor near the end of the session, when a great many other bills, equally suspect under careful analysis, are also awaiting passage. There is here the usual "logjam" of important legislation, with members impatient to get home to sweet-talk low-IQ voters. The "heat is on" for swift passage.

If anyone wishes, he may suggest amendments, which may or may not be voted down. The votes are there, the floor managers know, to pass the bill. The word is passed to the stalwarts, all ready to act. At the signal, the bill is easily pushed through.

The Senate Finance Committee in 1966, of which Russell Long, an Establishment stalwart, was chairman, consisted of 17 members. Six were identified by Senator Clark as of the Establishment core, 6 were from the South, 8 were from one-party states and 12 were from outside Metropolia. Only 7 were clearly non-Establishmentarians and only 6 would ordinarily be classified as liberals or rationalists.

The House Ways and Means Committee under the redoubtable Wilbur Mills of Arkansas had 11 members out of 25 from one-party states, many more from one-party districts, 8 from the South and 13 from outside Metropolia. The back country was clearly in the saddle. As the committee is under the mesmeric control of Mr. Mills, much like the New York

Philharmonic under Leonard Bernstein, it is not necessary to carry the analysis further. It is all an Establishment affair.

Oddly, what radicals call Wall Street tax laws are largely put into final form by men from the swamps, bayous, tundra, bogs, crossroads, pastures, plains, hills, ravines, badlands and backwoods of the country. These men with some exceptions have not attended fancy law schools or studied at the leading universities; there is about few of them any taint of sickly intellectuality. They are, one might say, as common as any drug-store loafer. Nor did any of them, so far as I can ascertain, ever have to meet a flabbergasting payroll in private business. None was ever a super-salesman, a super-lawyer or a big-time entrepreneur. One can safely say that none has had either firsthand or theoretical knowledge of economics, finance or business affairs. As far as taxes are concerned they only know what they may have alertly picked up by hearsay in their committee rooms from visiting monetary sophists.

Yet, when all is said and done, they are well able to distinguish campaign contributors from unsound, unkempt and uncouth, not to say openly literate, ivory-tower theorists.

The Pay-Off

Contrary to common supposition a *majority* of those in the House and Senate enjoy incomes vaulting far beyond their relatively modest salaries of $30,000 a year plus office expenses, travel allowances and other extras. Merely at this salaried minimal they are already in the upper 1 per cent of income receivers.[43] Income-wise they make members of the Mafia look like bashful Boy Scouts.

Much of this congressional income—by all signs probably most—is obtained in ways that, although technically legal, would be condemned by almost any citizen having ordinary claims to respectability and even by many of the more high-toned swindlers who comb the bistros for hard-to-get victims.

So many, indeed, are the ways on record congressmen have of funneling furtive lucre into their pockets that they defy description at any seemly length. Some attempt must be made, however, to comprehend what goes on among political entrepreneurs in order to understand the *weltaunschauung* of the men who confect our tax laws.

Congress is largely but not exclusively staffed by assiduous off-the-soil moneymakers who use government as a tool in their profit-seeking operations with the gusto of a pack of hypertonic pickpockets assailing a convention of paralytics. In so doing, manifestly, its members are engaging in wholly unfair competition with the business and professional classes, especially with the small and medium-sized portions. Most business people, high or low, and even Mafians, do not have such ready toll-free access to the inner valves and spigots of government.

I am far from contending that money-making congressmen (who must be distinguished from a civilized minority genuinely concerned about the fate of the Republic) are *primarily* athirst for lucre. So to say would involve me in a bootless squabble with degree-flaunting sages about the tenuous and wholly irrelevant question of primacy in motivation—of possible interest only to psychologists. Whether congressional absorption in money-making is first or last in order of emphasis it is patently *materially the largest* and *most assiduously pursued* of all congressional interests.

These possibly truistic prefatory remarks are inspired not by some hostile, foreign, pagan and blasphemous un-American influences such as the godless writings of Karl Marx, Nicolai Bakunin, V. I. Lenin or Leon Trotsky but by first-hand, on-the-scene, carefully put together reports in such solidly established, churchly bourgeois publications as the *New York Herald Tribune* and the *Wall Street Journal*. On the score of method it would be difficult to find sources more homey and comfy unless one had it all in the form of a unanimous opinion of the United States Supreme Court certified in blood by the National Association of Manufacturers.

A bastion of old-line conservatism that yearned for the return of the mansard roof and the Stutz Bearcat, the *Herald Tribune* was until its demise the nonpareil Republican organ of the country.* The *Journal* is to Wall Street what *Pravda* and *Izvestia* are to the Kremlin, although it is a tremendously better paper professionally. None of this, of course, is a guarantee of pinpoint accuracy. But neither publication could be suspected of unorthodox or vagrant leanings in politics or social conceptions. If there was error in the political facts it sprung from inadvertence rather than ignorance or un-American, pro-intellectual bias. Although ornaments of the corporate press (the *Tribune* was owned by John Hay Whitney, a vintage super-millionaire), they are not to be confused with the "mass media," the chief task of which is to portray the world as a never-ending sideshow while fostering mass illusions about the great day that is just around the corner, due to dawn right after the election of John ("The Louse") Outhouse.

Such publications belong to what sociologists modishly dub "the elite press." Of such there are some dozen to eighteen in the country (I myself

---

* The discontinuance of the valued *Herald Tribune* was announced as the consequence of a prolonged, complicated strike involving ten labor unions and two other newspapers. *New York Times,* August 13, 1966; 1:6–7.

lean to the first figure). Among hundreds this is not many but it represents the level of press seriousness. Although sections of this elite have been accused from time to time of editing news in favor of their own point of view, it has never been so much as whispered that they are "un-American" or anything but wholeheartedly committed to the Constitution, profits and godliness. Error, yes; heresy, never.

Even though these elite papers are corporate entities, and as such are subject to the usual reservations, in recent years their owners, who once felt safe under Mark Hanna and Calvin Coolidge, have become dimly but increasingly aware that they are insidiously threatened simply as flesh-and-blood by much that is taking place—by events internal, external and technical. As a screwball society of demoralized citizens gradually comes unglued under ideologically justified neglect by its repeatedly sworn dung-hill guardians, the wealthy and their family members are also affected. Long unable to trot their horses through Central Park owing to the descent upon it of hordes of the demented, they, too, in or near the vicinity of their homes now are increasingly robbed, assaulted, raped, kidnapped, blackmailed, swindled, intimidated by servants and plug-ugly labor leaders, assassinated, run down by unregulated cars, poisoned by offbeat drugs and foods full of additives, overcharged, misled, misdirected, engulfed in half-shot planes and the like. One could compile imposing lists of wealthy victims within just the past five years, some with prolonged pedigrees and valuable Roman numerals after their names.

Again, this isn't the half of it. They are now, wealth or no wealth, subject to common industrial hazards of the population as a whole: air pollution, smoke inhalation, water pollution, unpleasant regional odors, public-service strikes, gratuitous noise, equipment failures right and left, chemical leakages, explosions, water shortages, area "blackouts," public crowding, riots, radiation poisoning, possible atomic warfare and the like.

And if elected government officials are conveniently purchasable, it is always possible, even probable, that they will be purchased by adversely hostile interests burrowing under established cushy positions.

As there is no Stock Exchange quoting officials' prices (which would be a great convenience) one never knows for sure at what figures the political bidding begins and ends. Nor does one ever know when one has a firm acceptance. Bought men sell out again at higher figures—which makes sense. All of which promotes much displeasing uncertainty and anxiety even among general beneficiaries.

Established wealth, in order to realize its potentialities to the maximum, needs orderly, intelligent and principled government. It does not have that now, but is caught in something of a more efficient continuation of the catch-as-catch-can nineteenth century; government is now more systematically and organizedly wayward than it once was. Although after the Civil War the rising magnates engaged in plenty of funny business with the politicians, the latter had not yet organized on a rational semi-corporate basis to put the vacuum cleaner systematically on rich and poor alike. Hence, in part, the rising concern in what are, seen from the street, high places.

If government is thoroughly unprincipled and is at the same time pretty much out of control, if the butler and the rest of the help are freely helping themselves to the vintage stuff and giving their lip to their betters, established wealth is itself in some danger of being clipped. As the *Herald Tribune* somewhat primly observed, "An anarchistic moral climate prevails in Congress." The complaint is not, then, that the congressmen are Bolsheviks but that they are dedicated anarchists, which is surely just as bad or worse. If government men kick up their heels in wild abandon, the rule of the jungle, using government as a handy bludgeon, has returned and, as Thomas Hobbes said, life for everyone tends to become "nasty, brutish and short." If, as it turns out, government officials are surreptitiously enmeshed in a tangle of distractingly profitable involvements, where anyone comes out in the ensuing melée is chancy. Here the problem of government takes on particularly seamy hues, as much—in some ways, more—for the rich as for anyone else.

But if the elite press expected a public uprising on the heels of these probing exposures, recalling the best efforts of the old-time "muckrakers" such as the famed Lincoln Steffens, the editors showed little knowledge of the political system or the public. Proved money-grabbing by elected officials in the atomic age piques a disoriented public far less than the latest *amours* of the Hollywood set, ax murders in Brooklyn or the birth of two-headed quintuplets. As long as there seemed some possibility of sandwiching "call girls" into *l'affaire* Bobby Baker a few years ago, public interest momentarily stirred. It faded as soon as the impresarios failed to produce the cash-minded damsels in undress. Tabloid readers sulked at being deprived of an American Profumo Affair.

In what follows it should always be remembered that there is no question of illegality involved. Everything reported is strictly legal, just as Hitler's extermination of the Jews was legal—a little point I mention merely to suggest how much weight one may attach to the notion. And until further notice everything that follows is taken from the unreservedly patriotic *Herald Tribune* of June 9 through June 15, 1965.

"Anyone who wants any legislation, buys it with cold, cold cash. I don't mean you go up to a Senator and ask him if he'd like to make $5,000 by voting for your bill. That's out today. So are broads and booze."

The words were those of a well-known veteran Washington lobbyist who was explaining his modus operandi.

"What you do is arrange to meet him alone somewhere—but not at his office. I almost never go up on the Hill, except maybe to show friends or relatives around.

"You don't tell him what you want. He knows. You tell him you understand he has a tough campaign coming up—or he has had a tough campaign—and you'd like to help cover the costs. Then you leave an envelope with cash in it. The real reason you are giving the money is never mentioned.

"Of course, you can't do this with all Congressmen. But generally it takes only a couple of votes in subcommittee to swing a bill one way or another. After you've been here awhile you know who to deal with."[44]

As there are more than 4,000 registered lobbyists in Washington, nearly eight to a congressman, it is evident that there are plenty of paymasters. While bribes are illegal, random gifts are not; but to be fully legal they should be reported on income-tax returns. Presumably they are not. And presumably they come out of capacious expense accounts provided lobbyists by their principals, whoever they may be. "Campaign" contributions are legal but should be reported; many are not.

An *al fresco* way of receiving gifts was disclosed by T. Lamar Caudle, an assistant attorney general who was convicted in 1956 of tax-fraud conspiracy. Caudle told the FBI that he customarily parked his car with the window open and was always pleasantly surprised that "somebody kept putting presents" in the back seat. The *Herald Tribune* doubted that congressmen use this method, which seems overly conspiratorial; the congressional deals are more apt to be right over the counter, thus disarming untutored observers.

Lobbyists stand so high in Washington that they constitute an informal branch of government. Thus, Dale Miller, long a successful lobbyist, "is one of President Johnson's closest friends. The president accorded Mr. Miller, a fellow Texan, a signal honor by naming him chairman of the 1965 inauguration committee. Myron Weiner, lobbyist for the ocean freight forwarding industry, shared his Washington apartment for a while with Sen. Harrison Williams, D., N. J. During the Bobby Baker investigation it was disclosed that Mr. Weiner split a fee with Mr. Baker, even though the former Senate majority secretary reportedly performed no special service for it."

And so it goes. The *Herald Tribune* continued:

The relationship between Congressmen and lobbyists is based on reciprocity.

Lobby organizations are the big campaign contributors and the buyers of most seats at political fund-raising banquets. In an age of skyrocketting campaign expenses, Congressmen need the financial handouts which lobby groups offer. ["Campaign expenses," while real, are in part a euphemism. As Frank R. Kent mordantly noted long ago, campaign-fund collectors have "sticky fingers" —that is, they pocket part of the money and divide it with cronies. Frank R. Kent, *The Great Game of Politics*, Doubleday, Page & Co., N.Y., 1923, pp. 131-33—F.L.]

On their part, lobbyists require the support and votes of the lawmakers if their clients are to prosper in the fiercely competitive business world. [What happens when face-to-face competitors each bid for lawmakers' support was not inquired into.—F.L.]

Generally, lobbyists solicit aid through "persuasive education," stressing the merits of their position; by wining and dining lawmakers and their aides, and by subtly offering rewards.

The era of the outright bribe, when the little black bag stuffed with greenbacks was left on the desk, is fading with age.

Few lobbyists try brazenly to buy votes with cash across the table. Instead, the lobbyist seeks to make the Congressman beholden to him. Should the lawmaker be on the fence, uninformed or indifferent concerning a measure, it is presumed he will feel obliged to favor the stand promoted by his lobbyist friend.

One lobbyist said the latest ruse among his colleagues was to work through lawyers.

"The lawyer-client relationship keeps everything confidential. The lawyer, who is never registered as a lobbyist, simply calls up the Congressman and says he represents a client on a matter in which the Congressman might be interested."[45]

Corporation lobbyists have two main objectives: to influence legislation and to dampen enforcement of existing laws by federal corporate regulatory agencies such as the Federal Power Commission, the Federal Communications Commission and a long string of others the average rank-and-file nitwit believes to be standing vigilantly on guard. Simple inquiries by congressmen have the effect of deflecting the hand of law enforcement, because all these agencies are financed through appropriations voted by congressmen. The hostility of even one congressman can lead to severe reduction of an agency's needed funds, can even cause official heads to roll. In consequence, virtually all regulations on the books are only selectively applied.

As to legislation, it was brought out in 1963 that John R. O'Donnell, a promoter of Philippine sugar interests, had bankrolled more than twenty congressmen in 1960 to insure passage of a dubious $73-million Philippine war claims bill for which he expected a fat commission. (Cases cited are only typical examples from among many offered; this text does not profess to be an exhaustive treatise, which would fill volumes if it went back over more than two or three years.)

O. Roy Chalk, president of Trans Caribbean Airways, the D.C. Transit System and other projects, is a chum of Representative Abraham Multer, Democrat of New York, the *Herald Tribune* asserted. Multer achieved a certain amount of notoriety as an echo of Chalk's views, so much so that when a subway system to which Mr. Chalk is piously opposed in Washington was suggested Mr. Multer owlishly warned all and sundry that building it would surely increase the capital's crime rate.

Stanley L. Sommer, a Washington public relations man associated with Morris Forgash, head of U.S. Freight Forwarders, admitted, said the *Herald Tribune*, that "many Senators" have been entertained on board the Forgash yacht "Natamor." Among other tidbits which the paper said Mr. Sommer related, he had picked up the tab for Senator Everett M. Dirksen, Mrs. Dirksen and her sister for a frolicsome Labor Day weekend in 1963 at the Carousel Motel, Ocean City, Maryland. The hotel was owned by Bobby Baker, ousted former secretary to the Senate Democratic Majority of which Majority Leader Lyndon B. Johnson was a free-wheeling ringmaster.

It is noticeable throughout that it is mainly Establishment and fellow-traveling legislators who are enmeshed in this sort of far-ranging entrepreneurial activity. The Establishment forms the spiderweb out of which operations are conducted and to which the operator returns for protection. Men banding together for protection are one source of Establishment power.

Members of the House and Senate are of several economic categories. They are, first, of independent, partly or wholly hereditary means, well educated, who have acquired a general rational interest in government; some of the best ones, intellectually and morally, can be found in this group. In their various outlooks many of these recall the Founding Fathers, nearly all men of property. Unfortunately, they are greatly outnumbered by the dung-hill climbers whose political task it is to gyp their dung-hill constituents. There are, too, moderate-sized business and professional entrepreneurs, most of them unable to distinguish between their business and governmental duties; they use government as a tool of their businesses, a practice openly defended by the late Senator Robert Kerr of Oklahoma, an oil man who was often referred to as "The King of the Senate." There are, finally, those without means or firm business connections. Most of these, excepting only the conspicuously educated, are "on the make," looking upon the government much as brokers look upon the Stock Exchange: an opportunity to feather their nests and thus gain witless public esteem, status. A difference, however, is that brokers do not function under oath.

And it is because congressmen have taken an ostentatious oath that one is entitled, without listening to any sophomoric mush about "human failings" as the orchestra plays "Hearts and Flowers," to subject them to sharp scrutiny and judgment. What one might be inclined to overlook in a broker, or even a banker, one cannot sensibly treat as "just one of those things" in a legislator or other official if one values reasonable civil security.

In the passing of loaded legislation, many instances of which were cited by the staid *Herald Tribune,* the lawmakers manifestly act either for their own account or, as brokers, for the account of others. As the record shows, they function in both roles.

Apart from direct gifts of money, which perhaps are what give most Establishment congressmen their financial starts, the prime way outsiders, mainly corporations, mobilize their zeal is by means of retainers through their law firms. Of 435 representatives and 100 senators, the *Herald Tribune* noted, 305 are lawyers. The firms of nearly all are under lucrative multicorporate retainer.

While one cannot show in every case that a lawyer-congressman is supporting a client of his firm on the floor or in committees, it can be shown in many cases. In some instances one would be hard put to show a one-one connection between a client and a legislative beneficiary. The client-attorney relationships of the congressmen, however, show that both client and attorney are running out of the same corporate stables, flying the same battle flags. The congressmen, if not full-fledged corporate men, are so close to it in their thinking that they are indistinguishable from the officials of the United States Chamber of Commerce. Nobody has to tell the congressmen how to think, for example, on the subject of taxes if they think about them at all; they think that way spontaneously.

The law-retainer racket, often combined with threatened extortion, is very old and is touched upon by Charles Francis Adams II, one-time president of the Union Pacific Railroad, in his *Autobiography* (1916). In Washington on business for the railroad Adams at once encountered "a prominent member of the U.S. Senate" who was still alive, retired, when Adams wrote: ". . . he has a great reputation for ability, and a certain reputation, somewhat fly-blown, it is true, for rugged honesty. I can only say that I found him an ill-mannered bully, and by all odds the most covertly and dangerously corrupt man I ever had opportunity and occasion carefully to observe in public life. His grudge against the Union Pacific was that it had not retained him—he was not, as counsel, in its pay. While he took excellent care of those competing concerns which had been wiser in this respect, he never lost an opportunity of posing as the fearless antagonist of corporations when the Union Pacific came to the front. For that man, on good and sufficient grounds, I entertained a deep dislike. He was distinctly dishonest—a senatorial bribe-taker."

This sort of thing is virtually standard legislative practice in the United States and was the thought in the mind of the *The Nation* (June 26, 1967) when it charged that the nature of the case made against Senator Thomas Dodd before he was censured by the Senate had been largely a cover-up. John Stennis, chairman of the Ethics Committee, *The Nation* charged, had steered the Senate away from considering the more serious charges against Dodd: "that he had (1) threatened to investigate the movie industry but, after taking a political contribution from the Motion Picture Association, dropped the probe; (2) threatened to investigate the television industry, but dropped the matter after taking money from a major member of the industry; (3) taken money from insurance companies while supposedly investigating them; (4) taken money from the firearms industry, and thereafter cooled in his ardor to control interstate shipments of guns; (5) used an airplane belonging to McKesson & Robbins, the drug makers, while sitting on an antitrust subcommittee investigating the drug industry; (6) taken a gift from Westinghouse's lobbyist while sitting on a judiciary subcommittee probing price fixing in the electrical industry; (7) sought favors and jobs for a number of groups and individuals who had contributed to his seemingly bottomless need for money."

Dodd, in fact, was a fairly typical legislator, fitting right into the history of the American congressional system.

Apart from the incentives of surreptitious gifts, campaign contributions and law retainers, congressmen ferret out independent legislative and bureaucratic incentives strictly for their own account. Not only brokers, they are entrepreneurs and promoters as well. They are especially concentrated in the building-and-loan, television, insurance, local banking and credit fields, all subject to regulation and franchising by governmental agencies. Some are also personally interested in a variety of other government-regulated business activities, including the juggling of oil lands. They are, not to put too fine a point on it, estate builders. Estate building represents their philosophic horizon.

First a word about law firms.

Aware that some question of propriety might arise, some congressmen are related to two-name law firms. There is, first, their original firm. There is, also, a newer firm listing all partners' names except their own but occupying the same office, employing the same personnel, using the same telephone number and the two sets of names on the same door. The *Herald Tribune* photographed some of these novelties.

It is presumably through the newer firm that business about which there might be some question is siphoned. The congressman does not participate on the books in such business. But, also presumably, his partners in the old firm are grateful. Presumably he is given a compensatory share in the old firm, doing business with nongovernment-connected clients, and is excluded from direct participation in the juicy second firm. Thus appearances are preserved.

But, even so, the single-name law firm prevails. Most congressmen don't care about appearances.

As the *Herald Tribune* noted, Senator Everett Dirksen, a big Establishmentarian and like his close friend Lyndon B. Johnson an ardent public partisan of prayer and God, is a member of the obscure Peoria, Illinois, law firm of Davis, Morgan and Witherell. This little firm numbers among its clients the formidable International Harvester Company, Pabst Brewing Company, the National Lock Company and the Panhandle Eastern Pipeline Company, a sprawling giant.

"During a 1959 Senate debate on pending legislation to bar pressures on Federal regulatory agencies, Sen. Dirksen said he would continue contacting them for constituents until such time the law provided he could be 'put in jail for doing it.' "[46]

"In addition to his public chores, he is a . . . director of the First Federal Savings and Loan Association of Chicago. . . .

"Sen. Dirksen's business ties meshed neatly with his politics, earlier this year, with the appointment of Carl E. Bagge, a Chicago railroad attorney, as an industry-oriented member of the Federal Power Commission. It was on the Senator's recommendation that President Johnson appointed Mr. Bagge."[47]

The *Herald Tribune* then recalled that the Dirksen law firm represented Panhandle Eastern Pipe Line, which "falls within the jurisdiction of the FPC." Dirksen, therefore, is seen to play a variety of roles. Everybody—legislator, president, law firm, corporations, commissions and lobbyists—is rolled together in the same capacious bed.

Dirksen, although nominally a Republican, bobbed up in several parts of the *Herald Tribune* inquest. In 1962 he received, according to this rock-ribbed Republican newspaper, concentrated campaign contributions from members of the pharmaceutical industry: officials of the Warner-Lambert Pharmaceutical Company, the Olin Mathieson Chemical Corporation (Squibb) and G. D. Searle and Company, drug manufacturers.

"During this period," said the *Herald Tribune*, "Sen. Dirksen was leading the opposition against Sen. Estes Kefauver's campaign to regulate the cost and safety of consumer drugs.

"In his book, *The Real Voice*, on the late Sen. Kefauver's drug fight, author Richard Harris says that Sen. Dirksen became known as the defender of the medical and pharmaceutical interests."[48]

Representative Claude Pepper, Democrat of Florida, former senator, a practicing lawyer with three Florida offices, and an officer and director of the Washington Federal Savings and Loan Association of Miami Beach, in 1963 introduced two bills authorizing savings and loan associations to buy tax-exempt securities. He was at the time a member of the House Banking and Currency Committee which passed on the bills. Sitting on the board of Pepper's Savings and Loan Association was Arthur Courshon, one of the chief savings and loan lobbyists in Washington. One bill was enacted into sacred law in 1964.

Pepper lost his Senate seat in 1950 after fourteen years' incumbency in an election that achieved some fame owing to the novelty of the charges against him by George Smathers. The latter bawled to the swampwater electorate that Pepper had a sister who was a "thespian" and before his own marriage had "practiced celibacy." One wonders what would happen in the outlands if some candidate were ever accused of being a carnivore heterosexual and biped who had caused his wife to undergo parturition. Very probably he would be lynched before a dictionary could be ordered from Sears, Roebuck. Many congressmen, in sober fact, are paranymphs.

Not a few statesmen like Senator Smathers, Democrat of Florida, although no longer active as lawyers, nevertheless "promote legislation favorable to their law firm's clients. Over the years Sen. Smathers has supported bills beneficial to Standard Oil of New Jersey, International Telephone and Telegraph Corp., Pan American World Airways, the Florida East Coast Railway and several insurance companies, all clients of the Miami law firm which bears his name."[49] He is a real corporate fan.

Senator Sam J. Ervin, Jr., Democrat of North Carolina, a member of the Judiciary Committee which had held hearings on four of nine sitting Supreme Court justices, argued as a paid attorney against the government before the court for the Milliken textile interests.[50]

Two businessmen-Senators—Wallace F. Bennett, R., Utah, and Edward V. Long, D., Mo.—have successfully blocked the "truth-in-lending" bill which Sen. Paul Douglas, D., Ill., and a host of other Senators have been sponsoring since 1960 [said the *Herald Tribune*]. Sen. Bennett, former president of the National Association of Manufacturers, is head of an automobile distributorship and director of an insurance company. Sen. Long, a director of a St. Louis bank, has been a vocal supporter for savings and loan institutions since he served in the Missouri legislature. [More recently he has been shown tied up with James Hoffa's Teamsters' Union.]

U.S. Controller of Currency James Saxon once commented that about two-thirds of all Congressmen are involved in savings and loan associations. An aid later reported Mr. Saxon's estimate was somewhat exaggerated but that a substantial number of Congressmen were indeed connected with savings and loan groups.

He said that of the 1,200 or so inquiries which the Controller's office receives annually regarding bank charters and branch applications, at least half come from Congressmen. Most of the inquiries, the aid said, were simple requests for information without any suggestion of pressure.

But as pointed out by George B. Gallaway, author and government expert, "A telephone call from a Senator or Congressman can paralyze the will of a government executive and alter the course of national policy."

In other cases, Sen. Jennings Randolph, D., W. Va., an insurance company director, has taken an active role in debate on proposed medical insurance legislation. His deciding vote killed medicare in the Senate in 1962.

Rep. Multer, chairman of the subcommittee on bank supervision, is privately associated with banking operations.[51]

Senator B. Everett Jordan, Democrat of North Carolina, is chairman of the strategic Rules Committee and frequently has argued on the Senate floor against allowing increases in competing foreign textile imports as recommended by the Tariff Commission. Increasing such imports is part of a supposed national policy of knitting together a raveled world.

The senator is himself a domestic textile man, an officer and director of the Sellers Manufacturing Company of North Carolina.

It was before his committee that the case of Bobby Baker, hired secretary to the Senate Majority, was brought for investigation. Baker was accused of improperly using his position in personal out-of-bounds windfall money-making schemes. And it was Senator Jordan who abruptly closed the inquiry as the trail grew hot with the historic remark: "We're not investigating senators."

"Would Bobby Baker have been able to engage in shadowy business deals if his Senate bosses had been above reproach?" the *Herald Tribune* asked rhetorically.[52] Baker, in the view of sophisticates, merely paralleled the operations of his masters, from whom as a very young man he had learned everything he knew about anti-public skulduggery.

Alluding to the Bobby Baker case, the *Herald Tribune* said it "raised doubts about the moral fiber of the government right up to the steps of the White House."[53] It was, indeed, precisely as attention was directed toward the Senate group of which Lyndon B. Johnson had been a rabidly prayerful member that Senator Jordan abruptly closed off the tepid Baker investigation.

The television industry embraces many congressmen. It has been estimated that 75 per cent of congressmen have interests in television-radio broadcasting franchises. The *Herald Tribune* found that nine senators and fourteen representatives had direct or family-related interests in broadcasting stations. "While he was in the Senate, the family of Lyndon B. Johnson held the only television broadcasting license in Austin, Tex."

The Case of Lyndon Johnson: A Paradigm

According to the *Wall Street Journal,* Mr. Johnson's large-scale property-dealing activities began when he was a representative back in the 1930's.[54]

"Unofficial estimates," said the *Herald Tribune,* "pegged the President's fortune, accrued mostly through his radio-TV holdings, from nine to 14 million. Last August in a public statement he listed his net assets at $3,484,098. A month later, Mr. Humphrey, who sometimes refers to himself as an 'unemployed druggist,' reported his net worth as totaling $171,-396."[55]

Earlier Barry Goldwater, Republican presidential candidate, disclosed that he and his wife were worth $1.7 million mostly in stocks, all of it inherited money.

Johnson, by contrast, was a poor boy who made good—in politics. Back in the 1920's he worked on Texas road gangs as a laborer and was variously employed in catch-as-catch-can jobs until he went to Congress in 1934 after a brief stint as state director of the depression-born National Youth Administration. Those were lean days but, as the Democratic song promised, happy days were returning and soon everything would again be as it was before the dismal crash of 1929. Once on the government payroll Johnson, like many of his colleagues, was never pried loose.

The Johnson fortune, and the miracle of its growth despite the monkish immersion of its architect in steamy affairs of state, came in for a great deal of sudden press attention. What figures are available on it were unprecedentedly disclosed during the presidential campaign of 1964. This revelation resulted from many rumors of the vast magnitude of the Johnson holdings and particularly from a cold-eyed 7,000-word analysis in the *Wall Street Journal* of August 11, 1964. The editors of this elite *feuilleton* had assigned a three-man assault team of ace reporters to invade Texas and find out what caused all the aroma. Their report heightened the worst fears abroad in the land, leading to the later somewhat perfumed self-disclosure reported in the *New York Times* on August 20, 1964.

The *Journal* led off its findings with the following rollicking heading:

LYNDON'S PALS
HIS HOMETOWN COTERIE
WHEELS AND DEALS IN
LAND AND BROADCASTING
THEY BUY INTO AUSTIN BANKS,
TRADE PROPERTY WITH LBJ
AND PLAY SOME POLITICS TOO
DIRECT LINE TO THE WHITE HOUSE

What engages our attention here is not what might interest a political partisan: the fact that this was about the holder of the highest competitive office in the land. It would be a grave mistake to look upon Mr. Johnson's financial affairs as rarely exceptional. They are, rather, a baroque pattern of a Congressional Establishment man's affairs. I remarked earlier that none of these men operate alone. One man could not juggle all this stuff. Behind practically each Establishment figure is organization: a standard political organization of the Republican or Democratic variety and a personal political-financial organization of long-time cronies.

This area of our politics has not been studied, as far as I am aware, by our political scientists. What shows on the surface in Washington is only the tips of the various icebergs. These personal political-financial networks show what politics are about to most of their successful professional practitioners: chiefly a way of self-enrichment. The *pubpols* are trying to become junior *finpols*.

So, taking what the *Journal* found out as a paradigm of approximately what would be found in practically every Establishment case, there was disclosed the following:

The Johnson affairs revolved around the hitherto obscure Austin law firm of Clark, Thomas, Harris, Denius and Winters, "patronized by giant national corporations." A separate lawyer, A. W. Moursund of Johnson City, was found to be Mr. Johnson's personal attorney, realty partner and a key figure in his affairs. He was "linked by private telephone circuit to the LBJ Ranch and the White House." All the lawyers interviewed talked themselves down, jocosely. "I'm just a country lawyer," said Moursund. "I'm just a poor boy, born and raised in East Texas, trying to make an honest buck," said Don Thomas of the law firm. Said Mr. Ed Clark: "Spell my name right—I need the business."

Mr. Johnson, the Johnson family, these lawyers and other cronies, the *Journal* found, held parallel or interlocking interests in television-radio properties, vast tracts of land made valuable by federal electrification and Johnson-sponsored dam projects over the years and shares in clusters of Texas banks that gave the group enormous credit resources. Said the *Journal*: "According to experts of the American Bar Association it is unusual for law firms to invest substantially in bank stocks, but perfectly legitimate."

There was, first, the Texas Broadcasting Company, a name substituted for The LBJ Company when Mr. Johnson unexpectedly became president of the United States. This outfit owned the various radio and exclusive television stations of the Johnsons. A "competing" radio station, working out of the same address, had been long before set up by Johnson associates and employees: John Connally, now governor of Texas, Walter Jenkins, Merrill Connally, Willard Deason, Melvin Winters (the Johnson City contractor who is a trustee of the Johnson foundation), Robert L. Phinney (an old Johnson college roommate who became Austin's postmaster and more recently director of the Internal Revenue Service for the region), and various other Johnson employees or associates.

The *Journal* was piqued by two contrasting strands it found in Johnson affairs: the pattern of monopoly as in the television broadcasting station and concentrated bank holdings, and the pattern of apparent competition within the group itself.

The broadcasting enterprises are housed in a modern office building at Tenth and Brazos Street in Austin owned by the Brazos-Tenth Street Corporation, a holding company held in the name of Don Thomas of the law firm. Mr. Thomas denied point-blank that he was just a "front man" for LBJ. Yet he is also the secretary and a director of the broadcasting company, and a trustee of The LBJ Company Profit-Sharing and Incentive Plan and of the Johnson City Foundation, an LBJ creation.

The Brazos-Tenth Street Corporation, the *Journal* found, figures in baffling big land deals with Mr. Johnson. Court records showed that it bought property from The LBJ Company and resold it the same day to Lyndon B. Johnson in person. It engaged in a series of such land deals with the then vice president, as local records showed, and in some cases acted as the buyer-seller in deals between Mr. and Mrs. Johnson. The *Journal* explained them as possible tax maneuvers through a "conduit agency."

Other deals were recounted in which parcels of land were sold over the years in a circle extending through Johnson companies and employees and then winding up again in the hands of the original owner, Donald Thomas of the law firm.

Money for the various deals, said the *Journal*, was supplied by banks in which the "members of the Johnson inner circle have an interest and a voice."

Mr. Moursund himself was found to be a big dealer in land tracts, held fifty-fifty with The LBJ Company. According to Mr. Thomas, the president owned about 5,000 acres of land, most of it ranch land but 27 acres of it bought back in the 1930's for about $300 an acre and now worth about $20,000 an acre, a rise from $8,100 to $540,000. In addition to being a partner of LBJ in big land deals Mr. Moursund was a trustee of the broadcasting company stock and of the Johnson City Foundation, the philanthropic distributions in one year of which were found to total $8,000 out of $11,000 income and an increase of $89,000 in asset value.

Both Mr. Moursund and the law firm were found to be extensively interested in regional banks, and the *Journal* reporters found the belief strong in the muted region that Mr. Johnson was an *eminence grise* in the background. Mr. Moursund, his mother, his law partner, Mr. Thomas of Austin and the Brazos-Tenth Street Corporation acquired control of the Moore State Bank of Llano, Texas, soon after Messrs. Moursund and Johnson had paid it a visit.

"Lyndon's associates own or manage stock in all eight of Austin's banks," said the *Journal*. "Here in Johnson City, at about the time Lyndon Johnson was being inaugurated as Vice President, Brazos-Tenth acquired four-fifths of the stock of the town's only bank, Citizens State (resources: about $3 million). On the board sit Mr. Thomas, Mr. Moursund and another key member of the inner circle, Jesse Kellam, president of the Johnson broadcasting company." Kellam is a college chum of Johnson's, succeeded him in 1934 as Youth Administration director, helped him with his first congressional campaign, now owns stock in four Austin banks and is a director of one of the biggest, the Capital National.

But the big man at Capital National was Ed Clark of the law firm, a former Texas secretary of state, lobbyist and political and legal trouble-shooter for Mr. Johnson. Clark and his partners are big stockholders in Capital National.

Mr. Moursund is a director of the American National, another big Austin bank of which the Johnson Profit-Sharing Plan and the Johnson City Foundation are also stockholders. "The Johnson foundation also has holdings in three other Austin banks; its total of bank stock comes to roughly $137,000."

In Austin National, the biggest bank in the region, Brazos-Tenth has a stockholding foothold.

John Connally served as the first president of the ostensibly competing radio outfit, KVET. Connally had been secretary to Representative Johnson prior to 1948 and was manager of the presidential bid of LBJ in 1960. As governor of Texas he is now conceded to have complete Establishment control of the state, having routed the liberals. Connally originally subscribed to half of the new radio station's stock for $25,000, which he borrowed from Ed Clark's Capital National Bank. Mr. Clark was also a founder of the radio company that entered the field against the Johnsons' KTBC, headed by Mrs. Johnson.

The Federal Communications Commission, the *Journal* noted, apparently did not notice KVET had the same address as KTBC and numbered among its founders KTBC personnel. It is illegal for the owner of one station to hold even minority interest in a competing station in the same town. Walter Jenkins, later an administrative aid to President Johnson, was an early stockholder in the Connally station.

Difficulties in Washington connected with the new station were quickly cleared. Its bid for a wavelength held by a San Antonio station, seventy miles away, was quickly resolved by the FCC; KVET got the desired wavelength. "Then the Civil Aeronautics Administration complained erection of the 210-foot broadcasting tower would 'present an undue hazard for the safe operation of aircraft.' But two weeks later it changed its mind.

"KVET, like Lady Bird's KTBC, had no trouble getting network affiliation, signing up with Mutual. To this day these two remain the only network outlets in Austin, though the city now has seven radio stations."

Connally in 1955 became attorney for Sid Richardson, the multimillionaire Fort Worth oilman, thus cementing the relations of the group with the inner-circle depletion-allowance crowd, of which Mr. Johnson in the Senate was always an ardent supporter. At this time Mr. Connally turned over his control in KVET to Willard Deason, old Johnson school chum.

"Those who drop in to visit station president Deason nowadays can hear his cheerful view of competing with the Johnsons and his cozy recollections of how it all came about. They can see two pictures adorning his office. One is a brown-tone photo taken in 1932, of schoolmate Lyndon. The other is a large autographed portrait of the President of the United States."

It was hard on the heels of this instructive report that Mr. Johnson took an unprecedented step for a president of the United States by disclosing figures on his financial position. The principal assets shown consisted of the Texas Broadcasting Corporation and real estate. The total valuation placed on them was $3,484,098. Ownership titles were split among the family so that the president apparently held $378,081 of assets, his wife $2,126,298 and the two minor daughters close to $500,000 each. No mention was made of the Johnson City Foundation.

As the *Times* pointed out, original ground-floor costs were used in arriving at valuations and the auditors themselves noted that the method used was "not intended to indicate the values that might be realized if the investments were sold."

Unfeeling and obviously partisan Republicans called the valuations "incredibly low" and charged that the method used was "like the city of New York listing the value of Manhattan Island at $24," the original price supposed to have been paid to the Indians.

Financial analysts in general contended that merely the holdings shown were worth up to $15 million or more.

There were internal discrepancies in the report as published. Texas ranch properties listed among total balance-sheet assets were set at $502,-478, a figure carried forward from an erroneous computation that on the basis of the itemization given should have added up to $1,445,822. Either the total given is wrong or the items composing it are erroneously stated, as anyone may ascertain by consulting the *Times*.

In the preceding decade the family had received admitted cash income exceeding $1.8 million, irrespective of the *pro forma* quadrupling in value of assets. The original cost of the broadcasting enterprise was $24,850 in the period 1944–47. Undistributed profits of $2,445,830 after the deduction of purely potential capital gain taxes were solely used to bring its valuation to $2,470,680. Capital gain tax will never be paid unless the broadcasting enterprise is sold.

The broadcasting company, it was shown, is wholly owned by Mrs. Johnson and her two daughters. It owned or had an interest in broadcasting facilities in Austin, Waco, Bryan and Victoria in Texas, and in Ardmore, Oklahoma.

Both in type of personal holdings and those distributed among kin there was nothing to differentiate the statement from that of any Wall Street tycoon except the numerical details. The president and his wife held respectively $159,270 and $239,270 of tax-exempt state and local government bonds. Each held ranch properties valued at $227,114 and minor amounts of "other assets."

Properties owned by Mr. and Mrs. Johnson were placed in trust in November, 1963, immediately after he assumed the presidency. They will be so held until he no longer holds federal office. Yet, he held high federal office before the creation of this trusteeship, which has the sole effect of placing the properties under the management of nominees. It does not represent a divorce.

Knowing he is the beneficiary under this trusteeship, is the president's mind so free of property influence that he is likely to come out for, say, strict government regulation of television advertising or the end of tax-free oil? Is he likely to agree with Kennedy appointee Newton Minow that television is a "wasteland"?

Said the *New York Times* editorially on September 25, 1964, about this arrangement:

The property has been placed in trust while the President is in office, and Mr. Johnson will unquestionably take special pains to avoid any charge of improper influence over the F.C.C. But a conflict of interest remains as long as the nation's chief officeholder possesses a stake, direct or indirect, in a property he is charged with regulating.

This property was acquired when Mr. Johnson was in Congress. He was doing what many other Congressmen . . . have done. There is, unfortunately, no law against Congressmen owning television and radio facilities or having a financial interest in other franchises or businesses that are either regulated by Federal agencies or dependent on Government contracts. But the very fact that Mr. Johnson set up a trust when he assumed the Presidency indicates that ownership of Government-regulated business suggests a conflict—for members of Congress as well as for the occupant of the White House.

The *Times* suggested "divestiture" of the property as a way out, without suggesting the nature of such legerdemain. If it were sold the president would realize a handsome profit. If it were given away for charity it would defeat the intended purpose from the beginning.

The insight given by the Johnson financial statement, as far as it went, into the affairs of a big Establishmentarian and career politician who thirty years before was as poor as the proverbial church mouse enabled reflective observers to see where rhetoric leaves off and substance begins in the thinking of the Establishment. The energy devoted to putting together from scratch and sheltering these properties should be some guide to personal motivation. What was disclosed bore none of the earmarks of a part-time hobby.

What is even more strange is that even as President Mr. Johnson has continued large-scale land and cattle purchases through agents, paralleling value-bringing state highway and bridge-building projects, according to the *New York Times* in an extensive report of December 26, 1966 (23:2–3). This report of total holdings more recently of 14,000 acres in five separate ranches led Washington wits to say that Mr. Johnson has been the biggest real estate operator as president of the United States since President Jefferson's "Louisiana Purchase."

Despite his single-handed involvement of the United States in a big Asiatic land war, long held by the Chiefs of Staff as something to be avoided at all costs, Mr. Johnson is nevertheless hailed by many as the architect of "The Great Society," an apparition that is due to materialize no doubt at about the same time as grass-roots communism appears in Russia and the Soviet state "withers away." Just how much stock one should take in the Great Society fantasy was suggested at the annual get-together of the American Political Science Association in 1965, as reported by the *New York Times*:

Although a high proportion of them unquestionably voted for Mr. Johnson last fall, the comments of the political scientists indicated a shocking skepticism about Washington's earnest belief that this President has introduced—through his Great Society programs, his style of vigorous personal leadership and his invocation of the virtues of one "great big party"—a dramatic new element in American politics.

Nelson Polsby of Wesleyan University captured the prevailing view when he remarked:

"There's nothing new about all this. All you really have is a swollen Congressional majority, that Barry Goldwater handed the Democrats, passing programs that have been kicking around since New Deal and Fair Deal days."

A colleague from Wesleyan, Clement E. Bose, compounded the heresy, saying that the Johnson record "is not one of innovation, but of ratification of ideas that have been germinating since the time of Henry Wallace."[56]

So much for "The Great Society."

Other Political Horatio Algers

Before closing the books on the Horatio Algers in politics, some further nuggets from the valuable *Herald Tribune* series, put together by ace reporter Dom Bonafede, should be exhibited:

"Civic participation" by applicants is one of the yardsticks used by the Federal Communications Commission in granting TV licenses, and being a congressman is interpreted as "civic participation" given weight in licensing—a doctrine that Democratic Senator William J. Proxmire of Wisconsin called "an amazing proposition."[57]

Representative William E. Miller, Republican candidate for vice president in 1964, was on the payroll of the Lockport Felt Company while in Congress, where he had "openly promoted legislation favorable to the company on the floor." He was made a vice president of the company two weeks after leaving Congress.[58]

Senators Spessard Holland and George Smathers of Florida and B. Everett Jordan and Samuel J. Ervin, Jr., of North Carolina were co-sponsors of a bill in which the Florida Power and Light Company was "the prime mover" to exempt from federal regulation private utilities not directly linked with out-of-state transmission networks.[59]

Until he recently sold the bulk of his holdings, Sen. Warren G. Magnuson, D., Wash., the Commerce Committee chairman, was part owner of a Seattle broadcasting station. One of the committee's functions is to oversee operations of the FCC.

Sen. John L. McClellan, D., Ark., the famed rackets-buster, is chairman of the subcommittee investigating the Federal banking system, even though he is a bank director in private life. Another subcommittee member, Sen. Sam J. Ervin, D., N.C., also holds a bank directorship.

Rep. William C. Cramer, R., Fla., spoke against the Administration's war [sic!] on poverty almost from the program's inception. But his protests appear to have been muted ever since a laundry service he heads in St. Petersburg was awarded a contract with Women's Job Corps.[60]

Although the Corrupt Practices Act of 1925 requires congressmen to report campaign contributions and expenditures, limiting what can be spent to $5,000 for representatives and $25,000 for senators, large numbers of members of both Houses report "none" on the required forms after each election.[61]

Yet carloads of money are nevertheless spent, or at least collected, in congressional campaigns. Only $18.5 million was formally reported as collected for the 1962 "off year" campaigns, but an expertly estimated $100 million was collected.[62]

Political money is really tossed about in a large way.

"Newly elected Rep. Richard L. Ottinger, D., N.Y., a multi-millionaire in private life, spent almost $200,000 through 34 committees to win his seat. Yet, his campaign report lists expenditures of $4,500 and no contributions."[63]

Although there are criminal penalties prescribed for negligent failure to file a report or to file a false report, there has never been a prosecution under the Act of 1925.

"Ingenious methods of raising campaign funds are developed. . . . Card games are held in which a portion of the pot from each hand is set aside for a campaign committee. For many years, Rep. Michael J. Kirwan, of Ohio, House Democratic Campaign Committee Chairman, staged a St. Patrick's Day party for the purpose of soliciting campaign funds."[64]

Cocktail parties are a standard fixture where lobbyists are panhandled for handouts to support democracy. One lobbyist told the *Herald Tribune* that it usually cost him $100 for a single drink "and a cold shrimp on a toothpick," which was perhaps cheap.

A generally favored swindle is to run $100- to $1,000-a-plate testimonial dinners, production cost about $10 apiece, and to send twenty-five to a hundred tickets to various corporate people, who generally grab them like manna and distribute them to the office help. If the corporate boys fail to remit they suspect an undeserved demerit may be entered against their names in some little black book.

While a direct gift of money in excess of $3,000, except (as the courts have percipiently ruled) expensive presents to a lady friend, are subject to tax, a gift in recognition of "public service" is not so taxable. Although such gifts are not lavished on low-paid scientists, artists, military officers and profound cogitators, who may be supposed to have rendered some public service, they are rife in the case of officials, especially congressmen. It is not necessary to pass them money in some back alley. What is done is to stage a glittering public affair, with hundreds of well-heeled customers present, and to present the modest recipient with a large certified check as the cameras flash the scene for posterity. What results are photographs reminiscent of Renaissance paintings titled "Adoration of the Infanta." Diners leave with the vague semi-alcoholic feeling that they have participated in a religious ceremony, have at least paid homage to a glorious Republic once sadly betrayed by wicked, wicked, wicked Benedict Arnold.

Lest any strait-laced, dyspeptic methodologist charge that I am drawing my data from only two sources which, although highly orthodox, could be wrong or wrong-headed, let the future historian know that among many other sources on congressional skulduggery there are the nationally syndicated Washington columns of Drew Pearson, a practitioner of the journalistic craft for more than forty years.

Not only do we encounter many members of the cast we already are familiar with in the Pearson columns but a host of new names ooze into view week after week.

"Any pressure group that is rich and powerful enough can find a champion in Everett Dirksen," said Pearson. "It is his conviction that the special interests are entitled to a voice in the Senate. His office has been headquarters for almost every major group—the drug industry, gas and oil combine, food packagers, etc.—that has had a legislative problem.

"To no one's particular surprise, Dirksen's law firm in faraway Peoria,

Ill., has collected retainers from many a giant corporation whose interests the Senator has served in Washington."[65]

A few other nuggets from the Pearson columns—the nuggets alone would fill a book—are as follows:

Representative William H. Harsha, Jr., Republican of Ohio, has been a strong opponent of the Federal Mass Transportation Act, designed to develop rail and commuter services for clogged cities. His law firm represents the Greyhound Bus Lines. The congressman favors limiting imports of residual fuel oil. His firm represents Phillips Petroleum and Ashland Refining Company.[66]

Representative Charles Chamberlain, Republican of Michigan, introduced a bill to repeal the manufacturers' excise tax on cars and trucks. His law firm represented the United Trucking Service and the Detroit Automobile Inter-Insurance Exchange as well as the Panhandle Eastern Pipeline Company of Texas, which like other companies appears to make use of many congressional law firms.[67]

In the 1940's Representative Victor Wickersham, Democrat of Oklahoma, asserting "I am a poor man," advocated increased congressional salaries. Despite still moderate congressional salaries, he was more recently set on getting back into office. In an application filed with the Federal Communications Commission to buy radio station KREK in Sapulpa, he stated his current net worth at $1,579,789, placing him among some 90,-000 millionaires. Pearson traced various typical flourishes in the financial efflorescence of Wickersham over the years.[68]

Upon the impending retirement of Representative Oren Harris, chairman of the House Commerce Committee, to accept a presidential appointment as a United States judge, Pearson noted that Harris was a stockholder in Station KRBB of El Dorado, Arkansas, and as a close associate of Ham Moses of the Arkansas Power and Light Company "had introduced more special-interest legislation than any member of Congress."

Because of the inability to find a suitable replacement for Harris, said Pearson, the lobbyists asked Senator McClellan to intervene and hold up at the White House Harris's appointment for the stated reason of a "ticklish" election in Arkansas. The president obliged.

"This will help Madison Avenue, but it puts the President in a bad light in regard to his family radio-TV property in Texas. He has claimed that he has kept aloof from influencing the Federal Communications Commission; but now he continues in power the congressional chairman who has slapped down the commission on behalf of the big networks.

"Note—It's significant that Mr. Johnson has been very chummy with the big networks, as witness the repeated White House dinner invitations to network executives. . . ."[69]

How it may work out when anyone drives a high-placed official into a tight corner was shown in the case of Senator Thomas J. Dodd of Connecticut, as reported by Pearson. The FBI had been informed of documentary data in Pearson's hands and photographed and rephotographed it.

[Pearson's subaltern had] been working with half a dozen prospective witnesses, all former Dodd employees. . . . These were young people who had been shocked at what was happening in Dodd's office and departed. They felt under moral obligation to report what was happening.

The G-men called on the witnesses all right, but didn't ask a single question about Dodd, his conduct, whether he had diverted funds from testimonial dinners to his own pocket or whether he had acted on behalf of an agent for a foreign power, Gen. Julius Klein.

Instead, the FBI crossexamined these young people about the alleged theft of Dodd's documents. They also heckled them about other stories Jack Anderson and I had written.

As fast as the FBI discovered the identity of the witnesses, they were bullied and badgered, hounded and harassed. One lost his job on a House committee; the news of his dismissal came from Dodd's office. Another . . . since submitting his resignation . . . has been unable to find another job. Others have had their jobs threatened. One woman, seven months pregnant, was grilled by agents for three hours.

Agents hauled some witnesses right into Dodd's office for cross-examination and behaved as if they were working for the Senator. Other witnesses were alternatively soft-soaped and threatened with Federal prosecution.

I have been around Washington a long time, but have never seen such an example of police state operation.

Such investigations, of course, do not happen by accident. They usually go beyond the Attorney General, Mr. Katzenbach, an awfully nice guy but a bit wishy-washy when it comes to standing up to the White House or the Senate Judiciary Committee, of which Tom Dodd is a member.

Such investigations usually go right up to the President himself. Johnson has on his desk a direct private phone to J. Edgar Hoover. They are very old friends, dating back to the days when I used to visit in Johnson's home when he was a gawky young Congressman from Texas living just across the street from Hoover's well-appointed bachelor abode.

Johnson is not only a friend of Hoover's but he is a friend of Dodd's. It takes a real friend to make the two trips he made to Connecticut to speak at testimonial dinners which raised $100,000 for Tom's personal bank account.

Johnson did all right for Tom. He hoisted him to a choice position on the Senate Foreign Relations Committee, ahead of other Senators, a vantage point from which he was able to work more effectively for Gen. Klein. And he almost picked Tom to run with him for Vice President.[70]

While much more along the same line could be cited it is time to close the books on this phase of our quest for enlightenment. Suffice it to say that a *majority* of members in both Houses are tainted with what is euphemistically known as a "conflict of interest." There is, however, as readily seen, really no conflict of interest involved. The line of interest is clearcut and unambiguously pointed in one direction—to personal nest-feathering at public expense.

Nor are only overt Establishment people involved. Democratic Senator Thomas Dodd was never a recognized Establishment man, perhaps one reason he was made an object of gingerly inquiry by the Senate for actions little different from those of others except that he involved himself with a registered agent of unholy foreign interests and stepped into delicate areas subject to foreign policy and the jurisdiction of the Foreign Relations Committee under vigilant Chairman J. William Fulbright.

But where is the line to be drawn on congressional self-dealing? What difference does it make whether the havoc caused is international or domestic?

Some fairly feeble solutions have been proposed for this parasitism at the heart of the political system. One is that congressmen be required to disclose their personal financial holdings so that the public may evaluate their votes, thus determining whether they are cast on the merits of a case or for personal profit. This proposal has been supported by Senators Clark, Wayne Morse, Paul Douglas, Clifford Case, Jacob Javits, Kenneth Keating, Maurine Neuberger and others—all non-Establishmentarians. In the House it was supported by Edith Green, Ogden Reid and John V. Lindsay. Senators Clark, Hugh Scott of Pennsylvania, Stephen Young of Ohio, William Proxmire of Wisconsin, Morse of Oregon and Mike Mansfield of Montana have voluntarily disclosed their personal financial holdings and Paul Douglas rendered an annual public account of his income and expenditures. They have had few emulators.

Senator Dirksen predictably objected to the proposed law on the clownish ground that it would be "an invasion of privacy" and would make him a "second-class citizen" into whose private affairs every vagrant Peeping Tom could penetrate.

Apart from the fact that the Establishment, as a sovereign force effectively unchecked by any knowledgeable electorate, will never enact such a measure, if it did who would enforce it?

Hidden Holdings

Again, if congressmen disclosed their holdings, such disclosure would not portend much even if it was made annually. For the source of the poor-boy congressman's original stake consists in most cases obviously of under-the-counter gifts, ambiguous campaign contributions, legal retainers, public testimonial awards and benevolent bank loans. And all such, if subject to disclosure, could be kept in the names of wives, parents, daughters, sons, cousins and the like.

Actually, any man may have vast holdings with nothing set down anywhere in his name. A man can own a million shares in a big corporation without his name ever appearing on the books. The stock can be held by obscure paid nominees who have signed, in blank, stock transfer certificates allocating these shares to whoever holds and fills in the certificates.

Any person interested in concealing assets can do even better than this, as we are reminded by that old reliable, the *Wall Street Journal*, of recent decades a most informative newspaper. Money can be transferred to one's own neutrally named holding company, a "shell" company, in any one of a number of places—Lichtenstein, Luxembourg, Panama, the Bahamas—and deposited in a numbered Swiss bank account, the owner of which the bankers are forbidden by strict Swiss law to disclose. The Swiss bank, conducting all operations in its own name, can buy or sell securities, realty or other titles in any market without anyone knowing for whom it acts. Profits are transferred to the owner direct or to the "shell" company, which cashes checks and turns money over to the true owner. The "shell" is in charge of low-paid employees, glad to perform this less than onerous occasional service. The money, if wanted in the United States, is simply carried home in one's wallet or is brought back by couriers.

This method, as a device for evading American income, capital gains and inheritance taxes, is already used by many American business and professional men, Las Vegas gamblers, racketeers, some millionaires and owners of at least 10 per cent of some corporations' shares among executives, according to the *Wall Street Journal*. It estimates that hundreds of millions of dollars are so involved, perhaps billions.[71]

The stacking away of tax-shy assets abroad is not confined to marginal elements. As the *New York Times* informs in a special dispatch from Luxembourg:[72]

Along the Grande Rue and the Boulevard Royal, companies like du Pont Europa Holdings and Amoco Oil Holdings have nestled their "sièges sociales" (head offices) in filing cabinets next to 2,000 other Luxembourg holding companies.

With a few exceptions, the head office is the street address of a bank or a law firm. The lawyer or the banker may be a director of more corporations than are most captains of industry anywhere.

Some Luxembourg holding companies date back to 1929, when Parliament passed a law making it easy and inexpensive for them to be established and kept here. Not a few were or are facades for family businesses in nearby countries, shells to make possible the investment of income hidden from the tax collector.

Since this is not such an easy contrivance anymore, the reasons for setting up Luxembourg holding companies nowadays are likely to stem primarily from difficulties in carrying on essential business operations elsewhere.

This indeed has been the basis for the recent stir of holding-company activity by American corporate giants in this quiet, 999-square-mile Grand Duchy. With direct dollar sources of capital restricted by the American balance-of-payments restraints, Luxembourg has become a strategic base for raising needed investment capital in Europe.

Apart from basic tax advantages, the Duchy also provides a singular freedom from business regulation.

A holding company can be formed within weeks—days, says one American lawyer. The company is exempt from income and capital-gains taxes. Most important, Luxembourg requires no tax withheld [on payments to foreigners].

Actually, the only chance for a significant change in Congress and the stripe of elected officials generally is to get an altogether different type of person into active politics, perhaps men of the type of the non-Establishmentarians. Considering all factors, including the fuzzy mentality of the electorate, this will be very hard if not impossible to accomplish. The fundamental difficulty is institutional: the universal equal franchise that gives the vote to clods.

It is not for lack of precept that congressmen conduct themselves as they do while bringing a laudably strict set of standards to bear against appointees in the executive and judicial branches. Thomas Jefferson laid down the rule in 1801 when he was vice president and Senate presiding officer that "Where the private interests of a member are concerned in a bill of question he is to withdraw." This is just what a competent judge does if there is any question of his personal involvement in a case *sub judice*.

Such a rule assumes that the relevant body consists of gentlemen and, perhaps, scholars. The electorate, it is observable, does not usually support such when they appear.

For the latter-day comers up from bayous, swamps, gutters and sties the rule was broadened by House Speaker James G. Blaine of Maine, who in

1874 asserted astonishingly that a member might vote for his private interests if the measure was not for his exclusive benefit but for the benefit of a group. (Blaine was exposed in 1884 as a bribe taker in connection with the securing of land grants for the Little Rock and Fort Smith Railroad.)

Said the *Herald Tribune* significantly in concluding its valuable series:

"Frequently a Senator or Representative's outside income results directly from the fact that he is a member of Congress."[73]

Political Sources of New Fortunes

That the transfer of moneys to congressmen is a long-term, standard affair is attested by the *Wall Street Journal* of May 11, 1966, which says that "dozen" of congressmen "allow wealthy supporters to set up office funds or let lobbyists for business and labor sponsor testimonials, anniversary celebrations, birthday parties and other occasions or excuses for fundraising not necessarily related to campaign needs—namely, office, entertainment and travel expenses."

Few legislators, the *Journal* noted, reject such helpful emoluments, which come under the heading of perquisites of office. "But a majority of legislators," continued the Wall Street *Pravda*, "regard contributions made outside regular campaign fund-raising channels as perfectly proper, always assuming that the recipient doesn't mortgage his independence to the givers."

These statements come under the heading of "laying it on the line" by Wall Street for those multitudes who are under some illusion about how, and why, the government is operated.

It is always well to remember that existing laws, passed by Congress and Congress alone, do not prohibit these activities. In fact, in many ways it would be tedious to probe, they encourage them. Congress no more navigates under any canon of ethics than does the Politburo. In this respect both bodies are on all fours. As in the case of any true sovereign, Congress is richly privileged. So, indeed, is the president.

Whatever Congress and the president are not specifically, in detail and under penalty, prohibited from doing they may do. So they do it, whatever it is.

The simple enumeration of powers of Congress in Article I, Section 8, of the Constitution should show any doubter that, collectively, this is an awesomely powerful assembly. Any small group such as the Establishment leaders that can by intrigue (the supreme method of *practical* politics) manipulate this divided collectivity internally obviously has in its hands a formidable engine, with a wealth of modern technology at its service.

The only restraints upon Congress, largely theoretical as far as immediate or individual actions are concerned, are the Supreme Court and the president. The latter, if he wants cooperation from it, must cooperate with it.

Difficult though it is to build a fortune by engaging in new business ventures among the established corporate giants, there is a wide open road to wealth if one knows how to worm one's way into politics. By all present indications, really big new fortunes in the future will be more and more politically based, and we are already, perhaps, in the era of big emerging political fortunes. Should this become so, it will be evident that the United States is reenacting parts of Roman and later European history when fortune-building was the perquisite of men associated with sovereign powers rather than of men more directly related to the market place. Much of such political fortune-building, it is notable, was in the past related to the systems of taxation and government contracting.

Ex-Senator Paul Douglas, a careful student of congressional ethics, does not believe it would do any good to raise congressional pay but, looking at the fat rewards given high executives by corporations to keep their wonder boys in line, one pauses to reflect. If congressmen were each paid $200,000 per year plus $50,000 expenses, all tax-free, they would at least know whence their good fortune came. They would know for whom they were working. And such pay, by visibly exalting the office, might attract many others who under the present system do not wish to engage in the shabby dodges, the money grubbing, necessary to achieve substantial emoluments —that is, so-called financial security. The total public cost would be relatively slight, only $133,750,000 annually, a bagatelle compared with sums now voted for all manner of dubious projects, far less than the cost of elections.

Opposition to such a pay boost might be counted upon to come from two quarters—the frugal-minded rank-and-file citizens to whom the present $30,000 annually plus expenses is in itself an astronomic sum, and the very rich. The latter—or at least their advisers and lobbyists—would in many cases probably oppose the idea because such pay would make congressmen truly independent of the patronage of the rich. A senator who had served only six years could easily accumulate $1 million of his own and could thereafter safely afford to stick his tongue out at ubiquitous paymasters. True, such compensation would still not be enough for some, who would be up to the old tricks, perhaps even more flamboyantly. But threatened loss of the cushy job, as in the corporations, would be a big deterrent to skulduggery. Corporate officers, it can be shown, are personally far more straitlaced than most congressmen.

The Basic Deal

We are now in a position to understand the basic deal, arrived at by unconscious but instinctively sure stages, among *finpols*, *corp-pols* and *pubpols* in the welfare-warfare economy.

In return for substantial camouflaged tax (and other) concessions ranging up to complete exemption for very large incomes (these being constantly sought by the spokesmen for big wealth who appear before congressional committees) and for thoughtfully saddling most of the tax burden onto the politically illiterate lower labor force, the *pubpols* have been heavily financed on their road to financial independence by "campaign" contributions, testimonial gifts, law firm retainers and simple donations. Without such financing the poor-boys-who-made-good in politics would never have acquired the stake necessary to set themselves up as entrepreneurs under federal allocation of licenses (which they indirectly control), in building-and-loan operations, television-radio broadcasting, consumer loan sharking, local banking and insurance underwriting and subsidized speculation in oil and mineral lands. And without retainers from grateful corporate clients many lawyer-congressmen would be hard put to divert lucrative business from some of the less directly political law firms.

Just as the more impetuous racketeers when in difficult straits with the law turn to skillful high-fee pleaders like Edward Bennett Williams or Percy Foreman (in an earlier day they turned to the Max Steuers and Clarence Darrows), so the big corporations when they find themselves in a tight spot, legalistically speaking, turn to the big-league law firms of Wall Street, State Street and La Salle Street. While for routine matters the bush league of congressional law firms will do, when the action gets really serious it is necessary to bring the big guns of the big-name firms to bear. Before such luminaries, entranced judges sit properly spellbound at seeing it uncontrovertibly proved once again by law, logic and philosophy that wealth is virtue, poverty is crime. The lesser firms, however, are indispensable for routinely guiding legislation or softening the touch of regulatory commissions to a delicate *pianissimo* that would arouse the artistic envy of a Horowitz.

Naturally, with the big property owners given a large degree of accommodation up to complete exemption, with loopholes liberally carved in the imposing tax wall, it is necessary to saddle the rising costs of the welfare-warfare economy onto the shoulders of the rank-and-file in the labor force. Hence the lopsided tax structure, Wilbur Mills's "House of Horrors," that we have scrutinized in only slight detail.

The signal contribution of the democratic politician here (and this is well understood in such places as Wall Street) is that he is gifted with the ability to flimflam this large collection of taxpayers with stupefying rhetorical pyrotechnics and appeals to free-floating sentiment; he puts these gifts to work so that, even if not cheered, the public cannot grope its way out of the verbal barrage in which appear all the gems of stale oratory. In addition, to show he is friendly he kisses babies, smiles, shakes hands endlessly and gobbles strange foods thrust upon him by the local constituency.

His brain in something of a fog, grasping desperately at some notion of a lesser evil, the common man feels that the vote he is about to cast is the best thing, everything considered, that he can manage in the hairy circumstances. So, perhaps not too happy about the whole thing, he stoutly votes for Horace "Bugsy" Latrine, "The People's Friend," and against John "The Louse" Outhouse, who slipped and allowed himself to be photographed giving candy to a Negro baby, thus fomenting the sinister rumor that he keeps a harem of lascivious Negresses contrary to the laws of God and men.

Karl Marx, in an often quoted apothegm, thundered that "The State is the executive committee of the ruling class." Although this is merely redundantly truistic it is often disputed by bargain-counter sages. Yet the utterance has misled many self-styled Marxists to believe that the *finpols* or big capitalists issue direct whiplash orders to their docile minions in government, sometimes by picking up a phone in Wall Street and barking harsh instructions over the wire. Nothing could be further from the truth, even though direct wires from Wall Street to the White House have been known to exist during Republican Administrations up to the time at least of Herbert Clark Hoover.

The process through which the *finpols* induce the *pubpols* to march in lock-step with them is much subtler than this but not so Marxianly subtle as merely being common participants in a cultural climate; nor does it consist of winning them over by powerful logical arguments in favor of the free enterprise or capitalist system. The *finpols* insure that the *pubpols* will be likeminded by making it possible for the latter to become free—that is, government-licensed—entrepreneurs themselves. The fusion of thoughtways is achieved this simply. That the process is not more subtle anyone may observe by noticing how quickly a politician can change his outlook if the *quid pro quo* is not forthcoming. In such circumstances self-styled conservatives can be led to stand for quite radical measures, let the cultural climate be what it may.

It is noticeable that congressmen and spokesmen for the rich in general are much more impassioned in defense of the free enterprise system of government economic support than the prime beneficiaries. One seldom hears of a Rockefeller, Du Pont, Mellon, Ford or lesser luminary of great wealth bawling wildly to the countryside about the impeccable virtues of free and easy enterprise. This task is discreetly left to recent converts.

And while I believe there is much to be said for capitalism in some of the modified variegated forms it takes, particularly in Europe, and while I also believe there is little, humanistically speaking, to be said for the Leninist version of the vaguely outlined Marxist substitute, capitalism at its best can arouse in the sensitive observer at most a cool and moderate sort of admiration. It did not, contrary to the sly suggestion of its political friends, invent science and machine technology (industrialism), launch the Age of Discovery or put in their places the natural resources of the earth. Rather did it impress these into its service. Nor did it foster the population boom, which is greatest outside its confines. Even tried-and-true capitalist economists of any stature do not trace to capitalism all novel boons, whatever they may be, although anti-capitalists madly trace to it all evil.

It is left to recent off-the-street converts, beneficiaries of the big quick deal, the windfall, to discover overwhelming virtues in a system that, whatever its merits, is subject to evaluative analysis that brings to light not a few dubious aspects into which it is not edifying to delve.

Appreciations of capitalism by economists, it is always evident, are far more muted than those of its public political celebrants. For those who wonder at the emotional fervor of the politicos, the explanation is as simple as it is vulgar. Would not almost anyone except the rarely cultivated man be inclined to see, as in a Pauline revelation, vast merits in a system that suddenly, without any forewarning, showers down upon him personally, apparently from nowhere, vast rewards? Would not such a man—a Dirksen, perhaps—be dramatically and sincerely struck by the suddenly revealed beauties of the system? Would he not feel strongly impelled when the occasion presented itself to draw upon whatever eloquence he commanded to defend and extol that system? He was nothing, and he knows this; the system made him into something, perhaps a television pundit, perhaps a senator, even president. Here is ground for true belief.

There is a more immediate reason, too, for the *pubpols* to see extravagant merits in the system, which plays the role of the goose that repeatedly lays the golden eggs—for them. Many economists, some in dismay, have observed how Congress is inclined to starve the public sector of the economy (as government nonmilitary operations are somewhat ornately styled) and to favor the private or corporate sector. Congressmen in general show little enthusiasm for schools, parks, hospitals, sanatoria, low-income housing, libraries and the like but immoderate enthusiasm for, say, armaments entrepreneurs and bowling alley proprietors. While structures and programs in the public sector can be "milked" to a certain extent at their inception, as in the letting of contracts and buying land, the process cannot be repeated indefinitely as with going concerns in the private sector.

With a going concern, such as a bowling alley, it is different. It can, first, be taxed continuously—a great advantage; schools and the like pay no taxes but eat them up. Furthermore, the proprietor can be shaken down regularly for campaign contributions and off-the-cuff gifts in return for regulatory legerdemain. The proprietor is to a certain extent, at least as far as the courts will permit, at the mercy of the "democratic" politician and his little tin box.

And if the "democratic" politician has been thoughtful enough to intersect two new superhighways at the door of the bowling alley, with mandatory long-cycle traffic lights installed, he is obviously deserving of a testimonial donation for public service from the bowling alley proprietor. Hasn't the business generated boosted gross national product? A politician who can do this and at the same time gain public plaudits for his sagacity is obviously a statesman who should be concretely recognized.

Cooperation, it is evident, is necessary between *finpols* and *pubpols* if the system is to work as it does. Nor are showdowns between the two ever necessary because all that is usually required to bring most of the latter into line (if they stray) is money, the big grease of American politics. In saying this, one is not saying that *all pubpols* are susceptible to the monetary touch. It is not necessary to have *all* of them on the side of the big money. The entire operation, indeed, looks better if there are some honest dissenters, even vociferous dissenters. Such dissent appears to imply that positions have been taken, each way, on the merits of an argument. There are, perhaps, mysterious reasons on the side of the majority, which consists of sound down-to-earth men like Everett Dirksen and Lyndon Baines Johnson.

All that the big money needs is a "democratic" majority—of a subcommittee of 3 to a legislative committee, of a legislative committee of 15 to 25, of a caucus of 50 to 100, of a legislative body of 100 or 435. This is not much to achieve in a nation of some 200 million immortal souls. And even if there is not a majority on the side of the money interest, all is not lost because any suddenly flaring opposition can be blocked and stalemated by a minority under the rules. If the money interest cannot have its way, neither can anyone else unless there has been a rare political upheaval induced by nontypical circumstances.

So much has been written about the veritable misdeeds of the corporations, not without ample grounds, that there is a tendency among critics to overlook the indubitable fact that business enterprises sometimes, even often, like black sheep of a family, act quite legally, properly and even meritoriously and are nevertheless clipped below the belt by the *pubpols*. It would take hundreds of pages to detail all the harrowing cases in this vastly neglected area, so I cite a single recent major instance simply to remind the reader of what goes on.

L. Judson Morhouse, fifty-two, an authentic Anglo-Saxon and chairman of the Republican Party in New York State, was convicted and sentenced in June, 1966, to two to three years of penal servitude on two counts of bribery, a very serious offense. The judge could have imposed a sentence of twenty years and a fine of $9,000 but, as he explained, the defendant until his conviction had an "unblemished" reputation and "has many good friends in most high places who have willingly come forward to urge leniency." The judge also noted that Morhouse "was a man who wielded tremendous governmental power and influence" which, as the judge himself volunteered, he had "perverted" for "personal and private gain." According to the prosecutor, Morhouse was an "influence peddler"—not uncommon in politics.

The specific charge against Morhouse was that he induced former State Liquor Authority Chairman Epstein to accept an illegal $50,000 for granting the Playboy Club of Chicago a New York liquor license and that he, initiator of the deal, assisted the Playboy group in bribing Epstein. The Playboy Club was a legitimate taxpaying enterprise—not even a sweatshop —that sought to do legitimate taxpaying business in New York City. Yet it was required to pay toll to do legitimate business—a common occurrence as between small and moderate-sized businesses and politicians. This is one reason (rather than labor costs) many enterprises move from one part of the country to another, especially out of big cities, although after they get well settled in a new location they often have the "bite" again put on them by local politicos. Sometimes, though, the "bite" is smaller in one place than another so moving may be advantageous. One can refuse to pay and instead fight for one's rights in the courts, but experience has shown that this process can be so costly as to be ruinous.

Morhouse took his sentence stoically, although his lawyer said he had been punished enough by merely being put on trial (a strange doctrine). Against this contention, the prosecutor cited a long list of other instances in which Morhouse had received "fees" ranging up to $100,000 from enterprises engaged in legitimate endeavors, enough to give him success or what sociologists coyly refer to as "upward social mobility."

So it is not, very evidently, necessary for a company to be delinquent in some way in order to experience the exactions of politicians, although the big corporations are seldom hustled about in the way the Playboy Club was. Morhouse would never have acted as he did in this case if the Standard Oil Company of New Jersey had wished to put up a gas station or refinery in some unseemly place. When the big corporation wants anything out of the routine—and the Playboy Club did not even ask that—it simply states its case "on the merits" in high places and gets all or most of what it wants. As a matter of tactics it asks for a great deal more than it really wants in order to be roundly rejected in some way, thus making the regulatory commission, public executive or legislature look properly vigilant in the eyes of the public—a simple instance of *finpolitics*. The reason the big enterprises no longer resort to crude bribery, except perhaps through remote agents in minor situations where a local ordinance bars the road, is that they have the ways already thoroughly greased all along the line through "campaign" contributions, donations-for-public-merit, testimonials, law business, foundation grants to savants and other forms of patronage involving legal tender. The request, whatever it is, in substance slips through easily all the way up to and including Congress. But if some random individual made an analogous request, he would be hailed before the nearest psychiatrist or, perhaps, jailed for jarring the dust on some moth-eaten statute.

Morhouse, it should be made clear, did not suddenly suffer any loss of esteem among those "in the know." He had simply been caught working on a highly competitive street—New York City is Democratic and upstate New York Republican and hostile to the city; Morhouse in the city was somewhat out of the jurisdiction under his surveillance and up against rivalrous politicos. According to the well-understood rules of the game, he had to serve as a scapegoat, thereby helping to reassure the public. My own opinion of Morhouse did not change in the slightest when he was convicted because I always assumed, on the basis of a long line of similar cases, that as a state party chairman he was doing something of the sort—if not this then something else of a gamey order. What he did was hardly more than par for the course.

Just as the businessman is not in business for his health, the typical American politician is not in politics for his health, the pay of office or because he is enamored of the public. So to suppose would, in the light of much evidence, strain credulity beyond the breaking point.

Money in Politics

That a great deal of money is bandied about in politics is well known. On this topic many extensive studies have been written that need not be summarized here. All, fragmentary though they are, show a steady avalanche of money.[74]

What is now, today, causing concern about this telltale phase of American political life is the rising cost.

It was estimated, for example, by Dr. Herbert E. Alexander, an authority on election costs, director of the Citizens Research Foundation and Kennedy-appointed executive director of the President's Commission on Campaign Costs, that the 1964 national campaigns cost at least a whopping $200 million, not counting efforts by volunteers, unpaid efforts by public officials or amateurs and sideline commentary by telecasters, newspapers and other publications.[75] And campaign costs, as we have observed, are not the only items of political expenditure. The bill, it is evident, is running very high.

An incisive, brief updating of the situation was written by Victor Bernstein for *The Nation,* June 27, 1966, under the title of "Private Wealth and Public Office: The High Cost of Campaigning." As it was shown, political money is not put up by the rank and file of citizens. In all its forms it invariably comes from property owners and people of assured position—the upper 1 per cent of income receivers—apart from such money as has in recent decades filtered into the pot from labor leaders, themselves in the upper-income strata.

As Bernstein made clear, the electoral system, as distinct from the extra-legal politicians' system within government (another item of big expense), is extremely costly to operate. In the 1966 off-year, for example, $175 million were scheduled to be spent solely at the state levels. Again, a Senate seat, as Bernstein testifies, can cost a million or more, and $2 million were spent to make John Lindsay the able mayor of New York. This last leaves out of account what was spent to defeat him.

Noting that in order to be in politics one must be rich or have rich friends, some of the currently rich ones cited being the Kennedys, Harriman, the Rockefellers, Romney, Pell, Ottinger and Johnson (there are others), Bernstein raised the rather marginal question of whether democracy (by which he meant the rundown U.S. political system) is "better served by relatively penurious politicians who owe office to support by the rich" or by the rich in person. He did not note the fact, significant in my view, that Johnson like many others not mentioned grew rich while in, of, by and for politics.

Congressional Origins

Most congressmen, all now in the upper 1 per cent of income receivers, were at least originally impecunious. This is made crystal clear in Donald R. Matthews's thorough study, *U.S. Senators and Their World*. According to Matthews, all except a handful of senators were the sons of men in middle-class occupations.[76]

On the basis of the mainly blurry class indices he cites—professional, proprietor and official, farmers, low-salaried workers and industrial wage earners—I should rather say most came from lower-middle-class and middle-class occupational backgrounds. This is made evident, first by the fact that among 180 senators in the decade 1947–57 no fewer than 52 per cent were rural born[77] and at the time of their birth none of the criteria of upper-middle-class status such as relatively high income and prolonged schooling were ordinarily found in rural areas. "Places like Centerville, South Dakota; Isabel, Illinois; Ten Mile, Pennsylvania; Rising Sun, Delaware; and Honea Path, South Carolina, nurtured more senators [in the group studied] than all the cities of the United States combined."[78] Most of the remaining senators came from small towns, with the most overrepresented small-towners from places of 2,500 to 5,000 population.[79] The Senate, in brief, consisted largely of pure hicks, ruling an urbanized, mechanized society.

As to class origins, "The children of low-salaried workers, wage earners, servants, and farm laborers, which together comprised 66 per cent of the gainfully employed in 1900, contributed only 7 per cent of postwar senators. [Owing to the disparity of birth rates between the upper and lower classes, the disparity in political life-chances, as Matthews notes, was "actually greater than these figures indicate."—F.L.] Only two of the 180 men, Senators Wagner and O'Daniel, were the sons of unskilled, urban wage earners. Wagner's father was a janitor in a New York City tenement; O'Daniel's father was a construction worker. Senator Purtell was the son of a cigar-maker; McNamara, of a shipfitter; Daniel (S.C.), of a millwright; Welker, of a carpenter; Pastore, of a tailor; Cordon and Dirksen, of painters; Payne and Dworshak, of printers; Anderson, of a salesman; Myers, of a bookkeeper; Lennon, of a clerk; Margaret Chase Smith was the daughter of a barber."[80] There were no Negroes, although Negroes constituted 10 per cent of the population.

"Among the sons of farmers, some were born in relative poverty, yet it is virtually impossible to ascertain this in specific cases. It is still possible to conclude that very few senators were born in working-class and lower-class families."[81]

Yet 33 per cent of Democrats and 31 per cent of Republicans had fathers who were farmers.[82] Farmers have never been considered upper middle class. And 16 per cent of Democrats and 7 per cent of Republicans had fathers who were lawyers, not invariably an upper-middle-class index in the United States.

That most of these men are generically middle class, and as such likely to be upward strivers and admirers of entrepreneurial as distinct from rentier plutocracy, is also shown by the fact that just prior to their debut in the Senate 102 were job-holding political officials, 88 having started out as lawyers and 97 regarding the law as their principal nonpolitical occupation.[83] By percentages, 26 per cent of these pre-senatorial officeholders were in law-enforcement offices (prosecutors), 23 per cent in administrative offices, 17 per cent in state legislatures, 11 per cent in the House of Representatives, 9 per cent in the governor's chair, 9 per cent in local elective offices, 3 per cent in some statewide elective office and 2 per cent on the congressional staff.[84]

For those hoping for a better day in politics with new upcoming men, it should be noticed that the pipelines feeding high office are now filled with similar types. Anyone looking to the state legislatures for zeal in better government can get a glimpse of the future in Congress that will induce sober second thoughts.

While class origin may be broadly indicative of outlook it is not determining in every case, as is easily shown. Despite their humble origins Everett M. Dirksen and Margaret Chase Smith have all along been pillars of the Establishment which Joseph C. Clark and a number of other propertied patricians sharply oppose. Johnson, once literally dirt-poor, was a leader of the Establishment. Looking further afield one sees that some of the leading oppressors of all time were of lower-class origin: Hitler was a house painter, Stalin was a lower class theological student and Mussolini was a one-time school teacher. On the other hand, Thomas Jefferson, perhaps the modern world's most forceful exponent of democracy, and Frederick Engels, collaborator and financial angel of Karl Marx, were both wealthy. Nearly all the original Bolshevik leaders were middle-class and upper-class intellectuals; there was not a true proletarian among them nor, be it noted, did they produce a pro-proletarian government. Most of the Fabian Socialists and, indeed, socialists in general, have been middle class, upper middle class or aristocrats like Lord Bertrand Russell and many others duly certified as such in *Burke's Peerage*. Socialism is too remote in its aims for most workers to understand. Most lower-class people in politics, perhaps influenced by the cultural climate, act so as to deny their origins.

Although class origins, especially from the middle upward, do often have an influence on political outlooks, what should be rationally determining

in judging politicians is the set of propositions they are willing to implement in action. If they frame their working propositions rationally, in the
light of the evidence and according to critically refined values they are, as
I see it, jewels beyond price whether born and raised in a sty or a palace
and whether styled conservative, moderate, liberal or radical.

Digressing a bit, let it be noted that Matthews brings out that 84 per
cent of senators went to college, and of those attending college 31 per cent
went to the most highly rated institutions. No less than 45 per cent specialized in law. Of those specializing in law, 47 per cent went to law
schools of the highest type. As lawyers, then, many of these men were
theoretically capable of understanding what a new statute meant. They
could, if they wished, spot the loophole in a tax measure on first reading
as though it were the Empire State Building. The point is: The tax laws
are no accident or consequence of carelessness. They are as premeditated
by the Establishment as a bullet from a Colt .45, intended to kill. Most
senators, in other words, usually know precisely what they are doing.
What is in question is not their intelligence but their values-in-action.

Professor Matthews is carried away by misplaced enthusiasm, however,
when he notes that "Senators are among the most educated—in the formal
sense of the word—of all occupational groups in the United States," with
85 per cent of them having been to college against only 14 per cent in the
entire population.[85] It is true that he qualifies with the phrase "in the
formal sense of the word," which merely indicates they attended school.

But, thorough, Professor Matthews makes clear that of those who attended but did not necessarily finish college 69 per cent attended other
than Ivy League (20 per cent non-Ivy League eastern schools or the mid-
western "Big Ten" universities). While some of this 69 per cent may have
attended, finishing or not, rigorous schools, most of them, as *Who's Who*
shows, attended distinctly makeshift swampwater colleges.*

That many of the senators are in no sense educated men, whatever their
on-the-record schooling, I shall show by citing two salient cases.

---

* Matthews, in his discussion of senators and lobbyists, pp. 176–96, illustrates very
well the tendency of academic political scientists to avert their eyes from obvious unpleasant facts. He introduces his genteel discussion of this phase with a lobbyist's story
about two women watching a senator and a lobbyist conversing innocently in a Senate
waiting room. "O-o-h!" says one of the women, awed, "Is he bribing him now?" Although a very fine study, the Matthews book on this and similar phases we have examined reminds one very much of an old-time silent film drama in which the hero
chastely kisses the heroine, who thereupon proceeds to have a baby. That anything else
happened between kiss and the appearance of the little stranger was not suggested.
Similarly, legislation to this school of political science seems to be the consequence of
immaculate ratiocination. "Slush" is a word it does not recognize.

Senatorial Irrationality

Senator James Eastland, chairman of the powerful Judiciary Committee, whom *Who's Who* reports as having attended without finishing the University of Alabama and Vanderbilt University, in 1962 published an elaborate report prepared by his staff purporting that various of the justices of the Supreme Court had in scores of cases made "pro-Communist" decisions and that the court as a whole had made such decisions no less than forty-six times.[86]

In every instance the Eastland mode of logic adhered to the following form:

"Communist officials are politicians.

"Republican and Democratic officials are politicians.

"Therefore, Republican and Democratic officials are pro-Communist."

No educated man could seriously make such a carefully premeditated argument on a serious question.

Former Senate Majority Leader Lyndon B. Johnson since entering the White House has shown the same sort of elementary confusion, especially on the Vietnam question, thereby disturbing the professoriate from coast to coast. The Johnsonian whirligig arguments in favor of its Vietnam action have been notoriously confused, contrary and contradictory, thus destroying the entire ostensibly reasonable structure.

The initial Johnsonian logical error about Vietnam did not concern form but content.

The argument was as follows:

"If people are bombed they will negotiate.

"These people are bombed.

"Therefore, these people will negotiate."

Although valid in form this argument was completely unsound because its first premise was known to be factually false. Official studies of the behavior of people and governments in England, Germany, Russia and elsewhere in World War II, all known to the American military, showed in fact that if people are bombed their tendency to resist increases. Malta was bombed almost to extinction by the Germans yet never sued for peace.

The sound argument, dismissed out of hand by Johnson, who was probably not bright enough to grasp it, was as follows: "If people are bombed it is known they will resist more desperately (and not negotiate)."

This, in fact, happened, showing the value of logic—if one knows it and applies it.

Mr. Johnson's educational attainments, on the formal record, go beyond those of Mr. Eastland. Mr. Johnson holds a Bachelor of Science degree—from the Southwest Texas State Teachers College.

Not only does the Senate (and House) consist mainly of hicks but of poorly educated hicks even though they must be conceded to possess a certain low animal cunning. The main sin of the majority consists of simple presumption in presenting themselves as leaders of men.

Blue-Sky Limits

As to money in politics, Bernstein quotes Robert Price, one-time hard-headed deputy mayor of New York, very precisely to the point that beyond a certain small amount from the national and county committees a congressional candidate must rely on his own efforts. "If he commands a popular following, he can raise a substantial sum from the small contributions of many people through a broadcast or mail appeal," said Price. "But usually for the bulk of what he needs he must rely on friends, or friends of friends, or labor or business. *The biggest givers are likely to be firms with government contracts, or with hopes of getting one; they are what I call the predators—the guys who, if you win, will want something for their money.*" [Emphasis added.]

Noting that most campaigners are not so fussy as Mayor Lindsay of New York in turning down certain large offerings, Bernstein agrees with many observers that "the higher and more influential the office sought, the more likely is the contributors' list to be studded with the names of the wealthy." These give directly to many party committees, buy a full-page ad in a party pamphlet for $15,000 at a clip (until recently tax-deductible), join the President's Club for $1,000 or more and clamor to pay high rates for places at testimonial dinners.

Again quoting Mr. Price after reviewing the influence of money in politics, Bernstein continues:

"'It is in seeking the nomination,' says Robert Price, 'that wealth or access to it, counts most for the candidate. Once he wins the nomination, he already has the attraction of a winner, and he has the party apparatus at his disposal; until then, he is more or less on his own.'" John F. Kennedy's triumph over Hubert Humphrey in the West Virginia primaries is given as a case in point.

There are jungles of laws governing the use of money in the electoral process but, as Bernstein shows, they are full of holes, obviously premeditated.

A political committee is allowed to receive or spend only $3 million in any year, but the law applies only to committees operating in two or more states—not to state or local committees and not to *series* of interstate committees. A candidate could legally have a hundred committees collecting $3 million each, or $300 million in all. He could have a local committee that collected the whole $300 million.

Every political committee under federal jurisdiction must report to the House of Representatives all contributors of $100 or more and all recipients of $10 or more, but the reports are kept in Washington (for a period of only two years) and are not subject to check or audit.

Each Senate candidate may spend personally up to $25,000, each House candidate up to $5,000 but there is no limit on *contributions receivable* or on what others spend for him. Each can legally have an infinity of committees receiving unlimited amounts.

No national bank, corporation or labor union may contribute as much as a dime to the election, primary, pre-nomination convention or caucus campaign of any federal candidate *but* officers of such entities may legally contribute without limit and may form any number of "educational" and "non-partisan" organizations.

No government contractor may contribute to a federal candidate during the negotiations for or the life of his contracts *but* an officer of a contracting firm may legally contribute without hindrance or limit.

No individual whatsoever, in the entire universe, may contribute more than $5,000 to any one candidate or any one committee during any calendar year whatsoever *but*—any individual may make an infinite series of $5,000 gifts to as many candidates or as many *committees* for a single candidate as he likes.

What all this means, behind the legalistic verbiage, is that the sky is the limit and that any individual, corporation, bank, labor union or other entity whatever can contribute by various channels as much as it wants to any single man or collection of men seeking office. The laws governing the use of money in elections, like the laws governing the use of money in rewarding public officials, are pure balderdash as far as interfering with the practice. The sole purpose of the laws as drawn is, as in the case of the tax laws, to appease uninstructed public opinion and at the same time permit popularly irksome practices to continue without let-up.

And what all this shows most saliently is that influence over or ready access to the makers of public policy has very high cash value.

For readers who may feel that the sources I cite on this point are not sufficiently conservative and are therefore tainted, we may turn once again to the trusty *Wall Street Journal*, under date of September 20, 1960. There, on the subject of campaign money, it is duly set forth:

"Where does all the money come from? Despite growing stress on little gifts, fund-raisers still depend on wealthy contributors who give $500 or more. That's why Republican Chairman [Thruston] Morton made a special plea last week to the members of New York Union League Club, calling the party's financial problem 'most difficult.' And that's why some Democrats are worried over possible defections of Texas oil men. As a measure of concern, a Democratic team made up of Sen. Smathers of Florida and Rep. Ikard of Texas last month gathered 100 Houston oil men together to reassure them: Don't worry about the platform; the Democrats won't hurt you." Smathers and Ikard spoke truly.

One can always say this to people of wealth about both parties: Don't worry about the platform; you won't get hurt because the little old Establishment and, most likely, the president himself have everything under nice control. The platform is pure blarney.

What would happen if Congress, for instance, passed a thoroughly equitable tax law? For one thing, the members of Congress who voted for such a law would quickly find their extracurricular emoluments ended. The rich, it is well to note, make their political contributions out of part of their tax savings, thus serving to keep public policies as they want them and at public cost. Neat. . . .

A Note on Methodology

On the score of method many political scientists would no doubt be inclined to fault me for highlighting what they call the seamy side of politics. What they are almost uniformly inclined to do in their writings is to put it all "in perspective" by sandwiching in passing reference to these dealings among a vast mass of routine formal details. The story, as journalists say, gets lost. It is buried in the salad.

If sports writers used their method in reporting a prizefight, they would chronologically and even-handedly record every punch and movement from the beginning and terminate with the drab curt statement that the champion finally scored a knockout with an illegal punch on the back of the neck. The headline would read: FIGHT AT THE GARDEN. This would be "objectivity," but of a crazy sort.

Instead, able (and permitted) to sift the significant from the trivial, the seasoned sports writer is more apt to begin his account:

"Scoring a knock-out in the second minute of the ninth round with the illegal rabbit-punch, Plug-Ugly Muldoon last night retained the world's heavyweight championship as excited fans jeered and threw pop bottles. Apparently the referee did not see the illegal punch and therefore did not disqualify the champion although the blow was clearly visible from ringside.

"From the beginning it was a dirty fight with the loser, Ratsy Schlemiel, freely butting in the clinches and Muldoon levering in low blows of explosive force. Still, the referee, for whom many have suggested an eye examination or a long vacation, did not see although he twice warned each gladiator. . . ."

The headline on this masterpiece would read something like:

MULDOON RETAINS CROWN

IN DIRTY BRAWL AT GARDEN

SCHLEMIEL K.O.'D WITH FOUL BLOW

REFEREE BOOED

Newspaper reporting of Congress, however, ordinarily tends to follow the drab cue given by the political scientists.

If congressional reporting in general were as forthright as sports reporting, a headline on a congressional session might read somewhat as follows:

CONGRESS IN NEW TAX SWINDLE

CLIPS LABOR FORCE

AS STOCK PRICES SOAR

BONE THROWN TO BLIND VETS

DIRKSEN FORESEES

PROSPERITY FOR ALL

The text would be similarly to the point.

In Defense of the Politician

For any reader who is now ready to bring in a hanging verdict against the genus politician *Americanus,* let me interpose a restraining caveat.

Under the American theory of government the people are sovereign and have the right to boot out any officeholder in duly prescribed elections. "Throw the rascals out," has been the battle cry in many rousing elections, often coming from the throats of other rascals trying to squeeze in.

The assumption behind this apparent permissiveness is that the people (by definition good) know, or can sense mysteriously, who is deserving between two politicians. But as seasoned politicians know, meritorious service is not sufficient to retain the favor of the electorate.

This could be shown by the citation of scores of cases but I will here cite a single recent lamentable case. Senator Kenneth B. Keating, Republican incumbent, was defeated in New York in 1964 by Robert F. Kennedy, Democrat. The electorate had no particular distaste for Keating, who had functioned as a liberal, voted for all measures preponderantly favored by

New Yorkers and was roundly praised before and after his defeat by a wide spectrum of editorialists. As Senator Kennedy himself later analyzed his victory, Keating made a tactical mistake by not merely standing in dignity on his record. Instead, Keating in the course of the campaign launched a panicky attack on Kennedy as a carpetbagger from Massachusetts, thus opening the door to attention-getting verbal counter-blows by Kennedy which he could not otherwise have delivered with any good grace.

The downfall of the civilized but non-lustrous Keating showed once again that electoral tactics and the appearance of an attractive new face may count in an election more heavily than unquestioned merit in office.

Having seen this sort of thing happen many times, knowing the ditheriness of the electorate, the impecunious man in politics usually guards against it by clandestine counter-organizational measures and by seeing to it while in office that he gathers something of value to tide himself over in the event he is brusquely turned out. The politician, in the form of his personal profit enterprises, his organization and the various Establishments going up the line in a hierarchy, belongs to something very analogous to an underground trade union. Committed for life to the holding of public office, he does not intend to see himself unemployed or, if suddenly turned out, without ready means of self-support. He is, in brief, intelligent within his zany environment.

If arrangements similar to those affecting the politician applied to all employees they would be forced, every two, four or six years, to debate with rivals for their jobs before company stockholders, customers and assorted cranks. If these thought a new candidate looked fresher, younger, more clean-cut, sexier or was better spoken or more churchly they would vote him in. It is precisely to defend themselves against critical judgments of that kind that workers, whenever they succeed in organizing, vociferously stress job seniority and job security. The quixotic democratic idea that an officeholder, a man of no hereditary substance, dependent only upon his salary, should be subject to offhand dismissal every few years at the hands of the *hoi polloi*, thereupon to join the throng of job seekers in the open labor market, is one that has little appeal for the ordinary, up-from-no-where, jerk-water politician. He therefore guards against such a dire eventuality in every way he can think of, some highly aromatic and far out in left field.

What happens in the case of many successful politicians is that they are so intelligently careful about their many defensive measures, and so lucky, that they reap far more than job security and carryover money for life's arduous road. They become authentically rich, in a position to thumb their noses at the foolish public, which they freely if covertly do.

It should not be thought that I am offering an apology for the politician in thus presenting him, accurately, as a job-protecting specialized worker on his way up in the world. I am simply offering the perspective from his personal point of view. It is because of the position he occupies under oath, transcending in importance that of the physician-surgeon, that one holds him, after everything has been said on all sides, to the strictest accounting. When a physician-surgeon is able to enhance his own security by deviating from the highest canons of medical practice, as by performing unnecessary, high-fee operations, society and his peers do not forgive him merely because his financial problem is understood. In the same way we can safely condemn the typical off-the-soil politician: He is betraying his true responsibilities in order to achieve personal accommodation *vis-à-vis* the mob.

The Upside-Down Republic

In his great *Republic,* praised by some, derided by others, Plato laid out a reasoned scheme of government in analogy with what his primitive psychology comprehended of the individual. A man, as Plato saw it, consists chiefly of a head or rational function, the chest or spirited function (heart and lungs) and the stomach or appetitional function. People, as he saw them, were classifiable as these functions dominated their temperaments.

Because the head was presumptively the better (because rational) part of a man, Plato deduced that the head should rule the state. Hence a philosopher or man of learning should be king, assisted by similar men of learning. Should a ruler be a man of knowledge or an ignorant man? Obviously, he should be a man of knowledge. The safety of the state and its people required it. Who would deny it?

Subject to these rational, informed rulers—men of learning and intellectuals—would be men of the spirit, whom Plato called guardians and auxiliaries. Guardians corresponded to our civil service employees and auxiliaries to soldiers. As Plato saw them, both regarded personal honor or prestige (status) as the highest value just as the philosophers primarily valued knowledge and insight.

These strata in the Platonic Republic would lead very ascetic lives, would own no property, would never marry and would conduct sexual relations only on rare occasions when perfect children were desired. Women as well as men were equally to be guardians and auxiliaries. Children of these strata would be brought up by special teachers, would never be left under the corrupting influence of their doting parents.

Below these strata would be the common people, perpetual victims of their insatiable appetites, who would lead their confused catch-as-catch-can lives under rules laid down from above, although they might rise into the ascetic strata if they wished. The people of the appetites might own property, marry, have and mal-educate their own children and copulate blissfully with all the abandon of Hindus on a holiday.

It is from Plato that we derive our high ideals of the lawgiver, rarely approached in reality, as anyone can see.

But although Plato's scheme, intended only as a didactic device, is now widely ridiculed by trivial minds, it is worth noticing that what we have in the United States is its exact opposite—hardly an improvement.

The rulers, in our present scheme, are people of the largest appetites, to whom most public deference is paid. While appetites exist among all, their greatest strength is obviously among the most voracious acquisitors, the rich and their sycophants in office.

Rated considerably below these in public esteem are our guardians and auxiliaries: civil servants and soldiers.

And, popularly rated lowest of all, are our philosophers or men of learning. One must admit that the public is a bit ambivalent and confused on this score owing to some colossal breakthroughs scored in recent years by the learned and by no one else; but as between a plutocrat and a politician on the one hand and a professor or vagrant intellectual on the other any popular survey will show that the professor, proverbially absent-minded and inept, is low man in the totem-poll. He is in most schools kept on a tight leash held by trustees. He is rarely a free agent.

We are confronted, it is evident, with an exact inversion of the Platonic scheme. Yet some persons unreasonably expect the common people of the larger appetites installed at the top to conduct themselves like Platonic philosophers, guardians and auxiliaries, which is much like expecting a gorilla to conduct himself like a Lord Chesterfield.

Subversive Jeffersonianism

In voting, politicians have noticed, the American electorate is hardly attracted by any except the most general Jeffersonian propositions. If the inclination of the electorate were toward true Jeffersonianism, actually an inverted aristocratic doctrine, politicians would conduct themselves differently and speak differently. Any even slightly successful politician is fully aware that any office-seeker who liberally salted his speeches with specific Jeffersonian views, or composed his speeches of actual Jeffersonian quotations, would be lucky to escape with his life from the nearest functionally illiterate mob. Radicals and civil-righters of various stripes have tried it again and again and have been deluged with rotten eggs, overripe fruit, stones and local police attentions. The broad public is simply not democratic, would find Jefferson repugnant if they could read him. If any stray reader doubts this let him dip into Jefferson's writings here and there or select common topics from their indexes.

For Jefferson, extolled in the abstract at annual Jefferson Day fund-raising dinners of the Democratic Party, was very close to being a political bedfellow of at least one prominent side of the later-coming Karl Marx and practically the antithesis of Lyndon B. Johnson and almost every American president since Lincoln.

Even more than in the Declaration of Independence Jefferson elsewhere explicitly preached an inherent popular right to make revolution, by force and violence, without awaiting a green light from the Supreme Court. The Confederacy acted precisely according to this doctrine although it did not in its support of slavery (its true love) subscribe to the notion of equality. Nor is civil equality the ideal of the broad populace today, as one can see from popular reactions to the ordinary claims of Negroes, Puerto Ricans, Mexicans and a variety of other ethnic or national minority groups.

As anyone can readily detect, such sentiments are subversive and are hardly subscribed to by any discernible portion of the electorate, which instantly identifies them as akin to Bolshevism and unconducive to job security and quiet viewing of night baseball on TV.

Two unequal strains have been woven through American politics from the beginning. There has been patrician Jeffersonianism, largely given lip service except by patricians themselves here and there. And there has been Hamiltonianism. Alexander Hamilton (1757–1804), our first Secretary of the Treasury, was an ambitious poor boy in politics, a self-appointed spokesman for plutocracy and outright corruption in politics as a way of insuring its hold. Hamilton detested the common people with more fervor than is usual among those who have emerged from among them and did more than anyone else at the inception to give American economic affairs and much of political affairs their gamey flavor.

Slain in a duel with Aaron Burr, Hamilton fittingly lies buried in Trinity Churchyard at the head of Wall Street.

As far as ascendant trends are concerned, in the United States one openly talks John Locke and Thomas Jefferson but surreptitiously acts Alexander Hamilton.

A Plan for Improvement

It is not the duty of the critic to suggest ways of improving a bad show.

After he has pronounced upon it his job is finished. A wide public, however, thinks otherwise and believes it stymies a critic when it says: "How would you improve the script?" The presumption is that this would be difficult or impossible to do.

Many cut-rate sages on the political fringes adopt this attitude and say: "Democracy [meaning the present system] may be imperfect but it is the best system possible."

Denying this completely, I shall here, for the benefit of skeptical cogitators, sketch in a few strokes significant improvements that could easily be wrought in the American system, although such improvements would by no means produce everlasting salvation.

It cannot be denied that the best government would be that which was run by the most qualified men. As we see in the case of the medical profession, the greatest proportion of qualified men is produced by rigorous attention to their education and training. Standards are imposed which prospective doctors must meet—in the medical schools, in post-school training and in state licensing examinations. Nevertheless, some bad hats slip through even in the strictest jurisdictions, and some degenerate into bad hats, which cannot readily be guarded against.

If a set of proper educational standards for officeholders were adopted, those who met them could be assigned to a public panel from which all candidates of any party would have to be chosen. In reply to nitwit sages who will say that this bars poor boys, the instruments of major corruption in politics, my reply is: Poor boys unable to afford schooling might qualify merely by passing the examinations given to the schooled.[87]

Just as one would not think of licensing a man as a surgeon on his plea that he was too poor to afford medical school, so one would not in a well-ordered polity think of licensing a poorly schooled office-seeker.

Under the scheme I here propose bad hats would slip through but their number would be so significantly reduced that they would have a hard time finding enough fellow-travelers to caucus.

Again, no matter how strict the qualifications were, they would by no means intercept all inept politicians. While I can readily devise qualifications that would block out a Harding, a Coolidge, an Eisenhower, a Johnson and a horde in Congress, I do not, unfortunately, see any way of devising qualifications that would block out a Wilson or Hoover without at the same time blocking out some very good men.

In the matter of qualifications, law-school training would, as I view the prospect, count for very little but first-class degrees from first-class schools (the emphasis being on first-class) in social studies, humanities and general thought processes would be essential.

In the matter of improvement, attention should also be paid to those who select officeholders, those who vote. Improvement beyond the present level could here be attained by a simple scheme of weighted voting. Every citizen would have one vote, as at present. Those who finished grade school would have two votes, high school four votes and college sixteen votes. As the educated population is not evenly spread through all voting districts I would take the national average and re-weight the voting strengths in each election district so as to conform to the national average, distributing the voting power pro rata. Those who did not have the formal schooling might be admitted to higher voting brackets by passing the same examinations passed by the schooled.

An ancillary good effect of this scheme would be to enhance the status of learning in the populace by equating it with political power. Any two-vote citizen could readily convert himself into a four-vote citizen simply by meeting high school requirements through self-study or part-time attendance at any of the many schools. The four-vote citizen could similarly convert himself into a sixteen-voter.

The more sophisticated the voter the more able would he be to decide on candidates on the already thoroughly screened panel.

I would extend the scheme to jurors, who would be full-time professionals, publicly salaried, of specially educated men sitting on public panels. Six-man juries, judges of the facts in every case, could probably do the job. Barred would be the present catch-as-catch-can juries of the witless who return too many dubious verdicts. The trained jurors, all skilled in evaluating evidence under the law, would provide a reservoir of future aspirants to elective office.

Such a scheme would not eliminate interest biases and class biases from voting, but it would soften them and would tend to eliminate much of the present chicanery and gullibility from politics.

Let not any reader suppose that I believe these extremely excellent ideas, for which I obviously deserve a high decoration and an ample public pension, will be seized upon and put into effect by the powers-that-be, who have other fish to fry. I simply set these notions down to make it evident that the present system does not contain the ultimate in entirely workable and sensible political ideas. And, who knows, in some happier day they may bear fruit for the Republic.

Only those who would deny that the ascertainably most qualified persons should run the government and should have greater weight in selecting government personnel can rationally oppose this plan, which can be put into force without any great disturbance to fundamental institutions.

Thirteen ❧

THE CLEVERNESS
OF THE RICH

There is a lush literature, much of it monographic, on the creation of the modern world's large fortunes—most of them originated in and still concentrated in the United States, the self-advertised paradise of the common man. Almost always writers flatly claim or imply that the schemes of fortune-builders, legal or illegal, were extraordinarily clever, infinitely complicated and without supplemental support.

Actually, scrutiny of the way any very large fortune was put together shows that the method was simple, often but not invariably at least partly illegal, usually secret and sooner or later supplemented with the direct or indirect aid of sovereignty or its agents. One can show the creation of singularly few very large fortunes that was not aided by the stealthy support or benign tolerance of government agents. A preponderance of politicians, like flies around garbage, is always on the side where the money is.

Whatever cleverness was shown invariably lay in the transparent simplicity of the scheme. In the case of no known large fortune was there a complex scheme. Apart from three exceptions by type every large fortune is the consequence of a simple formative pattern, pursued in most cases in secrecy, in all cases with pertinacity and with the direct or indirect aid of sovereign power or its agents.

The three typical exceptions to the rule of secrecy are: Where the scheme involved a patent, land title or franchise that effectively kept other grabbers off the known valuable terrain. There is also the special case of a lawful operation that got such a head start out of gusher earnings others found it difficult or impossible to raise the capital to overtake it.

As to patents, themselves often covering complex processes, in virtually all instances the operative patent holders were not the inventors. The Mellons, for example, did not invent the aluminum extraction process although they took the lion's share for financing its beginnings with bank money, "other people's money"—a true case of "nothing down."

It is noticeable that whenever anyone puts into play a good commerical idea others (such is the widely distributed appetite for easy lucre) instantly copy it. Competitive copying is especially noticeable in the spheres of fashion and novelties although it extends to designs and innovations in almost everything. The person who first develops the idea does not derive full profit from its exploitation owing to the rapid appearance of panting interlopers. He is thus prevented from making a full killing but *in theory* a wide and infinitely deserving public is catered to at constantly lower prices by many avaricious sellers.

On the other hand, the man especially protected by the umbrella of sovereignty or its agents and who has a franchise, *effective* possession of a basic patent, or is working a good thing in secrecy with respect to potential competitors and the public, need not fear being forced to share with others. In the presence of fully established competition no one can build a fortune; competition divides the market, diminishes the share of each operator, impedes or prevents fortune-building.

But can this be true? the careful reader will ask. Is it not a fact that fortunes are being openly made or monumentally added to all around us today by giant competitive corporations, without benefit of special franchises as in public utilities, of effectively held patents or of operating secrecy?

The prime money-making factor for nearly all existing large corporations and many smaller ones—not merely legal monopolies like AT&T—is that they are parts of discreet monopolies. They only pretend to be competing. If they had to compete, they would be little better off than a fashion designer whose work is infringed overnight.

There is no need venturing to show here that the large corporations are monopolistic units within each industry. The job has been done many times. The reader is referred to a long line of analytic literature, much of it monographic and scholarly and dealing with specific monopoly situations, many formally adjudicated as monopolies under the laws and others not so adjudicated either because the purposely imperfect law does not prohibit their monopoly practices or has not been brought to bear owing to lack of zeal in law-enforcement officials.[1]

Earlier the illegal monopoly conspiracies in the electrical and steel industries were touched upon, each formally and solemnly adjudicated as such under the Great Seal of the United States in federal court. Until the time of exposure (an unfortunate occurrence to all corporate right-thinkers) such frequent conspiracies are secret—meeting one of the prime requirements of fortune-building here laid down. Analogous conspiracies seem to exist at all times in all American industries, although the facts are hard to produce. In Europe such cartel practices are legal, a triumph for candor if not for distributive justice.

The Rockefeller Story

As complicated a money-making scheme as any that led to a large fortune (and it was essentially a simple scheme) was that devised by John D. Rockefeller, the proverbial poor boy who became very rich almost overnight. As the high-pressure methods he diligently employed have been copiously recorded, there is no need to review them in detail. The methods were secret and conspiratorial at every step of the way—so much so that it took nearly forty years to bring even the earliest steps to light. Standard Oil was in its long formative period one of the world's biggest clandestine operations. And always there was assistance from the agents of sovereignty; for Standard Oil infiltrated its well-rewarded henchmen into strategic nooks and crannies of the political system as well as into the ranks of its competitors. It developed one of the earliest systems of industrial espionage, hardly gentlemanly.

Rockefeller's advantage, which he used to beat down thousands of producers and to force hundreds of rival refiners into his hands, was the consistently lower freight rates he obtained from railroads and pipelines as a large buyer of crude oil and shipper of refined oil. The railroad rebates and drawbacks, secretly granted by common carriers which under law were required to give everyone the same rates, were only one aspect of illegality that saturated Standard Oil up to the final paper dissolution by Supreme Court decision in 1911. But Rockefeller kept his holdings; and the constituent parts of the one-time trust remained intact, loosely united by stockholdings in foundations, trust funds and the hands of family members and partners. By his ability to control transportation rates unfairly with the connivance of railroads fighting each other for huge shipments, Rockefeller could force down the price of crude oil to him at the well-head and could undersell refineries outside his combination until they sold out to him at sacrifical prices or went under. By this process he became what Establishment writers joyously salute as an industrial statesman.

Rockefeller, after a sketchy education and a brief apprenticeship as a bookkeeper, started in business for himself in 1859 at the age of twenty. By the early 1880's, slightly more than ten years after the Standard Oil

Company of Ohio was founded to succeed the firm of Rockefeller, Andrews and Flagler, the company's portion of the national oil business, crude and refined, was rated at 85 per cent and the fledgling company was already extending its spiderweb into California and Texas. As early as 1883 the company took the output of 20,000 wells, held 4,000 miles of pipeline, used 5,000 tank cars and employed 100,000 people.[2] It was already an obvious monopoly, alluded to as such on the floor of Congress.

Apart from some new capital early brought into the coercive combination by investors such as whisky-distiller H. V. Harkness, most of the money for the expansion came from especially favorable secret transportation rates. These were always Rockefeller's hidden ace, his major source of growing capital.[3]

With variations of detail one will find a similar pattern of secrecy in the building of virtually every large fortune.

Why the Fortune-Builders Succeeded

The builders of the large fortunes succeeded, then, because the crucial part of their operations was kept secret. When attempts were made to uncover the inelegant facts, they were blocked by Horatio Alger officials under the purchased control or influence of the fortune-builders.

This last was true, for example, of the Standard Oil Company as of others. From a very early stage its partisans bloomed miraculously in the Ohio legislature and executive branch and in the Congress and the national executive branch. These "representatives of the people" at every turn nipped one attempt after the other at investigation, despite widespread indignation in Congress and among the then free-entrepreneurial newspapers.[4]

The question widely asked was: If there is nothing wrong, why will not the friends of Standard Oil permit an investigation?

When effective investigation finally took place, despite herculean opposition and proclaimed attempts to bribe officials such as the attorney generals of Ohio, there was indeed found much reason for concealment. In his annual report to the governor of Ohio in 1899, Attorney General F. S. Monnett detailed charges of six attempts to bribe his predecessor, David K. Watson, to withdraw a suit filed in 1890 against the Standard Oil Company of Ohio for participating illegally in the Standard Oil Trust.[5] Mr. Monnett also charged in court that he had been offered a bribe of $400,000 to quash a later suit to enforce the court decision in the first.[6] This and other suits brought by Monnett were abruptly quashed as soon as a successor took office in January, 1900, but not before enough information about the secret operations of Standard Oil had been developed to prepare the way for later federal dissolution suits.[7]

"It was a matter of constant comment in Ohio, New York and Pennsylvania that the Standard was active in all elections, and that it 'stood in' with every ambitious young politician, that rarely did an able young lawyer get into office who was not retained by the Standard."[8] This practice promoted by Rockefeller prevails among corporations today with their coast-to-coast chains of retained political law firms. As a result, most of our legislators in Washington and the state capitals are bluff and hearty corporation men, yet they speak in public in common accents, as though they were human.

It is evident, then, that although some elected officials perform their duties as required by law and the expectancies of constituents, a majority do not. For proof, turn to the tax laws. This prospect brings into range for consideration those who elect officials, the people themselves.

That the public in general through the shallow criteria it brings to bear in selecting its wayward officials makes possible the ostensible cleverness of the rich is, as far as I know, a thesis never before explicitly laid down and forthrightly argued. As we are interested in ascertaining how the lopsided distribution of the world's goods came about in so short a time in the United States and why it is likely to continue for the indefinite future, this phase is germane. For without a public and a system constituted in a certain way it would be impossible for anyone, clever though he might be, to become extremely rich in the ways that have been practiced.

Favorable Circumstances

Nobody, first of all, would be rich if he had not been favored by circumstances. Favoring general circumstances in the United States have been a naturally rich virgin continent, an enlarging widely skilled population, a basic law designed to facilitate private property under earlier purely agrarian-mercantile circumstances, an expanding machine technology that took multiplied advantage of agrarian-mercantile law and a plethora of purchasable officials.

Had Henry Ford been a Swiss, operating under Swiss law, he could never, no matter how shrewd, have developed the Ford Motor Company. Had Rockefeller been a citizen of England, France, Russia, Germany or China, functioning in any of those countries, he could never, by whatever hook, crook or cleverness, have developed the Standard Oil Company.

If one nevertheless insists that the fortune-builders were unusually clever men, entitled to their fortunes as a reward for performing vast economic services—and this is the line apologists do take—one cannot go on to argue equal cleverness in their heirs. For the performance of what service, for the display of what cleverness, do they hold their enormous riches and transcendent power? Does their cleverness consist of their pre-selection of ancestors?

In the case of either the originators or the inheritors the fortune was hardly derived by conspicuous cleverness but a set of fortuitous circumstances, one element of which (still bearing particularly on inheritance) was a body of pre-existing law reasonably designed to fit more modest cases, not designed to apply to huge international estates enjoying the application of machine technology in mass production. In the United States it is now common for heirs (sometimes quite stupid) to come into estates, largely untaxed, that make the inherited dukedoms decried by eighteenth-century republicans and democrats seem microscopic. No grand duchy ever came near the proportions of many American corporations and banks. The United States is the most exaggerated case of plutocracy in all history, eclipsing all others *combined*.

The Demon of Demos

A big factor in modern fortune-building, however, was unquestionably the state of popular opinion and understanding. This opinion has never been more than occasionally, in fits of temper, opposed to fortune-building. The common if languid supposition seems to be that everyone may have his fair chance in this inspiring game. As every clean-living, clear-eyed, pure-souled American boy may look forward to being at least president, so every American virgin may marry a millionaire. Those boys who fail to achieve the presidency may quite easily (one gathers in reading the *Wall Street Journal, Time* and *Fortune*) as consolation prizes become millionaires or marry an heiress. The films play about a good deal with this popular fantasy of heir-pauper marriage, blissfully passing over the fact that if every nubile scion of wealth each year married someone on the relief rolls there would be hardly more than a hundred such marriages a year. To look for the sociologists' precious Upward Social Mobility by this route is veritably to chase dancing moonbeams.

To understand fully how fortunes came to grow so profusely in the United States to grotesque, diseased dimensions and how they are so readily maintained in full panoply amid outlandish cries that they are being whittled away by taxation, one must give some attention to the general populace.

Referring to this populace, the profoundly experienced P. T. Barnum said: "A sucker is born every minute."[9]

The late H. L. Mencken referred to the common citizen as a boob and to the collectivity of common citizens, what sociologists now drably refer to as "the mass," as the booboisie, a thesis he tirelessly embellished with copious examples in voluminous brilliant writings over several decades. Mencken never tired of pointing to the obvious chicaneries and obscenities in the spectrum of phenomena which disoriented professors and clear-eyed politicians call democracy.

Expressing the purely operational as distinct from the formal attitude of American society, Texas Guinan, joyously echoed by W. C. Fields, whooped: "Never give a sucker an even break."[10]

There was hardly any need to give utterance to this thoughtful homily, which appears to have been ventured in gleeful satire at contemplation of the absurd American scene.

It would be advisable here, or so I suppose, to avoid such epithets born of anguished subjectivity and find some other meaningful term for the masses with reference to their inadequacies of judgment. I propose, therefore, that they be regarded, in varying degrees, as handicapped, crippled, unable to make sound judgments and decisions in their own self-interest. They live blindly in a system that offers wide although not unlimited free choice and they are unable to choose wisely. They are victims of their own choices. Nobody protects them from themselves!

What qualifies most of the mass for being regarded sympathetically as handicapped people, mental cripples, rather than astringently as willful suckers and boobs is their seemingly inherent infantile *gullibility*. The masses are handicapped in that they are ready believers in tales and promises of nimbler wits, prone to give credence to the improbable or very doubtful. They believe that some obvious charlatan—a preacher, a politician, a vendor of cheap merchandise—is going to do something very good for them, at only a slight fee or absolutely free. At their most extreme these people are the followers of astrologers, spiritualists, religious dervishes and messiahs of all kinds, very often political messiahs. They believe, for example, that installment selling is something contrived for their special advantage, rarely suspecting that it is elevating already high prices of shoddy goods by 14 to 30 per cent. "Nothing down"—and they buy happily. Furthermore, they tend strongly to resist whatever is objectively the case if it does not harmonize with their delusions. Tell most of them today that Lyndon B. Johnson, or anyone else, has no more serious intention of establishing the Great Society than he has of becoming sheriff of Buncombe County and they will want to report their veracious informant to J. Edgar Hoover as seditious, possibly a full-fledged heterosexual and viviparous.

Gullibility and muddle-headedness are functions of insufficient intelligence. The intelligent person is prone to make significant distinctions, to analyze, compare, reflect and seek out difficulties in proffered propositions whether flattering or promising to himself or not. Skeptical self-analysis is beyond the powers of the gullible because they already feel insecure, must (as they say) "believe in something" if only in believing. Intimations of any lack in their judgment are resisted. Hence it follows that they believe whatever ethnic, religious or national group to which they belong is inherently superlative. "If I belong it must be good; hence, I'm proud to be a Ruritanian." Having little sense of individual identity, they derive their identity from some extensive tribe—hence White Supremacy, Black Power, etc.

Sagging IQs

While all men may have been created equal, whatever that means, what strikes the most casual observer is their disparity of age, circumstance, capability and condition. And, considering people in general with respect to their judgmental powers, what is most unequal about them is their intelligence.

During World War II the government administered what was known as the General Education Test to nearly ten million men. A score of 100 represented the average. Approximately 50 per cent of all who took the test scored from 86 to 114; 25 per cent were below 86; and 25 per cent above 114. The method of grading was based on earlier inquiries of psychologists into the national distribution of intelligence. Of college graduates who took this test more than 81 per cent scored 115 or higher so that by present standards four out of five persons completing college have the ability suggested by the test score of 115 or higher. An IQ of 110 is the minimum required for admission to standard colleges and universities today, excluding at a stroke 75 per cent. Colleges, however, do not get all the high IQs.

Testing for IQ, although regularly done by government, universities and corporations in selecting personnel and admitting students, is a scientific practice as widely resisted today, and roundly condemned, as was the assertion by Copernicus and Galileo in the sixteenth century that the earth was spherical and revolved about the sun. IQ testing yields information generally unwanted because, among other things, it strikes at the basis of the democratic dogma: the doctrine of equality and the alleged ability of people to act with equal skill in their own interest.

Resistance to accepting the idea of an IQ is reinforced by its frequent presentation as something honorific, like having blue blood in the old days. Yet a person of lower IQ will often outachieve one of higher IQ who may, owing to adverse emotional factors, amount to nothing. However, everything else being equal (which it rarely is) the higher IQ will have the edge, and the very low IQs will never get into the running. Nonetheless at most levels IQs can be raised at least a few points—sometimes many points.

Although widely assailed by radicals as well as democrats as revealing nothing inherent (a doubtful contention) but only skills acquired in a certain cultural milieu, the methods of psychological testing are expertly defended by specialists. Children in the same family, subject to identical cultural influences although to different kinds of stress in the family constellation, often show wide variations in IQ. Cultural deficiency, therefore, although it often plays some role, cannot be designated the sole cause of low ratings. There is more than training in a Heifetz or Einstein. Tests have been devised, as a matter of fact, that bypass cultural influences in testing. They show no uniformity in intelligence.[11]

It is this utterly pathetic low state of IQness in much of the population that points up the observation made some forty years ago by an acute political observer that "Actually the great bulk of the 119,000,000 [citizens] are thoroughly muddy-minded about politics, swayed by feeling rather than reason, really incapable of clear-headed thought or understanding."[12]

Open elections, where they take place, are quite correctly cited as one of the hallmarks of a democratic system. But, considering the confused mentality of the mass, the two-party or multi-party electoral system is much like a formally fair duel between a man stricken with palsy (the general public) and a dead-shot duelist (the professional politician) or a chess match between a tyro and a master. Only one outcome is possible: the way of the politician.

What is the case, then, is that a largely incapable public exercises its judgment in validating the selection of its legislators and officials, with the melancholy results for that same public shown by the history of popular elections since before the Civil War. Voting behavior has been extensively studied. Although many new details have since been brought to light in various studies, nothing essential has been changed since Frank R. Kent made the foregoing observation in 1928.

Where the Public Goes Wrong

Where the voting public goes wrong is in whom it accepts in each jurisdiction as plausible candidates—not men of proven knowledge, ability and purpose but men who appeal to various unexamined prejudices: ethnic, religious, national-origin, occupational, aesthetic, regional, personal and the like. As Plato brought out in his dialogue *Gorgias* the politician uses rhetoric to flatter and seduce his public and to carry the decision even against the man of knowledge and sound judgment. People in general, it seems, are far more responsive to blandishment than to reason. They love obvious charlatans.

Although bemusingly capable men are by chance indeed elected occasionally, thereby serving as justification and embellishment for the system, in most cases the public elects flexible men who are prepared to betray it at the first sign of personal profit. Such officials have no more sympathy with the public, itself callous, than have Soviet commissars, possibly less. Each set, Soviet or U.S.-type democratic, is cut out of the same bolt, concerned only with advancing their own small-bore careers.

The electoral system, then, is the setting for a cat-and-mouse game between the greater part of the demoralized public and the professional politician, who knows what he wants for himself and usually gets it. One of the many outcomes of it all is seen in the tax laws. Here, of course, we find that the rich have indeed managed rather cleverly.

There has never been an even approximate correlation of level of IQ with voting statistics, but studies in the sociology of political participation show clearly that it is the socially lower and less skilled classes who most abstain from electoral voting. The largest voting turnouts in Europe and the United States are among higher income receivers—the more educated, businessmen, white-collar workers, government employees, commercial-crop farmers, miners, whites, people over age thirty-five, men, industrial workers in western Europe, older residents, married people and members of organizations. Lower voting turnouts are consistently seen among low-income receivers—unskilled workers, servants, service workers, peasants, subsistence farmers, Negroes (often barred), women, persons under age thirty-five, newer residents, industrial workers in the United States, unmarried people and isolated individuals. Voting in general tends to rise in crisis situations, and then the otherwise quiescent lower orders tend to vote more heavily but from authoritarian and anti-democratic points of view.[13] In crisis, extremism and strongarm tactics become *de rigeur,* appealing especially to the lowly, no doubt satisfying feelings of frustrated hostility.

Self-Defeat: The Lot of the Common Man

Just how and why the common man in the United States gets spun off the merry-go-round as he does is most precisely shown by systematic stages.

When it comes to voting the choice narrows down to two almost indistinguishable men. In Russia there is ludicrously only one man to vote for;

but it is hardly more absurd than voting for almost identical political twins like Johnson and Goldwater. Both systems are equally absurd.

Before an election the choice of candidates has already been made and almost always either one of two men is going to win although both may be absolutely undesirable—as undesirable, indeed, as a Russian might find a candidate on his single slate.

The crucially important political phase, then, as Frank R. Kent has pinpointed it, is when the candidates are selected. All the sociological analysis of partisan and class voting after this stage, as far as the American two-party system is concerned, is politically quite beside the point. The fundamental line has been pre-determined.

In almost all cases in the United States candidates are selected in primaries or by conventions of delegates themselves elected in primaries. Except in the South the choice of candidates—whether by primaries, caucuses or conventions—is determined wholly by political leaders, bosses, owing to the voluntary abstention of the public from serious political activity.

In Russia the bosses will not allow anyone else to present candidates. In the United States anybody may present candidates but usually fails to do so. Political bosses in the United States come into being by reason either of the political default of the people or of circumstances such as specialized nonpolitical occupation that keeps people from broad political activity. Politics, democratic or otherwise, is intrinsically a specialty.

Because in the South there is broader public participation in the primaries, although not very broad, in this respect the South seems more alert politically. But the candidates in the southern primaries usually differ from each other only in contending that each would be more diligent in repressing Negroes. The South, then, has been not only one-party but, stupidly, one-issue.

Where conventions determine the candidate, the bosses obviously have the determining role. But in the primaries, too, they determine the outcome because the broad public virtually boycotts the process. The participants are almost entirely political jobholders or patronage beneficiaries, informally compelled to vote and to vote in ways that enable them to hold their benefices. If it were not for this compulsory voting by beneficiaries, primaries could not be held in most cases.

It is the primaries that give the major parties their legal status. This is because the law of most states stipulates, with no broad dissent, that parties shall hold primaries participated in by party voters for nominating party candidates and officers. The only other way a candidate can get on the ballot is by petition, signed by a certain number of voters, and such a candidate does not run under a party label and has no established organization working for him.

"There could not be a greater mistake" than abstention from primaries, says the able Kent. It is this public abstention that gives the political machine its chance to control the situation, which it does through the precinct executives. "It actually permits the machine to run the country." Here is the veritable foundation for the various legislative Establishments and for legislation biased in favor of the propertied. It rests on pervasive popular ineptitude.

As there is no other effective way for candidates to get on the ballot, the primary is the political key that unlocks all doors.

"It ought to be plain, then," says Kent, "that so long as the machine controls the primaries, it is in a position to limit the choice of the voters in the general election to its choice in the primaries. That is the real secret of its power, and, so long as it holds that power, it cannot be put out of business. Defeating its candidates in the general election not only does not break its grip, it often does not make even a dent in it. . . . The only place a machine can be beaten is in the primaries."

As for the candidate who gets on the ballot by petition, "Nothing short of a political tidal wave or revolution can carry an independent candidate to success," Kent points out. "He may pull sufficient votes from one side or the other to bring about the defeat of one of the regular party nominees, but his own election is a thing so rare as to be almost negligible."

To the established party the primary, which validates it legally, is far more important than the election, which alone seems important to the public. Even if it loses the election, the party organization remains intact owing to patronage—federal, state, county and (over the long term) judicial—gained in past elections. The party organization can, indeed, survive many election defeats. Remaining organized, it is always a threat and draws some deferential attention from the ascendant party which, in fact, helps it out from time to time with "nonpolitical" and "bi-partisan" appointments. The legal parties have much in common, notably their tender joint concern and realistically proper solicitude for their angels, the propertied classes. There are many informal party intermediaries.

The Republican Party long survived in the Deep South despite endless election defeats, owing to its nourishment by federal patronage. Although it held primaries, where federal jobholders voted, it never won state elections or sent members to Congress. The party delegates, however, often played a determining role in the choice of presidential and vice presidential candidates at Republican national conventions. They had something to sell—their organizational votes.

Although the party organization can survive a long series of election defeats, it could hardly survive a defeat in the primaries and could absolutely not survive two primary defeats. If twice defeated it would be clear that it had been outwitted by rival organizers or an intelligent public to whom recipients of party patronage would turn for protection. Organizers able to outwit an entrenched machine are men obviously more capable of outwitting the opposing party in the coming election.

Sometimes factions contend in primaries—the Old Guard, Reformers and Independents. Each puts up a slate, for public office and party office. Each is committed to high-flown party principles, and contends that it can best implement those principles and achieve electoral success. On such a question the general voter in effect has the difficult job of a personnel manager for a large corporation. He must know principles and policy and he must pick out the electorally most plausible man. This, obviously, is usually hard to do. Information is lacking—all the men seem superficially good. If one seems better in some ways the others seem better in other ways. Whose side are they really on? What to do? Here the average voter, who isn't versed anyhow in the ins and outs of the situation, throws up his hands. The primary and its ends baffle him and he stays away. Yet here is the very heart of the electoral process and from now on nature takes its course.

Generally the Old Guard wins owing to its control of patronage. If enough patronage holders are discontented, owing to what the Reformers call poor leadership, they may vote with the Reformers or Independents. In this case party leadership changes, perhaps party policy. What change, actually, has been wrought? Usually it is nothing of broad importance— perhaps only a change from Anglo-Saxon to Irish candidates, from Irish to Italian, from Italian to Puerto Rican. In a changing electoral district the new candidates have more "political sex appeal," are more likely to entice more boobish voters.

An important feature of party primaries often is that they not only nominate party candidates but also party officials: county and state committeemen who elect chairmen. The party chairmen may or may not hold public office, but they are the main part of the continuing party machinery. They are, legally, the party, and they participate in party decisions, convey party views to officeholders. They are men who have immediate access to executive officials, legislators and judges. What they have to say is always very, very important, not to be lightly disregarded.

As Kent points out, by not participating in the primaries the general voter loses at least 50 per cent of the effectiveness of his franchise. He thereby assumes his actual political status—a second-class citizen. As few participate in primaries it may seem, by this token, that virtually everybody is a second-class citizen. But this is not so, for there are those, nonvoters in primaries, who recapture the first-class citizenship at a later stage by contributing to political campaign funds. They "buy in." They are politically first class. They are rich people in a plutocracy.

Nobody has chased the common man away from the primaries. He just does not feel up to participating. His democratic franchise here he finds just too much to handle. He does not, in fact, have anything to contribute; he is politically empty. As a result, the party apparatus and candidates on both tickets belong to professionals, often men never heard of in the community, usually men of limited outlook. They function behind the scenes. They have the party power. They are American versions of Gromyko, Kosygin, Brezhnev *et al.*[14]

The party managers must find men ready, able and willing to campaign and at the same time men who will be acceptable to a broad, culturally differentiated, intellectually and emotionally low-grade public—Mencken's boobs, Barnum's suckers, Kipling's "muddied oafs." The party managers are, contrary to common supposition, restricted to a very narrow potential group, with characteristics shared by less than 5 per cent of the population.

Men selected as candidates must, first, have independent financial means or be in occupations that will permit long leaves of absence. Persons dependent on an assured wage or salary would, even if approached, turn down the offer because they could not take a chance on being out of a job if they lost the election, nor could they take a chance on not winning the next election in two to four years. So, most of the labor force is automatically self-excluded. True, here and there somebody at times takes the long chance; but not many. Again, scientists, physicians, surgeons, scholars, engineers cannot be had because even if they won election they would not be able to keep abreast in their professions; only men willing to abandon their specialized life work might be obtained and they are virtually nonexistent among high-level practitioners. Again, successful corporation executives, unless retired, cannot be induced to run because if they won they would be automatically excluded from the line of corporate promotion and extravagant remuneration and if they lost they would probably be out of any job. They would be "controversial." As it turns out, most of the highly capable men in the country are in sober fact not available to stand as candidates for public office. Either personal economics or professional commitments keep them out.[15] Yet, the inferior types that predominate in politics seem to satisfy the propertied. One can easily make deals with them. They are purchasable.

The political manager, then, must go shopping under conditions of extreme scarcity for prospective candidates. He finds most of them among young lawyers, men with partners willing to see them take long leaves of absence and who, if defeated, can return to the practice of law. Thus Matthews found that among Democrats in the Senate, our supreme political body, 63 per cent were lawyers; among Republicans, 45 per cent. Those who defined themselves as businessmen were 17 per cent among the Democrats and 40 per cent among Republicans. Among the Democrats 7 per cent were farmers, 7 per cent professors and 5 per cent other professionals; among the Republicans 8 per cent were farmers, 1 per cent professors and 5 per cent other professionals.[16]

The up-and-coming men in politics, then, must be lawyers, men of independent means or in some business they can run by remote control as an adjunct to politics. The lawyers chosen are usually not at the top of their profession either as pleaders, brief specialists or jurisconsults but are men seeking to make their way, hopeful that their political participation will bring big retainers to their law firms—and it will! With nice corporate retainers in the office, however, these public officials develop a sound pro-corporate point of view. While rhetorically they may swing far to the left or right, when it comes to voting and deciding, they must see things as the corporations do. They must then follow the corporate "party line." They are at least corporate fellow travelers.

People in Politics: Pop Politics

People in politics all, contrary to popular supposition, work very hard. It is common for a citizen to walk into some public building and, noticing its rather soiled condition and easygoing atmosphere, make an invidious comparison with the trim premises of a tightly run corporation. Here is mute evidence of the difference, he thinks, between shoddy government enterprise and efficient private enterprise. Bank pens work smoothly, post office pens sputter.

The rank and file in the political organizations put in long hours and work hard, often at two or three jobs—and most of them put money in the bank every week, usually sufficiently honest money. Many of their tasks are boring. Others would not perform them. But, in some measure, they carry with them a heady something called power.

In the selection of candidates, however, the political organizer must be careful to select men who will not offend large blocks of voters. As experience has shown, the average mentally handicapped or boobish citizen, his brain in a scramble, attaches vast importance in candidates to religion, race or ethnic grouping, national origin, sex and generally conventional conformist outlook and behavior. He feels grimly punitive toward any sort of deviation from a fixed norm, a stereotype, in his mind. He wants, above all, no independent thinkers—freaks who emit horrible propositions about the importance of intelligence tests, read books—or use three syllable words.[17]

Politicians oblige. If the voters wanted men who spoke Sanskrit, dressed in kilts or used the language of mathematics, the politicians would procure them.

Voters, it has been found, are also partial to men against women, married men against bachelors, fathers as against the childless, the personable against the less personable, the fluent and expansive against the reflective— the generally reassuring, humorous and blandishing against the fellow who raises odd difficulties. They prefer Gorgias to Socrates. They will not, as politicians know, take anybody who lectures to them or even indirectly appears to be lecturing to them, although this is precisely what they need before anything else. They need hard instruction, prolonged, grueling, on the line.

The party leaders, to give them credit, do the best they can in selecting candidates. They do the best they can, too, in seeking to detect hidden aberrancies in a new man, such as penchants for reading, concert-going, tennis-playing or a compulsive desire to speak the exact unvarnished truth at all times—all of which in the budding statesman would spell trouble with the booboisie.

The Role of Money

With the organization now functioning smoothly, something else is needed: money. Here is where the affluent regain their first-class citizenship.

If the organization has not been very successful it must depend on its own resources, mainly "kickbacks" from its successful candidates and appointees. But with victory comes prosperity in the form of campaign contributions, always and almost only from the affluent and well positioned— the wealthy, corporation executives and lawyers, government contractors, brokers, influence-seekers, friends of the candidates, etc. Here and there trade unions are heard from, but for the most part the labor force is now quiescent, not in sight. It is at work, out at the beach or watching television.

Because it is almost entirely the affluent that put up party campaign funds, knowing that some lucre is going to stick to the fingers of political managers, we see here the reason both the Republican and Democratic Parties are, basically and primarily, the parties of the propertied classes—the corporations, the trade associations, the real estate lobbies, the millionaires, the big rich and the super-rich. This is the simple, nonscandalous fact. Money, big money, rules the roost from now on.

Leftist agitators have thundered about this thousands of times from soap boxes at gaping hinds, as though this ought not to be and as though it was sinful. This, as it happens, is the way babies are born in politics—or by even rougher methods as under totalitarianism. They are not brought in by the stork.

The electoral process, owing to the childish nature and behavior of the public, is expensive, and is really paid for by the public in elevated prices. Much is at stake in the public policy that will be made by officeholders—who will pay most of the taxes in an increasingly expensive welfare-warfare state, who will get contracts of $100 million, $500 million, $1 billion, where $200-million roads and dams will go and where they won't go, etc. This is obviously a game (as most participants see it) for big stakes, far from the pitifully petty concerns of the electorate about the religion of the candidates, whether they are divorced and whether they are hetero-, homo-, bi- or a-sexual.

As the public has the franchise, almost without restriction except for Negroes, if it does not like the way matters are arranged all some eighty million members of the labor force need do is (1) participate intelligently in all primaries and (2) contribute about $5 a year to their party, amounting to about $400 million a year in all. If it did this, the public might have more to say in determining policy—if it knew anything at all about policy.

This is an easy prescription but hard to apply to an engine with some eighty million separate parts. Not only does the public consist of many parts but many of these parts are mutually and irrationally antagonistic on grounds irrelevant to the welfare of each. Their various ethnic, religious, nationalistic, regional, occupational, class, caste and cultural differences have in most cases nothing to do with their personal and mutual welfare. Yet they enjoy indulging these irrelevant infantile predilections as though they mattered—and politicians are solicitously attentive. Where the constituency would not like a Ruritanian on the ticket there is no Ruritanian. Where a Ruritanian would help, there he is. Is he *pro-bono publico?* Maybe yes, maybe no, but it is electorally irrelevant. And so with all other types.

If the voters participated intelligently in the primaries, their spokesmen would need to find truly representative candidates—not too easy to do. Most likely persons would turn them down for more agreeable pastures.

In any event, the rank-and-file citizen prefers to accept the ready-made pre-financed, pre-fixed parties, in which in most cases he is permanently enrolled as in a religious brotherhood. Most voters ploddingly vote straight tickets, for one party, year after year. They are, as anyone can see, creatures of easy habit with little genuine political discernment. One can count most of their votes in advance. Politicians do.

But here, as elsewhere, he who pays the piper calls the tune. Although each of the major parties is usually (except when befogged by ideology) alert to whatever may transiently pull the handicapped boobs to their banners, they deliver in major matters, always and invariably, for their main financial supporters. Considering the way everybody performs politically and thinks privately, this is the only way it could possibly be. The idea of democracy first killed itself in ancient Greece. In modern times it did it again in the United States.

Left and Right

Much is made by such writers as Professor Seymour M. Lipset of Left and Right and of which of the major parties is the friend of the common man and which of Big Business.[18] In these respects, in fact, there is little to choose. The Democratic Party came by its latter-day reputation as a peculiar friend of the common man because of its purely sensible emphasis since 1932 on federal programs in sagging domestic affairs and on adjusting to some of the dislocations brought about by technological change. Earlier, this one-time party of the southern slave owners had made friends in the North by welcoming the European refugees of the immigration, each of whom had a vote, most of whom were politically snubbed by the well-washed Whigs and Republicans.

The Republican Party has tended, impolitically, to decry recent Democratic emphases and has consequently lost majority support, which it held from 1860 to 1932, as long as it was able to guarantee low-paid jobs. What money the workers were not paid in those days went, in general, into the sprouting fortunes and for the most part now rests comfortably in trust. The benign Carnegie paid $10 a week for seventy hours and more in the withering heat of the steel mills—a humanist!

But the aims of both political parties, declared and achieved, are to maintain the existing politico-economic system and the same relative distribution of its rewards. This is all Franklin D. Roosevelt ever said he sought to do and all he really did. His main promise was to get the system back in operation and this he did so thoroughly that the 1960's are little different in their externals from the 1920's.

All this is inevitable, as it must be when given the general low-level, don't-know-where-I'm-going-but-I'm-on-my-way outlook of the common citizen. He's bound to be short-changed.

The Dirty End of the Stick

Just what the common man gets by voting the prearranged preferences offered him in elections we may see by looking at the case of Negro Congressman William L. Dawson of Chicago.

Dawson's 90 per cent Negro First Congressional District contains one out of every three Negroes in the state of Illinois. Dawson has ruled it as a private fief for 24 years, and cooperative fellow politicians have continued to change the shape of the district as the Negro population keeps swelling and moving into white neighborhoods. If you are a Negro on the South Side, and you need a job, a favor or a bail bondsman, you see someone from Dawson's organization. His record in Congress is shabby; not a single Chicago journalist can remember a piece of legislation that bears his name. It doesn't matter.

"This man is not interested in politics as a means of helping his constituents," one political writer said. "What he is interested in is staying in power."

Dawson in power has obtained for his faithful constituents the worst housing conditions in the city, a soaring crime rate, an increase in heroin addiction and the spread of teenage gangs who flock together in vicious packs, preying on strangers, extorting money from businessmen, and killing each other out of boredom. It is a record so marvellous that it should qualify Dawson for an ambassadorship to Haiti. . . .

Dawson stays in power at an age when most men are writing memoirs because he commands an organization that makes good old Tammany Hall seem like a congregation of Ethical Culture teachers. Every one of the 446 precincts in the district has its own captain and two assistants, and if possible a worker for every street. There are seven wards in the district, and each ward office is responsible for controlling the precinct captains. The seven wards in turn answer to the people who run Dawson's own Second Ward office.

Dawson has plenty of what Chicagoans call "clout." He is vice chairman of the Cook County Democratic Central Committee, and Mayor Daley understands perfectly just how important Dawson and his organization are in the general scheme of Chicago politics. In 1963, Daley won reelection by 139,000. Dawson-controlled Negro wards contributed 115,000 of those votes.[19]

Representative Adam Clayton Powell, the Negro clergyman-sybarite, for more than twenty years ran a similar district in New York City.

The point here is not to highlight invidiously Negro personalities but to cite two extreme cases as models of what most people more or less get by voting along ethnic, religious, regional and national-origins lines. In almost every case of such widespread voting, it can be shown that the constituents in the home district or state are in some way getting the dirty end of the stick, not perhaps so blatantly as under Dawson and Powell but perceptibly nevertheless. They get it especially in taxes but also in many other ways. Catholics are rooked by Catholics, Protestants by Protestants, Irish by Irish, Negroes by Negroes, and so on, all very democratically.

In the better-grade suburban, city "silk-stocking," Jewish and advanced farm districts it is different. Only in a diluted sense are the alert constituents there ever let down. For the most part they are served as they intelligently if narrowly understand their interests.

An inflexible rule can be stated here: The further one moves down the socio-economic-cultural scale the less the sweet-talking political organizations deliver on behalf of the broad constituencies, which is one reason politicians are repeatedly found by pollsters to be in popular ill repute. People realize that, somehow, they are short-changed. But it is defective understanding in most of the people themselves in attempting to utilize the popular franchise that is considerably to blame, although plenty of teachers have offered to instruct them. Boobs will not heed, however. They just do not seem to get the point. They think it's great to be a Ruritanian and a communicant of the Hocus-Pocus Church.

Instances of Boobishness

As one out of many thousand instances of widespread boobishness one may cite the abrasively intrusive surveillance by the public over the private life of officials. A senator, photographed at a wedding holding a champagne glass, sought to have the picture suppressed owing to the painful impression it would make on constituents; he would not have minded if it had been a glass of whisky.[20] Deviations from local folkways are not tolerated in politicians by most American constituencies.

What can be done for a public who insist upon bringing irrelevant criteria to bear in voting for officials and who decline to participate in the basic task of seeking out and supporting suitable candidates?

Governor Nelson A. Rockefeller of New York is a case very much in point. Professor Lipset as of 1960 thought it more likely "that Nelson Rockefeller, the liberal Republican Governor of New York, will ultimately prove to be the true representative of the revived pattern of direct participation in politics by members of the upper class—participation through their traditional party, the Republican" rather than upper-class people like Franklin D. Roosevelt, Adlai Stevenson, G. Mennen Williams, John F. Kennedy and Averell Harriman in the Democratic Party. At the time all politicians conceded that Rockefeller, had he forced his own nomination as he could have, would have beaten John F. Kennedy hands down.

Yet Lipset's Republican hope was buried in political ashes for years owing largely to his subsequent divorce and remarriage. By reason of this purely personal action, which could not affect a man's managerial capability, a large section of the small-town Republican Party followership turned against him. As far as the presidency is concerned, Rockefeller was long pronounced dead by politicians but was at least tentatively exhumed as 1968 approached. Now many sophisticated observers such as Walter Lippmann and Gore Vidal began looking upon him as the nation's single hope of escape from Johnsonian *realpolitik*.

Wealthy party supporters proceed quite otherwise. If a man votes right in committees, on the legislative floor, makes the big decisions in favor of property, they are behind him no matter what he does privately. They could not care less if he maintained a string of supple mistresses of all colors, shapes, religions and sizes and smoked opium. All that would bother them about this sort of thing in a sound legislator or decision maker would be the danger of the public getting wind of it. But the man's private life, if he was politically on the beam, would be strictly his own business. He could listen to string quartets and detest baseball for all they cared. He could even be civilized!—the ultimate of extreme democratic tolerance.

The common run of voter, a person nobody pays any attention to most of his life, when it comes to casting his ballot suddenly feels that he has some power. Intolerant of all differences, he intends to use his paltry power to the hilt. As anticipated by the politicians, he looks the candidates over and compares them with a mental cartoon of the perfect philistine and asks himself these questions: Is he baptized? Does he belong to the right Christian sect? Does he go to church regularly? What is his race? Does he show the least sign of being superior, uppity, in any way, such as by seriously using long words? Does he seem to enjoy himself in some unorthodox way? Has he at any time stepped out of a petty conventional mold? Does he ever say anything original? The wrong answers to such questions, as politicians know, will usually swing large decisive blocks of votes and will cause ordinary boobs to break party regularity.

Aside from party regulars, most voters, in the belief of politicians, vote punitively. What they are voting against, furthermore, is not ordinarily some disliked policy but, usually, some personal characteristic of the man. He may, like Adlai Stevenson, be too witty. In this way the boobs, calling upon all other boobs to join with them, work off a good deal of their frustrated hostility. What their vote will do for them taxwise they have no idea. They don't know most of them are already paying 50 to 80 per cent more taxes under Democratic "leftism" than they ought to be paying under an equitable arrangement.

For some time to come, Negro politicians are going to have an easy task snaring boobish Negro votes. They are, borrowing a leaf from southern white colleagues, simply going to talk tough about the white man. They are not, however, going to overcome the white man. They are going to make deals with him, for their personal benefit, behind the scenes. Their Negro constituents meanwhile are going to continue more or less to eat humble pie in one form or other, like their white fellow-democrats. Adam Clayton Powell and William L. Dawson and the late Oscar De Priest of Chicago are merely precursors of a long line of coming Negro politicians who, under enlarging liberalized attitudes toward Negroes, will have found the road to Upward Social Mobility. They will have money in the bank, possibly a lively white mistress—or two—under the bed.

As to his ethnicity or national origin a politician cannot usually deceive his public. If he is a Ruritanian he has to admit it and bray loudly that he is inordinately proud of it, thus securing the votes at least of nitwit Ruritanians. On the score of religion, except for sect, it is another matter. Being for the most part intelligent men, most politicians, although conspicuous church-goers, unquestionably have no more conventional religious belief than Lenin, Marx or Robert Ingersoll. True, most of them probably believe also that organized religion is a good thing for keeping the boobs in line, joining here the thought of Plato in his *Laws*. But it is almost a certainty that, tested under the influence of a truth serum, most politicians would admit they themselves had little or no religious belief. Indeed, every significant action of their lives shows most of them are devoid even of natural piety. Not only do most of them have little genuine respect for people, hesitating not at sending tender youth into trackless jungles on sleeveless errands of death; they clearly show they have no respect even for the universe; they do not hesitate to pollute the atmosphere with lethal dust. They are simply low-grade technicians, in outlook so many plumbers (although it is probably an insult to hardworking plumbers to say so).

Quis Custodiet Ipsos Custodes?

Reasonably sure of most of their men after election, the propertied elements—inheritors, *nouveaux riches* and their many power-elite agents—unlike the general public do not sit back and wait to see what is brewing in the halls of government. Through lobbyists and other intermediaries they forcefully intervene at any and all times in the legislative and administrative processes, leaving nothing to chance.

They also prudently keep a close and constant watch at all times on their elected representatives through the medium of the corporate press, trade press and private reporters. Many trade associations and corporations maintain these private reporters in Washington and the state capitals, women as well as men who move about, mingle, socialize, listen, observe and write long regular reports. In distant files dossiers build up on all or on the key men in relation to general or special interests. Into these dossiers goes everything, including gossip, carefully labeled as such. All of this information is useful when it comes to making nominating or appointive recommendations, campaign contributions, "reaching" a man or developing a public offensive against some recalcitrant official. In a very real sense officials are captives of these elements.

Public office, said Grover Cleveland, is a public trust. But big property owners, having large stakes, do not allow their trust officers, either in finance or politics, to get far out of sight. Heeding Jefferson, they believe in being vigilant and forehanded in defense of their profitable liberties. As to trust officers in finance, although they are carefully selected, thoroughly screened and carefully watched by stages through the years, they are nevertheless heavily *bonded*. This ultimate precaution makes sense because one can be most thoroughly betrayed only by someone one trusts most implicitly. One can never tell when any man may slip a neuron and dip into the till or cook the books. Strange chemical reactions sometimes take place when a trust officer encounters a nymph or a betting agent.

Public officers, however, are not ordinarily bonded. They can, though, be carefully watched, monitored, consulted, instructed, advised and personally assisted—in brief, surrounded. This they are, but only with respect to the specific felt interests of the propertied. The ordinary public, members of the labor force, cannot maintain such close vigilance and must depend on newspapers and the occasional reports of large organizations. Most of the electorate, in fact, does not even read these, preferring the sports pages, comics, crime sensations. Roll-call votes do not interest them unless they are about school prayers.

What the public learns about its representatives is only what appears in the newspapers or hostile pamphlets. It may learn to its dismay that their senator loves "the purr of a Cadillac, the genial clink of ice cubes late at night, the company of lovely ladies. . . ."[21] By means of such trivia, which might easily have applied to George Washington (who liked fast horses rather than Cadillacs but was fond of the ladies and a touch of the grape), home sentiment is raised to an angry simmer.

Any legislator who, perhaps seeking higher office, levels a lance at some large propertied interest, like the late Senator Estes Kefauver, instantly raises against himself formidable under-the-surface forces. And crusades such as Kefauver's against politically protected crime syndicates, high drug prices and monopoly are, beyond doubt, educational, informative and entertaining, and they do produce some temporary modifications. But in the long run matters settle back pretty much as they were, awaiting the appearance of another nine-day giant-killer.

Most people in politics—organization types—do not aim at being the Number One Man. And most who do, know that the spot is more easily attained deviously than by appearing as a fierce tribune of the people. For this reason crusaders are few and far between. But anyone in politics who feels neglected can always step into the crusading role. For this reason, among others, the propertied interests try to see that nobody feels neglected, everybody instead feels facilitated. "Don't stir up the animals," is the working maxim.

It should always be remembered that the man in office, even before he is approached by minions of the propertied, does not feel angry at any established interest. He is, usually, already in some degree a man of property himself, perhaps with glowing prospects ahead. While public promises he may rashly have made may be forgotten or disregarded, there being nobody immediately present to hold him to his duty, he is always in contact with those to whom he has made private promises. These must always be kept unless he is "let off the hook" for good reasons he can show.

The common erroneous assumption of the voters is that anyone of their ethnic or national-origin number, class, fraternal order, religion or region is sympathetically inclined toward them. Such a representative, they believe, "understands" them better. Yet, as the record shows, such voters have pretty consistently been let down in their day-to-day interests all the way down the line. Money cancels all prior obligations.

It is not necessarily that the politicians intend it this way, which is merely the way the ball bounces, the cookie crumbles, the rainbow disintegrates. It is simply that intelligent pressure and attention directed on them come mainly from the propertied. The nonpropertied are either absent or are interested chiefly in a long line of irrelevant nonsense like school prayers and ritual conformity to shopworn shibboleths. What can one do for people who believe their true friends are characters like the Reverend Billy Graham, Norman Vincent Peale, Archbishop Fulton Sheen and Francis Cardinal Spellman? It costs a politician or his moneyed supporters nothing to declare in favor of school prayers; it may sound commendable to many. But, whether the prayers are held or not, they make no difference as between poverty and affluence.

It should not be thought, however, that a tight leash is kept on officials by the propertied. For it is not. The watchers are always sensitively aware that officials must play peekaboo with the larger public and must sometimes vote or act in ways that are thoroughly unsound from a propertied point of view. Such grandstand action is seldom resented by the watchers unless it is felt to be gratuitous and avoidable.

But any elected official who consistently goes against the grain of the propertied interests is quickly tagged "anti-business," tantamount to being labeled an anti-party deviationist in the Soviet Union. The man so labeled has been marked for political destruction, will have to fight to the hilt for his political life. Anti-labor he may be and live, anti-immigrant, anti-farmer, anti-intellectual and even anti-veteran. But if he consistently gives the watchful lobbyists a hard time he must depend strictly on his own resources and ingenuity to gain and hold electoral support. Very few have succeeded at it.

Public Discontent: How Deep Is It?

Most Americans, most of the time, nevertheless live in a state of mild semi-content in the substandard habitations that compose substandard residential areas of the richest industrial country on earth. Where there is positive discontent it is usually not very thoroughgoing and could usually be easily removed. Almost any person questioned, of course, would usually like a better job, perhaps a more lively or varied one; somewhat better pay but not necessarily a great deal more; a somewhat better neighborhood to live in, perhaps less noise, soot and crowding in the region; somewhat better schools for the children but nothing outstanding; a longer vacation; not necessarily shorter hours but perhaps somewhat lower taxes (but not very much lower); possibly somewhat lower prices in general; a new car (possibly a Thunderbird); a color television set or even two; maybe a little fishing shack in the country but nothing fancy; some new or additional electric appliances for the home; possibly less crowded transportation to and from work; some deferred dental work; and the like. There is little among an average American's visualized needs, including medical, that would not be taken care of by just a little more money. As to cultural quality there is little felt need. Culturally, everything is thought to be good enough.

I am not referring here, of course, to the lower 20 to 25 per cent, too stupefied by its condition to look for anything better or even to complain. Some at this level do remark plaintively, true enough, of rats infesting their scabrous homes or leaks in the roof and seem to hope that somebody will some day come and remove them. Unable to qualify for readily available jobs because of low intelligence, lack of training, psychic depression, uncouth manners or general debility (hereditary or acquired), lack of accurate information and personal neglect, often concentrated in regions to which they have earlier been enticed at temporarily good pay for now-abandoned mining or industrial processes under what economists blithely call Labor Mobility, they listlessly sit and vaguely hope that something new will turn up. What would suit them as well as anything else would be a first-class war for which they could get good wages making ammunition. In the meantime, forehanded fly-by-night, freedom-loving entrepreneurs extract from them whatever they may have in cash, usually public relief money, by means of conscientious overcharges for rent, food, clothing and dispensable gadgets dispensed on the basis of free misrepresentation.

Little noticed about the habitual poor is the fact that most of them are poorest of all in spirit. Most are from unusually large families in which they have been pointedly depreciated and "put down" by habitually irritated parents or, when such is not the case, they have come to see themselves as an operative cause of the harsh family condition—another troublesome mouth to feed. Contrasting with the low sense of self-esteem among the poor is a correspondingly high sense of quiet self-esteem among the established rich, a reflex to their having usually been catered to by parents and servants and always spoken of as entitled to the best—in clothes, in food, in schools, in marriage, in trips to Europe and the like. The habitual rich do not place a high value upon self merely because they have money (as is often thought) but because in most cases they have been conditioned to being highly valued or overvalued by everybody around them. In many among poor as well as rich there is a noticeable reaction-formation to these basic feelings of value and nonvalue. Many of the poor react by assertively proclaiming their high value (which they do not really feel) and respond approvingly to the assertions of clergy, democratic ideologists and politicians about their superlative value: "God must love the poor because He made so many of them." Some no doubt feel in their bones that it is a fairy tale—but it is a pleasant one. The rich, *per contra*, react by developing an outward mien of modesty, unassumingness, tentativeness and self-deprecation. Everybody remarks: "What a nice democratic guy! He'll talk with anybody, real friendly. Who'd ever think he was worth $100 million? A real gentleman."

But, whether overassertive or submissive in attitude, most of the poor feel marked down. From birth onward their entire experience, with only unusual exceptions, has underlined and emphasized their lowliness and dispensability. Here, indeed, is the purely human difference between most of the rich and the poor, which F. Scott Fitzgerald correctly sensed in noting that the rich were different and which Ernest Hemingway failed to register when he observed in response that the only difference was that the rich had more money. Money, indeed, is the least of the differences, man for man and pound for pound, between the rich and the poor, always allowing for exceptional cases on both sides of the fence. The broad difference lies in self-valuation—too low in one case, too high in the other.

Two things the working American dreads but seldom talks about: loss of his health and loss of his job, which loss of health by itself usually entails. "Thank God for your health," it is commonly said reprovingly to complainers unless they are on their last legs.

Without the ownership of income-producing property, holding at most some small savings, some life insurance and possibly some equity in a mediocre mortgaged home, 90 per cent of Americans (as we have seen) are completely dependent on wages or salary. Relatively few hold jobs under tenure or long-term contract. If the jobs are removed the jugular vein is severed, not only on the means of livelihood but on self-esteem. Most Americans out of a job, no matter how they got that way, feel beaten. If joblessness continues very long they begin to be looked at askance by family and friends. Are they flat tires in the land of success? They begin to wonder themselves.

Full-scale employment is a prime basic aim of American public policy, supported by both parties. It has been recognized since the massive lay-offs of the 1930's that here, if nowhere else, is a problem that could generate really big political upheaval. Although the labor force has grown with the population, unemployment remains and a number work part time as well as some at two jobs. Those the political managers have not been able to absorb into the labor force they have tried to provide for by (1) prolonged routine schooling, (2) the maintenance of a German-style standing army of more than three million men and (3) paid retirement at ages 62 to 65. Anyone retired, in the Wehrmacht, Luftwaffe or in school is obviously not unemployed. Yet approximately one-third cannot qualify for military service for physical or mental reasons; many of the same group plus others cannot absorb available schooling—a problem.

By way of providing for the inexorably growing labor force, the political parties foster schemes of government-subsidized capital expansion at home —"economic growth"—and investment abroad—"economic imperialism"— under military protection.

There is present, then, especially as population growth has not even been tardily curbed, an obviously explosive situation—what professors are prone to call "a dynamic configuration." This last implies only that almost anything can happen.

As long as they are employed at fairly reasonable wages Americans, far less politicalized than their European counterparts, are sufficiently content. Only low prices for farmers, low wages or unemployment, as history shows, can put a noticeable number of them into serious political motion and make them start thinking, reading and talking about their plight. Even then their political expression in the form of dissident parties has never amounted to a considerable percentage of the popular vote. As long as there seems any hope simply of bottom-level, hand-to-mouth employment, they remain glued to one of the prefabricated parties. In this they are very much like the diligent Germans who, as history attests, will go any way politically that the jobs lie. Perhaps this is only reasonable.

Popular Gratitude

Americans, moderately content (except for certain minority blocs in times of crisis), are almost to a man grateful for living in such a marvelous political and economic situation, extending liberty and equal justice to all—the last in part a reflex attitude to propaganda that begins early in the public schools. Those rank-and-file Americans who do not feel grateful tend to feel guilty over their lack of gratitude for such a reputedly fine system.

The intense gratitude felt by many is well illustrated by a case cited by Drew Pearson: Nick Galinfianakis, a lawyer, Duke University professor and member of the North Carolina state legislature, stood as a candidate for Congress in 1966 against Smith Bagley, young grandson of R. J. Reynolds, the tobacco tycoon. Pearson noted that Galinfianakis got into politics when friends put up $18 to file his name as a candidate for the state legislature. Said Galinfianakis to Pearson:

"With a name as monstrous as mine I thought it was a joke. I didn't think anyone would vote for a name like mine. However, my father was born in Crete and had a sense of gratitude toward this country. He used to run water out of a spigot and say, 'Look at the clean water we have to drink. We couldn't get that back in Greece.' My father ran a little hot dog stand, and he felt a deep obligation to this country. I feel that in the Legislature I've been discharging his obligation—and mine."[22]

This is far from an isolated instance but typifies, I have found, a general attitude especially among immigrant groups down to the third generation and among recent refugees from Soviet and Nazi totalitarianism. Second- and third-generation children of immigrant families have in millions of cases been told, when complaining of anything, to "be grateful you have a roof over your head," "be grateful you have something at all to eat." "Be grateful. . . ."

In most of the immigrant families, and among many of the earlier native frontier families, there remains a family tradition about some sort of distant, life-sapping and perhaps nameless hardship that has been narrowly escaped. The descendants of those who escaped that hardship, whatever it was, are repeatedly told to be grateful for living in a country of so many opportunities, such wide liberties, such bountiful fields, such clean water, such blue skies. The children owe gratitude above all to parents for choosing such a country. Examples of poor boys who have "made good," from Rockefeller and Carnegie to Everett M. Dirksen and Lyndon B. Johnson, are often cited and the mass media can run the list up into the thousands, the ten thousands. But, and here is the dazzling moment of truth, they can't run it up to a million, not to 500,000, not perhaps even to 100,000. There are enough showcase examples of "successes," however, who have it to become the biggest used-car-lot operator in all history, to overwhelm most dissenters. The unconvinced are merely carpers. Whatever is amiss, it is implied, will soon be rectified, perhaps after the next big election.

If times are bad or uncertain they will sooner or later improve. In any event, there is no need for anything drastic although many persons would no doubt agree it would be a boon if there were only guaranteed jobs or income, perhaps hereditary jobs.

In reading their newspapers Americans reinforce their attitudes by making note of wholesale death camps in Germany; concentration camps and secret police in Russia; mass slaughters in India, Turkey, China and Pakistan; famines in Greece and elsewhere; overpopulation; lack of water, and, in general, secret police, executions, a bad situation all over the earth. They little realize that foreign newspapers, with equal truth, regularly feature lynchings and riots in the United States, American unemployment and slums rivaled perhaps only by those of India, floods, soup lines, Hoovervilles, gangsters, periodic American depressions and recessions, McCarthyite cultural vigilantism, widespread American lawlessness, traffic jams, ugly cities, water and air pollution, advertising fakery, and other vile conditions. There is, evidently, widespread editorial selection all over precisely with the idea of fostering in-group feelings of complacency. Actually, things are varyingly bad in most places. All Utopias are bogus.

Not everybody, of course, has traditional grounds, however tenuous, for feeling grateful. There are, first, the Negroes—10 per cent of the population. Negroes provide clamorous evidence that the American system, whatever it is, is not benign in all its dispensations. Oddly, to those nurtured on myth, it has its Siberias.

There are, as a matter of fact, many others who seem to have little ground for gratitude; most of them appear to be of the politically apathetic strata that cannot even bring themselves to vote. As a financial writer for the *New York Post*, commenting on an analysis in the *Social Security Bulletin*, puts it:

The number of "poor" Americans—officially defined as having a yearly income of about $3,100 or less for a non-farm family of four—has been slashed a minimum of 6,000,000 since 1960. In the same period, the number of "near poor" just above this lowest income bracket has jumped at least 1,000,000. In totals today, 34,000,000 are living under the "poverty" line and 16,000,000 Americans are living right above it. These facts . . . are a warning of what even a slight economic recession could mean to 50,000,000 Americans. . . .

According to the Social Security yardstick, the poor individual today has 70¢ a day to spend on food plus $1.40 for rent, clothes, home maintenance, transportation, everything else. The near poor person has 93¢ a day for food, plus $1.85 for everything else. The fact is that one in four Americans (including 22,000,000 children under 18) now exist at these levels. The fact is that 43 per cent of all Americans over the age of 65 today are either poor or near poor.[23]

This is about what many smokers spend in a day on cigars.

Perhaps even most of these feel grateful for something. If they do not, their discontent is not translated into political action. Very possibly most of them are of low IQ, perhaps inordinately low owing to diet deficiencies and self-depreciation.

But if 25 per cent of Americans live in poverty and near-poverty another 50 per cent can hardly be said, in the light of official income statistics, to be living more than meagerly. Touches of "the affluent society" begin to be encountered only in the lower levels of the economically upper 25 per cent and do not amount to much until one gets into the upper 10 per cent of income receivers. The "affluent society" is really a not too thick veneer, mostly a surcharged installment-credit affair.

Educational Levels

According to the 1960 census, the formal schooling of Americans twenty-five years old and over was as follows:[24]

	Number	Per Cent
Total persons in this age range	99,024,000	100.
No schooling	2,251,000	2.3
One to four years of school	5,997,000	6.
Five to seven years of school	13,710,000	13.8
Eight years of school	17,397,000	18.
One to three years of high school	19,047,000	19.2
Four years of high school	24,330,000	24.5
One to three years of college	8,705,000	8.8
Four years or more of college	7,588,000	7.5

Impressive when compared with the data for Basutoland, as they sometimes are, these statistics, as educators warn, do not portend what they are
taken to portend owing to the general low quality of the American educational system, especially at the elementary and secondary levels and more
than half of the college level. Most formal education in the United States
is of the once-over-lightly, hit-and-run, masscult, bargain-counter and vocational variety so that even many college graduates have lingering difficulties about spelling, writing plain prose, identifying crucial historical
figures, events and ideas or reading beyond the level of *Reader's Digest*.
If one is seeking *effectively* schooled people one must reduce the high
school and college figures of a largely Potemkin-Village system by more
than half.[25] No other large country, however, has a better system.

Education, of course, is not to be confused with mere schooling. Eric
Hoffer, lightly schooled longshoreman-author of *The True Believer*,
stands out as a far more thoroughly educated man than, for example,
William F. Buckley, Jr., Yale graduate who wrote the grotesque *God and
Man at Yale*, as good a sample as any of the Buckley lucubrations. If one
concedes Buckley every one of his points against Yale—and a civilized
man would hold them to be positive virtues—one sees that he has unwarrantably built his case about a complex institution on few and untypical cases relating wholly to the minor undergraduate college, ignoring
the mountain for the mouse.

It should not, then, be supposed that I make a cult of schooling and
believe that even at its best it *necessarily* represents education. A cultivated
autodidact like Hoffer (and there are others) can, as it so happens, hold
his own with swarms of Ph.D.'s. A few topflight professors do not even
have a bachelor's degree—Lewis Mumford for one example.

George Gallup, the poll wizard, every so often makes a popular survey
on topics of immediate public interest. Invariably, on whatever is of trivial

interest he finds the public well informed, on whatever is of serious concern the vast majority is abysmally ignorant even though the newspapers have gone overboard on the subject. Few will know what a cyclotron is; nearly everyone will be quite expert on something like the Profumo Affair or mini-skirts.

If one gives credence to the bare school statistics, however, a considerable part of the population is sufficiently educated: 40.8 per cent over twenty-five as of 1960 had graduated from high school, with 7.5 per cent finishing four years or more of college and 8.8 attending college for one to three years, mostly one. There is obviously a weak base here for general intelligent political action. Statistically, the certified laggards outnumber the certified competents. Recalling the figures on the distribution of intelligence, knowing that formal completion of schooling in a loose system is not always indicative of solid knowledge and good judgment, it is evident why the populace is not able to select, elect and retain representatives who will act in their broad interests.

The Brain Drain

Educational attainment in the United States, indeed, is generally so low that this complex industrial nation must now increasingly draw much of its highly skilled personnel from abroad, often attracting from needier nations their people of great skill. Just as the United States now processes far more of the raw materials of the world than any other country so it seems well over the threshold of attracting to its shores by offers of higher salaries and better professional facilities most of the brains of the world. The process has been called "the brain drain." Immigration, once confined to the unskilled, now features the highly skilled.

According to *Foreign Affairs* on the subject of the "brain drain" to the United States, "the statistics that have been developed on the so-called 'brain drain' present a somber picture. According to one UNESCO report, 43,000 scientists and engineers emigrated to the United States between 1949 and 1961, 'many' of whom came from the less developed countries. Of the 11,200 immigrants from Argentina alone between 1951 and 1963, nearly half were technicians and professional people, 15 percent were high-level administrators and 38 percent skilled workers. In 1964–65, 28 percent of the internships and 26 percent of the residencies in U.S. hospitals were filled by foreign graduates—nearly 11,000 in all—and 80 percent of the foreign interns and 70 percent of the foreign residents were from developing countries. The drain from Asian nations, particularly

Taiwan and Korea, is the most serious: it is estimated that over 90 percent of the Asian students who come here to study never return home."[26]

Those who came to the United States as advanced students came under foreign assistance programs; but they remain to fill in gaps of higher personnel that are not filled by the native products of the American school system.

England, which itself drains the Commonwealth countries of talent, is alarmed at the drain of its own physicians, surgeons and scientists to the United States. It is losing physicians and surgeons in the proportion of one-fifth to one-third of the graduates of its medical schools each year, some of them intensively trained specialists.[27]

While the official unemployment rate hovers a little below 4 per cent and the extreme poverty rate around 25 per cent, the Department of Labor has advised that there are three million high-level jobs more or less permanently vacant in the country—for engineers, scientists, technicians, statisticians, administrators, nurses, physicians, teachers and the like. Neither the populace nor the educational system seems able to supply fully the needs of a technologically advanced system, partly because of native incapacity, partly because of educational shortsightedness and parsimony and partly because of low-level communal goals set by half-literate local community leaders and politicos.

Corporations, universities and government agencies compete madly with each other for well-schooled personnel. Local communities flounder and sink because men of informed judgment have been drawn away to distant points of the compass, leaving local Chamber of Commerce mentalities in charge.

These figures, true enough, can be interpreted in various ways. It can be said that technology has advanced so fast that it has left much of the population behind, breathless, which is strictly true. It can also be said that the population and communal institutions have not been adequate to meet rising needs, which is equally true.

Just as the level of educational attainment is not sufficient to meet the general needs of the time so, it is my argument, the level of educational attainment is not sufficient to meet the political needs of the people in selecting political personnel devoted to the needs of the nation. One gets instead the well-known variety of peanut politician, mainly exemplified at or near the top in streamlined hicks like Lyndon B. Johnson, Everett Dirksen, Orville Faubus and George C. Wallace, to name only a few of the currently most obtrusive and obnoxious.[28]

As politics is the realm productive of public policy, the troubles of the country trace back inevitably to politics. Here we find largely inadequate officeholders chosen by largely inadequate people on the basis of largely irrelevant criteria, always allowing for the fact that a minority of the officeholders and a minority of the people are fully adequate to their responsibilities.

The democratic system thus comes full circle and in the United States presents a parody of itself on the governmental level.[29] As a consequence the entire land is officially plunged into Madison Avenue nonsense. The system, it turns out, has been infiltrated and subverted by boobocrats.

While institutional inadequacy is involved it is (contrary to a long line of radicals, liberals and plain democrats) by no means the whole story. Although many Americans above age twenty-five are inadequately educated and schooled, *nobody at all is twisting their arms to make them remain that way.* The major cities are all heavily supplied with public night schools on every level from the primary grades to university postgraduate levels and anybody may rectify his educational defects very readily, usually free of direct charge. Some do; most don't. Again, most of the major cities have excellent libraries, very lightly patronized.

Where the interests of the broad public lie may be discerned on any weekend when they hit the roads in their cars. While this aimless driving about on superb highways may be cosmically innocent, like praying, it is not done by a populace seriously concerned about its destiny. It is done, in fact, by handicapped boobs.

The Market Place

What we have before us is an operative and a formal political-legal system. The latter, it should be perfectly understood, is quite well devised to respond in an orderly, systematic way to the collective will of the populace.

The operative system, the *real* system—control by corporation-subsidized politicians—quickly came into being and prevailed owing simply to the inability of the electorate to understand and use properly the system offered. This electorate consisted almost entirely of rustic Anglo-Saxon and Scotch-Irish hinds and, in the course of time, largely illiterate continental European immigrants.

With the spread of the popular franchise after 1830 the system decreasingly elevated characters like George Washington, John Adams, Thomas Jefferson and James Madison, the choices of an educated landed and mercantile enfranchised political elite, and instead pushed up from the soil confused Jacksons, Van Burens, Buchanans, Grants, McKinleys and more recently Hardings, Coolidges, Eisenhowers, Johnsons *et al.* The trend was even more marked on the lower levels and only exceptionally did men of genuine political grasp make their way upward. Many of this order simply did not make it and turned away from politics.

The operative system that came into being, then, was a reflex to popular rather than institutional inadequacy, an important distinction. It is the Marxist idea that all social evil is traceable to existing institutions. I deny this although I do not deny that existing institutions are often influences toward evil, especially as these institutions are distorted under usage. Beautiful parks are despoiled by ordinary people misusing them, not by their managers.[30]

In glancing at the market place, it will be observed that what is chiefly criticizable about it is that much of it, as in "democratic" politics, represents a genuine adjustment to the low-level understanding and goals of much of its public, the customers. It is also true, however, that much of this market place simply ignores the customer, the public, and goes about blithely frying its fish in its own way, as in the establishment of monopoly arrangements. In many ways the market and its institutions, as it turns out, pointedly do not exist to serve the public; the public exists to serve the market, to facilitate its operation.[31]

The American economist Thorstein Veblen developed the concept of economic surplus, most recently employed by the neo-Marxists Baran and Sweezy in computing it (for the first time) for 1929–63. It was Veblen's contention in *The Theory of Business Enterprise* and *The Theory of the Leisure Class* that much, perhaps most, of this surplus was wasted, purposely and conscientiously, so that it could not be used to improve institutions or the life of the people as a whole. The argument was: Capitalism establishes monopolies and uses advanced technology in order to increase surplus to a certain point and then wastes much or most of this surplus in order not to alter the necessary conditions for generating such surplus. Instead of operating to uplift and improve everybody and ameliorate the conditions of life, thus altering institutions, it was held it operated to keep everybody right where he was, which meant that the rich became richer and the poor remained poor or meagerly sustained.

The economic surplus, specifically, is the difference between what a society produces and the cost of producing it. The larger the surplus the more a society has to dispose of in various ways of its theoretical choice.

As derived by Baran and Sweezy with the assistance of Joseph D. Phillips from orthodox official data, since 1929 the American surplus has ranged from a low of 40.4 per cent of gross national product in 1934 to a high of 71.6 per cent in 1943; it stood at 56.1 per cent in 1963. It stood at 46.9 per cent in 1929 and has shown a definite tendency to rise over the decades. As estimates are used even in some of the official government figures employed, there is room for error. But even if error went as high as 10 per cent, or even 15 per cent, either way, the computations would be broadly indicative.

The major components of the surplus for 1963, for example, were as follows:[32]

Total property income	$104,618,000,000
(Corporate and noncorporate income, rents, interest, profit component of corporate officers, etc.)	
Waste in distribution (sales effort, trade advertising, etc.)	29,749,000,000
Nontrade corporate advertising	7,700,000,000
Surplus employees' compensation	17,650,000,000
(Finance, insurance, realty and legal services, which last cost only $870 million)	
Absorbed by government	168,008,000,000
Total surplus	$327,725,000,000
Percentage of Gross National Product	56.1

The direct return to property, then (out of gross national product of $589.2 billions-plus), amounted to more than 17 per cent, which accrued in all to not much more than 10 per cent of the populace by any reckoning and was concentrated most heavily in a thin upper level of this 10 per cent. With respect to the surplus itself, the take of property was nearly 30 per cent.

Waste in the Business Process

The components of waste in the business process shown in the Baran-Sweezy computation consist of expenditures for advertising, market research, expense-account entertaining, maintaining an excessive number of sales outlets, public relations and lobbying, salaries and bonuses of salesmen, maintenance of showy office buildings and business litigation. None of this adds anything to the value or utility of what is produced.[33]

There would be an element of waste in any system, but the argument here is that the waste under capitalism is institutionally determined in order to maintain capitalism itself rather than a high quality of social life. It does no good to argue with a Moscow-oriented Marxist that there is as much or more waste and irrationality in the Soviet system, because the defensive answer here would be that the Russian system was not an outgrowth of capitalism, as Marx stipulated that socialism should be, but is an originally backward system that must pass through a capitalist phase of labor exploitation and the like in order to establish an industrial base for socialism, which is something that will be ushered into being in due course. Those who believe this, in view of the rise of a Soviet vested political bureaucracy, must draw upon whatever credulity they possess. My own view with respect both to capitalism and to sovietism is: There is no Santa Claus. Under whichever system one has, workers, it seems, will work and administrators will administer, on terms more or less unequal in all cases unless administrators deliberately choose to play fair.

As to advertising, it is recognized by many economists of repute as an uneconomic aberration, introduced by corporations as a substitute for competitive pricing. The advertisements create the illusion of product differentiation among large varieties of essentially identical products. These essentially identical products are, it is true, differently styled and packaged but in most cases the "talking points" are irrelevant.

Economists agree that the ultimate consumer pays for the advertising which in turn defeats the ultimate consumer in his search for lower prices, maintains monopoly prices. The worst thing that can happen in the system, in the view of its managers, is price-cutting, which reduces surplus.

Continual advertising itself, by its overwhelming success, in some cases leads to a virtual monopoly of some products—for example, the *Gillette* among the wet-shave safety razors.

As the gilt-edged economist E. H. Chamberlin observed, "selling methods which play upon the buyer's susceptibilities, which use *against him* [my emphasis] laws of psychology with which he is unfamiliar and therefore against which he cannot defend himself, which frighten or flatter or disarm him—all of these have nothing to do with his knowledge. They are not informative; they are manipulative. They create a new scheme of wants by rearranging his motives."[34]

"Madison Avenue" has come in for a great deal of condemnation. It should be observed, however, that the irrational extravagances of advertising could not be employed if there were not a vast public unable to see through the transparently deceptive devices used. It is public response that sustains advertising.

It is not that the advertisements are false in general, although false advertisements, advancing direct claims that can be disproven, have been found in abundance by the Federal Trade Commission. But, even though not false, the advertisements are almost invariably grossly misleading. They are vague, ambiguous, irrelevant and often absolutely nonsensical. By freely using improper techniques, advertising effectively subverts the work of the schools in teaching the proper uses of language and clarity in thinking. The multitudes of handicapped are intellectually defenseless when they come to advertising, and the process of absorbing the nonsense of the free-ranging advertisers intensifies their intellectual handicap. Many people talk and think about the world the way Madison Avenue has vividly but zanily taught them.[35]

The logic of Madison Avenue is to employ language and pictures irrationally with a rational view to selling price-fixed goods and making money. It is able to do this because it carefully exploits human weakness —suggestibility and ignorance. In saying this, nothing is said about products or their quality—another story.

Reinvestment of Surplus

Whatever property owners do not consume or allocate to various self-serving nonprofit purposes they reinvest. Such reinvestment may be in already established areas or in new areas: new industries or foreign lands. Precisely what the propertied element consumes cannot be directly computed. Small property holders probably consume most of their income. In the case of large property holders, income cannot be consumed without resorting to colossal extravagances such as the maintenance of six large homes.

What is left for consumption and personal reinvestment one may obtain some glimpse of by taking account what is reinvested by corporations. In 1962, as Baran and Sweezy show, expenditures of surplus by nonfinancial corporations for research and development totaled $12 billion and for outlays on plant and equipment $32 billion, of which a fantastic 81.9 per cent was greedily charged as depreciation. Since 1953 the totals for research and development, plant outlays and abnormally exaggerated depreciation had climbed steadily and phenomenally. There was, thus, $48 billion reinvested out of total property income for the year of $99.2 billion, or nearly half.

There was, furthermore, the item of foreign investment, possibly not more than half of which represented actual flow of capital from the United States. The total of direct foreign investments increased from $11.8 billion in 1950 to $40.6 billion in 1963, an increase of $28.8 billion, according to official figures. Between 1950 and 1956 such investment each year ranged from half to three-quarters billion but thereafter in each year has usually far exceeded $1 billion and in 1957 exceeded $2 billion. It therefore seems safe to say that on the average at least half of property income is usually reinvested, with the proportions of what is reinvested increasing as one moves up the scale of property holders in point of individual magnitude. In general, the invested position of the propertied is steadily improving. Foreign investment is far more lucrative than domestic and the quest for foreign markets is what enables American industry to bypass in so many ways its own population.

Some of the approximate $50 billion that was left over may also have been reinvested as new personal investments. In any event, the property owners in that year had some $50 billion of unearned income at their personal disposition, roughly equivalent to the sum absorbed by the armed forces.

Yet, as Baran and Sweezy remark, the monopoly system tends to work at cross purposes with itself.

It tends to generate ever more surplus, yet it fails to provide the consumption and investment outlets required for the absorption of a rising surplus and hence for the smooth working of the system. Since surplus which cannot be absorbed will not be produced, it follows that the *normal* state of the monopoly capitalist economy is stagnation. With a given stock of capital and a given cost and price structure, the system's operating rate cannot rise above the point at which the amount of surplus produced can find the necessary outlets. And this means chronic underutilization of available human and material resources. Or, to put the point in slightly different terms, the system must operate at a point low enough on its profitability schedule not to generate more surplus than can be absorbed.[36]

Compensation for surplus or intermediary employees, as Baran and Sweezy admit, would exist in any system; but it is their argument, for which they cite good reasons, that under the American system much of it is excessive and wasteful. The intermediation of brokers and agents adds nothing to the value of products. A real estate or stock broker, for example, may mediate the sale of the same property many times a year, drawing a commission each time. Nothing new has been added.

Government Absorption of Surplus

The largest absorption of the surplus of the highly productive American system, however, takes place through government. Here, as official data show, absorption of surplus has risen steadily from $10.2 billion in 1929 to the level of $168 billion in 1963. Here is the statistical basis for the cry of statism against the welfare-warfare-subsidy state. From 1929 to 1961 government spending steadily rose from 9.8 per cent to 28.8 per cent of gross national product.[37]

It is common knowledge that some of government expenditure by anybody's standards represents waste, expenditure for socially unnecessary ends. The common notion of the congressional "pork barrel," with respect to which congressmen trade votes in order to get unnecessary expensive projects for their districts, supports the notion. The local folks are pleased but are postoffices in the form of Greek temples and colonial mansions necessary? Are various airfields and army posts necessary? Governmental absorption and spending of surplus, however, whether wasteful or not, "pumps" money back into the economy. The government, thus—local, state and federal—is the biggest customer in the marketplace and, if it considerably reduced or withdrew its patronage, the so-called private enterprise economic system would almost instantly collapse. By running Keynesian deficits it can push the economy ahead. By curtailing expenditures it can depress the whole structure.

Despite the outcries against statism, it has been mainly for the military establishment that government demands on the economy have been made. Whereas in 1929 less than 1 per cent of gross national product was devoted to military purposes, by 1957 it had risen to more than 10 per cent and accounted for approximately two-thirds of the aggregate expansion of all government spending. Government spending, then, is largely military spending.

Which government expenditures are socially necessary or sustaining and which are waste of surplus? We know already there is some waste, by common agreement; the question is only to determine how much there is, a difficult if not impossible task.

Whereas nondefense or civilian expenditures by government increased only from 7.5 per cent of gross national product in 1929 to 9.2 per cent in 1957, the military proportion increased by fifteen times. Transfer payments increased from 1.6 per cent to 5.9 per cent, less than four times.[38] Transfer payments comprise interest on government debt, subsidies minus surpluses of government enterprises, veterans' allowances, old-age pensions, unemployment benefits and the like.

Although some argue that military spending is not a prop to the economy and contend despite the 1930's that there would not be a depression if military spending were reduced (because with the reduction in military expenses there would presumably be a corresponding reduction in taxes and a compensating rise in private spending or in redundant investment), it seems inescapable that no scattered private spending or investment could replace the massive concentrated military effort which currently takes more than three million men out of the labor force and makes an effective demand for more than 10 per cent of the production of the labor force.

Instead of military spending, others argue, there could be an increase in socially necessary civilian spending as for hospitals, schools, sanatoria, playgrounds, health resorts, community centers, galleries, museums, lecture halls, libraries, public housing and the like. While such creations would indeed absorb surplus at as great a rate as one liked they would, clearly, be "socialistic." Such a civilian creation by government would in many directions, as in housing, medicine and other areas, conflict with profit enterprises and by supplying libraries, museums, lecture halls, playgrounds and the like would provide alternate uses for the free time of people, to the possible detriment of profit enterprises like TV, movies, automobiles and so on. All this is precisely what is not wanted by the vested interests who exert decisive political leverage. But if there were effective political leadership, overswollen military budgets could be trimmed for these domestic purposes.

Merely to staff a great expansion in such socially useful facilities would require the diversion of much upper-level personnel from profit-making enterprises.

Some percentage of the military establishment, by the testimony of all schools of thought, represents waste. Some of it is necessary waste, arising from unavoidable circumstances; some is avoidable waste. There are, again, those who would argue that, humanly speaking, it is all waste; we need not follow this line of thought in a highly imperfect world. Owing to continual technological advance, moreover, there is rapid obsolescence of much military equipment in a situation where it is felt, hysterically, that the nation must be prepared at any moment for a maximum military effort to save its very life.

Large portions of civilian outlay by government can also readily be interpreted as waste. The federal roadbuilding program, as indicated in Note 28, *supra,* is considered (I think rightly) a huge example of compounding social waste by Baran and Sweezy, who also interpret slum clearance as in good part a waste of public money. This last item of waste comes about in this way: Instead of utilizing low-cost open spaces, readily available, the slum-clearing programs buy up deteriorated properties at good prices to the owners and then supply contractor-promoters with huge sums and excessive tax rebates to construct new buildings that rent at such prices as to bar slum dwellers. Slum clearance thus becomes indirectly subsidized luxury building, a delight to politicians, many of them participants in the building syndicates.

Government expenditures for schools and hospitals, health and sanitary measures (water supply, sewage and garbage removal), conservation and recreation, housing and facilitation of commerce, police and fire protection, courts and prisons, legislatures and administrative offices are conceded by these writers to be socially necessary. Presumably they would agree that libraries, post offices, government printing and the maintenance of rivers and harbors are in the same category. But, as they point out, there has been little expansion of such services relative to the expansion of gross national product. Most expansion of governmental spending and allocation of funds has been in areas that are more or less, or entirely, socially and economically wasteful or rationally questionable.

Thus, while socially necessary services are skimped and held down with cries for "economy in government," the sluice gates are wide open for the military in repelling a Leninist communism held to be lapping at distant shores and in underwriting schemes of roadbuilding and urban renewal that not only facilitate huge profit-making enterprises but undermine those that are socially more efficient such as railroads.

In general, what Baran and Sweezy say here is true. The stake of property is steadily being increased under the camouflage of high depreciation write-offs. Persuasive advertising is wasteful and exploitative of credulity, a substitute for genuine competition. More surplus employees are utilized than is socially necessary, although not more than this kind of system requires. Much of what the government spends is indeed wasteful in various degrees and from various points of view and much of it, as in the approach to housing and the automobile complex, is positively harmful. In this last category we have, not merely social waste for profit, but positive, certifiable social *harm* for profit. Beyond the harm produced by the approaches of public policy to urban housing and the automobile complex there is the harm induced by misallocation of resources, as in military overspending for Over-Kill.

The prime virtue of capitalism in theory is that it provides a mechanism —the ostensible free market—for meeting the effective varied demands of people at the best prices. What happens, however, when people are deviously induced to make an effective demand for something they do not need (automobiles instead of houses) or something that will not meet some need (chewing gum instead of psychotherapy) is not embraced in the theory. People must know their need and how to satisfy it. Again, if the market is under monopoly, people cannot make effective demand at the best possible prices even for things they do not need—things that do not cater to necessity, convenience or comfort. Ideas of spurious need are inculcated by playing upon latent fears, such as that other people will ostracize them if they do not use deodorants and a long line of other products. Advertising, seen in this aspect, is obviously a vast booby trap, a legally condoned swindle for profit.[39]

Quality in the Consumer Economy

As to the quality of goods in the Consumer Economy, where consumption in and of itself is regarded by many public men as the remedy for all ills, there is a wide range. In order to appeal to the impecunious, much of what is offered is sleazy, saturated with built-in obsolescence. The case made by Ralph Nader about the Detroit automobile could in general be applied to many products, although in the automobile it was more serious than usual owing to the immediate life-and-death aspect.[40]

In order that at least the more literate portions of the middle classes may pick their way about among a large variety of substandard, overpriced and absolutely unnecessary products that cater at most to free-floating anxiety and suppressed restiveness, there have emerged successful private enterprises such as Consumer's Union and Consumer's Research. By means of regular reports these organizations, and others, advise subscribers of the results of product analysis and price comparison.

Strong in the production of capital goods (generally machinery designed for further production), the American productive system in the line of consumer offerings is about as uneven as the American school system. The main consideration all along the line is admittedly the rate of profit. Producers, it must be conceded, are entitled to fair returns for effort, but the object of business enterprise in general and of the American business system in all its parts is to obtain maximum possible return without regard for quality or social necessity, comfort or convenience. Do-nothing products, economic placebos, are quite common. Under the rubric of glorious freedom, if they make a big profit through misleading advertising as in the case of deodorants, they are justified. The vendor has given the customer what he has been frightened or cajoled into wanting and has given employment perhaps to thousands who are raising children to grow into another army of worker-consumers making null or below-par products—all, however, for somebody's profit.

Many products in the market, especially in pharmaceuticals and foods, are repeatedly found in government laboratories to be positively harmful. This is a long story in itself.

Just how little fear of authority producers feel under the skull-and-crossbones of freedom we learn from Admiral Hyman G. Rickover, of the Bureau of Ships of the Navy and known as "The Father of the Atomic Submarine," a really competent man. Rickover announced that work on many atomic submarines was being delayed because parts, upon which performance depended, were being delivered that did not follow specifications. He cited "the inability of American industry to meet the exacting demands for quality and reliability posed by modern technology" and charged that industrialists did not know what went on in their plants, which were left to administrators chiefly interested in getting more contracts. The National Aeronautics and Space Administration at the same time voiced similar complaints, which it later smothered in a tribute to the cooperation of industry. Rickover not only held to his position but has many times made it known in the same terms.[41] The deaths of three astronauts were ascribed to poor equipment.

Not all officials react disagreeably to treating the government as though it was a rank-and-file customer. The political authorities of Massachusetts, for example, accepted the Massachusetts Turnpike as constructed. Soon after completion the road was already crumbling over long stretches and was being extensively rebuilt. As one who has driven over this road many times and experienced its undulations, seen it pitted with holes and watched repair crews at work over its entire length, I can personally testify to its generally poor condition, especially as contrasted with the New York State Thruway, with which it connects. As soon as one travels on to the New York State road from the Massachusetts road one is aware of a dramatic transition from uncertainty and hazard to a well-engineered, well-built road. The ancient Romans built roads that are still used for heavy-duty purposes.

A very wide range of consumer goods conforms more to the standards of the Massachusetts Turnpike than to the New York State Thruway, all produced under the pressing motivation of a quest for maximum profits. Cheap goods, perhaps not paradoxically, are often socially expensive goods.

Institutions or People

The full-blown Marxist will have no difficulty putting his finger on the difficulty. He will say it is capitalism, or monopoly capitalism. With this convenient analytical abstraction, I do not agree.

Capitalist institutions, being oriented toward private profit in return for the commitment of private capital, no doubt facilitate and reinforce inherent selfish drives in the acquisitive-minded, encourage corner-cutting. It is part of self-serving capitalist theory that the driving self-interest of the entrepreneur indirectly serves society, with an invisible hand conferring benefits out of the process. Up to a point this may be true, or it may once under competitive conditions have come nearer the truth than it is under monopoly conditions. But as the screws are rationally tightened to generate more and more profits, more and more surplus, the gains in the productive sector of the economy are increasingly made at the expense of the consuming sector. And social welfare lies at least as much as or more in the consuming sector than in the producing sector. Production is merely the means, consumption the end. In dominant American thinking, this order is reversed. Again, much of what is termed capitalism has been simple illegality, outside the system.

If the general public were as rational as the producers and had at its fingertips as much knowledge and insight, and ability to apply knowledge and insight, all would perhaps be well. But a very large section of the public, a majority, is woefully handicapped through the possession of insufficient rationality, knowledge and insight. Its members are as amateur participants in a card game with experts. Not only are the politico-economic adversaries of the broad public highly expert but they are what is known among card players as sharpers, prone to violate the rules. These sharpers play a cooperative game with marked cards. Not only this but to some extent they are mind readers. Armed with a knowledge of psychological laws and backed up by computer technology, the large-scale entrepreneur knows in advance what plays the amateurs in elections and markets are bound to make. The amateurs, in fact, are inherently restricted in the plays they are able to make in their own defense. Even if they were pantologists they would not be able to make better choices than a mass-oriented monopoly market and complex political system offer.

In the selection and purchase of goods and services, the disorganized public is led in some cases by necessity, in others by the quest for convenience and comfort and, at times, by the attraction of dispensable diversion and luxury. Beyond these ends it may, too, as advertisers well realize, be led by the prospect of purely imaginary and illusory advantages, as that ladies will become intensely amorous at the sight of men who use certain pomades.

By Way of Summation

The cleverness of the rich, as I see it, has consisted largely of the fact that the acquisitors among them have been able to operate practically unhindered by law among multitudes of thoroughly confused people, who are readily victimized in politics and economics. The victims have at all times been left externally free to choose in their own way. The rich, whether they knew it or not, could always have been fortified in the thought that the handicapped will usually make the wrong choices under the rule of external freedom.

Approached from the standpoint either of IQ or formal education, far more than half the population has not had the knowledge, intelligence or ability to make choices in its own interests. It has merely drifted with the tide, trusting to its feelings, while others gathered in the hay. Nobody in most instances twisted the arms of this population to make it perform as it did in the polling booth and the market; on the other hand, rescue parties have been few and have not been understood as such by the victims, who regarded saviors such as Mrs. Sanger as enemies. A whole line of would-be saviors, including socialists such as Norman Thomas, have been rotten-egged for taking the trouble to make known their panaceas to this same population. Left and right, radicals, reformers, liberals and labor organizers have been bustled off to jails, not usually by capitalists or even by capitalist agents, but by the local rank and file of victims and their duly elected officers.

Underlying the low IQs and faulty education have been deliberately contrived cultural deprivation as in the case of Negroes and spontaneous, self-induced cultural deprivation as in the case of rural and small-town Protestants and urban Catholics. These, it is evident, have been self-designated victims in a game with rules the rank-and-file did not understand.

What is evidently the case is that a large section of the population is dependent—emotionally, intellectually, economically and politically—and is unable inherently or by conditioning to function in its own behalf under free institutions. A large section of the population, indeed, if it is to be properly served, should be regarded as public wards, ethically subject to rather close highly informed benign guidance in making life dispositions. No doubt much of this dependency arises from its conditioning, from its unreasonably inculcated faith that provision will be made for it, if not by man then by some remote deity. Perhaps a socialist sector of society should be established for it, perhaps true socialism itself is the ultimate answer.

As to socialism as the answer to social ills: I have never been a socialist simply because socialism has seemed to be a dispensation out of practical reach. As shown by the nonindustrial countries where it has been forced by revolutionary means, installed at a time of total social collapse, it can hardly be attained by force. The consequence is simple totalitarianism, with heavy-handed politicians in the saddle. Nor, as is evident from public indifference to it in the face of persuasive argument by a long line of intelligent men from G. B. Shaw to Bertrand Russell, can it be attained by persuasion. Socialism, which long antedates Karl Marx, who merely gave a distinctive romantic turn to the way of attaining it, is in fact an aristocratic doctrine, originated by a French count—Claude Henri de Rouvroy de Saint-Simon (1760–1825), who fought in the American revolution and was imprisoned during the French revolution. Like socialists in general, aristocrats were disdainful of men of business, who believed in turning everything, including all of society, into a profit-making scheme. As Veblen said, "Men whose aim is not an increase in possessions do not go into business."[42]

Not only is the profit-seeking way of the businessman distasteful to aristocrats, who long looked down on "people in trade," but it has been looked at askance by professionals from time immemorial. To the ancient Greeks, Hermes was not only the god of commerce but also of cunning and theft. While traders have perhaps been more influential than any other group in the diffusion of culture—more than the philosopher, theologian or writer—their influence here was no more than an unconscious byproduct of their intrusions into all corners of the world.

It was basically the existence of this sort of trusting, optimistic, dependent, happy-go-lucky population that made it possible within a single generation for the wealth of the nation to find its way into hands almost as few as in some of the long-established older countries. The cleverness of the American rich comes down to the fact that acquisitors found themselves, like delirious foxes in a chicken farm, turned loose among so many unprotected suckers and boobs—the handicapped. From this situation sprang the rule, the overriding operating principle of American society: Never give a sucker an even break.

The result was not brought about by capitalism, as the socialists claim, for such an abstraction has no power to do anything whatever. It was brought about by *individual* capitalists—that is to say, it was brought about by people seeking wealth, using convenient institutions, ideologies and strategies, versus less adroit people.

Human life, in truth, is less an affair of institutions and systems than of people and an interplay of motivations and abilities.

What I have said in this chapter, it is evident, reflects on the sagacity of most of the public, the darling of the democratic ideologue, who replaced God with "The People" as an object of veneration and faith. Any critical evaluation of the public usually is rejected as, somehow, unacceptable in the light of democratic dogma.[43]

The objective role of the democratic ideologue is precisely as follows: Out of his own inner need to see humanity liberated from the rule of others he preaches his ideology. Into the network of institutions and policies thereby generated steps the economic entrepreneur and the politician, who convert democratic institutions into something of vast profit—to themselves. It is time, by now, to see that most people are not capable of wielding this instrument of democracy in their own interests. They do not know by what standards to select representatives who will secure the popular interest. Perhaps, even, they do not care.

Fourteen 🌿

FINPOLITAN FRONTIERS

As the management of properties is considered by apologists to represent in itself a great social contribution (which may in some muted degree indeed be so), in this chapter there will be passingly considered this aspect—even though the management of personal holdings can hardly be considered a clearcut public contribution. At best it would be an ambiguous one. Just because a man runs his plantation well provides no ground in itself for immoderate public rejoicing (as public relations men insist), however much we may admire his adroitness and democratic bearing.

As to corporations, most of the big ones are run well. They are models of self-centered efficiency and rational planning. In some cases they are managed by dominant owners, in others by well-paid hired managers acting for dominant owners. But while laudable efficiency and rational planning —in their own self-oriented interests—mark the large corporations, the dominant public ideology sponsored by the leaders of these very corporations is that there should be no public planning. Planning is a wicked word when engaged in by government, for it allegedly leads to "statism," by definition a bad thing. But corporate planning for maximum profits is virtuous. The consequence is that only corporate policy is rational, in the interests of the corporation, and helter-skelter public policy is helpless to defend itself against the corporations. Such being the case it can only be incidentally that the well-managed corporation is publicly supportive; often it is discovered as overtly anti-social. Merely managing a corporation well, then, does not represent a social contribution. Such action may represent carefully contrived piracy. We can, therefore, forget about corporate management as *ipso facto* a social contribution even though it *may* be in some instances.

The Rockefeller Empire

The Rockefeller empire of contrapuntal profit and nonprofit enterprises is here taken, purely for illustrative purposes, as the central and conventionally most creditable of such ostensible contributions, with allusion later to lesser similar finpolitan complexes. Currently this empire is an international network of industrial, financial, cultural and political activities that for variety, quantity and quality put everything of a similar kind in the shade. The present third generation of ruling Rockefellers—five sons and a daughter of John D., Jr., without considering the independent branch of the founder's brother, William—has at its fingertips what is the quintessence of many great fiefdoms, worthy to be included in a modern Arabian Nights tale. All of it is bone and muscle, none either of fat or meagerness. It is not only quantitatively but qualitatively rich, like a Christmas fruit-nut-brandy cake.

The reigning Rockefeller brothers are John D. III (b. 1906), Nelson Aldrich (b. 1908), Laurance S. (b. 1910), Winthrop (b. 1912) and David (b. 1915). They have a sister, Mrs. Abby Mauzé, who figures in the gilt-edged sextette, according to reports by family friends, pretty much as a silent partner. All appear to be of good intelligence, not the least of their assets, although actually the intelligence at their disposal—the pooled family intelligence deriving from long experience with a mercurial world plus that of their large professional advisory and research staffs—greatly exceeds their personal intelligence. Like the ruler of a great state they have far more relevant information at their ready disposition than they carry with them in their own heads. As far as the contemporary world is concerned, they are thoroughly *informed*. They can, in fact, out-think most contemporaries.

The fourth, and even fifth, generation is being readied in the wings. At this writing there are twenty-three living members of the fourth generation. John D. III has one son and three daughters, Nelson four living sons and two daughters, Laurance one son and three daughters, Winthrop one son, David two sons and four daughters and Abby two children. Some of these offspring are now married and themselves have children of the fifth Rockefeller generation, members of an established world dynasty.

In Their Own Eyes

The self-image of the Rockefellers is quite different from that which a detached observer might arrive at, although it is a conception that many people now share through the power of public relations. "The boys' father," says Joe Alex Morris, "had been brought up with the feeling, which his mother emphasized, that the family's money belonged to God and that he was to be merely a steward. He impressed something of this idea on his sons. . . ."[1] They are, then, stewards of wealth. In this case the laudably humble role carries with it vast emoluments, privileges, immunities and intangible advantages and disadvantages.

Discussing foreign trade after World War II, Nelson remarked: "In the last century capital went where it could make the greatest profit. In this century, it must go where it can render the greatest service."[2] Noble words. . . .

Again, speaking of the financing of various enterprises in Latin America, Nelson said: "We're really setting up pilot plants. Our way of life is confronted with a lot of big problems that have to be solved. We hope that our pilot plant operations will demonstrate some of the things that American enterprise can do to help solve these problems that are vital to our everyday life and to our position in world affairs. Because we've got to master such problems if our system is going to survive."[3] Survival of "our system," then, is a matter of concern.

The Rockefellers, then, look upon themselves as stewards rendering service and helping solve big world problems in harmony with "our system." They are, in fact, problem solvers, within limits imposed by mass irrationality.

The Economic Base

"Any real clues as to the wealth of the brothers," says *Fortune*, "have been vigilantly guarded since their birth. None of the terms of the trusts established for them by their father has ever been revealed, and even the names of the trustees are known only to the family and a few key advisers. The great concentration of the brothers' wealth is in oil companies like Jersey Standard, Creole, and Socony-Vacuum, but the precise amount is still their secret since the holdings are not big enough for mandatory disclosure to the SEC."[4] Glimpses of some of the trust funds, however, were obtained from TNEC records as cited in Chapter Four. As the SEC does not require the reporting of stockholdings of less than 10 per cent in a company unless held by an officer, the six Rockefellers, none of whom is a Standard Oil officer or director, *could* (but certainly do not) own up to nearly 60 per cent of the stock of each of the many Standard Oil companies without the fact appearing on the public record.

"Though these circumstances make appraisal inordinately difficult, ap-

praisal is essential to an understanding of the material source of the brothers' power—their wealth," *Fortune* continued. "Their personal fortunes are
estimated at upwards of $100 million each [as of pre-boom 1955 and prior
to their father's death—F.L.]; the money is mostly tied up in trust funds,
yielding them individual incomes of probably $5 million a year before
taxes, but leaving control to trustees. Roughly $7 million is given away
each year to standard charities, or in gifts such as Laurance's recent offer
of one-half the island of St. John for a national park in the Virgin Islands.
Apart from the trusts, they have an asset of roughly $150 million in Rocke-
feller Center [an understatement, clearly, for the Empire State Building
alone recently sold for $100 million—F.L.]; some $15 million is put out as
U.S. venture capital; $12 million has gone into Latin-American enterprises
such as dairies, supermarkets, fisheries, hog farms. At a minimum, then,
the brothers are probably worth over $500 million. Even in 1955 dollars,
this does not compare too badly with the 1913 fortune of $900 million—
considering that the holdings of their father, their sister, and other Rockefeller kin are not included in the $500 million, considering all that has
been given away, and finally, considering taxes."[5]

Since the death of John D. Rockefeller, Jr., in 1960, the center of financial gravity has moved, manifestly, to the brothers. And inheritance
taxes have not whittled down the original Standard Oil fortune by much
because the original John D. transferred most of it to his son (and daughters) by gift, himself dying comparatively stripped of wealth, and the son
in turn transferred at least half of it by bits and pieces to his children,
thus incurring only gift taxes. As some was transferred in the 1930's at
depression prices, some no doubt nontaxable at birth, possibly by the
grandfather as well as the father, the gift taxes on highly elastic, dynamic
properties were minimal. Morris says: "With the third generation, the family's accumulated wealth is being dissipated on a great descending curve
by taxes, philanthropies and division among the heirs. . . ."[6]

Now, whatever else one may say, one cannot rightly say the Rockefeller
fortune is in any way being dissipated; it is, apart from that portion undeniably dedicated to public purposes, only being subdivided as to direct
beneficiaries but held together in concentrated form in properties. One can
dismiss the so-called tax bite out of hand. Owing to its trustification the
fortune left in private hands is intact, and a potent influence.

Precisely how much has been paid in inheritance taxes, even while many
publicists erroneously assert that taxes are breaking down big estates, can
easily be shown. John D. Rockefeller's estate after death in 1937 totaled
$26,410,837, of which $16,630,000 was paid in federal and state taxes.[7]
His son's estate totaled approximately $150 million, of which half went

to the Rockefeller Brothers Fund and half to his wife. The first half was nontaxable as a philanthropic contribution and the second half was nontaxable under the marital deduction of the tax law, a spouse receiving tax free under 1947 law half of any estate above the basic deduction of $60,-000.[8] There was some small real and personal property in the estate of the junior Rockefeller, and any of it that was not given to institutions would be subject to a minor tax, tax experts pointed out.

We see, then, that the Rockefeller fortune, estimated at $900 million in 1913, has to this date not paid much more than $16,630,000 in inheritance taxes.

Leaving it at this would be misleading because the 1913 dollar has depreciated by approximately 70 per cent to the Johnson dollar of August, 1966. In terms of the value of current dollars, as measured by the Bureau of Labor Statistics indexes of the cost of living, Rockefeller's fortune as of 1913 was worth approximately $3 billion, exclusive of what he had put into foundations before 1913. A man today would need to make $100 per week to equal in purchasing power $30 per week in 1913, when, moreover, he was not subject to a federal tax bite. Put another way, what cost 30 cents on the average in 1913 now costs $1, taxes sometimes added.

Fraternal Investments

The brothers' investments, apart from trust funds of which the capital is distributable only to their grandchildren (an example of serial entailment if the grandchildren replace the trusts with new trusts according to standard estate doctrine) are held through Rockefeller Brothers, Inc. There was also established by them in 1940 the Rockefeller Brothers Fund to finance nonprofit or philanthropic properties.[9]

None of the brothers is actively associated with the management of any of the Standard Oil companies, although most, like their father, held minor jobs with some of them upon emerging from college and some have for a time been directors. All are directors of Rockefeller Brothers, Inc., formed in 1946, and Rockefeller Center, Inc., and trustees of the Rockefeller Brothers Fund. David, for a short time secretary to Mayor Fiorello La Guardia of New York, is now chairman of the ultra-powerful Chase Manhattan Bank, one of the "Big Three" largest commercial banks in the world. His cousin James S. Rockefeller, of the William Rockefeller branch of the family, is chairman of the First National City Bank of New York, another of the "Big Three."

John D. III is chairman of the Rockefeller Foundation and the General Education Board as well as of the Lincoln Center of Performing Arts.

Laurance is chairman of Rockefeller Brothers, Inc., and Rockefeller Center, Inc., and styles himself a "venture capitalist." Nelson was chairman of Rockefeller Center before becoming governor of New York in 1958. Winthrop heads his own Winrock Enterprises in Arkansas and participates in the fraternal enterprises; he was elected Republican governor of Arkansas in 1966.

A division of labor has been worked out by the quintet. John D. III is generally in charge of nonprofit or philanthropic enterprises, David of banking and finance, Laurance of new investments, Nelson (and, lately, Winthrop) of direct political participation (all are indirectly in politics through financial participation in the Republican Party) and Winthrop to some extent in his own orbit although he is a participant in all the fraternal enterprises and his brothers may, too, be participants in some of his ventures.

Winthrop, for special reasons associated with his development in the family constellation and his childhood relations to his older brothers appears to be the more independent of family patterns, at least in shading. Although each brother is sharply individualized, which a psychologist would expect in view of their order in the family, Winthrop appears to be the most noticeably different, more ambient. Both intra-family and later experience, including severe combat experience in World War II during which he rose from enlisted private to lieutenant colonel and won the Purple Heart and Bronze Star with oak leaf cluster, no doubt set him somewhat apart. Although all the brothers except Nelson served in the armed forces, Winthrop's experience was sufficiently unique, following and presaging a persistent pattern, so that among the Rockefellers he is a bit of an odd-man out. As such, he provokes a more spontaneous kind of publicity. Actually, all the Rockefellers are far more individualistic than even some close admirers credit them with being. On policies, their intimates report, they often differ and argue strongly back and forth at quarterly meetings. How differences are settled, by majority vote or otherwise, is not indicated. Which one, if any, is dominant in the group is as much a mystery as in the Russian Politburo.

It would require a rather long catalogue to detail all the projects, profit and nonprofit, with which they are associated. Morris lists thirty-six boards and committees of which John D. III was a member over a period of eighteen years and suggests that one multiply the list by five to ascertain how many such formal connections the brothers have, excluding their club memberships. Some of these are permanent connections, some temporary. The Rockefellers, because of past unpleasant experience with deputies (as in the Colorado Fuel and Iron Company strike of 1913), always involve themselves with all projects with which they are financially associated; and the mere business of attending rounds of meetings occupies much of their time and energy. They are working diplomats, or *finpols*, who aim to eliminate unfavorable public repercussions to the often commendable application of great power.

The Enterprises in Closer View

Their major enterprises are as follows:

Trust funds, at least seventy-five, managed by family nominees, invested in corporations, mainly in Standard Oil companies. Precisely what is in the trust funds, precisely how many there are or what they are worth in the aggregate is not publicly known. As trust funds are usually managed, there is shifting of holdings, perhaps only in the way of selling out at higher prices and buying back at lower. Whether there has been such shifting of Rockefeller holdings is not known. If the trustees were omniscient and in every market phase sold out at top prices and repossessed at market lows, never making an error, the funds would today be worth far more than anyone believes them to be. As nobody can pick market highs and lows with perfect prescience, theoretically maximum results can never be attained. What seems more certain is that the relative value of the Rockefeller trusts has at least been preserved with respect to the performance of the economy. Whether they have out-performed the economy is not known, but it is a lively possibility considering the politically coddled oil industry.

A question of interest to a wide public is how the brothers stand with respect to control of the Standard Oil companies. The image projected by writers in the confidence of the family is that they are passive income-receivers, rentiers. Up to a point they may indeed be. But at any moment the massed family holdings can be mobilized into active dominance and control. This was shown cleanly in 1929 when a wayward chairman of the Standard Oil Company of Indiana, in which the Rockefellers were not active, took it into his head to seize control. The chairman was very popular with small stockholders, who had enjoyed unexpected extra dividends and the like. After rivalrous appeals to stockholders for proxies, at a special meeting the chairman was overwhelmingly voted out by the massed proxies of the Rockefeller family, philanthropic funds, family trust funds and *nonfamily* investment and trust funds. For investment managers throughout the world, after studying the issues, had decided to side with John D. Rockefeller, Jr. Mainly the small, purely dividend-oriented stockholders sided with the chairman. The Rockefellers held proxies for about 65 per cent of the stock when all the chips were down. A new management was installed. What was exemplified here was corporate *power*.

Who Controls the Corporations?

As there is a good deal of learned nonsense in circulation about who controls the corporations—nonsense placed into circulation by professors intent upon making a complex mountain out of a simple molehill—this is as good a place as any to dismiss the question. This nonsense was originally set in motion by Berle and Means in *The Modern Corporation and Private Property* (1932) and has since been embroidered upon by James Burnham in *The Managerial Revolution,* and others. Even such hard-bitten observers as the neo-Marxists Baran and Sweezy have to some extent been brought into the camp of those who believe corporations are dominated by managers, not by stockholders.[10]

When all the chips are down, which is not always the case, the stockholders, particularly the big stockholders or trustees managing big stockholdings, exercise broad control by *determining the composition of the management.* Basically, the stock controls. There are situations, however, where the generalized-ownership kind of influence Baran-Sweezy talk about comes into play.

Even with respect to small stockholders the formal power of the management is in any test restricted. Lindahl and Carter, in The Dartmouth Study, repeatedly point out, correctly, that the small stockholders have much legal power they do not use with respect to company policy.[11] Small stockholders are usually interested only in dividends, and as long as these keep flowing they are inert. But in many cases of record a single small stockholder has, by invoking the assistance of the courts, completely thwarted an established management, even a stockholding management. There is a great deal of law on the books on the side of the smallest stockholder. Most small stockholders feel they cannot take the time, trouble and expense to invoke this law; if they don't like the way the company is run they usually simply sell out, depressing the value of the stock to the chagrin of managers. They have an effect indirectly.

The big nonmanagerial stockholders hold the whip hand. So I believe it to be the case of the Rockefellers with respect to the Standard Oil empire, in which they are silent partners. If any issue arises with respect to which control needs to be asserted, they will unhesitatingly once again, as in the case of the Indiana company, assert that control. This fact—or assumption—is unquestionably part of the thinking of every high Standard Oil official in the world.

Even though we don't know precisely the amount of stock the Rocke-fellers own in the Standard Oil companies, it is known what stock is owned by the Rockefeller Foundation, the Rockefeller Brothers Fund *et al.* This stock, too, has voting power, and the trustees include the Rockefellers. The voting power of these foundation stocks combines with the precisely unde-termined stake of the family members to give a large, perhaps unexercised voice, in the determination of the company management. No company management is going to ride roughshod over or even politely ignore the interests merely of the foundation stock, formally a public possession. And so it is in other cases.

As I indicated, it is not known precisely what the participation of the Rockefellers is in the Standard Oil companies. When the master New Jer-sey company was ordered dissolved in 1911 it was separated into thirty-eight independent companies, and the stocks of thirty-three underlying subsidiaries as well as those of the parent companies were distributed pro rata to stockholders. The parent company then had outstanding 983,383 shares, of which John D. Rockefeller I owned 244,500 or almost 25 per cent, giving him working control. If this distribution had been maintained through the constituent companies the family would, clearly, now hold about 25 per cent evenly throughout the empire.

There is ample reason to believe, however, that this even ownership has not been maintained. First, the stocks in some companies appear to have been sold out, with more emphasis placed on other companies. Again, there has been distribution of assets on the philanthropic circuit, although where such distribution has been retained as principal the control power of the stock has remained in being, an important point.

During his later lifetime it was often reported that John D. Rockefeller, Jr., owned 10 per cent of the Standard Oil Company of New Jersey, an enormous holding in itself in the largest industrial company in the world in point of assets; but this percentage, as it was often assumed, did not necessarily exhaust the *family* participation in the company.

While soon after dissolution the Rockefeller share of the constituents of the New Jersey company was valued in the market at around $900 million, subsequent price movements showed that this was a gross undervaluation. For in the market the stocks, and this prior to the automobile age, were steeply marked up in price. It took the dissolution of the trust to reveal to investors something of what this company was worth. It was the greatest profit-generating mechanism the world has ever to this day seen. It made General Motors even as of today look small because it included with the New Jersey company, which alone tops General Motors in assets in the industrial field, the present-day Indiana, California, Mobil, Marathon and many other big companies.

What happened to this 25 per cent Standard Oil interest is that it was subdivided among family members and family foundations for the most part. Taxes, either inheritance or gift, have had little impact, and as to income taxes far from all income of the companies has been paid out. It has been retained and reinvested.

So much for the trust funds, corporate control and the Rockefeller position in Standard Oil companies.

Venture Capitalists at Work

Rockefeller Brothers, Inc., is the brothers' joint private investment company, into which they apparently put some of their income from Standard Oil sources, thus diversifying in an uncertain world. Its holdings are not reported. This enterprise, with Laurance as chairman, appears to concentrate in the area of modern advanced technology. Laurance himself, for his personal account, has invested in technologically advanced growth-type companies; and writers such as Morris leave it ambiguous whether some of his investments at different times also included his brothers. Sometimes he clearly acts for the brothers together, sometimes apparently alone.

In the first five years of its life the brothers put less than $4 million into ventures of Rockefeller Brothers, Inc., Morris reports, whereas their total investments of venture capital in that period came to $15 million.[12] The proclaimed intent of Rockefeller Brothers, Inc., is "to achieve social and economic progress as well as a fair profit on investment."[13] How much it is now worth does not appear on the record.

Laurance, the gadgeteer of the family, with ace flyer Eddy Rickenbacker in 1938 bought into North American Aviation, which was converted into Eastern Air Lines, a profitable venture. He then went into nonscoring Platt le Page, pioneer in building helicopters, and finally put in with the then limping J. S. McDonnell Aircraft Corporation, in which the brothers collectively after the war held 20 per cent of the stock on an original investment of $400,000 apart from any share Laurance antecedently held, put by Morris at an original modest $10,000. This company produced the advanced *Phantom* and *Banshee* jet fighters, which are thought to have enabled the United States to command the air in Korea in 1950–52 and which are still used in improved models. It is more recently deep in space-age technology.[14] But the Rockefellers, through their oil interests, were already an integral part of the front line of national offense-defense.

Other investments of the brothers were in Marquardt Aircraft Company of Los Angeles, manufacturer of ram-jet and pulse-jet engines and electronic air-navigation and control devices; the Laboratory for Electronics, Inc., of Boston, makers of cyclotron equipment, radar components, electric flight control and guidance systems; Airborne Instruments Laboratory, radar and electronic devices and target indicators; the Aircraft Radio Corporation, radar and other electronic instruments; Horizons, Inc., engineering development and research and (Laurance alone) $1 million as of 1952 in the Glenn L. Martin aircraft enterprise.[15]

Laurance, too, held an interest in Reaction Motors (21 per cent), Marquardt Aircraft (20 per cent), Wallace Aviation (27 per cent), Flight Refueling (30 per cent), Piasecki Helicopter (17 per cent), Airborne Instruments (24 per cent), Aircraft Radio (24 per cent), New York Airways (3 per cent), Horizons (5 per cent), and Nuclear Development Associates (17 per cent).[16]

Four out of five of these ventures, said *Fortune*, were successful.[17]

While the Rockefeller brothers clearly have decided to put a good part of their personal investments into the field of advanced technology, which may seem to them the wave of the investment future, some clue to their broader investment approach may be discerned in the portfolio of the Rockefeller Brothers Fund.

At the end of 1964 we find there $20,689,425 by market value of government and corporate bonds, $21,882,161 of corporate notes, $1,801,589 of preferred stocks and $161,608,512 of common stocks with a book or acquisition value of $88,157,570. The entire Fund was valued at $205,981,687.

Although the portfolio embraced a wide section of the investment spectrum, like any balanced investment fund, distinctive Rockefeller properties among the holdings were as follows:

	Shares	Book Value	Market Value
Standard Oil Co. (New Jersey)	684,220	$30,422,352	$61,665,328
Standard Oil Co. of California	244,333	10,388,607	17,927,934
Socony Mobil Oil Co.	199,900	8,482,656	18,340,825
Marathon Oil Co., a Standard Oil unit	31,200	1,074,958	1,996,800
Chase Manhattan Bank	167,168	6,949,897	12,203,264

All these stocks, naturally, represent corporate voting power which, in conjunction with other family holdings, represent still greater voting power. Additional smaller holdings were in Alcoa, AT&T, Armour, Bethlehem Steel, Chrysler, Du Pont, Eastman Kodak, Ford Motor, General

Electric, General Motors, Great A&P, IBM, International Nickel, International Paper, National Cash Register, Polaroid, Sears, Roebuck, Texaco, etc. As indicated by this Fund, then, the Rockefellers are diversified by investment throughout the American corporate structure.

Their private holdings presumably follow the same general line of distribution, although there may be differences of emphasis in different funds.

More recently at least, Laurance has had a large position in the Itek Corporation, formed in 1960 to concern itself with mechanical, electrical and electronic equipment and to develop optics with relation to photography and photocopying.

Some of these personal investments have been closed out. Where there has been a profit, the close-out required a capital gains tax of 25 per cent. These capital gains ventures of the Rockefellers are, in my opinion, on the basis of the theory of giving tax leniency to actual new ventures, fully justified and differ from capital gains leniency accorded buyers and sellers of stock and real estate in the open market, where there is not the shadow of any social contribution. Whether the brothers operate cyclically in the stock market, as their grandfather did over a broad spectrum, is not known, although the family Stock Exchange seat is still held.

The brothers, Morris reports, are "keenly interested" in making money but not by any means for the sake of mere possession or accumulation, only of "proving their ability."[18] To them, he says, money is a mere tool with which to build. They don't like to talk about money, which by reason of constant allusion in their presence must surely be boring, but will redirect pecuniary conversations to *value*. Unlike lesser mortals they are in a position where they can do this on the basis of authentic impulse. Their biggest problem about money is no doubt that they have had dumped in their laps so much of what most other people desire.

Contrapuntal Enterprises

The Rockefeller Brothers Fund is a foundation enterprise run by the brothers and the largest in a flotilla of others including the General Education Board, the Rockefeller Foundation, the Laura Spelman Rockefeller Memorial and the like. Out of the General Education Board were financed the University of Chicago and many other educational enterprises in whole or in part, including many southern Negro colleges. The Rockefeller Foundation has been more broadly engaged in financing medical, scientific, cultural and other enterprises in vast profusion, a work the Rockefeller Brothers Fund is continuing.

There is, quite evidently, a counterpoint going far back into the history of John D. I between profit-making enterprises, originally subject to much public and judicial disapproval, and nonprofit-making enterprises that have earned wide public approval. Anyone who does not like the way Rockefeller conducted his business affairs is, upon inquiring into his non-profit or philanthropic enterprises, brought up short. Here the signals become crossed, as in the case of Pavlov's experiments with dogs. Original feelings of pain or disapproval are now followed by feelings of pleasure and approval. Then, as one sits back to enjoy the pleasure, one suddenly again feels a stab of pain. Observers are confused, perhaps like the Pav-lovian dogs brought to a state of nervous breakdown or apathy.

There is room a-plenty here for feelings of ambivalence. Are the Rocke-fellers trying to improve the world? Or are they merely automatically milk-ing it?

These questions, which reflect the Rockefellers as controversial figures, require some sort of answer. There are many persons who would blandly and patronizingly dismiss such thoughts as the product of a presumptuous writer's overheated imagination. If there were nothing to the negative side then, one should ask, why did Winthrop, who never hurt a fly, when he went to work in the Texas oil fields in 1933 find it necessary to have body-guards and, when he returned in 1936, to get a permit to carry a gun for protection against "fanatics"?[19]

Point Counter Point

The contrapuntal Rockefeller style of operation is shown by the more recent enterprise of the brothers in the international field, especially in Latin America and the Middle East but also, of all places, in Russia. Two organizations, Morris reports, were established by them as an "experiment in international cooperation." One was the International Basic Economy Corporation (IBEC), originally started with $2 million in 1947 and soon capitalized at $10,824,000, "intended to help raise the standard of living in the localities involved—chiefly Latin America—and to return a profit, if possible, to the investors."[20]

Paralleling IBEC there was formed the American International Associa-tion for Economic and Social Development (AIA), with Nelson president of both at the inception. Because IBEC would be operating its profit enter-prises in poor if not primitive areas, AIA would engage in providing health, education, research and credit facilities. AIA was nonprofit. Opera-tions were begun in Brazil and Venezuela and later extended to other areas.

AIA put up Rockefeller funds but, following a settled Rockefeller policy, it involved others as well—at first various Venezuelan oil companies and the Corn Products Refining Company and later Pfizer Corporation do Brasil; Anderson, Clayton, Ltda; The Sulphur Institute; The Ford Foundation; and Price Waterhouse and Company. Then it called upon local governments to put up matching funds.

Since Morris reported on these enterprises they have grown, particularly in the profit area. IBEC as of 1965 had 9 plants in the United States and 135 stores in Latin America and 108 wholly or partially owned subsidiaries in various parts of the world. It had 297 common and 32 preferred stockholders and 10,090 employees. Its business included housing, retailing, credit and many other endeavors. Total assets at the end of 1965 were $142,227,662 and total sales $191,711,425. Profits for 1965 were $2,723,-007. The president was R. S. Aldrich and one of the vice presidents was Rodman C. Rockefeller, Nelson's son.[21] This has manifestly become a big operation.

AIA in 1961 had total assets of $752,585, received gifts of $908,207 for the year and expended $837,444.[22]

Early in 1967 it was announced (New York Times, January 16, 1967; 1:6–7) that IBEC was entering Russia and the Iron Curtain countries in a multi-billion-dollar operation. Joining 50–50 with Tower International, Inc., of the Cleveland Cyrus Eaton interests, it was announced that the joint enterprise would begin or complete already launched large hotels in Budapest, Belgrade, Warsaw, Prague, Sofia and Bucharest in a Rockefeller-Eaton version of an Iron Curtain Hilton chain. Also to be built were rubber plants in Russia costing considerably more than $200 million, a $50-million aluminum plant in Yugoslavia and a glass plant in Rumania. Highly profitable arrangements were announced to have been made in return for American financing and construction know-how and can-do; materials, labor and sites would be supplied by the Communist governments.

The entire deal was looked upon by the principals as the beginning of a highly useful "dialogue" between the capitalist West and the communist East, a really constructive thrust that can bring salvation to the ordinary run of mortals and, naturally, plenty of dollars to the promoters. Considering the stature of all the participants it was hard to see how the whole enterprise could fail to be a huge success.

These two ventures in the private development (exploitation?) of undeveloped world regions show the general emphasis. The tax-free AIA clears the way; IBEC earns the profits. The profits of IBEC more than nourish AIA. All spells "development," international fraternization.

Almost from the very beginning the Rockefellers have followed a policy, wherever they could, of requiring that others be brought in with matching funds. In this way they have succeeded in involving a broader section of the community of wealth in any particular nonprofit enterprise.

Thus, when John D. Rockefeller put up the money to get the University of Chicago started, Marshall Field I, the department-store tycoon, was prevailed upon to provide the land, and many rich Chicagoans—Armours, Swifts, Fields and others—have from time to time contributed funds to the university. In this way the Rockefellers have been, to a large extent, bellwethers or pilots in the field of philanthropolity.

Before World War I, after Andrew Carnegie financed Abraham Flexner in a study of the medical schools that led to profound valuable reforms and the elimination of a large number of shabby diploma mills, it was decided to give the University of Rochester a medical school. Flexner approached George Eastman, the Rochester camera magnate, and explained that the cost would be $10 million. Eastman offered to put up $2.5 million, which Flexner found inadequate. Eastman then sent word that he would put up $3.5 million, to which Flexner is said to have replied: "That would make it a Rockefeller school, not yours. It must be yours." Over this Eastman brooded for a few weeks and then called in Flexner, shaking his finger and shouting: "I'll put up five million—then I don't want ever to see your face again!"[23]

Enter Frederick T. Gates

In this and many other instances the way was by no means smooth in cooperative money-raising. Nevertheless, this pattern of the Rockefellers, originally devised by Rockefeller's close adviser, Frederick T. Gates, head of the American Baptist Education Society, has been rather faithfully adhered to throughout. They try to put up no more than half the funds for any project.

How Rockefeller became acquainted with Gates, why he decided to make him his philanthropolic adviser, is a revealing story. Gates, a clergyman stationed in Minneapolis, was called upon by George A. Pillsbury, the flour king, to help draw up his will, by which he intended to leave several hundred thousand dollars to a Baptist school. Pillsbury decided to give immediately only $50,000 and leave them to raise a like amount, thus insuring their close supervision of the money. Then he would leave an amount in his will. Gates succeeded in raising $60,000 additional for the Pillsbury Academy and was thereupon made head of the Baptist Education Society, which had a plan for establishing a big university in

Chicago or New York. In this guise he approached Rockefeller, a Baptist official, who invited him to pass a weekend with him, during which Gates did little talking.

The oil man became interested in him [says Morris] especially when he learned that Gates was acquainted with the Merritt family in Minneapolis which owned the vast Mesabi Range iron ore deposits. John D. knew that if he could buy Mesabi Range and develop it under the techniques he had developed in the oil business he could become the master of American steel and iron. Furthermore, the Merritts needed money.

Not long afterward Gates was instrumental in getting a large loan for the Merritts, who pledged the key railroad into the iron field as security. It was Rockefeller money, although the Merritts didn't know it, and in time John D. had the railroad, and forced the Merritt family to sell out to him at his own price. The steel men immediately took alarm when they saw the Mesabi Range fall into Rockefeller hands, but John D. apparently did not want a knockdown fight and he later leased the deposit to Carnegie for fifty years.[24]

The Multifacet Style

This was back in the late 1880's and early 1890's. The way Rockefeller scooped up Gates and the ultra-juicy Mesabi Range and started planning for the University of Chicago well illustrates the Rockefeller and the higher finpolitan style. This style is multifaceted.

The essence of a finpolitan project is that it be multifaceted, that it have aspects of profound profitability interlaced with do-gooding, philanthropy and favorable publicity. It must seem constructive, statesmanlike. The philanthropic thrust qualifies and protects the profit-making thrust. For this reason, almost any Rockefeller or emulatory higher finpolitan endeavor is very much like a rich four-decker sandwich: One layer is Big Business, the next layer is obviously vaguely philanthropic or cultural-scientific, the third layer represents favorable notoriety stemming both from profitability and from philanthropy and the fourth layer and the first three layers in combination represent cultural, social, political and economic *power*. It all adds up to power.

In the case of the Rockefellers as of others of the wealthy, there are plenty of persons ready to dispute such suggestions. Thus, Professor Nevins, writing of the elder Rockefeller, says: "Unlike James B. Duke, he never for a moment mingled private commercial interests with philanthropic acts."[25] I have no interest whatever in asserting that Rockefeller did or did not mingle commercial and philanthropic acts; what is at stake is simple intellectual clarity with respect to facts. On the basis of abundant evidence that Nevins himself is obliged to scan, Rockefeller did mingle profit and nonprofit activities; it would have been difficult if not impossible to avoid doing so.

The chief instrumentality of this mingling was Gates himself.

As Gates has written, owing to public reports coming out about his great wealth, Rockefeller at the time began to be "hounded almost like a wild animal" by people soliciting funds for plausible and implausible causes. Many simply wanted personal handouts.[26] From this pressure he wanted to escape, and Gates, now in Rockefeller's employ, was the man to whom solicitors were sent for screening.

"It has been customary to treat Gates as a minister who developed an interest in education and philanthropy," says Nevins. "Actually, Gates was essentially a businessman with a talent for large affairs, a keen interest in the power of money, and a passion for seeing it expended with the greatest possible efficiency. He was, in short, a man after Rockefeller's own heart . . . he was also shrewd, alert, aggressive, and capable of driving hard bargains. The time was not far distant when this former minister, coming to New York, would teach Wall Street itself some lessons."[27]

Subsequently Nevins notes, "The man whom Rockefeller thus selected as his principal aide in philanthropy was as remarkable as any of his partners in business. In sheer ability he matched Flagler, Rogers, and perhaps even Archbold . . . he possessed an unusual combination of gifts: insight, genuine imagination, analytical power, and vision, backed by unquenchable energy, courage, and an evangelistic fervor. . . . He was often impulsive and sometimes inconsistent. . . . At bottom, as we have said, he was a businessman rather than a minister or social worker, and he soon gained a reputation for cautious, adroit, and hard-headed conduct in business affairs."[28]

Gates, like many an underling, was as flinty as his master. At the time of the strike at the Colorado Fuel and Iron Company in 1913 (twenty-seven dead and two mines set on fire by desperate workers), Gates stood firmly against the strikers as Rockefeller, Jr., relented. Both had been directors of the company of which John D. Rockefeller was "a major stockholder" (Fosdick); and L. M. Bowers, the chairman, was the uncle of Gates.

Characterizing the strikers as "desperate and lawless," waging "organized and deliberate war on society," Gates said, "The officers of the Colorado Fuel and Iron Company are standing between the country and chaos, anarchy, proscription and confiscation, and in so doing are worthy of the support of every man who loves his country."[29] Actually, the strikers had been maddened with ill treatment. According to John T. Flynn, a biographer who presents a less genteel Rockefeller than Nevins, "When Henry C. Frick shocked the country by shooting down ruthlessly the striking iron workers at Homestead, John D. Rockefeller wrote him a letter approving his course and expressing sympathy."[30] Gates and the elder Rockefeller saw pretty much eye to eye.

So talented did Rockefeller quickly find Gates that "Inevitably, Gates was soon looking after Rockefeller's investments as well as his philanthropies."[31]

Although the Standard Oil Trust absorbed all of Rockefeller's time and energy, he had nevertheless already made extensive diversified investments—in mines, steel mills, paper mills, a nail factory, railroads, lumbering, smelting properties and the like.[32] On some of these he had been stuck, through bad advice; others were not being operated properly. Gates was sent on tours of the country to look into the properties underlying the entire investment portfolio. He reported back to Rockefeller on what he found, not always favorably. Then he was given *carte blanche* to reorganize, revise and to bring order out of chaos.

Gates stepped into a dual role as the first director of the Rockefeller philanthropic activities and as investment manager, and he was equally good in both roles.[33]

Beyond this the clergyman-humanitarian became a rabid and successful Wall Street speculator for his own account and an officer of various Rockefeller companies, notably the head of the Lake Superior Iron Ore Company. "Nothing could be stranger than the spectacle of this impecunious Baptist preacher setting out to raise funds for a religious college and winding up in a few years as the president of an iron mine and ore railroad company worth twenty millions, and finally the almoner of America's greatest multimillionaire, with the power of the purse over these vast treasures."[34]

For his role in negotiating the sale of Rockefeller ore properties to the embryo United States Steel Corporation, Gates resolutely demanded and received a commission from Rockefeller.[35] Gates had some idea of his worth in cash value.

Such being the case, the meaning of a statement is baffling when it indicates that Rockefeller never mingled philanthropy and business. There was such mingling in still further degree when he established endowments with Standard Oil stock, all of which carried company voting power.

What became the "Rockefeller style," then, was apparently not something reasoned out in advance. Gates and Rockefeller played everything "by ear," and the style slowly evolved. But from the moment Gates joined Rockefeller formally in 1891, both the philanthropies and the satellite investments were carefully thought about and supervised by Gates while Rockefeller tuned Standard Oil up to concert pitch. In the course of time the contrapuntal role of Gates took Standard Oil into its sweep and is well exemplified today in IBEC, AIA and other new Rockefeller enterprises.

Division of World Emphasis

Just as the brothers have evolved a division of labor among types of activities so, too, have they evidently (perhaps unconsciously) divided the world into spheres of individual influence. Latin America, where Nelson has a Venezuelan ranch, appears to be his particular domain; his son, thus, is a high official of IBEC. The Orient is the particular domain of John D. III. All areas are under the supervision of David as the head of a bank with more than 200 world branches. Laurance seems pointed toward Africa. Only Europe does not yet seem spoken for.

The chief chairmanships and directorships show the special orientations of interest.

John D. III, chairman of the Rockefeller Foundation, the General Education Board, the national council of the United Negro College Fund, was also as of 1966 a trustee of Princeton University, Harvard-Yenching Institute and chairman of Products of Asia, Inc., Products of India, Inc., and president of the Japan Society, Inc., and the Asia Society, Inc. He was a lieutenant commander in the United States Naval Reserve during World War II, special assistant to the under secretary of the Navy late in 1945, and was a consultant of the Dulles Mission to Japan on the peace settlement in 1951 and a U.S. delegate to the Japanese peace treaty conference in San Francisco in 1951. He holds the following decorations: Order of Auspicious Star of China (Kuomintang), Order of the British Empire, Grand Cordon of the Order of the Sacred Treasure of Japan, Grand Cordon of the Star of Ethiopia, Most Exalted Order of the White Elephant of Thailand and Commander of the Ordre des Millions d'Elephants et du Parasol Blanc of Laos.

Now, whatever else this worthy man is, taking into consideration many other directorships, trusteeships and chairmanships, he is more than any ordinary citizen with one vote at the polls. He is, also, manifestly more than a wealthy man. He is a *finpol*, intermeshing between governments, industries and cultural institutions.

"Because of their many friendships with missionaries, the Rockefellers had [as early as 1914] taken a keen interest in China," says Nevins.[36] There were others who churlishly believed the keen interest of the pecuniary wizard of Standard Oil related more to the fact that China was a huge market outlet for kerosene, of which Standard was then almost the sole supplier.

The Rockefellers were, at any rate, keenly interested in China, as they are now, without missionaries, interested in all of the Orient from Japan to India, where Standard Oil at least incidentally has large interests, and the General Education Board put up money to establish the China Medical Board and to build Peking Union Medical College. Up to 1952, Nevins says, the Foundation had put some $45 million into westernizing Chinese medicine, science and education. More recently, as the Communists took over China, the Rockefellers shifted Asiatic emphasis to Japan, India and other areas.

Nelson Rockefeller, three-time governor of New York, premier state of the Union, was president of Rockefeller Center from 1938 to 1945 and chairman from 1945 to 1953 and 1956 to 1958; Federal Coordinator of International American Affairs, 1940–44; Assistant Secretary of State, 1944–45; chairman of the International Development Advisory Board (Point Four), 1950–51; Special Assistant to the President of the United States, 1954–55; Under-Secretary of Health, Education and Welfare (HEW), 1953–54 and has at various times (when not helping run the government) been or remains director or trustee of various foundations, museums and organizations. A Phi Beta Kappan, he holds the Order of Merit of Chile, the National Order of the Southern Cross of Brazil and the Order of the Aztec Eagle of Mexico. Here, again, is no common person, no ordinary wealthy man, no run-of-the-mill politician. This is a *finpol*, a very wealthy man with an interlacing of high governmental and cultural *points d'appui*.

David Rockefeller, chairman of The Chase Manhattan Bank, worked his way quickly up through various jobs in the bank and is also chairman of The Chase International Investment Corporation, chairman of Morningside Heights, Inc., a big housing development, and a director of B. F. Goodrich Company, Rockefeller Brothers, Inc., and the vast Equitable Life Assurance Society. He was an army captain in World War II, is a director and trustee of various Rockefeller foundations and museums, and is an overseer of Harvard University, of which he is an alumnus. He holds a Ph.D. from the University of Chicago. He also holds the French Legion of Honor and the Legion of Merit. In 1940 he published *Unused Resources and Economic Waste*. Here again is a high personage, far from an ordinary citizen.

Laurance Rockefeller is a similar type of Higher Organization Man. He is chairman of Rockefeller Brothers, Inc., Caneel Bay Plantation, Inc.,

Rockefeller Center, Inc., and director of Filatures et Tissages Africains (Africa and the Caribbean are apparently his particular domains), Cape of Good Hope Corporation, Dorado Beach Hotel Corporation, president and trustee of Rockefeller Brothers Fund and trustee of the Conservation Foundation, chairman of the New York State Council of Parks, member of the corporation of Massachusetts Institute of Technology, a trustee of the YWCA, director of the American Committee of International Wildlife Protection, director of Resources of the Future, director of the American Planning and Civic Association and of the Hudson River Conservation Society, commissioner and vice president of the Palisades Interstate Park Commission, trustee and president of Jackson Hole Preserve, Inc., trustee of the Alfred P. Sloan Foundation, chairman of the Memorial Sloan-Kettering Cancer Center, trustee and vice president of Sealantic Fund, trustee and president of the American Conservation Association, trustee and vice president of the New York Zoological Society and director, trustee or officer of various other bodies. He is a Commandeur de L'Ordre Royal du Lion, Belgium, recipient of the Conservation Service award of the U.S. Department of Agriculture and of its Special Conservation award and a holder of the Horace Marder Albright Scenic Preservation medal. A lieutenant commander during World War II, he is a member of the Naval Air Reserve.

Winthrop trails somewhat in this august procession but is coming abreast fast via politics. Governor of Arkansas, he is also chairman of IBEC Housing Corporation and Winrock Enterprises, Inc., conducting vast agricultural and cattle-raising enterprises in Arkansas; a director of the Union National Bank of Little Rock, Rockefeller Brothers, Inc., and Rockefeller Center, Inc.; a trustee of Industrial Relations Counsellors; chairman of the board of Colonial Williamsburg, Inc., and Williamsburg Restoration, Inc.; chairman of the Arkansas Industrial Development Commission; trustee of the National Urban League, Rockefeller Brothers Fund and the National Fund for Medical Education. Since 1953 he has resided in Arkansas.

Among them all they cover a great deal of ground. As anyone can see, they are community-minded, but on an international scale that gives this term a new dimension. The world is their plantation.

The Foundation Thrust

Total outlays for philanthropic or nonprofit enterprises by the founder of Standard Oil are put by Raymond B. Fosdick at $446,719,371.22 capital sum and income therefrom of $850 million—in all well over a billion dollars.[37] Most of the income was expended in the form of grants, except in the case of Rockefeller Institute.

The capital sums were allocated as follows:

Rockefeller Institute for Medical Research, 1902 (now Rockefeller University)	$ 60,673,409.45
General Education Board, 1902	129,209,167.10
The Rockefeller Foundation, 1913	182,851,480.90
Laura Spelman Rockefeller Memorial, 1918–28	73,985,313.77
	$446,719,371.22

In recent years the capital funds of the General Education Board have been drawn down steeply for grants in the neglected field of education and the Laura Spelman Rockefeller Memorial was merged in 1928 with the Foundation. Funds for the University of Chicago came largely through the General Education Board. Coming up in place of the General Education Board has been the Rockefeller Brothers Fund.

Up to 1950 external grants by income and principal were as follows:[38]

Rockefeller Foundation		
From income	$325,754,751.35	
From principal	$125,773,613.93	
Total		$451,528,365.28
General Education Board		
From income	$132,339,912.86	
From principal	$164,427,148.34	
Total		$296,767,061.20
Laura Spelman Rockefeller Memorial		
From income	$ 27,839,809.74	
From principal	$ 27,500,000.00	
Total		$ 55,339,809.74
International Education Board		
From income	$ 6,495,807.82	
From principal	$ 11,837,482.00	
Total		$ 18,333,289.82
Grand Total		$821,968,526.04*

Here should be added $60,673,409.45 for Rockefeller University.

The International Education Board was established by John D. Rockefeller, Jr., in 1923 but, in a very real sense, all the Rockefeller moneys are derived from the founder because nobody in the family since him has been a fortune-builder or even a conspicuous moneymaker. The grandsons have enterprises under way that appear likely to become high profitable but not on any scale, as far as appears to date, resembling the original Standard Oil, the real honey-pie.

What remained of these funds at the end of 1950 was as follows:

Rockefeller Foundation	$158,103,332.13[39]
General Education Board	$ 24,624,493.01[40]
Rockefeller Brothers Fund (as of 1955)	$ 59,663,273.62[41]
	$242,391,098.76

Of the moneys in the Rockefeller Brothers Fund the late John D. Rockefeller, Jr., contributed $58 million in 1951 and bequeathed to it half of his estate. Reflecting part of this bequest in the amount of $65 million, at the end of 1960 the Fund showed total assets of $116,173,369.[42] Appreciation since then, as already shown, has been great.

Since 1950, of course, these funds have been generating more income, most of which has been allocated in the form of grants.

It is clear, then, that a truly stupendous sum was directed from the fortune of a single individual into various medical, educational, scientific and general cultural projects, both in the United States and abroad. As most of these moneys consisted of dollars of much greater purchasing power than the present dollar, it is evident that in dollars of current value the disbursements were of far greater weight.

That all this was part of a far-reaching plan is denied by spokesmen for the family such as Professor Nevins and Raymond B. Fosdick. To the charge of critics that the benefactions were established as "a shield against public censure," or, as some charged, "conscience money," Fosdick, following Nevins, points out that Rockefeller in his 'teens, as a pious Baptist, was already giving to the church as much as 6 per cent of his earnings. He kept a meticulous record down through the years of all such gifts, which amounted to more than $1,000 annually by 1865 and to nearly $6,000 by 1869—goodly sums in those days. He gave $558.42 in a lump to Denison University, for example, in the late 1860's.[43]

Rockefeller, in other words, gave money all along, even as he saved and acquired it, and, as it appears in the Fosdick-Nevins accounts, merely stepped up the rate when he became very wealthy. Yet, that there was more to it than a mere continuation of charitable giving, is shown when these writers quote Gates.

Mr. Rockefeller, a prudent man, apparently showed some doubt at first about proposals of large-scale largesse, if such it was. Says Fosdick:

"Mr. Gates, who could never be anything but candid and forthright, used to thunder at the elder Rockefeller, 'Your fortune is rolling up, rolling up like an avalanche! You must keep up with it! You must distribute it faster than it grows! If you do not, it will crush you and your children and your children's children.' "[44] These remarks are taken from Gates's autobiography and one wonders, if Rockefeller was such a freehanded routine giver, why Gates had to "thunder" at him to drive home the message.

What Rockefeller really thought even Gates, who described him as "a very reserved man" who revealed "little or nothing of his own innermost thoughts," did not profess to know.[45] He may have had no thoughts to keep in reserve—a plain man.

A Domesticated Machiavelli

To me it seems a disservice to the Machiavelli of Standard Oil, whom even an apologist like Nevins shows continually embroiled with business and political opponents one after the other down through the years, to attempt to domesticate him in terms of churchly estimates of genteel benevolence. As the history of Standard Oil by any author, pro or con, clearly shows, Rockefeller was of a deeply conspiratorial, scheming nature, always planning years ahead with a clarity of vision that went far beyond anything any of his associates had to offer. It seems to me far more in keeping with what we know of the man's character, as revealed by his business career, that he embarked on his large-scale philanthropies with at least some self-serving personal ends in view.

Until Gates took over, Rockefeller had been giving money away more or less helter-skelter, mainly to Baptist missionary societies. One gets the impression that some of this giving was merely to get rid of importunate suppliants, who, as Gates said, "beset" him.[46] When Gates joined Rockefeller, he very gradually converted the magnate to the idea of "scientific giving."[47] This "scientific giving" slowly took the form of the great foundations.

Rockefeller very early saw that he was getting some mileage from his Baptist patronage. As early as 1889 when a small Baptist publication criticized the Standard Oil Company, all of whose leading figures were Baptists, the company was stoutly defended by the *Examiner*, official organ of the Baptist Church.[48] Had Rockefeller and his Standard Oil colleagues all been Jews or Catholics one trembles to imagine what the anti-Rockefeller movement would have been like! It could not have escaped Rockefeller's notice that wherever his money had been bestowed he had staunch friends.

His gradual conversion by Gates, it seems to me, shows Rockefeller in a better light in terms of intelligent motivation than many of his apologists indicate. These latter show him only as a compulsive, mechanical giver from the very beginning. Actually, he was a thoroughly responsible man within the light of his own interests and his understanding of them. As the center of raging and constantly intensifying public controversy, which made him in his time "the most hated man in the world," Rockefeller might well have suspected that he was leaving a bitter inheritance to his children and grandchildren. Again, the torrent of public criticism against him, in part at least calumny, could not help but have some effect upon his wife and children however much he discounted it personally as attributable to envy. He prized his son especially, as many remarks showed, and was always deeply pained at any criticism of him. When both father and son were being publicly criticized he said: "They have no right to attack Mr. John. All my life I have been the object of assault. But they have no ground for striking at him!"[49] Possibly Mr. Rockefeller now saw some valid ground for attacks on himself.

His family was, indeed, Rockefeller's Achilles Heel and it is not at all difficult to see that he wanted to make a better public impression than the one currently dominant for the family's sake if not his own. Rockefeller, therefore, as I see him, put his mind coldly to the problem and saw that what Gates and others recommended might at least divide the forces against him, perhaps turn the tide. His first tentative ventures in large-scale philanthropy suggested that this view was valid. Rockefeller did not plunge into philanthropy. He was never a plunger, always made his moves in business, politics and philanthropy gradually and after careful thought.

Gradualism in Philanthropolity

That his large-scale entry into public philanthropy was very gradual and, after being undertaken, was spread out over a long period of time is shown by Nevins, who lists his donations for every year beginning with $2.77 for 1855. Rockefeller kept a record of his donations, which prior to 1880, says Nevins, was incomplete. But in no year through 1877 was as much as $10,000 recorded as donations and not until 1884 was more than $100,000 donated. In 1887 the figure jumped to $284,116.52 and in 1890 to $303,-542.78.

Up to the time when Gates joined him in 1891 his gifts had mainly been to the Baptists. In the 1890's his donations exceeded $1 million each in only five years. In 1892 his Ohio trust was dissolved by court order. Even though he had been comparatively generous, all this up to 1900 was no more than chicken feed; the flood from the secret recesses of Standard Oil was still to come. In 1900 he put up more than $2 million and again in 1901. But in 1902, when the General Education Board and Rockefeller Institute were launched, he contributed $5,407,856.78. Falling somewhat short of this amount for the next two years, in 1905, when public outcry against him was stupendous, he put up $13,602,820.78. Although he was never to miss a year until death in these benefactions, the really big years were as follows:

1907	$ 39,170,480.52
1909	71,453,231.15
1913	45,499,367.63
1914	67,627,095.87
1917	15,770,624.48
1919	138,624,574.61
1920	31,780,348.24
1928	19,964,455.38

Not only did such munificence top anything else of record (and until Rockefeller and Carnegie came along, public donations were meager indeed) but the Rockefeller benefactions went nearly wholly into projects of invariably high quality. To fault Rockefeller on the quality of his projects, one must fault the highly rated University of Chicago, Rockefeller University, the work of the Foundation in combating hookworm, yellow fever, malaria, typhus, influenza, tuberculosis, rabies, yaws, schistosomiasis and various other diseases, and the worldwide contributions to medical education, the financing of projects in experimental biology and other natural sciences, international relations and scores of other fields.

That kudos accrued to Rockefeller, particularly from the press and executive types in charge of projects in education, science and medicine, in place of the earlier brickbats, is not to be denied; but the seeking of praise for meritorious performance, if such was the case, is not in itself a fault. That Rockefeller preferred praise to adverse criticism is evident from the fact that Standard Oil early busily engaged itself in buying and surreptitiously financing newspapers.[50] The influencing of public opinion in his favor was a problem that Rockefeller long wrestled with before he found the right combination.

Prior to 1913 at least, the problem of taxes could not have influenced Rockefeller in his philanthropies because business and wealth were subject then only to piddling local taxes. Nor can it be held that the creation of the Rockefeller Foundation was a direct reflex to the advent of federal taxes in 1913 because the Foundation had long been planned, at least since 1905. The community of Big Business, it is true, was opposed to the new taxes and Rockefeller's chief attorney, Joseph H. Choate, had been the lawyer who in 1893 convinced the Supreme Court that income taxes were unconstitutional; it was therefore necessary to amend the Constitution to enact income taxes. However, even though the advent of federal taxes did not influence the idea of the Foundation, it was gradually noticed by others that there were distinct tax advantages in making philanthropic allocations. This fact is now part of standard tax doctrine, set down in many tax treatises. Gifts to philanthropic funds pay no taxes, the income on such funds pay no taxes, and there is no inheritance tax on such funds. Furthermore, stocks placed in such endowments carry corporate voting power—a nice point. It should be recalled here that it is power really, rather than money or property, that we are concerned with.

Considerations such as these may not have occurred to Rockefeller during tax agitation prior to 1913 but it is hard to see that they could have escaped the notice of his lawyers. At any rate, the size of his philanthropic allocations increased markedly beginning with the new tax laws. Whatever he did not allot to philanthropy was now going to incur income and estate taxes; and such taxes, he must have foreseen, would tend to increase rather than diminish.

As to the relation of taxes to philanthropolic capers the *Wall Street Journal* of August 2, 1967, points out that philanthropies would be sharply reduced if compensating tax reductions were reduced or repealed—an assertion made on the basis of a study by the Brookings Institution in collaboration with T. Willard Hunter, executive vice president of the Independent Colleges of Southern California. In this study there were interviewed 30 of 47 living philanthropists who in 1965 made 69 capital gifts of $1 million or more each for an aggregate of more than $93 million. The donors reported that $40 million, or 43 percent of all, would not have been given if there was no tax reduction allowed; they also reported that had deductions been limited to the original cost of securities rather than to an inflated price, as has been proposed, the donations or allocations would have been reduced by 46 per cent. The donors themselves rated tax savings as fifth on a list of twelve considerations controlling philanthropolic maneuvers.

Actually, it can be shown that in many cases a donor can obtain for himself more indirect in-pocket income by being a generous philanthropist than by holding tightly to direct investments. Among many possible illustrations are the cases of big chemical proprietors who have donated entire schools and laboratories of chemistry to big universities, at huge but tax-deductible costs. What the chemical proprietors have now derived from the schools in the way of new discoveries and trained research chemists has given them a constant return of many hundred per cent on the original "donation."

Peer-group esteem is gained on the *finpolic* circuit by such contributions that strengthen the entire *finpol* network. Rockefeller, *finpolically* speaking, was a very good neighbor, of vast benefit to all *finpols*.

On the basis of his own experience with legislators at the state and national level Rockefeller could not have felt reassured about what they might do with his money. He no doubt felt that he could make a more constructive disposition of it than they. With this view, if it was his, I concur. Even today one can have no rational confidence in the allocation of funds by any Congress the American people in their present low state of cultural development are likely to elect.

There were, at any rate, many advantages, perhaps foreseen and unforeseen, in the course he gradually adopted, not the least of which was wider public acceptance for himself and his family (for which he seems to me to deserve great credit), particularly at the hands of the educated and the middle classes. The high quality of most of the Rockefeller projects particularly commended the man, and still commends him, to the cultivated, and lends strong color to the view of him as a Robin Hood who took, not from the rich for the poor but from grasping business rivals, politicians and an oafish squandering public and, now under severe public criticism, turned a substantial and possibly major portion of the loot over to institutions closely identified with high civilization—a triumph of the sardonic over the indignantly sentimental, a twisting of the knife in the philistines.

Rockefeller, thus, is a paradox. The biggest, most assiduous, most successful, sufficiently unscrupulous and most condemned acquisitor converted himself into the most munificent high-level giver. Rockefeller, late in life and possibly suiting the word to his Lord Bountiful actions, himself enunciated the elvish principle that "A man should make all he can and give all he can."[51] If this was intended to mean (and it does not necessarily) that a man should try to make a great deal of money and give nearly all of it away, the program seems absurd to the point of the comical.

The Finpolitan Model

Although this chapter may appear, thus far, to be about the Rockefellers, it really is not. As I remarked at the beginning, the highly civilized Rockefellers are featured here, perhaps sacrilegiously, purely for illustrative purposes. For what has become the "Rockefeller style" is in essence the *finpolitan* style, which copies the Rockefeller style in a general way. Many others do or pretend to do about as the Rockefellers do, perhaps not with as much earnest conviction.

"If the rich are capitalism's aristocracy," as William Manchester observes, "the Rockefellers are its royalty."[52] One is constrained to agree. They not only show the way in *finpolitania*; they invented it and appear to be deeply convinced of the constructiveness of their role, not an unusual human trait.

Various aspects of the life of the wealthy have been depicted by assorted writers. Perhaps the most popular, representing the role most of the *hoi polloi* see for themselves as rich people, has been the wealthy as irresponsible playboys, spendthrifts and more or less graceful idlers. This view is well conveyed in the writings of Cleveland Amory and others of the same genre. The next most compelling aspect has been the wealthy as ruthless grabbers, as shown by Gustavus Myers and Matthew Josephson. Some attempt, of less wide interest but in my view more significant, has been made to show the wealthy as contemporary social power wielders, as I and C. Wright Mills have done. On the American scene Thorstein Veblen first delved in depth into the role of the wealthy as socially irresponsible power wielders and exorbitant consumers. Individual critical biographies, as by Harvey O'Connor and John T. Flynn, have touched on all these aspects.

But the modes of being of the more mature among the established wealthy have by no means been fully explored. These modes turn out to be distant emulations, not always convincing, of the Rockefeller style. Although academic sociologists anxiously inquire into the most minute, interstitial phases of contemporary society, it is instructive to notice that there is no systematic sociology of the wealthy. The academicians seem to sense through built-in radar that this is taboo terrain and allow unanointed non-award-winning journalists, publicists, free-lancers and miscellaneous literate and offbeat ideologists to dominate the field which, it is true, promises little in the way of academic promotion. A notable exception among the certified sociologists is the suave E. Digby Baltzell, author of *The Philadelphia Gentlemen* and *The Protestant Establishment: Aristocracy and Caste in America*, the latter a penetrating study.

"The real truth is that very few of the social scientists look very deeply

into the subject [of fortunes] for fear of being thought politically radical,"
says Professor Floyd Hunter in *The Big Rich and the Little Rich* (Doubleday & Co., N.Y., 1965, pp. 173–74). "There has been so much moralizing
about the division of power and wealth in world society that an earnest
consideration of what actually takes place in modern American economic
affairs, politically, is left largely to sterile theoretical conjecture. There is
no serious empirical study of socio-economic logistics of the distribution of
wealth. There is no forthright, open discussion of what the phenomena of
personal wealth really does for the community—or doesn't do."

It could be shown, indeed, that there is room for at least 200 interesting
books, as yet unwritten, in the field of the large American wealth-holders.
As it is, the subject is largely taboo, in accord with imposed canons of respectability. Who would be so foolish or reckless as to court the stigma of
disrepute by inquiring into the doings of the wealthy?

As C. Wright Mills discovered, not much material has been systematically
gathered on this general subject of the sociology of wealth and one must,
perforce, dig into whatever random outcroppings are left available; data
are systematically hidden. Nor do there appear to be comtemporary Bos-
wells like the late Clarence W. Barron of the *Wall Street Journal* to make
mordant secret notes on the inner doings of the contemporary tycoons. Perhaps some enterprise like that is going forward; if so, it has not yet come
to light.

Although contemporary wealth is associated with the term "capitalism,"
in the *finpolitan* model capitalism becomes something more like super-cap-
italism. The term "monopoly capitalism" is in any event self-contradictory
because capitalism does not allow of monopoly; it is competitive and its
companies can fail. The super-capitalist companies, potential claimants
to public subsidies, are permanently beyond failure, occupants of a politically protected haven. In search of a better term under the tyranny of old
meanings, it would perhaps be better to speak of financial syndicalism, for
the big *finpolitan* groups are in fact *syndicates* of concentrated yet widely
deployed private holders with governments at their beck and call.

And as to concentration of holdings, we have yet apparently seen nothing
like the destiny toward which the world is heading. In *Multinational Corporate Planning*, edited by George A. Steiner and Warren M. Cannon
(Macmillan, N.Y., 1966), it is pointed out that the big corporations are
now multinational. "In the light of present trends and future prospects,"
say these percipient writers, "it does not seem at all impossible that in
the next twenty years, six or seven hundred large multinational companies
will be doing most of the world's business. . . ." This will indeed be pan-
imperialist super-concentration.

The *finpolitan* corporation, or cluster of corporations, is a multinational corporation. Multinationality is a hallmark of *finpolity*.

Style Setters of Wealth

Rockefeller set at least two of the three major widely copied styles of operation for the American wealthy, and the *finpolitan* style just outlined is the one that is currently dominant, with variations.

The first Rockefeller exercise in style setting was the use of the trust as an instrument of corporate integration and monopolization. In 1872 when the Standard Oil Company of Ohio, the original company, secretly provided funds to acquire companies in other states, it placed the acquired stocks in the custody of one of its directors as a *trustee*. (Under law as it then stood it was illegal for any company to own other companies in another state.) But Rockefeller, like other rising tycoons, was not deterred by a detail like legality. Furthermore, the law on trusts at the time was suitably vague. By 1879 the system was devised of having three officials of Standard of Ohio act as trustees of the acquired stock. They were not, the company contended, legally trustees for Standard of Ohio but, if for anybody, for the thirty-seven underlying stockholders of Standard of Ohio. These stockholders could roundly deny, as they did even on the witness stand, that Standard of Ohio owned these companies. It was all these acquired companies, scattered in many states, that secretly composed what came to be called the Standard Oil Trust. As far as the public knew, these companies were all competitors of Standard.

As word seeped into business and legal circles about this handy new arrangement, which long preceded the New Jersey holding-company law of 1889, other industries organized into trusts until there were soon a Sugar Trust, Whiskey Trust, Tobacco Trust, Rubber Trust, Shoe Trust, Butcher Trust, Furniture Trust, Coal Trust, Cotton-Seed Trust, Gunpowder Trust and many others. These were all actually secret cartels to regulate the market and hold up prices in the interests of the owners. Standard Oil was the first of the giant trusts.

How readily the unpublicized device could be used to baffle people is shown by an affidavit filed by Rockefeller in a Cleveland law suit in 1880, that read: "It is not true . . . that the Standard Oil Company, directly or indirectly, through its officers and agents owns or controls the works of. . . ." Here followed the names in a long list of companies, the stock of which was secretly held by trustees employed by the Standard Oil Company of Ohio.[53]

"Legally, this statement might be defended," says Nevins, a vacuous remark because legally any action whatever is entitled to a defense. "The three trustees held ownership and Rockefeller could say they acted not for the Standard but its stockholders. Actually, to call the statement disingenuous would be putting the matter mildly; it was equivocation. Such evasive tarradiddles were then too common in American business."[54]

What is pointedly false about this assertion is that the "trustees held ownership." Trustees are not owners but agents. While it may be *said* that they were agents for the Standard stockholders, a closely knit group, they were in fact agents and *employees* of Standard of Ohio, whose stockholders held an interest in the acquisitions *in proportion to their share of ownership of Standard of Ohio*. Rockefeller's affidavit was perjury and a fraud on the court.[55]

At the time, Rockefeller owned 8,984 out of 35,000 outstanding shares of Standard Oil, Henry M. Flagler 3,000, Stephen V. Harkness 2,925, Charles Pratt 2,700, Oliver H. Payne 2,637, J. A. Bostwick 1,872, William Rockefeller 1,600, J. J. Vandergrift 500, John D. Archbold 350, J. N. Camden 200, C. M. Pratt 200 and Ambrose McGregor 118. The Cleveland group, comprising Rockefeller's Baptist cronies, held 19,146 shares, a majority.[56]

Each of the key Standard Oil units was duly found to be a law violator. First the Standard Oil Company of Ohio was held by the Supreme Court of Ohio in 1892 to be in violation of the law in its trust arrangement, was forbidden to continue it and ordered to pay the costs of the litigation. The assets were thereupon by an exchange of stock acquired by the Standard Oil Company (New Jersey), operating under the wide-open New Jersey holding company act of 1889, and to the Standard Oil Company of New York; these had approximately the same directors. Finally, in 1911, the U.S. Supreme Court found that the New Jersey company violated the Sherman Act and, tapping it lightly on the wrist, ordered it dissolved into its constituent corporate parts and the stock of each company distributed pro rata to each of its stockholders. Instead of owning one-quarter of one central company Rockefeller now owned one-quarter each of nearly two score companies!

Standard Oil in the foregoing was clearly guilty of noncapitalist behavior as, indeed, many of the fortune-builders have been. Critics of capitalism commonly lump together the behavior of strictly performing capitalists with that of operators outside the rules, thus making capitalism take the blame for much that is outside capitalism. This is not to say that capitalism, for its austerely stylized procedure, may not be the legitimate object of distasteful criticism; but capitalism surely should not be blamed for noncapitalist behavior. If a man robs a bank and is not caught, thus coming into the possession of a large sum of money, he has not according to the dicta of any school of economics acquired his money in a capitalist way.

Capitalism is an economist's ideal abstraction, concerned with aggregate results and average procedures. Many of the big fortunes, however, were built precisely because they departed in important respects from average procedures, precisely because their builders were anything but capitalists. Within capitalism, under the rules, one can lose; the fortune-builders never had any intention of submitting to disadvantageous rules that might land them in the bankruptcy courts. They had lawyers and legislators to assist them in avoiding the rough while benefiting from the smooth.

One learns little about the capitalism of the economists by studying the history of the big fortunes. John D. Rockefeller indeed became a capitalist, but not by practicing capitalism—at least not exclusively. Those who lost out to him, however, were often garden-variety capitalists.

A style Rockefeller neither set nor practiced, which was copied from an English innovator, was that of issuing "watered" stock in mushrooming corporate combinations. J. P. Morgan, William Rockefeller and almost the whole of the upper financial community went in for this exhilarating practice, through which patriotic investors were mulcted of billions and promoters either sold out or retained full control at no cost. This was not capitalism either. The Rockefeller companies were always closely held until the dissolution order of 1911, and Rockefeller never gypped fellow investors. In his acquisition of companies Rockefeller always tried to induce the sellers to take Standard Oil stock rather than cash, which most of them cannily refused to do and thus unwittingly threw away the chance of becoming incalculably wealthy. Sore losers, many of these later joined the accusing chorus against him.

But the successful style of how the well-tempered super-millionaire and his family should conduct themselves was definitely evolved by the hard-pressed Rockefeller and Gates. This style required the creation of foundation philanthropies and the involvement of members of the family in publicly approved cultural, scientific and socially supportive projects. Although widely imitated, as were the Rockefeller trust and the English watered-stock ideas, it is a style subject to great variations.

The foundation idea, as we have already seen, has come to be a widely utilized scheme of tax evasion while maintaining tax-exempt corporate control.

Capitalism as a Scapegoat

The idea that capitalism is to blame for everything irrational, and that failure to face up to basic problems derives only from pro-capitalist bias, comes largely from socialists, who, in their super-heated zeal, present a vastly over-drawn indictment of capitalism. Even if we agree that capitalism—particularly unregulated, automatic capitalism of the classic variety that allows no modifications in terms of human needs—is subject to rejection, it is not true that all social problems stem from the economic system. But according to many socialist (particularly Marxist) critiques, capitalism is to blame for all that is detestable or frightening about the contemporary world.

Actually no system, including socialism, will *automatically* produce good results. The contradictory is an unexamined notion that stems through the Physiocrats of the eighteenth century from the idea of a mechanical physical universe as given in Newtonian physics. Nature is automatic; whatever is automatic is natural; whatever is natural is good (itself a questionable notion). Therefore, a good economic system will be an automatic one, operating according to natural laws. Any viable socio-economic system whatever, as a matter of historical fact, needs constant modification from day to day at many points. Such being the case, any system is humanly troublesome, requiring constant revision and tinkering. Every system is bound to be far from perfect.

Without defending capitalism either in automatic or rationally modified form, one must nevertheless notice that capitalism contains within its theory no propositions directly or by implication stating support for racism, prostitution, ill treatment of criminal offenders, overpopulation, neglect of the mentally retarded, support of crime and the like. To this the socialist will reply: But capitalism, seeking only maximum profits, fosters callousness by seeing salvation only in profits; and, by directly and indirectly pressuring people through its profit-making machinery, induces much social havoc—alcoholism, emotional disturbance, delinquency and the like. Only infidelity between the sexes appears to have been left out of the indictment, although Marx included even this.[57]

Ills of Long Standing

Yet this long list of ills for which capitalism is blamed existed long before capitalism was ever heard of, although the ills were not as finely limned as now by modern statistical methods. The persistence of unsolved problems is cited gleefully by socialists; but the solutions of many problems, as of food supply, are not cited on the credit side for capitalism. I don't myself believe that capitalism is responsible for the improvement in food supply or the conquest of disease; credit here should properly go to modern scientific technology. But neither should capitalism be unwarrantably blamed for the persistence of old problems.

Where the blame mainly lies for failure to apply rational procedures to the solution of a legion of problems is shown, in fact, valuably and dazzlingly, by the reluctance of intelligent capitalist foundations to step into any except conventionally approved areas, even though retired foundation officials cite the need for intrusion into many neglected fields. It would not, with respect to most of the problems lying about, hurt capitalism as such to see these problems solved; indeed, capitalism might be benefited by having much sand removed from the social gears.

That the public itself offered no encouragement in basic problem-solving is shown primarily in the fact that ameliorative measures, with respect to many problems, were never adopted by Congress. Stone-faced, unsympathetic Demos barred the gate there.

The foundations, it is clear, must consider not only capitalism but the behavior of a certainly hostile public. This public opposes almost anything civilized.

Capitalism, although it thrust itself up into the world, did not create that world or its ideas. It modified that world; in some instances for good, in others for ill. The worst count against capitalists (not capitalism) is that in their insatiable drive for raw materials and markets they have fostered some of the most destructive wars and revolutions in history and seem likely to foster more. Here, as I see it, is a heavy count in an indictment, hardly requiring the critic to bring in topics like prostitution to bolster his case.[58] Beyond this capitalists simply neglect social problems, often in deference to public opinion.

But the very fact that capitalists (and socialists) are able to enlist a large populace on their side in a warmaking capacity, merely by waving the flag, shows there is more to it all than capitalism or socialism. There is, in fact, an irrational populace, ready to be mobilized for destruction by any bugle-blowing fuehrer. It is this irrational populace, as I see it, that impedes capitalists themselves, gives them pause, in advancing to the solution of many basic problems (leaving to one side the thorny question of war).

Barbarians in the Mass

The situation would be more readily understandable at a glance if the population were attired, in harmony with its basic emotional and intellectual organization, in suitable symbolic garb. Then more than 50 per cent of the people, perhaps up to 75 per cent, would be still dressed today in animal skins and sandals and would wear their hair long and unkempt. Businessmen and their assistants would be dressed, as now, in standard sack business suits. Professionals—lawyers, physicians, educators and savants—would be dressed, medieval-style, in long black robes; each might wear a distinctive hat. Many clerics, as suitable to shamans, would be outfitted in feathers, bones and bangles. Perhaps many people, politicians especially, would be garbed eclectically—part skins, part business suit, perhaps adorned with a feather or bone here and there. Some, representing a hard core, would no doubt be dressed in no more than loin cloths. Most of this populace would carry spears.

Generally, however, the majority of this symbolically garbed populace would be dressed in skins and sandals. These are the ones most responsive to religious and political dervishes—among the religious mercurially responsive to the hard-nosed Catholic hierarchy, Billy Graham and lesser Protestant luminaries and among the politicals to the likes of George Wallace, Lester Maddox, Theodore Bilbo, Strom Thurmond, Everett Dirksen and Huey Long (to say nothing of good old Lyndon B. Johnson and Barry Goldwater).

Here in skins, for all to see, would be the crowd that responds joyfully to all calls of a holy war against whatever is rational. Here is the crowd that not only well-tempered capitalists fear. This is the presumably democratic mass, toward whom philosophic democrats look with increasing dubiety for salvation. The doctrine of democracy no doubt made sense as a political device when it was a question of appealing against the despotic authority of unprogressive kings. Unfortunately, once the kings were overthrown, many self-hypnotized democrats began to take their doctrine about the essential right-mindedness of the populace seriously. Teach the people to read and write, they said, and they will automatically—that word again —turn to the best in literature and culture and soon lift themselves into the radiance of full humanity, with malice toward none.

This did not happen, as any demographic survey will show; most of these elements refuse to be budged from their irrational ruts, long hallowed by medicine men. It would require hundreds of thousands of psychiatrists and assistants to reorient them.

Karl Marx was a little more precise than the democrats when he found an unheeding constituency for socialist revolution in the working class, specifically factory workers. These persons, brought together under harsh conditions from field and farm, Marx saw as the battering ram of glorious socialist revolution, overthrowing the overreaching, exploiting capitalists. Yet the workers in no capitalist society behaved according to this vision, any more than people in general responded to the democratic vision. The most militant workers, indeed, banded themselves together in over-reaching trade unions, separating themselves from the bulk of workers. Neo-Marxists such as Baran-Sweezy now admit they cannot get revolutionary assistance from the production workers, who are rapidly being reduced in number by automation. Even if they were not being so reduced, however, they would on the basis of past performance show no support for socialism. In no instance has any considerable segment of the working class of any capitalist country supported socialist aspirations. There is little idealism on the working-class level.

The metaphorically skin-clad majority has no more than a confused conception of either democracy or socialism and has no interest in applying itself to get an improved conception. Prayer, imprecation and incantation remain its chief short-cut instrumentalities for dealing with reality.

It is here that opportunity beckons to the dervishes, religious and political. It is here that they find they are in business, in a position to mediate, at a price, between mass irrationality, which has its own claims, and rationality.

Transition to Capitalism

Capitalism in rising to the economic surface came into a world of many surviving historical currents. Focusing our attention on Europe, it will be noticed that most of the population was literally skin-clad and wholly illiterate as the Christian church thrust itself up in the fifth century, A.D., from the ruins of classic civilization in the Mediterranean. Whatever of civilization came into northern Europe came via the Church. Yet the feudal system, associated in time with the Church, was not born of the Church. It was simply a local secular system of boss and followers that came into being, first in Italy, with the decay of Roman imperial institutions. Feudalism, as the dominant economic-political system, is uncritically held in retrospect responsible for whatever one cares to focus attention on in this period, just as capitalism is held responsible by socialists for whatever happens today.

In the course of time the rise of cities and inter-regional trade gave birth to a growing merchant class, embryonic capitalists or bourgeoisie (city dwellers). These people differed from churchmen, lords and village vassals; they were businessmen and businesswomen. With the slow accumulation of wealth, this merchant class increasingly held the whip hand, and it finally asserted it most strongly in the successful French Revolution.

But although economic institutions were now increasingly looked upon as capitalistic rather than feudal, wages being paid for labor rather than service and protection, all the old cultural ways persisted and still flourish.

Marx, in *The Communist Manifesto*, recognized the capitalists as a new class, superior historically and functionally to peasants, vassals, lords, clergy and the like, but doomed to fall before the holy onslaught of the factory proletariat. Marx, obviously, wishfully accelerated the pace of history, and wrongly anticipated a turn that never took place. Marx's lumpish proletariat, actually, was heading nowhere beyond right where it stood. As matters now appear, it is heading toward liquidation, first split, then part pushed lower into a dismal subproletariat via automation and part pushed upward into the lower middle classes or beyond, perhaps into middle-classness. What made the capitalists superior to predecessors, although not wholly acceptable to Marx, was their greater rationality. But, as Marx saw it (correctly I believe), it was a rationality largely misplaced, wholly in the narrow service of self, to the dangerous neglect of society as a whole. Only the proletariat, oppressed under wage slavery, could in the Marxian view feel the necessity for equitable social arrangements all around. Such arrangements, as Marx thought (perhaps rightly), could be supplied only by socialism. The proletariat has obviously failed Marx and his followers just as the masses have failed the democrats. They represent lost hopes.

As any casual glance around the United States will show, the country is full of mentalities more appropriate to the old Teutonic forests, the Roman arenas and the medieval countryside than to a society of capitalist institutions. One can discard socialism completely. For verification of this view one hardly needs stray as far away as Nashoba County, Mississippi; Selma, Alabama; Cicero, Illinois; or even Bronx County, New York. One need only read speeches in *The Congressional Record*, where the free-ranging infantile Freudian id reveals itself in full baroque regalia.

The Finpolitan *World Preserve*

Any hut, any palace, the Kremlin itself is open to the *finpolitans*, who range the world in breadth and depth. These cannot, manifestly, be ordinary people. They put grand dukes comparatively into the shade.

"What we really have," said one of the Rockefellers to Morris, "is our name. That is our big asset. It opens doors and, as our money is dispersed, it is of far greater value than anything else as long as it remains a good name. Seeing that it does must be our first consideration. There is an old saying: 'Shirt sleeves to shirt sleeves in three generations.' Well, we have to avoid a third-generation anticlimax. We have to put our time and our money to work building something new."[59]

Aptly put. The Rockefellers, as any intelligent person might have suspected, do not feel they have been called upon to preside over the dissolution of the world's largest fortune. They are, like all the *finpols,* at work preserving and building something new. They have long-term projects. They intend to stay even as their public relations men, imaginatively anticipating socialist intentions, suggest they are disappearing.

As Laurance put it on another occasion, they are concerned "to see to it that the well doesn't run dry." Two of the fourth generation who have been earmarked to occupy themselves for this reason with family business affairs are Nelson's son, Rodman, and David Rockefeller, Jr.[60] "There are so many Rockefeller organizations extant that it is hard for outsiders to keep them straight."[61]

That their multi-faceted position is at times as confusing to them as it may be to outsiders is shown when Morris says elsewhere that "The Rockefellers always have their guard up against anyone who suggests that their name and wealth give them some special privilege."[62] Here, on different pages, one can have it either way: Their name alone has great weight in the world (page 36), their name confers upon them no special privilege (page 28). What is the case is that in ordinary behavior they are like anyone else, "democratic," standing in a long line to get a wedding license, eating in a college cafeteria to save pocket money or living as a common laborer in the oilfields on the first job. But when large objectives loom, the name alone opens difficult doors.[63] They appear to be Cinderellas, of lowly station one minute, up in the clouds the next.

The name, however sinister it may sound to leftists, is a primary asset of all the *finpols*—Du Ponts, Mellons, Fords, Pews, Hartfords, Rosenwalds *et al.*

Just what the cash value of the name is in each case would be difficult to determine with any preciseness. What, one may ask, would it be worth to a syndicate if converted into the designation of The Rockefeller National Bank and Trust Company, the Rockefeller Insurance Company or Rockefeller Enterprises, Inc.? Merely for the use of the name in some such enterprise the promoters would unquestionably be willing to assign a sizeable block of stock, the exact dimensions subject to negotiation. With the understanding that the Rockefellers would be associated with the management, bringing into the background their vast connections and holdings, the block of stock would be considerable apart from any contribution of capital by the Rockefellers. They need put up no money at all.

Beyond this, the name is of shadowy intangible value in a project-oriented world.

As to opening doors, indeed, the Rockefeller name is magic. (The names of all the American big-wealthy open doors all over the world.) Whenever the Rockefellers—or any of the other higher *finpols*—travel abroad, they are instantly enmeshed in the nets of upper-level governmental protocol. As key figures in American society, they instantly galvanize governmental attention.

Thus, says Kahn in the *New Yorker*, when David Rockefeller at forty-eight contemplated taking a trip to Russia, he paused to reflect; for he "had heard hints that if he should get to the USSR he would probably be invited to confer with Premier Khrushchev, and there was no telling how explosively the Communist leader might react to a confrontation, on his home ground, with a notorious international banker."[64]

Rockefeller decided to go, and in Leningrad "was told Khrushchev would like to see him the following afternoon at the Kremlin, in Moscow." There he went with his daughter Neva and for two and a half hours participated in what he later described as "the most intensive conversation I've ever had with anyone."[65] What the upshot of it all was has not been indicated, but within two years the United States had widened its trade relations with the Soviet bloc. Was there any connection?

As Kahn pointed out in the *New Yorker*, the Rockefellers cannot traipse into any country anywhere without ascertaining the political climate in advance. At the wrong time their appearance could cause riots. Thus in Ghana, to which the Rockefeller Brothers Fund had contributed a million-dollar program of developing small local industries, in 1963 they came under heavy ungrateful attack by the *Ghanaian Times* which said truculently: "Whilst the Governor of New York concentrates on changing the political climate in Washington to open up the trade in nuclear arms, the president of Chase Manhattan is mostly concerned with commodities like copper and bananas." The paper went on to charge that David was engaged in blocking the Organization of American States and the Alliance for Progress, trying to overthrow (apparently without success) the governments of Bolivia and Peru, providing Portugal and the Union of South Africa with arms, dominating the U.S. Congress with stooges and a kept press, and using the Central Intelligence Agency and the State Department as tools to supervise and protect his bank's ramified foreign investments.[66]

While all this sounded a bit far-fetched to the conventionally skeptical, the reserved *Christian Science Monitor* had earlier described Rockefeller as "a businessman who is listened to all over the world."[67] Apparently they were at least aware of this fact in Ghana.

As Kahn went on to point out, David Rockefeller travels a good deal all over the world, inspecting properties, meeting with the highest government officials—left, right or centrist.

In return, at home, David frequently entertains, in the city and at Pocantico Hills, potentates who visit the United States.

"David's always got an Emperor or Shah or some other damn person over here, and is always giving them lunches," grumbled the doughty Sidney J. Weinberg of Goldman, Sachs and Company. "If I went to all the lunches he gives for people like that, I'd never get any work done."[68]

Not only is he engaged in an interminable running series of conferences with the highest foreign movers and shakers at home and abroad but his schedule takes in without any party discrimination the highest American officials. All of this going and coming, hosting and guesting, may indeed be conducive to a more smoothly running world (and this one devoutly hopes) but it is not a line of activity familiar to ordinary mortals. This, in point of fact, is the way it is on the *finpol* circuit. This is beyond mere Big Business. This is Super-Business, where the line of demarcation between inner government and upper business is so blurred as to be indistinguishable. It isn't deals but concessions, protectorates and spheres of influence that are negotiated here.

Training for such a high-level life in the case of the Rockefellers began early. Whereas the aim of the routinely upcoming wealthy was merely to get into *The Social Register* or to marry impecunious nobility, the Rockefellers were early pointed toward much higher game: close-harmony association with the power-elite leadership of nations. *Declassé* nobility, whatever aura it carried from the past, never interested any of the Rockefellers; they always went directly for the man who was in charge *now*. He, they seemed to know through some sort of osmosis, was the fellow to know and understand, whatever his forebears or background. They aren't discriminatory; they would just as soon negotiate with an emperor as with an ex-peasant.

Thus Nelson, just out of college and just married, went on a trip around the world with his bride. He carried letters of introduction to "high officials and distinguished persons," and in India had interviews with the Viceroy, later Lord Halifax, and Mahatma Gandhi.[69] These were, to say the least, rather exalted companions for a collegian. But this was no ordinary collegian. It was a future high U.S. *finpol*.

With the possible exception of Winthrop, all the Rockefellers when they go abroad are knee-deep during their entire visit in power-wielders, power-elitists and their mentors, majordomos and public relations men. The same is true of other *finpols*, and of their representatives, the upper managers of the big corporations and banks. In the Orient John D. III is kow-towed to from teahouse to pagoda and palace.

This hobnobbing with the international bigwigs contrasts rather pointedly with Nelson's political campaigning at home, during which thousands of TV viewers have seen sweaty admirers pounding his back at Coney Island and other plebeian haunts and shouting, "Good old Rocky." There is apparently a difference of opinion between foreign leaders (including Khrushchev and the Emperor of Japan) and the American public about the precise status of the Rockefellers. Can it be that the foreign political sharks, as they muster out the palace guard and diplomats to greet them, are mistaken? My own view of them accords more with that of the foreigners. The *finpols* are ultra-bigwigs, super-megaton bigshots, Brobdingnagian commissars of affairs. In relation to them the average one-vote citizen is a muted cipher, a noiseless nullity, an impalpable phantom, a shadow in a vacuum, a sub-peasant.

Whereas at home the contact of these worthies with the *pubpols* is somewhat veiled, out of consideration for the illusions of the American booboisie, abroad the contact is more open. But for every contact with the power-brokers abroad there plainly are ten to a hundred with the domestic variety, all readily accessible by telephone. The *finpols* along with the *pubpols*, rising men of wealth, *churchpols*, *corp-pols* and top corporation lawyers, *lawpols*, are collectively engaged in running the world politico-economic system according to their own peculiar lights. Out of these ranks are drawn most appointed high government officials when such officials are not drawn from the ranks of electorally defeated *pubpols*.

Public policy is determined by this echelon in the sense that a given stated policy is either implemented or ignored. If it is ignored, like Prohibition, it is dead. Thus, in the 1950's anti-Communism was the policy publicly supported as a means of promoting a lucrative military-industrial complex, and many rank-and-file citizens gleefully joined in verbally strafing Communism and hunting out real and supposed Communists and deviant ideologists. In the 1960's, despite the escalation of the Vietnam war by President Johnson, anti-Communism was allowed to wane, as a diplomatic rapprochement gradually took place with the Soviet Union and trade relations were broadened with the Soviet bloc. The Vietnam war was waged not against Communism but against an amorphous "aggression." True, many stalwarts tried to pump life back into the anti-Communist crusade of the 1950's but they were more and more ignored by the upper financial-political echelons. These did not repudiate their former anti-Communist position, which might once again be useful; they simply abandoned it and chatted at length with Mr. Gromyko, possibly discussing The Chinese Menace. Soon, no doubt, it will be unpatriotic to eat chop suey and egg foo yung as it became unpatriotic to eat knockwurst, sauerkraut and hamburger (liberty steak) in 1917–18. And so it goes in a fabulous democracy.

So extensive are the affairs of the *finpols* that all the members of each *finpolitan* financial syndicate (*finsyn?*) require large personal staffs embracing far more than body servants. In the case of the exemplary Rockefellers, for example, "In addition to a special staff that each Rockefeller has to handle his personal affairs, the Rockefellers in mass have a general staff to handle their communal business. There are more than three hundred employees in this establishment, which includes a legal department, an investment department, a philanthropic department, a brigade of accountants, and a family archivist."[70] Many of these are people of arcane knowledge in near and remote fields, including a specialist on theological education in underdeveloped regions.

It is the general style of this *finpolitan* world that newcomers to big wealth will in time, whatever their current reservations, come to embrace through their children and grandchildren. Although the more recent Texas oil millionaires do not belong to this world, they are already getting ready for it as shown by their sprouting foundations. Once one has made the money, as old Judge Mellon recognized, it is necessary to hold on to it. And the *finpolitan* style is a way of becoming a permanent fixture, of weaving oneself into the warp and woof of the *status quo*. The *finpolitans*, it is evident, are far less concerned with today than with tomorrow.

Finpolitan Sociology

What any sociology of the *finpolitan* world would be devoted to, it seems to me, would be the outlining of point by point comparisons between the Rockefeller style and that of their contemporaries. There would be shown wherein the established big-rich copy the Rockefeller style and wherein they deviate from it. Variations of emphasis take place throughout. But, despite variations, basic similarities are visible, notably the presence of investments in huge slabs.

In one matter all the *finpolitan* groups resemble each other: None behaves as though it believed it had been called upon to preside over the dissolution of the family dukedom. All, like the man who came to dinner, act thoroughly at home and as though they intend to stay, even as mass-media propaganda trumpets that the great fortunes are being dissipated. Rather than being dissipated, they appear to be more permanently and acceptably entrenched from day to day. It is only a popular fantasy that the big fortunes are disappearing; but, perhaps like a bad dream, they disappear only in order to appear again.

Fifteen 🌿

THE DIVINE SPARK
AMONG THE RICH

Pretty much ignored by the public relations artists, who usually have more specific fish to fry, some of the American rich at least have individually performed in ways commendable from strictly critical points of view and in ways that at least occasionally draw indulgent, even maudlin, commendation from outside their class. They have by no means, contrary to leftist propaganda, all been grabbers, wastrels and self-aggrandizers. In what ways they have been brushed by the divine and semi-divine afflatus, as far as they are visible to mortal man, it is the purpose of this chapter to indicate.

Commendations of the rich are by no means rare, especially in the many media subject to their own control or influence. The task, however, is to evaluate them in the light of criteria more widely shared. Results then become somewhat modified.

The public relations fraternity argues that the founding, building up, assembling, directing and managing of any one of the large corporations or banks represent prima facie an important creative contribution to something called The American Economy, a contribution which in the aggregate is taken as comparable to the genetic labors of the Hebraic Jehovah over six prodigious days. While this may be so in some degree (the element of time to one side) there are a few obstacles to accepting this somewhat florid view—as, for example, whether the economy has been added to or subtracted from, accelerated or delayed. As far as that is concerned, many ingredients happily blended by economists into the potpourri of Gross National Product are pronounced by spoilsports as deleterious: whisky, cigarettes, gaseous industrial fumes, comic books, cheap films, ugly billboards, the traffic complex, misleading advertising, crumbling shelters, shoddy merchandise, slums and industrial wastes conscientiously dumped into natural waterways.

The public relations wizard points to corporation C and asks one to kowtow at least mentally to founder F for what is palpably a creative achievement, giving employment to X thousands of good and prayerfully parental souls of the Great Society who would, presumably, otherwise be living in trees and caves. This pretty much accords with the foolish popular view of the corporation: a job-giving, life-sustaining entity. Ordinarily left out of such considerations is the fact that corporation C in its majestic rise, by various ruses (some possibly adjudicated illegal), may have blocked the rise of other laudably life-sustaining entities. Until pressured by a slow-moving government to relinquish its absolute monopoly, Aluminum Company of America, for example, certainly stood in the way of the emergence of aluminum-making jobs now provided by Kaiser Aluminum, Reynolds Metals, Olin Mathieson and various others. Corporate managers have not always or solely been concerned about all-out production and full employment. Right now by means of automation they are eliminating jobs right and left. They have been at least occasionally interested in making money for themselves, at times by restricting production and jobs, at times by nonproductive but profitable manipulation at the top. Job creation has been quite incidental to the whole process, really has nothing to do with it.

The inimitable Beethoven, writing symphonies, did not have agents in the field impeding other symphonic writers, attempting to trip them up or cause them to write down sour notes. Like most creators he did his stuff and allowed others to do theirs. He did not hold patents on all possible combinations of musical notes, ready to direct his lawyers against other note jugglers. Much of corporate achievement, so-called, has involved sheer frustration of others, hardly creative. The sculptor, too, it is sometimes the riposte of nimble pro-corporate dialecticians here, destroys in order to create; he destroys pristine stone, reshaping its contours. But the sculptor does not destroy other sculptors! If he did he would indeed be the greatest living sculptor; but hardly on grounds of his own creativity.

The merging of companies, too, is usually hailed by the mass media as a stupendous creative act, a titanic generative copulation, which indeed it may in some cases be. It is, however, hardly creative in every single case or even in a majority of cases. What was created when a collection of existing steel companies were merged into the United States Steel Corporation by the elder J. P. Morgan other than a profitable opportunity to issue a vast quantity of watered stock? The constituent companies marched on under the triumphal arch of the new stock issue. The same is true of General Motors and many others.

While admitting there is creativity on the corporate circuit in peculiarly corporate matters (human creativity being hard to quell), I merely suggest that it should be specifically shown rather than uncritically assumed with respect to the panorama of corporations. Despite public relations puffery there are grounds to doubt there is much creativity in this quarter and instead much sedulous copying and overreaching (as shown by widespread corporate espionage), and I simply want to leave this phase out of consideration as a clear-cut social contribution. Most of what is remarkable about corporations, as I noted earlier, is specifically noncorporate, technological, and derives from science and engineering rather than the business and financial offices. What is alone generally impressive about corporations, despite the glamour of the executive washroom and the keys thereunto pertaining, is their purely engineering aspect.

It is, therefore, of some interest to notice that when corporations put themselves on display in their best party clothes at world's fairs and in conducted tours of their premises they provide, no doubt in all innocence, only an engineering display. The ordinary visitor innocently thinks, as he is innocently expected to think, "This is a marvel of Big Business. Wall Street is really great." The sophisticated observer, however, thinks, "What a marvelous exhibit of engineering skill! M.I.T. and Cal Tech are certainly great schools." To the latter observer the business side of it all is comparatively dull and uninteresting, heavy-handed and simple-minded.

In the case of the foundations the situation is much the same. Concrete contributions may indeed have been made by mobilizing funds at strategic points and times, as in the case of the Rockefeller foundations; but far from all foundations have made parallel contributions. Most have as their end financial manipulation behind a sentimental screen.

Corporations manufacture, distribute and sell lifesaving penicillin, at a profit. But no corporation discovered penicillin. Corporations never discover, invent or create anything—are never any more than tools, as often for ill as for good.

The Philosophers on Wealth and Power

While public relations virtuosi busily confect their tales to lull the broad public in its belief that everything is for the best in the best of all possible deliriously free worlds it may be of some interest to take note of the powerful cultural undertow these virtuosi, apparently unaware, are working against.

The rich, thanks in major degree to press agentry and the intellectual sinuosities of the mass media, currently appear to enjoy high status in the United States that will not diminish, presumably, as long as there is almost full general employment, the retention of which is a basic aim of national policy. As long as general employment keeps the populace moderately content, only a scattering of deviant and no doubt justly uncelebrated mentalities will be inclined to dissent from the image of the rich as public saviors and heroes. Hardly anyone except an obvious outcast or deviant presumes to venture doubts. From what quarter, if any, do these pathetic nay-sayers get their wrongheaded cues? What warrant have they for their nonadmiring and surely nonadmirable attitude? Have they indeed strayed from a nice, clean, healthy and wholesome disinfected Americanism owing to the insidious lucubrations of a tele-hypnotic, despicably fiendish Karl Marx sending aberrant messages from the documentary depths of the British Museum?

The simple fact is that the most reflective minds of western civilization, practically from inception, have looked with jaundiced eyes at the rich and the powerful. So to look is quite in harmony with the culture; to think otherwise is to step outside the intellectual boundaries of western civilization. All slick-paper public relations palaver in obeisance to the rich, indeed, is alien to the deepest currents of this civilization and represents nothing other than misbegotten ideological perversity, wrongheadedness of the nth degree.

Concededly one of the greatest minds of western civilization, teacher of Alexander the Great and still casting a broad shadow over us all, notably in his single-handed invention of logic, was Aristotle (384-322 B.C.). On the subjects of the wealthy and the powerful the great Aristotle resolutely put it into writing as follows (*Rhetoric*, Book II, Ch. 16, W. D. Ross trans.):

The type of character produced by wealth lies on the surface for all to see. Wealthy men are insolent and arrogant; their possession of wealth affects their understanding; they feel as if they had every good thing that exists; wealth becomes a sort of standard of value for everything else, and therefore they imagine there is nothing it cannot buy. They are luxurious and ostentatious; luxurious, because of the luxury in which they live and the prosperity which they display; ostentatious and vulgar, because, like other people's, their minds are regularly occupied with the object of their love and admiration, and also because they think that other people's idea of happiness is the same as their own. It is indeed quite natural that they should be affected thus; for if you have money, there are always plenty of people who come begging from you. Hence the saying of Simonides about wise men and rich men, in answer to Hiero's wife, who asked him whether it was better to grow rich or wise. "Why, rich," he said; "for I see the wise men spending their days at the rich men's doors." Rich men also consider themselves worthy to hold public office; for they consider they already have the things that give a claim to office. In a word, the type of character produced by wealth is that of a prosperous fool.

There is indeed one difference between the type of the newly-enriched and those who have long been rich: the newly enriched have all the bad qualities mentioned in an exaggerated and worse form—to be newly-enriched means, so to speak, *no education in riches.* The wrongs they do others are not meant to injure their victims, but spring from insolence or self-indulgence, e.g., those that end in assault or in adultery.

As to Power: here too it may fairly be said that the type of character it produces is mostly obvious enough. Some elements in this type it shares with the wealthy type, others are better. Those in power are more ambitious and more manly in character than the wealthy, because they aspire to do the great deeds that their power permits them to do. Responsibility makes them more serious: they have to keep paying attention to the duties their position involves. They are dignified rather than arrogant, for the respect in which they are held inspires them with dignity and therefore with moderation—dignity being a mild and becoming form of arrogance. If they wrong others, they wrong them not on a small but on a great scale.

Good fortune in certain of its branches produces the types of character belonging to the conditions just described, since these conditions are in fact more or less the kinds of good fortune that are regarded as most important. It may be added that good fortune leads us to gain all we can in the way of family happiness and bodily advantages. It does indeed make men more supercilious and more reckless; but there is one excellent quality that goes with it—piety, and respect for the divine power, in which they believe because of events which are really the result of chance.

This account of the types of character that correspond to differences of age or fortune may end here; for to arrive at the opposite types to those described, namely, those of the poor, the unfortunate, and the powerless, we have only to ask what the opposite qualities are.

Nor is the earnest inquirer given a less severe view if he turns to Plato, the other great cultural legislator whose shadow is imbedded integrally in western civilization. All European philosophy, said Alfred North Whitehead (no radical), is but a footnote to Plato. The "divine Plato" took an extremely dim view of wealthy people and personal wealth. Dipping into the excellent Hamilton-Cairns one-volume edition published by the Bollingen Foundation, a Paul Mellon enterprise, we find the following nuggets:

"So, when wealth is honored in a state, and the wealthy, virtue and the good are less honored. . . . Thus, finally from being lovers of victory and lovers of honor they become lovers of gain getting and of money, and they commend and admire the rich man and put him in office but despise the man who is poor." (*Republic*, 8.551b.)

As to democracy, "the insatiate lust for wealth and the neglect of everything else for the sake of money-making were the cause of its undoing." (*Ibid.*, 8.562b.)

The arts and crafts are corrupted by the co-presence of great wealth and poverty. (*Ibid.*, 4.421d.)

"Wealth and poverty" should be kept out of the good society "since the one brings luxury, idleness, and innovation, and the other illiberality and the evil of bad workmanship. . . ." (*Ibid.*, 4.422a.)

Those most successful in the pursuit of wealth become the targets of the drones, become "the pastures of the drones." (*Ibid.*, 8.564e.)

". . . it is the evil life commonly led by the sons of autocrats and men of extraordinary wealth. Such a training will never, never lead to outstanding goodness in boy, or man, or graybeard." (*Laws*, 3.695e.)

"But to be at once exceedingly wealthy and good is impossible, if we mean by the wealthy those who are accounted so by the vulgar, that is, the exceptional few who own property of great pecuniary value—the very thing a bad man would be likely to own. Now since this is so, I can never concede to them that a rich man is truly happy unless he is also a good man, but that one who is exceptionally good should be exceptionally wealthy too is a mere impossibility." (*Ibid.*, 5.742e.)

"One arises from the passion for wealth which leaves a man not a moment of leisure to attend to anything beyond his personal fortunes. So long as a citizen's whole soul is wrapped up in these, he cannot give a thought to anything but the day's takings. Any study or pursuit which tends to that result everyone sets himself eagerly to learn and practice; all others are laughed to scorn. Here, then, we may say, is one reason in particular why society declines to take this or any other wholly admirable pursuit seriously, though everyone in it is ready enough, in his furious thirst for gold and silver, to stoop to any trade and any shift, honorable or dishonorable, which holds out a prospect of wealth, ready to scruple at no act whatsoever—innocent, sinful, or utterly shameful—so long as it promises to sate him, like some brute beast, with a perfect glut of eating, drinking, and sexual sport." (*Ibid.*, 8.831c,d.)

A soul stung to savagery by unsatisfied lusts "is chiefly found concerned with that on which most men's longing is most permanently and sharply set—wealth, with the power wealth gets alike from native bias and pernicious wrong education to breed countless cravings for insatiate and unbounded possession of itself. And the source of this perverse education is the credit given to false praise of riches alike by Greek and non-Greek; they promote wealth to the first place among good things, whereas in truth it holds but the third, and thus they deprive not only themselves but their posterity." (*Ibid.*, 9.870a.)

Plato has a great deal more to say about the wealthy, most of it disparaging. His remarks, indeed, foreshadow the Aristotelian position that the best society is one dominated by a middle class of the moderately affluent, with neither extremely rich nor extremely poor. In both the Platonic and Aristotelian perspectives the United States is a monstrously lopsided entity, a veritable Gorgon, a chamber of horrors.

What is perhaps of paramount interest is that no subsequent major thinker has departed essentially from the script as laid down by these giant pundits. It may be that thinkers in following Plato and Aristotle here merely felt rivalrous toward those with a claim to power other than intellectual, as Plato indeed unquestionably felt rivalrous toward the poets. Yet intellectuals in general have not felt so uniformly against nonintellectual power rivals like soldiers, politicians, explorers, religious leaders or artists as they have against the rich, a feeling that by no means reached its apogee, as commonly supposed, in the writings of Karl Marx.

Marx has clearly been topped in the writings of Jean-Paul Sartre, the stylish French metaphysician, who refers to the wealthy and the respectable in general as *salauds* (filthy beasts) because he believes they have it in their power to produce alterations for the better but instead work assiduously to perpetuate ancient swindles while professing humane goals.

Sartre, like Aristotle and Plato, is rather remote from most Americans. Nearer home, a recent expression of the attitude, deeply etched into American radical and dissenting literature, can be sampled in the summary by the Marxist, Herbert Aptheker, of the non-Marxist C. Wright Mills's *The Power Elite* as "filled also with burning attacks—as passionate but not as muted as that of his mentor Veblen—upon the social and personal immorality of the rich, their coarseness, cruelty, hypocrisy, greed, and lustfulness."[1]

One could, it is true, assemble examples of the rich from the American scene who apparently fit different items of these characterizations. But, straying outside the circle of the rich, one could unquestionably find proportionately as many cases for each count in the indictment at all except the most refined levels of society. And seeking examples of virtuosic cruelty, one would find it impossible to discover any rival among the American rich to such a Marxist redeemer as Josef Stalin, to say nothing of Lavrenti Beria and a swarm of power-crazed leftist midgets from the lower depths. "Practical" Marxists like Dr. Aptheker, while launching their shafts of criticism, seem blissfully unaware of what their own affiliations and loyalties commit them to defend.

The Aptheker-Mills indictment of "the rich," as formulated above, is clearly far too broad and obviously loaded. It reveals and perhaps prescribes an attitude rather than describes.

But if one turns to the influential Alexander Hamilton among the Founding Fathers, one finds, contrary to Plato, Aristotle and almost every other considerable political thinker in western history, that government should belong to "the wealthy, the good and the wise." As to the last two, Plato and Aristotle would have agreed; as to the first, we know what they thought.

Social thinkers down through the centuries have all had favorite classes, which they took to be the instruments of deliverance. With Plato it was the intellectuals, with Aristotle the middle classes, with Jefferson the small farmers, with Marx the factory workers, with Hamilton the wealthy and so on. In this boxing of the class compass, one contemporary writer, Nelson Algren, has oddly found his favorite social group among what Marx called the *lumpenproletariat*—thieves, pimps, prostitutes and down-and-outers.

But, in his admiration of the wealthy, Hamilton, political father of the American plutocracy, virtually represented an historical minority of one among political thinkers.

The Problematic Rich

Who, in the first place, are "the rich"?

Included in the designation are trust-fund infants who at the moment of birth are incalculably rich (and presumably no more offensive than any other infants), trust-fund children of various ages, women young and old of mixed capabilities and outlooks and men ranging from inane idlers and wastrels through routine performers to the intensely but not always laudably active. Whatever else one can say about *most* of the rich, one cannot reasonably say they are especially coarse, cruel, greedy or more than commonly hypocritical or lustful. Money in a special place of high honor to one side, a person of ordinary sensibilities would much prefer to associate with many, perhaps most of them, than with the average run-of-the-mill politician, labor leader, advertising impresario or gospel-monger.

What Mills focused his attention on was the active rich, particularly the policy setters, and among these one could not deny the presence of the immoral (tax manipulators, for example), the coarse, the cruel, the hypocritical, the greedy and the lustful; but even among these, that *all* or most are of the order indicated can be easily shown to be fictional.

What is problematic about the rich is more as follows: The possession of wealth, inherited or acquired, itself informs the possessor that he is special, that he holds winning cards over most people in most social situations. He can, for one thing, finance a greater number of amorous episodes—a big advantage in the estimation of the simple-minded. He holds a social advantage over most others which, unluckily for him, may so turn his head as to give him delusions of inherent superiority, as is often the case in the possession of anything rare and desired. One hugs one's advantages—health, strength, intelligence, learning or wealth—and tends to take them as marks of invidious excellence: snobbism. In some rich families, the Rockefeller notably, the children are carefully reared in as middle class a way as possible to prevent their developing such common delusions; yet the fact cannot be concealed for long that they are special, that they hold a fistful of aces in worldly goods, and that others surely define them as different. They are different; they are rich—in effect, noble—in a society replete with poverty and degradation. Their wealth makes it possible for them to mobilize more effective power than most people at particular points, at times to their own undoing. Money is like a spirited horse in at least this respect: One must know how to ride it, which few really do.

Like anyone else, the rich person may experience frustrations and a sense of being unduly limited; but he does not usually feel it in as many ways nor as frequently or humiliatingly as the nonrich. He feels that he has, in general, more elbow room, a wider range of choice. And he has indeed more elbow room, geographic and psychological.

As to the active policy-making rich and their agents of the power elite (for these latter are mostly agents): Like nearly all people they are usually heedless of whatever is not before their eyes, either lack sufficient imagination (like reckless motorists) or have their attention fully absorbed (like nearly everyone else) by their personal problems and projects. The doers of the world all have projects, and one is either a doer or nondoer. And doers all derive an intense feeling of satisfaction from any project carried to success, whether it consists of writing a book, leading a revolution, creating or managing a corporation or winning an election. Absorption in one's own project, whether it is building a corporation or writing a poem, leaves one unable to play one's attention over other aspects of reality. Probably the greatest harm in the world comes of the simple fact that nobody is able to pay full attention to everything at once. One really should, yet it is impossible. Although this is so, it does not follow that attention cannot be focused on a wider horizon than immediate, specialized interests—a marked tendency of the rising rich at least. The basic offense of most of the active rich, if it is an offense, is that they usually pursue their own visions, skillfully or crudely, not only to the neglect of the rest of the world (as does the poet) but, at times, because they have power, against or indifferent to the needs and wishes of the rest of the world. Not only do they have power but, like most people, they are thoroughly egocentric.

Although now woven by means of large enterprises into the warp and woof of all society, the rich, like nearly everyone else, put their own enterprises first in the narrowly reasonable effort to preserve their social advantage, by means fair or seemingly questionable. Without that social advantage they would, like the common people, be at the beck and call of almost any self-appointed messiah presenting himself as the latest in the line of the Apostolic Succession or, perhaps, a spiritual representative of a freely prescribing Karl Marx or even, like Adolf Hitler, as the offspring of Wotan. Being rich is basically defensive in a rough world, although the defensive position has its own hazards.

What is perhaps most irksome about the rich to the intelligent nonrich, particularly to those with some other vision of how society should be arranged, is not actually what any rich individual may or may not do. True, by behaving outwardly like a gentleman the rich man may temper animosity; but he cannot, even by gentlemanly behavior, mollify persons like Plato, Aristotle, Marx, Sartre and others acutely aware of his necessary role, which is much like that of a character in a Greek drama enacting the capricious will of the gods.

The rich, the plain fact is, confront the rest of society as a solid, semicorporate phalanx, buttressed by law and public policy. By law they hold their positions legitimately and hence can feel complete rectitude. When the national anthem is being sung they can feel it is being sung in celebration of the legal system that supports them, for the aggrandizement of which every man, the poorer especially, may be called upon to offer his very life simply by presidential order, without any declaration of war by Congress. Beyond this, existing policies under the law favor them; they have been adopted largely by their agents with their corporate permission.

The existence of this solid phalanx is sharply noticeable only to those who have some proposal to make with a view to adjusting policy in order to accommodate some large number of people who are, in one way or the other, supposedly being unduly inconvenienced by any number of things. Whenever any public proposal is made for any change (however slight), it is bound to encounter opposition. Upon inquiry it turns out that the opposition ordinarily stems from one or more affluent or rich people, usually referred to euphemistically as Interests. While there are indeed many interests in a society, the most assertive is surely the property interest.

Even a case about a trivial question, adversely affecting only one propertied person, may have wide implications for many or all propertied because it may set a precedent upon which further more extensive similar actions may be taken. The entire phalanx of the propertied becomes agitated and makes its displeasure known to legislators, judges and other officials. After all, one cannot have unsound decisions approved. Again, the entire phalanx of the propertied may be committed by simply one among the propertied, who presses deviously for and obtains some tax concession. This concession thereafter applies to all, whether they asked for it or not.

Thus it happens that even minor, purely common-sense proposals for reforms often precipitate fierce political dogfights.

In a relevant case, early in 1966 C. Wright Patman, the powerful chairman of the powerful House Banking and Currency Committee, decided on the basis of a committee vote to investigate the entire question of how trust funds are used in corporate and bank control. When *subpoenas* began to go out to banks requesting information there was suddenly called on June 7 a meeting by 17 of 33 committee members, who required the recall of many *subpoenas*; on a showdown, however, the right of the chairman to issue *subpoenas* was upheld.

This checking of a committee chairman was a very unusual action, which obviously had its source in some of the entities being investigated. Not many citizens, it is true, are alert to this situation or probably care very much.

What the final outcome of the investigation will be, whether it will be muted or not, is not yet known. Whether light will be thrown on what Chairman Patman claims are some $215 billion of trust fund holdings one cannot yet tell; all this is *terra incognita* right now.

By the end of the year, at any rate, Chairman Patman on the basis of *subpoenas* already returned was able to announce that three-quarters of the banks of the country had at least 5 per cent of their stock held by other banks through trust funds managed for beneficiaries and that this percentage of stock ownership represented a long step toward control. The very largest banks, he said, operated under this sort of interlocking ownership, were all more or less in the same ownership bed—one big happy incestuous family.[2]

The information needed in this area is as follows: identifications of trust-fund holdings, book values and current market values, nature of trusts and length of time they run, beneficiaries of a multiplicity of trusts (reducing income taxes), cost of operation of trusts, validity of investment selections for trusts, etc. Whether the named beneficiaries or the managers benefit most is an undetermined question.

The propertied, for one thing, are mostly especially sensitive to anything about taxes—how much shall be the total levy and, more important, how shall the collection be proportioned? In general, the propertied interest in the United States, sheltered behind technician-spokesmen, has been opposed (whatever some individual property owners felt) to government levies for the sake of the domestic comfort, convenience and necessity of the broad public (its own comfort and convenience being apparently assured) but has been generously unstinting in any military or semi-military expenditures that gave government a strong argument abroad in assuring access to markets, raw materials and trade routes. At present, with military and space exploration budgets inflated to record proportions, the cities internally are literally falling apart. It has been estimated by insiders that 75 per cent of the military budget is rationally unjustifiable.

Beyond the desire to keep down tax totals (hence the fiscally sound objection to "reckless government spending") there is the collective desire of the propertied to shove a disproportionate part of the tax burden over onto the lower labor force which, imbued with patriotic ardor, is presumably happy to support a democratic paradise that freely allows them to go and listen to happy tidings of the afterworld from the likes of Billy Graham and Fulton J. Sheen and to rub elbows with the rich at Coney Island. As we have already seen how deftly this tax burden is shouldered onto the pious, patriotic and not-too-bright lower labor force, the point need engage our fascinated interest no longer.

Whatever the call may be for social adjustment will either cost tax money or intrude more or less adversely on some propertied interest—that is, upon the revenues of some collection of rich persons. More public housing will tread on the toes of private landlords. And as this call for adjustment is fought by the "interests," some proponents are irked. The purely common-sense proposal, for example, to place effective health warnings on cigarette packages was fought to a standstill and defeated in Congress, with the result that the tobacco industry through intensified advertising is selling more cigarettes than ever before in the teeth of repeated formal government findings that they are a clear menace to health. Similarly there was fought tooth and nail suggested mandatory automobile safety equipment and there have been fights in the state legislatures against attempts to limit in any way the free resale of unroadworthy second-hand cars. One could cite thousands of similar cases.

To be sure, when it is said that an "industry" opposes something, the source of the opposition is kept sufficiently abstract and remote. An industry is not something subject to sense experience. One cannot see it or feel it. "Industry" here boils down to no more than several boards of directors —perhaps fifty to a hundred men—who represent stockholders, mainly large stockholders—in brief, rich people. These latter are, somewhat poetically, as adversely affected by automobile air pollution as the poor although they can resort to air conditioning or retreat to remote fresh-air estates and ranches.

It is this consistent opposition to proposals for reasonable as well as unreasonable change that the propertied have offered down through history, opposition more effective than argument, that has caused the rich to be looked upon as problematic ever since Plato. It is not that they are necessarily vicious, as the Marxists often postulate; it is just that they are blandly or uncomprehendingly selfish, and not always very intelligently. The unpropertied person may be just as selfish but he has no telltale instrument such as property with which to reveal his selfishness so completely.

Like the small band of Greeks in the pass at Thermopylae the selfish rich hold back by their skill of maneuver in an entrenched position (always in the name of sound policy) huge disorganized armies of *sansculottes* and *descamisados* (among which, thoughtfully, they have their own friends haranguing on all manner of irrelevancies dear to the same *sansculottes* and *descamisados*). It is all much like a disciplined Roman legion against a barbarian rabble.

Because virtually everything has an economic aspect and because the rich, as we have seen, own and control the foundation and prime stages of the economic system, practically anything that anyone is likely to propose in the way of a new arrangement is going to strike some among the propertied and the rich adversely, and hence lead them to invoke the law defensively or work for a new self-serving public ordinance. Often the mere attempt to reroute traffic by local ordinance causes merchants to spring into tigerish opposition, presumably in defense of property rights.

Again, many individuals who engage in entrepreneurial action, hoping to become rich, find that the way is barred by persons, propertied or rich, already in established positions. As Henry J. Kaiser discovered, there is no room for another automobile manufacturer. True, there are interstices into which newcomers may insert themselves with success, particularly the area of new technology but, in the main, the road is blocked to all except the very clever—and lucky—among newcomers.

The rich, then, come to seem to those who have encountered their resistance like part of a single corporate entity, a special class, or, as the

Marxists say, *a class interest*. Because they are each part of this class interest, embalmed like a fly in plastic, there is not much they can do to earn credit in the eyes of critics. Owing to the saying of Jesus in *Matthew*, XIX, 24, that "It is easier for a camel to go through the eye of a needle, than for a rich man to enter into the kingdom of God," there was no way out for a rich man for hundreds of years except to give his property to the church. The result was that in the late medieval period the *churchpols* in the name of the church held tightly more than half the land of Europe; the latecoming kings were far less gullible than the earlier gentry. In the eyes of the Marxists there is nothing a rich man can do except, like Frederick Engels, devote his wealth to the promotion of Marxism; anything less will fail to gain credit. The rich could, to be sure, turn all their wealth over to the government where it would at the present time fall under the benign jurisdiction of Lyndon B. Johnson, in which circumstances few judicious moralists would see any particular gain for mankind.

Castigation of the rich, however, arises less from envy, as commonly supposed, than from people who have in some way been blocked or frustrated by the massed *class interest* of the rich. The rich man may be a really nice guy; but his very interests, indeed his whole being, force him to present himself in a certain stylized way. Most of the critics of the rich have themselves been power claimants, who know the rich and powerful can readily trump their cards. Plato, Aristotle and a long line of independent intellectuals have known that their carefully reasoned arguments are subject to political defeat less by sound counter-arguments than by the power of inertia, money and entrenched position. As any practical politician knows, in going before Congress on any question it is better to be backed by lucre than by a bullet-proof argument. Money will win almost every time on crucial questions, such as intruding from afar into World War I, and the only way apparently to defeat it is by some other brute power. Hence, as the Marxists say, revolution. The proffered cure here, though, except in cases of complete war-induced social collapse as in Russia in 1917 and China in the 1940's, is clearly worse than the disease because serviceable institutional restraints are swept away in the uproar and a clean slate is open to an unrestrained set of new power seekers, not at all squeamish (as history has shown) about how they apply their power. Leninist Communism is clearly a modern receivership in political bankruptcy.

Where those counts in the Aptheker indictment are best sustained is with respect to certain uneducated men of the poorer classes who have by hook or crook made themselves rich: the original grabbers. In this country these are the "Robber Barons" of the nineteenth century and later replicas. The record on these is by now fairly well known. While many of the established rich, normally lacking imagination and perhaps sufficient sapience, have been normally heedless, the clear-cut depredations of the rich have in most cases been carried out by founders, newcomers, in panicky flight from poverty. It is the ex-poor among the rich who have been the most active social offenders. This was the crowd Veblen largely wrote about in all their vulgarity.

All of which is not to say that there is nothing of an overbearingly objectionable nature about the general policies since World War II contrived by Mills's insidiously bland power elite on behalf of remote principals. Those policies have been, on the whole, immediately self-serving, broadly neglectful of visible internal social decay and in that sense actually inimical over the long term to basic upper-class interests. What there really is to the idea of a power elite consists of people—upper-crust lawyers, politicians, officials, journalists, public relations men and idea men—who in various ways recommend themselves to the rich and well positioned by formulating defensive stopgaps for immediate problems. A way to remunerative position in the United States is to get the nod from some one of the wealthy or their adjutants, and those who get this nod are invariably from lower levels of society, usually chimpanzee-bright men who have developed know-how and can-do for poulticing over difficult situations in the interests of established arrangements. This is the level where "urban renewal" and roadbuilding become new ways of generating windfall profits. Nobody, it is pertinent to notice, gets the nod who is in any way seriously opposed to the established order. Indeed, nobody gets the nod who is merely reflectively doubtful and hesitant. Such persons would only generate dissension or uncertainty in high places and impede a smooth-smooth administrative operation.

As nobody to my knowledge has attempted to pinpoint collectively the possibly laudable achievements of rich people, quite apart from their class interests, I here set myself this heretical task with a view both to rounding out the picture and to seeing concretely just what the achievements may amount to. How undeniably constructive and creative have the wealthy, more particularly the American wealthy, really been?

The Sacred Group

In seeking to isolate the achievements of the wealthy, it seems desirable to indicate the broad area within which one looks. Who, shall we say, are the wealthy?

Fortunately the Federal Reserve Board and Census Bureau, as noticed earlier, have come up with recent figures, the most precise on official record, to the effect that there were an estimated 200,000 nuclear families averaging three persons in the country as of December 31, 1962, in possession of net assets of $500,000 or more.[3] So, for these purposes, we shall take this last as the maximum figure representing a proto-wealthy family, although a person worth a few thousands less could hardly be considered impoverished. Naturally, the indicated small group includes everybody in possession of up to a heady billion dollars by value and beyond.

But even a group of this reduced size is cumbersome to inquire into and includes more than the definitively wealthy. This group of 200,000 nuclear families can be narrowed down somewhat, however. *U.S. News and World Report*, October 11, 1965, estimated on the basis of more recent Treasury figures that: "Today there are about 90,000 millionaires," by which it alluded to persons owning assets worth at least $1 million.[4] Some of these were in extended family clusters, and some families as we know (Du Ponts, Fords, Rockefellers, Vanderbilts *et al.*) contain many millionaires and millionaire nuclear families. Total holdings of the group were estimated in excess of $250 billion. As of 1948, the millionaire group totaled only 13,000 by the reckoning of this same source.

U.S. News pointed out that this 90,000 indicated that one family in every 625 was in the millionaire class, which meant approximately 1/6 of 1 per cent of families, a fraction of a sliver, had net assets of at least $1 million.

The sevenfold variation in number of millionaires between 1948 and 1965 stemmed from the fact that most wealth-holders concentrate their holdings in corporation stocks; and in 1948 stock prices were comparatively low, in 1964 and 1965 they were comparatively high. It does not indicate that new asset-nuclei were formed to this extent. Judging by the composition of estates in 1961, Treasury figures showed (as *U.S. News and World Report* acknowledged), that upper-class wealth was held as follows on the average: Stocks, 65.1 per cent; tax-exempt bonds, 8.5 per cent; real estate, 6.7 per cent; cash, 4.3 per cent; U. S. government bonds, 4.2 per cent; mortgages and notes, 1.8 per cent; insurance, 1.8 per cent; other bonds, .8 per cent; and miscellaneous, 6.8 per cent. Such being the case, any appreciable rise and fall of the stock market will alternately see-saw many suddenly up into the millionaire class or ease them down. The 1948 figure, in my view, is more indicative of the really heavy money than a 1965 figure. Better yet would be a 1932 figure.[5] As to the formation of new asset-nuclei, this is a far rarer occurrence than is regularly suggested in *Time*, *Fortune* and the *Wall Street Journal*.

As far as the achievements of the really wealthy are concerned, then, we may limit ourselves to looking within a contemporary group of very few families.

Not only will contemporary names be drawn from this property bracket but, at times, a retrospective view will be taken of individual achievers, always leaving out of consideration, for reasons stated, business organizers and managers as such. In order to read of their corporate deeds of derring-do one need merely turn to the pages of *Fortune*, which publishes a continual celebration of how well men run their own plantations.

Excluded will be any who have *entered* the indicated property bracket through achievements in the world of entertainment, sports and the arts— popular playwrights, actors, athletes, opera singers and virtuoso musicians. Those of whom note will be taken will be only those known to be in, around or about this property class *prior* to their achievement, not those who got into it through recognizable achievement. A financially successful once poor inventor would not be included.

Standards of Achievement

Anything that passes by worldly standards as achievement other than ambiguous corporate success will be counted as such. The operative phrase here is "by worldly standards," for much not applauded by the world as an achievement represents a great purely personal achievement as in the case of many persons, rich or poor, who daily force themselves up from a bed of pain and painfully perform daily duties or anyone, rich or poor, who becomes fairly civilized, a lamentably rare occurrence.

The commonly recognized areas of formal achievement, apart from business (which appears to rate high in popular esteem), are politics, law, the performing and creative arts, the sciences, scholarship, medicine, philosophy, religion, education, engineering, entertainment in the broadest sense, sports and journalism. In considering a sub-division of possibly 90,000 individuals and families we have considerable leeway, a large group to deal with although only a sliver of the population. But this, at least, is the area within which to look.

Psychologists generally consider 1/2 of 1 per cent of the population to be "gifted" in some way so that if the same ratio were preserved among 200,000 families owning $500,000 or more of property there would be at least 2,000 (two adults) "gifted" upper wealth-holders. Because not all the "gifted" bring their gifts to fruition there would not necessarily be this many outstanding achievers in the group; but there should be on the basis of the general distribution at least 500. Available data, however, do not enable one to assemble such a total, so that outstanding achievers are either proportionately fewer in the heavily propertied group, are somehow concealed from external view or are unpublicized. Yet it is in the nature of outstanding achievement sooner or later to call attention to itself.

It would be possible to identify all wealthy individuals only if one were provided with statements of net worth, which are not available; there are, however, indications in many cases, as already noticed. Achievement itself is notable and focuses public attention on the achiever and his background in an age of excessive publicity. As far as the very rich are concerned, we know pretty well who they are and can inspect them directly.

But I shall not, owing to the absence of precise data, be able to spot all, or nearly all, especially down near the lower levels of wealth-holding. There may be a wealthy man of considerable achievement, but if it is not shown on the record that his family has a certain net worth I cannot name him, much as I would like to. However, in the interests of an increase in knowledge, this is a game that others, privy to facts inaccessible to me, can play by supplementing my report. For, owing to the inattention of sociologists, we do not know with any precision the record of personal achievement or nonachievement of all large and largish property holders. The evidence only becomes clear as we ascend into the rarefied realm of the known very large property holders, the super rich.

Area of Greatest Impact

It is not, first, usually thought possible for a man of wealth to be any sort of achiever. "Inherited wealth is a big handicap to happiness," said William K. Vanderbilt in a press interview in 1905. "It is as certain death to ambition as cocaine is to morality."[6] As to the attainment of wealth through personal achievement, a universally spread view is summarized in an old Chinese proverb: "A man seldom gets rich without ill-got gain; as a horse does not fatten without feeding in the night."[7]

Yet the handicap indicated by Vanderbilt is sometimes overcome.

As the record shows, law combined with politics has been the area of greatest impact of propertied activists apart from corporate management. Not that legal practice as such, which in general is not extravagantly rewarded, has attracted big propertied people to any conspicuous extent. The rigors of either advocacy or jurisconsultation appear to have had few attractions for the wealthy, although the acquisition of a law degree and admission to the bar I take to be concrete achievements, whatever further steps are necessary to attaining distinction as a lawyer.

In general, lawyers from heavily propertied families do not enter into general legal practice, civil or criminal. Some members of lower wealth-holding lawyers do go into the practice of corporate law. As such they are, in general, necessarily defenders of the propertied position. Non-Establishment lawyers are, in general, defending criminal lawyers and plaintiffs' lawyers in civil actions, apart from a few affiliated with nonconformist causes such as constitutional rights. The Establishment, so-called, is usually interested either in prosecuting someone, rarely a member of the Establishment itself, or in defending some part of itself against not always valid individual claims.

While there may be lawyers from wealthy families who are non-Establishment practitioners, such a fact does not clearly show on the record.

In politics some of the more prominent of wealthy lawyers have been Franklin D. Roosevelt, Adlai Stevenson and members of the Taft family beginning with William Howard Taft, one-time president of the United States. The Tafts, in addition to law, have notably operated in real estate.

William Howard Taft became chief justice of the Supreme Court but he is one of the very few among latter-day big wealth-holders who have held a judgeship. Taft, of course, was a thoroughgoing Establishment judge. A less well-known but highly distinguished judge was Curtis Bok of the Supreme Court of Pennsylvania, who died in 1962. A grandson of Cyrus H. K. Curtis, the mass publisher, and Edward M. Bok, Curtis Bok was also a gifted and sensitive author who wrote *Star Wormwood, The Backbone of the Herring* and *I, Too, Nicodemus,* all worth reading. Over a long period of years he was an exceptionally fine public servant. There was, too, Judge Thomas Mellon, the founder.

Judges are quite rare, though, among families of notable wealth. One draws a comparative blank among the big-wealthy on judges although one would unquestionably find a few among some of more modest fortune if the data were available. Judges, of course, are often men of some modest property, acquired through the practice of law, inheritance or marriage except for those few who have made financial killings as members of political syndicates.

Wealthy men directly in politics are no special novelty in American history. George Washington, the first president, was considered perhaps the wealthiest man of his time in the country, an inheritor. Many of the nation's founders, relative to their time, were quite wealthy, including Thomas Jefferson—at least until his final years. They were nearly all men of property, usually landed, a fact pointedly reflected in the Constitution. But even on a relative scale their wealth did not attain the proportions of the latter-day industrial fortunes.

After the Civil War there were many, usually self-erected, former poor men, who sat in the United States Senate, there closely guiding their interests in railroads, oil, mining and lumbering; but that these held their seats in consequence of any political achievement or aptitude is open to serious question. Prior to 1913 senators were elected by state legislatures, many of which, staffed by dung-hill democrats, awarded Senate seats simply to the highest bidder. It did not take much in the way of political know-how to sit in "The Rich Man's Club," as the Senate was commonly called.

I will not, then, count any of the pre-1913 rich senators as political achievers simply on the ground of their presence in the Senate.

Although rich and budding rich men were always shuttling about in the shadowy background of both political parties, supplying "campaign funds" and pulling devious strings right and left, they were in the more recent period brought forward and given more direct participation by the Republican Warren G. Harding. A former senator, President Harding was a small-town newspaper publisher of no great wealth. However, he appointed as his secretary of the treasury Andrew W. Mellon, then one of the richest men in the world—an inheritor as well as acquisitor; self-created Herbert C. Hoover as his secretary of commerce; the corporation lawyer Charles Evans Hughes as his secretary of state; and Albert B. Fall, stooge of the oil industry, his secretary of interior. Since Theodore Roosevelt it had become pretty much the custom to install corporation lawyers as secretary of state and attorney general.

Franklin D. Roosevelt, a minor millionaire himself before becoming a popular tribune, went much further in this respect than either Harding or Hoover, who appointed multi-millionaire Ogden L. Mills to succeed Mellon. Roosevelt, believing that men of wealth and good schooling should serve in government rather than lounge about in their clubs, practically stacked his cabinets with men of wealth, while standpatters, reactionaries and presumed malefactors of great wealth shrieked that he was a Communist and a "traitor to his class," here validating in action a Marxist conception of class consciousness among the rich. He started off with William H. Woodin, head of the American Car and Foundry Company, as secretary of the treasury and replaced him with multi-millionaire Henry Morgenthau, Jr. When the world situation became gravely serious in 1940 he appointed Frank Knox, Republican newspaper tycoon, as secretary of the navy and later James V. Forrestal, partner of Dillon, Read and Company, Wall Street investment bankers. He appointed Edward Stettinius, Jr., son of a Morgan partner, secretary of state. He brought back the able Henry L. Stimson, Republican corporation lawyer and Hoover's secretary of state, as secretary of war. He made Jesse Jones, self-erected Texas Democratic big-league banker-politician, secretary of commerce and Francis Biddle attorney general. Down through the upper ranks of officialdom he drew freely upon men of great wealth, making Nelson A. Rockefeller the Coordinator of Inter-American Affairs; W. Averell Harriman, former partner of Brown Brothers Harriman & Co., his representative from the beginning in a variety of posts, mainly diplomatic; Joseph P. Kennedy head of the Securities and Exchange Commission, and so on. He gave both Harriman and Rockefeller their political starts.

Roosevelt, it is true, made many appointments from other quarters and, in fact, assembled a mixed bag. But, far from stacking his appointments with radicals or liberals, as recklessly charged, a far stronger case could be made that he drew most of his appointees from Wall Street, Newport, the corporate circuit and the big-city political machines. Scholarly liberals and radicals were brought in mainly as ideological window dressing in a time of great public discontent. Henry Wallace, considered a far-out radical in the bayou country, was himself a very wealthy man, at most a liberal conservative.

If results are what count, Roosevelt was not hostile to the private-property business system, which he found in self-induced crisis and left some years later revived and reinforced with government support. Remove Rooseveltian government economic subsidy, patronage, guarantee and support today, and the much-vaunted free-enterprise system, beloved of Chamber of Commerce orators, would collapse like a bullet-riddled toy balloon. How many depositors would trust the banks, for a simple example, if it were not for government insurance of deposits? How many would trust the one-time wide-open Stock Exchange if it were not for the SEC?

The fact that the rich were in politics, then, was nothing new. What is new is that, more recently, taking their cue from Roosevelt, the latter-day rich have increasingly taken a *direct* part, with some of them at least showing signs of becoming forthright public men. They have themselves stood for election, and have been elected, a favorable development from the point of view that those who own the country should take responsibility openly for running it rather than hiding behind stooges in Uncle Sam and Abraham Lincoln suits.

Very rich men, inheritors or corporate wizards, have taken to winning elections right and left despite ingrown Populist prejudices. The electorate appears to be growing tired of the old-time "friend of the people," shaggy with folksy duplicity and athirst for franchises or whatever else he can lay furtive patriotic hands on. Winning an election, I take it, may be counted an achievement whereas winning friendly appointment is not particularly. For the latter all one needs is the nod from some Mr. Big.

By his untypical election as governor of New York in 1928 Franklin D.

Roosevelt apparently led wealthy men to believe they too could be elected to that key office, although, as we have noticed, Theodore Roosevelt, Taft and Hoover were, earlier, in the wealthy class. Franklin Roosevelt was succeeded in the governorship by Herbert H. Lehman of the Wall Street banking family, who served from 1932 to 1942 before becoming a United States senator. Except for Thomas E. Dewey's twelve-year tenure after 1942 the governorship of New York has been held by wealthy men since 1928. In 1954, with strong labor support, W. Averell Harriman, later again in the State Department, became the first of the ultra-wealthy of later years to win an important election when he became governor of New York as a Democrat, opening the way psychologically for ultra-wealthy Nelson A. Rockefeller, also supported by labor, to succeed him in 1958 and to win reelection twice to date. As Roosevelt showed on several occasions, the electorate will not shy away from a man because he is wealthy. The voters, presumably, think he is less apt to tap the public till for himself than is an Horatio Alger boy from the grass roots and dung hills.

Outside of New York, too, wealthy men, some of whom got their political start under Roosevelt appointments, have also taken to winning elections. G. Mennen "Soapy" Williams, shaving soap and talcum powder dual heir, who began as a New Deal appointee in 1936, was the elected labor-supported governor of Michigan from 1949 to 1960 and thereafter was assistant secretary of state for African Affairs; a lawyer, he is also a doctor of jurisprudence. William W. Scranton, also a lawyer and scion of an old Pennsylvania coal fortune, was first an Eisenhower official, then a member of Congress and in 1963 was elected governor of Pennsylvania.

The Kennedys, of course, stand out as men of great wealth who have directly participated in politics, although they are really members of an old-line political family like the Lodges, Stevensons and Tafts. John F. Kennedy, a budding journalist and war hero, was first easily elected a member of the House from Massachusetts, then of the Senate. In 1961 he became president. His brother Robert, a lawyer, was first his attorney general and then became senator from New York while brother Edward, also a lawyer, followed John F. to the Senate from Massachusetts.

Senator Joseph S. Clark of Pennsylvania, whom we have noticed in his effort to democratize the Senate, is a wealthy as well as extremely able public-spirited man. Barry Goldwater, senator from Arizona before winning the Republican presidential nomination in 1964, inherited a substantial interest in a large department store, never had to work his way up from anywhere. The late Robert Taft, senator from Ohio and presidential aspirant, came of a wealthy family; and the same necessarily holds of his son, also directly concerned in Ohio politics.

This list could be extended—Theodore Green and Claiborne Pell of Rhode Island, the Saltonstalls and Peabodys of Massachusetts, Ogden Reid of New York and Rockefeller IV of West Virginia, Angier Biddle Duke, Governor Winthrop Rockefeller of Arkansas, Harrison Williams, Jr., of New Jersey, et al.—but the highlights have been indicated. While one might evaluate the political performances of each of these men differently, perhaps rating Roosevelt and Kennedy high and Goldwater and Taft low, or vice versa, each represents achievement on the ground that winning elections is itself a recognized achievement. Roosevelt I would call an outstanding achiever in politics.

In some quarters there is a tendency to downgrade the feat of a wealthy man in winning an election because he has had the use of his own funds. But money alone does not win elections, although it is in the plutocratic American system a necessary aid. Furthermore, nearly every man who wins an election is backed by money—his own, that of a moneyed group (like Richard Nixon and his oil backers in 1952) or of an established political machine. The few exceptions appear to be sheer flukes in American politics. Money from at least a small group is almost always behind the candidates, particularly the winner. Only here and there in political low-pressure areas an unfinanced amateur may sneak over the goal line.

A significant recent tendency has been the appearance of a number of successful high corporation officials in elective political office. Small and very medium-sized business people have been no great novelty in elective office, particularly at the state level; but men from the corporate big league have been pointedly absent. George Romney, former head of American Motors and twice elected governor of Michigan, launched a campaign as a 1968 Republican presidential aspirant; and Charles Percy, former head of Bell & Howell, was elected senator from Illinois in 1966. On the corporate circuit, these men were big guns. If more big managers of corporations thrust forward in politics, the country may see something of what cold corporate rationality can do applied to government, assuming that such men retain the corporate approach. Robert S. McNamara, former president of Ford Motor Company, conducted his own specialized exercise in corporate rationality with the Defense Department, but his best efforts there had not been able to out-general Ho Chi Minh on his batteries of Pentagon computers.

In any event, it would appear that a change is under way when the industrial rich, descendants of original tycoons, and corporate nabobs participate directly in politics instead of working through subsidized lower-class stooges. There is a gain here, in the first place, for candor. At least the fractional thinking part of the electorate can now evaluate what these candidates publicly stand for instead of voting for men presumably independent but secretly harnessed to the corporate juggernaut. What any of these men propose politically may not be approved by the observer, but the observer will nevertheless learn by noticing public performance precisely what he does stand for.

Personalities like Lyndon B. Johnson, although moderately wealthy, are not included in the foregoing because they were not wealthy when they came to politics but were politicians first, wealthy men later.

No claim is implied here that all the wealthy who are lawyers have been named, for that list would run into hundreds, or that the mere fact of being a lawyer is something wonderful. Quite a number of the wealthy and the well-to-do become lawyers although not so many, it appears, as become corporation executives, project promoters and nonprofit administrators.

The Ruling Class

That members of the wealthier classes do often become corporation executives, administrators, lawyers and appointed or elected officials, thereupon opening themselves to evaluation in terms of going standards of achievement, is hardly odd in the light of the concept in political science of a "ruling class." Activists among the rich do seem to drift primarily into directorial, managerial or similar executive-type functional posts. However, to suggest that the United States, where sovereignty in theory lies within the whole people, has a ruling class is ideologically heretical, repugnant to public-school alumni and is for the most part volubly and emphatically denied. It is, above all, quite contrary to public school indoctrination.

For my part, I do not insist that the United States has a tight ruling class because there is often some ambiguity about what public activists in general are up to. Some appear confused themselves.

Objections to the idea of an American ruling class generally seem to flow from misconceptions about the nature of rule, which in the United States is indirect, and also from the idea that a ruling class must be formally constituted, as by titled nobility with certain formal privileges and immunities. Objections also seem to stem from the notion that a ruling class, in order to exist, must be closed to outsiders (which, for example, the ruling class of England never was).

But if a ruling class consists of people whose members veritably rule, a class whose imperative wishes and criteria largely order society, then it seems to me a case can be made that there is such a class in the United States, partly hereditary as to property and position and partly open to conforming newcomers. While not every member of a ruling class exercises rule, some being no more than detached observers and more or less graceful idlers, it is from such an established class that rulers may be selected.

If rulers are those who lay down and enforce the rules, then it would seem that the United States has such a class. The only question remaining would be whether these rulers are publicly selected on the basis of sheer merit or attain their positions largely by means of wealth or hereditary position. Newcomers to rule in the United States, it will be noticed, must pretty much accept and implement already going values established by pre-existent rulers. A difference between being born into a ruling class and being accepted into it is that the newcomer must learn and adopt the general values of the ruling group. A man who works his way into the ruling group from the laboring class (and there have been and are such) does not ordinarily retain the values of his original class. He acquires, more or less, the values of his new associates. Like most converts he is often more orthodox than a pope. Everett Dirksen, once a journeyman baker, does not have the outlook today of a journeyman baker.

How, it may be asked, would one discern a member of a ruling class if there were such a class? The method, it seems to me, would be simple: One would notice whether or not he ruled and how much he ruled. In this sense there is certainly a ruling class in the United States; for radiating throughout the country are various wide-jurisdiction chains of command—political, economic, cultural and judicial—that always have someone at their heads. These head men are, or so seem to me, rulers.

That there is something improper *per se* about such rulership, as is either directly charged or strongly implied in much leftist analysis, may be flatly denied. Social organization of any kind requires rule, and the fact that certain executive types from a small group assume rule derives as much from the passivity and incoherence of the masses as from any impropriety or inequity in arrangements even though one concedes that anyone who has "influence," either through the possession of money or established position, does have an inside track when it comes to establishing himself in a position of rule. But under any possible version of socialism, for example, there would be similar rulers; and, despite all cant about a democratic socialism, such rulers would tend increasingly to be drawn from a semiprofessionalized self-perpetuating class, properly designated as privileged rulers.

The idea that we have rulers is somewhat obscured by phrase-makers who at least unconsciously are trying to hide the fact or to save the notion of popular sovereignty, which I unabashedly take to be simple nonsense in any possible social context. The vocabulary of concealment consists of words like "executive," "administrator," "decision maker," "public servant," etc.; the more direct and colloquial "boss" comes closer to the true state of affairs.

That the American people choose their own rulers (at least in the political sphere) is an idea that will die hard no matter how carefully one shows that the choice almost always narrows down to two not very different hand-picked men who have been long nurtured in the political pipeline, gradually rising to the top. That the American people as a whole "chose" any president or other official in the sense of selecting him from among many possible can be dismissed as a notion beneath notice. What there is to public choice of political officials is negative—and itself controlled. Anyone known, for example, to be an atheist, freethinker, socialist or (in many jurisdictions) a believer in divorce (or subject to a variety of other designations) will be rejected out of hand by the electorate because these words have been antecedently contextually placed as "scare" words. The public, without knowing it, is manipulated by its preconditioned emotional response to certain loaded words, often irrelevant to the man or issue. Such words are given their value content by dominant defining agencies, which are always in the hands of persons favoring the established order (members of a ruling class?). It is not that people select among candidates as they are told. They limit their selection as they have been conditioned by definitions containing concealed value judgments. They are, then, mostly ruled from within themselves but by others who have antecedently determined their reactions. Far from being free men, they are puppets, prisoners of their indoctrination.

Outside the directly political area, in corporations and private organizations, the case for the selection of rulers by popular choice has not even the most tenuous ground to stand on and nobody at all argues for it. Yet corporate rules affect more people directly and immediately than governmental rules. And in the Catholic Church, by way of large example, the members have nothing to say about the selection of its personnel.

As all rulers, men at the head of chains of command, either come from a class habituated to producing decision makers or are strivers from the swamps and bayous who learn the same ways and vocabulary either in big organizations or government, the case is strong for at least entertaining the notion that there is in the United States a partially open ruling class oriented around its own special values. Among others, this class by cultural fiat rules out socialists, atheists, agnostics, and freethinkers—that is, as to the latter, people who make judgments only according to evidence. If one's mind is known so to operate, without prior commitment, one is a political pariah by decree, a strange political fact in a supposed free country. Jefferson could not be elected dog catcher today.

In the United States, according to theory, one is only ruled with one's consent. Yet this is true only in the sense that, if one does not successfully resist, one consents. Nobody living ever had an opportunity to consent to the Constitution, to most of the laws on the books or to more than an infinitesimal fraction of the officials and rules to which he is subject. There is, it is said, an orderly mechanism for changing any feature one may not like about political reality. As to this, it is well known that the mechanism is so complicated and cumbersome that one can pretty much forget about timely orderly change. If the need for doing anything whatever in the world had to be determined by the processes for legally amending the United States Constitution, for example, we would live in an almost frozen universe.

Individual performance within a class, however, always differs; and even in a ruling class not all members are likeminded, a fact which gives rise to differences about emphasis or policy. It is the outcome of policy that determines political achievement. But the fact that a man of wealth is carrying the ball at all in the political arena seems to me to represent political achievement unless it can be shown that he is, as in the self-proclaimed case of the late Senator Robert Kerr of Oklahoma, simply looking after his own economic interests from the vantage point of public office.

Because the flood of hereditary wealth-holders into public office since Roosevelt has consisted largely of university men, it does seem to me that they have generally brought with them a broader conception of public interest than many hardbitten professional politicos or businessmen possess. Neither Roosevelt nor Kennedy played the narrow Wall Street game, although they were far from opposed to the general economic interests of wealth-holders. They were also far from socialists or even soft-headed do-gooders.

One will have to evaluate the performance of the rich in public office from one's own point of view. I say only that whatever they do (if they don't merely service themselves) represents effort and the assumption of responsibility, hence achievement. The fact that Winston Churchill was an upper-class Tory does not lessen the fact that he was a tremendous achiever beyond the call of ordinary duty. And the more like Churchill, Roosevelt or Kennedy any politician is the more of an achiever I take him to be. In saying a man is an achiever one does not necessarily approve his achievement. One is not required to like an artist's picture, no matter how great an artist he may be. But the alleged achievement must be more than mere activity carried on for one's self-interest. Although his occupation may be onerous, a navel-gazer (or so it seems to me) cannot be rationally rated an achiever any more than can a miser.

Beyond Politics

Publishing has attracted a number of the wealthy. Whether there is achievement here is determined (at least by me) in the light of whether the publishing has any constructive purpose beyond making money. Here one must look for some indication of intent as well as fulfillment. Where the intent is general enlightenment, and where this intent is to some appreciable extent attained, I would look upon the enterprise as an achievement of public value; where the intent is obscurantic or merely commercial, one may disregard it; although it is probably always better that people read something than nothing.

Publishing enterprises that have grown from scratch and that have made the owners wealthy, as in the cases of the Pulitzer, McCormick-Patterson and Ochs families, do not fall into the category of our interest.

As to newspapers, it seems to me that Dorothy Schiff with the *New York Post*, the Eugene Myers family with the *Washington Post* and the late Marshall Field III with the *Chicago Sun-Times* have taken over or started newspapers which they have inclined broadly toward civilized values. The late William Randolph Hearst, the wealthiest man ever in the newspaper field, seems to me to have turned in a negative achievement, for the most part pandering to mass weaknesses. John Hay Whitney, in a costly attempt to keep a revivified *New York Herald Tribune* afloat, made a particularly worthy effort in latter-day journalism, to be vanquished in 1966 by adverse circumstances. Under Whitney the *Herald Tribune* made notable contributions, to some of which allusion was made earlier.

Unfortunately, there is not much in newspaper publishing as a whole (or the mass media in general) subject to evaluation as contributory achievement. As the dean of the Columbia University Graduate School of Journalism reports:

Of the two hundred or so major papers, somewhere between ten and eighteen are generally ranked as excellent by such knowledgeable critics as reporters, editors, and journalism educators [with these figures I would concur—F.L.]. A few critics would raise the total to thirty or forty. Perhaps another fifty to eighty smaller dailies would be ranked as "very good for their size." All of these would be so ranked because they are reasonably complete, thorough, dependable, enterprising, and fair in their news columns, regardless of editorial-page views. At the other pole, a total of perhaps another fifty newspapers large and small, would be ranked as "bad" newspapers—some because of a tendency to distort news to conform with the owner's prejudices, others because of sheer incompetence in reporting and editing, some because of both faults. Between these extremes, at levels ranging from "poor" to "fair," lie the vast majority of American daily newspapers.[8]

Most of the big newspapers, good or bad, are self-generated enterprises, not dependent on a wealthy sponsor so much as on commercial support by corporate advertisers.

Marshall Field broadened his publishing effort by going heavily into the field of adult and children's reference and educational books, with notable success. More recently a number of wealthy people have gone into book publishing but, it seems to me, mainly for investment purposes. In the field of books in general during the past fifty years young men of some original small property have entered and achieved commercial as well as cultural publishing success, but as these have not until recently represented anything to be regarded as considerable established wealth they do not belong in this account.

In the early 1960's Huntington Hartford, enamored of Broadway, launched the elaborate magazine *Show*, a critical but not commercial success. It was soon relinquished.

Paul Mellon's Bollingen Foundation has published or reprinted many books in the field of art and the humanities—worthwhile books that would otherwise not have appeared and highly esteemed by a critical few. Praise seems to me due in such a case.

One of the most distinguished publishing enterprises founded and endowed by a wealthy man was the Loeb Classical Library of Greek and Latin classics with English translations on facing pages; it was established by James Loeb (1867–1933, Harvard, '88), a member of the banking firm of Kuhn, Loeb and Company until his retirement at the age of thirty-four. Loeb in 1905 also founded the Institute of Musical Art, now part of the Juilliard School of Music, and established in Munich a clinic for psychiatric study—a man far ahead of his time.

Many creative writers have been facilitated in the production of new works by fellowships issued for several decades by the Guggenheim Foundation, although this foundation would not be classifiable as a publishing enterprise.

Wealth-financed writings are far more extensive than the uncontrolled productions of Guggenheim fellows. Study grants are issued by many foundations, but one cannot uniformly regard the results as publishing achievements because, with the exception of occasional eye-opening works like Myrdal's *An American Dilemma* and Kinsey's two books on sexual behavior, they are often indirect apologies or rationalizations for existing states of affairs. Where contra-factual or misleading conclusions are put forth even unconsciously under the rubric of certified scholarship as links in a covert in-group celebration under a self-protecting mythology, they can be regarded, it seems to me, only very dubiously as achievements. There are such sponsored writings.

Publications that in their various ways have represented noncommercial contributions to political and social understanding have been *The Nation* and the *New Republic*. *The Nation* was subsidized for many years by wealthy inheritor-editor Oswald Garrison Villard and more recently published under James J. Storrow, Jr., son of the Boston banker; and the *New Republic* was assisted into being by Willard Straight of the J. P. Morgan firm. *The Reporter*, financed with Rosenwald money, has also turned in a distinguished noncommercial record. Dogmatic leftists tend to dismiss these publications because they are gradualist-reformist in tendency. It is interesting to notice, though, that the leftist publications pick up most of their grist from publications such as these and the better newspapers, subjecting it to their own ideological interpretation. Without the better publications to rely upon for information, the editors of the left would be completely blind.

Except for small enterprises run by artistic or intellectual groups there is little or nothing of value in daily, weekly or monthly publications that has not emerged as a consequence either of pure commercialism or of patronage by the more enlightened of the wealthy or affluent. Out of the masses themselves has come nothing in this line except fantastic religious, moralistic and political tracts. "The Face on the Bar-Room Floor" is an epic of this school.

While some of the rich have stood forth as publishers, not many, as in the case of Curtis Bok, have distinguished themselves as writers. John F. Kennedy, to be sure, instantly comes to mind as a writer who with his *Profiles in Courage* rang bells; he very evidently had it in him to function at least at the Lippmann-Reston level, or perhaps beyond, even had he been no more than a poor scholarship student in his youth. Money or no money, Kennedy was obviously a talented fellow; money simply gave him a longer reach. Talented himself, he could recognize talent, something successful politicians are often unable to do. His obvious admiration for political courage, too, seemed to augur something in his political future that political and economic climbers tended to fear, lending color to the disputed view that his assassination was the outcome of a rightist conspiracy.

If more than a very few of the wealthy have individually distinguished themselves as practicing journalists, I have not been able to pick up the trail from the dim record. There was, of course, Villard.

Six times married and divorced Cornelius Vanderbilt III (b. 1898) lists himself as an author, lecturer, cinematographer and televiser and has served as a working reporter and then founder, publisher and president of Vanderbilt Newspapers, Inc., which briefly issued illustrated newspapers in Los Angeles, San Francisco and Miami. He was associate editor of Hearst's *New York Mirror* from 1925 to 1929 and has since worked as a columnist for many newspapers and periodicals. He is the author of more than fifteen semi-popular, semi-autobiographical books, including *Farewell to Fifth Avenue* (1935).

As with most books by scions of the rich, readers appear to have been chiefly interested in Vanderbilt's autobiographical and "insider" revelations. This was true, too, in the case of Evelyn Walsh McLean's *Father Struck It Rich*.

Vanderbilt appears to me to have come the closest of one from a very rich family to being a professional writer and working editor; he was precisely that most of his adult life. I call anyone here a professional writer who habitually sets words down on paper for sale to the public. The definition implies no critical judgments.

The Literary Set

Mary Borden (Lady Spears), daughter born in 1886 of William Borden, the dairy-products tycoon, comes the closest known (to me) of any higher-strata American rich to being a critically extolled professional creative writer. Author of some twenty works, mostly fiction, "Her novels reveal a quiet but devastating wit" according to William Rose Benét's *The Reader's Encyclopedia* (1955). There have been writers in some abundance from the propertied middle class, in possession of some modest private unearned income (Henry James, Clarence Day, Willa Cather, Ellen Glasgow and others), but this is not the question. Anne Morrow Lindbergh, daughter of a Morgan partner, should also be noticed as a writer of considerable distinction.

Creative writers about the rich and the upper classes in the United States—Edith Wharton, Theodore Dreiser, F. Scott Fitzgerald, Frank Norris, Louis Auchincloss—have not themselves been of the very wealthy strata; although Edith Wharton was definitely upper class in that she was of the Rhinelander pre-Revolutionary family, wrote about some of the latter-day rich and was married to an affluent Bostonian. Auchincloss, as a big-firm Wall Street lawyer with Yale and Groton in the background, I would place in the cultivated upper middle class rather than the plutocracy.

Most writing, especially by scions of the post-Civil War industrial fortunes, has been in the form of memoirs, some of them emanating from literary ghosts. I conclude that few if any of the American big rich, excluding here descendants of early-established New England mercantile families, have distinguished themselves as writers; I do not, however, assert that none of them has authored a book of some sort or written an essay.

As to great editors—taking as par for this course Joseph Pulitzer, Maxwell Perkins, H. L. Mencken, E. W. Howe, Henry Watterson or almost anyone of a similar stripe—I would say the rich have produced none. Hearst would surely not rate.

Performing and Plastic Arts

In the performing and nonliterary creative arts, one can pick up a name here and there, mostly from lower levels of wealth, but the record is rather meager. Albert Spalding (1888–1953), a very fine violin virtuoso and composer, was a scion of the sporting-goods family; and Mary Cassatt (1845–1926), an esteemed painter especially of mothers and children, was the daughter of a banker and sister of the president of the Pennsylvania Railroad. Neither Spalding nor Cassatt, however, were from the top echelons of wealth.

In the upper level of wealth is Gerald Felix Warburg (b. 1901), son of Felix M. Warburg and Frieda Schiff and a distinguished performing cellist, formerly a member of the Stradivarius Quartet and known for his concertizing and involvement in musical enterprises. Here, too, should be mentioned James P. Warburg, son of Paul M. Warburg, the banker, and Nina J. Loeb (Kuhn, Loeb), who paralleled a career in investment banking and corporate management by authoring more than thirty books on aspects of economics, finance, politics and public affairs and found time to produce some books of verse—a literary geyser. There is, too, Edward M. M. Warburg (b. 1908), a social worker who has taught art, has participated in archaeological expeditions and more recently has taken a directorial role in various cultural and charitable enterprises. The Warburgs, offshoots of a cultivated Anglo-German Jewish banking family, seem to me an untypical case oriented more like certain descendants of earlier Boston mercantilists than latter-day industrialists, even though their center of activity has certainly been Wall Street. They were affluent, probably rich, before they came to the United States.

Beyond this one has to search carefully for more candidates. Gloria Vanderbilt has had "one-man" shows in painting. That there are creative sparks within the Vanderbilt clan is also suggested by the fact that Harold S. Vanderbilt, premier international yachting champion, around 1925 invented the game of contract bridge, which is an achievement of the same order that one would surely acknowledge to the unknown developers of games like chess, checkers and mah-jong.

Raymond Pitcairn, described in *Who's Who* as a lawyer, architect and philanthropist (1885–1966), president of the Pitcairn Company and a director of the family's inherited Pittsburgh Plate Glass Company, one of the larger of the nation's industrial enterprises, was the architect of the Cathedral of the Bryn Athyn (Pennsylvania) Church of the New Jerusalem (Swedenborgian). He is the father of eight children, including Nathan Pitcairn (born 1912), director of Pittsburgh Plate Glass and many other companies.

Alfred Victor du Pont (born 1900) has been a career architect since 1930. Irénée du Pont, Jr. (born 1920), is a mechanical engineer with the family company. Many of the contemporary Du Ponts, however, have had educations in science or engineering at schools such as Harvard, Yale and M.I.T., and many are ensconced in family enterprises. John du Pont presents himself as a marine biologist as well as an Olympic athlete.

In this book reference to the Du Ponts is only to the dominant owning group of E. I. du Pont de Nemours and Company, which since its reorganization in 1902 is what gave this group its money-power; members of this group have largely concerned themselves with business, finance and, indirectly, politics. In politics they provided the backbone of the opposition to Roosevelt's New Deal.

The family as a whole is much more extensive than the chemical kings and has been traced genealogically by two family members, obviously imbued with familial mystique.[9]

As of 1949 the genealogy showed 1,035 descendants of Pierre Samuel du Pont de Nemours, some of the eighth generation.[10] The first known ancestor of the line leading to Pierre Samuel, there being other branches, was Jehan du Pont, baptized at Rouen on February 22, 1565.[11] The French Du Ponts were inscribed generally on local roll-books as "bourgeois," so that the family may be said to have been officially middle class until the emergence of a section of it on the latter-day upper *finpolitan* circuit of plutocracy.

As a middle-class family it included a considerable number of nonbusiness achievers, a fact not germane to this inquiry about the wealthy of a later day. Nor is this inquiry concerned with any of the noncorporation Du Ponts, most of whom interestingly do not bear the surname of Du Pont at all. One would not, for example, associate the name of

Lawrence Sven Anderson (b. 1944) with that of Du Pont; yet his mother was Rosina du Pont, who traces back directly to Pierre Samuel (1739–1817). Nor would one at first blush be inclined to designate Washington Irving, Jr. (b. 1952) as a Du Pont; but he too, is a direct descendant of Pierre Samuel. And so it goes with many others who do not bear the Du Pont name.[12]

Medicine

In medicine we find William Larimer Mellon, a specialist in tropical diseases who has served the natives in the West Indies, and Henry Clay Frick II, grandson of the ironmaster, a physician and surgeon specializing in gynecology. If there are any other medical men from heavily moneyed strata, they have escaped my notice. As to medicine in general today (without any reference to those two valued practitioners), a variety of investigators has shown that it has become pretty much a lush prerogative of the middle class, members of which dominate it as a recently lucrative field. The great discoveries of selfless medical scientists have, by and large, been capitalized along conspicuously lucrative lines by striving middle-class people.[13] It is the belief of some investigators that the present need to finance a medical education privately out of middle-class resources operates to exclude men of genuine talent from lower levels of society and to proliferate business-oriented unthorough doctors whose strictly middle-class economic outlook obviously dominates the policies and expressions of the American Medical Association. Doctors, it is implied by many dicta of this association, should properly function on a strictly individual cost-plus-average-rate-of-high-profit basis—all the traffic will bear.

Although wealthy men sometimes marry their nurses I was unable to find any women from wealthy families serving as professional nurses, but such a fact might be difficult to detect. Some wealthy women do serve as nurses' aids in home communities and during wartime. Most nurses of whatever degree probably serve mainly out of economic necessity in an ill-rewarded field. Despite immoderate public expressions of esteem for them, nurses in the United States are generally treated as lower servants.

Public Performers

Wealthy men and women not infrequently marry theatrical performers and opera stars, but there are few cases of a wealthy man or woman becoming a professional performer. One of these few cases was Grace Kelly (born 1929) who became a prize-winning film star and then Princess

Grace of Monaco; she is the daughter of wealthy Philadelphia contractor John B. Kelly. More recently there has emerged film star Dina Merrill, daughter of cereal heiress Marjorie Merriweather Post. Similarly, wealthy people are sometimes sportsmen in the sense of following or bankrolling some sport such as horse racing or yachting, but one rarely finds one as a competitive participant like yachtsman Harold S. Vanderbilt in rough-and-tumble big-league action. Except for youngsters in college sports, hardly any stand forth under my scrutiny as athletes—Grace Kelly's father was a sculling champion—despite the newspaper-fostered national cult of athleticism. Many of the wealthy, of course, play golf and tennis; but they simply don't rate on the big-trophy circuit.

In general, the Hollywood, Broadway and athletic circuits are dominated by people who came up from the nonpropertied depths of nonentity. Some of these, of course, have hit it big financially and hobnob happily with the well-heeled in feverish Café Society.

Scientists, Scholars and Philosophers

Nobody from a conspicuously rich established family was found in a possibly imperfect search among scientists or scholars as these are listed in *American Men of Science: The Physical and Biological Sciences*, 3 vols., 11th edition (R. R. Bowker Co., New York, 1965); and *American Men of Science: The Social and Behavioral Sciences*, 10th edition (the Jaques Cattell Press, Inc., Arizona State University, Tempe, Arizona, 1962). In the four-volume *Directory of American Scholars* (R. R. Bowker Co., New York, 1963), there is listed Corliss Lamont, son of a one-time leading Morgan partner, as a writer on contemporary and philosophical affairs. Among various books he is perhaps best known for his *The Philosophy of Humanism*, 1957.

I would not deny that some—a few—scientists, scholars, philosophers or educators may have sprung from families of lesser property, perhaps up to $1 million by value, but I have been able to devise no system for readily locating them, especially those who trace a line of descent on the distaff side. In general, the record as I scan it suggests that few people of noticeable wealth go into science, scholarship, education, medicine, journalism, the judiciary, philosophy or the arts—that is to say, they shun subtle detail work all the way from managing their own accounting systems on upward. Some men-on-the-make, however, like the original Rockefeller, have a genius for detail that reminds one of extremely self-demanding artists.

Echelons of Command

Activists among the rich (as distinguished from the more or less graceful and here and there civilized idlers) tend to surge toward positions of broad command in corporations, nonprofit cultural, social and artistic organizations and in government, in this last recalling Aristotle's observation about the penchant of the rich for political office. There they do what they can to lay out and enforce broad lines of policy within which the detail work of others will bear the requisite fruit. The wealthy may finance the detail work that goes into the creation of an instrument like television and may finally finance its launching; they thereafter determine, in concert with up-and-comers, *how it shall be used*—as an instrument of general enlightenment or an instrument for selling merchandise at a profit. While compromises are worked out to meet the objections of churlish dissenters, anyone is free to see where the emphasis falls and what the level of appeal is.

From the universities to the corporations and cultural organizations, the wealthy and their chosen aides *supervise* the detail workers. In their various positions of command the supervisors are known as executives, administrators, directors, publishers, trustees, sponsors, officials, community leaders, philanthropists and public servants. I imply no criticism here, simply point to the fact that activity and achievement among the rich at any level usually boil down primarily to concern with ordering the surrounding state of affairs and directing detail work along soundly approved lines of profitability.

I do not deny but indeed assert, while pointing to Franklin D. Roosevelt and John F. Kennedy, that such concern may visualize improvement in the surrounding state of affairs rather than keeping them soundly headed toward the rocks. Yet, whether it represents improvement, deterioration (as C. Wright Mills contended) or the maintenance of the *status quo*, it shows the area of major interest. The active rich and upcoming rich, as far as one can judge from the available record, are far less interested in understanding, improving or embellishing the world than in running it, at times running it close to the rocks as when the German industrialists embraced Hitler, or as when American financiers thrust the United States into World War I.

The World of Celebrity

The Celebrity Register, edited by Cleveland Amory (Harper and Row,

New York, 1963), lists people as noteworthy according to the amount of space they are given in the mass media. Among the rich there mentioned one finds Douglas Dillon; Donald Douglas; Angier Biddle Duke; Doris Duke; Irénée du Pont; Cyrus Eaton; Henry J. Kaiser; Sherman Fairchild; Marshall Field IV (d.); Harvey S., Leonard, Raymond and Russell Firestone; Randolph and William Randolph (Jr.) Hearst; Henry, Benson, William C. and Mrs. Edsel Ford; Paul and Richard King Mellon; John Pillsbury; Alfred G., Cornelius, Jr., Gloria and Harold S. Vanderbilt; all the Rockefeller brothers and Jievute Paulekiute Sears ("Bobo") Rockefeller; Ogden Reid; Walter P. Chrysler; Amon Carter, Jr.; Dorothy Schiff; Lady and John Jacob Astor of England; Henry Crown; Lammot du Pont Copeland; August Busch; and a medley of others.

In combing through the list of the rich who are also celebrated by percipient editors one does not encounter any significantly additional names relating to notable personal achievement and, indeed, one notes many omissions.

The Question of Achievement

This question of achievement has arisen, I remind the reader, for two reasons: (1) It is part of standard public relations ideology that the big fortunes are used in all ways for public support and (2) the criteria of achievement are applied in general most forcefully by the rich to others. What I am doing, heretically, is applying the standards to them. I mention this because it should not be inferred that I myself value achievement as such, and in and of itself, very highly; there is much to be said along the line of Bertrand Russell's *In Praise of Idleness*. As far as people in general are concerned, I personally value them first for general amiability, which I consider beyond price, and after that for such higher cultivation as they may have acquired. A man both amiable and cultivated seems to me the limit of what one can ask for in a human being. If he is also creative he is, patently, ineffable.

The achiever, as it is now known, is usually a person psychologically programmed or impelled to function in a certain way and possessing the ability to satisfy his impulsion. It is, however, part of the middle-class cult of personality to celebrate immoderately the carrier of such often purely fortuitous programming. A man's specific achievement, as far as that goes, is often greater or lesser than he is, a fact sensed by those achievers who draw back from public acclaim not so much out of modesty as uneasiness with the personal judgment of which they are the objects.

Although achievement is a splashy middle-class value, it is applied most rigorously by the rich, who bring it to bear on others far more rigorously than I have applied it to them in this chapter, where at times I have inwardly quailed at the thought of how purists would look upon the free catholicity of some of my inclusions. As I explained initially, however, I do not pretend to be applying the canons in all their rigor but will take almost anything offered.

What the rich generally demand in all things of direct concern to them is perfection—from food, clothing, drink, raiment and shelter to expertise in all skills of which they feel need. This is readily seen in the food and service in their clubs and restaurants and in the arrangements in their own hospitals. Where the rich congregate and bestow their patronage everything is offered according to tiptop standards. It is the same when it comes to choosing skills for their cultural and economic enterprises. In the plastic arts what they clearly want is the best, for which they pay astronomic prices. On the cultural front standards, particularly technical, are most rigorously imposed, on students and faculty alike, in the key universities; as one traces the chain of command upward one arrives finally at the board of trustees, where the familiar names of the rich, absent farther down, begin to occur with frequency and regularity. The more prestigious the university the more frequently do outstanding names in science and scholarship appear among the faculty—Nobel laureates or men of comparable lofty stature. The higher one ascends among the graduates, from the *cum laudes* to the *magna cum laudes* and on to the *summa cum laudes* the more rigorous are the applied standards. It is the same among the big corporations, which skim the cream of the physicists, chemists and engineers. Who wishes to invest money in a skyscraper if it is going to turn out to be another Leaning Tower of Pisa?

In brief, only the best is wanted except perhaps in social analysis. Many are called, few are chosen.

Throughout society, ordered from on high, the screws are tight as to (1) technical standards of production and service and (2) rates of pay for all subordinates. The consequence is that the United States is a high-tension society, invisibly and almost insensibly imposing upon all achievers demanding standards of performance and upon the labor force minimal rates of pay in the name of strictest economy and efficiency. It would clearly be inefficient as well as uneconomical to pay more than was required according to the unbreakable "law" of supply and demand. Hence, when rare skills are required by the ruling group—at this point we can stop all fencing and notice that we are in fact confronted by a quite small ruling group—more bearers of these rare skills are produced, thus bringing into play the "law" of supply and demand. It would not do to have only 500 or so physicists in the country, each of whom could command an exorbitant salary comparable to that of a corporation chairman (and possibly tax exempt). It is better to produce thousands of physicists so that few can expect a salary above that of, say, an assistant bank cashier.

It is a curious fact in the United States that some of the rarest and most difficult skills—as of a creative mathematician—are paid for on a very low scale (Einstein, we recall, got $16,000) whereas far less rare skills, such as in the imposing of rules and standards, are relatively well rewarded. True savants in the United States are far more of the order of menial servants than they themselves suspect.

Although rejecting and resenting it when applied to themselves, the rich in general make full use of the instrument of criticism, in their own service. While this can be shown in many directions it appears most readily in the matter of politics. Not only is criticism sharp here but it is oriented not philosophically, according to reason, but along lines of naked and narrow self-interest. The politician who pursues under necessity some unfamiliar course, such as Franklin Roosevelt, is subjected to the most unsparing and ungenerous appraisal. No holds are barred. A Norman Thomas is hooted off the rostrum.

If it is one of the functions of criticism to encourage the performer to do better, it must follow that a function of criticism of the rich is to enable them to do better—as they expect everyone to do from waiters and bus boys on upward to presidents.

Achievement as a Value

The important value of achievement is directly imposed on American society largely by pushful products of the lower middle class who have received the nod from on high to occupy executive posts throughout the mass media, the great carriers of values in our day.

Any competent news editor can determine in a flash how noteworthy anyone is. His is an important function, for he decides how much valuable space can with maximum economic efficiency be allotted to anyone. He achieves his end by drawing upon wide background knowledge and evaluating how wealthy a person is, how elevated his position in the social hierarchy or the proper dimension of his apparent objective achievement. He believes he is governed by audience interest; that this is not so can be proved by showing that many of his emphases are of interest to no very wide audience. Attaining the presidency, winning a Nobel Prize, getting some championship, hitting a record number of home runs or writing a Broadway "hit" are instantly recognized pretty indiscriminately as big achievement; he has more difficulty in presenting some important scientific breakthrough. Not that many really care. As those know very well who make these measurements, not to have money, position or some approved tangible achievement to one's credit is to be a nobody, an employee at most, subject to downplay in the news columns unless one commits some titillating indiscretion or stupefying horror.

There are those moralists who carefully explain that such facile valuation is mistaken, that the widow suffering with lumbago and sciatica who rears six children to become solid citizens is as good as anyone, perhaps better. One may agree; but, as they say in electoral politics, if you have to explain just how good somebody really is you are lost. One either sees the point instantly against the background of accumulated values, as the news editor sees it, or never. Attention wanders as the moralists drone on hollowly that every person is invested with high human dignity and is of infinite inherent value. As anyone can see by looking about him, in terms of established going values this is just not so; operationally it is pure bunk. In terms of applied going values, most people are crashing nobodies.

Eccentrically applying this same scale of going values to the rich, as they are applied to everybody else, produces results approximately of the order I have indicated in this chapter. The activists among the rich are not achievers so much as commanders and through their intricate public-relations system project their positions of command as superlative achievements. A man is not an "industrialist" because he possesses some recondite skill denied to other men; he is an industrialist because he possesses and commands capital. And so it is with most of the roles the rich play. Put another way, give many other men the same cards and they could play the same hand, perhaps to better effect, surely not to worse.

Achievement and the Middle Class

Achievement in general appears to be a middle-class prerogative. The rich, as William H. Vanderbilt observed, do not appear motivated by any particular ambition, other than to rule. They are brought up to feel that they have already somehow made the grade. The poor and near-poor, having all they can do to keep their heads economically above water, cannot aspire even in fantasy to much in the way of achievement except possibly in sports or entertainment. Becoming a soft-shoe dancer or a professional ballplayer represents perhaps the zenith of aspiration among some of the more ambitious of the younger poor.

In the middle classes—lower middle class being those with nontaxable estates, higher middle with taxable estates up to whatever level one would consider wealthy, let us provisionally say $1 million—there is just enough feeling of scarcity to suggest that something more might be desirable and enough feeling of attainment to lead to the belief that more might be achieved along some line. It is in this social stratum that dreams are born of becoming big corporation executives, big lawyers, big scientists, novelists, college presidents, scholars, roving journalists and super-salesmen.

The middle classes invariably have something to begin with but often feel capable of more distinctive performance. Not, as it is commonly said, that they are mere status strivers, although there are those, too. They do, however, have a base from which to launch operations, if only in the direction of money-making or attaining position. The only way most of the poor feel they might make some money beyond the subsistence level is by winning against heavy odds in a sweepstakes, finding oil or robbing a bank. For the really poor man, imbedded in a poverty culture, the out-look for personal achievement is bleak. He needs constant help and en-couragement of the kind available to its members from within the middle class: "Sure you can be a big engineer. Look at So-and-So and So-and-So. All you need do is stick to your studies and pick up some good con-nections."

Both the rich and the poor lack the balanced tension for achievement found in the middle class, often to the undoing of its more taut members.

So, although I don't decry the slender evidences of achievement within the wealthier classes, some of whom are at least percipient enough to underwrite and finance achievement in others, it is a fact that it doesn't amount to very much and is concentrated within the less well-heeled middle classes. This conclusion has bearing from a different direction on the contention out of public relations metaphysics that the big fortunes in one way or the other are really great public benefactions, largely de-voted to public good works. That this contention is prevalent may be seen by noticing the designation by newspapers of nearly all wealthy men as philanthropists. Some may be here and there but surely not all.

As we have seen, only 8 per cent of all donation, in the neighborhood of an aggregate $10 billion annually, comes from foundations; 50 per cent of all public giving goes to religious institutions and amounts, in fact, to the price of support of untaxed church services. There remains 42 per cent, or about $4.2 billion, spread around among Community Funds and special-purpose charitable and medical organizations to which the public in general contributes.

Achieving saviors put forth from among the big fortune-holders, then, appear to be few. If there were any Mozarts or Pasteurs among them it would be evident that the public was receiving gifts beyond price; but I could find none although I stand ready to be corrected on the point by any one of the many articulate admirers and supported supporters of the rich.

While it may be that the American rich, compared with the European rich, have devoted more lucre to good works, it is nevertheless true that they have had more to parcel out and what they have parceled out has not been great proportionately. Even if one concedes without further ado the acts of the twelve largest foundation donors as unquestionably and unchallengeably disinterested and publicly supportive they, as it happens, do not turn out to be much in bulk.

Most of the cash revenues of the active and inactive among the rich seem to me devoted to supporting a life of luxury and ease amid surrounding conditions of pressing need. Not that what is devoted to luxurious living represents out-of-pocket deprivation of the poor or that the latter would be sustained if only they had these revenues. Such a contention would not stand up under analysis.

What fosters the great disparity between the wealthy few and the impoverished many is *public policy*. Although some of the wealthy disagree with important aspects of this public policy, the wealthy and the near-wealthy *as a class* use their considerable influence to maintain it *in their own interest*. It is not that they take from the poor what belongs to the poor but that they sponsor, support and underwrite public arrangements, such as the tax structure, that makes any different outcome impossible. With the tax structure, merely one detail among many (the price system is another), rigged against him the way it is, it is almost impossible now for any member of the labor force even to save his way into the economic middle class. The tax bite on earned incomes is much too great in the Garrison State.

Even with smaller taxes most members of the labor force would be unable to save their way out of it because, hazards apart, the system of advertising consumer goods often operates upon them with coercive effect. Able himself to resist the blandishments of the advertisers, an employee finds that his wife and children more readily succumb, importune him to make rash purchases for their delight and put him in the position of a niggardly churl for counseling prudence. "All the other families in the neighborhood have one; why should we be different?" Given the choice between being intelligent Economic Man or compliant Good Father, he usually chooses the latter role and becomes, as the news editors will say, Mr. Nobody. He complains, may console himself with strong drink but always gives in. In the end, he has not made the grade but is given a gold watch for forty years' service before being ushered off to live on less than $100 per month Social Security. His children often look on him as a flop, speak of him disparagingly.

In their influence over public policy the rich and their power-elite, then, are not successful merely through being devilishly clever or unscrupulous. They are usually successful because their natural victim (or, better perhaps, bystander) the mass-man about whom reformers are continually concerned, is passive, relaxed, psychologically conditioned to submission and usually broadly untutored. He irrationally favors, in fact, many aspects of policy that are most disadvantageous to him.

While there is much else to be said pro and con about mass-man, he nevertheless shows these broad characteristics:

1. Since infancy he has been indoctrinated by parents and parental substitutes to believe there is a supernatural power on which he can safely rely. "The Lord will provide," it is said, although it is not said just what provision He will make. Those who sincerely believe they are supernaturally protected do not apparently feel it necessary to rely on their own wits. Owing to the belief, probably well founded, that religion makes most people readily tractable, the State exempts religious institutions from taxation as an adjunct to its more direct police powers. Whatever is tranquilizing on the masses is generally approved by social managers.

Conservatives, standpatters and reactionaries invariably extol religious belief as a political support, and this was well exemplified in the inaugural address of Ronald Reagan as governor of California when he said: "Belief in and dependence on God is absolutely essential. It will be an integral part of our public life as long as I am Governor. No one could think of carrying on with our problems without the help of God."[14]

For this reason critics of the established order—radicals and many liberals who would wish to change or modify it—see religion as part of the *political* process of keeping the common man in chains and submissive to higher secularists, often in clerical garb. The issue as between conservatives and radicals is not whether God exists—for this question is of interest to neither—but what the effect is on the populace of belief or disbelief in God. Religion is seen by both equally as an adjunct to repression and inhibition.

What is perhaps most significant about sincere religious belief with respect to its influence on political and economic attitudes is this: If one, for example, can believe without any difficulty in the Virgin Birth of Jesus and that Jesus walked on the waters, changed water into wine and performed other unnatural acts then one will experience little difficulty in accepting Everett M. Dirksen and Lyndon B. Johnson, to name no others, as great statesmen, and little difficulty in believing that some fifty-nine-cent cosmetic will make one irresistible to the opposite sex. A social effect of religion, at least in its cruder forms, is that it fosters widespread public credulity, makes a wide public sitting ducks for political and economic short-change artists. As people joyfully sing "Washed in the Blood of the Lamb," they are beset by thousands of invisible vampires. Offended by this spectacle, the skeptic turns away.

2. He has been schooled to believe sincerely that he lives under a government as nearly perfect as the subtlest mind of man can devise. Indeed, the better his schooling and the more apt a student he has been in elementary and secondary grades on the subject of government, the more widely he has been misled. For what has been presented to him, at least in the best schools, has been razor-exact in its formalism. Although formally true, most of the lessons he has learned on the subject of government have been intrinsically and deeply false or at least misleading. The difference between government as he has learned about it and government as practiced is the difference between a battle plan on which troops have been briefed and the actual battle. What is in the latter that was not in the plan are blood, pain, pillage, destruction, cries of agony and death. The plan is neat; its execution is sheer havoc.

The American governmental system, I do deeply believe, is beautifully rational in its structure. It implicitly assumes that all will be well if everyone, equally endowed, is intelligently self-protective. What throws it askew, however, is that people are neither equally endowed by nature or law. Paradoxically, one might say that the system was devised by dogmatic, somewhat myopic rationalists.

3. On top of this religio-political indoctrination he is given most of his information about daily affairs not by experts but by the daily press, which many analyses have shown to be deficient. While a close reading of six to a dozen of the best newspapers at home and abroad will give one a close approximation to much relevant contemporary truth, few people can give the time to such reading and, even if they were fully intelligent, they would not always be well served. During World War I, for example, a close reading of all the best papers in the United States and Europe would not have given one so much as an inkling of the true causes, origins and aims of the war. Historians had to ferret out the facts later.

In consequence of the foregoing (among other things) we get Mencken's booboisie, Barnum's suckers, my own handicapped dependents.

The man of affairs, however, either rich or up-and-coming, usually has a different background. He has not, first, been successfully indoctrinated with the idea that he can rely on a Higher Power. He is more apt to believe that "the Lord helps those who help themselves," or that the Lord is a neutral referee.

As to schooling, he has usually pursued it further to the advanced level that introduces comparative government and problems in American government; or he has heard government talked about in skeptical terms at home. Whether he studies government in college or from the vantage point of a law school, he becomes aware there is much fine print about exceptions and variations to be absorbed. There are many "buts." The whole thing does not operate according to the broad strokes of elementary summaries. There are, as it turns out, "smoke-filled backrooms" where men of easy virtue bargain with tight abandon for imperial stakes.

Any high-level course in problems of American government quickly acquaints the student with the fact that the governmental system is shot through with difficulties and contradictions. In many situations and circumstances the system will no more save or protect the individual than the deity to which daily prayers are directed.

People of affairs, particularly wealthy people, do not rely on the newspapers, even the best newspapers, for information upon which to act. They employ their own research staffs and subscribe to many expensive informational services unknown to the general public. A clerk, for example, may read about a stock in some publication and decide to commit a large percentage of his slender capital to its purchase. A wealthy man has a staff or a specialist study such a stock and, if he buys at all, commits to it only a small portion of his capital, perhaps less than 1 per cent.

It is, then, natural that when any popular interest enters the public arena against any particular or combined money interest it is much like a muscle-bound amateur entering the ring against a lithe battlewise champion. It is only a question of what round the amateur will go down in or by what margin he will be outpointed. The champion can deliver the result any way, and on order. He can even, if this seems politically desirable, allow himself to be knocked out in some contest where the issue is minor, giving the popular faction a sense of triumph for a change. Such popular victories turn out to be "no title" contests. Winning or losing them makes no fundamental difference.

The dice, in brief, are loaded by (shall we say?) destiny.

Instead of the rich being irresistible exploiters, then, as Marxists present them, the situation as a whole is much more like a sadomasochistic process with one small group internally programmed for command and the other, much larger, for gratifying submission. While the outcome of submission is not widely relished, the process of submission itself appears to be pleasing to most people. In Barnum's words, they are born suckers. They like to salute.

Freud looked upon all civilization as a process of necessary repression. Most of this repression is achieved by psychological means through the uptraining of children in certain ways by parents and parental substitutes. Where such training fails and overt rebels against the system of repression appear, the police and the military stand ready. They carry out direct repression.

What happens within these systems of repression at different periods and places is that certain small classes arise, identify themselves with rule, and turn the whole mechanism of necessary repression to their personal advantage. Necessary repression, expressed in law, becomes the mechanism behind which they carry on repression in their own interests. Law and order, desirable in general, mean in the light of special emphases wealth or affluence for a few, poverty for many.

For the people in charge of the instruments of repression in time are emboldened to make more and more exceptions in their own immediate interests, as in the case of the medieval popes. What was forbidden to everyone else was allowed, off the record, to the pope. Who was there, after all, to say him nay?

Sixteen

THE CREAM OF THE QUEST

The various attitudes and dispositions of the wealthy coterie—the up-and-coming, the active and established, the playful and the idly parasitic (artistic contrast on the social scene to the lethargic parasitic poor)—obviously have some sort of general end-in-view or goal. For a man ordinarily seeks to attain or retain great wealth for some more tangible reason than simple social security, which the American rich have achieved to an absurd and perhaps self-defeating degree. As seems evident, the common reason for attaining and retaining wealth, as displayed in specific careers, is to lead some personally determined insulated version of the Good Life. Considerable independence of others is an invariable hallmark of the good life as delineated by the rich. Power itself creates a barrier between those who possess it and those who do not.

As all of the rich have far more choices open to them than the nonrich in selecting personal roles and scheduling their time, the way they live should at least shadow forth their conception of how one should properly live. Manifestly, if they thought it a hardship to sleep in a gold canopied bed in a mansion they could, exercising free choice, instead sleep in a Bowery doorway, under a haystack or in a cabin small by a waterfall; some, in fact, prefer to sleep, occasionally at least, in remote hunting lodges or on damp, unsteady yachts. As far as that is concerned, they could, exercising choice, retire to a monastery on a cold Himalayan slope or join (or even buy) a circus. A few, to be sure, have satisfied profound inclinations by buying Broadway shows and square-rigged sailing ships.

Yet, despite the wide range of material choices open to them, recipes for living among the rich are so restricted and familiar as to have become historical clichés. Their general style of living has changed little since the days of the Pharaohs, both absolutely and relatively to the rest of society.

The personal life of a rich man in truth is rather cut and dried and pretty much follows a longstanding script; it is about as stylized and full of surprises as a minuet. Within a rather narrow range one can accurately predict his moves from collecting expensive objects to breeding horses and dogs. To be rich and not a collector is to be a fairly rare bird.

Certain broad patterns of living can be clearly discerned among the rich, although one may be a total abstainer and another a sturdy boozer; one may prefer blondes and another exotic non-Caucasians. It is no doubt because life for the rich is historically routinized, holding few surprises either enchanting or terrifying, that so many of them become addicted to gambling, from the stock market to the casino and horse race. Except for those who play out their gambling drive in politics or forms of business rulership, many of them are patently subject to boredom, as many photographs show.[1]

While I would not go so far as to say that all of the rich are bored all of the time, boredom has historically been one of the occupational hazards of the upper classes; for people who have seen nearly everything and satisfied inclinations as much as they could each day acquire a considerable feeling of *déjà vu*. Unlike the common run of employee they have, for example, never had the unexpected thrill of being suddenly called to account. They have never suddenly been told: "You're fired," a dramatic experience known to thousands of poorer men, including university presidents.

Unlike the very poor they are not, even rarely, bemused by unexpected kindness or consideration; for they have learned to expect such attitudes from others, especially from officials and personnel, and might, perhaps, be diverted rather than otherwise moved by some rare outburst of rudeness that would annoy a humbler man. Some of the rich no doubt get some release from boredom by reading the overheated Marxist press and learning what aspiring back-alley commissars have in store for them. But such roaring historic adventure on the guillotine, they no doubt sadly realize, is not to be for them. They are fully aware of all the overlapping mechanisms of social control, from the Holy Ghost and the local schools to the police and the military, to say nothing of privately retained legislators and eager-beaver rank-and-file vigilantes ever ready to show their patriotic zeal by harassing bedraggled dissenters.

Whatever their orientation either as actives or passives on the social scene, the rich are all affected, almost without their knowledge, by the concentrated dynamic of money. Their assets, as it were, are constantly sending out invisible impulses to them to make some move, make some move, make some move. . . . To get away from the compulsively hypnotic influence of these assets is seemingly, for nearly all, virtually impossible. They are as Trilbys to the Svengali of their money.

This is readily seen in the cases, always fulsomely reported, of people who unexpectedly come into large properties, either by inheritance or by winning some sweepstakes. As soon as happy news of the good fortune is received there must be a celebration with champagne, cigars and immoderate quantities of delicatessen goodies. Under the questioning of reporters the lucky recipient, delivered from an impecunious hell, must relate what he intends to do with his windfall. He is sometimes baffled at first, but the world insistently demands an answer and it is clear that he must do something with the money. To refuse it out of hand would be manifest folly. So we see that the money is already prodding him, and will keep on prodding until the day it is all gone. He can spend it all rapidly (and some have done just this) or he can more prudently bank it and spend only the income, thus reserving its magic power for disposition over a wider section of space and time; if he does this he has almost insensibly moved upward in the socio-economic structure, joined the bourgeoisie.

No case has yet been reported, although there may have been one, of a man informed that he had just come into an unexpected $5 million who, making a note of it, nonchalantly sauntered off to keep a dental appointment and to pick up some chopped meat for his dog on the way home. Nor has any case yet been reported of a man, telephoning a friend, who near the end of the conversation says something like, "By the way, George, I've just been surprised to learn I've come into $5 million." Such recipients, to the contrary, usually start sending excited messages to all points of the compass.

Most of the rich, whether they arrived by their own scheming or have inherited, are not thus taken by surprise. It was always understood by most of them that they were going to be rich as soon as some older relative passed to his reward. While no great alteration is required in the style of life of such they, too, have it gradually borne in upon them by bankers, lawyers, wives and friends that they are under some irresistible compulsion to make moves in which their money plays a major role, something like the queen in a game of chess. Few new heirs, if any, find that they can ignore or even tranquilly contemplate from afar their newly acquired assets. They are suddenly burdened with problems: an investment problem, a tax problem, a political problem, a donation problem, a general living problem. Where to spend the summer? The winter? Spring and fall? And what of the difficult periods between seasons, where there is an overlap? And what to wear? What clothing? Who to see and not see?

A generalization that applies with hardly an exception to all of the rich is that asceticism is rarely if ever an ingredient in their personal scheme of affairs. Not that it should be; it just is not. Rather is it the case that however the life of one rich person may differ from that of another both live at the opposite pole from asceticism. The elder J. P. Morgan was quite a bon vivant, a swinger, and Rockefeller was a teetotaler and homebody; yet Rockefeller, among other things, maintained four palatial estates, one for each season of the year, from Maine to Florida. Although a tight-lipped Baptist elder, he was far from monkish.

The personal life of the rich, almost without exception, comes down to sensory gratification on a grand scale, gratification attained in the light of standards generally considered luxurious. A simplistic material determinism seems to rule their lives as by an iron law. Here and there, it is true, have been persons frugal to the point of miserliness, such as Hetty Green, but in general the rich are found to live according to popular conceptions of extreme luxury even though one may be comparatively restrained and another an obvious sybarite. They do, broadly, precisely what the average man in the street would do, neither more nor less, were he on their lofty pecuniary perch. What one may say in the most extreme criticism of them is that they are so ordinary, so common, so vulgar, yet placed in positions of extraordinary advantage. Far more than they themselves suppose, they are automatons, moved one way or the other almost always by considerations of money. To find a rich man, apart from an occasional eccentric inventor, living a life largely unmotivated by his money is, as I believe the record shows, a virtual impossibility. Successful inventors, yes; others, no.

The Gorgeous Setting

What unquestionably first strikes the most indolent observer about the personal lives of the rich compared with the nonrich is the opulence of their residential settings. These lush habitations, contrary to many hurried commentators, have more than a titillating value for outsiders. They are, I submit, deeply symbolic of a self-conception and of actual objective social status. They are, contrary to the eagle-eyed Veblen, more than an exercise in ostentatious display and conspicuous consumption. They are, in fact, a dead giveaway of what it is all about.

Since the time of the Pharaohs, and no doubt even before, the head man in the kingdom always had the biggest house, a palace, and with the advent of progress in utilizing labor he came to have many palaces suitable to the different seasons of the year and different moods. The supporting nobility and priesthood had lesser but sufficiently palatial habitations, and it was only as some of these came to have more to say in ruling the realm that their homes began to rival in size that of the monarch.

At the risk of provoking the bargain-basement sages into charging that I am oversimplifying, let me lay it plainly on the line: The people with the most say-so have always had the largest and most elaborate domiciles. Big house historically means big man in the realm; conversely, small house means nobody in the realm.

As direct survivals of this tradition, embellished by Roman emperors, Louis XIV, the czars and a few others, we today see the pope, spiritual ruler over some 500 million precious immortal souls, living in a series of huge palaces, one of which is set in his own small city. We see the figure-head kings and queens of England still housed in extraordinarily large houses, some approaching the size of the Kennedys' Merchandise Mart in Chicago. And we see the successors to the czars living in the Kremlin, no shack.

From time to time a vast residence has been awarded at the expense of the realm to someone who has been of signal service to the rulers, as in the case of huge Blenheim Palace in Oxfordshire, England, awarded in Queen Anne's reign to John Churchill, first Duke of Marlborough, for his victory in 1704 over the French and Bavarians at the decisive battle of Blenheim in Bavaria. Winston Churchill spent much of his boyhood in this truly imperial edifice.

A very big house, then, or a series of big houses, means historically that the inhabitant is either a ruler or one very closely associated with rule. It is never, never, never the case that anyone functionally or otherwise dissociated from rule, anyone such as an artist, philosopher, civil service official or scientist, inhabits such a big house except as a guest. The big houses, then, are the outward signs writ plain of a class habituated to rule, reminding us of the principle of Roman law: *Cui bono?*

As the United States does not have anything like a ruling class, according to an extensive assortment of fully housebroken professors, we are confronted here by an apparent anomaly: People who in theory have no more to say about governance than the ordinary truck driver somehow inhabit some of the choicest and most expensive establishments of all history. In American political theory, to be sure, the rulers are fundamentally the whole people, who from time to time duly elect their representatives. These latter, if anyone, are held to be the real rulers. Yet these putative real rulers, unless they already belong to the very rich class, never inhabit dwellings of comparable opulence even if they reach the White House, which is itself a comparatively modest affair with a short-term lease.

When American presidents leave office they almost invariably return to relatively unimposing dwellings—Eisenhower to a remodeled frame farmhouse in Gettysburg, Truman to a Victorian frame house in Independence and Lyndon B. Johnson eventually to a not very impressive ranch house in West Texas. With no intention of being disparaging, one can see that these ex-presidential habitations, comfortable enough to be sure, would hardly rate as servants' quarters on most of the larger estates. Members of the Supreme Court, as anyone can see, occupy nothing more substantial.

This is not to say that the president and members of Congress are not powerful for stipulated periods within constitutional limits. But their power, whether it consisted of Wilson steering the country far off center into World War I or Johnson by his own decision intervening massively in faraway Vietnam, was always exercised at the prompting and with the approval of the magnates. We know this, first, because the magnates publicly applauded and, secondly, not a single one of them seriously dissented. Except for certain features of policy under Franklin D. Roosevelt, when counsels in a crisis were divided, the magnates have been in general harmony with national policy all along. Either the magnates wanted that policy (and heavy documentation by Gabriel Kolko for 1900–12 in *The Triumph of Conservatism* shows them as the very source of policy) or the political managers have been clairvoyant enough to hit upon policies that would meet with the broad approval of the magnates even as many highly intelligent and informed nonmagnates dissented (as with respect to Johnson on the Vietnam policy).

Much policy deeply affecting the lives of most citizens, as far as that goes, is never submitted to the political powers for their rescript. For whatever is not specifically forbidden under the rule of freedom is permitted. As a single example, let us consider technological innovation, always embarked upon by private decision but invariably of vast public consequence. In pursuit of greater economy and efficiency, higher productivity per man employed and more substantial profits, the corporate managers, deputies of the big owners, constantly refine the technology of production. More particularly they have recently, without any prompting word from formal government, plumped heavily for labor-eliminating automation. And although the size of the labor force has steadily increased it has not increased parallel with population growth, thus dealing large sections of the populace out of it, notably the younger, the crudely skilled and those designated as superannuated at sixty-two to sixty-five years. No representatives, near or remote, of those dealt out ever passed on the policy that has had such effects. The measures were simply taken by private, unilateral decision in consonance with sound corporate practice, an example of veiled power that has wide effects.

More formally, now, with the social effects apparent, the young were bidden to remain in school, for which many have no stomach either because of personal incapacity or because a considerable segment of conventional schooling is plainly boring and irrelevant to any felt issue. Many simply cannot stand the dull routine. Again, many in a pecuniary milieu want to earn money so as to feel some illusory independence. As a consequence, the country now possesses a large section of disoriented young, neither at school nor at work and getting into a variety of headline-making mischief from congregating in unseemly hordes to sedulous extra-curricular copulation and drug addiction.

No elected representative ever passed on the decisions that produced these results. The decisions were made quietly by quiet men in quiet corporate boardrooms.

The big houses, in brief, are occupied by the basic decision makers, and this has been the rule down through history. A difference, however, is that in the United States the decisions are only indirectly and obliquely imposed.

It should not be supposed that the idea of this self-conception of rulership on the part of the rich is sustained only by the fact that they have a penchant for assorted ducal mansions and grounds. That this is the self-conception is shown, too, by the way many of them sign their names with Roman numerals appended, betokening an established family line in the style of European nobility. It is shown, furthermore, and more convincingly, in the affinity of the American rich, particularly with respect to their young women, for marriage with members of the European nobility.

Such marriages have taken place by the hundreds and I will not trouble once again to cite and update them. The most spectacular of them was the marriage of Consuelo Vanderbilt to the Duke of Marlborough, the two offspring of which are directly in the ducal Marlborough line. That the motivation in these marriages was the quest for titles, mainly on behalf of the mothers of daughters, is made clear by the fact that wealthy young American males rarely married a titled European female; for in that case the title was not shared.[2]

Almost always it was the case that marriage took place when the title could pass and the offspring, grandchildren of American commoners, could be authentically ennobled. "I am the mother of a genuine, 24-karat duke," the American woman could sigh in quiet idiotic joy.

It is obvious that the American industrial rich, not sharing the distaste of the Founding Fathers for titles, identified themselves with and saw themselves playing a role similar to European nobility and royalty.

True, a self-conception is not necessarily a reflection of reality; it could be pure fantasy. It is on other grounds, of actual rulership, that we see that the self-conception was not mistaken. The big-rich of the United States are in fact if not in form American dukes; the general populace pretty much enacts the role and has the outlook of peasantry, most of them quite gladly.

Patterns of Residence

While much has been written in detailed description of the opulent and vasty residences of the freedom-loving rich, and many photographs of them have been published, it has not been noticed as far as I am aware that they occur in distinct, different patterns.

These patterns are as follows:

1. The compound, or multiple estate, containing many large residences of different members of an extended family and sometimes including an entire village and much acreage.

2. The cluster or territorial grouping of separate estates of an extended family.

3. Scattered estates up to fifty or more of the different branches of an extended family.

4. The single country estate of a nuclear family, usually the mark of someone new to wealth.

In all cases it should be understood that the estate is merely the family center. There remain to be reckoned town houses, distant estates in non-urban terrain and foreign estates; many wealthy Americans own either European or Latin American estates and a few persons have them in northern Africa, particularly Morocco.

One function of the large estate, of course, is to instil awe and thereby place social distance between the owner and the clamorous *hoi polloi*.

The question of preserving social distance is important for a variety of reasons, not the least of which is that it would be awkward in many ways if rich and poor were closely mingled. It would certainly be socially awkward when the rich man sat down to a feast and the poor man turned to his stew and grits. As a matter of common sociability the rich man would be expected to offer some of his steak and endive salad to the poor man and to accept some of the stew. If it were only one or a few poor men asked to partake of a sumptuous repast it would be one thing; but if the participation were quite general it would be another. A man worth $100 million would be broke over night, for example, if he treated all the families in the country to a single steak dinner at his expense.

Social distance, then, is seen to come down, among other things, to a matter of economy. One cannot invite everybody into the plantation and remain rich for long. The visitors will literally eat one out of house and home, like invading locusts. That the rich man is not ordinarily this open-handed does not signify that he is especially ungenerous; he is merely prudent and posts his various signs: "Private, Keep Out." Privacy becomes a cult.

Examples of Residential Patterns

A prime example of the compound or multiple-dwelling arrangement is the Rockefeller estate, *Kykuit*, of 4,180 acres at Pocantico Hills, New York, just east of Tarrytown in the fabled Sleepy Hollow country. Such land in the region sells at $5 to $10 thousand per acre and higher. Until Winthrop left for Arkansas all the brothers had each a large house on this estate, where lived also Rockefeller I and II. The place has many scores of buildings, for maintenance and the housing of a large staff, and includes a $1 million playhouse (at cost many years ago) that holds bowling alleys, tennis court, swimming pool and squash court.[3]

The Rockefeller brothers also have New York City residences. John III and his wife share a large duplex apartment on the upper East Side and in 1950 built a house for guests near fashionable Beekman Place.[4] Nelson and his family occupy a triplex penthouse on Millionaire's Row of Fifth Avenue, facing Central Park.[5] David, Laurance, Rodman C. and Winthrop all have separate domiciles on New York's upper East Side, as shown in the telephone directory.

Nelson owns a large ranch in the highlands of Venezuela on which he sojourns at intervals, Laurance has a plantation in Hawaii and Winthrop has a palatial working plantation in Arkansas. It is not, however, necessary for the wealthy to own their separate places of residence; many of them lease large places from time to time in various parts of the world or take over entire floors in de luxe hotels as the occasion seems to require. They are, therefore, to be found now and again flitting in and out of Paris, London, the Riviera, the Bahamas or Puerto Rico.

Kykuit is bisected by a public road that affords views of dense forests and open fenced fields on either side for a stretch of many miles; this road is Route 117, connecting North Tarrytown with Pleasantville, New York.

Once entirely open to the public, only part is now open for hiking, horseback riding and hunting. But where the family homes are it is "as remote from the outside world as a fortified principality."[6] Tight security is maintained: "high stone walls, massive iron gates, alert guards, police dogs and miles of barbed-wire fences make the homes a sanctuary."[7] The home of David, however, is right on the main public road.

The main house, *Kykuit* itself, until his death occupied by John D. II and his wife, is a fifty-room granite structure in modified Georgian design with spacious views of the surrounding country. It has four stories with guest rooms on the third and fourth floors.[8]

More recently the widow of John D. II, finding this edifice too roomy, constructed elsewhere on the estate a modest $300,000 Georgian home of only ten bedrooms. The destiny of the big house has not apparently yet been decided.

Various price tags have been put on all this by different commentators but as the books of account have not been made public it is perhaps misleading to cite any. When Rockefeller I died the *New York Times* (May 24, 1937) said the single granite house had cost $2 million to build, while the estate took $500,000 a year at Depression prices to maintain. The entire affair required a staff then of 350. Standard equipment throughout are elevators, air conditioning and just about anything in the way of appurtenances, comforts and conveniences one cares to name. The domicile of no potentate is any better equipped.

This compound or multiple assembly style of dwelling was adopted by the numerous Kennedys for their summer residences at Hyannisport, Massachusetts. For more prolonged residence they appear to find the scatter-type of dwellings more suitable. Many families, indeed, have their summer estates in the compound form, a great many on coastal islands. In addition to the numerous Forbes family, whose places dot Naushon Island near Martha's Vineyard, there are many others of a similar nature. Islands appear to hold a great attraction for the rich, insuring complete privacy, and on them one finds the compound of estates and at times a collection of seasonal estates of many different high-ranking families, such as Jekyll Island off the Georgia coast was until the 1940's. The biggest island layout, of course, is Santa Catalina Island off California, owned by William Wrigley, Jr., the chewing gum king, for many years. This sort of thing, one might say, is really living, for with an island of one's own one is really the local sovereign.[9]

The more numerous Du Ponts provide the chief illustration of the cluster type of massed estates in northern Delaware and extending over into nearby Pennsylvania. Because of the many large Du Pont houses strewn about, the region has been dubbed by some as "America's chateau country" and "the du Ponts' duchy of Delaware."[10]

The largest of the Du Pont estates—Longwood, Nemours and Winterthur—have been given tax-free endowments as public museums so that the average citizen can now go and get some foretaste of what Valhalla is really like; but the names of two dozen others strew the countryside: Montchanin, Granogue, Chevannes, St. Amour, Louviers, Bellevue, Guyencourt, Owl's Nest, Bois des Fossés *et al.*[11]

Latterly many of the Du Ponts, according to a recent expert biographer, have taken to acquiring more modest habitations such as *Hexton* of Samuel Francis du Pont, which we are reassured "has dignity without formality, spaciousness without ostentation, ease without opulence."[12]

It should not be supposed that Du Pont residences are confined to Delaware. Lammot du Pont, who died in 1952, had a big summer place on Fisher's Island, New York, near the mouth of Long Island Sound. Many of the wealthy have summer *dachas* on this hallowed isle. Alfred I. du Pont moved to Florida, where he left the mammoth Nemours Foundation noticed earlier. Others have extra residences by the scores, city and country, tucked away elsewhere.

For a detailed description with photographs of a fabulously elegant Du Pont house the reader is referred to Folsom.[13]

The four third-generation branches of the Vanderbilt clan, less cohesive than either the Rockefellers or Du Ponts, scattered their many separate *palazzi* to all points of the compass.

The most ornate Vanderbilt place among many is the French Renaissance chateau of George W. Vanderbilt near Asheville, North Carolina, built when he had achieved hereditary success at the age of twenty-six. It contains 250 rooms and was set in 146,000 acres (now 12,000 acres) with a three-mile drive through 500 varieties of flora from the front gate to the house.[14] Inside views of the house show it to be, like many homes of the American rich, a quite literal variation on the themes of grandiloquent opulence expressed at Versailles and Fontainebleau. "As conceived by Mr. Vanderbilt, his new principality was typical of those developed by royal families in Europe hundreds of years earlier."[15] This place was inherited by his daughter Cornelia and, as of 1964, by her two sons, George and William Cecil. Here is an example, one among many, of an original name lost to view through a distaff marriage. The original cost of this place in 1895 was estimated at $7 million and its present value is set at $50–$60 million.[16]

Vanderbilt mansions, one after the other, used to dominate Fifth Avenue in New York but have since been torn down to make room for lucrative skyscrapers. Frederick W. Vanderbilt built a vast stone *palazzo* overlooking the Hudson River at Hyde Park, New York. Avoiding inheritance taxes, it was left to New York State and is now operated as a museum of high life in yesteryear. Cornelius Vanderbilt, another grandson of the founder, built *The Breakers* at Newport, with interiors that are practically replicas of royal French palaces. Other Vanderbilts played house with big houses elsewhere. Many presently occupied by authentic Vanderbilts are scattered about the country.

More usually a wealthy family has one or two single country estates and one or two town houses, such dispositions of course depending on the size of the family and the fortune.

Although the trend is now toward less ornate or more secluded places on distant shores, some of the original big houses, along with their large truly royal art collections, have since passed to public or educational use so as not to figure in testamentary estates for tax purposes.

Data, descriptions and dazzling photographs of a few among many ultra-elaborate chateaux are given by Folsom in the following: *Vizcaya*, of James Deering, Miami; *Marble Casa*, of Henry M. Flagler, Palm Beach; *Ca' d' Zan*, John Ringling, Sarasota; *Shadow Lawn*, Hubert T. Parson, former president of F. W. Woolworth Company, West Long Branch, New Jersey; Fifth Avenue mansion, Henry Clay Frick, New York City, lower floor now an art museum housing the Frick collection; Tudor mansion, Andrew W. Mellon, Pittsburgh, now Mellon Hall of Chatham College; *La Cuesta Encantada*, William Randolph Hearst, San Simeon, California; *San Marino*, Henry E. Huntington, San Marino, California; *Ophir Hall*, Whitelaw and Ogden Reid, Purchase, New York, now part of Manhattanville College of the Sacred Heart; *The Elms*, E. J. Berwind, Newport; various mansion-sized Newport "summer cottages" belonging to Dukes, Youngs, Mrs. Perle Mesta, Mrs. Stuyvesant Fish, Vanderbilts, Firestones, Jelkes, Van Rensselaers, Havemeyers and others; *Belcourt Castle*, O. H. P. Belmont, Newport; *Ochre Court*, Ogden Goelet, Newport, now part of Salve Regina College; *Stan Hywet Hall*, Frank A. Seiberling, Akron; *Fair Lane*, Henry Ford, Dearborn, Michigan, part now of Dearborn campus of the University of Michigan; *Meadow Brook Hall*, Mr. and Mrs. Alfred G. (Dodge Motors) Wilson, Rochester, Michigan, now part of East Lansing campus of Michigan State University; and English manor house, Edsel Ford, Grosse Point Shores, Michigan.

These, let it be understood, are only a very few samples among many.

While the ducal country and foreign estate is still part of the standard equipment of the very wealthy, the big town house has been largely replaced by the cooperative luxury apartment which in many cases amounts to a large town house sequestered behind the flat facade of an apartment building. The advantage of a cooperative apartment is that it need never become a taxable white elephant but can be sold at full value as it is or broken down into more saleable smaller apartments. Taxwise, the cooperative apartment is a liquid asset as the big town *palazzi* and their art collections failed to remain under post-1913 tax policy.

The Rockefeller estate at Pocantico Hills is almost certain to wind up either as a huge public park, a fashionable real estate development or as part of each. After having been forced to accept by testamentary bequest several large country properties that thus escaped figuring among taxable assets, New York passed a law requiring that all such bequests must first gain the consent of the state in order to escape the cash-draining tax net.

Dazzling Interiors

The interiors of most of these houses are more spectacular than the exteriors, which are mostly impressive in their dimensions. As photographs, liberally supplied by Folsom, show very well, rooms are often of palacelike proportions with the marble walls covered by expensive paintings and tapestries. Rare Oriental draperies and rugs, entire imported paneled rooms from European chateaux and expensive bric-a-brac and furniture are in most places strictly *de rigeur*. *Expensive* is the operational word. The National Gallery in Washington now houses the Andrew W. Mellon art collection and the Frick Museum shows what Frick collected. There is, too, the opulent J. P. Morgan Library of rare medieval illustrated books and manuscripts, once a private sanctuary. This sort of thing, as a matter of fact, is scattered all around.

The magnates were, and many remain, art-minded, and no doubt saw themselves secretly as latter-day versions of Renaissance princes. But a difference in their relation to art is that, while the princes and later kings subsidized working artists, the American wealthy usually merely bid up the prices of extant art. A few today, such as Nelson Rockefeller, collect modern art and thus may be looked upon as giving monetary encouragement to living artists. But, by and large, art dealers rather than artists benefited from the artistic interest of the American magnates, who were traders and collectors rather than art patrons.

The artistic impulses of most of the rich are recognized in their own circles as essentially pecuniary. Thus, the *Wall Street Journal*, January 3, 1967, impiously notes that a work of art is looked upon as "a growth stock, a whopping tax deduction—or an artful fake." Actually, says this authoritative publication, "it's possible for a painting to be all these things at once."

"The rise in prices has led many purchasers to view art primarily as an investment whose growth potential puts many a high-flying stock to shame," said the *Journal*. "According to dealers and others in the art world, some 'collectors,' who not long ago thought Modigliani was some kind of Italian dish, now move in and out of the art market like so many Wall Street speculators, hunting bargains, and then trying to resell them at a fancy profit."

Works of art, acquired at bargains, in other words have the potentialities of capital gains and do represent diversification of holdings in an always uncertain world. In any market they would always (unlike money) be worth something. This apart, as the *Journal* said, art works, whether genuine or fake, make possible huge tax deductions that offset actual money income. The way this works is as follows: a man buys a painting, genuine or fake, for $1,000, holds it a while and then donates it to a museum at a declared market value of $10,000, thus obtaining a net $9,000 deduction from taxable income for a tax-free gift to the always-to-be-considered public. If the museum spots it as a fake, it says nothing for fear of discouraging the later donation of genuine works. There is, thus, a ready market for palpable fakes.

In order to obtain tax benefits the operation requires only that the declared value of the gift exceed the cost, whatever it was.

"In surveying the appraisals used in justifying the tax deductions of 400 donated works," said the *Journal*, "IRS [Internal Revenue Service] found that the art objects had cost the donors a total of $1,471,502—but that their total declared 'fair market value' as deductions had climbed to $5,811,908." The ruse is profitable whether the art work is authentic or not.

Art works, too, may play other financial roles. A man may pay $10,000 for a painting and later bestow it as a gift on a friend or relative. As a gift of valuable property this is theoretically taxable, but gifts of portable objects are not ordinarily scrutinized and, as far as that goes, the tax courts have ruled that valuable gifts to, say, a lady friend, are not taxable; so to argue would check sentiment. An ardent admirer may give a series of such gifts to a lady and not be subject to a tax, thus building up her net worth tax free. The gifts, being valuable, may be used as collateral up to at least half their value against loans. And they may be sold privately for cash.

Art collecting, again, may be used to pay a large portion of inheritance taxes. Thus, as part of his general operation, a wealthy man, otherwise no aesthete, gradually builds up a collection of paintings of some artist or school; his very acquisitions have the effect of giving these paintings a scarcity value—and it is scarcity as well as vogue that gives these objects their appraisal value whether they are works of art, postage stamps, books and manuscripts or old coins. A collection that cost $10 million may ultimately have a market value of $50 million, which is recovered in careful sales and the proceeds used to pay inheritance taxes relating to revenue-producing properties as well. Two birds are thus killed with one tax stone: There is no capital-gain tax on the increment in value (death excluding capital gains under the tax law) and the proceeds pay all or a large part of taxes, thus preserving revenue-producing property for the inheritors.

Aesthetic objects thus play a dual decorative as well as pecuniary role.

Concluding this bit, it can be shown that the pecuniary approach to art has been thoroughly systematized for the benefit of a well-heeled clientele. For verification the reader is referred to two large-paged books: Richard H. Rush, *Art as an Investment*, Prentice-Hall, Inc., Englewood Cliffs, New Jersey, 1961, 418 pages, and Robert Wraight, *The Art Game*, Simon and Schuster, New York, 1965, 224 pages. The ins and outs, and the "angles," get full treatment here.

Apartment House Chateaux

Since World War II, even as more and more of the booboisie are found to be sleeping in subway trains, doorways, flophouses, parks and bus stations, there has been a surge of building large luxury apartment buildings in the larger cities: New York, Chicago, Boston, Philadelphia, etc. This building boom has, perhaps, been greatest in New York City where on central Manhattan there have been erected scores of luxury apartment buildings, many of them cooperatively owned by the well-heeled tenants.

As it would require a great deal of space to list and describe them all let us concentrate on an outstanding recent example, the United Nations Plaza, as described by the always staid *New York Times*.[17]

United Nations Plaza, of thirty-eight stories, is the tallest residential structure in the city and faces the United Nations headquarters from the north at 48th Street and the East River. The initial cost of each apartment is $25,900 for 3½ rooms to $166,000 for a nine-room duplex "with its own little elevator, wood-burning fireplace and curving stairs, and with carrying charges that range from $248 to $1,590 a month. . . . The cost of the apartment is only the beginning for a lot of tenants. Fully a third of them have taken down walls, put up new ones, installed circular columns or big square pillars, and otherwise altered the original floor plan. And it is taken for granted that a majority of the tenants will upgrade bathroom fixtures and kitchen appliances."

Although there were more than 335 basic apartments, some tenants acquired several and joined them together while enlarging rooms so as to have, in effect, a large townhouse behind a flat glass-and-aluminum facade. This is standard procedure in luxury apartment buildings. In many of the apartments metal fittings have been replaced with gold or sterling silver fittings.

Corner suites have seven-foot-high windows that stretch for forty-eight feet in the living-dining areas, and many look out over the East River. All apartments are air-conditioned and at the touch of a switch can be kept at any moderate temperature, winter or summer. Bathroom floors and walls are of Carrara marble, kitchens are eighteen feet long and a gourmet restaurant on the ground floor offers room service to tenants.

Luxurious to the nth degree, the edifice has tenants who are fully a match for the setting. At the time of making its report, said the *Times,* among the owners,

. . . there are no theater people, no familiar television faces, and only one writer, Truman Capote. What is filling United Nations Plaza, especially the East tower, is a sort of power elite.

Of the 71 per cent that quietly make wheels go 'round, 69 per cent are senior vice presidents, executive vice presidents, presidents or chairmen of the board.

In big business they include John Dickson Harper, president of Alcoa, the company that put up the building; William Johnstone, chairman of the finance committee of Bethlehem Steel; Chester Laing, president of John Nuveen & Co., investment bankers; and Lowell P. Weicker, president of Bigelow-Sanford, Inc.

In publishing they are Roy Larsen, chairman of the executive committee of Time, Inc.; Andrew Haiskell, chairman of the board of Time, Inc., and Mrs. Philip (Katherine) Graham, publisher of *The Washington Post* and president of *Newsweek* magazine.

The 9 per cent of the tenants who are lawyers include Christian Herter Jr., whose father was Secretary of State, and William Pierce Rogers, who was Attorney General under Eisenhower.

Eight per cent are classed as persons of independent means; a good many of them have sold homes and taken apartments to simplify living.

Among the 6 per cent embracing various professions are William S. Brown, a partner of Skidmore, Owings & Merrill, architects; Ross Claiborne, editor of the Dell Publishing Company, Inc.; and Bonnie Cashin, who designs clothes for Seventh Avenue. . . .

Among the 6 per cent of the tenants who are identified with government or with philanthropic foundations are Senator Robert F. Kennedy, Raymond Dinsmore and Mrs. Albert (Mary) Lasker, widow of an advertising tycoon. . . .

Mary Lasker, whose apartment will not be finished until early summer, and who wanted to be no higher than the 10th and 11th floors because otherwise she would "be too far above the trees, . . ." [will use her apartment] as a kind of annex to her house on Beekman Place—where she will continue to live. . . .

[She has an apartment of only five rooms] but it was actually made by taking three and a half apartments with a total of 22 rooms.

That the rich, as F. Scott Fitzgerald sensitively discerned, inhabit an altogether special reality is shown in what they designate a room. The dimensions of a living room in a lower middle-class home become in a rich man's house those of a dressing room, a mop room or a linen closet. Rooms, properly speaking, in a rich man's house are generally at least four times larger than average residential rooms, sometimes ten or even twenty times larger. . . . They are often of museum and ballroom calibre, as photographs show.

"To Bonnie Cashin, United Nations Plaza represents 'a whole new world. And moving into it is almost like going to a new country. . . .'"

Interiors and intimate methods of operation of United Nations Plaza have been shown on television. As there explained, the tightest security is maintained, both at the front door and with respect to deliveries. Deliverymen must show credentials at various guarded barriers in the basement, will be admitted only on explicit instructions from on high and must be checked in and out. Names of occupants are not listed on mail boxes. The security staff and supportive personnel have all had their backgrounds rigidly scrutinized before gaining clearance by standards reported to be more exacting than those of the FBI and CIA for their finely tuned personnel.

While by no means the only such place in the larger cities United Nations Plaza may be taken at least as the *dernier cri* in "compact," luxury urban living quarters even though some of its larger apartments are no more than annexes to and extensions of nearby town houses for overflow guests, power brokers and relatives.

Standard Equipment

Practically standard equipment in all the bigger houses of the super-wealthy are items like pipe organs, extensive gardens and hothouses, interior and exterior swimming pools, chapels, statuary and sculpture strewn about, inlaid imported wall paneling and ceilings and a full line of all gadgets known to modern man. Expense has not been spared, money is plentiful.

Whereas early this century most of the big-rich owned their own private railroad cars and later their fleets of chauffeured automobiles, more recently many own their own long-distance airplanes, standing ready at some nearby airport. Whereas upper corporation managers make free use of company planes to look in on plant operations in distant parts, the big stockholders have their private planes and crews.[18]

The random reader will be happy to learn that the government thoughtfully provides a subsidy of $160 million per year to provide services for private and corporate aircraft and that taxes on aviation gasoline now cover only 4 per cent of this cost; the rest is charged to the general taxpayers.[19] Actually the government underwrites the wealthy 100 per cent.

The private large cruising aircraft appears to have largely replaced the private railway car and ocean-going steam yacht of an earlier day, although sports yachts are still present in single-ownership fleets.

Entertainment and Parties

These elaborate residences are used a great deal for entertaining and partying. The rich do a good deal of entertaining for friends and acquaintances because they do not ordinarily congregate in public places. If they did not provide a great deal of room in their homes for many guests and servile personnel they would, in order to avoid monkish seclusion, be forced to congregate where the public gathers in so-called public luxury establishments that are, in fact, largely patronized by pushers, entertainers, people "on the make" and obvious fourflushers. One rarely, as a matter of fact, sees any of the very rich in the presumably fashionable *bistros*. Here and there, now and then, yes; generally, no.

Expensive parties to mark various occasions have long been a predilection of the American rich, with the costs ranging from $250,000 to $1 million or more per shindig. The debutante party, through which the rich man presents his nubile daughters to the world, was long a standard affair with double orchestras blending entrancing sounds in huge ballrooms and champagne and caviar pouring down the gullets of thousands of well-heeled democrats amid banks of imported flora. While these exhilarating affairs (which seemed to outside observers to be rubbing it in) are now rarer, they are by no means entirely outmoded. The big party in general has given way to more discreet entertaining in small groups. They are, however, still served to the queen's taste.

A History of Luxury Parties in America would require a book of many hundreds of pages, the main source being the High Society pages of the leading newspapers. That aspect of partying that exerts most fascination for the mythical man-in-the-street, however, is of the order of what is reported to have suited the staglike taste of the late T. Coleman du Pont, obviously a man of the people. "In 1912, in partnership with Charles P. Taft, the President's brother, Coly built the McAlpin Hotel in New York, and on its twenty-first floor he established his Manhattan *pied-à-terre*. His parties there soon became famous for their gaiety and their pretty girls; Coly often had half the chorus of a Broadway show among the forty or more guests at an after-theater party. 'The General is loyal to a myriad of pretty girls who are proud to claim him as a friend,' a New York newspaper said in a needling story, 'and no one, not even Mrs. T. Coleman du Pont, seems to raise an objection. In fact, some people imagine that Mrs. T. Coleman du Pont must be a myth. One never sees her, never hears of her.' "[20]

Dinner parties, sedate or hilarious, always were, and remain, a favorite form of entertaining eight to a dozen or so of the ranking gentry. While political figures from abroad are often present, no doubt useful in snagging distant concessions and other goodies, it is noticeable that local politicos are rarely on hand except in Washington, where political intrigue is the sole social interest. Generals and admirals, however, are much sought for a certain austere contrasting tone.

It would, in any event, be bad electoral image-making for a politician of the domestic variety to be counted among those present at some of the more rococo parties of the ultra-affluent, which smack to some of the more straitlaced in the constituencies of European royal revels simply because champagne (a high-class soda pop) out in the sticks connotes something exotically perverse.

A Map of American Wealth

If a map of the centers and nature of privately held wealth were drawn, it would show the larger corporations in their headquarters and principal plants as fortresses toward which raw materials are constantly moving and from which are streaming products. These fortresses would represent the "big business" factor.

The big banks, represented by a different symbol, would appear as special centers with influences radiating out into the world of "small business." For in general, as we have noticed, "small business" is to a large extent the loan-supported business of the big banks, upon which some of the larger corporations are no longer dependent. Small business, paradoxically, is really fractionized big business.

The map would then show the family estates of the principal owners, numbering several hundred.

There would be symbols to show the locations of the principal metropolitan clubs and the principal pleasure resorts of the wealthy.

Corporate headquarters and big banks would tend to be clustered in

New York City but plants, resorts and family estates would be more widely scattered, thinning out as one moved to the extreme west and south. In general, there would be considerable clustering around major urban centers and sparseness of symbols in nonurban areas.

Self-Image of the Rich

What all this shows, it would appear, is that the rich, despite the meagerness of their personal achievement as limned in the preceding chapter, believe they are entitled to opulent settings. A divinity was once thought to hedge a king and it seemed only common sense that a divine personage be given the most opulent setting conceivable to man. The same sort of thinking applied to *churchpols,* who were believed to be in the closest confidence of the Deity. Faced by uncouth, undivine "robber barons," public thought in Europe simply bowed to *force majeure.* It was difficult to dispute with armed gangsters.

The first thing that occurred to the newly emerged American rich was to ape the style of life of European nobility and royalty. The American rich, quite obviously, saw themselves playing the same relative roles as masters of the situation, "lords of creation" in the phrase of Frederick Lewis Allen. In the main, the style of life of the English and French higher gentleman became the style of life of the American rich, who took root in a country where, oddly, a powerful political symbol was still the log cabin.

Whereas European royalty and nobility played profound integral roles in European history, the latter-day American rich were more like hitchhikers who opportunistically climbed aboard a good thing. They produced neither the technology, the climate, the land, the people nor the political system. Nor did they, like many European groups (as in England), take over the terrain as invading conquerors. Rather did they infiltrate the situation from below, insinuate themselves into opportunely presented economic gaps, subvert various rules and procedures, and, as it were, ride a rocket to the moon and beyond, meanwhile through their propagandists presenting themselves, no less, as the creators of machine industrialism which was in fact copied from England and transplanted into a lush terrain.

Let this be added: The fortune-builders were indeed organizers in a virgin terrain of little or no organization. They organized economic affairs according to well-established European patterns, and for this service charged a fee that some commentators consider extortionate, others reasonable. What was it, really? It was extortionate, of course. Judging by their style of life they set a high value on their services which amounted to merely imposing their rule. If one evaluates their achievement in other than self-serving corporate terms, the great expense of maintaining their personal way of life begins to look very much like another instance of misallocation of resources. From my possibly jaundiced point of view, it does not seem to me that the country is getting any return for the wealth self-lavished on their style of living.

Lest anyone believe that I am particularly indignant about this prospect let me at once enter a disclaimer. I harbor no such indignation, not any more than I would have for a man who sees a particularly enticing meal outspread and sits down to enjoy it—a wholly natural thing to do. What indignation I have is reserved for those who contemplate the prospect and consider it in accord with the cosmic proprieties or even that a greater public show of deference is due. I would not wish to proclaim to the world that Americans are an especially slavish people; I do not believe such to be the case. But there is a considerable section of Americans, for reasons about which one can only speculate, who definitely are obviously slavish. They have been commented upon in the memoirs of visiting royalty and nobility taken aback by being advanced upon in the United States with alarming gesticulations of deference and extravagant signs and cries of voluntary submission.

My own explanation for this phenomenon is that the United States was largely settled by members of the lower classes of Europe in whom were deeply ingrained a sense of their class lowliness and fealty to the upper orders. Descendants of these still like to kowtow whenever they can, and the more affluent of them spend large sums of money so they can be presented at the English royal court, there to bow, curtsy and scrape, to any other royal or ducal ceremonial to which they can wangle admittance or to the Vatican where they can experience the ineffable ecstasy of kissing the pope's ring, joy supreme. Some of this ingrained tendency, as it is easy to see, plays out on the domestic scene and is focused at times on public figures like Governor Nelson A. Rockefeller who, as the television cameras show, is at times plainly amazed and perhaps puzzled by the ecstatic fervor of his enthusiastic public reception. That it is all pretty much of a preconditioned American mechanism, uncommitted to any particular object, is shown when it is directed, without partiality, at some former sausage-stuffer who has become a film star or at a toothsome female, obviously guilty of first-degree murder, who has just been released with cheers by a jury of her peers. Clamorous deference in such circumstances, as the newspapers regularly report, at times attains riotous proportions. What ensues is in fact a raving mass self-abasement.

In this purely American setting, the self-image of the rich is at times reflected back upon them in magnified dimensions, no doubt leading some of them to believe they have taken far too humble a view of themselves.

Deviants from the Norm

Among the wealthy there do not appear to be many who show the slightest tendency to deviate from the norm of being either a *finpol*, a *pubpol*, a *corp-pol* or a more or less graceful idler and rentier. The life of the rich, as we have noticed, is as patterned and stylized as the life of the poor, holding few surprises.

That this is the case is seemingly more and more clearly realized by at least some of them, of late notably by the pace-setting Rockefellers even though they have been outrun into healing by a Mellon and a Frick. The fourth generation of Rockefellers, however, seem to be deviating more than occasionally from the plush-lined ruts traveled by the general man of wealth. As a psychologist might say of them and a few contemporaries, they appear to be seeking an identity of their own by breaking into new ground, thus playing a role more original than that of mere descendants of John D. I, or even of travelers in his general trustified direction.

As one swallow proverbially does not make a summer one need not look upon what is happening in this quarter as a trend. It is perhaps, however, a portent that some of the descendants of the industrial rich may be about to retrace, if history grants them the chance, the path followed by the historically more distinguished descendants of the earlier and more modestly capitalized mercantile Boston and landed Hudson Valley gentry who were considerably eclipsed in wealth and central influence by the rise of the industrial rich.

Michael Rockefeller, twenty-three, son of Nelson A., was an aspiring anthropologist until he was lost at sea from a disabled power-raft in 1961 while on an expedition to Dutch New Guinea with a Harvard University-Peabody Museum Expedition. He was declared legally dead on February 2, 1964. The *Times* reported he left an estate of $660,000.[21] According to all accounts, he was a superior fellow who was going to make some sort of individual mark.

Steven Rockefeller, another son, has become a clergyman, expounding the Gospel in benighted Chicago.

More recently Laurance Rockefeller, Jr., twenty-two, has appeared in the news as a member of Vista (Volunteers In Service To America), sometimes referred to as the domestic Peace Corps. Newspapermen caught sight of him as he began an eight-week training period in East Harlem, beginning adult life literally among the dregs.

In the meantime John D. IV, whose father is John D. III, had moved into an impoverished neighborhood in West Virginia, started hobnobbing with the local *descamisados* and *sans-culottes* and was swiftly elected to the West Virginia House of Delegates. If other cases are any guide, he is on his way to becoming at least a governor or a senator, possibly president. The United States could very appropriately have a President John D. Rockefeller IV.

The various courses embarked upon by these four young Rockefellers are, though, obviously offbeat as far as most of the rich are concerned. Many more of the affluent young are to be found congregating at the nearest country club or yacht basin, as I have determined by personal anthropological observation in the field.

Cracks in the Compound Walls

What I have written thus far might tend to leave the impression that the rich are, relatively, in a cushy position. And so they are. But the enviableness of their position amid accumulating signs of storm on every hand can be easily exaggerated unless seen in perspective.

In saying that the rich are faced by difficulties I simply state sober fact, not trying to gain for them any feeling that they are as heroes and heroines in an enveloping Greek tragedy. C. Wright Mills was very careful to issue an elaborate caveat against pitying them when he wrote,

> The idea that the millionaire finds nothing but a sad, empty place at the top of this society; the idea that the rich do not know what to do with their money; the idea that the successful become filled up with futility, and that those born successful are poor and little as well as rich—the idea, in short, of the disconsolateness of the rich—is, in the main, merely a way by which those who are not rich reconcile themselves to the fact. Wealth in America is directly gratifying and directly leads to many further gratifications.
>
> To be truly rich is to possess the means of realizing in big ways one's little whims and fantasies and sicknesses. . . . The rich, like other men, are perhaps more simply human than otherwise. But their toys are bigger; they have more of them; they have more of them all at once.
>
> . . . If the rich are not happy it is because none of us are happy. Moreover, to believe that they are unhappy would probably be un-American. For if they are not happy, then the very terms of success in America, the very aspirations of all sound men, lead to ashes rather than fruit. . . . If those who win the game for which the entire society seems designed are not "happy," are then

those who lose the happy ones? Must we believe that only those who live within, but not of, the American society can be happy? Were it calamitous to lose, and horrible to win, then the game of success would indeed be a sad game, doubly so in that it is a game everyone in and of the American culture cannot avoid playing. For to withdraw is of course objectively to lose, and to lose objectively, although subjectively to believe one has not lost—that borders on insanity. We simply must believe that the American rich are happy, else our confidence in the whole endeavor must be shaken. For of all the possible values of human society, one and one only is truly sovereign, truly universal, truly sound, truly and completely acceptable goal of man in America. That goal is money, and let there be no sour grapes about it from the losers.[22]

Mills here is partly ironic because his whole book expresses a complete lack of confidence in the general American endeavor. There is, then, no reason why the rich from his point of view should be even theoretically regarded as happy. It is probably true, however, that on balance they are no unhappier than anyone else and probably have at least a greater number of euphoric interludes.

In speaking of the rich as of any collective group there is always the danger of tacitly assuming that all the units in the collection, because they share some characteristic, are as alike as peas. The rich, of course, differ among each other in age, constitution, temperament, intelligence and knowledge. They also differ as to source of wealth: inherited or self-accumulated, diversified or concentrated, held in the form of bonds, equities, real estate or a combination of all. Yet, despite individual differences, they are similar in that they are, most of them, held within the same social matrix, subject to the same external compulsions and pressures.

This fact is clearly brought into view when we consider that although the rich have much power, more than the common run of men surely, they also experience in general a deeper sense of frustration than most people owing to the fact that their greater power is exercised within the restraints of a certain system and under the scrutiny of other powerful people. This amounts to saying that, though great, their power has limits, often annoying limits.

We can see this at a glance by looking at the problem of air pollution. And New York City, financial center of the world, is fittingly held by experts to have the worst pollution problem in the country. True, the rich man can flee the city from time to time and has in his homes and offices the latest air filtration devices; he is not so badly off as the ordinary citizen who must breathe the lethal stuff without interruption. Yet he knows that his staff, to which he is as loyal as it is to him, is caught in the muck. And he knows various projects of interest to him—perhaps a big skyscraper promotion—are qualified in their attractiveness and even value.

Why, then, as he has power, does he not deal with the problem decisively?

He is unable to do so, no doubt to his chagrin, because of the very momentum and direction of the system. Although he may publicly deprecate stress on the health issue he understands it as well as anyone. He is, however, caught in the situation as depicted by Theodore B. Merrill, an editor of *Business Week,* who said in a comprehensive national survey as long ago as 1960 (and in the meantime the problem has become more urgent) that "Nobody is going to put in any kind of control devices that cost him money unless he has to. . . . It simply has to be unprofitable for an industry to pollute the air or else they are going to pollute it, because it is cheaper to use the air for a sewer than to pay for keeping it clean."[23] The same holds true of polluting waterways.

Here, it would seem, profit is being put before human life and health, a point made endlessly by nasty socialists. And it is not merely profit that is in question but the general standing of an institution, a particular company. Although a rich man may control this company and could instantly make it stop polluting the air, such unilateral action would not solve the pollution problem, to which other companies also contribute. Unless all the companies acted in concert the action of one would have little effect.

And if all the companies in a particular region agreed to undergo the expense of reducing air pollution their costs would rise and profits fall in relation to companies in less populated regions not burdened with such costs. The inter-company position of the social-minded companies would decline. At this point multitudes of investors, some of them large but not controlling, would perhaps begin selling the stock of the social-minded companies because the relative return was diminishing in comparison with that of unsocial-minded companies. Dutch, Swiss, South American and ordinarily prudent domestic investors would sell out, realizing that these social-minded companies have expensive profit-eroding problems.

Investors, high or low, do not feel sympathetically identified with a company's problems, do not "forgive" it for making a poorer financial showing in a good cause. They simply analyze the figures and prospects of various companies. Some of these investors live in the bracing air of distant mountain resorts, by the seaside, off on distant healthy pampas. All they know is that as between company A and company B the latter, not burdened with many social-minded expenses, shows an ascending line of profitability and that this is better for *them.*

Why not then, it may be asked, make all companies uniformly comply to the maximum with all social-minded regulations, thus putting them on all fours and passing additional costs on in price? Doing this, however, would raise national costs *vis-à-vis* industries in other countries, which could undersell the Americans. In the world market the lowest-cost producer, everything else being equal, has a profit advantage and most readily attracts new capital most cheaply. And the world market is an area of prime interest to capitalists.

It is, then, "The System," as socialists have long contended, that gives priority here to its own systemic needs over the larger question of human life and health in specific instances.

As many scattered stockholders begin selling out of a company with a declining relative level of profitability, the price of the stock, its value, declines, affecting multitudes, jeopardizing bank loans and inducing an endless train of economic troubles. And when it comes to new financing the capital is not readily available, must be obtained along the route of a fixed rate of high interest, itself damaging to profitability, rather than through the issuance of equities. Being unilaterally social-minded, then, is ruinous.

Although powerful, the rich man, even the grouping of all rich men, is not powerful enough to fly in the face of the requirements of the supporting system. Beyond a certain level they must all take the rough with the smooth as offered by that system, a point that no doubt makes disconsolate the more reflective of them.

We may, now, imagine that one of the many economists who devote their lives to extolling the beauties of this system, its contributions to "progress," is dying in a hospital of lung cancer or emphysema contracted because of pervading air pollution. A case of poetic justice, it will be said. Yet he, as insight-limited as most economists, fails to make the connection between his lamentable condition and the economic system he so much admires. He considers himself only the victim of genetics or "bad luck," and if pressed will probably echo rueful Adam Smith that there's a great deal of ruin in every system—surely an intellectually weak stance.

The rich man wants for his children, whom he often loves passionately, the best in the way of education. He sends them to special schools that have the choice of teachers for small groups that are carefully supervised from dawn to nightfall. Most of these children, many of whom sign the family name with coveted large Roman numerals suffixed, go on to the best available in the way of colleges.

Yet the rich and powerful man cannot forever shield from his own children knowledge that they are going into a society bristling with avoidable destructive problems that *it is unable owing to its corporate systemic requirements to solve.* Many of these problems have their horns pointed directly at the children of the rich man.

Let us look at this neglected aspect.

All general disturbing and life-threatening social problems—air and water pollution; crime; overpopulation; vexed race relations; traffic tangles; accumulated causes of civil disturbance such as slums, unemployment and extreme poverty—intrude upon the young rich with about as much force as upon the young poor. The rich young person may have better oases to which to retreat; but he is nevertheless adversely affected by the same accumulating, neglected phenomena.

Even in their oases the young rich are by no means safe. They, like others, are subject to narcotic addiction, alcoholism and psychological disorders—and an inventory of all their tribulations along this line would be impressive. They, too, in various ways are assailed by hard types. And let us remember that their fathers are powerful men.

Of crime, against their own persons and in its aspect of crime against property a rising, low-grade, guerrilla variant of Marxist class war, they are steady direct and indirect targets. As the *Wall Street Journal* in many articles during the 1960's made clear, there is a broad and steady determined assault on the merchandise and cash of the big companies by shoplifters and employees—crime carried out by noncriminal classes. Losses here, contrived by people whose appetites are stimulated beyond the reach of their means through the agency of voracious advertising, are passed on to the general public as much as possible in higher prices; but some of these losses, running into billions annually, must be absorbed. There are not sufficient jails to hold most of the offenders, many of whom when caught are let off with suspended sentences, dire threats from the bench, paroles, disgracing publicity, etc.

That the rich are as subject as anyone to misadventures in a wide-open society (kept wide-open in general so as to facilitate double-dealing in profitable particulars) can be shown by the citation of a number of salient cases, abstracted from among many.

In 1966 the young daughter of Charles Percy, former chairman of Bell & Howell, camera manufacturers, and now junior senator from Illinois, was wantonly murdered in her bed in the family home in exclusive Kenilworth, Illinois, on the Gold Coast north of Chicago. Her unknown slayer was not apprehended. Wealth, power and exalted position did not protect her in a jungle society.

In the same year a well-organized kidnapping plot against Leonard K. Firestone, rubber scion of Beverly Hills, California, was frustrated through the enterprise of an underworld tipster. The two plotters, one the tipster, were killed by eager police in the attempt. Had the plot been successful Mr. Firestone would have been abducted and held for ransom as a number of rich people have been, despite the severe "Lindbergh law" against kidnapping and despite the virtual impossibility of circulating ransom money. Such money, in whatever form, is subject to modern, high-speed photographic recording by the FBI and instantly becomes "hot" money, hardly worth the risk at ten cents on the dollar. It can even be treated and made radioactive, a dead giveaway when passed over Geiger counters.

Robberies in the homes of the rich are frequent and there is reason to believe they are not always reported. And this despite elaborate protective systems. While traveling, the rich are especially the targets of expert thieves, as in the case of Henry Ford II in New York City, also in 1966. His hotel suite was burglarized and jewels in the reported amount of $50,000 were taken. Servants in the homes of the affluent and rather wealthy, according to news reports, are pretty regularly trussed up by invading thieves and the premises ransacked. Burglaries are common in wealthy residential districts.

Grant-laden Establishment methodologists, exponents of a sterile sociological scholasticism, will no doubt charge that I have selected a few unrepresentative cases to make my point. Actually, I cite these as representative cases, available in any year. This is what is going on, all the time.

A close variation of the following *New York Times* headline (August 31, 1967; 22:4) is repeated every few months with respect to violent events in Connecticut, New York, New Jersey, Pennsylvania and elsewhere:

SOCIETY MATRON

BEATEN TO DEATH

It has become almost a standard story to read about women of property murdered in their isolated splendid homes by intruders, who as often as not are not caught. The only reason I don't list those of a recent year or two is that I don't want to use the space.

With respect to the high-toned village of Purchase, New York, a "three-square-mile domain of big homes, colorful gardens, private swimming pools, tree-shaded bridle paths, elegant country clubs and winding lanes" said the *Times* of August 13, 1967 (66:4-6), "Sixteen burglaries of estates have occurred in the last month. Some estimates of the loss in jewelry, antiques and cash run up to $250,000 but Harrison police detectives are dubious at the high estimates. . . ."

No police dubiety was expressed, however, about the amount of $780,-000 set as the value of jewels stolen from Mr. and Mrs. Cornelius Vanderbilt Whitney at Saratoga Springs, reported by the *Times* on August 6,

1967. The thieves missed $175,000 additional in gems only because Mrs. Whitney wore them to dinner.

What I want to say here for the methodologists is that the rich, almost as much as the poor in their slums, are the recurrent victims of violence in a cuckoo-clock political system. The profiteers and their poor-boys-who-made-good in the legislatures seem unable to give much protection to their own women and children, to say nothing of the women and children of the less well heeled.

The rich, like the rest of us, are as readily victimized by deleterious products: dentifrices, cosmetics, pharmaceuticals and various untested chemical applications to various parts of the body. After all, there is only a certain range of offerings of this kind; the rich have no more sophisticated choices open to them than the rest of the public in the way of deodorants, depilatories, mouth washes, unguents and the like. Their young gorge on rancid hot dogs and hamburgers at ball games like any other red-blooded, true-blue American.

That various of these products, including widely circulating food preparations, are dangerous to health is regularly made known by appropriate federal supervisory agencies, kept thoughtfully understaffed through the courtesy of a bought bucolic Congress. The rich here are often hoist by their own politico-economic petard.

For a resounding case—one among many—let us go back a few years, to 1932. In that year died after a long wasting illness Eben McBurney Byers, director of a number of companies and chairman of A. M. Byers Company, of Pittsburgh, makers of iron pipe. Mr. Byers, a Groton–Yale man, had been national amateur golf champion in 1906, came of a wealthy established family and was no small-bore personality. The medical diagnosis at Doctors' Hospital, New York City, was that he had a brain abscess, caused by radium poisoning. For three or four years he had been dosing himself with two to three two-ounce bottles per day of a widely advertised preparation containing minute quantities of radium. He was under the impression that the lethal stuff was doing him some good. Following testimony by one of his physicians, the Federal Trade Commission in January, 1932, issued a stupendous order prohibiting, no less, the Bailey Radium Laboratories from advertising Radithor as harmless. Not only had this product been so advertised, it was reported by the *Times*, but it had been recommended, said the *Times*, for 160 conditions and symptoms.[24] So ended Eben McBurney Byers, a man on the inside track of wealth.

That the rich are as gullible as anyone else in readily gobbling up and smearing themselves with whatever products are offered in the free-free-free market is readily apparent. Merely because a man is clever at conserving what he has inherited or is skillful in overreaching the public in the clinches affords no indication that he is clever enough to protect himself and his family in all aspects of the freedom-blessed American politico-economic jungle.

The situation is made clearer still in the case of the automobile. A rich man is obviously in a position to purchase the best there is in the way of automobiles and have his own private mechanics service them. But, as Ralph Nader has shown and as Detroit has more recently admitted through extensive recalls of delivered automobiles, many automobiles are not mechanically safe in a country crosshatched with roads literally clogged with cars. Even though a rich man may have a car that is in perfect working order, there is no guarantee that he will not be run into or run down by some automobile that is either mechanically defective or in the hands of a defective driver, of which numerous are disclosed from time to time. The rich man and his family, it is evident, are as exposed to the automobile menace as they are to poisonous smog. They are no better off in this respect, unless they remain permanently indoors, than the rest of society. And, sure enough, as newspaper reports from time to time show, top-drawer eminents and their children are from time to time cut down in the streets by cars or battered on the roads. A complete inventory of such cases would require many pages.

Although injured by avoidable accidents or made ill by detestable products, the rich man does have an edge in that he can procure, no matter where he is, the very best and most expensive medical services. But doctors cannot always save him, much as they would like to.

The rich are especially enamored of medicine, and give heavily to their own hospitals and to medical research. Plainly, like the rest of us, they are seeking mundane salvation. But their faith in the powers of the doctors at times passeth all understanding. What I mean is illustrated by a story told me some years ago by an eminent internist, who complained that he had been detained for several hours on a sleeveless errand while many patients were in need of attention. He had been summoned with some ten or a dozen other specialists to attend a wealthy New York banker in his eighties who was very ill. It was obvious at a glance that the man was dying and yet members of the family walked about on tiptoe, with bated breath, and looked upon the assembled doctors as a high priesthood capable of saving the wasted hulk—the patriarch and founder of the clan.

The fees for this consultation, my annoyed informant told me, were bound to be astronomical, and the whole gathering obviously futile, an instance of medical fetishism. As E. M. Byers discovered, expensive medical care cannot always save one.

One might suppose that a rich and powerful man, aware of the source of some patently deleterious influence, would take arms and gird himself against the common threat. Here we come to an aspect of inner *finpolitan* affairs to which most of the sociologists have turned a blind, uncomprehending eye. It is a *finpolitan* rule that one company does not take a public position against another—whatever it does—as long as it does not act directly as an adversary; and the members of one industry do not lead or join in the public denunciation of another industry. Each industry, each company is allowed to pursue its own way unless it tries to grab too big a share of the market.

Thus, when public criticisms gain momentum against one company or one industry, when that company or industry stands in the public dock, as it were, others preserve diplomatic silence. The mass media, too, stand aside if they do not offer outright defenses of the criticized practices. Thus we see the entire corporate world maintaining a studied silence as pharmaceuticals are criticized for pricing practices, automotives for safety factors, the oil industry for special tax shelters and any or all for monopoly, gouging prices, poor products or community pollution.

The reason for this impotent silence is simply that if one wealthy group opens fire on the cushy preserve of another wealthy group there will be retaliation in kind. For each industry has vulnerable points open to criticism. It is the need, then, to preserve some semblance of intramural harmony that causes the financial groups to maintain silence about the shortcomings of their various members. Higher capitalism is a little club holding within it diverse temperaments, true enough, but temperaments that must, under pain of direct reciprocal attack, preserve an appearance of outward solidarity to the world.

Lest anyone believe I am making a purely supposititious point let me make it clear that one capitalist often thoroughly detests another entire industry and that such detestation, properly financed, can lead to the root-and-branch destruction of the detested industry. John D. Rockefeller I, for example, disliked the liquor industry, and he opposed smoking, dancing and the theater as well. The liquor industry in the United States was for a time destroyed with heavy losses, through Prohibition, illustrating what can happen. I am not suggesting that it was Rockefeller who smashed the liquor industry; but he shared the point of view of the Prohibitionists in regarding liquor in general as a social menace, a blight on efficiency.

Rockefeller was by no means an exception in holding such straitlaced views about the propriety of certain entire industries. I once knew a successful Wall Street broker who always did whatever he could to dissuade his customers from buying shares in alcohol, cigarette, film and small-loan companies on the ground that he thought them socially harmful.

Yet such intramural antipathies, which usually have rational grounds (as in the widespread capitalistic detestation of the powerful domestic fire-arms industry), seldom lead to any effective action against the offenders; for everybody is, in a way, in the same boat and hence silent. As I used to argue to my moral broker-friend, his qualms were vain; customers could come into his office with money from any source, even from some illicit enterprise. What was gained if they now purchased only stocks in morally approved enterprises? Moral or immoral, the companies offering stocks were all legal entities in an economic system that does not discriminate between producers of fire-arms and producers of surgical instruments. All industries are created equal.

Being bound to keep quiet when he sees obvious destruction being wrought by some reckless peer, at least the intelligently reflective capitalist cannot, contrary to Mills, be entirely happy. And his unhappiness has an entirely different cause from that of most people. It is the unhappiness of a consciously powerful man who realizes he can do nothing effective against something he considers profoundly evil, cannot even fully protect his own children. Even though he may feel that his own enterprises are as far beyond criticism as ingenuity can make them, he knows that this is no defense against fabrications which can be circulated against him to his distress by powerful people his uncooperative crusading spirit has made angry.

It is for this reason, among others, that it is rare to find crusaders among capitalists, who all in one way or the other live in glass houses.

In the matter of divorce and broken families the rich are, if anything, worse off than most of the population; at least they are no better placed. For the divorce rate among the rich, with many of them such ardent believers in marriage that they remarry up to five and even ten times, is very much higher than the national rate. Divorce, even if one looks upon it as a desirable escape hatch from an untenable situation, is never taken as a sign of sound human relations; rather is it taken as an index of unresolvable interpersonal trouble.

If stable familial relations and intra-family continuity are desirable, as it is widely held, then divorce and the dispersion of family members, particularly the young, must be an index to failure. At least the children of divorced rich couples are not happy about the event. And this sort of failure is rife among the rich. Failure being the opposite of success, in this department of life the rich, however they got that way, cannot be looked upon as generally successful. Perhaps they are no more unhappy than others; yet they do not appear to be conspicuous winners in the marital sweepstakes. As in the case of most divorcing couples, they find each other unbearable—and not simply in one instance but, as the record shows, in a train of instances. Not to be able to find a single retainable marital partner in a number of attempts surely argues some sort of personal impoverishment in a culture that values marital stability.

Deficiencies and lacks of the kind we have looked at are not, as many suppose, purely subjective, the ills to which all men are heir. They are social, deriving from the general social situation, which has much to do in shaping the psychologies of people.

The rich, it is clear, are not immune to the general fallout from the existing socio-political system even though they may have compensations denied to others. Far from all the fallout upon the rich has been indicated and one could go on at considerable length about more. However, confining ourselves again to the young and innocent rich, it is clear that their minds are as subverted as those of poorer youth by the all-pervading influence of persuasive advertising.

If someone systematically splashed mud on the clothing of rich children their parents would soon take steps to see that the offender was laid by the heels. Yet the rich, for all their power, cannot protect their children from the subversive influence of advertisers who insistently confuse the intellect in various detectable ways. Most of the time they misuse language and pictures in the effort solely to sell.

True, the rich youth like the poor, if he makes his way into the higher and more recondite studies such as semantics, logic and epistemology, can overcome the enervating intellectual influences of advertising and homespun propaganda, thus possessing himself at least of his own mind. But few find their way to such rarefied studies and the result is that the rich usually have as confused a view of the world as the poor, subject to exploded notions (particularly in economics) and with about the same general world view as that of a postman or bartender. That this is so is readily seen in the public utterances of the more vocal of them. Among the self-erected we have cracker-barrel philosophers like Henry Ford I and H. L. Hunt and among the more educated we have the sagging economic views of David Rockefeller and, on a much lower level of wealth, the socio-cultural divagations of William F. Buckley, Jr., who asserts the presence of "eternal verities." A B-minus undergraduate in epistemology at Swampwater College knows better than that even though Buckley's public vowel movements are intently studied by a select circle of admirers.

One would think that a rich man, with money at his fingertips, would get smart and hire an epistemologist who would at least straighten him out from time to time about the grounds for rational belief. For we may well suppose that a rich man, always wanting the best, does not wish to go about in a scatterbrained condition hawking absurdities. He must want the true view just as he wants a livewire girl, a prime steak and a sound wine. Yet we find him apparently no better off in this respect than the common man. Nor, considering the baneful social influences to which they are subject will most of his prized children be better off. Madison Avenue vomits on their minds as freely as on the battered mind of the ordinary clod.

In this matter, however, the rich man is no doubt imbued with the un-justified self-pride of others as summarized by Descartes in the opening lines of his *Discourse on Method:* "Good sense is of all things in the world most evenly distributed among men, for each one believes himself so well endowed with it that even those who are the most difficult to please in all other things are generally satisfied with their share." (For our purposes we may ignore the *non sequitur* noticed by logicians between the warrant-ing reasons cited and the conclusion.) In any event, the rich man like the nonrich believes his own mind is as good as any and its way of operation to be in no particular corrigible; one can see this in the bland assurance with which the rich often express themselves publicly on recondite matters such as achieving the national destiny. In this belief, no doubt in the majority of cases, the rich are like others demonstrably self-deceived, vic-tims of self-pride, unless they have gone to herculean efforts to free them-selves from the free-market socio-cultural seepage all about them; they are as much off the track as T. W. K. Mits, the well-known man in the street.

The Successful Kennedys

Sufficient grounds have been stated, I believe, to suggest, contrary to sup-position among both the rich and their critics, that the rich are not so well off as they themselves sometimes suppose and are commonly supposed to be, even though they may be more advantageously placed than the average man in many selected areas. Their difficulties, furthermore, are not merely those common to the flesh of man but often derive from their own celebrated social system, from the propaganda-hallowed but rickety social structure itself. Such is the resistance of indurated dogma to reason-able refutation, however, that one could pile further proof on proof in the single well-known case of the successful Kennedys, dogged by socially induced tragedies; nor are they alone.

The first of the Kennedys to feel the blow of adversity was the eldest son, Joseph P., Jr., who had early been earmarked in the family circle as a future president of the United States. Aged twenty-nine, he was killed in action as an eager airman in Europe during the replay with special Hitlerian effects of World War I. Two weeks later Kathleen's ultra-British husband was also killed in action. And in 1948 Kathleen herself, flying in a private plane to join her father on the Riviera, was killed as the machine crashed in rain and fog over France.

With the election to the presidency in 1960 of John F. Kennedy, the second oldest son, the Kennedys' star seemed once again in the ascendancy; they were literally the darlings of the world. The abrupt assassination of the socially aware president in Dallas in 1963 by a publicly neglected, mentally disturbed ex-marine was especially ironic; a social system eroded by neglect struck down a potential statesman through one of its neglected cases.

The theme of violence in the Kennedy later history, which had almost finished JFK during the war in the South Pacific, showed itself again in the nearly fatal airplane crash of Senator Edward M. Kennedy in his own plane in 1964. As it was, his back was severely injured, necessitating the wearing of a brace.

The Airplane and The Rich

The airplane, it may be observed in this melancholy recital, is a special hazard of the rich and affluent. Few plane crashes, unless upon buildings, ever involve lower-class citizens; many tycoons have already met their end in the skies. And the bored rich, in their affinity for plane travel as for everything technologically novel and "advanced," are themselves the victims of a smooth statistical falsification given wide currency: that the *rate* of passenger fatalities in aircraft is lower than that on railroads. This falsification is achieved by comparing fatalities per passenger-mile. If, however, one properly takes into consideration all the relevant factors and makes the comparison on the basis of passenger-mile-*hours* (for time is an essential factor in measuring motion, which is a function of time as well as distance), then it is seen that the *rate* of fatality is tremendously higher in air travel. As far as that goes, in absolute figures passenger air fatalities are greater than passenger railroad fatalities.

We see here that the rich are as susceptible as anyone to being gulled by institutionalized propaganda (assuming that they are indeed misled by the claims of alleged superior safety in airplanes). Although airplanes may be sufficiently safe, considering all factors, they are self-propelled kites flying with heavy loads of volatile fuel, obviously highly vulnerable to serious mishap. In computing air fatalities the Federal Aviation Agency, for example, *excludes* deaths occurring in airborne dynamite explosions![25] Such are apparently not deemed statistically kosher.

The Curse of Prominence

Great prominence itself, as many of the wealthy know, carries with it special problems. In the case of the Kennedys this was shown in the wrangle over the wording of the originally authorized book by William Manchester about the assassination of the president. Said *The Nation* (February 6, 1967): "The subsequent attempts on the part of the Kennedys to control the text of the book and its serialization gave the impression of an arrogant use of money and power. They may have been within their legal rights, but that is not the point. Apparently most of what they objected to was of little moment one way or the other. The public was not in a mood to go along with them, whether they were right or wrong. The John F. Kennedy aura was blown away by the exchange of recriminations.

"At a given point of idolatry," *The Nation* continued, "the public turns from adoring its idols and begins to examine their feet. Once celebrities reach a certain level of overexposure, there is just as much mileage to be gained from cutting them down as there was from building them up. The writers and broadcasters who provide this sort of fare are familiar with the reaction, and when some of them sense the turning point, the others follow. All of the overexposed live in the shadow of an obloquy. It is one of the hazards of publicity."

What is less widely known is that scholarly John F. Kennedy himself, in 1959, successfully brought pressure to bear to exclude from the book *The Kennedy Family* by Joseph Dinneen three summary paragraphs about the attitude of his father toward Jews. Dinneen in 1944 had interviewed the elder Kennedy for the *Boston Globe* and had taken shorthand notes of the interview. Present also was Lawrence Spivak, then editor of *The American Mercury* and later a national television news panelist. The *Globe* decided not to publish the interview and Dinneen fifteen years later summarized it in his book, of which he sent a set of galley proofs as a courtesy to JFK. The president-to-be, disturbed, insisted over the telephone from Oregon that the prickly paragraphs be omitted even though the work was now in plates. Dinneen and the publishers after some resistance consented to the awkward deletion and substituted some inoffensive material.[26]

JFK, soundly from a public image point of view, recognized that the nature of the interview, far from settling the issue of anti-Semitism raised against his father, piqued critical interest and raised more questions than it resolved. From an electoral point of view, though the president-to-be was not at all anti-Semitic, even a brief summary of the interview could have been troubling by reason of association.

Cosmetic Images

In passing, it is standard although not universal *finpolitan* and *pubpolitan* practice to attempt to control or influence—that is, censor—writings and other expressions that becloud one's public image by suggesting something untoward or disturbing. What is wanted is a carefully retouched pleasant studio portrait of persons and events, not a candid catch-as-catch-can camera shot of some bigwig off guard and thus completely himself. For this reason writers and other commentators on public affairs are generally wooed, flattered, facilitated in various ways and, at times, subsidized, authorized, edited, lied to, intimidated or coerced by powerful public figures. While resorting to the courts to expunge nonlibelous matter from a text is rather unusual, the general attitude of those Kennedys involved in the Manchester controversy is not unusual among political and corporate people, whatever illusions the public may have about the free-wheeling independence of writers under the Star Spangled Banner.

Attempts to control the projected image extend even to photographs. Few politicians like to be photographed smoking cigars, perhaps because that typical act of politicians reminds the public of cartoons about paunchy, cigar-smoking ward bosses, concededly corrupt. Herbert Hoover had the plates confiscated from a photographer who snapped him cigar-smoking aboard a battleship, and Jack Kennedy, who smoked panetelas, did not like to be photographed in the act. Roosevelt, however, did not conceal that he smoked cigarettes, no doubt feeling that by doing it openly he projected an image of insouciance and self-sufficiency. Nor do politicians like to be photographed with a convivial glass in hand.

Franklin D. Roosevelt, always sensitively concerned about his image, worked carefully to see that it was not clouded. For a long time, although he was under close direct scrutiny, it was unknown by the general public that he was wholly paralyzed from the waist down and had to wear leg braces. Roosevelt himself went to herculean and physically exhausting lengths to keep the surely significant fact of this weakness from becoming generally known.[27] John F. Kennedy, too, kept from general circulation the fact that he suffered from Addison's disease.

Moreover, writers and photographers who offend by engaging in unauthorized image revision are thereafter rebuffed, barred, harassed, denounced, spied upon, rebuked, intimidated and otherwise made to feel remorse, regret or fear at having offended the higher powers, whose claim to kid-gloved handling is invariably based upon nothing more than money or position.

Ralph Nader, for presuming to question automobile safety in *Unsafe at Any Speed*, was subjected to close surveillance by General Motors, largest corporation by sales in the world, for which act a high GM official later publicly apologized. According to Nader, with General Motors denying the charge, the object was to obtain some bit of publicly inflammatory information of an irrelevantly derogatory nature.[28] True or not in this case, it is often true in many other cases because a largely confused philistine public believes that the truth of some statement is brought into serious question if it can be shown that its originator is a Communist, Socialist, atheist, homosexual, yogi, imbiber in strong waters, freethinker or one addicted to engaging in *crim. con.* with amiable ladies. Dedicated, sincere heterosexuality may itself be impugning.

Unsettling though it may be to many sturdy citizens, it is probably a fact that a majority of the scientists at work on the federal space-exploration program are thoroughgoing atheists or agnostics. For careful studies have shown that *most* American scientists (save us all!) are of this horrifying, cosmos-shattering orientation. Should, therefore, the space program not be canceled or its personnel changed? Should not, in the name of common safety, Billy Graham and Fulton J. Sheen be placed in charge? Why, the perturbed grass-roots citizen may well ask himself, cannot persons with a wholesome, dung-hill, 100 per cent American outlook be selected for this highly elevating work?

In one of his few but revealing *gauche* moves, President John F. Kennedy, deeply annoyed, canceled the White House subscription to the *New York Herald Tribune* and barred it from the sacred premises—an instance of Jove hurling the penultimate thunderbolt: banishment.

Concluding, although the difficulties encountered along life's way by the Kennedys and others can hardly be taken as par for the course among the rich and powerful they do show, in concentrated cases, what in varying degree all of the rich are up against in a highly turbulent irrationally structured society. The rich are by no means as well off as they are often imagined to be and as a sociologist such as C. Wright Mills imagines them to be. They have many troubles going far beyond those to which the flesh of man is heir. They are, in many ways, "on the spot." They have a lion by the tail.

Nowhere else is this better shown than in the matter of self-protection in the atomic age. The rich are individually as subject to nuclear holocaust as the poor in the brave new world's threatened nuclear democracy of all-encompassing death. And although many of the rich have constructed elaborate bomb shelters on their estates, complete with television (what station will be on the air?), among the more intelligent such contrivances must be clearly recognized as no more than tranquilizers for the women, children and servants. The world to which hypothetical shelter survivors would emerge would be one, according to all estimates, in which the dead would be looked upon with envy. The tycoons know this as well as does Herman Kahn.

The Fundamental Problem of the Rich

The fundamental difficulty of the rich has not yet been fully indicated. This difficulty consists of acquiring a sense of worthwhile function (and getting the world to agree with the self-estimate of this function) and, at the same time, of containing the many eruptions and breakdowns in a social system the obsolete structure of which is continually being strained by the introduction of new profit-making technology as well as by the rise of appropriately ferocious rivalry abroad. The situation in which the contemporary rich find themselves could be described by some pundit, brightly, as challenging.

As to function, it comes down largely to rule under various euphemistic rubrics. At times, as the pages of *Who's Who* attest, the claims to function are more flamboyant and see the subjects pathetically proclaiming themselves as financiers, investors, venture entrepreneurs, philanthropists and the like. After all, a financier is only a money lender, an investor is someone who owns something producing revenue for his own account, a venture entrepreneur a promoter for his own account and a philanthropist a lover of mankind. While being a lover of mankind may be laudable it does not bespeak any particular knack. For what is man or mankind but an abstraction? One never encounters man in experience, only men, women and children. What some testy observers ask is this: Will some of the self-proclaimed lovers of mankind kindly get off the necks of men, women and children?

Function, among the rich, as we have seen, is most often stated in terms that boil down to rule: executive, public official, administrator, trustee and the like.

In the modern world, function is closely related to self-identity because the question is no longer who one is but what one does. To the question "Who are you?" the answer is generally that one is a truck driver, clerk, teacher, performer or what-not of a certain name. "I am a tuba player named John Jones" is, at least for a beginning, a satisfactory designation (if true) of one's identity.

The rich, however, have difficulty in stating any function for themselves that is dissociated from rule. While terms like financier, investor, venture entrepreneur and philanthropist suggest commendable, nonintrusive and possibly supportive roles, terms such as executive, director, official, trustee and administrator and the like are clearly epitomized in a revealing term: boss.

In the contexts in which they are publicly advanced, all these terms hazily suggest synonyms for "hero," and at times a halo is also indicated for the heroic figure as in "international financier" and "upper-echelon executive." As one hears and reads of such, one is literally stunned by the superhuman vistas suggested. And when one reads that messages are being exchanged—actually exchanged—between the president of the United States on the one hand and international financiers and upper-echelon executives on the other (subject: something or other) one can imaginatively feel the world grinding on its hinges.

Whether the rich recognize it or not, in most public roles they seem to feel qualified to play they appear as bosses, however disguised, and not necessarily unbenevolent. In any other function they may elect to attempt —of a physicist, a ballplayer, a soft-shoe dancer, an artist, a writer or a philosopher—they find that their money gives them no edge at all. In roles of nonrulership, where the competition is extremely lively, if they decided to go in for poetry they find that par for the course is set by hard-to-beat T. S. Eliot or Robert Lowell, if for ballplaying by Mickey Mantle and Joe DiMaggio, etc. Most of the rich seeking active roles therefore drift, by default as it were, to corporations, banks, brokerage houses, nonprofit funds and various political jurisdictions. These are all organizational havens for imprecision even though they all harbor aspects where precision may be required of underlings, and appreciated.

In attempting to establish his unique identity through some unfinanced achievement, the rich man is pretty much in the position of anyone else, even a pauper. If his claim to competence is that he is very good at chess, all he need do to establish it is to beat a few lower-rung chess experts and then move higher. If his forte is science all he need do is gain the accolade of other scientists, hard to do. Normally finding such feats difficult, his next recourse is to get for himself one of the vaguely heroic current designations, crown it with an adjectival halo and project it into print: a public image. Most people will accept him, even applaud him, in his self-designation. The only ones who will ever question his bona fides will be dyspeptic churls, fit only for treasons, spoils and stratagems, perhaps to boot connoisseurs of pornography and arcane seances—in short, losers.

No matter what designation of puissance the rich man permits his media of publicity to allot him, however, there remains the harsh fact that he is operating within an increasingly obsolete social structure, politically designed for an agricultural and local commercial economy and culturally for the most part of even more antedated vintage. This social structure, under the impact of high-powered technology, is obviously increasingly inadequate to its supportive task, requires much change and is insulated against change by the resistance of many established economic groups, perhaps including his own.

What to do? One palliative after the other is embraced, resulting in an increasingly cross-stress, tension-producing patchwork. Where will it all lead? What will happen to the rich man's special stake, constantly threatened by science-derived innovations and requirements for more and more government intervention?

Obeying the maxim "If you can't lick 'em, join 'em," most of the rich appear increasingly to have joined forces with government in developing the welfare-warfare state, largely utilizing tax money from the labor force and thereby guaranteeing themselves one big profitable customer. Yet even this maneuver introduces endless new difficulties, and there remains to be contended with the rest of the terrestrial world exploding into smoggy industrialism.

The state of mind of a fully aware wealthy man, then, cannot be as tranquil as commonly supposed. And that it is not at all tranquil is shown by the endless fulminations of the various communications media against communism, socialism, statism, totalitarianism, radicalism, fascism, technocracy, liberalism, crime in the streets (where it clearly should not be), do-goodism, reformism, softism, sentimentalism, apathy, unpatriotism, unconstitutionalism, centralization, bureaucracy and the like, and by the stream of contributions to super-patriotic Pied Pipers. All persons who think seriously in terms of adjustment to modern conditions then find they must be extremely circumspect so as not to be suspected as subversive and un-American, in the ideological company of foreigners.

A constant danger now faced by the jumpy *finpols* is the possibility that someone among the *pubpols*, like a Roosevelt or a Kennedy, will really take the bit in his teeth and start running the ball in a different direction, perhaps change the nature of the whole game. For, in the shadow of the uncertainties of an old-line local business economy with high-speed technology grafted on to it, the *pubpols* appear to be slowly shaping a wider role for themselves as government is required to step supportively into various fissures of a misshapen society.

While it appears a bit early to assert that the days of the rich are numbered, as socialists like to believe, it does appear they are in for some stormy times and, perhaps, for eventual extinction at the hands of rising forces—a subject to be broached in the next and concluding chapter. The rich, in any event, are in a time of many troubles as their wealth increases, and I conclude that the more thoughtful among them cannot be feeling as complacent as the bland-bland exterior of their power elite may suggest.

For it is veritably written: "So foul a sky clears not without a storm."

Seventeen ❧

OLIGARCHY BY
DEFAULT

Latter-day discourses on the economic system as something separate merely
because it can be analytically isolated bypass the inescapable fact that
there is always present a *politico*-economic system: government with economic ramifications, an economy with political ramifications. Governments
and economic systems are never separate; they are opposite sides of the
same coin. As experience shows, their leading personnel are interchange-
able. Such being the case, in any study of economic and financial affairs
we are invariably concerned with some sort of system of coercion and
repression. For all government is universally conceded to rest at bottom on
systematized collective coercion and repression.

Such coercion and repression, to be sure, are necessary. Without them
life, in the words of a famous dictum, would be "solitary, poor, nasty,
brutish, and short." Without them anarchic individual coercion would
prevail in a social jungle.

In the long, turbulent course of history many cushions and restraints
were developed within governmental systems to protect the populace from
their fierce protector—that is, to soften some of the more outrageous aspects
of coercion the engine of government itself made possible. For the instrument of government was usually freely used by rulers—"the insolence of
office," "power corrupts," "to the victor belong the spoils"—for ulterior and
wholly private ends. Today, in the celebration of particular systems of
government, one finds that it is the imperfect restraints against self-serving
rulers and their friends that are really celebrated—Constitution, Bill of
Rights, written laws, half-measures of social support, the development of
equity in law, and the like.

Nevertheless, after all the fine print has been duly perused and applauded, coercive power (soothingly designated as sovereign power) re-

mains and is properly suspect. Behind their bland masks the most civilized of governments retain all the powers of any despotism, their application duly prescribed (and the prescriptions not infrequently violated). Taking into consideration all governmental powers and their usual application, there are in fact no genial governments at all. And in the interstices of even the most finely meshed restraints (those of the United States probably being less finely meshed than those, for example, of England, France or Sweden) there is much room for one-sided self-service by the rulers and those with clandestine privileged access to them. While one might balk at assenting to the proposition that government is the executive committee of the ruling class, it is a demonstrable fact that it is peculiarly at the service of the upper economic class, which accordingly is warrantably regarded as in effect a ruling class.

Lest such an observation be thought by provincials to give this exposition an unholy Marxist aura, let us in reverential solemnity quote such an austere Establishmentarian as Woodrow Wilson, who said (Franklin D. Roosevelt later concurring) in words as valid today as when first uttered:

"The masters [sic!] of the government of the United States are the combined capitalists and manufacturers of the United States. It is written over every intimate page of the record of Congress, it is written all through the history of conferences at the White House, that the suggestions of economic policy in this country have come from one source, not from many sources. The benevolent guardians, the kind hearted trustees who have taken the troubles of government off our hands have become so conspicuous that almost anybody can write out a list of them. . . .

"Suppose you go to Washington and try to get at your government. You will always find that while you are politely listened to, the men really consulted are the men who have the biggest stake—the big bankers, the big manufacturers, the big masters of commerce, the heads of railroad corporations and of steamship corporations. . . . The government of the United States at present is a foster child of the special interests."[1]

For the alleged violation of some of its peculiar, even minor, mandates any government whatever will execute any high-minded offender whether he be Jesus, Socrates, John Hus, Servetus, Thomas More, Joan of Arc or John Brown. Socrates was executed by a far more democratic system than any now even claims to be and in a more refined system of civilization than that of any modern country. Under threat of durance vile all governments require the payment of taxes, even unfairly apportioned taxes as in the United States with its packed poor-boy legislatures.

Again, any government even in a trivial or doubtful cause such as Vietnam may place the lives of its younger male citizens in extreme jeopardy by coercing them into the armed forces under the claims of routinely invoked patriotic duty and sending them into kill-or-be-killed situations. Most Americans have been astonished in recent years to see what was always known to the informed: that the president alone can send existing armed forces anywhere without consulting anyone, least of all the public or Congress. He could order an overnight assault against any country, thereby precipitating general war. He could, in full constitutionality, order all of the armed forces into the depths of the Congo and nobody could legally halt the operation. Congress, it is true, could refuse the money to continue the operation and thus be in the position of refusing to support helpless men who had only obeyed legal orders. And this is only a very little of what a fully constitutional American president can do—*without consulting anyone.*

Most of what a president does not ordinarily do—such as send secret police to citizens' doors late in the night—he does not do because he does not want to. He can do this sort of thing quite legally; there is no law saying at what hour police may call. And such a personally likeable man as President John F. Kennedy did indeed send out nocturnal police visitors in the squabble over steel prices.

Government power, wielded by officials, individual human beings, is evidently great power over others, not necessarily *for* others, and anyone who wields it, smiling or not, or has ready access to the wielders obviously has great power far beyond that of any man in the street. Moreover, this power with modern techniques is far greater than it ever was. By means of modern methods of communication, government can put its agents into action anywhere in a matter of minutes. It has been credibly reported that President Johnson, with far more power at his fingertips than all presidents combined up to Harry Truman, and more than either Truman, Eisenhower or Kennedy, personally designated overnight targets in North Vietnam for powerful air squadrons waiting to take off from remote, dawn-shrouded airfields. We possess today, in brief, pinpoint government. It can even listen in on conversations anywhere, and freely does so despite denials. It freely uses internal spies, especially in the matter of taxes on obscure citizens.

For these and other reasons it is now said by some students of the situation that we live under an elective despotism. Freely celebrating our condition in strictly American style, if we accept this dictum we could say we live under the greatest and most glorious elective despotism in history. Most people—well over 95 per cent of them—have no more power in this system, either immediately or ultimately, than has a rank-and-file Russian in the Soviet system, and this despite all the blandishing talk about government with the consent of the governed and the sovereignty of the people.

As to consent, which of my readers can step forward and say he was ever asked for his consent to the Constitution or any of its varied interpretations? The electorate of 1789 was asked for and gave such consent and we may readily agree that the majority of people in states asking for admission, at the time of admission, have so consented. But who else? When the people of the Confederacy, disliking the arrangement, pointedly withdrew the consent given by their forebears they were confronted by military force and after a sanguinary struggle were eventually subdued. As Lincoln said, the Union must be preserved, a proposition drawn from out of the air that flatly contradicts the doctrine of consent. Yet Lincoln was right; it is inherently of the nature of government that, like a tiger, it never voluntarily assents to its own dismemberment. The idea of consent *vis-à-vis* an established government is the purest of nonsense, written though it is into the American myth.

The American System

Treatises on American government often with scrupulous accuracy tell how the government operates *formally*—the federal system, separation of powers, checks and balances, popular election of officials, judicial review, administrative agencies and the whole remaining bit. None of these treatises depicts how the government actually works in the application of the forms, how it works *informally*. What really takes place constitutes a considerable deviation from the formal script. Rules are freely bent, especially in the conduct of the legislatures, which make their own rules. Police, too, function pretty autonomously. For a starter let us notice that most of the precious electorate in most elections—state, federal and local—do not vote at all. Many, even though unconstrained, have never voted; and these, under one possible interpretation, may be politically the most sensible of all. For most of those voting haven't the least idea what it is all about.

Power not exercised by dilatory members of any functioning organization will of necessity be exercised by more diligent members, a universal rule applying to corporations, fraternal societies and labor unions as well as to government. To a very considerable extent, then, we see in all organizations, including the government of the United States, rule by default, by a self-selected oligarchy. If the citizens won't run the show the endless procession of Bobby Bakers, W. Judson Morhouses, Everett Dirksens and Lyndon B. Johnsons will.

In what follows I shall first state summarily, with gloves off, precisely how government actually operates in the United States.

1. Officials (except judges) nominated by either one of two major parties are periodically elected at local, state and federal levels by a largely inept electorate that in most elections fails to participate to the full and in general turns out far below 50 per cent. Whether the electorate fully participates makes no operational difference because most of the candidates are handpicked by nominating caucuses of the two major parties rather than of one party as in Russia. These caucuses function in default of popular activity; the populace simply has no political drive of its own. It is politically inert. If Russia permitted a Socialist Party and a Communist Party (joined behind the scenes) it would be on all fours with the United States in respect of parties in the field; the candidates in the two parties might be politically identical twins, as is often the case in the United States (Johnson versus Goldwater). In those rare cases where policy is uppermost in the mind of the electorate it is usually a destructive policy, as toward Negroes in the South (and elsewhere). Policies promising to be injurious to minority groups such as Negroes, Catholics, foreigners, Jews, Mexicans, Chinese, intellectuals and, in fact, all deviants from fixed philistinish norms, usually attract a larger-than-usual supporting vote. Ordinarily, policies are beyond the comprehension of the electorate, which chooses between two handpicked candidates strictly on nonability factors: religion, race, appearance, age, marital status, region of origin, platform manner, synthetic public image and the like. Officials thus elected I have termed *pubpols*, public politicians, to distinguish them from the many other types of more specialized politicians in the American politico-economic system: *finpols, corp-pols, churchpols, lawpols* and *lab(or)pols*. A close examination of the roles of any of these will show that they differ only in quality, not degree or kind, from *pubpols*. Less perspicuously, such are ordinarily styled "leaders" or "executives"; sometimes "trustees" or theologians. They are in sober fact politicians, *primarily and exclusively* concerned about the operation of government and who gets—and doesn't get— what, when, where and how.

2. As the attainment of office gives officials access to the dread levers of government, including the levers of the hangman, people who already possess or are acquiring well-defined economic stakes are especially alert to the whole process. While the masses are distractedly mesmerized by the number 1 television program or the World Series, the moneymen are busily planning and discussing far ahead. Owing to the power leverage at stake, rivalry for office is in most jurisdictions keen. It gets keener the higher one ascends in the system. Because of the rivalrous electoral grab for power leverage, the struggle is expensive. Money is needed, and can be obtained

only from those relative few who have it to spare. Most of the labor force is too modestly compensated and improvident to contribute.

3. Money plays a large role in the manipulation of this system—much larger than is usually conceded, which means that persons who have money have a wide political edge over those who do not. First, there are the campaign contributions, always large and constantly getting larger. True, it takes money to run these campaigns wherein the issues are presumably being put before the people. But it was long known prior to the cases in 1967 of Senator Thomas J. Dodd before the Senate and of Bobby Baker in the courts that *much* of the money in probably *most* campaigns (although not all) is diverted to the private tax-free accounts of the politicians. As Frank R. Kent said decades ago, many politicians have what is known in the trade as "sticky fingers." The money they collect is not for justifiable campaign expenses but is a down payment on future influence in government. Some of this money must often be divided—the "split"—to gain the support of local newspapers and key figures who stand forth as "community leaders." Most campaign funds are, therefore, properly and soberly designatable as slush funds. Some represent slush, slush, slush all the way. The American system is a slushy system.

Officeholders know this and at times show their clear recognition of the facts. Thus, in the campaign of the natural gas industry in 1956 for exemption from federal regulation when an enabling bill was before Congress, already endorsed by President Eisenhower, eager-beaver hinterland lawyers for the industry turned up and offered a cash "campaign contribution" to veteran Senator Francis Case of South Dakota, who instantly took umbrage and publicized what he interpreted as a barefaced attempt to influence his vote. This untypical incident scuttled the bill, which was vetoed.[2] Most politicos gladly accept such offerings, say nothing about them.

(In England, campaign funds and the duration of campaigns are severely limited by law. Legislators are paid very modest salaries and are required to abstain from voting and discussion in matters affecting their private interests—the Jeffersonian rule.)

Lest I again be suspected of harboring Satanic leftish sentiments while setting down what is only God's own plain unvarnished fact, allow me to quote at some length Senator Russell Long, Establishment Democrat of Louisiana and Majority Whip, who in April, 1967, said on the Senate floor:

Most campaign money comes from businessmen. Labor contributions have been greatly exaggerated. It would be my guess that about 95 per cent of campaign funds at the congressional level are derived from businessmen. At least

80 per cent of this comes from men who could sign a net worth statement exceeding a quarter of a million dollars. Businessmen contribute because the Federal Corrupt Practices Act prohibits businesses from contributing. Funnelling contributions through their officers is a simple and safe way for business to accomplish what it cannot do directly.

A great number of businessmen contribute to legislators who have voted for laws to reduce the power of labor unions, to regulate unions, to outlaw the union shop.

Many businessmen contribute to legislators who have voted to exempt their businesses from the minimum wage.

Businessmen contribute to legislators who have fought against taxes that would have been burdensome to their businesses, whether the tax increase was proposed as a so-called reform, a loophole closer, or just an effort to balance the Federal budget.

Power company officials contribute to legislators who vote against public power and against expanding the Rural Electric Administration cooperatives. REA officers are also able to raise some money, although not nearly as much for those legislators who vote the other way around, although the real power of the REA cooperatives is to be found in the strong grassroots support they can generate against their enemies.

Bankers, insurance company executives, big moneylenders generally contribute to legislators who vote for policies that lead to high interest rates.

Many large companies benefit from research and development contracts which carry a guaranteed profit, a so-called fixed fee of about 7 per cent of the amount of the contract. Executives of such companies contribute to those who help them get the contracts or who make the money available. In recent years, quite a battle has developed over the desire of government research contractors to obtain and keep lush private monopoly patent rights on those things discovered with billions of dollars of government research money. The possibility of windfall profits in this area defies imagination. Research contractors contract to legislators who vote to permit them to have private patent rights on government research expenditures.

Drug companies are often able to sell brand-name drug products at anywhere from twice to 50 times the price of identical nonbranded products for welfare and medicare patients if the companies can prevail upon government to permit their drugs to be prescribed and dispensed by their private brand names rather than by the official or generic name of the product. Executives of drug companies will contribute to legislators who vote to permit or bring about such a result.

Many industries are regulated. This includes the railroads, the truckers, the airlines, the power companies, the pipelines, to name but a few. Executives of regulated companies contribute to legislators who vote to go easy on the regulation, and ask no more questions than necessary about their rates.

Companies facing threat of ruinous competition from foreign sources have executives who contribute to those who help protect them from competition by means of tariffs and quotas.

Many industries are subsidized. This includes the merchant marine, the shipbuilders, the sugar producers, the copper producers, and a host of others. Executives in such industries contribute to those who help keep them in business.

This list is merely illustrative; it could be elaborated upon and enlarged to include many more. . . . Merely by assiduously tending to the problems of business interests located in one's own state, a legislator can generally assure himself of enough financial support to campaign effectively for reelection.[3]

The Majority Whip in his unguarded ire here spoke the simple, unvarnished truth. The only detail on which I would question him is in his use of the term "businessmen." For these people, the big ones at least, are not businessmen in the senses commonly understood. They are *finpols* and *corp-pols disguised* as businessmen. They are actually rulers, like the dukes and barons of old. Business is not really their business; protected, nonrisk moneymaking is.

Scornfully rejecting the suggestion that some pontifical politicos did not accept campaign contributions, Senator Long said that "any person who is the darling of the newspaper publishers has much of his campaign covered in favorable news and editorial support they can afford. If his record has the overwhelming approval of the wealthy business people, if he has a consistent record of favoring penny-pinching economy when the needs of the sick and poor were involved, a consistent record of voting to protect management from the demands of labor, of protecting monopolies from the public rather than the other way around, he will find that the campaign expenses seem to take care of themselves. Radio and television broadcasts may be paid by unseen and unknown beneficiaries. The man may well find himself with a substantial campaign surplus and no place to spend it."[4]

Interrupting in the course of Long's speech, Senator Albert Gore of Tennessee reported that his study of campaign contributions in 1956 showed that the Republican Party collected more from the tiny island of Manhattan than from all the states combined, while the Democratic Party was not far removed from the same pattern.[5] This was not very astonishing as New York City is the financial capital of the country, the dog that wags the Washington tail. The slush comes from New York, the accommodating votes from the hinterland.

Long spoke in favor of retaining the short-lived law that allowed taxpayers to assign $1 of federal income taxes to campaign funds, which would be financed out of a common pool.

But money in American politics extends far beyond campaign contributions (largely supplied by corporations even though corporations are forbidden by law to contribute *directly*). As we have seen, once they are elected, politicians have many ways of collecting money or monetarily convertible equivalents. (1) It is brought to them by lobbyists in their offices in paper bags. (2) It is paid to them by corporations through their law firms for vague legal services or for self-serving intervention in governmental bureaus. (3) It is available to them as in the case of Bobby Baker in the form of easy bank loans and also takes the form of allotting them shares gratis or at cut-rate terms in going enterprises such as insurance and loan companies and banks. Baker was obviously a middleman.

The object of transferring money in this way is to avoid any implication of bribery, a word which politicians know has an ugly sound. Moreover, it is illegal. Although politicians are still bribed, and are sometimes convicted of accepting bribes (as in the recent case of highly placed W. Judson Morhouse), bribery after a distinguished history is now regarded as too cumbersome in the American system. But gifts with no explicit strings attached are not barred by law and are often conveyed in full public view in "testimonial dinners." Will the recipient of such gifts thereafter take a detached view of the special requests of the donors? To believe so is to be credulous beyond hope of redemption.

The newer ways of conveying money to officials in a pervasively corrupt governmental system have clearly been devised to salve their consciences against any gnawing belief that they are being bribed. Thus, Senator Dodd after the call for his censure by the Senate was able to protest publicly with every show of righteous indignation, his voice vibrant, that he was not conscious of having done anything wrong. In this contention he was supported by not a few politicos with whom he had no partisan connection.

On a separate occasion, speaking in defense of Senator Dodd, Senator Long charged that half the members of the Senate Ethics Committee that sat in judgment on Dodd "couldn't stand the investigation Senator Dodd went through" and, finally, that "half the Senate" was in the same boat. A few days later, Senator Long apologized. In making his for-the-record apology Senator Long now surprisingly described the members of the Ethics Committee as "six of the finest members who have ever served in this body."

"If I made a mistake and if I did wrong by saying what I said, I am here to offer them a public apology," said the Majority Whip. "If I have any complaint of this committee it is that their standards are too high."

Senator John Stennis of retrograde Mississippi, chairman of the Ethics

Committee, declined to shake hands with Senator Long after the trebly conditional apology.[6] This theatrical rebuke had much the same effect on public opinion as if Tweedledum had refused to shake hands with Tweedledee.

While it is by no means the case that all officeholders are thus beholden to outside moneymen, mainly *corp-pols,* it certainly appears to be the case that most legislators are. The conditions are evident in the legislatures of the largest industrial states where there is the most money, but they are most plainly evident in Congress. The case of Senator Dodd and the shenanigans of Bobby Baker to sophisticated observers merely represent instances of rather general practice floating inconveniently into view, like garbage at a fashionable swimming beach.

Contrary to common supposition, most officeholders act officially as they do not out of ideological or intellectual commitment but out of monetary devotion. They believe fervently, for example, in "the free enterprise system"—that is, capitalism. Why not? It is keeping them politically afloat on a sea of slush, as nonradical Senator Long lengthily attested.

These money transfers in politics, then, are largely payoffs or retainers to guarantee tractable political behavior. And they do ordinarily have this result.

Congress, which now operates pretty wide open on this sort of thing, applies much stricter criteria to appointees in the executive branch and the judiciary than it does to itself. Congressional committees often, with a great show of virtue, closely question presidential appointees about possible conflicts of interest between their properties and their assigned role in government. Usually Congress is satisfied if a man like the late Secretary of Defense Charles E. Wilson of General Motors sells his stock. President Johnson, not subject to Congress, did not even do this but appointed trustees for his properties. Is it likely that the trustees would make any decision adverse to the easily irked president? So to suppose would, it seems to me, be infinitely boobish.

In disclosures such as in the recent Bobby Baker, Dodd and Morhouse cases, the latest of thousands of analogous instances where the politico has been caught redhanded, his fingers streaming lucre, editorialists often piously refer to "corruption" and "venality." Such moralistic judgments, while understandable, conceal the true causes, and tend to support a widespread erroneous view that politicians are for some reason a special odious breed.

The precise reason there are so many lightfingered and readily purchasable figures in American political life traces directly to the politico-social structure. In the first place, in the American system to have money, however obtained, entitles one to special deference. Not to have it incurs ready contempt. This is straight free-enterprise doctrine, expressing the difference between success and failure, the elect and the damned. Next, and perhaps most importantly, with the opening of the free franchise and public office to all comers in the early nineteenth century in the name of democracy the procuring of impecunious purchasable politicians was in effect guaranteed.

For poor boys to make good in democratic politics was by definition as noble as for them to make good in anything else, part of the holy American vision. But it takes time and therefore money to be in politics, which made it inevitable that moneymen behind the scene retained more than a little to say. In the popular electoral system the electorate was supposed to pick (but not finance) its representatives, who would faithfully represent them; when the electorate was displeased it might vote them out in favor of new men. But it was early noted that the electorate more often than not endorsed men for superficial reasons and voted out faithful men for trivial reasons or for no other reason than a vague discontent about general conditions. In political landslides, for example, everybody went out, saints and sinners alike.

Career politicians, *pubpols*, early saw that it did little good to be a true "friend of the people," who had little insight into affairs or genuine concern about policy. Against the possibility that they might be abruptly voted out of office and livelihood through public caprice or vindictiveness, officeholders began to take prudent measures of self protection. One such measure was the development of local party organizations, "machines," the labor unions of politicians. Another was to use ingenuity in developing unorthodox sources of income with a view to providing nest-eggs that would tide meagerly paid officeholders over lean periods when they were out. (In the latter nineteenth century, the distinguished Charles Francis Adams II reports, he could not live on the $1,000 a year he was paid as mayor of Quincy, Massachusetts.) In many cases unorthodox income was illegal, as from bribes and extortion; in most cases it was questionable. But, up to a point, in all cases it was a practical necessity, although some politicos garnered more than enough under the rule of serendipity.

This broad consequence, which we see exemplified in most originally unpropertied career *pubpols*, in no way derived from the nature of politics as a black art but from the nature of a specific system raised on the unsupported (and, since, often disproved) theory that ambitious, self-willed, untutored men elected from among the people will be the respected, loyal, sympathetic, low-paid servitors of those same people—the democratic dogma. Some few will, as events have shown. Most won't, and the people are usually too inattentive, unperceptive or lacking in judgment to be able to distinguish potential friend from betrayer. They reelect their betrayers, again and again.

This system of popular elections, moreover, was not one devised by the perspicacious Founding Fathers but represented a later dubious embroidery on the basic constitutional system, an embroidery that most of the Founders would have rejected as absurd. Madison, for example, was astute enough to discern what would happen under the universal franchise. The Fathers, often hymned, had no confidence in a universal franchise that would elevate poor boys in urgent and continual need of funds to high office, there to be readily tempted and seduced and to acquire personal interests of their own that ran against those of the populace. But this result was in a few decades broadly achieved amid sentimental clamor for "democracy." Instead of obtaining a boon in the form of electoral democracy, as ideological democrats contended, the people insensibly had rigorous public demands made upon them by such a system—*demands they could not meet*, to their own undoing. In giving them electoral democracy, history played a dirty trick on the American people, most of whom actually want and need benevolent paternalism.

In getting electoral democracy, the American people had figuratively thrust upon them a political version of a Stradivarius violin. But they had not the least conception of how to play it. One result has been continual and avoidable disharmony. Emotionally committed though one may be to democracy, which on speculative grounds might be thought desirable, operationally it is as impossible as perpetual motion. For democracy is something that belongs to the psyche, to group interaction, not to outward forms. As an avalanche of evidence shows, people in general are not the least bit democratic at heart. True democracy, of course, can be learned; but only under carefully controlled favorable conditions such as are rarely present in the upbringing of most children.

That there is considerable disaffection with popular elections even at grass-roots levels is shown by the widespread growth of city managership this century in replacement of elected mayors. In no fewer than 40 per cent of municipalities, some of them rather large, city managers are now hired as trained administrators by the city council. This compares with 50 per cent of the cities that retain elected mayors and 10 per cent governed by commissions, town meetings or representative town meetings.[7] The idea could well be applied to the states which, like Nebraska, could also replace bicameral legislatures (baseless imitations of the federal model) with unicameral bodies.

Officeholding in the provision of the Founding Fathers was limited to property owners, as was most voting, an idea repugnant today but which in its operation in the eighteenth-century American context limited public office at least on the higher levels to men of considerable education and public responsibility. One would not, however, agree with the prescription of H. L. Hunt today that the vote now be limited to people of property; for too many propertied people now are uneducated and have the cracker-barrel grasp of H. L. Hunt.

What made the Founding Fathers and the signers of the Declaration of Independence so noteworthy was not that they were men of property; they were noteworthy because they happened also to be men of broad learning and insight, ready to defer to those of their own number like James Madison, Benjamin Franklin and Alexander Hamilton who showed especially sharp insight. True, among the signers of the Declaration some, such as Samuel Adams and Thomas Jefferson, were early optimistic democrats; most were not. In any event, this crowd was a far cry from the Everett Dirksens, Thomas J. Dodds, George A. Smatherses and a host of other once poor boys (later indifferent to the poor) who found affluence in politics and became, in sooth, cracker-barrel statesmen. The Founding Fathers were a historical fluke.

Among many areas of significance missed by sociologists in their frequent preference for the trivial is this one of the changes in the socio-financial condition of career politicians, either bosses or officeholders. Many, although originally poor and never in highly remunerative employment, like the late Mayor Frank Hague and President Lyndon B. Johnson, accumulate sizable estates. In the case of others, members of their immediate families suddenly blossom in effulgent prosperity. Clearly, most of them are financial entrepreneurs of no mean cut. Also omitted by the sociologists is a ground-up study of the relation between the corporate clients of legislators' law firms and the performance record of the legislators. Are legislators with oil companies in their law offices, for example, for or against special favors to the oil industry? Are legislators whose law offices represent banks in favor of more or less regulation of banks?

The Dance of the Pubpols, Finpols and Corp-pols

The essence of the way the American politico-economic system operates can be brought out most readily by means of employing two key words: *overreaching* and *patronage*. The term "patronage" here excludes reference in this text to governmental job appointments by political parties; such patronage, dwelt upon by newspapers, does exist but it is patronage in a distinctly minor form and of little relevance here.

The chief instrument of economic power in the United States is the corporation, more particularly the large corporation. The corporation is, at its best, a completely rational mechanism with a single overriding goal: the maximization of profits consonant with steady growth. From an internal point of view, everything about the successful large corporation is rational, which is one of the aspects that make it an attractive object of study to those who like to study something wholly rational in an irrational world. Corporate rationality, however, is wholly internal. It is at variance with social rationality and, in fact, the rational corporation takes advantage for itself of much social irrationality, as some corporations take advantage of the desire of many people to swill whisky and to smoke cancer-inducing cigarettes.

The United States, I am convinced, would be a vastly superior place in which to live if it were organized along corporate lines as a single corporation rationally committed to maximizing the welfare of all people. I don't have in mind here a fascist corporate state, although this is probably what the outcome would be if misguided idealists set about trying to install a benevolent political corporation. Short of such a goal, we have before us as a model the welfare capitalism of Sweden, disliked by rabid free-enterprisers athirst for tax exemption.

In its rationality the corporation does everything it can, including much that is illegal, to maximize its profits. It employs deceptive (and irrational) advertising, produces below-par goods even for vital military and space programs, resorts to deceptive packaging, evades taxes, abuses weights and measures, engages in monopolistic price-fixing, caters to popular irrationalities, overcharges, profiteers, and, in general, does whatever it can, evaluated as good or bad, legal or illegal, to maximize its position. To the outsider there is something questionable about one act or the other of the big business corporation. If the quality of the goods is excellent the price may be too high; if the price is low the quality suffers. In any event, it pays no taxes, merely collects them from customers. Again, much of corporate goods produced is of no utility other than in catering to free-floating anxieties, often stimulated by advertising. Here the rational corporation profits from irrational people.

Overreaching is not something new in history. But in its American systematization, complete with computers, it is distinctly new, and it affects every nook and cranny of society as well as of individual attitudes. It is seen, for example, in many of the formal and publicly defended economic policies of the medical profession; some doctors, alarmingly, are no more than overreaching businessmen and bad doctors to boot. It extends into the ghettos with their high prices and high installment interest rates for below-par merchandise. It is reflected in the terms and product given by builders to home buyers. It is freely practiced against the general labor force by the stronger trade unions. It stands out blatantly in advertising. Systematic overreaching of the weak, in sooth, is as American as apple pie. It is respectable. Rightly practiced it will lead one to membership in the country club, a zero in the infinite.

The rich themselves are in many ways the victims of this spirit of over-reaching and must be constantly on their guard against swindles, an involved story commended to the sociologists for further inquiry. As an example, although the best medicine is available to the rich they are in fact the victims of many medical rackets and in known instances un-scrupulous doctors play a cat-and-mouse game with them, prolonging their disabilities and, for all one knows, bringing them to premature avoidable ends. The rich get into this impasse on the theory that whatever costs most must be best, and there are doctors who do not hesitate to set especially high fees. There exists, among other things, a special tier of high-fee proprietary hospitals, physical and psychiatric, especially programmed to act as a vacuum cleaner on the pockets of those with ability to pay, and not markedly notable for sound medical results. The victims of such estab-lishments, however, can comfort themselves with the fact that there are being applied in medicine the most rigorous canons of free and unregu-lated private enterprise.

The *corp-pols* are the actual front line and cutting edge of capitalism. They represent the hard-nosed elements in the system and, during suc-cessful behavior, under the canons of strict business principles, are largely autonomous. As long as they run the corporation in harmony with hard business rationality, always with deference to public opinion (manip-ulated through public relations) they are in complete charge. True, if the big stockholders wished to interfere with operations they could.

The big stockholders, however, often but not always rentiers and some-times personally tender-minded, not up to conducting confrontations with nail-hard labor leaders and nagging politicos, not always well informed, do not interfere with the *corp-pols* unless there is a crisis in internal com-pany affairs or between the company and the outside world. In such instances the big stockholders can and often do intervene decisively, espe-cially against a runaway or berserk management. Ordinarily, though, the big stockholders let well enough alone, even endorsing judicially certified illegal conduct.

Big stockholders could, it is true, meddle into the affairs of corporate management and, theoretically, could insist upon strict social-minded policies. They do not do this, usually, not because they are of the despicable temperaments pictured by C. Wright Mills and others but because they are indifferent, diffident or are afraid to disturb a smoothly running profitable operation.

Some clarification of the roles of *corp-pols* and *pubpols* seems advisable here lest they be misrepresented. Despite adverse moral judgments often registered against them by critical commentators each of these types always does broadly what is inherently required by the system he serves. More significantly, each at all times implements to the best of his ability the chief operative value of American society: worship of William James's bitch-goddess, Success. In their various ways these men are all successes and exemplify in their dreary daily activity the American doctrine of success. As men who faithfully obey the inner rules of the game they merit and receive wide public approbation. If at times what they do appears messy under close scrutiny, this is only because the American idea of success is messy. At such times they may be called upon to act as scapegoats for the system, to take the blame as moral lepers. This they do, grimly.

It should be observed that, except for disaffected, out-of-step critics, there is no widespread rejection on the American scene of the ascendant notion of success. Not only does a broad public uncritically accept steamy monetary success as a proper life goal but it feels any questioning of this goal to be un-American, possibly traitorous or at least subversive and surely cowardly. Who but a coward would shrink from entering the glorious contest for success? The "unsuccessful" are regarded with contempt or pity, often even by themselves.

What we find, if we delve deeply enough, is a special value system at the root of it all.

The traditional value system, originated out of long and tragic human experience, was encapsulated in traditional religion. As religious mythology, cult and ritual were demolished by critical rationalism the values of which these were the virtually sole and fragile carriers also suffered, came into disrepute as goody-goodyness and were insensibly superseded by the harsh values of success, of which the mass media stood as the principal guarantors. Instead of the clergy now defining values for society the job was taken over by half-literate, often personally demoralized editors and publishers.

Religion, in the process, was reduced from a vital, widely shared world view to routine churchgoing on the part of the less educated. As the healthy baby of traditional values was thrown out with the dirty bathwater of myth and cult, the only repositories remaining for traditional values were the university and traditional philosophy, neither of which had much impact in the daily lives of people and both of which were strangers to the editors and publishers of the mass media, nearly all militantly ignorant men.

Because man by his very nature must always live by one set of values or the other, the new set of harsh values not only filled a vacuum but accorded with the experience of what had until recently been a frontier society. In that society difficult conditions at once highlighted the competent and the incompetent. The competent man was he who could take care of himself: the self-reliant man, the *successful* man.

The original American fortune-builders, the Robber Barons of the nineteenth century, it is well to notice, were all with hardly an exception faintly educated or illiterate lower-class men, none at all above the lower middle class and many from even further down: unskilled laborers, farmers, wandering adventurers. The American plutocracy, in truth, did not originate from within an aristocracy but came straight from the *hoi polloi* and implemented by far-ranging commercial action the narrow, culturally impoverished daily values of this *hoi polloi*. It was this element up from the lower cultural depths, making common cause with formerly poor boys in politics, that provided American society with personal proof of the worth of the new scale of values by enriching themselves. Expression of an inherent American point of view was given by the Rev. Horatio Alger, Jr., in his novels of successful economic derring-do on the part of poor boys.

These good-in-their-place frontier values, as much evidence now shows, are insidiously destructive in a more developed environment, even of their own votaries. While the bulk of attention is focused on the massive poverty sector of American industrial society, what is generally overlooked, except by a few close observers, is that affluent suburbia and much of the success-striving middle class is also engulfed in its own particular variety of emotional slum-ghettos. The very winners in the system, the affluent, are in different ways as malserved as the poor, a fact increasingly evident to educated middle-class youth.

That the values put to the fore by the success cult are destructive is seen most readily in the blighted personal lives even of winning strivers under the system. Within the reaches of the *Social Register* we see ample evidences of the blight reflected in a book such as Cleveland Amory's *Who Killed Society?* Lower down we find it in special reports.

"According to psychologists, physicians, family counselors and others," reports the *Wall Street Journal*, "companies now absorb too much of the time, energy and devotion of their rising young executives; exhausted by their jobs, they are mere shells at home, unable to function effectively as husbands and fathers.

"The result is seldom divorce, which is bad for the careers of young men on the go. Instead, marriages in name only are preserved between weary, indifferent men and women beset by all sorts of emotional ills, including chronic loneliness, sexual frustration, alcoholism and excessive dependence on their children."[8]

There followed an interesting, long, quasi-psychiatric analysis of emotional troubles on the suburbia executive success-circuit, about which there is a growing special literature.

In two surveys in the Chicago area on attitudes of women it developed that they saw their mates, not as persons, but in order of importance as breadwinner, father and husband; and saw themselves, again, not as persons but as mother, wife and homemaker. Few of the women had any interest in or knowledge of their husband's work but evaluated the man in terms of being "a good provider" or having "a good job." Commenting on this phenomenon Marya Mannes said: "Throughout their responses, the conclusion was inescapable that the wives cared far more about what their husbands *did* than about what they *were,* as persons. About one-third of the women not only put their own role as mothers first, but indicated that the husband was essentially outside the basic family unit of herself and her children." It is because men are primarily an accessory to the fact of the contemporary family "instead of half of a primary relation" that so many, in the opinion of Miss Mannes, finds ways outside the family of establishing the fact of their manhood. Said Miss Mannes mordantly: "Is a primary relationship between man and wife indeed possible in a society where secondary considerations—success, status, possessions, social acceptance, public opinion—impinge more and more on a family unit less and less tied together by common needs and bonds? . . . . If the illusion of a truly companionable marriage is to exist, women might start thinking of their husbands as men first, and accessories last. And vice versa."[9]

Financial deficiencies are blamed on the man; family deficiencies are blamed on the woman. As comparatively few individual incomes, only 10 per cent until the more recent Johnsonian inflation, exceed $10,000 a year, according to the cold statistics, it is evident that most American males are big flops incomewise and are wide open to cutting remarks from their success-oriented, status-craving wives wrestling with child care and household chores.

All, then, as one could easily show by citing a variety of sources, is not happy sailing in the alcohol-sustained, drug-propped affluent belt of society, which in its own way is as badly churned up as the city slums and ghettos. Children in this situation, of course, suffer most of all.

In passing, it is difficult for a habitual reader of the *New York Times*, the *Wall Street Journal*, the *Christian Science Monitor* and the *Washington Post* to avoid concluding that the United States shelters under the glorious Star Spangled Banner an extremely sick society, fundamentally made ill by the institutional implementation of a set of extremely destructive values.

Let us return, now, to the big corporation.

The management is the soul of any corporation. Without good management—that is, the rational application of unsentimental business principles as rigorously as possible in an imperfect world—the best corporation is bound to lose ground steadily to demonic rivals. And the importance of management is recognized in the many university courses and books and periodicals devoted to it. Management, in fact, is governance, rule. And within the modern corporation one finds the most rational and usually judicious application of rule in history, although for ends often extraneous to the general welfare. Corporate management fries its own fish and makes the best terms it can with cloudy public opinion and with government— that is, with *pubpols*. The men who run these corporate fiefdoms, managers, are actually rulers of vast domains, *corp-pols*. Although comparatively most of them are not extremely rich, the *corp-pols* are indispensable to the rich. Some become very rich.

A good management of a corporation is the equivalent of a John D. Rockefeller in the Standard Oil Company and performs a similar general role. As pristine Rockefellers are hard to find growing naturally, it is necessary to train them up. This uptraining is done on the chain of command, from the junior executives onward. Along this chain of command many are called, few ultimately chosen; some are dropped along the way, some shunted into corporation dead ends or cul-de-sacs, some lost to rivals. The hard, sharp, rational, dominant, smart and highly acquisitive are moved upward under the incentives of higher pay, more and more public deference and elevated social status. Emerging as executive vice president and president, a man is known to be a crashing success within the system. He is somebody to be reckoned with. He is a *corp-pol*, as powerful in his way as any senator, sometimes more powerful. As chairman he becomes something of an Elder Statesman, ready to tell congressional committees what is, and what is not, sound. For these are all, with few exceptions, sound men. They know the inner workings of affairs as many large stockholders do not.

What critics of the abstraction called capitalism rarely see is the impersonality of the actual system, allowing few involved in it to experience it in its fullness. Thus, owners in this system, unless they are also managers, have only remote impersonal relation to it. Absentees, they are seldom directly touched by it. As far as knowing precisely what goes on, most of them are as ignorant as the common man. Some do not wish to be put to the inconvenience of knowing, in which case the system also serves them well. Capitalists, at any rate, are rarely close students of capitalism and the way it works. All most of them know is that they are getting only what they believe they are in all plain justice cosmically entitled to, and this holds of many inheritors who never soiled a finger as well as of the self-erected. The courts agree to the hilt.

As to harsh characterizations of the rich as special hard types, it is easy to show that they are false. As Lampman showed, 40 per cent of the owners of taxable estates are women. As Professor James Smith showed, women predominate among the owners of estates exceeding $10 million, a figure more recently verified by Herman P. Miller, special assistant to the director of the Census Bureau.

As of 1958, millionaires by sex and average age, Miller found, were as follows:[10]

Amount (in millions)	Men	Age	Women	Age
Total	22,024	61	17,630	58
$1–2	16,336	59	11,063	60
2–3	3,156	62	3,048	56
3–5	1,124	68	1,320	63
5–10	1,073	63	541	67
10 and over	335	58	1,658	40

The predominant number of very big holders, then (five to one), are women of an average age of forty, who are in this category either as heirs, widows or as a consequence of estate splitting by older men, usually husbands. Most such female holdings, of course, are under the direction of male investment managers, lawyers, trustees, husbands or fathers. As far as that is concerned, some of the richest people are minors, children.

While some of the women are as dividend-hungry as any man, and some hungrier, by and large they are not hard types; nobody at all has ever suggested they are. At worst what one could say of most of them is that they are foolish, uninformed, self-centered, inexperienced, possibly insensitive, often childishly arrogant. Many of the men, given sheltered rearing under tutors and in hothouse schools, are as temperamentally detached from the workings of monopoly capitalism as the women. Usually products of the Ivy League, they are in all ways gentlemen, often highly civilized. They collect modern art, give money to universities and libraries, support unquestionably worthy causes and even give privately off the record for laudable ends.

The absurd self-image of at least some of these women, many of whom appear to consider critics of their forebears as guilty at least of *lèse majesté*, was publicly projected recently by Helen Clay Frick, the seventy-seven-year-old spinster daughter of the harsh ironmaster, partner of Carnegie, who died in 1919. Miss Frick in 1965 brought suit for libel against Dr. Sylvester K. Stevens, executive director of the Pennsylvania Historical and Museum Commission, for some unusually mild depreciative characterizations of the deceased Henry Clay Frick in Stevens's *Pennsylvania: Birthplace of a Nation*. In what must be considered the extreme of understatement he suggested that the rapacious Frick was hardly a model Christian gentleman but was rude and autocratic.

Frick, during and after his lifetime, had steadily been depicted by many writers as the prototype of a ruthless nineteenth-century Robber Baron, overreaching and ignorant, but Miss Frick, in bringing suit, denied ever having heard any of this, claimed to be shocked at the besmirching of her sire's reputation by a scholar and asserted that he had been libeled and she had been caused great anguish of spirit. Waiving damages, she asked that the book be suppressed and the record corrected.

After carefully listening to a great deal of testimony from both sides Judge Clinton R. Weidner of the Cumberland County (Pennsylvania) Court of Common Pleas, handed down a masterly fifty-one-page opinion that could have been written by Justice Oliver Wendell Holmes. The court's opinion was far more critical of Frick than the book had been. Not only were the alleged defamatory statements completely true, said the learned jurist, but they were milder than were warranted by the facts. Frick himself, in view of his stance as a lone wolf against the world, would have been proud of them.

As the *Times* pointed out, the judge's opinion, ventured in the face of as many as four plaintiff's lawyers at one time in the courtroom itself, "came close to calling her suit frivolous." Scolding the plaintiff, the court said she knew nothing whatever about her father's affairs and wanted nobody else to know about them.

"Dr. Stevens has written what he believes to be true and what the court believes to be true," said the court firmly.

In the ordinary case, this would have been the end. But some two and a half months later, upon the withdrawal of the baseless case by stipulation,

Miss Frick reopened it and thereby suddenly found herself in the role of defendant. She reopened it by absurdly expressing "delight" at the author's "retraction of false statements." Dr. Stevens at once characterized this statement of hers as "positively vicious and face-saving." He went on to say: "This whole thing, on the very day she has admitted her suit was groundless, is designed to make it look as though I am retracting something and Miss Frick is graciously consenting to withdraw."

The stipulation withdrawing the case was made "with prejudice," which meant that she lost the option of reopening her complaint. As the *Times* pointed out, the stipulation was signed by her attorney with the knowledge that subsequent editions of the book, after changes in two trivial references to fact, one being the suppression of the word "coal," would contain some new language sharply critical of her father.

Charging "deception" and "bad faith," attorneys for Dr. Stevens asked the court to revoke the dismissal of her suit and thrash out her claim that there had been a retraction of false statements. There the matter rests at this writing.[11]

What was of general interest about this case was the way it showed one of the reserve powers of the wealthy to harass in costly and timewasting legal actions writers who comment critically on their public actions, even on those dead. It was knowledge of such powers that led attorneys for the publisher of Professor Edwin Sutherland's *White Collar Crime* to require that the names of companies that had been repeatedly convicted of violating the law not be mentioned. Individuals who have been convicted of violating the law, especially in the commission of felonies, can be and are thereafter often for the rest of their lives referred to as "criminals." Any scribbler can refer to anyone of such as "ex cons." Although it might seem that one should by the same token be able to refer to a convicted corporation as a criminal corporation, the publisher's attorneys in the Sutherland case thought it the better part of prudence not to mention their names.

The situation is this: Can the Super-Cosmos Corporation, convicted in open court many times of felonies and thereupon subjected to penalties and restraining orders backed by sanctions, be referred to as a criminal corporation? Lawyers, as we have seen, advise against it, knowing that their client may soon be served by a summons sworn out by the law firm of King, Lord, Duke and Pontiff of 1 Wall Street. Hardly any judge in Anglo-Saxondom would dream of even entertaining a motion to dismiss an action brought by this pontifical firm, whose members look with basilisk eyes even upon Lowells and Cabots. The offender will surely be forced to prove that crime is crime.

Even individuals, always lower class, who have never been convicted of anything are open to unpleasant characterizations in the press. Persons frequently arrested by the police, or questioned, are thereafter often referred to as "police characters." By this token at least the top 1,000, and probably more, leading corporations are police characters; for they are constantly having run-ins with the authorities, are constantly being questioned about alleged violations, sometimes convicted. Yet to refer to any of them as police characters or as suspected outlaws might be costly. If not themselves sovereign they are so tightly interlaced with sovereignty that one is indeed guilty of *lèse majesté* in impugning them to the slightest degree. Like a king, they are hedged by divinity.

Beyond this there are "undesirable characters," rather *degagé*, unaesthetic types the police do not enjoy seeing lounge about in central city districts, with newspapers often concurring in the appellation. What, now, about composing a list of undesirable corporations, opening with whiskey and cigarette companies?

Yet, most of the rich today are not a demonic crowd. They are not ordinarily fanatics. Often quite "democratic," they will bandy pleasant words with almost anyone over drinks, will probably mildly fault their severer critics as persons who unaccountably "come on too strong." Some of this, of course, may be simple evasiveness.

Again, they are sufficiently numerous, random products, so that the law of large numbers applies to them. They range over the whole bell-shaped spectrum of the law of probability so that for every one with some unlovely characteristic there is a balancing personality with the opposite characteristic. There are not only Miss Fricks but diametrically opposite types. In the middle range of 50 per cent one finds more similarities, usually acceptably decorous along average lines neither great nor odious.

As I said, most of the rich, except possibly some of the self-erected, are not hard types.

The hard types in the system, the ones who make the system work like an automatic mouse-trap for the largely unconscious benefit of the rich, are, first, the *corp-pols* and, second, a plain majority of the *pubpols*. These upward-striving intermediaries are selected hard types in the same sense that a surgeon or a commando soldier is a hard type. They are decision makers, and the decisions they make are invariably devoid of sentiment. A surgeon does not refrain from cutting because it will draw blood, possibly induce death or leave a scar; a commando does not refrain from slitting a throat because he will be dispatching some kind mother's son, some worthy wife's husband, some innocent child's father. By training and temperament these are indeed special types, not subject within their group to the law of probability as to their functional characteristics. With each one it is possible to predict almost certainly how he will act in given circumstances.

The big stockholding rich, largely absentees, to a considerable extent women, have little direct contact with the *corp-pols*, their plantation overseers. Such little functional contact as there is takes place, if at all, through boards of directors; on these, however, many of the very rich do not sit.

The social meeting *ground* for them all—big male stockholders, *finpols* and *corp-pols*—is the metropolitan club, where there is on the whole a rather desultory mingling. Although glad to be present as evidence of their puissance, many of the intermediary *corp-pols* in this milieu look with some reserve, possibly even disdain, on some of the big stockholders and *finpols*. For the *corp-pols* are usually different, and know it, in that they for the most part came up the long, hard way. They feel pretty much as battle-hardened veterans do in the presence of inexperienced though superior officers. Many of the rich they no doubt look upon as pampered nonrealists. Some of the *corp-pols* did not finish high school because their families were too poor; others went to Jerkwater College—or to business college.

The human drive in the system clearly comes, for the most part, from the *corp-pols* and *pubpols*, men from comparatively deprived backgrounds hungry for position, money and deference. The system would work perfectly well if all the big stockholders were playboys and playgirls. The system does not really need the big stockholders who are, as it were, wards of the courts.

True, many of the rich no doubt see the situation pretty much as do the *corp-pols* and *pubpols*. They recognize that there should be money incentives and that "success," not public sustenance, is the proper goal. Whether they do or not, however, makes little difference as long as they keep hands off smoothly running operations. Difficulties are best handled by the highly paid *corp-pols* in concert with the *pubpols*, most of each category commando types.

Little is known of the direct relations between corporate managers and the big owners. "To what degree do these richest families or groups *use* their voting power to influence the operations of 'their' companies?" asks Robert Heilbroner. "We do not know. There exists a shroud of secrecy over the relation between the centers of inherited wealth and the determination of working policy in capitalism."[12]

Here, one must note, top management officers even after their retirement never produce revelatory memoirs of inner company affairs as do men who have served a stint in government. The latter, even high military officers, often finally "tell all," sparing nobody up to the president of the United States and his wife. Perhaps a reason such inner revelations about the corporations never appear is that the qualified writers are still on the payroll, drawing large retirement pay. By telling what went on they might be kicking the bottom out of their own boat. Thus the system automatically covers its most significant inner traces.

We are not, however, without some clues that the big hereditary owners have some direct influence in their corporations. One clue, as we have noticed, exists in the anti-Semitism of the metropolitan clubs, introduced there by rough-house nineteenth-century tycoons and echoed today in the personnel policies of the large corporations and the memberships of country clubs. In their respective outlooks, then, the big owners and the *corppols* are not strangers to each other. *Somebody* must initiate such a policy at the top, *somebody* must enforce it. The Founding Fathers were not anti-Semitic. Other policies may similarly be left-handedly, indirectly, imposed. Yet in this quarter all is very shadowy.

Nor, one may infer, are the very rich merely accidental beneficiaries of the one-sided tax laws. Parties of interest must have asked, *sub rosa,* for such preferential treatment. The *pubpols* could not have written such laws without some prompting. Had they done so they would be in the creative class of Franz Kafka.

What is probably true of many or most of the special benefits enjoyed by the rich is that at different times some one or a few of the rich utilized leverage available to them with amiable key *pubpols* and exerted their will with respect to some facet of the law. Whatever was of benefit to one then became of benefit to all in that category. As many at different times busied themselves with different facets of the laws, the result was a tremendously wide range of special benefits made available to a broad upper-income class. While the full range of the benefits looks as though it could only have resulted from a common conspiracy, each individual benefit was obtained by some individual go-getter exerting his political leverage. There is, then, nothing like a central *moneybund* calling all the shots, only individual go-getters exerting power through stooges that brings unsought benefits to others. Naturally, nobody objects to features of the law that he finds give him a favored outcome. This is only what is known in popular parlance as "getting the breaks." The rich get many such "breaks," for many of which most of them never asked. For most of them it is all pure serendipity.

Where the dominant rich enter the system most openly is through patronage, political and cultural. The political patronage comes from the rich directly in the form of campaign contributions and indirectly from their corporations that hand out largess through their overpaid officers in the form of campaign contributions and direct payments in the form of money from lobbyists and corporate retainers for political law firms. For sources of campaign funds, see Alexander Heard, *The Costs of Democracy*, University of North Carolina Press, Chapel Hill, 1960. Cultural patronage is exercised through the foundations and, sometimes, the trustee-controlled universities directly. Scholars and scientists whose work either contributes to the well-being of the existing establishment or provides justification and rationalization for it are supported with lavish grants and cushy appointments. Others, either critical or producing unwelcome or unusable findings, are not. It is as simple as that.

This sort of foundation patronage produces a double advantage for the donors for it is publicly designated not as patronage but as philanthropy. In some cases philanthropy may be truly involved; over the entire foundation panorama, as we have seen, it is not. The foundations serve many ulterior purposes, the very least of them philanthropic.

There is, too, the general patronage in the form of rich corporate advertising placements in the mass media, serving to keep these firmly on the side of the existing establishment at all times when the chips go down.

As far as the Establishment is concerned, there is convenient scholarship and inconvenient scholarship. Inconvenient scholarship, while tolerated, is simply neither supported nor promoted. Scholarship that validates the American Celebration, however, showing Uncle Sam *ueber alles*, is heavily supported.

What this amounts to, quite simply, is patronage, impersonally conferred.

Basically, what gains befuddled acceptance for the system generally, it will be noticed, is verbiage—political, social, economic and cultural. Elaborate quasi-metaphysical arguments are ready at every point to prove that the existing state of affairs is exactly as it inevitably should be—all factors, of course, taken into consideration. Everybody, in other words, is right where he ought to be in the social scale, including the foundation-supported professors who excel at such arguments. Anybody who says differently is a deviant, a kook, unsound, far out in left field and probably infected by some un-American ideology. The horror of horrors is for an academic to be an avowed Marxist, as Richard Nixon showed in campaigning rabidly up and down the state of New Jersey in 1965 to have a Marxist school teacher cashiered. The obtuse Nixon lost, probably because his intended victim bore a politically potent Italian name.

It would be extraordinary if the winners in the system did not believe, after the way they had obeyed its rigorous rules (including those of inheritance), that everything was as it properly ought to be. And it is the winners who monopolize the stage in evaluating the system.

The Role of the People

But neither overreaching nor patronage would get very far unless they were practiced within a population that was emotionally simple and not in possession of sound knowledge and realistic judgment. Most of the population, whatever one may say on its behalf, is of this order, is quite uninformed and readily susceptible of being emotionally worked upon, distracted.

A Harris poll, for example, has shown that 40 per cent of American Catholics believe that whenever the pope delivers himself of an opinion it has the status of a law, a bizarre claim that the Catholic Church itself is far from making.[13] Just as large a percentage of non-Catholics, if not larger, are under similar misapprehensions about facts relating to the Catholic and perhaps their own ecclesiastical establishments.

A vast majority of the white population south of the Mason-Dixon Line, and large numbers, probably a majority elsewhere, are firmly of the belief that Negroes are subhuman or only semihuman, despite the positive assertions of biology and anthropology to the contrary. Merely to argue the scientific findings in many quarters is to risk being assaulted by righteously indignant citizens who consider the speaker erotically irregular, a "nigger-lover."

A Louis Harris poll in 1966 showed that whereas 78 per cent of the more affluent and educated sections of the population believed Negroes are unfairly discriminated against, only 46 per cent of lower-income people thought so. "Almost three out of every four whites who earn less than $5,000 a year and never went beyond the eighth grade in school think the education available to Negroes is as good as that available to whites," said Mr. Harris. "What is more, about half of this group thinks Negroes are not discriminated against in general and that housing for Negroes is as good as it is for whites."[14]

Careful sociological studies have shown that the masses are poorly informed on vital topics despite a plethora of accurate information available and that they are politically illiberal and withdrawn in their attitudes. Astrology flourishes.

As noted earlier, the further one moves down the social scale the more authoritarian and illiberal become the individuals.

Professor Robert E. Lane on the basis of a comprehensive study concluded that:

The lesser degree of political participation and interest in lower status groups is partly accountable by the following factors: (1) Lower-strata women (but not men) have less leisure available for political activity. (2) Lower status persons have less economic security, and, partly for that reason, feel less of a sense of control over their (political) environment. (3) The threat of deprivation of upper-strata groups present in the politics of the welfare state provides greater motivation than the promise of reward to the lower-status groups.

The relation of public policy to the group stakes at issue in that policy is made more visible to upper-status groups than to lower-status groups.

Lower-status individuals can influence and benefit from governmental action only socially, by group activity and membership, while upper-class persons can influence and benefit from such action individually. Therefore, upper-class persons have a higher incentive to participate.

Lower-status people, feeling at a disadvantage compared to upper-class people, tend to avoid social contact in mixed groups, withdraw interest, defer to others in "difficult" matters, and generally reveal a lack of self-confidence. Actually, lack of experience and influence combined with pressures to be "opinionated" leads to unrealistic participation in some instances.

Child-rearing practices in the lower-status groups tend to provide a less adequate personality basis for appropriately self-assertive social participation.

The social norms and roles in the lower-status group tend to emphasize political participation less than do the norms and roles of the upper-status groups. There is a tendency for these political roles to be concentrated in middle-class rather than upper-class or working-class groups. . . .

Lower-status persons experience greater cross pressures with respect to (a) ethnic versus class identifications, (b) divergent political appeals of the media to which they are exposed, and conflict between media and status identification, (c) community leadership and own-group leadership, and (d) subjective versus objective class identification.

Lower-status persons belong to fewer formal organizations and have fewer intimate personal friends. However, union membership tends to modify this pattern.

Lower-status persons have less capacity to deal with abstract issues and less awareness of their larger social environment.

Lower-status persons are less satisfied with their lives and communities, leading, in a minimally class conscious society, to withdrawal from civic activities, or, alternatively, to participation in deviant politics.

Inter-class mobility tends to weaken the forces for political participation, a tendency modified by identification with upper-status (participant) norms by both upwardly mobile and downwardly mobile groups.[15]

None of this, however, accounts for greater lower-class response when politicians promise authoritarian repression of some segment of the populace. The promise by such as Joseph McCarthy and George Wallace that heads are going to roll never fails to galvanize the lower orders politically.

The lower-status groups—that is, those below the middle class—are, in other words, confused. And it is this element, peasantlike in outlook, that constitutes most of the electorate, accounting for the easy nomination and election of so many persons who in medical parlance would be designated as quacks or unqualified practitioners. Public office in the United States—and elsewhere—is full of them: quacks.

Politics, contrary to roaring democratic theory, is not something that can be readily practiced with proper success by anybody. Politics, like any other discipline, requires qualified specialists.

Here a note seems in order. There is theoretical as well as practical politics. The multi-vocal structure of theoretical politics is laid out in the works of Plato, Aristotle, Polybius, Aquinas, Hobbes, Locke, Montesquieu, Kant and many similar savants. A formal exercise in practical politics, based on actual political maneuver, is Machiavelli's *The Prince*. Biographies abound with additional material. Formally qualified people in career politics ought to be thoroughly acquainted with this whole literature and to be broadly grounded as well in logic, semantics, linguistics, epistemology, scientific methods, the social studies and the humanities. Simply by laying down such formal requirements I have disqualified practically every working politician on the American scene. But I have no hesitancy in saying that those who do not have some approach to such preparation are at the very least quacks. Quackery is of the very essence of being a politician on the American scene, a leader of the booboisie into fetid blind alleys.

This quackery shows itself most blatantly in the wild abuse of language by routine career politicians. Language in routine American politics is not used to inform or to analyze problems but to manipulate emotions and to obfuscate. Purely whimsical bandying of language, as in the case of Senator Everett Dirksen, can alone make one a national character in the eyes of the press. But the more sober use of language by politicians not given to the devious Dirksen's fanciful flights of bombinating rhetoric is equally misleading so that the nation literally, under President Johnson, fell into the position of the polity of George Orwell's *1984* where peace means war, defense means aggression, the Great Society means the Shabby Society, prosperity means recession and a "war on poverty" means befuddlement of the poor and the perpetration of financial skulduggery.

Few politicians use language warrantably. In a well-known dictum, they use it to conceal thought. The gobbledegook of endless government reports and political speeches furnishes proof without end. The *Congressional Record* is full of the stuff. Madison Avenue and the politicians are as one in this respect. Such use of language stamps the user an arrant quack, on a par with a healer who professes to cure disease with electric belts and charms.

The United States Senate no doubt contains the greatest concentration of professional political intelligence in the nation. Yet, leaving aside terms such as liberal, moderate and conservative and applying the loosest criteria possible, it is difficult to exempt more than a bare third of it from the rubric of quack. The House of Representatives is far more meagerly equipped, and in the state legislatures it is often a case of 100 per cent quackery among their various member lawyers, real estate and insurance brokers, loan sharks, undertakers and small-time dealers. The executive offices are for the most part filled by similar quacks, fugitives from anything resembling culture. Ghost writers fill the breach.

Still, the average officeholder is of a capability far superior to the average of the peasantlike populace he serves. The politician is not, as often supposed, of an inferior order comparatively. There is not the slightest doubt that Senators Stennis and Eastland, for example, are people superior in ability and drive to the population average in Mississippi. And the same holds true elsewhere. Again, officeholders, whatever one may say of them, meet the criteria of the broad electorate. They have what it takes to gain acceptance by the boobs. The "pork barrel," for which the politicos are castigated, is what gains them votes out in the spiritually barren home districts.

As Professor Lane remarks:

Most of the current criticism of popular rule does not emanate from the enemies of democracy, but rather from its saddened friends. It deals in part with the capacities of the people to make wise decisions in their own interest, the strength of their desire to participate in government, and the nature of the benefits they derive therefrom. On the basis of clinical research and public opinion polls, students of democratic government have concluded that the electorate is wanting both in vital information and in rational pursuit of enduring self-interest; the tasks have exceeded the capacities of the public to perform them. Thus, Walter Lippmann, continuing a line of argument he began so brilliantly in *Public Opinion* some thirty-five years ago, states that a central cause for the breakdown of democratic governments in modern times has been that "the assemblies and the mass electorates have acquired the monopoly of effective powers" and do not know how to use them. . . .

Erich Fromm, although he favors widespread social participation, has cast doubt upon men's desire for the burdens which such participation implies. Freedom implies choice, participation implies responsibility, and under stress the majority of the people may find choice painful and responsibility too weighty a load. Apathy, withdrawal, conformity, "pseudo-willing," result. . . .

It is said that the masses have not gained through their new political power because the sources of their trouble are not political but economic. Democracy is a mask for plutocracy, and the plutocrats remain entrenched in power. Thus the long struggle to enfranchise the masses of men has, so far, come to no avail; the franchise is useful only as it offers leverage to attack the real citadel of power.

[Commenting here, Lane says:] This idea is curiously at the confluence of three streams of thought. The first, liberal democracy, is illustrated by [Carl L.] Becker who says that "economic forces . . . brought about an increasing concentration of wealth and power in the hands of the fortunate few, and thereby nullified, for the majority of people, many of those essential liberties which provide both the theoretical justification and the necessary conditions for the practical success of democratic institutions." The second element in this confluence is contributed by Mosca and Pareto, both of whom identify democracy with plutocracy. And the third element, of course, is the Marxian interpretation of bourgeois democracy as a complex of institutions manipulated by the capitalist class.[16]

That the universal franchise and the wide open consumer market are, on the basis of their experience with it, now fully acceptable to the dominate orders has been seen in the massive and costly efforts of the Johnson Administration to force them upon the Vietnamese at the point of firepower. In the Johnsonian view even people to whom the idea of voting is bewildering, contra-cultural and perhaps repugnant, are to be forced to vote. This, the American Way, it is held, will lead to their liberation. Yet neither voting nor the open consumer market has led to the liberation of the masses in the United States; rather have they delivered them into the pincers of ignorance, poverty or near poverty and emotional deprivation. The masses are, literally, stupefied by the "opportunities" open to them.

Voting, unless there is ground-up, knowledge-based participation, cannot lead to popular deliverance. Only if the assumption were true that each participant is of fairly equal capability could the process work. But people simply are not of equal capability and motivation, contrary to the dream of the early democrats. They must lose out in the electoral game for a multitude of reasons, some of which have been cited. The shrewd manipulators —the *pubpols, corp-pols, finpols,* admen and *scholpols*—must come out on top every time just as the heavyweight champion must easily defeat every amateur who steps into the ring with him.

Democrats, liberals and radicals, have wasted millions of words and hours of their time trying to arouse the people in their own interests either to electoral or to revolutionary assault, and always without avail. Marx predicted, erroneously, that factory operatives, the workers, would take the lead in an assault on the owners; such an assault has never taken place in any industrial country. Marxist parties have taken power only under conditions of war-induced general social collapse, as in agricultural Russia and China, with only the most meager of Marxist proletarian support. Non-Marxist peasants in both cases were the revolutionary instrument. (Marx, *inter alia*, detested the peasantry, which he saw as reactionary.)

Nor have popular causes been more successful in the electoral arena, where splinter parties have long failed to gain even a foothold. For the mass does not vote for its objective interests; it always votes for some fantasy.

From Lincoln onward no more than two out of nineteen presidents are argued by anybody to have been oriented toward the popular interest and even those two are rejected by some experts as true paladins of the people. The people, very obviously, are not capable of wielding the electoral sword, thus accounting for the success of institutionalized overreaching and patronage. The rich, in plain fact, are rich because they cannot help it. They are playing marbles for big stakes against blind men, cannot help winning with little effort.

To the Marxists all these presidents were tools of the capitalist Establishment; but not to the people, to whom the Marxists look vainly as the instrument of social reconstruction. As to this, say the Marxists, the people are fooled by the mass media; but it is of the essence of politics, as of military affairs, not to be fooled. To be fooled in politics is to be conquered. In losing out so consistently by means of open elections the people, clearly, are being hoist by their own petard. They have not the least inkling what the elections are all about.

It would be difficult for any set of men, however qualified, to run so complexly ponderous a country as the United States really well. As it is, the United States is very, very poorly run, year after year, by the quacks, overreachers and patrons, as the accumulation and multiplication of social problems attest. At the same time, propagandic apologists continually bellow how well the country is run. Nothing, though, ever seems to get any better; everything gets demonstrably worse and worse, converging toward some awesome future crisis, some catastrophic reckoning. *Après nous, le deluge.*

So really bad is the situation that American sociologists have gradually developed a forbidding branch of their discipline labeled, simply, Social Problems, the equivalent of pathology in medicine. To this melancholy subject scores of textbooks are devoted, dealing with crime, its causes and its steady increase; rigging of courts and elections; poverty; racial and religious conflict; curtailments of civil rights; prison brutality; ill health and inadequate and profit-perverted medical care; mal-education, non-education and illiteracy; the prevalence of divorce and desertion; the excesses of pressure groups; faulty mass transportation; child mistreatment and abandonment; personal anomy; inadequate housing; social disorganization; widespread psychic disorder; slums, overcrowding and overpopulation in relation to available facilities; advertising and propaganda; unattended mental illness; commercialized alcoholism; gambling; drug addiction; traffic tangles; prostitution; pathological deviancies; war, etc., etc.[17] All of this bespeaks a very sick society, a poor political system.

What is most remarkable about all these problems is that despite the reports and recommendations of one public commission after the other none ever appears to be solved or even made more tractable. Each appears to be growing greater and new ones, such as water and air pollution and air traffic, are constantly being added. As the sociologists report, many causes are discernible but a general cause seldom mentioned is simple political neglect. Forthright confrontation of the problems is prevented by the various forms of political blockage at which the *pubpols* are most adept. Again, as much of the brains of the country are in the service of overreaching in the market place and political arena in pursuit of the dollar there are few competent people left in circulation to deal adequately with the problems. Money for social problem-solving, of course, is kept to a minimum as the public coffers are opened wide for the purchase of multi-redundant military hardware and space rockets to the moon: *Over-kill.*

Lavish in the money rewards given to *corp-pols* and *pubpols,* as we have seen, the going system becomes niggardly in the pay scales adopted for supportive personnel such as teachers, social workers, scientists, counselors, aides, nurses, engineers and the like. As a way of obtaining money and forthright action with respect to these problems the proper method would appear to place them all under the jurisdiction of the Defense Department, where they seem to belong. For what is the value of keeping the nation muscular on the outer frontiers while it is eroding at the core? In view of the rising tide of unsolved, gingerly tended social problems, what is it, precisely, that is being defended?

The Final Reckoning

Where will it all end? What will be the historical outcome of the concentration of wealth and power in the United States?

Although all answers to such questions must be speculative we have recently been provided with a brilliantly suggestive study along these precise lines by Robert L. Heilbroner in *The Limits of American Capitalism.*[18]

Heilbroner, in harmony with details laid out earlier in this text, is well aware of corporate dominance in American affairs. He notes that, out of some eleven million separate economic enterprises down to single news-stands, about a million companies do approximately 85 per cent of the busi-ness, and a half million corporations do 98 per cent of all corporate busi-ness and 75 per cent of all business. In turn, 1/10th of 1 per cent of the biggest industrial corporations, the 500 at the top, do about 33 per cent of all business in the corporate field. Furthermore, the top 50 industrial companies have sales as great as the next 450 while the profits of the top 10 are equal to those of almost half of the remaining 490. The 500th on the annual *Fortune* list has total sales of only $97 million, which is less than the profits of any of 26 of the 50 largest.[19]

By 1975, according to Willard Mueller, chief economist of the Federal Trade Commission, 200 corporations will own two-thirds of all American manufacturing assets compared with the same proportion owned by 500 corporations in 1962. The reason for this further concentration, it was indicated, is the renewed, Administration-sanctioned merger movement.[20]

We are confronted, in short, by corporate giantism. The backbone of political support comes from this corporate world.

A single company, AT&T, holds nearly 5 per cent of all nonbank cor-porate assets.

If only the top 150 companies with assets or sales at $1 billion or more were suddenly to stop doing business the entire economy would collapse. These companies compromise 50 industrials, 40 banks, 20 insurance com-panies, 10 merchandisers, 10 transportation lines and 20 public utilities.[21]

While the 100 top industrial corporations owned 25 per cent of all busi-ness assets in 1929, they owned 31 per cent in 1960. In 1963 they ac-counted for 53.8 per cent of total national income compared with 55.8 per cent in 1955.

Contrary to misleading propaganda about widespread ownership, in the 100 largest corporations the directors alone owned or controlled at least 10 per cent of the voting stock.

"Among the 150 super-corporations, there are perhaps as many as 1,500 or 2,000 operational top managers, but as few as 200 to 300 families own blocks of stock that ultimately control these corporations."[22]

Heilbroner, unlike Karl Marx, does not see the corporate system termi-nating in revolution although, sensitively aware of the vagaries of history, he does not absolutely rule out transitional phases of violence. Rather does he see the system very gradually and slowly changing just as the feudal manorial system was transformed gradually to the system of the open cash market, the citadel of bourgeois capitalism.

This being the probability, "Under the limits imposed by the present reach of business thought, the prospect is still for a society of narrow ambitions and small achievements, a society in which we belatedly repair old social ills and ungenerously attend to new ones."[23]

Although the present system is one, like feudalism, of lopsided privilege, Heilbroner in a keen insight points out that the legal basis of privilege now is screened as such even from the beneficiaries, who are not aware that they are privileged. This basis consists of the laws that permit private benefit to be derived from huge-scale production and allows free and untrammeled use of the national and international market place for private enrichment.

Therefore, "privilege under capitalism is much less 'visible,' especially to the favored groups, than privilege under other systems."[24] Under feudalism the privileges were harshly evident and explicitly known to all participants.

Instead of resisting encroachments upon privilege forthrightly, those who are privileged unconsciously resort to ideology, befuddling all but the well informed. Thus, attempts to deal with the periodic vast malfunctionings and slumps of individualistic capitalism by means of national planning (in place of egocentric planning on the part of huge corporations) are vociferously cried down as encroachments upon an abstraction called Freedom.

Because the system is now too deeply rooted and generally accepted it could not be violently or arbitrarily uprooted without enveloping the nation in prolonged chaos, as Heilbroner fully recognizes; and no responsible thinker any longer seriously proposes that it be uprooted.

How then, will it change, as all things involved in history do change?

The long-run threat to monopolistic capitalism, as Heilbroner sees it, is similar to the original threat to feudalism in that it is subtle and seemingly harmless. The manorial economy of feudalism was undermined by what was originally a cloud no larger than a man's hand: the cash market that established itself right in the shadow of the manorial walls. This cash market brought into being a new social type: the businessman. In his first guise the businessman was looked upon by the lords of the manor much as we today look upon a pushcart peddler—as a person of no economic, social or political consequence, at worst a mere nuisance. From this tiny seed, however, were to come the future original Rockefeller, Carnegie, Vanderbilt, Du Pont, Woolworth, Mellon, Ford *et al*. These men in their various ways were all pushcart peddlers grown to giant size under favoring conditions and laws.

The intangible, subversive threat to capitalism, as the cash market was to feudalism, Heilbroner sees as science and technology, without which modern capitalism cannot function but with which it cannot make its peace because it is constantly thrown into deep inner turmoil and confusion by them. For one thing, the composition of the labor force is constantly radically altered by technological change, first by the introduction of new machinery that converted agricultural workers into urbanized factory workers and more recently by automation which displaces factory workers into rising service industries, dumps them on the unemployment rolls or wastes them in huge and militarily unnecessary peacetime standing armies. Technology has even displaced the traditional foot soldier and cavalryman for all but relatively small-scale anti-insurrectionary operations, brush-fire wars, and replaced them by higher functional types like aviators, astronauts, rocketmen and a horde of advanced technicians. Warfare has been transformed into a vast engineering operation by which entire populations are exterminated. There is no longer, actually, much fighting in war. It has become mass slaughter. The mass destruction is the inverse of mass production.

The alteration in the labor force shows itself most spectacularly in the emergence of new elites, rising to share influence and authority with the business elite of *finpols* and *corp-pols*.

These new elites in Heilbroner's view consist of the new military policymakers (*milpols*), the professional expert from the academic world in the form particularly of specialists in the social and natural sciences, the highly trained new type of government administrator and possibly the administrators that have come into view with the emergence of the big labor unions. These labor administrators are of a type quite different from the old-line ward-boss variety of labor leader.

While few if any of these men are hostile to the existing system of monopoly capitalism, Heilbroner believes (in which belief I concur) that in the long run, over a span of 50 to 150 years, the differences in background, method and objectives of these elites from those of the business elite will generate frictions between them, as frictions were generated between the feudal lords and the rising business classes. The business elite has a single-minded objective: profit. Although the new elites are not opposed, now, to corporate profit aims, in part because they are accustomed to these aims as assumptions of the established system, what will be their reaction when, as and if the plans of the profiteers seriously conflict with their plans?

It should be pointed out that the members of the new—and indispensable —elites share a characteristic in common not shared with the business elite.

They are all problem-oriented and are, in fine, problem-solvers over a widely inclusive range of problems. Name almost any problem and one may be sure that at least one of them nurtures it as a pet project.

If it is argued that the *corp-pols* and *finpols*, too, are problem-solvers (which may indeed be the case), it is evident at once that they are concerned with a single overriding problem: profits. Such a single overriding aim is not to be found among any of the new elites who, although not men of the broad reach of the major philosophers or of diverse talents like Renaissance men, are nevertheless basically and incontrovertibly reflective intellectuals of some sort. They are all thoroughly infected by pervasive rationality, which in the long run seems of ill omen to the free-wheeling corporation.

There is already low-grade although tolerable friction in some quarters between some of these new types and members of the business elite. Unless big business radically alters some of its characteristic orientations it seems that one may expect increasing friction, with dominance no longer guaranteed to the business elite. The inherent social irrationality of the system of production chiefly for private profit, utilizing for the short run the increasingly powerful tools of science and technology, practically guarantees the long-run end of such dominance.

Marx saw socialism as something to be soon ushered into developed capitalist societies by revolution carried out by the new class of factory workers, led by history-conscious intellectuals. Heilbroner sees something very akin to socialism, or production-for-use in a rationally aspiring society, ushered in by a new class consisting of these intellectual elites. The revolutionary potential, in sum, resides in the intellectual middle classes, not in the passive, dependent proletariat, who have no "historical task."

I see one possible flaw in Heilbroner's reasoning, which to my somewhat skeptical eyes is tinged with historical optimism. History, contrary to the devotees of the idea of progress, rarely produces solutions in accord with ideal aims, a lamentable fact. Historical solutions are, somehow, always flawed.

The fly I discern in this particular mixture is the presence of the new military elite who, although men of a different order from the old-time military spit-and-polish drillmasters, are nevertheless military men. And the military in any instance that comes to mind have never allied themselves with a New Order as opposed to an Old Order. Military people are usually essentially conservative if not reactionary and are usually socially naive. Professor Morris Janowitz of the University of Chicago, who directed two large-scale studies, the first of 465 American generals appointed between 1898 and 1940 and the second of 761 Army, Navy and Air Force general and flag officers appointed between 1910 and 1950, found that as of 1954 only 5 per cent of the generals identified themselves as "liberals" but 68 per cent declared they were "a little on the conservative side" or plain "conservatives." "Such a finding will startle no one familiar with the published political views of retired generals," as one writer observed.[25] It may be that such characteristics do not inhere in the new computer-automation jet-propulsion type of military person, who may indeed be above and beyond the authoritarian master-servant mentality of the traditional military personality. If so, my doubts are beside the point.

But if the new military elite is anything like the old one it would, in any great crisis, tend to side with the Old Order and defend the *status quo*, if necessary, by force.

In the words of the standard police bulletin known to all radio listeners, "These men are armed—they may be dangerous."

Historically, the established military have always fought and thrown their influence against all rising new social orders, whether capitalist or socialist, and have always been strong supporters of reaction. Where they have retained influence after any revolution, peaceful or violent, they have been Bonapartists. Like all conservatives, they take a pessimistic view of the human enterprise, are partial to the heavy hand. Devotees of applied force, habituated to organizing their entire experience around its use, they are rarely men of peaceful persuasion and evolutionary transition.

As I freely admit, I may be wrong in thus looking at the new military elite, which by reason of the experience-broadening complex technology it now commands may be of an entirely new historical stripe. If it is, and no available evidence supports such a view, then Heilbroner's vision may be more penetrating than my own tentative doubts allow me to concede.

In any event, it cannot be denied that science and technology are already injecting much uncertainty into the demonic corporate thrust for profits. Allowed unrestrained and continued free play, that thrust cannot but disrupt the entire social system to an extent greater than yet ever seen.

Yet, as Heilbroner sees it, it is not the immediate needs of science and capitalism that are in conflict so much as a basic divergence of intent—of science to impose the human will on society and of capitalism to allow society to function by happenstance as if it were not subject to the will. Whereas science is socially active capitalism is socially passive and "In the end capitalism is weighed in the scale of science and found wanting, not alone as a system but as a philosophy."[26]

Savior of the World

American politicos, swelling with fatuous misbegotten pride, have increasingly taken to presenting the United States and the American people as the major guarantors of what remains of civilization in a world torn by shabby power struggles on every hand. Whatever else the foregoing pages may portend, they should suggest that anyone looking to the United States for the solution to world problems is depending on a huge but weak reed. With a thoroughly antiquated, distorted political system—formally 178 years old but with many later dubious additions such as the universal franchise—the United States is unable even to begin solving its own many very serious domestic problems. How, then, can it take on those of Asia, Africa, Europe and South America?

Not unless it underwent a considerable amount of basic politico-economic revision would the United States be in a position to play more than a palliative international role. And as its inept intrusion into Vietnam under the guidance of a strictly backwoods politician has shown very clearly, it may be capable of playing vastly destructive roles. What reasonable ground there is for believing that American presence in laggardly developed regions and political power-vacuums is more likely to achieve human gains than English, French, Japanese, Dutch or Russian presence has certainly not been shown.

If they prove nothing else the widespread American riots, increasing and spreading from the 1940's and 1950's into the 1960's, prove that the American ruling class, given the political instrumentalities of its rule through low-grade stooges, is unable to rule at home. The general cry goes out for law and order, yet there is steadily less and less law and order, more and more crime and insurrection as Lyndon B. Johnson calls for national days of prayer. For prayer rather than science or reason is the tool of the political medicine men. What is happening as the average citizen looks on in disbelief is that an outworn, patched politico-economic system is cracking, while no serious steps are taken to ascertain the causes and remedies. The causes of American insufficiency, at home and abroad, are political, not economic, or at least political before they are economic. Better put, they are cultural. Serious problems cannot be solved on the basis of a consensus of value-disoriented dolts.

APPENDIX A

LARGEST NET TAXABLE INCOMES SINCE 1940
(AFTER DEDUCTIONS)

	1940*	1945**	1950#	1955##	1960'	1961"
$1 million plus	49	71	219	267	306	398
$500,000 to $1 million	112	258	623	628	735	985
$300,000–$500,000	252	528	1,290	—	—	—
$200,000–$500,000	—	—	—	4,022	4,848	6,104
$150,000–$300,000	1,066	2,871	6,716	—	—	—
$150,000–$200,000	—	—	—	3,946	4,413	5,457
$100,000–$150,000	1,866	5,530	11,564	12,260	14,221	16,786
$ 50,000–$100,000	10,285	33,495	62,689	77,604	101,272	110,476
$ 25,000–$ 50,000	36,176	120,220	220,107	190,707	441,401	496,591
	49,806	162,973	303,208	289,434	557,196	626,797

In 1963 in New York State alone there were seventy-three incomes of $1 million or more (*New York Times*, February 20, 1965; 27:1).

AGGREGATE NET TAXABLE INCOME OF LARGEST INCOMES

	$1 Million-Plus Income	$500,000 to $1 Million Income
1940*	$ 87,746,000	$ 74,170,000
1945**	$105,184,000	$146,657,000
1950#	$374,670,000	$361,529,000
1955##	$452,713,000	$335,849,000
1960'	$455,501,000	$383,080,000
1961"	$589,220,000	$520,171,000

* *Statistics of Income for 1940*, Part I; United States Treasury Department, Bureau of Internal Revenue, p. 10.

* * *Statistics of Income for 1945*, Part I; United States Treasury Department, Bureau of Internal Revenue, pp. 21–22.

Statistics of Income for 1950, Part I (Preliminary); United States Treasury Department, Bureau of Internal Revenue, pp. 14–27.

Statistics of Income: 1955; United States Treasury Department, Bureau of Internal Revenue, pp. 18–24.

' *Statistics of Income: 1960* (Preliminary); United States Treasury Department, Bureau of Internal Revenue, pp. 15–21.

" *Statistics of Income: 1961* (Preliminary); United States Treasury Department, Bureau of Internal Revenue, p. 14.

The main sources of aggregate incomes exceeding $1 million are as follows (all references from the Treasury Department's *Statistics of Income* for each year):

	Salaries	Dividends	Interest	Partnership Profit
1940	$ 1,499,000	$ 60,561,000	$ 1,290,000	$ 1,301,000
1945	$ 1,752,000	$ 53,336,000	(included in dividends)	$ 8,013,000
1950	$ 7,693,000	$179,203,000	$ 6,148,000	$ 7,923,000
1955	$ 7,836,000	$286,158,000	$ 6,146,000	$ 11,613,000
1960	$12,766,000	$274,848,000	$ 9,648,000	$ 6,588,000
1961	$18,607,000	$259,574,000	$ 8,754,000	$ 10,503,000
1962	$13,789,000	$276,946,000	$ 9,490,000	$ 3,607,000

	From Trust Funds	Rents and Royalties	Business Loss	Capital Gain
1940	$27,624,000	$ 115,000	$ 1,711,000 (minimum)	$ 12,113,000
1945	$18,439,000	$ 1,940,000	$ 3,462,000 (profit)	$ 37,068,000
1950	$94,943,000	$ 4,846,000	$ 1,031,000 (profit)	$ 31,245,000
1955	$ 5,005,000*	$ 4,095,000	$ 3,208,000	$248,099,000*
1960	$ 3,966,000	$ 2,351,000	$ 7,345,000	$285,335,000
1961	$ 3,163,000	$ 2,371,000	$ 7,915,000	$434,272,000
1962	$ 3,431,000	$ 3,837,000	$ 3,289,000	$367,303,000

Main Sources of Incomes $500,000 to $1 Million

	Salaries	Dividends	Interest	Partnership Profit
1940	$ 3,110,000	$ 45,187,000	$ 1,994,000	$ 921,000
1945	$ 7,545,000	$ 58,476,000	(included in dividends)	$ 23,720,000
1950	$27,827,000	$158,822,000	$ 7,035,000	$ 3,848,000
1955	$31,409,000	$187,071,000	$ 6,483,000	$ 15,393,000

* Between 1950 and 1955 the Treasury Department changed its method of reporting trust-fund income. While it previously reported the capital gains of trust funds as part of trust-fund income, it decided to report such capital gains in the total of capital gains, thus diminishing the reported income of large trust funds. In order to show the full participation of trust funds, the capital gains accruing to them should be specifically shown. It will be noticed that in 1950 trust-fund income was three times all capital gain income but by 1955, with the removal of trust-fund capital gains to the capital gain column, trust-fund income was only about 2 per cent of capital gain income. Most of the sudden rise in capital gain totals came about because most of these capital gains came from trust funds.

1960	$31,674,000	$193,660,000	$10,620,000	$ 7,052,000
1961	$38,868,000	$216,469,000	$13,035,000	$ 21,662,000
1962	$37,378,000	$201,352,000	$13,898,000	$ 6,094,000

	From Trust Funds	Rents and Royalties	Business Profit	Capital Gain
1940	$20,291,000	$ 1,286,000	$ 1,958,000	$ 12,550,000
1945	$20,983,000	$ 1,004,000	$ 4,631,000	$ 53,451,000
1950	$64,426,000	$ 7,546,000	$ 3,848,000	$132,287,000
1955	$ 4,765,000*	$ 6,439,000	$ 6,964,000(L)	$171,594,000*
1960	$ 4,807,000	$ 5,314,000	$ 6,735,000(L)	$239,392,000
1961	$ 6,325,000	$ 4,554,000	$ 8,211,000(L)	$357,066,000
1962	$ 4,829,000	$ 9,460,000	$ 8,791,000(L)	$274,079,000

(Omitted: Sales of noncapital property, receipts from annuities and pensions and miscellaneous small items.)

APPENDIX B

COMPANIES WITH LARGEST TOTAL ASSETS

TNEC (1937)	Fortune* 1964	Dominant Family Groups—Fortune List (by TNEC and SEC source)
1. American Telephone & Telegraph	1. American Telephone & Telegraph	**
2. Standard Oil (New Jersey)	2. Standard Oil (New Jersey)	Rockefeller
3. Pennsylvania RR	3. General Motors	Du Pont
4. U.S. Steel	4. Ford Motor	Ford
5. Southern Pacific RR	5. U.S. Steel	Phipps, Haldane et al.
6. N.Y. Central RR	6. Texaco	Hill, Gates, Lapham et al.
7. Consolidated Edison (N.Y.)	7. Socony Mobil Oil	Rockefeller
8. General Motors	8. Gulf Oil	Mellon
9. Commonwealth & Southern (utility properties distributed)	9. Sears, Roebuck	Rosenwald
10. Baltimore & Ohio RR	10. Standard Oil of California	Rockefeller
11. Santa Fe RR (ATSF)	11. General Telephone & Electronics	Paine, La Croix et al.
12. Cities Service	12. International Business Machines	Watson-Smithers-Hewitt-Fairchild
13. Union Pacific RR	13. Standard Oil (Indiana)	Rockefeller
14. Socony Vacuum Oil	14. Consolidated Edison (N.Y.)	Brady et al.

* Fortune publishes these rankings in July and August of each year. These company names were taken from the 1965 issues reporting on 1964 performances under the categories of industrial, public utility, transportation and merchandising companies.

** Railroads and other types of public utility companies are generally dominated by small coalitions of several families, directly or through banks or other financial instrumentalities. This holds as well for many industrial companies.

TNEC (1937)	Fortune* 1964	Dominant Family Groups—Fortune List (by TNEC and SEC source)
15. Standard Gas & Electric (utility properties distributed)	15. General Electric	White, Gardner et al.
16. North American Co. (utility properties distributed)	16. Pacific Gas & Electric	Crocker et al.
17. Northern Pacific Ry	17. Pennsylvania RR	
18. American Power & Light (utility properties distributed)	18. Southern Pacific	Harkness, James, Dodge et al.
19. United Gas Improvement (utility properties distributed)	19. E.I. du Pont de Nemours	Du Pont
20. Great Northern Ry	20. Chrysler	Chrysler-Bache-Hutton-Hanna-Mellon
21. Standard Oil (Indiana)	21. Bethlehem Steel	Mellon-Grace
22. Bethlehem Steel	22. Tennessee Gas Transmission	Symonds, Stone & Webster
23. Ford Motor	23. New York Central RR	Kirby-Murchison et al.
24. American & Foreign Power	24. Shell Oil	(Royal Dutch)
25. E.I. du Pont de Nemours	25. Western Electric	
26. Electric Power & Light (utility properties distributed)	26. Union Carbide	Kenan-Acheson et al.
27. Commonwealth Edison (Chicago)	27. Santa Fe RR	
28. Chesapeake & Ohio Ry	28. Commonwealth Edison (Chicago)	
29. Illinois Central RR	29. Phillips Petroleum	Du Pont-Phillips
30. Pacific Gas & Electric	30. Southern Calif. Edison	Crocker
31. Texaco	31. Southern Co.	
32. Standard Oil of California	32. Union Pacific RR	Harriman-Goelet-Vanderbilt

		Dominant Family Groups—*Fortune* List (by TNEC and SEC source)
TNEC (1937)	*Fortune** 1964	
33. Columbia Gas & Electric	33. American Electric Power	
34. Anaconda	34. Public Service Electric & Gas	
35. Southern Ry	35. International Telephone & Telegraph	
36. Gulf Oil	36. International Harvester	McCormick-Deering
37. Niagara Hudson Power	37. Sinclair Oil	
38. Public Service Electricity & Gas	38. Aluminum Co. of America	Mellon
39. National Power & Light (utility properties distributed)	39. Norfolk & Western Ry	(Pennsylvania RR)
40. Int'l Hydro-Electric System (utility properties distributed)	40. Westinghouse Electric	Mellon *et al.*
41. International Telephone & Telegraph	41. Cities Service	Rockefeller Foundation *et al.*
42. United Light & Power (utility properties distributed)	42. Continental Oil	
43. Norfolk & Western Ry	43. Monsanto	
44. Louisville & Nashville RR	44. Columbia Gas & Electric	Pitcairn *et al.*
45. American Gas & Electric (utility properties distributed)	45. El Paso Natural Gas	
46. International Harvester	46. Goodyear Tire & Rubber	(Sears, Roebuck)
47. General Electric	47. Procter & Gamble	Procter-Gamble
48. Empire Gas & Fuel Co. (utility properties distributed)	48. Eastman Kodak	U. of Rochester, M.I.T., Philipp, Clark, Carter *et al.*
49. Middle West Corporation (utility properties distributed)	49. Anaconda	Connor, Gimbel, Guggenheim

TNEC (1937)	Fortune* 1964	Dominant Family Groups—Fortune List (by TNEC and SEC source)
50. Philadelphia Electric	50. Republic Steel	Mather
51. Reading	51. Dow Chemical	Dow
52. Shell Union Oil	52. Consumers Power	
53. Pacific Telephone & Telegraph	53. Philadelphia Electric	Rosengarten
54. Republic Steel	54. Niagara Mohawk Power	Schoelkopf, Machold, Easton, Lewis et al.
55. New England Power Association	55. General Public Utilities	
56. American Water Works & Electric (utility properties distributed)	56. Firestone Tire & Rubber	Firestone-Rieck-Woodworth
57. Southern California Edison	57. Allied Chemical	Meyer, Weber, Nichols et al.
58. Kennecott Copper	58. Radio Corp. of America	
59. Consolidated Oil	59. International Paper	Phipps-Mills
60. Koppers	60. Texas Eastern Transmission	Brown & Root
61. Engineers Public Service (utility properties distributed)	61. Celanese	
62. Atlantic Coast Line RR	62. Detroit Edison	
63. Philadelphia Company (utility properties distributed)	63. Armco Steel	Payson et al.
64. Armour (Illinois)	64. Texas Utilities	
65. Swift	65. Reynolds Metals	Reynolds
66. Western Union Telegraph	66. National Steel	M. A. Hanna
67. Detroit Edison	67. Northern Pacific Ry	†
68. Union Carbide	68. R. J. Reynolds Tobacco	Reynolds
69. Sears, Roebuck	69. Tidewater Oil	Getty
70. American Tobacco	70. Great Northern Ry	†

† In both these companies a strong interest was held by the late Arthur Curtiss James, who died without heirs. The late Vincent Astor was also a leading stockholder in Great Northern Railway.

TNEC (1937)	Fortune* 1964	Dominant Family Groups—Fortune List (by TNEC and SEC source)
71. New York, Chicago & St. Louis RR	71. American Natural Gas	
72. United Gas	72. American Can	Moore
73. Northern States Power	73. Olin Mathieson Chemical	Olin
74. Pullman	74. Atlantic Refining	Rockefeller
75. International Paper	75. Sun Oil	Pew
76. New England Telephone & Telegraph	76. Inland Steel	Block-Mather-Ryerson
77. Missouri-Kansas-Texas RR	77. Southern Ry	
78. West Penn Electric	78. Middle South Utilities	
79. Aluminum Co. of America	79. Consolidated Natural Gas	
80. Consumers Power	80. Jones & Laughlin Steel	Laughlin-Horne-Jones
81. Allied Chemical	81. Kaiser Aluminum	Kaiser
82. Westinghouse Electric	82. Virginia Electric & Power	
83. Delaware & Hudson RR	83. Union Oil of California	Matthews-Stewart-Earl
84. F. W. Woolworth	84. Kennecott Copper	Guggenheim-Penrose et al.
85. Youngstown Sheet & Tube	85. W. R. Grace	Grace-Phipps
86. Jones & Laughlin Steel	86. Louisville & Nashville RR	(Atlantic Coast Line RR)
87. Montgomery Ward	87. Sperry Rand	
88. Phillips Petroleum	88. Deere	Deere
89. Armour (Delaware)	89. Montgomery Ward	Ward, Thorne, Avery, McLennan
90. Lehigh Valley RR	90. F. W. Woolworth	Woolworth-McCann-Donohue-Kirby
91. National Steel	91. Chicago, Burl. & Quincy RR	
92. Tidewater Oil	92. Continental Can	
93. National Dairy Products	93. Caterpillar Tractor	

TNEC (1937)	Fortune* 1964	Dominant Family Groups—*Fortune* List (by TNEC and SEC source)
94. Duquesne Light Co.	94. Youngstown Sheet & Tube	Mather
95. Phelps Dodge	95. Singer	Singer-Clark
96. Goodyear Tire & Rubber	96. Pacific Lighting	Miller-Volkman-Schilling
97. Chrysler	97. National Dairy Products	Rieck-Breyer-McInnerney
98. Central & South West (utilities)	98. American Tobacco	Elkins-Widener
99. United Fruit	99. U.S. Rubber	Du Pont
100. Atlantic Refining	100. Great Atlantic & Pacific Tea	Hartford
101. Great Atlantic & Pacific Tea	101. Peoples Gas Light & Coke	
102. Liggett & Myers Tobacco	102. Union Electric (St. Louis)	
103. R. J. Reynolds Tobacco	103. American Cyanamid	Bell-Darby Biddle-Duke
104. Eastman Kodak	104. Pittsburgh Plate Glass	Pitcairn-Mellon
105. U.S. Rubber	105. Transcontinental Gas Pipe Line	Stone & Webster
106. Pure Oil	106. Minnesota Mining & Mfg.	McKnight
107. American Can	107. Pure Oil	Dawes *et al.*
108. Warner Brothers	108. Ohio Edison	
109. Federal Water Service	109. Burlington Industries	
110. Lackawanna RR (absorbed by Erie RR)	110. New England Electric System	
111. Peoples Gas Light & Coke	111. Florida Power & Light	
112. Central RR of N. J.	112. Illinois Central RR	
113. Western Maryland Ry	113. Duke Power	Duke
114. Firestone Tire & Rubber	114. American & Foreign Power	(Electric Bond & Share)

TNEC (1937)	Fortune* 1964	Dominant Family Groups—*Fortune* List (by TNEC and SEC source)
115. American Radiator & Std. Sanitary	115. United Air Lines	
116. Union Oil of California	116. General Foods	Post-Davies-Hutton-Woodward-Igleheart
117. Boston Edison	117. Northern States Power	
118. Singer	118. American Airlines	
119. Inland Steel	119. Northern Natural Gas	
120. Duke Power	120. Weyerhaeuser	Weyerhaeuser-Clapp-Bell-McKnight
121. Pere Marquette Ry (absorbed by Chesapeake & Ohio Ry)	121. Crown Zellerbach	Zellerbach
122. Virginian Ry	122. Marathon Oil	Rockefeller
123. Pacific Lighting	123. Chicago, Mil. & St. Paul RR	
124. American Smelting & Refining	124. Pacific Power and Light	
125. Consolidated Gas, Electric Light & Power of Baltimore (name changed)	125. Allegheny Power System	
126. American Rolling Mill (Armco)	126. B. F. Goodrich	Goodrich, Raymond *et al.*
127. Glen Alden Coal	127. Borden	Borden-Milbank-Horton
128. Procter & Gamble	128. Boeing	
129. Loew's, Inc.	129. Pan American Airways	
130. Weyerhaeuser	130. Brunswick	
131. Pittsburgh (Consolidation) Coal	131. Long Island Lighting	Phillips-Olmsted-Childs
132. Ohio (Marathon) Oil Co.	132. J. C. Penney	Penney-Ginn-Sams
133. B. F. Goodrich	133. Erie-Lackawanna RR	
134. Continental Can	134. Georgia-Pacific	Cheatham-Pamplin

TNEC (1937)	Fortune* 1964	Dominant Family Groups—Fortune List (by TNEC and SEC source)
135. Kansas City Southern Ry	135. Federated Department Stores	
136. Long Island Lighting	136. Swift	Swift
137. Lone Star Gas Corp.	137. National Distillers	Panhandle Eastern Pipeline
138. Sun Oil	138. Sunray DX Oil	
139. Hearst Consolidated Publications, Inc.	139. Trans World Airlines	Howard Hughes
140. Cincinnati Gas & Electric	140. General Dynamics	Henry Crown
141. United Shoe Machinery	141. Baltimore Gas & Electric	
142. Cleveland Electric Illuminating	142. Panhandle Eastern Pipe Line	
143. National Biscuit	143. United Aircraft	
144. Wheeling Steel	144. Chicago & North Western Ry	
145. S. S. Kresge	145. Pennsylvania Power & Light	
146. Borden	146. Atlantic Coast Line RR	Walters-Newcomer-Jenkins
147. Hudson & Manhattan RR	147. Potomac Electric Power	
148. Paramount Pictures	148. St. Regis Paper	
149. American Sugar	149. North American Aviation	
150. Pittsburgh Plate Glass	150. Joseph E. Seagram and Sons	Bronfman
151. Western Pacific RR	151. May Department Stores	May
152. Brooklyn Union Gas	152. Corn Products	Milbank-Allen-Moffett et al.
153. Allis-Chalmers	153. General Tire & Rubber	
154. Corn Products	154. Owens-Illinois	Levis, Allied Chemical
155. Crane	155. FMC	

TNEC (1937)	Fortune* 1964	Dominant Family Groups—Fortune List (by TNEC and SEC source)
156. Deere	156. Coca-Cola	Woodruff-Candler- Whitehead-Lupton
157. Crown Zellerbach	157. Safeway Stores	Skagg-Lynch-Merrill
158. Continental Oil	158. Allis-Chalmers	Milbank-Falk-Albright
159. General American Transportation	159. Lockheed Aircraft	
160. National Lead	160. Signal Oil & Gas	
161. R. H. Macy	161. Wisconsin Electric Power	
162. New England Gas & Electric	162. Western Union Telegraph	Vanderbilt-Astor- Geddes-Schiff
163. American Car & Foundry	163. Kimberly-Clark	Kimberly
164. Anderson, Clayton	164. Public Service of Colorado	
165. Wilson	165. Houston Lighting & Power	
166. Morris & Essex RR	166. General American Transportation	Mellon-Epstein- Bernheim
167. Radio Corp. of America	167. Borg-Warner	
168. New Jersey Zinc	168. Public Service of Indiana	
169. Owens-Illinois	169. Honeywell	
170. Richfield Oil	170. Standard Oil (Ohio)	Rockefeller
171. Cudahy	171. Armour	Armour-Prince
172. International Shoe	172. Cleveland Electric Illuminating	
173. Marshall Field	173. Illinois Power	
174. Gimbel Brothers	174. Southern New Eng- land Telephone	
175. Philadelphia & Reading	175. Chicago, Rock Island & Pac. RR	
176. Schenley Distillers	176. Kroger	
177. J. C. Penney	177. Martin Marietta	
178. Climax Molybdenum	178. Schenley Industries	Rosenstiel-Jacobi- Wiehe-Schwarzhaupt- Gerngross

TNEC (1937)	Fortune* 1964	Dominant Family Groups—Fortune List (by TNEC and SEC source)
179. Lehigh Coal & Navigation	179. Seaboard Air Line RR	
180. Standard Brands	180. Phelps Dodge	Hanna-Dodge
181. Coca-Cola	181. American Smelting & Refining	Deering
182. Kansas City Power & Light	182. National Cash Register	
183. General Foods	183. Richfield Oil	Atlantic Refining (Rockefeller)
184. S. H. Kress	184. National Lead	Cornish
185. International Business Machines	185. American Metal Climax	Hochschild-Loeb-Sussman-Selection Trust
186. National Supply	186. J. P. Stevens	Stevens, Duke
187. General Telephone	187. Charles Pfizer	Pfizer
188. Safeway Stores	188. Consolidation Coal	Mellon-Hanna
189. U.S. Smelting	189. Spiegel	
190. American Cyanamid	190. Colgate-Palmolive	Colgate
191. Colgate-Palmolive-Peet	191. Campbell Soup	Dorrance
192. Carolina Clinchfield & Ohio Ry	192. Philip Morris	
193. American Metal	193. American Machine & Foundry	
194. Boston & Albany RR	194. Kaiser Industries	Kaiser
195. California Packing	195. Bendix	
196. Mid-Continent Petroleum	196. Kaiser Steel	Kaiser
197. American Woolen (now Textron)	197. United Merchants & Mfrs.	
198. U.S. Gypsum	198. Litton Industries	Ash
199. National Distillers	199. American Motors	
200. Texas Gulf Sulphur	200. Douglas Aircraft	Douglas, J. S. McDonnell
	201. Scott Paper	
	202. Allied Stores	Prudential Insurance Co.

Fortune does not rate these companies by assets but by total sales or operating revenues. It does, however, indicate on its four lists of nonfinancial companies—industrial, railroad, public utility and merchandising—the assets of each company. For the list above the categories have been blended, by size of assets, into a single list that is comparable with the TNEC list. Both lists are based on the same type of data: assets.

NOTES

CHAPTER ONE

1. It was thirty years ago that I wrote of the United States: "Yet most of its people are, paradoxically, very poor; most of them own nothing but a few sticks of furniture and the clothes on their backs." *America's Sixty Families*, hereafter coded as *ASF*, Vanguard Press, N.Y., 1937. Those lines, which some critics accepted only as extravagant hyperbole, were written during a vast economic depression but the statement holds literally true of boom periods too, which are different only in that people have low-paid jobs.

2. Carl Bakal, *The Right to Bear Arms*, McGraw-Hill, N.Y., 1966, p. 1.

3. Jack Anderson, *Washington Exposé*, Public Affairs Press, Washington, D.C., 1967, pp. 447–58.

4. For a preliminary insight into the extent of the American military-industrial establishment, see Fred J. Cook, *The Warfare State*, Macmillan, N.Y., 1962. As to the effects of the military-industrial establishment, see Seymour Melman, *Our Depleted Society*, Holt, Rinehart and Winston, N.Y., 1965.

5. Studies of the concentration of wealth have been: G. K. Holmes, "The Concentration of Wealth," *Political Science Quarterly*, December, 1893, pp. 589–600; C. B. Spahr, *The Present Distribution of Wealth in the United States*, N.Y., 1896; W. R. Ingalls, *Current Economic Affairs*, York, Pa., 1924, and *Wealth and Income of the American People*, York, Pa., 1924, using income-tax data for the first time; W. I. King, "Wealth Distribution in the Continental United States at the Close of 1921," *Journal of the American Statistical Association*, June, 1927, pp. 135–53; Frederick R. Macaulay, *Income in the United States*, II, National Bureau of Economic Research, N.Y., 1922, pp. 424–25; Lewis Corey, *The Decline of American Capitalism*, N.Y., 1934; W. L. Crum, *The Distribution of Wealth*, Boston, 1935, study of estate-tax returns, 1916–33; R. R. Doane, *The Measurement of American Wealth*, N.Y., 1933; Maxine Yaple, "The Burden of Direct Taxes as Paid by Income Classes," *American Economic Review*, December, 1936; Fritz Lehmann (with Max Ascoli), *Political and Economic Democracy*, N.Y., 1937; Charles Stewart, "Income Capitalization as a Method of Estimating the Distribution of Wealth by Size Groups," *Studies in Income and Wealth*, III; and Mary S. Painter, "Distribution of Wealth in Estates and Estate Tax Yield," unpublished ms., NBER, 1946. These historical sources are cited by Lampman (q.v.).

6. The National Bureau of Economic Research, sponsor of the study, was founded in 1920 as a nonpartisan, nonprofit organization to study economic problems. Its many studies have been executed by economists of impeccable repute. Among its directors are Marion B. Folsom, director of the Eastman Kodak Company; Crawford H. Greenewalt, chairman of E. I. du Pont de Nemours and Company; Gabriel Hauge, president of the Manufacturers Hanover Trust Company of New York; Albert J. Hettinger, Jr., partner of the international banking house of Lazard Frères and Company; and Charles G. Mortimer, chairman of the General Foods Corporation, as well as others. The big enterprises are interested in such data as part of market research; for there are absolute financial limits to the market for products of various kinds, particularly costly items like houses, cadillacs, yachts, airplanes, world cruises and fall-out shelters but also for many relatively inexpensive mass-processed products.

7. Robert J. Lampman, *The Share of Top Wealth-Holders in National Wealth, 1922–1956*. A Study by the National Bureau of Economic Research. Princeton University Press, Princeton, N.J., 1962, p. 14.

8. *Ibid.*, p. 23.

9. *Ibid.*, pp. 23, 192–93.

10. *Ibid.*, pp. 202, 204, 209.

11. *Ibid.*, p. 213.

12. *Ibid.*, p. 220.

13. *Ibid.*, pp. 86–87.

14. *Ibid.*, p. 84.

15. *Ibid.*, pp. 84, 276.

16. *Ibid.*, p. 217.

17. A. A. Berle, Jr., *The American Economic Republic*, Harcourt, Brace & World, N.Y., 1963, p. 221. Professor Berle finds even more sunshine than this in the Lampman text. Lampman set it forth, as Berle notes, that the top 1.4 per cent received 14.2 per cent of all income though they held more than 25 per cent of wealth and that the top 1 per cent of adults, though they held 25 per cent of personally owned wealth, Berle said, are "only able to save 15 per cent of all saving." Apart from the fact that this 15 per cent of savings is disproportionately large, not subject to rapid depletion for personal emergencies, and hardly deserving of the diminishing qualification "only" (at this same rate the upper 8.4 per cent would have 90 per cent of all savings!), Berle does not let on that dividend income paid to stockholders in the aggregate represents less than half of corporate earnings; the balance is ploughed back into the companies but accrues to the account of the owners and can be personally captured by the sale of some stock. Income received by wealth-holders, then, is only part of income actually accrued to their accounts. Such accrued undistributed corporate income amounts in effect to concealed personal income. Berle asserts happily that the United States "has gone a considerable distance toward socializing income," although what this means other than something mysteriously and vaguely pleasant is far from clear.

18. James D. Smith and Staunton K. Calvert, "Estimating the Wealth of Top Wealth-Holders from Estate Tax Returns," Proceedings of the American Statistical Association, Philadelphia annual meeting, September, 1965, 19 pp.

19. Lampman, *passim*. Lampman brings out, for example, that the median age of top wealth-holders in 1953 was 54 years, with more than half 40 to 60 years old. The median age of the entire adult population was 44 years. Of the top wealth-holders 72 per cent were married, 16 per cent were widowers or widows, 3 per cent were divorced or separated and 9 per cent were single. About 85 per cent of the men were married; only about half the women. ". . . the wealth-holders form a larger part of the widow and widower population than of any other marital status group" (p. 100). While there were more women than men with over $1.5 million of gross estate, women held only 40 per cent of the wealth. "The information on top wealth-holders furnishes little support for the popular idea that women own the greater part of American wealth" (p. 20). Many women appear among the top wealth-holders because of the practice of estate-splitting that has developed since the introduction of the income tax and the estate tax. They are also heirs of wealthy fathers and husbands—in brief, few made it by economic efforts of their own. But only 25 per cent of all aged couples received any income at all from assets in 1951 (p. 91). Succinctly, only one in four aged Americans succeeded in making even meager provisions for retirement. Occupation was found to be an important determinant of income, with nearly three-fourths of the upper 2 per cent of income recipients independent professionals, businessmen and executives, and one-tenth farmers (presumably operators of large-scale industrial-type farms).

20. "Survey of Consumer Finances," *Federal Reserve Bulletin*, 1953, Supplementary Table 5, p. 11.

21. *Statistical Abstract of the United States*, 1964, Michigan Survey, p. 474.

22. *Ibid.*, p. 473.

23. *New York Times*, May 2, 1965; IV, 4:1.

24. *Statistical Abstract*, 1964, p. 474.

25. Temporary National Economic Committee, 76th Congress, 3rd session, *Survey of Shareholdings in 1,710 Corporations with Securities Listed on a National Securities Exchange*, Government Printing Office, Washington, D.C., 1941. Monograph No. 30, p. 241.

26. Lewis H. Kimmel, *Share Ownership in the United States*, Brookings Institution, Washington, D.C., 1952, pp. 43, 46.

27. J. Keith Butters, *et al.*, *Effects of Taxation—Investment by Individuals*, Harvard Business School, Boston, 1953, p. 85.

28. *Survey*, cited in text, p. 151.

29. *Ibid.*, p. 148.

30. *Ibid.*, p. 151.

31. *Ibid.*, p. 136.

32. *Ibid.*, p. 96.

33. Gabriel Kolko, *Wealth and Power in America*, Praeger, N.Y., 1962, pp. 49, 70, 89–91, 94, 109, 130–31.

34. *Ibid.*, p. 34.

35. *Ibid.*, p. 48.

36. W. J. Cash, *The Mind of the South*, Knopf, N.Y., 1954, p. 115.

37. *Statistical Abstract*, 1964, p. 336.

38. *New York Times*, May 3, 1965; 24:3.

39. *New York Times*, May 27, 1965; 4:5.

40. Kathleen M. Langley, "The Distribution of Capital in Private Hands in 1936–38 and 1946–47," Parts I and II, *Bulletin of the Oxford University Institute of Statistics*, December, 1950, Table XIII, p. 352; February, 1951, Table XVB, p. 46. Cited by Lampman, pp. 211, 216.

41. *London Times* dispatch cited in Felix Greene, *A Curtain of Ignorance*, Doubleday, N.Y., 1964, pp. 112, 141.

42. The great amount of intermarriage among wealthy Americans, and with titled Europeans, is given considerable discussion in *ASF*, pp. 9–18.

43. Associated Press dispatch to the *New York Times*, December 26, 1960.

44. Paul Woodring, *A Fourth of a Nation*, McGraw-Hill, N.Y., 1957.

45. Cleveland Amory, *Who Killed Society?*, Harper, N.Y., 1960, p. 476.

46. *Ibid.*, index.

CHAPTER TWO

1. *New York Times*, June 22, 1965; 24:1–3.

2. The late C. Wright Mills in *The Power Elite*, Oxford University Press, N.Y., 1956, a book which has its merits, involved himself in several methodological snarls in a vain attempt to get some precision into the figures about the big owners. "To list the names of the richest people of three generations, I have had to do the best I could with such unsystematic sources as are available" (p. 375). He settled "mainly [as] a matter of convenience" on $30 million upward for a large fortune (the criterion of *America's Sixty Families*), which yielded him 371 names. But he had to throw out 69 of these because no sources gave any information about them (p. 379). Thus he had left 302 names to play with. The sources of these were books he cites by Gustavus Myers, Matthew Josephson, Frederick Lewis Allen, Ferdinand Lundberg, Dixon

Wecter, Stewart H. Holbrook, and Cleveland Amory; he also had recourse
Fortune and *The World Almanac.* He accepted as generally accurate the compu
tions of *America's Sixty Families,* based on 1924 income-tax revelations, because t
subsequent probate of various wills attested to their close accuracy. He neverthel
suspected (and justifiably) that with the passage of time there was more to be know
He thereupon set out upon a frantic and confessedly vain quest for new informatic
"In order to obtain information about people now alive," Mills wrote (p. 37
"the following agencies and government bureaus were contacted—various officials
each of them gave us such information as they could, none of it 'official,' and none
much use to us: The Federal Reserve Board [sic] of New York; the Securities a
Exchange Commission; U.S. Department of Commerce, Bureau of Domestic Co
merce; and the Bureau of Internal Revenue's Statistical Division and Informati
Division. Individuals were also contacted in the following private organizations: D
& Bradstreet; The National Industrial Conference Board's Division of Business E
nomics; *The Wall Street Journal; Barron's; Fortune;* The Russel Sage Foundatic
U.S. News and World Report; Brookings Institution; Bureau of National Affairs; F
eral Savings and Loan; and two private investment houses. People seen in these
ganizations could only refer us to sources of which we were already aware. Some b
never thought much about the problem, others seemed slightly shocked at the idea
'finding out' about the top wealthy people, others were enchanted with the idea b
helpless as to sources." Yet *Fortune,* only a year later, perhaps inspired by Mil
report of his massive difficulties, in its issue of November, 1957, was able to reel c
albeit with some exaggeration, the names of a goodly number of fairly new but the
tofore not obscure heavy-money men that Mills's dragnet was apparently not f
enough to catch. And this reminds us of the no doubt over-inclusive observation
the novelist James T. Farrell that a sociologist is a person who will take a grant
$100,000 and a staff and pinpoint in a year the location of the brothels in a giv
city area, missing only a few, while the ordinary man will get complete information
five minutes by asking for it from the cop on the beat.

Mills, for most of his contemporary information, was forced back to the 1924 t
figures as analyzed in *America's Sixty Families* but he worked up a number of obscu
quarrels with their derivation. His first methodological refinement was to add the N
York Herald Tribune to the *New York Times* as a source although, if he was goi
to do this, why did he not take all metropolitan newspapers? He took note anew in t
way of the fact reported in *America's Sixty Families:* "The release of this data v
so administratively sloppy that one paper published data about a man whom anotl
paper ignored, some errors were printed, and in some cases all journalists missed t
names of people who were known to have paid large taxes." The point, actually,
that none of the papers provided relevant information going beyond the *Times.* Mil
thanks to his combing of the *Herald Tribune* (with which as a former staff meml
I was hardly unfamiliar), was able to come up with two new names: J. H. Brewer a
L. L. Cooke. But he was unable to identify them and after pulling them out of t
lists like a joyous Jack Horner he never referred to them again. As Mills notes th
like a number of people, "paid much higher taxes in 1924 than many of the peop
named by Lundberg, but who are not included in his listing of '60 families.'"

Mills seemed to believe that the names for the sixty families were drawn from t
tax lists. Although most of them were there, the lists did not determine their inclusic
for which the simple criteria of social presence sufficed (the cop on the beat). Fr
time to time various people, of no great financial or political account, have "windfa
incomes, subject to large taxes; passingly noteworthy, they cannot be considered p
of any financial elite, and in *America's Sixty Families* their general existence w
noted and thereafter ignored. Mills remarks further that *America's Sixty Famil*
includes families in the top sixty that "do not even appear among the rich wh
individuals [my emphasis—F. L.] are concerned." Why they should when it is a qu

tion of families Mills did not make clear. A family with a hundred members each getting $100,000 a year (the pattern of some actual families), all from the same source, certainly bulks larger financially than an individual getting $2 million a year. There are family investment companies set up in this way and, although the individual incomes are widely dispersed and of little significance, the investment and political influence of the managing members is of the reach of about $200 million as compared with about $50 million for the recipient of a $2 million income. On concentrated size alone the family group has the stronger punch.

Again, Mills remarks enigmatically, "Ferdinand Lundberg, in 1937, compiled a list of '60 families' which, in fact, are not all families and which numbers—as 'families'—not 60, but 74. But he does not analyze them systematically. By 'systematic' I understand that similar information is compiled for each person on the list and generalizations made therefrom" (p. 377). As to this Mills is correct in a certain trivial way for there were two *groups* of families listed as belonging, respectively, to the Morgan and Rockefeller camps, adding up in each case to stupendous holdings. Yet each single family was sufficiently impecunious to remain probably below the $30-million level at 1924 prices. "What Lundberg does," Mills summarizes, "is (1) generalize blood relations—sometimes cousinhood only—into power and financial cliques. [For the financial and political importance of cousinhood "only" one might study the Mellons and Du Ponts.—F. L.] We do not wish to confuse [!] the two. In addition (2), we cannot go along with the list he has abstracted from the *New York Times*, which is not uniformly made up of families or individuals or companies but is a miscellany." But Mills produces no better or more systematized list, unless his adding of the mysterious J. H. Brewer and L. L. Cooke yields one. Again, the *Herald Tribune* list was no less an unsystematic as well as duplicative miscellany.

Mills himself generalizes the individual possession of $30 million or more into power eliteness, which is hardly tenable in view of the fact that some such possessors are in homes for mental deficients and others are playboys—what newspapers call sportsmen, clubmen or explorers when they feel they cannot plausibly apply the terms philanthropist, financier or industrialist. Mills, again, going against the brute facts of history in his search for symmetry, boldly casts out the names of people whose holdings do not seem to exceed $30 million but who have nevertheless played strong public roles. Thus, he discards Tafts, Lehmans and De Forests as well as Deerings (intermarried with the McCormicks) even though at the time he wrote they certainly included individuals worth more than that. If one accepts the thesis of a functioning "power elite" as constructed by Mills (which I do not, for reasons to appear later in the main text), one cannot so cavalierly dismiss Tafts, Lehmans and Deerings from the cast. Mills finally approached the symmetrical world of his own making (p. 380): "For each generation I took the 90 richest people. We are thus considering the 90 or so *most prominent* and richest in each of three historical epochs. This gives us a total of 275 cases for concentrated analysis, which is the upper 74 per cent of the 371 cases mentioned by all sources known to us. Of the 90 cases elected as Group I, the median year of birth is 1841; the median year of death, 1912. The year when the median age is 60 is therefore 1901; hereafter Group I is identified as the 1900 generation. Of the 95 cases selected from Group II, the median year of birth is 1867; the median year of death, 1936. The year when the median age is 60 is therefore 1927; Group II thus consists of the 1925 generation. Of the 90 cases in Group III, the median year of birth is 1887; and most of these were still alive in 1954. On the average there were 60 in 1947; thus Group III is thus the 1950 generation."

Mills does not list the names for inspection or actually produce a concentrated analysis. He proceeds to draw very precise percentages for his text (Chapter 5) about class origins, nativity, schooling, rentier-activist status, Social Register listing and so on. And it is these percentages, perpetrating the fallacy of misplaced precision, that need to be looked upon with some questioning. One can, *faut de mieux*, live with them; they make no difference to any open issue. As to his conclusion that most of the wealthy now largely come from the wealthy classes in contrast with an earlier day, Professor Pitirim Sorokin of Harvard pointed this out in 1925 (cited at page 21, *ASF*). Mills's tight divisional categories present certain problems: Is a man rentier or accumulator whose income derives half from inherited trust funds and half from creative scheming? Are the Du Ponts (some of whom run their companies, others of whom apparently only cash dividend checks) rentiers or activists? Actually, all of the inheritors are rentiers most of the way. On the basis of their rentier status they may then be playboys or playgirls, or active in corporate affairs and politics. Mills's misplaced precision—for the field is no more subject to such statistical precision than is the wreckage of a battlefield after the battle—leads him to conclude that "men have always held from 80 to 90 per cent of the great American fortunes" (p. 110). But as we have already learned from Professor Lampman (Chapter I), working with complete official figures, women constitute very certainly about 40 per cent of all holding more than $60,000 of property. They could, of course, only be holding the lesser estates but, as most big wealth now is inherited and the incidence of women inheritors is about the same as men, there is no visible reason why the Lampman distribution should not prevail approximately in all strata. On Mills's showing, the number of very wealthy women in his contemporary group of 90 would range from 9 to 18. But much wealth is held in family trust funds, with males and females participating equally. Women, moreover, belong more than passively to any hypothesized "power elite," as the physical presence of Perle Mesta, Clare Boothe Luce, Cissy Patterson and similar female politicos shows. Mills inclines to accord women, by reason of such butterflies as Barbara Hutton and Doris Duke, a purely passive role in his mythical elite.

Actually, according to a study made in 1958 by Professor James Smith, an economist with American University, about 40 per cent of all owners of property valued at $1 million were women, but about 80 per cent of owners of the estates valued at $10 million or more were women. Two careful studies, then, show Mills to have been very wrong on the relationship of men and women to propertied wealth, although in most cases women became proprietors through men: fathers, grandfathers, uncles, brothers and husbands. They usually outlive husbands, thus becoming heirs; often they are the much younger second and third wives of tycoons.

By some misstatement of theses owing to inattentive reading, Mills is able to supply pseudo-corrections, as when he says that "Sixty glittering, clannish families do not run the American economy. . ." (p. 147). Nor did anyone ever say they did. *America's Sixty Families*, to which he thus alludes, opens with this paragraph: "The United States is owned and dominated today by a hierarchy of its sixty richest families, buttressed by no more than ninety families of lesser wealth. Outside this plutocratic circle there are perhaps three hundred and fifty families, less defined in development and in wealth, but accounting for most of the incomes of $100,000 or more that do not accrue to members of the inner circle." While this statement would require some revision today, it is not the statement Mills represents it to be.

With a view to commenting finally upon the methodological difficulties of work in this field, since Mills saw fit to bring them up, let me say that *America's Sixty Families* began as a study of just a few of the very rich families, with a view to finding common characteristics, but this intention had to be abandoned owing to lacunae in the record of each. Where data were available for one, they were lacking for the other. The study was therefore broadened to bring in more families and more data just as statisticians enlarge a sample. As with Mills, a cut-off point had to be determined on what was considered big wealth, and the figure of $30 million was arbitrarily decided upon— even though I didn't think a man worth $29.5 million was qualitatively less worthy of consideration. It was found that sixty fortunes of varying size fit that category, taking the Rockefeller and Morgan satellites as each constituting a group (because it was known on other grounds that they belonged in the picture), although it was pointed out that there were two lower strata of 90 and 350 each that would be resorted to for characteristic behavior when data were lacking for the top 60. This procedure was perhaps more systematic than the situation warranted but a book is a systematic discourse and some organizing principle is necessary.

Even leaving aside the question of an organizing principle (of which Mills's "power elite" is one such) and simply calling it all "history," and therefore "open" in organizing principle, would not have solved the problem. For written histories are themselves tightly organized. They are not as "open" as historical events but are put in some sort of theoretical matrix. To this extent at least they may be misleading. But, leaning now toward more "openness," I have titled the present work simply *The Rich and the Super-Rich.* I still believe that the family is the significant unit of holding wealth for the simple reason that it is through the family that the laws of inheritance and the transmittal of money power takes place.

3. "The Fifty-Million-Dollar Man," *Fortune*, November, 1957.

4. *New York Times*, July 3, 1961; 9:2.

5. *Ibid.*, November 27, 1962; 43:7.

6. *Ibid.*, May 9, 1964; 28:6.

7. *Ibid.*, December 6, 1958; 14:1.

8. J. Paul Getty, *My Life and Fortunes*, Duell, Sloan and Pearce, N.Y., 1963, p. 258.

9. *Ibid.* pp. 55, 122–29.

10. *Ibid.*, 127–29, 135, 138–46.

11. *New York Times*, September 13, 1963; 35:3–7.

12. Getty, pp. 259–60.

13. Hunt's wealth has been estimated as high as $3 billion, according to Arnold Forster and Benjamin R. Epstein, *Danger on the Right*, Random House, N.Y., 1964, p. 136. No evidence I have been able to find lends credence to any such figure or even to the more frequently cited figure of $1 billion.

14. Information about H. L. Hunt was obtained mainly from Robert G. Sherrill, "H. L. Hunt: Portrait of a Super-Patriot," *The Nation*, February 24, 1964; Cleveland Amory, "The Oil Folks at Home," *Holiday*, February, 1957; "The Land of the Big Rich," *Fortune*, April, 1948; "The World's Richest Men," *New York Times Magazine*, October 20, 1957; "Venture in Pakistan," *Newsweek*, September 26, 1955; *New York Times*, August 17, 1964; 1:3; August 23, 1964, III; 1:3; *Washington Post*, February 15–19, 1954; and "World's Richest Man Is a Texan," *Pacific Coast Business and Shipping Register*, August 16, 1954.

15. John Gunther, *Inside U.S.A.*, Harper and Brothers, N.Y., 1947, p. 816.

16. Information about these men has been gleaned from "Big Wheeler-Dealer from Texas," *Fortune*, January–February, 1953; "Henry Holt and the Man from Koon Kreek," *Fortune*, December, 1959; "Murchisons and Allen Kirby," *Life*, April 28, 1961; "Kirby's Fight to Hold Allegheny," *Fortune*, April, 1961; and *Holiday*, February, 1957.

17. Cleveland Amory, "The Oil Folks at Home."

18. "Why Things Went Sour for Louis Wolfson," *Fortune*, September, 1961.

19. Stewart Alsop, "America's New Big Rich," *Saturday Evening Post*, July 17, 1965.

20. See, for example, "The Paper World of Karl Landegger," *Fortune*, November, 1964.

21. Forster and Epstein, p. 244. The figure was first used by Dan Wakefield, *Esquire*, January, 1961, and has been repeated many times in newspapers from coast to coast.

22. *New York Times*, October 6, 1958; 31:1.

23. *Time*, March 4, 1957; 69:7.

24. *New York Times*, October 6, 1958; 31:1.

25. *Moody's Industrial Manual 1964,* p. 2079.

26. *Ibid.,* p. 2528.

27. *Ibid.,* p. 2040.

28. Forster and Epstein, pp. 242–43.

29. Arthur Schlesinger, Jr., "A Thousand Days," *Life,* July 16, 1965, p. 36.

30. *Who's Who in America,* Vol. 33, 1964–1965.

31. *Ibid.*

32. *Ibid.*

33. *Ibid.*

34. Julian Dana, *A. P. Giannini, Giant in the West,* Prentice-Hall, Inc., N.Y., 1947, pp. 221, 342–43.

35. *National Cyclopedia of American Biography,* Vol. 41, p. 11.

36. *New York Times,* July 31, 1957; 10:3.

37. *National Cyclopedia of American Biography,* Vol. 47, p. 42.

38. Cleveland Amory, *The Proper Bostonians,* E. P. Dutton & Co., Inc., N.Y. 1947, p. 315.

39. Information on De Golyer in greater detail is to be found in the *National Cyclopedia of American Biography,* Vol. 43, pp. 12–14; and in *Biographical Memoirs,* Vol. XXXIII, National Academy of Sciences of the United States of America, Columbia University Press, N.Y., 1959.

40. *New York Times,* December 15, 1956; 26:1.

41. Cleveland Amory, "The Oil Folks at Home."

42. *Biographical Memoirs,* p. 67.

43. *Fortune,* November, 1957, p. 236.

44. *New York Times,* October 19, 1950; 31:6, and October 26, 1950; 21:2.

45. *National Cyclopedia of American Biography,* Current Volume F, p. 46.

46. *New York Times,* September 2, 1956; 26:1.

47. *National Cyclopedia of American Biography,* Vol. 43, p. 486.

48. Details about William Danforth are taken from Gordon M. Philpott, *Daring Venture: The Life Story of William H. Danforth,* Random House, N.Y., 1960, an appreciative biography obviously written with the deep personal feeling of a happy associate. Although Danforth was listed in *Who's Who* he is, oddly, not mentioned to date in the *National Cyclopedia of American Biography,* the *Dictionary of American Biography* or *Current Biography, 1940–65.* On his death the *New York Times,* December 25, 1955; 48:7, gave him not very extended notice; but it was just like Danforth to die on Christmas Eve. Easter was his only other option.

49. The saga of these men, once-reputed fortune-builders, is outlined in Earl Sparling, *Mystery Men of Wall Street,* Greenberg, N.Y., 1930.

50. *New York Times,* July 23, 1936; 19:6. The unblaze of unglory at Cutten's end may be traced through the *Times,* March 11, 1936; 6:2; June 25, 1936; 21:3; December 29, 1936; 7:4; January 10, 1937; 30:7; April 15, 1937; 42:7; May 20, 1937; 15:2; September 21, 1937; 26:2 and June 13, 1940; 25:6. Although this last item is indexed by the *Times,* it is not on that page.

51. The flamboyant career and downfall of Zeckendorf are extensively noticed in the *New York Times,* May 8, 1965; 1:2, and May 19, 1965; 1:5. Zeckendorf's career began in 1938 when he joined the obscure real estate firm of Webb & Knapp, which soon bloomed as a high-powered promoter. To obtain money for his gaudy ventures Zeckendorf was said to pay as high as 24 per cent interest.

52. *The New Millionaires and How They Made Their Fortunes,* by the editors of the *Wall Street Journal,* McFadden-Bartel Corporation, N.Y., 1962.

53. *Ibid.,* p. 9.

54. *Ibid.,* p. 10.

55. *Ibid.,* p. 9.

56. *Ibid.,* pp. 17–24.

57. *Ibid.,* pp. 25–32.

58. *Ibid.*, pp. 33–39.
59. *Ibid.*, pp. 40–46.
60. *Ibid.*, pp. 54–61.
61. *Ibid.*, pp. 62–70.
62. *Ibid.*, pp. 70–75.
63. *Ibid.*, pp. 75–80.
64. *Ibid.*, pp. 85–89.
65. *Ibid.*, pp. 90–98.
66. *Ibid.*, p. 90.
67. *Ibid.*, pp. 113–22.
68. The discovery of the astute Goldman and Di Lorenzo is extensively reported in the *New York Times*, April 26, 1965; 1:7,8, and their names should be included on any future *Fortune* $75-plus million list unless something untoward should happen, such as a jerk in the business cycle.
69. "Non-Poverty Program: Millionaires Are a Dime a Dozen," *New York Times Magazine*, November 28, 1965, p. 50.
70. Alfred P. Sloan, Jr., *My Years with General Motors*, Doubleday and Company, Inc., N.Y., 1964. "Mr. Brown defined return on investment as a function of the profit margin and the rate of turnover of invested capital. (Multiplying one by the other equals the per cent of return on investment . . . you can get an increase in return on investment by increasing the rate of turnover of capital in relation to sales as well as by increasing profit margins" (pp. 141–42). Brown's method of financial analysis, which Sloan describes in reverent detail, enables General Motors to determine at any instant the current profitability of any nook or cranny in its vast maze. For Brown was not analytically interested in the rate of return on *total* invested capital, a fuzzy figure that conceals many financially inefficient operations. It doesn't tell one where to go to eliminate inner drags on profitability. General Motors can probably determine precisely the rate of return at any moment on any department, machine or individual down to an office boy or night watchman.
71. Robert E. Lane, *Political Life*, The Free Press, N.Y., 1965, p. 106.

CHAPTER THREE

1. Estes Kefauver, *Crime in America*, Doubleday & Co., N.Y., 1951, pp. 139–40.
2. *Ibid.*, p. 140.
3. *Ibid.*, p. 138.
4. Robert F. Kennedy, *The Enemy Within*, Harper and Brothers, N.Y., 1960, pp. 215–38.
5. *Ibid.*, p. 216.
6. *Ibid.*, pp. 217–18.
7. *Ibid.*, p. 218.
8. *Ibid.*, p. 222.
9. Daniel Bell, *The End of Ideology*, The Free Press of Glencoe, N.Y., 1960, Chapter 7.
10. *Ibid.*, p. 116.
11. *Ibid.*, p. 117.
12. *Ibid.*, pp. 117–18.
13. *Ibid.*, p. 119.
14. *Ibid.*, p. 128.
15. *Ibid.*, pp. 128–29.
16. *Ibid.*, pp. 130–33.
17. *Ibid.*, pp. 134–35.
18. *New York Times*, February 17, 1965; 45:1.

19. Ferdinand Lundberg, *Imperial Hearst*, Equinox Press, N.Y., 1936, pp. 43, 103-4, 110-11, 133-36, 142, 153-64, 169-71, 291-301, 346. The newspaper-war story is followed in many of its subsequent strange ramifications on the basis of court proceedings to the highest levels in government through the tracing of the careers of two of its leading figures, the late Max and Moe Annenberg, in John T. Flynn, "Smart Money," *Collier's*, January 13, 20, 27 and February 3, 1940. This is a pure star-spangled American success story.

20. Kefauver, p. 86.

21. Edwin H. Sutherland and Donald R. Cressey, *Principles of Criminology*, J. B. Lippincott Company, Philadelphia, 1955, Chapter 3.

22. Edwin H. Sutherland, *The Sutherland Papers*, edited by Albert Cohen, Alfred Lindesmith and Karl Schuessler, Indiana University Press, Bloomington, 1956, p. 46.

23. As it was put by Willis J. Ballinger, economic adviser to the Federal Trade Commission, "For 48 years in this country we have been trying to deter economic murderers with 10-cent penalties for each mass killing."—Testimony on S. 10 and S. 3072 "Federal Licensing of Corporations" before a Subcommittee on the Judiciary, United States Senate, March 10, 1938.

24. Sutherland and Cressey, pp. 86-87.

25. Edwin H. Sutherland, *White Collar Crime*, with a foreword by Donald R. Cressey, Holt, Rinehart and Winston, N.Y., 1961 edition.

26. *Ibid.*, p. 9.

27. Sutherland, *The Sutherland Papers*, p. 63. An extended discussion of this definition, cited by Sutherland, is in Jerome Hall, "Prolegomena to a Science of Criminal Law," *University of Pennsylvania Law Review*, LXXXIX, 1941, pp. 549-80; "Interrelations of Criminal Law and Torts," *Columbia Law Review*, XLIII, 1943, pp. 735-79, 967-1001; "Criminal Attempts—a Study of the Foundations of Criminal Liability," *Yale Law Review*, XLIX, 1940, pp. 789-840.

28. Sutherland, *The Sutherland Papers*, p. 51.

29. Sutherland and Cressey, pp. 40-41.

30. Sutherland, *White Collar Crime*, pp. 253-56.

31. Sutherland, *The Sutherland Papers*, p. 77.

32. *Ibid.*, p. 66.

33. *Ibid.*, p. 67.

34. Sutherland, *White Collar Crime*, p. 17 *et seq.*

35. The reader interested in identifications will have some difficulty reconstructing Sutherland's list even if he obtains the two original lists, taking sixty-eight top companies after excising public utilities (including transportation and communications), unless he deduces that the omitted industry is the oil industry. Later the reader will be referred to the *Fortune* lists of 500 corporations (published in July of each year) and of banks and utility companies (published in August of each year). These lists are made up from the same data scattered through Moody's and Poor's corporation reference manuals but are presented by *Fortune* in handy tabular form. None of these readily available lists is reproduced here, in order to conserve space for other material. Their availability to the reader is assumed.

36. Remuneration of top corporate executives—salaries plus stock bonuses and other perquisites—ranges between $100,000 and $750,000 per year. Drawing figures from *United States Census of Population, 1950: Occupational Characteristics*, Table 19, and the same publication for 1960, Table 25, we find that the median incomes in some strategic occupations are as follows:

	1949	1959	1969*
Natural scientists	$4,245	$ 7,965	$15,000
Chemists	4,091	7,245	12,800

Social scientists	4,446	7,868	13,900
College faculty, deans and presidents	4,366	7,510	12,900
Teachers	3,465	5,709	9,400
Civil engineers	4,590	7,773	13,100
Electrical engineers	4,657	8,710	16,300
Mechanical engineers	4,594	8,497	15,700
Metallurgical engineers	4,657	8,639	16,100
Lawyers and judges	6,284	11,261	20,200
Actors	3,260	5,640	9,800

* The figures for 1969 are a provisional extrapolation of those for 1959, applying the inflationary rate of 1949–59 increase. They are taken from a compilation prepared by Professor A. T. Finegan for the Industrial Relations Section of Princeton University: *Memorandum*, May 21, 1964, "Income of Men in 48 Professional Occupations: 1949 and 1959." The entire table of all groups is reproduced in *Bulletin of the American Association of University Professors (AAUP Bulletin)*, June, 1965, p. 251.

37. Chic Conwell and Edwin H. Sutherland, *The Professional Thief*, University of Chicago Press, Chicago, 1937.

38. Sutherland and Cressey, pp. 38–47.

39. Sutherland's work on the concept of white collar crime and other aspects of crime has been accepted and incorporated into general works of criminology by leading criminologists and has stimulated much additional individual research and countercriticism. It has been the most fruitful single concept in criminology in a long time. Some of the general works in which it is treated are: Harry Elmer Barnes and Negley K. Teeters, *New Horizons in Criminology*, Prentice-Hall, Inc., Englewood Cliffs, N.J., 1959; Robert G. Caldwell, *Criminology*, Ronald Press, N.Y., 1956; Ruth S. Cavan, *Criminology*, Crowell, N.Y., 1955; Mabel A. Elliott, *Crime and Modern Society*, Harper and Bros., N.Y., 1952; Richard R. Korn and Lloyd W. McCorkle, *Criminology and Penology*, Holt-Dryden, N.Y., 1959; Walter C. Reckless, *The Crime Problem*, Appleton-Century-Crofts, N.Y., 1961; Donald R. Taft, *Criminology*, Macmillan, N.Y., 1956; and George B. Vold, *Theoretical Criminology*, Oxford University Press, N.Y., 1958. Some of the many monographs that have followed the trail blazed by Sutherland on white collar crime alone are Marshall B. Clinard, *The Black Market: A Study of White Collar Crime*, Rinehart, N.Y., 1952; Clinard, "Criminological Theories of Violations of Wartime Regulations," *American Sociological Review*, June, 1956; Clinard, "Sociologists and American Criminology," *Journal of Criminal Law and Criminology*, January-February, 1951; Frank E. Hartung, *Law and Social Differentiation*, University of Michigan Press, Ann Arbor, 1949; Hartung, "White Collar Offenses in the Wholesale Meat Industry in Detroit," *American Journal of Sociology*, June, 1950; Hartung, "White Collar Crime: Its Significance for Theory and Practice," *Federal Probation*, June, 1953; Donald R. Cressey, *Other People's Money*, The Free Press of Glencoe, N.Y., 1953; Vilhelm Aubert, "White Collar Crime and Social Structure," *American Journal of Sociology*, November, 1952; Robert E. Lane, "Why Businessmen Violate the Law," *Journal of Criminal Law, Criminology, and Police Science*, July-August, 1953. Two critics of Sutherland are effectively refuted by Cressey in the foreword to the 1961 edition of Sutherland's *White Collar Crime*.

But as Professor Walter Reckless of Ohio State University observes, "Most American sociologists have accepted the principal tenets of Sutherland's formulation with respect to white-collar crime." (Reckless, *The Crime Problem*, p. 225.)

No court has formally passed on the question: Is "white collar crime" crime?; it might be expensive, win or lose, to find out. As Cressey, now at the University of California, states in a footnote to his foreword to the 1961 edition of *White Collar Crime*: "The original *White Collar Crime* manuscript contained court and commission citations and, thus, identified the various corporations involved. The original publisher's attorneys advised Sutherland that a corporation might sue the publisher and author on the ground that calling its behavior criminal is libelous. Sutherland withdrew the manuscript and prepared the present one. Had the original manuscript (which Mrs. Myrtle Sutherland still holds) been published, and had a libel suit been initiated, then Sutherland's contention that the listed offenses are in fact crimes might have been tested in a court of law—a corporation might have argued that the statement is libelous because its behavior is not crime, with Sutherland giving the arguments in this volume. I was one of Sutherland's research assistants at the time, and I urged that the original manuscript be published for this reason, if for no other. However, my idealistic desire to see a scientific principle tested in a court of law was not tempered by any practical consideration such as having money riding on the legal validity of the scientific principle. This was not the case with either the publisher or Professor Sutherland."

40. Communication from the Federal Trade Commission, dated September 8, 1965.

41. These figures were compiled from the annual reports of the Federal Security Agency, 1945–52, at pages 62, 63, 560, 570, 550, 228, 217 and 251 respectively (separate reports of the Food and Drug Administration for 1945, 1946, 1951 and 1952 are cited) and from the annual reports of the Department of Health, Education and Welfare, 1953–61, at pages 226, 220, 180, 222, 213, 214, 216, 260 and 354 respectively.

42. United States Securities and Exchange Commission, *Twenty-six Annual Report,* year ended June 30, 1960, p. 187.

43. *Ibid.*

44. National Labor Relations Board, *Twenty-ninth Annual Report,* 1964, p. 201.

45. Responding to inquiry about the number of findings against employers, the National Labor Relations Board in a letter dated September 1, 1965, says that such data are not available extending back to 1945 but are available beginning with 1953. "During the period July 1, 1953, through June 30, 1964 (11 years)," says the Board, "a total of 6,581 unfair labor practice cases were brought to the Board on contest over either the facts or application of the law. The Board found violations in 5,229 cases, or 79 per cent. Of the 6,581 contested ULP cases, 4,570 were 'CA' cases (charge against employer). The Board made findings of unfair labor practices against employers in 3,727 cases, or 82 per cent of the 4,570 contested 'CA' cases."

46. The preceding four paragraphs are a mild and sketchy version of the gangsterlike way in which the late Henry Ford ran the Ford Motor Company. A more detailed presentation may be found in the solidly documented book by the University of Minnesota Ph.D., Keith Sward, titled *The Legend of Henry Ford,* Rinehart and Company, Inc., N.Y., 1948, pp. 327–429. More extended sources are to be found in lengthy volumes of nine hearings before the National Labor Relations Board. The methods of the Ford strong-arm men, the NLRB commented in the Dallas case, were those of "organized gangsterism." While this is all history now, I refer to the late Henry Ford as one example of a man who ran his company by methods of unbridled violence and underhanded subterfuge because there is perhaps more popular illusion about him as a benevolent industrialist than about any other. In reading about Ford it is difficult to see why there should be any particular worry about a Mafia infiltrating a big company other than concern that there might be new recruits to evil practices. The original Henry Ford, one is forced to conclude as one reads the record,

had nothing to learn from any Mafia. He had, indeed, a close business association with Joe Adonis, since deported to Italy. Adonis, a notorious Mafia gangster, held the truck-hauling contract from Ford's Edgewater, New Jersey, plant and for this work from 1932 to 1940 was reputed to have received at least $3 million (Sward, pp. 299–300). Speaking of the Mafia. . . .

47. These data are supplied in a memorandum accompanying a letter to the author from the United States Department of Justice, dated August 20, 1965. The writer states: "I am sorry I do not have the workload statistics available for public distribution as far back as 1945." The writer further states: "In answer to your second question the Division does not have readily available statistics showing a breakdown of monopoly and restraint of trade charges. You may obtain this information from several legal publications that publish resumes of antitrust cases as they are instituted and terminated. You will find activities in Government cases reported weekly in Trade Regulation Reports, published by Commerce Clearing House. Accounts of important antitrust cases and matters are also reported weekly in Antitrust & Trade Regulations Report published by the Bureau of National Affairs. I am sure you will find either of these publications helpful." I surely appreciate the Washington writer's desire to be helpful, but his remarks reflect the official statistical slackness that prevails wih respect to corporate crimes.

48. John Herling, *The Great Price Conspiracy*, Robert B. Luce, Inc., Washington, D.C., 1962, p. 320.

49. Detailed treatment of the electrical-industry case is given in Herling's, *The Great Price Conspiracy*. John G. Fuller, *The Gentlemen Conspirators*, Grove Press, N.Y., 1962, may also be consulted. A more compressed account is in "The Incredible Electrical Conspiracy," *Fortune*, April–May, 1961. There is a subtle, balanced, rue-fully gracious analysis of the ethical nuances of the case in Walter Goodman, *All Honorable Men*, "Business: A Way of Life," Little, Brown and Company, Boston, 1963, pp. 9–99.

50. This case is reported in the *New York Times*, July 24, 1965; 1:8.

51. *New York Times*, July 27, 1965; 1:2.

52. *Ibid.*, January 8, 1961; 63:1.

53. *Ibid.*, October 24, 1966; 1:4; *New York Post*, May 15, 1967. The latter medium said that members of the Council were not only continuing to support the war despite escalation but were preparing to back Mr. Johnson for reelection in 1968 against any Republican yet named as a possible presidential contender. Mr. Johnson, in fact, commands more Big Business support than any president since William McKinley.

54. Allan Nevins, *Study in Power: John D. Rockefeller; industrialist and Philanthropist*, Charles Scribner's Sons, N.Y., 1953, Vol. II, p. 426. Reviewing this book in *The Nation*, May 30, 1953, Keith Hutchison observed that Nevins depicts Rockefeller "as a good man who committed many evil acts usually from the best of motives and with generally healthy consequences. This paradox leads to some strange conclusions."

55. *New York Times*, September 20, 1953; 67:1.

56. This subject is extensively treated in ASF, pp. 133–48, 186–202 and *passim*.

57. Sutherland, *The Sutherland Papers*, pp. 92–93.

CHAPTER FOUR

1. Cabot's obituary notice was in the *New York Times*, November 3, 1962; 25:4. He is extensively noticed in the *National Cyclopedia of American Biography*, Vol. 14, p. 251, and Vol. 34, p. 13, in which many other entries relate to the taciturn Cabot

family and its offshoots. Up to this writing no public report of dispositions under Cabot's will has come to my attention.

2. *New York Herald Tribune*, October, 2, 1965; 18:3.

3. William H. A. Carr, *The Du Ponts of Delaware*, Dodd, Mead & Company, N.Y., 1964, p. 2.

4. *Moody's Bank and Finance Manual*, 1964, p. 648. Other financial details about Christiana Securities are available at this source.

5. *Ibid.*, p. 648.

6. *New York Times*, June 3, 1962; 12:3.

7. Temporary National Economic Committee (TNEC), United States Securities Exchange Commission, *Investigation of Concentration of Economic Power*, U.S. Senate, 76th Congress, 3rd session, Monograph No. 29, 1940–1941, 1557 pp. At p. 867 it is shown that Christiana held 27.56 per cent of E. I. du Pont common, with the Du Pont family holding 74 per cent of Christiana or 20.39 participation in E. I. du Pont through this single channel alone. But this was far from the whole story. For at p. 869 it is shown that the Du Ponts personally and through a network of family subholding companies and trust funds held altogether 43.93 per cent of E. I. du Pont common, enough to insure absolute control. This without taking into consideration family holdings of preferred and debenture stock. These data are now, to be sure, somewhat dated. But what they show of contemporary relevance is the pattern of Du Pont holdings. Since the ownership position in General Motors was increased it is reasonable to infer that the general situation is no different in E. I. du Pont and in Christiana Securities. Later data will be cited showing the position to be about the same. See also *ibid.*, p. 107.

8. Carr, p. 2.

9. *Ibid.*, p. 348.

10. *Foundation Directory*, 1964, pp. 136, 138.

11. *New York Times*, May 23, 1961; 32:6.

12. TNEC, *Investigation . . .* , p. 869.

13. *Ibid.*, pp. 1510–11.

14. *Ibid.*, pp. 869, 1441.

15. *Ibid.*, p. 1511.

16. *Ibid.*, p. 1512.

17. *New York Times*, April 27, 1964; 49:1.

18. Carr, p. 299.

19. Max Dorian, *The Du Ponts: From Gunpowder to Nylon*, Little, Brown and Company, Boston, 1961, pp. 278–79. Carr, pp. 293–94.

20. Carr, pp. 191–94.

21. *Ibid.*, p. 241.

22. *Ibid.*, p. 243.

23. *Ibid.*, p. 244.

24. *Ibid.*

25. *Ibid.*, p. 245.

26. *Ibid.*

27. Edward W. Proctor, *Anti-Trust Policy and the Industrial Explosives Industry*, doctoral dissertation, Harvard University, 1961. Cited by Carr, pp. 245–46.

28. Carr, p. 246.

29. *Ibid.*, pp. 286, 334.

30. *Ibid.*, p. 285.

31. *Ibid.*, p. 288.

32. *Ibid.*, p. 299.

33. Cited by Carr, pp. 333–34.

34. TNEC, *Investigation . . .* , pp. 1514–21.

35. *Ibid.*, pp. 628–31, 964–65, 1010–13.

36. Harvey O'Connor, *Mellon's Millions*, The John Day Company, N.Y., 1933, pp. 52–53.

37. *Ibid.*, p. 100. The ins and outs of the Mellons's complicated wheeling and dealing that finally gave them fingers in more than 100 well-known companies are carefully traced by Harvey O'Connor.

38. *New York Times*, May 20, 1960; 1:2, and May 21, 1960; 25:8.

39. *Ibid.*

40. TNEC, *Investigation* . . . , pp. 1324–29 and *passim*.

41. *Ibid.*

42. *Ibid.*, p. 129.

43. *New York Times*, July 21, 1937; 21:2.

44. TNEC, *Investigation* . . . , 126–31. A word on the money-value given for these holdings may perhaps be in order here. The 1937 values of the big oil company holdings are those given by TNEC. The December 31, 1964, values are the result of my own computations, conducted as follows: The closing prices of stocks for 1964 were taken from *The Commercial and Financial Chronicle*, January 3, 1965. These were computed against the entire outstanding stock issue of each company as given in *Moody's Industrial Manual*, 1965; *Moody's Public Utility Manual*, 1965; and *Moody's Transportation Manual*, 1964. For the industrials and public utilities the stock outstanding at the end of 1964 was taken, and for the railroads the stock outstanding at the end of 1963. The prices were multiplied with the outstanding stock issue and then the TNEC percentages were extracted. While tedious, this computation was not complicated except in the case of the Middle West Corporation, a public utility holding company later dissolved by government order. The constituent company stocks were in this case apportioned according to the break-up formula and the computation was made, taking into consideration later stock splits but not the issuance of rights to subscribe to new stock; nor was cognizance taken of later stock sales by the constituent companies to reduce indebtedness because they did not appear to dilute existing equities. Also, a capital distribution of $4.50 in cash per share of Middle West was added. While the Middle West Corporation figure is the most approximate in the column, it appears to be closely representative of what the stock would have been worth in the market had the company continued to exist. But owing to the noncomputation of subscription rights throughout and the ignoring of tax advantages accruing from stock dividends and stock split-ups, the final figure, while not intended to indicate the total of any existing investment portfolio, represents if anything an understatement of the total Rockefeller funds as surveyed by TNEC.

45. *New York Times*, April 18, 1947; 23:3; April 19, 1947; 1:4.

46. Sward, p. 464. Henry Ford is something of a folk hero. He is popularly thought of as the once-poor, small-town bicycle mechanic who not only showed the city slickers a thing or two, by cracky, but who brought a cheap automobile into the price range of the deserving common man. He was all of this. But, as Dr. Sward incontrovertibly shows, he was also extremely ignorant, narrow-minded, bigoted, slow to learn, dictatorial, grasping, unsympathetic and unimaginative. His spectacular success probably enhanced his natural anxieties as it thrust him more and more into a complex world where the trusty maxims of the cracker barrel were continually set at naught.

47. Dwight Macdonald, *The Ford Foundation: The Men and the Millions*, Reynal & Company, N.Y., 1955, p. 3.

48. *Ibid.*

49. *Ibid.*, p. 4.

50. "Estate Planning," *Federal Estate and Gift Tax Reporter*, Commerce Clearing House, Inc., N.Y., p. 7553, insertion no. 287–5, dated August 18, 1960.

51. ASF, pp. 286–373.

52. *New York Times*, October 29, 1948; 22:6.

53. *Ibid.*, June 4, 1943; 26:3.

54. *Ibid.*

55. Some readers may wonder why the Fords did not keep their 10 per cent of voting stock and simply sell 90 per cent of nonvoting stock to get tax money. They could not have done this because experienced buyers shy away from nonvoting stocks, and the stock for tax purposes would obviously have been worth less than claimed. There is, then, a factor of value about the voting power of a stock. But the Fords could meet legal requirements by retaining initial 100 per cent voting power in their stock and giving the foundation nonvoting stock with equal dividend rights, provided they made the foundation stock eventually salable by allowing it some voting rights after sale or transfer. However, the Ford stock retained by the family, even though it is technically possible for it to be reduced to equality with the common, is worth more, share for share, than either the Class A or common stocks. This greater worth would be displayed only if a substantial block of the B stock were ever publicly offered, which will presumably never happen. A further element of astuteness in the way chosen to market the common stock was in deferring the time with its sale and making it possible to sell it gradually. Had 90 per cent of voting stock of Ford Motor been offered for sale between 1948 and 1950 the prices realized would have been very low in an unfavorable market. Sophisticated operators, when they have a choice, sell stock only in rising markets; the unsophisticated do just the opposite.

56. TNEC, *Investigation . . .* , pp. 1330–31.

57. *Moody's Industrial Manual,* June, 1966, p. 537.

58. John T. Flynn, *God's Gold,* Harcourt, Brace and Company, N.Y., 1932, p. 449.

59. Such is the power of propaganda that the name of Wilson for most people still suggests liberalism and progressivism. Wilson, in fact, was a standpat southern conservative, opposed to trust-busting and every kind of social reform. His administration was little more than an adjunct to J. P. Morgan and Company, whose representatives had little difficulty switching him from a policy of neutrality with respect to the European war to one of belligerency. For data on Wilson the reader should consult the definitive Arthur S. Link, *Wilson,* 4 vols., Princeton University Press, Princeton, 1946–1954, and *Woodrow Wilson and the Progressive Era,* Harper, N.Y., 1954. Thorough analysis of the misnamed progressive era is also to be found in Gabriel Kolko, *The Triumph of Conservatism,* The Free Press of Glencoe, N.Y., 1964; as to Wilson see pages 190–278 and especially 205–6. For essentially the same conclusions but without so much specialized documentation see *ASF,* pp. 106–48, "The Politics of Pecuniary Aggrandizement: 1912–1920." For a recent brief treatment of the way the United States was unceremoniously switched into belligerency in 1917 see Robert Sobel, *The Big Board: A History of the New York Stock Market,* The Free Press, N.Y., 1965, pp. 206–21.

60. Richard F. Hamilton, "Conviction or Convenience: The Trap of the Great Society," *The Nation,* November 22, 1965.

61. *New York Times,* November 22, 1965; 57:4.

CHAPTER FIVE

1. TNEC, *Investigation. . . .*

2. *Ibid.,* pp. xvi–xvii.

3. *Ibid.,* p. 116.

4. *Ibid.*

5. *Ibid.,* p. 117. The holdings were listed at this place.

6. *Ibid.,* pp. 105–7.

7. *Ibid.,* p. 641.

8. *Ibid.,* pp. 107–8.

9. *Ibid.*
10. *Ibid.*, pp. 107–8, 846–51.
11. *Ibid.*, pp. 852–53.
12. *Ibid.*, pp. 107, 125, 1489.
13. *Ibid.*, p. 1489.
14. *Ibid.*, pp. 1017, 1489.
15. *Ibid.*, p. 108.
16. *Ibid.*, pp. 108–9.
17. *Ibid.*, p. 109.
18. *New York Times*, August 6, 1964; 31:1. The original sum was $26 million, but with income and appreciation rose to $96.35 million.
19. TNEC, *Investigation* . . . , p. 109.
20. *Ibid.*, pp. 112–13.
21. *Ibid.*, p. 1341.
22. *Ibid.*, pp. 1455–82.
23. ASF.
24. TNEC, *Investigation* . . . , p. xvi.
25. Amory, *The Proper Bostonians*, pp. 32–35.
26. Stanley Silverberg, Senior Economist, Department of Banking and Currency Research, Office of the Comptroller of the Currency, "Bank Trust Investments in 1964," *The National Banking Review*, United States Treasury, Washington, D.C., June, 1965, Vol. 2, No. 4, p. 483.
27. *Ibid.*, pp. 483–84.
28. *Ibid.*, pp. 486–87.
29. *Ibid.*, p. 487.
30. *Ibid.*
31. *Ibid.*, p. 488.
32. *Ibid.*
33. *Ibid.*, p. 489.
34. *Ibid.*, p. 490.
35. *Standard Federal Tax Reporter, Income Tax Index*, Sec. 195, p. 12,033, 1964, Commerce Clearing House, N.Y.
36. Source of data: U.S. Treasury Department, Internal Revenue Service, *Statistics of Income: 1958–59*, pp. 175–76.
37. Stated at insertion No. 517–3, January 11, 1965, p. 7002, "Estate Planning," *Federal Estate and Gift Tax Reporter*, Vol. 2. Mellon's deathless words, there set down for the prudent, were: "According to my experience, it is more difficult to keep wealth when you have it than to accumulate it. Fluctuations in value, panics, maladministration of justice, frauds, accidents and the constant grinding of taxation and other influences, tend constantly to the disintegration of wealth. More especially so at a period of life when the master spirit is weakened and the stimulus of success no longer allures to renewed exertion; and we are more inclined to repose than activity. In that condition we are more likely to lose than gain. I now no longer wonder at many of my business contemporaries having acquired wealth in the prime of life and letting it slip through their fingers in old age. Without prudent children, or others competent to guard it, it is a natural consequence that a man's wealth will begin to waste away with his mental and physical energies."
38. Martin L. Lindahl and William A. Carter, *Corporate Concentration and Public Policy*, Prentice-Hall, Inc., Englewood Cliffs, N.J., 1959, p. 85 *et seq.*

CHAPTER SIX

1. Anyone who wishes may ascertain for himself what the ownership situations are

by consulting the *Official Summary of Security Transactions and Holdings* of the Securities and Exchange Commission. For a particular company it is best to begin with the latest monthly issue and trace it back in its alphabetized order through each year. Immediately after stock splits and stock dividends is a good time to look for the entire roster of officers, directors and those holding more than 10 per cent of the stock. There is little difficulty about this procedure as long as only one or a few companies are traced. But considerable time is required if one wishes to trace the big holdings in the major companies. It took me 165 hours to trace all the companies listed back through 1960 and the following from 1945 to 1960: Aluminum Co. of America, Atlantic Refining, Du Pont, Ford Motor, Ohio Oil, Sears, Roebuck, Socony and the various Standard Oil companies. But considerable time was taken to make note of many holdings and some time was taken for certain additional companies prior to 1960.

2. TNEC, p. 867.

3. TNEC, *Investigation* . . . , pp. 214–15.

4. *Ibid.*, Appendix III, No. 3, facing p. 242.

5. *Ibid.*

6. *Ibid.*, No. 1 facing p. 242.

7. *Ibid.*, Appendix III, facing p. 242.

CHAPTER SEVEN

1. *Statistical Abstract*, 1964, Table No. 654, p. 487.

2. *Ibid.*, Table No. 655, p. 488.

3. *Ibid.*, Table No. 433, p. 321.

4. *Ibid.*, Table No. 662, p. 492.

5. *Ibid.*, Table No. 668, p. 495.

6. *Ibid.*

7. *Ibid.*, Table No. 662, p. 492.

8. *Ibid.*, Table No. 668, p. 495. These computations are made on the basis of the U.S. Treasury categories set forth for active corporations. The industrial and trading corporations are those in the mining, construction, manufacturing, transportation, communication, electric, gas, sanitary and wholesale and retail trade groups, which are differentiated from other groups of active corporations.

9. *Ibid.*, compiled from Table No. 668, p. 495.

10. 12,000 *Leading U.S. Corporations*, by the editors of *News Front*, Inc., N.Y., 1963, p. 7.

11. *Statistical Abstract*, Table No. 680, p. 501.

12. *Ibid.*, Table No. 683, p. 502.

13. *Ibid.*, Table No. 682, p. 502.

14. *Ibid.*, Table No. 684, p. 503.

15. Lindahl and Carter, pp. 60, 61, 102.

16. Desmond Smith, "AT&T: The Folksy Octopus," *The Nation*, January 3, 1966, p. 16.

17. *Wall Street Journal*, October 28, 1965; 1:6.

18. Federal Trade Commission, *Report on Corporate Mergers and Acquisitions*, U.S. Government Printing Office, 1955, pp. 10–11.

19. *Ibid.*, p. 13.

CHAPTER EIGHT

1. Ritchie P. Lowry, *Who's Running This Town?* Harper and Row, N.Y., 1965, pp. xviii–xxii.

2. *ASF.*, pp. 9–22, offers a rather extensive catalogue of leading family inter-marriages up to the 1930's but the source to which one must turn for a more extended treatment and detailing of such marriages (and divorces) as well as of the private lives of the rich and near-rich is Amory, *Who Killed Society? passim.; The Proper Bostonians, passim.;* and *The Last Resorts*, Harper, N.Y., 1952, *passim.* Amory, an hereditary insider himself, from Boston, is a sharp if at times near-the-surface observer who encapsulates a good deal of genially corrosive social criticism in a constant flow of amusing anecdotes. His books are irreverently informative on all sorts of above-stairs details and are entertainingly readable. His central theme is that the claims to superiority of an earlier work-minded New England elite, to some extent justifiable, have given way to crass vulgarity and decadent frivolity among the latter-day metro-politan bourgeoisie, the *rentier* elements of which are largely useless to self as well as others. Amory, alienated from his hereditary class, writes of a low-life upper-class of pretended gentility, the nonfunctional elements of which are personally disoriented and indeed victimized by the possession of too much easy money. They can be looked upon as denizens of a gilt-edged slum, and observation shows that many of the *rentiers* behave little differently from delinquent ghetto-dwellers. Those elements of the mon-eyed class who do not fit into the world of corporate affairs or politics are usually thrust aside by the dominant men and given overgenerous palliative allowances or trust funds. Thereafter they dig themselves ever deeper into their tangled private hells. Dixon Wecter in *The Saga of American Society*, Charles Scribner's Sons, N.Y., 1937, gives a much less mordant, rather superficial historical treatment of the same stratum as an example of social aspiration.

3. *New York Times*, December 17, 1965; 1:6.

4. Amory, *Who Killed Society?* pp. 59–106.

5. *Ibid.*, unnumbered appendix. Amory lists more than 500 of these armorial fami-lies, of which Washington is genealogically listed as No. 1 and Zinzendorf as No. 521. Some families are entitled, impressively, to double registration. But, unfortunately, as Amory notes (p. 104) in the quest for a coat of arms the Fords, the Deerings "and hundreds more have tried and failed." There was once suggested, says Amory at the same place, a coat of arms for the Crane plumbing family of Chicago. "The shield was divided into four parts, including, in each section, a sink, a bathtub, etc. Over all was a hand gripping the handle of a chain—with the inevitable motto, '*Après moi le deluge.'* " In St. Louis, Amory avers, the motto translates into "*Après moi le Desloge*" in honor of the Desloge family of the St. Joseph Lead Company. This family is credited with piously building an underground ballroom, a crypt of merriment, con-taining statues of many saints, leading local wits to say, "They've got every saint in there but St. Joe Lead."

6. Mills, pp. 63–68.

7. Recently at Harvard, members of the freshman class were surprised to notice that some of their number were receiving invitations to fancy-dress parties and cotil-lions in nearby Boston from hostesses they did not know. It was soon deduced that the invitations came to freshmen who had attended private schools, with the single exception of one who had attended a public high school which was designated as an "academy." The names had been hurriedly culled from the university directory. Here the private-school boys were singled out to meet Social Register daughters, presumably with a view to future correct matchmaking, although it may be that the mothers in charge simply reasonably wanted to be sure the unknown male guests knew correct social deportment and dress. This rough screening process would miss any future Alfred P. Sloans and similar uncut diamonds. But statistically the hostesses were on the right track. The incident serves to show how private-school status can be socially deter-mining in unexpected ways.

8. Mills, pp. 58, 64–69, 106–7.

9. Amory, *Who Killed Society?* p. 212.

10. *Ibid.*, p. 370.

11. *Ibid.*, p. 211.

12. *Ibid.*, p. 206.

13. *Ibid.*, p. 198, and E. Digby Baltzell, *The Protestant Establishment: Aristocracy and Caste in America*, Random House, N.Y., 1964, *passim*. Professor Baltzell delves thoroughly into this facet in various parts of his masterly analysis. Through the metropolitan clubs, it is Baltzell's thesis, there is imposed a caste rule from the top of American society. This society, indeed, is bounded by caste at top and bottom; the bottom caste, as shown in Gunnar Myrdal, *An American Dilemma*, Harper and Bros., N.Y., 1939, consists of the Negro. The top caste is voluntary, the bottom caste involuntary. In between, induced reactive castes emerge, although there is a parallel stratified class society, as many sociological analyses show. This is not a simple Marxian stratification of capitalists and proletarians but a much more complex kind, with factions within classes and castes. What gives the whole at times a Marxian appearance is that none of the classes below the top sliver own productive property to any appreciable extent. But the caste structure includes more than Negroes and upper propertied elements; for the whites who are most active in holding Negroes down (mostly southerners), present themselves as an anti-Negro caste. Their claim to distinction is solely that they are not Negroes; their castemark is the lightness of their skin. Again, the propertied caste at the top has its own supporters, who accept its values, and these function as a subcaste. Jews are themselves forced into a castelike mold by exclusion. The United States, in other words, is not only a great deal more like the Banana Republics than it likes to think itself; it is also a great deal more like India, one of the most backward nations in the world, than most of its citizens suspect. Despite trumpetings about equality it is both a caste society and a class society, with emphasis upon the negative features of both. Ideologically derived propaganda, however, presents it to its own people and to the world as an egalitarian or opportunitarian society.

14. Baltzell, p. 84. Professor Baltzell sketches in some detail the Dillon background, pp. 83–86, and the difficulty the recent secretary of the treasury had in getting into the caste-iron Chevy Chase Club in Washington particularly.

15. *Ibid.*, pp. 35–37.

16. John Slawson and Lawrence Bloomgarden, *The Unequal Treatment of Equals: The Social Club . . . Discrimination in Retreat*, Institute of Human Relations, AJC, N.Y., 1965, pp. 20–21.

17. As to the case of the Merchants Club see Benjamin Epstein and Arnold Forster, *Some of My Best Friends . . .* , Farrar, Straus and Cudahy, N.Y., 1963, p. 34. Concerning the Duquesne Club, see Baltzell, pp. 362–63.

18. Osborn Elliott, *Men at the Top*, Harper and Brothers, N.Y., 1959, pp. 166–67.

19. Baltzell, p. 365.

20. *Ibid.*, p. 367.

21. *Ibid.*, p. 137.

22. *Ibid.*, pp. 7–8.

23. *Ibid.*, p. 7.

24. *Ibid.*, pp. 362–68.

25. Elliott, pp. 164–71.

26. The University of Michigan, Institute for Social Research, Survey Research Center, *Discrimination Without Prejudice: A Study of Promotion Practices in Industry*, Ann Arbor, 1964, p. 1.

27. Vance Packard, *The Pyramid Climbers*, McGraw-Hill Book Company, N.Y., 1962, p. 36.

28. *Ibid.*, p. 37.

29. Pinpoint studies and magazine commentaries thereon are as follows: *Report of the Philadelphia Chapter of the American Jewish Committee on the Relations of Jews to Major Life and Fire and Casualty Companies in Philadelphia*, June 25, 1965,

shows that in 6 companies under scrutiny, of 187 senior officers only 1 was Jewish and of 109 directors only 1 was Jewish; with respect to 10 companies, out of 81 officers in 73 departments, 2 were Jewish in one company and 1 was Jewish in another. The same pattern prevailed among junior officers. *Patterns of Exclusion from the Executive Suite: The Public Utilities Industry*, Institute of Human Relations, AJC, N.Y., 1963, reports that of 755 officers in the 50 utility corporations designated by *Fortune* as the largest, only 8 (about 1 per cent) "appear to be Jews"; 43 of the corporations appear to have no Jewish officers at all. This same report cites the fact that in 1961 less than 0.6 per cent of the officers of 6 leading banks in an eastern city were Jews. *The Mutual Savings Banks of New York: A Survey of the Exclusion of Jews at Top Management and Policy Making Levels*, Institute of Human Relations, AJC, N.Y., 1965, shows that 82 per cent of New York City's 50 mutual savings banks have no key Jewish officers at all, and 60 per cent have no Jewish trustees; less than 2.5 per cent of the more than 400 officers and under 3.5 per cent of the approximately 750 trustees are Jews. Yet almost 25 per cent of the population of New York City and 50 per cent of its college graduates are Jewish! See also: Lewis B. Ward, "The Ethics of Executive Selection," *Harvard Business Review*, March-April, 1965; "Invisible Persuader on Promotions," *Business week*, December 12, 1964; and "How Does Religion Influence Job Choice?" *Business Week*, April 17, 1963. A more recent study by the American Jewish Committee of the 50 largest American commercial banks found that Jews, who in popular myth are monopolists of banking, hold only 1.3 per cent of senior officer positions and 0.9 per cent of middle-management positions; but in New York City with its very heavy Jewish population Jews hold only 0.6 per cent of senior officer positions (*New York Times*, September 2, 1966; 40:5-6).

30. *New York Times*, November 14, 1965; 85:3.
31. Cited by Baltzell, p. 43.
32. *Ibid.*, pp. 40-41.
33. Amory, *Who Killed Society?* pp. 544-51.
34. Dana, p. 162.
35. *Ibid.*
36. *Ibid.*, p. 163. Dana erroneously spells the name "Bartou."
37. *Ibid.*, pp. 163-64.
38. *Ibid.*, pp. 196-240.
39. Elliott V. Bell, "The Decline of the Money Barons," in *We Saw It Happen*, edited by Hanson W. Baldwin and Shepard Stone, Simon and Schuster, N.Y., 1938, pp. 135-37.
40. Nevins, p. 269.

CHAPTER NINE

1. "The nobles were subject in principle to the *vingtièmes* and the capitation (pool-tax), from which the clergy were exempt. The peasants alone paid the *taille*." The *vingtième* was "A tax of a twentieth, levied, in theory, on the whole income, but in practice only on certain kinds of income" while "the *taille*, one of the principal sources of the national revenue, was originally levied for military purposes; hence the nobility, whose profession was that of arms, was exempt, as well as the clergy." Mathiez, p. 20. Mathiez is a French historian of high repute.

2. Louis Eisenstein, *The Ideologies of Taxation*, The Ronald Press Company, N.Y., 1961, p. 11. This valuable and probing book, a logical analysis of the unconsciously comic but seriously intended rationalizations and excuses for American taxation by a keenly perceptive Washington, D.C., tax lawyer, should be read as an extension in depth of this chapter. Our main sources are the tax laws, the annual *Statistics of Income* published by the Internal Revenue Service, the mordant Eisenstein study,

Randolph E. Paul's *Taxation in the United States*, Little, Brown and Company, Boston, 1954, and Philip M. Stern's *The Great Treasury Raid*, Random House, N.Y., 1964, a briskly readable popular treatment mainly of the data unfolded by Eisenstein but without Eisenstein's delineation of the ideological subterfuges. Paul was special tax consultant to the president and the Treasury Department from 1937 to 1941, special assistant and tax adviser to the secretary of the treasury in 1941 and 1942 and general counsel of the Treasury and acting secretary of the Treasury in charge of Foreign Funds Control from 1942 to 1944. Stern was deputy assistant secretary of state in the Kennedy Administration and is a former Harvard and Rockefeller Fellow who became legislative assistant to Senators Henry M. Jackson and Paul H. Douglas. All these books contain extensive bibliographies, Paul's mainly along historical lines. Paul acknowledges his indebtedness to a seminal paper by Eisenstein in 58 *Harvard Law Review* 477 (1945).

3. Ideology helps obscure from the initiators themselves the injustice involved. As Eisenstein remarks (pp. 11–12), under a putative democracy, "Reasons have to be given for the burdens that are variously proposed or approved. In time the contending reasons are skillfully elaborated into systems of belief or ideologies which are designed to induce the required acquiescence. Of course, if an ideology is to be effective, it must convey a vital sense of some immutable principle that rises majestically above partisan preferences. Except in dire circumstances, civilized men are not easily convinced by mere appeals to self-interest. What they are asked to believe must be identified with imposing concepts that transcend their pecuniary prejudices." Three ideologies he regards as primary are then considered as seemingly high-minded interpretations of the tax laws: the ideologies of ability to pay, of barriers and deterrents to general economic well-being and of equity. But as he also points out (p. 15) the ideologist is "nicely flexible" from time to time in which ideology he subscribes to. He speaks as a believer through principle when he speaks for the bar as a whole but he becomes a believer from "direct interest or compensation" when he speaks for a client. "Since he is then stimulated by monetary rewards, he is a believer through compensation as well as conviction." But, as a taxpayer himself, the ideologist may also be a believer through self-interest. "One of the major achievements of the [American Bar] Association is that it enables tax lawyers to serve in several capacities without fear of embarrassment." Whatever ideology is espoused from time to time one may always be sure it is believed in the deepest sincerity, the paving material for the well-known road to Hades. Clients, too, are equally sincere. The reader should never forget that we are concerned at all times in this study with people who are always thoroughly and unshakably sincere, true believers in what they do.

4. Eisenstein, p. 181.
5. *Ibid.*
6. *Ibid.*, p. 127.
7. Mathiez, p. 21.
8. Eisenstein, pp. 55–56. As the scholarly and deeply learned sources I cite draw their data from the period of the pre-1964 tax rates it is necessary to notice that those rates have been revised. Instead of rates ranging from 20 per cent to 91 per cent, the formal rates were reduced to 16–77 per cent in 1964 and to 14–70 per cent in 1965. But early in 1966 it was proposed that the new rates be raised by one or the other percentage in order to pay for President Johnson's personally initiated *pubpolic* large-scale intrusion in the Vietnam religious and civil war. A rise of 7 per cent proposed by Johnson would restore 16 per cent of the reduction. Corporation rates were reduced from 52 to 50 per cent in 1964 and to 48 per cent in 1965. Income from foreign operations pays much less and huge special credits are allowed for new investments. As there is constant tinkering with the tax structure, usually to the disadvantage of the lower brackets, it is only the continuing pattern that is of interest. Readers who wish to apply current rates to cases cited need simply ascertain their difference, as I have

done in some cases, whatever they may be after the latest go-round in Congress. It would, in any case, be impossible to give rates that will be precise throughout the life of a book, although one may be sure the essential tax structure and relative differences will be unchanged at least until Birnam Wood starts moving toward Washington.

9. Although Mr. Stern's book, *The Great Treasury Raid,* is recommended to readers who wish to be led in easy style into many incredible but true details, an objection must be registered against its catchy title, which is not a little misleading. There has been no raid on the United States Treasury, direct or indirect. Each year the government sets the total of money it wants for operations and dispensations and it always gets what it sets out to obtain. What aspect of raid there is is directed by the big property holders and their tax lawyers and lobbyists, with the connivance of *pubpols,* against the powerless average man, often a very unmoneyed man and usually job-dependent, moderately circumstanced and thoroughly gullible. Whatever the major financial beneficiaries of the system are able to avoid paying—and protests by any of them against the process are yet to be heard—is necessarily pushed over on the shoulders of the powerless who, as Mr. Eisenstein observes, are patriotic and uncomplaining.

10. *Statistical Abstract, 1964,* p. 412.

11. *Ibid.,* p. 387.

12. *Wall Street Journal,* May 5, 1958, p. 1. There is a good editorial in this issue on the tax structure as an economic impediment.

13. Quoted by Eisenstein, p. 107.

14. Lewis H. Kimmel, *Taxes and Economic Incentives,* Brookings Institution, Washington, D.C., 1950, p. 182.

15. *Fortune,* July, 1965, p. 155. Observations in the text are confined to very large corporations. If one takes the range of corporations, especially the 7,129 with more than 100 employees each, one finds as of 1961 some truly astonishing rates of return. St. Paul Ammonia apparently led with 286.7 per cent, Southern Nitrogen had 102.4 per cent, Gillette 40.1 per cent, Alberto-Culver 39.6 per cent, American Photocopy 33.2 per cent and Avon Products 32.6 per cent. Source: *12,000 Leading U.S. Corporations.*

16. The National Industrial Conference Board, *The Economic Almanac,* 1964, reports a series of many leading industries from 1925 through 1960 at pp. 274 and 276.

17. Adolph A. Berle, Jr., *Power Without Property,* 1959, pp. 32–47.

18. Stern, p. 199.

19. "War and the Clergy," *New York Times,* February 15, 1966; 2:3–4.

20. Guenter Lewy, *The Catholic Church and Nazi Germany,* McGraw-Hill Publishing Company, N.Y., 1964, *passim.*

21. Stern, pp. 62–63.

22. Stern in *The Great Treasury Raid* deals with various on-the-record cases of income splitting by means of family partnerships, multiple trust funds and multiple corporations at pp. 71–80.

23. *Statistical Abstract, 1964,* Table 465, p. 342.

24. "In making their judgments the committee members evaluate test scores, academic record, qualities of leadership, extracurricular activities, and other pertinent information submitted by the student and his school." *Student Information Bulletin, National Merit Scholarship Qualifying Test, Spring 1966,* Science Research Associates, Inc., Chicago, 1966. Better put, above, it might be ". . . and a variety of irrelevant information. . . ."

25. *The Handbook of Basic Economic Statistics, February, 1966,* Economic Statistics Bureau, Washington, D.C., pp. 230–31.

26. *Ibid.*

27. Eisenstein, p. 53.

28. Stern, pp. 198–99.

29. Stern, p. 191.

30. *Statistical Abstract, 1964*, p. 405. Additional bonds are partially tax exempt.

31. See Eisenstein for opinions pro and con, pp. 69–75.

32. Stern, p. 112. Various similar cases of the expense of luxurious living being deducted before taxes, thus reducing the tax bill, are cited in *ASF, passim.*

33. *Ibid.*

34. *Ibid.*

35. *Ibid.*, pp. 113–14.

36. Cited by Stern, p. 113.

37. *Ibid.*

38. *Ibid.*, p. 124.

39. All these cases are reported by Stern, pp. 181–83.

40. Stern gives the pros and cons of these arguments, pp. 183–90.

41. *Ibid.*, p. 184.

42. Edwin Sutherland, "Crime of Corporations," *The Sutherland Papers*, p. 89.

43. Eisenstein, p. 127.

44. Stern, pp. 18–19. But in this exposition generally I am following Eisenstein, pp. 124–25.

45. Eisenstein, p. 124.

46. *Ibid.*

47. *Ibid.*, p. 125.

48. Stern, pp. 143–60.

49. *Ibid.*, p. 143.

50. *Ibid.*, p. 148.

51. *Ibid.*, p. 88.

52. *Statistical Abstract, 1964*, p. 400.

53. Stern, pp. 144–45.

54. *Ibid.*, p. 45.

55. These specially tailored tax laws, obtained through influence in Congress, are rather thoroughly discussed by Stern, pp. 44–61. Some of the cases are quite amusing.

56. *Ibid.*, p. 254.

57. Anderson, pp. 223–33. Anderson reports many cases and much harrowing detail.

58. William Surface, *Inside Internal Revenue*, Coward-McCann, Inc., N.Y., 1967, pp. 76–77.

59. *New York Times*, July 13, 1967; 26:1.

60. Stern, pp. 15–16.

61. *Statistical Abstract, 1964*, p. 397.

62. *Ibid.*, p. 395.

63. Mr. Stern in his final chapter presents a plan for reforming and simplifying the income tax in the spirit of the Sixteenth Amendment, taxing income "from whatever source derived," uniformly and at rates only half as high as the pre-1963 rates. Under this plan all receipts with purchasing power constitute income. Congress would then set deductions for self and each dependent. There would also be deducted all costs in obtaining the income. From the result in each case would be computed the tax at rates of 11 to 50 per cent. But this is the last we may expect to hear of this or any other plan of reform; for what it does is to put all income and costs on an absolutely equal footing. There would be no partial or total exemptions, no special deductions and no special dispensations such as have been insidiously worked into the law in secret sessions of the congressional tax committees. The reason the country will not get such a reform—at least not by act of Congress—is that the privileged beneficiaries of the present tax structure—and its victims as well—do not want it. They will fight it. And those few who would favor such a reform do not have the power to defeat them, are political nullities.

CHAPTER TEN

1. That many of those hailed as philanthropists in the public prints because they have financed foundations have not in their lifetimes shown any love for man in the concrete was pointed out in *America's Sixty Families*, p. 336; some of them ran their industrial plants under cover of machineguns in the hands of certified gangsters. If there was any philanthropic disposition shown in his lifetime by the late Henry Ford, for example, it has escaped the notice of biographers who, indeed, stress opposite inclinations and explicit expressions. If the word has any meaning at all, Ford, like many contemporaries, was as nonphilanthropic as any common man. Yet he established the largest foundation of all!

2. The Stock Exchange firm of Paine, Webber, Jackson & Curtis in its publication, *Charitable Foundations*, N.Y., 1956, pointed out that "Since the charitable foundation may remain under the direction of the creator either directly or indirectly, its assets may be used to complement the general financial activities of the creator while still achieving specific desirable charitable goals."

According to the Commerce Clearing House *Federal Tax Service*, N.Y., July 18, 1962, "Perhaps the greatest advantage [of foundations] is afforded closed corporations. Through the use of a foundation the operator of a closed corporation may be able to keep voting control of the corporation in the family after the death of the principal stockholder. Estate and gift taxes are frequently so high that sale of the stock is necessary in order to pay them, the result being that the family loses control of the corporation. However, the principal stockholder can avoid this result by granting or bequeathing nonvoting stock in the corporation to the foundation. Since such a gift or bequest is deductible for estate or gift tax purposes, the result may be that the taxes will then be small enough so that they can be satisfied out of other estate assets without selling the voting stock." All this is part of standard financial doctrine.

Representative Wright Patman cites (*Tax-Exempt Foundations and Charitable Trusts: Their Impact on Our Economy*, Select Committee on Small Business, House of Representatives, Government Printing Office, 1962, p. 17) broad legal opinion written by Berman & Berman, tax attorneys, in the *Cleveland-Marshall Law Review* to this effect:

What can be accomplished by creating a foundation:

1. Keep control of wealth.
2. Can keep for the donor many attributes of wealth by many means:
   (a) Designating the administrative management of the foundation.
   (b) Control over its investments.
   (c) Appointing relatives as directors of the foundation.
   (d) Foundation's assets can be used to borrow money to buy other property that does not jeopardize its purposes. Thus, foundation funds can be enhanced from the capitalization of its tax exemption.
3. The foundation can keep income in the family.
4. Family foundations can aid employees of the donor's business.
5. Foundations may be the method of insuring that funds will be available for use in new ventures in business.
6. We can avoid income from property while it is slowly being given to a foundation by a combination of a trust and the charitable foundation.
7. We can get the 20 per cent charity deduction in [now 30 per cent—F.L.] other ways:
   (a) By giving away appreciated property to the foundation, we escape a tax on the realization of a gain.
   (b) We can give funds to a foundation to get charitable deduction currently in our most advantageous tax year.

(c) Very often local personal and real property taxes can be avoided.

(d) We can avoid speculative profits.

(e) We can give away valuable frozen assets, white elephant estates, residences, valuable works of art, and collections of all arts.

This general perspective of foundation purposes, as far as the record shows, was most recently prior to the Patman inquiry offered to public view in *America's Sixty Families*, 1937, pp. 320–73. This is basically what foundations are for, not for improving the world and its people.

A more prevalent attitude among the pseudo-knowledgeable is reflected in a report of an unidentified young sociologist quoted by Dwight Macdonald, p. 20, *infra*. "The French seem totally unable to understand the Ford Foundation," he wrote from Paris where he was working on a Ford-financed project. "The 'inside-dopesters' are sure of the explanation of such an otherwise incredible institution—to 'cheat' the government out of tax money. This appears to be the residue of some unfortunate American's effort to explain the relationship of our tax system to the rise of the private foundation. [Note: This thesis was set forth in *America's Sixty Families*, although I cannot be sure I was the "unfortunate American" who carried the tidings to France—F.L.] . . . Some suspect that these foundations are some sort of quasi-official intelligence agencies working for the State Department under cover of scientific respectability." As more recently it has been disclosed in massive detail that foundations as well as universities have widely acted as "covers" for the CIA, it appears that the young sociologist at the time he wrote still had much to learn and the French had their wits about them. Macdonald himself cogently discusses (pp. 42 and 132) the tax-evading features of the foundation and its relation to the tax laws.

The original master source for extended critical analysis of foundations is to be found in the record of hearings and exhibits under Frank P. Walsh of the Commission on Industrial Relations created by act of Congress, August 23, 1912. They are reported in Senate document 415, Vols. VIII and IX, 64th Congress, first session, Government Printing Office, 1916, pp. 7429-8480. Here for more than 1,000 pages were anticipated the broad results found to be the fact in the Patman hearings some fifty years later.

3. For a general analysis of the purely correct empty formalistic character of the so-called social sciences see, for a beginning, *Knowledge for What?* by one of the leading figures in the field, Robert S. Lynd (Princeton University Press, Princeton, N.J., 1939). For penetrating remarks on the uses of historiography as a propagandist part of what he calls "the American celebration," see Mills, *The Power Elite*, pp. 330–36, 411, and also his *The Sociological Imagination*, Evergreen, N.Y., 1961. "The American celebration," in general, uses the Founding Fathers, the Constitution, Daniel Boone, Washington, Jefferson and Lincoln (or whoever is handier) as a background to validate questionable features of the present, which are offered as natural (hence laudable) historical outgrowths. General Motors, thus, is nothing but a later massive institutional version of Benjamin Franklin's interest in applied science and is properly subject to solemn celebration as such. Henry Ford is Daniel Boone writ large in industry. The institutional historians are not financed by foundations to produce books titled "The American Past and Present: A Study in Frightening Contrasts."

4. *Foundation Directory*, p. 10.

5. *Ibid.*, p. 11.

6. *Ibid.*, p. 17.

7. *Ibid.*, p. 13.

8. *Ibid.*, p. 18.

9. Source for all except the terminal clause of this paragraph: *Tax-Exempt Foundations and Charitable Trusts: Their Impact on Our Economy*, Second Installment, Select Committee on Small Business, House of Representatives, October 16,

1963, p. 15. Source for concluding clause, *ibid.*, Third Installment, March 20, 1964, p. iii. The Patman reports are issued under the above title at different dates in three installments. There is also a published transcript of hearings under title of *Tax-Exempt Foundations: Their Impact on Small Business*, U.S. Government Printing Office, 1964. Hereafter references to the first-mentioned series will be to *Patman I*, *Patman II* and *Patman III*. References to the report of hearings will be designated *Patman Hearings*.

10. The most comprehensive public listing of leading foundations and their financial details are found in Schedule 5, *Patman I*, pp. 86–113, many very large but with obscure names such as the Surdna Foundation of New York with stated assets of $60,774,209, the Max C. Fleischmann Foundation of Nevada with assets of $69,038,-632, the Louis W. and Maud Hill Foundation of Minnesota with assets of $59,542,-735, etc.

11. *Patman I*, p. v.

12. *Patman I*, Schedule 2, pp. 38–46.

13. *Ibid.*, pp. 14–15.

14. *Ibid.*, pp. 38–46.

15. *Ibid.*, p. v.

16. *Ibid.*, p. 74.

17. *Ibid.*, p. v.

18. *Ibid.*, p. 4.

19. *Ibid.*, p. 71.

20. *Ibid.*, pp. 114–28.

21. *Ibid.*, pp. 3–5.

22. *Ibid.*, pp. 7–8.

23. *Ibid.*, pp. 8–9.

24. *Ibid.*, pp. 9–11.

25. *Ibid.*, pp. 10–12.

26. *Ibid.*, p. 12.

27. *Ibid.*, p. 16.

28. *Ibid.*, p. 71.

29. *Ibid.*, pp. 129–31.

30. *Ibid.*, pp. 74–77.

31. *Ibid.*, p. 79.

32. *Ibid.*

33. *Ibid.*, p. 80.

34. *Patman II*, p. 19.

35. *Ibid.*, p. 20.

36. *Ibid.*

37. *Ibid.*

38. *Ibid.*, p. 41.

39. *Ibid.*, p. 43.

40. *Ibid.*, pp. 61–88.

41. *Patman III*, p. 1.

42. *Ibid.*

43. *Ibid.*

44. *Ibid.*, p. 2.

45. The foregoing assets and the quotation are cited *ibid.*, pp. 2–3.

46. Dwight Macdonald, *The Ford Foundation: The Men and the Millions*, Reynal & Company, N.Y., 1956, most of which appeared originally in the *New Yorker* in 1955. Mr. Macdonald appends a useful but incomplete bibliography; it does not mention the voluminous report of the United States Industrial Commission, which he discusses briefly in his text (pp. 22–25) nor (necessarily) the later Patman reports. Although he lists some of the periodical literature there is more—for example, an in-

cisively critical article by Abraham Epstein in the *American Mercury*, May, 1931; nor does he list congressional hearings and debate on the bill introduced in 1910 in the Senate that would have granted a federal charter of unrestricted powers to the proposed Rockefeller Foundation, which was chartered under New York laws in 1913. The federal charter plan was buried largely on the basis of a devastating analysis by Jacob Gould Schurman, president of Cornell University and a Carnegie Foundation trustee; Schurman is quoted in *Patman I*, p. 74.

47. Macdonald, p. 178. Mr. Macdonald indicated his belief, mistaken, that foundation secrecy was now all in the past. *Ibid.*, p. 159.

48. *Patman I*, pp. 5–7.

49. *Ibid.*, p. 2.

50. *Ibid.*

51. *Patman II*, p. 6.

52. *Foundation Directory*, 1964, p. 11.

53. *Patman I*, p. 51.

54. *Foundation Directory*, 1964, p. 29.

55. *Ibid.*, p. 30.

56. *New York Times*, April 27, 1966; 28:7.

57. *Ibid.*, September 3, 1964; 10:3–8. More recently the beneficiaries of these eight mysterious foundations were found to be the American Friends of the Middle East, "an anti-Zionist, pro-Arab, organization," and the Cuban Freedom Committee, "sponsor of 'Free Cuba Radio' and certainly the most belligerent anti-Castro radio series broadcast out of this country, whose advisory board includes several galloping right wingers." See Robert G. Sherrill, "Foundation Pipelines: The Beneficent CIA," *The Nation*, May 9, 1966, pp. 542–44. I would disagree that the American Friends of the Middle East is either anti-Zionist or pro-Arab; it is only pro-oil, *pro-finpol*.

58. *Foundation Directory*, p. 35.

59. *Ibid.*, p. 17.

60. *Ibid.*, p. 42.

61. *Ibid.*, p. 41.

62. Macdonald, p. 169.

63. *Ibid.*, p. 16.

64. *Ibid.*, p. 27.

65. *Ibid.*, p. 28.

66. *Ibid.*, p. 29.

67. *Ibid.*, p. 34.

68. See Kolko, *The Triumph . . .* , *passim*.

69. Abraham Flexner, *Funds and Foundations*, Harper and Brothers, N.Y., 1952, pp. 125–41.

70. The inception and development of this report are traced by Macdonald, pp. 137–42.

71. Dwight Macdonald gives good brief accounts of all these activities in their early phases.

72. Macdonald, pp. 148–49.

73. *Ibid.*, p. 117.

74. *Ibid.*, pp. 46–47. Flexner, in *Funds and Foundations*, gives an excellent historical summary of the work of the Carnegie and Rockefeller funds.

75. Macdonald, p. 81.

76. See *America's Sixty Families*, pp. 338–44, for an analysis of the maldistribution of medical advances and an insight into the self-serving character of much medical research on medical problems peculiar or of special interest only to the rich. That the situation is little changed in thirty years can be quickly ascertained from a recent thorough survey, Elinor Langer, "The Shame of American Medicine," *The New York Review*, May 26, 1966, p. 6. See particularly Langer's authoritative bibliography.

77. Lest the careful reader conclude that this deduction of *finpol* support on the basis of the endorsement of one man is brashly drawn from too slender a premise, let it be noticed that President Lyndon B. Johnson toward mid-1966 was given unreserved endorsement by some 100 chairmen and presidents of the largest corporations, constituting the Business Council, a private organization that periodically advises the government on what to do (*New York Times*, May 16, 1966; 1:1). In a follow-up dispatch from Washington, the *Times* (May 22, 1966; IV, 6E, 1–3) reported: "The nation's big business executives, to the surprise of all, including themselves, still love Lyndon Johnson in May as they did a year ago in November. . . . They feel comfortable with him, and they see him often, as they have felt comfortable with no President in their lifetimes; not even General Eisenhower." Widely referred to as "Mr. Johnson's War," Vietnam military intervention nevertheless from the beginning had the virtually unanimous endorsement of Big Business—that is, hereditary *finpolitans*. In reflection of this top-level consensus neither the Republican Party nor the corporate press showed significant opposition, although the Democratic Party was inwardly torn to its vitals. Cued by the corporate press, the sketchily educated masses always, when polled, preponderantly expressed loyal support for the president, who was widely reported to be agonized at all the destruction of life he was obliged out of a high sense of dedicated duty to be responsible for. Mr. Johnson, the press made clear, suffered far more than the troops in the field or the Vietnamese people and, it is reported, tragically had to resort to copious doses of tranquillizers.

78. *Patman I*, pp. 133–35.

79. *New York Times*, August 19, 1967; 42:3.

CHAPTER ELEVEN

1. Arch Patton, *Men, Money and Motivation*, McGraw-Hill Book Company, N.Y., 1961, p. 39.

2. "Cormorant," *Encyclopedia Britannica*, Vol. 6, 1958, p. 449.

3. *New York Times*, July 31, 1965; 25:2.

4. Mills, *The Power Elite*, p. 282.

5. *Ibid.*, pp. 288–91.

6. The idea of a privileged managerial elite apparently traces back to *The Mental Worker*, Geneva, 1905, by Waclaw Machajski, a Polish Marxist who asserted that eliminating capitalists would "substitute for the capitalists a class of hereditary soft-handed intellectuals, who would perpetuate the slavery of the manual workers and their offspring." (Quoted by Max Nomad, *Rebels and Renegades*, The Macmillan Co., N.Y., 1932, p. 208). This happened under Leninism with the rise of a privileged bureaucracy of nonowners, as shown by Milovan Djilas, *The New Class*, Praeger, N.Y., 1957. But capitalism, too, it seems, had its managerial elite, who were elbowing the owners aside just as the Communist managerial elite elbowed the ever-deserving workers. This thesis was argued with much flourishing of statistical tables by A. A. Berle, Jr., and Gardiner C. Means in *The Modern Corporation and Private Property*, The Macmillan Company, N.Y., 1933. Management control, said Berle-Means, is strongly tending to displace ownership control, p. 124 and *passim*. As later shown in TNEC Monograph #29 this was not so, although the thesis, once stated, turned out to have a fascinating life of its own. The notion was popularized and greatly extended by James Burnham, *The Managerial Revolution*, The John Day Co., N.Y., 1941, and was extended over even larger areas by C. Wright Mills; it was always at variance with ascertainable facts. Leninist societies are obviously directed by managers; there are no owners apart from the state. In a capitalist society there are owners, and their ranks are limited to a few of power and consequence in the United States. These owners are not only free of rule by their own managers but have as much

to say over the temporary political managers in the long run as the political managers have over them in the short run. Nonowning managers have little independent power in this situation; they have no independent power base.

7. Mills, *The Power Elite*, p. 277.

8. *Ibid.*, p. 346.

9. *Wall Street Journal*, May 26, 1966; 1:6.

10. Patton, p. 198.

11. Osborn Elliott, pp. 21–23.

12. David R. Roberts, *Executive Compensation*, The Free Press, Glencoe, Ill., 1959, pp. 115–16.

13. *Ibid.*, pp. 130–31.

14. *Ibid.*, p. 129.

15. *Ibid.*

16. Daniel Bell, pp. 40–41.

17. *Ibid.*, p. 42.

18. W. Lloyd Warner and James C. Abegglen, *Big Business Leaders in America*, Harper and Brothers, N.Y., 1955. This book is based on a more fundamental study by the same authors, *Occupational Mobility in American Business and Industry, 1928–1952*, University of Minnesota Press, Minneapolis, 1955. Methods and techniques used are fully discussed in this latter work.

19. Warner and Abegglen, *Big Business Leaders . . .* , p. 15.

20. *Ibid.*, p. 48.

21. *Ibid.*, pp. 50–51.

22. *Ibid.*, p. 51.

23. *Ibid.*, p. 57.

24. *Ibid.*, p. 210.

25. *Ibid.*, p. 211.

26. *Ibid.*, pp. 215–16.

27. *Ibid.*, pp. 214–15.

28. *Ibid.*, p. 111.

29. *Ibid.*, pp. 225–26.

30. Alan Harrington, *Life in the Crystal Palace*, Alfred A. Knopf, N.Y., 1959, p. 12.

31. *Ibid.*, p. 39.

32. *Ibid.*, p. 71.

33. *Ibid.*, p. 96.

34. *Ibid.*, p. 209.

35. *Summary of American Science Manpower*, 1964, National Register of Scientific and Technical Personnel, National Science Foundation, Washington, D.C., March, 1966, p. 1.

36. *Ibid.*

37. *Ibid.*

38. *New York Times*, December 18, 1965; 1:3; February 8, 1966; 1:3–4.

39. *New York Times Magazine*, May 15, 1966, pp. 50–51.

40. "Can Executives Be Taught to Think?" *Fortune*, May, 1953.

41. Joint Economic Committee for the Council of Economic Advisers, *Economic Indicators*, May, 1966, U.S. Government Printing Office, p. 5.

42. *Wall Street Journal*, June 21, 1966; 12:3.

43. Dr. Turfboer's analysis appeared originally in *Sales Management, the Magazine of Marketing* and was largely reproduced in *The National Observer*, May 31, 1965; 18:1–2.

44. *New York Times*, July 18, 1965; III, 5:4.

45. Mabel Newcomer, *The Big Business Executive: The Factors That Made Him, 1900–1950*, Columbia University Press, N.Y., 1955, p. 149.

46. *Ibid.*, p. 151.

CHAPTER TWELVE

1. *Statistical Abstract, 1965*, p. 384.
2. *Ibid.*, p. 386.
3. *Ibid.*
4. *Ibid.*, p. 385.
5. Quoted by Joseph S. Clark, *Congress: The Sapless Branch*, Harper and Row, N.Y., 1964, p. 32. Senator Clark initiated his public analysis with *The Senate Establishment*, Hill and Wang, N.Y., 1963. Hereafter these books are cited as *Congress* and *Senate*.
6. *Congress*, p. 17.
7. *Ibid.*, p. 20.
8. *Ibid.*, pp. 22–23.
9. *New York Times*, April 11, 1965; IV, 6:4.
10. Richard L. Madden, Martin J. Steadman and associates, in the *New York Herald Tribune*, August 5–18, 1963; the series of articles titled "Our Sideline Legislators," dealt at considerable length and in detail with the entrepreneurial and suspect pecuniary activities of leading members of the New York State Legislature, the second most powerful legislative body in the western hemisphere. A great deal of sordid under-the-counter stuff—such as the acquisition by gift or at a bargain of interests in banks, insurance companies, loan companies, etc., that either did business with the state or obtained special favors from it—was found on every hand. The series should be read by students of government as a model of what goes on in all the state legislatures and as showing what the true interests are of average American politicians. Their last interest, it should be asserted, is the proper operation of government. The *Harvard Law Review*, April, 1963, published an important long, unsigned article titled "Conflicts of Interest of State Legislators."
11. Austin Ranney and Wilmoore Kendall, *Democracy and the American Party System*, Harcourt, Brace & Co., N.Y., 1956, pp. 157–66.
12. *Congress*, p. 112.
13. *Ibid.*, pp. 112–13.
14. *Ibid.*
15. *Ibid.*, p. 212.
16. V. O. Key, *Politics, Parties and Pressure Groups*, Crowell, N.Y., 1958, p. 347.
17. Drew Pearson, "Washington Merry-Go-Round: Congressmen's Clients," *New York Post*, June 22, 1966, p. 46.
18. *Congress*, p. 114.
19. *Ibid.*, p. 173.
20. *Ibid.*, pp. 186–87.
21. *New York Times*, July 15, 1965; 10:1.
22. *Congress*, p. 118.
23. *Ibid.*
24. *Ibid.*, p. 119.
25. *Ibid.*, p. 189.
26. *Ibid.*
27. *Ibid.*, p. 191.
28. *Ibid.*, p. 192.
29. *Senate, passim.* For two whole days Senator Clark doggedly presented his objective analysis on the floor of the Senate, subject to correction and emendation by other senators. Except for niggling about some minor points by Senators Long and Mansfield, the Establishment made no effort at refutation. Indeed, Clark's presentation was irrefutable. It cited the cold record throughout.
30. *Congress*, p. 183.

31. *Ibid.*, p. 181.
32. *Senate*, p. 105.
33. Eisenstein, p. 215.
34. *Ibid.*, p. 216.
35. *Ibid.*, pp. 216–17.
36. *Ibid.*, p. 218.
37. *Ibid.*, p. 220.
38. Stanley S. Surrey, "The Federal Income Tax Base for Individuals," *Columbia Law Review*, 815, 829; 1958. Cited by Eisenstein, p. 220.
39. Eisenstein, p. 126.
40. *Ibid.*
41. *Ibid.*, p. 200.
42. *Ibid.*, pp. 203–4.
43. From words such as "majority," "almost all," "nearly all" or "with few exceptions" in what follows, the reader should not conclude that the text reflects some *a priori* bias against Congress. It is the consensus of seasoned down-to-earth observers on the point made here that most congressmen garner incomes ranging far above their salaries. As stated in the *New York Herald Tribune*, June 16, 1965; 10:7–8, "The great majority of Congressmen combine public service with private profit. They earn outside incomes from private business and professions, despite their $30,000-a-year income, plus expenses and lavish fringe benefits." Many other highly respectable sources could be cited for the same conclusion.
44. *New York Herald Tribune*, June 11, 1965; 16:1.
45. *Ibid.*
46. *Ibid.*, June 13, 1965; 14:1.
47. *Ibid.*, June 10, 1965; 1:5.
48. *Ibid.*, June 15, 1965; 10.
49. *Ibid.*, June 13, 1965; 14:1.
50. *Ibid.*
51. *Ibid.*, June 13, 1965; 14.
52. *Ibid.*, June 14, 1965.
53. *Ibid.*
54. *Wall Street Journal*, August 11, 1964; 1:6.
55. *New York Herald Tribune*, June 10, 1965; 1:5.
56. *New York Times*, September 12, 1965; 46:1.
57. *New York Herald Tribune*, June 14, 1965.
58. *Ibid.*, June 10, 1965.
59. *Ibid.*
60. *Ibid.*, June 14, 1965.
61. *Ibid.*, June 15, 1965.
62. *Ibid.*
63. *Ibid.*
64. *Ibid.*
65. *New York Post*, June 7, 1966; 34:3–5.
66. *Ibid.*, June 22, 1966; 46:3–5.
67. *Ibid.*
68. *Ibid.*, April 29, 1966; 46:3–5.
69. Philadelphia *Evening Bulletin*, December 18, 1965.
70. *New York Post*, April 25, 1966; 32:3–5.
71. *Wall Street Journal*, July 14, 1966; 1:6.
72. *New York Times*, July 7, 1966; 3:2–3.
73. *New York Herald Tribune*, June 16, 1965.
74. The reader who wants to acquaint himself with the historical background of campaign collecting should consult Louise Overacker, *Money in Elections*, The

Macmillan Co., N.Y., 1932; and *Presidential Campaign Funds*, Boston University Press, 1946; and Jasper B. Shannon, *Money and Politics*, Random House, N.Y., 1959. There have also been many fully recorded congressional investigations and many informal writings on the same subject.

75. *New York Times*, October 27, 1964; 31:4.

76. Donald R. Matthews, *U.S. Senators and Their World*, The University of North Carolina Press, Chapel Hill, 1960, p. 19.

77. *Ibid.*, p. 15.

78. *Ibid.*, p. 14.

79. *Ibid.*, pp. 15–17.

80. *Ibid.*, p. 19.

81. *Ibid.*, p. 20.

82. *Ibid.*, p. 21.

83. *Ibid.*, p. 282.

84. *Ibid.*, p. 283.

85. *Ibid.*, pp. 25–26.

86. *New York Times*, May 3, 1962; 1:1.

87. On the score of poor boys in politics there are those who will say that the Senate was most corrupt prior to the popular election of senators when rich men fairly openly bought their seats from pliant state legislatures and the Senate was widely known as "The Millionaire's Club." To this I reply: Every one of the indubitably corrupt pre-1913 millionaire senators was a self-erected poor boy, and many were functionally illiterate. A poor (or rich) boy in politics who has not been subjected to a great deal of educational correction or who has not devoted himself to a great deal of intellectual self-improvement (as Lincoln did) is as dangerous to the public, the poor included, as a rattlesnake. Melancholy though it is to record, it is a fact that could be shown by thousands of pointed instances, with few in exception. After forty years of close observation, whenever I hear of the poverty-stricken beginnings of some candidate, unless the record also shows some considerable successful intellectual strivings on his part, alarm bells start going off throughout my nervous system. The odds, I know, are overwhelming that he is no Lincoln or even Truman, is more probably another Dirksen or Johnson.

CHAPTER THIRTEEN

1. The literature of merely recent monopoly is so vast that the reader is referred to the central index of the Library of Congress, the New York Public Library, the Widener and Baker libraries at Harvard University and to other metropolitan and university libraries. "When the supply of a product is controlled so that purchasers cannot buy it elsewhere and are forced to meet the terms of sale laid down by the owner, a monopoly exists," according to the definition of monopoly in the one-volume *Columbia Encyclopedia*. The English common law has long outlawed all monopolies except those expressly conferred by the state, and since 1624 Parliament has greatly curtailed state monopolies. That we in the United States live under huge private-profit monopolies anyone can readily ascertain by noticing the uniform regional pricing of identical and nearly identical commodities and services, the prices set by manufacturers and enforced through privately licensed dealers, and by noticing the high rates of return of the sellers. Prices are not set by market interplay or bargaining, according to conventional economic theory, but are dictated and frozen by the cartelized sellers. A recent penetrating analysis of American monopoly is *Monopoly Capital* by Paul A. Baran and Paul M. Sweezy, Monthly Review Press, N.Y., 1966. Embodying a neo-Marxist approach, it would be intellectually more satisfying if it brought Soviet Russia and China under its critical guns as instances of obvious state-monopoly capitalism.

As it is, the writers regard Soviet Russia as on the road to a free Utopia of the common man, a sad delusion. If the whole book were recast in the following tenor, where words in brackets have been added by me, it would in my view gain in intellectual stature: "It is not that armed force under capitalism [and sovietism] is used only in the international sphere. In every capitalist [and soviet] country, it is used to dispossess, repress, and otherwise control the domestic labor force." (P. 179.) And so on. Nevertheless, this book is an excellent tough-minded analysis of *American* monopoly as a whole, disregarding the *ex parte* references to international capitalism as though the term excluded the Soviet bloc and China (and with such exclusion all normal wickedness from these entities), and its attribution of all social difficulties to capitalism.

2. Albert Z. Carr, *John D. Rockefeller's Secret Weapon*, McGraw-Hill Book Co., N.Y., 1962, p. 62.

3. The literature on Rockefeller and Standard Oil is extensive; every general book on the subjects contains an extensive bibliography. Virtually all follow the original pattern laid down by Ida M. Tarbell in *The History of the Standard Oil Company*, originally published in 1904 after magazine serialization, republished from the original plates in 1925 by The Macmillan Company and still the basic study in the field. The most pretentious resurvey of the same field is Professor Allan Nevins's *Study in Power*, an unconvincing public-relations attempt to touch up or explain away as many as possible blemishes exposed by Tarbell in her brief for the prosecution. Although ostentatiously flaunting all the outward trappings of demure scholarship and widely offered by libraries on their open shelves as a standard reference work, a signal-flare for the serious student must be sent up on the Nevins study, which is thematically inconsistent and in various places consists of very thin ice or no ice at all. A single instance from among many: Professor Nevins writes of Tarbell, p. 341, Vol. II, "She treated rebating as the special sin of the Standard, not as an almost universal practice, with her much-praised independents as eager to get rebates as anybody." This statement, among various others by Nevins on crucial matters, is blatantly false because Tarbell scrupulously points out, repeatedly, that rebating was a general practice, with Rockefeller as the biggest shipper owing to his secret combination getting the biggest rebates. In the identical 1904 and 1925 editions, p. 101, Vol. I, Tarbell writes: "Of course Mr. Rockefeller must have known that the railroad was a common carrier, and that the common law forbade discrimination. But he knew that the railroads had regularly granted special rates and rebates to those who had large amounts of freight. That is, you were able to bargain with the railroads as you did with a man carrying on a strictly private business depending in no way on a public franchise." She explicitly dwells on the point again in Vol. I, pp. 33–34, 48–49, 52, 119, 132–33 and 152. Rockefeller went further than this and demanded, and received, secret "draw-backs" and "rake-offs" on shipping payments of competitors—a point that still retrospectively annoys many otherwise sympathetic businessmen who are willing to concede him his rebates as just ordinary smart business. He made money, in brief, on the shipments of others, without their knowledge! Nevins, developing a Madison Avenue pettifogger's defense brief at every point he can for Rockefeller, presents Tarbell's as an excellent pioneering but biased and shakily evidential study; yet most of his accusations along this line are seen upon reference to the heavily documented Tarbell text to be false or misleading. However, the Tarbell account is by no means complete or balanced, because she wrote about a largely, until then, secret operation. But even when facts withheld from Tarbell are in part revealed as in the cooperation of the successor Standard Oil Company of New Jersey with the writing of *Pioneering in Big Business: 1882–1911* by Ralph W. and Muriel Hidy, Harper and Bros., N.Y., 1955, there is plenty of room for complaint about incompleteness and lack of balance. The Hidys confine their discussion of Standard Oil's political activities to 7 out of 839 pages (pp. 205, 213, 663–670), gingerly touching upon such bold subversion of the formal political process as they are unable to deny.

By way of exculpating Rockefeller, the Hidys plead that the practices were quite general, institutionalized and not unique to Standard Oil. Nevins adopts the same line with respect to Rockefeller. Nearly everybody was doing it and, as we have seen, is still in one way or the other doing it. With this I agree. Rockefeller neither made nor dishonored a loose system ready-made for his purposes; he simply harmonized with it to a superlative degree. It was partly for this reason that he was made to bear the brunt of the purely verbal attack against it.

4. See Tarbell, I, pp. 56, 58, 70–71; II, pp. 112–19 and *passim*.

5. *Ibid.*, II, pp. 145–46.

6. Carr, pp. 109–10.

7. Tarbell, II, p. 264.

8. *Ibid.*, II, 112.

9. H. L. Mencken, *A New Dictionary of Quotations*, A. A. Knopf, N.Y., p. 1159.

10. *Ibid.*

11. See a succinct defense of intelligence tests by David Wechsler, professor of clinical psychology at New York University School of Medicine, the *New York Times Magazine*, June 26, 1966, p. 12, under the title "The I. Q. Is an Intelligent Test." The literature on the subject is large. IQ tests are used by intelligent people and institutions for intelligible purposes. What the IQ measures is the ability to discern distinctions rapidly and accurately. Rapidity may be overstressed. Colleges generally have found that, although good test results do not invariably foreshadow academic success, in conjunction with past good academic performance and cooperative attitude they broadly point at least to academic success in a great majority of cases. Adverse emotional experiences, it is known, may mar a predicted and extrapolated high performance pattern. The General Education Test alluded to in the text was, as a matter of fact, not very thorough-going and did reflect cultural factors, to the detriment of the culturally deprived. What makes that test worth citing as suggestive, however, is the large group exposed to it, enabling one to hypothesize that a more finely articulated test individually applied to as many cases would show broadly similar relative results in accordance with the law of distribution of characteristics in large groups.

12. Frank R. Kent, *Political Behavior*, William Morrow and Company, N.Y., 1928, p. 8.

13. Seymour Martin Lipset, *Political Man*, Doubleday & Co., N.Y., 1960, p. 184, and Chapter 4.

14. See Frank R. Kent, *The Great Game of Politics*, Doubleday, Page & Co., N.Y., 1923, Chapter II, "Why the Primaries Are More Important Than the General Election."

15. Matthews, p. 34.

16. *Ibid.*, p. 36.

17. Moses Rischin, *Our Own Kind—Voting by Race, Creed or National Origin*, The Fund for the Republic, N.Y., 1960.

18. In *Political Man*, pp. 285–309, Professor Lipset analyzes voting in the United States by social classes, pinpointing the social bases of the electorate, and he has no difficulty in showing that the lower classes have tended strongly "leftward" by voting for the Democratic Party, both before and after 1932. Such a strictly European use of the left-right differentiation is definitely misleading, however; impassable barriers on each side are firmly established by basic law and court decision. Neither party, nor any party, can move beyond a certain point soon reached without a change in the Constitution and its interpretation, and *radical constitutional change is not on the program of either party*. What is *counted* as leftism and rightism is clearly important here. At its most extreme, leftism in the economic realm calls for the abolition of privately owned productive property and in the political sphere for unrestricted political and civil liberty. Economically, Russian and Chinese Communism conform formally to the leftist prescription completely, but politically and culturally they are as far to

the right as Nero, Hitler and Caligula (a circumstance confusing to many). In other than Leninist revisions of Marxist leftism, only basic industries are to be government-owned, with or without due compensation to the owners, or productive property is to be owned collectively by unions or *syndicates* composing the labor force: syndicalism. None of this has anything whatever to do with the Democratic Party. At least in their proselytizing stages, all leftist groups strongly stress individual civil and political liberties, which are suppressed as ruthless political managers, as in the Soviet and Chinese blocs, take over the direction of putative collective ownership. No even faintly libertarian noncapitalist regime has yet emerged anywhere. As to producing basic change by peaceful processes, which even the great, great Founding Fathers were unable to do, it is often pointed out that extreme leftists, mainly Communists, under free choice have never won an election; note is not taken, on the other hand, that anti-Communists have never won an election in a Communist country. Who controls and lays down the rules of the electoral system obviously determines at least the broad out-come of elections. The Communists win under their rules by requiring people to vote only one way. The capitalists win under their rules by allowing everybody and any-body to vote or not, knowing that the mass is confused and at odds within itself. Those who seek by the electoral process, socialism, or any other basic change, obviously recommend a procedure that has slight likelihood of ever succeeding. When leftists seem on the way to achieving such change by fair electoral means, they are simply suppressed by military force, as in Spain and elsewhere. And as elected Socialists were once thrown out of the New York State Legislature.

As to rightism, the furthest right any considerable thought yet extends in the United States is to require much less government intervention in social and economic affairs, leaving the field clear to money-chasing entrepreneurs as prior to 1932. Then workers, possibly forbidden to organize and strike, can again be paid a purely subsistence wage, and small entrepreneurs can become affluent. While sufficiently rightist this prospect is not very far right—say to the possible point of institutionalizing arrangements in a Corporate State of formalized working serfs with few civil liberties. Here would be a pure private capitalist counterpart to Soviet Russia and China. When it comes to seeing leftism in the New Deal one must grasp at straws. TVA, true enough, is govern-ment enterprise; hence presumably leftist. But it supplies unusually cheap power to a host of private-profit industries, surely not leftism. The labor laws, establishing the large unions, are also seen by some as leftism. But leftists themselves, such as Socialists, who ought to know left from right, claim that these laws made the union into cooper-ative adjuncts of the large corporations, whose general policies the unions endorse. Social Security is often cited as an example of New Deal leftism. Yet, upon examina-tion it is nothing but collective forced insurance for old age, wholly at popular ex-pense, which most of the population was incapable of accomplishing for itself. Many voters, it is true, believe they are voting left when they vote Democratic, "the party of the common people." Thus "leftist" immigrant groups, as Lipset notes but fails to ponder, voted for Wilson in 1916 on the ground that he kept the country out of war. Yet immediately upon his re-election Wilson rushed the unwilling country into World War I on falsely stated grounds, which is precisely what rightists and "pro-gressives" like Theodore Roosevelt, William Howard Taft and Charles Evans Hughes intended to do. Again, many self-styled leftists voted for Democratic Lyndon B. John-son in 1964 because, a man of peaceful palaver, he said he had no intention of making war in Vietnam. Yet even as he protested, Johnson was readying forces faster than Republican Barry Goldwater promised to do—immediately. Johnson's intervention, with no declaration of war from Congress, was swiftly endorsed by Richard M. Nixon, Barry Goldwater, Nelson A. Rockefeller and other Republicans.

Professor Lipset makes quite a point of arguing that the major parties are far from identical, as often charged. He is right, but for reasons other than he gives. First, when the chips are down, on major issues, there is usually no serious dispute between the two parties; they tend to define each situation as one or the other faction of big property holders defines it. As part of his untenable thesis that they are really upper- and lower-class parties, Lipset cites the fact (p. 287) that "based on interviews with a systematic sample of one thousand such men, [it was] found that even within this upper economic group, the larger the company of which a man was an officer, the greater the likelihood that he was a Republican." As he showed, in the largest corporations 84 per cent of the executives voted Republican. Professor Lipset unaccountably leaves the story hanging there after citing the true observation of Charles Beard that *the center of gravity* of wealth is with the Republicans, of poverty with the Democrats. Professor Lipset never cites the overshadowing, eye-filling, knock-down fact of consistently large campaign contributions. If science should take account of all relevant factors, this is surely odd social science as applied to politics. When one looks to campaign contributions *at any time*, one finds the heavy money backing *both* parties and sometimes the same interests contributing impartially both ways. Company executives may vote preponderantly Republican, thereby displaying respectability, but many of the largest stockholders contribute huge sums to the Democrats; and in wealthy families some toss big money one way, some another way. Their respectability assured, these elements need not make public ritual displays. Thus in 1928 when tenement-born, proletarian, Irish Catholic, man-of-the-people, friend-of-all-races, down-to-earth, plain-talking Alfred E. Smith reached for the presidency on the Democratic ticket as boobs cheered and jeered, some of his leading campaign contributors were William F. Kenny, president of the W. F. Kenny Contracting Company ($125,000); multi-millionaire Thomas Fortune Ryan; John J. Raskob of Du Pont and General Motors, and banker Herbert H. Lehman ($110,000 each); Jesse H. Jones, Texas multi-millionaire banker and wheeler-dealer ($75,000); multi-millionaire Pierre S. du Pont; multi-millionaire Harry Payne Whitney (Standard Oil); and M. J. Meehan, razzle-dazzle stockmarket manipulator ($50,000 each); Bernard Baruch ($37,590); Robert Sterling Clark and William H. Todd, shipbuilder ($35,000 each); John D. Ryan, chairman of Anaconda Copper ($27,000); and $25,000 each from Nicholas Brady, public utility tycoon; Francis P. Garvan of Allied Chemical; Peter O. Gerry, Rhode Island political millionaire whose ancestor inspired the term "to gerrymander"; Oliver Cabana, president of the Liquid Veneer Corporation; Arthur Curtiss James, millionaire railroad operator whose estate ultimately came to $96 million; Edith A. Lehman of the banking family; George W. Loft, candy entrepreneur and stock market operator; Nicholas M. Schenck, movie producer; William H. Woodin, director of General Motors and president of the American Car and Foundry Company; and many similar rich "fat cats." (See *America's Sixty Families*, pp. 179–80.) This was neither a leftist nor lower class crowd. Nor was it a crowd that usually spent its money under misapprehensions of the nature of the transaction. It was not even preponderantly Catholic. A similar line-up for the Democrats appears in every election; and behind Lyndon B. Johnson stand as heavy contributors big-rich Sid Richardson, Clint Murchison, H. L. Hunt, billed as "the richest man in the world," and the rest of the post-1920 Texas depletion-allowance oil crowd plus many more of the current big-money operators such as government-contractor George Brown of Brown and Root, Inc. All are deft soft-shoe dancers when it comes to taxes. As the point seems to give difficulty even to big-league professors, it should be explained that the sole genuine difference between the two parties in their social bases is that from the top down the Republican Party is the party of established people, and the Democratic Party (except for traditional professional Democrats) the party of persons of greater relative newness and insecurity of position—economic, political and cultural. Old-rich tend to be Republican; new-rich Democratic. Old-established in the farm belt, the small towns and the white-collar circuits tend to be Republican; newcomers in the cities tend to be Democrats. Persons with insecurity of position, no matter how wealthy, need more room for maneuver; they are more dependent on flexibility of public policy in securing their personal interests and even safety. Such being their position they also need popular votes, hence party flexibility before the public. They will concede an inch to gain a mile whereas Republicans have often fought for an inch and lost a mile. But to interpret such differences in terms of revolutionary and counter-revolutionary European politics is entirely misleading and fails to show the true dead-center nature of American two-party politics. It is often pointed out that all the changes suggested in the Socialist platform of 1900 except government production have been enacted into law and are now operative. Is this leftism? I would say hardly because all reasonable reforms (though many unimaginative conservatives would not agree) benefit the existing system, strengthen the basic established position. Thus women's suffrage, fought for madly by leftists, opposed bitterly by conservatives, was finally legalized. Then it was found that the women's vote was a great conservative political force because women, basically unadventurous, tend very strongly to vote for the *status quo*. Many conservatives, too, were violently opposed to government regulation of corporations. But such regulation, always tender, proved to be a conservative boon. See Kolko, *The Triumph of Conservatism*.

19. Pete Hamill, "Man of the People," *New York Post*, August 26, 1966, pp. 5, 45.

20. Matthews, p. 79.

21. *Ibid.*

22. Drew Pearson, *New York Post*, May 27, 1966; p. 46.

23. Sylvia Porter, "16,000,000 'Near Poor,'" *New York Post*, June 9, 1966; p. 46.

24. *Statistical Abstract, 1964*, p. 112.

25. High-level criticisms of American formal education are numerous and caustic. For the evidence see: Theodore Caplow and Reece J. McGee, *The Academic Market Place*, Basic Books, N.Y., 1958; James B. Conant, *The American High School Today*, McGraw-Hill Book Company, N.Y., 1959, and *Slums and Suburbs: A Commentary on Schools in Metropolitan Areas*, McGraw-Hill, N.Y., 1961; Paul Woodring, *A Fourth of a Nation*, McGraw-Hill Book Company, N.Y., 1957; Nevitt Sanford (ed.), *The American College*, John Wiley & Sons, N.Y., 1962; Arthur E. Bestor, *Educational Wastelands*, Alfred A. Knopf, N.Y., 1953; Robert M. Hutchins, *The Higher Learning in America*, Yale University Press, New Haven, 1936; Thorstein Veblen, *The Higher Learning in America*, B. W. Heubsch, N.Y., 1918; Ralph Lazarus, *We Can Have Better Schools*, Committee on Economic Development, N.Y., 1960; H. G. Rickover, *Education and Freedom*, E. P. Dutton, N.Y., 1959; Mortimer Smith, *The Diminished Mind*, H. Regnery Co., Chicago, 1954; *et al.* For a sharp neo-Marxist summation see Baran and Sweezy, pp. 305–35.

26. James A. Perkins, "Foreign Aid and the Brain Drain," *Foreign Affairs*, July, 1966, p. 617.

27. *New York Times*, September 16, 1966; 1:8.

28. Baran and Sweezy in *Monopoly Capital* (pp. 170–73) make the excellent point that the United States really has two school systems—a good one to produce personnel almost sufficient for the operation of the society in the interests of private profit and a poor one. The good one consists of the topflight secular private colleges and universities, secular private schools and the public elementary and high schools of the better suburbs; the poor one, except for state universities designed to catch straggling lower-class potential high-level performers, consists of everything else. The division is indirectly secured by fastening the burden of school support on each penny-pinching philistine local community, thus "respecting" local autonomy, and by "respecting" religious convictions by allowing religionists glorious freedom to trap their helpless children in inferior schools. While billions of dollars are appropriated for the building of more automobile roads, thereby catering to a highly profitable industry that directly and indirectly accounts for about 20 per cent of the economy, there is adamant resistance to federal appropriations for floundering schools. As these writers

skillfully point out, the favored automobile complex is not only in large measure wasteful of resources but is severely destructive socially in its effects of air pollution, urban congestion, traffic jams, noise and confusion, high accident rate (50,000 dead annually, 1,500,000 killed since the introduction of the automobile), proliferation of garages, parking lots and filling stations, and undermining the efficient alternative of railroads. In pointing to the disreputable state of housing in the United States (pp. 289–300) these same writers do not take note of the fact that popular expenditure which should have been directed into healthful housing has been enticed to the destructive automobile. Every rat-infested slum—a point Marxists do not note—has its streets lined, day and night, with automobiles, many of them late models and of the more expensive types. There are so many that one can instantly discern that they cannot all belong to landlords, local politicos, dope peddlers and procurers. Many families in the United States that live substandard nevertheless own cars, often good ones, which they have purchased on the installment plan, meanwhile denying themselves many amenities. The American automobile is a toy for people who are properly evaluated as boobs or as mentally handicapped. It represents an enormous misallocation of resources for largely frivolous purposes. The same elements often have, also, TV and radio sets, etc.

29. I use the term "democratic system" as presented in Henry Mayo, *An Introduction to Democratic Theory*, Oxford University Press, N.Y., 1960, especially in his Chapter IV. That is, I take it merely as a method of choosing and installing policymakers without reference to the quality either of policy or the underlying society.

30. Baran and Sweezy, p. 155, quote Karl Marx on the "contradiction" inherent in a specific democratic electoral system. Writing of the democratic French constitution of 1848, Marx said: "The most comprehensive contradiction of this constitution consisted in the following: the classes whose social slavery the constitution is to perpetuate—proletariat, peasants, petty bourgeois—it puts in possession of political power through universal suffrage. And from the class whose social power it sanctions, the bourgeoisie, it withdraws the political guarantees of this power. It forces its rule into democratic conditions, which at every point help the hostile classes to victory and jeopardize the very foundations of bourgeois society." (Marx, *The Class Struggles in France: 1848–1850*, International Publishers, N.Y., 1934, pp. 69–70.) Whatever contradiction there is here represents a contradiction with Marx's theory that the "exploited classes" are exploited through arrangements deliberately contrived against them, either consciously or unconsciously. Yet an open electoral system has never been construed as contrived against the lower classes. Such a system, as Marx noted, gives these classes the means to victory, enables them by their vote to "jeopardize the very foundations of bourgeois society." Yet these lower classes, both in the United States and Europe, have never shown the slightest inclination to use their franchise to replace existing institutions with institutions more favorable to their own comfort, convenience and necessity. They cannot even obtain an equitable tax system, do not even realize that they live under a grossly inequitable tax system that ridiculously favors "the bourgeoisie." The missing ingredient in the lower classes is knowledge, understanding and, above all, *determination* to work at all times to secure their own interests. They childishly expect some political good fairy to do this for them, and thus stand forth as *dependents*. Although many conservatives originally opposed the popular franchise on the ground that the populace would vote all wealth into its own hands, experience has shown that this fear was ungrounded—so much so that the dominant political-economic classes are now literally forcing the franchise upon people to whom the whole idea is utterly bewildering and repugnant as in South Vietnam and elsewhere. The people, thus far at least, have been no more able to master the open electoral system than to master calculus or classical Greek. It is still, not only in the United States but also in England and France, quite beyond their powers. They do not even know where to begin, or what to do when, as and if they begin, nor what

specifically to aim for after they start doing something. They are at sea in their own confusion, entangled in their own entrails.

31. This aspect of the market is shown not only in such matters as built-in obsolescence and arbitrary style changes to insure rapid turnover (for the profit of the supplier) but also in many arrangements supposedly catering to public convenience and comfort but really more or less unpleasant.

32. Baran and Sweezy, p. 389. The reader new to Marxism will find a balanced critical analysis in Henry B. Mayo, *Introduction to Marxist Theory*, Oxford University Press, N.Y., 1960.

33. As Baran and Sweezy supply lucid justifications for regarding these components as economic waste, drawing on a large number of entirely conservative economists for support, I do not reproduce any part of their arguments, although the reader should remember I do not agree that institutional arrangements determine what happens in society and how people act and think. This fundamental Marxist credo, were it true, would have made impossible Marx's own sharp economic analysis and *non sequitur* political programming, which goes against the grain of established institutions.

34. E. H. Chamberlin, *The Theory of Monopolistic Competition*, Harvard University Press, Cambridge, Mass., 1931, p. 119. Cited by Baran and Sweezy, p. 117.

35. In the teaching of logic and semantics for many years at New York University I required elementary classes as an exercise to apply techniques they had learned to common advertisements with a view to finding, if they could, a single intellectually sound ad. Apart from purely notificatory advertisements of the nonpersuasive variety, no student was ever able to produce an ad that the classes did not utterly demolish analytically. All ads submitted were either untrue, misleading or nonsensical in the sense of speaking of round squares, finely rounded squares and the most finely rounded squarish rounds.

36. Baran and Sweezy, p. 108. The interested reader is referred to Baran and Sweezy for arguments and data sources. They, like other socialists, are convinced there would be a better utilization of resources under socialism, a purely conjectural notion. They also, unlike many socialists, consider the anti-libertarian state capitalism of Soviet Russia to be socialism, with bureaucratic types such as Gromyko, Kosygin, Brezhnev and Khrushchev more reliable world influences than the Rockefellers, Du Ponts, Fords, Mellons *et al.*, against whose agencies they are openly pitted in many parts of the world. A virtue of these latter as against the former, however, is that they do not make life miserable for artists like Boris Pasternak and cultural creators in general. At most they may ignore them. The Russian "socialist" official believes he has the right to total intervention in the life and thought of even superior types of individuals and acts upon that belief with all the power of state institutions—all in the overpowering name of socialism. Naturally, others than artists and thinkers are subjected to the same sort of heavy-handed, bovine repression, including ordinary workers in the mass. In their often percipient analysis of the American system Baran and Sweezy bring to bear an ethical value base they do not apply to the Soviet Union, as when they say truly (p. 209) that "militarization fosters all the reactionary and irrational forces in society, and inhibits or kills everything progressive and humane. Blind respect is engendered for authority; attitudes of docility and conformity are taught and enforced; dissent is treated as unpatriotic or even treasonable." Yet it is in the militarized Soviet Union rather than the United States that we see enforced to the hilt blind respect for authority, the inculcation of attitudes of extreme docility and conformity, with dissent of any kind absolutely forbidden.

37. *Ibid.*, p. 146.

38. Source: F. M. Bator, *The Question of Government Spending*, 1960. Tables 1 and 2. Cited by Baran and Sweezy, p. 152.

39. For those who always ask the critic what he would do by way of rectification

(as if no rectification were possible or as if the critic was supposed to think for everybody), there would be a simple semi-solution to the automobile-housing tangle, as follows: Nobody might be allowed to purchase or rent an automobile, new or secondhand, unless he was certified as adequately housed. An immediate advantage in the proposal would be a reduction in automobiles on the road. Economically, however, there would not necessarily be much improvement in housing because many, perhaps most, of those denied the right to buy an automobile (or motorcycle) would not necessarily use money in down payment on a house or apartment; they would probably fritter it away before they had accumulated enough. While not all of the poor housing in the United States is attributable to the purchase of cars and other gadgets, much of it clearly is. Rather than live in better quarters many people freely choose cars, thus providing the base for housing statistics that in turn provide fuel for many critics of capitalistic housing. It isn't capitalism that is at fault here so much as people. As between housing and cars, many people have clearly and childishly chosen cars. Capitalism caters to consumer childishness.

40. Ralph Nader, *Unsafe at Any Speed*, Grossman, N.Y., 1965.

41. *New York Times*, October 7, 1963; 1:7.

42. Thorstein Veblen, *The Theory of Business Enterprise*, Charles Scribner's Sons, N.Y., 1932, p. 20.

43. I know this from the remarks of liberal critics about a book I published in 1954, *The Treason of the People*, Harper and Brothers, N.Y., which analyzed the inept political performance of the public in the light of democratic theory. A number of critics took the view that whatever failure the public experienced in securing its own interests was attributable less to its own misfeasance and nonfeasance and more to the wiles of its oppressors. The major portion of the public, in fact, is largely victimized by its own incapacity for self-government and self-defense. As a case in point, I again refer to the tax laws.

CHAPTER FOURTEEN

1. Joe Alex Morris, *Those Rockefeller Brothers*, Harper and Brothers, N.Y., 1953, p. 16.

2. *Ibid.*, p. 180.

3. *Ibid.*, p. 171.

4. *Fortune*, February, 1955, p. 140.

5. *Ibid.*

6. Morris, p. 34.

7. Nevins, II, p. 424.

8. *New York Times*, May 21, 1960; 25:8.

9. *Ibid.*, p. 48. Most of the many magazine articles on the brothers, and some later books, draw heavily upon or are modeled on the Morris book, to which I am greatly indebted for information. Some of the magazine articles on the brothers collectively or individually have appeared in *Fortune*, February and March, 1955; *The Economist*, June 6, 1959; *U.S. News & World Report*, February 1, 1960, and April 1, 1963; and the *New Yorker*, January 9 and 16, 1965. There was also William Manchester, *A Rockefeller Family Portrait*, Little, Brown and Co., Boston, 1959, much of which appeared originally in *Holiday* magazine. The brothers make good periodical and newspaper "copy."

10. Baran and Sweezy, p. 34.

11. Lindahl and Carter, *passim*.

12. Morris, p. 162.

13. *Ibid.* What "progress" and "fair" mean depends upon one's own interpretation.

14. *Ibid.*, p. 166.

15. *Ibid.*, p. 169.
16. *Fortune*, March, 1955, p. 116.
17. *Ibid.*
18. Morris, p. 33.
19. *Ibid.*, pp. 109–10.
20. *Ibid.*, pp. 180–81.
21. *Moody's Industrial Manual*, June, 1966, p. 1609.
22. *Foundation Directory*, 1964, p. 424.
23. Morris, p. 144.
24. *Ibid.*, p. 136. The vexed later relations of Rockefeller with the Merritts were recounted by Gates in a pamphlet, *The Truth About Mr. Rockefeller and the Merritts,* New York, 1911.
25. Nevins, II, p. 401.
26. *Ibid.*, p. 199.
27. *Ibid.*, p. 166.
28. *Ibid.*, p. 200.
29. Raymond B. Fosdick, *John D. Rockefeller, Jr.: A Portrait,* Harper, N.Y., 1953, p. 144.
30. Flynn, *God's Gold*, p. 458.
31. Nevins, II, p. 202.
32. *Ibid.*, p. 203.
33. *Ibid.*, pp. 200–12.
34. Flynn, *God's Gold*, pp. 310–11.
35. Nevins, II, p. 274.
36. *Ibid.*, p. 391.
37. Fosdick, p. 122.
38. Raymond B. Fosdick, *The Story of the Rockefeller Foundation,* Harper and Brothers, N.Y., 1952, p. x.
39. The Rockefeller Foundation, *Annual Report*, 1950, p. 306. Securities were carried in this report at a ledger value of $152,241,857.35 but were also stated to have a quoted market value of $270,711,218.38, which gave the entire fund at the time a market value of $276,572,693.16. Increases in market value add to the dollar worth of holdings even though grants are made out of principal.
40. General Education Board, *Annual Report*, 1950, p. 58. Securities then carried at $19,012,162.04 had a market value of $20,396,565.63, giving assets a slightly higher total than stated in my text. The Board, in a *Review and Final Report*, 1902–64, marking the termination of its activities, reported a total expenditure in its career of $324,632,958. Of this, $129,209,167 was an original gift from John D. Rockefeller; $128,848,570 was income from investments; $50,703,024 was capital gain; and $15,872,197 represented other receipts of principal and income. Grants consisted of $208,204,853 to universities and colleges; $62,675,363 to all levels of Negro education, including collegiate; $25,799,262 to "science of education"; $8,433,541 to non-Negro public education; $6,669,255 to miscellaneous educational activities; $2,642,690 to fellowships and scholarships; and $10,207,994 to administration.
41. Rockefeller Brothers Fund, *Annual Report*, 1954–1955, no page number.
42. *Ibid.*, 1960, pp. 10, 23.
43. Fosdick, *The Story* . . . , pp. 4–5.
44. *Ibid.*, p. 3.
45. *Ibid.*, p. 2.
46. *Ibid.*, p. 7.
47. *Ibid.*
48. Flynn, *God's Gold*, p. 296.
49. Nevins, II, p. 409.
50. Flynn, *God's Gold*, p. 293.

51. Fosdick, *The Story* . . . , p. 6.
52. Manchester, p. 10.
53. Nevins, I, pp. 386–87.
54. *Ibid.*, p. 387.
55. The tension observed to exist between Big Business and the intellectuals derives in part from attitudes toward the Constitution. The intellectuals as good students absorbed a great respect for James Madison and the Founding Fathers in the course of their public school career. Businessmen, on the other hand, have shown a marked tendency to twist the Constitution in the service of their own needs. In so doing business people did only what many other groups did or tried to do. Owing to their greater power they were better able to get away with inroads on the Constitution and to make them deeper. Hence, other reasons apart, there is widespread distrust of business people, successful exponents of a self-servingly flexible Constitution, by intellectuals seriously committed to the spirit of the Constitution. To get off this hook of public reprobation for being "anti-business," intellectuals manifestly should take the Constitution less seriously.
56. Nevins, I, p. 386.
57. That the socialist critique of capitalism is vastly overdrawn out of emotional zeal can easily be shown in hundreds of items. As an instance, socialists and communists long contended that racial antipathy was fostered in the United States by capitalists in order to divide the working class and thus impede the benign revolution. Yet a large number of precise recent studies shows a preponderance of the educated and the heavily propertied supporting the Negro claim to full social equality, while among the white working class and the lower middle class the stiffest opposition to Negro claims is registered. Many large labor unions simply bar Negroes, thus preventing their employment in certain lines of work. What the capitalist attitude really was to the Negro represented merely an opportunistic accommodation (as now toward labor unions) with noncapitalist agrarian southern whites, whose political support was wanted for capitalist legislative schemes.
58. The similarity in form but difference in specific content between pro-socialist and pro-capitalist arguments is interesting. The modes of thought in each case are those of the synthesizing English and French classical economists. Pro-capitalist elements, for example, never tire of depicting communism as a cohering, monolithic international structure, operated from a single center. But socialists have long held to the view, which Baran-Sweezy subscribe to, that capitalism is an interlocked, international, basically monolithic entity, operated under identical rules in all its parts. Both arguments are thoroughly unsound. So-called socialism and so-called capitalism are significantly different from country to country. As to capitalism the differences are spelled out for different countries in Andrew Shonfield, *Modern Capitalism*, Oxford University Press, N.Y., 1965. Similarly, socialists argue that capitalism impedes all progress toward the solution of world problems, while capitalists claim that capitalism is identical with progress. Both arguments are false. Indeed, there is a similar degree of falsity and accuracy in the arguments pro and con of the proponents of each purely abstract system. The intellectual problem is to select from each side what is objectively valid. Many criticizable features of the politico-economic system have no necessary connection with capitalism as such—for example, the tax structure, which differs in rates and modes from country to country. The depletion allowance and various of the other tax loopholes written into the law with the consent of Congress and the president, while sought and obtained by various individual capitalists for their own benefit at the expense of fellow citizens, are not prescribed for or required by capitalism. If all the tax loopholes were eliminated, capitalism would not only continue but would probably give a more balanced account of itself. A pure capitalist would want a strictly equitable tax law. The tax laws derive from individual greed, not capitalism. And Stalin's concentration camps had nothing to do with socialism.

59. Morris, p. 36.
60. E. J. Kahn, Jr., "Profiles: Resources and Responsibilities—II," *New Yorker*, January 16, 1965, p. 61.
61. Morris, p. 42.
62. *Ibid.*, p. 28.
63. *Ibid.*
64. E. J. Kahn, Jr., "Profiles: Resources and Responsibilities—I," *New Yorker*, January 9, 1965, p. 37.
65. *Ibid.*
66. *Ibid.*, pp. 38, 40.
67. *Ibid.*
68. *Ibid.*, p. 46.
69. Morris, pp. 57–58.
70. Kahn, II, p. 41.

CHAPTER FIFTEEN

1. Herbert Aptheker, *The World of C. Wright Mills*, Marzani & Munsell, Inc., N.Y., 1960, p. 17.
2. *New York Times*, June 3, 1966; 53:5; June 8, 1966; 66:4; June 10, 1966; 70:2; and December 30, 1966; 38:4.
3. Federal Reserve Board and Bureau of the Census, *Survey of Financial Characteristics of Consumers*, Board of Governors of the Federal Reserve System, August, 1966, pp. 148, 151. Library of Congress Catalog Number 66–61695.
4. *U.S. News and World Report*, October 11, 1965, p. 119.
5. *America's Sixty Families* took as indication of really heavy money the figure of $30 million projected by names from 1924 tax returns. While amounts below that level were not construed as pittances, only sixty families appeared to exceed it. In all, it was estimated that there were 500 significantly wealthy families in the country; this figure, allowing for slippages and newcomers, I believe to be still fairly correct although Robert L. Heilbroner in his brilliant *The Limits of American Capitalism* places the figure at 200 to 300 families (p. 26). Top wealthholders, owing to preemption of position, do not increase proportionately with either population growth or economic expansion. But even if one were wrong by a 50-per cent underestimation and top wealthholders numbered 1,000 families, or even 2,000, how significant would the higher figure be in a population of 200 million?
6. Mencken, p. 1277.
7. *Ibid.*
8. Columbia University, Graduate School of Journalism, Fiftieth Annual Report of the Dean, *That the People Shall Know*, 1963, p. 13.
9. See H. A. du Pont, *The Early Generations of the Du Pont and Allied Families*, National Americana Society, N.Y., 1923, two volumes; and *Genealogy of the Du Pont Family, 1739–1949*, copyright by Pierre S. du Pont, Wilmington, Delaware, 1949, two volumes. The latter publication is in loose-leaf and is added to from time to time in copies available in major public libraries.
10. Pierre S. du Pont copyright, p. iv.
11. H. A. du Pont, pp. 8–9.
12. Pierre S. du Pont copyright, Charts 72 and 88b. See the index for all Du Ponts, including the large number, fully authentic, who do not bear the family name.
13. See Richard Carter, *The Doctor Business*, Doubleday, N.Y., 1958; and Martin L. Gross, *The Doctors*, Random House, N.Y., 1966.
14. *New York Times*, January 6, 1967; 18:1–2.

CHAPTER SIXTEEN

1. Professor John Tebbel in *The Inheritors*, G. P. Putnam's Sons, N.Y., 1962, makes particular note in captions to photographs of the obvious boredom shown by some of the rich even in their pleasure haunts. Note photographs inserted between pages 232 and 233, especially the slack expressions on the faces of Mr. and Mrs. William K. Vanderbilt, who had recently arrived in Miami on their yacht *Ara* and were snapped watching the races at Hialeah; on the face of John Jacob Astor VI at a big film premiere; on the Belmonts at Belmont Park; and on Marshall Field III and his third wife. In this collection only Mr. and Mrs. Cornelius Vanderbilt Whitney seem buoyed up by some private glimpse of the comic. As is the case in many of their public photographs, Rockefeller I and II and Morgan I and II merely look formidably glum, as though they were having trouble with the help.

2. Note is taken in *America's Sixty Families*, pp. 14–17, of the intermarriage of wealthy American young women with European nobility. Somewhat greater pains are taken there in subsequent pages to show that the American big-rich already in 1937 consisted very considerably of a cousinage. When one refers to almost any combination of the big inheritors one is, more often than not, referring to cousins. This cousinage of wealth firmly bridges the Atlantic today.

3. Merrill Folsom, *Great American Mansions and Their Stories*, Hastings House, N.Y., 1963, pp. 203–6.

4. Morris, p. 31.

5. *Ibid.*

6. Folsom, p. 204.

7. *Ibid.*

8. *Ibid.*, p. 205.

9. *America's Sixty Families*, pp. 432–33.

10. William H. A. Carr, p. 2.

11. *Ibid.*, p. 326, and *passim*.

12. *Ibid.*, pp. 343–44.

13. Folsom, pp. 93–100.

14. *Ibid.*, p. 55.

15. *Ibid.*, p. 57.

16. *Ibid.*, p. 62.

17. *New York Times*, February 16, 1966; 38:1–5.

18. In *America's Sixty Families*, pp. 408–46, there was presented an extensive catalogue of the yachts, pipe organs, airplanes, horses, automobile fleets and assorted appurtenances of the freedom-loving American rich; in these pages I forebear burdening the reader with similar formidable lists. Interested readers can check on such ownerships in catalogues on file in major public libraries—on yacht ownership in *Lloyd's Register of American Yachts*, on airplane ownership in standard registers of the Civil Aeronautics Board, on paintings in various art registers, etc. Suffice it to say here that all such stuff is pretty much standard equipment of the rich denizens of the greatest democracy in history.

19. James Reston, "Washington: The Fat Cat Subsidies," *New York Times*, December 7, 1966, 46:5–8.

20. William H. A. Carr, p. 268.

21. *New York Times*, January 16, 1964; 17:8; February 3, 1964; 67:6.

22. *The Power Elite*, pp. 163–64.

23. "Pollution in the Air We Breathe," *Consumer Reports*, August, 1960, p. 406.

24. *New York Times*, April 1, 1932; 1:2; 11:1.

25. *Statistical Abstract*, 1964, p. 587. See footnote No. 2, Table 814.

26. This story is told in Whalen, *The Founding Father*, pp. 387–90, where the

original unpublished *Globe* interview appears in its entirety. As a denial of alleged anti-Semitism, the interview as written conveys an impression of a man threading his way through a difficult subject in which care must be exercised not to concede too much one way or the other. Kennedy made it clear that he did not dislike *all* Jews, only *some* Jews, and that he certainly was opposed to anything extreme like their outright extermination. Anti-Semitism, he maintained, is sometimes promoted by Jews in their very efforts, futile, to combat it, while some Jews take unfair advantage of the persecution against them; furthermore, some Jews in public life ascribe justified personal criticism to anti-Semitism. "I try to see the whole problem in its proper perspective," the ex-ambassador asseverated with fine judiciousness.

27. John Gunther, *Roosevelt in Retrospect,* Harper & Bros., N.Y., 1950, pp. 235–40, 267–68.

28. For information about how writers who offend those on high are chivvied about see, for a beginning, Jack Anderson, *Washington Exposé,* Public Affairs Press, Washington, D.C., 1966, pp. 9–44, 110, 162 and *passim.*

CHAPTER SEVENTEEN

1. Woodrow Wilson, *The New Freedom,* Doubleday and Co., N.Y., 1913, pp. 57–58. Demagogue though Wilson was, these speeches of his first presidential campaign were an accurate portrayal of the state of affairs in the United States, then and now.

2. Robert Engeler, *The Politics of Oil,* Macmillan, N.Y., 1961, pp. 403–7, 412–15. This book is a treasure trove on political skulduggery by the oil industry.

3. *Congressional Record,* April 4, 1967, p. S4582.

4. *Ibid.,* p. S4586.

5. *Ibid.,* p. S4577.

6. *New York Times,* May 5, 1967; 22:2–5.

7. *Municipal Year Book, 1966,* The International City Managers' Association, Chicago, 1966, p. 95.

8. *Wall Street Journal,* May 10, 1967; 1:6.

9. Marya Mannes, "I, Mary, Take Thee, John, as . . . What?", *New York Times Magazine,* November 14, 1965, p. 52.

10. Herman P. Miller, "Millionaires Are a Dime a Dozen," *New York Times Magazine,* November 28, 1965, p. 50.

11. The report of the court's decision is in the *New York Times,* May 26, 1967; 1:2. The actions leading to the reopening of the case are reported in the *Times,* August 10, 1967; 39:8, and August 11, 1967; 29:6.

12. Robert L. Heilbroner, *The Limits of American Capitalism,* Harper and Row, N.Y., 1965, p. 26.

13. *Newsweek,* March 20, 1967; 60:3.

14. *New York Post,* August 15, 1966; 7:1–2.

15. Lane, *Political Life,* pp. 233–34. For an extended factual inquiry into the political deficiencies of the general public, see Ferdinand Lundberg, *The Treason of the People,* Harper & Bros., N.Y., 1954.

16. Lane, pp. 35–36.

17. For a beginning consult Paul B. Horton and Gerald R. Leslie, *The Sociology of Social Problems,* Appleton-Century-Crofts, N.Y., 1955.

18. This book is strongly recommended to the serious reader.

19. Heilbroner, pp. 8–11.

20. *Wall Street Journal,* April 6, 1967; 1.

21. Heilbroner, p. 11.

22. *Ibid.,* p. 26. In *America's Sixty Families,* 1937, p. 3, the top plutocracy was

set forth as consisting of three asset/income layers of 60, 90 and 350 families, or approximately 500 families in all.

23. Heilbroner, pp. 59–60.
24. *Ibid.*, p. 72.
25. William H. Honan, "Meet the Generals (Yes, Sir!)," *New York Times Magazine*, December 18, 1966, p. 50.
26. Heilbroner, p. 133.

Index

(Asterisks indicate a wealthy individual or an extended family of wealth)

NOTE

Hundreds of names not indexed are cited in the text. There are so many that a selection necessarily had to be made to avoid having an index resembling a small telephone directory in size. It is the author's hope that the selection offered will be found useful by serious readers.